Essential Symbols

B	Market price of a firm's debt (in Chapter 19, it stands for benefits)
β	Beta; a measure of an asset's nondiversifiable risk
CAPM	Capital asset pricing model
CF	Cash flow after tax
CFBT	Cash flow before tax
D	Cash dividends paid by a firm
Δ	Delta; means "the change"
Dep	Depreciation
EBIT	Earnings before interest and taxes
EPS	Earnings per share
FV	Future value factor
FVA	Future value factor for an annuity
g	Compound percentage growth rate (in cash dividends)
I	Interest in dollars on a bond (or interest rate)
IRR	Internal rate of return
k	A percentage required rate of return or discount rate
k_b	Rate of return on a bond; before-tax cost of a bond
$k_{effective}$	Actual interest rate based on compounding frequency
k_i	After-tax cost of debt; $k_b(1 - T)$
k_M	Expected rate of return on the market portfolio
k_{nom}	Stated interest rate
k_{ps}	Cost of preferred stock
k_{RF}	Risk-free rate of return
k_s	Required return on common stock; cost of common equity

$\bar{K}_p$	Expected return on a portfolio		S	Market value of a firm's equity
M	Maturity (or par) value of a bond		T	Firm's marginal tax rate
n	Number of periods		t	Time
NPV	Net present value		V	Market value of firm $(S + B)$
P	Market price per share of stock		V_c	Call option value
P/E	Price/earnings ratio		V_L	Value of levered firm
PMT	An annuity		V_p	Put option value
PV	Present value factor		V_U	Value of unlevered firm
PVA	Present value factor for an annuity		W	Weight, or proportion of the total
σ	Standard deviation (lowercase sigma)		WACC	Weighted average cost of capital
σ_p	Standard deviation for a portfolio		X	Exercise price
Σ	Summation; "take the sum of" (uppercase sigma)			

ESSENTIALS OF FINANCIAL MANAGEMENT

THIRD EDITION

George E. Pinches

The University of Kansas

HarperCollins*Publishers*

To Carole, Susan, and Bill

Sponsoring Editor: John Greenman
Project Editor: Bonnie Biller
Art Direction: Lucy Krikorian
Text Design Adaptation: Caliber Design Planning Inc.
Cover Coordinator: Lucy Krikorian
Cover Design: Hudson River Studio
Production: Kewal K. Sharma

ESSENTIALS OF FINANCIAL MANAGEMENT, Third Edition

Library of Congress Cataloging-in-Publication Data

Pinches, George E.
    Essentials of financial management / George E. Pinches.—3rd ed.
      p.   cm.
      Includes bibliographies and index.
    ISBN 0-06-045198-X (Student Edition)
    ISBN 0-06-045168-8 (Teacher Edition)
      1. Business enterprises—Finance.   2. Corporations—Finance.
    I. Title.
    HG4026.P57   1990
    658.15—dc20   89-35403
                                                              CIP

90 91 92   9 8 7 6 5 4 3

Brief Contents

Detailed Contents

PART FOUR   Long-Term Investment Decisions   207

Financial Management Today Topics

International Finance Sections

Preface

Management of the activities that bear on financial decision making is a rapidly changing field. A growing body of theory, empirical findings, and practice is helping us understand and respond effectively to evolving financial needs, institutions, and instruments. Increasingly, the essentials must be studied as they apply not only to large, profit-oriented firms, but also to small firms, governmental units, and international organizations. With this in mind, these distinguishing features of *Essentials of Financial Management* have been maintained or strengthened in the third edition:

1. A consistent framework is used throughout, based on the magnitude, timing, and riskiness of expected cash inflows and outflows.
2. The text links all financial decisions to the concepts of risk and required return in order to emphasize the goal of maximizing the value of the firm. All major financial decisions, even in such often neglected areas as working capital management, are examined in terms of value maximization and the net present value framework.
3. An introductory text in the subject must be as up-to-date as financial management itself. The world we live in is changing so rapidly that current trends in financial practice, along with recent developments in relevant theory and empirical studies, must be—and have been—incorporated.
4. Step-by-step illustrations and examples have been provided so that students will see all relevant calculations used in the decision-making process.
5. Most financial management texts fail to show students how firms actually plan for the future. Chapter 23 of this text demonstrates how financial officers use the techniques presented previously for financial planning and strategy.
6. Relevant international material is interspersed wherever it is appropriate, and now also receives concentrated attention in Chapter 24. This way of introducing international finance has the advantage of meeting the requirements of the American Assembly of Collegiate Schools of Business (AACSB) without disturbing the logical sequence. (See the list of international sections following the detailed contents.)
7. Each chapter is self-contained to provide greater flexibility in chapter sequence and permit the inclusion or exclusion of particular chapters. By covering or omitting sections noted in various chapters, and including or excluding appendixes, the level of coverage can be easily adjusted, while maintaining the emphasis on the essentials of financial management.
8. Most financial management texts have grown in size in recent years. My approach is to cut material as new material is added, in order to maintain the proper

balance among coverage, depth, and length. **It should be noted that the first six parts of the book— excluding Chapters 11 and 17—provide a comprehensive first course for schools on the quarter system.**

Changes in the Third Edition

In designing the third edition I had three basic objectives. First, a determined effort was made to streamline the book and keep it to a manageable length. Second, a continuing aim was the systematic introduction of new concepts at the forefront of financial management, including fresh ideas from financial theory, empirical studies, and practice. My third aim was to enhance learning through a dedicated commitment to making the treatment more intuitive, emphasizing sound pedagogy, and avoiding errors.

Major Changes

I made significant changes in the third edition to improve the coverage and flexibility of the text as follows:

1. The use of the "pie" concept of the firm as an integrating idea ties various elements of the text together, and helps students conceptualize what is happening. The emphasis is now on maximizing the total value of the firm, which is comprised of the claims of both stockholders and bondholders.
2. The event time study methodology, in very simplified form, is introduced in Chapter 2. It is then used later in the text to report and illustrate the findings of several recent empirical studies.
3. Over 40 new "Financial Management Today" inserts, one or two per chapter, facilitate coverage of current topics of interest, results of empirical studies, small business practices, and other items.
4. The chapter on stock and bond valuation (Chapter 6) has been relocated so it now comes right after Chapter 5, on the time value of money.
5. Chapter 7, on risk and return, has undergone a major revision to expand coverage of both the capital asset pricing model and the efficient market hypothesis. In addition, an appendix has been included on calculating covariances and correlation.
6. A major revision of Chapter 10, on risk and capital budgeting, makes it more up-to-date via the introduction of the economic break-even analysis concept, coverage of simulation, and elimination of this chapter's duplication of material on required rates of return found elsewhere.
7. An entirely new chapter (Chapter 11) on the Black–Scholes option pricing model and its use in making capital budgeting decisions has been added, along with simplified tables that enable students to easily calculate the value of call or put options.
8. Chapter 14 has been retitled and its emphasis shifted from the concept of marginal cost of capital to the concept of appropriate required rates of return. In addition, the weighted average cost of capital is now employed.
9. A major expansion of the capital structure chapter, Chapter 15, provides greater development of the role of personal taxes and the impact of other factors on the capital structure decision. Substantial new theoretical and empirical work has been incorporated into this chapter.

10. The chapter on mergers, Chapter 22, has been extensively revised and retitled "Mergers and Corporate Restructuring," to reflect recent developments in the corporate world and the growing importance of restructuring, leveraged buyouts, leveraging-up, and divestitures as firms streamline their operations.
11. To provide additional flexibility and coverage, a new chapter (Chapter 24) on international financial management has been added. This chapter now expands and rounds out the topic-linked coverage already provided in other chapters throughout the text.
12. The number of appendixes has been reduced substantially, and to improve the flow of material those that remain have been placed at the back of the book.

Other Coverage Modifications

In addition to those changes noted above, other significant extensions of coverage include:

- agency costs (Chapters 1 and 15)
- historical return data on stocks and bonds (Chapters 2 and 6)
- different ways of calculating earnings per share (Chapter 3)
- statement of cash flows (Chapter 4)
- simplified notation that is more consistent with financial calculators (Chapter 5)
- broader coverage of the risks of and calculations necessary for bonds, preferred stock, and common stock (Chapter 6)
- simplified notation, clarification, and introduction of the incremental internal rate of return (IRR) concept (Chapter 8)
- option pricing approach for valuing the firm (Appendix 11A)
- information on initial public offerings, underpricing, and issuing stock (Chapter 12)
- material on debt financing, convertibility, and financial distress (Chapter 13)
- introduction of signaling theory and the pecking order theory (Chapters 15 and 16)
- more on spontaneous sources of short-term financing (Chapter 18)
- incorporation of taxes in all calculations, and recent developments in the money market (Chapter 19)
- emphasis on the annual percentage rate (APR) for calculating interest rates (Chapter 21)

Pedagogical Features

As was true in the first and second editions, I have made a major attempt to enhance learning through a variety of pedagogical features:

1. Each chapter begins with an overview that highlights the major issues.
2. Chapter introductions. The key elements of each chapter are introduced, with relevant real-world examples, in a special section at the beginning of each chapter.
3. Key terms appear in italics on their first mention in the text and are included in a glossary at the end of the book.
4. Numerous real-company examples are used in the chapters, and J. C. Penney is employed in a number of places to illustrate the actual calculations involved.

5. "Financial Management Today" sections have been included in each chapter to provide current information on a number of different issues.
6. Each chapter has a summary for easy review.
7. The first question at the end of each chapter highlights all terms introduced in that chapter, and provides a convenient means for students to check their understanding of these terms.
8. Each chapter concludes with an extensive problem set that has been class tested. An "Answers to Selected Problems" section is provided at the end of the book.
9. Over 65 self-test problems are included. These exercises foster students' ability to set up problems in ways that yield proper financial decisions. Step-by-step solutions now appear at the back of the book, rather than right after the problems, as they previously did, so that students do not inadvertently read the answers before they think about the problems.
10. Selected current references are included at the end of each chapter.

Ancillary Materials

Essentials of Financial Management, Third Edition, offers a complete set of supplements designed to maximize student understanding and the mastery of financial management.

Instructor's Manual

I have prepared a complete Instructor's Manual, consisting of answers to all the chapter questions and complete solutions to all problems in the text. In addition, handouts on the use of Lotus and adjusted present value (APV), which can be reproduced and distributed to students, are included. This manual also describes alternate sequences for presenting the text material.

Test Bank

A separate Test Bank prepared by Kathryn M. Kelm, University of Kansas, and myself consists of over 1,800 multiple-choice and true–false questions and problems, as well as over 200 additional longer problems. The multiple-choice and true–false questions are also available on Harper Test, a user-friendly computerized test generation package.

Study Guide

An extensive Study Guide prepared by David C. Ketcham, University of Tennessee, and myself supplements, explains, and extends the material in the text. Its key elements include topical outlines stressing the main features of each chapter, summaries of key equations, "What to Look For" sections that discuss and elaborate on important or difficult concepts, completion questions that test understanding, and over 100 additional problems with step-by-step solutions especially designed to bring out the key analytical concepts of each chapter.

Pinches Problem-Solving Disk

Available free to adopters, this user-friendly disk, prepared by Larry W. Courtney, introduces the power of spreadsheet programs to the teaching of financial management. Compatible with Lotus 1–2–3®, versions 1A, 2.0, 2.01, and the Student Version of Lotus, this disk prompts students to perform sensitivity analysis on over 20 in-text problems that are identified by the disk symbol: ■. Multiple copies can be made and handed out to students.

LOTS: Lecture Outline and Transparency System

A completely new supplement for this edition is LOTS (Lecture Outline and Transparency System) prepared by Stuart E. Michelson, University of Kansas, Robert M. Hull, Emporia State University, and myself. This is an entirely new concept that provides over 20 pages per chapter of lecture outlines that can be used as teaching transparency masters. LOTS may be used by instructors for a quick review of material before they go to class. It may also be used to make transparencies for an outstanding course that strengthens student comprehension, recall, and note-taking. This item will be of assistance to all instructors, but is especially designed for use in large sections, and for coordinating activities among sections when numerous instructors are teaching the course. These materials have been class tested and provide an unusual new kind of support for all instructors.

Lotus 1–2–3®

Lotus 1–2–3® for Financial Management, by George E. Pinches and Larry W. Courtney, Harper & Row, 1989, provides step-by-step guidance for students and faculty wanting to use Lotus in financial management. The first eight lessons are designed so students, without any help from instructors, can work their way through the main concepts of Lotus and develop an understanding of how it is used in financial management. Then the 17 models, or templates, are discussed and the enclosed diskettes enable students to use already developed models for simple, or more complex, analysis. All of the templates can be modified, if desired. This package, available at a nominal cost, is designed for both the first course in finance and also for later courses. It can be used throughout a student's career.

Zero Error Goal

To students and instructors alike, the presence of errors can be distracting and impede the learning process. My commitment is to provide the most error-free text and ancillaries possible. In line with this zero error goal, I offer a reward of $10.00 per error (misspelled word, arithmetic mistake, and the like) to the first person who finds an error in *Essentials* and reports it to me. In addition, I offer $5.00 per error to the first person who finds a spelling or math error in any of the ancillary materials (Instructor's Manual, Test Bank, Study Guide, Pinches Problem-Solving Diskette, or LOTS). In all cases any error that has follow-through effects will be counted as a maximum of two errors. My goal is not only to have zero errors in this edition, but in all subsequent editions. Please report any errors to me and I will see that your assistance in improving the quality of the *Essentials* teaching package is immediately recognized, in hard cash. My address is:

Professor George E. Pinches
School of Business
University of Kansas
Lawrence, Kansas 66045

Acknowledgments

Essentials of Financial Management, Third Edition, has been class tested, and the comments, criticism, and encouragement given freely (and often vocally) by students contributed in no small way to the development and refinement of this text. I would like to thank the individuals who reviewed and provided comments and suggestions on the first two editions:

Tom Berry	Laura Hoisington	Lawrence C. Rose
Harry Blythe	Mike Joehnk	Bill Sartoris
John Boquist	Eldon C. Johnson	Carl Schwendiman
Phil Cooley	Christopher G. Lamoureux	Jaye Smith
Benoit Deschamps	Rick LeCompte	Carl Stern
Art DeThomas	Hyong J. Lee	Gary Tallman
Peter DeVito	John Legler	Martin Thomas
Norman S. Douglas	Leo P. Mahoney	A. Frank Thompson
Gene Drzycimski	Paul Malatesta	John Traynor
David Dubofsky	Mary Kay Mans	Gary Trennepohl
Ed Dyl	Stephen G. Marks	Keith Van Horn
Dave Ewert	Lalatendu Misra	Jerry Viscione
Al Frankle	Eric Moon	Nancy Wiebe
Stephen Gardner	Prafulla G. Nabar	Jimmy B. Williams
Larry Gitman	Gary Noreiko	Bob Wood
Manak C. Gupta	Robert A. Olsen	B. J. Yang
Hal Heaton	Larry G. Perry	Mike York
Ronald Hennigar	Robert W. Phillips	Kent Zumwalt
Larry Hexter	Verlyn Richards	

I also thank the professors who provided detailed comments and suggestions that materially improved the third edition:

Mary Helen Blakeslee, Rollins College
Mary Ellen Butcher, formerly of Providence College
Thomas J. Coyne, John Carroll University
Wilfred L. Dellva, Villanova University
Kendall P. Hill, University of Alabama at Birmingham
Pearson Hunt, Rollins College
O. Maurice Joy, University of Kansas
Ravindra R. Kamath, Cleveland State University
David B. Lawrence, Drake University
Ginette M. McManus, Cleveland State University
Emmanuel S. Santiago, Kansas State University
David L. Scott, Valdosta State College

In addition, a number of other individuals made important contributions to this edition. Alfred H. R. Davis, of Queen's University, my coauthor for *Canadian Financial Management*, contributed in no small way to my thinking on some of the revisions for this edition. Narendra Khilnani provided research assistance and helped in finding some of the "Financial Management Today" inserts; Bruce D. Bagamery, Shirly A. Kleiner, Laurian Lytle, and Tarun Mukherjee also made important contributions. The typing support provided by Paul Toepfer and Karla Wallace is greatly appreciated. In addition, Dorothy J. Jones did her usual superb job in typing and proofing the Instructor's Manual. The staff members at Harper & Row, especially Bonnie Biller, John Greenman, Steve Pisano, and Suzy Spivey, did their usual outstanding job.

Finally, I must acknowledge the continued love and support of my family. Without their understanding, neither the first two editions nor this revision could have been completed.

To the extent I have succeeded in writing a clear introduction to the essentials of financial management, I owe a large debt of thanks to the help and criticism I have received from others. I encourage all users to continue to provide me with comments, suggestions, and criticisms. All are most welcome in my attempt to provide an ever-improving means of learning the essentials of financial management.

GEORGE E. PINCHES

P A R T   O N E

The Financial Management Environment

1

Why Financial Management Matters

Overview

- Financial management involves the acquisition, management, and financing of resources for firms by means of money, with due regard for prices in external economic markets.

- The primary objective is to maximize the value of the firm.

- The fundamental determinants of the value of the firm are the magnitude of future cash flows, their timing, and their riskiness. As investor perceptions of these change, so will the value of the firm.

- The chief financial officer of most firms is the financial vice-president. Many others within the firm are also directly involved in making and carrying out financial decisions with consequences for the future well-being of the firm.

eneral Motors is investing $3.5 billion to build a totally integrated automobile plant for its Saturn line of high-quality, price-competitive small cars. The facility in Tennessee will be almost twice as large and five times as expensive as any other GM plant. It's easy to see why: The plant will be highly automated. It will allow GM to manufacture many of the cars' components locally. When complete, it should produce 400,000 to 500,000 cars annually—twice as many as any existing GM plant.

On the other side of the world, many U.S. firms had sizable investments in South Africa. That country's apartheid policies are no longer just a moral issue; U.S. internationals are increasingly concerned about the deteriorating economic climate, the continued violence, and the political deadlock in South Africa. A few years ago there were about 300 U.S. firms in South Africa with a total investment of some $2.5 billion. But now firms are pulling out, reducing their presence, or shrinking their exposure by selling controlling interests to South Africans.

Businesses continually face decisions like these, decisions with important financial implications. Every day firms choose to move into new lines of business, replace equipment, change suppliers, reorganize operating structures, start new advertising campaigns, or automate inventory systems. The financial consequences of these and many other actions may be direct or indirect, but they cannot be ignored. In this book, we examine the financial aspects of a firm's ongoing business decisions. We see how and why firms plan investments, financing, and operations. As we move along, you will become familiar with terms and concepts that are constantly in the news; but more important, you will gain the tools and theory, along with the rationale, goals, and strategies, that will enable you to be an effective decision maker in your own business activities.

Why Financial Management Is Important

Corporations measure their performance and check their progress with financial tools. They also create financial incentives, such as executive stock options, profit-sharing plans, and employee stock purchase plans. More top executives have a financial background than almost any other form of business training. And because of increasing worldwide competition, deregulation, and slower growth in the American economy, financial management is more important than ever before. Everyone associated with a firm benefits from effective financial management; likewise, everyone suffers from poor decisions.

Consider, for example, these three cases. For years General Electric has stressed effective financial management and has provided a comprehensive financial training program for junior executives. The result has been not only the continued growth and strong financial performance of General Electric, but also the prospering of its finance subsidiary, General Electric Credit Corporation (GECC). GECC has become an important and innovative supplier of financing to businesses. Equally important for GE's owners, because of GECC, General Electric's effective corporate tax rate has been among the lowest of major profitable firms. Another example of the importance of financial management is the revitalization of Chrysler Corporation after its brush with financial disaster in the early 1980s. Chrysler was able to survive by securing federal loan guarantees, by restructuring its operations, and by managing its financial affairs in a forthright manner in order to secure the cooperation of over 20,000 suppliers and 400 banks. Chrysler not only survived, it has again become profitable and paid back its government-guaranteed loans early. Without government assistance and expert financial management, Chrysler surely would have gone under.

Revco, once a fast-growing chain of discount drug stores, got itself into such financial difficulties that it had to seek protection under Chapter 11 of the Bankruptcy Code. In July 1988 it earned the dubious distinction of being the first big *leveraged buyout (LBO)* to go into Chapter 11. In an LBO a firm goes from a publicly owned firm to a private one—through the use of massive amounts of debt to buy the outstanding common stock. But, due to overly optimistic projections, slow asset sales, and poor management, the cash flow Revco needed to sustain the debt load was not there. Effective financial management could have made a difference.

What Is Financial Management?

Finance is the word used to describe both the money resources available to governments, firms, or individuals, and the management of these monies. Our focus is on the second aspect, management. For our purposes, *financial management* is the acquisition, management, and financing of resources for firms by means of money, with due regard for prices in external economic markets. Let's look at this definition part by part.

First, our focus is on the acquisition, management, and financing of resources needed by the firm. Resources are generally physical, such as cash, inventory, accounts receivable, equipment and machinery, or manufacturing and distribution facilities. But they also include people—the employees of the firm. The money for these resources comes from a variety of sources, such as borrowing, leasing, stock issues, and the internal cash flow generated by the firm's activities. The firm's goal is to provide and manage these resources as efficiently as possible—to balance needs against risks and returns.

Second, firms keep track of resources in terms of dollars. They could use production runs, tons, boxcar loads, or any other unit, but it is far simpler for all firms to use a single standard. That standard is money, and the unit is dollars. The results of almost any activity considered by the firm can be expressed in dollars. For example, one firm might consider acquiring another firm for stock. The value of the transaction can still be expressed in dollars, even though stock is used to finance the deal.

The third point is that our primary concern is the firm and its operations. But no firm, like no person, exists in a vacuum; performance is affected by a variety of external factors, such as the health of the economy, taxes, interest rates, international tensions, and the prevailing political and regulatory moods. In fact, as we will see, the performance of the firm is ultimately judged by the investment community—another external factor.

The financial tools, concepts, and techniques we discuss apply to all kinds of firms and individuals. But our focus here will be on corporations, rather than proprietorships or partnerships. A *proprietorship* is an unincorporated business owned by one individual. In a *partnership,* two or more individuals own the business. While a proprietorship or partnership is easy to set up, most successful ones are eventually converted into corporations. A *corporation* is a legal entity given the power to act as an individual and has limited liability. This means that owners can lose no more than the money they have invested in the corporation, even if the business goes bankrupt.

Ownership in a corporation is evidenced by shares of *common stock*. Corporations can readily issue and sell their common stock, which allows them to raise capital. Corporations can also obtain funds by selling *bonds,* which are long-term debt instruments bought by creditors. Finally, corporations are taxed differently from partnerships or proprietorships.

The Objective: Maximizing Stockholder Wealth

To achieve the goal of acquiring, managing, and financing resources efficiently, the firm must have an objective—a purpose. To understand this objective, or purpose, it is helpful, as in Figure 1.1, to think of the firm as a pie. The ingredients that go

Figure 1.1 The Firm as a Pie

Depending on the assessment of a firm's decisions made by the investment community (via the financial markets) the size of the pie can be enlarged or shrunk, often dramatically.

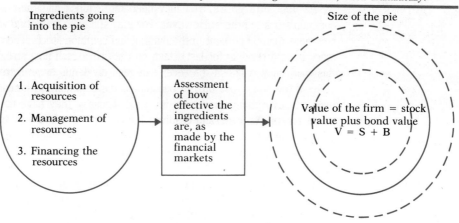

Ingredients going into the pie

1. Acquisition of resources
2. Management of resources
3. Financing the resources

Assessment of how effective the ingredients are, as made by the financial markets

Size of the pie

Value of the firm = stock value plus bond value
$V = S + B$

into the pie include the basic factors that financial management stresses—the acquisition of resources for the firm and the management and financing of these resources. How effectively these resources are used, however, is not determined solely by the firm and its managers. Rather, how effectively they are used is determined by *how much someone else is willing to pay for a claim on them.*

Thus, the financial markets, where the firm's stock and bonds are traded, come into play. The size of the pie, or the value of the firm, is ultimately determined by these financial markets. If the firm does an excellent job with its ingredients the financial markets will recognize this and the size of the pie will increase. Conversely, if the firm does a lousy job, the size of the pie will decrease. The point to remember is this: You can't fool the financial markets for long.

The total value of the firm, V, or size of the pie, is a function of the claims of both stockholders and bondholders on the firm,

$$V = S + B \qquad (1.1)$$

where S is the market value of the stock and B is the market value of debt. Our objective is to maximize V. For simplicity we assume this can be accomplished by maximizing S. Throughout this book then, *the primary objective of the firm is to maximize the value of stockholder claims on the firm.* An alternative way of stating the maximization of S involves denoting the price of a single share of common stock by P, and using a zero (0) subscript to show we are talking about time today, or at time t = 0. The objective then becomes that of maximizing P_0. This objective of *stockholder wealth maximization* should underlie all financial decisions.

Constraints: Stockholders Versus Management

It's easy to see why our basic premise is that it is the common stockholders whose benefit is most important. Think of a small business where you are the owner and also the manager of the firm. Your primary goal is to earn a good income, or to maximize your wealth. When the firm is small, you supply all the capital and you take nearly all the risks. The bank or some other institution or person may have lent you money, but the ultimate rewards of good performance go to you, as do the major risks of bad performance.

As your firm grows, you may need more funds and thus decide to sell some common stock to others. However, you may still keep majority ownership by controlling more than 50 percent of the outstanding common stock. The owners of common stock have a residual (or last) claim on the firm's cash flow stream. In good times, this claim may result in the receipt of cash dividends or an increase in the market price of the stock, or both. In bad times, the common stockholders (including you) may lose everything they have invested, because they have the last claim on the firm's assets. As owners of the firm, the common stockholders' benefit must always be paramount in financial decisions. That is why the objective of the firm is stated in terms of maximizing the value of stockholder claims on the firm, or maximizing stockholder wealth.

In large corporations, there is separation of management and ownership. The management of the firm can be thought of as the *agent* of the owners. Stockholders delegate decision-making authority to the managers to act on their behalf. To ensure that management acts in the interest of all stockholders, the firm must incur *agency costs*. These may take the form of monitoring devices, such as reporting requirements or outside audits. Or they may take the form of expenditures, through bonus or salary plans tied to stock performance, so that possible undesirable managerial behavior is limited. Or they may be opportunity costs, such as bypassing a risky but potentially beneficial new investment because management prefers a safer project.

Ultimately, management's performance is judged in the financial marketplace and is reflected in the price of the firm's common stock. Poor management, or a continually low stock price, makes the firm vulnerable to unwelcome interference such as takeover by another firm in an unfriendly merger, or *proxy fights*[1] by stockholders. The effect of either of these actions, if successful, may cause some or all of the managers to lose their jobs.[2] So, although the interests of management and stockholders do not necessarily coincide, through monitoring devices, compensation plans, and the financial marketplace, forces are at play to align their interests. Nevertheless, to the extent that management interests differ from those of the owners of the firm, the firm's objective may not be fully realized.

Constraints: Stockholders Versus Creditors

Firms raise funds from creditors as well as from common stockholders. *Creditors* are all parties that hold fixed-type financial claims against the firm: long-term debt (bonds, mortgages, leases), short-term debt (bank loans or commercial paper), accounts payable, wages and salaries, and pension liabilities. This creates a second type of agency cost, because of potential conflicts between stockholders and creditors.

---

[1] A proxy fight is an attempt by some group other than the firm's current management and board of directors to obtain control of the firm by electing a different board of directors. This is done by soliciting a proxy from each stockholder, which is an authorization given by a stockholder to let someone else exercise his or her voting right at a stockholders' meeting. By securing enough proxies, the group could elect a different board of directors, which might lead to changes in the firm's operation and management.

[2] Managers can also lose their jobs if the firm is very successful and is purchased by another firm. In situations such as this, however, the acquiring firm generally makes every effort to retain the successful management.

Whose Company Is It?

In most large firms the management runs the firm and owns a small percent of the outstanding shares of common stock. The rest is held by other shareholders. One way to look at corporations is in a principal–agent relationship, where the shareholders are the principals and they hire managers who act as their agents. The job of the agents is to run the firm and maximize the value of the shareholders' wealth. Not all actions by managements, however, are necessarily in the shareholders' best interest.

Some large institutional investors have recently become increasingly concerned about certain management actions and practices.[1] One of these is a lack of open voting, scrutinized by an outside independent source, at annual meetings. Another is that some companies have instituted "supermajority" requirements for voting on mergers, where up to 80 percent of the stock may have to vote in favor of merger for it to be approved. More than in recent years, corporate America's annual meetings increasingly pit management against shareholders on a number of issues that govern the way companies are run. Institutional investors, such as the New York City Employees' Retirement System, College Retirement Equities Fund, and California Public Employees' Retirement System, are bringing a number of these measures before the firms' annual meetings. These include open voting, supermajority issues, as well as others, such as poison pills, which are enacted to slow potential takeovers, and greenmail, where management buys back stock at a premium from potential acquirers. It's clear there is growing shareholder activism that extends far beyond social issues such as divestment in South Africa. Management is going to have to learn to live with investors who want to exercise more control on the issues facing corporations.

[1] "Whose Company Is It, Anyway?" *Business Week* (April 25, 1988).

Consider a firm that, in order to undertake the acquisition of another firm, issues a large amount of new debt. If this new debt is perceived by the financial marketplace to have increased the risk of bankruptcy to existing bondholders, the market value of the existing bonds will fall. In such a case the stockholders would be expropriating wealth from the firm's creditors. To protect against such expropriation, constraints are often written into debt instruments. If constraints are not present, new debt holders will attempt to protect themselves from expropriation by requiring higher than normal rates of return. Either way, the firm incurs additional agency costs due to the conflicts between stockholders and creditors.

Finally, the firm has to deal with many other parties, who are sometimes referred to as stakeholders. These include the firm's employees, customers, suppliers, and the community at large. Because of the possibility of conflicts of interests between the goal of stockholder wealth maximization and the desires of other interested parties, constraints exist. These constraints are reflected in the form of agency costs (related to managers or creditors) and requirements imposed by the government (for employees and communities) if stockholders attempt to expropriate wealth from the firm's stakeholders. Even so, the goal of stockholder wealth maximization, subject to these constraints, is still the appropriate goal for the firm.

The Objective in Practice

In practice, the overall objective of maximizing the value of the firm has three important messages. First, it is theoretically correct and provides the proper basis for making decisions. Second, since there are obviously some constraints on this objective, firms can maximize value only subject to those constraints. Third, even if there are constraints, the objective provides a clear and precise frame of reference within which to judge decisions. In other words, it provides a standard of comparison and allows us to determine if the decisions are the best ones under the circumstances. It also permits us to measure how much value the firm is giving up if decisions are not in accordance with the objective.

How to Achieve the Objective

Now that we know the basic objective is to maximize the value of the firm, or, for simplicity, to maximize S, the next point to consider is how firms go about attempting to achieve it. Our interest is in the value of the firm in the financial marketplace, not in its *book value* (assets minus liabilities in an accounting sense) or in some other figure like its replacement value. We, as managers or investors, are interested in the highest market value of the firm's stock. How do we go about valuing a firm? Theoretically, *the value of the firm is determined by (1) the magnitude of the future cash flows to be received; (2) the timing of these cash flows; and (3) the risks involved.* These three factors influence the value placed on any asset, and hence the market value of the firm.

By *cash flows,* we mean actual cash to be received or paid. This is not the same as earnings or net income in an accounting sense. As we will see in Chapters 3 and 4, there is a fundamental difference between accounting and financial decision making. As students who have studied accounting, you will be able to use some of this knowledge in the study of finance. But the focus is quite different: *The accountant looks at earnings; in financial management we use cash flows.* Earnings are only a clue to the ability of the firm to generate cash flows. Earnings can, in fact, be misleading, since their purpose is to match revenues and expenses in the proper time period based on historical costs. *The accounting system is not designed to report the inflow and outflow of cash.*

One of the fundamental concepts in finance relates to the timing of the cash flows. By *timing,* we mean when the cash is to be received or disbursed. If you have the choice of receiving $100 today or $100 a year from now and you are rational, you will take the $100 today. This is true even if you do not need the $100 until a year from now, because by investing the money now you will have more than $100 in one year. Firms want to speed the receipt of cash inflows and delay, to the extent practical, the outflows.

A second concept relates to *valuation,* the process of determining the worth of an asset based on its risk and returns. Risk is the third basic concept in finance. By *risk,* we mean the uncertainty of something happening, or the possibility of a less than desirable outcome. Other things being equal, rational investors require a

Figure 1.2 Interaction of Demand and Supply to Determine the Price and Quantity (or Volume) of a Common Stock

As investors in the aggregate perceive lower cash flows, a longer time before receipt of cash flows, or more risk, their actions will cause the demand curve to shift to the left, resulting in a lower market price, P_0'. A shift to the right in the demand curve will have exactly the opposite effect.

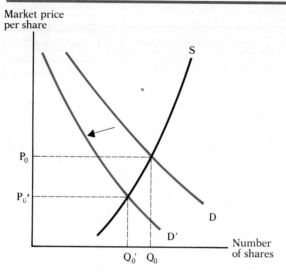

higher return for exposing themselves to higher risk. In financial management, this risk–return relationship is fundamental.

The interaction of the magnitude, timing, and riskiness of expected cash flows, as perceived by the financial market, influences the demand and supply curves that determine the market price of common stock. In Figure 1.2, the interaction of supply and demand determines the initial price P_0 and quantity Q_0 for a specific stock.[3] If perceptions change because of a decrease in the magnitude of the expected cash flows, a delay in the receipt of the cash flows, or increased risk, the demand curve would shift to the left (to D' in Figure 1.2), with the result that the new market value of P_0' would be lower than the original market value. Changes in the opposite direction would cause the demand curve to shift to the right, resulting in an increase in the market value of the firm's common stock.

These are the various factors that affect the price of the firm's stock. But how does management actually achieve the objective of maximizing the value of stockholder claims? Figure 1.3 depicts the factors at work. First in importance are external factors such as the financial markets (where firms raise funds), government regulations, the tax structure, competition, and the state of the economy. The firm has only indirect influence over these—through lobbying in Congress and market positioning,

---

[3] The exact shapes of the supply and demand curves is open to debate. However, at any given point in time, their shapes can be approximated by Figure 1.2. For simplicity, no shift in the supply curve is assumed.

Figure 1.3 Factors Affecting the Firm's Stock Market Price

Firms cannot do much to affect the external environment, but through their strategic and policy decisions they can have a significant impact on many factors that largely determine the magnitude, timing, and riskiness of the firm's expected cash flows. Management actions do have a significant impact on the firm's common stock price.

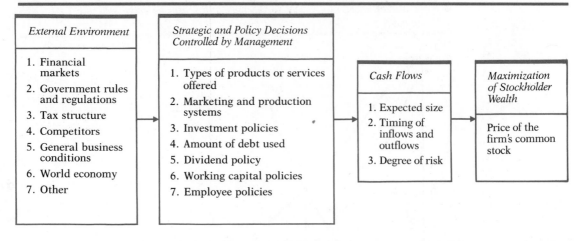

for instance. Next are the strategic policy decisions directly under management control. These include the choice of products or services offered; marketing, and production systems; investment, financing, and dividend policies; and employee practices.

Many of these strategic factors may appear fixed in the short run, but over the long run all can be changed by management. These policies directly determine the magnitude, timing, and riskiness of future cash flows. Only those management decisions that improve the magnitude or timing of future cash flows or reduce their riskiness will be perceived favorably in the financial markets and lead to an increase in the value of the firm's stock. So the important variables to focus on, and the ones we stress throughout, are cash flows—their magnitude, timing, and riskiness.

The Finance Function

The term *financial manager* is often used to refer to anyone directly engaged in making or implementing financial decisions. Except in the smallest firms, many individuals are ordinarily responsible for financial activities. In most large firms, the person ultimately responsible is the financial vice-president, who is the *chief financial officer* (*CFO*) of the firm. The chief financial officer is deeply involved in financial policy making, as well as in corporate or strategic planning.

Typically, at least two individuals report directly to the CFO. The *treasurer* is usually the person responsible for seeing that the firm obtains funds as needed, for making sure cash is collected and invested, for maintaining relations with banks and other financial institutions, and for seeing that bills are paid on time. In some organizations, the treasurer also oversees credit management, capital budgeting decisions, and other items such as inventory control. The *controller* is responsible for preparing

Super Predictions

Can the outcome of the Super Bowl actually foretell the stock market? The prediction goes like this: Whenever a team with roots in the old National Football League wins the Super Bowl, the stock market will end that year higher. If a team from the old American Football League wins, stocks will fall. The majority of teams have roots in the old NFL. When the leagues merged in 1970, the NFL's Colts, Steelers, and Browns shifted to the American Conference; but keeping to the roots (and counting each conference's expansion teams with its predecessor league) there are 17 old NFL teams to 11 old AFL teams. So the odds are that the Super Bowl indicator will call for an up market 61 percent (17/28) of the time. How has it done?

Year	Winner	Roots/call	DJIA	S&P 500
1967	Packers	NFL ↑	+15.2%	+20.1%
1968	Packers	NFL ↑	+4.3	+7.9
1969	Jets	AFL ↓	−15.2	−11.4
1970	Chiefs	AFL ↓	+4.8*	+0.1*
1971	Colts	NFL ↑	+6.1	+10.8
1972	Cowboys	NFL ↑	+14.6	+15.6
1973	Dolphins	AFL ↓	−16.6	−17.4
1974	Dolphins	AFL ↓	−27.5	−29.7
1975	Steelers	NFL ↑	+38.3	+31.6
1976	Steelers	NFL ↑	+17.9	+19.2
1977	Raiders	AFL ↓	−17.3	−11.5
1978	Cowboys	NFL ↑	−3.2*	+1.1
1979	Steelers	NFL ↑	+4.2	+12.3
1980	Steelers	NFL ↑	+14.9	+25.8
1981	Raiders	AFL ↓	−9.2	−9.7
1982	49ers	NFL ↑	+19.6	+14.8
1983	Redskins	NFL ↑	+20.3	+17.3
1984	Raiders	AFL ↓	−3.7	+1.4*
1985	49ers	NFL ↑	+27.7	+20.5
1986	Bears	NFL ↑	+22.6	+20.2
1987	Giants	NFL ↑	+2.3	+2.0
1988	Redskins	NFL ↑	+11.9	+12.4
1989	49ers	NFL ↑		

* Exception to the rule.

Up through 1988 the Super Bowl indicator has been right 20 out of 22 times—91 percent accuracy! While it's obviously a coincidence, and there is no reason to believe there's any economic significance associated with it, it's still uncanny. Who's going to win the Super Bowl next year, and what is the market going to do?

Table 1.1 Major Financial Management Functions

The financial management functions encompass the entire spectrum of the firm's activities. Financial management is important not only for individuals in finance, but also for those in other areas, since these decisions, directly or indirectly, influence the fortunes of the firm.

Investment in and management of long-term assets through the capital budgeting process

Evaluating, securing, and servicing long-term financing from within the firm or from financial market instruments such as common or preferred stock, debt, leases, warrants, or convertibles

Determination of the required rate of return through attention to the firm's capital structure and alternative sources of funds

Distribution of funds to the firm's stockholders via a cash dividend policy

Securing, managing, and investing in current assets such as cash, accounts receivable, and inventory

Obtaining short-term financing from creditors or the financial markets

Assessing the viability of growth via merging, and ensuring the economic vitality of the firm

Planning for the ongoing activities of the firm and ensuring that the firm responds to the changing financial and economic environment

---

financial statements, for cost accounting, for internal auditing, for budgeting, and for the tax department.

The principal finance functions, and the ones we will study throughout the book, are listed in Table 1.1. Note that the thrust of financial management is on the acquisition, management, and financing of resources—exactly as specified in our definition. Because of the importance of financial decisions to the long-run profitability and success of the firm, major decisions are often made by the board of directors or the executive committee. For example, major capital expenditures, proposed financing changes, and dividend payment policies are decided at the highest level in the firm. However, authority for less important decisions, such as small- or medium-sized investments, credit policies, and cash management changes, are often delegated to division managers or others at lower levels in the firm. Financial managers are all those individuals whose decision-making responsibility affects the financial health of the firm.

International Financial Management

Roughly 25 percent of the assets of U.S.-based manufacturing firms are located outside the United States. Moreover, the rate of growth of international investment exceeds the growth rate of aggregate U.S. domestic investment. At the same time, major changes are taking place all over the world. The Japanese now have direct investment of over $35 billion in the United States, and export at least $85 billion a year to this country. Likewise, the recent treaty between the United States and Canada will remove all remaining tariffs on trade between the two countries within 10 years. The pact should spur growth on both sides of the border by creating a unified, continent-wide market. One likely result will be increasing cross-border integration of regional economics, linking states and provinces with North–South flows of products.

Equally important are the changes taking place in the European Common Market where many of the trade restrictions between those 12 countries will be lowered by 1992. For firms already operating in the European Community, they will have to develop international strategies much sooner. As the head of one firm has stated, "You have to be everywhere to know what your competition is doing." Likewise, there is growing evidence that as these nations strive to eliminate trade restrictions among themselves, they will also transfer many of them to foreigners—effectively ushering in a complex era of broad European protectionism. These developments, which may have major implications for non-European internationals, are designed to protect European companies and penalize outsiders. It is an attempt to see that outside competitors don't take advantage of the unified marketplace before European firms have the opportunity to benefit from this profound restructuring. As long as the policy is followed, non-European firms and governments will have to adopt strategies to cope with it, or risk being shut out of one of the biggest markets in the world.

Speaking of big markets, the market value of Japanese firms dominates the global marketplace. While U.S.-based firms typically report more profits, the market value of major Japanese firms easily outweighs that of major U.S. firms. The reason is not hard to see. Since the Tokyo Stock Exchange reopened in 1947, the market value of stocks listed on it have increased an astounding 16,000 percent in the 39 years to 1988! Tokyo now is the home of the best performing stock exchange in the world. In 1988, 55 of the top 100 firms in the world (ranked by market value) were Japanese firms. The impact of the Japanese, in terms of investment in new plant and equipment, competition for customers, and even an individual's personal investment strategy, has never been greater.

All of these developments have profound implications for financial management. More than ever it is a worldwide economy. Most firms, whether large or small, need to think globally both in terms of exporting to other countries and in terms of positioning themselves so that foreign competition does not erode their marketplace. Effective financial management is a key underpinning of a firm's global strategy. While our primary focus is on financial management in the United States, we will explore certain aspects of international financial management throughout the book. In addition, Chapter 24 is devoted exclusively to international financial management.

Overview of the Text

This text is divided into seven parts, each dealing with a major topic:

The financial management environment

Financial analysis

Fundamental concepts for financial management

Long-term investment decisions

Long-term financing decisions

Working capital management

Financial strategy

In Part One, we consider why financial management matters, and what our objective is in making financial decisions. Then we examine the domestic financial system, interest rates and their importance, and certain tax aspects important for financial management. The purpose of Chapters 1 and 2 is to provide background for the rest of the book.

Financial analysis is considered in Part Two. First, in Chapter 3, we review the accounting process used by firms to keep basic financial records. Then in Chapter 4 we consider cash flow, forecasting, and why cash flow, not accounting net income, is the focal point for making financial decisions. These chapters provide essential information for effective decision making.

Part Three examines the fundamental concepts of financial management in detail. We begin by considering the time value of money. The next topic is valuation—that is, how bonds and stocks are valued. Finally, we consider risk and the required rate of return on financial assets like bonds and stock. Chapters 5, 6, and 7 provide basic concepts employed throughout the book when financial decisions are considered.

The investment in long-term, or capital, assets is the topic of Part Four. We start by considering how to determine the relevant cash flows and the basics of capital budgeting. Then we consider replacement decisions and other more advanced aspects of the capital budgeting process. We then examine how risk affects the decision. These three chapters, 8, 9, and 10, examine techniques used widely in making capital investment decisions. Finally, for those wanting more advanced treatment, Chapter 11 introduces the ideas of options and option pricing theory, in order to understand more about capital budgeting decision making.

Part Five focuses on five very important topics. First is understanding more about obtaining long-term funding using common stock or debt (Chapters 12 and 13). The second is determining the appropriate required rate of return to use for financial decision making (Chapter 14). Then we examine the topic of how much debt versus equity the firm should have (Chapter 15). We then consider the internal generation of cash by the firm and how this relates to the cash dividend decision (Chapter 16). Finally, the topic of leasing is considered in Chapter 17.

In Part Six, our attention shifts to short-term assets and financing. First, we consider what working capital is, and how changes in current assets or current liabilities affect it. Then we examine cash and marketable securities, accounts receivable, inventory, and short-term financing. Chapters 18, 19, 20, and 21 are important, because of the tremendous size of working capital for most firms. Its management is an ongoing, day-to-day activity of the firm.

Part Seven deals with financial strategy. In Chapter 22 we examine the fascinating topics of mergers and corporate restructuring. Then in Chapter 23 we consider financial planning and strategy, along with how firms attempt to accomplish this important task. In Chapter 24 we consider various aspects of international financial management, in addition to the selected coverage provided in prior chapters.

Summary

Financial management involves the acquisition, management, and financing of resources for firms by means of money, with due regard for prices in external economic markets.

It is concerned with the efficient utilization of resources. The firm, however, does not operate in a vacuum, and is directly affected by its external environment in two primary ways: (1) by paying the amount required to secure both short-term and long-term financing; and (2) by having the ultimate success of the firm determined by how the financial marketplace values the firm. The stock price, which indicates the firm's economic value in the marketplace, is the ultimate indicator of how effective the firm is.

Three variables influence the determination of the firm's value in the marketplace: (1) the magnitude of its cash flows, (2) the timing of those cash flows, and (3) the risks involved. The study of financial management is built on these ideas, along with the concept of valuation. Financial management is of concern to everyone, because only if the firm acquires, manages, and uses its resources efficiently will owners, managers, employees, and society as a whole benefit to the fullest.

Questions

1.1 Define or explain the following:

a. Leveraged buyout (LBO)
b. Finance
c. Financial management
d. Proprietorship
e. Partnership
f. Corporation
g. Common stock
h. Bond
i. Stockholder wealth maximization
j. Agent
k. Agency cost

l. Proxy fight
m. Creditors
n. Book value
o. Cash flow
p. Timing
q. Risk
r. Valuation
s. Financial manager
t. Chief financial officer (CFO)
u. Treasurer
v. Controller

1.2 Explain what is meant by the statement "Financial management is the acquisition, management, and financing of resources for firms by means of money, with due regard for prices in external economic markets."

1.3 How can the firm be viewed as a pie? Make sure to distinguish between the ingredients that go into the pie, and the factors that determine the ultimate size of the pie.

1.4 Comment on the following statement, overheard in the executive suite: "Chris, I'm on the horns of a dilemma since I'm going to be judged by the common stockholders on the basis of market price, over which I have absolutely no control. In fact, I can't even control sales or earnings per share as well as I'd like, and they are the primary determinants of the market price."

1.5 What is meant by the terms "agency relationships" and "agency costs"? How do they relate to the idea of constraints on the objective of maximizing the value of stockholder claims on the firm?

1.6 There are agency costs related to both managers and creditors. How do they differ from each other? What is their effect?

1.7 Explain how cash flows, timing, and risk relate to the firm's objective of maximizing the value of stockholder claims on the firm.

1.8   Why does the firm have to be concerned about external economic conditions and the perceptions of the financial marketplace as it considers and makes financial decisions?

References

For more on financial theory, decision making, and its effect, see

COOLEY, PHILIP L., AND J. LOUIS HECK. "Significant Contributions to Finance Literature." *Financial Management* 10 (Tenth Anniversary Issue, 1981), pp. 23–33.

COPELAND, THOMAS E., AND J. FRED WESTON. *Financial Theory and Corporate Policy,* 3rd ed. Reading, Mass.: Addison–Wesley, 1988.

RAPPAPORT, ALFRED. *Creating Shareholder Value: The New Standard for Performance.* New York: Free Press, 1986.

Information on agency and other stakeholders can be obtained in

BARNEA, AMIR, ROBERT A. HAUGEN, AND LEMMA W. SENBET. *Agency Problems and Financial Contracting.* Englewood Cliffs, N.J.: Prentice-Hall, 1985.

CORNELL, BRADFORD, AND ALAN C. SHAPIRO. "Corporate Stakeholders and Corporate Finance." *Financial Management* 16 (Spring 1987), pp. 5–14.

JENSEN, MICHAEL, AND WILLIAM H. MECKLING. "Theory of the Firm: Managerial Behavior, Agency Costs, and Ownership Structure." *Journal of Financial Economics* 2 (October 1976), pp. 305–360.

Managerial salaries and related topics are discussed in

Symposium on "The Distribution of Power Among Corporate Managers, Shareholders, and Directors," a special issue of the *Journal of Financial Economics* 20 (January/ March 1988).

BAKER, GEORGE P., MICHAEL C. JENSEN, AND KEVIN J. MURPHY. "Compensation and Incentives: Practice vs. Theory." *Journal of Finance* 43 (July 1988), pp. 593–616.

MURPHY, KEVIN J. "Top Executives Are Worth Every Nickel They Get." *Harvard Business Review* 64 (March-April 1986), pp. 125–132.

NARAYANAN, M. P. "Managerial Incentives for Short-term Results." *Journal of Finance* 40 (December 1985), pp. 1469–1484.

2

The Financial System, Interest Rates, and Taxes

Overview

- The financial system consists of financial markets and institutions. Its goal is to provide an effective means of bringing together suppliers and demanders of funds.

- Interest is the cost paid by a borrower or the return earned by a supplier of funds. Expected inflation and risk premiums directly affect interest rates.

- Our financial markets are reasonably efficient. This means market prices rapidly reflect all known information, including risk considerations. Exposure to additional risk increases the required return.

- Taxes directly affect cash flows; therefore, they are an important consideration in many financial decisions.

In the face of lower earnings, ITT announced it was cutting its cash dividend by nearly two-thirds so it could afford heavy investments in the U.S. telecommunications business. By the end of the day, the price of ITT's common stock had dropped by roughly a third. This dramatic decline in price was due in large part to the actions of institutional money managers, who control more than $1 trillion in holdings and an estimated 60 percent of corporate stocks and bonds. Some people are concerned about the influence these relatively few managers can have on bond and stock prices.

During the past few years federal regulators have had to step in and rescue many banks and savings and loan associations. All we seem to hear is the bad news—but the Federal Deposit Insurance Corporation can point to a major success with Continental Illinois Bank. Their stake in Continental, obtained in 1984 in the largest financial bailout to date, has recently dropped as ownership was resold to the public. In the process of achieving this turnaround, Continental Illinois shed its retail banking units to concentrate on institutional investors and midsize and smaller companies. As major changes sweep the financial industry, other financials will have to make equally tough choices to survive and prosper.

Recently, American Express joined a number of other firms—such as McDonald's, Philip Morris, 3M, and Walt Disney—in having its common stock listed on the Tokyo Stock Exchange. "We think," Amex said in explanation, "it broadens the market for American Express stock with investors around the world, and will enhance our reputation in Japan because there will be a lot of publicity surrounding the listing." Japan is the second largest economy in the world. Obviously, American Express is hoping to increase use of its credit card and other services in Japan.

As we know from Chapter 1, a firm does not operate in a vacuum. Its financial performance, cash flows, and ability to raise and invest funds are determined by its actions within the financial environment of markets, institutions, and interest rates. Understanding the financial environment is important for effective financial decision making.

Our Financial System

The fundamental goal of our financial system is to help transform the savings (income minus consumption) of individuals, firms, or governments into investments (the purchase of assets to produce goods or services) by others. If one individual, Frank Thomas, and Xerox both have excess funds, the function of the financial system is to channel these funds to governments, individuals, and firms. This transfer of funds almost always results in the creation of financial assets by the suppliers of funds, and of financial liabilities by the demanders of funds. The purpose of the financial system is to provide an effective means of bringing together suppliers and demanders of capital. The basic relationships are shown in Figure 2.1. Note, however, that not only are suppliers and demanders part of the system, but so are the financial institutions and financial markets that have evolved to increase the efficiency and smoothness of the system.

Financial Institutions

Financial institutions, or *financial intermediaries* as they are called, often come between suppliers and demanders of funds. Intermediaries accept savings, and in return the suppliers of funds acquire claims against the intermediaries. Then the intermediaries make loans or investments to the demanders of funds. As a reward for entrusting savings to a financial intermediary, the supplier expects some return in the form of interest or cash dividends. Among the advantages of handling money transfers through financial institutions are that they (1) provide flexibility and liquidity, (2) are convenient, (3) provide expertise, and (4) spread the risk.

The major institutions in our financial system include these:

1. Commercial banks, the traditional department stores of finance. Because of the deregulation of interest rates[1] and certain other changes, the role of banks is undergoing fundamental change.

---

[1] Under the Depository Institutions Deregulation and Monetary Control Act of 1980, the Depository Institutions Deregulation Committee phased out the ceiling on interest rates thrift institutions could pay depositors.

Figure 2.1 Relationship Among Suppliers and Demanders of Funds, Financial Institutions, and Financial Markets

Funds are supplied through the financial markets directly or by going through financial institutions. A well-developed network of financial institutions and effective financial markets are important for financial management.

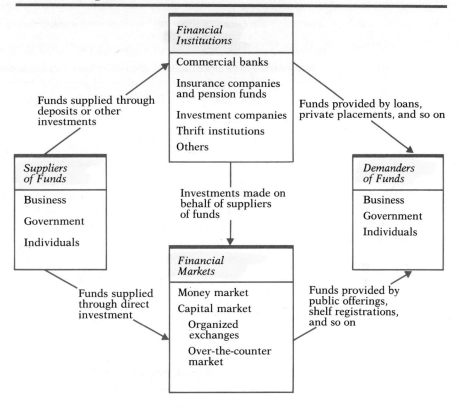

2. Insurance companies and pension funds, including life insurance companies, fire and casualty companies, and private and government retirement plans.
3. Investment companies, including various mutual funds in which investors pool their funds into a large fund managed by an investment advisor.[2] Mutual funds have traditionally invested in stocks and bonds; a more recent innovation is money market mutual funds, which grew rapidly because they provided investors higher returns than either banks or savings and loan associations. However, as financial deregulation has progressed, and as interest rates have fallen, the assets of some money market funds have also fallen.
4. Thrift institutions, including savings and loan associations, mutual savings banks, and credit unions.

[2] Mutual funds are sometimes called "open-end" investment companies because they continually sell and redeem shares. A much smaller number of investment companies are "closed-end"; they do not sell and redeem their shares.

5. Other financial organizations including finance companies, mortgage companies, and real estate investment trusts.

Financial institutions are currently undergoing a profound restructuring. The primary causes behind this trend include (1) the deregulation of interest rate ceilings, allowing financial institutions to broaden their services; (2) interstate banking; and (3) entry or expansion of firms into the financial institutions business. Financial institutions provide a substantial portion of the funds available to corporations and other demanders of funds. Commercial banks have been the largest supplier of funds in recent years. Financial institutions often purchase stocks or bonds through the financial markets. Firms may also approach a financial institution to make a *private placement* of a new stock or bond issue. If Georgia Pacific, for example, needs to raise additional funds, it might approach the New York State retirement system directly for private placement of a new issue of bonds. Whether the financial institutions interact directly with the demanders of funds through loans or private placements, or indirectly through the financial markets, the important point to remember is that these institutions play a major role in assuring the smooth flow of funds in our economy. In fact, a hallmark of most developed countries is an extensive set of financial institutions, or some other mechanism (such as government agencies or trading groups of interrelated companies) for seeing that suppliers and demanders of funds are brought together.

In the United States, *investment bankers* provide assistance to firms needing funds. The investment banker often purchases new stock or bond issues from the firm and immediately resells them to investors—the suppliers of funds. Investment bankers bring suppliers and demanders together by providing the firm with expertise and marketing capabilities. Without investment bankers (see Chapter 12), the financial markets would not operate as smoothly as they do.

Financial Markets

Financial markets exist whenever a financial transaction takes place. For our purposes, it is helpful to divide financial markets into two general types—the money market and the capital market. The *money market* is the market for short-term (one year or less) debts. It also includes securities originally issued with maturities of more than one year but that now have a year or less until maturity. The tremendous growth of the money markets in the last decade created opportunities for both investors and firms. Investors have a wide variety of short-term investments to choose from, while firms (and other demanders such as the government) can secure short-term financing more easily than ever before.

In contrast to the short-term or money market is the *capital market,* which is the market for long-term bonds or stocks. Included in the capital markets are (1) long-term U.S. government notes or bonds; (2) longer-term government agency issues;[3] (3) municipal bonds; (4) various forms of debt issued by firms; and (5) common and *preferred stock*[4] issued by firms. The primary distinguishing feature of

---

[3] A government agency is one sponsored or created by the federal government to serve some public purpose. Many of these agencies can issue bonds and notes, although the issues are not directly backed by the federal government.

[4] Preferred stock represents ownership that has a prior but limited claim on assets and income before common stock. Cash dividends usually cannot be paid on common stock until after they have been paid on preferred stock.

the securities that comprise the capital markets is their life—they all have an anticipated life of longer than one year. They may range from a 5-year note issued by the government or some business to common stock that has no specified maturity date.

All securities when they are originally offered—that is, with the proceeds of the sale going to the issuer of the securities—are issued in the *primary market*. (This applies to both money market and capital market securities.) By primary, we are saying that the proceeds go to the principal, which is typically some government unit or corporation. After the securities begin to trade between individuals and/or institutional investors, they become part of the *secondary market*. In the secondary market, the original issuer has no part in the transaction. This market exists to facilitate investor trading.

A well-developed secondary market is important for two reasons. First, by creating the mechanism for trading, it enables investors to add to or liquidate holdings easily. If an institution wishes to sell 10,000 shares of McDonald's common stock, the transaction can be made quickly and efficiently because of the existence of a fully developed secondary market. The second reason secondary markets are important is that they make issuing additional securities by firms (or governments) easier. Since investors know they can buy and sell securities easily, they will be more likely to purchase the original issue. The existence of a well-developed secondary market therefore has important implications for financial management. Without secondary markets, firms would have to use very different financing strategies because issuing both short- and long-term securities would be much more difficult. We might have smaller firms that financed most of their capital needs with internally generated funds. Another alternative would be for more direct government financing of firms, as is true in countries that have less well-developed secondary markets.

Transactions in the secondary market occur on *organized security exchanges* or in the over-the-counter market. Among organized exchanges, the New York Stock Exchange (NYSE) is the second largest (in total dollar volume) secondary market for stocks in the world. Approximately 1,500 common stocks and numerous preferred stocks are listed on the NYSE (or the Big Board, as it is often called). It accounts for about 70 percent of the total dollar value of all stock outstanding in the United States. The next largest is the American Stock Exchange, which has more than 1,300 stocks listed. Other stocks are traded on various regional stock exchanges. If they are unlisted, they trade in the *over-the-counter (OTC) market*. OTC is the term used to describe all buying and selling activity that does not take place on an organized exchange. The OTC market is made up of security dealers or brokers who, using telecommunications, interact to create a market for various securities. In addition to the common stock of many smaller companies, most bonds are also traded in the OTC market. All government securities are traded in the OTC market. The one exception is that corporate bonds issued by large firms are usually traded on the New York Exchange.

The Government's Role

Although it does not appear in Figure 2.1, the federal government has a major impact on the domestic financial system. (1) It provides regulation and support; (2) it has statutory authority over the Federal Reserve system; and (3) it makes fiscal policy.

America's Secondary Equity Markets

Stocks in the United States are traded either on exchanges or in the over-the-counter (OTC) market. The primary exchange is the New York Stock Exchange (NYSE); the other exchanges are the American Stock Exchange (AMEX) and the regionals—the Boston Stock Exchange (BSE), the Cincinnati Stock Exchange (CSE), the Midwest Stock Exchange (MSE), the Pacific Coast Stock Exchange (PSE), and the Philadelphia Stock Exchange (Phlx). Trading in the OTC market is through the National Association of Securities Dealers Automated Quotation (NASDAQ) system. In 1987 the share and dollar volume for these trading places were as follow:

	Share Volume		Dollar Volume	
	(In millions)	Percent	(In millions)	Percent
NYSE	47,801	49.0%	$1,873,597	69.0%
AMEX	3,506	3.6	52,548	1.9
Regionals (BSE, CSE, MSE, PSE, and Phlx)	7,156	7.3	247,516	9.1
NASDAQ	37,890	38.9	499,855	18.4
NASDAQ/OTC trading in listed securities	1,170	1.2	43,489	1.6
Total	97,523	100.0%	$2,717,005	100.0%

In both share and dollar volume the New York Stock Exchange dominates the trading in the United States. NASDAQ, however, is second in both share and dollar volume, followed by the regionals and then the American Stock Exchange. To give you some idea of the differences in the number of issues and firms, for the New York Stock Exchange the trading was made up of 2,244 issues for 1,647 companies. For NASDAQ it comprised 5,337 issues for 4,706 companies. Finally, for the AMEX it was 1,072 securities issued by 869 companies.

Regulation and Support

The U.S. government regulates or supports many activities of the domestic financial system. The issuance of securities in the primary market, unless they are privately placed, is regulated by the Securities and Exchange Commission (see Chapter 12). The Comptroller of the Currency regulates certain aspects of banking, and the Federal Reserve system plays a major role in shaping monetary policy. The Federal Deposit Insurance Corporation insures deposits in banks, and the Federal Home Loan Bank system has regulated savings and loan associations. Many other government agencies, such as the Federal Housing Administration and Farm Credit Administration, also affect the financial system.

The Federal Reserve System

The *Federal Reserve system,* or the Fed, has at its disposal an array of tools that can influence the operations of commercial banks and, therefore, the entire financial system. A powerful Fed tool, and the one used least, is to change the reserve requirement (the percentage of deposits member banks must keep on reserve at the Fed). Two other important tools are (1) to change its pattern of open-market operations, or (2) to change the discount rate. Through purchases or sales of securities, the open-market operations of the Fed can expand or shrink the amount of money in the public's hands. Likewise, by raising or lowering the discount rate (that is, the rate charged to commercial banks when they borrow at Federal Reserve banks), the Fed can affect the cost of funds and signal its intentions as economic conditions change. All these actions can affect the availability and costs of funds provided through the financial system.

Fiscal Policy

In addition to monetary policy, the fiscal policy followed by the federal government also has a great impact on the cost and availability of funds. In recent years, with large government deficits and increased defense spending, fiscal policy has tended to stimulate the economy. However, to finance these deficits, the federal government has had to issue more Treasury bills, notes, and bonds. The impact of high government deficit financing on the American economy has been twofold. First, it has increased the demand for funds; this, other things being equal, has tended to keep interest rates up. Second, corporations have been "crowded out" at times because not enough funds have been available to supply their needs after the demands of the federal government have been met. This happens when big new government issues temporarily lower government security prices and raise the rate of interest the government pays. Even if the funds are available, the cost rises because of the government's action.

International Financial Markets

In addition to the domestic financial market, the financial marketplace is now world-wide. Large U.S. firms routinely issue bonds or secure short-term financing overseas. Some even list their stock on foreign stock exchanges. While many of the same forces are at work world-wide, there are two fundamental differences. First, the role of a single government, or governmental unit such as the Fed, is diminished since funds tend to flow fairly freely between many countries. Second, exchange rates can and do change between various currencies. As discussed in Chapter 24, understanding exchange rates is important for financial managers who deal in international financial management transactions.

Why Is the Financial System Important?

You may already see the need to know about financial institutions and markets. Here are some of the reasons:

1. The financial system provides an effective means of bringing together suppliers and demanders of funds. It enables firms that have excess funds, or firms that need funds, to make transactions quickly and cheaply.
2. The financial system includes the crucial secondary market. By facilitating the buying and selling of outstanding securities, an organized secondary market makes it easier for a firm to raise external debt or equity capital.

3. The financial system changes rapidly, affording new opportunities. Every year new institutions, securities, and markets appear. These allow astute firms to use new sources or securities for raising capital.
4. The value of the firm is determined in the financial markets. That value depends on the interaction of supply and demand in the financial marketplace—given the external business environment and management's strategies and policy decisions. The welfare of the firm—and its employees, managers, owners, and creditors—rests directly on the value of the firm's stock as determined in the financial markets.

Interest Rates and the Required Rate of Return

In a free economy, capital is allocated by means of the price system—that is, through the interaction of supply and demand. The cost of debt capital is reflected in the interest rate paid by the firm, while the cost of equity capital is a function of both cash dividends and the price of the stock. In this section, we seek to understand how rates, inflation, and risk interact.

Interest Rates

Interest rates are the prices paid when an individual, firm, or governmental unit borrows funds. *Interest* is the cost incurred by demanders of funds when they use debt financing. From the suppliers' standpoint, interest is what they earn when money is loaned to someone else. So, interest is both a cost and a revenue—it just depends on whether we are a demander or a supplier of funds. Interest is generally stated on a percentage per year basis. If you borrow $1,000 (the *principal*) and agree to repay $1,080 (principal plus interest) in one year, you are paying 8 percent interest for the use of the funds. Even if you borrow or lend for periods longer or shorter than one year, the interest is almost always stated on an annual basis.

Real Rate of Interest

In a perfect world with no expected inflation, or risk premiums, the cost of funds would be determined solely by the interaction of the supply of loanable funds from savings and the demand for loanable funds for investment. As shown in Figure 2.2, the *real rate of interest*, k_{real}, is an equilibrium rate that is a function of the aggregate supply of and demand for capital. This real rate of interest is not static, but fluctuates over time as actions by suppliers, the Federal Reserve Board, and others determine the amount of loanable funds available for investment. The demand for funds comes from firms, individuals, and government. As the need for funds strengthens or weakens, the demand curve for loanable funds shifts. As the supply of funds decreases or the demand increases (and assuming no other changes), the real rate of interest rises. Correspondingly, an increase in supply or a reduction in demand results in lowering the real rate of interest. The real interest rate is thus a function of the actions of the government and the state of the economy since both influence the supply and demand for funds.

Figure 2.2 Supply of and Demand for Loanable Funds

In a perfect market, the real rate of interest is an equilibrium rate resulting from the intersection of the supply of loanable funds (savings) and the demand for loanable funds (for investment purposes).

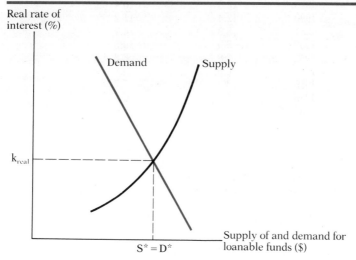

Real rate of interest (%)

Demand

Supply

k_{real}

$S^* = D^*$

Supply of and demand for loanable funds ($)

Expected Inflation

Inflation refers to a change in purchasing power as reflected by changes in the price level. Expected inflation has a direct impact on interest rates because suppliers of funds will demand a higher rate to make up for being paid back in dollars that have less purchasing power. The result is that interest rates rise when a high rate of inflation is expected and fall when the rate of expected inflation is low (*disinflation*).

There is a relationship between the expected rate of inflation and the observed (or nominal) rate of interest, called the *Fisher effect:* The *nominal interest rate,* k_{nom}, is equal to the real rate of interest, plus an *inflation premium* so that

$$\text{nominal rate of interest} = \text{real rate of interest} + \text{expected rate of inflation} \tag{2.1}$$

U.S. *Treasury bills,* which are short-term borrowings of the U.S. government, are the best proxy we have for the short-term nominal rate of interest. This rate is often called the *risk-free rate,* k_{RF}. We can rewrite Equation 2.1 as follows:

$$\text{risk-free rate} = \text{real rate of interest} + \text{inflation premium} \tag{2.2}$$

The risk-free rate encompasses both the real rate of return plus a premium for expected inflation.

The real rate of interest is thought to be around 1 to 2 percent. Thus, we would predict the risk-free rate, k_{RF}, to be 1 to 2 percent above the expected rate of inflation. To see if this is true, look at the following, which compares the rate of interest on U.S. Treasury bills with changes in inflation.

Year	Consumer Price Index (Percent Change)	Yield on U.S. Treasury Bills
1978	9.0	7.2
1979	13.3	10.4
1980	12.4	11.2
1981	8.9	14.7
1982	3.9	10.5
1983	3.8	8.8
1984	4.0	9.8
1985	3.8	7.7
1986	1.1	6.2
1987	4.4	5.5
Mean	6.5	9.2

SOURCE: Ibbotson, Roger G., and Rex A. Sinquefield. *Stocks, Bonds, Bills, and Inflation* (SBBI), 1982, updated in *Stocks, Bonds, Bills and Inflation 1988 yearbook.*™ Ibbotson Associates, Chicago. All rights reserved.

Over the period from 1978 to 1987, the nominal rate of return on Treasury bills was 9.2 percent, while the rate of inflation was 6.5 percent. Interest rates and inflation did not move exactly together, nor was the nominal rate of interest 1 to 2 percent greater than actual inflation. Why? There are at least three reasons: (1) Some of the inflation may not have been expected. (2) Inflationary expectations tend to lag behind actual inflation. (3) The movement of interest rates may be slow to adjust to changes in expected inflation. But regardless of the failure of nominal interest rates to reflect inflation exactly, there is an important relationship between expected inflation and interest rates.

Maturity Premium

So far we have considered the real rate of interest and the effect of expected inflation on interest rates. The security examined, U.S. Treasury bills, has an initial maturity of 3 months, 6 months, or occasionally a year. Now we examine longer-term debt offerings of the U.S. government. As we will see in Chapter 6, the market prices of long-term bonds decline much more sharply than market prices of short-term bonds whenever overall interest rates rise. This gives rise to a *maturity premium* to compensate for this additional risk. The effect is to raise the rates on long-term bonds relative to those on short-term bonds. In recent years the maturity premium on long-term government bonds has been one to two percentage points.

The Term Structure of Interest Rates

U.S. Treasury securities are free of any default risk, since there is virtual certainty that the government will pay interest on the bonds, and redeem them in full and on time when they mature. Thus, the nominal return on any government security is equal to the real rate of interest, an inflation premium, and a maturity premium. The nominal rates of return for U.S. Treasury securities as of December 1980 and December 1987 are plotted in Figure 2.3. The lines are called *yield curves,* and the graphs depict the *term structure* of interest rates for a given risk class of securities.

Figure 2.3   The Term Structure as of December 1980 and December 1987

A downward-sloping yield curve occurs when inflation is expected to decrease. An upward-sloping yield curve occurs when inflation is expected to increase. (SOURCE: Federal Reserve *Bulletin, various issues.*)

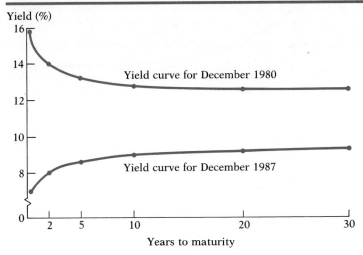

The risk class we are examining is Treasury securities; a similar but higher yield curve exists for various classes of corporate debt. A downward-sloping yield curve, such as that in December 1980, indicates lower expected rates of inflation. An upward-sloping yield curve, like that in December 1987, indicates higher inflation expected in the future. Here are some observations concerning yield curves:

1. They fluctuate depending on the general supply and demand for funds.
2. Their shape changes from downward-sloping, to being flat, to upward-sloping depending on the future rate of inflation expected by investors.
3. Yield curves for firms will be above those of the government. The more risky the firm is perceived to be, the higher the yield curve.

The yield curves plotted in Figure 2.3 also embody the maturity premium. This maturity premium increases with the length to maturity of any bond. The effect can be seen in Figure 2.4, where the solid line depicts the nominal yield curve, which encompasses both the inflation and maturity premiums along with the real rate of interest. The dashed lines, which lie below the nominal yield curve, indicate what the yield curves would look like if no maturity premium existed.

Default Premium

The risk that a corporate borrower will not pay interest and principal on a bond is greater than the risk of the U.S. government not meeting its obligations. This additional risk is called default risk, and is shown by the *default premium*. Corporate bonds are rated as to their investment quality from triple A, the highest rating for very sound firms, to C or below, for bonds in default. The higher the quality of a

Figure 2.4 Effect of the Maturity Premium on Yield Curves

Maturity premiums, which arise due to the heightened interest-rate sensitivity of longer-term bonds, increase with the maturity of the bond.

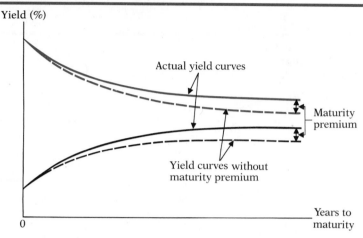

bond, the higher its rating and the lower its nominal interest rate. Here are some recent interest rates:

U.S. Treasury, 20-year	9.02%
Aaa corporate	9.82
Aa corporate	10.06
A corporate	10.34
Baa corporate	10.90

The difference between the yield on a Treasury bond and a corporate bond of equal maturity is its default premium.[5] For the data above, the default premium on high-quality Aaa corporate bonds was 0.80% (9.82% − 9.02%) while it increased with Baa bonds to 1.88% (10.90% − 9.02%).

The "Risk Premium"

So far we have examined three risk premiums for bonds—those related to expected inflation, maturity, and default. But there are other sources of risk for corporate securities. Two risks in particular are the liquidity of the security, and its nature and characteristics. The *liquidity premium* arises for securities for which there is no active market, so liquidity cannot be assured. For example, assume you own 100 shares of Jose's Bakery, a small local firm. If you decide to sell the stock, you may face some time delay or receive less from the buyer due to the lack of a readily available secondary market. While it is difficult to measure liquidity premiums, they may be between 1 and 2 percent for illiquid versus liquid issues.

A second type of risk relates to the basic nature and characteristics of the security. This *issue-specific premium* arises from the types of securities (and the provisions attached to them) that firms issue. As discussed in Chapter 13, the presence or

---

[5] This assumes there is no liquidity or issue-specific premium, both of which are discussed in the next section.

absence of certain issue-specific features—such as callability, convertibility, or sinking fund provisions—is present with bonds. Likewise, consider investing in a long-term bond of Kroger versus investing in Kroger common stock. With the bond, you have a legal claim on the firm that must be met before any cash flows go to pay cash dividends. If you invest in Kroger common stock, you have the last claim on the firm's cash flows, and Kroger does not legally have to pay you a cash dividend. You may become rich if Kroger prospers; on the other hand, you may receive nothing. So there is more issue-specific risk with the common stock of a firm than with its long-term debt.

The term *risk premium* in finance is used to reflect the risks over and above the risk-free rate, k_{RF}. The risk premium is equal to

$$\text{risk premium} = \frac{\text{maturity}}{\text{premium}} + \frac{\text{default}}{\text{premium}} + \frac{\text{liquidity}}{\text{premium}} + \frac{\text{issue-specific}}{\text{premium}} \qquad (2.3)$$

The investors' *required rate of return*, k, is equal to (1) the risk-free rate, and (2) the risk premium. Thus,

$$\text{required return} = \text{risk-free rate} + \text{risk premium} \qquad (2.4)$$
$$k = k_{RF} + \text{risk premium}$$

Short-term debt securities, such as some issued by General Motors, will have a very small risk premium (over the risk-free rate). On the other hand, if you hold the common stock of Jose's Bakery, you carry a substantial risk. Other things being equal, you will require a higher rate of return from investing in Jose's Bakery than from investing in General Motors.

Required Rates of Return, Business Decisions, and Stock Prices

Required rates represent the return expected by investors and the cost incurred by the firm. While we usually think of required rates being associated with the interest cost of debt, the same relationship between return and cost also exists for common equity. Here are some key points related to required rates:

1. If the term structure is downward-sloping, long-term debt is cheaper than short-term debt. This suggests that long-term debt may be a better or more likely financing source. However, that is not always so. Firms may choose intermediate (3- to 7-year) term debt when faced with a downward-sloping yield curve because they feel the whole term structure may decline dramatically in the near future. If it subsequently does decline, long-term debt financing can then be obtained at substantially lower rates.
2. As inflation wanes, the whole term structure generally shifts downward. Short-term rates drop more than long-term rates, resulting in an upward-sloping yield curve at a lower level than previously existed.
3. Interest rates on bonds tend to fall during recessions.
4. Interest, as discussed shortly, is a tax-deductible expense for the firm.
5. Common stock, because of its greater risk premium (when compared with debt), costs the firm more. Stated another way, because of the greater risk associated with common stock, investors have a higher required return when they make a common stock investment. Also, since cash dividends are not a tax-deductible expense, they have to be paid out of the firm's after-tax cash flows. These factors—

increased risk and the tax consequences—make common equity more expensive than debt to the firm.

6. Stock prices are generally moved by two forces—changes in interest rates and changes in the firm's cash flows or risk. Typically, stock prices rise when interest rates fall. This occurs because with falling interest rates, investors switch their money into stocks. This buying pressure tends to move the market price of stocks up. However, if interest rates are falling because of a recession, the upward pressure due to falling interest rates is offset, at least in part, by lower expected cash flows for the firm.

Risk, Return, and Market Efficiency

Risk and Required Return

While the topic of risk and the return required by investors is explored in more depth in Chapter 7, it is important to establish this fundamental relationship here. It is also the relationship between risk and cost to the issuer. Looking at it from the investor's viewpoint, if you expose yourself to more risk, you expect a higher return. This higher return has to come from somewhere, and in this case it comes from the higher costs of raising capital borne by the firm.

To understand more about risk and return, let us examine data for the 1961–1987 period. Figure 2.5 shows graphically the growth of a dollar invested in small company common stocks, common stocks, long-term corporate bonds, and long-term government bonds. All results assume reinvestment of dividends or interest, and no taxes. Each of the indexes is initiated at $1.00 at the end of 1960. The figure shows that the return from small common stocks—over this time period—was far greater than the other securities shown. If $1.00 had been invested in small common stocks at the end of 1960, it would have grown to $41.74 by the end of 1987. Likewise, for common stocks $1.00 would have grown to $12.23, while a dollar invested in long-term corporate or government bonds would have grown to only $5.24 and $4.39, respectively. For comparison, inflation is also graphed. What we purchased for $1.00 at the end of 1960 required an expenditure of $3.87 by the end of 1987. While all four securities outperformed inflation, small common stocks were the big winner.

This return is not without substantial risk, however. In Figure 2.6 the annual percentage returns for the four securities are presented. Note that the variability of return for small common stocks is much greater than for common stocks. Likewise, the variability of returns for both long-term corporate and government bonds are less than for common stocks. Finally, note that the direction and magnitude of the returns are not consistent across the four securities, or over time.

These two figures visually demonstrate that higher return and higher risk typically go hand-in-hand. As risk increases for different classes or types of securities, so does the return demanded by investors. This tradeoff is depicted in Figure 2.7. To increase their required, or expected, return, investors must increase their exposure to risk. This relationship between risk and return (or the cost to the firm) is very important and will be pursued throughout this book. For now, all you need to remember is this: If a firm increases its risk exposure, it increases the return demanded by

Figure 2.5 Return Indices, 1960–1987

The vertical scale is logarithmic; equal distances represent equal percentage changes any place along the scale. Small stocks were the big winners over this time period. SOURCE: *Ibbotson, Roger G., and Rex A. Sinquefield.* Stocks, Bonds, Bills, and Inflation *(SBBI), 1982, updated in* Stocks, Bonds, Bills, and Inflation 1988 Yearbook.™ *Ibbotson Associates, Chicago. All rights reserved.*

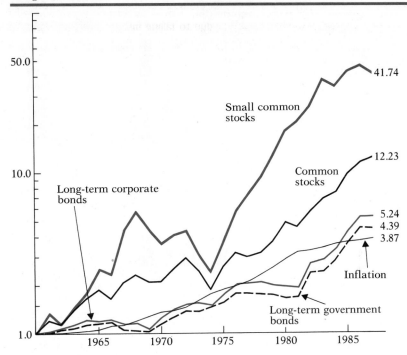

investors, and hence its costs. *There is no free lunch; increases in risk cause increases in costs.*

Two other points should be mentioned here. First, what is the relevant measure of risk will be examined in detail in Chapter 7. Second, while small common stocks outperformed common stocks in general for the 1961–1987 period, this relationship does not hold for all possible time periods. For example, from the end of 1983 to the end of 1987, common stocks substantially outperformed small common stocks. It is important to remember that for any specific subperiod, the results for any of the securities may deviate dramatically from those illustrated in Figure 2.5.

Market Efficiency

An *efficient market* is one in which security prices (of stocks, bonds, etc.) adjust rapidly to the announcement of new information so that current market prices fully reflect all available information regarding the security. For markets to be efficient, the following conditions must hold:

1. A large number of profit-maximizing individuals must analyze and value securities, and act independently of one another.

Figure 2.6   Annual Percentage Returns, 1961–1987

Common stocks, especially small stocks, exhibit much more volatility in their returns than do bonds. SOURCE: *Ibbotson, Roger G., and Rex A. Sinquefield. Stocks, Bonds, Bills, and Inflation (SBBI), 1982, updated in* Stocks, Bonds, Bills, and Inflation 1988 Yearbook.™ *Ibbotson Associates, Chicago. All rights reserved.*

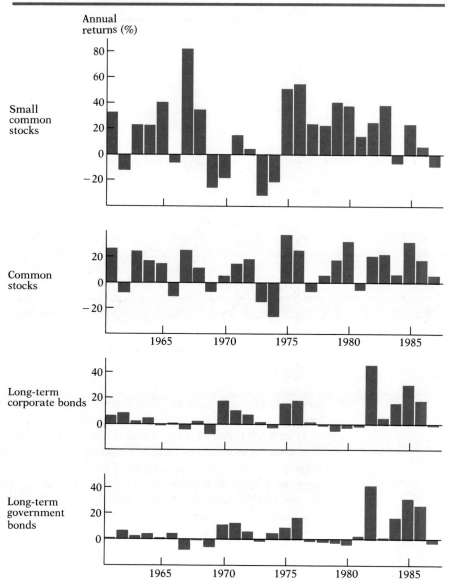

Figure 2.7 Relationship Between Required Return (or Cost to the Issuer) and Risk

U.S. Treasury bills provide a risk-free return. As risk increases, as evidenced by maturity, default, liquidity, or issue-specific premiums, the returns required by investors increase; so do the costs to the issuer.

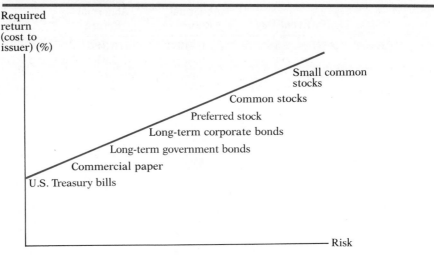

2. New information about the securities must arrive in a random fashion.
3. Investors, by reacting to new information quickly, must cause security prices to change so they reflect the influence of all the information available.

The implication of market efficiency is that prices always provide an unbiased indication of the worth of the security. It is unbiased because sometimes it may overadjust and at other times it may underadjust, but no one knows which it will be. In an efficient market, security prices reflect all available information, including risks. Over the last two decades, many tests of market efficiency have been conducted. The general conclusion is that security markets in the United States are reasonably efficient, and that prices tend to reflect both the information known and the risks involved.

To gain additional understanding of the concept and importance of market efficiency, let us examine the results of a recent study[6] focusing on the stock market reaction to the adoption of stock purchase plans. In the most common type of stock purchase plan, the firm lends the employee funds to purchase the stock at its fair market value. In another variety of stock purchase plans, the employee pays for only part of the stock and the firm contributes the remainder. The question addressed in this study was whether there was any stock market reaction to the announcement of these plans. That is, did these plans impact the value of the firm, and, if so, how much and in what direction?

[6] Bhagat, Sanjai, James A. Brickley, and Ronald C. Lease. "Incentive Effects of Stock Purchase Plans." *Journal of Financial Economics* 14 (June 1985), pp. 195–215.

Table 2.1 Abnormal Returns for Stock Purchase Plans

Day zero (0) is when the plans were announced. All returns reflect both dividends and market price movements. SOURCE: Bhagat, Sanjai, James A. Brickley, and Ronald C. Lease. "Incentive Effects of Stock Purchase Plans." *Journal of Financial Economics* 14 (June 1985), p. 205.

Event Day	Abnormal Return	Cumulative Abnormal Return
−5	0.34%	0.34%
−4	0.59	0.93
−3	0.32	1.25
−2	−0.83	0.42
−1	0.53	0.95
0	1.81	2.76
1	1.62	4.38
2	−0.01	4.37
3	−0.04	4.33
4	−0.23	4.10
5	−0.74	3.36
2-day announcement period (−1, 0)		2.34

To determine the stock market reaction to the announcement of new information, numerous empirical studies have employed an approach that focuses on abnormal returns for stocks. An *abnormal return* is simply the difference, on any given day, between the actual stock market performance for a firm (or group of firms) and its expected performance.[7] In efficient markets a stock's abnormal returns on any given day should be sensitive to the release of new information. If relevant new information is released that has not previously been accounted for in a stock's market price, then the abnormal return should be positive (i.e., the price goes up) or negative (i.e., the price goes down). *Event studies* focus on the examination of whether new information causes prices (as reflected by abnormal returns) to increase or decrease.

The basic results of this study on the announcement of stock purchase plans are shown in Table 2.1. Day zero (0) is the date the information was made public. The abnormal returns are listed for days before and after day zero. In addition, the *cumulative abnormal returns,* which are just the cumulative sum of the daily abnormal returns, are also listed.

In the absence of any impact of the announcement on stock market prices, the cumulative abnormal returns should fluctuate around a return of zero. In Figure 2.8 we see that the cumulative abnormal return is above zero, signifying a positive stock market reaction to the announcement of the stock purchase plan. Also, at the bottom of Table 2.1 we have shown that the 2-day *announcement period* (day$_{-1}$ and day$_0$) return was 2.34 percent. Studies often focus on this 2-day return; if an announcement appears in print on day zero, the first public announcement typically had to have been made the day before. This 2-day announcement period often captures the market impact of the release of new information.

---

[7] In determining expected performance, the risk of the firm and the performance of the stock market as a whole are normally taken into account.

Figure 2.8 Cumulative Abnormal Returns for Stock Purchase Plans

In the absence of any impact, the cumulative abnormal returns would fluctuate around zero.
SOURCE: *Bhagat, Sanjai, James A. Brickley, and Ronald C. Lease. "Incentive Effects of Stock Purchase Plans."* Journal of Financial Economics *14 (June 1985).*

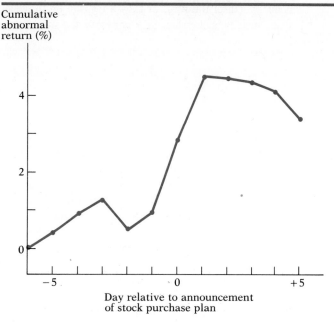

Day relative to announcement
of stock purchase plan

The authors of the study on stock purchase plans concluded that their announcement (1) had a positive impact on stockholder wealth; and (2) helped to align manager and shareholder interests. As such, stock purchase plans are viewed as a positive step by the financial markets.

Due to market efficiency, where prices react quickly and in an unbiased manner to new information, numerous other studies have investigated similar events. In our study of financial management we will consider some of the results of these studies and the impact of alternative managerial actions on the value of the firm.

The existence of reasonably efficient markets has a number of implications for managers. First, it bears a relation to the goal of maximizing the value of stockholder claims. If the security price is an unbiased indicator of the value of the firm, it provides an unbiased assessment of the performance of the firm. If managers want to perform well in the eyes of owners, they can be confident that the market price of the firm's stock provides a valid and reliable indicator. Second, trying to influence investors by providing lavish annual reports, briefings for financial analysts, or campaigns to "sell" the company to investors are likely to have no long-run effect on the value of the firm.[8] It could be argued that the firm would be better off if managers saved the money and time required of such persuasion and devoted themselves

---

[8] This is true unless there is some information value.

solely to improving the operating performance of the firm. This may have a much more important and lasting impact on the value of the firm. Third, comments by executives to the effect that their firm is "undervalued" are caused by a misunderstanding of the importance of the current market price as the primary indicator of the economic worth of the firm; or they are made on the basis of some other concept of value, such as book value. In either case, the statements reflect basic misconceptions.

Taxes[9]

The value of any financial asset—stocks, bonds, or even whole firms—depends on the stream of usable cash flows produced *after taxes are paid*. Because taxes reduce usable cash flows, effective tax planning is a major corporate responsibility. Any important undertaking, from a merger with another firm to the acquisition of a new fleet of trucks, affects the taxes the firm must pay. Any business, whether large or small, needs professional assistance in dealing with taxes. While state and local taxes also play a role in determining after-tax cash flows, we ignore their specifics, since they differ across the country. Moreover, the tax code is complex and ever-changing. We present only the essential elements.

Individual Income Taxes

Individuals pay federal income tax on their wages and salaries, on investment income, and on any proprietorship or partnership income. (Investment income includes dividends, interest, and profits from the sale of financial assets.) The amount of tax paid is based on the individual's taxable income; here are the 1989 rates for single taxpayers:

Individual's Taxable Income Increment*	Marginal Tax Rate
First $18,550	15%
18,551 to 44,900	28
Over 44,900	33 (due to a 5 percent surcharge)

* Taxable income = adjusted gross income minus exemptions and itemized deductions, or the standard deduction.

Highlights of the tax rates are:

1. Federal tax rates are somewhat progressive. This means that the higher the taxable income, the higher the tax rate.
2. The *marginal tax rate* is the tax on the last dollar of income. This rate ranges from zero percent (for those who do not have any taxable income) to 33 percent.
3. You can also use the table to calculate the *average tax rate*. For example, if your taxable income is $20,000, your tax bill is ($18,550)(0.15) + ($20,000 − $18,550)(0.28) = $2,782.50 + $406 = $3,188.50. Your average tax rate is therefore $3,188.50/$20,000 = 15.9 percent, which is *not* the same as the marginal tax rate of 28 percent. If you now receive a $2,000 raise, you still have to pay

[9] This section may be omitted without loss of continuity.

Financial Management Today

Bloody Monday

On Friday, October 16, 1987 the Dow-Jones Industrial Average (DJIA) closed at 2246.74. The following Monday on October 19, 1987 the Dow-Jones closed at 1738.74— a drop of 508 points! This drop of 22.6 percent on a single day dwarfed the 12.8 percent 1-day drop in October of 1929.

Some have contended that efficient market theory is dead since it cannot fully explain how a drop of this magnitude could take place. Others believe it was a rational and reasonable response to a series of negative announcements and information that had been hitting the market in the period immediately preceding the fall. Two other items need to be considered. The first is that information now is transmitted around the world literally in seconds. With instantaneous communication it means investors all around the world have quicker access to information—both good and bad. Equally important is that many large investors, using sophisticated computer techniques, are ready to buy or sell enormous amounts of stock almost instantaneously. Once institutions started selling, trading was fast and furious on Bloody Monday.

To put this into perspective, the DJIA on October 19, 1987 was as follows:

Time	DJIA	Volume in Thousands of Shares (Hourly, Except for the Last Interval, Which Is Half-Hourly)
Open	2046.67	—
10:30 A.M.	2153.55	97,919
11:30 A.M.	2124.02	116,460
12:30 P.M.	2070.00	87,870
1:30 P.M.	2053.04	77,660
2:30 P.M.	1961.16	81,220
3:30 P.M.	1867.00	82,780
Close	1738.74	60,340

As the table shows, when the market opened on Monday the disaster was well under way. The first trades on Monday put the Dow at 2046.67 for a weekend loss of 200 points. During the day the Dow rallied some, after which it fell through the rest of the day.

Prior to Bloody Monday, the NYSE volume had exceeded 300 million shares only twice in history, and one of those days was the preceding Friday. On Bloody Monday more than 600 million shares were traded, doubling the previous record. Undoubtedly many factors came into play, but the volume signifies the massive amounts of shares large investors were moving during the course of Bloody Monday.

28 percent of it, or $560, in additional taxes; your effective increase in after-tax cash flow will be only $1,440.

Taxes on Dividend and Interest Income

Dividend and interest income is fully taxed at the going rate—with one exception. Interest on state and local government bonds (municipal or tax-exempt bonds) is generally not subject to federal income tax. We can see that an individual in the 28 percent marginal tax bracket would receive as much after-tax cash flow from owning a 7.2 percent municipal bond as from a 10 percent corporate bond:

$$\text{tax-exempt yield} = (\text{taxable yield})(1 - \text{marginal tax rate})$$
$$= (10\%)(1 - 0.28) = 7.2\%$$

Capital Gains

Stocks and bonds are defined in the tax code as capital assets. If you buy a capital asset and later sell it for more than the purchase price, the increase in value is known as a *capital gain*. If you sell it for less, the decrease in value is a capital loss. Prior to the Tax Reform Act of 1986, capital gains were taxed at a lower rate than ordinary income. That differential has now been removed and the same rate— 15 or 28 percent—is applied to both kinds of income.

Corporate Income Taxes

Like individuals, corporations pay income taxes on their net taxable income (or earnings before taxes, EBT) on a somewhat progressive scale. The corporate tax structure is relatively simple, as shown below:

Firm's Taxable Income Increment	Marginal Tax Rate
first $50,000	15%
next 25,000	25
over 75,000	34

Hence, if a firm has taxable income of $200,000, its income tax due is ($50,000)(0.15) + ($25,000)(0.25) + ($200,000 − $75,000)(0.34) = $7,500 + $6,250 + $42,500 = $56,250. This results in an average tax rate of 28.1 percent ($56,250/$200,000), even though the marginal tax on the last $125,000 is 34 percent. Because of special tax provisions that on the one hand can lower the effective tax rate, and state and local taxes that on the other hand can raise the effective tax rate, we employ marginal corporate tax rates of between 30 and 40 percent throughout the text.

Interest and Dividend Income

Interest received by a firm is taxed as income at the ordinary tax rate. However, for cash dividends received from another domestic firm, the Revenue Act of 1987 sets up the following exclusions, based on the percent the receiving firm owns of the dividend-paying firm:

Receiving Firm Owns	Percent of Dividend Excluded from Taxation
20%-or-more	80%
Less than 20%	70

Thus, for a firm owning less than 20 percent of the dividend-paying firm, and assuming a 34 percent marginal tax rate, cash dividends received are subject to only a 10.2

percent [(30%)(34%)] tax. If the receiving firm passes after-tax cash flows on to its stockholders in the form of cash dividends, the income is ultimately subject to triple taxation: (1) The corporation originally distributing dividends pays taxes. (2) The receiving corporation pays taxes. (3) The individual investor receiving the dividend also pays taxes. This is the reason for the exclusion.

Tax Loss Carrybacks and Carryforwards

If a firm experiences operating losses, it first carries them back and then, if necessary, it can also carry them forward for tax purposes. An operating loss is first carried back 3 years and then forward for up to 15 years. This provision allows firms to receive a refund if losses are carried back, or a reduction in future tax liabilities (assuming the firm returns to profitability) if losses are carried forward. *Carrybacks* or *carryforwards* can therefore reduce cash outflows due to taxes. For simplicity we ignore this aspect of the tax code, although it is important in certain financial decisions.

Depreciation, Capital Gains, and the Investment Tax Credit

If a firm purchases a piece of equipment, it must depreciate it—that is, treat part of the original cost as a yearly expense—over a specified period of time. Depreciation serves to reduce taxable income, reported profits, and the firm's tax bill. We will defer discussion of the specifics of depreciation until Appendix 8A, where we consider long-term investment decisions. However, it is important to note one point concerning depreciation. Depreciation as specified by the tax code is different than depreciation specified by accountants. *We will always focus on depreciation as specified by the tax code.* Finally, the investment tax credit, which resulted in a direct dollar-for-dollar reduction in a firm's tax liability, was repealed by the Tax Reform Act of 1986.

Consolidated Tax Returns

If a firm owns 80 percent or more of another corporation's stock, it can consolidate income from both firms and file only one tax return. Consolidated returns may be beneficial if one firm has a loss.

Tax Payment Dates

Firms make payments periodically of their estimated tax liability. They must pay at least 90 percent of their estimated tax liability in this manner. For firms operating on a calendar-year basis, the payment dates are April 15, June 15, September 15, and December 15. Substantial underpayment may result in fines being levied against the firm. For simplicity we generally consider that taxes are paid only once a year, but, in fact, the payment procedure makes it essentially a pay-as-you-go proposition.

Subchapter S Corporations

Subchapter S of the Internal Revenue code permits small businesses meeting certain requirements to be incorporated. A *subchapter S corporation,* which can have no more than 35 stockholders, can thus escape the double taxation of dividends. However, many tax advantages do *not* apply to subchapter S corporations. In particular, their proceeds, like those of proprietorships and partnerships, are subject to taxation at the individual income tax rate.

International Tax Considerations

As complicated as domestic tax planning can be, the planning for international firms is even more complex. Effective integration of domestic and international tax planning requires adjusting to different laws, customs, and currencies. The starting point is that the U.S. government taxes U.S.-based internationals on their worldwide income. Using the idea of domestic tax neutrality, the government attempts to tax a dollar earned domestically at the same rate as a dollar equivalent earned abroad. In addition, to prevent double taxation, the United States and most other countries grant tax credits for income taxes paid in various countries. For U.S. firms with incorporated affiliates abroad, the foreign income often is not taxed until it is actually remitted as a dividend to the parent firm. The advantage, of course, is that the tax is deferred until the parent firm actually receives the income.

Because of these complications, many internationals attempt to reinvest the earnings of a foreign subsidiary in the country where the earnings were generated. In addition, there are often tax advantages if the subsidiary pays licensing fees or other "expenses" to the parent firm, instead of repatriating funds in the form of cash dividends. Unlike dividends from a domestic corporation, which are partially exempt from taxes, dividends received by a U.S. firm from a foreign subsidiary are fully taxable. These and many other considerations make the tax aspects of international operations a challenging and important topic for managers.

Summary

The financial system provides the basic framework within which managers operate to maximize the value of the firm. Sophisticated financial markets and institutions have developed over the years to provide an effective means of bringing together suppliers and demanders of capital. The entire financial system is influenced by many factors, including international developments, the economic climate in the United States, and monetary and fiscal policies. Effective managers must have some understanding of how these various forces affect the firm.

Interest rates reflect the cost of borrowed funds to demanders of capital, or the return earned by suppliers. The sum of the real rate of return and a premium for expected inflation is called the risk-free rate, k_{RF}. An indication of expected rates of inflation can be obtained by examining the yield curve, or term structure of interest rates.

Other premiums relate to maturity, default, liquidity, and issue-specific factors; the sum of these individual premiums is called the "risk premium." The return expected from owning any security is equal to the risk-free rate plus a risk premium. Increases in required returns and increases in risk go hand-in-hand.

Considerable evidence exists to suggest that financial markets in the United States are reasonably efficient. In an efficient market, new information is assimilated quickly and in an unbiased manner so that security prices reflect all available information, including the risks involved. Finally, taxes have a direct impact on the firm's cash flow. As such, they have an important role to play in many financial decisions.

Questions

2.1 Define or explain the following:

a.	Financial intermediaries	u.	Risk-free rate
b.	Private placement	v.	Maturity premium
c.	Investment banker	w.	Yield curve
d.	Money market	x.	Term structure
e.	Capital market	y.	Default premium
f.	Preferred stock	z.	Liquidity premium
g.	Primary market	aa.	Issue-specific premium
h.	Secondary market	bb.	Risk premium
i.	Organized security exchange	cc.	Required rate of return
j.	Over-the-counter (OTC) market	dd.	Efficient market
k.	Federal Reserve system	ee.	Abnormal return
l.	Interest	ff.	Event study
m.	Principal	gg.	Cumulative abnormal return
n.	Real rate of interest	hh.	Announcement period
o.	Inflation	ii.	Marginal tax rate
p.	Disinflation	jj.	Average tax rate
q.	Fisher effect	kk.	Capital gain
r.	Nominal interest rate	ll.	Carryback (carryforward)
s.	Inflation premium	mm.	Subchapter S corporation
t.	Treasury bills		

2.2 Explain in terms of Figure 2.1 how financial institutions and financial markets interact to bring suppliers and demanders of funds together. Why are financial institutions so important in this process?

2.3 Distinguish between primary and secondary markets. Why is a well-developed secondary market important even though the firm does not actively participate in it?

2.4 Explain how the federal government influences the domestic financial system.

2.5 How is a yield curve constructed? Can both U.S. government and corporate securities be used to determine a single yield curve? How does expected inflation and the risk premium affect the yield curve?

2.6 Explain the concepts of risk premium and required return. What fundamental relationship exists between risk and required return?

2.7 What does market efficiency mean, and why is it important for managers?

2.8 Explain the difference between average and marginal tax rates.

2.9 How are cash dividends treated when one firm owns stock in another firm?

2.10 What are the key points to remember concerning international tax considerations?

Self-Test Problems (Solutions appear on page 712.)

Taxable Versus Nontaxable Income

ST 2.1 Fritz Singleton is single and has taxable income of $30,000 before considering the income he receives from investments. Currently he has $20,000 invested in a corporate bond paying $9\frac{1}{2}$ percent interest per year.

a. Calculate Fritz's total tax liability considering both his regular taxable income and his investment income.

b. Fritz has the opportunity to exchange the $20,000 in corporate bonds for $20,000 in tax-free municipal bonds with an interest rate of 7 percent. In terms of his after-tax cash flow, is Fritz better off with the corporate bond or the municipal bond?

c. What taxable yield would Fritz have to receive to make him indifferent between the municipal bond and a corporate bond?

Bond Versus Stock Financing

ST 2.2 Joehnk Hotel has taxable income (cash inflows) of $14 million and taxable expenses (cash outflows) of $8 million. It can obtain $30 million in long-term financing by selling common stock or by using bonds. If it issues stock, the firm expects to pay a cash dividend of 6 percent per year [($30 million)(0.06) = $1.8 million]. If debt is used, the interest rate is expected to be 8 percent. If Joehnk employs a flat 40 percent tax rate and its taxable income and other expenses remain the same, which plan produces the higher after-tax cash flow? (*Note:* Ignore the progressive feature and just use 40 percent throughout.)

Problems

Term Structure

2.1 The following data exist on U.S. Treasury securities at three different points in time:

Maturity	4 Years Ago	2 Years Ago	Today
3-month	6%	10%	17%
1-year	7	11	16
5-year	8	11	15
10-year	9	11	14
20-year	9	11	14

a. Plot the three yield curves on the same graph.

b. Describe the shape of each yield curve and then, assuming that the real rate of interest at each point in time was 2 percent, discuss what has happened to inflationary expectations over the last 4 years.

Yield Curves

2.2 Assume that the real rate of interest is 1 percent and that investors expect inflation to be 6 percent in 1 year, 8 percent in 5 years, and 9 percent in year 10 and thereafter. A maturity premium on Treasury securities exists as follows: zero percent in 1 year, 0.25 percent in 5 years, and increasing by 0.25 percent every 5 years.

a. Determine the nominal interest rate for years 1, 5, 10, 15, and 20 for these Treasury securities.

b. Plot these to form a yield curve.

c. Suppose now that Shell Oil (a triple A firm) and Alfred's Air Balloons (a very risky firm) are both attempting to estimate their yield curves. Plot each in relation to the Treasury yield curve and explain how each is similar to or different from your original yield curve.

Risk Premiums, Risk, and Required Returns

2.3 The following information exists for four securities:

	Treasury Bills	Long-Term Treasury Bonds	Listed Corporate Bonds	Risky OTC Common Stocks
Real rate of interest	2.5%	2.5%	2.5%	2.5%
Expected inflation	6.5	6.5	6.5	6.5
Maturity premium	—	1.0	1.0	—
Default premium	—	—	3.0	2.0
Liquidity premium	—	—	—	1.0
Issue-specific premium	—	—	—	5.0

a. Calculate the risk-free rate, k_{RF}, and then calculate the risk premiums and required returns for Treasury bonds, corporate bonds, and risky common stocks.

b. If you were to plot the data, what general relationship would exist between risk and required return? Why?

Average Tax Rate for Individuals

2.4 Kerry Fortune and her brother, Doug, earn taxable incomes of $42,000 and $24,000, respectively. Determine the tax liability for each of them, as well as their respective average tax rates.

Average Tax Rate for Corporations

2.5 Select Printing has taxable income of $140,000, while Thompson Cleaners has taxable income of $650,000. Calculate the average tax rate for both firms.

Taxation of Dividend Income

2.6 Sartoris Industries is a miniconglomerate that in recent years has acquired an interest in a number of other firms. (This interest is less than 20 percent in each case.) Based on a flat marginal tax rate of 34 percent, its tax liability from operations (before considering any taxes due on cash dividends received) is $456,000. The following stocks are owned by Sartoris Industries:

Firm	Shares Owned	Cash Dividend Paid per Share
Kelley Music Co.	200,000	$1.80
Quaker Products, Inc.	525,000	0.40
Central Railroad Co.	405,000	2.65
Trans-Bay International	1,200,000	0.92
Goldfarb Aeroquip	280,000	2.28
Mississippi Industries	600,000	1.34

What is the total tax liability for Sartoris Industries?

References

Many general references on financial institutions and markets exist; here are two:

DOUGALL, HERBERT E., AND JACK E. GAUMNITZ. *Capital Markets and Institutions,* 5th ed. Englewood Cliffs, N.J.: Prentice-Hall, 1986.

KIDWELL, DAVID S., AND RICHARD L. PETERSON. *Financial Institutions, Markets, and Money,* 3rd ed. Hinsdale, Ill.: Dryden, 1987.

More detailed information on interest rates and the Fed is contained in

BERNARD, VICTOR L. "Unanticipated Inflation and the Value of the Firm." *Journal of Financial Economics* 15 (March 1986), pp. 285–321.

PEARCE, DOUGLAS K., AND V. VANCE ROLEY. "Firm Characteristics, Unanticipated Inflation, and Stock Returns." *Journal of Finance* 43 (September 1988), pp. 965–981.

REICH, CARY. "Inside the Fed." *Institutional Investor* 18 (May 1984), pp. 137 ff.

ROSE, ANDREW K. "Is the Real Interest Rate Stable?" *Journal of Finance* 43 (December 1988), pp. 1095–1112.

VAN HORNE, JAMES C. *Financial Market Rates and Flows,* 3rd ed. Englewood Cliffs, N.J.: Prentice-Hall, 1984.

Market efficiency has been studied extensively. Some works, including Fama's classic article, are these:

BREALEY, RICHARD A. *An Introduction to Risk and Return from Common Stocks.* 2nd ed. Cambridge, Mass.: MIT Press, 1983.

FAMA, EUGENE F. "Efficient Capital Markets: A Review of Theory and Empirical Work." *Journal of Finance* 25 (May 1970), pp. 383–417.

KEIM, DONALD B. "The CAPM and Equity Return Regularities." *Financial Analysts Journal* 42 (May–June 1986), pp. 19–34.

LARCKER, DAVID F., LAWRENCE A. GORDON, AND GEORGE E. PINCHES. "Testing for Market Efficiency: A Comparison of the Cumulative Average Residual Methodology and Intervention Analysis." *Journal of Financial and Quantitative Analysis* 15 (June 1980), pp. 267–287.

See Model seventeen in *Lotus 1–2–3® for Financial Management* by Pinches and Courtney for a template that performs alternative event studies.

Information on taxes is contained in

Federal Tax Course. Englewood Cliffs, N.J.: Prentice-Hall, published annually.

HAUGEN, ROBERT A., AND LEMMA W. SENBET. "Corporate Finance and Taxes: A Review." *Financial Management* 15 (Autumn 1986), pp. 5–21.

PART TWO

Financial Analysis

3 Analyzing Financial Statements

Overview

- Financial analysis involves analyzing financial statements prepared in accordance with generally accepted accounting principles to ascertain information concerning the magnitude, timing, and riskiness of future cash flows.

- Common-size statements and financial ratios should be analyzed over time and compared to the industry. And they should form the basis for asking further questions about the firm.

- Financial ratios can be grouped into five categories—liquidity, asset management, debt management, profitability, and market.

- The du Pont system focuses attention on the firm's profitability, asset utilization, and financial leverage.

Saddled with aging, inefficient plants and an undernourished line of small appliances, Black & Decker suffered a $158.4 million loss in 1985. But, with an aggressive cost-cutting program and new products, by 1988 it reported a profit of almost $100 million. All publicly owned firms regularly announce their profit or loss for the last year or quarter. Analysts for brokerage and advisory firms make stock and bond purchase or sale recommendations for institutional investors based on these reports. Individual investors analyze these reports for clues to a firm's progress, react to recommendations provided by investment advisors, or make decisions based on articles in the Wall Street Journal, Forbes, Business Week, USA Today, or other publications.

Financial data are reported based on a set of generally accepted accounting principles determined by the Financial Accounting Standards Board (FASB), a private standards-setting body. The FASB, in effect, sets the standard for thousands of American corporations. By adopting a position (or not acting at all), the FASB can have a major impact on items such as reported profits, the amount of inventory or other assets shown on balance sheets, or the amount of long-term debt or other fixed liabilities reported. Not surprisingly, many parties are concerned about the FASB and its role. A recent article commented: *"Accountants increasingly accuse the FASB of moving too slowly—and of producing little of substance when it finally does act. Some security analysts gripe that the FASB has ducked accounting changes that would have improved financial disclosures by public companies. Businessmen say that many of the accounting rules are unnecessarily complex and costly."*

Accounting statements are the primary source of historical financial information about the firm for managers, employees, creditors, and investors; our interest lies in using this information to gauge past performance and make projections about the future.

Different Statements for Different Purposes

In Chapter 1 we used the pie concept to visualize what is important in financial management. We found that the ingredients going into the pie are only part of the process; what is ultimately important is to maximize the size of the pie, which is equivalent to maximizing the value of the firm in the financial marketplace, or maximizing V. Accounting numbers are one measure of the size of the pie; unfortunately they are not the correct measure of the economic worth of the firm. In trying to maximize the size of the pie, too often managers focus on accounting figures of sales, assets, liabilities, stockholders' equity, and net income. While it is important for financial experts to understand these accounting ideas, we must be careful not to confuse maximizing accounting numbers with maximizing the value of the firm in the financial marketplace. The purposes of Chapters 3 and 4 are to make sure we (1) understand the accounting process, and (2) realize that we can't focus simply on the accounting numbers. Conceptually, maximizing accounting numbers is not equivalent to maximizing the economic worth, or value, of the firm:

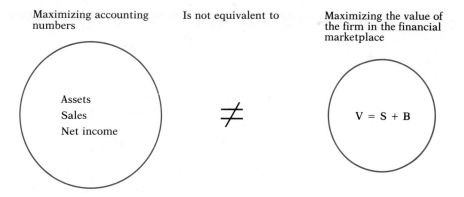

Maximizing accounting numbers — Is not equivalent to — Maximizing the value of the firm in the financial marketplace

Assets
Sales
Net income

$\neq$

$V = S + B$

Chapter 3 focuses on accounting-based ideas, while Chapter 4 emphasizes the primary importance that cash flow, *not* net income, plays in financial management.

More than one kind of financial statement may be prepared and used. The three used by most firms are

1. Financial statements prepared according to *generally accepted accounting principles* (*GAAP*). These data are presented in various financial publications and reported to the firm's stockholders in the *annual report.*
2. Tax reporting statements. Because of differences between what is allowed for tax reporting (Internal Revenue Service regulations) and what is required for GAAP purposes, separate tax statements are prepared. Tax consequences are of vital concern because the payment of taxes is a direct cash outflow for the firm.
3. Reports for internal management. Firms often develop their own internal financial reporting requirements, which are based on divisions, cost centers, or some other unit. Included are such items as direct costing, contribution margin analysis, standard costs and variances, and transfer pricing.

Our interest is in financial statement analysis, but we must specify *which* financial statements. The statements we are interested in are those prepared for external use based on generally accepted accounting principles. The objective of these principles is to provide a consistent and objective account of the firm's financial status based on historical costs, where revenues and expenses are matched over the appropriate time periods. There are three reasons for focusing on GAAP statements. First, because these are prepared for the public, it is by analyzing GAAP statements that investors, creditors, and others gauge the financial performance of the firm. Second, unless we are employed by the firm, the GAAP statements are all we have; neither tax nor internal management statements are made public. Third, you already have some knowledge of GAAP accounting statements. By starting here, we begin on familiar ground.

The Basic Financial Statements

The annual report that a firm issues to stockholders contains important financial information. The primary financial statements are the income statement and the balance sheet. The *income statement* records the flow of revenue and related expenses through the firm over some period of time, typically a year. The *balance sheet* is a snapshot of the firm's assets, liabilities, and owner's claims as of a specific point in time—the end of its fiscal year. These, along with the *statement of cash flows* (discussed in Chapter 4) and the footnotes to the statements, provide an accounting picture of the firm. Typically, an annual report provides statements for 2 or 3 years, along with summary financial information for several more years.

Financial statements report what happened to the firm in terms of sales, assets, liabilities, earnings, dividends, and so forth, over time. This information is one of the inputs investors and the general investment community use to form expectations about the required returns and riskiness of the firm. As investors form or revise their expectations about the magnitude, timing, or riskiness of the firm's returns, the market price of the firm's common stock will be affected. Understanding the annual report is therefore important for investors and for the firm's management.

The financial analysis we will make here is based on J. C. Penney Company,

Inc. (Penney), a major retailer.[1] Its primary operations consist of large and small retail stores, and catalog sales.

The income statement presents a summary of revenues and expenses for the firm during the last year. Table 3.1 presents the last 3 years' income statements for J. C. Penney. Here are some highlights of the income statement:

1. Sales minus cost of goods sold equals *gross margin.* The gross margin indicates what the firm sells goods for in relation to the cost of the goods.
2. *Operating profit* measures the earnings of the firm after all expenses except interest and taxes, and before any adjustments.
3. Adjustments for Penney include income from its unconsolidated subsidiaries.
4. The net operating income, or *earnings before interest and taxes* (*EBIT*), reflects the firm's earnings before the costs of financing and income taxes.[2]
5. Subtracting interest expenses results in *earnings before taxes* (*EBT*). By then

Table 3.1 Income Statement for J. C. Penney (In millions)

The format of this statement differs from that reported in the Penney annual report, primarily due to breaking out interest as a separate item. Typical of retailers, Penney's fiscal year ends on the last Saturday in January; the 1987 fiscal year, for example, actually ended on January 30, 1988.

	For Fiscal Year		
	1987	1986	1985
Net sales	$15,332	$14,740	$13,747
Cost of goods sold*	10,152	9,786	9,240
Gross margin on sales	5,180	4,954	4,507
Selling, general and administrative expenses	3,955	3,731	3,454
Operating profit	1,225	1,223	1,053
Adjustment: Income from unconsolidated subsidiaries	+39	+33	+11
Earnings before interest and taxes (EBIT)	1,264	1,256	1,064
Interest	300	350	370
Earnings before taxes (EBT)	964	906	694
Income taxes	356	428	297
Net income	$ 608	$ 478	$ 397

* Includes $241, $229, and $212 in depreciation expense in 1987, 1986, and 1985, respectively; and $444, $443, and $435 in lease expenses, respectively.

[1] The information on J. C. Penney came from its 1987 annual report. Some minor adjustments have been made to simplify the presentation and to improve consistency. In addition to the annual report, information can be obtained from the firm's 10-K report, which must be filed annually with the Securities and Exchange Commission. Annual reports and 10-Ks can be obtained by writing to most companies; many libraries have them—often on microfilm or microfiche.

[2] For financial purposes, it is important to present the income statement in a slightly different manner than that used by accountants. Since interest is a cost of financing and we are concerned about various financing alternatives, interest is broken out separately.

subtracting income taxes, we arrive at net income, or *earnings after tax (EAT)*. Note that if the firm has preferred stock outstanding, cash dividends on it have to be subtracted from net income to arrive at the *earnings available for common stockholders (EAC)*.

6. Since GAAP statements are prepared on an accrual, not a cash, basis, the $608 million in net income in 1987 does not mean that J. C. Penney earned $608 million in cash.

In Table 3.1, we see that Penney's net sales and net income increased in both 1986 and 1987.

One item of interest is the *earnings per share (EPS)*. By putting earnings on a per share basis, the effects of changes in the number of shares of common stock outstanding can be held constant, giving a better picture of the firm's fortunes from an investor's standpoint. Earnings per share is calculated as follows:

$$\text{EPS} = \frac{\substack{\text{earnings available for} \\ \text{common stockholders}}}{\substack{\text{number of shares} \\ \text{of common stock} \\ \text{outstanding}}} = \frac{\text{net income} - \substack{\text{cash dividends on} \\ \text{preferred stock} \\ (\text{if any})}}{\substack{\text{number of shares of common} \\ \text{stock outstanding}}} \tag{3.1}$$

For J. C. Penney in 1987, this was $608/138.4 = $4.39.[3] During 1986 it was $3.20, whereas in 1985 it was $2.66. After adjusting for differences in the number of shares of common stock outstanding, Penney's earnings per share increased in 1986 and 1987.

There are actually three EPS figures that could be reported, depending on whether any convertible securities are employed by a firm. *Convertible securities* are convertible bonds or convertible preferred stock (see Chapter 13) originally issued as debt or preferred stock. They can be exchanged for common stock of the issuing firm at the discretion of the investor.

1. SIMPLE EPS. The first is *simple EPS* as calculated using Equation 3.1.
2. PRIMARY EPS. Another is *primary EPS,* in which the earnings available for common stockholders are divided by the number of shares that would have been outstanding if all "likely to be converted" securities were converted.
3. FULLY DILUTED EPS. Finally, there is *fully diluted EPS,* in which the earnings available for common shareholders are divided by the total number of shares of common stock that would be outstanding after total conversion of the issue. Penney does not have any convertible securities outstanding. Also, since our interest is in financial management, not accounting, we focus in "simple EPS," or just EPS.

Balance Sheet

The balance sheet provides a record of the firm—its assets, liabilities, and resulting stockholders' equity—as of the end of its fiscal year. In looking at a balance sheet

---

[3] There were 138.4 million shares of stock outstanding at the end of 1987, 149.6 million at the end of 1986, and 149.2 million at the end of 1985. Penney employed the average number of shares of common stock outstanding, and the annual report presents EPS figures based on continuing operations, excluding operations that have been closed. Consequently, the EPS figures reported here differ slightly from those Penney reported.

Earnings Releases

When firms announce earnings early that's good news; when they announce it late, however, it can have a negative impact. That was the conclusion from a recent study looking at the timeliness of interim and annual earnings announcement releases.[1] Timeliness was defined as the difference between the actual release date and the expected release date based on the normal pattern of when a firm had previously released their earnings. In a sample of 100 NYSE firms over the 1970–1976 period, the following 2-day (t_{-1}, t_0) abnormal returns were found:

Interim Earnings Releases		Annual Earnings Releases	
Days Early	Announcement Period Abnormal Return	Days Early	Announcement Period Abnormal Return
≥ 9	1.29	≥ 23	1.53
6 to 8	1.00	16 to 22	4.21
4 to 5	0.35	10 to 15	0.01
2 to 3	−0.18	7 to 9	0.16
0 to 1	0.16	3 to 6	0.76
−1 to −2	−0.26	0 to 2	0.35
−3 to −4	−0.08	−1 to −3	−0.61
−5 to −6	−0.77	−4 to −7	1.01
≤ -7	−0.72	≤ -8	−1.10

The most striking result is firms that report their earnings releases earlier than expected have positive abnormal returns in the period surrounding the actual release date. Thus, unexpectedly early reports convey good information. Likewise, when firms delay reporting earnings there is a negative relationship. In fact, the very act of delaying a report appears to convey negative information to the capital markets.

[1] Anne E. Chambers and Stephen H. Penman. "Timeliness of Reporting and the Stock Price Reaction to Earnings Announcements," *Journal of Accounting Research* 22 (Spring 1984).

(Table 3.2), it is important to recognize that the figures are presented in terms of historical costs and do not reflect market values, the effects of inflation, or other current information. A balance sheet thus provides, at best, only a very rough idea of the value of the firm.[4] Here are some of the key aspects of the balance sheet:

[4] A figure often reported is *book value per share,* which is calculated as:

$$\text{book value per share} = \frac{\text{stockholders' equity}}{\text{number of shares of common stock outstanding}}$$

For Penney in 1987, this was $4,173/138.4 = $30.15. In 1986, it was $29.01; in 1985, it was $27.15. Book value per share is seldom a meaningful figure because it does not represent (1) the market value, (2) the replacement value, or (3) the liquidating value of the firm.

Table 3.2 Balance Sheet for J. C. Penney (In millions)

The balance sheet lists assets, liabilities, and resulting stockholders' equity, or net worth, of the firm at a specific point in time. Since it is based on historical cost, it is not indicative of the market value of the firm.

	January 30, 1988	January 31, 1987	January 25, 1986
Assets			
Current assets			
Cash and marketable securities	$ 112	$ 639	$ 158
Accounts receivable	4,536	4,614	4,504
Inventory	2,350	2,168	2,298
Prepaid expenses	132	111	117
Total current assets	7,130	7,532	7,077
Long-term assets			
Gross property and equipment	4,256	4,194	3,963
Less: Accumulated depreciation	1,346	1,275	1,151
Net property and equipment	2,910	2,919	2,812
Investment in unconsolidated subsidiaries	381	406	372
Other	421	331	261
Total long-term assets	3,712	3,656	3,445
Total assets	$10,842	$11,188	$10,522
Liabilities and Stockholders' Equity			
Current liabilities			
Accounts payable	$ 525	$ 555	$ 424
Notes payable*	955	1,081	740
Accruals and other	1,206	1,076	1,559
Total current liabilities	2,686	2,712	2,723
Long-term liabilities			
Long-term debt	2,395	2,431	2,865
Lease obligations	213	224	234
Deferred taxes	1,375	1,481	649
Total long-term liabilities	3,983	4,136	3,748
Stockholders' equity			
Preferred stock, no par†	0	0	0
Common stock, par value, 50¢: 500 million			
shares authorized	69	75	75
Additional paid-in capital	891	886	854
Retained earnings	3,213	3,379	3,122
Total stockholders' equity	4,173	4,340	4,051
Total liabilities and stockholders' equity	$10,842	$11,188	$10,522

* Includes current maturities of long-term debt.
† Twenty-five million shares have been authorized, but none have been issued.

1. The assets are divided into current (less than or equal to one year) and long-term (more than one year). Note that property and equipment is presented on both a gross basis and a net basis. The net basis reflects accumulated GAAP depreciation charged over the years as an expense in order to match expenses with associated revenues.

2. For simplicity, we have included "investment in unconsolidated subsidiaries" and "other" as long-term assets. Sometimes it is preferable to use another category for intangible assets.

3. Liabilities are also divided into current and long-term. The lease obligations account represents the present value of the long-term capital lease commitments of the firm. A corresponding dollar amount is also included in the property and equipment account to show the use of assets acquired by long-term capital leases. *Deferred taxes* represent the difference in the taxes actually paid to the Internal Revenue Service and those reported for GAAP purposes. (This topic is discussed further in Chapter 4.)
4. Both preferred and common stock are shown in the stockholders' equity section. Although Penney has preferred stock authorized, none is currently outstanding. The additional paid-in capital account represents the difference between the *par value* of the common stock and what the firm actually realized when it was issued.
5. *Retained earnings* is an account that reflects the sum of the firm's net income over its life less all cash dividends paid and any other adjustments. In a sense, it is a balancing account that (1) ties together the income statement and the balance sheet, and (2) allows assets to equal liabilities and stockholders' equity. It is important to recognize that *retained earnings is a claim on assets,* not an asset account. The retained earnings account *does not contain any cash;* the only cash is in the current asset account entitled "cash and marketable securities."

Table 3.2 shows that Penney has increased its long-term assets while current assets have fluctuated over the 3-year period. On the other side, the current liabilities, long-term liabilities, and stockholders' equity fluctuated some over this same period.

While not reported directly on its financial statements, Penney paid total cash dividends of $204.8 million in 1987.[5] Using the total cash dividend figure and knowing the number of shares of common stock outstanding, we can calculate the *dividends per share*. This is the dollar amount of cash dividends paid to investors during the year.

$$\text{dividends per share} = \frac{\text{total cash dividends paid to common stockholders}}{\text{number of shares of common stock outstanding}} \qquad (3.2)$$

For 1987, it was $204.8/138.4 = $1.48 per share. This compares with $1.24 in 1986 and $1.18 in 1985. Penney thus increased its cash dividends in 1986 and 1987.

Financial Statement Analysis

A firm's balance sheet reports its assets, liabilities, and stockholders' equity at a point in time; the income statement reports operations over the period of a year. For the investor, careful analysis of these statements can provide some clues about future cash flows. For management, careful analysis can help it plan for and anticipate the future. The point of financial analysis is to help diagnose trends that are indicative of the magnitude, timing, or riskiness of the firm's future cash flows.

When conducting an analysis, we need to keep four ideas in mind:

1. It is necessary to look at trends; generally 3 to 5 years worth of data are necessary to ascertain how the firm's financial performance is changing over time.

[5] Slight adjustments have been made in the total cash dividends paid by Penney for consistency and simplicity.

2. It is helpful to compare the firm's performance to that of the industry (or industries) in which it operates.[6] Although industry averages may not indicate where a firm wants to be because of different markets, management philosophy, or whatever, the comparison is helpful in analyzing trends.

3. *The importance of carefully reading and analyzing the annual report—including the footnotes to the financial statements—cannot be overemphasized.* Often these will point to other factors—such as contractual obligations, past and future financing policies, plans for further expansion or restructuring, or the sale of part of the firm's assets—that significantly affect the entire financial analysis.

4. The analysis may raise further questions for which additional information is needed. Sometimes this information can be obtained from the in-depth analysis of the annual report. At other times, questions may need to be asked of the firm. The important point is not to view the financial analysis as an end in itself.

Common-Size Statements

Income Statement

One of the simplest and most direct ways to analyze changes over time is to calculate a *common-size statement.* A common-size income statement is constructed by dividing the various components of the income statement by net sales. Hence, net sales equals 100 percent, and everything else is presented as a percentage of net sales. Penney's common-size income statement is presented in Table 3.3. Note that two financial ratios, the *gross profit margin* and the *net profit margin,* are listed as items (a) and (b) in the table. An analysis of this statement indicates that Penney decreased its cost of goods sold and interest, while selling, general, and administrative expenses increased over these 3 years. Comparing Penney and the retail industry, we see that Penney has a lower relative cost of goods sold but higher expenses, with the consequence that net income has been slightly higher for Penney than for the industry.

Balance Sheet

A common-size balance sheet can be calculated in the same manner, except that all the statement components are divided by total assets to put them on a common percentage basis. Penney's common-size balance sheet is presented in Table 3.4. An analysis of this statement indicates that Penney's current assets remained relatively constant. Compared to other retailers, Penney carries substantially more accounts receivable but less inventory.[7] Examining the investment in long-term assets, we see that Penney is maintaining its investment in property and equipment, but is still well below the industry. Also, due to Penney's financial subsidiary, it has slightly more investment in "other" assets than the industry.

An analysis of the liabilities indicates that Penney has fewer accounts payable, but more notes payable and accruals than the rest of the industry. Penney has reduced its reliance on long-term debt and now is close to the industry average. Deferred taxes (as discussed in Chapter 4) are much higher for Penney than the

---

[6] It is often difficult to find comparable industry data. If good industry data are unavailable, it is generally best to use one or more similar firms for comparison. We used K mart and May Department Stores to generate "industry" data.

[7] Receivables and inventory are considered in Chapter 20.

Table 3.3 Common-Size Income Statement for J. C. Penney and the Retail Industry

A common-size income statement is calculated by dividing the various components by net sales; that is the reason net sales equals 100 percent. Penney has relatively lower costs than the industry, and hence a higher relative net profit margin.

	J. C. Penney			Retail Industry		
	1987	**1986**	**1985**	**1987**	**1986**	**1985**
Net sales	100.0%	100.0%	100.0%	100.0%	100.0%	100.0%
Cost of goods sold	66.2	66.4	67.2	72.1	72.0	72.0
(a) Gross margin (gross profit margin)	33.8	33.6	32.8	27.9	28.0	28.0
Selling, general and administrative expenses and adjustments	25.6	25.1	25.0	20.9	21.3	21.8
Earnings before interest and taxes (EBIT)	8.2	8.5	7.8	7.0	6.7	6.2
Interest	1.9	2.4	2.7	1.2	1.3	1.6
Earnings before tax (EBT)	6.3	6.1	5.1	5.8	5.4	4.6
Income tax	2.3	2.9	2.2	2.4	2.4	2.3
(b) Net income (net profit margin)	4.0%	3.2%	2.9%	3.4%	3.0%	2.3%

Table 3.4 Common-Size Balance Sheet for J. C. Penney and the Retail Industry

All assets, liabilities, and stockholders' equity accounts are expressed as a percentage of total assets. The relative percentages in accounts receivable, inventory, long-term assets, and short-term liabilities are highlighted by the use of a common-size statement.

	J. C. Penney			Retail Industry		
	1987	**1986**	**1985**	**1987**	**1986**	**1985**
Assets						
Current						
Cash and marketable securities	1.0%	5.7%	1.5%	3.4%	6.2%	5.5%
Accounts receivable	41.9	41.2	42.8	15.1	14.5	15.6
Inventory	21.7	19.4	21.9	37.1	35.7	34.8
Other	1.2	1.0	1.1	0.5	1.0	0.4
Total current	65.8	67.3	67.3	56.1	57.4	56.3
Long-term assets						
Property and equipment, net	26.8	26.1	26.7	38.1	36.8	38.4
Other	7.4	6.6	6.0	5.8	5.8	5.3
Total assets	100%	100%	100%	100%	100%	100%
Liabilities and Stockholders' Equity						
Current liabilities						
Accounts payable	4.9%	5.0%	4.0%	22.0%	21.4%	19.6%
Notes payable	8.8	9.7	7.1	0.4	2.6	3.0
Accruals and other	11.1	9.5	14.8	5.4	6.1	8.2
Total current	24.8	24.2	25.9	27.8	30.1	30.8
Long-term						
Long-term debt and leases	24.0	23.7	29.4	23.7	22.8	26.4
Deferred taxes	12.7	13.3	6.2	6.6	7.0	5.3
Stockholders' equity	38.5	38.8	38.5	41.9	40.1	37.5
Total liabilities and stockholders' equity	100%	100%	100%	100%	100%	100%

retail industry. Overall, Penney has slightly higher current and long-term liabilities, with the result that they rely more on creditors for financing than other retailers.

Ratio Analysis

Another useful approach is to compute financial ratios. These ratios compare financial variables, and draw from both the income statement and the balance sheet. Although many different ratios can be calculated, we will focus on a basic set. The financial ratios are grouped into five categories, as follows:[8]

1. Liquidity ratios, which indicate the firm's ability to meet its short-run obligations.
2. Asset management ratios, which indicate how efficiently the firm is using its assets.
3. Debt management ratios, which deal with the amount of debt in the firm's capital structure and its ability to service (or meet) its legal obligations.
4. Profitability ratios, which relate net income to sales, assets, or stockholders' equity.
5. Market ratios, which indicate what is happening to the firm's relative market price, earnings, and cash dividends.

Liquidity Ratios

Liquidity ratios measure the firm's ability to fulfill its short-term commitments out of current or liquid assets. These ratios focus on current assets and liabilities and are often of lesser importance when considering the long-run viability and profitability of the firm. The two primary liquidity ratios are the current ratio and the quick ratio.

The *current ratio* measures the ability of the firm to meet obligations due within one year with short-term assets in the form of cash, accounts receivable, and inventory. It is calculated as follows (for J. C. Penney in 1987):

$$\text{current ratio} = \frac{\text{current assets}}{\text{current liabilities}} = \frac{\$7,130}{\$2,686} = 2.7 \tag{3.3}$$

The current ratio assumes a regular cash flow and that both accounts receivable and inventory can be readily converted into cash. A current ratio of 2.0 is sometimes employed as a standard of comparison. Current ratios of 1.0 and less are typically considered very low and indicative of financial difficulties. Very high ratios suggest excess current assets that probably are having an adverse effect on the long-run profitability of the firm.[9]

By subtracting out inventory, which often is not highly liquid, the *quick ratio* measures the firm's ability to meet its short-term obligations with cash, marketable securities, and accounts receivable:

---

[8] These five groups are convenience groupings which indicate that analysts might use them in combination to examine some aspect of the firm's operations. The ratios presented are general-purpose ratios applicable to most manufacturing and retail firms. However, some are not very useful or relevant in the financial, public utility, transportation, and service industries.

[9] Any interpretation of financial ratios is relative—either to the firm itself over time, or to the industry in which the firm operates. Also, knowledge of management's intent may be necessary. Consequently, what is "high" or "low," or "satisfactory" or "unsatisfactory" can be determined only in the context of a specific detailed analysis. Notice that too high a ratio may be just as indicative of a problem as too low a ratio. However, the action required is often far different.

$$\text{quick ratio} = \frac{\text{current assets} - \text{inventory}}{\text{current liabilities}} = \frac{\$7,130 - \$2,350}{\$2,686} = 1.8 \qquad (3.4)$$

Also called the *acid test ratio,* this is a measure of the near-term ability of the firm to meet its current liabilities without using its inventory. Quick ratios of less than 1.0 are not alarming in and of themselves. Very high quick ratios suggest excess cash, a credit policy that needs revamping, or a change needed in the composition of current versus long-term assets.

Asset Management Ratios

Asset management ratios are sometimes called activity ratios. They look at the amount of various types of assets and attempt to determine if they are too high or too low with regard to current operating levels. If too many funds are tied up in certain types of assets that could be more productively employed elsewhere, the firm is not as profitable as it should be. Four basic asset management ratios are the average collection period, inventory turnover, long-term asset turnover, and total asset turnover.

The *average collection period* estimates how many days it takes on average to collect the sales of the firm. By dividing sales (in the denominator) by 365, we determine average sales per day. Then, when receivables are divided by average sales, we can determine how many days it will take to collect the receivables:

$$\begin{matrix}\text{average}\\ \text{collection}\\ \text{period}\end{matrix} = \frac{\text{accounts receivable}}{\text{sales}/365} = \frac{\$4,536}{\$15,332/365} = \frac{\$4,536}{\$42.01} = 108.0 \text{ days} \qquad (3.5)$$

This ratio, which can also be calculated using average accounts receivable for the year, provides an indication of how effective the credit-granting and management activities of the firm are. If credit sales are available, it would be preferable to employ that figure rather than total sales. A very high collection period probably indicates many uncollectable receivables. A low ratio may indicate that credit-granting policies are overly restrictive, thus hurting sales.

The second asset management ratio is the *inventory turnover* ratio.

$$\text{inventory turnover} = \frac{\text{cost of goods sold}}{\text{inventory}} = \frac{\$10,152}{\$2,350} = 4.3 \qquad (3.6)$$

This ratio can also be calculated using an average of the year's beginning and ending inventories. The higher the inventory turnover ratio, the more times a year the firm is "moving," or turning over, its inventory. Other things being equal, and assuming that sales are progressing smoothly, a higher inventory turnover ratio suggests efficient inventory management. Low inventory turnover figures often indicate obsolete inventory or lack of effective inventory management.

The *long-term* (or *fixed*) *asset turnover* ratio provides an indication of the firm's ability to generate sales based on its long-term asset base. For some industries, this figure is important; in others, like banking and many service industries, it is of questionable value. It is calculated as follows:

$$\text{long-term asset turnover} = \frac{\text{sales}}{\text{long-term assets}} = \frac{\$15,332}{\$3,712} = 4.1 \qquad (3.7)$$

By comparing long-term assets (primarily property and equipment) to sales, this ratio provides an indication of how effective the firm is in using these assets. The higher the ratio, other things being equal, the more effective the utilization. Alternately, a low ratio may indicate that the firm's marketing effect or basic area of business requires attention.

Total asset turnover provides an indication of the firm's ability to generate sales in relation to its asset base. For Penney, it is

$$\text{total asset turnover} = \frac{\text{sales}}{\text{total assets}} = \frac{\$15,332}{\$10,842} = 1.4 \tag{3.8}$$

A high total asset turnover normally reflects good management, while a low ratio suggests the need to reassess the firm's overall strategy, marketing effort, and capital expenditure program.

Debt Management Ratios

Debt management ratios focus attention on the right-hand side of the balance sheet and the income statement.[10] Three primary ratios are total debt to total assets, times interest earned, and fixed charges coverage. The *total debt to total assets* ratio is calculated as follows:

$$\frac{\text{total debt}}{\text{to total assets}} = \frac{\text{total debt}}{\text{total assets}} = \frac{\$2,686 + \$3,983}{\$10,842} = \frac{\$6,669}{\$10,842} = 0.62 \tag{3.9}$$

This ratio attempts to measure how much of the total funds are being supplied by creditors. Total debt includes all current debt plus long-term debt, lease obligations, and so forth. A high ratio indicates the use of *financial leverage* to magnify earnings, while a low ratio indicates relatively low use of creditor funds. Chapter 15 discusses the use of financial leverage. Penney has 62 percent of its capital structure in debt-type instruments and thus it appears that owners are supplying less than half of the capital employed by the firm.

The second debt management ratio, *times interest earned*, provides an indication of the firm's ability to meet its interest requirements. For Penney, its times interest earned is

$$\begin{matrix}\text{times} \\ \text{interest} \\ \text{earned}\end{matrix} = \frac{\text{earnings before interest and taxes (EBIT)}}{\text{interest}} = \frac{\$1,264}{\$300} = 4.2 \tag{3.10}$$

The ability of the firm to meet its interest payments (on both short- and long-term debt) is measured by this ratio. It shows how far EBIT can decline before the firm

---

[10] An important ratio for creditors is *days purchases outstanding:*

$$\text{days purchases outstanding} = \frac{\text{accounts payable}}{\text{credit purchases}/365}$$

which provides an idea of how prompt the firm is in paying its bills. Accounts payable can be obtained for virtually all firms. (For Penney, reference to the footnotes in the annual report is required to separate accounts payable from accruals, which Penney reported together.) The problem comes with credit purchases, which are virtually never reported in financial statements. If total purchases are available, they are often used instead. Otherwise, some annual reports provide sufficient information so that a percentage of the cost of goods sold, such as 60 percent, may be employed as an estimate of purchases. For Penney, a thorough analysis of its annual report fails to provide any information on purchases—credit or otherwise.

How to Hide Debt

The Financial Accounting Standards Board has tried for a number of years to plug the holes in accounting procedures, but there are still many ways to hide a firm's liabilities. One old standby is to lease assets instead of purchasing them outright. Under a lease the firm has a long-term liability, but if it qualifies as an "operating" lease for accounting purposes the firm only has to report it in the footnotes of the financial statements. A key test is whether the residual value of the asset is at least 10 percent of the value of the asset. Another tactic is the use of a joint venture. Say a company has to build a big plant and it enters into a joint venture to go 50–50 with a partner, and it lets the partnership do the borrowing. The only record the company has to report is to disclose the debt in a footnote, if it's a "material" amount and if the company guarantees it. A third way is the use of "mandatory redeemable preferred stock," which sounds like equity but costs like debt. On the balance sheet it belongs someplace between the liabilities and equity sections. Companies therefore are reporting it between these two, and simply not labeling it as either.

Maneuvers like these, and others, continue to be used by many firms. Whether the effort is worth it is another question; the issue is whether investors and analysts see through these accounting maneuvers. By their very cleverness, however, companies have at least sensitized the market to watch for sleight-of-hand acts like these.

probably will have trouble servicing its interest obligations. A high ratio is indicative of a "safe situation," but perhaps not enough financial leverage is being used. A low ratio may call for immediate action.

The *fixed charges coverage* ratio provides a more comprehensive picture of the firm's ability to meet its legal financing requirements. While variations of this ratio exist, the one we calculate is

$$\text{fixed charges coverage} = \frac{\text{EBIT} + \text{lease expenses}^{11}}{\text{interest} + \text{lease expenses}} = \frac{\$1,264 + \$444}{\$300 + \$444} = \frac{\$1,708}{\$744} = 2.3 \quad (3.11)$$

This is a more comprehensive ratio than times interest earned and includes lease expenses, which are also a fixed legal obligation. Leasing is essentially like debt in that it (1) results in a fixed cost to the firm,[12] and (2) uses up some of the firm's debt capacity. By *debt capacity,* we mean the amount of fixed-cost financing the

[11] *Lease expense is an income statement account that is often found only in the footnotes to a firm's financial statements.* Do not confuse it with "lease obligations" or "capitalized lease obligations" accounts that show up on a balance sheet.

[12] Many leases have a required payment and then a contingent payment based on sales. In addition, much of the debt being issued by firms is not strictly fixed, but may "float" as general interest rates change. However, both of these are still fixed-cost types of financing since they (1) have a legal claim on income, and (2) do not share in the final distribution of earnings, as do common stockholders.

firm can service. To be even more complete, the denominator may also include sinking fund payments on long-term debt, and preferred dividends multiplied times $[1/(1 - \text{tax rate})]$. A high fixed charges ratio is more desirable than a low one, other things being equal. However, the question of financial leverage still needs to be considered.

Profitability Ratios

Three profitability ratios, which focus on the profit-generating ability of the firm, are net profit margin, return on total assets, and return on equity. The net profit margin, as discussed when we calculated a common-size income statement, is

$$\text{net profit margin} = \frac{\text{net income}}{\text{sales}} = \frac{\$608}{\$15,332} = 0.040 = 4.0\% \tag{3.12}$$

A low net profit margin indicates that (1) the firm is not generating enough sales relative to its expenses, (2) expenses are out of control, or (3) both. It is a widely used ratio of the efficiency of management. Net profit margins vary considerably by industry, with jewelry stores (for example) having much higher profit margins than grocery stores.

The second profitability ratio, *return on total assets,* provides an indication of the ability of the firm to earn a satisfactory return on all the assets it employs. It is calculated as follows:

$$\text{return on total assets} = \frac{\text{net income}}{\text{total assets}} = \frac{\$608}{\$10,842} = 0.056 = 5.6\% \tag{3.13}$$

Also known as *return on investment,* this ratio tells us how effective the firm is in terms of generating income, given its asset base. It is an important measure of the efficiency of management. The higher the ratio the better, since this provides some indication of future growth prospects.

The last profitability ratio is *return on equity,* which is

$$\text{return on equity} = \frac{\text{net income}}{\text{stockholders' equity}} = \frac{\$608}{\$4,173} = 0.146 = 14.6\% \tag{3.14}$$

This ratio, often called ROE, provides an accounting-based indication of how effective management is from the stockholders' point of view. It is directly affected by the return on total assets and the amount of financial leverage employed. This ratio, although helpful, does not focus on the returns that actually flow to the investor in terms of cash dividends and/or market appreciation. For this reason, *return on equity is not a reliable measure of returns from the investors' standpoint.*

Market Ratios

The last set of ratios is somewhat different, since they focus more on the investors' viewpoint. These ratios are the price/earnings ratio, dividend yield, and dividend payout. The *price/earnings (P/E)* ratio indicates how much investors are willing to pay for the firm's current earnings. It is calculated as follows:

$$\text{price/earnings} = \frac{\text{market price per share}}{\text{earnings per share}} = \frac{\$51.50}{\$4.39} = 11.7 \text{ times} \tag{3.15}$$

High expected growth firms tend to have high P/E ratios, while those with little or no growth prospects have low ratios. P/E ratios indicate how investors view the future prospects of the firm. Since P/E ratios fluctuate over time, it is helpful to look at trends for both the company and the stock market in general.

The second ratio is the *dividend yield;* for Penney in 1987 it is

$$\text{dividend yield} = \frac{\text{dividends per share}}{\text{market price per share}} = \frac{\$1.48}{\$51.50} = 0.029 = 2.9\% \qquad (3.16)$$

Since returns from investing in stocks come from *cash dividends* and appreciation or loss in market price, this is part of the total return expected by investors. Generally firms with high growth prospects have relatively low cash dividends and a relatively high market price, meaning they have a low dividend yield. Conversely, firms with low growth prospects typically have higher dividend yields.

Finally, the *dividend payout* ratio provides an indication of how the firm is splitting its earnings between common stockholders and reinvesting them in the firm. It is calculated as follows:

$$\text{dividend payout} = \frac{\text{dividends per share}}{\text{earnings per share}} = \frac{\$1.48}{\$4.39} = 0.337 = 33.7\% \qquad (3.17)$$

High-growth firms typically reinvest most of their earnings instead of paying them out, resulting in low payout ratios. Slow-growth firms in stable industries typically pay out a much higher percentage of their earnings. Dividend payout ratios are an important part of the cash dividend policy decision, as noted in Chapter 16.

The financial ratios for Penney and for the retail department store industry for 1985 to 1987 are presented in Table 3.5.

The du Pont System

In an attempt to improve its financial analysis, du Pont introduced a system which presents information in a manner that highlights relationships that might otherwise be missed. As Figure 3.1 on p. 64 shows, the *du Pont system* ties together three ratios—net profit margin, total asset turnover, and total debt to total assets. The return on total assets is thus seen to be

$$\begin{array}{l}\text{return on} \\ \text{total assets}\end{array} = \left(\begin{array}{l}\text{net profit} \\ \text{margin}\end{array}\right)\left(\begin{array}{l}\text{total} \\ \text{asset} \\ \text{turnover}\end{array}\right) = (\,3.97\%\,)(\,1.41\,) = 5.60\% \qquad (3.18)$$

The importance of breaking out the net profit margin and total asset turnover as components of the return on total assets, instead of calculating return on total assets directly, is that it focuses attention on the separate ideas of profitability and asset utilization. Penney's profitability as measured by net profit margin is probably acceptable, but its asset utilization needs improvement.

The bottom part of Figure 3.1 focuses on the capital structure, or financial leverage, employed. Penney is using 61.5 percent debt in its capital structure. Return on equity can be calculated by

$$\text{return on equity} = \text{return on total assets} \Big/ \left(1 - \frac{\text{total debt}}{\text{total assets}}\right) \qquad (3.19)$$

$$= 5.60\%/(\,1 - 0.615\,) \approx 14.6\%$$

Table 3.5 Financial Ratios for J. C. Penney and the Retail Industry

By comparing Penney and the retail industry over time, we can ascertain trends that may not be evident when only 1 year is examined.

Ratio	Calculation	J. C. Penney			Retail Industry		
		1987	1986	1985	1987	1986	1985
Liquidity							
Current	current assets / current liabilities	2.7	2.8	2.6	2.0	1.9	1.8
Quick	current assets − inventory / current liabilities	1.8	2.0	1.8	0.7	0.8	0.7
Asset Management							
Average collection period	accounts receivable / sales/365	108.0 days	114.3 days	119.6 days	31.3 days	30.9 days	34.4 days
Inventory turnover	cost of goods sold / inventory	4.3	4.5	4.0	4.3	4.3	4.1
Long-term asset turnover	sales / long-term assets	4.1	4.0	4.0	4.6	4.6	4.4
Total asset turnover	sales / total assets	1.4	1.3	1.3	2.0	2.0	1.9

Debt Management

Total debt to total assets	$\dfrac{\text{total debt}}{\text{total assets}}$	0.62	0.61	0.61	0.58	0.60	0.63
Times interest earned	$\dfrac{\text{EBIT}}{\text{interest}}$	4.2	3.6	2.9	6.1	5.1	4.3
Fixed charges coverage	$\dfrac{\text{EBIT} + \text{lease expenses}}{\text{interest} + \text{lease expenses}}$	2.3	2.1	1.9	3.1	3.6	2.7

Profitability

Net profit margin	$\dfrac{\text{net income}}{\text{sales}}$	4.0%	3.2%	2.9%	3.4%	3.0%	2.3%
Return on total assets	$\dfrac{\text{net income}}{\text{total assets}}$	5.6%	4.3%	3.8%	6.7%	5.8%	4.0%
Return on equity	$\dfrac{\text{net income}}{\text{stockholders' equity}}$	14.6%	11.0%	9.8%	16.0%	14.4%	10.3%

Market

Price/earnings	$\dfrac{\text{market price per share}}{\text{earnings per share}}$	11.7 times	11.4 times	11.6 times	12.4 times	12.8 times	11.2 times
Dividend yield	$\dfrac{\text{dividends per share}}{\text{market price per share}}$	2.9%	3.4%	3.8%	1.5%	1.3%	1.7%
Dividend payout	$\dfrac{\text{dividends per share}}{\text{earnings per share}}$	33.7%	35.0%	44.4%	34.9%	36.5%	58.0%

Figure 3.1 Determinants of Return on Equity for J. C. Penney

The du Pont system of analysis provides a framework for seeing how the firm's activities interrelate to affect its performance. Anything that changes net profit margin, total asset turnover, or total debt to total assets will affect return on equity.

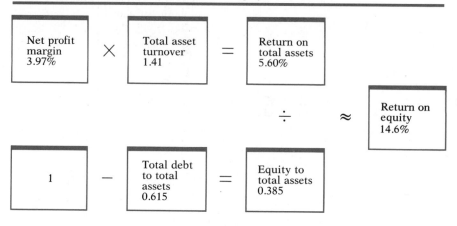

instead of calculating it directly, as we did earlier. Using this approach, we see that return on equity is influenced by (1) net profit margin and total asset turnover, which jointly affect the return on total assets; and (2) the financial leverage employed. In order to improve return on equity, a firm has three choices: increase the profit margin, increase total asset turnover, or use more debt. Correspondingly, reductions in the net profit margin, total asset turnover, or using less debt will lower the firm's return on equity.

Conclusions from the Penney Analysis

Based on the common-size statements, the financial ratios, and the du Pont system, we observe that

1. Penney's liquidity has remained constant in the last 3 years and is better than that of the industry as a whole. This suggests Penney has adopted a more conservative working capital policy position than the retail industry.
2. Its receivables are far above the industry average. However, this is due in part to Penney's policy of carrying its own receivables; others in the same industry do not. On the other hand, inventory is less than that of the industry. While Penney carries less total inventory than the industry, it turns it over just as fast.
3. Penney's long-term and total asset turnover have both stayed constant in recent years. In comparison to the retail industry, however, Penney is generating fewer sales from its asset base.
4. Penney's debt is slightly above that of the industry, and its coverage ratios are lower than the industry.
5. Comparing Penney's net profit margin to that of the industry, we see it is outperforming the industry. But its return on equity is lower than that of the industry.

In terms of the du Pont system, while Penney's net profit margin may be acceptable, it is underperforming the retail industry due to a low fixed asset turnover.

6. Finally, Penney's P/E ratio is slightly lower than that of the industry, suggesting that the firm is regarded as somewhat riskier than most, or as having poorer growth prospects, or both. In addition, Penney has paid out about the same percentage of its earnings as dividends. However, because of its lower market price, it provided a higher dividend yield to investors in 1987.

In 1983 Penney unveiled a plan designed to turn itself from a drab, middle-market retailer into a chain where shoppers would feel comfortable buying more expensive and fashionable merchandise. In the process, it discarded such products as big appliances and bargain-basement garments, remodeled many of its stores, added designer clothes, and stocked more name brands. At the time of the financial analysis, it was continuing to sharpen its focus on lines it believed offered superior profit opportunities: women's, men's, and children's apparel and soft home furnishings. The net result of these shifts are not fully known but it has made it more imperative that Penney be able to respond quickly to shifts in consumer demand and taste.

Our financial analysis suggests that Penney has had some problems. It has adopted a slightly aggressive financing position, has higher receivables, is generating lower revenues per dollar of assets, and is turning over its assets less frequently than the retail industry. At the same time it has improved its profit margin and is attempting to bring its return on equity up to the industry average. Penney is also increasing its reliance on long-term debt, and is repurchasing some of its common stock. The net result has been a transformation of Penney from a full-line retailer, to one that focuses on fashion merchandising. This may have increased the growth and cash flow prospects for Penney, but it has also increased its riskiness.

Limitations of Financial Statement Analysis

Our in-depth analysis of Penney provided many insights into the firm's financial condition. But any financial analysis has limitations:

1. The basic data arise from the accounting process and are therefore based on historical costs. Since one of the main purposes of financial accounting is to match revenues and expenses in the appropriate period, there may be little or no *direct* relationship to the firm's cash flows, especially in the short run.

2. The accounting process allows for alternative treatment of numerous transactions. Hence two identical firms may report substantially different financial data by employing alternative GAAP treatments.

3. "Window dressing" may appear in financial statements. For example, by taking out a long-term loan before the end of its fiscal year and holding the proceeds as cash, a firm could significantly improve its current and quick ratios. Once the fiscal year has ended, the firm could turn around and pay back the loan—but the transaction has already served its purpose.

4. Many firms are multidivisional, and sufficient data are generally not reported so that outsiders can examine the performance of the various divisions. Also, it is often difficult to find comparable industry data for multidivisional firms.

5. Inflation and disinflation can have material effects on the firm that are not fully accounted for in financial statements. This is especially true for inventory and long-term assets, which may be seriously understated when inflation is present.

The comparability of data within a firm over time, and also between firms, is therefore limited.

6. For firms with substantial international operations, other reporting problems exist in addition to those faced by domestic firms.
7. Industry averages are generally *not* where the successful firm wants to operate; rather, it wants to be at the top end of the performance ladder. Also, finding an appropriate industry for comparison is not as simple as it sounds.

In addition to the data contained in financial statements, many other sources of financial data exist. Some of these are listed in Table 3.6.

International Accounting Aspects

Financial analysis of firms with international operations presents additional problems, since the result of these foreign operations must be reported. Until fairly recently, firms were governed by FAS No. 8[13] under which "unrealized" foreign exchange gains and losses were reported each year on the parent firm's income statement, even though that amount might never be realized or might be reversed at a later date. FAS No. 8 was criticized because of its alleged distortion of the parent's income and its lack of reality.

Under FAS No. 52,[14] which became effective in 1983, companies must use the *functional currency*—that is the primary currency in which the foreign subsidiary operates—as the basis for computing and translating adjustments. All balance sheet items of the subsidiary are translated at the exchange rate prevailing on the final day of the parent's fiscal period, and any resulting gain or loss is reported both as an asset and in a special equity account on the parent's balance sheet. However, nothing flows through to the parent's income statement, thus eliminating the former roller coaster effect on earnings.

To see the impact of this new accounting procedure, consider an example where a West German subsidiary purchases equipment for 100 marks (M) when 1 M = $0.50. If the functional currency is the mark, the historical cost of the equipment is 100 M. If the functional currency of the subsidiary is the U.S. dollar, the historical cost of the equipment is $50. Assume that at a later date the exchange rate is 1 M = $0.80. If the functional currency is the mark, the historical cost is still 100 M, but the translated amount is now $80. This $80 will be reported on the parent's balance sheet as an asset and in a special equity account recording the foreign currency translation adjustment. If the dollar is the functional currency, the historical cost is $50 regardless of any changes in the exchange ratio. Thus, only $50 would be reported on the parent's balance sheet.

From the standpoint of financial analysis, the new requirement may make the numbers less meaningful, since (1) the parent's assets and equity change every year, depending on exchange rates; (2) firms facing similar situations may report

[13] FAS No. 8 stands for *Statement of Financial Accounting Standard No. 8,* "Accounting for the Translation of Foreign Currency Transactions and Foreign Currency Statements" (Stamford, Conn.: FASB, 1975).

[14] *Statement of Financial Accounting Standard No. 52,* "Foreign Currency Translation" (Stamford, Conn.: FASB, 1981).

Table 3.6 Sources of Financial Data

There are a great many sources of financial data. When in doubt about the availability of these or other sources, check with the reference librarian at your library.

Publication	Type of Information
Annual reports of companies	Individual company data
Bank and Quotation Record	Prices and yields of securities
Barron's	Security markets, individual securities, and analysis of individual companies
Business Week	General coverage, current and individual company trends
Cash Flow	General coverage of cash and working capital trends
Commercial and Financial Chronicle	Prices and yields of securities
Dun's Business Month	General coverage, current trends
Dun & Bradstreet's Key Business Ratios	Industry financial ratios
The Economist	General coverage of international developments
Federal Reserve Bulletin	Aggregate financial data
Forbes	General coverage, analysis of individual companies
Fortune	General coverage, size rankings of firms
Inc.	General coverage, especially of smaller firms
Institutional Investor	General coverage of financing trends and corporate security issues
Leo Troy's *Almanac of Business and Industrial Financial Ratios*	Industry financial ratios
Mergers & Acquisitions	General coverage of mergers, foreign involvement, and divestitures
Moody's Finance, Industrial, OTC and *Transportation* Manuals	Individual company data
Quarterly Financial Report of Manufacturing Corporations	Industry financial statements
Robert Morris Associates' *Annual Statement Studies*	Industry financial ratios
Standard & Poor's *Corporation Records*	Individual company data
Standard & Poor's *Industry Surveys*	Industry data
Statistical Bulletin of the Securities and Exchange Commission	Stock market activity and corporate security issues
Survey of Current Business	Aggregate financial data
Value Line Investment Survey	Individual company data
Various trade associations	Industry financial data
Wall Street Journal	General coverage, prices and yields of securities

different results, depending on the functional currency employed; and (3) firms are not required to provide information in the annual report concerning the functional currency employed. These and similar problems make the analysis of financial statements for an international firm even more difficult and challenging than for a firm doing all its business within the United States.

Summary

Financial statements are derived from a historical cost-based accrual accounting system employing generally accepted accounting principles. The two primary statements are the income statement and the balance sheet. By converting these statements to common-size statements and employing financial ratios, a financial analysis may be performed. When performing a financial analysis, it is important to remember that (1) the analysis should be done over a number of years, (2) industry data should be employed, and (3) the analysis may raise additional questions that require further probing. One way to tie together much of financial analysis is through use of the du Pont system. The process becomes more complex when an international firm is considered.

The primary point to remember about financial analysis is that its purpose is to provide clues to the magnitude, timing, and riskiness of expected cash flows. Since these three items are the fundamental determinants of the value of the firm, and since it is the maximization of the firm's market price that is our fundamental objective, financial analysis is useful only if it provides additional information regarding these three variables.

Questions

3.1 Define or explain the following:

a. Generally accepted accounting principles (GAAP)
b. Annual report
c. Income statement
d. Balance sheet
e. Statement of cash flows
f. Gross margin
g. Operating profit
h. Earnings before interest and taxes (EBIT)
i. Earnings before tax (EBT)
j. Earnings after tax (EAT)
k. Earnings available for common stockholders (EAC)
l. Earnings per share (EPS)
m. Convertible securities
n. Simple EPS

o. Primary EPS
p. Fully diluted EPS
q. Book value per share
r. Deferred taxes
s. Par value (of a stock)
t. Retained earnings
u. Dividends per share
v. Common-size statement
w. Gross profit margin
x. Net profit margin
y. Current ratio
z. Quick ratio
aa. Acid test ratio
bb. Average collection period
cc. Inventory turnover
dd. Long-term (or fixed) asset turnover
ee. Total asset turnover

ff.	Days purchases outstanding	nn.	Return on equity
gg.	Total debt to total assets	oo.	Price/earnings (P/E)
hh.	Financial leverage	pp.	Dividend yield
ii.	Times interest earned	qq.	Cash dividend
jj.	Fixed charges coverage	rr.	Dividend payout
kk.	Debt capacity	ss.	du Pont system
ll.	Return on total assets	tt.	Functional currency
mm.	Return on investment		

3.2 Financial statements may be prepared (1) under generally accepted accounting principles, (2) for tax purposes, or (3) for internal management purposes. Explain why we focus on those prepared under GAAP, and what the strengths and/or weaknesses of GAAP statements are.

3.3 If preferred stock is outstanding, the numerator of the earnings per share calculation is earnings available to common stockholders (net income − cash dividends on preferred stock), whereas it is simply net income if there is no preferred stock outstanding. Explain why this adjustment is necessary.

3.4 Book value per share, which is widely quoted in public utility rate hearings and often referred to when "touting" a common stock investment, is calculated by dividing stockholders' equity by the number of shares of common stock outstanding.

a. Based on your knowledge of the accounting process, why do you think that book value per share is generally not indicative of the value of the common stock?

b. Can you think of some specific situations when book value provides a reasonable estimate of value?

3.5 Explain in detail why

a. net income does not reflect cash.

b. retained earnings do not include any cash.

3.6 Explain why common-size statements may focus attention on items often overlooked when examining the firm's financial statements directly.

3.7 Anna Montgomery has been asked to conduct a complete financial analysis of the ability of Westbrook Enterprises to service its long-term financing obligations. In doing so, she determined that the firm has the following fixed-charge obligations over the next few years:

a. Interest of $2 million per year for each of the next 3 years.

b. Sinking fund payments of $1 million per year for each of the next 3 years. (A sinking fund is a required obligation often present when bonds are issued in order to retire some of the bonds before maturity.)

c. Lease payments of $1.5 million per year for each of the next 3 years.

d. Cash dividends on preferred stock of $1 million per year for each of the next 3 years. (The tax rate is 30 percent.)

How would you advise Anna to proceed with the financial analysis? Should any new financial ratios be calculated?

3.8 Financial leverage arises from the use of financing sources that require a fixed-cost type of financing. By employing financial leverage, we may be able to magnify gains (and losses) to common stockholders. Which one of these situations has the most (least) financial leverage? Why?

	A	B	C	D	E	F
Short-term debt	$ 0	$ 0	$ 0	$ 20	$ 20	$ 0
Long-term debt	0	0	50	0	30	20
Leases	0	0	0	20	0	30
Preferred stock	0	50	0	10	0	0
Common stock	150	100	100	100	100	100

3.9 Explain what the price/earnings (P/E) ratio is and why it is important to investors.

3.10 The du Pont system has been widely employed to provide a framework for the analysis of financial ratios. Comment on its usefulness; list its strengths and weaknesses.

3.11 Explain the impact of FAS No. 52 on an international's financial statements. Does this pose any additional problem for financial analysis?

Self-Test Problems   (Solutions appear on pages 712–714.)

Missing Financial Data **ST 3.1** Ed Phillips lost some financial data and is attempting to reconstruct the following balance sheet:

Cash	$ _____	Current liabilities	$	400
Accounts receivable	500	Long-term debt		_____
Inventory	_____	Common stock		_____
Net plant and		Retained earnings		300
equipment	_____	Total liabilities		
		and stockholders'		
Total assets	$ _____	equity	$	_____

Based on the following data, help Ed complete the balance sheet:

Collection period (365-day year)	10 days
Gross margin (as a percent of sales)	0.20
Inventory turnover	29.2
Quick ratio	2.0
Net income	$200
Return on total assets	0.08
Return on equity	0.20

The du Pont System **ST 3.2** Gem Products has total assets of $5 million, a total asset turnover of five times for the year, net income of $500,000, and a total debt to total asset ratio of 0.20.

a. What is its (1) net profit margin, (2) return on total assets, and (3) return on equity?

b. By making $1 million in investments to replace outmoded equipment (thereby increasing total assets by $1 million), Gem can increase its net profit margin to 3 percent. If sales remain the same, as does the total debt to total asset ratio, what is the new (1) return on total assets and (2) return on equity?

c. How could Gem have achieved the same return on equity obtained in (b) by changes in the ratio of total debt to total assets, instead of increasing total assets and the net profit margin?

Problems

Preparing Statements **3.1** The PCG Company is a diversified manufacturing and retailing firm. From the list of items that follow, prepare its balance sheet and income statement for the year ending November 30.

Accounts and notes payable	$ 65,377
Accounts receivable	63,836
Accumulated depreciation	69,467
Accrued expenses	81,797
Cash	17,542
Common stock	22,776
Cost of goods sold	875,727
Deferred taxes (long-term)	11,372
Interest expense	14,122
Inventory	156,230
Long-term debt and leases	108,962
Other current assets	13,675
Property, plant, and equipment (gross)	188,900
Retained earnings	?
Sales	1,093,611
Selling, general and administrative expenses	170,505
Taxes	15,230

Balance Sheet

3.2 Complete the balance sheet and sales and net income information below, given the following data:

Long-term asset turnover	4.0
Total asset turnover	2.4
Total debt to total assets	0.6
Current ratio	2.0
Quick ratio	1.0
Net profit margin	5.0%
Average collection period (365-day year)	15.208

Cash	$_____	Current liabilities	$_____
Accounts receivable	_____	Long-term debt	_____
Inventory	_____	Common stock	100
Net plant and		Retained earnings	_____
equipment	600	Total liabilities	
		and stockholders'	
Total assets	$_____	equity	$_____
Sales	$_____	Net income	$_____

Current Assets

3.3 K. J. Hibbard & Associates has the following financial data:

long-term asset turnover = 3.5

total asset turnover = 2.0

What percentage of total assets are current assets?

Changes in Current Assets

3.4 Wiebe Industries has a gross profit margin (gross margin/sales) of 25 percent on sales of $500,000 (all credit). Cash and marketable securities are $10,000, accounts receivable are $40,000, inventory is $50,000, and the current ratio is 2.0.

a. What is Wiebe's average collection period (use a 365-day year), inventory turnover, and quick ratio?
b. How much should inventory be if management wants the inventory turnover to increase to 10 times a year?
c. What would the accounts receivable be if management wants the average collection period to be 21.9 days?

Financial Ratios

3.5 Wallace Systems, Inc., is applying for a bank loan. It has given the bank the following financial data:

Balance Sheet

Cash	$ 40,000	Accounts payable	$ 5,000
Accounts receivable	40,000	Notes payable	20,000
Inventory	70,000	Long-term debt	75,000
Net plant and equipment	225,000	6% preferred stock	25,000
Total assets	$375,000	Common stock ($5 par)	150,000
		Retained earnings	100,000
		Total liabilities and stockholders' equity	$375,000

Sales	$390,000
Net income	$ 61,500
Dividends per share on common stock	$0.80
Market price per share of common stock	$60

As part of your analysis of the firm's request for a loan, you have decided to calculate the following ratios: (1) the number of shares of common stock outstanding, (2) earnings per share of common stock, (3) dividend payout, (4) return on total assets, (5) return on equity, (6) current ratio, and (7) quick ratio.

a. What are the ratios?

b. What can you conclude about the past profitability of Wallace Systems based on these ratios? Lacking any other information, would you recommend approving or disapproving the loan request?

Financial Analysis **3.6** The following data are taken from the financial report of Delux Drug Stores. In addition, relevant industry data are provided.

a. Compute the ratios for Delux corresponding to the industry ratios.

b. What are its strengths (weaknesses) compared to the retail drug industry?

Delux Drug Stores
Balance Sheet as of January 31
(Thousands of dollars)

Cash	$ 8,143	Accounts payable	$ 54,449
Receivables	5,596	Notes payable	7,711
Inventory	148,554	Accrued expenses	28,823
Other current	11,608	Deferred income taxes	20,347
Net long-term assets	132,609	Long-term debt and leases	103,662
Total	$306,510	Stockholders' equity	91,518
		Total	$306,510

Delux Drug Stores
Income Statement for Year Ended January 31
(Thousands of dollars)

Sales		$761,734
Cost of goods sold		550,930
Gross profit		210,804
Selling, general, and		
administrative expenses	$156,070	
Depreciation	10,784	166,854
EBIT		43,950
Interest		15,245
EBT		28,705
Taxes		12,056
Net income		$ 16,649

Retail Drug Industry Ratios

Current	2.00	Total asset turnover	3.20
Quick	0.50	Total debt to total assets	0.43
Average collection period		Times interest earned	3.00
(365-day year)	12 days	Net profit margin	3.33%
Inventory turnover	4.00	Return on total assets	10.60%
Long-term asset turnover	8.00	Return on equity	18.40%

Liquidity Analysis

3.7 Hickory Mills has applied to your firm for credit for future purchases it wants to make. As a first step, you calculated the following financial information:

	Year 1	Year 2
Current ratio	2.00	2.00
Quick ratio	1.25	1.34
Cash/total assets	10.00%	15.45%
Accounts receivable/total assets	15.00%	15.00%
Inventory/total assets	15.00%	15.00%

a. *Based on just this information,* do you believe credit should be granted to Hickory Mills? Why or why not?

b. Upon further analysis, you gather the relevant financial data for the 2 years, which is

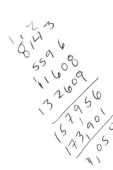

	Year 1	Year 2
Cash	$ 100	$ 170
Accounts receivable	150	165
Inventory	150	165
Total assets	1,000	1,100
Accounts payable	100	200
Notes payable	100	50
Sales	3,000	2,000
Cost of goods sold	1,800	1,500
Credit purchases	1,300	1,200

Calculate the following: (1) average collection period, (2) inventory turnover, and (3) days purchases outstanding. [*Note:* As given by footnote 10, days purchases outstanding equals accounts payable/(credit purchases/365).] Based on this further analysis, what conclusion do you reach now?

Impact on Ratios

3.8 Indicate the impact of the following transactions on the current ratio, total debt to total assets, and return on total assets. Use a plus sign (+) to indicate an increase, a minus sign (−) to indicate a decrease, and a zero (0) to indicate either no effect or an indeterminant effect. Assume the initial current ratio was greater than 1.0.

		Current Ratio	Total Debt to Total Assets	Return on Assets
a.	Cash acquired through a short-term bank loan			
b.	Accounts receivable are collected			
c.	Payment made to creditors for previous purchases			
d.	Cash acquired through issuance of additional common stock			
e.	Cash dividend declared and paid (the dividend has not been shown as an accrual)			

Financial Ratios and the du Pont System

3.9 The following are the balance sheet and income statement for Decca Components:

Balance Sheet

Cash and marketable securities	$ 100,000	Accounts payable	$ 50,000
Accounts receivable	650,000	Notes payable	350,000
Inventory	1,050,000	Long-term debt	2,000,000
Property, plant and equipment	6,000,000	Common stock	1,000,000
Less: Accumulated		Retained earnings	2,400,000
depreciation	(2,000,000)	Total liabilities and	
Total assets	$5,800,000	stockholders' equity	$5,800,000

Income Statement

Sales	$16,000,000
Cost of goods sold	10,000,000
Gross margin	6,000,000
Other expenses	3,000,000
EBIT	3,000,000
Interest	300,000
EBT	2,700,000
Income taxes	1,080,000
Net income	$1,620,000

a. Calculate the following ratios: (1) current, (2) quick, (3) total debt to total assets, (4) net profit margin, and (5) total asset turnover.

b. Using the du Pont formula, calculate return on equity.

(Do only if using Pinches Disk.)

c. (1) Now suppose Decca Components has decided to reduce its risk of running out of cash. To accomplish this, it will issue $1,000,000 in long-term debt and add the same amount to its cash and marketable securities account. This debt will be financed at a

10 percent yearly rate. (*Note:* Total interest will now equal $300,000 plus interest on the new debt.) What is the impact of this transaction on the ratios calculated in (a) and (b) above?

(2) Now suppose Decca wishes to issue new stock instead of long-term debt to increase the amount of cash and marketable securities on hand. Again, what is the impact of this transaction on the ratios calculated in (a) and (b) above?

(3) Now recalculate (1) and (2) above as before with the additional assumption that the cost of goods sold has increased by $1,000,000.

(i) What is the impact of this transaction on the ratios calculated in (a) and (b) above?

(ii) What is the impact on return on equity for all of these transactions? Why?

Effect on Return on Equity

3.10 The following data apply to Stern Products:

Sales	$1,000,000
Cost of goods sold	800,000
Net income	50,000
Total debt	250,000
Preferred stock	100,000
Common stock	100,000
Retained earnings	50,000
Average collection period (365-day year)	36.5 days
Inventory turnover	5

a. Determine: (1) total asset turnover, (2) net profit margin, (3) return on total assets, and (4) return on equity.

b. If sales and cost of goods sold are constant and all the following events occur *simultaneously,* what is the new net income, total debt, total stockholders' equity, and return on equity?

(1) Inventory turnover increases to 10.

(2) The average collection period decreases to 18.25 days.

(3) Return on assets increases to 15 percent.

(4) There are no changes in long-term assets; any reduction in assets causes an equal dollar-for-dollar reduction in the firm's debt.

Market Data

3.11 An abbreviated balance sheet is shown below:

Total assets	$800
Current liabilities	$ 50
Long-term debt	150
Common stock ($1 par)	100
Retained earnings	500
Total liabilities and stockholders' equity	$800

a. If return on equity equals 10 percent, find net income and return on total assets.

b. What is the firm's earnings per share?

c. If it pays out one-quarter of its current earnings as cash dividends, what are the dividends per share?

d. If the market price of the firm's common stock is $9 per share, what is the price/earnings (P/E) ratio and the dividend yield?

Investment and Financing Effects

3.12 Drake Motors has the following balance sheet and income statement:

Balance Sheet

Total assets	$2,500,000	Total debt	$1,000,000
		Stockholders' equity	1,500,000
		Total liabilities and stockholders' equity	$2,500,000

Income Statement

Sales	$5,000,000
Cost of goods sold	3,500,000
Gross margin	1,500,000
Operating expenses	900,000
EBIT	600,000
Interest	100,000
EBT	500,000
Income taxes (35%)	175,000
Net income	$ 325,000

a. If Drake has 50,000 shares of common stock outstanding, determine its present (1) total debt to total assets, (2) return on total assets, (3) return on equity, and (4) earnings per share.

b. Drake Motors is considering whether to renovate one of its existing plants for $1 million. (*Note:* This will add $1 million to total assets.) The renovation will reduce the cost of goods sold by $300,000 per year no matter which plan is adopted. Two possible plans have been considered for financing the renovation. Plan I keeps the existing ratio of total debt to total assets, requires 20,000 additional shares of common stock to be issued, and the new level of *total* interest paid is $150,000 per year. Plan II employs all debt financing, no common stock is issued, and the new level of *total* interest is $225,000 per year.

(1) Determine total debt to total assets, return on total assets, return on equity, and earnings per share under plans I and II.

(2) Based on your analysis, do you think Drake Motors should renovate the plant? If yes, should plan I or plan II be used?

Currency Translation and Return on Equity

3.13 Kramer Industries is based in the United States and has one plant in France. The firm has net income of $500, U.S. assets of $4,000, and U.S. equity of $1,000. The French subsidiary just started this year and bought equipment worth 10,000 francs when the exchange rate was 1 franc = $0.15. Hence, the cost of the purchase in U.S. dollars was $1,500 [i.e., (10,000) ($0.15)]. At the end of the firm's fiscal year, the rate of exchange was 1 franc = $0.30. In reporting the results of its operations, Kramer must report the subsidiary's assets along with its U.S. assets. These results appear both as assets and as a part of the firm's equity.

a. If the functional currency of the subsidiary is the dollar, what are Kramer's total assets and its stockholders' equity? Its return on equity?

b. If the functional currency is the franc, what are Kramer's total assets and its stockholders' equity? Its return on equity?

c. What will happen next year if the functional currency is the franc and everything remains the same except that the exchange rate changes?

References

Some useful books on the analysis of financial statements include

BERNSTEIN, LEOPOLD A. *Analysis of Financial Statements,* rev. ed. Homewood, Ill.: Dow Jones-Irwin, 1984.

HELFERT, ERICH A. *Techniques of Financial Analysis,* 6th ed. Homewood, Ill.: Irwin, 1987.

Financial ratio patterns and their usefulness are examined in

FOSTER, GEORGE. *Financial Statement Analysis,* 2nd ed. Englewood Cliffs, N.J.: Prentice-Hall, 1986.

GOMBOLA, MICHAEL J., AND J. EDWARD KETZ. "Financial Ratio Patterns in Retail and Manufacturing Organizations." *Financial Management* 12 (Summer 1983), pp. 45–56.

PINCHES, GEORGE E., KENT A. MINGO, AND J. KENT CARUTHERS. "The Stability of Financial Patterns in Industrial Organizations." *Journal of Finance* 28 (May 1973), pp. 389–396.

PINCHES, GEORGE E., J. CLAY SINGLETON, AND ALI JAHANKHANI. "Fixed Coverage as a Determinant of Electric Utility Bond Ratings." *Financial Management* 7 (Summer 1978), pp. 45–55.

Some additional topics of interest are discussed in

BALL, JR., BEN C. "The Mysterious Disappearance of Retained Earnings." *Harvard Business Review* 65 (July–August 1987), pp. 56–63.

BLACK, FISHER. "The Magic in Earnings: Economic Earnings versus Accounting Earnings." *Financial Analysts Journal* 36 (November–December 1980), pp. 19–24.

BRILOFF, ABRAHAM J. "Cannibalizing the Transcendent Margin: Reflections on Conglomeration, LBOs, Recapitalizations and Other Manifestations of Corporate Mania." *Financial Analysts Journal* 44 (May–June 1988), pp. 74–80.

CALLARD, CHARLES G., AND DAVID C. KLEINMAN. "Inflation-Adjusted Accounting: Does It Matter?" *Financial Analysts Journal* 41 (May–June 1985), pp. 51–59.

COOPER, ROBIN, AND ROBERT S. KAPLAN. "Measure Costs Right: Make the Right Decisions." *Harvard Business Review* 66 (September–October 1988), pp. 96–103.

See Model one in *Lotus 1–2–3® for Financial Management* by Pinches and Courtney for a template that calculates common-size statements and financial ratios.

The Emphasis on Cash Flows

Overview

- Cash flows are used in financial management because they are theoretically correct, unambiguous, and essential to the financial well-being of the firm.

- Cash flow and net income will not be equal. One reason is that depreciation for tax purposes differs from GAAP depreciation. The difference leads to the deferred taxes account.

- Cash budgeting, perhaps supplemented by pro forma analysis, is the main method of forecasting cash flows and financing needs or excesses.

- Because of uncertainty about the future, scenario analysis is an important part of the firm's cash flow forecasting procedure.

C orporate raider Irwin L. Jacobs and his company, Minstar, Inc., successfully took over AMF, a firm twice Minstor's size. To accomplish this, Jacobs offered $24 per share—$300 million in cash—for just over half of AMF's common stock; he acquired the remaining shares by issuing 10 percent bonds. Much of the $300 million was cash on hand, but Jacobs borrowed the rest ($58 million) and then repaid it from AMF itself. Could AMF afford to give up $58 million in cash—more than four times its prior year's earnings? Jacobs pointed to many ways of generating more cash flow, such as selling facilities, cutting costs, or running a more decentralized operation. Meanwhile, Phillips Petroleum was also in the cash flow spotlight. It closed down an overfunded pension plan and made a $900 million early debt repayment, thus reducing interest cash outflows to "only" $332 million per year.

A recent newspaper article noted that security analysts are now keeping a close eye on cash flows when advising investors: "Cash flow gives a clearer picture of company health," the analysts say, and "gets around some of the Mickey Mouse accounting that distorts earnings." The most important single item for the success of the firm is its cash flow—the actual amount of cash moving into and out of the firm. With sufficient cash inflows, a firm can make new investments; pay suppliers, employees, and investors; and repay borrowing. When cash flow is inadequate, firms must cut production and *employees, extend or refinance borrowing, cut or eliminate dividends, and even freeze or lower executive salaries. In this chapter we focus on the "macro," or firmwide, cash flows. Later chapters, especially Chapter 8, will show how to estimate other cash flows for good financial decision making.*

Cash Flow Versus Net Income

To understand the difference between cash flow and net income, we need to explore the role played by (1) depreciation, (2) taxes charged for accounting purposes versus taxes actually paid by the firm, and (3) various other adjustments.

What Is Depreciation?

Depreciation, in accordance with generally accepted accounting principles (GAAP), is an annual charge that attempts to reflect the wear and tear (or wasting away) of plant and equipment used by the firm in production, distribution, and selling. In calculating accounting depreciation, the firm makes an estimate of an asset's useful life and the pattern of expected use over time. For example, suppose a machine costs $200,000, has an accounting life of 10 years, and has an estimated salvage value of $20,000 at the end of the 10 years. This cost must, according to the matching concept, be charged against the income attributable to it over its 10-year life or the firm's profits will be overstated. If straight-line depreciation is appropriate, $18,000 [($200,000 − $20,000)/10 years] will be charged as an expense on the firm's income statement for each of 10 years.

This is deducted along with the cost of goods sold, selling, general and administrative expenses, interest, and taxes in arriving at accounting net income. However, depreciation is not a cash outlay; if the firm paid cash for the machine, $200,000 of cash went out at one time, when the machine was purchased. Thus, the $18,000 charged each year for the 10 years is a *noncash* charge; no money is changing hands.

To see the difference between cash flow and net income, consider the example in Table 4.1. Assume for simplicity that all sales are for cash, all expenses other than depreciation are cash expenses, and there were no changes in any other asset or liability accounts. Warner Manufacturing's abbreviated income statement, presented in column 1, shows that reported net income was $5.2 million. While depreciation is not a cash flow, its presence influences the firm's cash flows. As an expense, depreciation reduces earnings before tax (EBT), thereby reducing taxes (which *are* a cash outflow) owed by the firm. So, depreciation is important because it influences the amount of taxes paid by the firm. Without it, profitable firms would pay more taxes.

To calculate the cash flow of a firm, we must state it on an after-tax basis. We use the terms *cash flow after tax (CF)* to refer to the after-tax cash flows and *cash flow before tax (CFBT)* for the before-tax cash flows. Here is one method of estimating the after-tax cash flow:

cash flow after tax = cash flow before tax − taxes

$$CF = (\text{cash inflows} - \text{cash outflows}) - \text{taxes}$$

$$= CFBT - \text{taxes} \tag{4.1}$$

Table 4.1 Net Income and First Estimate of Cash Flow for Warner Manufacturing (In millions)

Since depreciation is a noncash item, it does not show up as a cash outflow; hence our first estimate is $9.2 million.

	GAAP Income Statement (1)	First Estimate of Cash Flow (2)
Sales	$50.0	$50.0
All costs and expenses except depreciation	36.0	36.0
Depreciation	4.0	
Earnings before interest and taxes (EBIT)	10.0	
Interest	2.0	2.0
Earnings before taxes (EBT)	8.0	
Taxes (35%)	2.8	2.8
Net income	$ 5.2	
First estimate of cash flow		$ 9.2

Applying this to Warner Manufacturing, we have (from column 2 in Table 4.1) a first estimate of cash flow:

CF = [$50 million − ($36 million + $2 million)] − $2.8 million

= ($50 million − $38 million) − $2.8 million = $9.2 million

Another calculation that highlights the impact of taxes and the tax shield arising from depreciation recognizes that

$$\text{taxes} = (\text{CFBT} - \text{Dep})T \tag{4.2}$$

where Dep is the depreciation and T is the firm's marginal tax rate. Substituting Equation 4.2 into Equation 4.1, we have:

$$\begin{aligned} CF &= \text{CFBT} - (\text{CFBT} - \text{Dep})T \\ &= \text{CFBT} - \text{CFBT}(T) + \text{Dep}(T) \\ &= \text{CFBT}(1 - T) + \text{Dep}(T) \end{aligned} \tag{4.3}$$

Equation 4.3 is employed throughout this book. Applying it to Warner Manufacturing, we have:

CF = ($50 million − $38 million)(1 − 0.35) + $4 million(0.35)

= ($12 million)(0.65) + $4 million(0.35)

= $7.8 million + $1.4 million = $9.2 million

Because the $4 million of depreciation is a noncash expense, it reduces the firm's taxes by $1.4 million from what they would be otherwise, thereby resulting in a

Table 4.2 GAAP, Taxable Net Income, and Resulting Actual Cash Flow for Warner Manufacturing (In millions)

Because virtually all firms employ different depreciation methods for tax purposes than for GAAP, the cash flow from operations may be higher than an initial examination of the firm's financial statements would suggest.

	GAAP Income Statement (1)	Taxable Income Statement (2)	Actual Cash Flow (3)
Sales	$50.0	$50.0	$50.0
All costs and expenses except depreciation	36.0	36.0	36.0
Depreciation	4.0	6.0	
Earnings before interest and taxes (EBIT)	10.0	8.0	
Interest	2.0	2.0	2.0
Earnings before taxes (EBT)	8.0	6.0	
Taxes (35%)	2.8	2.1	2.1
Net income	$ 5.2	$ 3.9	
Actual cash flow			$ 9.9

first estimate of the after-tax cash flow of $9.2 million.[1] Notice, from the first term of Equation 4.3, that if no depreciation had been charged, the cash flow after tax would be only $7.8 million.

Deferred Taxes

In addition to the impact of depreciation, a second complication affecting cash flows is that different depreciation methods and/or periods are employed for GAAP financial statements and tax purposes. The problem can best be illustrated by going back to Warner Manufacturing. In Table 4.1, we calculated a first estimate of Warner's expected cash flow based on the accounting depreciation method and period being employed. This GAAP depreciation was $4 million. Suppose, however, that because of a shorter depreciation period and/or different depreciation methods, Warner actually charged off $6 million for tax purposes. As shown in column 2 of Table 4.2, the net income reported for tax purposes was only $3.9 million, versus net income of $5.2 million for GAAP statement purposes. Also, because Warner was allowed $6 million in depreciation for tax purposes, actual cash outflow for taxes was $2.1 million, not the $2.8 million previously reported. This $0.7 million reduction in outflow raises

---

[1] A third approach is to add back depreciation to net income. For Warner, this would be $5.2 million + $4 million = $9.2 million, the same as before. This approach conveys the mistaken impression that depreciation is a "source of funds." As we know, depreciation does not provide any funds; it simply shields the firm from paying additional taxes if the firm is profitable. The folly of calling depreciation a source of funds can be seen by examining any firm that is operating at a loss. Although such a firm continues to charge off depreciation, there is no reduction in cash outflows associated with taxes. Hence, depreciation is not, and should not be considered, a source of funds.

When using Equation 4.3 to determine the firm's *total* after-tax cash flows, we include interest as part of the before-tax cash outflows. In Chapters 8, 9, and 20, however, we will *exclude* interest when calculating after-tax cash flows for capital budgeting purposes.

Now That's Tax Treatment!

Carl Ichan has developed the reputation over the years for being a corporate investor/raider and also a very shrewd businessman. In early 1989, Mr. Ichan's firm owned over 16 percent of Texaco. As part of a corporate restructuring Texaco agreed to pay all shareholders an extra, or special, dividend of $8 a share. The $8 dividend was structured to be paid out in two $4 increments—one in June and another in September of 1989.

If the entire $8 had been paid together, under tax law it would have been considered an "extraordinary dividend" because the $8 amount would have equaled or exceeded 10 percent of Texaco's share price. Extraordinary dividends paid to companies tend to get taxed at the maximum corporate tax rate of 34 percent. On the other hand, the two $4 dividends (since they were paid more than 85 days apart) were simply treated by the tax code as ordinary dividends. As such, 70 percent of the dividends were excluded from taxation, and the maximum effective tax rate paid by any firm—including Mr. Ichan's—was only 10.2 percent [i.e., $(0.34)(1 - 0.70)$].

The entire dividend paid out by Texaco was $1.95 billion. With Mr. Ichan's company holding over 16 percent of Texaco, it received about $300 millions in dividends. Due to the two-step dividend procedure, the difference between the 34 percent tax rate and the 10.2 percent tax rate saved Carl Ichan roughly $70 million!

the actual cash flow from operations to $9.9 million, instead of the first estimate of $9.2 million reported in Table 4.1.

Using Equation 4.3, we can calculate this actual cash flow figure as follows:

$$CF = CFBT(1 - T) + Dep(T)$$

$$= (\$50 \text{ million} - \$38 \text{ million})(1 - 0.35) + \$6 \text{ million}(0.35)$$

$$= \$12 \text{ million}(0.65) + \$6 \text{ million}(0.35)$$

$$= \$7.8 \text{ million} + \$2.1 \text{ million} = \$9.9 \text{ million}$$

The cash flow difference of $0.7 million ($9.9 million versus $9.2 million) is due to the difference in the tax shield based on the second term in Equation 4.3 ($2.1 million versus $1.4 million). In financial management we are interested in depreciation for tax purposes, so $9.9 million is the actual after-tax cash flow estimate.

As we note in Chapter 8, tax lives are generally much shorter than the lives used under GAAP when depreciating assets. Firms use different depreciation methods and periods for GAAP statement purposes than for reporting to the Internal Revenue Service (IRS). The difference between the two is accounted for by creating an account entitled deferred taxes, which shows up as a liability on the balance sheet. Note that the difference between the two taxes does not relieve the firm from any liability; what it does is delay the time when the firm actually pays the taxes.

Two implications of this difference should be mentioned. First, from the firm's standpoint, the important taxes are those due the IRS because of the legal liability associated with the actual cash outflow (or payment). Because of this, throughout the remainder of the book *we assume it is depreciation for tax purposes that is important.* All future references to income statements or depreciation, unless otherwise noted, employ depreciation as required for tax purposes. Second, because of these differences, financial analysis becomes somewhat less precise. This is another reason why financial statements prepared under GAAP cannot provide a completely accurate description of cash flows—the item managers are ultimately most interested in.

Other Factors Affecting Cash Flow

Many other factors also influence cash flows. The method of inventory valuation, the use of completed-contract accounting, and the installment method of reporting all influence the payment of taxes and hence the firm's actual cash flow. For firms with natural resources such as oil, minerals, or timber, there is depletion. This is a deduction allowed for tax and accounting purposes to encourage investment in, and development of, natural resources. The impact of depletion is similar to that of depreciation: It is a noncash expense that serves to reduce the tax liability if the firm is profitable.

Other items that may affect GAAP net income and actual cash flow differently are prepaid purchases, accrued expenses, and joint ventures. In addition, certain other major cash inflows or outflows, such as borrowing and repayment, issuing equity securities, or replacing debt with equity, also need to be considered, even though none of these show up on the firm's income statement. Given these complications, it should be obvious that actual cash flow and GAAP-reported net income are not the same, and that the financial statements do not tell all.

In December 1987 a new accounting standard for deferred taxes was announced.[2] This was scheduled for implementation for all financial statements issued after December 15, 1988. But late in 1988 a year's delay was made because many firms complained about the tremendous costs of implementing the new guidelines, especially when compared with what they perceived to be very marginal improvements in the quality of the data reported. This new accounting requirement for deferred taxes has two primary effects. First, it will tend to reduce the size of the deferred tax amounts shown on a firm's balance sheet. Second, and most important for our purposes, it will cause greater accounting-induced volatility in the taxes reported on a firm's income statement. As such, effective tax rates reported in GAAP financial statements will depart even further from statutory (i.e., IRS) rates than before enactment of the new requirement. This simply underscores the complex issues that arise when using a firm's financial statements, which focus on net income and historical cost, instead of cash flows.

Why Cash Flow?

We have emphasized that cash flows are important to a firm, but we haven't really said why. The reason is that cash flow is theoretically correct, unambiguous, and essential to the well-being of the firm. Also, you can't spend net income.

---

[2] *Statement of Financial Accounting Standards No. 96,* "Accounting for Income Taxes" (Stamford, Conn.: FASB, 1987).

Financial theory has its roots in economics; in fact, the theoretical study of finance is often called financial economics. Based on economic considerations, the value of the firm at any point in time is equal to the discounted present value of the expected cash flows. Likewise, the value of a share of stock to an investor is equal to the discounted present value of the expected cash dividends and/or terminal selling value. Only if cash flows are employed will the firm and investors be in a position to determine if actions taken are consistent with the goal of maximizing the value of stockholder claims on the firm by maximizing the current market price, P_0.

By emphasizing cash flow, we have an unambiguous measure of the returns coming to the firm. This would not be true if we used net income as determined by generally accepted accounting principles. Under GAAP, different inventory, depreciation, or other generally accepted alternatives can result in differences in reported net income for two firms that are otherwise the same. Alternatively, two firms can report the same net income, but have vast differences in actual cash flows for the period. The use of cash flow instead of net income removes the ambiguities.

Finally, the flow of cash is essential to the well-being of the firm. Firms may have high profits but inadequate cash flow, or low profits but high cash flow. To illustrate this idea, consider the example in Table 4.3. This firm is projecting its

Table 4.3 Difference Between Net Income and Cash Flow

Cash flow and net income are never the same. In some situations, cash flows far exceed net income; in others, they fall short. For this reason, our emphasis must be on cash flow.

Accounting Balance Sheet as of December 31

Assets		Liabilities and stockholders' equity	
Cash	$ 200	Short-term debt*	$ 200
Other assets	800	Long-term debt	300
Total	$1,000	Equity	500
		Total	$1,000

Projected Income Statement for 3 Months Ending March 31

Sales (50% cash)	$2,000
Cash expenses	1,500
Depreciation	100
EBT	400
Taxes (30%)	120
Net income	$ 280
Cash dividend	$ 60

Cash Flows

For the next 3-month period, the projected cash inflows and outflows are as follows:

Cash Inflows		Cash Outflows	
Sales for cash	$1,000	Cash expenses	$1,500
Cash on hand	200	Taxes	120
Total	$1,200	Cash dividend	60
		Repay short-term debt	200
		Total	$1,880

Resulting cash shortage = $1,880 − $1,200 = $680

* Due in 2 months.

income statement and cash needs for the next 3 months. With net income of $280, the situation appears stable until we realize that only half of the firm's sales of $2,000 will be for cash, and that $1,500 in cash expenses must be paid, along with taxes of $120, a cash dividend of $60, and repayment of a $200 short-term loan. Even after drawing its cash account down to zero, the firm has projected cash outflows that exceed projected inflows by $680. Over time, as the credit sales are collected, the firm's cash flow problem will probably be corrected. But it will suffer from a shortage of cash during the next quarter.

One additional point needs to be emphasized. Even though cash flow is the proper focus for financial decision making, in practice many firms concentrate on growth in sales, market share, or earnings. Too much attention is given to these aspects, and not enough to how they relate to cash flows. By focusing on cash flow, we are striving to serve the interests of both the owners and the managers of the firm. If cash flows are maximized, the accounting numbers (over time) will reflect this, and the value of the firm will be maximized. If the cash flows are inadequate, this will also be reflected in the firm's market price and financial statements. In an efficient capital market, managers have to pay attention to the magnitude, timing, and risks associated with the firm's expected cash flows. The firm pays a price if they ignore, or pay too little attention to, cash flows. That price is an opportunity cost equal to the attainable maximum market value of the firm minus the actual value of the firm.

Cash Flow Analysis

Now that we understand how cash flow differs from net income and why cash flows are so important, we need to know how to estimate them. Figure 4.1 shows that a firm's cash inflows arise from its operations (sales and collection of receivables), its investments in securities or subsidiaries, and its financing through bonds and stock or taking out loans. The firm's outflows, also shown in Figure 4.1, go to its operations (materials, wages and salaries, rent, taxes, and so forth), to meeting its working capital and long-term investment needs, and to its financing needs through the payment of interest and dividends, and the repayment of loans and bonds.

Statement of Cash Flows[3]

In recognition of the importance of cash flows, a statement of cash flows[4] must now be reported along with a firm's balance sheet and income statement. This new cash flow statement replaces the former statement of changes in financial position. The statement of cash flows for J.C. Penney is shown in Table 4.4 on pp. 87. Note that it is broken into the three basic categories discussed—operating activities, investing activities, and financing activities. We see that Penney generated $733 million in cash from operations in 1987, used $359 million for investing activities, and used $901 million for financing activities. The net result was a $527 million drop in the cash and marketable securities account. While not relevant for Penney, for international

[3] This section may be omitted without loss of continuity.

[4] *Statement of Financial Accounting Standards No. 95*, "Statement of Cash Flows" (Stamford, Conn.: FASB, 1987).

Figure 4.1 Sources of Cash Inflows and Outflows

Inflows will not equal outflows over any period of time except by chance. The excess of inflows (outflows) over outflows (inflows) results in an increase (decrease) in the firm's cash account.

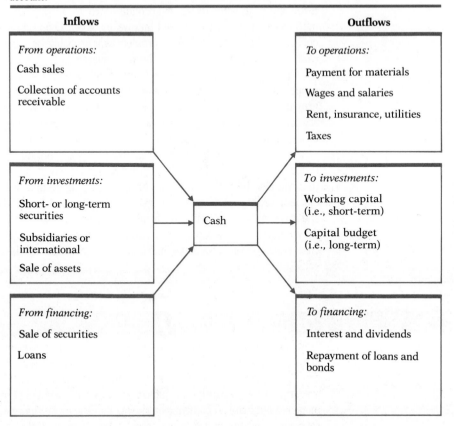

firms the effect of changes in exchange rates from one year to the next would be reported on the statement directly after the financing activities, but before the line entitled "Increase (Decrease) in Cash and Marketable Securities."

Advantages of the Statement of Cash Flows

The statement of cash flows is an improvement over the statement of changes in financial position, primarily for the following reasons.

1. The specific focus on the three separate activities of operations, investments, and financing is beneficial. This is especially so given that these are the three main functions of all firms.
2. The statement removes the effect of accruals and restates such items as collectibles or salaries to a cash basis.
3. The statement breaks out gross, as opposed to net, figures for such items as long-term debt transactions.

Table 4.4   Statement of Cash Flows for J.C. Penney (In millions)

Penney uses the indirect approach for estimating cash flows from operating activities. Many other firms also use this approach, even though the direct approach provides more useful cash flow information

For the Year	1987	1986	1985
Operating Activities			
Income before unconsolidated subsidiaries and extraordinary charge	$ 569	$ 497	$ 386
Deferred taxes	(112)	273	288
Depreciation	241	229	212
Amortization of original issue discount on debt	52	46	39
Nonrecurring items	172	—	—
Changes in cash from:			
Accounts receivable	70	(51)	(449)
Inventory	(170)	261	111
Other assets and liabilities	(89)	(38)	67
Net cash provided by operating activities	$ 733	$1,217	$ 654
Investing Activities			
Capital expenditures	(376)	(348)	(422)
Investments in and advances to unconsolidated subsidiaries	72	20	(33)
Other investments	(55)	(11)	(97)
Net cash used in investing activities	$(359)	$ (339)	$(552)
Financing Activities			
Increase (decrease) in short-term debt	427	(143)	(62)
Issuance of long-term debt	202	597	352
Payments of long-term debt	(728)	(618)	(252)
Extraordinary charge on retirement of long-term debt	—	(39)	—
Common stock issued (retired)	(589)	(11)	7
Dividends paid*	(213)	(183)	(176)
Net cash used in financing activities	$(901)	$ (397)	$(131)
Increase (Decrease) in Cash and Marketable Securities	(527)	481	(29)
Cash and marketable securities—beginning of year	639	158	187
Cash and marketable securities—end of year	$ 112	$ 639	$ 158
Supplemental Cash Flow Information			
Interest paid	$281	$ 325	$ 350
Interest received	24	27	22
Income taxes paid	402	95	21

* Cash dividends do not agree with those reported in Chapter 3 due to slight adjustments made, as noted in footnote 5, in Chapter 3.

Disadvantages of the Statement of Cash Flows

At the same time it provides the advantages listed above, the statement does not fully convert all items to cash flows, and introduces some additional confusion in other areas. The main problems are:

1. The operating activities part of the statement of cash flows can be presented in one of two ways—the direct approach, or the indirect approach. Under the direct approach the operating activities portion of the statement might look like the following:

Operating activities	
Collections from customers	$ 600,000
Payments to suppliers	(300,000)
Payments to employees for salaries	(180,000)
Payments to creditors for interest	(15,000)
Miscellaneous payments	(10,000)
Payments for taxes	(20,000)
Net cash flow provided by operating activities	$ 75,000

The alternative method (i.e., the indirect approach) starts from the firm's net income and then makes adjustments as needed. Comparing the direct approach (above) for determining the cash flow from operating activities against the indirect approach employed by Penney in Table 4.4, we see that the direct approach provides much more useful information in terms of determining the source and use of cash from operations. While FAS No. 95 strongly recommends the direct method, most firms appear to be adopting the indirect method. This choice reduces the usability of the statement of cash flows.

2. The statement does not reconcile the differences between taxes as reported on the firm's income statement with what was actually paid. Comparing the supplemental cash flow data for Penney from Table 4.4 with its income statement (Table 3.1), we see the following figures (in millions) for taxes paid:

	1987	1986	1985
Per income statement	$356	$428	$297
Per supplemental data to cash flow statement	402	95	21

The magnitude of the difference between the taxes reported as paid on the income statement against what was actually paid is—at least to us—astounding!

3. The statement permits but does not require separate disclosure of the cash flows associated with discontinued operations and extraordinary items.

4. Noncash investing and financing activities (such as capital leases, debt/equity swaps, and asset exchanges) are not included on the statement. They are simply reported in a supplemental statement, or in narrative form.

5. Interest or dividends received by the firm, as well as interest paid, are treated as operating activities; however, dividends paid by the firm are treated as a financing activity. This inconsistency in treatment is, at best, misleading.

The statement of cash flows is a step in the right direction. Even ignoring some of its deficiencies, however, it has one other disadvantage—it simply reports what has happened in the past. While firms could simply react to whatever cash flows occur, most plan for the future by estimating inflows and outflows. To do this, firms use cash budgets and pro forma financial statements.

Forecasting Cash Budgets

An important part of the forecasting process is the development of the firm's *cash budget,* which is just a detailed statement of the expected inflows and outflows. Cash budgets can be estimated for any period of time—often a month, a quarter, or a year. These budgets serve two purposes. First, they alert the firm to future cash needs or surpluses. Second, they provide a standard against which subsequent performance can be judged.

In preparing a cash budget, it is necessary to include all inflows and outflows expected by the firm. To do this, a detailed analysis of past cash flows is needed. Although the future cannot be expected to be exactly like the past, a thorough examination of past cash flow trends is the first step in effective cash flow forecasting by means of cash budgets.

The major items to be considered when estimating a cash budget are the following:

Cash Inflows	Cash Outflows
Cash sales	Cash purchases
Collection of accounts receivable	Payment of accounts payable
Income from investments	Wages and salaries
Income from subsidiaries or	Rent, insurance, and utilities
dividends from international	Advertising, selling, and other
ventures	related cash expenses
Sale of assets	Taxes (local, state, federal, and
Sale of securities	international)
Loans	Capital investments
	Interest and dividends
	Repayment of loans

A six-step procedure can be used to develop a cash budget.

1. Develop a scenario with an explicit set of assumptions.
2. Estimate sales.
3. Determine the cash inflows expected from operations.
4. Calculate the cash outflows expected to arise from operations.
5. Estimate any other expected cash inflows and outflows.
6. Determine the expected financing needed or surplus available.

Developing Different Scenarios

The first step in developing a cash budget is to determine the assumed conditions, or the scenario the cash budget is to cover. Since we are dealing with the future, which is uncertain, this is an important step. Assumptions concerning the state of the economy, competitor actions, conditions in the financial markets, and similar factors need to be spelled out in detail to set the stage for the rest of the analysis. Then another set of assumptions can be specified and the analysis redone to see the impact on the firm's cash flow position. This process is often called *scenario analysis.* Its purpose is to see how sensitive cash flows are to changes in the input data (or assumptions).

It is far better to allow for a range of outcomes instead of relying on a single estimate. A firm that develops only a single estimate is likely to be caught short if there is a large deviation from the expected outcome. Likewise, managers can determine which estimates have the most impact on the firm's expected cash flows.

Calculating Cash Flow

Even with the new cash flow statement it's often difficult for an outsider to get an accurate handle on a firm's cash flow. There are a number of approaches, however, for estimating a firm's cash flow. The most straightforward method is simply taking net income and then adding back charges such as depreciation, amortization, and depletion, all of which reduce net income without taking any cash out of the till. A more involved method, and one that has gained some attention in the financial community, is often titled "free cash flow." In this approach you start with cash flows defined above and then deduct only those capital expenditures that are needed to maintain the firm at its existing level. Free cash flow, then, is a measure of what could be paid out (or used in some other form) while leaving the firm intact in its current position.

A somewhat broader definition of cash flow might be entitled "raider cash flow." Since corporate raiders normally want the broadest measure of cash flow, they start with pre-tax, not after-tax, income, then they add back interest expense and deduct the necessary capital expenditures.

In addition to measuring the quantity of the cash flow, the "quality" of the cash flow is also critical. If most of the cash flow is coming from depreciation, then it's probably not as solid a figure as when most of it is coming from income. While firms are now required to prepare a cash flow statement as part of the accounting process, they are not allowed to report cash flow per share. Hence, accountants while recognizing the importance of cash flows, make sure they do not sanction the reporting of any measure of cash flow on a per share basis.

Then they can spend more time and money, if necessary, trying to improve these estimates. Finally, the longer the planning period, the more important the analysis of a number of sets of assumptions becomes. By doing these analyses, managers can gain an understanding of the possible consequences different events could have on the firm's cash inflows, outflows, risk, and required returns.

Forecasting Sales

The key element in developing an accurate cash budget is the sales forecast, which provides the basis for determining the size and timing of many of the forecasted inflows and outflows. The sales forecast can be based on an internal or an external analysis. Here are some forecasting techniques and their strengths and weaknesses:

Method	Time Period (Short, Medium, Long)	Accuracy	Reflects Changing Conditions?
Internal			
Linear extrapolation	S, M	Depends	No
Sales force composite	S, M	Depends	Yes
Time series	S, M, L	Often highly accurate	Yes, but often slow

Method	Time Period (Short, Medium, Long)	Accuracy	Reflects Changing Conditions?
External			
Market survey	M, L	Depends	Yes
Multivariate regression analysis	S, M, L	Depends	Yes, if built in

Three popular internal methods are linear extrapolation, using a sales force composite, and time series analysis. Linear extrapolation takes past sales and projects them into the future without any adjustment. The sales force composite method bases expected sales on estimates provided by sales personnel and the firm's marketing department. Consistency of forecasts is a major concern when the sales force composite method is employed. Forecasted sales might be the sum of separate forecasts made by managers of many of the firm's units. Left to their own, these managers will make different assumptions about inflation, growth in the economy, growth in market share, and so forth. Therefore, some method of maintaining consistent assumptions is crucial. Finally, many time series methods are available for forecasting expected sales based on past sales. These methods require more statistical expertise, but they are often best for generating accurate forecasts based on past data.

An external sales forecast, on the other hand, starts with factors outside the firm. This could be done by contracting with a firm to do a marketing research study or contacting other firms like Data Resources or Chase Econometrics, which specialize in preparing macroeconomic and industry forecasts. A statistical model that relates the firm's past sales to the projected level of gross national product, automobile sales, or whatever is most relevant might also be developed. Most firms use a variety of methods for forecasting sales, and often start the forecast on a divisional basis to obtain better accuracy. Once these divisional forecasts are made, they are combined into an overall forecast of expected sales.

Assume we use a very simple approach to sales forecasting based on linear extrapolation and information obtained from a sales force composite approach. Bartley Instruments, a robot components firm, begins with an analysis of its past sales (see Figure 4.2). Examining the data for 19X1 through 19X6, we see that Bartley has an upward trend in sales, but the growth has not been steady. Employing simple extrapolation techniques (see Appendix 4A), we project Bartley's 19X7 sales to be $4.685 million. This information is supplemented by the sales force composite forecast, along with taking into account what Bartley knows about the actions of the competition and the estimated performance of the economy in the next year. Based on this analysis, Bartley arrives at an estimate of sales of $4.5 million.

Bartley is interested in both the expected level and the potential variability of sales. If the expected variability is small, Bartley will have more confidence in its forecast. In that event, its operating plans can be relatively simple. If the sales forecasts are not so solid, Bartley will want to build a lot of flexibility into its plans, and to monitor trends closely.

Cash Inflow from Operations

Once sales have been estimated, expected cash inflows can be determined. Because most firms sell (at least in part) on credit, the collection pattern must be examined. First, Bartley "distributes" its estimated sales over the months of the

Figure 4.2 Projected Sales for Bartley Instruments

Bartley has experienced slow but reasonably steady growth since 19X2. The 19X7 projection assumes an "average" rate of growth—slightly higher than last year, but lower than the year before that.

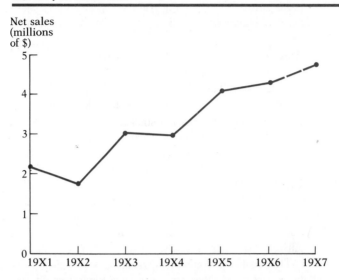

year. This may be done by using a historical percentage of the sales that occur each month. For example, assume February has historically accounted for 4.4 percent of total yearly sales. The estimated February sales are then $(0.044)($4.5 \text{ million}) = \$198,000 \approx \$200,000$. The estimated monthly sales for February through August are shown in Table 4.5.

Bartley knows that 30 percent of its sales are cash sales, and the remaining are credit sales. The collection of sales made on credit is estimated to occur as follows: 42 percent of total sales are credit sales that will be collected in the month following the sale; the remaining 28 percent are credit sales that will be collected 2 months

Table 4.5 Estimated Cash Inflows from Operations for Bartley Instruments (In thousands)

With a lag in the collection of accounts receivable, the cash inflow from sales ends up being less volatile than the sales pattern.

	February	March	April	May	June	July	August
1. Total sales	$200.00	$300.00	$430.00	$500.00	$440.00	$400.00	$300.00
2. Collections—1-month lag (42% of total sales)		84.00	126.00	180.60	210.00	184.80	168.00
3. Collections—2-month lag (28% of total sales)			56.00	84.00	120.40	140.00	123.20
4. Total collections (2 + 3)			182.00	264.60	330.40	324.80	291.20
5. Cash sales (30% of total sales)			129.00	150.00	132.00	120.00	90.00
6. Total operating cash inflow (4 + 5)			$311.00	$414.60	$462.40	$444.80	$381.20

after the sales are made. For simplicity, we assume there are no bad debts. In April, Bartley's sales are $430,000, of which $129,000 are for cash. In addition, Bartley expects to collect 28 percent of the sales made 2 months ago ($56,000), and 42 percent of last month's sales, for another $126,000. The operating cash inflows are estimated to be $311,000, which is substantially less than April's expected sales of $430,000. This difference is due to the delayed receipt of cash because of credit sales.

Cash Outflow from Operations

Next comes the forecast of expected cash outflows from operations. This begins with an estimate of the materials and related supplies needed in the production process. For Bartley, this is estimated to be 40 percent of expected sales, with the purchases made 2 months ahead of the anticipated sale. Of these purchases, Bartley pays cash for 20 percent, and the other 80 percent becomes an account payable. Bartley has a policy of paying all accounts payable in the month after they arise. In April, Bartley has total purchases of $176,000 (0.40 times June's expected sales of $440,000), of which $35,200 are for cash (see Table 4.6). In addition, $160,000 in accounts payable from the preceding month must be paid. Bartley also has other cash outflows related to operations. For simplicity, these can be broken into three categories. The first is wages, rent, selling, and other cash outflows. The other two are interest and taxes. The reason for breaking out the last two separately is that they may vary from month to month. Income taxes are payable on the fifteenth of April, June, September, and December, while payroll and other taxes are payable monthly. Total expected cash outflows related to operations are $389,500 in April.

Other Cash Inflows or Outflows

Once all cash flows from operations are determined, we can turn our attention to other possible inflows or outflows. Bartley has two other expected inflows and three other expected outflows. The inflows are from the sale of assets and cash

Table 4.6 Estimated Cash Outflows from Operations for Bartley Instruments (In thousands)

Many different classifications of cash outflows from operations can be employed. The specific ones that are most appropriate depend on the firm making the cash forecast.

	March	April	May	June	July	August
1. Total purchases (40% of expected sales; purchased 2 months ahead)	$200.00	$176.00	$160.00	$120.00	$100.00	$ 80.00
2. Credit purchases (80% of total purchases)	160.00	140.80	128.00	96.00	80.00	64.00
3. Payment of credit purchases (1-month lag)		160.00	140.80	128.00	96.00	80.00
4. Cash purchases (20% of current month's total purchases)		35.20	32.00	24.00	20.00	16.00
5. Wages, rent, selling and other cash expenses*		146.30	186.00	188.80	168.00	145.50
6. Interest*		8.00	32.00	8.00	8.00	32.00
7. Taxes*		40.00	5.00	30.00	5.00	5.00
8. Total operating cash outflow (3 + 4 + 5 + 6 + 7)		$389.50	$395.80	$378.80	$297.00	$278.50

* As estimated by the firm based on past and expected trends.

dividends received from a small foreign subsidiary. The outflows arise from the payment of cash dividends, repayment of a loan, and from capital investments. After all these other inflows and outflows are estimated, they are netted to produce the following monthly figures (in thousands):

	April	May	June	July	August
Net other inflow (+) or outflow (−)	−$45.00	−$98.00	−$55.00	−$95.00	$52.00

The Cash Budget   Once we know all anticipated cash inflows and outflows, we can determine the expected net cash inflow or outflow each month and see if additional financing will be needed. As shown in the top part of Table 4.7, Bartley is projecting that total cash outflows will exceed total cash inflows by $123,500 in April. The bottom part of the table shows that Bartley has $70,000 cash on hand on April 1, and has a minimum cash balance of $20,000 that it needs to maintain. This results in an estimated final cash position of −$73,500 at the end of April.

In Table 4.7 we see that Bartley has a negative cumulative expected cash position for the months of April, May, June, and July. In August the expected cash position is positive. The worst month is May, when the cash position is estimated to be −$152,700. Obviously, Bartley must do something—cut production, reduce other expenses, increase collections, or secure short- or long-term financing to cover the expected shortfall. Armed with the information obtained from the cash budget, Bartley

Table 4.7 Net Cash Flow and Financing Needed or Surplus Available for Bartley Instruments (In thousands)

Note that row 1 in the bottom part of the table, cash and marketable securities at the start of period, is carried over from the previous month's end-of-period cash figure from row 3.

	April	May	June	July	August
Calculating Net Cash Inflow or Outflow					
1. Total operating cash inflow	$311.00	$414.60	$462.40	$444.80	$381.20
2. Total operating cash outflow	− 389.50	− 395.80	− 378.80	− 297.00	− 278.50
3. Other net inflow (+) or outflow (−)	− 45.00	− 98.00	− 55.00	− 95.00	+ 52.00
4. Net cash inflow (+) or outflow (−) (1 + 2 + 3)	−$123.50	−$ 79.20	$ 28.60	$ 52.80	$154.70
Calculating Short-Term Financing Needed					
1. Cash and marketable securities at start of period	$ 70.00	−$ 53.50	−$132.70	−$104.10	−$ 51.30
2. Change in cash balance (net cash inflow or outflow)	− 123.50	− 79.20	28.60	52.80	154.70
3. Cash at end of period (1 + 2)	− 53.50	− 132.70	− 104.10	− 51.30	103.40
4. Minimum cash balance required	− 20.00	− 20.00	− 20.00	− 20.00	− 20.00
5. Cumulative short-term financing needed (−) or surplus (+) (3 + 4)	−$ 73.50	−$152.70	−$124.10	−$ 71.30	$ 83.40

can plan for the future. If borrowing is planned, the lender can be notified and appropriate plans made. When excess cash is available, its investment can be planned. These are topics of other chapters. But the basis for borrowing or investment decisions is the firm's expected cash position as estimated by its cash budget.

Effective management is enhanced by the development of cash budgets, which help managers plan and control. Once the cash budget is determined, many firms employ a *rolling forecast* that is updated every week, month, or quarter. But some care is in order. First, the cash budget estimated for Bartley Instruments was based on a set of specific assumptions—from the sales forecast on. Since events will differ in the future, the ability to do scenario analysis is essential. Second, cash needs may fluctuate *within* the budgeting period. Even though there may be plenty of cash on hand by the end of the period, different inflow and outflow patterns may leave the firm short of cash within the period.

Pro Forma Financial Statements

Pro forma statements project the firm's expected revenues, expenses, and financial position at the end of a forecast period.[5] While less detailed than cash budgets, these forecasts are often required by current and prospective lenders. There are two basic approaches to developing pro forma statements:

1. One approach takes as its input the projections arising from the cash budget. These projections are then modified to account for differences between the firm's cash flows and its GAAP accounting data.
2. The second is the *percentage of sales method,* which starts with the historical relationship of sales to various income statement and balance sheet items. Pro forma statements and financing needs or surpluses are then estimated. This procedure may be naive if it assumes that all the firm's costs are variable and vary directly with sales. In practice, some costs are fixed; therefore judgment is employed when estimating how some expenses are expected to change.

We use the percentage of sales method to estimate financing needs based on pro forma financial statements. Note that since it starts with accounting data, this method is not as precise as a cash budgeting approach to projecting cash flows and financing needs. However, its simplicity and its focus on the impact of the future on reported financial statements may make it a supplement to the more elaborate cash budgeting process. We will use Smith Products, a manufacturer of specialty tools, to illustrate the use of the percentage of sales method. Smith's best estimate of next year's sales is $22 million. If sales are substantially higher or lower, the pro forma statements will be off.

Pro Forma Income Statement

The next step is to estimate the historical relationship of expenses to sales for Smith. This is done by dividing Smith's cost of goods sold, selling, general and administrative expenses, interest expenses, taxes, and cash dividends by sales. If we use this information directly in a naive manner, Smith Products' estimated, or

---

[5] Pro forma statements can also be constructed for some past time period. Comparison with actual past performance may best show the effect of some planned major event, such as a proposed merger.

Table 4.8   Present and Pro Forma Income Statement for Smith Products If Expenses Are Projected Naively (In thousands)

This naive approach ignores fixed costs and often produces an estimate of net income that is biased low.

	Actual for Last Year	Basis of Projection	Pro Forma for Next Year
Sales	$20,000	*each 10* x	$22,000
Cost of goods sold	13,500 ÷ 20,000	Percentage of sales	14,850*
Gross margin	6,500		7,150
Selling, general and administrative expenses	4,500 ÷ 20,000	Percentage of sales	4,950
EBIT	2,000		2,200
Interest	600	Percentage of sales	660
EBT	1,400		1,540
Taxes (40%)	560	Percentage of sales	616
Net income	840		924
Cash dividends	300	Percentage of sales	330
Transferred to retained earnings	$ 540		$ 594

* $14,850 = ($13,500/$20,000)($22,000). The other percentage of sales estimates were calculated in the same manner.

pro forma, income statement is as shown in Table 4.8. Based on this approach, Smith Products would expect net income to be $924,000; with projected cash dividends of $330,000, $594,000 would be shown as a transfer from the income statement to retained earnings on the firm's balance sheet.[6] The new retained earnings amount is equal to the previous years' retained earnings plus the amount transferred from the pro forma income statement.

After further analysis, Smith Products decides that all expenses and outflows will *not* vary directly with sales. Specifically, the firm estimates that the cost of goods sold will be 66 percent of sales, that selling, general and administrative expenses will be 23 percent of sales, and that cash dividends will be $350,000. The same interest of $660,000 and 40 percent tax rate will be assumed. Smith Products' pro forma income statement is shown in Table 4.9. This analysis shows that net income is expected to be $1.056 million, and the estimated amount transferred to retained earnings will be $706,000. With these estimates, we can now proceed to estimate the balance sheet and obtain a rough approximation of the financing needed to support this expected increase in sales.

Pro Forma Balance Sheet and Financing Needed

Smith's present balance sheet is given in Table 4.10 on p. 98, along with the projected asset and liability accounts, assuming most of them maintain their historical relationship to sales. Net long-term assets are projected based on the firm's current capital investment plan. Note that three items are not projected: notes payable, long-term debt and lease obligations, and common stock are negotiated items that do not change

[6] Since the naive approach assumes all costs are variable, it generally produces an estimate of net income that is *biased low*. This results from ignoring the presence of fixed operating costs that are spread over more sales dollars as sales increase. However, if sales are decreasing and fixed operating costs are actually present, the naive percentage of sales method produces an estimate of net income that is too high.

Table 4.9 Pro Forma Income Statement for Smith Products Based on the Percentage of Sales Method (In thousands)

By taking account of fixed costs, Smith Products obtains a more realistic estimate of its expected net income.

	Basis of Projection	Pro Forma for Next Year
Sales		$22,000
Cost of goods sold	Judgment: 66% of sales	14,520
Gross margin		7,480
Selling, general and administrative expenses	Judgment: 23% of sales	5,060
EBIT		2,420
Interest	Percentage of sales	660
EBT		1,760
Taxes (40%) 1760×.40	Historical tax rate	704
Net income		1,056
Cash dividends *given*	Management forecast	350
Transferred to retained earnings		$ 706

as sales fluctuate. All other balance sheet items, except for net long-term assets and retained earnings, are assumed to change proportionally as sales change. Based on this procedure, Smith Products can obtain a rough estimate of its financing needs of $984,000. This is calculated as follows:

Total assets	$16,000,000
Less: Total liabilities and stockholders' equity	15,016,000
Additional financing needed (or surplus available)	$ 984,000

This, of course, assumes the estimated increase in retained earnings is exactly equal to Smith's internally generated funds. In addition, it is based on maintaining the cash account at its forecasted level of $440,000.

A slight modification can be made if a firm plans to draw down its cash account to meet part of its needs. To illustrate, assume Smith plans to draw its cash account down by $240,000. The financing needed is:

Total assets	$16,000,000
Less: Total liabilities and stockholders' equity	15,016,000
Additional financing needed	984,000
Less: Cash drawn down	240,000
External financing needed	$ 744,000

One additional caveat needs to be raised about the use of pro forma analysis to estimate financing needs. Many of our students have used this approach to estimate potential financing needs for real firms. Rarely does their analysis indicate *any* need for additional external financing. This continued indication of no external financing need makes us uneasy.

Now, of course, Smith Products must decide how to finance the needed expansion.

Table 4.10 Forecast of Changes in Balance Sheet Items for Smith Products (In thousands)

In this example, judgment was used to estimate the long-term assets while the naive percentage of sales method was used to forecast the other items.

	Actual for Last Year	Basis of Projection	Pro Forma for Next Year
Assets			
Cash	$ 400	Percentage of sales	$ 440*
Accounts receivable	2,100	Percentage of sales	2,310
Inventory	3,000	Percentage of sales	3,300
Total current	5,500		6,050
Net long-term assets	8,500	Judgment	9,950
Total assets	$14,000		$16,000
Liabilities and Stockholders' Equity			
Accounts payable	$ 1,300	Percentage of sales	$ 1,430
Notes payable	900	n.a.†	900
Accrued wages and taxes	1,200	Percentage of sales	1,320
Total current	3,400		3,650
Long-term debt and lease obligations	3,800	n.a.	3,800
Deferred taxes	600	Percentage of sales	660
Total long-term liabilities	4,400		4,460
Common stock and additional paid-in capital	3,000	n.a.	3,000
Retained earnings	3,200	Pro forma income statement	3,906‡
Total stockholders' equity	6,200		6,906
Total liabilities and stockholders' equity	$14,000	Total	15,016
		Additional needed	984
		Total to balance	$16,000

* $440 = ($400/$20,000)($22,000). The other percentage of sales estimates were calculated in the same manner.
† Not applicable.
‡ $3,200 from last year plus transfer to retained earnings of $706 from Table 4.9.

To illustrate the basic elements, assume that Smith decides to finance the total $984,000 by issuing $1 million in additional long-term debt.[7] As Table 4.11 shows, this results in Smith's long-term debt and lease obligations account increasing by $1 million to $4.8 million, and the difference between the $984,000 needed and the $1 million obtained ($16,000) is added to the firm's cash account.[8] Obviously, other plans and many factors have to be considered when firms plan for the future. We need to learn more before we return to financial planning in Chapter 23.

[7] It issues $1 million instead of $984,000 due simply to rounding the financing off to the nearest million dollars.

[8] Actually, the income statement should be reestimated to take into account additional interest above the existing $660,000 due to Smith's increasing its debt by $1 million. This would affect the size of the transfer to retained earnings. For simplicity, these secondary effects are ignored.

Table 4.11 Pro Forma Balance Sheet for Smith Products (In thousands)

By increasing its ratio of total debt to total assets from 55.7 percent (Table 4.10) to 56.9 percent, Smith can meet the proposed increase without additional common equity financing.

Assets		Liabilities and Stockholders' Equity	
Cash	$ 456	Accounts payable	$ 1,430
Accounts receivable	2,310	Notes payable	900
Inventory	3,300	Accrued wages and taxes	1,320
Total current	6,066	Total current	3,650
Net long-term assets	9,950	Long-term debt and lease	
Total assets	$16,016	obligations	4,800
		Deferred taxes	660
		Total long-term debt	5,460
		Common stock and additional	
		paid-in capital	3,000
		Retained earnings	3,906
		Total stockholders' equity	6,906
		Total liabilities and	
		stockholders' equity	$16,016

Forecasting in Practice

Inflation and Disinflation

Inflation can have a profound impact on the cash flows of the firm. The whole forecasting process must be reexamined in times of rapid inflation or disinflation. This is necessary because very different strategies may be necessary, and because the firm may not be able (or want) to pass the effects of inflation or disinflation on to its customers. Accounting problems make the pro forma approach to estimating cash needs more inexact. This occurs because reported profits, asset values, and even liabilities are further distorted in periods of high inflation.

The presence of inflation and disinflation also causes suppliers of funds to change strategies to protect themselves from its effect. They may provide only variable rate financing, in which the interest rate charged on a bond or loan is adjusted over time. Most banks now lend primarily on a variable rate basis. By doing so they try to match their assets and liabilities, thereby protecting themselves from losses due to inflation.

All these factors, and many more, make the cash flow estimation process more difficult. The consequence is to reduce the reliability of the forecast, and make close monitoring and evaluating various scenarios even more important.

The Growing Firm

As firms grow, their sales increase. Since most firms sell, at least in part, on credit, the firm will need to finance a larger amount of accounts receivable. Likewise, larger inventory levels will be necessary. As growth continues, the firm will have to expand its plant and facilities, requiring additional investment in long-term assets. The funding for some of these increased needs can be provided by increased accounts payable—which will also grow with the firm. The rest, however, has to come from two main sources—internally generated funds that are not paid out to the stockholders, and new external financing.

High rates of growth may put a firm in a cash bind. This is because it cannot finance the rapid cash needs with internally generated funds. As one step, most high-growth firms have low or zero cash dividend payouts. They simply have too many internal needs to use any cash for dividends. The solution to the cash needs of a growing firm is to acquire additional financing in the form of long-term debt, or additional common stock financing. While growth is generally desirable, it places a strain on the cash needs of the firm that must be planned for. Failure to do so is one of the primary shortcomings of many growing firms.

Spreadsheets

Although the forecasting techniques described in this chapter can be done by hand, more and more firms, small and large, are turning to computerized approaches. These range from sophisticated models based on econometrics or mathematical programming developed especially for specific firms to models that employ Lotus 1–2–3® or other *spreadsheet programs*. The key feature of all these approaches is the ability easily to conduct a scenario analysis. The beauty of spreadsheets is that they allow us to change a few assumptions and rerun the analysis. In addition, they provide the ability to update forecasts quickly and easily.

Throughout this book we examine many different factors that affect the magnitude, timing, and riskiness of expected cash flows. As these change, so does the value of the firm's stock. Properly designed and used, spreadsheets allow management to assess the effects of changes on the firm's expected cash flows. Spreadsheets are playing an ever-increasing role in financial management.

Summary

Cash flow, rather than accounting net income, is important for effective decision making. The thrust of financial management is different from that of accounting in several ways. First, financial management focuses on decision making and is future-oriented, whereas financial accounting attempts to provide a record of what has happened in the past. Second, financial management focuses on cash flows, whereas financial accounting emphasizes matching revenues and expenses. Third, financial management stresses valuation of the firm in the marketplace, whereas financial accounting provides asset, liability, revenue, and expense figures. While the accounting process is important, its main contribution to financial management is to provide information for managers, and investors who, through their actions in the marketplace, determine the value of the firm's common stock.

Because firms calculate depreciation differently for accounting than for tax purposes, they often pay less in taxes than is reported under generally accepted accounting principles. The difference is recorded on financial statements in the deferred taxes account. Such accounts have grown substantially in recent years. The statement of cash flows goes part of the way toward providing financial managers with usable cash flow information.

The primary means of forecasting cash flows relies on the cash budget, which includes all operating, investment, and financing cash inflows and outflows. The cash budget may be supplemented by pro forma financial statements, but, accounting-based projections provide only rough estimates of future cash flows. The usefulness of cash forecasts depends on accurate sales forecasts. Yet the future is inherently uncertain. Cash forecasting must therefore include the ability to ask alternative questions. Accurate, yet flexible, forecasts are a valuable tool in financial management. They give the best indication of the likely effect of future business conditions and decisions on the magnitude, timing, and riskiness of expected cash flows.

Note: There is an appendix to this chapter, "Appendix 4A: Linear Forecasting," at the back of the book.

Questions

4.1 Define or explain the following:

a. Depreciation	**f.** Rolling forecast
b. Cash flow after tax (CF)	**g.** Pro forma statements
c. Cash flow before tax (CFBT)	**h.** Percentage of sales method
d. Cash budget	**i.** Spreadsheet program
e. Scenario analysis	

4.2 Explain: (a) what tax depreciation is, (b) how it influences the firm's expected cash flows, and (c) why it is incorrect to call it a source of funds.

4.3 Two ways of figuring the after-tax operating cash flows of the firm are given by Equation 4.1, CF = CFBT − taxes, and Equation 4.3, CF = CFBT(1 − T) + Dep(T). Why do they both provide the same answer? Do both still work if the firm is operating at a loss?

4.4 What are some of the more significant ways in which GAAP financial statements and those prepared for income tax purposes differ?

4.5 Explain both the advantages and disadvantages of the statement of cash flows in terms of providing useful cash flow information.

4.6 Explain the various components of a firm's cash budget. How can sales be estimated? Why may a cash budget not be sufficient for planning *within* a given period?

4.7 What are the strengths and weaknesses and the differences between the cash budget and the percentage of sales method of forecasting future cash flows?

4.8 Gates Electronics is considering making the following policy changes. In each case, indicate whether *in the next period* the move will provide more cash inflows and/or reduce outflows (+), provide more outflows and/or less inflows (−) or have an indeterminate or no effect (0).

a. The firm becomes more socially responsible. _____
b. Increased competition is leading to price cutting and increased promotional expenses. _____
c. The firm decides to sell only for cash; previously some sales had been on credit. _____
d. By shifting to more debt, the firm expects its return on equity to increase. _____
e. The firm decides to change its inventory method from one GAAP method to another GAAP method. _____
f. The firm's dividend payout ratio is reduced.
g. Congress changes the tax laws, resulting in longer depreciation lives for tax purposes. _____

Self-Test Problems   (Solutions appear on pages 715–716.)

(Solutions appear on pages 715–716.)

Depreciation, Taxes, and Cash Flow

ST 4.1   Parkwest Hotel has the following income statement for financial reporting purposes:

Income Statement

Revenues	$180,000
All operating expenses except depreciation	142,000
Depreciation	15,000
EBIT	23,000
Interest	11,000
EBT	12,000
Taxes (30%)	3,600
Net income	$ 8,400

Assume that all revenues and expenses are for cash. The firm uses accelerated depreciation for tax purposes, so the actual depreciation charged is $20,000, not $15,000. Given the difference between GAAP financial statements and those prepared for tax purposes, what is Parkwest's actual cash flow from operations?

Cash Budget: Scenario Analysis

ST 4.2   Debbie Miller of CRF, Inc., is preparing a cash budget. Under the most likely case, sales (cash inflows) are estimated to be $100,000, $120,000, $140,000, and $100,000, respectively, for the four quarters. Cost of goods sold are $40,000 plus 20 percent of sales per quarter; selling, general and administrative expenses are $10,000 plus 5 percent of sales per quarter; and interest expenses are $5,000 per quarter. Taxes (at a 40 percent marginal rate) are paid quarterly on the above inflows and outflows. Other net cash inflows (+) or outflows (−) per quarter are +$10,000, −$50,000, −$60,000, and +$20,000, respectively. Cash on hand at the beginning of quarter 1 is $20,000, and a minimum cash balance of $15,000 must be maintained. Under its loan agreement, CRF can borrow funds during the year, but must be out of debt by the end of quarter 4.

a. Help Debbie prepare a cash budget for the next four quarters for CRF. Will CRF violate its loan agreement?
b. With a pessimistic forecast, sales will be $20,000 less *each* quarter, and other net cash outflows will be cut to −$40,000 in quarter 2 and −$50,000 in quarter 3. Will CRF violate its loan agreement?
c. With an optimistic forecast, sales will increase by $20,000 *each* quarter. Can CRF increase its other net cash outflows to a total of −$70,000 in quarter 2 and −$75,000 in quarter 3 and still meet its loan agreement?

Pro Forma Balance Sheet

ST 4.3   Given the following information, prepare a pro forma balance sheet for Ciliotta, Inc.:

Next year's projected sales	$50,000
Cash as a percentage of sales	5%
Accounts receivable as a percentage of sales	15%
Inventory as a percentage of sales	20%
Net long-term assets as a percentage of sales	30%
Current liabilities	A current ratio of 2 times
Long-term debt	$5,000 in current year; can go to $20,000
Common stock	$5,000 in current year; none planned
Retained earnings	$10,000 in current year
After-tax profits as a percentage of sales	5%
Dividend payout ratio	40%

Problems

Depreciation and
Cash Flow

4.1 Frankle Enterprises wants to assess the impact of different depreciation methods on its net income and cash flow. It can select an accelerated method that provides $40,000 in depreciation in the current year, or straight-line, which provides $15,000 in depreciation writeoff. Other relevant data are these:

Sales	$400,000
Cost of goods sold	$200,000
Interest expense	$ 40,000
Operating expenses (excluding depreciation)	$ 80,000
Cash dividends on common stock	$ 15,000
Cash dividends on preferred stock	$ 4,000
Shares of common stock outstanding	10,000
Marginal tax rate (T)	40%

Assume all of the figures above, except for depreciation, represent actual cash inflows or cash outflows.

a. For both the $15,000 and $40,000 depreciation figures, calculate (1) net income, (2) earnings per share (EPS), (3) amount transferred to retained earnings, and (4) cash flow. [*Note:* If you employ Equation 4.3 to calculate cash flow, modify it as follows: CF = CFBT(1 − T) + Dep(T) − cash dividends.]
b. In light of your findings in (a), explain why most firms maintain two sets of records—one under GAAP for financial reporting purposes and a second for tax (IRS) purposes.

Deferred Taxes

4.2 King Aviation (a new firm) has asked you, its controller, to determine the impact of using accelerated depreciation for tax purposes, while using straight-line depreciation for GAAP accounting purposes, on its deferred tax account. You estimate that King will have income before depreciation and taxes of $105 per year for the foreseeable future. The firm plans to purchase assets for $200 that will be depreciated via straight-line depreciation over their 8-year accounting life to a value of zero. But for tax purposes the firm will depreciate the assets to a value of zero as follows: first year, 20 percent of original cost; second year, 32 percent; third year, 19 percent; fourth year, 15 percent; and fifth year, 14 percent. If King Aviation's marginal tax rate is 30 percent, what is the total in its deferred taxes account on the balance sheet at the end of 5 years? (*Note:* This is simply the *cumulative sum of the difference* in taxes reported for GAAP purposes, and taxes actually paid to the IRS.)

Cash Shortage

4.3 Mott's Transit has run into some cash flow problems due to rapid expansion. Kevin Mott, the chief financial officer, is making plans for the next 6 months. Assume it is December 31. The balance sheet for the year just completed and the firm's projected income statement (both for accounting and tax purposes) for the first half of next year are as follows:

Balance Sheet as of December 31		Projected Income Statement for Next 6 Months	
Assets	$300	Sales	$500
Liabilities and equity		Expenses	360
Current debt	$100	Depreciation	30
Long-term debt	50	EBIT	110
Equity	150	Interest	25
Total	$300	EBT	85
		Taxes(40%)	34
		Net Income	$ 51

In addition, Kevin notes the following:

a. Eighty dollars of the $100 in current debt comes due in the first half of next year, and the bank has indicated it will not renew the loan.

b. A long-term debt issue of $50 is planned for the first half of next year.

c. Seventy percent of the sales projected for the first half of next year will be received in cash by June 30; the remainder will not be collected until the second half of next year.

d. Forty dollars in cash will be received during the first half of next year from sales in the last half of this year. (Thus, this is an account receivable that will be collected.)

e. Ninety percent of the estimated expenses for the first half of next year will be paid in cash during the period; the remainder can be paid in the second half of next year.

f. Taxes and interest must be paid in full during the first half of next year. Also, cash dividends of $16 are payable during the first half of next year.

g. The cash account cannot be reduced from its present level.

Prepare an estimate of Mott's expected cash inflows and outflows for the next 6 months. Do you foresee any problems? What actions might Kevin take to secure the additional cash needed?

Statement of Cash Flows

4.4 The statement of cash flows for Amoco Corp. for 1985, 1986, and 1987 was as follows (in millions):

	1987	1986	1985
Cash flows from operating activities:			
Net income	$ 1,360	$ 747	$ 1,953
Depreciation, depletion, amortization, and retirements and abandonments	2,295	2,418	2,059
Decrease (increase) in receivables	(197)	672	(73)
Decrease (increase) in inventories	(34)	75	17
Increase (decrease) in payables and accrued liabilities	331	(1,367)	159
Deferred taxes and other items	257	297	603
Net cash provided by operating activities	$ 4,012	$ 2,842	$ 4,718
Cash flows from investing activities:			
Capital expenditures	(2,332)	(2,256)	(3,881)
Proceeds from dispositions of property	129	97	185
Distribution of cash of Cyprus Minerals Co.	—	—	(23)
New investments and advances	(42)	(192)	(42)
Proceeds from sale of investments	119	131	25
Other	141	(32)	(11)
Net cash used in investing activities	$(1,985)	$(2,252)	$(3,747)
Cash flows from financing activities:			
New long-term obligations	3	1,153	334
Repayment of long-term obligations	(259)	(979)	(375)
Cash dividends paid	(847)	(849)	(872)
Issuances of common stock	603	161	127
Acquisitions of common stock	(443)	(363)	(937)
Increase (decrease) in short-term obligations	(9)	(263)	324
Net cash used in financing activities	$ (952)	$(1,140)	$(1,399)
Increase (decrease) in cash and marketable securities	1,075	(550)	(428)
Cash and marketable securities—beginning of year	441	991	1,419
Cash and marketable securities—end of year	$ 1,516	$ 441	$ 991

Supplemental Cash Flow Information

The effect of foreign currency exchange fluctuations on total cash and marketable securities balances was not significant. Net cash provided by operating activities reflects cash payments for interest and income taxes as follows:

	1987	1986	1985
Interest paid	$398	$408	$ 459
Income taxes paid	861	877	1,368

(*Note*: They also reported some information related to 1985 for Cyprus Minerals Company.)

a. Analyze the 3 years and comment on the primary sources of cash, the primary uses of cash, and any apparent trends. How else (in terms of a general approach) could the operating section of the statement be constructed?

b. What else would you like to know that is not reflected or apparent on Amoco's statement of cash flows?

Basic Cash Budget

4.5 Richmond Products has forecast its cash flows for the next two months as follows:

	First Month	Second Month
Total operating cash inflow	$210 million	$150 million
Total operating cash outflow	−140 million	−135 million
Other net inflow (+) or outflow (−)	−30 million	−90 million

Richmond's beginning cash balance is $15 million, and its minimum cash balance is $10 million. Determine Richmond's cumulative financing needed (−) or surplus (+) for both months.

Cash Budget

4.6 Sydney & Sons is in the process of developing its cash budget for the months of January, February, March, and April. Twenty percent of sales are for cash; 50 percent of total sales are for credit and collected the next month. The remaining 30 percent are for credit and collected in 2 months. There are no bad debts.

Purchases of raw materials are made in the month prior to the expected sale and average 45 percent of expected sales. They are paid for in the month following their purchase. Wages, rent, and selling expenses are $300,000 in January and will increase by $50,000 per month. Interest of $25,000 is payable every month. Taxes of $75,000 are payable in January, and $150,000 is due in April. Cash dividends of $100,000 are payable in February. Finally, capital expenditures of $200,000 are forecast for January, and another $50,000 are expected in April.

Actual sales for November and December and forecasted sales for the next 5 months are as follows:

November	$1,000,000	March	$1,800,000
December	900,000	April	2,300,000
January	1,000,000	May	2,500,000
February	1,400,000		

Cash on hand on January 1 is $100,000, and a $50,000 minimum cash balance is required each month.

a. Prepare a cash budget for January, February, March, and April.
b. What is the maximum level of short-term financing required?
c. Suppose sales receipts come in uniformly over the month, but all outflows are paid by the tenth of the month. Discuss the effect this would have on the cash budget. Would the cash budget just completed be valid? If not, what could be done to adjust the budget?

(Do only if using Pinches Disk.)

d. (1) Now suppose Sydney & Sons re-estimates its forecasted sales as follows:

January	$ 800,000	April	$1,900,000
February	1,100,000	May	2,200,000
March	1,500,000		

What is the effect of this on Sydney & Sons cash budget in (a)? What is the maximum level of short-term financing now required?

(2) Suppose Sydney & Sons not only re-estimates its sales forecasts as in (1), but also expects cash flow from collections to change as follows:

Collections: 1-month lag	40%
Collections: 2-month lag	45
Cash sales	15

Purchases of raw materials are also expected to increase to 50 percent. How has this affected the cash budget originally prepared in (a)? Has the maximum level of short-term financing changed?

Cash Budget (More Difficult)

4.7   The Shapiro Company is preparing plans for the next 6 months. The firm's special concern is a $2.5 million note that comes due in September. Sales (actual for May and June and forecast for the rest) are as follows:

May	$3,400,000	October	$1,800,000
June	3,500,000	November	1,500,000
July	4,000,000	December	1,400,000
August	2,500,000	January	1,500,000
September	2,000,000		

Sales are 10 percent for cash, 75 percent credit collected in 1 month, and 15 percent credit collected in 2 months. There are no bad debts. Purchases of raw materials are made as follows: 20 percent of sales 2 months ahead, paid in the month following the purchase; and 30 percent of sales expected 1 month ahead, paid in the month following the purchase.

Wages, selling and administrative expenses are estimated to be as follows:

July	$1,000,000	October	$700,000
August	900,000	November	700,000
September	800,000	December	700,000

In addition, there are lease payments of $100,000 per month. Interest payments on long-term borrowing of $300,000 in both August and November are required. Taxes of $325,000 are payable in September and December. Finally, there is the short-term note of $2,500,000 payable in September. There are no cash dividends or other inflows or outflows. Shapiro's beginning cash balance is $430,000 on July 1, and its required minimum balance is $400,000.

a.   Prepare a monthly cash budget for the last 6 months of the year.
b.   Will Shapiro be able to pay off the $2,500,000 note in full and on time?
c.   Suppose that due to a recession sales fall off, but production does not decline as rapidly. Also, customers take longer to pay their bills. What effect might this have on Shapiro's ability to repay the note?

Pro Forma Income Statement

4.8   Blakeslee Company's condensed income statement as of December 31 is:

(In millions)

Sales	$4,841.4
Operating expenses	4,333.5
Income from operations	507.9
+ Other income	37.9
EBIT	545.8
Interest	180.7
EBT	365.1
Taxes	83.5
Net income	$ 281.6

a.   If we had perfect foresight and knew next year's sales were going to be $5,432.2 million, estimate next year's income statement employing the percentage of sales method.

b. What differences exist between your pro forma income statement and Blakeslee's actual income statement for the year, listed below?

(In millions)	
Sales	$5,432.2
Operating expenses	4,823.7
Income from operations	608.5
+ Other income	70.0
EBIT	678.5
Interest	185.9
EBT	492.6
Taxes	124.9
Net income	$ 367.7

c. Do you believe some of these differences could be anticipated to obtain a more accurate pro forma income statement? Why or why not?

Pro Forma Balance Sheet and Financing Needs

4.9 Franklin Company's estimated sales for next year are $30 million. The percentage of sales for items that vary directly with sales for Franklin is given below:

Cash	5%	Accounts payable	15%
Accounts receivable	25	Accruals	10
Inventory	30	Net profit margin	5

Its net long-term assets are $6 million, notes payable are $2 million, long-term debt is $2 million, and common stock is $5 million. Franklin's present retained earnings are $5.1 million, and its dividend payout ratio is 40 percent.

a. Prepare a pro forma balance sheet and indicate the estimated amount of additional financing needed. Assume that long-term debt will be used to finance any shortfall.

(Do only if using Pinches Disk.)

b. (1) What happens if Franklin's sales are $40 million and its long-term assets increase to $8 million? If long-term debt is used, how does the ratio of total debt to total assets in (b) compare with the same ratio for (a)?

(2) Recalculate (1) assuming the percentage of sales for each balance sheet item that varies directly with sales for Franklin changes as follows:

Cash	5%	Accounts payable	25%
Accounts receivable	30	Accruals	15
Inventory	20	Net profit margin	10

How do these changes affect the pro forma balance sheet and the ratio of total debt to total assets?

c. If the ratio of total debt to total assets in the same industry is 50 to 55 percent, what can we conclude about the riskiness of Franklin Company in (b)? Its potential effect on Franklin's market price per share?

Financing Growth

4.10 El Rancho, Inc., has decided to embark on a rapid expansion. Its most recent income statement and balance sheet are as follows:

El Rancho, Inc.
Income Statement
Year Ending March 31
(In millions)

Sales	$30.0
Cost of goods sold	15.0
Selling, general, and administrative expenses	6.0
EBIT	9.0
Interest	1.0
EBT	8.0
Taxes (30%)	2.4
Net income	5.6
Cash dividends	3.0
Transferred to retained earnings	$ 2.6

El Rancho, Inc.
Balance Sheet
March 31
(In millions)

Current assets	$ 6.0	Accounts payable	$ 2.0
Long-term assets	14.0	Notes payable	2.0
Total assets	$20.0	Long-term debt	6.0
		Common stock	3.0
		Retained earnings	7.0
		Total liabilities and stock-holders' equity	$20.0

In attempting to determine its financial condition and needs, El Rancho believes the following will happen:

Sales	$40.0
Cost of goods sold	Same percent of sales as current year
Selling, general and administrative expenses	$ 9.0
Interest	$ 1.0 (initially, before additional financing)
Taxes	Same percent of EBT as current year
Cash dividends	$ 3.0 (initially)
Current assets	$ 7.0
Long-term assets	$23.0
Accounts payable	$ 3.0
Notes payable	$ 2.0
Long-term debt	$ 6.0 (initially)
Common stock	$ 3.0

a. Based on these estimates, prepare a pro forma income statement and balance sheet for El Rancho. How much additional financing (regardless of where it comes from) do you estimate it needs?

b. What happens if El Rancho acquires sufficient additional long-term debt financing to keep its ratio of total debt to total assets at its current level? Assume interest expenses increase by $500,000.

c. By cutting its cash dividends in addition to the step taken in (b), can El Rancho finance all its cash needs? What do you think will happen to the market price of El Rancho's common stock if it cuts cash dividends? Do you see any alternative means of raising the needed funds?

References

For some of the accounting problems, see

KNUTSON, PETER H. "FAS 96—Implications for Analysts." *Financial Analysts Journal* 44 (November–December 1988), pp. 17–18.

McGOLDRICK, BETH. "The Controversy over Deferred Taxes." *Institutional Investor* 18 (September 1984), pp. 249 ff.

SONDHI, ASHWINPAUL, GEORGE H. SORTER, AND GERALD I. WHITE. "Cash Flow Redefined: FAS 95 and Security Analysis." *Financial Analysts Journal* 44 (November–December 1988), pp. 19–20.

Cash flow, and its usefulness, is discussed in

CASEY, CORNELIUS J., AND NORMAN J. BARTCZAK. "Cash Flow—It's Not the Bottom Line." *Harvard Business Review* 62 (July–August 1984), pp. 61–66.

DAMBOLENA, ISMAEL, AND JOEL M. SHULMAN. "A Primary Rule for Detecting Bankruptcy: Watch the Cash." *Financial Analysts Journal* 44 (September–October 1988), pp. 74–78.

DRTINA, RALPH E., AND JAMES A. LARGAY. "Pitfalls in Calculating Cash Flow from Operations." *Accounting Review* 60 (April 1985), pp. 314–326.

GENTRY, JAMES A., PAUL NEWBOLD, AND DAVID T. WHITFORD. "Predicting Bankruptcy: If Cash Flow's Not the Bottom Line, What Is?" *Financial Analysts Journal* 41 (September–October 1985), pp. 47–56.

LARGAY, JAMES A., AND CLYDE P. STICKNEY. "Cash Flows, Ratio Analysis, and the W. T. Grant Company Bankruptcy." *Financial Analysts Journal* 36 (July–August 1980), pp. 51–54.

STANCILL, JAMES McNEILL. "When Is There Cash in Cash Flow?" *Harvard Business Review* 65 (March–April 1987), pp. 38–49.

For some information on economic and sales forecasts, see

BERNSTEIN, PETER L., AND THEODORE H. SILBERT. "Are Economic Forecasters Worth Listening To?" *Harvard Business Review* 62 (September–October 1984), pp. 32–40.

PAN, JUDY, DONALD R. NICHOLS, AND O. MAURICE JOY. "Sales Forecasting Practices of Large U.S. Industrial Firms." *Financial Management* 6 (Fall 1977), pp. 72–77.

GEORGOFF, DAVID M., AND ROBERT G. MURDICK. "Manager's Guide to Forecasting." *Harvard Business Review* 64 (January–February 1986), pp. 110–120.

See Models two, three, and four in *Lotus 1–2–3® for Financial Management* by Pinches and Courtney for templates that calculate various time series forecasts of sales, cash budgets, and pro forma financial statements and estimated financing needs or surpluses.

PART THREE

Fundamental Concepts for Financial Management

5

Time Value of Money

Overview

- Future value is the value at some future date of a given amount of money today compounded at a certain percentage rate. Present value is the value today of some future amount of money discounted at a given percent. Present value and future value are simply the inverse of each other.

- Given an amount today (i.e., the present value) and some future value or series, the interest rate that equates the two can be determined.

- Four examples of time value are (1) compound growth rates, (2) future sums, (3) loan payments and amortization schedules, and (4) effective interest rates.

- This book generally assumes annual compounding or discounting. More frequent compounding or discounting alters the effective rate of interest.

D uring a recent 10-year period, the price of Boeing's common stock increased at a 19 percent annual compound growth rate. In the same period Marriott increased at 21 percent, Shoney's at 23 percent, Wal-Mart at 38 percent, and Digital Equipment at 25 percent. To compare the performance of these companies, investors and managers must understand compounding and be able to calculate compound growth rates. From the stock market to your savings account, knowing the performance of your investment over time is essential to effective financial decision making.

Suppose Smithkline Beckman approached a group of banks—Wachovia, Chase Manhattan, First Chicago, and Wells Fargo—for a $20 million loan. After discussion, the parties agreed on the length of the loan, the rate of interest, and the frequency of repayments. The question remained: How much would the payments be? Part of each payment would go to pay back the original $20 million, part to pay interest on the loan—but just how much? Questions like this are basically the same questions you face when you obtain a car or home loan. Money is being borrowed, and interest is paid over time. We can answer these questions with present value techniques.

Finally, assume that American Airlines is planning its future fleet of planes. The capital budgeting group proposes that American spend the enormous sum of $7.5 billion over the next 5 years to replace a portion of its current fleet with newer, more fuel-efficient planes. The savings is expected to be $900 million per year for the 20-year average life of the new planes. Should American make the investment? What additional information is needed to make an intelligent, informed decision?

All these topics, and many more, require an understanding of the time value of money. Time value is important whenever cash flows occur at various times. In this chapter we learn how to account for time differences in the inflow or outflow of cash.

Basic Concepts

To maximize the size of our pie, or firm, it is essential to have the proper ingredients. Also, it is important to understand that how these ingredients are mixed together influences the size of the pie. In this part of the book we concentrate on three basic concepts: (1) the timing of when the cash flows (or ingredients) occur, (2) how to value bonds and stocks (or determine the size of the combined pie), and (3) how risk (or the mix of ingredients) affects the size of the pie. To maximize the size of the pie we must understand the impact that the magnitude, timing, and riskiness of the cash flows have on the pie. Holding other things constant, we can visualize this as follows:

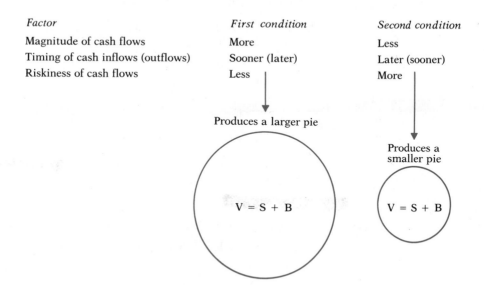

Factor	First condition	Second condition
Magnitude of cash flows	More	Less
Timing of cash inflows (outflows)	Sooner (later)	Later (sooner)
Riskiness of cash flows	Less	More

Produces a larger pie

$V = S + B$

Produces a smaller pie

$V = S + B$

It is to these topics we now turn our attention.

Finding the *future value*, or *compounding*, involves taking an amount today and determining what it will be worth sometime in the future if it earns a return of k percent interest per year. Calculating the *present value*, or *discounting*, involves finding the value today of an amount to be received in the future discounted at k percent per year. When compounding is employed, k is the *compound rate*. When discounting is employed, k is the *discount rate*. We begin by discussing both ideas; then see how they are related.[1]

Future Value

If you purchase a security worth $500 today that pays 10 percent interest compounded annually, how much will it be worth in 1 year? To determine this, let's define the following:

PV_0 = the present, or today's, value of the amount, $500
k = the annual interest rate, which is 10 percent, or 0.10
I = dollars of interest earned during the period = $k(PV_0)$
FV = the future, or ending, value of the amount
t = the number of periods or years, which can vary from zero to infinity but is a whole number, n

In our example the number of years, n, is 1; so the future value in 1 year, FV_1, is

$$FV_1 = PV_0 + I$$
$$= PV_0 + k(PV_0) = PV_0(1 + k)$$

We can now use this relationship to find out how much your security is worth at the end of 1 year:

$$FV_1 = \$500(1 + 0.10) = \$500(1.10) = \$550$$

The interest earned is $50, and the future value in 1 year is the sum of the original principal of $500 plus the interest of $50. This can be depicted using a timeline as follows:

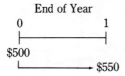

End of Year
0   1
$500
→ $550

What about the value of your investment at the end of 3 years? For a 3-year period, we have

$$FV_3 = PV_0(1 + k)^3$$
$$= PV_0(1 + k)(1 + k)(1 + k)$$
$$= \$500(1.10)(1.10)(1.10) = \$500(1.331) = \$665.50$$

---

[1] In this chapter, and throughout the book, it is assumed all students have a basic calculator. However, many financial calculators are inexpensive, and they make present value calculations extremely simple. Any finance or accounting major should invest in a financial calculator; it will pay for itself quickly in time saved and greater accuracy. The footnotes in this chapter will assist you in using a financial calculator.

This may be represented with a timeline as

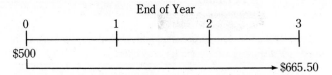

In general, the future value at the end of n periods is

$$FV_n = PV_0(1 + k)^n \tag{5.1}$$

The two cases just solved simply use Equation 5.1 with $n = 1$ and $n = 3$, respectively. With a calculator it is easy to compute the future value of any amount for any period of time.[2] We have tables, however, that provide *future value factors* ($FV_{k,n}$) for the quantity $(1 + k)^n$ in Equation 5.1. Table 5.1 is a portion of the more complete Table F.1, given at the end of the book. In terms of future value factors, Equation 5.1 can be rewritten

$$FV_n = PV_0(FV_{k,n}) \tag{5.2}$$

Suppose we solve for the future value of $500 in 3 years compounded at 10 percent using the appropriate FV factor from the table. We then have

$$FV_3 = PV_0(FV_{10\%,3yr}) = \$500(1.331) = \$665.50$$

The same future sum, $665.50, is obtained using Equation 5.1, or Equation 5.2 and the FV table.

One point should be mentioned. In the table we refer to *periods*, not *years*. While we typically talk about years, compounding and discounting can be done quarterly, monthly, or for any other period. This is discussed later in the chapter.

Present Value

So far we started with some amount today ($t = 0$) and then solved for a future value. Let's turn the situation around. Given a future value at time period $t = n$, what is the present value today? If you need $550 exactly 1 year from now, how much would you have to put aside today if you can earn 10 percent on the funds? The present value is given by

$$PV_0 = \frac{FV_1}{(1 + k)^1}$$

Substituting, the present value today of $550 to be received 1 year from now discounted at 10 percent is

$$PV_0 = \frac{\$550}{(1.10)} = \$500$$

[2] To solve for the value $(1.10)^3$ using a basic calculator, it is necessary to use the exponential function, y^x. In this problem $y = 1.10$, $n = x = 3$, $y^x = 1.331$, and $FV_3 = \$500(1.331) = \$665.50$. If you have a financial calculator, simply punch in $n = 3$, $k = i = 10$, $PV = 500$, and then hit the FV button to obtain the answer of $665.50.

Table 5.1 Future Value Factors for $1 Compounded at k Percent for n Periods:

$$FV_{k,n} = (1 + k)^n$$

A more extensive table is presented as Table F.1. Tables with four or five decimal places can be obtained if greater accuracy is needed.

Period, n	Compound Rate, k						
	7%	8%	9%	10%	11%	12%	13%
1	1.070	1.080	1.090	1.100	1.110	1.120	1.130
2	1.145	1.166	1.188	1.210	1.232	1.254	1.277
3	1.225	1.260	1.295	1.331	1.368	1.405	1.443
4	1.311	1.360	1.412	1.464	1.518	1.574	1.630
5	1.403	1.469	1.539	1.611	1.685	1.762	1.842
6	1.501	1.587	1.677	1.772	1.870	1.974	2.082
7	1.606	1.714	1.828	1.949	2.076	2.211	2.353
8	1.718	1.851	1.993	2.144	2.305	2.476	2.658
9	1.838	1.999	2.172	2.358	2.558	2.773	3.004
10	1.967	2.159	2.367	2.594	2.839	3.106	3.395

This can be depicted as follows:

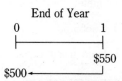

What if you need $665.50 in 3 years? How much would you have to put aside today at 10 percent compound interest to end up with the $665.50? Proceeding as before, we solve for the present value, PV_0, where

$$PV_0 = \frac{FV_3}{(1+k)^3} = \frac{\$665.50}{(1.10)(1.10)(1.10)} = \frac{\$665.50}{1.331} = \$500$$

to obtain the answer.[3] Graphically, this is

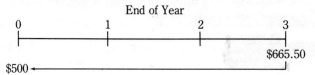

The general equation for the present value of an individual amount to be received n periods in the future, discounted at k percent, is

$$PV_0 = \frac{FV_n}{(1+k)^n} \tag{5.3}$$

In the preceding examples we used Equation 5.3, first for n = 1, then for n = 3. Equation 5.3 may also be written as follows: $PV_0 = FV_n[1/(1 + k)^n]$. The term in

---

[3] With a financial calculator, you punch in n = 3, k = i = 10, FV = 665.50, and then hit the PV button to determine the answer, which is $500.

The Value of Manhattan

According to popular legend, Manhattan island was purchased from the Canarsee Indians in 1626 for a price of 60 guilders, or about $24. Who won and who lost on this transaction? It's really a question of the time value of money. The purchase occurred 364 years ago (1990 − 1626), so we can use Equation 5.1 to find the value of the original $24 under different interest rate assumptions. The equation is

$$1990 \text{ value} = \$24(1 + k)^{364}$$

The value of the $24 in 1990 is as follows:

k	$24(1 + k)^{364}$
0.02	$32,410
0.04	38,049,307
0.06	39,043,270,000
0.08	35,193,150,000,000
0.10	27,999,390,000,000,000

It's hard to know the rate of interest that the Canarsee Indians could have received, or the value of Manhattan today, but some comparisons can be made. If they received a rate of 6 percent, the value in 1990 will be more than $39 billion; at 8 percent it will be in excess of $35 trillion. For comparison, the population of the United States is approximately 250 million. At a 6 percent compound rate, the present value in 1990 of the original $24 would allow $156 to be given to everyone in the U.S. At 8 percent it would be worth about $140,000 to each person, while at 10 percent it would be worth about $112 million to each person in the United States. Now that's compounding!

brackets is called the *present value factor* $(PV_{k,n})$. Table 5.2 lists some of them; the more complete Table F.3 may be found at the end of the book. Using PV factors, the basic present value equation (Equation 5.3) can be rewritten

$$PV_0 = FV_n(PV_{k,n}) \tag{5.4}$$

To find the present value today of $665.50 to be received 3 years from now, discounted at 10 percent, we proceed as follows:

$$PV_0 = FV_3(PV_{10\%,3yr}) = \$665.50(0.751) = \$500$$

Thus, from either Equation 5.3 or 5.4, the present value is $500.

Comparing Future Value and Present Value

Because a thorough understanding of future value versus present value is essential, let's pause for a moment and make sure we know that these two concepts are simply the inverse of each other. If we start with the fundamental equation of compounding, which is Equation 5.1,

$$FV_n = PV_0(1 + k)^n$$

Table 5.2 Present Value Factors for $1 Discounted at k Percent for n Periods:

$$PV_{k,n} = \frac{1}{(1 + k)^n}$$

PV factors for any period greater than zero are always less than 1. They decrease as the time period lengthens or the discount rate increases.

Period, n	Discount Rate, k						
	7%	8%	9%	10%	11%	12%	13%
1	0.935	0.926	0.917	0.909	0.901	0.893	0.885
2	0.873	0.857	0.842	0.826	0.812	0.797	0.783
3	0.816	0.794	0.772	0.751	0.731	0.712	0.693
4	0.763	0.735	0.708	0.683	0.659	0.636	0.613
5	0.713	0.681	0.650	0.621	0.593	0.567	0.543
6	0.666	0.630	0.596	0.564	0.535	0.507	0.480
7	0.623	0.583	0.547	0.513	0.482	0.452	0.425
8	0.582	0.540	0.502	0.467	0.434	0.404	0.376
9	0.544	0.500	0.460	0.424	0.391	0.361	0.333
10	0.508	0.463	0.422	0.386	0.352	0.322	0.295

we see that by dividing through by the quantity $(1 + k)^n$ and simplifying, we have the basic equation for present value, Equation 5.3, $PV_0 = FV_n/(1 + k)^n$.

In terms of future value versus present value factors, the $PV_{k,n}$ is the reciprocal of the $FV_{k,n}$ for the same discount rate and time period, so that

$$PV_{k,n} = \frac{1}{FV_{k,n}}$$

For example, the PV factor of 0.751 for 10 percent and 3 years is simply the comparable FV factor divided into 1, or

$$PV_{10\%,3\,yr} = \frac{1}{FV_{10\%,3\,yr}} = \frac{1}{1.331} = 0.751$$

This corresponds to the 10 percent, 3-year PV factor presented in Table 5.2.

These relationships hold for all comparable rates and time periods. So it should be easy to see that compounding to find future values, and discounting to find present values, are simply the inverse of each other. Future values will always be higher than the initial amount; as shown in Table 5.1, FV factors increase both with time and with the compounding rate. Likewise, when we are discounting, the present value is always less than the future value. The PV factors, as shown in Table 5.2, decline with both time and the discount rate employed. This relationship between FVs, PVs, interest rates, and time is shown in Figure 5.1. Note the effect that both time and the interest rate have on both FV and PV factors.

Figure 5.1 Relationships Among $FV_{k,n}$, $PV_{k,n}$, Interest Rates, and Time

Due to compounding, FV factors become steeper and steeper over time, indicating that the future values grow larger the longer the period and the higher the rate. Likewise, due to discounting, PV factors become flatter and flatter over time.

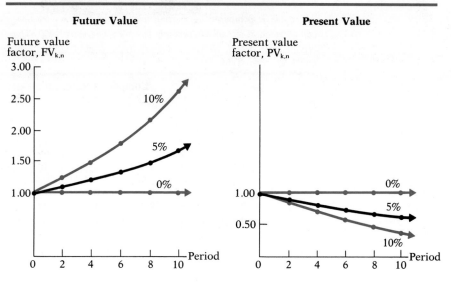

Multiple Cash Flows

Up to now we have considered only individual cash flows. It is even more important, however, to be able to deal with a series of cash flows that extend over time. Let's begin by discussing the future value or present value of an *annuity*, which is a series of payments of a fixed amount for each of a number of periods. Then we'll consider the discounting of an uneven series of cash flows. Finally, we will look at a *perpetuity*, where constant payments continue to be made indefinitely.

Future Value of an Ordinary Annuity

Consider the case in which a promise is made to pay $600 at the *end* of each of 4 years. (When the payments occur at the end of each period, this is an *ordinary annuity*.) If you receive the $600 at the end of each year and immediately invest it at 10 percent, how much will you have at the end of the 4 years? A graphic depiction of the steps necessary to determine the future value of the annuity is as follows:

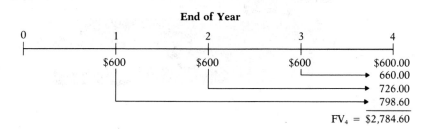

Table 5.3 Future Value Factors for an Annuity of $1 Compounded at k Percent for n Periods:

$$FVA_{k,n} = \sum_{t=0}^{n-1} (1 + k)^t = \frac{(1 + k)^n - 1}{k}$$

This table is computed by starting with 1.000. This occurs because the last payment is not compounded at all, and accordingly has a FV factor of 1.000. Then FV factors from Table 5.1 are added to 1.000. Hence, the 4.641 figure is calculated by adding 1.000 plus 1.100, 1.210, and 1.331 from Table 5.1.

Period, n	Compound Rate, k						
	7%	8%	9%	10%	11%	12%	13%
1	1.000	1.000	1.000	1.000	1.000	1.000	1.000
2	2.070	2.080	2.090	2.100	2.110	2.120	2.130
3	3.215	3.246	3.278	3.310	3.342	3.374	3.407
4	4.440	4.506	4.573	4.641	4.710	4.779	4.850
5	5.751	5.867	5.985	6.105	6.228	6.353	6.480
6	7.153	7.336	7.523	7.716	7.913	8.115	8.323
7	8.654	8.923	9.200	9.487	9.783	10.089	10.405
8	10.260	10.637	11.028	11.436	11.859	12.300	12.757
9	11.978	12.488	13.021	13.579	14.164	14.776	15.416
10	13.816	14.487	15.193	15.937	16.722	17.549	18.420

Since the payments start 1 year from now, the first payment of $600 is compounded for 3 years (t = 4 minus t = 1 equals 3 years). Likewise, the $600 received at the end of year 2 is compounded for 2 years; that received at the end of year 3 is compounded for 1 year; and the $600 received at the end of year 4 is not compounded at all. Repeated use of either of the previous future value equations (5.1 or 5.2) produces a future value of $2,784.60. Thus, $600 received for each of 4 years beginning 1 year from now will be worth $2,784.60 at the end of 4 years if the annual compound rate is 10 percent.

Algebraically, the approach just discussed can be expressed as follows:

$$FV_n = PMT \sum_{t=0}^{n-1} (1 + k)^t \tag{5.5}$$

where[4]

FV_n = the future value of an annuity of PMT dollars to be received for each of n periods

Σ = sigma, which means "take the sum of"

PMT = an annuity that starts at time period 1 and extends to time period n

k = the compounding rate

n = the number of periods, or life, of the annuity

[4] See Appendix 5A for the derivation of Equations 5.5 and 5.6.

Although Equation 5.5 can be used, a simpler expression for use with a calculator is[5]

$$FV_n = PMT\left[\frac{(1+k)^n - 1}{k}\right] \tag{5.6}$$

The part in brackets is simply the future value [i.e., $(1 + k)^n$] minus 1, divided by the compound rate, k.

Alternatively, *future value factors for an annuity* ($FVA_{k,n}$) have been calculated for the bracketed portion of Equation 5.6. These are presented in Table 5.3; more complete is Table F.2. In terms of the table values, the future value of an ordinary annuity is

$$FV_n = PMT(FVA_{k,n}) \tag{5.7}$$

We can now solve our annuity problem using Equation 5.7:

$$FV_4 = \$600(FVA_{10\%,4yr}) = \$600(4.641) = \$2,784.60$$

Either Equation 5.6 or 5.7 produces exactly the same value as determined by the step-by-step procedure using Equation 5.5; the advantage is the savings in time and/or accuracy.

Future Value of an Annuity Due

While our primary concern is with ordinary annuities, what if the four cash inflows in the problem above had occurred at the *beginning* of each period, not the end? This is the case of an *annuity due.* Each of our payments is shifted to the left one period, so they now occur at t = 0, t = 1, t = 2, and t = 3. Since each payment is compounded for an extra year, Equations 5.6 and 5.7 can be modified as follows:

$$FV_n(\text{annuity due}) = PMT\left[\frac{(1+k)^n - 1}{k}\right](1+k) \tag{5.6a}$$

and

$$FV_n(\text{annuity due}) = PMT(FVA_{k,n})(1+k) \tag{5.7a}$$

Solving the earlier problem as an annuity due, we have[6]

$$FV_4(\text{annuity due}) = \$600(4.641)(1.10) = \$3,063.06$$

---

[5] Solving via a calculator, we have for the quantity $\frac{(1+k)^n - 1}{k}$ the following:

$$\frac{(1.10)^4 - 1}{0.10} = \frac{1.4641 - 1}{0.10} = \frac{0.4641}{0.10} = 4.641$$

The future value of the annuity is $600(4.641) = $2,784.60, just as before. Using a financial calculator, we can punch in n = 4, k = i = 10, PMT = 600, and then hit the FV button to produce the same answer of $2,784.60.

[6] An alternative way to solve this problem is to look up the FVA factor for (n + 1) periods, and subtract 1.0 from it. The $FVA_{10\%,5yr}$ is 6.105. Subtracting 1.0, the FVA factor for a 10 percent, 4-year annuity due is 5.105. Calculating the future value of the annuity due, we have:

$$FV_4(\text{annuity due}) = \$600(5.105) = \$3,063.00$$

which is the same answer as above except for a 6 cents rounding difference.

The future value of an annuity due is larger than the future value of an ordinary annuity because of the extra year's compounding; hence, other things being equal, an annuity due is more valuable.

Present Value of an Annuity

As we did for individual cash flows, let's consider a different situation in which you are offered an investment that will pay $600 per year for each of 4 years beginning *exactly 1 year from now*.[7] How much would you be willing to pay for the investment if you expected a 10 percent annual return on your money? Now stream PMT, the constant (ordinary) annuity, represents the $600 to be received for each of n periods. In this case, n equals 4 years and PV_0 is the present value of this annuity. To determine how much we would pay involves determining the present value of this expected cash stream. As shown, there are four $600 amounts.

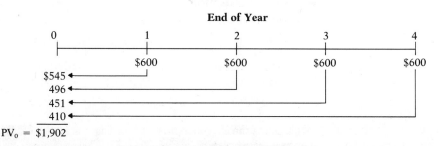

The first, received at the end of year 1, is discounted back 1 year at 10 percent, the second is discounted back 2 years at 10 percent, and so forth to produce a present value of $1,902. This is the amount you would be willing to pay if you required a 10 percent annual compound return on the investment.

Appendix 5A shows that the step-by-step process for determining the present value of an annuity just discussed is equivalent to calculating

$$PV_0 = PMT \sum_{t=1}^{n} \frac{1}{(1+k)^t} \tag{5.8}$$

$$= PMT \left\{ \frac{1 - [1/(1+k)^n]}{k} \right\} \tag{5.9}$$

The term in braces is simply one minus the present value [i.e., $1/(1+k)^n$], divided by the discount rate, k. Using Equation 5.9, the term in braces yields 3.170 for our problem;[8] therefore, the present value at 10 percent of $600 to be received each of 4 years is

$$PV_0 = \$600(3.170) = \$1,902$$

[7] This is an ordinary annuity. All future references mean ordinary annuities, unless otherwise specified. To determine the present value of an annuity due, see footnote 9.

[8] Solving Equation 5.9, we have

$$\frac{1 - [1/(1+k)^n]}{k} = \frac{1 - [1/(1.10)^4]}{0.10} = \frac{1 - (1/1.4641)}{0.10} = \frac{1 - 0.6830}{0.10} = \frac{0.3170}{0.10} = 3.170$$

Using a financial calculator, we punch in n = 4, k = i = 10, PMT = 600, and then hit the PV button. The result is $1,901.92. The 8 cents difference is due to rounding.

Table 5.4 Present Value Factors for an Annuity of $1 Discounted at k Percent for n Periods:

$$PVA_{k,n} = \sum_{t=1}^{n} \frac{1}{(1+k)^t} = \frac{1 - [1/(1+k)^n]}{k}$$

This table can be constructed directly from Table 5.2. For example, the PVA factor for 10 percent and 4 years is simply the sum of the 1-, 2-, 3-, and 4-year, 10 percent PV factors, from Table 5.2. Thus, 0.909 + 0.826 + 0.751 + 0.683 = 3.169, which, except for a rounding difference of 0.001, agrees with the 3.170 given below.

Period, n	\multicolumn{7}{c}{Discount Rate, k}
	7%	8%	9%	10%	11%	12%	13%
1	0.935	0.926	0.917	0.909	0.901	0.893	0.885
2	1.808	1.783	1.759	1.736	1.713	1.690	1.668
3	2.624	2.577	2.531	2.487	2.444	2.402	2.361
4	3.387	3.312	3.240	3.170	3.102	3.037	2.974
5	4.100	3.993	3.890	3.791	3.696	3.605	3.517
6	4.767	4.623	4.486	4.355	4.231	4.111	3.998
7	5.389	5.206	5.033	4.868	4.712	4.564	4.423
8	5.971	5.747	5.535	5.335	5.146	4.968	4.799
9	6.515	6.247	5.995	5.759	5.537	5.328	5.132
10	7.024	6.710	6.418	6.145	5.889	5.650	5.426

Instead of using Equation 5.9, tables are available for the bracketed portion in the equation, which are called *present value factors for an annuity* ($PVA_{k,n}$). Table 5.4 illustrates these; Table F.4 is more complete.

In terms of the table, the present value of an annuity is

$$PV_0 = PMT(PVA_{k,n}) \tag{5.10}$$

Our problem now becomes

$$PV_0 = \$600(PVA_{10\%,4yr}) = \$600(3.170) = \$1,902$$

Just as for the future value of an annuity, there are alternative ways to determine the present value of an annuity.[9] All are correct; just use the method you feel the most comfortable with, and that you make the fewest errors with!

Present Value of an Uneven Series

Because present values are so important for later applications, it is necessary to spend a little more time discussing how to proceed when we have an uneven series of cash flows. First, consider the case in which the cash flows are $100 at year 1,

---

[9] To calculate the present value of an annuity due we make the same basic adjustment, involving the factor $(1 + k)$, that we made to calculate the future value of an annuity due. Thus,

$$PV_0 (\text{annuity due}) = PMT \left\{ \frac{1 - [1/(1+k)^n]}{k} \right\} (1+k) \quad \text{or}$$

$$= PMT(PVA_{k,n})(1+k)$$

For our example, the present value if it is an annuity due is $600(3.170)(1.10) = \$2,092.20. With the payments made in advance, the present value of an annuity due is more valuable than if it is an ordinary annuity.

$150 at year 2, $325 at year 3, and the discount rate is 12 percent. Graphically the cash flows are:

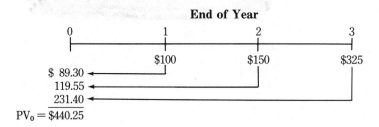

End of Year

Using Equation 5.4, each successive year's cash flow is multiplied by the appropriate 12 percent PV factor, with the result that the present value of this uneven stream is $440.25.[10] The general equation to find the present value of any uneven series of cash flows is

$$PV_0 = \sum_{t=1}^{n} \frac{FV_t}{(1+k)^t} = \sum_{t=1}^{n} FV_t(PV_{k,t}) \tag{5.11}$$

Now consider another example in which the cash flows are $100 at year 1, $150 at year 2, and then $325 for *each* of years 3 through 8. The discount rate remains 12 percent. This problem could be solved in eight separate steps using single-year PV factors, but time can be saved by using the techniques we have learned for annuities. To solve, we proceed as follows:

1. Determine the present value of the annuity of $325 to be received in years 3 through 8. Since this annuity is for 6 years (years 3, 4, 5, 6, 7, and 8), the use of a 6-year PVA factor is required. Employing $PVA_{12\%,6yr}$ and multiplying ($325)(4.111) results in $1,336.08. The present value of $1,336.08 represents the value of the annuity stream at the *end of year 2*.
2. The lump sum of $1,336.08 is then discounted back to time t = 0, which is $1,064.86 [i.e., ($1,336.08)($PV_{12\%,2yr}$) = ($1,336.08)(0.797)], as shown in Figure 5.2.[11]
3. Discount the $100 to be received at the end of year 1 and the $150 to be received at the end of year 2 back to time t = 0. The resulting amounts are $89.30 and $119.55, respectively.
4. Sum the values from steps 2 and 3. Thus, $89.30 + $119.55 + $1,064.86 = $1,273.71. This is the present value of the entire series discounted at 12 percent.

---

[10] Financial calculators have the ability to read in the three cash inflows, and k = i = 12. Punching the present value button (typically called NPV) will produce the answer of $440.19. The 6 cents difference results from rounding.

[11] An alternative way to obtain the present value of the annuity portion is to multiply the annuity stream PMT by the difference in an 8-year PVA factor minus a 2-year PVA factor. Thus, $325[($PVA_{12\%,8yr}$) − ($PVA_{12\%,2yr}$)] = $325(4.968 − 1.690) = $325(3.278) = $1,065.35. Except for a rounding difference of 49 cents, this is the same result for the annuity portion of the example obtained from the 2-step procedure described in steps 1 and 2 above. Using a financial calculator, the final present value is $1,274.08

Figure 5.2 Present Value of an 8-Year Uneven Series Incorporating an Annuity, Discounted at 12 Percent

When annuities are incorporated in an uneven series, it is quicker to use PVA factors to assist in the solution.

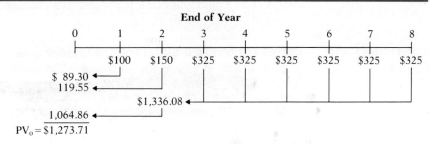

Year	Cash Flow	$\times$	$PV_{12\%,n}$	=	Present Value of Cash Flow
1	$ 100		0.893		$ 89.30
2	150		0.797		119.55
2	1,336.08*		0.797		1,064.86
					PV_0 = $\overline{\$1,273.71}$

*Years	Cash Flow	$\times$	$PV_{12\%,6\ yr}$	=	Present Value of Years 3–8 Cash Flows, at End of Year 2
3–8	$325		4.111		$1,336.08

Perpetuities

Most annuities have a finite life, but some may go on to infinity. An infinite annuity is called a perpetuity. The value of a perpetuity (see Appendix 5A) is found as follows:

$$\text{present value of a perpetuity}_0 = \frac{\text{annual receipt}}{\text{discount rate}} = \frac{PMT_1}{k} \qquad (5.12)$$

Thus, if we had a perpetuity of $140 per year *beginning 1 year from now* discounted at 7 percent, its present value would be $140/0.07 = $2,000.

To illustrate what happens as the life of an annuity is extended, consider the following, where the discount rate is still 7 percent:

Length of Annuity	Cash Flow Per Year, PMT	$\times$ PVA$_{7\%,n}$ =	Present Value of Annuity
20 years	$140	10.594	$1,483.16
30	140	12.409	1,737.26
40	140	13.332	1,866.48
50	140	13.801	1,932.14

This shows the present values of 20-, 30-, 40- and 50-year annuities of $140 per year discounted at 7 percent. When the length of the annuity is 50 years, its present value is $1,932.14, versus $2,000 if it had been a perpetuity. Thus, as the life of an annuity increases, its present value can be *approximated* by employing Equation 5.12 for a perpetuity.

Determining Interest Rates

In many cases both the present value at time t = 0 and the future cash flows and timing are known, but the interest or discount rate is not. We begin by determining interest rates for individual cash flows, and then consider annuities and the case of a series of uneven cash flows.

Individual Cash Flows

Suppose you borrowed $1,000 today and agreed to pay the interest and principal (of $1,000) back in a lump sum in 5 years. The agreed payment at that time is $2,012.07. What annual rate of interest are you paying on the loan? To answer that question, we start with the present value formula given by Equation 5.4, $PV_0 = FV_n(PV_{k,n})$, and solve for the present value factor, which is

$$PV_{k,n} = \frac{PV_0}{FV_n} \tag{5.13}$$

To determine the interest rate, we simply solve Equation 5.13 for the PV factor, and then look up the value of the PV factor in Table F.3 for the appropriate year. Thus

$$PV_{?\%,5yr} = \frac{\$1,000}{\$2,012.07} = 0.497$$

Looking across the row for year 5, we find the value of 0.497 in the 15 percent column.[12] Thus, the annual rate of interest on a $1,000 loan that will be paid back as a lump sum of $2,012.07 in 5 years is 15 percent.

Annuities

Precisely the same approach can be used when an (ordinary) annuity is being considered. Suppose you borrow $2,124.90 today and agree to repay it at the rate of $900 at the end of each of the next 3 years. What is the annual rate of interest you are paying on the loan? To determine this, we solve Equation 5.10, $PV_0 = PMT(PVA_{k,n})$, for the PVA factor, which is

$$PVA_{k,n} = \frac{PV_0}{PMT} \tag{5.14}$$

$$PVA_{?\%,3yr} = \frac{\$2,124.90}{\$900} = 2.361$$

Looking across the row for year 3 in Table F.4, we find the PVA of 2.361 under the 13 percent column. Thus, the annual interest rate on the loan is 13 percent.[13]

In both examples the interest rates turned out to be whole percents—15 percent in the first case, 13 percent in the second. In practice this rarely happens, and you are left with one of three alternatives: (1) determine the interest rate to the nearest

---

[12] A financial calculator makes this an easy problem to solve. By punching in n = 5, PV = 1,000, and FV = 2,012.07, and then hitting the k = i button, the answer is 15.008 percent. Since present value and future value are mirror images, this problem could be solved using future value factors instead of PV factors. The future value (FV_n) would be divided by the present value (PV_0) and the FV table used.

[13] With a financial calculator, we punch in PV = 2,124.90, PMT = 900, n = 3 and then hit i (for interest rate, or IRR, for internal rate of return) to solve for the exact rate of 13.004 percent.

percent, (2) use a financial calculator, or (3) "eyeball" where between two rates it falls.

Uneven Series

Unfortunately, determining the interest rate becomes more difficult if the series is uneven. Essentially you are left with two options—a trial-and-error approach, or using a calculator that has an internal rate of return function. Chapters 6, 8, and 9 discuss internal rates of return in detail both for determining the yield to maturity on a bond and for capital budgeting purposes. To illustrate the trial-and-error approach, suppose you invest $352.31 today, and the series of payments promised is $80 at t = 1, $125 at t = 2, and $225 at t = 3. What is your expected annual percentage return? With this approach, it is necessary to determine what set of PV factors associated with a specific interest rate *causes the present value of the cash inflows to exactly equal the initial present value,* PV_0. We want to determine what interest rate causes the present value of $80 at year 1, $125 at year 2, and $225 at year 3 to exactly equal the present value of $352.31. As shown in Table 5.5, at a 12 percent discount rate the present value of $331.26 is too low, so the discount rate must be lowered. If we use 8 percent, the present value of $359.85 is greater than the PV_0 of $352.31, so the discount rate must be raised. The actual interest rate that equates the present value of the expected cash inflows with $352.31 is 9 percent. And the annual interest rate, or return, on the investment is 9 percent.[14] Normally, with uneven cash flows the interest rate does not come out to be exactly equal to some whole percent. In that case eyeballing is required if the trial-and-error approach is employed.

Applications in Financial Management

The concept of time value of money may still seem a bit abstract. In fact, it has numerous practical applications in financial management. We will discuss four important applications—growth rates, future sums, loan amortization, and effective interest rates—but many other uses will appear throughout the book.

Growth Rates

It is frequently useful to estimate growth rates from financial data. For example, suppose Emery Brothers had sales of $15 million in 19X2 and estimates that by 19X6 its sales will be $35 million. What compound annual rate of growth is Emery predicting?

---

[14] If the trial-and-error approach is used, the question often asked is, "What interest rate should I start with?" One approach is to calculate a "simulated" annuity by summing the inflows and then dividing by the number of periods. Thus, ($80 + $125 + $225)/3 = $430/3 = $143.33. Dividing the present value of $352.31 by the simulated annuity of $143.33 gives a PVA factor of 2.458, which indicates what the rate would be if the series were in fact an annuity. Looking across the row for year 3 in Table F.4 indicates the simulated annuity interest rate is between 10 and 11 percent. *Then you have to proceed by trial-and-error from scratch,* as in Table 5.5, to determine the exact answer. The advantage of the simulated annuity approach is that it provides a reasonable first guess.

With a financial calculator, punch in the present value (PV) of 352.31, and the future values of 80, 125, 225. Then hit the k = IRR (internal rate of return) button to determine the interest rate of 9.005 percent.

Table 5.5 Solving for the Interest Rate in an Uneven Cash Flow Series with the Trial-and-Error Method

The trial-and-error method can be time-consuming. Two recommendations: First, make the initial estimate some "reasonable" number, perhaps between 10 and 20 percent. Second, when adjusting interest rates for a new trial, jump as much as 5 to 10 percent the first time or two in order to bracket the actual rate. Once the rate is bracketed, you can "eyeball" it and solve for the actual rate fairly quickly.

Decision Rule: Find the discount rate that equates the present value of the cash inflows with the present value, PV_0.

Step 1: Try 12 Percent

Year	Cash Inflow	$\times$ $PV_{12\%,n}$	= Present Value of Cash Inflow
1	$ 80	0.893	$ 71.44
2	125	0.797	99.62
3	225	0.712	160.20
			$331.26

Since the present value of the inflows of $331.26 is *less* than $352.31, the discount rate must be *lowered*.

Step 2: Try 8 Percent

Year	Cash Inflow	$\times$ $PV_{8\%,n}$	= Present Value of Cash Inflow
1	$ 80	0.926	$ 74.08
2	125	0.857	107.12
3	225	0.794	178.65
			$359.85

Since the present value of the inflows of $359.85 is *greater* than $352.31, the discount rate must be *increased*.

Step 3: Try 9 Percent

Year	Cash Inflow	$\times$ $PV_{9\%,n}$	= Present Value of Cash Inflow
1	$ 80	0.917	$ 73.36
2	125	0.842	105.25
3	225	0.772	173.70
			$352.31

Since the present value of the inflows of $352.31 *exactly equals* $352.31, the discount rate is 9 percent.

First, we need to determine the number of time periods by subtracting 19X2 from 19X6. There are 4 years *between* the two dates. (*Note:* There are not 5: be sure not to count both the first and the last years.) Then we simply employ a modification of Equation 5.13 (for determining interest rates):

$$PV_{?\%,4yr} = \frac{\text{beginning value}}{\text{ending value}} = \frac{\$15 \text{ million}}{\$35 \text{ million}} = 0.429$$

Reading across the row for year 4 in Table F.3, we find that a PV factor of 0.429 lies between 23 and 24 percent. The rate is a bit closer to 24 percent, so call it

23.6 percent.[15] Obviously, Emery Brothers expects rapid sales growth over the next 4 years.

Future Sums

Another application of time value is accumulating to a future sum. Consider Consolidated Electronics, which, as an inducement to retaining its president, has promised a bonus of $10 million on retirement, which will be in 7 years. If Consolidated can earn 8 percent on its money and plans to start making annual payments to fund the retirement bonus 1 year from now, how much will each payment have to be?

The first step is to recognize that this is a future value of an annuity problem. We therefore employ Equation 5.7:

$$FV_n = PMT(FVA_{k,n})$$

$$\$10 \text{ million} = PMT(FVA_{8\%,7yr})$$

$$PMT = \frac{\$10 \text{ million}}{8.923} = \$1,120,699.32$$

Thus, Consolidated Electronics will have to set aside over $1.1 million every year to fund the retirement bonus.[16]

Loan Amortization

Many loans are *term loans,* payable on what is called an amortized basis. The purpose of the amortization is to see that principal and interest are paid off on some predetermined time schedule. To illustrate, suppose Frankie's Chicken borrowed $48,040 on a 3-year loan to be repaid in three equal annual installments. The rate of interest is 12 percent on the declining principal balance of the loan. This 12 percent is the before-tax cost to Frankie's; it is also the before-tax return to the lender. What is the size of each of the payments? To solve this problem, we must first recognize that it is a 3-year, 12 percent annuity involving a present value, PV_0, of $48,040. Using Equation 5.10, we have

$$PV_0 = PMT(PVA_{k,n})$$

$$\$48,040 = PMT(PVA_{12\%,3yr})$$

$$PMT = \frac{\$48,040}{2.402} = \$20,000$$

Hence, Frankie's must make three equal annual payments of $20,000 to repay the loan.[17] The *amortization schedule,* which breaks the payments down between principal and interest, is presented in Table 5.6. For tax purposes, Frankie's reports the interest as a deductible cost of doing business, while the lender reports the same amount as taxable income. Note that more of the payment goes to pay back the

---

[15] With a financial calculator we punch in PV = 15, FV = 35, n = 4 and then hit the k = i button to determine the growth rate of 23.59 percent. This approach must be used with caution, since it assumes the series does not behave in an erratic manner. Since present value and future value are mirror images, this problem could also be solved using FV factors.

[16] Using a financial calculator, the size of the annuity (PMT) is $1,120,724.01 per year. The difference between this and the $1,120,699.32 determined above is due to rounding.

[17] The amount of the payment is calculated as $20,001.40 using a financial calculator. Most loans of this type are actually payable monthly or quarterly.

Table 5.6 Principal and Interest Amortized over Three Annual Installments at 12 Percent

Typical of many term (or installment) loans, the last payment differs from the earlier ones.

Year	Payment	Interest*	Principal Repayment	Remaining Balance
1	$20,000.00	$5,764.80	$14,235.20	$33,804.80
2	20,000.00	4,056.58	15,943.42	17,861.38
3	20,004.75†	2,143.37	17,861.38	0

* First-year interest is (0.12)($48,040); for the second year it is (0.12)($33,804.80); and for the third year it is (0.12)($17,861.38).
† This last payment is the sum of the remaining balance of $17,861.38 and the interest of $2,143.37.

principal as the years go by. Home mortgage or car loans typically employ exactly the same approach.

Effective Interest Rates[18]

The last and most complicated application of the concept of time value of money involves finding the effective rate of interest. From the standpoint of the borrower, this is the effective before-tax percentage cost; from the standpoint of the lender, it is the effective before-tax percentage return. To determine the effective cost, we need first to consider different compounding intervals. Then we examine both nominal versus effective interest rates and the use of 360- versus 365-day years.

Compounding Intervals

So far we have assumed that the interest (or discount) rate was calculated on an annual basis. Although for simplicity this is the approach used throughout much of this book, in practice semiannual, quarterly, monthly, daily, and even continuously compounded or discounted interest rates are common. The general formula to apply when dealing with more frequently compounded situations is this:

$$FV_n = PV_0\left(1 + \frac{k}{m}\right)^{mn} \tag{5.15}$$

where

k = the annual compound (or interest) rate in decimal form
m = the number of times *per year* interest is compounded
n = the number of years

Note that m, the number of compounding periods per year, is used twice in Equation 5.15—it must be the same in both places.[19] The equation for yearly compounding given previously, Equation 5.1, is simply a special case of Equation 5.15 when $m = 1$. To see the effect of the compounding interval, consider the future

[18] This section may be omitted without loss of continuity. Future value or present value tables should not be used since the calculations performed take the place of the tables.

[19] To use the FV table, we convert Equation 5.15 to $FV_n = PV_0(FV_{k/m,mn})$. While this works for simple cases, in general it is necessary to use a calculator with an exponential function, y^x, to solve more frequent than yearly compounding or discounting problems.

Figure Your Car Payments

Instead of employing the equations in the chapter, a rough-and-ready approach to determining the monthly payment on a car can be calculated as follows. The table below shows the payment per $100 borrowed for loans of various terms.

Payment per $100 Borrowed

Term	7%	8%	9%	10%	11%	12%	13%	14%	15%
3 years	$3.09	$3.13	$3.18	$3.23	$3.27	$3.32	$3.37	$3.42	$3.47
4 years	2.39	2.44	2.49	2.54	2.58	2.63	2.68	2.73	2.78
5 years	1.98	2.03	2.08	2.12	2.17	2.22	2.28	2.33	2.38

To see how this works, let's use an example. Say you need an $11,000 loan and know you can get financing at 10 percent. To find the monthly payments on a 4-year loan, find the figure at which the rate and the term intersect—$2.54. That figure is per $100, so the payment on an $11,000 loan would be $279.40 [i.e., ($11,000/$100)($2.54)]. If you stretch the payments over 5 years, the monthly payment falls to $233.20 [i.e., (110)($2.12)].

If you're working with a budget, the table can help you determine the maximum loan you can afford. Divide the monthly payment budgeted by the payment per $100 for the term and rate you expect to receive. Then multiply the result by 100 and you'll know how much you can borrow. Assume $300 per month is the most you want to commit to car payments and you can secure a 4-year loan at 12 percent. The payment per $100 on such a loan is $2.63; dividing $300 by $2.63 gives you $114.07. Multiplying by 100 then fixes the borrowing ceiling at $11,407.

While these figures are approximate, they are close enough to estimate the impact of different terms and rates on your monthly payments.

Enjoy your car!

value in 2 years of $50 today if the annual rate of interest per year is 8 percent and the compounding interval changes as follows:

$$FV_2(\text{annual, m} = 1) = \$50\left(1 + \frac{0.08}{1}\right)^{1(2)} = \$50(1.08)^2 = \$58.32$$

$$FV_2(\text{semiannual; m} = 2) = \$50\left(1 + \frac{0.08}{2}\right)^{2(2)} = \$50(1.04)^4 = \$58.49$$

$$FV_2(\text{quarterly; m} = 4) = \$50\left(1 + \frac{0.08}{4}\right)^{4(2)} = \$50(1.02)^8 = \$58.58$$

$$FV_2(\text{monthly; m} = 12) = \$50\left(1 + \frac{0.08}{12}\right)^{12(2)} = \$50(1.006667)^{24} = \$58.64$$

$$FV_2(\text{daily}; m = 365) = \$50\left(1 + \frac{0.08}{365}\right)^{365(2)} = \$50(1.000219)^{730} = \$58.67$$

$$FV_2(\text{continuously})^{20} = \$50(2.71828)^{0.16} = \$58.68$$

As we can see, the more frequent the compounding period, the greater the future value. This occurs because by more frequent compounding we are able to earn more interest on interest—thus increasing the return.

The same idea applies to finding present values when interest is compounded more often than once a year. Rearranging Equation 5.15 gives the general present value formula for more frequent periods:

$$PV_0 = \frac{FV_n}{[1 + (k/m)]^{mn}} \tag{5.16}$$

where all the terms are as defined previously. To illustrate, let's calculate the present value of $300 to be received 4 years from now if interest is compounded twice a year and the appropriate annual rate is 16 percent. Substituting, we have

$$PV_0 = \frac{\$300}{[1 + (0.16/2)]^{2(4)}} = \frac{\$300}{(1.08)^8} = \$162.08$$

Thus, $300 in 4 years has a present value of $162.08 today if an interest rate of 16 percent, discounted semiannually, is employed.

Nominal Versus Effective Interest Rates

The annual rate at which many loans and financial instruments are quoted is the nominal interest rate. Thus, you may make an investment that pays interest at a nominal annual rate of 8 percent. The *effective interest rate* adjusts the nominal rate based on the frequency of compounding employed and the number of days assumed in a year. The effective rate is

$$k_{effective} = \left(1 + \frac{k_{nom}}{m}\right)^m - 1 \tag{5.17}$$

where

$k_{effective}$ = the effective annual rate of interest
k_{nom} = the nominal annual rate of interest
m = the number of compounding intervals per year

From a decision-making standpoint, the effective rate should be employed when evaluating costs and returns. Otherwise, important cost (yield) differences may be overlooked.

As long as there is only one compounding interval per year ($m = 1$), the effective rate is equal to the nominal rate. But as the compounding interval decreases, the effective rate increases. To see this relationship between nominal and effective interest

---

[20] With continuous, or instantaneous, compounding, the equation becomes $FV_n = PV_0(e)^{kn}$, where e is defined as 2.71828 . . . . Using a financial calculator, punch in 0.16 followed by the e^x key. Then multiply by 50 to get $58.675544 \approx \$58.68$.

rates, consider the impact of the compounding period on a 12 percent annual nominal rate:

Compounding Interval	Effective Rate $k_{effective} = \left(1 + \dfrac{0.12}{m}\right)^{m} - 1$
Annually (m = 1)	12.000%
Semiannually (m = 2)	12.360
Quarterly (m = 4)	12.551
Monthly (m = 12)	12.683
Daily (m = 365)	12.747
Continuously[21]	12.750

Often the interest rate banks and depository institutions quote on savings accounts are effective rates. But for most other instruments—including bonds, mortgage loans, and commercial loans—only the nominal rate may be stated. Managers and investors must therefore be especially careful when comparing different rates.

Assume, for example, that your firm wants to borrow money for a period of 1 year. Essex National Bank quotes a nominal annual rate of 12.5 percent compounded quarterly. Southern National Bank quotes a nominal annual rate of 12.2 percent compounded daily. Which way is your firm better off in terms of the lowest effective before-tax cost?

Employing Equation 5.17, from Essex National Bank the effective cost is

$$k_{effective} = \left(1 + \frac{0.125}{4}\right)^{4} - 1 = (1.03125)^{4} - 1 = 13.098\%$$

From Southern, the effective cost is:

$$k_{effective} = \left(1 + \frac{0.122}{365}\right)^{365} - 1 = (1.00033425)^{365} - 1 = 12.973\%$$

After adjusting for the difference in the compounding intervals, we see that the effective cost of the loan from Southern National Bank is 12.973 percent, while it is 13.098 percent from Essex National. Other things being equal, we want the cheapest financing available. Therefore, you would recommend that the loan be obtained from Southern National Bank.

Number of Days Assumed in a Year

In the preceding example, we saw that the compounding interval had an important impact on the effective yield or cost. It was assumed that the nominal interest was earned, or charged, over 365 days. Another approach used by many banks and for some money market instruments is based on a 360-day year. This increases the effective yield to a saver, or the cost to a borrower.

Consider a 1-year $1,000 deposit at a nominal annual interest rate of 11 percent. Using a 365-day year, the saver has $1,110 after 365 days. Under the 360-day method, the saver has $1,110 after just 360 days. Reinvesting the original principal

---

[21] For the continuous case, the effective rate is $k_{effective} = e^{k_{nom}} - 1 = 2.71828^{0.12} - 1 = 12.750\%$. Using a financial calculator, hit 0.12 followed by e^{x}, and then subtract 1 to produce $0.127497 \approx 12.750\%$.

for the extra 5 days (6 days in a leap year) at 11 percent produces additional interest of ($1,000)(0.11)(5/360) = $1.53. Thus, the total interest earned over the 365 days is actually $111.53. This increases the effective yield over the 365-day method.

When calculating an effective yield, the nominal rate must be adjusted if a 360-day year is employed. With $k_{360\ nom}$ being the 360-day nominal interest rate, we have

$$k_{nom} = k_{360nom}(365/360) \tag{5.18}$$

In the example above, an 11 percent nominal rate with a 360-day year produces a nominal rate of 0.11(365/360) = 11.153 percent. To determine the effective rate when a 360-day year is employed, Equation 5.17 is used again. Assuming daily compounding in the above example, the effective rate is

$$k_{effective} = \left(1 + \frac{0.11153}{365} \right)^{365} - 1 = 11.797\%$$

The saver benefits from the use of a 360-day year. From the standpoint of a borrower, the use of a 360-day year raises the effective cost of a loan.

Summary

In this chapter we examined one of the fundamental concepts in finance—the time value of money. This concept has its foundation in the simple observation that a dollar today is worth more than a dollar in the future. The future value of an individual cash flow was found by $FV_n = PV_0(1 + k)^n$ or $FV_n = PV_0(FV_{k,n})$. The present value of an individual cash flow was then seen to be the mirror image of future values. Thus, $PV_0 = FV_n/(1 + k)^n$ or $PV_0 = FV_n(PV_{k,n})$.

In considering the future value of an annuity, we saw that it was simply the summation of a series of single-period future values. Likewise, the present value of an annuity was seen to be the summation of a series of single-period present values. When the future stream is uneven in its magnitude, then each year (or sometimes groups of years) must be discounted back to the present to find the present value of the stream. Finally, for perpetuities, the present value is equal to the constant annuity of size PMT divided by the discount rate, k.

To determine the interest rate that equates a present value and a future value for individual cash flows, first solve for the $PV_{k,n}$. Then find an amount equal to the calculated factor in the appropriate row of the PV table. The percentage listed in the appropriate column is the interest (or discount) rate. The same procedure can be employed for finding the interest rate for annuities. If the cash flow stream is uneven, however, a trial-and-error method (or a calculator with an internal rate of return function) must be used.

Applications of time value techniques in financial management are numerous. All require that you recognize whether individual cash flows or annuities are involved, and whether future or present values are appropriate. When determining effective interest rates, more frequent than yearly compounding or discounting is required. Throughout this book, you will see that understanding time value concepts is a prerequisite for making correct financial decisions.

There is an appendix to this chapter, "Appendix 5A: Deriving Time Value Equations," at the back of the book.

Questions

5.1 Define or explain the following:

a. Future value (compounding)
b. Present value (discounting)
c. Compound rate
d. Discount rate
e. Future value factor $(FV_{k,n})$
f. Present value factor $(PV_{k,n})$
g. Annuity
h. Perpetuity
i. Ordinary annuity

j. Future value factor for an annuity $(FVA_{k,n})$
k. Annuity due
l. Present value factor for an annuity $(PVA_{k,n})$
m. Term loan
n. Amortization schedule
o. Effective interest rate

5.2 Present value and future value are said to be the inverse, or mirror images, of each other. Explain why this is true. Then demonstrate how present value and future value factors relate to each other.

5.3 Explain the relationship between present value factors and present value factors for an annuity.

5.4 For positive interest rates, is it true that the following hold?

a. $FV_{k,n}$ is equal to or greater than 1.00.
b. $PV_{k,n}$ is less than 1.00.
c. $FVA_{k,n}$ is equal to or greater than the number of periods the annuity lasts.
d. $PVA_{k,n}$ is less than the number of periods the annuity lasts.

5.5 The following series of cash flows exists:

Time Period	Amount
t_1	$300
t_2	200
t_3	100
t_4	100

It is your job to find the present value of this stream. Show at least four different ways you could set up the cash flow stream to solve for this present value. (*Note:* Remember to use annuities when possible.)

5.6 A firm's earnings are expected to increase by 50 percent, from $200,000 at the end of t_3 to $300,000 at the end of t_8. Show why the compound (or annual) growth rate is less than 10 percent per year.

5.7 In a loan amortization schedule, the last payment will never be equal to the prior payments. Is this statement true or false? Why?

5.8 Explain why you are not indifferent to having your money invested in a bank that may, at its discretion, compound annually, semiannually, quarterly, monthly, or daily. (*Note:* Assume everything else stays the same.)

5.9 The effective interest rate is a function of the compounding interval and the number of days assumed in the year. Explain how both influence the effective rate.

Self-Test Problems   (Solutions appear on pages 716–718.)

Future Value and Compounding

ST 5.1   Suppose you put $1,000 into a savings certificate today that will pay 11 percent annual interest for 6 years.

a. What will the savings certificate be worth in 6 years? How much of this is interest?
b. If you withdraw the interest each year and spend it immediately (i.e., do not let it accumulate), how much will the $1,000 certificate be worth in 6 years? How much interest will you have withdrawn?
c. Explain why the total interest in (b) is less than in (a).

Present Values

ST 5.2   Find the present value of each of the following cash flow streams when the discount rate is 11 percent.

	Stream	
	A	B
1	$100	$400
2	200	400
3	200	100
4	300	100
5	300	100

What is the present value of each stream at a zero percent discount rate?

Uneven Series

ST 5.3   Scott's friend just told him about a great investment. By putting in $5,893 today, Scott should receive $3,000 in one year and $5,000 in two years. What is the projected compound annual percentage return on the investment?

Principal Repayment on a Loan

ST 5.4   Avis Products has borrowed $70,250 on a term loan with annual interest at the rate of 13 percent. The length of the loan is 20 years. What is the principal repayment in the third year?

Interest Rate with Cash Discount

ST 5.5   Linda Jackson recently took out an $80,000 loan at 12 percent when she purchased a new house. The loan will be paid back in 30 equal annual installments. However, the lender charged fees and closing costs that amounted to $5,552. Consequently, Linda received only $74,448 ($80,000 − $5,552). What is the yearly percentage cost of the loan?

Different Discounting Periods

ST 5.6   What is the present value (at t = 0) of $750 to be received 5 years from now if the discount rate is 20 percent per year, and the discount period is (a) annually, (b) semiannually, or (c) quarterly?

Effective Interest Rate

ST 5.7   What is the effective interest rate if the nominal rate is 9 percent per year, a 365-day year is used, and the compounding period is (a) yearly, (b) quarterly, (c) daily, or (d) hourly?

Problems

Direct Calculation Versus Tables

5.1   Solve the following (1) *without using tables* and (2) *with tables* (as a check). (*Note:* There will be slight differences due to rounding.)

a. The future value in 1 year of $200 today (at t = 0) at 8 percent.
b. The future value in 3 years of $200 today (at t = 0) at 8 percent.
c. The present value of $200, due 1 year in the future, at 8 percent.
d. The present value of $200, due 3 years in the future, at 8 percent.

FV$_{k,n}$ and FVA$_{k,n}$	**5.2** Use the tables to find the future value of the following amounts:

a. An initial $325 compounded at 12 percent for 4 years.
b. An initial $650 compounded at 6 percent for 9 years.
c. An annuity of $150 per year for each of 6 years compounded at 10 percent.
d. An annuity of $480 per year for each of 3 years compounded at 17 percent. |
| Future Value | **5.3** Your firm has a retirement plan that matches all contributions on a one-to-two basis. That is, if you contribute $1,000 per year, the company will add $500 to make it $1,500. The firm guarantees an 8 percent return on the funds. Alternatively, you can "do it yourself," and you think you can earn 11 percent on your money by doing it this way. The first contribution will be made 1 year from today. At that time, and every year thereafter, you will put $1,000 into the retirement account. If you want to retire in 25 years, which way are you better off? (*Note:* Ignore any tax considerations.) |
| Doubling Your Money | **5.4** Kathy Logan presently has $3,000 and wants to know how long it will take her to double this, assuming annual compounding at (a) 5 percent, (b) 10 percent, and (c) 15 percent. How long (to the nearest year) will it take? (*Note:* You should be able to solve this problem simply by looking at the FV table under the appropriate percentage.) |
| Future Value of an Annuity | **5.5** You plan to deposit $250 in a savings account for each of 5 years starting 1 year from now. The interest rate is 9 percent compounded annually. What is the future value in each of the following cases?

a. At the end of 5 years?
b. At the end of 6 years if *no additional deposits* are made? [*Note:* This just requires you to take your calculation in (a) one year further.]
c. At the end of 5 years, as in (a), if an *additional* $250 is deposited today (i.e., at t$_o$), so there are six deposits of $250 each? |
| Future Values | **5.6** Walt Adams is planning for retirement. He plans to work for 25 more years. For the next 10 years, he can save $3,000 per year (with the first deposit being made 1 year from now), and at that time he wants to buy a weekend vacation home he estimates will cost $40,000. How much will he have to save in years 11 through 25 so that he has exactly $300,000 saved up when he retires? Assume he can earn 10 percent compounded annually for each of the next 25 years. (*Note:* Ignore any tax implications. Drawing a time line helps with this problem.) |
| Ordinary Annuity Versus Annuity Due | **5.7** Henderson, Inc., is establishing a fund to pay off a $200,000 lump sum loan when it matures in 10 years. The funds will earn 8 percent interest per year. What is the size of the yearly payment in each case below?

a. The payment is made at the end of the year.
b. The payment is made at the beginning of the year. |
| PV$_{k,n}$ and PVA$_{k,n}$ | **5.8** Determine the present values (at t = 0) of the following:

a. A single cash flow of $1,142 at time t = 6 discounted at 8 percent.
b. An annuity of $300 per year to be received for each of 7 years discounted at 15 percent.
c. An annuity of $400 per year to be received for each of 5 years followed by a single cash flow of $1,000 in year 6, discounted at 20 percent.
d. An annuity of $200 for each of 6 years followed by an annuity of $800 for years 7 through 10, all discounted at 12 percent. |
| Present Value and Future Value | **5.9** Calculate the present value (at t = 0) and then the future value at the end of year 4 for the following series. The appropriate rate is 14 percent. (*Note:* In series B, simply retain the negative sign associated with the cash flow for year 3, and then proceed as usual.) |

		Series	
Year	A	B	C
1	$100	$300	$400
2	300	100	0
3	200	−100	50
4	50	200	100

Present Value

5.10 Guardian Electric has a line of small motors that no longer fits its corporate image. It is attempting to determine the minimum selling price for the small motors line. Guardian presently receives $250,000 per year after taxes in cash flows from the line. If the required rate of return (or discount rate) is 16 percent, how much should Guardian ask if it thinks the life expectancy of the line is as follows?

a. 10 years
b. 20 years
c. Infinity

Present Value of Uneven Series

5.11 Solve for the present value of the following series at least three different ways. The appropriate discount rate is 14 percent.

$1,000	$1,000	$4,000	$4,000	$4,000	$6,000
1	2	3	4	5	6

Interest Rates

5.12 Find the interest rates implied by the following:

a. You lend $500 today and receive a promise for repayment 8 years from now of $595.23.
b. You invest $500 today and have a promise of receiving $197.55 for each of the next 3 years.
c. You invest $1,400 today and will receive $2,592.59 back at the end of 3 years.
d. You lend $1,400 today and the repayments will be $281.80 for each of the next 8 years.

(Internal) Rate of Return

5.13 Richards Placement Enterprises has decided to automate to increase efficiency. By purchasing word processing equipment costing $6,627.60, it can save $1,800 per year for each of 10 years in labor costs. What is the (internal) rate of return on the word processing equipment?

Cash Down Payment

5.14 Stan Olsen purchased a new home for $75,000. He paid $20,000 down and agreed to pay the rest in 20 equal annual payments that include the principal payment plus 9 percent compound interest. The payments are at the end of each year. What will the payments be?

Loan Interest Rates

5.15 DeThomas Industries has been shopping around for a loan. The firm has four possibilities, as follows:

Loan	Principal	Annual Yearly Payment	Life of Loan (In years)
A	$125,000	$32,972.83	5
B	125,000	27,864.47	6
C	125,000	21,750.48	8
D	125,000	26,528.01	7

By calculating the yearly percentage interest rate, determine which loan is best. (*Note:* Assume the length of any of the loans is acceptable.)

Present Values (More Difficult)

5.16 You are a lucky winner in the Big East Lottery. As a result, you have a choice between three alternative payment plans.

Plan I: A lifetime annuity of $60,425 annually, with the first payment 1 year from now.
Plan II: A $70,000 annual annuity for 20 years, with the first payment 1 year from now.
Plan III: $800,000 today.

Your life expectancy is 45 more years. Ignoring any tax effects, determine the following:

a. At what interest rate would you be indifferent between plans I and III?

b. At what interest rate would you be indifferent between plans II and III?

c. At what interest rate (to the nearest whole number) would you be indifferent between plans I and II? (*Note:* It is easier to solve this by trial-and-error, rather than algebraically.)

d. What if (c) is now changed so you know the interest rate for both plans I and II is 12 percent for the first 20 years? What rate would you have to earn on the remaining 25 years of the $60,425 annuity to be indifferent between plans I and II?

Uneven Cash Flows

5.17 Determine the interest rate for the following series of cash flows:

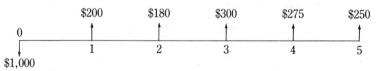

Interest Rate for an Uneven Stream

5.18 Consider the following set of annual cash flows: $t_1 = \$200$, $t_2 = \$200$, $t_3 = \$200$, $t_4 = \$500$, and $t_5 = \$500$.

a. Find the present value of this series if the discount rate is 12 percent.

b. If you could acquire the right to receive this series of cash inflows by paying $1,000 today, what would the compound percentage return be on your investment?

Perpetuity

5.19 After graduating from college you make it big—all because of your success in financial management. You decide to endow a scholarship for needy finance students that will provide $3,000 per year indefinitely, beginning *1 year* from now. How much must be deposited *today* to fund the scholarship under the following conditions?

a. The interest rate is 10 percent.

b. The interest rate is 8 percent.

c. For both 10 and 8 percent, if everything stays the same except that the first disbursement will not be made until *3 years* from now.

Growth Rates

5.20 In each of the following cases, calculate the compound growth rate implied by the figures.

a. It is now t_0. By time t_7, ACX Corporation expects to triple sales.

b. Susan bought a stock for $26 today and hopes to sell it at the end of 4 years for $100.

c. Canadian Paper Products, had net income of $262,000 at the end of t_1, and expects to have net income of $1 million at the end of t_7.

Loan Amortization Schedule

5.21 Lynne Industries is negotiating for a $129,360, 5-year, 11 percent term loan.

a. Determine the size of the yearly payments and the loan amortization schedule. (*Note:* Round all figures to the nearest dollar.)

(Do only if using Pinches Disk.)

b. You have also been given a monthly amortization schedule on the Pinches Disk: What advantages in terms of total payments and total interest paid does monthly amortization offer over yearly amortization? Why?

c. (1) Determine the size of the payment and the loan amortization schedule in (a) if the yearly interest rate is 9 percent. What is the impact of this change on both the yearly and monthly amortization schedules? Are there still clear-cut advantages to monthly payments?

(2) Now suppose Lynne Industries needs to add a computer system to update its accounting system. This system will require an additional $100,000 of financing. (*Note:* You will need to add $100,000 to the original loan amount.) If the total loan is financed at an 11 percent annual rate for a 5-year term, what will be the affect on the amortization schedules?

(3) Finally, while negotiating the loan in (2), the possibility of a 10-year payment period was discussed. What is the affect of a 10-year repayment period on the individual payments, the total payments, and the total interest paid? What can we conclude about shorter versus longer loan repayment periods?

Term Loan: After-Tax Cash Outflow

5.22 South Park Products is taking out an 8-year, $43,440 term loan, with an interest rate of 16 percent per year. Interest is paid annually, and the firm's marginal corporate tax rate is 40 percent.

a. What is the size of the yearly payment?

b. Determine the loan amortization schedule. (*Note:* Round all figures to the nearest dollar.)

c. Determine the net cash outflow per year to service both principal and interest after taking into account the tax deductibility of interest for tax purposes. (*Note:* Round to the nearest dollar.)

Cost of Alternative Loans

5.23 San Jose Winery needs $500,000 for expansion of its warehouse. The company plans to finance $100,000 with internally generated funds but wants to secure a loan for the remainder. The contracting firm's finance subsidiary has offered to provide the loan based on six annual payments of $97,299.93 each. Alternatively, San Jose Winery's bankers will lend the firm $400,000 to be repaid in six equal annual installments (covering both principal and interest) at a 15 percent interest rate. Finally, an insurance firm would also loan the money; it requires a lump sum payment of $747,663.55 at the end of 6 years.

a. Based on the respective annual percentage costs of the three loans, which one should San Jose select?

b. What other considerations might be important in addition to cost?

Compounding Periods

5.24 If $1,000 is invested today, how much will it be worth in (a) 5 years or (b) 10 years, if interest is at 12 percent and compounded annually, semiannually, or quarterly?

Future Value: Semiannual

5.25 If you invest $80 every 6 months for the next 7 years (beginning 6 months from now) and these funds earn an annual rate of 8 percent (compounded semiannually), what will be the value of this investment at the end of the *8th* year?

Automobile Loan

5.26 Liz has decided to purchase a newer car; the net amount to be financed is $3,400. The financing will be at 12 percent per year (or 1 percent per month) for 18 months. What is the size of the monthly payment?

Add-On Interest

5.27 Todd York has recently taken out a $2,000 loan from Community Finance Company. The interest rate was quoted as a "low" 13.45 percent for 24 months. Todd's payments were determined as follows:

annual interest = 13.45% of $2,000 = $269 per year
total due = $2,000 + 2 years($269) = $2,538
monthly payment = $2,538/24 months = $105.75

This method of calculating interest is called *add-on*. What is the annual rate of interest (to the closest percent) Todd is paying? (*Remember:* Any figure you calculate will be on a monthly basis and must be multiplied by 12 to convert it to an annual rate.)

Effective Interest Rates

5.28 First Bank offers a nominal rate of 10 percent per year, compounds interest daily, and uses a 360-day year. Mahoney Bank offers a nominal rate of 10.25 percent per year, compounds interest monthly, and uses a 365-day year. By calculating the effective rate of interest for both banks, determine where you should place your money. (*Note:* Assume it is not a leap year.)

Finding Interest Rates (More Difficult)

5.29 Gardner National Bank has decided to offer a $10 gift certificate to any depositor who puts at least $400 into a new or existing savings account.

a. Suppose you open a 7 percent savings account with a deposit of $500 and immediately cash the $10 gift certificate so that the bank receives a net amount of $490 from your deposit. If interest is compounded daily based on a 365-day year and the funds stay in the bank for exactly half a year, what is the annual percentage cost of the funds to the bank?

(Do only if using Pinches Disk.)

b. To entice even larger depositors the bank offers a $30 certificate for deposits of $1,000 or more. What would the new annual percentage cost of the funds to the bank be if you deposited $1,000, instead of $500?

c. Now suppose in order to compete with other local banks Gardner is compelled to pay 7.5 percent on savings accounts of less than $1,000, and 8 percent on those of $1,000 or more. What is the cost of the funds to the bank in both (a) and (b) at the new rate?

d. What would be the effect on the cost of funds to the bank in (a), (b), and (c) if the funds were left on deposit for 5 years, instead of for only half a year? [*Note:* The interest rate in (a) and (b) is 7 percent, and the rate is 7.5 and 8 percent respectively in (c).]

References

For more on future and present value, see

BRICK, JOHN R. *Commercial Banking.* Haslett, Mich.: Systems Publishers, 1984, Chap. 3.

CISSELL, ROBERT, HELEN CISSELL, AND DAVID C. FLASPOHLER. *Mathematics of Finance,* 6th ed. Boston: Houghton Mifflin, 1982.

VICHAS, ROBERT P. *Handbook of Financial Mathematics, Formulas, and Tables.* Englewood Cliffs, N.J.: Prentice-Hall, 1979.

Uses of your calculator are covered in sources such as these:

GREYNOLDS, ELBERT B., JR., JULIUS S. ARONOFSKY, AND ROBERT J. FRAME. *Financial Analysis Using Calculators: Time Value of Money.* New York: McGraw-Hill, 1980.

HEWLETT-PACKARD, HP-12C, *Owner's Manual and Problem Solving Guide,* 1983.

More on term loans is provided in

ARNOLD, JASPER H., III. "How to Negotiate a Term Loan." *Harvard Business Review* 60 (March–April 1982), pp. 131–138.

See Lesson four in *Lotus 1-2-3® for Financial Management* by Pinches and Courtney for more on future and present values, especially when using Lotus 1-2-3®.

Bond and Stock Valuation

Overview

- The market value of any financial asset is equal to the expected cash flows coming from the asset, discounted at the investor's required rate of return.

- The yield to maturity on a bond is the compound rate of return that causes the present value of the future interest and maturity amounts to equal its current market value.

- A no growth or a constant growth model is often used to value common stocks.

- The relationship between financial management decisions, valuation, the market value of the firm, and its required rate of return is continuous and ongoing.

D uring 1988 the common stock of Cyprus Minerals traded between $36 and $19 3/4, while that for Tiffany & Co. was between $44 1/2 and $21. Damon Biotech had a high of $5 and a low of $7/8, while Quantum Chemical traded between $108 1/4 and $55 1/4. At the same time, the common stock of J.C. Penney closed one week at $51 5/8, while during the preceding 52 weeks it had traded as high as $55 3/4 and as low as $38. Also, a long-term Penney bond was quoted at 102 1/2, or $1,025 per $1,000 par bond. But, only a couple of years earlier the same bond was selling for a little over $800. These examples indicate the substantial price fluctuations that both stocks and bonds can experience.

Every day, economic conditions change. Government agencies issue statistics and pronouncements, bond and stock analysts offer the latest predictions, and firms declare good or bad news. And the market prices of bonds and stocks change. To understand why securities prices change, we need to know how risk, required return, and price are related. In other words, we must understand how bonds and stocks are valued.

It is easy to see why investors must understand the basics of valuing stocks and bonds. But it is equally important that we see why managers understand how bonds and stocks are valued. Many of the firm's investment *and financing decisions are directly influenced by current and anticipated prices and returns for securities. Some of the most important decisions turn on the investor's required rate of return. So, managers must understand how risk, required return, and market prices are related.*

Determining Bond Values and Yields

A bond is a promissory note issued by a firm or government. Some bonds are relatively short-lived, but most have an initial maturity of 10 to 30 years. Bonds are one of the primary sources of funds for corporations. We discuss them before considering common stocks, because as a fixed-income type of security, their valuation is straightforward. To understand bond valuation, we need to define the following terms:

1. PAR VALUE. The stated or face value of a bond is its *par (or maturity) value—* usually $1,000. It represents how much the firm has promised to pay to the bondholder at its maturity date.
2. COUPON INTEREST RATE. The *coupon interest rate* is the interest, as a percentage of par, that will be paid every year. An 11 percent coupon-rate bond will pay $110 [(i.e., 0.11)($1,000)] in interest per year. Interest is normally paid every 6 months; but, for simplicity, we typically assume it is paid annually.
3. MATURITY. The length (or term) of a bond, expressed in years, is its *maturity.* At maturity, the firm is legally obligated to redeem a bond at its par value.
4. NEW ISSUES VERSUS OUTSTANDING BONDS. A new bond issue is one that is sold in the primary market, with the proceeds of the issue going to the issuing unit. At the time bonds are initially sold, they are typically priced so they sell close to their par value. Outstanding bonds, on the other hand, refer to all bonds that have previously been issued and are still outstanding. They may be bought or sold in the secondary market, and their price may be close to or far away from the par value.

Bond Valuation

The market price of a bond is equal to the present value of the series of interest payments to be received over the bond's life, plus the maturity value of $1,000, all discounted at the required rate of return for the bond. Thus, a bond's value is equal to

$$\text{value} = B_0 = \sum_{t=1}^{n} \frac{I}{(1 + k_b)^t} + \frac{M}{(1 + k_b)^n} \tag{6.1}$$

$$= I(PVA_{k_b,n}) + M(PV_{k_b,n})$$

where

B_0 = the current market price of the bond
I = the dollar amount of interest expected to be received each year (or par value × coupon interest rate)
n = the number of years to maturity for the bond

k_b = the required rate of return for the bond

M = the par or maturity value of the bond

To see how the equation works, let's consider a $1,000 par bond that has a 12 percent coupon rate and a 25-year maturity. If this bond has a required rate of return of 12 percent and pays interest annually, its value is

$$B_0 = \frac{\$120}{(1.12)^1} + \frac{\$120}{(1.12)^2} + \cdots + \frac{\$120}{(1.12)^{25}} + \frac{\$1,000}{(1.12)^{25}}$$

$$= \$120(PVA_{12\%,25yr}) + \$1,000(PV_{12\%,25yr})$$

$$= \$120(7.843) + \$1,000(0.059) = \$941.16 + \$59.00$$

$$= \$1,000.16 \approx \$1,000$$

In this example the bond has a current market value of $1,000, which is exactly equal to its par value. Thus, if the required rate of return is equal to the bond's coupon rate, the current market value of a bond is equal to its par value.[1] The bond then sells at its par value of $1,000.

Interest Rates and Bond Prices

Bonds generally do not sell for their par value. Instead, they sell for more or less than $1,000, depending on current market conditions. To see why, let's use what we learned about interest rates in Chapter 2. The required return on a bond for an investor is equal to the risk-free rate plus a risk premium, or

$$k_b = k_{RF} + \text{risk premium}$$

where k_b is the required return and the risk-free rate, k_{RF}, is a function of the real rate of interest plus expected inflation. The risk premium is

$$\frac{\text{risk}}{\text{premium}} = \frac{\text{maturity}}{\text{premium}} + \frac{\text{default}}{\text{premium}} + \frac{\text{liquidity}}{\text{premium}} + \frac{\text{issue-specific}}{\text{premium}}$$

Putting this all together, the return required by bond investors is a function of six factors—the real rate of interest, expected inflation and premiums related to maturity, default, liquidity, and issue-specific characteristics. For the moment, let's consider long-term bonds issued by the U.S. government. In this case we can ignore the last three premiums, and say that

$$k_{\text{treasury securities}} = \frac{\text{real rate}}{\text{of interest}} + \frac{\text{expected}}{\text{inflation}} + \frac{\text{maturity}}{\text{premium}}$$

$$= k_{RF} + \text{maturity premium}$$

Expected Inflation

Assume that the 25-year bond discussed above is a U.S. government bond. At the time it is issued, investors hold expectations as to future inflation. Suppose that

---

[1] Bonds actually sell at their current market price plus accrued interest. For a new issue there is typically little or no accrued interest. However, if it was one-fourth of the way through the year, then the actual cost of purchasing the bond would be $1,000 + ¼($120), or $1,030. Another type of bond is a zero-coupon bond. These are considered in Chapter 13.

after the bond is issued, expected inflation jumps by 4 percent. This jump will cause market interest rates for new bonds of similar quality and maturity to increase from 12 to 16 percent. This change in market interest rates will also cause the required rate of return on *all outstanding bonds of similar quality and maturity* to increase—again, to 16 percent. This occurs because investors considering the 12 percent coupon rate bond will not be willing to settle for less than they can receive in newly issued securities of comparable quality but with a higher coupon rate. What would the market value of these U.S. government bonds be? To determine this new market price, the interest and principal are discounted at the new required rate of return of 16 percent so that[2]

$$B_0 = \$120(\,PVA_{16\%,25\text{yr}}\,) + \$1,000(\,PV_{16\%,25\text{yr}}\,)$$
$$= \$120(\,6.097\,) + \$1,000(\,0.024\,) = \$731.64 + \$24.00 = \$755.64$$

An investor purchasing this 12 percent coupon rate bond for $755.64 and holding it for 25 years receives a compound return of 16 percent.[3] This return is composed of two parts—the 12 percent coupon, which is expected to provide $120 per year, plus the expected capital appreciation of $244.36 ($1,000 − $755.64).[4] The difference between the $1,000 par value and the current market price of $755.64 is called the *discount* on the bond.

Bonds may also sell at a *premium.* To continue our example, if market interest rates drop to 8 percent on bonds of comparable quality and maturity, the current market price of the 25-year, 12 percent coupon rate bond becomes

$$B_0 = \$120(\,PVA_{8\%,25\text{yr}}\,) + \$1,000(\,PV_{8\%,25\text{yr}}\,)$$
$$= \$120(\,10.675\,) + \$1,000(\,0.146\,) = \$1,281 + \$146 = \$1,427$$

Because the coupon rate of 12 percent is greater than the current market interest rate of 8 percent, investors pay a premium of $427 ($1,427 − $1,000) for the bond. The relationship between the current market yield and the market price is graphed in Figure 6.1. The fundamental point to remember is this: *The price of a bond and general market interest rates move inversely.* If the market interest rate is less than a bond's coupon rate, the bond will sell at a premium. If market interest rates are greater than the coupon rate on a bond, the bond will sell at a discount.

Interest Rate Risk and Maturity Premiums

Bond prices are influenced not only by market interest rates, but also by the term to maturity of the bonds. To see this relationship, consider what happens to

---

[2] Using a financial calculator, we punch in the cash flows (24 at 120 and one at 1,120), $k_b = i = 16$, and then hit the NPV button to produce the answer of $756.12. Rounding causes the 48 cents difference.

[3] This statement assumes the investor can reinvest the periodic interest payments at the promised return—16 percent in this case. If the interest received from this bond is reinvested at a rate lower than 16 percent, the actual return will be less than the promised return of 16 percent.

[4] This gain of $244.36 will not be realized all in 1 year. Instead, if the market interest rate (or term structure) remains constant over the entire period, the market price of the bond will increase each year. Since market interest rates do not stay constant, bond prices fluctuate from year to year depending on both their maturity and the current market interest rate for securities of comparable quality and maturity.

Figure 6.1 Relationship Between a Bond's Market Price and the Current Market Rate of Interest

As market interest rates fall, the bond price rises. Similarly, a rise in the market rate of interest causes bond prices to decline.

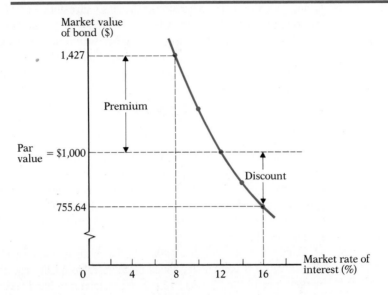

Figure 6.2 Relationship Between a Bond's Market Price, the Current Market Rate of Interest, and Bond Maturity

The market price of shorter-maturity bonds fluctuates substantially less than for longer-maturity bonds as the market rate of interest changes.

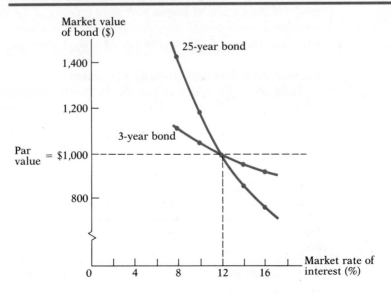

the current market price of our 12 percent U.S. government bonds if they have only 3 years to maturity instead of 25. As Figure 6.2 shows, the 3-year bonds' market prices adjust substantially less to changes in market interest rates than do the prices of 25-year bonds. This tendency of prices on short-term bonds to fluctuate less in response to interest rate changes is called *interest rate risk.* It is because of interest rate risk that, as we observed in Chapter 2, long-term government bonds typically have a maturity premium (or higher interest rate) over short-term government bonds.

Default, Liquidity, and Issue-Specific Premiums

Up to now we have discussed the relationship between the prices on U.S. government bonds, required returns, expected inflation, bond maturity, and bond prices. Corporate bonds are subject to additional risks arising from the possibility of default, liquidity, or issue-specific features. One impact of these other risks is to increase the whole structure of interest rates for corporate bonds versus governments as investors demand a higher return to compensate them for the additional risks. How might some of these factors affect the value of a firm's bonds? Consider what happens if Herman's Carpets is close to bankruptcy and files for protection under the federal bankruptcy laws. Since default risk is great, the required rate of return demanded by investors increases, leading to lower market prices for Herman's outstanding bonds. The same effect results if the bond is not very liquid (i.e., there is a "thin" market with few potential buyers), or if the bond differs in terms of its features, thus making it more risky than other bonds of comparable maturity. The result in all three cases will be a higher return required by investors.

Two other sources of risk exist. One is *reinvestment rate risk,* which is the risk that an investor's income may fall if there is a need to reinvest in another bond issue. Suppose you own a bond that pays a 14 percent coupon rate, while bonds of comparable risk provide an 8 percent return. If your bond matures, or is called by the issuing firm, you will now receive only $80 per year, or, in other words, you have lost $140 − $80 = $60 in interest per year.[5]

Another source of risk is *event risk,* where a drastic change in circumstances changes a "safe" bond into a "risky" one. This can be illustrated by looking at the leveraged buyout of RJR Nabisco in 1988. Before the buyout, RJR Nabisco had about $5 billion in bonds outstanding. To fund the leveraged buyout another $16 billion in borrowing took place. Overnight the possibility of default went up, and investors demanded a higher return to compensate themselves for the increased risk. The market value of the existing RJR Nabisco bonds dropped 20 percent. This is an example of a completely new kind of risk that most bondholders are not protected against. It also involves risk shifting, where part of the potential value created by the leveraged buyout was, in fact, created by the shift in risk from owners to bondholders.

Many factors can affect bond prices. The key point to remember is that as risk increases, market price decreases, and vice versa. This is true no matter what specific factors cause the investor's required rate of return to increase or decrease.

---

[5] This topic is examined in self-test problem ST6.2 and in problem 6.5.

Determining the Yield to Maturity

Instead of being given the required rate of return on a bond, suppose you are told that a 15-year maturity, $1,000 par bond with a 7 percent coupon rate sells for $914.13. What is the compound rate of return, called the *yield to maturity (YTM)*, you would earn if you purchased the bond and held it for the entire 15 years? To solve this problem, we have to find the unknown discount rate, as follows:

$$B_0 = I(PVA_{k_b,n}) + M(PV_{k_b,n})$$

$$\$914.13 = \$70(PVA_{?\%,15yr}) + \$1,000(PV_{?\%,15yr})$$

Our job is to find the discount rate (or $PVA_{k,n}$ and $PV_{k,n}$ for the same number of time periods) that makes the present value of the interest of $70 per year and the maturity value of $1,000 equal to the current market price of $914.13. Before we start, one point should be obvious. Since the market price of $914.13 is *less* than the par value of $1,000, the appropriate discount rate will be *greater* than the coupon interest rate of 7 percent. This is because as we increase the discount rate, the bond price decreases. We know the discount rate must be greater than 7 percent.

If we try 9 percent, the present value is

$$B_0 = \$70(8.061) + \$1,000(0.275) = \$564.27 + \$275 = \$839.27$$

which is too low. Lowering the discount rate to 8 percent, we get

$$B_0 = \$70(8.559) + \$1,000(0.315) = \$599.13 + \$315 = \$914.13$$

The yield to maturity, which represents the investor's expected return by buying it at $914.13 and holding the bond to maturity, is 8 percent.[6] If the present value does not come out to exactly equal the current market value of $914.13, then eyeballing can be used to estimate the yield to maturity.[7]

Bond Values with Semiannual Interest[8]

Most bonds pay interest semiannually. To value bonds with semiannual interest payments, Equation 6.1 is modified as follows:

$$\text{value with semiannual interest} = B_0 = \sum_{t=1}^{2n} \frac{I}{2}\left[\frac{1}{1 + (k_b/2)} \right]^t + M\left[\frac{1}{1 + (k_b/2)} \right]^{2n} \tag{6.2}$$

$$= \frac{I}{2}(PVA_{k_b/2,2n}) + M(PV_{k_b/2,2n})$$

Note that the yearly interest, I, is divided by 2 in order to determine the semiannual interest payments. Also, the required rate of return, k_b, is divided by 2 and the number of periods, n, is doubled to 2n.

---

[6] Using a financial calculator, we solve for the yield to maturity using the internal rate of return (IRR) function by punching in 914.13 at t = 0, 70 for t_1 through t_{14} and 1,070 for t_{15}, and then hitting the IRR button to produce the yield to maturity, k_b, of 8.003 percent.

[7] If the bonds can be called by the firm and retired prior to maturity, it is often helpful to compute the *yield to call (YTC)*, which is the unknown k_b such that $B_0 = I(PVA_{k_b,n}) + $ call price$(PV_{k_b,n})$, and n is the number of years until call. The call price will be greater than (or occasionally equal to) the bond's par value.

[8] This section may be omitted without loss of continuity.

To illustrate bond valuation with semiannual interest payments, consider the earlier example of a 25-year, 12 percent coupon rate bond. When the required rate of return was 16 percent and interest was paid annually, the current value of the bond, B_0, was $755.64. With semiannual interest, the value of the bond is

$$B_0 = \$120/2(\,PVA_{16\%/2,2\times25}\,) + \$1,000(\,PV_{16\%/2,2\times25}\,)$$
$$= \$60(\,PVA_{8\%,50}\,) + \$1,000(\,PV_{8\%,50}\,)$$
$$= \$60(\,12.233\,) + \$1,000(\,0.021\,) = \$733.98 + \$21.00 = \$754.98$$

Note that in this example semiannual interest causes the bond's value to be slightly less than the $755.64 with annual discounting. This results from assuming semiannual instead of annual interest (and discounting).

What if we want to determine the yield to maturity when interest is paid semiannually? Assume the current market value of the bond, B_0, is $1,054.09, the coupon interest rate is 11 percent per year, interest is paid semiannually, and the bond has a maturity of 8 years. As before, we divide the coupon interest rate in half, so it becomes 5.5 percent per 6 months, and double the maturity to 16 periods. The yield to maturity is found by solving for the unknown discount rate, where

$$\$1,054.09 = \$55(PVA_{?\%,16\ periods}) + \$1,000(PV_{?\%,16\ periods})$$

At 5 percent and 16 periods we have $55(10.838) + $1,000(0.458) = $1,054.09. The YTM on an annual basis is (5 percent)(2) = 10 percent. By paying $1,054.09 for the bond, with interest paid semiannually, the expected yield to maturity is 10 percent per year.

Consols and Preferred Stock

A *consol* is a perpetual coupon rate bond. These got their name from the famous British consols, issued to help finance the Napoleonic wars in the early nineteenth century. The value of a perpetual bond is

$$\begin{matrix}\text{value of} \\ \text{perpetual bond}\end{matrix} = B_0 = \frac{I_1}{k_b} \qquad\qquad (6.3)$$

If the required rate of return is 9 percent, and the coupon interest rate is 4 percent, then a $1,000 par value perpetual bond would be worth $40/0.09 = $444.44.

The valuation of preferred stock is similar to consols. As such, the same approach can be employed using dividends, instead of interest, in Equation 6.3. If the preferred stock has an $80 par value, and the dividend is 9 percent per year, the yearly dividend is ($80)(0.09) = $7.20. If the required rate of return is 12 percent, the the value of the preferred stock is $7.20/0.12 = $60.

Bond Valuation and Financial Management

In recent years bond yields (as shown in Figure 6.3) have fluctuated widely, primarily because of wide swings in actual and expected inflation. Since bond yields and prices are inversely related, bond prices have also been volatile. This relationship is important because debt is one of the firm's main sources of capital. To determine the firm's required rate of return, or cost of capital (the topic of Chapter 14), and its capital structure (Chapter 15) requires a thorough understanding of bond valuation and pricing. Managers must also compare the costs and risks of financing with coupon-paying

Figure 6.3 Relationship Between Long-Term Corporate Bond Yields and Changes in the Consumer Price Index

Market interest rates and inflation tend to move together. In recent years, inflation has declined much more rapidly than bond yields. SOURCE: Federal Reserve Bulletin *and* Monthly Labor Review, *various issues.*

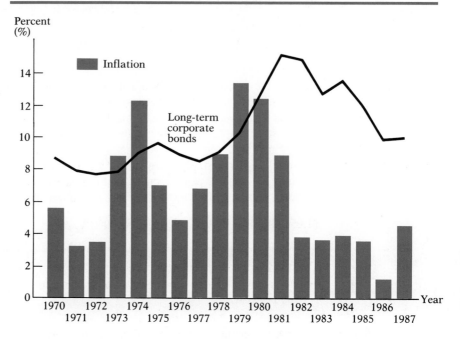

versus zero-coupon bonds (Chapter 13), and with other intermediate or long-term sources such as term loans (Chapter 5) and leases (Chapter 17).

The term structure, investor expectations, and required rates of return also become important when comparing the risks and costs of using short-term debt (discussed in Chapter 21) with those for long-term debt. Finally, managers must understand the interaction of risk, returns, and costs when deciding whether to replace an outstanding bond issue with a new one (these refunding decisions are examined in Appendix 13A). Hence, we see that there are many situations in financial management where knowledge of the valuation and pricing of bonds is important.

Determining Common Stock Values

The valuation of common stocks, although similar conceptually to bond valuation, has some additional complications because neither the cash dividends nor the ending values are constant (as the interest and maturity value are for bonds). Common stock represents residual ownership in the firm. The following definitions are needed to understand common stock valuation:

D_t = the annual amount of cash dividends expected to be received at the end of the tth year. D_0 is the current dividend just paid, D_1 is the cash dividend expected 1 year from now, and so forth.[9]

k_s = the required rate of return on the stock

n = the number of time periods, or years, which in some cases will be infinity

P_t = the market price of the stock at the end of year t. P_0 is the price today *right after* the receipt of the cash dividend D_0. P_1 is the price 1 year from now *right after* receiving the dividend D_1, and so forth

g = the expected (compound) *growth rate* in the cash dividends. We also assume this is the rate of growth in the market price.

Dividend Valuation

To start, let us think of common stock valuation as being like bond valuation. The current market value of a share of common stock is equal to the present value of the expected cash dividends and future market price, where

$$\text{value} = P_0 = \sum_{t=1}^{n} \frac{D_t}{(1 + k_s)^t} + \frac{P_n}{(1 + k_s)^n} \tag{6.4}$$

The current market value of a stock that will pay cash dividends of $1.00 at t = 1, $1.50 at t = 2, and $2.00 at t = 3, and have a market value of $40.00 at t = 3 can be determined in a straightforward manner. If the required rate of return is 14 percent, the value of this stock is[10]

$$
\begin{aligned}
P_0 &= \frac{D_1}{(1 + k_s)^1} + \frac{D_2}{(1 + k_s)^2} + \frac{D_3}{(1 + k_s)^3} + \frac{P_3}{(1 + k_s)^3} \\[2mm]
&= \frac{\$1.00}{(1.14)^1} + \frac{\$1.50}{(1.14)^2} + \frac{\$2.00}{(1.14)^3} + \frac{\$40.00}{(1.14)^3} \\[2mm]
&= \$1.00(PV_{14\%,1yr}) + \$1.50(PV_{14\%,2yr}) + \$2.00(PV_{14\%,3yr}) \\
&\quad + \$40.00(PV_{14\%,3yr}) \\[2mm]
&= \$1.00(0.877) + \$1.50(0.769) + \$2.00(0.675) \\
&\quad + \$40.00(0.675) \\[2mm]
&= \$0.88 + \$1.15 + \$1.35 + \$27.00 = \$30.38
\end{aligned}
$$

If an investor pays $30.38 for the stock, and the cash flow stream of dividends and market price occur as projected, the rate of return realized on the stock will be 14 percent.[11]

What if we keep adding more years of dividends to Equation 6.4 so that we can think of the cash dividends going on forever? In that case, we get to the fundamental

[9] In practice, most firms pay cash dividends on a quarterly basis (see Chapter 16). However, for simplicity we assume they are all paid at one time—the end of the year.

[10] We could add together the $2 cash dividend in year 3 and the market price of $40; however, for clarity they are kept separate.

[11] This assumes, similar to the interest received on bonds, as noted in footnote 3, that the cash dividends received at t = 1 and t = 2 can be reinvested for 2 years and 1 year, respectively, at 14 percent. With a financial calculator you enter t_1 = 1.00, t_2 = 1.50, t_3 = 42.00, k_s = i = 14, and then hit the NPV button to produce the value of $30.38.

Brokerage Fees

When investors buy or sell stocks, they typically use a brokerage firm. The brokerage firm can be either full-service or discount. Brokerage fees are "negotiated" between the individual and the firm, but two main factors drive the size of the fee paid; the number of shares traded, and the price per share.

The table below shows the average brokerage commission and percent of the total trade value (in parentheses) for a group of five full-service and five discount brokers in 1988.[1]

Number of Shares	Share Price					
	$5		$20		$70	
	Full-Service	Discount	Full-Service	Discount	Full-Service	Discount
25	$ 27.00	$34.80	$ 39.05	$ 34.85	$ 56.50	$ 39.40
	(21.6%)	(27.8%)	(7.8%)	(7.0%)	(3.2%)	(2.3%)
100	$ 39.18	$35.40	$ 62.81	$ 40.00	$101.83	$ 43.89
	(7.8%)	(7.1%)	(3.1%)	(2.0%)	(1.5%)	(0.6%)
1,000	$194.24	$76.20	$390.88	$113.27	$721.09	$183.47
	(3.9%)	(1.5%)	(2.0%)	(0.6%)	(1.0%)	(0.3%)

Brokerage fees (with the exception of 25 shares at $5) are less when using a discount broker. That's because the function of a discount broker is simply to execute trades; a full-service broker will execute trades and provide other support or advice. Note that brokerage fees as a percent of the trade value drop dramatically as both the number of shares and the price per share goes up. While we often ignore brokerage commissions in finance, for the small investor their impact cannot be ignored.

[1] Barbara Donnelly. "Small Customers Are Targeted by Full-Service Brokers." *Wall Street Journal* (October 3, 1988); and Barbara Donnelly. "Discount Brokerage Fees Creep Upward." *Wall Street Journal* (October 10, 1988).

common stock model—the *dividend valuation model*—which states that the market value of a share of common stock is equal to the present value of all future dividends:

$$\text{value} = P_0 = \frac{D_1}{(1 + k_s)^1} + \frac{D_2}{(1 + k_s)^2} + \cdots + \frac{D_\infty}{(1 + k_s)^\infty}$$

$$= \sum_{t=1}^{\infty} \frac{D_t}{(1 + k_s)^t} \tag{6.5}$$

In Equation 6.4, the second term is $P_n/(1 + k_s)^n$, where P_n represents the market price at time t = n. But what determines the market price at time n? It is simply the present value of all cash dividends expected to be received *from period n + 1 to infinity,* discounted at the required rate of return of k_s. Equation 6.4 is simply a special case of the more general Equation 6.5. This relationship will prove useful when we consider valuing stocks that are expected to have nonconstant growth in future cash dividends. However, before doing that, we want to consider the simpler cases of (1) no growth in cash dividends, and (2) constant growth in cash dividends.

No Growth in Cash Dividends

In the special case of no future expected growth in cash dividends, assume that the stock will pay a constant dividend of, say, $2 per year from now until infinity. Although the *no growth model* is obviously unrealistic, it provides a convenient benchmark and vastly simplifies our computations. In such a case, the dividend valuation equation (Equation 6.5) is simply a perpetuity. For a common stock with a constant expected cash dividend from t_1 to infinity, its current market value is given by

$$\text{value with no growth} = P_0 = \frac{D_1}{k_s} \tag{6.6}$$

If we have a stock that is expected to pay a cash dividend of $2 per year from time $t = 1$ until infinity, and the required rate of return is 16 percent (or 0.16), then its current value, P_0, is $2/0.16 = $12.50. A rational investor would pay no more than $12.50 for this stock if his or her required rate of return is 16 percent.

Constant Growth in Cash Dividends

In another special case, consider what happens if cash dividends are expected to increase at a constant (percentage) rate each year. To find the present value of this stream of constantly growing dividends, we can use Equation 6.7, which is the *constant growth model:*[12]

$$\text{value with constant growth} = P_0 = \frac{D_1}{k_s - g} \tag{6.7}$$

In using this equation for a constantly growing series of cash dividends, we must use *the cash dividends expected 1 year hence,* or D_1. If we have a stock whose current

---

[12] To see this relationship, first convert Equation 6.5 to the following, where g is the constant compound growth rate:

$$P_0 = \frac{D_0(1+g)}{(1+k_s)} + \frac{D_0(1+g)^2}{(1+k_s)^2} + \cdots + \frac{D_0(1+g)^n}{(1+k_s)^n} \tag{i}$$

If we multiply both sides of Equation (i) by $(1 + k_s)/(1 + g)$ and subtract Equation (i) from the product, we obtain

$$\frac{P_0(1+k_s)}{(1+g)} - P_0 = D_0 - \frac{D_0(1+g)^n}{(1+k_s)^n}$$

As the number of years, n, approaches infinity and if k_s is greater than g, the second term on the right-hand side goes to zero. Consequently,

$$P_0\left[\frac{1+k_s}{1+g} - 1\right] = D_0 \qquad P_0(k_s - g) = D_0(1+g)$$

$$P_0\left[\frac{(1+k_s) - (1+g)}{1+g}\right] = D_0 \qquad P_0 = \frac{D_1}{k_s - g}$$

If the growth rate is greater than k_s, the market price will be infinite. While g may be greater than k_s for a few years, it cannot continue that way for long periods of time. Whenever we employ Equation 6.7, we assume k_s is greater than g.

cash dividend (at time t = 0) is $2, the constant compound growth rate in dividends is 10 percent per year, and the required rate of return is 16 percent, the value of this stock is

$$P_0 = \frac{D_1}{k_s - g} = \frac{D_0(1 + g)}{k_s - g} = \frac{\$2\,(1.10)}{0.16 - 0.10} = \frac{\$2.20}{0.06} = \$36.67$$

Note that this current price of $36.67 is substantially higher than the $12.50 when no growth in future cash dividends was assumed. This is as we would expect since, other things being equal, an investor would value a growing cash flow stream at a higher rate than a nongrowing stream. While growth rates for firms are not often constant, Equation 6.7 is still useful because of its simplicity.

Nonconstant Growth in Cash Dividends[13]

The last situation we will consider is when a firm grows at a fast rate for a few years and then reverts to a constant or no growth situation. This might occur because a firm made previous investments that produced high cash flows, but increasing competition, as in the computer software area, is expected to reduce the future growth rate. For example, if the required rate of return was 16 percent, consider how we would value this situation: (1) Dividends at time t_0 = $2; (2) followed by 10 percent growth in dividends for each of years 1, 2, and 3; (3) followed by 3 percent compound growth thereafter until infinity. This set of cash flows is graphed in Figure 6.4.

The following four-step procedure can be employed to solve this problem:

1. Determine the cash dividends until the series reverts to either constant growth to infinity, or no growth. Thus

$$D_1 = D_0(FV_{10\%,1yr}) = \$2.00(\,1.100\,) = \$2.200$$

$$D_2 = D_0(FV_{10\%,2yr}) = \$2.00(\,1.210\,) = \$2.420$$

$$D_3 = D_0(FV_{10\%,3yr}) = \$2.00(\,1.331\,) = \$2.662$$

2. Determine the first year's dividend *after* the growth rate changes to either constant growth to infinity, or no growth.

$$D_4 = D_3(FV_{3\%,1yr}) = \$2.662(\,1.030\,) = \$2.742$$

Since the growth rate changed to 3 percent (from 10 percent), the new growth rate of 3 percent must be used in this step.

3. Determine the market price of the stock as of time t = 3 for the constant or no growth period.[14] Thus

$$P_3 = \frac{D_4}{k_s - g} = \frac{\$2.742}{0.16 - 0.03} = \frac{\$2.742}{0.13} = \$21.0923$$

---

[13] This section may be omitted without loss of continuity.

[14] If there was no growth in cash dividends expected after year 3, $P_3 = D_4/k_s = \$2.662/0.16 = \$16.6375$. Discounting this back to time zero at 16 percent and adding it to the discounted value of the cash dividends to be received for periods 1, 2, and 3, produces a market price of $16.07.

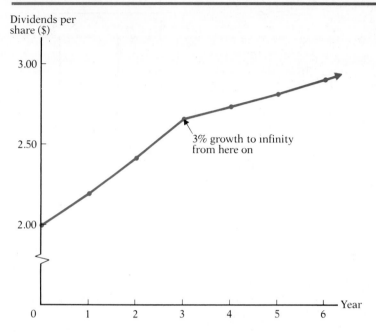

Figure 6.4 Cash Dividend Series Growing at 10 Percent for 3 Years Followed by 3 Percent Growth to Infinity

Due to the compounding effect, the lines between years 0 and 3 and between years 3 and 6 are not quite straight.

Note that (1) the growth rate is the constant one expected from time t = 3 until infinity, and (2) the market price is as of time t = 3.

4. Using Equation 6.4 and the required rate of return of 16 percent, discount both the expected cash dividends from step 1 and the expected market price from step 3 back to the present. As shown in Figure 6.5, the present value of this stream of expected cash flows is $18.92. Thus, the current market value of the stock should be $18.92.

To see the relationship between the growth rate in expected cash dividends and the current market value of a stock, consider Table 6.1, which summarizes our calculations. In the case of no growth in future cash dividends, the market price is $12.50, whereas it is $36.67 at a 10 percent compound rate to infinity. Finally, growth at 10 percent for 3 years followed by low or no growth thereafter produces market prices of $18.92 and $16.07, respectively. Clearly, *the rate and length of the expected growth rate in cash dividends has a major impact on the market price of a common stock.* This is why accurate estimation of expected growth rates is an important aspect of common stock valuation.

Non-Dividend-Paying Stocks

We have discussed stock valuation when the firm pays cash dividends, but not all firms do so. How should we value non-dividend-paying stocks? There are three ways. The first is to estimate *when* the firm will start paying dividends, their size, growth rate, and so forth. Then simply proceed as we have discussed. The second

Figure 6.5 Time Line and Solution for Nonconstant Dividend Series

The dividend in year 4 equals $2.662(FV_{3\%,1yr})$. The market price determined using D_4 is the price at time $t = 3$. It must be brought back to time zero, as are the cash dividends for years 1, 2, and 3, by discounting at 16 percent.

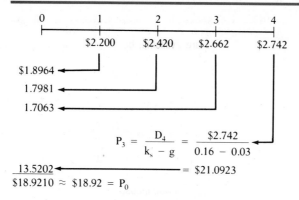

is a variation of the first, except you must estimate some future market price, and then discount it back to the present as we have done previously. The final approach employs earnings, and multiplies (or capitalizes) them by some factor (based on perceived growth, risk and/or estimates derived by looking at "similar" firms) to arrive at an estimated value.

Stock Valuation and Financial Management

To see why valuation is so important, first let's define returns, then consider actual versus expected returns, and, finally, discuss its relevance for effective financial management.

Table 6.1 Relationship Between Expected Growth and Market Value

There is a direct relationship between the amount and length of expected growth in cash dividends and a stock's market value.

Condition*	Resulting Market Value (P_0)
No future growth in expected cash dividends	$12.50
10 percent compound growth in expected cash dividends for $t = 1$, $t = 2$, and $t = 3$, followed by no future growth†	16.07
10 percent compound growth in expected cash dividends for $t = 1$, $t = 2$, and $t = 3$, followed by 3 percent compound growth to infinity	18.92
10 percent compound growth in expected cash dividends to infinity	36.67

* $D_0 = \$2$ and $k_s = 16$ percent for all conditions.
† From footnote 14.

Stock Indices

Many stock indices are available, both for United States stocks and those around the world. The earliest stock index in the United States was the Dow-Jones Industrial Average (DJIA), started in 1884. It now contains 30 of the largest firms in the United States. The Dow-Jones Industrial Average is a price-weighted average. Under price weighting the prices of one share of all the securities are added together. With this weighting method, higher-priced stocks carry more weight than lower-priced stocks. The DJIA, because of price weighting and since it does not adjust for stock dividends of less than 10 percent, has some deficiencies as an index. However, it's probably the most widely followed index in the United States.

In 1923 Standard & Poor's started some indices. The major one, the S&P 500 Stock Index, is now composed of 400 industrials, 40 public utilities, 40 financial institutions, and 20 transportation companies. All Standard & Poor's indices are value weighted. That is, both the price and the number of shares of each stock are recognized; therefore, stocks with larger total market values exert the most influence. Because of its broad range and its value weighting, the S&P is one of the better general-purpose indices in the United States.

In 1966 the New York Stock Exchange started its own index, called the NYSE Composite Index. It covers all stock listed on the Exchange. It also is value weighted, so its movements are dominated by stocks of larger companies. Oftentimes when listening to the news, you'll hear the comment that the price of an average share of stock on the NYSE went up or down so many points. When said in this manner, the commentator is referring specifically to the NYSE Composite Index.

There are many other indices such as the Value Line Index, the ASE (American Stock Exchange) Index, the NASDAQ (National Association of Security Dealers Automated Quotation) Index, the Wilshire 5000 Equity Index, and more academic indices such as the CRSP (Center for Research in Security Prices) value-weighted and equally weighted indices. There are also many stock indices available for narrower sectors of the country or economy. These are useful for special-purpose comparisons when a general index is too broad.

Returns

The *return* from investing in any financial asset comes from one of two sources: (1) income from interest, dividends, and so forth; and (2) capital gains or losses—that is, the difference between the beginning and ending market values. For common stocks, these returns are (1) cash dividends received during the period and (2) capital appreciation or loss. For any period (e.g., month, year, etc.) we can define the return on a stock as

$$\text{return} = k = \frac{D_1 + P_1 - P_0}{P_0} \tag{6.8}$$

If a firm expects to pay cash dividends of $3.50 per share at time t = 1, the present market price is $40, and the expected price at time t = 1 is $42, then the return is

$$k = \frac{\$3.50 + \$42 - \$40}{\$40} = \frac{\$5.50}{\$40} = 0.1375 = 13.75\%$$

In the example, this is an *ex ante* (*expected*) *rate of return*; it is what investors anticipate receiving *before* the fact. Their *ex post* (*realized*) *rate of return* over the period (calculated using Equation 6.8, but with historical data) may differ from the forecasted return if cash dividends are more or less than $3.50 or if the ending market price is different from the $42 projected.

Returns from bonds or from any other financial asset can be computed in exactly the same manner using appropriately specified values in Equation 6.8. In practice we can measure returns over any time period, but a year is typical. Also, note that we can calculate *ex post* returns whether or not we actually sell the financial asset. To illustrate this, suppose an investor purchased the stock in our example and held it for 1 year. If the actual cash dividend received was $3.50 and the actual ending market price was $42, then the return over that period was 13.75 percent—whether or not the investor actually sold the security. If the investor holds the stock, then for the next period $42 represents the initial price, and any capital gain or loss for the period is measured against the $42 figure. This process is repeated over and over again, and a series of *ex post* returns exist for as long as the stock is owned by the investor.

Actual Versus Expected Returns

An investor's *ex post,* or realized, return may differ from his or her *ex ante,* or expected, return. In theory, expected returns are always positive, since investors will not expose themselves to risk without the prospect of appropriate returns over and above the risk-free rate. But an examination of Figure 6.6 shows, similar to what we saw in Chapter 2, that *ex post* common stock returns have not always been positive. While the dividend component is relatively stable, the capital (or price) appreciation or loss is not. Over this time period about 40 percent of the total return on common stocks came from dividend income; the remainder was due to changes in the market price of common stocks. Of course, even in bad years some firms do well; there are always "winners" and "losers." In subsequent chapters we will examine many actions managers can take to increase the chance that their firm will be a winner, not a loser.

Importance for Financial Management

Risk, return, stock price, and managerial decisions are closely related, as Figure 6.7 depicts (see p. 160). Beginning at the top left, we start with financial management decisions. These affect the magnitude, timing, and riskiness of the firm's expected cash flow. Next, investors (based on all the information coming to them about the firm, economy, etc.) assess the perceived risk for the firm—which, as we know, directly affects the investor's required rate of return. These actions determine the size of the pie (or the market value of the firm). Based on the performance of the firm's stock and bonds and the firm's required rate of return, additional financial management decisions are made: The relationship between financial management decisions, valuation, the market value of the firm, and its required rate of return is continuous and ongoing.

Figure 6.6 Total Returns, Dividend Income, and Capital Appreciation for Common Stocks, 1960–1987

Returns from dividends are much more dependable from those attributed to price appreciation or loss. SOURCE: *Ibbotson, Roger G., and Rex A. Sinquefield,* Stocks, Bonds, Bills, and Inflation *(SBBI) 1982, updated in* Stocks, Bonds, Bills, and Inflation 1988 Yearbook™, *Ibbotson Associates, Inc., Chicago.*

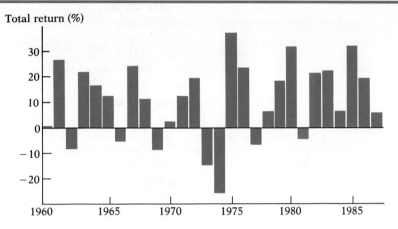

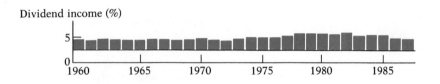

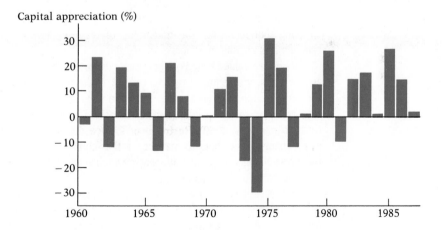

Figure 6.7 Relationship Between the Firm's Financial Management Decisions, Investors' Actions, and Valuation

Because of the interrelated and circular nature of (1) the decision-making process, (2) investors' actions, and (3) the value of the firm, managers must understand the common stock valuation process.

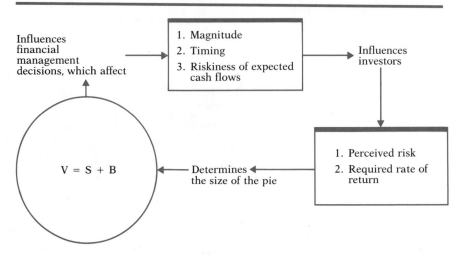

Summary

Valuation is the second fundamental concept of financial management. The valuation of financial assets provides the foundation for making effective financial decisions. Anything that reduces the magnitude of the expected cash inflows, delays their receipt, or increases their risk reduces the value of a financial asset. Likewise, anything that increases the magnitude of the cash flows, speeds their inflow, or reduces risk results in an increase in value.

Bonds are valued based on their expected interest and maturity values, discounted at the investor's required rate of return. If the market interest rate is higher than the bond's coupon interest rate, the bond sells at a discount. If the market interest rate is lower than the coupon rate, the bond sells at a premium. The longer the term to maturity, the more the bond's price fluctuates as general market interest rates change. The yield to maturity is that compound rate of return which equates the present value of future interest payments and the maturity value to the bond's current market value.

The market value of common stock is equal to the present value of all expected cash dividends, where the investor's required rate of return is employed as the discount rate. For simplicity, we often employ a no growth or constant growth dividend valuation model to value common stock.

Expected (*ex ante*) returns and realized (*ex post*) returns are not equal. However, the greater the risk, the greater the return expected by investors. The relationship between financial management decisions, valuation, the market value of the firm, and its required rate of return is continuous and ongoing.

There is an appendix to this chapter, "Appendix 6A: Reading the Financial Pages," at the back of the book.

Questions

6.1 Define or explain the following:

a. Par (maturity) value
b. Coupon interest rate
c. Maturity
d. Discount
e. Premium
f. Interest rate risk
g. Reinvestment rate risk
h. Event risk
i. Yield to maturity (YTM)
j. Yield to call (YTC)

k. Consol
l. Growth rate (g)
m. Dividend valuation model
n. No growth model, $P_0 = D_1/k_s$
o. Constant growth model, $P_0 = D_1/(k_s - g)$
p. Return
q. *ex ante* (expected) rate of return
r. *ex post* (realized) rate of return
s. Bid price
t. Asked price

6.2 Using both stocks and bonds, explain why their current market value is equal to the present value of the future cash flows expected by investors, discounted at their required rate of return.

6.3 Why is it that bonds do not typically sell at face value? How do fluctuations in market interest rates and the length of time to maturity influence bond price fluctuations?

6.4 The rate of return you will receive on a bond if you buy it today and hold it until maturity is its yield to maturity (YTM). (*Note:* In answering these questions, ignore any reinvestment problem associated with the future interest to be received.)

a. What happens to the YTM as market interest rates change?
b. Will you receive any more, or any less, if interest rates change as long as you hold the bond to maturity? Why?
c. Will you receive any more, or any less, as interest rates change if you are forced to sell before maturity? Why?

6.5 Explain the difference between determining the value of a bond, or its yield to maturity, employing annual versus semiannual discounting. With semiannual discounting, why do we adjust for the number of periods not only for the coupon interest, but also for the maturity value?

6.6 The following formula is applicable where dividends have been estimated for a few years, at which time the estimated future market price is then employed:

$$P_0 = \sum_{t=1}^{n} \frac{D_t}{(1 + k_s)^t} + \frac{P_n}{(1 + k_s)^n}$$

Explain where the term P_n comes from.

6.7 Carl is in the process of valuing a common stock under various circumstances, as follows:

Conditions	Estimated Stock Price
Required return = 15%; D_0 = $1.00; g = 0; period = ∞	$ 6.67
Required return = 15%; D_0 = $1.00; g = 10%; period = ∞	22.00
Required return = 15%; D_0 = $1.00; g = 10% for each of 5 years followed by 5% from there to infinity; period = ∞	10.00
Required return = 15%; D_0 = $1.00; g = 5%; period = ∞	10.50

One of his answers does not make sense. Which one? Why?

6.8 Carolyn believes she can understand financial management without knowing bond and stock valuation. Explain to her why this isn't true by providing specific examples of how bond and stock valuation are important for effective decision making.

Self-Test Problems (Solutions appear on pages 718–719.)

Bond Valuation

ST 6.1 What is the current market price of a $1,000 par, 12 percent coupon rate bond if interest is paid (1) annually, or (2) semiannually, there are 10 years to maturity, and the required rate of return is (a) 12 percent, (b) 14 percent, (c) 8 percent?

Realized Return on a Bond

ST 6.2 Five years ago Homer Hennigar purchased for $1,000 a 20-year, 14 percent coupon rate bond with a par value of $1,000. Interest on the bond is payable semiannually. For the past 5 years market interest rates have stayed constant, but now they have fallen to 10 percent. They are expected to stay at 10 percent for another 5 years and then fall to 8 percent for the final 10 years. Assume that all cash flows received for the first 5 years can be reinvested at a 14 percent annual rate until maturity; those received during the second 5 years can be reinvested at a 10 percent annual rate until maturity; and those received during the last 10 years can be reinvested at an 8 percent annual rate. What will Homer's realized rate of return be if he holds the bond for the entire 20-year period?

Nonconstant Growth

ST 6.3 Cavalier Industries has a current (D_0) cash dividend of $2 per share. You estimate that cash dividends will grow at 12 percent per year for each of 3 years ($t_1, t_2,$ and t_3), and then at 6 percent per year for each of 2 more years (t_4 and t_5). After t_5, you expect them to grow at 2 percent per year to infinity.

a. What is the current market value of Cavalier Industries common stock if the required rate of return is 14 percent?

b. What is the market price if everything is the same as in (a) except that after year 5 there is no expected growth in cash dividends?

Problems

Bond Prices

6.1 Compton Computer bonds pay $80 annual interest, mature in 10 years, and pay $1,000 at maturity. What will their value be if the market rate of interest is (1) 6 percent, or (2) 10 percent, and interest is paid (a) annually, (b) semiannually?

Bond Price Changes and Time to Maturity

6.2 Find the current market value of a 20-year, 9 percent coupon rate bond with a par value of $1,000, if interest is paid annually if current market rates are (a) 11 percent, or (b) 7 percent. What are the current market prices if everything is the same except the bond has only·(1) 10 years to maturity, or (2) 2 years to maturity? What can we say about the relative influence of changing market interest rates on the market prices of short-term versus long-term bonds? Can you speculate on why this is so?

Yield to Maturity

6.3 Greenman Engineering has some 15-year $1,000 par bonds outstanding, which have a coupon interest rate of 9 percent and pay interest annually. What is the yield to maturity on the bonds if their current market price is:

a. $1,181.72?
b. $795.99?
c. Would you be willing to pay $795.99 if your minimum required rate of return was 11 percent? Why or why not?

Yield to Maturity Versus Yield to Call

6.4 A $1,000 par value bond has a 12 percent coupon rate, pays interest annually, and has 15 years remaining until it matures.

a. If B_0 = $1,151.72, what is its yield to maturity (YTM)?
b. If the bond can be called in 6 years at $1,030, what is the bond's yield to call (YTC)? Why is the YTC in this problem lower than the YTM? Would this always be true?

(Do only if using Pinches Disk.)

c. What would the YTM and YTC be in (a) and (b) if the coupon rate was 10 percent instead of 12 percent and all other values remained the same? Is the YTC still lower than the YTM? Why or why not?
d. Now suppose the years remaining until maturity changes to 20 and the years to call changes to 10, while the other values remain the same as in (a) and (b). What are the new values for YTM and YTC? Why do they differ from those calculated in (a), (b), and (c)?
e. Finally, repeat the calculation in (d) except the coupon rate is now at 10 percent instead of 12 percent, the call price is $1,070, and the years to call is 15. What are the values for YTM and YTC? How do these compare with your answers in (a), (b), (c), and (d)?

Realized Return on Bond

6.5 Five years ago Mary Yang purchased twenty 15-year, 14 percent coupon rate bonds at their par value of $1,000 each. The bonds pay interest once a year. At the end of 5 years the issuing firm called the bonds at $1,050 each, so she received $21,000 in total.

a. What was Mary's expected yield to maturity (YTM) when she purchased the bonds?
b. Based on what she received, what was her actual annual percentage return over the five years if she reinvested the interest payments received at 14 percent?
c. What would have been her actual percentage return if everything had been the same as in (b), but interest rates had fallen immediately so that she could have reinvested the interest payments received at only 12 percent?

Yield to Maturity: Annual Versus Semi-annual Interest

6.6 Kamath Brothers has a $1,000 par, 9 percent coupon rate bond outstanding. The bond has 14 years to maturity.

a. If the current market value of the bond is $1,200, and interest is paid annually, what is the bond's yield to maturity?
b. What if everything is as in (a), but interest is paid semiannually? [*Note:* Unless you are using a financial calculator, you may not find any appreciable differences in the answers to (a) and (b).]

Preferred Stock

6.7 You are interested in buying 100 shares of a $60 par value preferred stock that has an $8\frac{1}{2}$ percent dividend rate.

a. If your required return is 11 percent, how much would you be willing to pay to acquire its 100 shares?
b. What if no dividends will be paid until t = 3? At the same required return, how much would you now be willing to pay?

Implied Growth Rate 6.8 Smith Supermarkets' common stock is selling at $54, the cash dividend expected next year (at time t = 1) is $3.78 per share, and the required rate of return is 15 percent. What is the implied compound growth rate (to infinity) in cash dividends?

Different Growth Rates 6.9 A stock currently pays cash dividends of $4 per share ($D_0 = \$4$), and the required rate of return is 12 percent. What is its market value in the following cases?

a. There is no future growth in dividends.
b. Dividends grow at 8 percent per year to infinity.
c. Dividends grow at 5 percent for each of 2 years; and there is no growth expected after D_2.

(Do only if using Pinches Disk.)
† d. Growth will be 10 percent for each of 2 years (n = 2), after which growth will be 5 percent per year until infinity.
┼ e. Recalculate (d) where growth is now 7 percent for 5 years (n = 5), after which growth will be 3 percent per year until infinity.
┼ f. Finally, now suppose the required rate of return is 15 percent and $D_0 = \$2.50$. Recalculate (a), (b), (d), and (e) with these new values.

Declining Growth Rate 6.10 Siegel Mines' ore reserves are depleted. Hence, the expected future rate of growth in the firm's cash dividends is −5 percent. (That is, the cash dividends will decline 5 percent per year.) The cash dividend at time t = 0 is $4.40, and the required rate of return is 11 percent. What is the current market value of the stock if we assume dividends decline at 5 percent per year until infinity?

Constant Versus Nonconstant Growth 6.11 Steve Dubofsky is contemplating the purchase of a small, one-island service station. After-tax cash flows are presently $20,000 per year, and his required rate of return is 14 percent.

a. What is the maximum price Steve should pay for the service station if he expects cash flows to grow at 4 percent per year to infinity?
b. If Steve decides he needs a 15 percent return, and there will be no growth in after-tax cash flows for 3 years, followed by 10 percent per year for years 4 and 5, followed by 3 percent growth to infinity, how much is the maximum he should pay?

Nonconstant Growth: Delayed Start 6.12 Nontraditional Energy is a new enterprise that is not expected to pay any cash dividends for the next 5 years. Its first dividend (D_6) is expected to be $2, and the cash dividends are expected to grow for the next 4 years (through t = 10) at 25 percent per year. After that, cash dividends are expected to grow at a more normal 5 percent per year to infinity. If $k_s = 18$ percent, what is P_0? (*Note:* Carry the calculations to three decimal places.)

Common Stock and Length of Holding Period 6.13 Jane Nelson is considering purchasing stock and holding it for 3 years. The projected dividends (at a 5 percent growth rate) and market price are: $D_1 = \$4.20$; $D_2 = \$4.41$; $D_3 = \$4.63$; and $P_3 = \$97.23$. Her required rate of return, given the risk involved, is 10 percent.

a. What is the maximum price Jane should pay for the stock?
b. If the dividends for years 1 and 2 remain at $4.20 and $4.41, respectively, and are expected to grow at 5 percent per year to infinity, what would the market price have to be at the end of the second year if Jane sold the stock but still demanded a 10 percent return?
c. What is the discounted present value (the current price) of the dividends from years 1 and 2, and the market price you determined in (b) above?
d. Why are your answers the same for (a) and (c), aside from any rounding errors?
e. Is the value of the stock today dependent on how long Jane plans to hold it? Does its price today depend on whether Jane plans to hold the stock for 2 years, 3 years, or any other period of time?

6.14 Cassady Enterprises is a no growth firm that pays cash dividends of $8 per year. Its current required rate of return is 12 percent.

a. What is Cassady's current market price?

b. Management is considering an investment that will convert the firm into a constant growth firm, but it requires stockholders to forgo cash dividends for the next 6 years. When cash dividends are resumed in year 7, they will be $8 *plus* the expected constant growth of 11 percent [i.e., ($8)(1.11)] from year 6 to year infinity. If its new required return is 16 percent, will the stockholders be better off? (*Note:* Calculate the current price, P_0.)

c. What happens if everything is the same as in (b), except that the growth rate is only 10 percent?

6.15 Suppose you believe that Legler Products common stock will be worth $144 per share 2 years from now. What is the maximum you would be willing to pay for a share if it pays no cash dividends, and your required rate of return is 16 percent?

References

For a comprehensive analysis of returns on stocks, bonds, and inflation, see

Stocks, Bonds, Bills and Inflation. Chicago: Ibbotson Associates, published yearly.

Bonds, their valuation and duration, are covered in

FONG, H. GIFFORD, AND FRANK J. FABOZZI. *Fixed Income Portfolio Management.* Homewood, Ill.: Dow Jones-Irwin, 1985.

FONS, JEROME S. "The Default Premium and Corporate Bond Experience." *Journal of Finance* 42 (March 1987), pp. 81–97.

GRANITO, MICHAEL R. *Bond Portfolio Immunization.* Lexington, Mass.: D. C. Heath, 1984.

JAHANKHANI, ALI, AND GEORGE E. PINCHES. "Duration and the Nonstationarity of Systematic Risk for Bonds." *Journal of Financial Research* 5 (Summer 1982), pp. 151–160.

The dividend discount model is considered in

DONNELLY, BARBARA. "The Dividend Discount Model Comes into Its Own." *Institutional Investor* 19 (March 1985), pp. 1977 ff.

CARLETON, WILLARD T., AND JOSEF LAKONISHOK. "Risk and Return on Equity: The Use and Misuse of Historical Estimates." *Financial Analysts Journal* 41 (January–February 1985), pp. 38–47, 62.

RAPPAPORT, ALFRED. "The Affordable Dividend Approach to Equity Valuation." *Financial Analysts Journal* 42 (July–August 1986), pp. 52–58.

Some interesting recent articles include

DE BONDT, WERNER F. M., AND RICHARD THALER. "Does the Stock Market Overreact?" *Journal of Finance* 40 (July 1985), pp. 793–805.

FAMA, EUGENE F., AND KENNETH R. FRENCH. "Dividend Yields and Expected Stock Returns." *Journal of Financial Economics* 22 (October 1988), pp. 3–25.

HASBROUCK, JOEL. "Stock Returns, Inflation, and Economic Activity: The Survey Evidence." *Journal of Finance* 39 (December 1984), pp. 1293–1310.

KEIM, DONALD B., AND ROBERT F. STAMBAUGH. "Predicting Returns in the Stock and Bond Markets." *Journal of Financial Economics* 17 (December 1986), pp. 357–390.

STICKEL, SCOTT E. "The Effect of Value Line Investment Survey Rank Changes on Common Stock Prices." *Journal of Financial Economics* 14 (March 1985), pp. 121–143.

See Models five and seven in *Lotus 1-2-3® for Financial Management* by Pinches and Courtney for templates that calculate bond and stock values.

7

Risk and Return

Overview

- Risk arises from four sources—the state of the economy, inflation or disinflation, firm- and issue-specific factors, and the international scene.

- Portfolios are subject to diversifiable risk and nondiversifiable risk, but diversifiable risk can be eliminated. Nondiversifiable risk, as measured by beta, is therefore the relevant measure of risk for assets held in a diversified portfolio.

- The capital asset pricing model describes the required rate of return on a security as a function of the return on a risk-free security, plus a risk premium that incorporates beta.

- Capital markets are reasonably efficient; consequently, securities prices react quickly and unambiguously to new information.

In 1985 Phillips Petroleum was faced with a problem. Two different groups wanted to take over, then sell out to someone else or dismantle the firm. To repel them, Phillips needed cash quickly. It soon more than tripled its debt to a peak of $8.9 billion. And oil prices, already in their worst slump in 50 years, were falling. As a Phillips executive commented: "Prices are a major topic of conversation around here. . . . The price of our principal commodity is going southward and the debt tends to magnify that risk." However, by the end of 1988 Phillips had already reduced its debt to $4.9 billion.

Phillips was experiencing risk from two primary sources: declining oil prices—which affected it very directly—and its decision to increase substantially the use of debt financing. But all firms face risks. For Mack Trucks and Westinghouse Electric, both of which do substantial overseas business, a major source of risk has been fluctuating exchange rates between different currencies. Extremely volatile exchange rates can be much more dangerous to American companies than a strong dollar; they increase risk, and make planning, controlling, and monitoring international operations more difficult and expensive.

Risk cannot be avoided in financial decision making. Along with cash flows and time value, risk affects the value of any asset. We must learn what *causes risk and how it should be measured. Then we can study its impact on required returns. Without understanding risk, managers cannot make effective decisions.*

The Meaning of Risk

Whenever you are in a situation where the outcome is unknown, you are exposed to risk, or *uncertainty.* We use these terms interchangeably to mean that the outcome is subject to chance and not definitely known, or in which there is exposure to possible loss. If you gamble in the casinos in Atlantic City or in Nevada, you bear risk. Investing in stocks, bonds, real estate, or gold bullion also exposes you to risk. Most of the decisions a business makes—to raise prices, to expand production, or to bring out a new product—exposes the firm and its owners to risk. Thus, although the firm's managers make the decision, it is the firm's securities holders who, along with the firm, experience the risk. Risk arises from many different sources and has a number of different meanings in practice. For this reason, it is helpful to group the major sources of risk into four categories: (1) general economic risk, (2) inflation and disinflation risk, (3) firm- and issue-specific risk, and (4) international risk. Let's consider each of these sources of risk in turn.

General Economic Risk

One major source of risk is *general economic risk.* The prospect of a recession affects most firms; they often reduce production and employment as they attempt to maintain profitability. Also at work are the monetary and fiscal policies of government, tax adjustments, transfer payments, and many other factors that stimulate or hold back the economy. As all these forces operate, businesses, consumers, and investors become more or less optimistic or pessimistic about the future of the economy. This overall optimism or pessimism is reflected in the degree of *risk aversion* that influences the returns expected by investors. The first source of risk is the general economic environment and how it is reflected in the degree of risk taking or risk aversion prevalent in the economy as a whole.

Inflation and Disinflation Risk

A second source of risk is represented by *inflation risk* and *disinflation risk.* For businesses, inflation causes increased uncertainty about pricing policies, financing costs, and costs of labor and material. It also tends to raise the effective corporate tax rate. Some firms may benefit from inflation; others may be severely hurt by it due to the combination of higher costs and an inability to pass on increases to consumers. Although these effects are not constant across industries, the clear picture is that inflation, particularly unanticipated inflation, increases the risks to business. When firms become accustomed to inflation, disinflation may also be a source of risk. This has been particularly true in the last few years as some firms have found that policies adopted during the high rates of inflation in the late 1970s and early 1980s simply did not produce the profits and cash flows expected when inflation fell dramatically. All of this causes additional risk.

Firm- and Issue-Specific Risk

A third source of risk is *firm- and issue-specific risk.* For convenience, we break this down further into the three categories of (1) business risk, (2) financial risk, and (3) issue-specific risk.

Business Risk

The general market the firm operates in is a source of risk. The technological stage of development of the industry, the competition and the degree of fixed versus variable costs of production, and sales and marketing techniques all influence the amount of risk to which a firm is exposed.

Although this risk is often related to the nature of the industry, it is more appropriate to view *business risk* as the inherent uncertainty regarding the earnings before interest and taxes (EBIT) of the firm. This subject of business risk, which is a fundamental source of risk among firms, is discussed in more detail in Chapter 15.

Financial Risk

Another kind of risk at the firm level is financial risk. *Financial risk* depends on the amount of financing provided by creditors. The use of debt, leases, or preferred stock exposes the firm to more risk. This risk arises from imposing the fixed costs of financing, which have a prior claim on the firm's cash flows, before the common stockholder receives anything. Financial risk is discussed in detail in Chapter 15. The point to remember here is that a firm with little or no fixed-cost financing has little or no financial risk. Conversely, firms with a lot of debt, leases, and/or preferred stock have a larger amount of financial risk.

Issue-Specific Risk

In addition to business and financial risk, additional risks arise because of the type of securities (and the provisions attached to them) that firms issue. A firm's common stock is more risky to an investor than its bonds because the bondholder has (1) a legal claim, and (2) a prior claim over the common stockholders. Likewise, the specific provisions attached to a bond regarding sinking funds, call features, and so forth influence the risk of the specific issue. These issue-specific risks, while often less important than business or financial risk, are still significant when it comes to assessing the riskiness of various security issues.[1]

International Risk

International risk is another important source of uncertainty. The American auto industry, for example, faces considerable risk because of intense international competition. Firms engaged in manufacturing and/or selling in other markets face risks that are not present when their operations are restricted to the United States. Equally important is the impact international monetary crises, oil prices, wars, and the like have on the economy. All firms may face some international risk, but it obviously is more important to those that compete on an international basis.

The important point to remember is this: As firms face risk, so do their owners—the common stockholders. If the firm's risk increases the common stockholder's risk also increases. The firm and its owners are intertwined, so that risks that affect the firm also affect its stockholders.

---

[1] In Chapter 2 we discussed three other sources of risk that could be relevant here—maturity risk, default risk, and liquidity risk. Maturity risk is more related to bonds. Default risk and liquidity risk can exist for both bonds and stocks. Likewise, reinvestment rate risk and event risk, discussed in Chapter 6, could also be relevant here:

Table 7.1 Probability Distributions for Houston International and American Chemical

The rates of return are those expected to occur under various states of the economy. These rates could be given in decimal form, but we employ percentages throughout.

State of the Economy (1)	Probability of State Occurring (2)	×	Associated Rate of Return (3)	=	Mean or Expected Rate of Return (4)
Houston International					
Boom	0.30		60%		18.0%
Normal	0.40		20		8.0
Recession	0.30		−20		−6.0
	1.00		expected rate of return = k̄ =		20.0%
American Chemical					
Boom	0.30		25%		7.5%
Normal	0.40		15		6.0
Recession	0.30		5		1.5
	1.00		expected rate of return = k̄ =		15.0%

Measuring Risk

Now that we understand some of the sources of risk, we need to learn how to measure it. We begin with individual securities and then move to *portfolios,* which are just groups of securities. For our purposes, let's suppose we are interested in measuring the risk associated with two common stocks—Houston International and American Chemical.

Probability Distributions

The *probability* associated with an event is the chance the event will occur. In column 1 of Table 7.1 the possible states of the economy are given,[2] followed by the estimated probabilities associated with the various states in column 2. The probability of a boom during the next period is 0.30, the probability of a normal state of the economy is 0.40, and the probability of a recession is 0.30. Note that the probabilities must sum to 1.00.[3] In column 3, the estimated outcomes are given. One point should be stressed: Finance has a future orientation; our interest is in the expected rate of return. Since the future is uncertain, there is risk associated with owning either Houston International or American Chemical common stock.

The probability distributions presented in Table 7.1 and graphed in Figure 7.1 are called discrete probability distributions. By discrete we simply mean that the probabilities are assigned to specific outcomes. Another type of probability distribution is continuous. In this book, we emphasize discrete distributions.

[2] We deal with only three states of the economy—boom, normal, and recession—although more could be used if desired.

[3] More formally, the following three conditions hold. First, all outcomes must be accounted for. Second, each individual probability must be greater than or equal to zero. Third, the probabilities must sum to 1.00.

Figure 7.1 Discrete Probability Distributions for Houston International and American Chemical

A discrete probability distribution means that a spike occurs at each specific outcome. A continuous probability distribution would show a smooth curve.

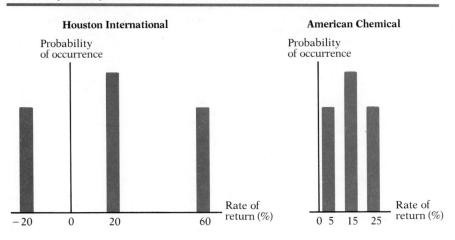

Expected Rate of Return

Two measures are typically employed to summarize information contained in probability distributions. The first is the *mean* or *expected value*. This is calculated by multiplying the probabilities of occurrence by their associated outcomes, so that

$$\text{expected value} = \bar{k} = \sum_{i=1}^{n} k_i P_i \qquad (7.1)$$

where

$\bar{k}$ = the expected value or expected return
n = the number of possible states
k_i = the rate of return associated with the ith possible state
P_i = the probability of the ith state occurring

Thus, the expected return is the weighted average of the possible outcomes (k_i values), with the weights being determined by the probability of occurrence (P_i values).

The expected returns for both firms are presented in Table 7.1. Houston International's expected return is 20 percent; American Chemical's is 15 percent. As we noted in Chapter 6, these expected rates of return will generally not be equal to the actual, or *ex post*, rate of return. The actual rate of return depends on which specific state of the economy occurs.

Standard Deviation

The second summary measure arising from probability distributions is a measure of risk or variability in the possible outcomes. Risk is a difficult concept; one measure that is helpful is the *standard deviation,* which is a measure of *total risk*. It measures how "tightly" the probability distribution is centered around the expected value. Looking back at Figure 7.1, it is easy to see that American Chemical's possible rates of return are much more tightly bunched than Houston International's. However, it is hard to say much else about the riskiness of the two stocks without some

Table 7.2   Calculation of Standard Deviations for Houston International and American Chemical

Calculating standard deviations is easy following this procedure, as long as there are not too many possible outcomes.

$(k_i - \bar{k})$	$(k_i - \bar{k})^2$	$\times$	P_i	$=$	$(k_i - \bar{k})^2 P_i$
Houston International					
$(60 - 20)$	1,600		0.30		480
$(20 - 20)$	0		0.40		0
$(-20 - 20)$	1,600		0.30		480
			variance	$= \sigma^2 =$	$\overline{960}$

standard deviation $= \sigma = \sqrt{\sigma^2} = \sqrt{960} = 30.98\%$

American Chemical					
$(25 - 15)$	100		0.30		30
$(15 - 15)$	0		0.40		0
$(5 - 15)$	100		0.30		30
			variance	$= \sigma^2 =$	$\overline{60}$

standard deviation $= \sigma = \sqrt{\sigma^2} = \sqrt{60} = 7.75\%$

measure that allows us to determine the spread of the distribution. The standard deviation is such a measure. It is defined as

$$standard\ deviation = \sigma = \sqrt{\sum_{i=1}^{n} (k_i - \bar{k})^2 P_i} \qquad (7.2)$$

where

σ = sigma or the standard deviation (the bigger the spread of the distribution, the larger the standard deviation)[4]

k_i = the outcome associated with the ith state

$\bar{k}$ = the expected value or expected return

P_i = the probability associated with the ith outcome

To calculate the standard deviation, the steps shown in Table 7.2 are employed.[5] We see that the standard deviation for Houston International is 30.98 percent and 7.75 percent for American Chemical. These results confirm our observation from looking at Figure 7.1 that American Chemical's rates of return are much tighter compared with Houston International's. There is more total risk associated with Houston International because it has a larger standard deviation.

---

[4] The square of the standard deviation, σ^2, is the *variance* of a distribution.

[5] Although our concern is primarily with the chance of a loss, indicating that only downside risk is important, the standard deviation measures risk on both sides of the expected value. Because standard deviations are relatively easy to calculate, and because of the theoretical developments to follow, we use the standard deviation. If the distribution is skewed, with a long tail in one direction or the other, both the expected value and the standard deviation may be deficient. In those cases, some other measure is often needed. These complications are ignored. Sometimes it is useful to calculate the *coefficient of variation* (*CV*), which is the standard deviation divided by the mean. This is a measure of risk *relative* to the mean and is useful when two or more means are not the same.

Two additional points should be made concerning standard deviations. First, the scale of measurement for the standard deviation is exactly the same as the original data and the expected value. In our example the original unit of measure was the percentage rate of return per unit of time. Both the expected value and the standard deviation are expressed in exactly the same unit. Thus, we can summarize the information contained in a probability distribution simply by reporting its expected value and standard deviation.[6]

The second point is that as long as we are talking about single securities, the standard deviation, which measures total risk, is the appropriate measure of risk. If that security is part of a nondiversified portfolio, the standard deviation is still a valid measure of risk. (A nondiversified portfolio might contain two securities, with 95 percent represented by one security and only 5 percent of the portfolio invested in the second security.) However, *when we consider a security that is in a diversified portfolio with a number of other securities, the standard deviation is not the most appropriate measure.*

Portfolio Risk and Diversification

Up to now we have been examining risk for single securities. However, most individuals do not hold just one asset; they hold a portfolio of assets. If you hold only one asset, you suffer a loss if the return turns out to be very low. If you hold two, the returns on both must be low for you to suffer a loss. By *diversifying,* or investing in more than one asset where the assets do not move proportionally in the same direction at the same time, you reduce your risk. The important point to remember is this: *For the investor, it is the total portfolio risk and return that is important. The risk and return of individual securities should not be analyzed in isolation; rather, they should be analyzed in terms of how they affect the risk and return of the portfolio in which they are included.*

Portfolio Returns

Measures of risk and return for a portfolio are exactly the same as for individual securities—the expected return, or mean, and the total risk as measured by the standard deviation. The *expected return on a portfolio,* $\bar{K}_p$, is simply the average of the returns for the securities weighted by the proportion of the portfolio devoted to each security. We can write this as

$$\bar{K}_p = W_A\bar{k}_A + W_B\bar{k}_B + \cdot \cdot \cdot + W_Z\bar{k}_Z \tag{7.3}$$

where

$$\bar{K}_p = \text{the expected rate of return on a portfolio}$$
$$W_A \cdot \cdot \cdot W_Z = \text{the proportion of the portfolio devoted to security A through security}$$
$$\text{Z (the sum of the W's} = 1.00, \text{ or } 100\%)$$
$$\bar{k}_A \cdot \cdot \cdot \bar{k}_Z = \text{the expected rates of return on securities A through Z}$$

---

[6] This statement assumes that the probability distributions are relatively normal. This assumption, although not strictly true for securities, allows considerable simplification. Also, for groups of securities in a portfolio, the portfolio returns tend to be approximately normal.

To illustrate, consider three stocks, A, B and C, with expected returns of 16 percent, 12 percent, and 20 percent, respectively, in a portfolio comprised of 50 percent stock A, 25 percent stock B, and 25 percent stock C. The expected return on this portfolio is

$$\bar{K}_p = W_A\bar{k}_A + W_B\bar{k}_B + W_C\bar{k}_C$$
$$= 0.50(\ 16\%\ ) + 0.25(\ 12\%\ ) + 0.25(\ 20\%\ ) = 8\% + 3\% + 5\% = 16\%$$

Portfolio Risk

Unlike the expected return, the portfolio risk, as measured by its standard deviation, is (with the exception of one special case) *not* a weighted average of the standard deviations of the securities making up the portfolio. To understand why, we must consider the concept of *correlation*. Correlation (Corr) measures the degree with which two variables, such as the returns on two securities, move together. Corr takes on numerical values that range from +1.0 to −1.0. The sign (either + or −) indicates whether the returns move together or inversely. If the sign is positive, the two securities *tend* to move up and down together. If it is negative, the securities move inversely, that is, when the return for one stock decreases, the return on the other increases. The magnitude of the correlation coefficient indicates the strength (or degree) of relationship between the returns on the two securities. If the correlation is +1.0, the returns on the two securities move up and down together so that the relative magnitude of the movements is exactly the same. If Corr is between 0.0 and +1.0, the returns usually move up and down together, but not all the time. The closer it is to 0.0, the less the two sets of returns move together. When the correlation is exactly 0.0, there is no relationship between the returns; they are independent of each other. Similarly, when the Corr is negative the closer it is to −1.0, the more the returns on the two securities tend to move *exactly opposite* to each other. These general relationships are shown in Figure 7.2.

Two-Security Portfolios

To see the impact of different degrees of correlation on the portfolio standard deviation, consider the case of two stocks, F and G. As shown in Figure 7.3 on p. 175, we

Figure 7.2   Correlation Coefficient Under Three Different Conditions

If the correlation were perfectly positive (+1.0), all the points in (a) would lie on a straight line with an upward (to the right) slant. Likewise, perfectly negative correlation (−1.0) would result in all points in (b) plotted on a straight line with a downward slant.

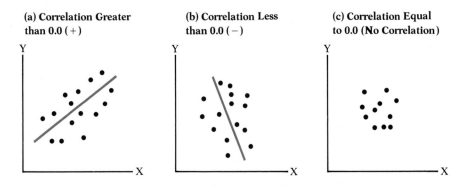

(a) Correlation Greater than 0.0 (+)

(b) Correlation Less than 0.0 (−)

(c) Correlation Equal to 0.0 (No Correlation)

start with historical returns for both stocks for the years 19X3, 19X4, 19X5, and 19X6. The average return for stock F of 10 percent is simply its mean, while its standard deviation is 16.83 percent.[7] For stock G its average return is 20 percent, while its standard deviation is the same as stock F's—16.83 percent. Looking at both the rate of return graphs (a) and the rate of return data (b) in Figure 7.3, we see that the two securities moved *exactly* together. The only difference is that stock G had a 10 percent higher rate of return in each year than stock F. Since they moved exactly together, their Corr was +1.00. A portfolio composed of 50 percent F and 50 percent G has a return of 15 percent, and a standard deviation of 16.83 percent (as also shown in Figure 7.3). When the correlation between two securities is +1.00, or perfectly positive, there is *no* reduction in portfolio risk. *This is the only situation where forming portfolios does not provide risk reduction to an investor;* the portfolio standard deviation for this special case is a weighted average of the standard deviations of the securities making up the portfolio.

Now consider the other extreme—where two securities move exactly opposite to each other, which means they have a perfect negative correlation of −1.00. What happens to the expected return and risk of a portfolio in this case? As shown in Figure 7.4 on p. 176, for the same two stocks, F and G, with the same expected returns and standard deviations, the portfolio expected return, $\bar{K}_p$, is still 15 percent. But look carefully at what has happened to the portfolio standard deviation. Because the returns on the two securities move exactly opposite to each other, when one goes up the other goes down, with the result that the standard deviation, our measure of portfolio risk, became 0.0. Obviously, this is the best of all possible worlds; we have maintained our 15 percent portfolio expected return but reduced the risk. Why? Because the correlation between the two stocks was perfectly negative.[8]

What happens to the portfolio risk when we have positive, but less than perfectly positive, correlation between the returns? As shown in Figure 7.5 on p. 177, for our two stocks F and G, when the correlation between their returns is +0.44, the

---

[7] To calculate the standard deviation when *historical returns over some past period* are available, the following formula is employed:

$$\sigma = \sqrt{\frac{\sum\limits_{t=1}^{n} (k_t - \bar{k})^2}{n - 1}}$$

For stock F, with yearly returns of 5, 30, −10, and 15 percent, we proceed as follows:

$$\bar{k} = \frac{\sum\limits_{t=1}^{n} k_t}{n} = (5 + 30 - 10 + 15)/4 = 10\%$$

$$\sigma = \sqrt{\frac{(5 - 10)^2 + (30 - 10)^2 + (-10 - 10)^2 + (15 - 10)^2}{4 - 1}}$$

$$= \sqrt{\frac{25 + 400 + 400 + 25}{3}} = \sqrt{\frac{850}{3}} = \sqrt{283.3333} = 16.8325 \approx 16.83\%$$

Note that we use 4, since there are four years, in figuring the mean, but only 3 (n − 1) in calculating the standard deviation.

[8] The elimination of all the risk in this example is a direct result of how it was constructed. This topic will be discussed further in the next section.

Figure 7.3 Rate of Return for Two Securities and Portfolio FG (Perfect Positive Correlation: Corr$_{FG}$ = +1.0)

When the correlation is perfectly positive, the portfolio standard deviation is simply the weighted average of the individual securities' standard deviations.

(a) Rate of Return Graphs

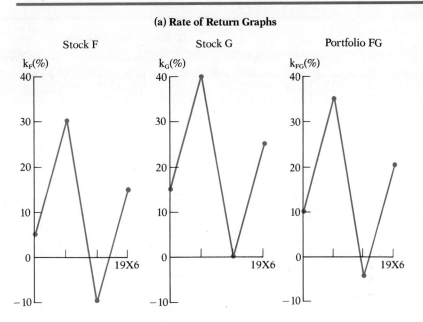

(b) Rate of Return Data

Year	Stock F k_F	Stock G k_G	Portfolio FG k_{FG}
19X3	5%	15%	10%
19X4	30	40	35
19X5	−10	0	−5
19X6	15	25	20
Average return	10%	20%	15%
Standard deviation	16.83%	16.83%	16.83%

portfolio return remains at 15 percent, while the portfolio standard deviation is now 14.29 percent. Remember that when we had perfectly positive correlation (Figure 7.3), the portfolio standard deviation was 16.83 percent. With positive but less than perfectly positive correlation in the returns, *some* risk reduction has occurred. The primary finding is that, since the portfolio standard deviation is less than the weighted average of the individual security standard deviations, portfolio diversification led to a reduction in total portfolio risk. In recent years, the standard deviation of the average stock on the New York Stock Exchange (NYSE) has been approximately 30 percent, while the standard deviation of the market portfolio of all NYSE stocks has been about 15 percent. We conclude that in practice investors can reduce, or diversify away, part of their risk.

Figure 7.4 Rate of Return for Two Securities and Portfolio FG (Perfect Negative Correlation: Corr$_{FG}$ = −1.0)

With perfect negative correlation, the portfolio standard deviation is reduced substantially, but typically not to zero. The zero standard deviation is a direct result of how the example was constructed.

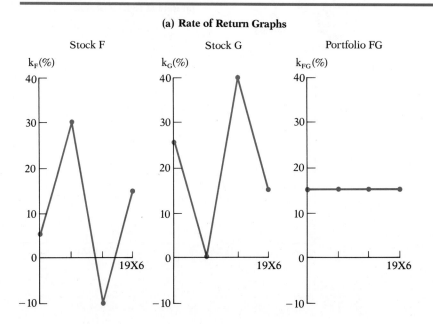

(a) Rate of Return Graphs

(b) Rate of Return Data

Year	Stock F k_F	Stock G k_G	Portfolio FG k_{FG}
19X3	5%	25%	15%
19X4	30	0	15
19X5	−10	40	15
19X6	15	15	15
Average return	10%	20%	15%
Standard deviation	16.83%	16.83%	0.00%

The previous examples show that portfolio risk depends not only on the risk of the individual securities in the portfolio but also on the relationship (correlation) between their returns. Instead of using the procedure shown in those examples we can calculate portfolio risk, σ_p, for a two-security portfolio by using the following equation.

$$\sigma_p = \sqrt{W_A^2 \sigma_A^2 + W_B^2 \sigma_B^2 + 2 W_A W_B \sigma_A \sigma_B Corr_{AB}} \qquad (7.4)$$

where

W_A, W_B = the proportion of the total portfolio devoted to security A and to security B, respectively

Figure 7.5 Rate of Return for Two Securities and Portfolio FG
(Partially Positively Correlated: Corr$_{FG}$ = +0.44)

When the correlation between two securities is less than perfectly positive, total risk, as measured by the portfolio standard deviation, is reduced.

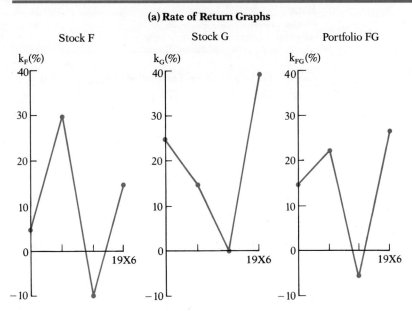

(a) Rate of Return Graphs

Stock F Stock G Portfolio FG

(b) Rate of Return Data

Year	Stock F k_F	Stock G k_G	Portfolio FG k_{FG}
19X3	5%	25%	15%
19X4	30	15	22.5
19X5	−10	0	−5.0
19X6	15	40	27.5
Average return	10%	20%	15%
Standard deviation	16.83%	16.83%	14.29%

σ_A^2, σ_B^2 = the variances for securities A and B

Corr$_{AB}$ = the degree of correlation between the returns on securities A and B

σ_A, σ_B = the standard deviations for securities A and B

$\sigma_A \sigma_B$Corr$_{AB}$ = the *covariance* or co-movement between securities A and B[9]

If the two securities are perfectly positively correlated (Corr = +1.0), as in Figure 7.3, the portfolio standard deviation is simply the weighted average of the two individual security standard deviations. Thus,

$$\sigma_p \text{ (when Corr} = +1.0) = W_A\sigma_A + W_B\sigma_B \qquad (7.5)$$

[9] Calculation of covariances is discussed in Appendix 7A.

Table 7.3 Standard Deviation for a Two-Security Portfolio as the Degree of Correlation Changes

With perfect positive correlation, the portfolio standard deviation is the weighted average of the two securities' standard deviations. In all other cases, the portfolio standard deviation is less.

Data:

Houston International $\quad \sigma_{HI} = 30.98\%$

American Chemical $\qquad \sigma_{AC} = 7.75\%$

$$\sigma_p = \sqrt{W_{HI}^2\sigma_{HI}^2 + W_{AC}^2\sigma_{AC}^2 + 2W_{HI}W_{AC}\sigma_{HI}\sigma_{AC}Corr_{HI:AC}}$$

Case 1: Perfect Positive Correlation, $Corr_{HI:AC} = 1.0$

$$\sigma_P = \sqrt{(0.50)^2(30.98\%)^2 + (0.50)^2(7.75\%)^2 + 2(0.50)(0.50)(30.98\%)(7.75\%)(1.00)}$$

$$= \sqrt{(0.25)(959.7604\%) + (0.25)(60.0625\%) + (0.5)(30.98\%)(7.75\%)(1.00)}$$

$$= \sqrt{239.9401\% + 15.015625\% + 120.0475\%} = \sqrt{375.003225\%} = 19.365\%$$

Case 2: Positive Correlation, $Corr_{HI:AC} = 0.5$

$$\sigma_p = \sqrt{239.9401\% + 15.015625\% + 2(0.50)(0.50)(30.98\%)(7.75\%)(0.50)}$$

$$= \sqrt{239.9401\% + 15.015625\% + 60.02375\%} = \sqrt{314.979475\%} = 17.748\%$$

Case 3: No Correlation, $Corr_{HI:AC} = 0.0$

$$\sigma_p = \sqrt{239.9401\% + 15.015625\% + 2(0.50)(0.50)(30.98\%)(7.75\%)(0)}$$

$$= \sqrt{239.9401\% + 15.015625\% + 0\%} = \sqrt{254.955725\%} = 15.967\%$$

Case 4: Negative Correlation, $Corr_{HI:AC} = -0.5$

$$\sigma_P = \sqrt{239.9401\% + 15.015625\% + 2(0.50)(0.50)(30.98\%)(7.75\%)(-0.50)}$$

$$= \sqrt{239.9401\% + 15.015625\% - 60.02375\%} = \sqrt{194.931975} = 13.962\%$$

Case 5: Perfect Negative Correlation, $Corr_{HI:AC} = -1.0$

$$\sigma_P = \sqrt{239.9401\% + 15.015625\% + 2(0.50)(0.50)(30.98\%)(7.75\%)(-1.00)}$$

$$= \sqrt{239.9401\% + 15.015625\% - 120.0475\%} = \sqrt{134.908225\%} = 11.615\%$$

Otherwise, the portfolio standard deviation is less than the weighted average of the two individual security standard deviations.

To see these relationships, once again, let us continue our example of Houston International and American Chemical common stocks. Recall that Houston International had an expected rate of return of 20 percent and American Chemical had an expected return of 15 percent. What is the portfolio expected return if we create a portfolio composed of equal amounts of both stocks? Employing Equation 7.3, we have

$$\bar{K}_p = W_{HI}\bar{k}_{HI} + W_{AC}\bar{k}_{AC}$$

$$= 0.50(20\%) + 0.50(15\%) = 17.5\%$$

Houston had a standard deviation of 30.98 percent and American Chemical's was 7.75 percent. In case 1 of Table 7.3, the portfolio standard deviation is calculated when the correlation between the returns for the two securities is +1.0. As shown, the portfolio standard deviation is 19.365 percent. Because the correlation is perfectly positive, this same result could have been obtained by taking the simple weighted average of the two security standard deviations and employing Equation 7.5 as follows:

$$\sigma_p \text{ (when Corr} = + 1.0) = 0.50(30.98\%) + 0.50(7.75\%)$$

$$= 15.490\% + 3.875\% = 19.365\%$$

The important item to observe is that when two securities returns are perfectly positively correlated, there are no diversification benefits to be achieved through reducing the portfolio standard deviation.

However, what happens as the correlation coefficient decreases? In case 2 the Corr is +0.5, and the resulting portfolio standard deviation of 17.748 percent is less than the 19.365 percent obtained earlier. Similarly, when the returns of the two securities are independent of each other (when Corr = 0.0), we see in case 3 that the portfolio standard deviation is still lower at 15.967 percent. The portfolio standard deviation continues decreasing as the correlation between the two sets of returns becomes negative (case 4). Finally, when the Corr = −1.0 (case 5), the lowest portfolio standard deviation of 11.615 percent is determined. As long as the returns for two securities are not perfectly positively correlated, we can eliminate part of the risk as measured by the portfolio standard deviation. This is the diversifiable risk.

The Efficient Frontier

The foregoing shows that, given a particular pair of weights, the standard deviation of the portfolio's returns decreases as the correlation between the securities return decreases. However, an investor is not restricted to investing only one fixed amount in each security. Table 7.4 shows a sample of the many portfolios of Houston International and American Chemical that can be formed, and their expected return and standard deviation for various correlations.

Figure 7.6 graphs the set of all possible portfolios that can be formed from

Table 7.4   Portfolio Expected Returns and Standard Deviations for Various Correlations and Weights

With perfect positive correlation there is no benefit to diversification because the portfolio standard deviation is a weighted average of the two securities' standard deviations. With perfect negative correlation there is one portfolio that has a standard deviation of zero. Most securities are positively, but not perfectly positively, correlated; therefore, forming portfolios of these securities can reduce, but not eliminate, risk.

| Weight | | | Portfolio Standard Deviation Given Corr$_{HI:AC}$ | | | | |
HI	AC	Return	1.00	0.50	0.00	−0.50	−1.00
0.00	1.00	15.0%	7.75%	7.75%	7.75%	7.75%	7.75%
0.10	0.90	15.5	10.07	8.93	7.63	6.05	3.87
0.20	0.80	16.0	12.39	10.73	8.76	6.20	0.00
0.30	0.70	16.5	14.72	12.89	10.76	8.09	3.87
0.40	0.60	17.0	17.04	15.26	13.24	10.84	7.75
0.50	0.50	17.5	19.36	17.75	15.97	13.96	11.62
0.60	0.40	18.0	21.69	20.32	18.85	17.25	15.49
0.70	0.30	18.5	24.01	22.94	21.81	20.62	19.36
0.80	0.20	19.0	26.34	25.60	24.84	24.05	23.24
0.90	0.10	19.5	28.66	28.28	27.90	27.51	27.11
1.00	0.00	20.0	30.98	30.98	30.98	30.98	30.98

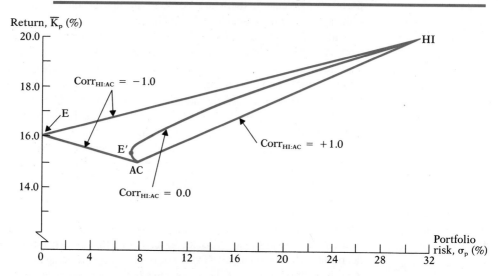

Figure 7.6 **The Feasible Sets of Portfolios That Can Be Formed from Houston International and American Chemical If the Correlation Between Them Is −1.0, 0.0, or +1.0**

The feasible set for a two-security portfolio is a straight or curved line.

these two securities when the correlation between their returns is +1.0, 0.0, and −1.0, respectively. The set of all possible portfolios for a given correlation is called the *feasible set,* which for a two-security portfolio is either a straight line or a curve. For example, if the correlation is +1.0, the feasible set is a straight line from AC, where 100 percent of portfolio funds are invested in American, to HI, where 100 percent is invested in Houston, and the standard deviation of each portfolio in this feasible set is a weighted average of the standard deviations of two securities making up the portfolio. If the correlation is −1.0, the feasible set is made up of two straight-line segments, and there is one portfolio in the set (in this case, portfolio E) for which the risk of the portfolio is zero. If the correlation is zero we have a feasible set that is a curve. This situation is more representative of the majority of portfolios, because risk can be reduced but not eliminated.

The objective behind forming portfolios is not simply to reduce risk but, rather, to select efficient portfolios. An *efficient portfolio* is one that provides the lowest possible risk for a given level of expected return, or the highest possible expected return for a given level of risk. Thus, we see that not all portions of the feasible sets in Figure 7.6 represent efficient portfolios. If the correlation between Houston and American is −1.0, we see that the portion of the set from E to HI dominates the portion from AC to E because it offers a higher return for risk (σ_p) levels between zero and 7.75. Thus, E to HI represents the *efficient frontier* of portfolios when the correlation is −1.0. Similarly, E′ to HI is the efficient frontier of portfolios when the correlation is zero. Thus a rational investor will choose the portfolio from the efficient frontier that best suits his or her personal preferences.

The two-security portfolio case can be generalized to the N-security case. How-

Figure 7.7 The Efficient Frontier for an N-Security Portfolio

The feasible set for a many-security portfolio is a space, not a straight or curved line. All portfolios to the left of the space are unattainable.

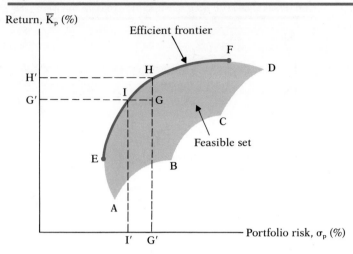

ever, in the case of many securities the feasible set is no longer a line or a curve but a space, as represented by the shaded area, and its boundary, in Figure 7.7. The feasible set represents the infinite number of portfolios (and their respective risks and returns) into which the N securities can be formed. The curve EF represents the efficient frontier of portfolios. All portfolios on this curve dominate the rest of the feasible set because they offer the highest expected return for a given level of risk, or the lowest risk for a given level of expected return. To see this, consider portfolio H on the efficient frontier and portfolio G in the feasible set. Although they both provide the same level of risk, H has the higher expected return; therefore, portfolio H dominates portfolio G. Other portfolios on the efficient frontier could be determined in the same manner or by minimizing the level of risk for a given return, as could be done between portfolios I and G. *Because portfolios on the efficient frontier dominate all others they would be preferred by investors.*

Diversifiable and Non-diversifiable Risk

Our discussion up to now can be summarized as follows:

1. If the securities are perfectly positively correlated, there is no reduction in risk from forming a portfolio.[10] When the returns on stocks of Houston and American were perfectly positively correlated (+1.0), the portfolio standard deviation was always a weighted average of the individual security standard deviations.
2. When the correlation between the security returns is less than +1.0, there are benefits from diversifying in terms of risk reduction. Thus, when the correlation is less than +1 the portfolio standard deviation is always less than it is when

---

[10] For simplicity, we are assuming no short selling is allowed. It can be shown that under certain conditions, risk reduction can be accomplished even when the correlation between the two sets of returns is +1.0.

Figure 7.8 Impact of the Number of Securities on Portfolio Risk

By the time 20 to 30 securities are in a portfolio, most of the diversifiable risk has been eliminated, leaving only nondiversifiable (i.e., market or systematic) risk. The benefits of diversification arise from reducing the exposure to diversifiable risk.

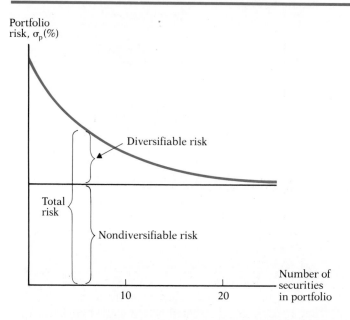

the correlation is equal to $+1$. The only exception to this is when all portfolio funds are invested in only one asset. For example, when $W_A = 1$, Equation 7.4 reduces to $\sigma_p = \sigma_A$; because there is only one security in the portfolio, the portfolio's standard deviation must equal that of the security.

3. The maximum risk reduction is achieved when the returns on two securities move exactly opposite to each other so their correlation is -1.0 (or they are perfectly negatively correlated). Table 7.4 shows that with a correlation of -1 and 20 percent invested in Houston and 80 percent in American, respectively, the standard deviation of the portfolio is zero.

4. Returns on most securities are positively (but not perfectly positively) correlated. This occurs because the returns on most assets tend to move, to a greater or lesser degree, with the general movements in the economy. For stocks the correlation tends to be between $+0.40$ and $+0.75$.

5. The results of the two-asset case can be generalized to N-assets.

Because it is unusual to find firms with extreme correlations (i.e., $+1$ or -1), risk can be reduced but not eliminated by forming portfolios. But just how much risk reduction can we achieve? The answer has been provided by a number of studies, as shown in Figure 7.8. The total portfolio risk, measured by its standard deviation, declines as more securities are added to the portfolio. Adding more stocks to the portfolio can eliminate some of the risk, but not all of it.

The total risk can thus be divided into two parts: (1) diversifiable risk (sometimes

Diversification's Not Always Beneficial

Fenced in by more stringent regulators and reluctance on the public's side to pay higher and higher utility rates, many public utilities have diversified into unregulated industries. An example is the former Arizona Public Service, which has been renamed Pinnacle West Capital. During the last few years they decided to mine uranium, invest in high-tech companies and land, buy a savings and loan, and even purchase a piece of the Phoenix Suns basketball team.[1] But things haven't turned out the way Pinnacle West anticipated. Their savings bank, MeraBank, lost millions in 1988 and had to close 33 branches and cut nearly 700 jobs. According to one analyst the MeraBank purchase was the worst single diversification a utility has ever made. What's more, sales from their uranium mining unit fell off and land prices in the Phoenix area dropped dramatically.

In early 1989 the company acknowledged the severity of the situation by charging off between $75 and $100 million on its accounting statements. In addition, it cut dividends and its stock price dropped by 50 percent from where it was a year earlier. But their troubles weren't over since Moody's Investors Service downgraded their bonds—causing Pinnacle West to pay more for future debt financing.

While Pinnacle West obviously thought diversification was the means to higher growth and higher returns, they have suffered from biting off more than they could chew and diversifying into the wrong areas at the wrong time. Diversification, while often positive, can have very negative consequences for firms that make the wrong decisions. At best, it is a two-edged sword when firms move into areas outside of their sphere of expertise.

[1] "A Bundle of Bad Deals Has Pinnacle West Reeling." *Business Week* (January 30, 1989).

called "company-specific" or "unsystematic" risk), and (2) nondiversifiable ("market" or "systematic") risk; so that

$$\text{total risk} = \text{diversifiable risk} + \text{nondiversifiable risk} \qquad (7.6)$$

Diversifiable risk relates to events that affect individual companies, such as strikes, product development, new patents, and other activities unique to an individual firm. Because these events occur somewhat independently, they can be largely diversified away so that negative events affecting one firm can be offset by positive events for other firms. The second type, *nondiversifiable risk,* includes general economic conditions, the impact of monetary and fiscal policies, inflation, and other events that affect all firms simultaneously. Because these risks remain whether or not a portfolio is formed,

Relevant risk = nondiversifiable risk

The only risk a well-diversified portfolio has is the nondiversifiable (market or systematic) portion. Therefore, the contribution of any one security to the riskiness of a portfolio is its systematic risk.

Figure 7.9 The Efficient Frontier When Borrowing and Lending Are Allowed

The inclusion of borrowing and lending possibilities changes the efficient frontier from the curve (arc) EF to a straight line $k_{RF}ML$.

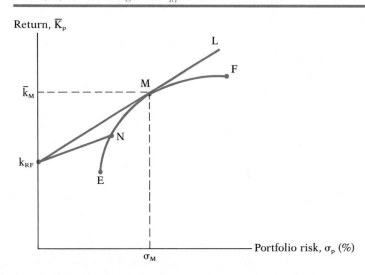

The Capital Asset Pricing Model

The two fundamental ideas of (1) risk reduction via diversification and (2) risk premiums associated with more risky investments have led to the development of the *capital asset pricing model (CAPM)*.[11]

The Capital Market Line

The ability of investors to borrow or lend at the risk-free rate is crucial to the development of the CAPM. This means that an individual can invest not only in a portfolio of risky securities but also in a risk-free security (e.g., Treasury bills). The inclusion of this risk-free security completely alters the shape of the efficient frontier that we saw in Figure 7.7 for the N-security case.

Figure 7.9 shows the efficient frontier of risky assets, EF, from Figure 7.7, and also the risk-free security. Because a risk-free security is defined as one that has a known return, k_{RF}, and a standard deviation of zero, its return plots on the vertical axis. Investors can now combine this riskless security with portfolios on the efficient frontier of risky portfolios to obtain combinations of risk–return payoffs

---

[11] The major assumptions of the CAPM are: (1) all investors are expected wealth maximizers who evaluate portfolios on the basis of means and standard deviations; (2) all investors can borrow or lend an unlimited amount at the risk-free rate, k_{RF}, and there is no restriction on short sales; (3) all investors have homogeneous expectations concerning expected returns and risks on securities; (4) the market is frictionless, and there are no taxes (or taxes do not affect investment decisions); and (5) all investors are price takers and cannot, based on their buying or selling, influence the market price. Even though these assumptions may appear to be very limiting, all of them can be relaxed without seriously affecting the basic conclusions derived from the model.

that did not exist before. For example, the line $k_{RF}N$ represents all possible portfolios formed by buying various combinations of the risk-free security and the risky portfolio N. All portfolios along this line dominate the part of the efficient frontier below N (i.e., E to N) because all points on the line $k_{RF}N$ provide a higher return for a given level of risk.

Portfolios can also be formed between the risk-free security and risky portfolios that lie higher up on the efficient frontier. They would be represented by lines drawn from k_{RF} to successively higher points on the efficient frontier, with each successively higher line dominating all previous lines. This process stops when the line drawn from k_{RF} is tangent to the efficient frontier. This occurs at point M in Figure 7.9. All portfolios on the line segment between k_{RF} and M represent lending portfolios, because when an investor buys a riskless asset such as a Treasury bill, he or she is lending to the government at the risk-free rate. In addition, remember that investors are able to borrow at the risk-free rate. Consequently, any investor who is willing to accept higher risk (than σ_M) to obtain higher return (than $\bar{k}_M$) may borrow at k_{RF} and invest the borrowings plus their initial funds in the risky portfolio, M. These borrowing portfolios are represented by the line segment that extends from M to L in Figure 7.9.

We have established that all investors are better off by holding portfolios that are linear combinations of the risk-free security (either lending or borrowing) and one risky portfolio, M. This portfolio M is called the *market portfolio* (k_M) and is a value-weighted portfolio of all risky securities.[12] That is, in equilibrium, it must contain all risky securities in proportion of their market value to the total market value of all securities. Accordingly, if the market value of IBM represents 5 percent of the market value of all risky securities, then IBM would constitute 5 percent of the market portfolio.

Thus, by allowing investors to borrow and lend at the risk-free rate, we see that they are able to attain portfolios that were previously unattainable. As shown in Figure 7.9, the *new* efficient frontier represents linear combinations of the risk-free asset and the market portfolio. It is depicted by the line $k_{RF}ML$ and represents the risk-return trade-off for efficient portfolios. Once presented with this new efficient frontier, each investor chooses the point on the line that corresponds to his or her preferences.

The straight line $k_{RF}ML$ in Figure 7.9 is called the *capital market line (CML)*. It shows the capital market equilibrium relationships between risk and return for efficient portfolios consisting of various combinations of the risk-free asset and the market portfolio. We know that this line has an intercept of k_{RF}, which represents the return on the risk-free security. If investors are to invest in risky securities they must receive a risk premium to compensate for the added risk. We see from Figure 7.9 that for an investor to invest in the (risky) market portfolio he or she must receive a return of k_M. Thus, the amount ($k_M - k_{RF}$) represents the risk

---

[12] The theory calls for the market portfolio to contain all risky financial assets (e.g., stocks, bonds, options, etc.) and all risky real assets (e.g., precious metals, jewelry, real estate, stamp collections, etc.). However, such a market is not observable. Therefore, in practice, a broad-based stock index like the NYSE index is used as a proxy for the market portfolio.

premium, or excess return over the risk-free rate, expected for incurring the risk associated with the market portfolio, σ_M. Therefore

$$\text{slope of the CML} = \frac{k_M - k_{RF}}{\sigma_M} \qquad (7.7)$$

The slope of the CML is called the *market price of risk* and can be thought of as the equilibrium expected reward per unit of risk. Because the CML shows the trade-off between return and risk for efficient portfolios, the unit of risk must be the portfolio standard deviation. Therefore, the equation for the CML is written as:

$$\bar{K}_p = k_{RF} + \left(\frac{k_M - k_{RF}}{\sigma_M}\right)\sigma_p \qquad (7.8)$$

where

$\bar{K}_p$ = the required rate of return on any efficient portfolio on the CML

k_{RF} = the risk-free rate of return, which is generally measured by the return on Treasury bills

k_M = the expected rate of return on the market portfolio

σ_M = the standard deviation of returns on the market portfolio

σ_p = the standard deviation of the returns on the efficient portfolio being considered

Because all efficient portfolios must lie on the CML, Equation 7.8 states that the required return on an efficient portfolio in equilibrium is equal to the risk-free rate plus the market price of risk multiplied by the amount of risk on the portfolio being considered. It is important to remember that *only efficient portfolios made up of various linear combinations of the risk-free security and the market portfolio lie on the CML.*

Beta as a Measure of Risk

The CML applies only to efficient portfolios. We would now like to extend the analysis to individual securities. Individual securities bear the same direct relationship between risk and return as we observed for portfolios. Therefore, the fundamental question is: How do we measure risk for an individual security?

For securities held in a diversified portfolio the contribution of any one security to the riskiness of a particular portfolio is its nondiversifiable, or market, risk. Therefore, for securities in a diversified portfolio, risk can best be measured by how their returns move, or are correlated with, the returns of the portfolio as a whole. If the portfolio is reasonably well diversified, we can, for simplicity, talk about the returns for securities in general, not just for the portfolio in question. An example might help us see this idea. Harold Levitz has a diversified portfolio of 25 stocks. If he wants to find the riskiness of any of the 25 stocks in the portfolio, he could relate the returns of each stock to the returns on the total portfolio of 25 stocks. However, we know that if the portfolio is well diversified, its returns are going to move very much in line with the returns for all stocks in the market. So, instead of worrying about the returns of the 25-stock portfolio, Harold can just as easily consider how his individual stocks move in relation to the market portfolio of stocks.

This market portfolio is often measured by some broad-based stock index, like the New York Stock Exchange (NYSE) Index. The important point is that *for diversified investors, the appropriate measure of risk is how the return on an individual stock moves relative to the returns for the market portfolio.* Nondiversifiable risk is measured by *beta,* β_j, where the subscript j refers to the jth security. Beta reflects the nondiversifiable risk remaining for stock j after a portion of its total risk has been diversified away by forming portfolios. The beta coefficient, β_j, is the measure of the asset's volatility in relation to the riskiness of the market portfolio as a whole—in other words, it measures what the returns on the asset are expected to be relative to the returns on the market. The stock market as a whole is our frame of reference; it has a beta of 1.0. The beta for an individual stock indicates the expected volatility of that stock in relation to the volatility of the market portfolio. Any stock whose returns fluctuate over time exactly as the market does is an average-risk stock and also has a beta of 1.0. Risky stocks (see Figure 7.10), such as airlines and high-technology firms, whose returns tend to move up and down faster than the general market's returns, are more volatile and have betas greater than 1.0.

We can be more specific: The returns on a stock with a beta of 1.40 will, on average, increase 40 percent faster than the market in up markets, and will decrease 40 percent faster in down markets. Lastly, as also shown in Figure 7.10, conservative firms with very stable cash flows and returns, such as some banks and public utilities, fluctuate less than the market and therefore have betas of less than 1.0.

Betas for a select group of stocks are listed in Table 7.5. The range of beta values in the table from 0.55 to 1.85 is indicative of the general range of betas in practice. Examining this table we see that General Motors, IBM, and McDonald's, had betas close to 1.00. Their returns were of average volatility. On the other hand, Apollo Computer, with a beta of 1.85, had very volatile returns, whereas Green Mountain Power's returns were very stable, as indicated by its beta of 0.55.

Figure 7.10   Beta, Volatility, and Returns

High-beta stocks have much greater volatility in their returns relative to market portfolio returns over time than do low-beta stocks.

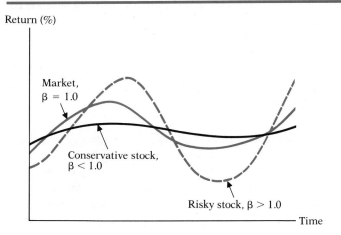

Table 7.5 Beta Coefficients for Selected Firms

Beta is a measure of the volatility of the firm's returns versus the market's returns. It measures risk for individual stocks in well-diversified portfolios. (SOURCE: Value Line Investment Survey, *January 6, 1989, various pages. Reprinted by permission of the publisher. Copyright, Value Line, Inc.)*

American Express	1.35	IBM	0.95
Apollo Computer	1.85	K mart	1.15
Champion Spark Plug	1.10	May Department Stores	1.25
Commerce Bancshares	0.65	McDonald's	1.00
Emery Air Freight	1.30	Penney	1.15
General Motors	0.95	Texas Air	1.60
Green Mountain Power	0.55	Xerox	1.20

Portfolio Betas

We have been examining betas for individual stocks. A portfolio of stocks also has a beta. This *portfolio beta* is a weighted average of the betas of individual securities:

$$\beta_p = \sum_{j=1}^{n} W_j \beta_j \tag{7.9}$$

where

β_p = the portfolio beta or volatility of the entire portfolio relative to the market
n = the number of securities in the portfolio
W_j = the percent of the total value of the portfolio in security j
β_j = the beta for security j

Depending on the composition of the portfolio, the beta can be more than 1.0, equal to 1.0, or less than 1.0.

Suppose you have $10,000 invested in each of 10 stocks so that your total investment is $100,000; the amount invested in each stock is 10 percent, or 0.10. If all the stocks have a beta of 1.20, the portfolio beta is also 1.20. What happens if you sell one of the stocks and reinvest in another stock with a different beta? If the new stock has a beta of 0.60, the new portfolio beta will be

$$\text{new portfolio beta} = \beta_p = \sum_{j=1}^{n} W_j \beta_j$$
$$= 0.90(1.20) + 0.10(0.60) = 1.08 + 0.06 = 1.14$$

Similarly, if the new stock has a beta of 2.00, the portfolio's new beta will be 1.28 [0.90(1.20) + 0.10(2.00)].

Security Market Line

We have seen that the best measure of a stock's relevant or nondiversifiable risk is its beta and that it is distributed around 1.0, the beta of the market. To obtain the return relationship for an individual security, we reformulate the trade-off of Figure 7.9 now using beta on the horizontal axis, as shown in Figure 7.11. Once again this figure shows that if an investor wants a higher return, he or she must incur more

Figure 7.11 The Security Market Line (SML)

The security market line is a graphic representation of the capital asset pricing model (CAPM).

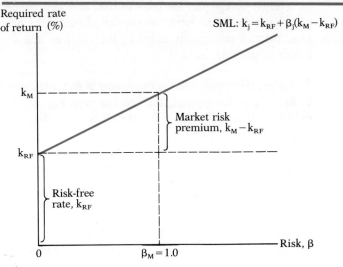

risk.[13] The line shown in Figure 7.11 is called the *security market line (SML)* and shows the risk–return trade-off for an individual security or asset.

The equation for the SML relationship depicted in Figure 7.11 is

$$k_j = k_{RF} + \beta_j(k_M - k_{RF}) \tag{7.10}$$

where

k_j = the required rate of return on any risky asset j held in a diversified portfolio

k_{RF} = the risk-free rate of return, which is generally measured by the return on Treasury bills

β_j = the beta coefficient for the asset

k_M = the expected rate of return on the market portfolio

$(k_M - k_{RF})$ = the market risk premium required to encourage investors to invest in the market portfolio as opposed to investing in some risk-free security

$\beta_j(k_M - k_{RF})$ = the risk premium for the stock in question. This premium is greater than or less than the market risk premium depending on the size of β_j, which measures how the returns on stock j move in relation to the returns for the market portfolio.

The security market line, Equation 7.10, when graphed as in Figure 7.11, shows that the required rate of return on any stock is equal to the return of a security

---

[13] This assumes the beta is positive, as it is for the vast majority of assets. Only occasionally are there assets whose returns move counter to the returns on the market. An example of a negative beta stock might be a gold mining company.

that has no risk, k_{RF}, plus a risk premium $\beta_j(k_M - k_{RF})$. In other words, the required rate of return on an asset is equal to the price of time (including expected inflation) as depicted by k_{RF} plus the price of risk, or a risk premium. In a risk-free world, only the price of time would be relevant. Because the investor's world is not risk-free, the risk premium is added to the risk-free rate to determine the required return on any risky asset.[14]

Using the Capital Asset Pricing Model

To employ the capital asset pricing model to estimate rates of return, it is necessary to have three elements: (1) the risk-free rate, k_{RF}; (2) the expected return on the market portfolio, k_M; and (3) the stock's beta, β_j. At any point in time, these might be estimated as follows:

RISK-FREE RATE, k_{RF}

1. This variable is primarily a function of expected inflation and economic conditions. Typically the rate on Treasury bills is employed as a proxy for k_{RF}. Let's assume it is 7 percent.

EXPECTED RETURN ON THE MARKET PORTFOLIO, k_M

2. The expected return on the market can be estimated by relying on econometric forecasts, or by viewing the expected return on the market as a function of three items: (1) expected inflation, (2) real growth in the economy, and (3) a risk premium commanded by stocks over bonds.[15] Thus, if the expected (not historical) rate of inflation is 5 percent, real growth (in constant dollars) in gross national product is expected to be 3 percent, and the risk premium of stocks over bonds is 4 percent (which is about what it has been historically), we would estimate $k_M = 12$ percent.

BETA, β_j

3. We could estimate the stock's riskiness by relying on published betas by *Value Line*, Merrill Lynch, or other investment advisory services. Alternatively, employing the techniques discussed in Appendix 7B, we could estimate β_j based on historical returns for the stock and the market.

Assume we estimate beta to be 1.40. To find the required return on the stock, we could plug these values into Equation 7.10. However, we can also plot the relationship as follows. The first step is to specify the security market line (SML) as in part (a) of Figure 7.12. The second step is to take the beta for the security in question (1.40 in our case) and read up to the SML and across to the rate of return axis. Doing this indicates that the required rate of return is 14 percent, shown in

---

[14] In Chapter 2 (Equation 2.3) we defined the risk premium to be equal to a maturity premium, a default premium, a liquidity premium, and an issue-specific premium. The capital asset pricing model, as specified by Equation 7.10, is a formal theoretical model for specifying this risk premium—and one that is especially applicable for common stocks. Further, Equation 2.4 was an intuitive statement of the CAPM.

[15] An alternative would be to use the historical or expected market-risk premium, which is simply the difference between the returns on the market portfolio, k_M, and the risk-free rate, k_{RF}. This would then be added to the risk-free rate, as estimated by Treasury bills, to obtain an estimate of the expected return on the market.

Figure 7.12 Use of the Security Market Line to Estimate the Required Rate of Return for a Stock with a Beta of 1.40

In (a) the SML is determined by estimating the risk-free rate and the expected return on the market portfolio. In (b), by knowing the stock's beta, we can determine its required rate of return.

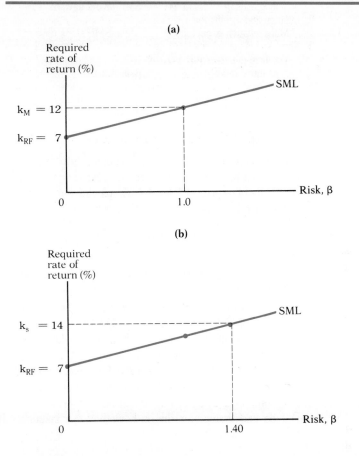

(a)

(b)

(b) of Figure 7.12. Alternatively, we could use Equation 7.10 to find the required rate of return, as follows:

$$k_j = k_{RF} + \beta_j(k_M - k_{RF})$$
$$= 7\% + 1.40(12\% - 7\%) = 7\% + 7\% = 14\%$$

Either way, we get the same result. This approach can be used to find the required rate of return for any stock, or portfolio of stocks.

The CAPM can assist us to see what happens to the required rate of return, and the market price of the firm's stock, as risk changes. Earlier in the chapter we discussed four basic sources of risk; general economic risk, inflation and disinflation risk, firm- and issue-specific risk, and international risk. An increase in any of these has the following effects:

Risk	SML Effect	Required Return, k_j	Stock Price, P_0

1. General economic
   Pessimism; risk aversion
   increases
	SML pivots upward	↑	↓

2. Inflation and disinflation More inflation expected	whole SML shifts upward	↑	↓

3. Firm- and issue-specific
   The firm is perceived
   as more risky
	β_j increases	↑	↓

4. International
   a. Increased marketwide
      risk
	a. whole SML shifts up-
	   ward
		↑	↓

b. Firm has more inter- national risk exposure	b. β_j increases		

To illustrate the price impact, suppose a firm is expecting a constant growth in dividends of 8 percent per year, the current cash dividend (at t = 0) is $3, and the required rate of return is 16 percent. Employing the constant growth formula (Equation 6.7), the current market price of the stock is

$$P_0 = \frac{D_0(1 + g)}{k_s - g} = \frac{\$3.00(1 + 0.08)}{0.16 - 0.08} = \frac{\$3.24}{0.08} = \$40.50$$

What happens if, because of changes in risk, the investor's required rate of return increases to 18 percent or decreases to 13 percent, while everything else remains unchanged? With an increase in risk and required return, the new market value falls to P_0 = $3.24/(0.18 − 0.08) = $32.40. Likewise, a decrease in risk and required return results in an increase in market value to P_0 = $3.24/(0.13 − 0.08) = $64.80. We see that, other things being equal, *increased risk lowers the market value of the firm's stock and reduced risk increases its value.* Thus, risk has a major impact on the value of the firm. Managers must always be aware of the impact of their actions on the perceived riskiness of the firm's cash flows, as well as on their magnitude and timing, for this is how they can influence the market value of the firm.

The Equilibrium Nature of the CAPM[16]

The capital asset pricing model specifies what the required rate of return on any asset should be. In equilibrium, the required rate of return on an asset such as a stock equals its expected return. What happens if this is not the case? Consider Figure 7.13, which shows a security market line based on investor beliefs about the relationship between required rates of return and nondiversifiable risk. For some reason, suppose our two stocks, Houston International and American Chemical, are improperly priced. Houston is underpriced; American Chemical is overpriced. This occurs because Houston International's expected rate of return is greater than its required rate of return (as specified by the SML), and therefore the stock is *underpriced.* Likewise, American Chemical's expected rate of return is less than the required return; consequently, it is *overpriced.*

---

[16] This section may be omitted without loss of continuity.

Figure 7.13 Process When Securities Are Not in Equilibrium

Houston International is underpriced and therefore providing an excess (risk-adjusted) return; the opposite is true for American Chemical. The price of Houston will increase and that of American Chemical will decrease until their expected and required returns are equal.

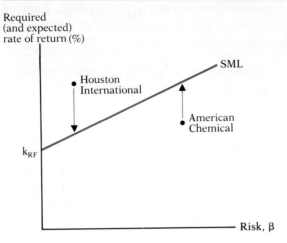

To solidify our understanding, let us use an example. Assume Houston does not pay cash dividends, its current market price, P_0, is $20, and its expected market price, P_1, is $28. Using Equation 6.8 to calculate the expected return we have

$$k = \frac{D_1 + P_1 - P_0}{P_0} = \frac{0 + \$28 - \$20}{\$20} = \frac{\$8}{\$20} = 0.40 = 40\%$$

If Houston's required return, as given by the security market line (SML) is only 25 percent, what will happen to the current market price? It will increase as investors see that Houston is undervalued. How much? We can determine that by setting k equal to 25 percent and solving for the new equilbirium price as follows:

$$k = \frac{P_1 - P_0}{P_0}$$

$$0.25 = \frac{\$28 - P_0}{P_0}$$

$$1.25(P_0) = \$28$$

$$P_0 = \$28/1.25 = \$22.40$$

We see that if the price increases from $20 to $22.40, the expected and required rates of return for Houston will be equal, at 25 percent.

Exactly the opposite will happen to American Chemical. Since its expected return is below its required return, investors will sell American Chemical, driving the market price down. This will continue until the expected and required rates of return are equal; that is, until they are in *equilibrium*.

A Word of Caution	The capital asset pricing model is simple and logical; its assumptions can be relaxed without invalidating the model; and it describes in a formal manner the major factors investors consider when making financial decisions. Even so, some caution needs to be employed when using it.

1. The model is based on *ex ante,* or expected, conditions; yet we have only *ex post,* or realized, data. To use historical data without adjustment for future expectations invites trouble. Future, not past, risk and return are the items of concern.
2. Evidence exists that certain stocks provide *ex post* returns greater than could be expected based on the CAPM. Three of these "anomalies" relate to small stocks, low P/E stocks, and certain seasonal effects.

The capital asset pricing model is the simplest, yet most comprehensive, model available at present that depicts the relationship between risk and return. While certain other models are gaining support in the world of finance (such as arbitrage pricing theory discussed briefly later in the chapter, or the Black–Scholes option pricing model developed in Chapter 11), the CAPM is our general frame of reference. It provides both a conceptual and empirical way of relating risk and return. Used wisely, it is a powerful tool for both investors and managers. However, like any other tool, improper use can lead to unexpected or unintended consequences.

The Efficient Market Hypothesis

Extensive empirical evidence suggests that stocks, especially those of large NYSE companies adjust rapidly to disequilibrium situations. Consequently, equilibrium ordinarily exists, and, in general, required and expected returns are equal. Stock prices certainly change, sometimes violently and/or rapidly, but this simply reflects changing economic or firm-specific conditions and expectations. Stock prices may also continue to react over longer periods of time to favorable or unfavorable information. This is to be expected since as new information becomes available, the market adjusts to the new information.

An efficient market is one where information is widely and cheaply available to all investors, and where all relevant and ascertainable information is already reflected in security prices. The notion that capital markets are efficient has been around for about 20 years—it is now an accepted part of the study of finance. The *efficient market hypothesis* states that prices react quickly and unambiguously to new information. By unambiguously we mean that sometimes the price may overreact while other times it may underreact, but on net the magnitude of the reaction will be "on target."

There are three forms of the efficient market hypothesis depending on the set of information that is assumed available to investors.

1. *Weak-form efficiency* is based on the past record of stock prices; thus, current stock prices reflect all information contained in past stock prices.
2. *Semistrong-form efficiency* takes as the information base all publicly available information. Thus, information about earnings, dividends, new products, mergers, and so forth, constitute publicly available information.
3. *Strong-form efficiency* is based on all information, whether public or privately held.

Over the years there has been extensive testing of the efficient market hypothesis. This testing indicates that (1) stock prices react quickly to new information; (2) there are no abnormal (or excess risk-adjusted) returns after transactions costs based on using past price data; (3) there are few abnormal returns after transactions costs based on using all publicly available information; and (4) there may be abnormal returns after transactions costs when private information is employed. These findings suggest that the stock market is highly efficient in the weak form, and reasonably efficient in the semistrong form. However, capital markets may not be efficient in the strong form, so abnormal profits (or returns) may be available to those who possess inside information.

There is a very important lesson we need to learn based on the concept and testing of market efficiency; that is, *you can trust market prices since they impound all available information about the value of a security.* For the investor this means there is no way for most of them to achieve consistently superior rates of return. To do so you have to know *more* than is publicly available; you have to have access to (or generate) unique private information beyond that available to other investors. Does that mean you should despair? No, not at all. What is important in an efficient market is to determine the amount of risk you are willing to bear. If markets are efficient, which they are close to, then to increase your return you must increase your risk exposure. The most important decision is to determine how comfortable you are with a higher versus a lower risk exposure. If you can't tolerate much risk, that dictates the type of investments you will make, and the returns you can expect (or require).

The efficient market hypothesis has two important messages for managers. First, in an efficient market you should expect to pay an equilibrium rate for financing obtained, commensurate with the riskiness of your firm as perceived by investors. Second, in making investment decisions, the only way to increase the value of your firm is to find superior investments whose expected return is greater than the required return. This latter idea can be illustrated by considering the process a firm goes through when it acquires another firm where the management considers the other firm undervalued. On approximately half of the occasions the stock of the acquired firm really will be undervalued. But, on the other half it will be overvalued. On average the value will be correct, so that the acquiring company comes out even, except for the costs of the acquisition.

Efficient markets are hard for some people to accept. However, investors and managers are increasingly realizing the important implications of security markets that are reasonably efficient. These are as follows:

1. On average, expected and realized returns are equal.
2. Prices react quickly to new information.
3. Abnormal (risk-adjusted) returns require private information.
4. Without private information, increased returns require exposure to additional risk.
5. The best estimate of the value of the firm is what someone else is willing to pay for it. Hence, the primary value to be concerned with is the market value of the firm, V. To maximize our pie, or V, we must maximize the market value of the stock, S, and the market value of the bonds, B.

Arbitrage Pricing Theory[17]

An alternative to the CAPM, the *arbitrage pricing theory* (*APT*), is receiving considerable attention. The APT requires fewer assumptions than the CAPM; likewise, the market portfolio does not play a special role. The return for an individual stock, j, in the APT is assumed to be a linear function of a number of factors common to all securities

$$k_j = a_j + b_{j1}F_1 + b_{j2}F_2 + \cdots + b_{jN}F_N + e_j \qquad (7.11)$$

where

---

[17] This section may be omitted without loss of continuity.

k_j = actual return on security j

a_j = the expected return on security j if unaffected by all factors

$b_j's$ = the sensitivity of security j to factors $1 \cdots N$

F's = factors common to the returns of all securities being considered

e_j = unique affects on the return of security j

Like the CAPM, the APT is only interested in nondiversifiable risk. The APT theorizes, however, that the risk premium associated with this nondiversifiable risk is a function of a number of factors rather than solely the expected returns on the market portfolio. This means that the risk premium is actually the sum of a set of risk premiums. Thus, in equilibrium the required rate of return on security j is written as

$$k_j = k_{RF} + \sum_{n=1}^{N} b_{jn}(k_n - k_{RF}) \qquad (7.12)$$

where

$$k_n = \text{the required rate of return on the } n^{th} \text{ factor}$$
$$(k_n - k_{RF}) = \text{the market price of risk for the } n^{th} \text{ factor}$$
$$\sum_{n=1}^{N} b_{jn}(k_n - k_{RF}) = \text{the risk premium for security j}$$

The APT is more general than the CAPM. However, a problem with the APT is that the underlying factors are not known *ex ante*. If only one factor affects a security's return, and that factor is the market portfolio, then Equation 7.12 reduces to Equation 7.10, the SML equation of the CAPM. Furthermore, empirical testing indicates that return on the market portfolio appears to be the most important risk variable for the majority of firms. That being the case, the CAPM continues to be a useful model for representing the relationship between risk and required rates of return for large, actively traded firms.

Summary

Dealing with risk in financial management requires us to understand both its sources and its meaning. The sources of risk are general economic, inflation and disinflation, firm- and issue-specific, and international. As factors change in any of these areas, risk may change; further, as risk changes, so will the investor's required rate of return.

An asset's total risk is measured by its standard deviation. This standard deviation is a good measure of an asset's risk when it is held in isolation, or when it is part of a nondiversified portfolio. In a diversified portfolio, risk can be divided into two components: diversifiable risk and nondiversifiable risk. Since diversifiable risk is eliminated in the portfolio, the appropriate measure of the remaining (or relevant risk) is nondiversifiable risk as measured by beta, β_j. Beta indicates the sensitivity of the asset's returns relative to the market's expected returns as follows:

1. If $\beta_j = 1.0$, the risk is equal to the market's risk.
2. If $\beta_j = 2.0$, the risk is twice as great as the average risk.
3. If $\beta_j = 0.5$, the risk is only half as great as the average risk.

The capital asset pricing model relates risk and required return for all securities via the security market line, which is $k_j = k_{RF} + \beta_j(k_M - k_{RF})$. The required rate of return on any security in equilibrium is equal to the risk-free rate, plus a risk premium based on the asset's nondiversifiable risk. Although securities are occasionally out of equilibrium, this is not generally the case; the expected rate of return and the required rate of return are typically equal.

In an efficient market prices react quickly and unambiguously to new information. The capital market in the United States is reasonably efficient. This has important implications for both financing and investment decisions of the firm. Managers need to understand these implications, and the preeminence of the market value of the firm as the basis for effective decision making.

There are two appendixes to this chapter, "Appendix 7A: Calculating Covariances and Correlations," and "Appendix 7B: Calculating Security Betas," at the back of the book.

Questions

7.1 Define or explain the following:

a.	Uncertainty	u.	Feasible set
b.	General economic risk	v.	Efficient portfolio
c.	Risk aversion	w.	Efficient frontier
d.	Inflation risk	x.	Diversifiable risk
e.	Disinflation risk	y.	Nondiversifiable risk
f.	Firm- and issue-specific risk	z.	Capital asset pricing model (CAPM)
g.	Business risk	aa.	Market portfolio, k_M
h.	Financial risk	bb.	Capital market line (CML)
i.	International risk	cc.	Market price of risk
j.	Portfolio	dd.	Beta, β_j
k.	Probability	ee.	Portfolio beta
l.	Mean (expected value)	ff.	Security market line (SML)
m.	Standard deviation	gg.	Underpriced
n.	Total risk	hh.	Overpriced
o.	Variance	ii.	Equilibrium
p.	Coefficient of variation	jj.	Efficient market hypothesis
q.	Diversifying	kk.	Weak-form efficiency
r.	Expected return on a portfolio, $\tilde{K}_p$	ll.	Semistrong-form efficiency
s.	Correlation	mm.	Strong-form efficiency
t.	Covariance	nn.	Arbitrage pricing theory (APT)

7.2 What are the four primary sources of risk? Are any of these specific to individual firms and hence sources of risk that can be diversified away in a well-rounded portfolio?

7.3 In what situation is an asset's standard deviation an appropriate measure of risk? Why is this so?

7.4 Security A has a mean of 25 and a standard deviation of 15; security B has a mean of 40 and a standard deviation of 10.

a. Which security is more risky? Why?
b. What if the standard deviation on security B was 15? 20? (*Note:* In answering this part,

you must consider whether it is absolute risk as measured by the standard deviation, or relative risk as measured by the coefficient of variation, that is important.)

7.5 Explain how forming a portfolio may result in a reduction in risk. What is the necessary condition for this risk reduction to occur?

7.6 Explain the ideas behind the efficient frontier concept. What does the efficient frontier look like if we are considering (a) only risky assets, and (b) a risk-free asset and the market portfolio of risky assets?

7.7 The primary outcome of the capital asset pricing model (CAPM) is the security market line (SML) equation, which is $k_j = k_{RF} + \beta_j(k_M - k_{RF})$. What do all these terms mean? How can they be estimated?

7.8 Why is it that most stocks have positive betas? What would be the required rate of return, relative to the risk-free rate, on a stock that had a negative beta?

7.9 Security j has a beta of 0.90, the risk-free rate is 8 percent, and the expected return on the market is 16 percent. What will happen to the required rate of return on security j under the following conditions (assume each part is independent)?

a. Inflation is expected to increase by 3 percent over the next couple of years.
b. Due to stringent monetary and fiscal controls, the government is shrinking its deficits and encouraging additional optimism for industry, consumers, and investors.
c. The company just won an unexpected victory in a major lawsuit concerning patent infringement.
d. International competition is increasing rapidly in the firm's market areas, leading to increased risk.
e. The government has decided to place an excess profits tax, amounting to 50 percent, on all corporate profits.

7.10 The capital asset pricing model indicates the relationship between risk and the required rate of return. However, occasionally securities get out of equilibrium, and their expected rate of return is greater or less than their required rate of return.

a. What process occurs to bring the expected rate of return back into equilibrium so it equals the required rate of return?
b. How does the idea of market efficiency relate to this process?

7.11 Explain the efficient market hypotheses, being sure to distinguish between the three forms of market efficiency. What important implications does market efficiency have for investors, and for managers?

Self-Test Problems   (Solutions appear on pages 719–720.)

Returns, Standard
Deviation, and CAPM

ST 7.1 Returns for the next period for two stocks, A and B, and the market, M, are given by the following probability distribution:

State of the Economy	Probability of State Occurring	Associated Rate of Return		
		A	B	M
Boom	0.2	40%	50%	40%
Normal	0.5	0	5	15
Recession	0.3	−10	−5	−15

a. Calculate the expected rate of return for stocks A and B individually. Then calculate (1) the associated rates of return for a portfolio comprised of 50 percent A and 50 percent B and (2) the expected rate of return for the portfolio AB.

b. Calculate the standard deviation for stock A, stock B, and the portfolio AB (carry to two decimal points). By comparing the average of the individual stock's standard deviations versus the portfolio's standard deviation, what can we say about the correlation between the two stocks?

c. Calculate the expected return on the market.

d. If the risk-free rate is 5 percent, and the market is efficient so that the expected and required returns for portfolio AB are equal, what is the beta for portfolio AB?

Required Rate of Return

ST 7.2   The expected return on the market portfolio is 12 percent, and the risk-free rate is 6 percent. If an asset is 60 percent riskier than the market, what is the required rate of return for the asset?

Risk and Return

ST 7.3   Find the required rate of return on security j under the following conditions:

a. $k_{RF} = 6\%$, $k_M = 12\%$, and $\beta_j = 1.20$
b. Inflation increases by 3 percent so that $k_{RF} = 9\%$, $k_M = 15\%$, and $\beta_j = 1.20$
c. Risk aversion increases so that $k_{RF} = 6\%$, $k_M = 15\%$, and $\beta_j = 1.20$
d. $k_{RF} = 6\%$, $k_M = 12\%$, and beta (1) increases to 2.00 or (2) decreases to 0.50

Disequilibrium and CAPM

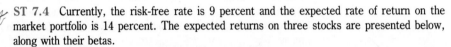

ST 7.4   Currently, the risk-free rate is 9 percent and the expected rate of return on the market portfolio is 14 percent. The expected returns on three stocks are presented below, along with their betas.

Stock	Expected Return	Beta
Miller Aviation	18%	1.7
India Imports	11	0.6
Royal Communications	15	1.2

Which stocks are over-, under-, or correctly valued in the market?

Problems

Expected Value and Standard Deviation

7.1   The following information is available about Boquist Transit.

Probability	Return
0.20	40%
0.40	20
0.40	10

Compute Boquist's expected return and standard deviation.

Expected Value and Standard Deviation

7.2   A firm is considering investing in one of two projects, which have the following returns and probabilities of occurrence:

Probability	Project A	Project B
0.10	40%	50%
0.20	20	20
0.40	10	5
0.20	0	−20
0.10	−20	−40

a. Calculate the expected return for each project. Which is more profitable?
b. Calculate the standard deviation for each project. Which is more risky?
c. Which project is preferable?

Portfolio Risk

7.3 Securities A, B, and C have rates of return and probabilities of occurrence as follows:

	Security Return (%)		
Probability	A	B	C
0.30	60	50	10
0.40	40	30	50
0.30	20	10	90

a. Calculate the probability distribution of expected rates of return for a portfolio composed 50 percent of security A and 50 percent of security B. [*Note:* First convert the individual security returns for securities A and B to a single series of returns via $0.50(60) + 0.50(50) = 55$, which has a 0.30 probability of occurrence. Do the same for A and B for the other two probabilities.] Now do the same for a portfolio composed of 50 percent security A and 50 percent security C.
b. Calculate the expected value (or mean) and standard deviation for portfolios AB and AC from (a). [*Note:* Once you have the probability distributions in (a), then you can treat the returns like that of a single security. Equations 7.1 and 7.2 are appropriate.]
c. Which portfolio has the highest expected return? Lowest risk? Which portfolio is preferable?
d. What if everything remained the same, except assume the standard deviation calculated for portfolio AC was 21 percent. Which portfolio would now be preferable? Why?

Portfolio Risk Using Historical Data (More Difficult)

7.4 Stocks A and B have the following historical cash dividend and price data:

	Stock A		Stock B	
Year	Cash Dividend D_t	Year-End Price P_t	Cash Dividend D_t	Year-End Price P_t
19X2	$ —	$40.00	$ —	$15.00
19X3	2.00	43.00	—	22.00
19X4	2.50	38.50	0.50	18.50
19X5	2.50	48.00	0.50	14.00
19X6	3.00	44.00	0.50	28.50

a. Calculate the yearly returns for stock A, stock B, and a portfolio comprised of 50 percent A and 50 percent B. (*Note:* Carry the calculations to four decimal places; then convert the returns to percentages with two decimal places for use in the rest of the problem.)
b. Calculate the mean for stock A, stock B, and the portfolio AB. Do the same for the standard deviation. (*Note:* Use the equations for the mean and standard deviation given in footnote 7.)
c. Take the average of the two individual stocks' standard deviations [(standard deviation A + standard deviation B)/2] and compare this with the portfolio standard deviation AB. Based on the extent to which the portfolio has a lower risk than the average of the two stocks' standard deviations, what would you estimate the correlation to be between the returns on stock A and stock B? More specifically, if you were told the correlation was either +0.85 or −0.45, which one would you choose? Why?

Three-Security Portfolio

7.5 Securities D, E, and F have the following characteristics with respect to expected return, standard deviation, and correlation among them:

Security	Expected Return $\bar{k}$	Standard Deviation σ	Correlation
D	8%	2%	$Corr_{DE} = +0.40$
E	16	16	$Corr_{DF} = +0.60$
F	12	8	$Corr_{EF} = +0.80$

What is the expected return and standard deviation of a portfolio comprised of 50 percent D, 25 percent E, and 25 percent F? (*Note:* For three securities, Equation 7.4 becomes:

$$\sigma_P = \sqrt{W_D^2\sigma_D^2 + W_E^2\sigma_E^2 + W_F^2\sigma_F^2 + 2W_DW_E\sigma_D\sigma_ECorr_{DE} + 2W_DW_F\sigma_D\sigma_FCorr_{DF} + 2W_EW_F\sigma_E\sigma_FCorr_{EF}.})$$

Correlation and Standard Deviation

7.6 Consider two stocks, A and B, with their expected returns and standard deviations, as follows:

	A	B
Expected return, $\bar{k}$	15%	10%
Standard deviation, σ	10	8

a. What is the expected return if the portfolio contains equal amounts (0.50) of each security?
b. What is the standard deviation for the equally weighted portfolio in (a) if the correlation between the security returns is: (1) $Corr_{AB} = +1.00$, (2) $Corr_{AB} = +0.50$, (3) $Corr_{AB} = -0.50$.
c. How does the decrease in the portfolio standard deviation (as the correlation between the security returns drops) relate to diversifiable and nondiversifiable risk?

Portfolio Risk, Return, and Efficient Frontier

7.7 You have estimated the following probability distribution of returns for two stocks:

Stock N		Stock O	
Probability	Return	Probability	Return
0.2	8%	0.2	26%
0.3	4	0.3	12
0.3	0	0.3	0
0.2	-4	0.2	-4

a. Calculate the expected rate of return and standard deviation for each stock.
b. If the correlation between the returns on the two stocks is -0.40, calculate the portfolio return and standard deviation for portfolios containing 100 percent, 75 percent, 50 percent, 25 percent, and 0 percent of security N, respectively.
c. Plot the results from (b). Which portfolios lie on the efficient frontier?
d. If there is no risk-free asset, which portfolio would *you* prefer? Why? Would other individuals necessarily choose the same portfolio?

Efficient Frontier

7.8 The following portfolios are available for selection:

Portfolio	Return, K_p	Risk, σ_p
1	16%	16%
2	14	10
3	8	4
4	12	14
5	9	8
6	10	12
7	7	11
8	5	7
9	11	6
10	3	3

a. By plotting the data determine which portfolios lie on the efficient frontier.

b. Which portfolio would *you* prefer? Why? Would other individuals necessarily choose the same portfolio?

c. Independent of (b), now assume a risk-free asset exists that returns 10 percent. What is the market portfolio of all risky assets? Which portfolio would *you* now prefer? Why?

CAPM

7.9 The risk-free rate is 8 percent and the expected return on the market portfolio is 14 percent. What are the required rates of return for the four stocks listed below:

Stock	R	S	T	U
Beta	2.0	0.6	1.0	−0.2

What can we say about the volatility of each stock relative to the market's volatility?

Graph of SML

7.10 If the risk-free rate of interest is 8 percent and the expected return on the market portfolio is 15 percent, graph the security market line.

a. Explain why beta of the market is equal to 1.0.

b. What is the approximate required rate of return (reading from your graph) on a security that has a beta of 0.75, or 1.50?

c. Calculate the required rates of return for the two securities in (b) employing the SML equation. How similar are your answers to those estimated in (b)?

Required Rate of Return

7.11 Larry Lewis is attempting to estimate the required rate of return for Davidson Steel. The risk-free rate is 7 percent. Based on the analysis provided by a number of investment advisory firms, Larry estimates the expected return on the market portfolio is 15 percent, and beta for Davidson Steel is 1.25.

a. What is the required rate of return for Davidson Steel?

b. Larry decides to estimate the expected return on the market himself. He believes expected inflation is 6 percent, the real rate of growth in the economy is 3 percent, and the risk premium of stocks over bonds is 4 percent. The risk-free rate remains at 7 percent and beta is still 1.25. What impact does this have on Larry's estimate of Davidson's required rate of return?

Portfolio Required Return

7.12 Haber Fund has a total investment in five stocks as follows:

Stock	Investment (Market Value)	Beta
1	$3.0 million	0.50
2	2.5 million	1.00
3	1.5 million	2.00
4	2.0 million	1.25
5	1.0 million	1.50

The risk-free rate, k_{RF}, is 7 percent and the returns on the market portfolio are given by the following probability distribution:

Probability	k_M
0.1	8%
0.2	10
0.3	13
0.3	15
0.1	17

What is Haber Fund's required rate of return?

7.13 Suppose two securities lie exactly on the security market line (SML) with the following characteristics.

Security	k_j	β_j
A	19.6%	2.25
B	16.8	1.75

a. What are k_{RF} and k_M? (*Note:* Solution involves solving simultaneous equations.) What does the graph of the SML look like?

(Do only if using Pinches Disk.)

b. What are the values of k_{RF} and k_M if the securities have the same betas as in (a), but required returns of 22.75 percent for security A and 19.25 percent for B? How does this compare graphically with the SML graph in (a)?

c. Now suppose the betas for the two securities again remain the same, but the required returns are 22.6 percent for A and 19.8 percent for B. Now what are the values of k_{RF} and k_M? How does this SML graph differ from the original in (a)? Why?

d. Finally, what are the new values of k_{RF} and k_M if security A has a required return of 23.8 percent and a beta of 3.00, and security B has a required return of 18.2 percent and a beta of 2.00? What does this new SML graph look like? How does it differ from the original SML in (a)? Why?

7.14 Hoisington Investments has the following portfolio:

Stock	Investment	Stock's Beta
A	$20 million	0.90
B	40 million	1.40
C	10 million	2.00
D	30 million	1.20

a. What is the portfolio's beta coefficient?

b. If the risk-free rate is 8 percent and the return on the market portfolio is 15 percent: (1) What is the equation for the SML? (2) What is the (percent) return Hoisington should be earning on the portfolio if its risk–return pattern puts it right on the SML?

c. Hoisington has just received $25 million in additional funds and is considering investing it in security E, which has a beta of 1.80 and an expected return of 19 percent. (1) Should stock E be purchased? (2) If not, at what rate of return would it be suitable for purchase (if its beta remains at 1.80)?

7.15 Brad Lawrence has the following investments:

Stock	Required Return, $\bar{k}_j$	Portfolio Weight, W_j	β_j
Chicago Power & Light	7.5%	0.40	0.60
Uptown	12.7	0.30	1.40
Summit Industries	10.3	0.30	1.10

a. What is the required return on the portfolio?

b. What is the portfolio beta?

c. Brad has decided to take on some more risk in order to increase his return. He sold some of the Chicago Power & Light stock and invested the proceeds into the other two stocks already held. If the new portfolio's required return is 11.06 percent, and the new portfolio beta is 1.165, how much is now invested in each of the three stocks? (*Note:* Solution involves solving simultaneous equations. Let X equal the proportion of the portfolio invested in Chicago Power & Light, and Y equal the proportion of the portfolio invested in Uptown. Since the sum of all three proportions equals 100 percent, or 1.0, then $1 - X - Y$ equals the proportion of the portfolio invested in Summit Industries.)

Interaction of Required Rate of Return and Common Stock Valuation

7.16 Zumwalt Products has dividends today, D_0, of $2 per share, an expected growth rate of 9 percent per year to infinity, a beta of 1.40, $k_M = 13\%$, and $k_{RF} = 8\%$.

a. What is the required rate of return?

b. What is the current market price of Zumwalt's common stock?

c. Zumwalt is contemplating the divestiture of an unprofitable but stable revenue-producing division. The effect will be to increase the growth rate in cash dividends to 11 percent, and also increase beta to 1.60. What will be the new market value?

d. Instead of (c), Zumwalt could merge with another firm that is a steady cash producer, but is less risky. The effect would be to lower beta to 1.20 and reduce the growth rate in dividends to 8 percent. What would be the market value now?

e. Instead of either (c) or (d), a new, aggressive management could be brought in. Beta would go to 2.00, and the growth rate in dividends would be 13 percent. Now what would be the stock price?

f. Is Zumwalt better off staying where it is, or moving to one of the plans outlined in (c), (d), or (e)? Which plan should the firm choose? Why is that the best plan?

Risk and Stock Price

7.17 Ohio Electronics' common stock is expected to pay a dividend of $3.15 next year, D_1; the growth rate is 5 percent; its beta is 1.50; $k_M = 15$ percent, and $k_{RF} = 7$ percent.

a. What is the current market value of Ohio Electronics' common stock?

b. The combined actions of the Federal Reserve system and the U.S. Treasury cause the risk-free rate to drop to 5 percent. (*Note:* At every beta, the SML is 2 percent less than before.) What is the new market price?

c. *In addition to the change in* (b), risk aversion has decreased so that the return on the market is now 11 percent. What is the current market price?

d. Finally, *in addition to the changes in* (b) *and* (c), the firm closes some of its marginal operations. Beta decreases to 1.333, while D_1 is $3.12 and g decreases to 4 percent. What is the current market value for Ohio Electronics?

Risk, Correlation, and Stock Price

7.18 Landmark Industries is in the process of evaluating the effect of different factors on its market value. Landmark expects to pay dividends of $3 a year from now ($D_1 = \$3$), and the growth rate in its dividends is 4 percent per year until infinity. Landmark estimates the following: $k_{RF} = 6\%$, $k_M = 11\%$, $\sigma_j = 16\%$, $\sigma_M = 10\%$, and $Corr_{jM} = 0.50$.

a. What is the required rate of return for Landmark and the current market value of its stock? (*Note:* As shown in Appendix 7B, $\beta_j = [(\sigma_j)(Corr_{jM})/\sigma_M]$.)

b. What is Landmark's required rate of return and stock market value if everything stays the same, except that its correlation with the market increases to 0.75?

c. If all the conditions are as in (a) except that σ_j increases to 64 percent and σ_M increases to 20 percent, what is the required rate of return and market price for Landmark?

d. If all the conditions are as in (a) except that σ_j decreases to 8 percent, what is the required rate of return and market price for Landmark?

Disequilibrium and CAPM

7.19 The risk-free rate is 5 percent and the expected return on the market portfolio, k_M, is 10 percent. The expected returns and betas for four stocks are listed below:

Stock	Expected Return	Beta
Steelman Zinc	12.0%	1.3
Rose Paint	9.5	0.8
Natural Automotive	10.5	1.1
Blythe Electronics	13.0	1.7

a. Which stocks are over- or undervalued?

b. In an efficient market, what occurs to bring expected and required rates of return back into equilibrium?

c. Which are over- or undervalued if the risk-free rate increases to 7 percent, and the expected return on the market portfolio goes to 11 percent?

References

For information on portfolio theory, the CAPM and efficient markets see

FAMA, EUGENE F. *Foundations of Finance*, New York: Basic Books, 1976.

HAUGEN, ROBERT A. *Modern Investment Theory*, Englewood Cliffs, N.J.: Prentice-Hall, 1986.

There is a tremendous amount of material on risk and return. Some recent items include these:

ANG, JAMES S., AND DAVID R. PETERSON. "Return, Risk, and Yield: Evidence from Ex Ante Data." *Journal of Finance* 40 (June 1985), pp. 537–548.

BEY, ROGER P., AND GEORGE E. PINCHES. "Additional Evidence of Heteroscedasticity in the Market Model." *Journal of Financial and Quantitative Analysis* 15 (June 1980), pp. 299–322.

BREALEY, RICHARD A. *An Introduction to Risk and Return for Common Stocks*, 2d ed. Cambridge, Mass.: MIT Press, 1983.

GESKE, ROBERT, AND RICHARD ROLL. "The Fiscal and Monetary Linkage Between Stock Returns and Inflation." *Journal of Finance* 38 (March 1983), pp. 1–33.

KEIM, DONALD B. "The CAPM and Equity Return Regularities." *Financial Analysts Journal* 42 (May–June 1986), pp. 19–34.

TINIC, SEHA M., AND RICHARD R. WEST. "Risk and Return: January vs. the Rest of the Year." *Journal of Financial Economics* 13 (December 1984), pp. 561–574.

Research on the arbitrage pricing theory is expanding rapidly. See, for example:

LEHMANN, BRUCE N., AND DAVID M. MODEST. "The Empirical Foundations of the Arbitrage Pricing Theory." *Journal of Financial Economics* 21 (September 1988), pp. 213–254.

CONNOR, GREGORY, AND ROBERT A. KORAJCZYK. "Risk and Return in an Equilibrium APT: Application of a New Test Methodology." *Journal of Financial Economics* 21 (September 1988), pp. 255–289.

See Model sixteen in *Lotus 1–2–3® for Financial Management* by Pinches and Courtney for a template that calculates beta using historical data.

PART FOUR

Long-Term Investment Decisions

Capital Budgeting Techniques

Overview

- Only by accepting positive net present value (NPV) projects can the firm maximize its value.

- The capital budgeting process has four phases: (1) search and identification; (2) estimating the magnitude, timing, and riskiness of cash flows; (3) selection or rejection; and (4) control and postcompletion audit.

- The relevant cash flows are the incremental after-tax cash flows for the initial, operating, and terminal periods.

- Both net present value (NPV) and internal rate of return (IRR) are measures consistent with the goal of maximizing the value of the firm. Most experts favor the use of NPV because of possible multiple internal rates of return and ranking problems.

Federal Express, which supplies overnight delivery of letters and small packages, first offered its stock to the public in 1978. By early 1989 the market price per share of the Memphis-based air courier had grown from $3 to $52, a compound rate of growth of around 30 percent per year. Federal Express achieved this dramatic result by revolutionizing the private delivery of packages and mail. While other private courier services depended on scheduled airlines, Federal Express made a crucial investment decision: It bought its own planes, thus gaining control over shipments and ensuring speedy, reliable service. Today, it owns over 230 planes. To ensure its international presence, in December 1988 it paid $880 million to buy Tiger International, the world's largest heavy-cargo airline.

However, a large capital investment alone is no guarantee of ultimate profitability. Exxon found this out, after 10 years and a capital investment of at least $500 million. It discovered that oil (its primary business) and producing and selling office products do not mix. Exxon pulled the plug on its office systems division because of chronic losses and an unwillingness to invest more money in a highly competitive, rapidly changing industry.

All firms, whether large or small, continually invest in new long-term, or capital, assets. The profitability of these investment decisions directly *affects the value of the firm. Effective capital budgeting procedures for making long-term investment decisions are therefore a key ingredient for success. Successful firms, as evidenced by increases in market value, make good capital budgeting decisions. Let's see how they do it.*

Capital Budgeting and the Value of the Firm

The primary goal of the firm is to maximize its value, or to maximize the size of the pie. While many things contribute to maximizing the value of the firm, it is our belief that the most important single factor is the investments the firm makes. These investments determine the direction of the firm since, over time, how the firm has positioned itself (in terms of its products or services, its position in its industries, and so forth) is a direct function of its past investment decisions. Also, it is important to emphasize at the outset that good investment decisions build on the unique aspects and advantages a firm has vis-à-vis its competitors.

If we think of the value of the firm as being a function of its investment decisions, its financing decisions, and its operating decisions (that is, the day-to-day management), then

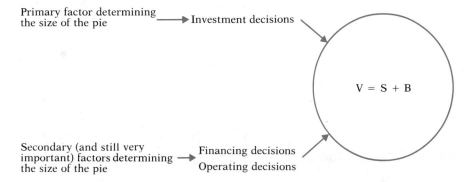

So, to maximize $V = S + B$, the first step is to make good investment decisions. That is the subject of Chapters 8 through 11.

Capital budgeting techniques are used to evaluate proposed investments in long-term assets. Long term is taken to mean any investment for which returns are expected to extend beyond 1 year. An investment can be as small as the purchase of some office furniture, or as large as a complete new plant. The *capital budget* contains estimates of cash flows for long-term projects. *Capital budgeting* is the process by which long-term investments are generated, analyzed, and placed in the capital budget.

Project Classification

Capital budgeting projects can be categorized into three broad categories: (1) expansion, (2) replacement, and (3) regulatory. *Expansion projects*, as discussed in this chapter, are those designed to improve the firm's ability to produce or market its products. If a firm decides to add a new line of machine tools, the plant necessary to produce the tools is an expansion project. A *replacement project* (see Chapter 9) is one designed to take the place of existing assets that have become obsolete. Finally, there are *regulatory projects*. These provide no direct cash benefits to the firm, but must be completed for the firm's operations to continue. For example, the Occupational Safety and Health Administration and the Environmental Protection Agency can require firms to spend billions of dollars to improve the health and safety of the work environment.

Another method of classifying projects is to view them as (1) *mutually exclusive* or alternatively, (2) *independent.* When two projects are mutually exclusive, the acceptance of one precludes the acceptance of the other. A proposal to purchase one computer precludes a proposal to acquire another computer if only one is needed. The two proposals are mutually exclusive. However, a proposal to acquire a computer and another proposal to build a new warehouse are independent. The cash flows are unrelated, and the firm may choose one, both, or neither.

Value Maximization

There is a relationship between the steps followed in valuing bonds or stocks, discussed in Chapter 6, and the basic capital budgeting decision-making criterion. In security analysis, we determine the present value of the expected cash inflows and compare it to the current market value. In capital budgeting, we calculate the *net present value (NPV)*, which is equal to the present value of the expected cash flows, discounted at the required rate of return, and then subtract the initial cash investment required.

Accepting positive NPV projects has a direct impact on the value of the firm. To understand this, consider an all-equity firm that has a current market value of $5 million. That includes $1 million in cash that can be invested in new long-term investment projects. You have to decide whether to invest the $1 million in a proposed capital investment, or keep it in cash. The choice is as follows:

	Market Value (In millions)	
Asset	Reject New Project	Accept New Project
Cash	$1	$0
Other	4	4
New project	0	PV
	$5	$4 + PV

Clearly the new project is worthwhile if its present value, PV, is greater than the $1 million required investment. This occurs only if the NPV is greater than zero, since when the NPV is zero, the discounted cash inflows from the project would *just equal* the initial investment of $1 million.

What happens, for example, if the proposed project has a net present value of $1.5 million? Your firm will receive its $1 million investment back plus an additional $1.5 million (both after discounting). What will happen to the value of the firm? It will increase as investors recognize the impact of the capital investment decision. This simple example provides us with an important message: *Only by accepting positive NPV projects can a firm increase its value; accepting projects with negative NPVs leads to a decrease in the value of the firm.* This fundamental decision criterion will be employed throughout our study of financial management.

Capital Expenditures

Unexpected "good" news is incorporated swiftly into stock prices. Likewise, unanticipated "bad" news is also incorporated rapidly. A recent study examining capital expenditure announcements sheds some light on the information associated with increases or decreases in an industrial firm's capital budget.[1] The study found the following performance over the two-day (t_{-1} and t_0) announcement period window.

Sample	Announcement Period Abnormal Return
All budget increases	1.21%
Increases from previous year's budget	1.22
Increase from current year's previously announced budget	1.19
All budget decreases	−1.52
Decreases from previous year's budget	−1.64
Decrease from current year's previously announced budget	−1.19

These data indicate that announcements of increases in planned capital expenditures are associated with significant positive returns. Likewise, decreases in planned capital expenditures are associated with negative abnormal returns. This suggests firms that have positive net present value projects and are making additional investments convey that information to the markets with their capital expenditure increases. Likewise, firms that don't have good investment projects also signal that information to the markets by reducing their planned capital expenditures.

[1] John J. McConnell and Chris J. Muscarella. "Corporate Capital Expenditure Decisions and the Market Value of the Firm." *Journal of Financial Economics* 14 (September 1985).

The Capital Budgeting Process

While the impact of accepting positive NPV capital projects is simple and straightforward, complications develop when we put our knowledge to work. To see why, it is important to understand that capital budgeting is a process involving a number of somewhat separate but interrelated activities. The *capital budgeting process* can be broken down into four steps:

1. Search and identification
2. Estimation of the magnitude, timing, and riskiness of cash flows

Figure 8.1 The Capital Budgeting Process

Capital budgeting is an ongoing process in which effective feedback should assist in improving decision making for subsequent capital investments.

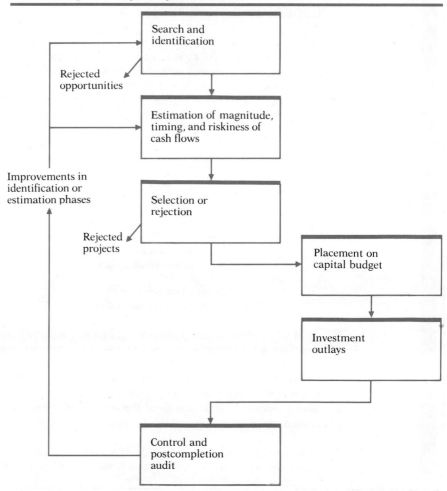

3. Selection or rejection
4. Control and postcompletion audit

The relationships among these steps are shown in Figure 8.1.

Search and Identification

The search and identification stage involves actively searching for new investment opportunities within the firm's expertise *or* identifying problems that need attention. It is a triggering process: The thrust of this phase is not to analyze and solve well-defined problems, but to identify possibilities for capital investment.

In the broadest sense, there is a direct connection between the search and identification stage and the firm's overall strategic objectives. There must be a fully integrated and consistent relationship between long-term strategic objectives and the capital budgeting process. Too often, this is not the case. The decision to enter a new market or adopt a new production technology is often just the first in a long series of investment decisions. Then either additional investments are made because they "are necessary" given the previous decision, or the capital budgeting decision-making process is employed only *within* the previously defined strategic plan.

Either way, the firm has the cart before the horse. It should be the firm's capital budgeting techniques, employing discounted cash flows and fully considering the risks and expected returns, that determine the firm's long-run strategic decisions—not the other way around!

Estimating the Magnitude, Timing, and Riskiness of Cash Flows

Once opportunities or problems have been searched for and identified, the next step is the development of alternative courses of action and the estimation of the magnitude, timing, and riskiness of the cash flows associated with each one. This is often the most difficult part of the entire process. It requires extensive knowledge, hard work, and an understanding of how possible competitor actions will affect cash flow projections. The estimation phase tends to become narrower in focus than the search and identification phase. This is because the desired outcome is detailed and specific: a set of alternative capital budgeting projects and associated cash flows, risk estimates, and specification of the key assumptions incorporated into the forecasts.

Selection or Rejection

After the necessary estimates have been made, next comes selection. The important points to remember about this phase are these:

1. The methods used to select or reject projects must be consistent with the objective of maximizing the value of the firm.
2. The key underlying assumptions (concerning the techniques employed and the data used) must be understood by the firm's capital budgeting specialists as well as by senior management.
3. Alternative courses of action, changes in risk, and actions of competitors must be considered.

Control and Postcompletion Audit

The final phase is that of control and postcompletion audit. Control can be thought of as the process by which the actual cash flows are compared with the projections. In addition, this phase should involve the subsequent reevaluation of the economic merits of ongoing projects—in order to determine whether to continue them. Evaluating the performance of ongoing capital investments is important for any complete capital budgeting process. A successful program (1) suggests needed revisions in the identification procedure, (2) provides information to improve future estimates of cash flows and risk, and (3) indicates ongoing projects that should be abandoned. Effective control and postcompletion audits are vital to maximizing the value of the firm.

All four steps are important; but we will focus on the second and third—estimation of the magnitude, timing, and riskiness of cash flows, and project selection. *Throughout this chapter and Chapter 9, we assume that all projects being considered are equally risky.* That is, their risk is equal to the firm's overall level of risk. Although this is obviously unrealistic, it allows us to focus on the essential elements of the capital budgeting process. Assuming all projects are equally risky means we can use a single *hurdle* (or discount) *rate* throughout. This rate is the required rate of return, designated as k. As discussed in Chapter 14, the required rate of return for projects of average risk is the firm's market-determined cost of capital.

How to Estimate Cash Flows

To accurately estimate the relevant cash flows, we must understand how corporations treat depreciation and taxes under the Internal Revenue Service code. The specifics of the modified Accelerated Cost Recovery System (ACRS) of depreciation and corporate taxes as specified by the Tax Reform Act of 1986 are reviewed in Appendix 8A. Table 8.1 provides a summary of the major depreciation and tax items necessary for capital budgeting.

Three points should be mentioned in estimating cash flows. First, as noted in Chapter 4, we are interested in cash flows (both inflows and outflows) as stated on an after-tax basis. Since taxes are an important determinant of cash flows, we are interested in looking at cash flows after all taxes have been taken into account. These are called cash flows after tax (CF) to distinguish them from cash flows before tax (CFBT). Second, we must guard against carelessly counting costs or benefits that should not be considered. A classic example is the treatment of overhead costs by accountants. If these overhead costs are fixed and their total amount does not change as a result of implementing a project, they do not affect the cash flows and are irrelevant for decision-making purposes. Finally, it is helpful to divide the cash flows into three segments:

1. The *initial investment* is the net after-tax cash outflow that typically occurs at the start (i.e., at time t_0) of the project under consideration.
2. The *operating cash flows* are the relevant net after-tax cash flows expected over the economic life of the project.
3. The *terminal cash flow* is the net after-tax inflow or outflow that occurs when the project is terminated.

The Initial Investment

The initial investment, CF_0, is the net after-tax cash flow that occurs at time zero. For an expansion project, it is calculated as follows:

1. Cost of equipment, facilities, and land purchased
2. All other costs related to the investment (transportation, installation, additional personnel, and so forth, net of taxes)
3. Additional net working capital required[1]
4. Opportunity costs (e.g., land used for this project that could have been sold)

Although the initial investment in many complex projects is spread over a number of years, for simplicity we treat it as occurring at the present (t = 0). When after-

---

[1] *Net working capital* is the difference between current assets and current liabilities. Often a project requires an increase in accounts receivable or inventory, thus increasing the firm's investment in the project. At the end of the project's life the additional working capital is no longer needed, and current assets and current liabilities may return to normal levels.

Table 8.1   Major Depreciation and Tax Assumptions

Although there are many more complexities, these are the basic concepts necessary for capital budgeting.

Category	Item	Assumption
Depreciation	Method	Simplified ACRS percentages in Table 8A.2 (or Table F.5), or straight-line over the normal recovery period
	Life	3, 5, 7, 10, 15, or 20 years
	Resale value	Not relevant under tax code when calculating depreciation
	Real estate	Not dealt with
Corporate taxes	Marginal corporate tax rate	30 to 40%
	Tax loss	Direct reduction in tax liability (assumes firm as a whole is profitable)
	Firm in loss position	No taxes paid
	Carryback or carryforward of losses	Ignored
	Tax payment date	Tax paid or credit received immediately; at time t_0

tax cash outflows occur beyond $t = 0$, they are treated like other CFs, except that the negative sign is retained.

Operating Cash Flows

The second part of the cash flow stream, operating cash flows, are the net cash flows that occur while the asset is in operation. They begin in year 1 and continue throughout the project's useful life. These operating cash flows are typically positive, although there may be occasional years when the outflows are greater than the inflows. Operating cash flows are calculated by taking the difference in the cash inflows minus the cash outflows to provide the cash flow before tax, CFBT, attributable to the proposed project. IRS depreciation then enters into the picture, since it is a deductible expense for tax purposes and serves to reduce taxes. Operating cash flows for an expansion project, as originally given in Chapter 4, are

$$\text{operating CF}_t = (\text{ cash inflows}_t - \text{ cash outflows}_t)(1 - T) + \text{Dep}_t(T)$$

$$= \text{CFBT}_t(1 - T) + \text{Dep}_t(T) \tag{8.1}$$

where T is the firm's marginal corporate tax rate. In calculating depreciation, remember that land cannot be depreciated and all assets are depreciated to zero for tax purposes.[2]

Depreciable Life Versus Economic Life

Under ACRS depreciation, the *depreciable lives* (as specified by the normal recovery period) have been shortened for virtually all assets. The result is that the normal recovery period is generally less than the asset's useful *economic life*. In such a case, cash inflows and outflows may occur every year, while the effects on the operating CF from depreciation will occur only in the early years of the project's life.

---

[2] As noted in Chapter 4 (footnote 1), now we *exclude* interest as part of the before-tax cash outflows.

Table 8.2 Depreciation and Operating Cash Flows for Sunbelt Industries

The approach employed to calculate the operating cash flows was originally given by Equation 4.3.

Depreciation

Year	Original Cost	× Simplified ACRS Factors	= Depreciation
1	$200,000	0.20	$40,000
2	200,000	0.32	64,000
3	200,000	0.19	38,000
4	200,000	0.15	30,000
5	200,000	0.14	28,000

Operating Cash Flows

Year	CFBT	CFBT(1 − T)*	+ Dep(T)*	= CF
1	$25,000	$16,250	$14,000	$30,250
2	25,000	16,250	22,400	38,650
3	25,000	16,250	13,300	29,550
4	25,000	16,250	10,500	26,750
5	25,000	16,250	9,800	26,050
6–10	25,000	16,250	0	16,250

Cash Flow Stream

$30,250 $38,650 $29,550 $26,750 $26,050 $16,250 each

1   2   3   4   5   6   7   8   9   10

* The tax rate equals 35 percent.

Consider the example of Sunbelt Industries, which is contemplating the purchase of a new machine with a 5-year tax life, or normal recovery period, but with a 10-year economic life. If the machine costs $200,000, cash flow before tax, CFBT, is $25,000 for each of 10 years, and the tax rate is 35 percent, then the ACRS depreciation and operating cash flow stream are as shown in Table 8.2. Notice that because depreciation occurs in the first 5 years, the cash flows in the early years are greater than in the later years.

Opportunity Costs

Opportunity costs are a special type of cash flow. An *opportunity cost* is the cost of a forgone opportunity. For example, suppose a firm is analyzing a project that would employ warehouse space currently being rented out for $4,800 a year. If the company decides to expand, it loses the benefit of $4,800 per year in rental income. The loss in rental income is an opportunity cost and must be deducted from each year's operating cash flows. Similarly, if a car manufacturer decides to market a new subcompact model, sales of the firm's other models may decline. Cash inflows lost from the decline in sales of the other models is an opportunity cost of the new subcompact project.

Terminal Cash Flow

Terminal cash flows are the after-tax cash flows other than the operating cash flows that occur in the last year of the project's life. For an expansion project, they are calculated as

Funds realized from the sale of the asset plus a tax benefit if it is expected to be sold at a loss, or minus a tax liability if it is expected to be sold at a gain[3]

Release of net working capital

minus

Disposal costs (net of taxes)

The terminal cash flow typically is positive, but it may be negative.

Selecting Capital Budgeting Projects

Firms use a variety of techniques to determine whether to accept proposed projects. The payback period is a naive, or nondiscounted, technique. The net present value (NPV) and internal rate of return (IRR) techniques both employ discounting to deal with the magnitude, timing, and riskiness of the cash flow stream.[4]

Payback Period

The *payback period* is the number of years it takes for the firm to recover its initial investment in a project. Payback occurs when the cumulative net cash inflows minus the initial investment equals zero, or

$$\text{payback is the time, T, such that} \left(\sum_{t=1}^{T} CF_t - CF_0 \right) = 0 \tag{8.2}$$

The decision rule for the payback period is as follows:

1. If T is less than required T—accept.
2. If T is greater than required T—reject.
3. If T is equal to required T—you are indifferent.

Consider the two projects in Table 8.3. Project A has an initial investment of $442 and cash inflows of $200 for each of 3 years. Project B requires an initial investment of $718 followed by cash inflows of $250, $575, and $100 for the 3 years. For project A, which is an annuity, the payback period can be found simply by dividing the initial investment by the annual CF. Thus, $442 divided by $200 yields a payback period, T, of 2.21 years. For project B, the payback is found by determining how many years are needed to recoup the initial investment of $718. In the first year $250 is recovered, and by the end of the second year $825 is recovered. So, the payback period is between 1 and 2 years. Table 8.3 shows that the payback period is actually 1.81 years. Thus, project B has the shorter payback period. If a firm's maximum acceptable payback period is 2 years, it would accept project B and reject project A.

The payback period has three advantages. First, it is simple to calculate. Second, it is easy to understand, and can be explained easily. Third, it provides a rough indicator of the riskiness of the project, since projects that pay back sooner are

---

[3] Assuming the firm is profitable.

[4] Two other techniques are the average (or accounting) rate of return and the profitability index. Given our understanding of the deficiencies of accounting data for effective decision making, we should be wary of any attempt to make capital investment decisions with the average rate of return. The profitability index is discussed in Chapter 9 (footnote 13).

Table 8.3 Calculation of the Payback Period for Projects A and B

When the cash inflows are unequal, as in project B, interpolation (or eyeballing) is employed to determine the payback period.

Cash Flow Streams

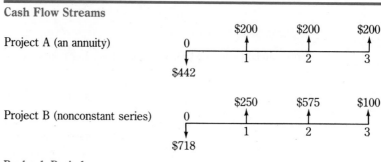

Payback Period
Project A: T = $442/$200 = 2.21 years

$$\text{Project B: } T = 1 \text{ year} + \frac{\$718 - \$250}{\$825 - \$250} = 1 \text{ year} + \frac{\$468}{\$575} = 1.81 \text{ years}$$

often viewed as being more liquid and hence less risky than those with longer payback periods.

At the same time it has three significant disadvantages. The first is that the required (i.e., maximum acceptable) payback is arbitrary; that is, it is set without any economic justification. Second, it does not take into account the timing of the cash flows, since discounting is not employed. Third, it does not deal with any cash flows that occur beyond the payback period. Suppose we had two projects with cash flows as follows:

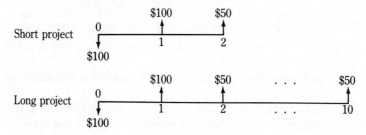

It is obvious that the longer project is better than the shorter one. However, both projects have the same payback of 1 year. Because of these disadvantages, the payback period is not an appropriate decision-making criterion.[5]

Net Present Value

The second selection technique we consider is net present value (NPV). The NPV is determined by discounting the cash inflows back to the present (t = 0) at the required rate of return, k, and then subtracting the initial investment, so that

---

[5] Some firms calculate a discounted payback period to overcome the timing disadvantage, but the other problems remain.

$$\text{net present value (NPV)} = \sum_{t=1}^{n} \frac{CF_t}{(1+k)^t} - CF_0 \qquad (8.3)$$

The decision rule for net present value is as follows:

1. If NPV is greater than zero—accept.
2. If NPV is less than zero—reject.
3. If NPV is equal to zero—you are indifferent.

When the NPV is greater than zero, the firm is in the position where it is generating funds above and beyond those necessary to (1) repay the initial investment and (2) provide it with a return of k percent on its investment. This incremental return represents the funds generated by the project that can be used for other purposes by the firm. Assuming the required rate of return for projects A and B is 12 percent, their net present values are calculated as in Table 8.4. Since both projects have positive NPVs, both should be accepted. Notice that the net present value criterion says project A is preferable (since it has a larger NPV), whereas the payback criterion (from Table 8.3) indicates project B was preferred. If we were choosing between the two projects, the net present value would lead us to make the correct decision; the payback period would lead to an erroneous decision.

In addition to solving for a project's NPV, it is often useful to depict the capital

Table 8.4 Calculation of the Net Present Value for Projects A and B

The discount rate employed was 12 percent. Since both NPVs are positive, both projects assist in maximizing stockholder wealth.

Cash Flows Streams

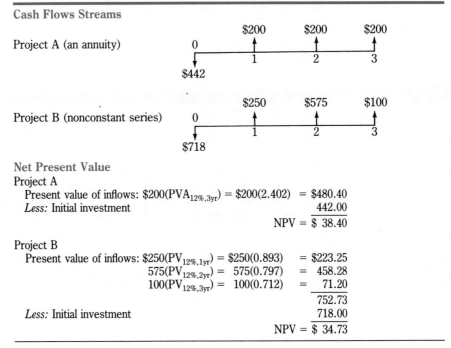

Net Present Value

Project A
  Present value of inflows: $200(PVA_{12\%,3yr}) = \$200(2.402)$ = \$480.40
  Less: Initial investment   442.00
                                        NPV = \$ 38.40

Project B
  Present value of inflows: $250(PV_{12\%,1yr}) = \$250(0.893)$ = \$223.25
                          $575(PV_{12\%,2yr}) = 575(0.797)$ = 458.28
                          $100(PV_{12\%,3yr}) = 100(0.712)$ = 71.20
                                           752.73
  Less: Initial investment   718.00
                                         NPV = \$ 34.73

Figure 8.2 Present Value Profile for Project A

A present value profile shows what happens to the NPV as the discount rate changes. The internal rate of return occurs where the present value profile line intersects the horizontal axis (or discount rate).

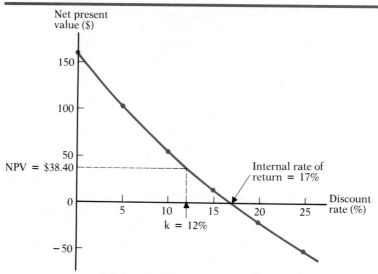

budgeting decision graphically. When a variety of rates are employed to discount a project's cash flows, a *present value profile* may be constructed. For project A, employing various discount rates results in the following net present values:

Discount Rate	Net Present Value
0%	$158.00
5	102.60
10	55.40
15	14.60
20	−20.80
25	−51.60

Plotting these values produces the present value profile shown in Figure 8.2. The present value profile provides a pictorial representation of the sensitivity of NPV to the discount rate employed. The steeper the slope of the present value profile, the more sensitive the NPV is to the rate employed.

Internal Rate of Return

The *internal rate of return (IRR)* is the discount rate that equates the present value of the cash inflows with the initial investment. The internal rate of return is found by solving for the unknown IRR such that Equation 8.4 holds

$$\sum_{t=1}^{n} \frac{CF_t}{(1 + IRR)^t} = CF_0 \qquad (8.4)$$

This internal rate of return for a project is then compared with the hurdle rate, k, which is the required rate of return. The internal rate of return decision rule is as follows:

1. If IRR is greater than k—accept.
2. If IRR is less than k—reject.
3. If IRR is equal to k—you are indifferent.

The steps for determining the IRR are exactly the same as those presented in Chapter 5 for determining an interest rate.[6] As shown in Table 8.5, the calculated IRR for project A is 17 percent, whereas it is 15 percent for project B. Since the hurdle rate is 12 percent, both projects would be accepted by this criterion.

Another way to think about the IRR can be seen by going back to the present value profile in Figure 8.2. The point where the present value profile intersects the horizontal axis is the internal rate of return on a project. Hence, one way to determine the IRR on a project, at least approximately, is to construct a present value profile. As shown in Figure 8.2, the profile line intersects the horizontal axis at 17 percent. So with either the graphic or the more precise numerical method, the IRR for project A is 17 percent.

Which Is Best: NPV or IRR?

Both net present value and internal rate of return are consistent with our objective of maximizing the value of the firm. Projects with NPVs greater than zero or IRRs greater than the hurdle rate add to the value of the firm. If a project has a negative NPV, or if the IRR is less than the hurdle rate, acceptance would lead to a reduction in the value of the firm.

The IRR tends to be widely employed in practice, presumably because it is easier to understand. For example, an NPV of $25.34 does not have the same intuitive appeal of an IRR of 16.5 percent. However, most experts, when asked which is best, would choose net present value. To understand why this is so, it is necessary to consider two additional topics—multiple internal rates of return and ranking problems.

Multiple Internal Rates of Return

One problem that occasionally occurs when the IRR is calculated is that there may be more than one return. *Multiple internal rates of return* may occur when a nonsimple cash flow series occurs. A *simple cash flow* sequence is one in which there is an initial investment (which is negative) followed by a series of positive cash inflows:

Since there is only one change of sign, from negative to positive, there can be only one IRR.[7] However, a *nonsimple cash flow* series has more than one change in the cash flow sign:

---

[6] The yield to maturity (YTM) on a bond calculated in Chapter 6 is also an internal rate of return.

[7] Mathematically this is a result of Descartes' rule of signs, which implies that every time the sign of the cash flows change, there will be a maximum of one real new root.

Table 8.5   Calculation of the Internal Rate of Return for Projects A and B

Since both projects have internal rates of return that exceed the hurdle rate of 12 percent, both would be selected.

Cash Flow Streams

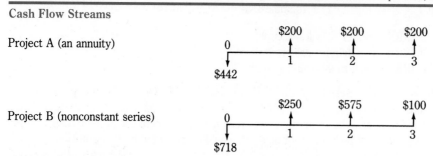

Project A (an annuity)

Project B (nonconstant series)

Internal Rate of Return

Project A

Step 1   Divide the initial CF by the annual operating CF to determine a PVA factor: $442/$200 = 2.210.

Step 2   Find the closest PVA factor from the row appropriate to the number of years from Table F.4. In the 3-year row the closest PVA factor is exactly 2.210 at 17 percent. Hence, the IRR is 17 percent.*

Project B

Step 1   Calculate the average annual operating CF to get a "simulated" annuity.† ($250 + $575 + $100)/3 = $308.33 ≈ $310.

Step 2   Divide the initial CF by the simulated annuity to determine a PVA factor: $718/$310 = 2.316.

Step 3   Find the closest PVA from the row appropriate to the number of years from Table F.4. This is an "approximate" IRR which provides a starting point for further analysis. The closest 3-year PVA factor is 2.322 at 14 percent so the IRR is approximately 14 percent.

Step 4   Use the discount rate from step 3 as a starting point. The present value of the cash inflows is determined using PV factors from Table F.3. If this present value is greater than CF_0, raise the discount rate; if it is less than CF_0, lower the rate.

Year	CF	PV at 14%	Present Value
1	$250	0.877	$219.25
2	575	0.769	442.18
3	100	0.675	67.50
			$728.93

Since the present value of the inflows at 14 percent is greater than the initial investment of $718, raise the discount rate to 15 percent.

Year	CF	PV at 15%	Present Value
1	$250	0.870	$217.50
2	575	0.756	434.70
3	100	0.658	65.80
			$718.00

Since this present value of the cash inflows exactly equals the initial investment, the IRR is 15 percent.*

---

* If the value falls between two factors, eyeballing will be needed.

† This approach is unnecessary if you have a financial calculator. For those without such a calculator, the simulated annuity approach generally saves time by providing an approximate IRR that serves as a starting point for the final calculations.

In this case, there are three changes in sign, and there may be [...] of return. None is meaningful for decision making. Graphically, [...] of this three-sign-change multiple-IRR problem might appear [...]

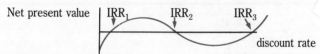

Under circumstances such as these, the IRR criterion is inappropriate for [...] making, and the net present value approach should be used.

Ranking Problems

The net present value and internal rate of return always make the same accept–reject decision for independent projects.[9] They can be used interchangeably. However, when two (or more) mutually exclusive projects are considered, the firm can select only one. That one should be the project that contributes most to the value of the firm. Unfortunately, the IRR and NPV methods do not always provide consistent rankings of which of a group of mutually exclusive projects is "better." Consider two projects, F and G, with cash flows as follows:

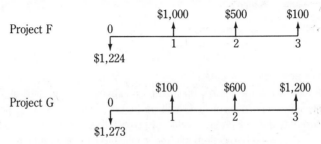

The net present values for these two projects at 11 percent are $156.10 for project F and $181.50 for project G. According to the NPV criterion, we should select project G. But the internal rate of return for project F is 21 percent, whereas it is 17 percent for project G. According to the IRR criterion, we should select project F. Obviously, a conflict exists.

We can calculate the net present values at various discount rates, as follows:

Discount Rate	Project F	Project G
0%	$376.00	$627.00
5	267.90	403.20
10	173.10	214.70
15	89.80	57.20
20	13.90	−78.50
25	−52.80	−194.60

[8] The present value profile could have other shapes and still be consistent with three sign changes. For example, the profile could be just the opposite and still have three intersections with the discount rate line. Alternatively, it could also be tangent to (or just touch) the discount rate line and then go back up (down). Finally, it could turn back up (down) before reaching the discount rate line, in which case the roots are imaginary.

[9] Excluding the possibility of multiple internal rates of return.

Figure 8.3 Conflicting Rankings Between Net Present Value and Internal Rate of Return

According to NPV you would select project G; however, project F has a higher IRR.

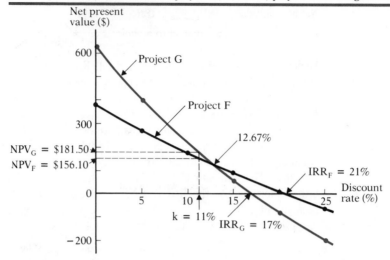

We now have the data necessary to plot their present value profiles in Figure 8.3. As shown in the figure, up to the crossover discount rate of 12.67 percent, the net present value of project G will be higher than the NPV of project F. Above 12.67 percent, the net present value of project F is greater than that of project G.

There are two conditions under which conflicting rankings can occur with mutually exclusive projects:

1. When the size of the initial investment for one project is considerably different from the initial investment for the other.
2. When the timing of the two projects' cash inflows differ significantly.

Looking at the cash flow streams for projects F and G, we see that the timing of their cash inflows differs significantly.

The ultimate factor that causes the difference in rankings is due to implicit reinvestment rate assumptions incorporated into both the NPV and the IRR formulas. The NPV method assumes that intermediate cash flows (those from years 1 and 2 for projects F and G) are reinvested at a rate equal to the required rate of return. In our example the implicit reinvestment rate for the NPV method is 11 percent for both projects. The IRR method assumes these same intermediate cash flows can be reinvested at the projects' internal rate of return. Under the IRR method, the implicit reinvestment rate assumption is 21 percent for project F and 17 percent for project G.

Which reinvestment rate assumption is better—the required rate of return in the NPV approach, or the project's IRR in the internal rate of return method? Most would argue for the required rate of return, since (1) it is a market-based rate that is the same across all projects of similar risk; (2) any project that returns more than it costs is contributing to the maximization of the value of the firm; and (3) it allows us to maximize dollars, not percents.

Reconciliation of IRR and NPV[10]

From the previous example we see that choosing the mutually exclusive project with the higher IRR may lead to a choice that is inconsistent with the NPV criterion. Now we will show how to use the IRR method properly, so that the selection from both criteria is the same.

The IRR method will rank mutually exclusive projects such as F and G in the same order as the NPV method if we apply the *incremental IRR approach*. This approach is used to make choices between two projects by carrying out the following steps:

STEP 1: Calculate the IRR for both of the projects under consideration. Using projects F and G, this is 21 percent and 17 percent, respectively.

STEP 2: Select the project with the higher IRR and compare it to the required rate of return, k. If the project's IRR is less than k, both projects are rejected. If the project's IRR is greater than k, the project is set up as the "defender." In our example, the IRR for project F is 21 percent, and this is greater than the required rate of return of 11 percent. Therefore, F is our defender.

STEP 3: Calculate the incremental cash flows of the "challenger," project G, over the defender. The incremental cash flows in our example are:

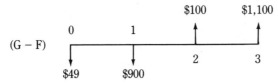

STEP 4: Calculate the IRR for these incremental cash flows. In our example the IRR for (G − F) is 12.67 percent.[11]

STEP 5: Compare the IRR for the incremental cash flows to the required return, k. If it is less than k, the defender should be chosen; if it is greater than k, the challenger should be chosen. In our example, the IRR of 12.67 percent is greater than 11 percent; therefore, project G, the challenger, should be picked. This is the same choice that the NPV provides.

This five-step procedure has reconciled the IRR and NPV methodologies. It shows us how we can properly apply the IRR methodology to mutually exclusive projects. In effect the procedure has broken project G into two parts. One is equivalent to project F and has an IRR of 21 percent, and the other is project (G − F) with an IRR of 12.67 percent. Thus, the firm has undertaken a package of projects, consisting of F and (G − F), that provides the highest total NPV of the two projects under consideration.

---

[10] This section may be omitted without loss of continuity.

[11] Note that the IRR for (G − F) of 12.67 percent is the same as the crossover rate of return in Figure 8.3. This is because the crossover rate of return, known as the Fisher rate, is the rate of return that makes the NPV of the two projects equal to each other. Thus, this must be the same rate of return that makes the NPV of the difference between the projects equal to zero.

Toddler University

In just 4 years a new children's footwear manufacturer, Toddler University, grew from a shoestring operation to estimated 1988 sales of $25 million.[1] One of the keys to their success is they have designed a radically new shoe. For children's shoes there typically are 11 sizes and 5 widths, so retailers needed to stock 55 pairs of shoes. However, Toddler's shoes are designed so that a removable insert can be used to adjust the width. By patenting a shoe with 5 inserts for width Toddler has reduced the inventory problem from 55 sizes to 11 sizes. In addition, their design, which features soft-stitched and built-to-last rubber toes and heels, enables them to sell the shoes at a much higher price than ordinary children's shoes.

The design by itself didn't solve the problem, because once sales started to move, Toddler needed to find equity financing. They secured more than $13 million from investors including the following:

Toddler U's Biggest Equity Investors	Millions of Dollars
Marketing Corporation of America	5.4
Harvard University	3.5
Morgan Stanley	1.5
Rouse Company	1.0

Finally, they had delivery problems. With a prod from investors, Toddler in 1987 hired a new president. Deliveries started improving dramatically and a good measure of financial know-how was brought to the company.

Small businesses can succeed, but it takes a combination of quality product, adequate financing, and effective management to bring the whole thing off. Toddler is an example of some of the issues that face small businesses if they're to succeed.

[1] "At Toddler University, the Chairman Is Getting A's." *Business Week* (January 16, 1989).

This procedure has been applied to projects with timing differences in their cash inflows; however, it can be applied equally well to projects that differ significantly in initial investment. In such a case, step 2 is replaced by setting up the lower costing project as the defender. The other steps are followed as outlined. In either case this procedure can be applied to many mutually exclusive projects by considering them two at a time.

An Expansion Project Example

To refine our understanding of the capital budgeting process, let us consider an expansion project. Ideal Industries is contemplating the purchase of some special equipment with a total cost of $120,000 to increase the efficiency of its production force. It will be depreciated via ACRS to zero over its 3-year normal recovery period. However, Ideal estimates it will have a resale value of $15,000 in 3 years. The cash inflows and cash outflows are $75,000 and $20,000 per year, respectively. The firm's marginal tax rate is 30 percent, and the market-based required rate of return is 14 percent. The first step is to calculate the depreciation schedule as follows:

Year	Original Cost	×	Simplified ACRS Factors	=	Depreciation
1	$120,000		0.33		$39,600
2	120,000		0.44		52,800
3	120,000		0.23		27,600

Then the initial, operating, and terminal cash flows can be calculated, as shown in Table 8.6. The initial outflow is $120,000. Then the operating cash flows of $50,380,

Table 8.6 Calculation of the After-Tax Cash Flow Stream and Net Present Value for an Expansion Project

Although the NPV method was employed, the IRR approach could have been used. With an IRR of 16.25 percent (via financial calculator) and a hurdle rate of 14 percent, the decision remains the same. All these calculations assume the firm is profitable.

Initial Investment
Cost of special equipment, $CF_0 = \$120,000$

Operating Cash Flows

Year	Cash Inflows	−	Cash Outflows	=	CFBT	$CFBT \times (1 - T)^*$	+	Dep(T)	=	CF
1	$75,000		$20,000		$55,000	$38,500		$11,880		$50,380
2	75,000		20,000		55,000	38,500		15,840		54,340
3	75,000		20,000		55,000	38,500		8,280		46,780

Terminal Cash Flow

Estimated resale value	$15,000
Less: Tax on sale	4,500
Net terminal cash inflow	$10,500

Cash Flow Stream

$46,780
+10,500
$50,380 $54,340   =$57,280

```
0        1        2        3
|_____|_____|_____|
|        ↑        ↑        ↑
$120,000
```

Net Present Value

$$NPV = \$50,380(PV_{14\%, 1yr}) + \$54,340(PV_{14\%, 2yr}) + \$57,280(PV_{14\%, 3yr}) - \$120,000$$

$$= \$50,380(0.877) + \$54,340(0.769) + \$57,280(0.675) - \$120,000 = \$4,634$$

* The tax rate is 30 percent.

$54,340, and $46,780 are calculated, as shown. Finally, the terminal cash inflow is calculated. Since all equipment is depreciated to zero for tax purposes and the estimated resale value in 3 years is $15,000, Ideal must pay taxes on the $15,000. At a rate of 30 percent the taxes are $4,500, resulting in a net terminal cash inflow of $10,500. This $10,500 is added to the third year's operating cash inflow of $46,780 to produce a total cash flow of $57,280 in the third year.

Finally, the net present value is calculated: It is $4,634. Ideal Industries should proceed with the acquisition of the special equipment, since the NPV is greater than zero. By doing so it is contributing to an increase in the value of the firm.

What Leads to Positive NPVs?

We have concluded that long-term investments having a positive net present value should be accepted. By doing so, the firm is maximizing its value. But what are the characteristics of projects with positive net present values?

Think back to our discussion (in Chapters 1, 2, and 7) of market efficiency, risk, and required return for financial assets such as stocks and bonds. Look again at some of our results:

1. The market for stocks and bonds is reasonably efficient.
2. In efficient markets, securities are fairly priced based on their risk and return, so the expected and required rates of return are equal and thus are in equilibrium.
3. If they get out of equilibrium, market forces (due to investors buying and selling securities) will drive the expected and required returns back together.

We can now see that our earlier discussion was based implicitly on the following idea: The NPV from investing in a stock or a bond is equal to zero. Stated another way, the actual market price and the theoretical market price are equal. We thus assume that, in general, no excess risk-adjusted returns are available in the financial markets.

Now carry these same general ideas over to capital budgeting decisions. If the product and labor markets are efficient and perfect, competition will quickly bid prices down or costs up to a level where the NPVs are equal to zero. That is, competitors will continue to enter the market until prices allow no more than the minimum acceptable return on capital, k. Hence, for a capital budgeting project to have a positive net present value, one of two situations must exist:

1. There are imperfections in the product and labor markets.
2. We have estimated the data incorrectly—overstating the magnitude or timing of the cash inflows, understating the outflows, or employing too low a discount rate.

Let's examine these items one by one. First, while financial markets are reasonably competitive and efficient, there is evidence that the labor and product markets are not. Less efficient product and labor markets may result from numerous causes—

unique advantages in quality or cost (perhaps due in part to the special ;
the firm's management and employees, or using nonunion employees), a
imposed barriers to competition (such as patents). Other possible source
consistent technological leadership, economies of scale that provide a c
cost advantage, an established distribution and marketing system, or brand loyalty
and trusted product warranties. All these barriers serve to accomplish one important
goal—they delay the effective response of competitors and provide opportunities
for firms to capture positive net present values before they erode away. But unless
there are legal or other effective barriers to entry, others will become aware of the
excess return (evidenced by positive NPVs) and devote the resources necessary to
become effective competitors. Hence, effective capital budgeting procedures must
(1) recognize the limited life potential of virtually all projects for producing positive
NPVs and (2) include an analysis of market imperfections, unique capabilities of the
firm, and barriers to entry that form the keystone of positive NPV projects.

The second possible reason for positive NPVs is due to estimation problems.
Several studies, along with discussion with a number of managers, suggests that in
practice we tend to be overly optimistic in formulating cash flow and risk estimates.
Depending on the approach taken, this tendency can be traced to many different
factors—such as the inherent optimism of managers, statistical problems, peer pressure, or ineffective performance and measurement systems. Whatever the cause,
the result is that the input data used in the capital budgeting process may be deficient.
The old saying "garbage in, garbage out" is clearly applicable to the capital budgeting
process. No matter how sophisticated the selection technique, if the estimated cash
flows or discount rate are incorrectly specified, the resulting net present value will
also be incorrect.

Other Capital Budgeting Issues

Thus far we have examined the basic procedures by which most medium and large
firms make capital investment decisions. We have examined how cash flows should
be estimated and what selection technique to employ, and we have considered how
positive NPVs arise. However, capital budgeting is a complex subject. Among other
important issues are these:

1. REPLACEMENT DECISIONS. In this chapter we considered a firm's decision to expand. However, additional problems, particularly with cash flow estimation, must
   be considered when assets that are already owned are replaced. Replacement
   decisions, along with unequal lives and interrelated projects, are discussed in
   Chapter 9.
2. INFLATION AND DISINFLATION. As discussed in Chapter 9, inflation can affect both
   the cash flows and the discount rate employed.
3. ABANDONMENT. Firms not only acquire assets, they must also abandon them.
   This topic is considered in Chapter 9.
4. CAPITAL RATIONING. Many firms and divisions have only a fixed amount of capital
   to allocate to capital projects during a given time period. It is conceivable a firm

may end up with positive NPV projects that have to be bypassed, or at least deferred. This topic is also discussed in Chapter 9.

5. PROJECT OR DIVISIONAL RISK. Thus far we have assumed that all projects are equally risky. That is not always the case, as we see in Chapters 10 and 14.

6. OPTIONS EMBEDDED IN CAPITAL PROJECTS. Many capital projects also contain an option that allows—but does not require—the firm to take some action. This exciting, but complex, topic is examined in Chapter 11.

7. REQUIRED RETURN, OR COST OF CAPITAL. In decision making using NPV, the market-determined cost of capital is the required rate of return for projects of average risk; in the IRR approach it is the hurdle rate the project must clear. The significance of the required return, or cost of capital, and methods for estimating it are discussed in Chapter 14.

8. INTERRELATIONSHIPS BETWEEN THE SIZE OF THE CAPITAL BUDGET AND THE REQUIRED RETURN. Up to now we have assumed that these two figures are independent. Some circumstances in which they are interrelated are discussed in Chapter 14.

Summary

The analysis of proposed capital expenditures is one of the most important topics in financial management. The capital budgeting process has four phases: (1) search and identification; (2) estimating the magnitude, timing, and riskiness of cash flows; (3) selection or rejection; and (4) control and postcompletion audit. Our attention has focused on the second and third phases, but the importance of the other two cannot be overemphasized.

In this chapter we examined expansion projects, where a firm is investing in new assets and expanding into new products or markets. Managers must estimate after-tax cash flows using ACRS depreciation and be aware of important tax ideas. The cash flow stream is broken into three segments—initial investment, operating cash flows, and the terminal cash flow.

Techniques relying on the net present value (NPV) or the internal rate of return (IRR) provide results consistent with the objective of maximizing the value of the firm. Managers using either technique will be led to the same accept or reject decision. The two methods may rank mutually exclusive projects differently, however, because they implicitly assume different reinvestment rates. Because of the possibility of multiple internal rates of return, and ranking problems, most experts favor the NPV criterion. Positive NPVs arise from inefficiencies in the product and labor markets, or inaccurate cash flow or risk forecasts.

The capital budgeting process forces managers to ask relevant questions concerning the magnitude, timing, and riskiness of cash flows. Without an effective capital budgeting process it is difficult to consistently make decisions that maximize the value of the firm.

There is an appendix to this chapter, "Appendix 8A: Important Depreciation and Tax Ideas," at the back of the book.

Questions

8.1 Define or explain the following:

a.	Capital budget	o.	Depreciable life
b.	Capital budgeting	p.	Economic life
c.	Expansion project	q.	Opportunity cost
d.	Replacement project	r.	Payback period
e.	Regulatory project	s.	Present value profile
f.	Mutually exclusive projects	t.	Internal rate of return (IRR)
g.	Independent projects	u.	Multiple internal rates of return
h.	Net present value (NPV)	v.	Simple cash flow
i.	Capital budgeting process	w.	Nonsimple cash flow
j.	Hurdle rate	x.	Incremental IRR approach
k.	Initial investment	y.	Accelerated Cost Recovery System (ACRS)
l.	Operating cash flows	z.	Normal recovery period
m.	Terminal cash flow	aa.	Investment tax credit (ITC)
n.	Net working capital		

8.2 Eddie does not understand how security valuation and capital budgeting are (a) similar and (b) related. Explain it to him.

8.3 A firm is considering the construction of two projects. Project A is a new receiving dock for supply trucks. Project B is a rail car receiving dock that will accept supplies by rail. Are projects A and B (a) mutually exclusive, (b) independent, or (c) interdependent? Why?

8.4 Trace the important relationships between the four phases of the capital budgeting process. Irrespective of Figure 8.1, indicate how all four phases could be related to one another.

8.5 Explain the differences between the initial investment, operating cash flows, and the terminal cash flow.

8.6 Explain the idea of opportunity costs. How do they relate to the notion of the operating CF stream?

8.7 The three decision criteria examined in this chapter were (a) payback period, (b) net present value, and (c) internal rate of return. Why are the NPV and IRR methods appropriate techniques, whereas the payback period is not?

8.8 What does it mean when the NPV is zero? What decision should be made? What is the IRR when the NPV is zero?

8.9 What causes the internal rate of return occasionally to have multiple rates? Are any of these rates useful for decision making?

8.10 Under what conditions do the NPV and IRR methods provide different rankings? Explain the cause of the difference between the two.

8.11 How are positive NPVs, the product and labor markets, and good data related?

Self-Test Problems   (Solutions appear on pages 720–722.)

IRR and NPV   ST 8.1   Each of two mutually exclusive projects involves an investment of $120,000. The estimated CFs are as follows:

Year	X	Y
1	$70,000	$10,000
2	40,000	20,000
3	30,000	30,000
4	10,000	50,000
5	10,000	90,000

The firm's required rate of return is 11 percent. Calculate the NPV and IRR for both projects. Which project should be chosen? Why?

CFs and NPV

ST 8.2 Norris Electronics is a manufacturer of electronic devices. Sales have recently been lost because of the inability to store sufficient finished goods inventory, even though Norris has the capability of increasing production. The solution under discussion is to increase production to create a larger finished goods inventory so that lost sales will not occur in the future. To increase the inventory, Norris estimates the following will be required:

1. The finished goods inventory needs to be expanded by $150,000.
2. Existing vacant warehouse space is available for storing the additional inventory. However, new equipment costing $80,000 with a 5-year normal recovery period is required. Straight-line depreciation will be employed, and Norris's marginal tax rate is 40 percent. Additional wages will be $40,000 per year.
3. The sales and production people estimate that the increased sales will result in a net cash inflow to the firm (after all production costs, but before considering the additional warehouse expense and taxes) of $100,000 per year.
4. In 5 years the equipment will have a resale value of zero. The $150,000 buildup in inventory can be liquidated at that time.

   a. If the required rate of return is 13 percent, should the expansion take place?
   b. What decision should be made if everything remains the same as in (a), except that warehouse space is currently rented out for $50,000 (before taxes) per year?

Problems

Initial Investment

8.1 Western, Inc., is preparing for an expansion of its accounts receivable and credit department. The present level of accounts receivable is $800,000; the proposed level is $1,300,000. New equipment costing $900,000 will be purchased. Additional before-tax cash outlays include $50,000 freight and installation and $20,000 for retraining of employees. (*Note:* Both cash outflows occur at the present, but they are tax deductible.) If Western's marginal tax rate is 40 percent, what is the initial investment?

Overhead and Opportunity Costs

8.2 Roberts Stores is considering opening a new store in Seattle. Gross cash inflows are expected to be $1,000,000 per year, and cash outflows are predicted to be $800,000 per year. In addition, Roberts' cost accounting department estimates that overhead costs of $75,000 per year should be charged to the new store. These costs include the store's share of the firm's management salaries, general administrative expenses, and so forth. Finally, the new store is expected to reduce CFBTs by $50,000 per year from one of the firm's existing stores. Roberts' marginal tax rate is 30 percent. (*Note:* For simplicity, ignore any impact of depreciation.)

   a. If all the overhead consists of fixed costs that will be incurred whether or not the new store is opened, what is the relevant operating CF?
   b. What if $50,000 of the overhead consists of variable costs related to the new store, and $25,000 consists of fixed overhead costs? What is the relevant operating CF now?

Relevant Cash Flows

8.3 A firm is considering an investment requiring the purchase of a machine that will cost $800,000 and be depreciated via straight-line depreciation over its 5-year normal recovery period. The firm's marginal tax rate is 35 percent. The cash inflows expected over the 5-year life of the project are $240,000 per year, cash expenses are $80,000 per year, and the reduction in the before-tax cash inflows from other machines currently owned will be $20,000 per year if this new machine is purchased. Finally, the new machine will require a one-time increase in accounts receivable of $15,000, and in inventory of $25,000. At the end of 5 years the machine will be worthless, and the firm will not replace it because it will be emphasizing other products by then. What is the relevant CF stream?

Payback Versus NPV

8.4 Cash flow streams for two mutually exclusive projects are given below.

After-Tax Cash Inflows

Year	Project A	Project B
1	$300	$600
2	400	200
3	50	100
4	50	700

Project A requires an initial investment of $600, and project B requires a $1,000 initial investment.

a. Use the payback period to determine which project should be selected.
b. If the required rate of return is 8 percent, determine the net present value for both projects.
c. Which project should be chosen? What are the drawbacks of the payback period method?

Unequal Depreciable Versus Economic Life

8.5 Metropolitan Hospital is a private hospital that has an opportunity to purchase a generator. The generator costs $98,000 and will be depreciated to zero under straight-line depreciation over its 7-year normal recovery period. The tax rate is 30 percent, and the cash flows before taxes over its 9-year economic life follow:

$$CF = CFBT(1-T) + Dep(T)$$

	Years				
	1	**2**	**3**	**4–5**	**6–9**
CFBT	$10,000	$12,000	$16,000	$20,000 each	$30,000 each

If the required rate of return is 17 percent, should the generator be purchased?

Opportunity Costs

8.6 CG Fashions is contemplating bringing out a new line of sweaters to add to its existing lines. The projected initial investment is $100,000, CF is expected to be $40,000 per year for each of 5 years, and the required rate of return is 15 percent.

a. Should the new line of sweaters be produced?
b. What happens if you discover that introducing the new line of sweaters will reduce CFs from existing sweater lines by $12,000 per year?
c. Why must the possibility of opportunity costs always be considered when the cash flow stream is being estimated?

Present Value Profile

8.7 Trennepohl Production is contemplating the acquisition of a new multiperson word processing system for $90,000. The system has a 5-year normal recovery period and will be depreciated via straight-line depreciation to zero. The corporate tax rate is 35 percent, cash inflows are estimated to be $56,000 per year for each of 5 years, and cash outflows are $26,000 per year for 5 years.

a. What is the net present value of the system if the discount rate is 0, 5, 10, 15, or 20 percent?
b. Graph the project's present value profile. What is the project's approximate IRR?

8.8 The initial cash outlay for a machine is $300,000. Its life is 5 years; ACRS depreciation will be used; it has no anticipated resale value in 5 years; and the marginal tax rate is 40 percent. If the operating cash flows before-tax (CFBT) are $110,000, each year, what is the project's internal rate of return (IRR)?

8.9 Projects A and B both require a $20,000 initial investment and have projected cash inflows as follows:

After-Tax Cash Inflows

Year	Project A	Project B
1	$10,000	$7,000
2	8,000	7,000
3	6,000	7,000
4	4,000	7,000

a. Calculate each project's net present value if the required rate of return is 12 percent.
b. Calculate the internal rate of return for each project.
c. Should either project be rejected if they are independent?
d. Which project should be selected if they are mutually exclusive?

8.10 A mining company can open a new strip mine for an initial investment of $24 million (at t = 0). In year 1, the mine produces a net cash inflow of $78 million. In year 2, the land must be returned to its original state, which requires an outflow of $60 million.

a. Find the net present values not calculated below.

Rate (%)	NPV (millions)
0	$_____
25	_____
50	_____
75	0.980
100	0
125	−1.185

b. Construct a present value profile with the data from (a).
c. Should the mine be built if the firm's required rate of return is 20 percent?

8.11 Richardson Home Products is analyzing two mutually exclusive projects. Both require an initial investment of $65,000 and provide cash inflows as follows:

After-Tax Cash Inflows

Year	Project C	Project D
1	$40,000	0
2	30,000	0
3	20,000	$104,200

a. If the required rate of return is 10 percent, which project would Richardson choose if NPV is employed?
b. Calculate the internal rate of return for both projects. Which project should be selected according to IRR? Why does the difference in rankings occur?

(Do only if using Pinches Disk.)
c. Now assume the required rate of return increases to 14 percent. Plot the present value profiles. Is there still a conflict in rankings? What are the crossover IRR and NPV values?
d. Recalculate (a), (b), and (c), except now the initial investment for project C is $70,000

and for project D $75,000. Has this caused any change in the rankings? Have the crossover IRR and NPV values been affected? Why or why not?

X **e.** Finally, recalculate (d), except now in years 4 and 5 project C has equal cash flows of $5,000 per year and project D has equal cash flows of $8,000 per year. How has this affected the rankings of the projects?

Conflicting Rankings:
Crossover Discount
Rate

8.12 Miles Equipment is considering two mutually exclusive projects, each with a 5-year life. Project P requires an initial cash outlay (CF_0) of $20,000 and has CFs of $6,540.22 for each of 5 years. Project Q has an initial investment of $100,000 and CFs of $29,832.94 for each of 5 years.

a. Calculate the IRR for each project and select the preferred project.

b. Assuming the projects are of equal risk, and the required rate of return is 13 percent, which project is preferable? Defend your decision.

c. At what specific discount rate would the firm be indifferent between the two projects?

Incremental IRR

X **8.13** Two mutually exclusive projects have after-tax cash flows as follows:

	Project X	Project Y
t_0	−$50	−$30
t_1	15	35
t_2	85	15

a. If the discount rate is 10 percent, what are the NPVs for the two projects? Their IRRs? Which project should be chosen?

b. Using the incremental IRR approach, determine which project should be chosen.

c. Why does the incremental IRR approach provide the same ranking as NPV for mutually exclusive projects?

Expansion

X **8.14** New equipment that has a 5-year life costs $40,000. Freight is $1,000, and site preparation costs are $5,000. Both the freight and site preparation costs occur at t_0, but they are tax deductible. Cash inflows are $23,000 per year for each of 5 years, and cash outflows are $6,000 per year. Straight-line depreciation (based on the cost of $40,000) to a value of zero in 5 years will be employed. However, in 5 years it is estimated that the equipment can be sold for $10,000, less $2,000 in dismantling costs. (*Note:* Take the tax on the $8,000, since the dismantling costs are tax deductible.) The firm's tax rate is 30 percent, and the required rate of return is 15 percent. Should the equipment be acquired?

Expansion: ACRS
Depreciation

8.15 Kelm, Inc., has a proposed project for $200,000 of research and development equipment that falls under the 3-year category. ACRS depreciation will be employed, and a $40,000 addition to net working capital will be required. The estimated benefits, CFBT, are $90,000 per year for each of 3 years; the equipment has an estimated resale value of $50,000 in 3 years; the firm's tax rate is 35 percent; and Kelm estimates that a 20 percent return is required for this project. Should the new equipment be acquired?

Expansion: Longer

8.16 Dyl Fabrication is considering converting a warehouse to enable the firm to increase production. The renovation will require the purchase of $4,200,000 worth of equipment. The equipment will be depreciated over 7 years via the straight-line method. The warehouse is presently being rented out for $150,000 per year.

The converted facility has an expected economic life of 12 years with no resale value. Because of the increased production capacity, Dyl expects additional cash inflows (before taxes) of $3,000,000 in year 1, and these are expected to increase by 5 percent *per year* thereafter. Fixed operating costs (cash outflows before taxes) are $100,000 per year, and variable cash outflows before taxes are 50 percent of expected cash inflows. If the marginal tax rate is 40 percent and the required rate of return is 20 percent, should the warehouse be renovated? (*Note:* Round all figures to the nearest dollar.)

References

For general information on capital budgeting, see, for example, the following material

BIERMAN, HAROLD, JR., AND SEYMOUR SMIDT. *The Capital Budgeting Decision.* 7th ed. New York: Macmillan, 1988.

GORDON, LAWRENCE A., AND GEORGE E. PINCHES. *Improving Capital Budgeting: A Decision Support System Approach.* Reading, Mass.: Addison-Wesley, 1984.

PINCHES, GEORGE E. "Myopia, Capital Budgeting and Decision Making." *Financial Management* 11 (Autumn 1982), pp. 6–19.

Some current articles on relevant topics include these

DORFMAN, ROBERT. "The Meaning of Internal Rates of Return." *Journal of Finance* 36 (December 1981), pp. 1011–1021.

MILLER, EDWARD M., "The Competitive Market Assumption and Capital Budgeting Criteria." *Financial Management* 16 (Winter 1987), pp. 22–28.

NARAYANAN, M. P. "Observability and the Payback Criterion." *Journal of Business* 58 (July 1985), pp. 309–323.

POHLMAN, RANDOLPH A., EMMANUEL S. SANTIAGO, AND F. LYNN MARKEL. "Cash Flow Estimation Practices of Large Firms." *Financial Management* 17 (Summer 1988), pp. 71–79.

PRUITT, STEPHEN W., AND LAWRENCE J. GITMAN. "Capital Budgeting Forecast Biases: Evidence from the Fortune 500." *Financial Management* 16 (Spring 1987), pp. 46–51.

Two studies on the impact of capital budgeting on a firm's market value are these

HAKA, SUSAN F., LAWRENCE A. GORDON, AND GEORGE E. PINCHES. "Sophisticated Capital Budgeting Selection Techniques and Firm Performance." *Accounting Review* 60 (October 1985), pp. 651–669.

MCCONNELL, JOHN J., AND CHRIS J. MUSCARELLA. "Corporate Capital Expenditure Decisions and the Market Value of the Firm." *Journal of Financial Economics* 14 (September 1985), pp. 399–422.

See Model nine (and Lesson four) in *Lotus 1–2–3 ® for Financial Management* by Pinches and Courtney for a template that performs capital budgeting calculations.

9 Replacement Decisions, Cash Flows, and Capital Rationing

Overview

- For replacement decisions, the proper cash flows are the incremental (new minus old) CFs.

- For interrelated projects, the after-tax cash flow stream and NPV of all possible combinations must be considered. Unequal lives are a factor only for mutually exclusive projects.

- Proper decision making requires that inflation or disinflation and abandonment, but not financing costs, be considered in the after-tax CF stream.

- Under capital rationing, the firm should select the set of positive NPV projects that maximizes total NPV and stays within the budget constraint.

Firms do not make capital investments just to expand into new product and market areas. They also replace existing assets. Routine replacements that occur as machines wear out are capital investments. So are significant technologically driven decisions to improve a firm's competitive position. Recently, Timken invested $500 million to build a superclean steel mill. Timken needed better-quality steel for its tapered roller bearings—the antifriction devices it invented—if it was to ward off Japanese competitors. Timken made that investment while experiencing one of its worst periods ever, but the alternative was to lose an increasingly large portion of its business to the Japanese.

In Chapter 8 we ignored an important fact of life that must be considered when making capital investment decisions: inflation or disinflation. Either can have a major impact on the ultimate benefits of investment decisions. Look at the oil and oil services industries. Many of these firms undertook major acquisitions or expansions when oil prices were high. Things were fine—until prices broke. When inflation is high, many capital expenditures look desirable; but when prices cannot be raised, other strategies often come into play. As one CEO observed: "Increased productivity and new products are the key ways to keep profits up in times of disinflation. New products help market penetration. And new products generally have a higher profit margin, at least in the early growth stages before pricing becomes competitive."

In this chapter we seek to broaden our understanding of the capital budgeting process. We do this by focusing on replacement decisions, estimating cash flows, and capital rationing. We also examine interrelated projects and how and when to be concerned with projects that have unequal lives.

Replacement Decisions

Replacing assets is often necessary. Effective replacement decisions, like the decision to expand existing capacity, require understanding the capital budgeting process. Determining the cash flows for a replacement project can be especially complicated. These are *incremental cash flows*—that is, the cash flows related to the new equipment less the cash flows related to the old equipment. While the idea seems straightforward, it is fundamental to effective decision making.

Incremental Cash Flows

Consider Bits & Bytes, a computer software firm that produces a popular computer game called Spacelords. It estimated after-tax operating cash flows (CFs) over a 3-year period as follows:

Spacelords initial CF estimate

$600,000 $500,000 $300,000

       1   2   3

The estimated cash flows decline due to an anticipated increase in competition and the development of more complicated and challenging games. Bits & Bytes planned, therefore, to withdraw Spacelords from the market after 3 years.

Recently, Bruce Douglas and his associates at Bits & Bytes came up with a new computer game called Rampagers. Although similar to Spacelords, Rampagers has many features that make it more challenging. The estimated initial investment and subsequent cash inflows were estimated to be as follows:

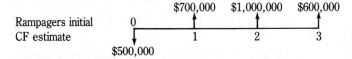

Rampagers initial CF estimate — 0 | $700,000 (1) | $1,000,000 (2) | $600,000 (3); $500,000

Given the favorable cash flow estimates,[1] Bits & Bytes developed and is now marketing Rampagers. All indications are that the projected CFs appear accurate, but a strange

[1] The IRR is 142.75 percent via financial calculator.

thing is happening—Spacelords sales have fallen off dramatically. What did Bruce and his associates forget to consider when they developed the after-tax CF estimates for Rampagers?

The answer should not surprise you. The two games have overlapping markets, with the result that the products are viewed as being partial substitutes for each other. Instead of buying Spacelords, many would-be purchasers are now acquiring Rampagers, so the cash flows from Spacelords have declined sharply. The newly revised cash flows for Spacelords are these:

Spacelords revised CF estimate

$100,000 $100,000   0

1   2   3

The problem arose because in making the initial estimate of the CFs attributed to Rampagers, Bits & Bytes did not properly evaluate the incremental cash flows. It is the incremental (denoted by a delta, Δ) cash flows that are important. The relevant incremental operating cash flow stream (ΔCF) Bits & Bytes should have considered before introducing Rampagers is calculated as follows:

	Year		
	1	2	3
Original CFs, Rampagers	$700,000	$1,000,000	$600,000
Less: Decrease in CFs, Spacelords	500,000	400,000	300,000
Incremental (Δ) operating CFs	$200,000	$ 600,000	$300,000

Based on this more complete analysis, the incremental cash flow stream for the new product should have been estimated as follows:

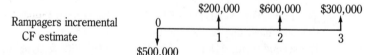

Rampagers incremental CF estimate

$200,000 $600,000 $300,000

0   1   2   3

$500,000

Even with this revised set of after-tax CFs, the IRR is over 48 percent, so Bits & Bytes should still come out ahead on its investment. But the message is clear: To make effective investment decisions, managers must focus on the incremental cash flow stream. This involves an analysis of the cash inflows and outflows related to the new investment, minus the anticipated inflows and outflows associated with an existing investment.

Often it is important to ask: "What will happen to the existing (or anticipated) cash flows if we do not make the investment?" In today's highly competitive and rapidly changing environment, managers cannot simply assume that existing cash flows will continue. Price cutting, product or marketing innovations, and the like can undermine a profitable investment. For this reason, managers need to know what to look for when calculating incremental cash flows.

Estimating Incremental Cash Flows

To calculate incremental after-tax cash flows, we proceed (as in Chapter 8) by breaking them into three parts—(1) initial investment, (2) operating cash flow, and (3) terminal cash flow. We make our capital budgeting decision by focusing on the difference between the new and the existing cash flows. Any other cash flow stream is erroneous and may lead to incorrect replacement decisions.

The Initial Investment

The incremental initial investment, ΔCF_0, is calculated as follows:

Cost of new equipment, facilities, and land purchased

All other costs related to the investment (transportation, installation, additional personnel, and so forth, net of taxes)

Additional net working capital required

Opportunity costs

minus

Funds realized from the sale of replaced assets plus tax benefit if it is expected to be sold at a loss, or minus tax liability if it is expected to be sold at a gain.[2]

As with expansion projects, we assume the initial investment occurs at time t = 0; in practice, however, it may be spread out over a number of time periods.

Operating Cash Flow

The incremental operating after-tax cash flow, ΔCF, must take into consideration the difference in the cash flows before tax (CFBT) for the new and the old projects, as well as the depreciation on both the new and old assets. To calculate the incremental operating cash flows, we have the following:

$$\text{incremental operating CF} = (CFBT_{new} - CFBT_{old})(1 - T)$$
$$+ (Dep_{new} - Dep_{old})(T)$$
$$\Delta CF = \Delta CFBT(1 - T) + \Delta Dep(T) \tag{9.1}$$

The first term, $\Delta CFBT(1 - T)$, is the change in the cash flows expected, ignoring the tax shield due to depreciation. The net effect on the tax shield is captured in the second term, $\Delta Dep(T)$. As we saw in the Bits & Bytes example, it is especially important to consider the exact nature of the cash flow before tax (CFBT) stream expected from the old (or existing) asset. Often a good deal of interchange between the marketing department, the production department, and the capital budgeting group will be required to arrive at reasonable estimates of both the new and the old CFBT streams. In addition, opportunity costs must also be taken into consideration.

Terminal Cash Flow

Finally, we need to estimate the incremental after-tax terminal cash flow that occurs in the last year of the replacement project's life. The incremental terminal after-tax cash flow, ΔCF_n, is calculated as follows:

Funds realized from the sale of the new asset plus tax benefit if it is expected to be sold at a loss, or minus tax liability if it is expected to be sold at a profit[3]

Release of net working capital (assuming the project will be terminated at time period n)

---

[2] Assuming the firm is profitable.

[3] Assuming the firm is profitable.

minus

Disposal costs for new asset (less disposal costs on old asset, if any, net of taxes)

Funds realized from the sale of the replaced asset plus tax benefit if it is expected to be sold at a loss, or minus tax liability if it is expected to be sold at a profit[4]

An Example

Consider Phoenix Industries, which is investigating replacing an existing assembly line with a new automated one. The existing assembly line was installed 3 years ago at a cost of $500,000. It is being depreciated for tax purposes via straight line to a zero value over its normal recovery period of 5 years. The straight-line depreciation is $100,000 per year, and the present depreciated book value is $200,000. Since 3 years have already elapsed, depreciation will continue for only 2 more years on the old machine. The old equipment will last 5 more years, at which time its resale value will be zero, but it could be sold now for $40,000.

The main benefit of the project would be to reduce yearly expenses from $510,000 on the existing line to $200,000 for the newer automated line. However, the new line would require a $20,000 increase in inventory. The new line would cost $1 million and be depreciated via simplified ACRS over its 5-year normal recovery period.[5] Due to increasing technological innovation, the estimated resale value of the new assembly line in 5 years is zero. Phoenix's tax rate is 40 percent, and the required rate of return for this project is 16 percent.

In solving this replacement problem, it is useful to begin by calculating the depreciation on the new assembly line equipment, less the depreciation on the old assembly line, as follows:

Year	Original Cost	×	Simplified ACRS Factors	=	New Depreciation	−	Depreciation on Old Assembly Line	=	Incremental Depreciation
1	$1,000,000		0.20		$200,000		$100,000		$100,000
2	1,000,000		0.32		320,000		100,000		220,000
3	1,000,000		0.19		190,000		0		190,000
4	1,000,000		0.15		150,000		0		150,000
5	1,000,000		0.14		140,000		0		140,000

Now we can proceed to calculate the incremental initial investment and operating cash flows. As shown in Table 9.1, the incremental initial investment is the $1 million for the new assembly line, less $40,000 to be received from selling the old assembly line, less $64,000 due to the tax consequences of selling the existing equipment at a loss. This last item arises because the old assembly line has a current depreciated book value of $200,000, but it could be sold for only $40,000, producing a $160,000 tax loss. Since the equipment was underdepreciated, we can write off the full $160,000 in the year of replacement and reduce taxes by $64,000 [i.e.,

---

[4] Assuming the firm is profitable.

[5] For simplicity, the lives of the old and new assembly lines are both 5 years. If the lives were unequal, then a modified approach, discussed later in the chapter, would need to be employed.

Table 9.1 Calculation of Incremental After-Tax Cash Flow Stream and Net Present Value for Replacement Project

Again, the internal rate of return could have been used instead of the net present value. With an IRR of 11.81 percent versus a hurdle rate of 16 percent, the decision would be to reject the proposed replacement.

Initial Investment

Cost of new assembly line	$1,000,000
Plus: Additional net working capital	20,000
Less: Sale of old assembly line	−40,000
Tax savings on sale of old assembly line*	−64,000
Incremental initial investment, $\Delta CF_0 = $	$ 916,000

Operating Cash Flows

Year	Cash Outflows (Old)	−	Cash Outflows (New)	=	Incremental CFBT	Incremental CFBT × $(1 - T)$†	+	Incremental Dep(T)†	=	Incremental CF
1	$510,000		$200,000		$310,000	$186,000		$40,000		$226,000
2	510,000		200,000		310,000	186,000		88,000		274,000
3	510,000		200,000		310,000	186,000		76,000		262,000
4	510,000		200,000		310,000	186,000		60,000		246,000
5	510,000		200,000		310,000	186,000		56,000		242,000

Terminal Cash Flow
Release of net working capital: $20,000

Incremental Cash Flow Stream

$242,000
+20,000

$226,000 $274,000 $262,000 $246,000   = $262,000

0

1   2   3   4   5

$916,000

Net Present Value

$$NPV = \$226,000(PV_{16\%,1\,yr}) + \$274,000(PV_{16\%,2\,yr}) + \$262,000(PV_{16\%,3\,yr}) + \$246,000(PV_{16\%,4\,yr})$$

$$+ \$262,000(PV_{16\%,5\,yr}) - \$916,000$$

$$= \$226,000(0.862) + \$274,000(0.743) + \$262,000(0.641) + \$246,000(0.552) + \$262,000(0.476)$$

$$- \$916,000$$

$$= \$194,812 + \$203,582 + \$167,942 + \$135,792 + \$124,712 - \$916,000 = -\$89,160$$

* (IRS depreciated book value of old asset − selling price)(tax rate), or ($200,000 − $40,000)(0.40) = $64,000.
† The tax rate is 40 percent.

($160,000) (0.40)], provided that the firm is profitable. Finally, the cost of the additional net working capital (due to the increase in inventory required) must be treated as part of the initial investment. So the net incremental investment needed to replace the existing assembly line is $916,000.

Next we calculate the incremental operating cash flows. The old assembly line had cash outflows of $510,000 a year, whereas the new one has cash outflows of $200,000 per year. The incremental savings (or $\Delta CFBT$) from the replacement is $310,000 per year. Taking this and the incremental depreciation, we can calculate

Financial Management Today

Ill-Advised Investments?

During the 1970s and early 1980s the oil industry underwent dramatic change. As oil prices rose dramatically consumption eventually fell, but profits remained high. One estimate placed the 1984 cash flows of the 10 largest oil companies at $48.5 billion, which was 28 percent of total cash flows of the top 200 firms in *Dun's Business Month*.[1] To use these extra cash flows, oil firms engaged in both diversification and a good bit of exploration and development.

In a study on capital expenditures the following was found for the 2-day (t_{-1} and t_0) announcement period.[2]

Intended Use of Funds	Announcement Period Abnormal Return
A. Budget Increases	
All budget increases	1.21%
Unspecified	1.49
General plant and equipment	1.80
Exploration and development	−0.55
B. Budget Decreases	
All budget decreases	−1.52
Unspecified	−1.72
General plant and equipment	−1.68
Exploration and development	1.49

As these data indicate, when capital expenditure increases are announced most firms experience positive returns; and when they cut back the stock price reaction is negative. However, oil and gas exploration and development announcements during the 1975–1981 period were associated with significant decreases in returns; likewise, cutbacks in exploration and development resulted in positive returns. Many, like T. Boone Pickens of Mesa Petroleum, contended it was much cheaper to buy reserves on the open market simply by acquiring another firm, instead of drilling for them. These results indicate the capital markets also viewed additional exploration and development expenditures as ill-advised.

[1] Michael C. Jensen. "Agency Costs of Free Cash Flow, Corporate Finance, and Takeovers." *American Economic Review* 76 (May 1986).
[2] John J. McConnell and Chris J. Muscarella. "Corporate Capital Expenditure Decisions and the Market Value of the Firm." *Journal of Financial Economics* 14 (September 1985).

the incremental operating cash flows, as shown in Table 9.1. Finally, the release of the $20,000 of additional net working capital is treated as a terminal cash inflow in year 5.[6] Given the incremental after-tax CF stream shown in Table 9.1 and the

[6] This assumes that the project terminates at this point in time. In reality, net working capital often is an ongoing commitment and cannot be assumed to be released.

16 percent required rate of return, the NPV is −$89,160. The decision is to reject the new line and continue to use the existing one in order to maximize the value of the firm.

Replacement decisions are an important part of the capital budgeting process. Following the steps outlined, and making sure we understand incremental cash flows, the proper decisions can be made to maintain the firm's competitive advantage and maximize its value.[7]

Interrelated Projects

In Chapter 8 we classified projects as either mutually exclusive or independent. A more accurate picture would show a continuum of relationships among projects, as in Figure 9.1. At one end stand *complementary projects.* If one of several complementary projects is undertaken, the cash flows of all related projects also increase. An example is a self-service gasoline station and a convenience store; combining both in one operation generally produces incremental business beyond the simple sum of what each would generate separately. In the extreme case, the cash flows and success or failure of the projects are so closely related that a decision has to be made to accept or reject a *systemwide project.* The entire system must be evaluated, since accepting only part of it produces nothing of value.

At the other end of the continuum are *substitute projects.* In this case acceptance of one project reduces the cash flows from another. If the effect is pronounced enough, the projects are said to be mutually exclusive; that is, accepting one precludes accepting others. A special case, lying between systemwide and mutually exclusive projects, is that of independent projects. In this case acceptance of one has no appreciable impact on the cash flows of other independent projects.

Finally, as shown in Figure 9.1, we have a broad spectrum of *interrelated projects,* where the acceptance of one project can partially affect—either positively or negatively—the cash flows of other possible projects. *The joint cash flows for two (or more) interrelated projects must be analyzed together.* Suppose Wilson Paint, which as part of its activities manufactures paint sprayers, is evaluating the desirability of producing two new models—the Quik Painter and the Quik Painter II. The firm has the choice of producing and selling either or both paint sprayers. The initial investment, cash inflows, and NPVs for both are as follows:

	Producing and Selling Only Quik Painter	Producing and Selling Only Quik Painter II	Producing and Selling Both
Initial investment	$200,000	$250,000	$400,000
After-tax cash flows for each of 10 years	50,000	60,000	70,000
Net present value at 13%	71,300	75,560	−20,180

[7] Some additional tax complications arise if presently owned equipment is traded in on new equipment. For simplicity, these complications are ignored.

Figure 9.1 Degree of Dependence Among Capital Budgeting Projects

A continuum of projects exists from those that are perfect complements to those that are perfect substitutes. Knowing the degree of dependence is necessary for effective decision making.

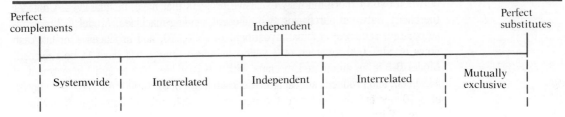

At the firm's required rate of return of 13 percent, both projects considered independently have positive net present values and should be selected.

But look what happens if Wilson decides to introduce both sprayers. Wilson's combined initial investment is slightly less than the sum of the two separate outlays, so there are some economies from producing both. The total after-tax cash flows, however, increase only slightly when both sprayers are introduced. Why? Because the two paint sprayers are really substitutes. A customer needs only one of the sprayers, and two different models provide very little in the way of incremental sales. The cash inflows are interrelated, so the total NPV from producing both paint sprayers is negative. Obviously, Wilson doesn't want to introduce both sprayers—and since the Quik Painter II has the higher NPV, it should be produced and sold.

This example suggests a basic procedure to be followed when interrelated projects exist:

1. Identify all possible combinations of interrelated projects. Assume three projects, A, B and C, are interrelated. In addition to analyzing A, B, and C separately, the combinations of (1) A and B, (2) A and C, (3) B and C, and (4) A and B and C must also be evaluated.
2. Determine the initial investment and after-tax cash flow stream for each project and combination, along with the total NPV of each project and combination.
3. Choose the individual project or combination of projects that has the highest total NPV.

One could argue that all projects within a firm are somewhat related. If this is the case, then the analysis of any project is a tremendous chore, since all possible combinations have to be considered. However, many projects are mutually exclusive, independent, or systemwide. The key, then, is to make sure that proper analysis has been done to determine the appropriate relationship, if any, between proposed capital budgeting projects. When the analysis has been done correctly, the proper projects are considered, the proper cash flows are identified, and the proper decisions will result.

Unequal Lives

In addition to considering interrelated projects, firms must often make a decision between two or more mutually exclusive projects that have unequal lives. Consider the choice between purchasing two different sanding machines. Model A-3 is semi-automated, requires an initial investment of $320,000, and produces after-tax cash flows of $160,000 for each of 3 years, at which time it will have to be replaced. Model B-6 is an automated machine with a 6-year life, has an initial investment of $420,000, and produces annual after-tax cash flows of $120,000. As Table 9.2 shows, at a 10 percent discount rate the net present value of the automated machine is greater. With an NPV of $102,600, it appears that model B-6 should be chosen.

But the net present value is a function of the life of the project. Although this does not matter when projects are independent, it does when they are mutually exclusive, and when future replacement is expected (i.e., it is *not* a one-shot investment). To make a valid comparison, it is necessary to equalize the lives of the two projects. There are a number of ways to do this. We will consider the equivalent annual NPV method.[8]

The *equivalent annual NPV* approach to the unequal life problem converts the original NPVs to yearly net present value figures. The effect is to assume the existing projects will be replicated over and over, with the result that the NPV can be stated as a yearly figure. The equivalent annual NPV is as follows:

$$\text{equivalent annual NPV} = \frac{NPV_n}{PVA_{k,n}} \tag{9.2}$$

where

NPV_n = the project's net present value over its original life
$PVA_{k,n}$ = a present value factor for an annuity based on the required rate of return and original life of the project

The equivalent annual NPVs for the two models are

Model A-3 $\qquad \dfrac{\$77,920}{PVA_{10\%,3yr}} = \dfrac{\$77,920}{2.487} = \$31,331$

Model B-6 $\qquad \dfrac{\$102,600}{PVA_{10\%,6yr}} = \dfrac{\$102,600}{4.355} = \$23,559$

Since Model A-3 has the highest equivalent annual NPV, *it contributes the most to the firm's goal of stockholder wealth maximization per year.* It should be chosen.

Three points should be stressed. First, we sometimes get the impression that different lives have to be taken into account for *all* projects. This is not true: *Unequal lives must be dealt with only for mutually exclusive projects.* For all independent projects, the NPV criterion already takes into account timing differences. By selecting indepen-

---

[8] There are two other methods. The replacement chain approach requires replicating the two projects until their lives are equal, which will occur at the least common denominator of their original lives. The second method is the infinite replication approach, which converts both projects to perpetuities. All three methods result in the same decision concerning which project should be selected.

Table 9.2 Net Present Value for Two Mutually Exclusive Projects Ignoring Their Unequal Lives

Other things being equal, Model B-6 would be chosen since it has the highest NPV. However, since NPV is a function of the life of the project, it is necessary in mutually exclusive cases to adjust for differences in lives.

Cash Flow Streams

		$160,000	$160,000	$160,000			
Model A-3	0						
		1	2	3			
	$320,000						

		$120,000	$120,000	$120,000	$120,000	$120,000	$120,000
Model B-6	0						
		1	2	3	4	5	6
	$420,000						

Net Present Value

Model A-3 NPV = $160,000(PVA$_{10\%,3\,yr}$) − $320,000

$\qquad$ = $160,000(2.487) − $320,000 = $77,920

Model B-6 NPV = $120,000(PVA$_{10\%,6\,yr}$) − $420,000

$\qquad$ = $120,000(4.355) − $420,000 = $102,600

dent projects with the largest NPV, we are making the correct decision without having to adjust for unequal lives. Second, the equivalent annual NPV approach does not allow for differing rates of inflation or disinflation and other changes (such as new technology). The best way to handle complications such as these is to build the effects of expected inflation, new technology, and so forth, into the CF estimates. Then the lives of the two projects will have to be equalized—perhaps by assuming some common termination point and considering the resale value at that point in time for each project. The NPVs for the two points can be calculated and compared.

Finally, in many unequal life cases the benefits are the same between the two projects, in that the after-tax cash inflows are the same for both. Only the cash outflows differ. In this case we can ignore the cash inflows and simply determine the equivalent annual cost of the two alternatives. Since our objective is to minimize cash outflows, we would then select the alternative with the *lowest* equivalent annual cost.

More on Cash Flow Estimation

In Chapter 8 and so far in Chapter 9 we have focused on three primary topics—the capital budgeting process, estimating the cash flows, and understanding the net present value (NPV) and internal rate of return (IRR) decision criteria. Now we need to consider (1) inflation and disinflation, (2) why financing costs are excluded, and (3) abandonment. We will conclude this section with a checklist for estimating cash flows.

Inflation and Disinflation	Often cash flows are estimated on the basis that they are not expected to change much over the life of the project. During the last few years, however, inflation and disinflation have become more important in the United States and all over the world. So we need to be sure these effects are properly accounted for in the capital budgeting process. In only one special case do the effects of inflation or disinflation cancel each other out and not affect the decision—when both the CFs and the required rate of return properly anticipate and adjust for the same percentage rate of inflation. *If this special case occurs, then inflation and disinflation do not have to be considered as a separate issue.*

A more likely occurrence, however, is for the required rate of return to reflect expected inflation or disinflation, while the cash flows do not. As we noted in Chapters 2 and 7, investors incorporate expectations of inflation into their required rates of return. Since this is so, the firm's cost of capital (which is based on the investor's required rates of return) also reflects expected inflation. But what about the estimated cash flows? If inflation is taken into account in the discount rate, but not in the after-tax CFs, the calculated NPV will be biased downward. Alternatively, if low expected inflation is reflected in the discount rate employed but a higher inflation estimate is built into the CFs, the NPV will be biased upward.

To see the importance of adjusting for inflation, consider the Sullivan Paper Company. Table 9.3 shows that the firm calculated the net present value of a proposed capital expenditure to be $2,971.50 at its required rate of return (which incorporates expected inflation) of 15 percent. The project should be selected, since it returns

Table 9.3 Cash Flows and Net Present Value for Sullivan Paper Project Without Adjusting for Inflation

The $21,000 investment was depreciated to zero over 3 years. Hence, the depreciation is $7,000 per year. The IRR for this project is 23.38 percent.

Initial Investment
$21,000

Operating Cash Flows

Year	Cash Inflows	−	Cash Outflows	= CFBT	$\text{CFBT} \times (1 - T)^*$	+ Dep(T)*	= CF
1	$20,000		$8,000	$12,000	$8,400	$2,100	$10,500
2	20,000		8,000	12,000	8,400	2,100	10,500
3	20,000		8,000	12,000	8,400	2,100	10,500

Terminal Cash Flow
None

Cash Flow Stream

```
              $10,500      $10,500      $10,500
     0           ↑            ↑            ↑
     ├───────────┼────────────┼────────────┤
     │           1            2            3
   $21,000
```

Net Present Value
NPV = $10,500($PVA_{15\%, 3\,yr}$) − $21,000 = $10,500(2.283) − $21,000 = $2,971.50

* The tax rate is 30 percent.

Table 9.4 Cash Flows and Net Present Value for Sullivan Paper Project Taking Account of Inflation

The IRR has dropped to 14.78 percent, which is less than the firm's 15 percent required rate of return.

Initial Investment
$21,000

Operating Cash Flows

Cash	Cash Inflows	−	Cash Outflows	=	CFBT	CFBT × (1 − T)*	+	Dep(T)*	=	CF
1	$20,000		$ 9,000		$11,000	$7,700		$2,100		$9,800
2	20,000		10,000		10,000	7,000		2,100		9,100
3	20,000		11,000		9,000	6,300		2,100		8,400

Terminal Cash Flow
None

Cash Flow Stream

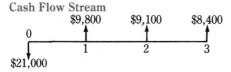

Net Present Value

$$\text{NPV} = \$9,800(\,PV_{15\%,1\,\text{yr}}\,) + \$9,100(\,PV_{15\%,2\,\text{yr}}\,) + \$8,400(\,PV_{15\%,3\,\text{yr}}\,) - \$21,000$$

$$= \$9,800(\,0.870\,) + \$9,100(\,0.756\,) + \$8,400(\,0.658\,) - \$21,000 = -\$67.20$$

* The tax rate is 30 percent.

more than the 15 percent required. But what happens if because of an increase in expected inflation not considered previously, the cash outflows are projected to increase by $1,000 per year? At the same time, due to depressed retail conditions, Sullivan does not anticipate that it can pass the increased costs on to its customers. The expected cash inflows will remain constant over the project's useful life. As Table 9.4 shows, the project's NPV is now −$67.20, which changes Sullivan's decision. Now it should reject the project.

Anticipating inflation or disinflation is not easy, but it is important if the proper capital budgeting decisions are to be made. Managers should remember the following:

1. Be consistent—make sure the inflation or disinflation consequences are built into the cash flows, since they are already incorporated in the discount rate (unless a real instead of a nominal discount rate is employed).
2. Even if cash inflows and regular cash outflows change in line with the general rate of inflation, CFs generally do not because of the tax structure. Taxes tend to increase more than proportionately as cash inflows rise. Also, inflation often requires an increased working capital investment above and beyond that required with little or no inflation.
3. Inflation is not constant across different sections of the economy. Therefore, it may *not* be reasonable to use a general price index to incorporate the effects of changing rates of inflation on expected CFs for a project.

4. Differential price changes may occur due to supply and demand considerations. These effects, which are due to factors other than the rate of inflation, can also have a significant impact on the CFs and must be taken into account.

Exclude Financing Costs

We have ignored one cash flow that a firm incurs when undertaking a capital budgeting project—the financing costs. Suppose a firm is evaluating whether to build a new plant. If the firm decides to employ debt financing, should we recognize the after-tax interest and principal repayments as ongoing cash outflows? Similarly, if equity is employed, should any costs related to it be treated as part of the ongoing cash outflow stream? *In both cases, the answer is no!* The capital budgeting decision should be separated from the financing decision.[9] The investment decision is based on the economic desirability of the project, irrespective of how it is financed; the financing costs are built into the required rate of return, as considered in Chapter 14. Should financing costs be deducted from the after-tax cash flows, they would be double-counted (once in the numerator of the NPV and again in the denominator, as part of the required rate of return, k) and the project's net present value would be underestimated.

Has Abandonment Been Considered?[10]

One of the most difficult problems in estimating cash flows is to make sure all the options are examined. Consider a manufacturing firm reevaluating an ongoing machine line. Assume the machine line has a 3-year life, and the expected after-tax cash inflows are as follows:

$30,000	$30,000	$45,000
1	2	3

Looking at this cash flow stream, we might be tempted to conclude that the machine line has a positive NPV. But what happens if you discover the machine line could be sold today for $85,000 after taxes? This $85,000 is an opportunity cost that must be considered. The choice now is between $85,000 today or the stream of expected after-tax cash flows, as follows:

	$30,000	$30,000	$45,000
0			
$85,000	1	2	3

Assuming the appropriate discount rate is 14 percent, the NPV is

$$NPV = \$30,000(PV_{14\%,1yr}) + \$30,000(PV_{14\%,2yr}) + \$45,000(PV_{14\%,3yr}) - \$85,000$$

$$= \$30,000(0.877) + \$30,000(0.769) + \$45,000(0.675) - \$85,000$$

$$= \$26,310 + \$23,070 + \$30,375 - \$85,000 = -\$5,245$$

[9] Project financing is an exception to this statement. For a few projects, financing is such an integral part of the opportunity it must be considered. One example is where the financing of a plant is tied directly to the investment. For example, when considering a new plant in Mexico, very cheap debt financing may be provided by a government-sponsored agency, so it becomes a direct part of the proposed investment and cash flow analysis. Many real estate projects furnish another example. In these cases, the financing cash flows must be directly included in the analysis.

[10] This section may be omitted without loss of continuity.

With this additional knowledge, the machine line has a negative NPV.

In the absence of any further information, the proper decision would be to abandon the project. This *abandonment decision* would maximize the value of the firm.[11] Let's assume, however, the option to modernize the machine line exists and the cash flows associated *solely* with the modernization are as follows:

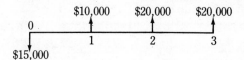

While this project obviously has a positive NPV, the *relevant set of cash flows for decision making is the combination of the existing and the new cash flows.* Assuming the cash flows are additive (that is, not complements or substitutes), the relevant cash flows for this abandon versus modernization decision are

	t_0	t_1	t_2	t_3
Existing machine line	−$ 85,000	$30,000	$30,000	$45,000
Plus: Modernization	− 15,000	10,000	20,000	20,000
Relevant CFs	−$100,000	$40,000	$50,000	$65,000

At a discount rate of 14 percent, the NPV is

$$NPV = \$40,000(\,0.877\,) + \$50,000(\,0.769\,) + \$65,000(\,0.675\,) - \$100,000$$
$$= \$35,080 + \$38,450 + \$43,875 - \$100,000 = \$17,405$$

Based on the relevant set of cash flows, the firm should keep and modernize the machine line. The second best alternative is to abandon the present line. The worst path is to continue operating the machine line as it is. By doing so, the firm passes up the opportunity of modernizing or abandoning—both of which are preferable.

A Cash Flow Checklist

In Chapter 8 we examined expansion projects and their cash flow estimation; replacement projects and other cash flow topics have been considered in this chapter. Based on all these items, we present a cash flow checklist in Figure 9.2. Note that all the topics we have considered are incorporated: (1) expansion versus replacement; (2) mutually exclusive, systemwide, interrelated, and independent projects; (3) equalizing the lives for mutually exclusive projects; (4) incremental after-tax CFs for replacement decisions; (5) inflation and disinflation; (6) ignoring financing costs; and (7) the question of abandonment. With this step-by-step approach to project identification and cash flow estimation, the proper questions are asked and all relevant cash flows are considered. When that is done, the most difficult part of the capital budgeting process has been completed. Actual acceptance or rejection, using NPV or IRR, is straightforward.

[11] The decision to keep or divest some division of a firm, as discussed in Chapter 22, is another example of an abandonment decision.

Figure 9.2   Checklist for Cash Flow Estimation

Note that opportunity costs are not identified directly on the checklist. They need to be incorporated when appropriate to ensure that the relevant cash flow stream is employed.

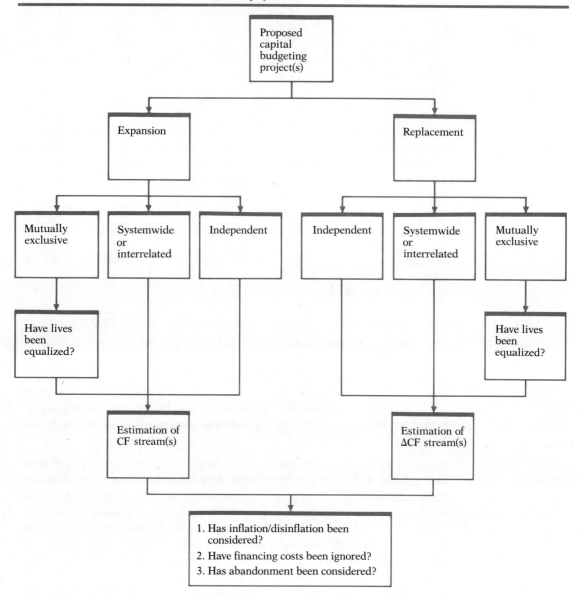

Figure 9.3 Effect of Capital Rationing on the Firm's Investment Decision

In the absence of capital rationing, the firm takes projects L, M, and N, since each provides a return above the firm's required rate of return. With capital rationing, it can select only projects L and M.

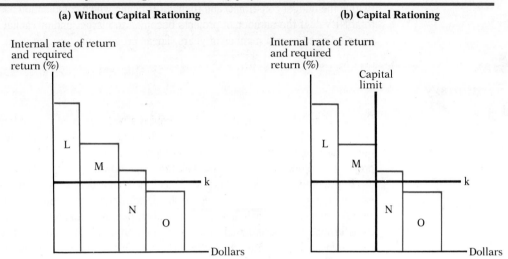

Capital Rationing

Unfortunately, all acceptable projects cannot always be undertaken. This is the case of *capital rationing:* A limit is placed on the size of the capital budget. It generally arises because of (1) internally imposed constraints on the amount of external funds a ·will raise, or (2) because of dollar limits imposed on the capital expenditures various divisions of firms can undertake. These can be thought of as "soft" capital rationing constraints; they are limits adopted by management as a financial control aid. Another type of capital rationing is the "hard" variety. In this case, the firm cannot raise any more funds in the capital markets. Theoretically, "hard" capital rationing does not exist if the proposed project has a positive NPV, because additional funds should be available (at some cost) to finance the project.[12]

To see the effect of capital rationing, consider Figure 9.3(a), which depicts four projects along with the required rate of return, k. Since the internal rate of return on the first three projects—L, M, and N—exceeds the required return, they would be accepted. However, notice what happens when a limit is placed on the amount of capital available for investment. In this case, shown in Figure 9.3(b), only projects L and M are accepted, even though project N still provides a return above the firm's required return.

Capital rationing leads to suboptimal decisions because it does not allow the firm to attain its maximum value. It is an opportunity cost that reduces the value of

---

[12] The interaction of the cost of capital and project selection in such a case is considered in Chapter 14.

the firm if positive NPV projects are bypassed. In the face of capital rationing, the goal is to *maximize the total net present value over all projects accepted.* If there are not too many projects, this can be accomplished by listing all feasible combinations (within the budget constraint) and then determining which combination has the largest total NPV.[13] If the number of projects becomes too large, and/or capital is expected to be rationed over a number of years, linear programming can be used.

Summary

Effective capital investment decisions require a well-designed capital budgeting process, knowledge of the proper selection techniques, a thorough understanding of the nature of the projects under consideration, including interactions with other projects, and determination of the relevant cash flows.

Replacement decisions arise when a firm is considering the option of replacing existing equipment, products, and so forth, with new equipment and products. For all three parts of the cash flow stream—initial, operating and terminal—it is essential to determine the incremental (new minus old) after-tax cash flows. Failure to do so results in an incomplete and faulty analysis. This same general idea of looking at the net CFs is also required when a firm is evaluating interrelated projects. Only by considering all possible combinations of projects can the firm make the proper decision. Finally, unequal lives have to be formally considered when mutually exclusive projects are being evaluated.

The required rate of return already takes into account expected inflation or disinflation. Failure to incorporate the effect of inflation on the CF stream therefore leads to biased figures, and possibly wrong decisions. Financing costs are not incorporated into the cash flow stream; the investment, or capital budgeting, decision and the financing decision should be made separately.

Often one of the most important aspects of the capital budgeting process—whether to consider the possible abandonment of present projects—is forgotten. Since capital budgeting is an ongoing process, reexamination of the economic desirability of already accepted projects is required to maximize the value of the firm. In the face of capital rationing, however, the firm (by definition) cannot maximize its value.

---

[13] An alternative selection criterion, the *profitability index* (*PI*), is often recommended when a one-period capital rationing constraint is considered. The profitability index is

$$PI = \frac{\sum\limits_{t=1}^{n} \dfrac{CF_t}{(1+k)^t}}{CF_0}$$

Since the discounted after-tax operating and terminal cash flows are divided by the initial investment, CF_0, the PI is a *relative* measure of economic desirability. Projects are ranked from highest to lowest, and all those with PIs greater than 1.0 are selected up to the dollar limit. With a one-period capital rationing constraint, this approach selects the best set of projects only *if all the funds available for investment (up to the capital constraint) are expended.* Since the total NPV approach is not affected by this problem, it is a more appropriate selection criterion.

Effective capital budgeting decisions require more than simple knowledge of the selection techniques. It can be difficult for managers to identify the proper after-tax cash flows to use, the questions to ask, and the comparisons to make. The topics discussed in this chapter assist managers in maximizing the value of the firm.

Questions

9.1 Define or explain the following:

a. Incremental cash flows	**f.** Equivalent annual NPV
b. Complementary projects	**g.** Abandonment decision
c. Systemwide project	**h.** Capital rationing
d. Substitute projects	**i.** Profitability index
e. Interrelated projects	

9.2 By comparing the calculations necessary for determining ΔCFs of replacement decisions with the calculations given in Chapter 8 for determining CFs for expansion decisions, identify the *specific* differences that exist for the initial, operating, and terminal cash flows.

9.3 Which of the following should be considered when calculating the incremental CFs associated with a new warehouse? Assume the firm owns the land, but that existing buildings would have to be demolished.

a. Demolition costs and site clearance

b. The cost of an access road built a year ago

c. New forklifts and conveyer equipment for the warehouse

d. The market value of the land and existing buildings

e. A portion of the firm's overhead

f. Lost earnings on other products due to managerial time spent during the construction and stocking of the new warehouse

g. Future IRS depreciation on the old buildings and equipment

h. Landscaping for the warehouse

i. Financing costs related to the bonds issued to build the new warehouse

j. The effects of inflation on future labor costs

9.4 Explain the difference between complementary and substitute projects. How are they related to (a) systemwide projects, (b) interrelated projects, (c) independent projects, and (d) mutually exclusive projects?

9.5 Many firms calculate the equivalent annual NPV of mutually exclusive projects when making capital budgeting decisions. In what circumstances does (doesn't) this lead to sensible investment decisions?

9.6 How does inflation affect the capital budgeting process?

9.7 Differentiate between financing and investment decisions. Why are financing costs excluded when calculating the CFs necessary for capital investment decision making?

9.8 Evaluate the following: "For a firm to remain in business, it must keep and update its equipment and processes. Hence, abandonment decisions are not relevant in practice."

9.9 Define capital rationing and explain why it does not lead to the maximization of the value of the firm.

Self-Test Problems (Solutions appear on pages 722–723.)

Replacement: ACRS Depreciation

ST 9.1 Meadowland Enterprises is contemplating the replacement of an existing asset with a higher-capacity model. The existing asset was purchased 2 years ago for $80,000 and is being depreciated over 5 years via straight-line. Right now it can be sold for $72,000, or it can be kept and will remain in use for the next 5 years. (*Note:* It has 3 years of life left for tax purposes, but has a 5-year economic life.) Its resale value (in either 3 or 5 years) is zero. The new model costs $120,000 and will be depreciated over 5 years using ACRS. Additional working capital of $5,000 is required, the tax rate is 40 percent, and the required rate of return is 15 percent. Meadowland estimates the new asset will reduce cash outflows, ΔCFBT, by $22,000 per year.

a. What is the depreciated book value of the existing asset?
b. Calculate the incremental initial investment.
c. Determine the incremental depreciation. Then determine the incremental operating cash flows.
d. What are the incremental terminal cash flows?
e. Should Meadowland replace the old asset?

Interrelated Projects

ST 9.2 Pisano Industries is considering two possible capital projects. Project I has the following CFs:

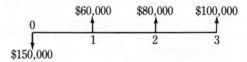

Project II can be undertaken only if the $150,000 initial outlay for project I has been made. The *additional* CFs for project II are as follows:

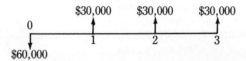

However, since projects I and II are partial substitutes, the CFs from project I will decrease by $10,000 in each of years 1, 2, and 3 if project II is also undertaken. If the required rate of return is 14 percent, what should the company do?

Problems

Incremental Initial Investment on Replaced Asset

9.1 A $32,000 machine with a 5-year normal recovery period was purchased 2 years ago. The machine will now be sold for $24,000 and replaced with a new machine with a 5-year normal recovery period costing $40,000. Straight-line depreciation is employed for both machines and the marginal corporate tax rate is 30 percent.

a. What is the remaining book value for tax purposes on the old machine?
b. What is the tax liability from selling the old machine, and the net proceeds considering both the selling price and the tax?
c. What is the gross outlay for the new machine by itself?
d. What is the incremental initial investment that is determined by subtracting the net proceeds on the old machine (b) from the gross outlay on the new machine (c)?

Incremental
Depreciation

9.2 Three years ago, Springfield Paper Products bought a $21,000 machine that is being depreciated via straight-line over its 7-year normal recovery period. Now Springfield has decided to replace the machine with a new $28,000 machine that will be depreciated via ACRS over its 7-year normal recovery period. What is the incremental (new minus old) depreciation on a *year-by-year basis* for each of the next 7 years?

Replacement

9.3 Century Investments has moved into new quarters and wants to replace its office equipment. The existing equipment is fully depreciated, but it can be sold today for $40,000. In another 5 years it will have a resale value of zero. The new equipment costs $250,000, has a 5-year life, and it has zero resale value in 5 years. Straight-line depreciation will be employed, the tax rate is 35 percent, and the required rate of return is 12 percent. Due to increased worker productivity and morale, the estimated benefits before tax, ΔCFBT, are $65,000 per year.

a. Determine the relevant cash flows.
b. Should the equipment be replaced?

Replacement

9.4 Swift Trip bought a $145,000 piece of equipment 2 years ago; its present depreciated book value is $87,000. It can be sold today for $125,000 (before taxes). If kept, however, it will last 5 more years and produce expected cash flows (CFBTs) of $13,000 for each of 5 years. A replacement machine costs $180,000, and it is expected to produce CFBTs of $28,000 for each of 5 years.

a. Assume neither machine has any resale value in 5 years. If the marginal tax rate is 34 percent, and the discount rate is 10 percent, should the equipment be replaced, assuming straight-line depreciation?
b. Would your decision change if ACRS depreciation is used for both pieces of equipment? (*Note:* This also changes the depreciated book value for the 2-year-old piece of equipment from the $87,000 figure.)

(Do only if using Pinches Disk.)
c. Suppose the old equipment was originally purchased for $155,000 with a resale value of $30,000 expected in 5 years and the new equipment has an expected resale value of $50,000. Should the equipment be replaced under the conditions in (a) and (b)?
d. Now suppose the discount rate has changed to 8 percent, a replacement machine would cost $150,000 instead of $180,000, and the old machine can be sold for $115,000 (before taxes). Should the equipment be replaced if everything else remains the same as in (c)?

Replacement: ACRS
Depreciation

9.5 Marshall Interiors is considering replacing its two trucks. The models being used have been fully depreciated to zero, but can be sold today for $3,000 *each*. In 5 years these two trucks can be sold for $500 *each*. The two new trucks will cost $20,000 *each*, have a 5-year ACRS normal recovery period, the firm's marginal tax rate is 35 percent, and these trucks are expected to have a resale value of $3,500 *each* (before taxes) 5 years from now. Because of the efficiency of the new trucks, the total benefit will be a reduction in after-tax operating costs [i.e., (CFBT)(0.65)] of $9,000 per year. Should these new trucks be purchased if the required rate of return is 12 percent?

Replacement: ACRS
Depreciation on Both

9.6 Courtney Toy is contemplating the replacement of one of its machines. The new machine costs $1,400,000, has a 10-year economic life, and is expected to save $250,000 (before taxes) in operating expenses each year. It will be depreciated under ACRS over its 7-year normal recovery period. The old machine cost $950,000, has a 10-year economic life remaining, but is being depreciated for tax purposes with the 7-year ACRS method. It was purchased 2 years ago, so there are still 5 years of depreciation remaining on the existing machine. The incremental initial investment (ΔCF) is $1,100,000, but the incremental operating cash inflows have yet to be calculated. At the end of 10 years, neither machine will have any resale value.

The discount rate is 14 percent, and the marginal tax rate on ordinary income is 30 percent. Should Courtney replace its old machine?

Interrelated Projects

9.7 West Coast Developers has designed an apartment building that will cost $7 million and produce after-tax cash inflows of $1.5 million for each year of its 10-year life. The firm also has plans for a recreation center that would cost $3.2 million and produce after-tax cash flows of $600,000 per year for 10 years. The firm owns land near Los Angeles and must decide which project to build. The land is large enough to accommodate both projects. West Coast Developers believes that if both projects are built next to each other, the residents of the apartment building will use the recreation center and increase its expected cash inflows to $700,000 per year. If the required rate of return is 14 percent, what should the company do?

Equivalent Annual NPV

9.8 Consider a firm in need of a stamping machine to print its logo on each product. It has the option to buy a one-speed machine that requires an initial investment of $350 and produces after-tax cash inflows of $300 for each of 2 years, or it can purchase a three-speed machine that costs $1,200 and produces cash inflows of $500 for each of 4 years. Neither machine has any resale value, and the required rate of return is 16 percent. Which machine should be purchased?

Equivalent Annual NPV

9.9 Either of two new molding machines that makes drinking glasses requires an initial investment of $2,000. Model 3SR produces short glasses and has a 5-year life. Model 3TR produces tall glasses and has a 9-year life. CFs expected from the purchase of model 3SR and model 3TR are $700 and $500 per year, respectively. If the required rate of return is 13 percent and there is no resale value, which model should be purchased?

Mutually Exclusive: IRR and NPV

9.10 Constantia, Inc., is contemplating replacing its existing boiler, which is worn out and has no resale value. One of two boilers will be chosen; both offer increased operating efficiency. The after-tax cash flows are as follows:

Year	Short-Life Boiler	Long-Life Boiler
Initial investment	$5,000	$8,000
1	2,500	2,750
2	2,500	2,750
3	2,500	2,750
4		2,750
5		2,750

a. Calculate both the internal rate of return and net present value for both boilers over their original lives. The required rate of return is 18 percent.
b. Which boiler should be chosen? Why?

Inflation

9.11 A project has an initial investment of $30,000, CFBT of $18,000 for each of 3 years, and a required rate of return of 13 percent. Straight-line depreciation will be employed, and the firm's marginal tax rate is 40 percent.

a. What is the project's NPV? Should it be accepted?
b. Due to inflation, the CFBTs in years 2 and 3 were overstated. It should be $16,000 in year 2, and $14,000 in year 3. Does this information cause you to change the decision made in (a)?

Abandonment

9.12 Noreiko Instruments sells a number of specialized product lines. Due to increasing competition, the CFs for its Gamma product line are estimated as follows:

$350,000 $250,000 $150,000 $100,000

1   2   3   4

A competitor has approached Noreiko and offered $650,000, after taxes, for the product line. If Noreiko Instruments' required return for this product line is 17 percent, what should it do?

Abandonment Versus Modernization

9.13 Hill's Products is considering abandoning a product line. The line could be sold for $50,000 after taxes, or it could be kept and it will produce after-tax cash flows of $17,500 for each of 4 years. In addition, the possibility of modernizing the line with after-tax cash flow consequences solely for the modernization is as follows:

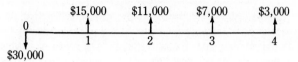

Should Hill's abandon, replace, or modernize if the discount rate is 14 percent?

Abandon, Overhaul, or Replace

9.14 A machine belonging to Clifton, Inc., is worn out. It can be sold today for scrap for $300 (after taxes). Alternatively, it can be overhauled completely for $900 and will produce the following stream of CFs:

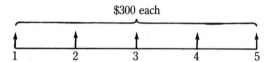

Finally, it can be replaced for $2,500. The economic life of the machine is 5 years if it is overhauled or replaced; the resale value at the end of 5 years is zero. If it is overhauled, the $900 is a tax-deductible expense that cannot be depreciated. If it is replaced, however, the new machine will be depreciated via the straight-line method over 5 years. If it is replaced, the operating cash flows for each year will equal $600 + Dep(T). If the marginal tax rate is 40 percent, and the required rate of return is 15 percent, what should Clifton do?

Capital Rationing

9.15 Aqua-Products has the following independent investments under examination.

Project	Initial Investment	After-Tax Cash Flows per Year	Life of the Project (In years)
A	$100,000	$39,000	4
B	50,000	12,000	6
C	80,000	39,000	3
D	60,000	15,000	7
E	75,000	25,000	5
F	90,000	25,000	6

Aqua-Product's required rate of return is 14 percent.

a. In the absence of capital rationing, which projects should be selected? What is the size (total dollars) of the capital budget? The total NPV of all of the projects selected?

b. Now suppose a limit of $250,000 (maximum) is placed on new capital projects. Which projects should be selected? (*Note:* Be careful, since there are three combinations that are almost equally acceptable.)

c. What is the total NPV determined in (b)? What is the loss to Aqua-Products due to the capital rationing constraint?

Profitability, Taxes, and Capital Budgeting

9.16 A project requires an initial investment of $300,000 and is expected to produce CFBTs of $95,000 for each of 5 years. Straight-line depreciation will be used over the 5-year normal recovery period. No-Tax Company has substantial tax losses and does not expect to pay any taxes in the foreseeable future. Tax Company has a marginal tax rate of 35 percent.

a. If both companies have a required rate of return of 14 percent, to which company is the investment worth more? (*Note:* No carryback or carryforward of the tax credit is feasible.)

b. Is it reasonable to use the same required rate of return for both companies? Why or why not?

References

For more on cash flow estimation and the effects of inflation, see

BRENNER, MENACHEM, AND ITZHAK VENEZIA. "The Effect of Inflation and Taxes on Growth Investments and Replacement Policies." *Journal of Finance* 38 (December 1983), pp. 1519–1528.

KROLL, YORAM. "On the Differences Between Accrual Accounting Figures and Cash Flows: The Case of Working Capital." *Financial Management* 14 (Spring 1985), pp. 75–82.

MEHTA, DILEEP R., MICHAEL D. CURLEY, AND HUNG-GAY FUNG. "Inflation, Cost of Capital and Capital Budgeting Procedures." *Financial Management* 13 (Winter 1984), pp. 48–54.

RAPPAPORT, ALFRED, AND ROBERT A. TAGGART, JR. "Evaluation of Capital Expenditure Proposals Under Inflation." *Financial Management* 11 (Spring 1982), pp. 5–13.

Some related topics are covered in

BALDWIN, CARLISS Y. "Optimal Sequential Investment When Capital Is Not Readily Reversible." *Journal of Finance* 37 (June 1982), pp. 763–782.

EMERY, GARY W. "Some Guidelines for Evaluating Capital Investment Alternatives with Unequal Lives." *Financial Management* 11 (Spring 1982), pp. 15–19.

GORDON, LAWRENCE A., AND GEORGE E. PINCHES. "Sophisticated Methods of Capital Budgeting: An Economics of Internal Organization Approach." *Managerial Finance* 14 (No. 2/3 1988), pp. 36–41.

STATMAN, MEIR, AND DAVID CALDWELL. "Applying Behavioral Finance to Capital Budgeting: Project Terminations." *Financial Management* 16 (Winter 1987), pp. 7–15.

TAGGART, ROBERT A., JR. "Allocating Capital Among a Firm's Divisions: Hurdle Rates vs. Budgets." *Journal of Financial Research* 10 (Fall 1987), pp. 177–189.

WEINGARTNER, H. MARTIN. "Capital Rationing: n Authors in Search of a Plot." *Journal of Finance* 32 (December 1977), pp. 1403–1431.

Other ways of calculating NPV, including the adjusted present value (APV) and equity residual value, exist; see

FRANKS, JULIAN R., JOHN E. BROYLES, AND WILLARD T. CARLETON. *Corporate Finance: Concepts and Applications.* Boston: Kent, 1985.

MARTIN, JOHN D., SAMUEL H. COX, JR., AND RICHARD D. MACMINN. *The Theory of Finance: Evidence and Applications.* Hinsdale, Ill.: Dryden, 1988.

PINCHES, GEORGE E., AND LARRY W. COURTNEY. *Lotus 1-2-3®for Financial Management.* New York: Harper & Row, 1989.

10

Risk and Capital Budgeting

Overview

- Using any discount rate above the risk-free rate assumes implicitly that risk increases over time.

- Project-specific or divisional required rates of return should be employed for more- or less-risky projects.

- Sequential analysis can be employed when risk changes over the economic life of a project. Sensitivity analysis is also widely used.

- Breakeven analysis should be conducted based on discounted cash flows, not GAAP accounting numbers. Simulation can also be used.

S *ears, Roebuck is accustomed to thinking big. From the world's tallest building, the largest retailer decided to become a financial-services supermarket. They forged into real estate, securities brokerage, banking, and credit cards. However, things have not turned out as they planned. None of the moves became big winners, so in 1988 and 1989, Sears shifted gears. They sold their Sears Tower headquarters in Chicago, along with some of their financial services business. And, to win customers back to their retail operations, they switched to a discount (everyday low) price strategy with greater emphasis on national brands. What started out looking like smart investment decisions turned out to be much less than expected.*

Investment decisions can have unforeseen consequences, and it is not easy to conduct a capital budgeting analysis in the face of a continuing stream of future investment opportunities. As an executive of a major firm recently stated: "You simply can't put a dollar sign on a technological future that may have a tremendous payoff." He noted that quantitative analysis is complicated by uncertainty. Which opportunities should be pursued, and which neglected? Which will prove successful, and which will fail? What is the probability of each potential outcome?

In Chapters 8 and 9 we ignored risk by assuming that all projects are equally risky. Now we examine how managers should make capital budgeting decisions in the face of uncertainty.

Risk and Strategic Decisions

We know that risk and expected return are positively related. To improve expected return, investors must expose themselves to more risk. Exactly the same relationship holds for capital budgeting decisions. For a firm to increase its expected return, it must increase its exposure to risk. Yet many questions remain. We shall find that managers must use judgment whenever there is risk.

Basic Sources of Risk

Risk relates to variability in returns, particularly returns that are less than those expected. For financial management purposes, we noted earlier that risk arises from four general sources—general economic, inflation and disinflation, firm- and issue-specific, and international. These sources also apply to risk in the capital budgeting decision.

General Economic

General economic conditions influence the actual cash flows for most capital budgeting decisions. For example, cost savings resulting from remodeling and improving the efficiency of a firm's production facilities will, to some extent, depend on the state of the economy. Since it requires a minimum production crew to run the facility no matter what the state of the economy, it is more cost effective in good economic times as opposed to recessionary times. Although some projects are more sensitive than others, virtually all have their returns influenced by economic conditions.

Inflation and Disinflation

The second source of risk relates to both expected and actual inflation. If a firm made its cash flow projections based on low expected inflation, and subsequently inflation heats up dramatically, the actual cash flows derived from the project may be affected. If inflation primarily affects cash outflows, the returns may be less than projected. Alternatively, if the firm is able to pass most of the impact of inflation on to its customers, the actual effect of inflation may be minor. It is not the rate of inflation in general that is the source of risk; rather, it is the specific inflation affecting the cash flows of the project that is important. Because of alternative rates of inflation in different sectors of the economy, at any point in time some projects, divisions, firms, or industries have more exposure to inflation and disinflation risk than others.

Project-Specific

The third source of risk in capital budgeting decisions is project-specific risk. This can be thought of as risk that arises because of the specific capital budgeting decision being considered. Suppose a firm is considering investing in a new, highly automated plant employing advanced state-of-the-art technology. Due to the technological considerations involved in such a project, there may be project-specific risk not shared by other projects being considered by the firm. New technological advances are needed, as well as developments on the job, to solve unforeseen problems as they arise. Hence, project-specific risks are important for some projects and not for others.

International

Investments made outside the boundaries of the United States have their own unique risks. Currency exchange rates will almost always differ between the time the investment is made and the cash inflows from the project are received. If the dollar loses value relative to the foreign currency, cash inflows coming to the parent will be lower than expected. In addition, various countries have rules with respect to when and how cash can be withdrawn from the country. Finally, political risks exist, especially in countries where the government is highly unstable, debts have piled up, or expropriation is possible.

The important point about all these different sources of risk is that they influence the cash flows from projects. In addition, unforeseen events may force the firm's investment to increase dramatically from what was expected at the time the project was approved. Witness what has happened to virtually every nuclear power plant constructed in the United States. Due to a variety of factors, the actual investment has been generally two to three times what was anticipated. Instead of taking 5 or 6 years, completion has generally taken 10 years or more. Thus, much of the risk relates to the variability of the cash flows, especially those that are substantially different than expected. Only if these risks are addressed and discussed at the time of the original decision will the firm be in a position to make decisions consistent with its objective.

Strategic Decisions

All sources of risk are important for the capital budgeting process because of their effect on cash flows. But cash flows are not the only reason for uncertainty. Managers must also consider the firm's strategic position in its segment of the industry and market. Unfortunately, when considering strategic and risky decisions, firms may find reasons to ignore the capital budgeting techniques described in Chapters 8 and 9. One is the inherent complexity of some projects—especially when future investments may be contingent on the success or failure of an initial investment. Another is the difficulty, both in practice and in theory, of effectively identifying and quantifying which of the risks should be considered in analyzing prospective capital budgeting projects. Taking risk into account is one of the most difficult tasks in the capital budgeting process, but it cannot be ignored. To do so is simply to invite further problems.

Risk Can Be Beneficial

Risk can also be a positive factor in project selection. That may seem strange, but remember that higher expected returns are possible only from exposure to additional risk. "If you know everything there is to know about a new product," said an executive of a major firm, "it's not going to be good business. There have to be some major uncertainties to be resolved. This is the only way to get a product with a major profit opportunity." This executive has learned an important lesson: if the firm is to prosper, it must find new product areas that have the potential to increase the value of the firm significantly. That is, it must find positive net present

When It Gets Too Costly

Texas Instruments and Hitachi have joined forces to design and produce 16-megabit dynamic random-access memory (DRAM) super memory chips, which are expected to be the workhorse of the computer industry for the mid-1990s.[1] One 16-meg DRAM will hold 2 million characters, or nearly 500,000 words. Texas Instruments decided to join with Hitachi because the combined costs of developing both a new design and the new manufacturing technology to produce these DRAMs were growing prohibitive. It is estimated that a single plant to turn out the 16-meg DRAMs will cost around $400 million. Even for a $6 billion outfit like Texas Instruments, that's a lot of money! One complication is that firms are compelled to gamble on the long odds of simultaneously developing a new design and new production methods before it can be certain whether they'll work together. A further complication is that with the growing change in the computer chip industry, you have to have at least three such DRAM generations in the pipeline. A small misstep can exact a big penalty—if you don't get to market within 6 months of the first company to do so, you probably won't make *any* money on that entire generation of chips. Each generation of DRAMs enjoys a meaningful sales life of around 5 years.

To play the game, Texas Instruments had to ante up. They really had no option; DRAMs are the proving ground for the new design and manufacturing techniques that permeate the entire integrated circuit market. The way to play the game, and at the same time cut some of the risk, was through a cooperative arrangement. In many rapidly changing and high-cost industries, joint efforts of this type probably are going to be seen more and more in the future.

[1] "What's Behind the Texas Instruments–Hitachi Deal." *Business Week* (January 16, 1989).

value projects where the firm can earn excess returns due to its competitive advantages. To find these areas, the firm must expose itself to risks above and beyond the average risks it faces. Is that additional risk exposure bad? No—not unless the firm does a poor job of evaluating and considering the risks.

Most significant, profitable investments and innovations—the Prudhoe Bay oil and gas field in Alaska, VCRs, fast food restaurants, and many more—all faced high risks. But higher expected returns accompanied those higher risks. Of course, not all high-risk capital investments pan out. But managers must foster an environment within the firm that does two things: (1) encourages the development and consideration of high risk–high expected return projects; (2) provides a proper format for adequately considering and evaluating these high-risk projects. Otherwise, the environment will either not encourage risk taking, or lead to making high-risk, complex capital investment decisions based on seat-of-the-pants analysis. Either result can have serious—and perhaps fatal—long-run consequences for the firm.

A Common Mistake

Many managers believe they must increase the required rate of return to account for the greater riskiness of the more distant cash flows. This is wrong. *The use of any discount rate (above the risk-free rate) automatically recognizes that more distant cash flows are proportionally more risky.* The discount rate is a function of both the risk-free rate and a risk premium. That is:

$$\begin{matrix} \text{required} \\ \text{return} \end{matrix} = \begin{matrix} \text{risk-free} \\ \text{rate} \end{matrix} + \begin{matrix} \text{risk premium based on} \\ \text{project risk} \end{matrix} \qquad (10.1)$$

If the risk-free rate is 6 percent and the risk premium for the project is 8 percent, for a total of 14 percent, both the 6 percent and the 8 percent compound over time. The compounding of the 6 percent adjusts solely for differences in the timing of the cash flows—in the absence of risk. The compounding of the 8 percent risk premium recognizes that more distant cash flows for the project are more risky. Thus, if cash flow distributions become more risky over time (as shown graphically in Figure 10.1), discounting implicitly takes account of some or all of this increase.

The use of a discount rate that embodies a built-in risk premium compensates for the *risk borne per period.* The more distant the cash flows, the greater the number of periods, and hence the greater the adjustment for risk. The only question is how much more risky the more distant cash flows are. If they are highly risky, then a higher discount rate, embodying a higher risk premium, may be needed. The point to remember is this: Some, and perhaps all, of the increase in riskiness of more distant cash flows is already accounted for by simply using the required

Figure 10.1 Increasing Risk over Time

As the dispersion increases, the riskiness increases. Using any rate above the risk-free rate in the discounting process implicitly compensates for some increases in risk.

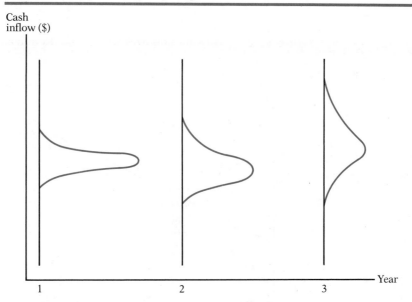

rate of return. (Another way of looking at increasing risk over time, and the topic of certainty equivalents, is discussed in Appendix 10A.)

Required Returns for Capital Budgeting Decisions

Once we start considering risk adjustment, we need to distinguish between two different situations. The first are those where *both initially and over time* the risks are above or below the average risk of the projects considered by the firm. The second involves projects where *initially the risks are above the average risk of the firm, but after some initial period the risks decrease.* Since different approaches are needed to deal with these two cases, we examine them separately. In this section we first consider required returns for capital budgeting projects, then we examine possible portfolio effects, and finally we consider situations where risk is expected to decrease after an initial start-up period.

Firm, Divisional, and Project Required Returns

In Chapters 8 and 9 we assumed, for simplicity, that risk was the same for all projects faced by the firm. But, we know this cannot be true. Some projects have to be more risky, while others are probably viewed as being very safe. In cases where risk differs significantly from the firm's overall level of risk, the use of a firmwide required rate of return results in the misallocation of resources. Consider Figure 10.2, which depicts the effect of using a single firmwide required rate of return when risk is not uniform across projects. If the firm's required rate of return is employed, project A will be rejected while project B will be accepted. However, if project A is less risky than the average project faced by the firm, a lower discount rate (as given by the sloped project-specific required rate of return line) should be employed. Since project A has an IRR greater than its appropriate required return,

Figure 10.2 Firmwide and Project-Specific Required Rates of Return

Use of a firmwide required rate will overallocate funds to risky projects (like project B) and underallocate them to safe projects (project A).

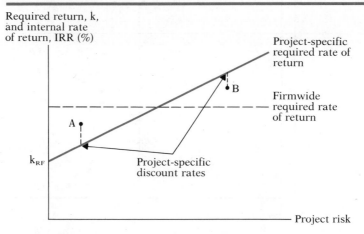

it should be accepted. Conversely, project B is more risky and, accordingly, a required return higher than the firm's overall required rate of return should be employed. Since the anticipated IRR on project B is less than its project-specific required return, it should be rejected. It is easy to see the effect of using a single rate for discounting all capital budgeting proposals—we overallocate resources to risky projects while we underallocate resources to safer projects. The impact of such a mistake is to reduce the value of the firm.

As noted previously, the required rate of return appropriate for evaluating any capital budgeting project is equal to:

$$\begin{array}{c} \text{required} \\ \text{return} \end{array} = \begin{array}{c} \text{risk-free} \\ \text{rate} \end{array} + \begin{array}{c} \text{risk premium based on} \\ \text{project risk} \end{array}$$

There are, in fact, three different approaches (as discussed in more detail in Chapter 14) to specifying what this required rate of return should be. The first, based on the firm's *weighted average cost of capital (WACC)*, provides a single firmwide required rate of return. This rate is appropriate for use when considering most replacement projects for a firm, or when the firm is homogeneous in terms of its projects and is not investing in any high- (or low-) risk projects.

The second approach is embodied in the form of *divisional costs of capital.* For example, an integrated oil company may have four divisions—domestic exploration, international exploration, refining, and marketing. Based on perceived risks in the different areas, the firm may establish divisional costs of capital (or required rates of return) as follows:

Domestic exploration	20%
International exploration	30
Refining	16
Marketing	12

These are the discount rates used for the NPV approach, or the hurdle rate for projects in each division if the IRR method is employed. (The calculation of divisional costs of capital is discussed in Chapter 14.) The use of divisional required rates of return may be thought of as a way station between the use of a single firmwide return, or, alternatively, different required rates of return for each project. Many firms in practice employ some type of divisional required returns for capital budgeting purposes.

Finally, a project-specific discount rate, or required rate of return, can be employed based on the risk associated with an individual project. Often the capital asset pricing model, CAPM, is employed to estimate these project-specific rates of return. Based on the nondiversifiable risk, a project's required rate of return using the CAPM would be

$$k_{project} = k_{RF} + \beta_{project}(k_M - k_{RF}) \tag{10.2}$$

where

$k_{project}$ = project's required rate of return

k_{RF} = the risk-free rate of interest

$\beta_{project}$ = the project's nondiversifiable risk as measured by its beta coefficient

k_M = the expected rate of return on the market portfolio

Figure 10.3 Alternative Required Rates of Return

Use of appropriate required rates of return, based on the risks and foregone opportunities, is essential for effective capital budgeting decision making.

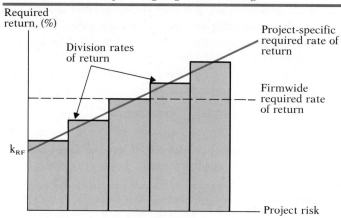

If the firm is all equity-financed, the project-specific return based on the CAPM is given by the security market line, SML, introduced in Chapter 7. (Calculation of project-specific required rates of return is also covered in Chapter 14.) These three approaches to estimating the required rate of return are depicted in Figure 10.3.

Two points should be emphasized with the use of required rates of return that consider the risk of capital budgeting projects. First, is the *stand-alone principle*. This principle says that a proposed project should be accepted or rejected by comparing it with the returns that could be secured based on investing in a similar risk project. The foregone returns from the bypassed investment are captured by using the appropriate required return for the project. For example, if an equally risky investment involves investing in securities that would provide an expected return of 20 percent, the proposed capital investment must return at least 20 percent. Otherwise the firm should reject the proposed capital project and invest in the securities. This stand-alone principle is important for all capital investment decisions made by the firm.

Second, as discussed in Chapter 14, the estimation of required rates of return is part science, and part judgment. While no method of dealing with risk is entirely precise, it is an important step that managers must take if they want to maximize the value of the firm. Failure to do so results in the same effect the ostrich achieves by burying its head in the ground—the world continues to spin and change while the ostrich (or firm) maintains its naive view that all is well.

What About Portfolio Effects?

Should firms concern themselves about the possible interaction between the cash flows expected from a new project and those from existing projects? The answer to that question is generally "no," but it is more complicated than that. *First and foremost,* if a new project is expected to have any positive or negative effect on cash flows associated with existing projects, these must (as noted in Chapter 9) be treated as opportunity costs or benefits and incorporated into the cash flows estimated for the new project.

The bigger question is this: Are there risk-reducing benefits that arise when a firm undertakes a project whose returns are less than perfectly positively correlated with those of the firm? That is, should the firm consider itself a portfolio and attempt to accept projects that reduce the risk (or standard deviation) of the portfolio returns? In an efficient market, the answer is "no." The reason is that investors are able to diversify on their own; they do not receive any incremental benefits from having the firm diversify. In effect, the firm is performing a redundant service.

If markets are not completely efficient, there may be some risk reduction (in terms of volatility of the firm's cash flows, probability of bankruptcy, and so forth) that can be achieved. It is very hard, however, to measure this benefit, and very easy to overestimate its impact. For this reason, projects should be considered on their individual merits, without attempting to quantify any benefits from risk reduction. Then, if it appears to be very important, possible portfolio effects can be introduced into the decision-making process.

When a Single Discount Rate Cannot Be Used

Up to now we have considered how to deal with risk that is above or below the firm's risk over the entire economic life of the project. But what about the situation where risk is high at first but then decreases? Consider the proposed development and marketing of "Clean-Ez," a portable electric car washer. In making its capital budgeting decision, the firm estimated that the preliminary phase, involving a small pilot plant and test marketing, would require a $7 million initial investment at time t_0. If the preliminary phase is successful, a $40 million cash outlay will be required to build the plant at time $t = 1$; then for the next 9 years (t_2 through t_{10}), the after-tax cash inflows will be $12 million per year. Thus, the estimated cash flow stream is as follows:

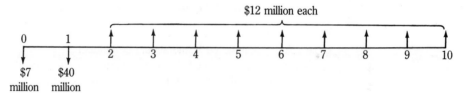

Because of the high risk of the project, a 20 percent return (versus the firm's required rate of return of 12 percent) was used. Based on a 20 percent discount rate, the NPV was

$$\text{NPV} = \$12,000,000(\text{PVA}_{20\%,\,9\,\text{yr}})(\text{PV}_{20\%,\,1\,\text{yr}}) - \$40,000,000(\text{PV}_{20\%,\,1\,\text{yr}})$$
$$- \$7,000,000$$

$$= \$12,000,000(\,4.031\,)(\,0.833\,) - \$40,000,000(\,0.833\,) - \$7,000,000$$

$$= \$40,293,876 - \$33,320,000 - \$7,000,000 = -\$26,124$$

Since the NPV is negative, the initial decision was to reject Clean-Ez.

However, Kay, one of the finance staff, asked: "Have we accurately considered the riskiness of Clean-Ez? If risk decreases after the preliminary phase, then the use of a 20 percent discount rate over the entire life of Clean-Ez unnecessarily penalizes more distant cash flows." After some discussion, it was determined that there was only a 50–50 probability the second investment (of $40 million) would be made at t_1. If the test marketing in the preliminary phase was below expectations, the additional funds would not be spent. On the other hand, if the preliminary phase was a success, Clean-Ez would be of average risk, and a 12 percent required rate of return would be appropriate over its remaining life.

Based on this additional information, Kay proceeded to employ *sequential analysis* as follows. First, she pointed out that there are two separate parts to the proposed project. The $7 million for the preliminary phase will be spent regardless. Depending on the results of that phase, there is a 50 percent chance that a $40 million cash outflow will be made in 1 year for a project of average risk. Likewise, there is a 50 percent chance that no additional investment will be made. So

$$\text{Success (50\%)} \quad NPV = \$12,000,000(\,PVA_{12\%,9\,\text{yr}}\,) - \$40,000,000$$
$$= \$12,000,000(\,5.328\,) - \$40,000,000$$
$$= \$63,936,000 - \$40,000,000 = \$23,936,000$$

Preliminary phase

$$\text{Failure (50\%)} \quad NPV = 0$$

The *expected NPV* in year 1 is simply 0.50($23,936,000) + 0.50(0) = $11,968,000. But this NPV is for a project starting at t = 1, and we have not considered the $7 million initial investment. Looking at the NPV of the total project from its inception, it is

$$NPV = \$11,968,000(\,PV_{20\%,1\,\text{yr}}\,) - \$7,000,000$$
$$= \$11,968,000(\,0.833\,) - \$7,000,000 = \$2,969,344$$

Based on this analysis, Kay concluded (correctly, we might add) that the Clean-Ez project has a positive NPV and should be funded.

One often hears executives or other critics of the present value approach say it unnecessarily penalizes long-term projects. As we have just seen, that does not have to be the case. By treating the decision as a sequential investment, we can handle the risk adjustment question. However, if we simply use a high required rate of return, we *will* be guilty of penalizing long-term projects if risk is not consistently at the higher level.

Information About the Riskiness of Projects

Up to now we have discussed risk in general as it relates to capital budgeting projects, and then considered how differences in risk can be dealt with through the use of a firmwide required rate of return, divisional required rates of return, or project-specific required returns. In all three cases differences in perceived riskiness are compensated for by adding an appropriate risk premium to the risk-free rate. Before making capital budgeting decisions it is important to examine the critical variables and assumptions that are expected to affect the project's success or failure. To do so we can employ sensitivity analysis, break-even analysis, and simulation.

Sensitivity Analysis

Sensitivity analysis does not formally attempt to quantify risk. Rather, it focuses on determining how sensitive the output (NPV or IRR) is to changes in any of the input variables. To understand sensitivity analysis, let's consider the example of the project in Table 10.1. The project requires an initial investment of $51,000, has after-tax CFs of $24,800 for each of 3 years, the tax rate is 40 percent, and the required rate of return is 13 percent. Calculating the NPV of $7,553 provides us with the base case net present value. To conduct a *sensitivity analysis,* it is necessary to change one of the input variables to determine how sensitive the NPV is to changes in that particular variable. The input data can be changed by a certain percentage, or by a given dollar amount.

To see how sensitive the NPV is to changes in the initial investment and the cash inflows, we changed them each by 10 percent. This results in a NPV of either $2,453 or $12,653 for a 10 percent increase or decrease in the initial investment. Likewise, the NPV is either $14,636 or $470 if the cash inflows increase or decrease by 10 percent. In Figure 10.4, this information is plotted against the base case NPV. The steeper the slope, the more sensitive the project's NPV is to a change in the input variable. We see that this project's NPV is more sensitive to a 10

Table 10.1 Cash Flows and Base Case Net Present Value for Sensitivity Analysis

Sensitivity analysis does not attempt to quantify risk; rather, it focuses on determining how sensitive the resulting NPV is to changes in the input variables.

Initial Investment
$51,000

Operating Cash Flows

Year	Cash Inflow	−	Cash Outflow	=	CFBT	CFBT × (1 − T)*	+	Dep†(T)*	=	CF
1	$50,000		$20,000		$30,000	$18,000		$6,800		$24,800
2	50,000		20,000		30,000	18,000		6,800		24,800
3	50,000		20,000		30,000	18,000		6,800		24,800

Terminal Cash Flow
None

Cash Flow Stream

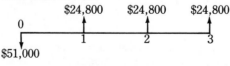

Net Present Value
base case NPV = $24,800($PVA_{13\%,3yr}$) − $51,000

$$= \$24,800(2.361) - \$51,000 = \$58,553 - \$51,000 = \$7,553$$

* The tax rate is 40 percent.
† Straight-line depreciation = $51,000/3 yr = $17,000 per year.

Figure 10.4 Sensitivity Analysis of 10 Percent Change in Initial Investment and Cash Inflows

The steeper the slope, the more sensitive the NPV is to a change in the input variable.

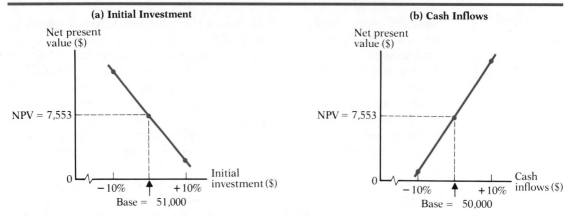

percent change in cash inflows than to a 10 percent change in its initial investment. Sensitivity analysis is widely employed in practice. This is especially true with the increasing use of spreadsheet programs such as Lotus 1–2–3® and online capital budgeting computer systems.

Break-Even Analysis

When undertaking a sensitivity analysis of a project, we are asking how serious it would be if some factor (i.e., cash inflows, life of the project, and so forth) turns out far worse than expected. Managers sometimes prefer to rephrase this question and ask how bad sales (and therefore, cash inflows) could get before the project loses money. This approach is known as *break-even analysis;* the break-even point occurs where the present value of the inflows equals the present value of the outflows, so the net present value is zero.

To illustrate break-even analysis, assume that Whiz-Bang Motors is projecting net income and cash flows for its new product line as shown in Table 10.2. Under simplifying assumptions, where sales equal gross cash inflows, there are no accruals, and tax and GAAP depreciation are the same, we see Whiz-Bang estimates that when sales are $300, net income will be $54. Based on an initial cash outflow of $1,000, a 10-year life, and a required rate of return of 15 percent, the per year cash flows after tax, CF_t, are $154 and the net present value is equal to −$227.07. With the same assumptions, if sales are zero, or, alternatively, $600, the net income, cash flows, and net present values are as follows:

	Sales of 0 per Year	Sales of $600 per Year
Net income	− $90	$198
Cash flow per year, CF_t	10	298
NPV	− 949.81	495.66

Table 10.2 GAAP Net Income and Cash Flow for Whiz-Bang

For simplicity we assume the equipment costs $1,000 and is depreciated to zero via straight line for both accounting and tax purposes over 10 years. Also, we assume there are no accruals, and that sales and costs are all collected (or incurred) so they are equal to cash inflows and outflows. As we have discussed previously, the reality of these assumptions is tenuous in practice.

	GAAP Income	Cash Flow
Sales	$300	$300
Variable costs (20% of sales)	60	60
Fixed costs	50	50
Depreciation	100	
Earnings before tax (EBT)	90	
Taxes (40%)	36	36
Net income	$ 54	
Cash Flow		$154

$$\text{NPV} = \$154(\text{PVA}_{15\%,10\text{yr}}) - \$1,000$$

$$= \$154(5.019) - \$1,000 = \$772.93 - \$1,0000 = -\$227.07$$

We see the NPV is highly negative when sales are zero, moderately negative when sales equal $300, and positive when sales equal $600 per year. Clearly, the zero NPV point occurs between $300 and $600 in sales.

To solve for the zero NPV level we proceed as follows:

$$\text{Zero NPV} = \text{PV of inflows} - \text{PV of outflows} = 0$$

$$CF_t(\text{PVA}_{15\%,10\text{yr}}) - \$1,000 = 0$$

$$CF_t(5.019) = \$1,000$$

$$CF_t = \$1,000/5.019 = \$199.25$$

The sales (or before-variable cost, fixed cost, and tax cash inflow) needed to generate after-tax cash inflows of $199.25 for each of 10 years is obtained as follows, where X is the unknown sales level:

$$\text{Sales} - (\text{variable} + \text{fixed costs}) - \text{taxes} = \$199.25$$

$$X - (0.20X + \$50) - (X - 0.20X - \$50 - \$100)(0.40) = \$199.25$$

$$X - 0.20X - \$50 - 0.40X + 0.08X + \$20 + \$40 = \$199.25$$

$$0.48X + \$10 = \$199.25$$

$$X = \$189.25/0.48 = \$394.27$$

This relationship is plotted in Figure 10.5. The present value of the cash inflows and the present value of the cash outflows cross at sales of $394.27. This is the point where the project has a zero NPV. As long as sales are greater than $394.27 per year, the project has a positive NPV.

Figure 10.5　Break-Even Chart Based on Total Present Values

This is just a form of sensitivity analysis, allowing sales (or the present value of the cash inflows) to change.

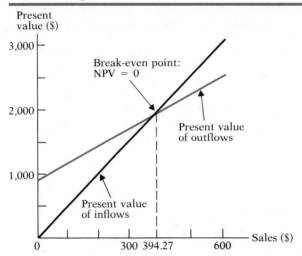

Instead of working with the present value of the cash inflows and outflows, we can work equally well with the equivalent annual inflows and outflows.[1] The annual cost of the project includes the recurring costs (i.e., variable costs, fixed costs, and taxes) *plus* the equivalent annual cost of the initial investment of $1,000. This equivalent annual cost is determined by dividing the initial cash outlay of $1,000 by the 10-year PVA factor:

$$\text{equivalent annual cost} = \frac{\text{initial investment}}{PVA_{k,n}} \qquad (10.3)$$

$$= \$1,000/5.019 = \$199.25$$

In Table 10.3 we show the equivalent annual cash inflows and outflows for our three levels of sales; the difference between the equivalent annual inflows and outflows is then shown in column 7. As long as the difference is positive, the project has a positive NPV.

This relationship is graphed in Figure 10.6. As you should expect, except for the change from the present value of the total inflows and outflows, to the equivalent annual inflows and outflows, the results are exactly the same as shown in Figure 10.5. The zero NPV still occurs when sales are $394.27 per year. It makes no difference whether we work with the total present values, or the equivalent annual inflows and outflows in order to determine the financial break-even point. Whiz-Bang does not want to introduce the project unless sales are expected to be at least $394.27 per year. To do so will lower the value of the firm.

---

[1] This is exactly the same concept introduced in Chapter 9 when we determined the equivalent annual NPV, so that mutually exclusive projects with different lives could be compared.

Table 10.3 Equivalent Annual Cash Inflows and Outflows for Whiz-Bang Motors

We assume that if the project operates at a loss, the firm can use the loss to reduce its tax bill. Thus, when sales are zero, the project produces a tax saving.

Sales; Gross Cash Inflow (1)	Cash Outflows					Net Equivalent Annual Flow (1) − (6) (7)
	Variable Costs (2)	+ Fixed Costs + (3)	Taxes + (4)	Equivalent Annual Cost (5)	= Total (6)	
$ 0	$ 0	$50	−$ 60	$199.25	$189.25	−$189.25
300	60	50	36	199.25	345.25	−45.25
600	120	50	132	199.25	501.25	98.75

Instead of employing present values, many managers calculate their break-even point based on GAAP net income. In Figure 10.7 we have plotted this relationship; it shows that the accounting-based break-even point is at a sales level of only $187.50 per year. Remember that Figures 10.5 and 10.6, based on present values, showed a financial break-even point of $394.27. The difference in the two approaches hinges on the depreciation of $100 per year that is deducted for GAAP accounting purposes, and the required rate of return of 15 percent for the project. By treating break-even analysis in an accounting manner, managers are ignoring the opportunity cost of the $1,000 investment outlay. We must allow for the fact that the $1,000 could have been invested elsewhere to earn a return of 15 percent. Depreciation thus understates the true cost by ignoring the foregone opportunity to earn a return on

Figure 10.6 Break-Even Chart Based on Equivalent Annual Cash Flows

We can redraw Figure 10.5, but now it is based on the equivalent annual inflows and outflows. The break-even NPV remains at the same level of sales of $394.27.

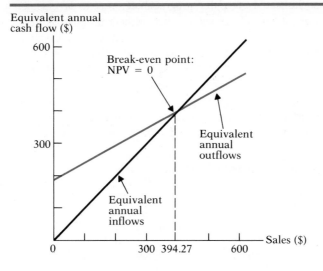

Figure 10.7 Break-Even Chart Based on GAAP Net Income

By ignoring the opportunity costs associated with investments, net income-based break-even analysis seriously understates the financial break-even point.

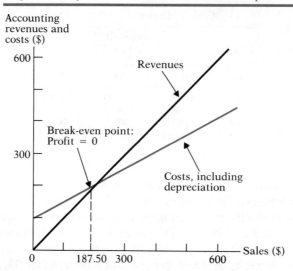

the $1,000 initial outlay. Companies that break even on an accounting basis are really losing money—they are losing the opportunity cost of their investment.

Simulation

Sensitivity analysis allows you to consider the effect of changing one variable at a time. A more refined approach, scenario analysis, is based on changing a limited number of possible combinations. A further refinement is *simulation* (often called *Monte Carlo simulation*), which is a technique for considering the effect of changing *all* of the relevant variables in an analysis. While simulation used to require relatively sophisticated computer programming, recent developments in computer software make it easy to use within a spreadsheet program like Lotus 1–2–3®.

The first step in a computer simulation is to specify the relevant variables, and the probability distributions associated with each variable. For example, in our Whiz-Bang example the relevant variables (at a minimum) are sales, the relationship of variable costs to sales, the initial investment, and the economic (as opposed to tax) life of the project. In fact, as any business executive will testify, this is a very short list of relevant variables. To illustrate simulation, suppose the probability of Whiz-Bang's sales associated with this new project have been estimated as follows:

Sales (1)	Probability (2)	Associated Random Number (3)
$ 0	0.05	00–04
150	0.25	05–29
300	0.40	30–69
450	0.25	70–94
600	0.05	95–99

The sales may be between $0 and $600, with the probabilities as indicated in column 2. Also, the associated random variables, as shown in column 3, are recorded.[2] Once this probability distribution of possible outcomes is estimated for sales, we then proceed to estimate probability distributions for all of the other relevant variables that are likely to change. While specifying the variables and their probabilities is not easy, it is often easier than the next step.

The second step involves specifying the interdependencies between variables, and across time. Specifying the interdependencies is the hardest, and also the most important, part of a simulation. If all of the components of a project's cash flows are unrelated, then the simulation is easy.

Once the variables, probabilities, and interdependencies have been specified, the simulation proceeds as follows:

1. Computers, through random number generations, will select a possible outcome for each variable. For sales, let us assume the random number 73 comes up.
2. For each variable, the random number selected determines the value to be employed for that variable. The 73 associated with sales means that the appropriate sales level for the first run of the simulation is $450. Values for all of the other variables are set in a similar manner.
3. Once a value has been established for each of the variables, the computer generates a NPV or IRR for the first run of the simulation.
4. This NPV or IRR is then stored, and the computer runs the second analysis. Here a different set of random numbers, and therefore a different set of values for the variables, is selected. The NPV or IRR is then computed and stored. This procedure goes on for 250 to 500 (or more) runs.
5. Once the 250 or 500 runs are completed, the frequency distribution of NPVs or IRRs, the expected value, and the standard deviation are all printed out. Often a graph is presented much like that shown in Figure 10.8.

Simulation, though complicated, has the obvious merit of compelling the decision maker to face up to uncertainty and interdependency. Once the model is constructed, it is simple to analyze what would happen if the probability distribution changed for any one variable, or if the degree of interdependency increased or decreased from that specified. Thus, simulation has the potential to enable us to ascertain many facets of the risk associated with proposed capital budgeting projects. Before we jump on the bandwagon, however, and conclude that simulation solves all of our ills, we need to consider a few of the problems with simulation.

The main problems are as follows:

1. Cost and time. Until recently it was very difficult to do realistic computer simulations on PCs. While new computer software is changing that, it must be recognized that big, complex projects still require significant amounts of time to set up and run. Equally important, unless the end users have been instrumental in setting up the simulation, they may not have confidence in the results and/or the specific assumptions underlying the simulation.

---

[2] For simplicity, we assume sales are a discrete variable that takes on only five values. This is solely for illustrative purposes; computer simulations routinely deal with continuous distributions.

Figure 10.8 Probability Distribution of NPVs or IRRs

By calculating the probability of success, information is provided about the likelihood of accepting a project that has the potential to increase the value of the firm.

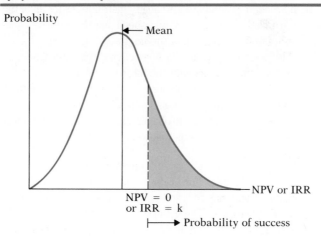

2. Interdependencies. As indicated previously, specifying the interdependencies between variables, and over time, is the most difficult part of any simulation. Here, it is crucial for knowledgeable managers to pool their resources and collective wisdom, to come up with reasonable, and educated, guesses as to interdependencies. Then these assumptions should be tested in the simulation, and communicated to the final decision makers.
3. Interpreting the results. In capital budgeting techniques considered up to now, the outcome has been a single NPV or IRR. This simplifies the analysis, and decision making, even though it may be unrealistic. But simulation goes to the other extreme. It provides a whole distribution of possible outcomes that can be converted into the probability of success. This *probability of success,* as shown in Figure 10.8, indicates what the chances are the project will have a positive NPV, or an IRR that is greater than the required rate of return. Not all managers are comfortable, however, with this additional information. They may have too much information, or too little guidance as to what are acceptable probabilities of success, or risk levels.
4. Finally, there are some peculiar problems related to probability distributions of NPVs or IRRs. If the NPV approach is employed, then the appropriate discount rate may not be the project's required rate of return. Rather, all of the risk may be captured by specifying the probability distributions of the relevant variables. If all the risk is incorporated into the probability distribution the NPV is calculated by *discounting at the risk-free rate,* k_{RF}. Once this step is taken, however, the resulting probability distribution of NPVs is very different than typically encountered. This is because we normally discount at the required rate of return, not at the risk-free rate. Hence, calculating NPVs in a simulation may lead to as many problems as it solves.

An alternative is to calculate the IRR on each project, and then present the probability distribution of IRRs. This gets around the potential problem of discounting at the risk-free rate with NPVs, but it raises a problem of its own. What do you think it must be? If you said a reinvestment rate problem (see Chapter 8), you are right! When dealing with a probability distribution of IRRs, each separate simulation run will come up with a different IRR, and therefore will make a different implicit reinvestment rate assumption. This causes a slight modification in the shape of the probability distribution of IRRs compared to the probability distribution of NPVs.[3] Even though this problem exists, the ultimate impact in practice is relatively minor. Therefore, it is often best to use the probability distribution of IRRs, recognizing that a slight bias exists. This may be more palatable, and produce less confusion, than attempting to deal with a probability distribution of NPVs based on a required rate of return equal to the risk-free rate, k_{RF}.

Where do we stand on using simulation for dealing with risk in capital budgeting decisions? While many theoretical and empirical advances have been made in using probability distribution approaches to make capital budgeting decisions, their use by firms has been very limited until recently. The recent developments in terms of more powerful PCs and good simulation software are, however, refocusing attention on using simulation to help get a better handle on risk. Used wisely, with a knowledge of both its strengths and limitations, simulation can aid effective decision making. While no panacea, it has progressed to the point where it can help decision makers gain a better understanding of the importance different variables, assumptions, and interactions have on capital budgeting decisions. As such, we view it as a reasonable addition to a good capital budgeting program.

A Risk Checklist

In this chapter we have identified a number of different ways of handling risk. Figure 10.9 provides a checklist for the items that need to be considered when dealing with risk in capital budgeting. In examining this figure, note that the question of how much risk the project has must be considered. If the project is of average risk, the capital budgeting decision can be made employing the techniques described in Chapter 8 or 9—with or without the use of sensitivity analysis or simulation. If risk is greater or less than the average project risk for the firm, then a project-specific or divisional required rate of return, or sequential analysis, should be employed. Finally, with or without risk adjustment, sensitivity analysis and/or simulation can be employed.

Since risk comes from many sources, it is difficult to generalize about it. One thing is certain, however: Effective managers must make a determined effort to probe for possible risks associated with capital budgeting projects. By proceeding in the manner described, they are ensuring that the right questions about risk are asked at the right time, and that reasonable methods of dealing with it are being employed.

[3] See the references at the end of the chapter for more on this problem.

Figure 10.9   A Risk Checklist for Capital Budgeting

Above- or below-average-risk projects require the use of project-specific or divisional required rates of return, or sequential analysis. The dashed line indicates that sensitivity analysis or simulation can be used with any of the approaches.

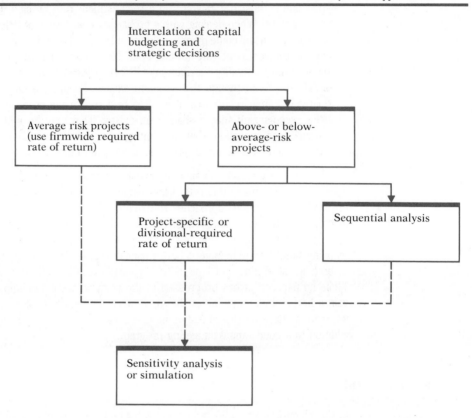

Summary

The effective treatment of risk is both difficult and important in capital budgeting decisions. Managers must be aware of general economic risk, risk due to inflation or disinflation, project-specific risk, and international risk. In recent years some firms have employed a strategic approach without fully understanding the use of discounted present value in making wealth-maximizing capital budgeting decisions. Failure to do so is dysfunctional and leads to a decline in the value of the firm.

For projects of average risk, a firmwide required rate of return is appropriate. But, for other projects a project-specific or divisional required rate of return should be employed to account for the above- or below-average risk. These approaches assume implicitly that risk is above or below the average risk of the project for its entire economic life. Although portfolio risk-reduction effects may occasionally occur, their importance is often overstated, and they are best ignored. For those projects where risk differs over time, the use of a sequential analysis is appropriate. Thus, later cash flows are not inappropriately penalized as they would be by using a single required rate of return.

Sensitivity analysis, where one input variable is changed at a time, is often employed in analyzing capital budgeting projects. A specific case in point is the use of break-even analysis. Note that it is inappropriate from a wealth maximizing standpoint to conduct a break-even analysis based on GAAP net income. Simulation, where all of the relevant variables are allowed to change, may also be employed in order to deal with risk when capital budgeting decisions are made.

There is an appendix to this chapter, "Appendix 10A: Certainty Equivalents," at the back of the book.

Questions

10.1 Define or explain the following:

a. Weighted average cost of capital (WACC)
b. Divisional cost of capital
c. Stand-alone principle
d. Sequential analysis
e. Expected NPV

f. Break-even analysis
g. Sensitivity analysis
h. Simulation (Monte Carlo simulation)
i. Probability of success
j. Certainty equivalent

10.2 Explain how general economic, inflation or disinflation, project-specific, and international sources of risk relate to capital budgeting projects.

10.3 Mike Larson, the CEO of Larson Enterprises, believes that the risk of a proposed capital budgeting project increases over time. As a result, a project-specific or divisional required rate must be chosen. As Larson's chief financial officer, explain to Mike when this strategy is not appropriate.

10.4 The divisional required rate of return approach to capital budgeting employing categories of projects with different risks might be graphed as follows:

Internal rate
of return (%)

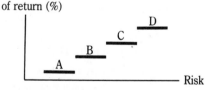

Risk

Explain how the divisional required return captures many of the risk return ideas of the capital asset pricing model. In what significant ways do the two differ?

10.5 Explain the importance of the stand-alone principle. Why are opportunity costs (or the foregone returns from bypassed investments) so important in making wealth maximizing capital budgeting decisions?

10.6 Should the firm be concerned primarily with diversifying its investment (or asset) portfolio? Why or why not?

10.7 How should you proceed when risk changes over time substantially faster or slower than accounted for by using a single required rate of return? Explain.

10.8 Adam believes that sensitivity analysis is a viable way to deal with risk. Do you agree with him? Why or why not?

10.9 Why does break-even analysis, when conducted employing GAAP accounting numbers, result in understating the economic break-even point? Can you see any redeeming features of an accounting-based break-even analysis?

10.10 Explain both the strengths and the weaknesses of simulation.

Self-Test Problems (Solutions appear on pages 724–725.)

CAPM: Determining k_M

ST 10.1 M. A. Munson Co. is considering the purchase of a new printing machine. The CFs are as follows:

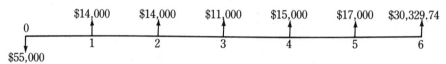

If k_{RF} = 8 percent and $\beta_{project}$ = 1.25, what is the return on the market portfolio, k_M, such that the firm is indifferent to the project?

Coefficient of Variation and Required Rate of Return

ST 10.2 Campbell Corporation is evaluating two mutually exclusive proposals—buying a word processing system or a microcomputer system. The after-tax cash flows are as follows:

	Word Processing System		Microcomputer System	
Initial investment	$215,000		$270,000	
CFs and probabilities of occurrence	0.20	$70,000	0.20	$120,000
for *each of five years*	0.60	60,000	0.60	80,000
	0.20	30,000	0.20	20,000

Campbell uses the following equation to estimate the project-specific required rate of return:

$$\frac{\text{required}}{\text{return}} = \text{risk-free rate} + 18\%(\text{ coefficient of variation }) = 8\% + 18\%\ CV_{project}$$

a. Which project is riskier, based on its coefficient of variation? (*Note:* The coefficient of variation is standard deviation/mean.)
b. Which, if either, of the projects should be selected, based on the required return calculated above? (*Note:* Round the required return to the nearest whole percent.)

Expected NPV

ST 10.3 Albany Enterprises is evaluating whether to build an exclusive resort on the island of St. Vincent in the Caribbean. The CFs are estimated to be $23 million for each of 15 years, the initial after-tax outlay is $150 million, and the appropriate discount rate is 10 percent.

a. Should Albany proceed with the project?
b. Upon further investigation, Albany decides that the CFs could be better characterized by the following probability distribution:

Condition	Probability	CFs per Year
Economy great	0.2	$30 million
Economy average	0.7	23 million
Hurricane: resort demolished	0.1	0

Does this new information affect your decision?

Problems

10.1 Norton Industries employs the capital asset pricing model to estimate project-specific required rates of return for capital budgeting decisions. The risk-free rate is 7 percent, the expected return on the market portfolio is 15 percent, and the project's beta is 1.50. The cash flow stream is as follows:

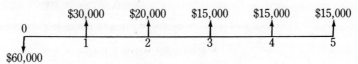

a. Should Norton undertake the proposed project?
b. Can you see any problems associated with using the capital asset pricing model to estimate project-specific required rates of return for capital budgeting decision making.

CAPM: Determining Beta

10.2 Hexter, Inc., is considering the investment in some new equipment. The CFs are as follows:

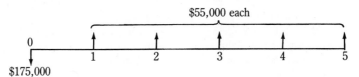

The CAPM approach will be employed to estimate the appropriate project-specific required rate of return; k_{RF} = 7 percent, $\sigma_{project}$ (standard deviation of the project's returns) = 32.20 percent, $Corr_{project, M}$ = +0.60, and the distribution of the market's return is:

Probability, P_i	Market Return, k_{Mi}
0.20	30%
0.20	20
0.30	15
0.30	−5

a. What is the project's beta? (*Note:* Carry to two decimal places. From Appendix 7B, $\beta_{project} = \sigma_{project} Corr_{project, M}/\sigma_M$.)
b. Should Hexter purchase the equipment?

Required Rates of Return

10.3 Texas Bar-B-Q plans to open two new fast-food stores, one in Dallas and one in Oklahoma City. The Dallas operation is estimated to be a riskier project and is assigned a risk premium of 3 percent above the firm's required rate of return as given by its weighted average cost of capital, WACC, versus the 1 percent risk premium assigned to the Oklahoma City store. Expected after-tax cash flows for each store are estimated below:

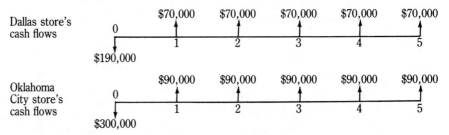

If the firm's weighted average cost of capital is 15 percent, should the Dallas store be opened? The Oklahoma City store?

10.4 Your firm is considering two mutually exclusive projects with the following CFs:

	Project A		Project B	
Initial investment	$120,000		$150,000	
CFs and probabilities of occurrence for *each of 6 years*	0.30	$35,000	0.30	$60,000
	0.40	30,000	0.40	40,000
	0.30	20,000	0.30	30,000

The following equation is employed to estimate the project-specific required rate of return:

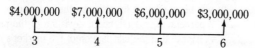

$$\begin{matrix}\text{required} \\ \text{return}\end{matrix} = \begin{matrix}\text{risk-free} \\ \text{rate}\end{matrix} + 10\%(\text{coefficient of variation}) = 11\% + 10\%CV_{\text{project}}$$

a. Which project is riskier, based on its coefficient of variation? (*Note:* The coefficient of variation is the standard deviation/mean.)

b. Which, if either, of the projects should be selected? (*Note:* Round the required return to the nearest whole percent.)

10.5 Berry Foods has developed chocolate marbles. The product will be test marketed in the southeastern United States for 2 years, requires an initial investment of $2 million, and because of heavy promotional expenses is not expected to generate any positive CFs during the first two years. There is a 60 percent chance that demand for the chocolate marbles will be satisfactory; if that is so, an $8 million after-tax cash outflow will be incurred at t = 2 to market the chocolate marbles in the eastern half of the United States. Subsequent CFs are as follows:

$4,000,000	$7,000,000	$6,000,000	$3,000,000
3	4	5	6

If the test market results are unfavorable (a 40 percent chance), the chocolate marbles will be withdrawn from the market. Once consumer preferences are known, Berry Foods considers chocolate marbles an average-risk project requiring a 14 percent return. During the test marketing phase a 25 percent return is required. What decision should Berry make?

10.6 Greentree Products is considering investing in a capital budgeting project where the CFs are as follows:

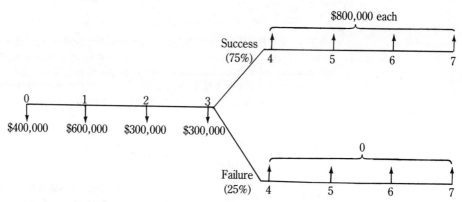

The cash investment (CF) in year 3 will be made *only* if the project is deemed successful (the upper branch). For the first 3 years, the appropriate required rate of return is 30 percent; after that, it drops to 10 percent. (*Note:* The cash flows at t_1, t_2, and t_3 are negative, just like at t_0.) What decision should Greentree make?

10.7 Rainbow Painters would like to purchase a mixing machine for an initial investment of $11,000. It would last 5 years and produce after-tax cash flows of $3,900 per year. The required rate of return is 16 percent.

a. If each of the following conditions is considered independently, decide whether the company should purchase the mixer if:
(1) The estimates are correct.
(2) The machine only lasts 4 years.
(3) Operating cash flows for each year decrease by 10 percent.
(4) The required return is 3 percent too low.
To which variable is the accept-reject decision most sensitive?

(Do only if using Pinches Disk.)
b. Suppose the mixing machine cannot be purchased for $11,000, but instead will cost $15,000. Recalculate the cases in (a) under this circumstance.
c. Now suppose the required return is determined to be 12 percent, while everything else is as given in (a). How will this affect the purchase decision in the first three cases in (a)?
d. Should the company invest in the mixer if all of the following conditions exist simultaneously?
(1) Machine cost = $13,000
(2) Required return = 15 percent
(3) Marginal tax rate = 33 percent
(4) Terminal resale value (before tax) = $2,000
(5) Machine will last 10 years
(6) Operating cash flows increase each year by 25 percent.

10.8 The board of directors of Peninsula Industries has just received a proposal that requires an initial investment of $1 million and is expected to produce cash flows before tax, CFBT, of $300,000 for each year of its life. As presented, the project has a 7-year economic life, but the initial investment will be depreciated by ACRS over its 5-year normal recovery period. The required rate of return is 15 percent, and the firm's tax rate is 35 percent.

a. Should Peninsula's board recommend acceptance of the project?
b. After discussing the project, certain members of the board feel the economic life will be only (1) 5, or (2) 6 years, not 7. Does this new information change the previous decision?

10.9 Ewert, Inc., is considering the extension of an existing product line. The incremental initial investment is $1.4 million, and the rest of the assumptions are as follows:
1. Depreciation for tax purposes to zero will occur over 7 years via straight line; the economic life is also 7 years.
2. Variable costs are 30 percent of estimated sales.
3. Fixed costs are $100,000.
4. The tax rate is 40 percent and the required rate of return is 20 percent.

What is the per year economic break-even level of sales?

10.10 McManus Systems has developed a whole new concept in large-scale fast-food restaurants. Excluding land costs the new restaurants require an initial outlay of $4 million per location. The following conditions apply:
1. Depreciation for both GAAP accounting and for tax purposes will be to a value of zero over 10 years.
2. Variable costs are 50 percent of sales.
3. Fixed costs are $300,000 per year.
4. The firm's marginal tax rate is 30 percent, and the required rate of return is 18 percent.

Excluding land costs, what is the accounting break-even point per year? The economic-break-even point (also excluding land costs)? Why does the accounting break-even point underestimate the volume of sales necessary to produce a zero NPV project?

Replacement Decision and Break-Even Initial Investment (More Difficult)

10.11 Costs have decreased and Indiana National is considering replacing their existing refrigeration system. To help them in negotiating the final purchase price they have hired a consultant—you! The relevant facts are:

Existing system
Purchased 5 years ago for $800,000.
Being depreciated to zero employing straight-line over 10 years. (*Note:* Five years have already elapsed.)
Will last 10 more years if retained.
Resale value if sold today is $150,000; resale value in 10 more years is $20,000.

New System
Will be depreciated to zero employing straight-line over 10 years.
Will last 10 years.
Resale value in 10 years is $50,000.
Benefits are a before-tax reduction in operating costs of $75,000 per year.

a. If the tax rate is 35 percent, and the required rate of return is 15 percent, what is the initial purchase price on the new system so that the NPV equals zero? (*Note:* Assume the firm is profitable so it receives the tax benefit from selling the existing system at a loss.)

b. Explain why the information calculated in (a) is important for effective decision making.

Simulation Analysis

10.12 The Campbell Corporation employs simulation analysis when evaluating major capital budgeting projects. After running a recent analysis they arrived at a probability distribution of possible outcomes as follows:

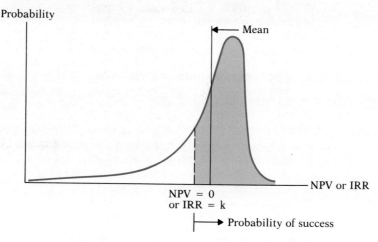

a. Based on this probability distribution, what do we know about the project?
b. What are the strengths and the limitations of simulation when making capital budgeting decisions?

References

Basic information on capital budgeting and uncertainty can be found in

Crum, Roy L., and Frans G. J. Derkinderen, eds. *Capital Budgeting Under Conditions of Uncertainty.* Boston: Martinus Nijhoff, 1981.

MARSHUETZ, RICHARD J. "How American Can Allocates Capital." *Harvard Business Review* 63 (January–February 1985), pp. 82–91.

Other topics of interest include

ANG, JAMES S., AND WILBUR G. LEWELLEN. "Risk Adjustment in Capital Investment Project Evaluations." *Financial Management* 11 (Summer 1982), pp. 5–14.

CRUM, ROY L., DAN J. LAUGHHUNN, AND JOHN W. PAYNE. "Risk Seeking Behavior and Its Implications for Financial Models." *Financial Management* 10 (Winter 1981), pp. 20–27.

GEHR, ADAM K. "Risk-Adjusted Capital Budgeting Using Arbitrage." *Financial Management* 10 (Winter 1981), pp. 14–19.

HODDER, JAMES E., AND HENRY E. RIGGS. "Pitfalls in Evaluating Risky Projects." *Harvard Business Review* 63 (January–February 1985), pp. 128–135.

KWAN, CLARENCE C. Y., AND YUFEI YUAN. "Optimal Sequential Selection in Capital Budgeting: A Shortcut." *Financial Management* 17 (Spring 1988), pp. 54–59.

SICK, GORDON A. "A Certainty-Equivalent Approach to Capital Budgeting." *Financial Management* 15 (Winter 1986), pp. 23–32.

More on simulation and other related approaches is contained in

CHEN, SON-NAN, AND WILLIAM T. MOORE. "Investment Decisions Under Uncertainty: Application of Estimation Risk in the Hillier Approach." *Journal of Financial and Quantitative Analysis* 17 (September 1982), pp. 425–440.

GIACCOTTO, CARMELO. "A Simplified Approach to Risk Analysis in Capital Budgeting with Serially Correlated Cash Flows." *Engineering Economist* 29 (Summer 1984), pp. 273–286.

GITMAN, LAWRENCE J., MICHAEL D. JOEHNK, AND GEORGE E. PINCHES. *Managerial Finance.* New York: Harper & Row, 1985, Chapter 14 and Appendix 14B.

ROBICHEK, ALEXANDER A. "Interpreting the Results of Risk Analysis." *Journal of Finance* 30 (December 1975), pp. 1384–1386.

11 | Options and Investment Decisions

Overview

- A call option is a right to buy, while a put option is a right to sell.

- An option's value depends on the price of the underlying asset, the exercise price, the time to expiration, the risk-free rate, and the standard deviation of the underlying asset.

- In the absence of risk, the value of a call option is equal to the maximum of (1) the market price of the stock minus the present value of the exercise price, or (2) zero.

- Capital budgeting decisions, abandonment, and guarantees all contain options that must be accounted for if they are to be valued correctly.

*A*n option is a right to buy or sell a particular good for a limited time at a specified price. The most familiar options are stock options—options to buy or sell shares of common stock. The development of options has been a major financial success story. Since they were first developed and traded on the Chicago Board Options Exchange (CBOE) in 1973, options have grown to become one of the biggest markets in the world. Option trading now takes place on a number of exchanges. In addition to options on common stock, there are also options on stock indexes, bonds, commodities, and foreign exchange rates.

Some of the major U.S. options exchanges and the options traded on them are the following:

> Chicago Board Options Exchange
>> Individual stocks
>> General stock market indices
>> Treasury bonds
> American Exchange
>> Individual stocks
>> General stock market indices
>> Oil and gas index

> *Transportation index*
> *Treasury bills*
> *Treasury notes*
> *Philadelphia Exchange*
> *Individual stocks*
> *Foreign currencies*
> *Gold and silver indexes*

Other exchanges also list options, and new options are introduced over time. At the same time, some options cease to exist if demand for them wanes.

Options

Option trading is a specialized business and its participants speak a language all their own. Why, then, should a financial manager be interested in options? The answer is because managers routinely encounter securities, or situations, that have options embedded in them. Only by understanding the basics of options will financial managers be in a position to recognize, understand, and value these often hidden options. Our focus in this chapter is twofold. First, to present the basics of options and option pricing theory. Second, to apply this knowledge to understanding the options imbedded in many long-term investment and abandonment decisions. This is an exciting, yet complex, new area that extends and builds upon the NPV-based approach to capital budgeting developed in Chapters 8–10.

In order to discuss options we need to understand certain basic terms. These include:

1. EXERCISING AN OPTION. The act of buying or selling the underlying asset via an option contract is called exercising the option.
2. EXERCISE PRICE (OR STRIKE PRICE). The fixed price stated in the option contract at which the underlying asset may be purchased or sold is the *exercise* (or *strike*) *price*.
3. EXPIRATION DATE OR MATURITY. The maturity date is when the option expires. After this date the option is worthless.
4. CALL OPTION VERSUS PUT OPTION. A *call option* provides the owner of the option the right to buy the underlying asset. Conversely, a *put option* provides the owner with the right to sell the asset.
5. AMERICAN OPTION VERSUS EUROPEAN OPTION. An *American option* may be exercised anytime up to and including the expiration date. On the other hand, a *European option* can only be exercised at the expiration date.

If you picked up the *Wall Street Journal* and looked at the listed options quotations for IBM, you might see the following:[1]

---

[1] In some places the letters "r" or "s" appear. An "r" means the option was not traded on that day. An "s" indicates that no option exists. At any point in time investors typically have the opportunity to purchase any of three different call or put options—that mature in one of three different months.

Option & N.Y. Close	Strike Price	Calls—Last			Puts—Last		
		Oct	Nov	Jan	Oct	Nov	Jan
IBM	100	14	s	s	$\frac{1}{4}$	s	s
112⅝	105	9⅛	s	11½	⅝	s	2⅛
112⅝	110	5⅛	6	8⅛	1⅝	2⅝	3¾
112⅝	115	2⅛	3⅛	5¼	3¾	5⅛	5⅞
112⅝	120	11⁄16	1½	3⅜	7½	r	9⅛
112⅝	125	¼	s	2 1⁄16	10⅞	s	13⅜
112⅝	130	⅛	s	1⅛	17¾	s	18

Beneath "IBM," the first column lists the closing price of IBM stock for the day. The second column lists the exercise (or strike) prices available. These exercise prices are kept fairly close to the prevailing market price of the stock. For volatile stocks more exercise prices will be available; likewise, as the stock price changes new exercise prices are opened for trading, at $5 intervals. Each contract is written for 100 shares, but the option prices are quoted per share as shown in the last 6 columns. Upon purchase of an option an investor would have the right to purchase (a call option) or sell (a put option) 100 shares of IBM at the exercise (or strike price).

For example, if you purchased the October call option with a strike price of $110, you would pay (100 shares)(5⅛) = $512.50, plus any commission fee. Once you own the call, you can exercise it by paying (100 shares)($110) = $11,000. The writer of the option is obligated to sell you 100 shares at $110 per share, providing you exercise the option before the expiration date.

The right to buy IBM at a specific exercise price as indicated in the call option is valuable. Likewise, put options also exist that provide the owner the right to sell shares at a fixed exercise price. How valuable the option is depends on five specific factors to be discussed shortly. Before moving into the formal valuation of options, let us examine their value at one specific point in time—at the date of expiration.

For simplicity, we will restrict our discussion to European options.[2] The value of a call option on the expiration date can be summarized as follows:

Condition	Value of Call Option
If market price of stock is greater than the exercise price	= market price − exercise price of the stock
If market price is less than the exercise price	= 0

This relationship can be shown as in Figure 11.1. Let us define P_0 as the current market price of the stock, X as the exercise (or strike) price, and V_c as the value of the call option. We see that as long as the market price of the stock *at the expiration date* is below the exercise price, the option is worthless. But, if the market price of the common stock is greater than the exercise price, then the value of the call option is equal to $P_0 - X$. The colored line in Figure 11.1 indicates the lower limit on the call option's value.

[2] Much of what follows applies equally well to American call options. For nondividend paying stocks, the market price of an American call option is always greater than the value it would have if exercised immediately. Rational investors will not exercise American call options early; hence, their value is the same (on nondividend paying stocks) as that of a European option. But more complications exist when valuing American put options. These are beyond the scope of our treatment.

Figure 11.1 Value of a Call Option at Expiration

If the market price of the stock, P_0, is greater than the exercise price, X, then the value of the option (as given by the 45° line) is $P_0 - X$. Otherwise, the call option is worthless.

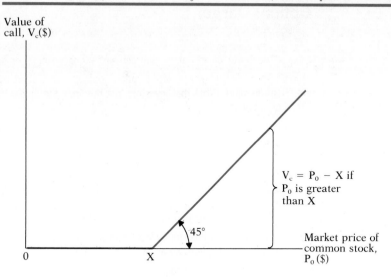

Value of call, $V_c($\$$)$

$V_c = P_0 - X$ if P_0 is greater than X

45°

Market price of common stock, $P_0 ($\$$)$

0   X

For example, assume you purchased the October call option on 100 shares of IBM with an exercise price of $110 and the expiration date has arrived. If the market price of IBM common stock had increased and is now $125, while the exercise price is $110, you can exercise the option—purchase 100 shares at $110 per share—and immediately sell the shares at $125. Your profit is [(100 shares)($125 − $110)] = $1,500, less what you paid for the option of $512.50. Ignoring the commission fee on the option, your profit is $1,500 − $512.50 = $987.50. Alternatively, if the market price of IBM common stock at the expiration date is only $105 per share, you will throw the option away and incur a loss of $512.50. The value of the IBM call option, V_c, at expiration is

$100(P_0 - X)$ if P_0 is greater than X

0 if P_0 is less than X

Thus, we see that the relationship of the stock price to the exercise price determines whether an option has any value at the expiration date of the option. This condition is true for both call options and for put options.

Valuing European Call Options

In the last section we determined what a European call option was (i.e., an option to buy that can be exercised only at maturity). Now we need to determine how options are valued at times other than the expiration date. At these times the value of the option will be greater than at expiration. This occurs because there is risk in that we don't know whether *at expiration* the stock price will be above or below the exercise price. Thus, the actual value of a call option *prior to the expiration date* will lie above the lower limit (given by $P_0 - X$, if P_0 is greater than X, or 0, if P_0 is less than X) shown previously in Figure 11.1.

Options Jargon

Long: The buyer of an option contract has a long position, or holds the contract long.

Short: The seller, or writer, of an option contract has a short position, or has sold the option short. (Note that investors, not the firms the option is on, are the "creators" of options.)

In-the-money: An option is in-the-money if by exercising the option it would produce a gain. A call option is in-the-money if the market price of the stock, P_0, is *greater* than the exercise price, X. Conversely, a put option is in-the-money if the market price of the stock, P_0, is *less* than the exercise price, X.

Out-of-the-money: An option is out-of-the-money if by exercising the option it would produce a loss. A call option is out-of-the-money if P_0 is less than X, while a put option is out-of-the-money if P_0 is greater than X.

Naked position: An investor holds a naked position if he or she holds only one of the following: the underlying asset, a single call option, or a single put option.

Hedged position: A hedged position is held if the investor holds the underlying asset and either a call or a put option written on the asset.

Straddle: A straddle is a position involving a call and a put on the same underlying asset and having the same expiration dates and exercise prices. To buy (or go long in) a straddle, an investor purchases both a call and a put; to go short a straddle, an investor writes (or sells) both a call and a put.

Basic Determinants

The factors that determine an option's value can be broken down into two basic sets. The first are those that relate to the option contract itself, while the second are related to the underlying asset (or stock). The three factors related to the option contract that affect the option's value are (1) the exercise price, (2) the expiration date, and (3) the level of interest rates, as indicated by the risk-free rate.

1. EXERCISE PRICE. Other things being equal, the higher the exercise price, the lower will be the value of a call option. This makes sense since the higher the exercise price, the less likely it is that the market price of the underlying asset will be above the exercise price at the expiration date. As long as there is some probability that the price of the underlying asset will exceed the exercise price, however, the call option will have value.

2. EXPIRATION DATE. The longer the time until expiration, the higher the value of the call option. Thus, other things being equal, if you hold a 6-month option, and also a 1-year option, the 1-year option will be more valuable because there

is more time for the market price of the underlying asset to fluctuate. This increase in time provides greater opportunity for the stock price to move, and hence increases the value of the option.

3. RISK-FREE RATE. The level of interest rates also affects the value of call options. This is because the market price of the asset, P_0, is in today's dollars while the exercise price is in future dollars. These must be stated at the same time, which is today, t_0. Based on the time value of money the present value of the exercise price is less when the risk-free rate is high, and the present value of the exercise price is more when the risk-free rate is low. Since the value of the call option is equal to at least the stock price, P_0, minus the present value of the exercise price a call option is more valuable the higher the risk-free rate. Thus, the value of a call option is positively related to the level of interest rates as measured by the risk-free rate.

In addition, two other factors that are related to the underlying asset also affect the value of call options. These are the stock price, and the variability (or riskiness) of the stock price.

1. STOCK PRICE. Other things being equal, the higher the stock price, the more valuable the call option. This occurs because at maturity the owner of the option will reap a larger return the more the stock price is above the exercise price.

2. STANDARD DEVIATION OF THE STOCK PRICE. Finally, the greater the variability of the underlying asset, the more valuable a call option will be. To see this it is important to remember a call option is only valuable when the market price of the underlying asset is greater than the exercise price. Call options on stocks with greater price volatility will therefore be worth more, other things being equal. Consider two 6-month call options, both with an exercise price, X, of $60, and a current stock market price, P_0, of $65. Let's assume the volatility of stock A is more than that of stock B. The call option on stock A will be more valuable, because with a higher stock price volatility, there is more likelihood that the value of the underlying asset may be above the exercise price than for stock B. As a consequence, *no matter what the degree of risk aversion of an individual investor, we find high variability in the underlying asset desirable when valuing options.*

To summarize, the value of a call option is a function of five variables:

1. Price of the underlying asset, P_0
2. Exercise price, X
3. Time to expiration, t
4. Risk-free rate, k_{RF}
5. Standard deviation of the underlying asset, σ

Thus, the value of a call option, V_c, is

$$V_c = (P_0, X, t, k_{RF}, \sigma) \tag{11.1}$$

where the plus (minus) sign by the variable indicates the effect of an increase in that variable on the price of the call option:

		Effect of an Increase of Each Factor on V_c
Stock price	P_0	+
Exercise price	X	−
Time to expiration	t	+
Risk-free rate	k_{RF}	+
Variability of stock's return	σ	+

As long as it is before the expiration date, an increase in the stock price, P_0, the time to expiration, t, the risk-free rate, k_{RF}, or the standard deviation, σ, will cause the value of the call option to go up. Thus, increases in any of these four variables will cause the actual option value to be further above the lower limit. This is shown graphically by the dashed line in Figure 11.2.

The Black–Scholes Model

The valuation of options is straightforward if we are willing to accept some complicated-looking equations. The Black–Scholes option pricing model gives the correct expression for the value of an option before the expiration of the option, assuming continuous compounding. While continuous compounding is not often employed in finance, it is required in the Black–Scholes model. Otherwise, a binomial approach, or numerical approximation, is required. The Black–Scholes model is designed for European options, which can be exercised only at their expiration date. It consists of three main equations; the primary one for valuing call options is:

$$V_c = P_0 N(d_1) - \frac{X}{e^{k_{RF}t}} N(d_2) \tag{11.2}$$

where

- V_c = the value of the call option
- P_0 = the current price of the stock
- X = the exercise (or strike) price
- t = time remaining before expiration of the option (expressed in decimal form as a proportion of a year)
- k_{RF} = continuously compounded risk-free rate of interest (in decimal form)
- e = natural antilog of 1.00 or 2.71828
- N(d) = the probability that a standardized normally distributed random variable will have a value less than or equal to d

The two subsidiary equations are

$$d_1 = \frac{\ln(P_0/X) + (k_{RF} + 0.5\sigma^2)t}{\sigma\sqrt{t}} \tag{11.3}$$

$$d_2 = d_1 - \sigma\sqrt{t} \tag{11.4}$$

where

ln( ) = the natural logarithm of the number in parenthesis[3]

---

[3] When using your calculator to determine option values, be sure to note that ln means the LN key, as opposed to e in Equation 11.2, which means the e^x key.

Figure 11.2 Value of a Call Option Before Expiration

The lower bound on the value is given by the solid colored line. But, other things being equal, the higher the stock price, P_0, the longer the time to expiration, t, the higher the risk-free rate, k_{RF}, or the greater the standard deviation, σ, the higher will be the value of the option, V_c, as indicated by the dashed line.

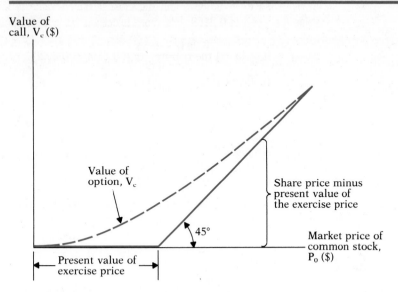

$σ$ = the standard deviation of the continuously compounded annual rate of return on the stock

We will discuss d_1 and d_2 more, but first let us use the three equations to value a call option.

To understand how to use this model, it is best to start with an example. Assume the data are as follows:

P_0 = \$100 (current price of the stock)
X = \$90 (exercise price)
t = 6 months, or 0.50 (maturity of the option)
k_{RF} = 10 percent, or 0.10 (annual risk-free rate)
e = 2.71828 (natural antilog of 1.00)
$σ$ = 28 percent, or 0.28 (risk on a continuously compounded annual basis)

STEP 1: Calculate d_1 and d_2, rounding the answers to four decimal places:

$$d_1 = \frac{\ln(P_0/X) + (k_{RF} + 0.5\sigma^2)t}{\sigma\sqrt{t}}$$

$$= \frac{\ln(100/90) + [0.10 + 0.5(0.28)^2]0.50}{0.28\sqrt{0.50}}$$

$$= \frac{0.10536 + 0.06960}{0.19799} = \frac{0.17496}{0.19799} = 0.8837$$

$$d_2 = d_1 - \sigma\sqrt{t} = 0.8837 - 0.1980 = 0.6857$$

STEP 2: Compute $N(d_1)$ and $N(d_2)$ using a cumulative normal distribution function table. (See Table 11.1; this is reproduced as Table F.6.)

To use this table, locate the number closest to the value of d in the d column. In our case $d_1 = 0.8837$, and the closest tabled value is for 0.90, which gives a value for $N(d_1)$ of 0.8159. For more precision we can interpolate as follows:

$$N(d_1) = 0.8023 + \left(\frac{0.8837 - 0.85}{0.90 - 0.85} \right)(0.8159 - 0.8023)$$

$$= 0.8023 + 0.0092 = 0.8115$$

Similarly, $d_2 = 0.6857$, and the closest tabled $N(d)$ value (for 0.70) is 0.7580. Again, we can interpolate and get

$$N(d_2) = 0.7422 + \left(\frac{0.6857 - 0.65}{0.70 - 0.65} \right)(0.7580 - 0.7422)$$

$$= 0.7422 + 0.0113 = 0.7535$$

STEP 3: Determine the value of the call option, V_c. This is done using the main equation (Equation 11.2) as follows:

$$V_c = P_0 N(d_1) - \frac{X}{e^{k_{RF}t}} N(d_2) = \$100(0.8115) - \frac{\$90}{e^{0.10 \times 0.50}}(0.7535)$$

$$= \$81.15 - \left(\frac{\$90}{1.05127} \right)(0.7535) = \$81.15 - (\$85.61074)(0.7535)$$

$$= \$81.15 - \$64.51 = \$16.64$$

The value of this call option with 6 months to maturity is $16.64.

In the Black–Scholes option pricing model the value of an option is determined by the five variables discussed earlier: the current stock price, P_0, the stated exercise price, X, the current risk-free rate, k_{RF}, the time to expiration of the option, t, and the standard deviation of the stock price, σ. The price, stated exercise price, and time to maturity are known. The current risk-free rate can be estimated based on the yield on U.S. Treasury bills with approximately the same time to maturity as the option. The only unknown is the standard deviation of the stock price, for which a starting value is typically estimated by determining the past variance, σ^2, of the stock's daily rate of return. This daily variance is converted to a yearly figure by multiplying it by 365. By taking the square root of the yearly variance, we have the standard deviation.

The most difficult part of the option pricing model to understand is given by Equations 11.3 and 11.4. Once these calculations are made, they are then used to estimate probabilities of occurrence. This is exactly the part of the Black–Scholes model that takes account of risk, and allows the model to give good estimates for option prices.

The Black–Scholes model (i.e., Equation 11.2) says that

$$V_c = P_0 N(d_1) - \frac{X}{e^{k_{RF}t}} N(d_2)$$

Table 11.1 Cumulative Normal Distribution Function

Because this is a cumulative distribution function, the values can be used directly in the Black-Scholes equations.

d	N(d)	d	N(d)	d	N(d)
		−1.00	0.1587	1.00	0.8413
−2.95	0.0016	−0.95	0.1711	1.05	0.8531
−2.90	0.0019	−0.90	0.1841	1.10	0.8643
−2.85	0.0022	−0.85	0.1977	1.15	0.8749
−2.80	0.0026	−0.80	0.2119	1.20	0.8849
−2.75	0.0030	−0.75	0.2266	1.25	0.8944
−2.70	0.0035	−0.70	0.2420	1.30	0.9032
−2.65	0.0040	−0.65	0.2578	1.35	0.9115
−2.60	0.0047	−0.60	0.2743	1.40	0.9192
−2.55	0.0054	−0.55	0.2912	1.45	0.9265
−2.50	0.0062	−0.50	0.3085	1.50	0.9332
−2.45	0.0071	−0.45	0.3264	1.55	0.9394
−2.40	0.0082	−0.40	0.3446	1.60	0.9452
−2.35	0.0094	−0.35	0.3632	1.65	0.9505
−2.30	0.0107	−0.30	0.3821	1.70	0.9554
−2.25	0.0122	−0.25	0.4013	1.75	0.9599
−2.20	0.0139	−0.20	0.4207	1.80	0.9641
−2.15	0.0158	−0.15	0.4404	1.85	0.9678
−2.10	0.0179	−0.10	0.4602	1.90	0.9713
−2.05	0.0202	−0.05	0.4801	1.95	0.9744
−2.00	0.0228	0.00	0.5000	2.00	0.9773
−1.95	0.0256	0.05	0.5199	2.05	0.9798
−1.90	0.0287	0.10	0.5398	2.10	0.9821
−1.85	0.0322	0.15	0.5596	2.15	0.9842
−1.80	0.0359	0.20	0.5793	2.20	0.9861
−1.75	0.0401	0.25	0.5987	2.25	0.9878
−1.70	0.0446	0.30	0.6179	2.30	0.9893
−1.65	0.0495	0.35	0.6368	2.35	0.9906
−1.60	0.0548	0.40	0.6554	2.40	0.9918
−1.55	0.0606	0.45	0.6736	2.45	0.9929
−1.50	0.0668	0.50	0.6915	2.50	0.9938
−1.45	0.0735	0.55	0.7088	2.55	0.9946
−1.40	0.0808	0.60	0.7257	2.60	0.9953
−1.35	0.0885	0.65	0.7422	2.65	0.9960
−1.30	0.0968	0.70	0.7580	2.70	0.9965
−1.25	0.1057	0.75	0.7734	2.75	0.9970
−1.20	0.1151	0.80	0.7881	2.80	0.9974
−1.15	0.1251	0.85	0.8023	2.85	0.9978
−1.10	0.1357	0.90	0.8159	2.90	0.9981
−1.05	0.1469	0.95	0.8289	2.95	0.9984

The term $X/e^{k_{RF}t}$ is simply the present value of the exercise price when continuous discounting is employed. This means that the value of a call option is

$$V_c = P_0 N(d_1) - (\text{present value of } X) N(d_2)$$

The terms involving cumulative probabilities are the terms that take account of risk. If the stock had little or no risk (i.e., a very small standard deviation, σ), the calculated values for d_1 and d_2 would be large, and the probabilities would both approach the value of 1. If $N(d_1)$ and $N(d_2)$ both equal 1, then the option pricing model can be simplified to

$$V_c = P_0 - \text{present value of X}$$

which, as shown in Figure 11.2, is the lower bound on the value of a call option before the expiration date. (As always, if P_0 is less than the present value of X, the option has a value of zero.) Thus, the expressions $N(d_1)$ and $N(d_2)$ capture the risk involved in the option. They are what cause the actual value of the option (as shown previously by the dashed line in Figure 11.2) to be greater than the lower bound (i.e., the solid colored line).[4]

To derive their model, Black and Scholes made a number of assumptions:

1. There are no transactions costs or taxes.
2. The risk-free rate is constant over the life of the option.
3. The stock market operates continuously (both day and night).
4. The stock price is continuous; that is, there are no sudden jumps in price.
5. The stock pays no cash dividends.
6. The option can be exercised only at the expiration date (i.e., it is a European option).
7. The underlying stock can be sold short without penalty.
8. The distribution of returns on the underlying stock is log-normal.

Even with these assumptions, the Black–Scholes model has been found to be a good predictor of actual option prices. Upon first acquaintance with the Black–Scholes option pricing model, many think it is too complicated to be useful. Nothing could be further from the truth. The option pricing model has gained wide acceptance, especially among investors and traders in options. Programs can easily be written to calculate the value of options, and some calculators even have subroutines available for determining the value of options. In addition, tables are available for classroom use.

Short Cuts for Calculating Call Option Values

The Black–Scholes formula is precise, but requires considerable calculation, as shown in the three-step procedure discussed earlier. However, if our objective is to determine an *approximate* value of an option, it is simpler to use tables. Consider the same example used earlier in which

$P_0 = \$100$	$k_{RF} = 0.10$
$X = \$90$	$\sigma = 0.28$
$t = 0.50$	

A simple procedure can be employed to find the approximate value of this call option:

STEP 1: Calculate the standard deviation times the square root of time:

---

[4] While beyond our treatment, it should also be noted that the value given by $N(d_1)$ is the hedge ratio necessary to construct a perfect hedge. Thus, a portfolio comprising a short position of one call option and a long position (i.e., where a sale has occurred) of $N(d_1)$ shares of stock will have a total value that will not change for small fluctuations in the price of the stock.

$$\sigma\sqrt{t} = 0.28\sqrt{0.50} = 0.1980$$

STEP 2: Calculate the market price divided by the present value of the exercise price.

$$\frac{P_0}{X/e^{k_{RF}t}} = \frac{\$100}{\$90/e^{0.10 \times 0.50}} = \frac{\$100}{\$85.6107} = 1.1681$$

STEP 3: Using the two values from steps 1 and 2, determine the tabled factor and multiply it by the share price.

For a call option, Table F.7 provides a value of 0.1626 for a calculated standard deviation times the square root of time of 0.20, and a market price divided by the present value of the exercise price of 1.16. Multiplying the stock price of $100 by 0.1626 from the table we have an estimated value of the price of the call option, V_c, of $16.26. This corresponds to the more precise value of $16.64 determined earlier. Although these tables are not completely precise, they are often close enough, because our primary emphasis is on understanding the essential elements of option pricing and valuation.

Put Options

Up to now we have focused on call options, which are options to purchase. We also know that put options, which are options to sell an underlying asset at a specific price for a predetermined period of time, also exist. The same five factors discussed previously for call options—the market price of the underlying asset, P_0, exercise (or strike) price, X, time to expiration, t, risk-free rate, k_{RF}, and standard deviation of the underlying asset's returns, σ—also affect the value of a put. The value of a put, V_p, *at maturity* is shown in Figure 11.3. As can be seen, the value of the put option at expiration is:

0 if P_0 is greater than X

X − P_0 if P_0 is less than X

Hence, for a put option the relationship is just the reverse of a call option. The put option only has value at its expiration date if the value of the stock is *less* than the exercise price.

The same five factors discussed earlier affect the value of a put option. The relationship of an increase in a variable, and its impact on the value of the put is somewhat different, however, as follows:

		Effect of an Increase of Each Factor on V_p
Stock price	P_0	−
Exercise price	X	+
Time to expiration	t	Either[5]
Risk-free rate	k_{RF}	−
Variability of stock's return	σ	+

Just like a call option, the actual value of a put option, V_p, will be above the lower limit depicted in Figure 11.3 except at its expiration date.

[5] As t increases, normally V_p increases; but if the stock price, P_0, is a good deal below the exercise price, X, then as t increases, V_p decreases.

Figure 11.3   Value of a Put Option at Expiration

If the market price of the stock, P_0, is less than the exercise price, X, then the value of the option (as given by the 45°line) is $X - P_0$. Otherwise, the put is worthless.

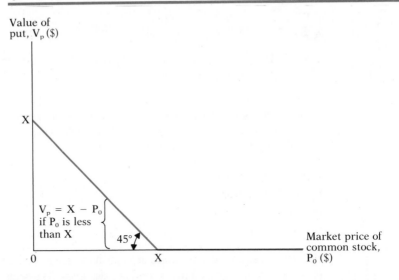

Valuing European Put Options

A put option is simply an option to sell. Once you know the value of a call option, determining the value of a put option is easy.[6] It is given by

$$V_p = V_c + \frac{X}{e^{k_{RF}t}} - P_0 \tag{11.5}$$

where V_p is the value of the European put option, and the rest of the terms are as defined before. For our example, with a call option value of $16.64, the value of a put option (with everything else the same) is

$$V_p = V_c + \frac{X}{e^{k_{RF}t}} - P_0$$

$$= \$16.64 + \frac{\$90}{e^{0.10 \times 0.50}} - \$100 = \$16.64 + \$85.61 - \$100 = \$2.25$$

The reason for the relatively low value of the put option is due to the relationship of the market price of the stock to the exercise price. The call option can be exercised (i.e., has value) as long as the market price remains above the exercise price of $90. However, this put option becomes valuable only if the current market price

---

[6] The put call parity states that the value of a call option, plus the present value of the exercise price, equals the value of the put option plus the market price of the stock, or

$$V_c + \frac{X}{e^{k_{RF}t}} = V_p + P_0$$

Therefore,

$$V_p = V_c + \frac{X}{e^{k_{RF}t}} - P_0$$

The Futures Trading Sting

Ending a 2-year undercover operation in early 1989, the FBI brought charges of widespread cheating of customers, market manipulation, fraud, and tax evasion resulting from Chicago's futures industry. Chicago's two futures exchanges, the Chicago Board of Trade and the Chicago Mercantile Exchange, are among the largest in the world.

The FBI investigation struck at the essence of futures trading. A futures contract is an agreement to deliver or take delivery of a commodity at a set price and time. The way futures are traded is through an open outcry system, which purports to deliver to investors the best available price. With open outcry, traders stand in an octagonal-shaped pit, buying and selling futures contracts among themselves by waving their arms and flashing hand signals. Independent floor brokers can trade both for their own accounts and for customers' accounts. This practice, called dual trading, leads to the possibility of engaging in an activity called "bucket trading."

In a bucket transaction an independent floor broker gets a customer's order to buy a futures contract at the best possible price. That's known as a "market order." Instead of executing the order immediately the floor broker signals a confederate known as a "bagman" to buy the contract. The bagman does and the broker continues to hold the customer's order. If the price rises within the next minute or two the floor broker then executes the customer's order at the higher price and buys the contract from the bagman. The bagman may make $3,000 or $4,000 on this transaction; the profit is split between the bagman and the floor broker. If the futures price goes down while the broker is holding the order, the broker simply repurchases the contract from the bagman at the old price. That way the loss is bucketed into the customer's account.

As a result of this sting operation, reform is on the way. New procedures have already been implemented to reduce some abuses of this type. They may even lead to a complete revamping of how futures are traded.

drops by more than $10 so it is below the exercise price of $90. In our example the market price of the common stock is above the exercise price; consequently, the put option is not very valuable.

Instead of employing Equation 11.5 to value the put option, Table F.8 can be employed. From our earlier calculations $\sigma\sqrt{t} = 0.1980$ while $P_0/(X \div e^{k_{RF}t}) = 1.1681$. Going to Table F.8, the tabled value is 0.0246. Multiplying by the market price of $100 produces $2.46, which compares closely with the $2.25 calculated earlier.[7]

---

[7] We can also value European options on dividend-paying stocks. If only one known cash dividend is expected to be paid before the expiration of the option, the equations are

$$V_c^* = \left(P_0 - \frac{D}{e^{k_{RF}t^*}} \right) N(d_1) - \frac{X}{e^{k_{RF}t}} N(d_2)$$

and

An Example: Valuing Warrants[8]	Now that we understand the basic features of options, and how to value them, let's apply that knowledge to valuing warrants. Before starting, it is important to emphasize that options are created by investors themselves (i.e., the firm in which the option is written is *not* involved in creating options). Warrants, on the other hand, are created by the firm.

A significant amount of privately placed debt, and a far smaller percentage of public offerings, occurs in packages where warrants are issued along with debt. Warrants are also sometimes given to investment bankers as compensation for underwriting services. (See Chapter 12 for a discussion of issuing securities.) A *warrant* is an option that provides the investor with the right to buy a specific number of shares of common stock at a predetermined price for a certain time period. Warrants are almost always detachable, which means that shortly after the package of securities is issued, the bonds and the warrants can be sold separately.

From the preceding discussion it is clear that warrants are similar to call options. In fact, from the investor's standpoint, a warrant is exactly the same as a call option on the common stock of the issuing company.[9] Consider the example of First America Bancorp which has issued some 5-year warrants with an exercise price of $40, and the current stock price is $31. Based on what we learned about call options, the lower limit on the value of this warrant (or option to buy a share of First America Bancorp) can be depicted as in Figure 11.4. Like any call option, however, the warrant will actually trade above the lower limit on its value. The height of the actual warrant price (given by the dashed line in Figure 11.4) above the lower limit will depend on the following:

Stock price, P_0

Exercise price, X

Risk-free rate, k_{RF}

Time to maturity, t

Standard deviation of the stock's return, σ

These are the same factors that determine the value of any call option.

Once a warrant is designed and issued, the exercise price is set. Also, for simplicity, let's hold the stock price, P_0, constant for a minute. In this case, the height of the actual warrant price above the lower limit depends on three things—the risk-free rate, k_{RF}, the time to maturity, t, and the standard deviation of the stock's return, σ. Of course, as time runs out, the actual price of the warrant snuggles closer and closer to the lower limit. On the final day of its life, its price hits the lower limit. If

---

$$V_p^* = V_c^* + \frac{X}{e^{k_{RF}t}} - P_0 + \frac{D}{e^{k_{RF}t^*}}$$

where

D = the cash dividend that will be paid before the expiration date

t* = the time (in decimal form) in years until the dividend is expected to be paid

and the rest of the terms are as defined before. If more than one cash dividend is expected before the expiration of the option, the expression $D/e^{k_{RF}t^*}$ must be modified to reflect the present value of all known dividends to be paid before expiration of the option. Cash dividends tend to reduce the value of call options and increase the value of put options.

[8] This section may be omitted without loss of continuity.

[9] Another call option is stock rights, which are briefly discussed in Chapter 12.

Figure 11.4 Relationship Between Market Value of Warrant and Its Lower Limit

Until expiration the actual market value of the warrant (given by the dashed line) will be greater than the lower limit (given by the solid colored line).

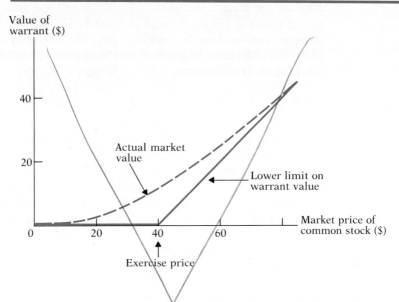

the warrant allows the purchase of more than one share of stock per warrant the lower limit is

$$\text{lower limit} = \left(\begin{array}{c}\text{market price of}\\\text{common stock}\\\text{–exercise price}\end{array}\right)\left(\begin{array}{c}\text{number of shares}\\\text{purchased with}\\\text{one warrant}\end{array}\right) \qquad (11.6)$$

The valuation of the First America warrants is straightforward. Assume that the firm does not pay any dividends on its common stock, the risk-free rate is 0.08, and the volatility of the stock returns is 0.40. With a maturity of 5 years, an exercise price of $40 and a current market value of the underlying common stock of $31, we can use Table F.7 to value the warrant as follows:

STEP 1: Standard deviation times the square root of time:

$$\sigma\sqrt{t} = 0.40\sqrt{5} = 0.8944$$

STEP 2: Market price divided by the present value of the exercise price:

$$\frac{P_0}{X/e^{k_{RF}t}} = \frac{\$31}{\$40/e^{0.08 \times 5}} = \frac{\$31}{\$26.8128} = 1.1562$$

STEP 3: Multiply tabled value by the stock price. From Table F.7, the value is approximately 0.3964, so that value of the warrant is $31(0.3964) = $12.29.

Thus, even though the current stock market price is less than the exercise price, due to the long time to maturity, the warrant has considerable value.[10]

---

[10] Two complications, which are beyond our treatment, exist—cash dividends, and the fact that additional common stock is issued when the warrants are exercised.

Options in Capital Investments

Options exist in many of the investment and financing decisions that a firm makes. It is for this reason that understanding how options are valued is becoming more important for financial managers. We will now examine some of the uses of option pricing theory in helping to make investment decisions; it should be emphasized, however, that we do so in a simplified (i.e., Black–Scholes) world. The same basic ideas, but with more complications, can be employed to more accurately determine the values than we illustrate.

Options to Invest

An example of a call option is an option to buy another firm. Assume your firm is privately held and is embarking on some exciting new developments. If these developments are successful you will need extensive marketing experience you do not presently have. The outcome of the current developments should be known within a year. To protect yourself you enter into an option to purchase Associated Wholesalers. The current market price of Associated is $56 per share, the risk-free rate is 0.11, the estimated standard deviation of Associated's stock is 0.20, and the exercise price (or contingent purchase price in 1 year) is $66. The first thing we need to do is recognize that this has all of the elements of any other option. In addition, it is a call option since we have the opportunity, but not the requirement, to buy Associated Wholesalers in 1 year.

What is the value per share of this call option? To find out, we employ our three-step procedure as before:

$$\sigma\sqrt{t} = 0.20\sqrt{1} = 0.2000$$

$$\frac{P_0}{X/e^{k_{RF}t}} = \frac{\$56}{\$66/e^{0.11 \times 1}} = \frac{\$56}{\$59.12505} = 0.9471$$

The tabled value from Table F.7 is approximately 0.0542, so the value of the option to invest is $56(0.0542) = $3.035 per share. That is the price you should pay per share in order to have the option of buying Associated Wholesalers in 1 year.

Another option is illustrated by the capital investments undertaken by a firm. These investments are generally not irrevocable, but the project can be expanded upon, modernized, replaced, or abandoned. Decisions such as these are contingent on the present values of the future cash flows that result if the options are exercised. Thus, *if capital expenditures are made now, they often create opportunities to make additional capital expenditures in the future.* These future opportunities are in effect options that will exist only if the current capital project is undertaken. As such, many capital expenditures may be viewed as call options.

Consider the example of Sanders Electronics, which is eyeing the rapid developments in automated nuances. If it invests now the NPV of a 2-year project at the appropriate discount rate is −$45 million. Hence, Sanders' decision is to reject the move into automated nuances. However, you point out that if Sanders does not make the present investment, expertise and opportunity may be lost—due to competitors getting the jump on Sanders. You project that in 2 years a new generation of automated nuances can go on-stream—the NPV of this additional, or contingent, project that would be undertaken in two years is $60 million, based on discounted cash inflows of $800 million and an initial investment of $740 million. In this light, the initial investment in the original negative NPV project that could be made now is simply a call option. If the results from the first 2 years are great, Sanders exercises the follow-on investment option and proceeds; otherwise, it walks away from automated nuances. If Sanders doesn't act now, however, the costs and time delays may be prohibitive in the future.

The key to the decision turns out to be how accurate the second NPV (in 2 years) of $60 million is. Since automated nuances may be highly risky, the actual NPV realized could be substantially more or less than $60 million. To consider this investment, first assume that the risk of automated nuances is low, with a standard deviation of 0.10. Also, the risk-free rate is 0.09. The decision is then based on the following analysis.

First, we estimate the value of the call option. The time is 2 years, the value of the follow-on investment *today* (i.e., P_0) is the cash inflow of $800 million (expected in 2 years) discounted back to the present at the required rate of return of 0.20, or $800/e^{0.20 \times 2} = \$536.26$ million.[11] The exercise price in this case is the investment required in 2 years, which is $740 million. Thus, we see that

$$P_0 = \$536.26 \text{ million} \qquad k_{RF} = 0.09$$

$$X = \$740 \text{ million} \qquad \sigma = 0.10$$

$$t = 2 \text{ years}$$

Using our three-step procedure the value today of this call option to invest in two more years is

$$\sigma\sqrt{t} = 0.10\sqrt{2} = 0.1414$$

$$\frac{P_0}{X/e^{k_{RF}t}} = \frac{\$536.26}{\$740/e^{0.09 \times 2}} = \frac{\$536.26}{\$618.10} = 0.8676$$

From Table F.7, the tabled value is 0.0133, and the value of the call option (to expand in 2 years) is $536.26 million(0.0133) = $7.13 million.

The total value of the investment opportunity to investment in automated nuances is the sum of the first NPV that exists today plus the option to make the second investment in 2 years, or

$$\text{value of opportunity} = \text{original NPV} + \text{call option} \qquad (11.7)$$

$$= -\$45.00 \text{ million} + \$7.13 \text{ million} = -\$37.87 \text{ million}$$

If the variability of the returns from the second investment in automated nuances is expected to be low, Sanders should not enter this field.

Consider what happens, however, if the variability of expected returns from the second investment has a standard deviation of 0.32 (instead of 0.10 assumed previously). Using our three-step procedure, we have

$$\sigma\sqrt{t} = 0.32\sqrt{2} = 0.4525$$

$$\frac{P_0}{X/e^{k_{RF}t}} = \frac{\$536.26}{\$740/e^{0.09 \times 2}} = \frac{\$536.26}{\$618.10} = 0.8676$$

---

[11] For consistency we will use continuous discounting to move the cash inflows and cash outflows around in this chapter. The *only* use of continuous discounting in this book is when the Black–Scholes model is employed.

From Table F.7 the tabled value is 0.1216 and the value of the option to expand is $536.26 million(0.1216) = $65.21 million. The total NPV = original NPV + call option = −$45 million + $65.21 million = $20.21 million. In this case, Sanders should proceed with the investment in automated nuances.

What should you finally recommend? It all depends on how valuable follow-on opportunities are expected to be. The key variable, and one that is hard to determine, is just how risky the follow-on opportunity is. Other things being equal, the more the variability in the follow-on opportunity's returns, the more valuable that call option becomes. Thus, as we noted in Chapter 10, risk may be beneficial in many capital budgeting decisions. Once an option pricing framework is employed, we see that greater risk (as shown by a larger standard deviation in the underlying assets' returns), leads to a higher option value.

Abandonment Decisions and Guarantees

In addition to call option applications, put options also exist in making investment decisions. An example of a put option is when a firm has the option to abandon a capital investment. Assume that your firm is making the investment in a new division (at time t_0) that is expected to have a positive net present value. But if cash inflows are low at the end of the first year, the firm will abandon (i.e., sell) the project for an after-tax cash inflow of $5 million. The present value at time t_0 of the cash flows expected after year 1 is $6.5 million, the risk-free rate is 0.12, and the standard deviation of the project, assuming no abandonment, is 0.55. Thus,

$$P_0 = \$6.5 \text{ million} \qquad k_{RF} = 0.12$$

$$X = \$5 \text{ million} \qquad \sigma = 0.55$$

$$t = 1 \text{ year}$$

Using our three-step procedure, the value of the option to abandon (i.e., a put option) is

$$\sigma\sqrt{t} = 0.55\sqrt{1} = 0.5500$$

$$\frac{P_0}{X/e^{k_{RF}t}} = \frac{\$6.5}{\$5/e^{0.12\times1}} = \frac{\$6.5}{\$4.43460} = 1.4657$$

From Table F.8, the tabled value is 0.0666, and the value of the option to abandon is $6.5 million(0.0666) = $432,900. The ability to get out of the proposed project has value. This has to be taken into consideration when calculating the project's net present value.[12] The total value of the opportunity when abandonment exists is

$$\text{value of opportunity} = \text{original NPV} + \text{abandonment (i.e., a put) option} \qquad (11.8)$$

Finally, let's consider another put option example. This is more difficult, but the general approach is widespread since it deals with the topic of guarantees. A guaran-

[12] In general, the valuation of abandonment options becomes more complicated because they may be exercised at the end of year 1, year 2, and so forth. This more general approach views the option to abandon as an American put on a dividend-paying stock, in which both the dividend payments and exercise price are uncertain. Numerical approximation techniques are required to value the general abandonment option.

tee—whether granted by a firm or a government—provides a floor, or exercise price, under which the cash flows can't fall. As such, there are many examples of guarantees that creep into financial transactions. Consider Megamarkets, Ltd. who is planning to divest its textiles division to Modern Fabrics. To facilitate the sale, Megamarkets guarantees that the cash flows from the textiles division will not fall below $6 million for each of the next 3 years. The question is, how much extra should Megamarkets charge for this cash flow guarantee?

To determine this we need two main items. First, we need the actual forecasted cash flows and related information. Second, we need to recognize that the cash flow guarantees are simply a *series* of put options where $6 million is the exercise price. If the forecasted cash flows are as follows, and the appropriate discount rate for the guarantees is 25 percent, then the present value, P_0, for each of the forecasted cash flows is

Year	Forecasted Cash Flow (In millions)	Present Value (at 25 percent) of Forecasted Cash Flows Employing Continuous Discounting (In millions)
1	$4.50	$4.50/e^{0.25 \times 1} = $3.50
2	5.50	5.50/e^{0.25 \times 2} = 3.34
3	8.00	8.00/e^{0.25 \times 3} = 3.78

If the standard deviation of the annual cash flow changes is 0.40 per year and the risk-free rate is 0.09, then,

Year (1)	Standard Deviation Times the Square Root of Time (2)	Price (or Asset Value) Divided by the Present Value of the Exercise Price (3)	Value of Guarantee (In millions) (4)
1	$0.40\sqrt{1} = 0.4000$	$\dfrac{\$3.50}{\$6/e^{0.09 \times 1}} = 0.6383$	$(0.6910)(\$3.50) = \$2.42$
2	$0.40\sqrt{2} = 0.5657$	$\dfrac{\$3.34}{\$6/e^{0.09 \times 2}} = 0.6665$	$(0.5289)(3.34) = 1.77$
3	$0.40\sqrt{3} = 0.6928$	$\dfrac{\$3.78}{\$6/e^{0.09 \times 3}} = 0.8253$	$(0.4038)(3.78) = \underline{1.53}$

Value of guarantee = $5.72

Using Table F.8 for valuing put options, the tabled values are entered in column 4 and multiplied by the present value (or current market value) of the cash flow guarantees. In pricing the textile division, Megamarkets should add $5.72 million to the price quoted because of the cash flow guarantees provided to Modern Fabrics. Failure to do so results in an underpricing of the worth of the textiles division and associated guarantees.

Numerous other illustrations of call options, put options, or combinations of options occur in finance. One of these—determining the value of the firm's stock and bonds—is examined in Appendix 11A. The ability to provide estimates of the worth of these options is an exciting new development—and one that is vitally important for effective financial management.

Summary

Options provide the right to buy (a call option) or sell (a put option) a particular good for a limited time at a specified price. For European options, which can be exercised only at maturity, their value is determined by the price of the underlying asset, P_0, the exercise price, X, the time to expiration, t, the risk-free rate, k_{RF}, and the standard deviation of the underlying assets returns, σ. Using the Black–Scholes option pricing model, the value of call and put options can easily be determined.

Warrants are long-lived options to purchase stock, which are issued by the firm. Numerous options exist in capital expenditure decisions. An option to purchase an asset or firm in the future is a call option. Likewise, many capital projects embody options—to expand on them, or alternatively abandon them, in the future. Finally, any type of guarantee has option features that make it valuable. Only by understanding option pricing theory can we develop the techniques and experience necessary to value these important financial options.

There is an appendix to this chapter, "Appendix 11A: Valuing the Firm Using the Option Pricing Model," at the back of the book.

Questions

11.1 Define or explain the following

a. Exercise (strike) price
b. Call option
c. Put option
d. American option
e. European option
f. Warrant

11.2 What five factors affect the value of a call option? How would a decrease in their level, other things being equal, affect the value of a call option?

11.3 Explain why risk is desirable when investing in options. How do the terms $N(d_1)$ and $N(d_2)$ capture this risk?

11.4 How do puts differ from calls? Why is a decrease in the market price of the stock desirable if you hold a put option, but not desirable if you hold a call option?

11.5 Explain how an increase in any of the five factors determining a put option's value affects the value of the put option.

11.6 How do cash dividends affect the value of a call option? A put option? (*Note*: See footnote 7.)

11.7 Compare and contrast warrants and options from the firm's and the investor's standpoints.

11.8 Why are capital budgeting projects, and the opportunity to abandon a project, closely related to call and put options?

11.9 Explain how to value guarantees, and why guarantees—whether provided by firms or governments—are valuable.

Self-Test Problems (Solutions appear on pages 725–726.)

Option Valuation

ST 11.1   The following applies for a call option:

$P_0 = \$35$ $t = 0.65$

$X = \$40$ $\sigma = 0.20$

$k_{RF} = 0.11$

a. Determine the value of a call option on the stock.
b. What is the value of a put option?
c. What is the value of the call option if the time to maturity drops to 0.30?

Percentage Return with Warrants

ST 11.2   A warrant allows you to purchase two shares of common stock at $10 each. The stock price when you purchased the warrant was $15 per share; it is now $35 per share. Based on the lower limit of the warrant value, your percentage return (ignoring taxes) is how much?

Guarantees

ST 11.3   Santiago, Inc. is attempting to sell its electronics division to its current management in a leveraged buyout. To effect the sale, Santiago will guarantee the free cash flows (i.e., cash flows over and above those required to meet normal outflows and make certain capital investments) of the electronics division will be a minimum of $6 million the first year, $7 million the second year, and $8 million the third year. Santiago estimates the free cash flow will actually be $5.5 million, $9.5 million, and $12 million, respectively, and that 25 percent is an appropriate discount rate for the estimated cash flows. If the standard deviation of the annual free cash flow changes is 0.32 per year, and the risk-free rate is 0.11, how much should Santiago ask over and above the "normal" price for the division due to the cash flow guarantees?

Problems

Option Prices

11.1   Prices for Compaq Computers options appeared as follows in the *Wall Street Journal*:

Options & N.Y. Close	Strike Price	Calls—Last			Puts—Last		
		Oct	Nov	Jan	Oct	Nov	Jan
Compaq	45	r	s	12¼	⅛	s	1
54½	50	5⅞	r	8½	¾	1⁵⁄₁₆	2⅛
54½	55	2⁹⁄₁₆	3⅞	5½	2⅝	r	4⅛
54½	60	⅞	1¾	3¼	5¼	6	r
54½	65	¼	s	1¾	9¼	s	r

Note: r, not traded; s, no option.

a. For October calls, explain why the call price decreases as the exercise price increases. For October puts, why does the put price increase as the exercise price increases?
b. For both calls and puts, explain why the option price increases as the maturity increases.
c. What other factors influence option values? In what direction?

Valuing Call Options

11.2   The common stock of Martin Co. is selling at $80.
a. If the exercise price is $70, $k_{RF} = 0.12$, and $\sigma = 0.26$, what is the value of (1) a 3-month call option, and (2) a 6-month call option?
b. If the common stock price remains at $80, k_{RF} at 0.12, and σ at 0.26, what is the value of a *3-month* call option on Martin if the exercise price is (1) $60, or (2) $80?

11.3 The base case for Herculas Western is as follows:

$$P_0 = \$34 \qquad t = 0.60$$

$$X = \$30 \qquad \sigma = 0.20$$

$$k_{RF} = 0.10$$

a. Calculate the base case value of a call option on Herculas Western.

b. Calculate the value of a call option on Herculas Western if the price increases by 50 percent. Do the same if each variable, (i.e., X, k_{RF}, t, and σ) increases by 50 percent *while the rest* of the variables remain as in (a). To which variable is the call price of Herculas Western most sensitive to a 50 percent increase? Least sensitive?

c. What is the value of the call option if all the variables in (a) *simultaneously* increase by 50 percent?

Valuing Put Options

11.4 The common stock of Michelson Mutual is selling at $50.

a. What is the value of a 3-month put option on Michelson if the risk-free rate is 0.08, a similar call option is valued at $2, and the exercise price is $60?

b. What is the value of the put option if everything remains the same as in (a), except the risk-free rate increases to 0.16?

c. What if everything is the same as in (a), except the current stock price is only $45?

Dividend Paying Stocks

11.5 Hyper, Inc. is a risky stock that just started paying cash dividends. The stock's price is $60, the exercise price is $55, the risk-free rate is 0.14, σ is 0.80, and the maturity of the option is 0.40 of a year. The next cash dividend will be $1 and will be paid in 0.20 of a year.

a. What is the value of a call option on Hyper (1) without cash dividends and (2) with cash dividends? (*Note:* See footnote 7 for the proper equations when cash dividends are present.)

b. What is the value of a put option on Hyper (1) without and (2) with cash dividends?

(Do only if using Pinches Disk.)

c. What is the value of a call option and a put option (both with and without cash dividends) if the time until the dividend payment is 0.30 instead of 0.20? Do more distant cash dividends have more, or less, influence on the value of options?

d. What if everything is as in (a) and (b) except now the cash dividend is $3.00? (*Note:* Remember to change the time until the dividend is paid back to 0.20.) What impact does the size of the cash dividend have on the value of call and put options?

e. What if everything is the same as in (a) and (b) except the time until expiration of the option is now 0.70 instead of 0.40? What effect does a longer option life have on the value of options on stocks that pay cash dividends versus options on stocks that do not pay cash dividends?

f. Finally, what is the value of both call and put options, with and without cash dividends, under the following conditions?

$$P_0 = \$120 \qquad \sigma = 1.20$$

$$X = \$140 \qquad D = \$2.00$$

$$t = 0.40 \qquad t^* = 0.35$$

$$k_{RF} = 0.12$$

Warrant Valuation

11.6 Bryan Steel's common stock price is $34. A new warrant is being issued with an exercise price of $38, its life is 3½ years, the risk-free rate is 0.10, and the volatility of Bryan's common stock is 0.45 per year. What is the value of the warrant?

| | | | | b |

Warrant Premium

11.7 Warrants for Gitman Industries allow the holders to purchase 10 shares of common stock at the exercise price of $35. The market price of the common stock is $37.50, and the market price of a warrant is 15 percent greater than its lower limit value.

a. What is the market price of a warrant?
b. At what dollar premium over its lower limit value is the warrant selling?

Purchase Option

11.8 Kleiner Designs is considering a number of acquisitions. On three of them, Kleiner wants to take out an option, pending further evaluation and developments. The three are as follows:

Firm	Current Market Price	Purchase (Exercise) Price	Terms of Option	Volatility of Stock
Green and Sons	$74	$72	30 days	0.15
Feldman	41	45	100	0.40
Rapidready	67	80	182	0.85

If the risk-free rate is 0.12, what is the cost (or value) per share of each of the options? (*Note:* Use a 365-day year.)

Investment Option

11.9 A project has a NPV of −$80,000. By accepting this project, however, in 2 more years you could make a subsequent investment of $250,000 and receive a present value (at $t = 2$) of $300,000. (Therefore, the NPV of the project at $t = 2$ is $50,000.) The standard deviation of the subsequent project is 0.25, $k_{RF} = 0.08$, and the appropriate discount rate for bringing the cash inflows of $300,000 back to time $t = 0$ is 0.20.

a. Should you make the investment?
b. What would the standard deviation have to be so you would be indifferent between accepting and rejecting the project?

Investment Option (More Difficult)

11.10 NextSource is at the forefront of the developments in using lasers as a cost-effective alternative source of energy. To proceed further requires an outlay of $200 million today— the results will not be known until sometime in the future. NextSource estimates that under the most optimistic circumstances (with a probability of 0.20) the results will be known in 2 years. But a more realistic estimate (with a probability of 0.40) is that it will take 3 years for the results to be known. Finally, under the worst case (with a probability of 0.40) the results will not be known for 4 years. Their best estimate of the timing and cash flows are as follows:

Year	PV of Inflows (In millions)	−	Outlay (In millions)	=	NPV (In millions)	Standard Deviation
2	$1,500		$700		$800	0.50
3	1,200		800		400	0.50
4	800		900		− 100	0.50

NextSource has determined that the appropriate rate to discount the future inflows back to time $t = 0$ is 0.25 and the risk-free rate is 0.10. Should they proceed? (*Note:* All three outcomes are independent of one another. Also, do *not* take a weighted average of the input variables and then calculate a single option value. Instead, calculate one option value for each year and then weight them by the probability of occurrence.)

Value of Abandonment

11.11 A project can be abandoned at the end of 1 year; the proceeds would be $100,000. If the project continues, the present value (at $t = 0$) of the future proceeds past year 1 would equal $160,000. The risk-free rate is 0.10, and the volatility (standard deviation) of the project's cash flows, assuming no abandonment, is 1.30.

a. What is the value of the option to abandon?

b. If everything stays the same as in (a) except the standard deviation drops to 0.20, what is the value of the option to abandon? Why does this occur?

Guarantees

11.12 Your firm is buying the chemical division of Savewest Chemical. Two alternative 4-year guarantees of the cash flows from the chemical division are being offered as follows:

Year	Guarantee One	Guarantee Two
1	$ 8.0	$ 4.50
2	9.0	7.00
3	9.0	11.00
4	10.0	13.00

The forecasted cash flows for the 4 years are as follows: year 1 = $10, year 2 = $13, year 3 = $15, and year 4 = $20. The appropriate discount rate for the cash flows is 0.20, the risk-free rate is 0.11, and the volatility of the cash flows is 0.50. If it does not affect the price you pay, which guarantee should you accept—one or two?

References

For a discussion of the Black–Scholes model, and some recent empirical results, see

BLACK, FISCHER, AND MYRON SCHOLES. "The Pricing of Options and Corporate Liabilities." *Journal of Political Economy* 83 (May–June 1973), pp. 637–654.

GULTEKIN, N. BULENT, RICHARD J. ROGALSKI, AND SEHA M. TINIC. "Option Pricing Model Estimates: Some Empirical Results." *Financial Management* 11 (Spring 1982), pp. 58–69.

HAUGEN, ROBERT A. *Modern Investment Theory*. Englewood Cliffs, N.J.: Prentice-Hall, 1986, Chs. 17 and 18.

JACOB, DAVID P., GRAHAM LORD, AND JAMES A. TILLEY. "A Generalized Framework for Pricing Contingent Claims." *Financial Management* 16 (Autumn 1987), pp. 5–14.

JOHNSON, HERB, AND DAVID SHANNO. "Option Pricing When the Variance is Changing." *Journal of Financial and Quantitative Analysis* 22 (June 1987), pp. 143–151.

Some of the more theoretical aspects of warrants are examined in the following:

CONSTANTINIDES, GEORGE M. "Warrant Exercise and Bond Conversion in Competitive Markets." *Journal of Financial Economics* 13 (September 1984), pp. 371–397.

EMANUEL, DAVID C. "Warrant Valuation and Exercise Strategy." *Journal of Financial Economics* 12 (August 1983), pp. 211–235.

GREEN, RICHARD C. "Investment Incentives, Debt and Warrants." *Journal of Financial Economics* 13 (March 1984), pp. 115–136.

Information on investment decisions in an option pricing framework is contained in

BRENNAN, MICHAEL J., AND EDUARDO S. SCHWARTZ. "A New Approach to Evaluating Natural Resource Investments." *Midland Corporate Finance Journal* 3 (Spring 1985), pp. 37–47.

KESTER, W. C. "Today's Options for Tomorrow's Growth." *Harvard Business Review* 62 (March–April 1984), pp. 153–60.

MYERS, STEWART C. "Finance Theory and Financial Strategy." *Midland Corporate Finance Journal* 5 (Spring 1987), pp. 6–13.

MAJD, SAMAN, AND ROBERT S. PINDYCK. "Time to Build, Option Value, and Investment Decision." *Journal of Financial Economics* 18 (March 1987), pp. 7–27.

TRIGEORGIS, LENOS, AND SCOTT P. MASON. "Valuing Managerial Flexibility." *Midland Corporate Finance Journal* 5 (Spring 1987), pp. 14–21.

See Model eight in *Lotus 1–2–3® for Financial Management* by Pinches and Courtney for a template that calculates the value of call or put options.

PART FIVE

Long-Term Financing Decisions

12

Obtaining Long-Term Financing and Common Stock

Overview

- The vast majority of the financing needs of firms is met by internally generated funds. Less than 25 percent is provided by new long-term issues, of which bonds play the largest part.

- Shelf registration lowers the cost to the firm and increases the speed and flexibility of obtaining long-term financing.

- Par value, book value, and market value are all quoted on a per share basis for common stock. Only market value has any economic meaning.

- Firms issue new common stock only infrequently; studies indicate they suffer a loss in market value when they do issue common stock.

In 1980, after a number of years of sustained growth, Apple Computer, Inc., sold over $90 million in common stock to the general public. For the first time Apple's common stock, which had been owned solely by its founders and several venture capital firms, was publicly traded. As firms become larger, many find they need to acquire outside common equity capital. "Going public" generally involves the use of investment bankers, specialists in raising capital and advising firms on their financing needs and trends.

Even with the help of investment bankers, however, firms occasionally run into trouble. An example is Fruehauf, the Detroit-based maker of trailers and brake parts. Fruehauf went private in a leveraged buyout in 1986; some investment bankers secured fat fees in the process. By early 1989 Fruehauf had cash flow problems. The bond and preferred stockholders battled for better terms in a proposed restructuring. Finally, even with the help of investment bankers, Fruehauf sold off its assets, and although the name remains on trailers, the firm was liquidated.

Recent years have witnessed a tremendous increase in the number of different types of financing instruments available to help firms raise capital. To help Arley Merchandise go public, an investment banking firm came up *with a special $6 million common stock offering. Investors were given the right to sell their stock back to the firm during the first 2 years at the original purchase price of $8—but not necessarily for cash. Another new twist occurred when General Motors acquired Electronic Data Systems (EDS) for $2.5 billion by issuing a new class E common stock. Cash dividends on the class E General Motors stock, and hence market performance, were linked to the future performance of EDS. These are just a few of the many new developments in ways of raising long-term capital.*

Raising External Long-Term Funds

In Chapter 1, we decided the primary objective was to maximize the size of our pie, where its size, V, is composed of the value of stock, S, plus the value of debt, B. In Part 5 we focus on raising long-term funds externally by issuing common stock or debt or by leasing. We also examine how firms determine their firmwide, divisional, or project-specific required rates of return. Then we explore two very important issues as they relate to maximizing the size of the pie. The first is the firm's capital structure and whether alternative capital structures directly influence the size of the pie. Finally, we examine dividend policy and whether it influences the size of the pie. Throughout, we will see that financial managers must focus on market values and market reactions, if they are concerned with maximizing the total market value of the firm.

Firms have two primary sources of funds. They can generate funds internally from continuing operations, or they can secure them externally from creditors or investors. Financing in the form of internally generated cash flows provides the vast majority of the average firms' needs, and short-term (1 year or less) external financing provides another source. The remainder comes from net external long-term sources. It is these sources we focus on now. Our attention in this chapter and Chapter 13 will be primarily on the two main vehicles used by firms to raise external long-term capital—common stocks and bonds.

When Do Firms Need External Funds?

Firms always need external funding to supplement funds generated internally. These financing needs tend to be linked, however, to the level of economic activity, as shown in Figure 12.1. In general, firms need external financing more when economic activity begins to turn down. As sales decline, so do internally generated funds, but the level of labor costs and the investment in capital equipment and inventory continues until firms can adjust to the slowdown in economic activity. Conversely, firms coming out of a recession have a lower need for external funds. This is because they have streamlined their activities and are typically operating below capacity, so that even a fairly small increase in sales can lead to a sharp increase in internally generated cash flows. In addition, the need for external funds increases relatively slowly, since plant expansion is not immediately needed. And inventory levels are kept in check, or even drawn down further, thereby freeing cash. In short, while individuals often need more funds in bad times, for corporations the relation is generally reversed.

Figure 12.1 Relationship of External Financing Needs and Economic Activity

Firms generally have higher financing needs at and after the peak of economic expansion, while their lowest needs come after the bottom (or trough) of a recession.

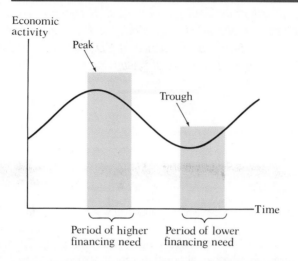

Means of Raising External Funds

Firms have a number of means of securing financing. These are shown in Figure 12.2. The first point to note is that the vast majority of funds are secured from the firm's ongoing internally generated funds. Once the firm decides it has to raise funds externally,[1] it has three basic options. First, it can use a *public offering.* The two main types available are (1) a *general cash offering,* which is made to investors at large, or (2) a *rights offering* (or privileged subscription), which is available only to the firm's current stockholders. Second, if the securities are not offered to the general public, then a private placement is made. The securities are sold to one or more institutional investors such as insurance companies, banks, or pension funds. Finally, a recent modification of the offering procedure, called *shelf registration,* is available to large, creditworthy firms. We will look at the basic features of all these methods, and at the role played by investment bankers.

General Cash Offering

Firms can issue common stock, preferred stock, or long-term debt through a general cash offering. Table 12.1 indicates the amount of funds raised using these three securities between 1980 and 1987. Note that the vast majority of funds raised in general cash offerings involve long-term debt. This is not surprising, since firms can generate substantial equity capital internally, but can secure debt financing only by going to the public markets or through private placements.

Most firms making a general cash offering of securities use the services of an investment banker, who does the actual selling. An investment banker serves as an intermediary between the financial markets and firms needing capital. Firms generally prefer to have the new issue *underwritten:* The investment banker purchases the issue from the firm at a fixed price and then resells it. When an issue is underwritten,

---

[1] This determination is made based on cash budgets or pro forma statements as discussed in Chapter 4.

Figure 12.2 Methods of Securing Financing

Since its introduction, the shelf registration option has become important for most large firms.

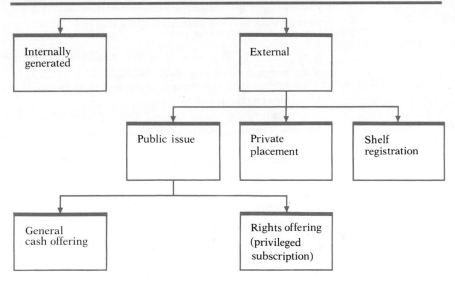

Table 12.1 New Publicly Issued Securities (In billions)

Bonds have typically dominated the new issue market. (SOURCE: Monthly Statistical Review, *Securities and Exchange Commission, various issues.*)

Year	Common Stock	Preferred Stock	Debt	Total
1980	$12.7	$ 3.2	$ 44.6	$ 60.5
1981	14.2	1.7	39.0	54.9
1982	13.4	5.0	44.8	63.2
1983	29.7	7.7	49.3	86.7
1984	8.6	4.2	59.6	72.4
1985	18.4	6.9	89.7	115.0
1986	33.5	11.6	172.6	217.7
1987	37.7	11.5	185.3	234.5

the risk of it not selling is borne by the investment banker—that is, the selling firm is guaranteed a fixed dollar amount. Another approach is for the investment banking firm to take the issue on a *best efforts* basis, under which the securities are sold for a fixed commission, but any unsold securities are the responsibility of the selling firm, not its investment banker. This method is often used by large, well-known firms that feel the issue will sell easily, or by very small firms when the risks and costs are too great for underwriting. Finally, some firms sell securities via *direct placement* (generally a rights offering to their stockholders) without using the services of investment bankers. For 1987, the relative use of these three methods was as follows:

	Underwritten	Best Efforts	Direct
Bonds	96.1%	3.3%	0.6%
Preferred stock	94.0	1.7	4.3
Common stock	74.2	17.9	7.9
Average[2]	86.4	9.5	4.1

Notice that over 85 percent of all securities were underwritten, but only 74 percent of the common stock was underwritten.

The Underwriting Process

To understand the investment banking process, it is helpful to trace the steps required. Our focus is on the negotiated underwritten process.

Preunderwriting Conference. Members of the issuing firm and the investment banker hold preunderwriting conferences at which they discuss how much capital to raise, the type (or types) of security to employ, and the terms of the agreement. The investment banking firm then begins the underwriting investigation. In addition to its own investigation of the issuing firm, a public accounting firm is called in to audit the firm's financial condition and to assist in preparing the registration statement that must be submitted to the Securities and Exchange Commission (SEC). Lawyers are required to rule on the legal aspects of the proposed issue.

After the investigation is completed, an underwriting agreement is drawn up. This agreement, which may be changed by subsequent approval of the parties, contains all the details of the issue except its price.

Registration and Pricing. The *registration statement,* or *prospectus,* is then filed with the SEC. This statement presents all the pertinent facts concerning the firm and the proposed issue. During a waiting period, the factual adequacy of the information is judged. The SEC assesses only the accuracy of the information; it does not judge the investment quality of the security. The first part of the registration statement, often called a *red herring* because of the statement printed on it that the securities have not been approved or disapproved by the SEC, can, however, be distributed.

Once the issue has cleared registration and an offering price has been determined, a "tombstone" advertisement listing the names of the underwriting firms from whom the prospectus may be obtained is often made. Figure 12.3 shows an example of a tombstone for à Sallie Mae common stock issue that involved a number of underwriters.

Underwriting Syndication and Selling. The lead investment banking firm the issuing firm has dealt with does not typically handle the purchase and distribution of an issue by itself. Instead, a *syndicate* is formed for the purpose of underwriting (or buying and then reselling) the issue. Syndicates often have between 10 and 60 underwriters in addition to the managing investment banker. The primary reasons for underwriting syndicates are to spread the risk and ensure national marketing capability.

Costs. The *flotation cost* to the issuing firm of selling securities includes the underwriting fee and all the other expenses related to the offering. These other

---

[2] Based on actual dollar amounts, not the percentages listed above.

Figure 12.3 Tombstone for Sallie Mae Common Stock Issue

Advertisements like this one appear in many financial sources, such as the Wall Street Journal *and* Institutional Investor.

This advertisement is neither an offer to sell nor a solicitation of an offer to buy these securities.
The offer is made only by the Offering Circular.

March 8, 1989

2,000,000 Shares

SallieMae

Student Loan Marketing Association

Nonvoting Common Stock
(par value $.50 per share)

Price $93.75 per Share

Copies of the Offering Circular may be obtained in any State only from such
of the undersigned as may lawfully offer these securities in such State.

MONTGOMERY SECURITIES

THE FIRST BOSTON CORPORATION

GOLDMAN, SACHS & CO.

MORGAN STANLEY & CO.
Incorporated

expenses include accounting and legal fees, an SEC registration fee, and printing costs. Total flotation costs are the difference between what the securities are sold to investors for (the gross proceeds) and what the issuing firm actually receives (the net proceeds). Thus, if a $50 million par bond issue is sold to the public for $50.5 million and the issuing firm receives only $49.5 million, the flotation costs are $1 million, or slightly under 2 percent ($1 million/$50.50 million = 0.0198 = 1.98 percent).

For common stock, flotation costs range from 3 percent for large, well-known firms to over 10 percent for smaller firms. This high direct cost for small issues is a function of the risks involved and the higher actual distribution expenses, since more effort is required to sell small common stock issues. For bonds and preferred stocks, the costs to the issuer are usually less than 2 percent. This is due to the lower degree of risk involved compared to common stocks, and because bonds and preferred stock are usually sold in large blocks to institutional investors, whereas thousands of investors may purchase common stock.

Private Placements

Private issues have some advantages over public ones. For example, the issuing firm is spared the time, expense, and trouble of having to register the issue with the SEC. Moreover, the firm can maintain a lower profile, since it does not have to disclose the financial and other data required in the registration process.

However, private issues also have some disadvantages. First, the lender may monitor the firm's activities more closely, either directly or through provisions in the loan agreement. If common stock financing is used, often the new investor is likely to gain substantial influence or even control of the firm. Also, the cost of privately placed debt is generally *higher* than for public issues. Finally, it is more difficult to raise large amounts via private placements, although this problem is not as serious as it once was, since groups of institutional investors often participate in large private placements.

Shelf Registration

In 1982, the Securities and Exchange Commission modified its registration procedure for some types of offerings by adopting Rule 415, or what is called shelf registration. To register under this new rule, a firm must file a relatively short form describing its financing needs and the securities it intends to issue over the next 2 years. When they think market conditions are favorable, they can take part of the issue "off the shelf" in a matter of minutes, without further disclosure being necessary, and offer them to investors. This procedure was made permanent in November 1983, but was amended so that firms having less than $150 million worth of stock held by outside investors were not allowed to employ shelf registration.

The increased flexibility provided by shelf registration has been welcomed by chief financial officers at large corporations. In recent years over half of all securities registered with the SEC were marketed through the shelf registration method. This rapid acceptance of shelf registration is due to its reduced cost and increased convenience—both of which are important when firms raise external capital. As a by-product of the shelf registration procedure, more and more security issues—both bonds and stocks—take the form of private placements, rather than general public offerings.

Common Stock: Rights and Privileges

Now that we understand some of the issues related to raising external funds, let's turn our attention to the first source of funds for most firms—common stock. The common stockholders are both the owners of the firm and one of its suppliers of long-term capital. This capital may be in the form of funds invested in the firm directly in exchange for new shares of common stock, or it may occur through the action of the firm's board of directors by retaining funds rather than authorizing them to be paid out in the form of cash dividends.

Income

Common stockholders have a residual right to the income of the firm in that the claims of creditors, lessors, the government, and preferred stockholders must be met before common stockholders receive cash dividends. Thus, if a firm has earnings before interest and taxes (EBIT) of $200,000, interest payments of $50,000, and taxes (at 35 percent) of $52,500, earnings after taxes (EAT) are $97,500. Assuming that cash flows are sufficient, firms typically pay out some proportion of their earnings in the form of cash dividends. They are not obligated to do so, and some firms, such as Digital Equipment, Commodore International, and Federal Express, do not currently pay dividends. The risk and potential returns are greater for common stock investors, since, in our example, if EBIT drops to $50,000, with interest payments of $50,000, earnings after taxes are zero. On the other hand, if EBIT increases to $600,000, with interest of $50,000 and taxes of $192,500, EAT is $357,500 and larger cash dividends may be paid out. The cash not paid out to common stockholders can be reinvested in the firm. As a consequence, the value of the firm's shares should increase and stockholders should benefit from any cash dividends, if paid out, and the increase in the price of the stock (or capital gains). Along with greater risk comes the possibility of larger returns.

Control

The firm's stockholders elect the members of the board of directors each year. Although in theory the stockholders control the firm through this election process, in practice control is often limited. This is especially true in large, publicly traded firms, since any individual stockholder generally owns only a small fraction of the firm's stock. Sometimes an outside or dissident group may challenge management by proposing its own slate of directors. Proxy fights, although rare in the past, represent one of the more effective means of attempting to turn the fortunes of a firm around. Recently, more proxy fights have been initiated, including some involving major firms. Obviously, it is only in firms that are providing lackluster performance (in terms of market price, dividends, and/or earnings) that successful proxy fights are possible.

Depending on the corporate charter or the law of the state in which the firm is incorporated, the board of directors is selected under a *majority voting* or a cumulative voting system. Under the former system, each stockholder has one vote per director for each share of stock owned. Directors are elected if they secure one more vote than 50 percent of the votes cast. Under *cumulative voting* the total number of votes each stockholder can cast is determined first. If there are five directors to be elected, and a stockholder owns 60 shares of stock, he or she can cast $(5)(60) =$

300 votes. By casting all of the votes for only one director, cumulative voting allows minority participation that is often precluded when majority voting is employed.

In addition to voting on the board of directors, stockholders are frequently asked to approve the selection of the firm's accounting auditor for the next year, and to vote on issues such as authorizing additional shares of common stock or approval of a common stock–financed merger if the firm is selling out to another firm.

Claim on Assets

As in the case of income, common stockholders have a residual claim with regard to the firm's assets in case of liquidation. Although some changes have occurred because of the new bankruptcy code that went into effect in 1979, creditors, bondholders, and preferred stockholders all have a prior claim on assets and will be paid something before common stockholders receive anything in liquidation. This residual claim increases the risk to common stockholders.

Limited Liability

An attractive feature of common stock is the separation of the stockholders from the liabilities of the firm. Because corporations are distinct entities under the law, stockholders have no responsibility for the debts incurred by the firm. Although this shield is not impenetrable in the case where stockholders use the firm for illegal acts, by and large stockholders are protected from liability for the firm's debts.

Preemptive Right

The *preemptive right* is a provision that may exist in the corporate charter, or be required by state statute, which grants stockholders the right to purchase new shares of common stock in the same proportion as their current ownership. Although this right used to be widespread, it is less so now because many firms have amended their charters to eliminate the preemptive right. One of the primary reasons is to provide the firm with more freedom to use common stock for mergers and acquisitions or other corporate purposes.

When the preemptive right exists, current stockholders have first claim on any new shares to be issued. For example, if a firm had 100,000 shares of stock outstanding and decided to issue 25,000 new shares, a stockholder owning 1,000 shares would have the opportunity to purchase 250 new shares. By doing so, the stockholder would maintain his or her current percentage ownership of 1 percent of the firm's outstanding shares.

Right of Transfer

Common stockholders generally have the right to transfer ownership to another investor. All that is required is for an investor to sell the stock to another person and sign the stock (endorse it on the back of the stock certificate) over to the buyer. If the stock is publicly traded, the stockholder may use the services of a securities broker to sell the stock. The purchaser of the stock (or the broker) sends the stock certificate to a transfer agent representing the firm. The transfer agent then issues a new certificate under the purchaser's name and records the transaction in the firm's records. At this point, the new owner is entitled to receive cash dividends (as discussed in Chapter 16) and has any other rights or privileges associated with owning the common stock.

Features of Common Stock

Authorized, Outstanding, and Treasury Shares

The firm's charter specifies the number of authorized shares—that is, the maximum number that can be issued without amending its charter. Additional shares can be authorized by a vote of the common stockholders. For convenience, most firms have more authorized shares than they currently have issued. For example, in Table 12.2, Texaco, at the end of 1987 is shown to have 350 million shares authorized, but only some 274 million have been issued. The outstanding shares are those held by the public; the firm can buy back issued stock and hold it as treasury stock. The number of shares outstanding is $274,293,417 - 31,441,423 = 242,851,994$.

Par and Book Value

Common stock can be issued with or without a par value. The par value of a share of common stock is stated in the firm's charter, but is of no economic significance. Firms with a specific par value for their common stock try to issue new stock at prices higher than par, since the stockholders are liable as creditors for the difference between the issuance price, if below par, and the par value of the stock. For this reason, most par values are very low. Texaco, for example, has a par value of $6.25 per share of common stock.

If the firm uses no par stock, it specifies the stated value that it uses for accounting purposes. The difference between the issuance price and the par (or stated) value is recorded on the firm's balance sheet as additional paid-in capital. Texaco has

Table 12.2   Stockholders' Balance Sheet Accounts and Related Information for Texaco, Inc., as of December 31, 1987 (In millions)

Remember there is no cash in the retained earnings account, and that book value is a meaningless figure. (SOURCE: Texaco, Inc., 1987 Annual Report.)

Common stock, $6.25 par; 350,000,000 shares authorized, 274,293,417 shares issued	$ 1,714
Additional paid-in capital	657
Retained earnings	8,294
	10,665
Less: Treasury stock (31,441,423 shares at cost)	1,494
Total stockholders' equity	$ 9,171

earnings per share = net income (millions)/shares of common stock outstanding (millions)

$$= -\$4,407/(274.293 - 31.441) = -\$18.15$$

dividends per share on common stock = $0.75

book value per share = total stockholders' equity (millions)/shares outstanding (millions)

$$= \$9,171/(274.293 - 31.441) = \$37.76$$

market price per share = $40.00 to $26.88
  (range for the year)

$657 million recorded as additional paid-in capital. Likewise, it has $1.714 billion in the common stock account, which reflects the number of shares issued (both outstanding and treasury) times the par value of $6.25 per share. Finally, Texaco has retained earnings (which have been transferred from the firm's income statements over the years) of $8.294 billion. The total of the preferred stock, common stock, additional paid-in capital, and retained earnings accounts, less the treasury stock, is equal to total stockholders' equity. For Texaco, this is $9.171 billion.

Book value of a share of common stock reflects the "accounting-recorded" worth of the firm and is calculated by dividing the stockholders' equity (or, equivalently, total assets minus total liabilities) by the number of shares of common stock outstanding. In the absence of inflation, and if the firm's balance sheet reflected the current economic worth of the firm, book value would indicate the current liquidation value of the firm. However, this is not the case, and there is no economic meaning that can be attached to book value per share.[3] Texaco had a book value of $37.76 per share at the end of 1987, but its stock traded between $40.00 and $26.88 during that year. One other unusual point should be noted about Texaco. In 1987 they filed for protection under Chapter 11 of the bankruptcy code—and had to settle a case with Pennzoil by paying $3 billion. This accounts for the earnings per share of −$18.15.

Forms of Common Stock

Most firms have only one type of common stock, but some have more than one class. Where two classes exist, one is often sold to the general public and the other is retained by the founders, with all or part of the voting rights reserved for the founders' group. Two examples will help to illustrate the use of different classes of stock. Ford has two classes of stock, both of which have voting privileges. As of December 31, 1987, the issued shares (in millions) were as follows:

	Shares Issued
Common	469.8
Class B	37.7
	507.5

Class B stock is owned by members of the Ford family and constitutes 40 percent of the voting power of the firm.[4] The common stock is held by the general public and has 60 percent of the total voting power. Each share of common stock is entitled to one vote. To maintain their 40 percent voting power, class B shares have more than one vote per share. As of December 31, 1987, each class B share had

$$\left(\frac{469.8}{37.7}\right)\left(\frac{0.40}{0.60}\right) = 8.31 \text{ votes}$$

Although each share of both classes participate equally in cash dividends or in case of liquidation, each class B share has more voting power than a similar share of common stock.

A second example concerns Adolph Coors. Coors has two classes of stock:

---

[3] An exception may occur for financial institutions or other similar firms where the recorded book value may be a reasonable estimate of the current liquidation value of the firm.

[4] If the number of class B shares is below 30,374,940 but equal to or greater than 16,874,966, the voting power drops to 30 percent.

class A, which is held by the founders and has voting power; and class B, which is held by the general public and, except for certain situations, has no voting power. Shares of both classes participate equally in dividends or liquidation.

Common Stock Financing

Although not the major external source of financing, common stock is often employed to raise external capital. So it is important to understand more about the use of common stock as a means of raising long-term capital.

Issuing Equity and the Value of the Firm

In recent years a number of studies have examined the market impact of firms issuing common stock. The results, at first glance, have been surprising. When firms issue common stock, their stock price declines. For industrial firms in the United States the decline amounts to about 3 percent. While that may not sound overwhelming, the fall in the market value represents a dollar amount equal to almost one-third of the money raised by the issue. Thus, the net increase in the value of the firm, ΔS, due to issuing new common stock for cash is equal to the net proceeds from the issue *minus* the decrease in the value of the outstanding stock. Stated another way, the cost of issuing common stock includes the direct flotation costs plus the indirect costs captured by the loss in value of the firm's outstanding stock.

How can we account for this result? In an efficient market investor expectations are built into the share price. These expectations may change as the firm issues new common stock. Consider two reasons why the price of the firm's stock may fall.

1. INFORMATION ASYMMETRY. Management always has some information about the firm which is not available to shareholders. What if this information allows them to determine when the firm is overvalued in the marketplace, and when it is undervalued? It will then attempt to issue new shares only when the firm is overvalued. This benefits existing stockholders, but potential new stockholders are not stupid. They will anticipate this and discount it by offering to pay less for the stock at the new issue date.
2. INVESTMENT PROSPECTS. Investment demands exist for most firms, sometimes due to "great" projects with high NPVs, other times for not so great projects. What if informed investors interpret the issuance of new common stock as a negative signal about the firm's investment projects? After all, if the new projects are really great, why should the firm let new stockholders in on them? It could simply issue debt and let existing stockholders capture all the gain. Again, new investors are not stupid, and will offer a lower price for the common stock on the new issue date.

While we don't know which, if either, of these explanations account for the decline in stock prices when common stock is sold, we do know the decline occurs. Alternatively, stock prices decline little if at all when the firm issues new debt. Effective managers must keep these findings in mind when contemplating how to raise long-term financing.

IPOs and Underpricing

When a firm first goes public with its common stock, it is referred to as an *initial public offering (IPO)*. A number of studies have examined initial public offerings. By calculating the difference in the offering price, and the price shortly after offering, these studies have examined the issue of *underpricing*. Underpricing is a real, but hidden, cost incurred by any firm when it first goes public. These studies have estimated the magnitude of underpricing with IPOs is high—15 to 20 percent. As such, the cost of underpricing often exceeds the other issuance costs for firms going public. Why does this underpricing occur? Probably for at least two reasons. The first is that both the investment banker and the issuing firm have some vested interest in seeing that the issue is fully sold. One way—but an expensive one—to ensure that the issue is all sold is to underprice it. The second is that determining the market worth of a firm that has never been traded is more of an art than a science.

Pricing a New Issue

When a firm already has stock outstanding and is issuing additional shares, they are typically priced a few dollars below the closing price the day before the stock is sold. If the firm is making an initial public offering, however, the pricing decision is much more difficult.

One way to go about establishing this selling price is to determine what the total value of the firm should be after the issue, and then divide this value by the number of shares of common stock to be outstanding. For example, if we assume that United Transport is estimated to be worth $3.5 million and 350,000 shares of common stock will be outstanding, the estimated selling price is $3,500,000/350,000 = $10 per share. Note that we are interested in the total number of shares to be outstanding, including any privately held or founders' shares not issued to the public. If United Transport decides to sell 150,000 shares, the offering would consist of 150,000 shares priced at $10 each for gross proceeds (before flotation costs and other direct issuance expenses) of $1,500,000. To employ this approach, however, we must answer the following question: How do we determine the total value of the firm of $3,500,000?

One way to do this is to use the valuation approach described in Chapter 6. For the constant dividend growth situation, the value of the total firm can be estimated by[5]

$$S = \frac{D_1}{k_s - g} \tag{12.1}$$

where

  S = the value of an all equity firm
  D_1 = total cash dividends expected to be paid to stockholders next year (at
      $t = 1$)
  k_s = the equity investors' required rate of return
  g = the expected (compound) growth rate in cash dividends

Suppose United expects earnings after taxes of $700,000 and plans to pay 50 percent out in the form of cash dividends, so that $D_1 = $350,000. Also, the firm expects

---

[5] It is assumed no debt exists.

Financial Management Today

Elimination of the Preemptive Right

When a firm offers equity to its existing shareholders, it is a rights offering. This is a preemptive right that typically existed in the corporate charter or was granted to shareholders by common law. Corporations have the power, however, to amend their articles of corporation to eliminate this right. To do so they have to amend their charters formally and have shareholders vote on the amendment to eliminate the preemptive right.

A recent study examined the impact of eliminating the preemptive right on the wealth of shareholders.[1] In 211 cases where preemptive rights were eliminated, the study found there was a small negative impact on stock returns during the event day which was the proxy mailing day (t_0) and the day after the proxy was mailed. However, later when the shareholders actually voted on the amendment, there was no impact on returns. The study goes on to conclude that the removal of preemptive rights from corporate charters, on average, decreases shareholder wealth. While this elimination may increase the flexibility of management, in terms of having alternative ways of raising equity capital without going first to the existing shareholders, this study indicates management action of this type may not be in the best interests of shareholders.

[1] Sanjai Bhagat. "The Effect of Pre-Emptive Right Amendments on Shareholder Wealth." *Journal of Financial Economics* 12 (November 1983).

its earnings and dividends to grow at approximately 7 percent per year for the foreseeable future. We have estimated D_1 and g in Equation 12.1; all that is needed now is an estimate of k_s. Estimating k_s, however, is not easy, especially for a firm that has never been publicly traded. United's investment banker can supply an estimate of k_s, we can use the k_s for some comparable publicly traded firm, or use some approach like adding a risk premium to the expected interest rate on long-term corporate bonds. If the rate on long-term bonds is expected to be 9 percent and the risk premium is determined to be 8 percent, our estimate of k_s is 17 percent. With this we can estimate the value of United Transport to be

$$S = \frac{\$350,000}{0.17 - 0.07} = \frac{\$350,000}{0.10} = \$3,500,000$$

In practice, an ad hoc approach based on comparative price/earnings (P/E) ratios is often employed. To use this approach, United's investment banker might examine price/earnings ratios for publicly traded firms in the same industry, as well as the P/E ratios of firms that have recently gone public. Other pertinent information, such as United's financial condition, growth prospects, quality and stability of management, and size are also compared. Once a P/E ratio for the firm is estimated, the total market value is determined by

$$S = (\text{net income})(\text{estimated P/E of stock}) \tag{12.2}$$

Continuing our example of United Transport, let's assume United's investment banker determines the stock's estimated P/E ratio is five times. The total value of United would be ($700,000)(5) = $3,500,000. Once the total value of the firm is determined, the pricing of the new shares to be issued proceeds as described previously. With either the dividend valuation or comparative P/E approach, the pricing of new issues is an imperfect and subjective process.

Recording a Stock Issue

Once stock is issued, it must be recorded on the firm's balance sheet. To see how this occurs, let's continue with United Transport. It currently has 200,000 shares of $2 par value common stock outstanding. The value recorded in United's common stock account is $400,000[i.e., (200,000 shares)($2 per share)]. United now sells 150,000 additional shares of common stock and receives $10 per share (ignoring flotation and other issuance costs). The entries are (1) an increase in the common stock account of $300,000 [i.e., (150,000 new shares)($2 per share par value)]; (2) an increase in the additional paid-in capital account of $1,200,000 (150,000 shares times the difference between the issuance price of $10 per share and the par value of $2 per share); and (3) an offsetting entry indicating that the cash account has increased by $1,500,000. The before and after balance sheets for United Transport are presented in Table 12.3.

Rights Offerings[6]

Rights offerings involve the issuance of new shares of common stock, with the firm's current stockholders having the first option of buying the issue. Their importance has tended to diminish over the years as many firms have eliminated the preemptive right and with the increasing popularity of dividend reinvestment plans (Chapter 16) and the introduction of shelf registration procedures.

When a firm has a rights offering, each stockholder receives one right for each share of stock presently owned. To understand a rights offering, consider the example of Wimpey Aviation, which has decided to raise $5 million in additional funds by selling common stock at $10 per share. The $10 is the subscription price for the rights offering. Wimpey currently has 1,000,000 shares of common stock outstanding with a market price of $11.50 per share. If the company elects to employ a rights offering, the firm is concerned about the following:

1. How many rights are required to purchase one additional share of stock?
2. What is the value of each right?
3. What effect does the rights offering have on the market price of each existing share of stock?

Number of Rights Needed to Purchase an Additional Share

The number of additional shares to be issued, if Wimpey has not already determined it, is given by:

$$\text{number of additional shares} = \frac{\text{funds to be raised}}{\text{subscription price}} = \frac{\$5,000,000}{\$10} = 500,000 \text{ shares} \qquad (12.3)$$

The next step is to divide the number of additional shares into the number of existing shares to obtain the number of rights needed to subscribe to one additional share:

[6] This section may be omitted without loss of continuity.

Table 12.3   Balance Sheet of United Transport Before and After Stock Issue

The $1,500,000 is split between the common stock and additional paid-in capital accounts on the basis of the par value and the issuance price. An offsetting entry is made indicating that the firm's cash account has increased by $1,500,000.

	Before the Issue	After the Issue
Assets		
Cash	$ 200,000	$1,700,000
Other	1,800,000	1,800,000
Total assets	$2,000,000	$3,500,000
Liabilities and Stockholders' Equity		
Liabilities	$1,000,000	$1,000,000
Stockholders' equity:		
Common stock ($2 par)	400,000	700,000*
Additional paid-in capital	200,000	1,400,000
Retained earnings	400,000	400,000
Total liabilities and stockholders' equity	$2,000,000	$3,500,000

* 350,000 shares at $2 par.

$$\begin{array}{l}\text{number of rights} \\ \text{to buy one} \\ \text{additional share, N}\end{array} = \frac{\text{existing shares}}{\text{additional shares}} = \frac{1{,}000{,}000}{500{,}000} = \text{two rights} \qquad (12.4)$$

Therefore, stockholders of Wimpey have to surrender $10 plus two rights in order to purchase one additional share of stock during the rights offering.

Value of Stock and Rights

When a firm undertakes a rights offering, a sequence of events takes place. First, the firm announces the proposed financing. For Wimpey Aviation, suppose this occurs on May 20. Shortly thereafter, trading begins for the rights on a when-issued basis. This simply means that a market exists for the new security with delivery of the security (the rights in this case) to take place when it is received. Subsequently, on June 24, the record date occurs; all stockholders of Wimpey's common stock on the record date receive one right for each share of common stock held. Similar to cash dividends, stock splits, or stock dividends, discussed in Chapter 16, the ex day is set four business days before the record date. This is June 18 for Wimpey's rights offering.[7] All stock traded before June 18 trades with the rights passing on to the purchaser (rights-on). Purchasers on or after June 18, however, acquire the stock without the rights (or rights-off). On the record date, the rights are actually mailed to the firm's stockholders. On July 22 the rights will expire. This sequence of events is illustrated in Figure 12.4.

    Rights-On. It is clearly worth something to be able to purchase additional shares of a firm's common stock at a price below its existing market price per

[7] Because there is a weekend included, the ex rights day is June 18, not June 20.

Figure 12.4 Timetable for Common Stock Rights Offering by Wimpey Aviation

The value of the stock drops by 50 cents on the ex rights day when the rights trade separately. The investor who does not exercise or sell his or her rights by July 22 (the expiration date) suffers a loss.

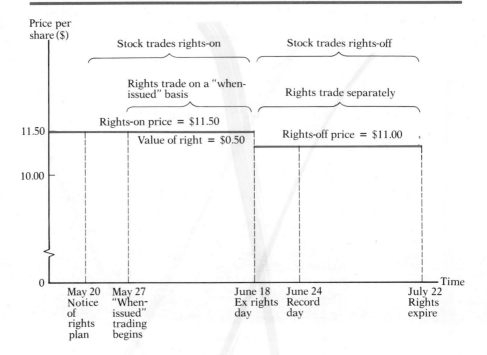

share. To determine the value of one right, the following formula can be employed:

$$\text{value of one right} = \frac{\text{market value of stock, rights-on} - \text{subscription price}}{\text{number of rights needed to purchase one share} + 1} \qquad (12.5)$$

$$v_r = \frac{P_0 - P_s}{N + 1}$$

where

v_r = the value of one right

P_0 = the rights-on market price per share

P_s = the subscription price

N = the number of rights needed to purchase an additional share of stock

Substituting the appropriate values for Wimpey Aviation:

$$v_r = \frac{\$11.50 - \$10.00}{2 + 1} = \frac{\$1.50}{3} = \$0.50$$

Valuing the Equity of a Closely Held Firm

The value of publicly traded firms can be determined simply by looking at the total market value of the firm's stock. When the firm is closely held, however, determining a value is both more difficult and more subjective. Three approaches that are often used are (1) the net asset approach, (2) the discounted cash flow approach, and (3) the earnings multiple approach.

The net asset valuation approach simply takes the appraised (or sometimes book) value of the firm's assets minus the claims in terms of liabilities and preferred stock. This may be useful if most of the assets are relatively liquid and their market value can be easily determined. A variation of this is a liquidation value approach, where the estimated liquidation value of the assets (in a fairly short time period) net of any costs associated with the liquidation is employed.

The discounted cash flow approach is very similar to the dividend valuation model discussed in Chapter 6. Cash flows are projected for a series of periods along with some estimated residual value of the firm; then these are discounted at an appropriate required rate of return. The senior claims are then subtracted to determine the estimated value of the firm's equity.

The third approach is the earnings multiple approach where adjusted after-tax earnings (net of any extraordinary gains or losses) are multiplied by some appropriate estimated price/earnings ratio, or multiple. This multiple is often determined by looking at other similar type firms. A variation of the earnings multiple approach is simply the capitalized earnings method; the adjusted after-tax earnings are divided by (or capitalized at) an appropriate required rate of return.

While each of these three methods has strengths and weaknesses, the results may differ substantially depending on who's doing the estimation and what approach is used. In one case, 15 "experts" were given the same data for a firm. The average firm value given by the 15 was about $11 million, but the high was $17.5 million while the low was $6 million. Obviously, there's a lot of judgment involved, no matter what method is used in valuing closely held firms.

In Figure 12.4 we see that up to the ex rights day, the market price of the common stock is $11.50 per share. However, after the rights offering is announced, the price is composed of two distinct elements—the value of the stock itself and the value of the right to purchase additional shares of the firm's common stock at a price below its current market value.

Ex Rights. On the ex rights day, the stock and rights begin trading separately. The theoretical value of the right after the stock goes ex rights can be solved by employing

$$\text{value of one right} = \frac{\text{market value of stock, ex rights} - \text{subscription price}}{\text{number of rights needed to purchase one share}} \qquad (12.6)$$

$$v_r = \frac{P_x - P_s}{N} = \frac{\$11.00 - \$10.00}{2} = \$0.50$$

where P_x is the ex rights stock price per share and the other symbols are as defined previously. Other things being equal, the value of Wimpey's stock will drop by $0.50, the value of one right, to $11 on the ex rights day.[8]

Effect on the Position of Stockholders

Stockholders have the choice of exercising their rights, selling them, or letting them expire. As long as they take some positive action, stockholders do not suffer any loss from a rights offering. However, if they take no action and let the rights expire, a loss is incurred. Consider a stockholder who owns 100 shares of Wimpey's common stock before the rights offering. Because of the rights offering, the investor can purchase 50 additional shares of common stock (remember it takes two rights for every share) at $10 each. The investor now owns 150 shares, which have a market value of $1,650 [i.e., (150 shares)($11)]. Subtracting the $500 paid for the 50 additional shares, the investor is back to his or her original value of $1,150. Thus, the investor is no better or worse off after exercising the rights.

Alternatively, the investor can sell the 100 rights for $0.50 each for a total of $50.[9] He or she now owns 100 shares of stock at $11 each, for a total of $1,100. The $1,100 market value of the stock plus the $50 received from the sale of the rights is exactly equal to the original value of the stock of $1,150. Finally, if the investor does not exercise or sell the rights, the investment is worth only $1,100; $50 was "thrown away" by not doing something with the rights. Clearly, investors should always take some positive action when they receive rights.

Listing the Stock

In addition to selling stock to raise additional capital, publicly held firms must also make a decision concerning whether the stock should be listed on an organized stock exchange. Small firms are typically traded in the over-the-counter market, since there is simply not enough activity to justify listing. As a firm gets bigger, it may decide to apply for listing on one of the regional stock exchanges. A West Coast firm might apply to the Pacific Coast Stock Exchange; one located in Milwaukee might apply to the Midwest Stock Exchange. With continued growth, the firm may decide to apply for listing on the American Stock Exchange, or if it is one of the nation's largest firms, it may apply to the big board—the New York Stock Exchange.

To apply for listing, the firm must meet certain conditions, a listing application must be filed with both the exchange and the SEC, and a fee must be paid. The minimum characteristics a firm must possess if it wants a listing on the NYSE are presented in Table 12.4. After a firm is listed, it must meet certain exchange require-

---

[8] The ex rights stock price can be calculated directly via:

$$P_x = \frac{(P_o)(N) + P_s}{N+1} = \frac{(\$11.50)(2) + \$10.00}{3} = \frac{\$33}{3} = \$11.00$$

[9] This assumes there is no brokerage, or selling, commission.

Table 12.4 New York Stock Exchange Listing Requirements for Common Stock

Other considerations include the degree of national interest in the firm, position in the industry, and prospects for both the firm and the industry. (SOURCE: New York Stock Exchange Fact Book, *1988*.)

Profitability

Earnings before taxes (EBT) for the most recent year must be at least $2.5 million. For the two preceding years, EBT must have been at least $2 million.

Assets

Net tangible assets of at least $16 million, but greater emphasis is placed on the aggregate market value.

Market Value

The market value of the publicly held stock must be at least $16 million.*

Public Ownership

At least 1 million shares must be publicly held, and there must be at least 2,000 stockholders who each own at least 100 shares.

---

* This requirement might conceivably be as low as $8 million depending on the level of the NYSE Index of Common Stock prices. Presently it is $16 million.

ments in order to continue its listing. The SEC also requires that both quarterly and annual financial reports be published by listed firms.

Since firms have to apply for listing, and additional financial reporting requirements are placed on them, why do they do it? By listing, the firm is assured of a continuous secondary market for its common stock. This may make the stock more attractive to some investors and may even make it easier for the firm to issue more common stock in the future. In addition, firms receive a certain amount of free advertising and prestige; many firms feel their position has been established once they have secured a listing on the New York Stock Exchange.

Regulation of Public Issues

Up to 1933, regulation of the securities markets was done entirely by the individual states. One of the earliest state security laws was enacted by Kansas in 1911. A member of the Kansas legislature remarked that the new law would prevent sellers from promising the "blue sky" to unsophisticated investors; hence, state regulations are referred to as *blue sky laws*. But state regulation was spotty, and when the security markets collapsed in 1929, it became evident that many securities had been misrepresented. Today, state laws continue to exist, but the primary laws governing the securities markets have been enacted at the federal level.

Primary Market Regulation

The new issues or primary market is governed by the Securities Act of 1933. The basic objective of this act is to provide full disclosure of all pertinent information; it does not attempt to prevent a firm from issuing highly questionable or risky securities. To accomplish this objective, the following means are employed:

1. The act applies to all interstate offerings to the public except for very small issues ($500,000 to $5 million, depending on the circumstances); short-term issues (maturing in 270 days or less); or those regulated by other federal agencies (such as railroads, banks, and public utilities).
2. Securities must be registered for a minimum number of days before there is a public offering. The registration statement supplies financial, technical, and legal information about the issue and the firm. Any misleading or incomplete information may cause a delay in the registration.
3. After the registration has become effective, the securities can be offered for public sale if accompanied by the prospectus.
4. Under shelf registration, however, a firm may register all securities needed over a 2-year period, and then issue them as desired during that period.

Secondary Market Regulation

Once securities have been issued, they are traded between investors in the secondary market. This market is regulated by the Securities Exchange Act of 1934. The primary provisions of this legislation are as follows:

1. It created the Securities and Exchange Commission. (For 1 year, the Federal Trade Commission administered the Securities Act of 1933.)
2. Major securities exchanges, such as the New York Stock Exchange and the American Stock Exchange, must register with the SEC. In addition, firms whose securities are listed on these exchanges must file periodic reports with both the exchange and the SEC.
3. Corporate insiders who are officers, directors, or major stockholders must file monthly reports. Any short-term profits from holding the firm's stock less than 6 months are payable to the firm.
4. Manipulative practices are prohibited.
5. Margin requirements[10] are set, and may be changed as desired, by the Federal Reserve system.

Regulation of the securities market has important consequences for managers. Because of this regulation, both the primary and the secondary markets are viewed as being both orderly and efficient. Firms can issue securities with full confidence that the issue will be sold in a manner that secures the needed capital and provides investors a ready market for resale. Without the development of an extensive investment banking community and efficient and orderly security markets, the costs and risks involved in issuing long-term securities would rise, increasing the firm's required rate of return, and through the capital budgeting process, influencing its investment decisions.

Summary

Firms acquire the majority of their financing from internally generated funds; bonds are the most important source of long-term external financing. Firms generally need

---

[10] Instead of paying the full amount initially, an investor can buy on margin and borrow the remainder from a securities dealer.

more funds at the peak of the business cycle and less in the trough of a recession. Public offerings involve either general cash offerings or, to a far lesser extent, rights offerings. Most bond and preferred stock public offerings are underwritten by investment bankers, while most stock issues are handled on a best efforts basis. Underwriting transfers the risk from the issuing firm to the underwriting syndicate formed to sell the issue.

An alternative to the public offering is private placement. The major advantages of private placements are the speed with which they may be effected and elimination of the registration procedure. In addition, terms can be tailored to meet the needs of both issuer and investor. Since it was created in the early 1980s, shelf registration has become a widely used way of selling new security issues. Shelf registration allows large firms to lower their issuing costs, and it also increases the speed and flexibility of the issuing process.

Common stockholders are the residual owners of the firm; as such, they have last claim on earnings in the form of cash dividends and assets in case of liquidation. They are exposed to more risk and accordingly have higher required returns than the firm's bondholders. Although stockholders generally have voting power, their major influence comes through their collective ability to affect the market price of the firm's stock by buying or selling it.

The financial decision with regard to the size and timing of a new stock issue will depend on the use for which the proceeds will be employed, market conditions, and the firm's capital structure. Empirical evidence indicates that the value of the firm's stock falls as new common stock is issued. If preemptive rights exist, they allow current stockholders to purchase additional shares before they are offered to outsiders. Finally, publicly held firms must also decide whether to apply to have their stock listed on an organized exchange.

Questions

12.1 Define or explain the following:

a. Public offering	**j.** Syndicate
b. General cash offering	**k.** Flotation cost
c. Rights offering	**l.** Majority voting
d. Shelf registration	**m.** Cumulative voting
e. Underwritten	**n.** Preemptive right
f. Best efforts	**o.** Initial public offering (IPO)
g. Direct placement	**p.** Underpricing
h. Registration statement (prospectus)	**q.** Blue sky laws
i. Red herring	

12.2 Since large firms often have extensive and well-trained finance staffs, they appear to be incurring extra costs by employing the services of investment bankers. What reasons can you give for engaging the services of investment bankers?

12.3 Before entering into an underwriting agreement, investment bankers make a careful investigation of the firm, especially if it is making its initial public offering. Since investment bankers quickly resell the securities, why the extensive investigation?

12.4 For underwritten common stock issues of less than $5 million in size, total issuance costs average about 15 percent. Does this mean the cost of external common equity is roughly 15 percent higher than the cost of internally generated funds for these firms?

12.5 List the rights or privileges of common stock ownership. For each, indicate whether it invariably attaches to the common stock or may be present for the stock of one firm and absent for another.

12.6 Explain the difference between majority and cumulative voting. What are the advantages or disadvantages of the two plans from (a) the firm's standpoint, and (b) the viewpoint of minority stockholders?

12.7 Differentiate between par value, book value, and market value per share. Why is market value generally the only important figure? Under what limited circumstances may par value or book value be of some importance? Explain.

12.8 The market price of a firm's common stock falls by about 3 percent when it issues additional shares of common stock. What possible reasons can we advance for this rather surprising finding?

12.9 Explain the direct and indirect costs of issuing common stock. Are there differences for firms that already have stock outstanding as opposed to those engaged in an initial public offering?

12.10 How might firms proceed when pricing a new issue of common stock? What makes this decision important?

12.11 The primary purpose of the preemptive right is to allow stockholders to maintain their proportionate ownership and control of a firm. How important do you believe this right is for the following:

a. The average stockholder of a firm listed on the New York Stock Exchange?
b. An institutional investor such as a mutual fund or a pension fund?
c. The stockholders of a closely held firm? Explain.

12.12 What advantages (are they real or imagined?) exist when a firm decides to list its common stock?

12.13 How do the Securities Act of 1933 and the Securities Exchange Act of 1934 attempt to regulate activities in the primary and secondary capital markets?

12.14 Each month, the Securities and Exchange Commission publishes a report of corporate insider purchases and sales in their own firms' equity securities. Why is such a report issued?

Self-Test Problems (Solutions appear on pages 726–727.)

Selling Costs

ST 12.1 In an $80 million bond issue by Consumers Power, the bonds were purchased by the underwriting group from Consumers Power at 99.125 percent of par and sold to the public at par, which was $1,000 per bond.

a. What was the total amount Consumers Power received from the issue?
b. What were the total underwriting costs? What were the underwriting costs as a percentage of the gross proceeds? What were the underwriting costs per $1,000 bond?
c. If an underwriting firm was also the seller, it received all the commission. Otherwise, other security dealers (not in the underwriting group) could buy the bonds and sell them for a commission of $2.50 per bond. If a dealer bought 50 bonds, how much in total did the dealer make, and how much did the dealer pay to the underwriters for the bonds?

ST 12.2   J. B. Eagen is a new firm that needs to raise $16,560,000 to begin operations. No debt will be used. Eagen's common stock is expected to pay a $4 cash dividend next year, and dividends and earnings are expected to grow at 9 percent per year for the forseeable future. If k_s is 19 percent and the cost of issuing the stock is 8 percent of the gross proceeds from the sale, how many shares must be issued and sold?

ST 12.3   Pantle Electronics is selling shares of common stock through a rights offering. Prior to the offering, the firm had 200,000 shares of common stock outstanding. Pantle plans to issue 20,000 shares at a subscription price of $12. After the stock went ex rights, the market price was $16. What was the price of Pantle Electronics' common stock just prior to the rights offering?

Problems

12.1   Evergreen Products recently sold a $30 million bond issue at par. The underwriting fees were 1.2 percent, and additional issuance costs were $125,000.

a.   How many dollars did Evergreen Products net from the sale?

b.   What were the fees (including both underwriting and other issuance costs) as a percentage of the gross proceeds of the bond issue?

12.2   Precision Computers, a new and rather speculative firm, wishes to raise additional capital by selling stock and going public. The firm's investment banker has suggested two alternatives. Plan I includes an underwritten offer of 1 million shares at $7.50 per share, with an underwriting fee of 8 percent of the gross proceeds. Plan II is a best efforts offering at $7.75 per share, subject to an underwriting commission of 3 percent of the expected gross proceeds sold, plus a $150,000 fee. The "best guess" is that 95 percent of the issue would be sold under plan II.

a.   Based on the net proceeds to the firm, which plan should Precision choose?

b.   Does your answer change if only 90 percent of the issue can be sold under the best efforts plan?

c.   All things considered, which plan would you recommend? Why?

12.3   Thomas, Inc., is planning a private placement of 60,000 new shares to an institutional investor at a 10 percent discount from the present market price of $40. There are presently 300,000 shares outstanding. If the current book value of the stockholders' equity is $6,000,000, calculate (1) book value per share both before and after the private placement, and (2) the market price per share after the private placement. Are existing stockholders better or worse off after the new shares are sold? Defend your answer, given your calculations.

12.4   Sports Enterprises is planning its first public offering of common stock. The CFO estimates that the equity investor's required rate of return is between 11 and 14 percent. Earnings and cash dividends are expected to grow at 6 to 9 percent per year for the forseeable future, while cash dividends to be paid next year (D_1) are $800,000.

a.   What is the range of possible total current market values for the stock of Sports Enterprises?

b.   If 500,000 shares of stock are authorized and outstanding, but 300,000 will be held by the founders, what is the maximum and minimum selling price per share and maximum and minimum total proceeds from the issue?

12.5   Granbe Enterprises is a new firm that needs to raise $6,412,500 through the issuance of 1 million shares of stock. No debt will be employed. Next year's cash dividends are expected to be $0.60 per share, and cash dividends and earnings are expected to grow at 8 percent per year for the foreseeable future. If k_s is 16 percent and the cost of issuing the stock is 10 percent of the gross proceeds, what percent of the issue must be sold in order for Granbe to obtain the $6,412,500? (*Note:* Any unsold shares will be distributed among the firm's owners so a total of 1 million shares will be outstanding.)

Pricing a New Issue:
Comparative P/E and
Dividend Valuation
Approaches

12.6 Spartan Energy is planning its first public offering. Its past growth in cash dividends and earnings has averaged 10 percent per year. Based on the number of shares Spartan is planning to issue, cash dividends and earnings per share for next year (t = 1) are expected to be $0.90 and $2, respectively. The firm's investment banker, Lindsay & Sons, has recommended that the stock be issued at a price of $15 per share. (Ignore any flotation or issuance costs.)

a. What is the P/E ratio implied by the recommended market price?

b. Two firms similar to Spartan Energy have the following characteristics:

	Firm Y	Firm Z
Expected EPS	$ 1.50	$ 3.00
Expected DPS	0.80	1.25
Expected growth rate per year	7%	9%
Market price	$15.00	$45.00

For firm Y and firm Z, determine (1) their P/E ratios and (2) their implied k_s. Then calculate an estimated market price for Spartan Energy using first the separate P/Es and k_ss, and then an average of them. Based on these comparable firms, what range of prices is implied for Spartan?

c. What required rate of return, k_s, is implied by the price of $15 if investors' expectations of the future are consistent with the past?

d. You believe the required rate of return calculated in (c) is high; it should be between 11.5 and 13 percent. The expected growth rate of 10 percent is okay. What issue price is implied, given these estimates?

e. Based on your analysis in (a) through (d), how would you respond to the Lindsay & Sons proposal?

Recording a Stock
Issue

12.7 Pennsylvania Paper is planning to issue 500,000 additional shares of common stock at an offering price of $12 each. Show the net effect of the transaction on the firm's balance sheet. (Ignore any underwriting or other issuance expenses.)

Assets		Liabilities and Stockholders' Equity	
Cash	$ 3,000,000	Liabilities	$25,000,000
Other	62,000,000	Common stock ($2 par)	4,000,000
Total	$65,000,000	Additional paid-in capital	10,000,000
		Retained earnings	26,000,000
		Total	$65,000,000

Common Equity

12.8 Payne & Sons has 200,000 shares of common stock authorized. Its common equity shown on the firm's balance sheet is as follows:

Common stock ($2 par)	$300,000
Additional paid-in capital	95,000
Retained earnings	600,000
	995,000
Less: Treasury stock (3,000 shares)	25,000
Common stockholders' equity	$970,000

a. How many shares are issued?

b. How many are outstanding? Explain the difference between (a) and (b).

c. How many additional shares can be issued without the approval of Payne & Sons stockholders?

d. If the firm issues 5,000 more shares at $15 each, prepare the new common stockholders' equity accounts.

Rights Offering

12.9 Hawkeye Banks has decided to employ a rights offering to raise $5 million. Currently (before the rights offering), there are 500,000 shares of common stock outstanding, the market price per share is $68, and the subscription price has been set at $50 per share.

a. How many additional shares of common stock will Hawkeye issue via the rights offering?

b. How many rights will be necessary to purchase one additional share?

c. What is the approximate value of each right?

d. When, and by how much, will the stock drop in price?

Rights Valuation and Timing

12.10 Manhattan Industries is planning a rights offering of 50,000 shares at $40 each. The following timetable is planned:

Date	Action
August 4	Announcement
September 11	Ex rights
September 17	Record date
October 15	Rights expire

The market price on August 4 is $50 per share, and four rights are required for each additional share to be purchased. Assume there are no changes in market value except due to the rights offering.

a. What is the value of one right?

b. Can you infer how many shares of stock Manhattan had outstanding before the rights offering?

c. Trace the market price per share from August 4 to October 15.

Rights Offering and Stockholder Wealth

12.11 Optics, Inc., has decided on a rights offering to raise $5.2 million for new equipment and working capital. The current market price per share before the offering was $84, the subscription price was set at $52, and seven rights are required to buy one more share.

a. Determine the value of the right and the ex rights price of the stock.

b. After announcing the offering, you receive a call from an irate stockholder who owns 700 shares of stock. The stockholder believes a personal loss will be suffered, since Optics decided to issue additional stock at a price substantially below the current market value. To convince this stockholder otherwise, you promise to send a statement showing the effects of a rights offering on stockholder wealth, assuming: (1) the stockholder exercises the rights; (2) the rights are sold (ignore brokerage costs); (3) the rights expire. Prepare such a statement.

References

For more on investment banking, equity financing, and shelf registrations, see

BARCLAY, MICHAEL J., AND ROBERT H. LITZENBERGER. "Announcement Effects of New Equity Issues and the Use of Intraday Price Data." *Journal of Financial Economics* 21 (May 1988), pp. 71–99.

BARON, DAVID P. "A Model of the Demand for Investment Banking and Advising and Distribution Services for New Issues." *Journal of Finance* 37 (September 1982), pp. 955–976.

HANSEN, ROBERT. "Evaluating the Costs of a New Equity Issue." *Midland Corporate Finance Journal* 4 (Spring 1986), pp. 42–55.

IBBOTSON, ROGER N., JODY L. SINDELAR, AND JAY R. RITTER. "Initial Public Offerings." *Journal of Applied Corporate Finance* 1 (Summer 1988), pp. 37–45.

JOHNSON, JAMES M., AND ROBERT E. MILLER. "Investment Banker Prestige and the Underpricing of Initial Public Offerings." *Financial Management* 17 (Summer 1988), pp. 19–29.

KIDWELL, DAVID S., M. WAYNE MARR, AND G. RODNEY THOMPSON. "SEC Rule 415: The Ultimate Competitive Bid." *Journal of Financial and Quantitative Analysis* 19 (June 1984), pp. 183–195.

RITTER, JAY R. "The Costs of Going Public." *Journal of Financial Economics* 19 (December 1987), pp. 269–281.

ROGOWSKI, ROBERT J., AND ERIC H. SORENSEN. "Deregulation in Investment Banking: Shelf Registration, Structure, and Performance." *Financial Management* 14 (Spring 1985), pp. 5–15.

SMITH, CLIFFORD W., JR. "Investment Banking and the Capital Acquisition Process." *Journal of Financial Economics* 15 (January–February 1986), pp. 3–29.

Voting rights and other topics of interest are discussed in

COOPER, S. KERRY, JOHN C. GROTH, AND WILLIAM E. AVERA. "Liquidity, Exchange Listing, and Common Stock Performance." *Journal of Economics and Business* 37 (February 1985), pp. 19–33.

DEANGELO, HARRY, AND LINDA DEANGELO. "Managerial Ownership of Voting Rights: A Study of Public Corporations with Dual Classes of Common Stock." *Journal of Financial Economics* 14 (March 1985), pp. 33–69.

LEASE, RONALD C., JOHN J. MCCONNELL, AND WAYNE H. MIKKELSON. "The Market Value of Differential Voting Rights in Closely Held Corporations." *Journal of Business* 57 (October 1984), pp. 443–467.

PARTCH, M. MEGAN. "The Creation of a Class of Limited Voting Common Stock and Shareholder Wealth." *Journal of Financial Ecomomics* 18 (June 1987), pp. 313–339.

13

Liability Management

Overview

- Bonds and preferred stock take many different forms. These alternatives assist firms in raising long-term funds as cheaply as possible while providing features that appeal to investors.

- Bond ratings are the best indication of the quality of bond issues. Other things being equal, the lower the rating, the higher the coupon rate and the higher the required rate of return.

- As interest rates fluctuate, zero-coupon bonds change in market price relatively more than similar coupon (or interest-bearing) bonds.

- Firms have increasingly begun to practice active liability management. Tactics include bond refundings (or buybacks), defeasance, and interest rate swaps.

Virtually every day firms turn to the long-term markets to raise large amounts of new capital. A glance at a few current issues of the Wall Street Journal *shows the following: Mark IV Industries was raising $200 million with 10-year subordinated debentures. Pitney Bowes Credit was issuing 10-year notes. Security Pacific Corporation was raising $250 million with notes offering floating interest rates. The Student Loan Marketing Association (Sallie Mae) went to the corporate debt market for the twelfth time in less than a year. And commercial banks, among others, have turned to new kinds of securities in recent years, including adjustable-rate preferred stock. What a mere 10 or 15 years ago was the dull, conservative field of debt and preferred stock financing has changed dramatically. Now firms rely on liability management—the aggressive manipulation of fixed and variable rate long-term financing.*

Look at how firms now take advantage of differences in worldwide interest rates. Thanks to heavy overseas demand, U.S. corporations have occasionally been able to issue securities called zero-coupon bonds in the Eurobond market at favorable interest rates—about 1 percent lower than the rate on U.S. Treasury bonds of comparable maturity. By then investing the proceeds of the bond issue in U.S. Treasuries, the firm can earn the 1 percent interest rate differential. It's a complex story. Zero-coupon bonds do not pay periodic interest, and the Treasury bonds are actually "stripped" of their coupons. This kind of transaction is new for most corporations, but it is indicative of the changes that are taking place in liability management.

Long-Term Debt

Long-term debt and preferred stock obligate the firm to pay a fixed annual return—interest on debt, and cash dividends on preferred stock. (They are thus often called fixed-income securities.) To secure funds at the lowest cost with the least risk, astute managers choose from among the various kinds of long-term securities depending on world markets, what investors are currently interested in, and the firm's current financial position. This chapter focuses primarily on the two main types of long-term securities—bonds and preferred stock. A third possibility—term loans—was examined in Chapter 5 when we calculated an amortization schedule.

Bond Terms

When a firm borrows with bonds, it issues a long-term promissory note to a lender. The contract between the firm and the lender is called a bond *indenture.* A copy of the indenture is included in the registration statement filed with the Securities and Exchange Commission. It is a legal document specifying all the provisions attached to the bond. One specific provision states that the lenders will receive regular interest payments, generally semiannually, during the term of the bond, and will receive the par or maturity value of the bond upon maturity. For example, if IBM issues a 20-year, $100 million bond with a coupon rate of 12 percent, it will pay $12 million per year in interest each year until maturity. The interest will be paid in two semiannual installments of $6 million each. On the maturity date in 20 years, IBM would then repay the $100 million.

Trustee

Bonds are not only of long duration, they are typically of substantial size. Issues of $50 to $500 million are not uncommon, and some are even larger. To ease communication between the issuing firm and the lenders, a trustee is appointed for all public issues of long-term debt. The primary responsibilities of the trustee (typically a bank) are as follows:

1. To see that all the legal requirements for drawing up the bond indenture are met before issuance.
2. To monitor the action of the issuing firm to see that its performance is in agreement with the conditions specified by the indenture.
3. To take appropriate action on behalf of bondholders if the firm defaults on interest or principal payments.

Security and Seniority

Bonds come with many types of provisions. As Figure 13.1 shows, one primary distinction is between secured and unsecured bonds. We will discuss them in order.

Forms of Secured Debt

The vast majority of secured debt consists of *mortgage bonds,* which may be first mortgage bonds if they have a primary claim on assets in the event of default, or second mortgage bonds whose claim is subordinate to that of the first mortgage bondholders. Some mortgages have a closed-end provision that prohibits the firm from issuing additional debt with equal priority against the pledged assets. No specific limit on the amount of debt secured by the firm's assets exists with an open-end provision. In between is a limited open-end mortgage in which some limited amount of additional debt may be issued. To strengthen the position of the bondholder, the

Figure 13.1 Types of Bonds

Many other variations exist, but these represent the primary types. Note that other features, such as adjustable rates or zero coupons, can be incorporated with any of these bonds.

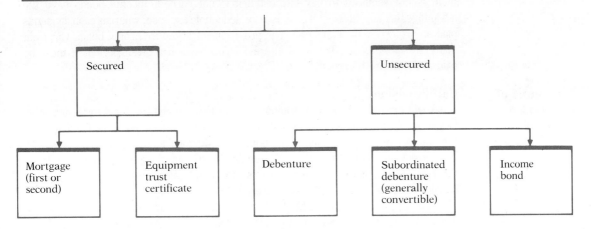

indenture also may contain an after-acquired property clause. This provision specifies that any property acquired by the firm in the future will also serve as collateral for the bonds.

A second form of secured debt is the *equipment trust certificate.* These frequently are used to finance railroad cars, trucks, buses, and airplanes. Here, the trustee acquires formal ownership of the asset in question. The issuing firm arranges to purchase the equipment and provides a down payment of 10 to 25 percent; the remainder is provided by the purchasers of the equipment trust certificates. The certificates are issued with varying maturities, often ranging from 1 to 15 years. After the entire issue is paid off, title to the equipment passes to the firm. Because the trustee holds title to the pledged equipment, equipment trust certificates provide good security to their purchasers.

Unsecured Debt

Unsecured bonds or *debentures* have no specific assets pledged as collateral. Instead, they are backed by the full faith and credit of the issuing corporation. Large firms with excellent credit ratings, such as Procter & Gamble, Exxon, and Shell, use debentures almost exclusively. Most debentures have a claim on assets in the event of default that comes after that held by bank loans, short-term debt, the government, and any mortgage bonds.

Although asset security may be considered important, in the final analysis it is the firm's cash flows that determines the attractiveness of a bond issue. Debentures frequently contain a negative pledge clause, which prohibits issuing new debt with a priority over the debentures' claim on assets. This generally applies to assets acquired in the future as well as those already owned by the issuing firm.

Subordinated debentures, which have a claim on assets inferior to that of other debentures in the case of liquidation, are widely used in raising long-term debt capital. Subordinated debt allows the issuing firm to increase its borrowing without jeopardizing the security position of its other long-term debt.

One last form of unsecured bond is the *income bond,* which requires interest to be paid only to the extent that it is earned by the firm. Income bonds typically arise out of reorganizations. They are somewhat like preferred stock in that management is not required to pay interest if it is not earned. Income bonds have the advantage that any interest, if paid, is a tax-deductible expense, whereas cash dividends paid on preferred stock are not. The provisions attached to income bonds vary, but many are *cumulative;* that is, if interest is not paid in a given period, it must be paid in the future if earned.

Provisions of the Bond Indenture

Call Provision

A *call provision* gives the issuing firm the right to call the bond for redemption before it matures. This provision states that the firm must pay an amount greater than the par or maturity value of the bond; the additional amount is the *call premium.* For most long-term bonds, the call premium starts out close to the coupon rate on the bond. Thus, if the firm wants to call the bonds soon after issuance, it pays a penalty of about 1 year's additional interest. This rate declines over time.

The call provision is valuable to the firm but potentially detrimental to investors. The problem for investors is that the call provision enables the issuing firm to substitute bonds with a lower coupon rate for bonds with a higher rate.[1] That is why so many bonds now carry a 5- to 10-year nonrefundable provision if the coupon rate on the new bonds will be below the current coupon rate on the bond to be refunded.

Sinking Fund

A *sinking fund* provision requires the firm to retire a given number of bonds over a specified time period. The logic behind sinking funds is to encourage firms to adopt a systematic pattern for retiring the largest portion of the debt before the maturity date. Generally bonds are redeemed for the sinking fund at par. While it is called a sinking fund, it should be emphasized that a separate fund is *not* set up and accumulated over the years. Rather, a given number of bonds *are actually retired each year.*

In most cases, the firm has an option on how to meet the sinking fund provision. If market interest rates have increased, causing the price of the bonds to fall below the par or sinking fund price, the firm can buy sufficient bonds on the open market to meet the requirement. But if market interest rates are low (and therefore bond prices are high), the firm will call the bonds by lottery at par. This option obviously benefits the issuing firm.

If the bonds are privately placed, this option is omitted because the bonds must be redeemed at par. Instead of having sinking funds, *serial bonds* consist of a package of bonds that mature in different years. A package of serial bonds is similar to a bond with a sinking fund provision, since both provide for the periodic repayment of the firm's debt. But the serial bond does not give the issuing firm an option—the bonds must be redeemed at par.

Convertibility

Some bonds, and an even smaller percentage of preferred stock, contain another feature–convertibility. Convertible securities are convertible bonds or convertible

---

[1] Refunding a bond issue involves calling one issue and replacing it with another. Refunding is considered later in the chapter and in Appendix 13A.

preferred stock originally issued as debt or preferred stock. They can be exchanged for common stock of the issuing firm at the discretion of the investor. There is no charge for making this exchange, and the exchange can be made whenever the investor wishes.

Consider a $1,000 par convertible bond that has a stated conversion price of $50. The number of shares the bond can be converted into (or exchanged for) is $1,000/$50=20 shares. A few other characteristics of convertible bonds are as follows. First, convertible bonds are typically debentures, and they are subordinated. Thus, virtually all convertible bonds are *convertible subordinated debentures*. Second, when convertible bonds are designed and issued, (1) their stated coupon interest rate is less than that required on nonconvertible bonds of similar quality and maturity, and (2) their conversion price is set above the current market price of the firm's common stock.

Convertible securities combine elements of both equity and fixed-income securities. As such, it is not surprising that the return required by investors falls between that required on bonds and on common stock. One important aspect of convertibles is that the firm has the ability to call the security at its discretion. This action may benefit the firm, but be detrimental to investors if they were not ready to convert, or "cash out," their investment.

Financing with Long-Term Debt

The frequency with which firms issue long-term debt varies considerably. At one extreme are large electric utility firms, which may issue debt every few years. Other firms issue long-term debt only infrequently. But however often they employ it, there are special considerations managers must be aware of when they use long-term debt.

Pricing and Selling the Bond Issue

Many large bond issues are underwritten, although an increasing number are being offered through the shelf registration procedure. The coupon interest rate is determined shortly before the bonds come to market so that they may be sold at a price close to par. Most bonds are issued in denominations of $1,000 in *fully registered* form. This means that the registration agent for the issuing firm (often a bank) will record the ownership of each bond, so that both interest and principal are paid directly to the owner of the bond. Until the last few decades, most bonds were issued in *bearer form*. When bearer bonds are employed, the certificate is the primary evidence of ownership. The owner must send coupons in for payment of interest, and the bond itself must be returned upon maturity for repayment of principal. Because of the risk of loss and the time and inconvenience involved in "clipping" coupons, most corporate bonds are now issued in fully registered form.

The price of a bond is expressed as a percentage of its par value. Thus, a price of 99.5 means 99.5 percent of its $1,000 par value, or $995. When a bond is sold the price is quoted net of accrued interest. This means the purchaser pays not only the purchase price, but also any interest that may have accrued between interest payment dates.

Bond Ratings   The most widely employed method for examining the relative quality of bonds is *bond ratings*, which reflect the probability of payment of both interest and principal. Two bonds with similar ratings and the same maturity have approximately the same yield to maturity.[2] The two major rating agencies are Moody's Investors Service and Standard & Poor's Corporation. Their ratings are described in Table 13.1.

The Aaa[3] and Aa bonds are of high quality; A and Baa bonds are also viewed as being of "investment grade." These four top grades may be held by banks and other institutional investors. Ba and B bonds are more speculative with respect to payment of interest and principal; bonds rated below B are either in default or have other characteristics that make them highly speculative.

Many factors influence the determination of bond ratings, but some of the most important are these:

1. Financial ratios such as the debt/equity ratio, times interest earned, and various profitability ratios, which provide evidence of the financial strength and riskiness of the firm.
2. The current status of the firm in terms of its competitiveness and management. In addition, the industry or industries in which the firm is engaged often will be a factor.
3. If the firm is in a regulated industry such as public utilities, the attitude of the appropriate regulatory authorities.
4. Specific provisions or characteristics of the bonds. For example, first mortgage bonds generally carry a rating one level higher than debentures for the same firm, and debentures are often rated one level higher than subordinated debentures.

When originally issued, most bonds are awarded a rating of B or above, with the highest-quality bonds carrying an Aaa rating. Aaa bonds are viewed by the rating agencies as having the lowest probability of default, so the issuing firms have to pay the least for debt financing. Table 13.2 indicates that between 1979 and 1987, the yield to maturity on Aaa-rated bonds was about 1.5 percent below that for Baa bonds. The differences in yields to maturity, although for bonds already outstanding, illustrate the differences in coupon rates attached to bonds in different rating groups.

Notice in Table 13.2 that even the Aaa corporate bonds are not viewed as riskless and hence have a higher yield to maturity than long-term U.S. Treasury bonds. As one proceeds down the rating scale, the bonds become more risky. Yield spreads between bonds vary over time. In 1982, for example, long-term U.S. Treasury bonds had a yield to maturity of 12.23 percent, whereas corporate Baa bonds were yielding 16.11 percent, for a difference of 3.88 percent (or 388 basis points). However, just three years later, in 1985, the difference in yields between the same two bond categories was 1.97 percent (12.72 − 10.75).

These differences, or yield spreads, fluctuate over time. The yield spread between Baa corporates and U.S. Treasury bonds for 1979 to 1987 is plotted in Figure 13.2 on p. 351. Note that in 1982 the yield spread was wide, but it was much narrower

---

[2] Exceptions occur when we compare bonds issued by industrial firms and those issued by public utilities. Because of different provisions and demand, the yields on utilities are typically higher than those of similarly rated corporate bonds.

[3] In the text we use Moody's codes, but they imply the corresponding Standard & Poor's rating.

Table 13.1 Bond Rating Classifications

Generally, both Moody's and Standard & Poor's rate a bond similarly, although differences in rating can and do exist. Bonds in the top four classifications (Aaa-Baa or AAA-BBB) are considered "investment grade." (SOURCES: Moody's Bond Record *and Standard & Poor's* Credit-week.)

	Moody's		**Standard & Poor's**
Aaa	Best quality, "gilt edge"	AAA	Highest rating
Aa	High quality	AA	Very strong
A	Upper medium grade	A	Strong
Baa	Medium grade	BBB	Adequate
Ba	Have speculative elements	BB	Least speculative of BB to CCC bonds
B	Lack characteristics of a desirable investment		
		B	More speculative
Caa	Poor standing; may be in default	CC	Still more speculative
		CCC	Most speculative
Ca	High degree of speculation; often in default	D	Income bonds in default
C	Extremely poor prospect of ever attaining any real investment standing		

Note: Aa to B bonds carry a 1, 2, or 3 to designate the top, middle, and bottom range of the rating.

Note: AA to BB bonds may be modified by the addition of a plus or minus sign to show relative standing.

Table 13.2 Yield to Maturity on Long-Term U.S. Treasury and Corporate Bonds

The differences in yields approximates the differences in coupon rates required by the issuing firm. Hence, other things being equal, firms strive for as high a rating as possible to reduce their interest costs. (SOURCE: Federal Reserve Bulletin, *various issues.*)

Year	U.S. Treasury Bonds	Corporate Bonds			
		Aaa	**Aa**	**A**	**Baa**
1979	8.74%	9.63%	9.94%	10.20%	10.69%
1980	10.81	11.94	12.50	12.89	13.67
1981	12.87	14.17	14.75	15.29	16.04
1982	12.23	13.79	14.41	15.43	16.11
1983	10.84	12.04	12.42	13.10	13.55
1984	11.99	12.71	13.31	13.74	14.19
1985	10.75	11.37	11.82	12.28	12.72
1986	8.14	9.02	9.47	9.95	10.39
1987	8.64	9.38	9.68	9.99	10.58
Average	10.56	11.56	12.03	12.54	13.10

Bond Rating Changes

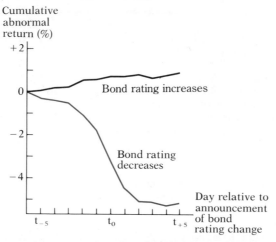

Do changes in a firm's bond rating have any information that is reflected in the returns of the firm's common stock? A recent study using daily data looks at the impact of changes in bond ratings and changes on the returns of the firm's stock.[1] As shown in the figure, in the 10 days surrounding the announcement of a bond rating change where the bonds were upgraded (signifying less risk), there is a very minor, but not statistically significant, impact on common stock returns. When the rating was changed downward (signifying more risk), however, there was approximately a 5 percent reduction in the returns (or value) for the firm's common stock. These results indicate that bond rating decreases contain information for common stock investors; bond rating increases, however, do not. This suggests that rating agencies provide some information for the capital markets.

[1] Robert W. Holthausen and Richard W. Leftwich. "The Effect of Bond Rating Changes on Common Stock Prices." *Journal of Financial Economics* 17 (September 1986).

three years later. In 1982 investors in "risk-free" U.S. Treasury bonds demanded a higher return due to higher inflation and other factors affecting market interest rates. But investors in Baa-rated corporate bonds demanded a substantial yield spread over and above the rate on U.S. Treasury bonds to compensate them for the additional risk. For firms entering the bond market, the going interest rate on outstanding issues of similar maturity and quality provides a good point of reference for estimating the coupon interest rate (and hence the before-tax cost) for a new bond issue.

Debt Financing and the Value of the Firm

In Chapter 12 we saw that firms issuing new equity experience a decrease in the value of their outstanding common stock. Thus, the value of the firm decreases apparently because of the "bad news" associated with the equity financing. Does this same pattern hold for firms that issue new publicly placed bond issues? That is, does the value of these firms' common stock fall? The answer is "maybe yes," but it falls much less than when a firm issues common stock.

Figure 13.2 Yield Spreads

Yield spreads vary over time, depending on (1) the general level of interest rates and (2) specific factors affecting the market for corporate or Treasury bonds.

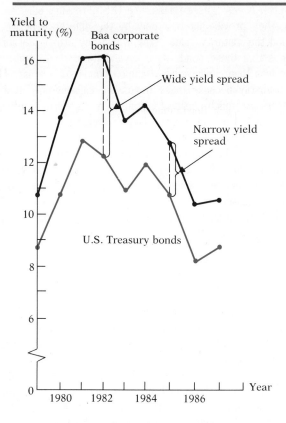

As an alternative to a public bond issue, firms, especially smaller ones, also rely on bank borrowings. The mechanics of these borrowings, as discussed in Chapter 5, often take the form of amortized loans. Firms that borrow from banks are typically smaller than firms that raise funds through a public bond issue, and the maturity (or length) of financing is shorter. In addition, some evidence exists that suggests when firms borrow from banks, they do not suffer the "bad news" effect in the form of a decrease in the value of the firm. It may be that banks have an advantage over other lenders in terms of evaluating and monitoring the borrowing firm—in large part because of their ongoing relationship with the firm. As such, borrowing from a bank—because of their closer relationship with and monitoring of the firm—may be good news, not bad news.

Financing in the 1990s

Because of dramatic shifts in the rate of inflation, innovations in the financial markets, and the development of worldwide capital markets, the degree of sophistication required for raising long-term capital has increased greatly. Firms now use many different forms of debt financing.

Zero-Coupon Bonds

In 1981 Martin Marietta sold $175 million of 30-year bonds with a 7 percent coupon rate at 54 percent of par for an effective yield to maturity of 13.25 percent. These were one of the first *deep discount bonds*. Subsequently, many firms have issued *zero-coupon bonds*. These bonds, like U.S. Treasury bills, are issued at a discount; that is, they provide interest only by the difference between their original issue price and the maturity value. Why would any firm issue zero-coupon bonds? The answer is that these bonds have a yield (or cost) to maturity of approximately 1 percent less than similar-quality coupon bonds sold at par. The cost to the firm is lower primarily because these bonds are callable only at a substantial premium. Purchasers are much surer of locking in a long-term return that will not be called by the issuing firm, and so are willing to accept a lower return.

Zero-coupon bonds have some unusual characteristics that differentiate them from the coupon-bearing bonds we valued in Chapter 6. To illustrate, assume that Anderson Products is going to issue a $100 million par value, 10-year, 12 percent zero-coupon bond. Assuming (for simplicity) that interest is compounded annually, we can use present value techniques to determine how much the firm will receive when the bond is issued. The net proceeds, B_0, from the bond (ignoring flotation costs) are equal to

$$B_0(\text{ zero coupon }) = \text{par}(\,PV_{kb,n}\,) \tag{13.1}$$
$$= \text{par}(\,PV_{12\%,10\,\text{yr}}\,) = \$100,000,000(\,0.322\,) = \$32,200,000$$

Anderson will receive approximately $32 million from the bond issue, and in 10 years it will repay $100 million to the purchasers of the bonds. While annual cash interest payments are not made, the Internal Revenue Service has ruled that *both the firm issuing the bonds and investors purchasing them* must impute and report interest (for tax purposes) just as if cash had changed hands. The actual amount of interest declared, as shown in Table 13.3, increases each year due to the compounding involved. Notice in the table that the total amount of interest (per $1,000 par value bond) of $678.03 is just equal to the difference between the par (or maturity) value of the bond and its original price of $321.97 per $1,000 bond. If market interest rates were to remain constant over the entire 10-year period, the values given in column 1 of Table 13.3 show the market value at time $t = 1$, $t = 2$, and so forth.

So far, so good! Zero-coupon bonds seem simple and straightforward. Now let us compare them with a similar coupon (or interest-bearing) bond. We will see that when market interest rates change, the *percentage* price change on a zero-coupon bond is greater than that on a coupon bond. This makes perfect sense: With the zero-coupon bond, nothing is received (or paid) until maturity, while with a coupon bond the current market value is a function of both the periodic coupon interest payments and the bond's par value.

Consider Figure 13.3 on p. 354, which shows the percentage change from the original price for the Anderson Products 12 percent zero-coupon bond and a similar 12 percent interest-bearing 10-year bond. If the market interest rate on the bonds is 12 percent, the coupon bond will sell at its par value of $1,000 (par bond), while the zero-coupon bond sells at $322 per bond. Assume you are an investor who has an equal dollar amount to invest in either bond. For simplicity, assume this is $322,000.

Table 13.3 Present Value and Interest per Year for 12 Percent $1,000 Par Zero-Coupon Bond

The interest on zero-coupon bonds is determined using the present value techniques discussed in Chapter 5.

Year	Present Value (12%) at End of Year* (1)	Present Value (12%) at Beginning of Year (2)	Interest (1) − (2) (3)
1	$ 360.61†	$321.97‡	$ 38.64
2	403.88	360.61	43.27
3	452.35	403.88	48.47
4	506.63	452.35	54.28
5	567.43	506.63	60.80
6	635.52	567.43	68.09
7	711.78	635.52	76.26
8	797.19	711.78	85.41
9	892.86	797.19	95.67
10	1,000.00	892.86	107.14
			$678.03

* For more precision, a financial calculator was used instead of Table F.3.
† For year 1, $321.97(1.12) = $360.61; for year 2, $360.61(1.12) = $403.88. The rest were computed in a similar manner.
‡ The original selling price is simply the present value of $1,000 discounted at 12 percent for 10 years. Using a financial calculator, you punch in FV = 1,000, n = 10, k = i = 12, and then hit the PV button.

With that you can buy 1,000 ($322,000/$322) zero-coupon bonds or 322 ($322,000/$1,000) coupon interest-bearing bonds. If market interest rates increase from 12 to 16 percent, which choice exposes you to more interest rate risk? To see, let's calculate the new market price for both bonds.

From Equation 6.1 for the 322 12 percent coupon bonds, each with a par value of $1,000, we have

$$B_0 = \$322,000(0.12)(PVA_{16\%,10yr}) + \$322,000(PV_{16\%,10yr})$$

$$= \$38,640(4.833) + \$322,000(0.227) = \$259,841.12$$

The 4 percent increase in interest rates lead to a decrease in value of $62,158.88 ($322,000 − $259,841.12), or a 19.30 percent decrease.

From Equation 13.1 for the 1,000 zero-coupon bonds with a total par value in 10 years of $1,000,000, we have

$$B_0(\text{zero coupon}) = \$1,000,000(PV_{16\%,10yr}) = \$1,000,000(0.227) = \$227,000$$

Now the same 4 percent rise in interest rates leads to a decrease in value of $95,000 ($322,000 − $227,000), or a 29.50 percent decrease. These figures, when calculated for a number of other market interest rates and plotted (as in Figure 13.3), demonstrate the increased price volatility or interest rate risk investors experience with zero-coupon as opposed to coupon bonds. By buying zero-coupon bonds, investors expose themselves to greater price fluctuations as market interest rates change.

So far we have considered a zero-coupon bond with 10 years to maturity. What happens to the interest rate risk (as evidenced by its price volatility) as the maturity

Figure 13.3   Percentage Price Fluctuations for Zero-Coupon Versus Coupon Bonds

This figure is based on 10-year, 12 percent bonds selling at their original price. However, the general relationships hold for all similar zero-coupon and coupon (interest-bearing) bonds.

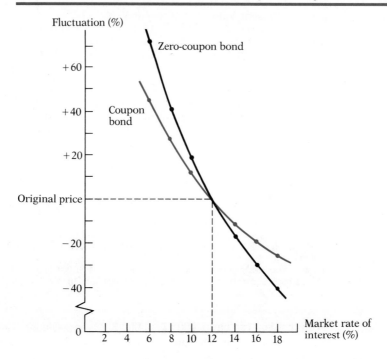

is shortened? As Figure 13.4 shows, the shorter the maturity, the lower the interest rate risk. This is due to the reduced impact of discounting with short- versus long-maturity bonds. From the issuing firm's standpoint, the primary attraction of zeros is their reduced cost vis-à-vis similar coupon bonds. For investors, their primary advantage is that they lock in the return when compared to coupon-bearing bonds.[4]

Junk Bonds

Junk bonds (or high-yield bonds) are those rated Ba and below. While traditionally they have not been a major financing source, that has changed in recent years. Starting in the mid-1970s, the investment banking firm of Drexel Burnham literally built junk bonds into a major part of the bond market. Today, junk bonds represent over 10 percent of all new bonds issued. They are also widely employed in financing mergers and leveraged buyouts.

Junk bonds are issued by firms with low credit ratings that are willing to pay 3

---

[4] In Chapters 6 and 8 we discussed the reinvestment rate assumption that is built into any IRR calculation. If you purchased the 10-year, 12 percent coupon bond at par, your expected return is the bond's yield to maturity, which is 12 percent. However, *you will realize the 12 percent only if you can reinvest each of the nine annual interest payments* (received at t_1 through t_9) *at 12 percent*. This is illustrated in self-test problem ST 13.4 and problem 13.5 at the end of the chapter. With a zero-coupon bond, investors do not have to worry about the reinvestment rate on the interest payments received.

Figure 13.4 Relationship of a Zero-Coupon Bond's Price Fluctuation, the Current Market Rate of Interest, and Bond Maturity

This relationship for zero-coupon bonds is exactly the same as that shown in Figure 6.2 for coupon (interest-bearing) bonds.

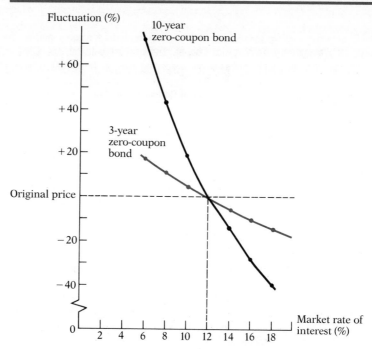

to 5 percent more to raise long-term debt than a triple A-rated firm. These are often growing firms that would rather borrow from the public than from banks or other financial institutions. Among the firms that have issued junk bonds are MCI, Golden Nugget, and Coastal Corporation. Due to their greater riskiness, these firms pay higher interest rates than many other firms; but the cost is still less than if they borrowed privately. While some question the growth of the junk bond market, in most cases the firm is simply securing financing by a public offering instead of through the institutional investors who traditionally supplied their long-term debt capital.

Variable Rates

The majority of loans made by commercial banks are now variable rate loans. That is, the interest rate may vary over the life of the loan. Often the rate is expressed as some fixed percentage over the prime interest rate.[5] For example, the loan agreement may specify that the rate will be "2 percentage points over prime." This means that if the current *prime rate* charged by the bank to its best customers is 13 percent, the interest rate on the loan will be 15 percent. Since interest is typically changed

---

[5] As noted in Chapter 21, prime is an artificial (or administered) rate. Some firms can actually borrow at rates below prime.

Copper Bonds

While bonds come in many different sizes, shapes, and flavors, an unusual one has been used by Magnum Copper. The interest paid on this $200 million issue is tied to average copper prices in the preceding quarter. The structure is as follows:

If Copper Prices Are	Bond Pays
$2 and above	21%
1.80	20
1.60	19
1.40	18
1.30	17
1.20	16
1.10	15
1.00	14
0.90	13
0.80 or less	12

In Magnum's case they don't mind paying for expensive financing if the price of copper is high.

If copper prices fall, however, the minimum guarantee of 12 percent may be illusory, because the 12 percent holds only if Magnum remains profitable. If copper prices fall and Magnum's quarterly profits drop below 1.5 times the total interest it has to pay, the 12 percent minimum interest rate disappears. The company can then pay 50 percent of the interest with more copper bonds. Both the firm and investors benefit if copper prices are high; if copper prices fall, however, the investor suffers, and the firm has some flexibility due to the reduced cash outflows for interest in a period where cash flows are inadequate.

every time the prime rate changes, the bank in effect varies the total payment required each period to pay the principal and interest on the loan.

International Financing

Both U.S. firms and their foreign subsidiaries raise funds in various international markets. However, considerable differences exist in these markets compared to those in the United States. One of the biggest is the much broader role played by banks in the international market. Commercial banks in Europe, the Middle East, and Asia have more flexibility and often combine commercial banking, investment banking, and direct investment. In addition, the banks often work closely with the country's government and may even be partially government-owned. In the United States, commercial banks were required to divest their investment banking operations by the Banking Act of 1933.

The *Eurodollar* system that operates in the international capital markets was developed in the 1950s as banks located outside the United States began to accept interest-bearing deposits in U.S. dollars. Although most of the early activity was centered in Europe, the system (which is often called the *Eurocurrency system*) is now worldwide and includes many different currencies. Eurodollar loans are typically in multiples of $1 million and have maturities lasting from a few days to 15 years or more. Generally these loans are unsecured, but they may contain certain restrictive provisions on the borrowing firms' activities. Large loans may be syndicated, with many banks participating; the lead bank coordinates the syndicate, structures the loan, and provides servicing when needed.

The model for such loans is the U.S. domestic multibank floating-rate term loan. The interest rate is usually stated as some fixed percentage above the *London Interbank Offered Rate* (*LIBOR*), with adjustments at predetermined intervals. Since LIBOR reflects the rate on liquid funds that move among the developed nations' money markets, it dampens borrowing based on interest rate speculation. LIBOR is usually more volatile than the U.S. prime rate because of the sensitive nature of supply and demand for Eurodollar deposits. Accordingly, it may be more difficult to project the cost of a Eurodollar loan.

When long-term debt is needed, the firm may also borrow internationally. An *international bond* issue is one sold outside the country of the borrower; it can be a Eurobond or a foreign bond. A *Eurobond* is one underwritten by an international syndicate and sold primarily in countries other than the country in which the issue is denominated. Thus, a Eurobond could be denominated in the U.S. dollar, the West German mark, or some other currency, but it would be sold mainly outside the country in which it was denominated. Although centered in Europe, the Eurobond market is truly international in scope and includes the Middle East and Asia. A *foreign bond* is one issued by a foreign borrower, but underwritten, sold, and denominated in one country. For example, a U.S. firm might float a foreign bond in Switzerland, underwritten by a Swiss syndicate and denominated in Swiss francs.

The Eurobond market has a number of distinguishing features:

1. Most bonds pay interest only once a year instead of semiannually.
2. Virtually all bonds are issued in bearer form, as opposed to the registered form prevalent in the United States, because of investor desire for anonymity.
3. Almost all Eurodollar issues are listed on one or more recognized stock exchanges— generally in London, Luxembourg, Frankfurt, or in Switzerland.

In addition to the possibility of lower interest rates, firms employing the Eurobond market avoid registration with the U.S. Securities and Exchange Commission. In recent years, many more U.S.-based firms have been turning to foreign capital markets to secure funds.

Managing Long-Term Debt

Until recently, liability management consisted simply of deciding what securities to issue. Debt was left to mature, then retired—perhaps with the proceeds from a new bond issue. High and volatile interest rates, the growth of international financial markets, and innovative investment banking firms have changed all that, and the management of long-term liabilities has taken a dramatic turn. Let's consider some of the techniques now available.

Refunding

A few years ago, when interest rates were high, many firms issued long-term debt. What happened when market rates fell? To astute managers, a fall in rates provided the opportunity to replace (or refund) the older, high interest rate bond with a similar bond offering a lower coupon rate. In a bond *refunding,* the firm calls all the old bonds at a fixed price and simultaneously issues new, lower coupon-rate bonds. The bond owners have no choice; when a bond is called it must be surrendered, for the firm stops paying interest on it. This process is discussed in detail in Appendix 13A. The decision to refund depends on the net amount required to call the existing bond and the present value of the future incremental cash flows. It is thus just another use of the net present value, NPV, framework developed in Chapters 8 and 9.

However, two complications can arise. First, how does the firm decide on the best time to refund? The answer depends primarily on the relationship of current market interest rates to forecasted interest rates next month, in 3 months, and so forth. The firm may benefit from a refunding today, but it must also consider whether it would be better off waiting in the hope that interest rates will fall further.

To protect investors, many bonds now carry a provision that prohibits them from being called for refunding for a period of 5 to 10 years. This brings us to the second complexity. What can the firm do if it wants to refund a bond issue but is prohibited by some provision in the bond indenture?

Alternatives to Refunding

Three alternatives are available when a firm is prohibited from refunding a bond issue.

1. One alternative is a public *tender offer.* This is an offer to the current bondholders to sell their bonds back to the firm at a predetermined price—one that ideally is attractive to investors and yet ultimately saves the firm money. This may not result in the retirement of the entire issue, but it can substantially reduce the size of the issue in question.

2. An alternative to the public tender offer is a *private market purchase.* Here the firm approaches one or several institutional investors who own a large amount of the firm's bonds and offers to buy them back. Again, the essence of the tactic is to save the firm future interest costs while benefiting the investor. Another alternative sometimes employed is to swap debt for some of the firm's common stock.

3. Instead of retiring some or all of the bonds, other firms are employing a tactic called *defeasance,* which means to "render null and void." To do this the firm enters into an arrangement with a trustee, usually a bank. The obligation for the bond is passed on to the trustee along with a portfolio of securities, typically U.S. Treasury bonds. The deal is structured so that the interest and principal proceeds from the portfolio of Treasury bonds will exceed those required to service the bond issue in question. Hence, for all intents and purposes the debt has been retired— and removed from the firm's balance sheet—without actually calling the bond issue before it was due. Exxon was one of the first to use defeasance when in 1982 it removed $15 million of debt from its balance sheet.

Interest Rate Swaps	*Interest rate swaps* are also increasingly used, especially with the widespread use of floating (or variable) rate financing. The idea is to separate the interest payments from the principal payments for long-term financing. The firm raises funds wherever it can as cheaply as possible—and then converts from floating to fixed rate, or vice versa, depending on the desires of the firm and expectations about the trend of future interest rates. This is accomplished by agreeing to swap interest payments (but not the principal) with another party. For example, if you expect interest rates to go up substantially, and that movement has not been fully anticipated by the market, then you want to swap into a fixed rate interest payment. Conversely, if you expect rates to go down, then being in a floating rate position will reduce the firm's interest charges. These and many other tactics are being used by more and more firms as they move from a passive to an active liability management policy.

Preferred Stock

Preferred stock is an intermediate form of financing between debt and equity that is relatively infrequently employed as a long-term financing vehicle except by public utility firms. Preferred stock generally has a par value—typically $25, $50, or $100—like debt, and also pays a fixed return like debt. But preferred stock legally is a form of ownership; cash dividends paid on preferred stock are similar to cash dividends on common stock in that they are not a tax-deductible expense for the issuing firm.

When preferred stock is issued, the selling price is set close to par. When a $100 par value, 13 percent preferred stock is issued, it will sell close to par and pay cash dividends of $13 [i.e., ($100)(0.13)] per year. The market price on preferred stock fluctuates; if the market yield (where yield = dividends per share/market price per share) on preferred stocks goes up, the market price of outstanding preferred stocks decreases. Because preferred stock is viewed by investors as being similar to bonds, the market yield on preferred stocks tend to move in much the same manner as the yield to maturity on bonds. Hence, as market interest rates on bonds rise, the market yield on preferred stocks also rises due to the declining price of the latter.

If the firm does not have sufficient cash flow to pay dividends on its preferred stock, it can omit the payment. Unpaid dividends on preferred stock are called *arrearages*. Most preferred dividends are cumulative; all past or present dividends must be paid before any further cash dividends are paid on the firm's common stock. Managers view dividends on preferred stock like any other fixed obligation and fully intend to pay the preferred dividends on time. However, preferred stock does provide a safety valve if the firm needs it.

Like common stock, preferred stock does not have any fixed maturity date. However, many recent issues of preferred stock make a provision for periodic repayment via a sinking fund. Virtually all preferred stock is callable at the option of the issuing firm. If a firm goes out of business, the claim of preferred stockholders is junior to that of any debt, but senior to that of common stockholders.

The use of preferred stock, like the issuance of long-term debt, may result in additional restrictions being placed on the firm in the form of limitations on the payment of cash dividends for common stock, maintenance of a minimum level of common equity, or a minimum requirement for the ratio of net working capital to the total debt and preferred stock of the firm. The primary function of these restrictions is to ensure that the firm can make cash dividend payments to its preferred stockholders. Although many preferred stocks have only limited voting rights, the tendency in recent years has been toward fuller voting rights.

From the firm's standpoint, preferred stock has certain advantages:

1. Since the returns to preferred stockholders are limited, financial leverage (see Chapter 15) is possible, because any extraordinary cash flows accrue only to common stockholders.
2. Nonpayment of cash dividends on preferreds does not throw the firm into default.
3. Control of the firm generally remains with the common stockholders.

The primary disadvantage of preferred stock is that cash dividends paid to service the preferred stock are not an allowable deduction for tax purposes. Thus, unlike debt, which it approximates in many respects, dividends on preferred stock must be paid out of after-tax earnings. This treatment makes the cost of most preferred stock much higher than the cost of debt.[6]

In the 1980s a new twist in preferred stock financing was introduced—*adjustable rate preferred stock*. Instead of paying a fixed cash dividend, the dividend rate is tied to a U.S. Treasury security index and adjusted quarterly. The appeal of adjustable rate preferred stock is twofold. First, it allows the issuing firm to issue preferred stock at a lower dividend rate than otherwise. Second, by doing so, the firm adds to its equity base (thereby improving the ratio of total debt to total assets) without issuing additional shares of common stock. From the buyers' standpoint, who are often other corporations, the appeal is the after-tax return coupled with the stability of the market value that results from the adjustable-rate nature of the dividend.

Long-Term Financing and Financial Distress

Differences and conflicts always exist between stockholders and bondholders. Stockholders want to maximize their return—this means that other things being equal, they want the firm to strive for higher returns. But, as we know, higher returns and higher risks go hand-in-hand. Bondholders, however, thought they purchased a much safer security. They become upset when the firm engages in activities that causes this safety to be eroded away.

An interesting way to think about the claims and positions of stockholders and bondholders is to recognize what happens under two very different conditions—the firm prospers, or it fails. If the firm prospers, the common stockholders will see that the bondholders are paid off, and then they claim everything else for themselves. Alternatively, if the firm fails, the stockholders (because of limited liability) walk away from the firm and turn it over to the bondholders.[7] While the stockholders lost their initial investment, at least they aren't liable for any further losses. We can summarize the effects as follows:

---

[6] This is discussed in Chapter 14.

[7] This topic is discussed more formally in Appendix 11A.

The Firm Prospers	The Firm Fails
Bondholders are paid off	Stockholders walk away
Stockholders claim the rest	Bondholders may receive something

Of course, there are many intermediate positions. We need to examine them briefly.

The term *financial distress* has a variety of economic contexts; we use it to mean the firm does not have enough cash on hand, or readily available, to meet current financial obligations. This may be a temporary situation, or it may be far more serious.

A firm facing financial distress has a number of options open to it, depending on the severity of the situation. The fundamental decision is whether to modify the firm, or to liquidate it. Within each option are out-of-court and in-court procedures. These are as follows:

OUT-OF-COURT OPTIONS

1. An *extension* involves nothing more than the creditor's agreeing to delay the payments due from the firm; that is, it extends the payment schedule. Hopefully, with a little more time, the firm can right itself, and proceed on its way.

2. A *composition* is more serious because creditors will receive only a pro rata settlement on their claims. Generally, creditors will agree to composition only when it appears they will receive more from accepting the settlement than from forcing the firm into bankruptcy, with its legal expenses and complications.

3. A "voluntary" liquidation is called an *assignment*. It is often more efficient, can be effected faster, and provides creditors a higher settlement than an in-court liquidation. One problem, however, is getting all creditors to agree to the assignment.

IN-COURT OPTIONS

The in-court options are covered by the Bankruptcy Reform Act of 1978. The basic options for firms are as follows:

1. In a *liquidation* the assets of the firm are sold under the direction of the courts, with the proceeds going to pay claimants based on a general order of priority spelled out in the Act.

2. In a *reorganization* the firm is actually put back on its feet, typically after extensive modifications both in terms of its businesses, and in terms of the claims of creditors and ownership. Typically, former stockholders end up with very little ownership in the reorganized firm.

Although somewhat different in detail, the liquidation versus reorganization decision is no different conceptually than keeping or divesting assets, or divisions, of a firm (as discussed in Chapters 9 and 22). The issue is whether the parties (primarily the creditors) are better off (i.e., have a higher NPV) under liquidation or reorganization.

Summary

Long-term debt and preferred stock are fixed-income-type securities, because both obligate the issuing firm to a series of payments over time. (The one exception is zero-coupon bonds, which obligate the firm to a lump-sum payment when the bond matures.) Bonds and preferred stock are issued with many different provisions and features. They help firms secure financing as cheaply as possible by providing securities that cater to different investor needs and desires.

When coupon-bearing bonds are issued, they are generally priced close to par and carry a coupon interest rate approximately equal to the going market interest rate on similar risk and maturity bonds. The primary measure of the riskiness of bonds is the bond rating. Other things being equal, the higher (lower) the rating, the lower (higher) the required return on the bond.

Zero-coupon bonds are sold at a discount and do not provide cash interest payments; rather, the interest provided is the difference between the original discounted selling price and the maturity value of the bond. As market interest rates fluctuate, the market price of zero-coupon bonds fluctuates more than the market price of similar coupon bonds. Other recent innovations include junk bonds and variable rate bonds.

Increasingly, firms have begun to practice long-term liability management with tactics such as bond refunding, buybacks, defeasance, and interest rate swaps. Preferred stock, due to its higher cost to the issuing firm, has traditionally been used rarely except by public utilities. The creation of adjustable rate preferred stock, however, has lowered the cost and broadened the appeal of preferred stock.

Conflicts exist between bondholders and stockholders since what benefits one may cause the other to suffer a loss. These conflicts are intensified during periods of financial distress.

There is an appendix to this chapter, "Appendix 13A: Refunding a Bond or a Preferred Stock Issue," at the back of the book.

Questions

13.1 Define the following terms or phrases:

a.	Indenture	u.	Eurocurrency system
b.	Mortgage bond	v.	London Interbank Offered Rate
c.	Equipment trust certificate		(LIBOR)
d.	Debenture	w.	International bond
e.	Subordinated debenture	x.	Eurobond
f.	Income bond	y.	Foreign bond
g.	Cumulative	z.	Refunding
h.	Call provision	aa.	Tender offer
i.	Call premium	bb.	Private market purchase
j.	Sinking fund	cc.	Defeasance
k.	Serial bond	dd.	Interest rate swap
l.	Convertible subordinated debenture	ee.	Arrearages
m.	Fully registered	ff.	Adjustable rate preferred stock
n.	Bearer form	gg.	Financial distress
o.	Bond rating	hh.	Extension
p.	Deep discount bond	ii.	Composition
q.	Zero-coupon bond	jj.	Assignment
r.	Junk bond	kk.	Liquidation
s.	Prime rate	ll.	Reorganization
t.	Eurodollar		

13.2 In recent years, when interest rates were very high, a number of large firms issued 5-year-maturity notes. These notes payed interest periodically, and the principal was repaid when the notes matured. Why do you think firms issued these notes instead of obtaining similar-maturity term loans?

13.3 As corporate treasurer, how would the following conditions influence your willingness to include a sinking fund provision and the need for a call feature in a new bond issue?

a. Market interest rates are expected to fall.

b. Your firm anticipates heavy cash outflows in relation to its cash needs in the next 5 to 10 years.

c. Market interest rates are expected to fluctuate substantially, both above and below the coupon rate on the new issue.

13.4 Explain the difference between fully registered and bearer bonds. What advantages, if any, exist for the firm by issuing fully registered bonds? For the investor?

13.5 Explain why investment bankers require a bond to be rated by Moody's and Standard & Poor's before it is underwritten. How specifically does the rating influence the cost to the issuing firm?

13.6 The percentage price fluctuation of zero-coupon bonds is (1) greater than the percentage price fluctuation of similar coupon bonds as market interest rates fluctuate; and (2) greater the longer the maturity of the zero. Explain why this is so.

13.7 Many firms issue zero-coupon bonds in the Eurobond market. Explain the motivation for issuing zero-coupon bonds in general and also why a firm might choose to do it through the Eurobond market instead of in the domestic bond market.

13.8 What are the primary differences between the Eurobond market and the bond market in the United States?

13.9 When might a firm want to refund a bond issue? How might it proceed if the bond indenture prohibits refunding for another 8 years?

13.10 Preferred stock often is called a hybrid security. Why? It can be said that preferred stock combines the worst features of both common stock and bonds. Explain why this might be so.

13.11 If the corporate income tax were abolished, would we expect to see more, or less, debt? More, or less, preferred stock? Why?

13.12 When a firm is in financial distress, what out-of-court and in-court options exist?

Self-Test Problems   (Solutions appear on pages 727–729.)

Restriction on Additional Debt

ST 13.1 Michigan Corporation has earnings before interest and taxes (EBIT) of $200,000 per year. The firm has $160,000 of 10 percent coupon-rate bonds presently outstanding. The indenture of these bonds places a restriction on the amount of total bonds issued by specifying that EBIT must be at least four times greater than total interest paid on the firm's bonds. What is the maximum amount (par value) of new 8 percent coupon-rate bonds that Michigan can issue?

Sinking Funds

ST 13.2 Huron Cement has just issued $30 million of 10 year, 10 percent coupon-rate bonds. A sinking fund provision requires equal payments to be made at the end of each of the next 10 years to actually retire one-tenth of the bonds each year. Huron's tax rate is 35 percent.

a. How large must the annual sinking fund payments be to retire the bond in 10 equal installments over the life of the bond? (*Note:* The bonds will be retired at their par value.)

b. What is Huron's *annual* after-tax cash outlay to meet the interest and sinking fund obligations each year? [*Remember:* (1) interest payments are tax-deductible, but sinking fund payments are not, and (2) no interest is paid on bonds once they are retired.]

Bond Provisions and Financing Costs

ST 13.3 Portable Products needs to raise approximately $10 million by issuing 20-year bonds. The following options are available:

a. A public offering of $10 million of 8 percent coupon-rate bonds at a price to net the firm $9,850,000.

b. A private placement of $10 million in bonds at par with an 8.5 percent coupon rate and no flotation costs.

c. A public offering of a deep discount bond that will pay $400,000 in interest each year and have a maturity value of $25 million. The firm will net $9,800,000 from the bonds.

d. A private placement of zero-coupon bonds that will net the firm $9,900,000 and have a maturity value of $45 million.

Interest payments are annual and the principal will not be repaid until maturity. Which bond has the cheapest percentage cost to maturity? (*Note:* To solve this, calculate the IRR for each of the four options.)

Expected Versus Realized Return

ST 13.4 Three years ago Pam purchased a 3-year, $1,000 par, 16 percent coupon-rate bond issued by Mason Manufacturing at par. The bond pays interest annually. Immediately after purchasing the bond, market interest rates fell to 6 percent and remained there throughout the 3 years.

a. What was Pam's expected yield to maturity (YTM)?

b. What was her actual (or realized) compounded percentage return? (*Note:* The interest received at t_1 and t_2 must be reinvested at 6 percent and compounded forward to t_3. You can then solve for her percentage return.)

Problems

Restrictions on Additional Debt

13.1 The Long Island Corporation has no short-term debt, but it does have a $10 million, 10 percent coupon-rate mortgage bond outstanding with a limited open-end provision. Additional 10 percent mortgage debt can be issued as long as all the following restrictions are met:

a. Ratio of debt to equity remains below 0.4.

b. Interest coverage (EBIT/I) is at least 5.

c. The depreciated value of the mortgaged assets is at least 2.5 times the mortgage debt.

The firm has a depreciated value of mortgage assets of $60 million, equity of $80 million, and earnings before interest and taxes (EBIT) of $12 million. Assuming that half the new bond issue would be used to add assets to the base of mortgaged assets, how much additional debt can Long Island issue?

Calling a Bond Issue

13.2 Carolina Paper has a $50 million bond issue outstanding with a 12 percent coupon rate. The current market interest rate on comparable quality bonds is 11 percent. The bonds have 25 years to maturity, but can be called with a premium equal to 1 year's interest.

a. What is the market price of the bonds?

b. How much is the call price on the bonds?

c. Should Carolina Paper call these bonds or purchase them? In explaining your answer, remember to consider any other factors that might influence purchasing the bonds.

13.3 Nabar International has determined that it can issue debentures at a base rate of 10 percent. The final coupon rate can be influenced by altering the terms and indenture provisions as follows: (1) issuing a mortgage bond instead of a debenture reduces the rate by 20/100th of a percent, or 20 basis points; (2) making the debentures subordinated increases the rate by 15 basis points; (3) including a sinking fund provision reduces the rate by 10 basis points; (4) making the bond noncallable for 5 years reduces the rate by 5 basis points; (5) issuing a Eurobond reduces the rate by 30 basis points; (6) making it a zero-coupon bond reduces the rate by 40 basis points. Given this information, from each pair of bonds below select the one with the lowest effective cost to Nabar International. (*Note:* If a condition is not mentioned, assume it is *not* a part of the issue.)

a. A zero-coupon debenture versus a Euro debenture with a sinking fund.
b. A mortgage bond with a sinking fund versus a mortgage Eurobond.
c. A zero-coupon subordinated debenture with a 5-year call delay, versus a mortgage bond with a sinking fund and a 5-year call delay.
d. A mortgage Eurobond with a sinking fund and a 5-year call delay, versus a zero-coupon Euro subordinated debenture with a 5-year call delay.

13.4 Davis Industries has two alternative $10 million bonds it can issue. If the bond carries a fixed coupon-rate, the interest rate will be 11 percent. If a variable rate bond is used, the rate will be pegged 1.5 percent above prevailing rates on 1-year U.S. Treasury bills and adjusted annually. In both cases interest is paid annually. A sinking fund of $1 million per year will begin at the end of year 1 for either bond. The firm's marginal tax rate is 40 percent.

a. Determine the year-by-year after-tax cash flows Davis will incur for each bond if 1-year U.S. Treasury bill rates turn out to be as follows:

Year	Prevailing 1-Year U.S. Treasury Bill Rate
1	10.0%
2	9.5
3	9.0
4	10.0
5	10.5
6	12.0
7	13.0
8	12.0
9	11.5
10	11.0

b. Without discounting the cash flows, does it appear that one bond would be preferable if Davis knew what interest rates would be? Why?

13.5 Five years ago, Karen Stephens purchased $20,000 of 15-year, 14 percent coupon rate bonds at par. The bonds pay interest annually. At the end of 5 years the issuing firm called the bonds at a call price of 105, so that Karen received $1,050 per bond, or a total of $21,000.

a. What was Karen's original expected yield to maturity (YTM)?
b. If interest rates remained at 14 percent over the 5-year period, what was Karen's actual compound percentage return? [*Note:* You do *not* have to compound the intermediate interest payments forward to t_5 to answer this part. Simply calculate the yield to call (YTC).]
c. If interest rates immediately dropped to 10 percent and remained there for the 5 years, what was Karen's actual compound percentage return? (*Note:* Now you *must* compound the intermediate interest payments forward to t_5.)

13.6 Swing-Along is planning to issue $100 million par value of 15 year zero-coupon bonds at a yield of 14 percent.

a. If interest is assumed to be paid annually, (1) what is the initial value, B_0, of the bonds, and (2) the appropriate interest for year 2?

b. What happens to your answers for (a) if interest is assumed to be paid semiannually? Why do your answers to (a) and (b) differ?

(Do only if using Pinches Disk.)

c. Recalculate (a) and (b) if the maturity of the bond issue is only 3 years. How does this change your answers to (a) and (b)? Graphically, which bond (15-year or 3-year) would result in the least percentage price fluctuations from the initial value as market interest rates change?

d. Now suppose the market discount rate drops to 10 percent before the bond is issued. How are your answers in (a), (b), and (c) affected by this event?

e. Finally, the firm has decided to issue $300 million in par value zero-coupon bonds. Which of the above scenarios would provide it the greatest initial inflow of funds?

13.7 Chancey Industries needs to raise $7.8 million through an issue of preferred stock. The preferred will have a $60 per share par value and pay an 8 percent dividend. Assume there are no flotation costs, that the preferred will be outstanding for a long time (so it can be treated as a perpetuity), and that it will be sold to yield purchasers a 9.6 percent return.

a. What price will Chancey receive per share?

b. How many shares will Chancey have to issue?

c. Why might Chancey choose preferred stock instead of debt?

13.8 Queen's Railroad needs to raise $9.5 million for capital improvements. One possibility is a new preferred stock issue. The 8 percent dividend, $100 par value stock would be sold to investors to yield 9 percent. Flotation costs for an issue of this size amount to 5 percent of the gross proceeds. These costs will be deducted from the gross proceeds in determining the net proceeds of $9.5 million. Assume the preferred stock will be outstanding for a long time so it can be valued as a perpetuity.

a. At what price will the preferred be offered to investors? (Carry to three decimal places.)

b. How many shares must be issued to net $9.5 million? [*Note:* Net proceeds = 0.95(gross proceeds); so, gross proceeds = net proceeds/0.95.]

13.9 Misra, Inc., needs to raise $600,000. It has the following alternatives: (1) sell common stock at $50 per share; (2) sell 8 percent preferred stock at par ($100 par); or (3) sell 9 percent debentures at par ($1,000 par). Assume there are no flotation costs. The firm expects EBIT to *increase* by 20 percent after the additional funds are secured and investments made. Partial balance and income statements for Misra are as follows:

Balance Sheet		Income Statement	
Current liabilities	$ 100,000	EBIT	$200,000
Common stock ($3 par)	300,000	Interest	20,000
Retained earnings	600,000	EBT	180,000
Total liabilities and		Taxes	63,000
stockholders' equity	$1,000,000	EAT	$117,000

a. What is the current EPS *before* the new financing is undertaken?

b. What is the estimated EPS under each of the financing plans, assuming that EBIT has increased?

13.10 Cooley Industries is a fast-growing conglomerate operating in the mid-Atlantic states. Although it has used only short-term debt previously, Cooley is in the market for long-term financing. Based on its investment banker's recommendations, two plans are being considered, as follows:

Plan I	Plan II
$20 million of straight debt issued at par (ignore flotation costs)	$20 million preferred stock issued at par (ignore flotation costs)
Par is $1,000 per bond	Par is $80 per share
12% coupon rate	11.5% dividend rate
Expected common stock P/E = 12 times	Expected common stock P/E = 13 times

EBIT is estimated to be $14 million; short-term interest (under either plan) is $1 million; the tax rate is 30 percent; and there are 3 million shares of common stock outstanding.

a. For plans I and II, determine the expected EPS.
b. If Cooley wants to maximize its market price per share, P_0, which plan should it choose?

References

Bond and preferred stock provisions are examined in

Brennan, Michael J., and Eduardo S. Schwartz. "The Case for Convertibles." *Journal of Applied Corporate Finance* 1 (Summer 1988), pp. 55–64.

Dunn, Kenneth B., and Chester S. Spatt. "A Strategic Analysis of Sinking Fund Bonds." *Journal of Financial Economics* 13 (September 1984), pp. 399–423.

McDaniel, William R. "Sinking Fund Preferred Stock." *Financial Management* 13 (Spring 1984), pp. 45–52.

Fabozzi, Frank J., and Irving M. Pollack (eds.). *The Handbook of Fixed Income Securities.* Homewood, Ill.: Dow Jones–Irwin, 1983.

Perry, Kevin J., and Robert A. Taggart, Jr. "The Growing Role of Junk Bonds." *Journal of Applied Corporate Finance* 1 (Spring 1988), pp. 37–45.

Thatcher, Janet S. "The Choice of Call Provision Terms: Evidence of the Existence of Agency Costs of Debt." *Journal of Finance* 40 (June 1985), pp. 549–561.

Bond ratings have been studied extensively. See, for example,

Pinches, George E., and Kent A. Mingo. "A Multivariate Analysis of Industrial Bond Ratings." *Journal of Finance* 28 (March 1973), pp. 1–18.

Pinches, George E., and Kent A. Mingo. "The Role of Subordination and Industrial Bond Ratings." *Journal of Finance* 30 (March 1975), pp. 201–206.

Pinches, George E., and J. Clay Singleton. "The Adjustment of Stock Prices to Bond Rating Changes." *Journal of Finance* 33 (March 1978), pp. 29–44.

The relationship between bond ratings and beta is examined in

Fabozzi, Frank J. "A Note on the Association Between Systematic Risk and Common Stock and Bond Rating Classifications." *Journal of Economics and Business* 34 (April 1982), pp. 159–163.

Schwendiman, Carl J., and George E. Pinches. "An Analysis of Alternative Measures of Investment Risk." *Journal of Finance* 30 (March 1975), pp. 193–200.

Current developments in liability management are discussed in

ARNOLD, TANYA A. "How to Do Interest Rate Swaps." *Harvard Business Review* 62 (September–October 1984), pp. 96–101.

FINNERTY, JOHN D., ANDREW J. KALOTAY, AND FRANCIS X. FARRELL, JR. *Evaluating Bond Refunding Opportunities.* Cambridge, Mass.: Ballinger, 1988.

JAMES, CHRISTOPHER, AND PEGGY WIER. "Are Bank Loans Different? Some Evidence from the Stock Market." *Journal of Applied Corporate Finance* 1 (Summer 1988), pp. 46–54.

LEWELLEN, WILBUR G., AND DOUGLAS R. EMERY. "On the Matter of Parity Among Financial Obligations." *Journal of Finance* 35 (March 1981), pp. 97–111.

MARR, WAYNE, AND JOHN TRIMBLE. "The Persistent Borrowing Advantage of Eurodollar Bonds: A Plausible Explanation." *Journal of Applied Corporate Finance* 1 (Summer 1988), pp. 65–70.

PETERSON, PAMELA, DAVID PETERSON, AND JAMES ANG. "The Extinguishment of Debt Through In-Substance Defeasance." *Financial Management* 14 (Spring 1985), pp. 59–67.

TURNBULL, STUART M. "Swaps: A Zero Sum Game?" *Financial Management* 16 (Spring 1987), pp. 15–21.

Selected material on financial distress is contained in

ALTMAN, EDWARD I. "A Further Empirical Investigation of the Bankruptcy Cost Question." *Journal of Finance* 39 (September 1984), pp. 1067–1089.

PINCHES, GEORGE E., AND JAMES S. TRIESCHMANN. "The Efficiency of Alternative Models for Solvency Surveillance in the Insurance Industry." *Journal of Risk and Insurance* 41 (December 1974), pp. 563–577.

QUEEN, MAGGIE, AND RICHARD ROLL. "Firm Mortality: Using Market Indicators to Predict Survival." *Financial Analysts Journal* 43 (May–June 1987), pp. 9–26.

See Models six and seven in *Lotus 1–2–3® for Financial Management* by Pinches and Courtney for templates that value bonds (including yield to call) and zero-coupon bonds.

14 Required Returns for Companies and Projects

Overview

- The required return is a function of the opportunities bypassed and the costs incurred.

- Debt is typically the least expensive source of financing, common equity capital the most expensive. This is because of tax considerations and the risk and return requirements of investors.

- The WACC is a weighted average of the expected future costs of funds. The weights are given by the market-value proportions of the firm's capital structure.

- If a firm substantially increases its level of financing, the after-tax cost of some or all of its sources of capital will increase. As that happens, the cost of capital, or required return, will increase.

he Wall Street Journal *reported that Philadelphia Electric was applying for an increase in the electric rates it is allowed to charge its customers. Philadelphia Electric, like other public utilities, is a regulated firm. It is permitted to charge rates designed to allow it to recover its operating costs and provide reasonable compensation for its providers of capital. Investors in stocks and bonds weigh their risk preferences and returns: The more the risk, the higher the required return. But a higher return to investors means higher costs to the firm. It's not surprising, then, that a major area of testimony—and controversy—in hearings before utility commissions is the cost to the firm of various sources of capital. Company witnesses argue that the firm's costs of capital are high, so higher rates are needed to compensate the providers of capital. Opponents, on the other hand, argue that the firm's capital costs are lower, and hence lower rate increases (or even rate decreases) are desirable; otherwise the firm's providers of capital will be overcompensated for the risks taken. Ultimately, the regulatory authorities, by setting the allowable rates, determine the amount of revenue public utilities will have for operating expenses and returns to the providers of capital.*

A nonregulated firm is not subject to the rate hearing process, but it too needs sufficient cash flows to cover the costs of operations and ensure a suitable return to investors. Knowing the cost of capital enables successful firms to make capital investments that provide adequate returns. If too low a cost estimate is employed, firms will make capital investments that provide inadequate returns, and the value of the firm will decrease, since the costs exceed the returns.

The Required Return Concept

To maximize the size of our pie, or the value of the firm, V, it is important to make good long-term investment decisions. This involves a thorough understanding of capital budgeting techniques, as discussed in Chapters 8–10. Another important part of the decision involves the use of the proper required rate of return as the discount rate for NPV decisions, or the hurdle rate when the IRR is employed.

To keep things simple we start with projects that can be viewed as being equal in risk to the firm as a whole. The proper rate to employ can be viewed in one of two ways.

1. THE OPPORTUNITY COST OF CAPITAL. When viewed as the *opportunity cost of capital,* the required rate is what the funds could earn in a similar risk investment. If a firm has a million dollars and it could be invested externally to yield 15 percent, then an internal (i.e., capital budgeting) project with equal risk should also return 15 percent. Otherwise, the value of the firm will fall.
2. THE WEIGHTED AVERAGE COST OF CAPITAL, WACC. This is simply the average after-tax cost of all funds available for investment by the firm. For example, if the firm's average after-tax cost of funds is 15 percent, then it must earn at least 15 percent (after taxes) or the value of the firm will fall.

While these two concepts may seem to be separate and distinct from one another, in an efficient market they are really flip sides of the same coin. Consider a zero NPV project. The rate the firm could earn on the project, given its degree of risk, is the same rate that the funds should cost. Why? Because investors have the same opportunities and they will not be willing to provide funds to a firm at any lower rate than what they could earn elsewhere. Hence, for average-risk projects we can use the terms required rate of return, opportunity cost of capital, or weighted average cost of capital interchangeably. Whatever it is called, it is the minimum rate the firm must earn to ensure that the value of the firm does not fall. Because of its wide acceptance, we use the term weighted average cost of capital, or cost of capital for short, in this chapter and in Chapter 15. But remember, it's simply the firm's required rate of return for projects of average risk.

Accurate estimation of the firm's required rate of return (when dealing with projects whose risk is equal to the firm's risk) is important. In terms of our pie, we have the following:

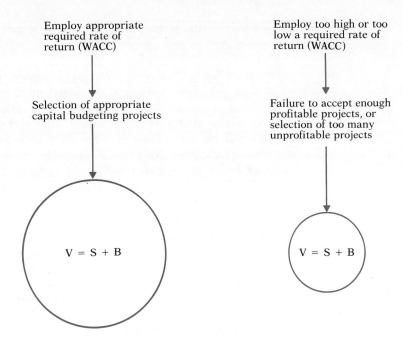

We begin by determining how to calculate the firm's weighted average cost of capital. Then we will consider how to proceed when the risk of proposed capital budgeting projects differs from the firm's average risk.

Definitions and Calculations

Before calculating the firm's weighted average cost of capital, we begin by defining some terms we will use throughout:

WACC = weighted average cost of capital. This is the weighted average of the cost of the last dollar of capital expected to be raised by the firm.

k_b = the before-tax cost of new debt issued by the firm. Ignoring flotation costs, this is equal to the yield to maturity (YTM) expected by investors, as defined in Chapter 6.

$k_i = k_b(1 - T)$, the after-tax cost of new debt issued by the firm, where T equals the firm's marginal corporate tax rate.

k_{ps} = the after-tax cost of new preferred stock issued by the firm.

k_s = the after-tax cost of equity capital. This k_s is identical to the k_s defined in Chapter 7, where it was called the investor's required return on common stock.

W_i = the weights that indicate the future financing proportions to be employed by the firm.

The firm's cost of capital is a weighted average of the various sources of new capital. Note that the costs are expressed on an after-tax basis. This is to ensure consistency for decision-making purposes with the cash flows, CFs, which are also calculated on an after-tax basis. If a firm raises capital with debt, preferred stock, and internally generated common equity, the WACC would be

$$WACC = k_i W_{debt} + k_{ps} W_{preferred\ stock} + k_s W_{common\ equity} \tag{14.1}$$

where the W's indicate the proportions of funding to be raised by each specific source.

Basic Assumptions

To use the weighted average cost of capital for decision-making purposes, two basic conditions must be met. First, the risk of the project under examination must be approximately equal to the risk of all new projects being undertaken by the firm. Although, as we discuss in Chapter 10, the precise estimation of project risk is not easy, our concern is that the risk not be substantially above or below that of the other projects being undertaken. When risk differs significantly, a divisional or project-specific required return (as discussed later in the chapter) should be employed. Second, it is important that the firm not materially change its financing policies as a result of the investments it undertakes. Since these proportions directly affect the WACC, as the financing mix changes, so will the cost of capital.

At this point, we are assuming that the firm's target capital structure (or desired debt/equity mix) will be constant. The reason for making this assumption is that different capital structures may influence the firm's cost of capital.[1] Our concern here is with determining a firm's weighted average cost of capital, assuming it is at the appropriate target capital structure. In Chapter 15 we examine the firm's capital structure.

Before proceeding, it is important to recognize that the WACC is a marginal cost. What is meant by the term "marginal"? We are using "marginal" in the economic sense of the cost of raising the last dollar of funds. For each of the components—debt, preferred stock, and common equity—we are interested in the cost of the last dollar of additional funds. As discussed later in the chapter, if these costs increase, so does the firm's WACC. Calculation of the firm's cost of capital has a future orientation. The WACC is a weighted average of the after-tax costs of various future sources of capital; any past or historical costs are irrelevant. The only reason to consider historical costs when calculating a cost of capital is to obtain some idea of the future-oriented estimates that must be made. But, in general, it is best to ignore them, since considering historical costs or proportions often leads to wrong conclusions.

Calculating Costs and Financing Proportions

In this section, the explicit costs of three types of financing—debt, preferred stock, and common equity—will be considered first, and then we will consider the specific financing proportions. The cost of common equity is the most difficult to calculate and the most important element in estimating a firm's cost of capital.

Cost of Debt

The cost of debt to be employed for cost of capital purposes is the before-tax cost, k_b, adjusted for the tax "subsidy" provided by the government to profitable firms, since interest is a tax-deductible expense. The after-tax cost of debt, k_i, is

---

[1] In addition, we are assuming that risk does not change, and that the firm's cash dividend policy is constant. If either of these change, some of the component costs might change, affecting the whole decision-making process.

Program Trading

Program trading is a term that has gained a lot of attention in the last few years. It basically means the rapid buying and selling of massive amounts of stock, often through the NYSE's high-speed order system known as SuperDot. Developed in the early 1980s, computer-assisted program trading is a popular way for big institutions to make rapid changes in their portfolios.

One form of program trading—called index arbitrage—combines the buying and selling of stocks with offsetting trades in stock-index futures. (An index future is tied to some stock index, like the S&P 500.) Traders look for small gaps between stock prices and futures prices, then buy whichever is cheaper and sell whichever is more expensive. By so doing they make a profit, and at the same time ensure that major deviations between stock prices and stock-index futures prices do not exist.

A buy-or-sell order touched off by a single index arbitrage program typically involves $25 million of trading—and sometimes far more. The impact of program trading is twofold. First, it increases the volume of transactions. It is estimated that on a typical day between 1 and 19 percent of the volume of shares traded on the NYSE are due to program trading. The second effect is much more controversial, and that is whether program trading can, by itself, cause wider gyrations in stock prices. Critics of program trading contend it is a major factor behind the increased volatility of the stock market. Supporters contend that even if there are temporary fluctuations, what it does is to drive prices to where they are going anyway, but at a faster rate. No matter what the critics contend, and even though there's been some scaling back of program trading, the technology exists, and without major restructuring we will continue to see program trading affect the stock market.

$$\text{after-tax cost of debt} = k_i = k_b(1 - T) \tag{14.2}$$

where

k_b = the before-tax cost of debt
T = the firm's marginal corporate tax rate

To calculate the before-tax cost, we solve for the expected yield to maturity (YTM) with Equation 6.1. The before-tax cost to the firm, k_b, is found by solving for the unknown discount rate:

$$B_0 = I(PVA_{k_b,n}) + M(PV_{k_b,n}) \tag{14.3}$$
$$= I(PVA_{?\%,n}) + M(PV_{?\%,n})$$

where

I = dollar amount of interest paid on a bond each year
M = the par or maturity value of the bond (typically $1,000)
n = the number of years to maturity for the bond

Consider the example of Ambassador Corporation, which plans to issue a new 20-year bond that has a $1,000 par value, carries a 12.75 percent coupon rate, and pays interest annually. The firm expects to receive $980. The before-tax cost to Ambassador is

$$\$980 = \$127.50(\text{PVA}_{?\%,20\text{yr}}) + \$1,000(\text{PV}_{?\%,20\text{yr}})$$
$$k_b = 0.13035 \approx 13\%^2$$

The before-tax cost is 13 percent.[3] The after-tax cost, calculated using Equation 14.2 with a tax rate of 40 percent, is

$$k_i = k_b(1 - T) = 13\%(1 - 0.40) = 7.8\%$$

The after-tax cost of debt is used because it is, in fact, the cost to the firm. Although the before-tax cost is 13 percent, as long as the firm is profitable, interest is a deductible expense for tax purposes. So, the after-tax cost with a 40 percent tax rate is only 7.8 percent.

Remember that we are interested in the cost of new debt financing. The coupon rate on existing debt is not relevant, nor are any costs connected with existing debt. The explicit cost of debt tends to be the least expensive of the three sources we consider, for two reasons. First, from the investor's standpoint, there is a fixed legal claim; bondholders have greater security than preferred or common stockholders. On a risk-return basis, we would expect bond investors to demand less return than stockholders—which they do. Second, the tax status of interest also makes debt cheaper than other sources, as long as the firm is profitable.[4]

Cost of Preferred Stock

The cost of preferred stock is calculated in much the same manner as the cost of debt, except for one basic difference. Since dividends on preferred stock are paid out of after-tax earnings, no tax adjustment is required. Thus, the cost of preferred stock, k_{ps}, is[5]

$$\text{cost of preferred stock} = k_{ps} = \frac{D_{ps}}{P_0} \tag{14.4}$$

where

[2] Using the PV and PVA tables, the present value (at 13 percent) of the interest payments and principal is $982.69, which indicates k_b is slightly over 13 percent. Via financial calculator, k_b is 13.035 percent.

[3] The before-tax cost can be approximated by

$$\text{approximate before-tax cost of debt} = \frac{I + (M - B_0)/n}{M + 0.6(B_0 - M)}$$

This approximation is more accurate than the typical bond yield approximation used. See the Hawawini and Vora end of chapter reference. The 0.6 in the denominator is a constant and has nothing to do with any tax adjustment; the impact of taxes is treated by Equation 14.2. This approximation does not work well with deep discount or zero-coupon bonds.

[4] If a firm is operating at a loss, its marginal tax rate is zero. For a firm that does not expect to pay any taxes for a long time, there is no tax subsidy for using debt, and $k_i = k_b$.

[5] Equation 14.4 assumes the preferred stock is a perpetuity. If it is expected to be called or retired in a specific number of years, a closer approximation can be obtained by using Equation 14.3 after adjusting to reflect preferred stock instead of debt.

D_{ps} = the cash dividends paid on the preferred stock each year

P_0 = the proceeds from the sale of the preferred stock

If Ambassador is planning to issue a \$50 par preferred stock that pays \$6 in dividends per year and the firm expects to realize \$48 per share, the after-tax cost of the preferred stock is

$$k_{ps} = \frac{D_{ps}}{P_0} = \frac{\$6}{\$48} = 0.125 = 12.5\%$$

In comparison with the 7.8 percent cost of debt calculated above, we see that the cost of preferred stock is higher. This occurs primarily because of the non-tax-deductibility of dividends on preferred stock.

Cost of Common Equity

The final cost to be considered is common equity. Actually, there are two possible costs here—one if the firm uses internally generated funds, and the other if it expects to issue additional shares of common stock. *Internally generated funds* are those cash flows that arise as a function of the firm's ongoing activities and that can be reinvested in the business. Because internally generated funds typically supply most of the common equity, we focus primarily on their cost.

Like the cost of debt and preferred stock, the cost of equity capital is also a function of the returns expected by investors. To estimate the cost of equity, k_s, it is necessary to estimate the returns demanded by investors. As with preferred stock, there is no need to adjust for taxes, because cash dividends on common stock are paid out of after-tax earnings. The difficulty in estimating the cost of equity capital arises because, unlike debt or preferred stock, there is no stated interest or dividend rate. In addition, due to the ability to share in both the good and bad fortunes of the firm, common stock may incur substantial price changes. So, estimating the cost of equity capital is more difficult than estimating the cost of debt or preferred stock. We examine three approaches for estimating the cost of common equity—the dividend valuation approach, the capital asset pricing model (CAPM), and an ad hoc method using bond yield plus a risk premium.

The logic behind assigning a cost to internally generated funds involves the opportunity cost concept again. Management faces a choice with the funds generated by the firm. It can distribute them to the firm's owners (its common stockholders) in the form of cash dividends, or reinvest them in the firm on behalf of the same common stockholders. The decision to reinvest funds instead of paying them out involves an opportunity cost. Stockholders could have taken the funds and reinvested them in something else. The firm must earn a return on the reinvested funds equal to what common stockholders could have earned in alternative investments of comparable risk.

What return is this? It's simply k_s, which is the return investors require on investments with comparable risk. If the firm cannot earn a return of at least k_s on the reinvested internally generated funds, it should distribute the funds to investors so they can invest them in other assets that provide an expected return equal to k_s.

Dividend Valuation Approach. In Chapter 6, we saw that one approach to determine the value of a share of stock was the dividend valuation model, which states the market value, P_0, is equal to the present value of the future dividends, $D_1 \ldots D_\infty$, where the discount rate, k_s, is the investor's required rate of return. Thus:

$$P_0 = \frac{D_1}{(1 + k_s)} + \frac{D_2}{(1 + k_s)^2} + \cdots + \frac{D_\infty}{(1 + k_s)^\infty} \qquad (14.5)$$

If the growth rate in dividends, g, is expected to be constant and less than k_s, Equation 14.5 reduces to

$$P_0 = \frac{D_1}{k_s - g} \qquad (14.6)$$

where D_1 is the cash dividend expected 1 year from now, k_s is the investor's required rate of return, and g is the constant percentage growth rate in cash dividends. Solving Equation 14.6 for k_s, we have one way of estimating the investor's required rate of return (which is the firm's cost of common equity). Thus:

$$\text{dividend valuation approach} = k_s = \begin{array}{l} \text{expected} \\ \text{dividend} + \text{expected growth} \\ \text{yield} \end{array} \qquad (14.7)$$

$$= \frac{D_1}{P_0} + g$$

Investors expect to receive a dividend yield, D_1/P_0, plus a capital gain (or loss) of g, for a total return of k_s.

To illustrate, assume the present market price on Ambassador's common stock is $25, dividends to be paid in 1 year, D_1, are $1.75, and the expected growth rate in dividends is 9 percent per year. The dividend valuation approach[6] to estimating the cost of equity capital yields

$$k_s = \frac{D_1}{P_0} + g = \frac{\$1.75}{\$25} + 9\% = 0.07 + 9\% = 7\% + 9\% = 16\%$$

The estimation of the expected growth rate in cash dividends is the most difficult aspect of applying the dividend valuation approach. We could start by analyzing past growth rates. That information is generally supplemented, however, by projections made by the firm itself or by security analysts. And it is the future growth rate that is important.

Capital Asset Pricing Model (CAPM) Approach. The second approach to estimating the cost of common equity employs the capital asset pricing model (CAPM). As described in Chapter 7, the CAPM states the investors' required rate of return is equal to the risk-free rate plus a risk premium, so that

$$\text{CAPM approach} = k_s = \text{risk-free rate} + \text{expected risk premium} \qquad (14.8)$$

$$= k_{RF} + \beta_j(k_M - k_{RF})$$

---

[6] If the expected growth rate in cash dividends is not constant, the nonconstant growth valuation approach discussed in Chapter 6 will have to be employed.

where

k_{RF} = the risk-free rate of return
β_j = the beta of security j
k_M = the expected rate of return on the market portfolio

The risk-free rate is generally measured by the yield on U.S. Treasury bills. Betas can be obtained by reference to *Value Line,* Merrill Lynch, or many other investment advisory services. Although the expected rate of return on the market cannot be measured directly, it can be approximated. We can add three components: (1) expected inflation, (2) expected real growth in the economy, and (3) an expected risk premium commanded by stocks over bonds.[7]

To illustrate the CAPM approach, assume Ambassador's beta is 0.95, the yield on Treasury bills is 11 percent, expected growth in the economy (as measured by projected GNP growth in constant dollars) is 3 percent, and the expected risk premium of stocks over bonds is 4 percent. Adding the last three components together provides an estimate of the future returns on the market of 11 + 3 + 4 = 18 percent. The investor's required rate of return, which is the cost of common equity, is

$$k_s = 11\% + 0.95(18\% - 11\%) = 11\% + 6.65\% = 17.65\%$$

This second approach to estimating the cost of common equity provides a figure of 17.65 percent versus the earlier figure of 16 percent estimated by the dividend valuation approach. The dividend valuation and CAPM approaches should provide approximately the same answer, unless some drastic differences in assumptions are made. Our difference is not too large and should give us some confidence in the reliability of the estimates.

Bond Yield Plus Expected Risk Premium Approach. The third approach to estimating the cost of common equity is an ad hoc method that states the investor's required rate of return is equal to what he or she could get on the bonds of the firm plus a premium for risk, so that

$$\text{bond yield plus expected risk premium approach} = k_s = \text{bond yield} + \text{expected risk premium} \qquad (14.9)$$

This method is useful when the firm does not pay any cash dividends, so the dividend valuation approach is not applicable, or when the common stock is not traded, so that neither the dividend valuation or CAPM approaches can be employed. To continue our earlier example, the before-tax bond yield of Ambassador was 13 percent, and the risk premium of stocks over bonds was expected to be 4 percent.[8] The required rate of return is then

$$k_s = \text{bond yield} + \text{expected risk premium} = 13\% + 4\% = 17\%$$

---

[7] Another way would be to add the expected market risk premium ($k_M - k_{RF}$) to the risk-free rate. Research indicates that risk premiums are not constant over time. Hence, use of historical risk premiums is generally not appropriate.

[8] This risk premium is firm-specific and may be more or less than the market risk premium employed in Equation 14.8. For simplicity, we assume the two risk premiums are equal.

Putting It All Together. For Ambassador, we have three estimates of its cost of common equity, as follows:

Approach	Estimated k_s
Dividend valuation	16%
CAPM	17.65
Bond yield plus expected risk premium	17

All differ slightly, but they are close. Taking everything into account, we would estimate Ambassador's cost of common equity is between 16 and 17.65 percent. A simple average of these estimates is 16.883 percent [(16% + 17.65% + 17%)/3]. We will round this to 17 percent for use below when calculating Ambassador's weighted average cost of capital.

Although the use of three different approaches may seem unduly complicated, it is useful in practice. By taking a number of alternative approaches to estimating the cost of common equity, managers are forced to consider which estimates are most useful. Estimating the cost of equity capital requires both judgment and an understanding of what the firm's common stockholders expect.

The cost of common equity is higher than the cost of debt or preferred stock. This occurs because from the investor's standpoint, there is more risk with common stock than with debt or preferred stock. Investors therefore have a higher required rate of return for common stock. But since the investor's required rate of return is the firm's cost, we see that the cost of common equity has to be the most expensive form of financing to the firm.

New Common Stock and Flotation Costs

If a firm has to issue common stock to raise additional equity capital, it will have to sell the stock at a price below its current market price. This means that P_0 in Equation 14.7 would have to be replaced by some lower price to reflect the underpricing required to sell the stock. The effect is to raise the cost of equity capital when the dividend valuation approach is employed. To illustrate this idea, assume Ambassador has used up its internally generated common equity funds and had to issue new common stock. The dividends next year are still $1.75, but in order to sell the new shares, a discount (or underpricing) of $4 per share is necessary. Hence, P_0 for new external common equity capital is $25 − $4 = $21. Also, the growth rate is still 9 percent. Using Equation 14.7 we have:

$$k_s \text{ (external common equity)} = \frac{\$1.75}{\$21} + 9\% = 8.3\% + 9\% = 17.3\%$$

This is higher than the 16 percent we estimated earlier for internally generated common equity. Once this adjustment is made we calculate the firm's WACC in the same manner as before, using Equation 14.1.

While this underpricing adjustment is straightforward for the dividend valuation approach, it is not as simple for either the CAPM or bond yield plus expected risk premium approaches. This is because the price of common stock does not appear directly in Equations 14.8 or 14.9. The best one can do using Equation 14.8 or 14.9 is to make a slight subjective adjustment if new common stock is to be issued.

Another possible concern involves flotation costs that are incurred when securities are sold. Some finance experts argue that the dollar amount of flotation costs should

The Penny Stock Scam

Legions of smooth-talking brokers are working out of boiler rooms from Florida to California to New York selling stocks for pennies—stocks that are worth less than that. With efficient telemarketing, computerized dialing, and cheap long-distance phone rates, what was once a nuisance may be turning into a much larger nationwide problem.[1] It has been estimated that the fraud in penny stocks is costing the public hundreds of millions of dollars a year in cold cash. What happens is that investors make an investment and then the brokers and companies either fold or simply disappear. To make matters worse, often when investors try to sell they simply cannot do so. Part of the problem is that the market for penny stocks is typically controlled by only one broker, so there are few checks and balances in the system. Moreover, the prices of most penny stocks cannot be found in any newspaper.

What can be done to deal with this? The Securities and Exchange Commission has launched a task force to fight frauds. In addition, many states—particularly where there are massive abuses like Florida and New Jersey—are beefing up their efforts to control and eliminate some of the abuses. One of the main problems, however, is that even though they bring a complaint in an attempt to force a firm out of business, the broker ends up reappearing in another form and continues right on enticing investors. The availability of more information about the prices of penny stocks would also help investors. The only price data are in the "pink sheets" published daily by the National Quotation Bureau. Ultimately, however, the most effective means of fighting the penny stock scam may be, using the words of our former first lady, Nancy Reagan, to "just say no" when a slick-sounding stock salesman calls.

[1] "The Penny Stock Scandal." *Business Week* (January 23, 1989).

be incorporated as an additional cash outflow when estimating the initial cash outflow, CF_0, for capital budgeting purposes. Conceptually, they are probably right, but the problem is that the firm is estimating the cost of a pool of funds raised over time, and invested in numerous capital projects. Also, the NPV approach rests on the premise that the investment (or capital budgeting) decision and the financing (or raising funds) decision are separate and distinct activities. Therefore, it is both impractical (or impossible) to ascribe specific flotation costs to specific projects, and it is also unnecessary (if we are to separate the investment and financing decisions). If flotation costs are small, our preference is to ignore them. If they are larger, we typically reduce the proceeds received from the specific financing employed. It can be shown that this latter treatment produced a biased low estimate of a projects' NPV. We prefer that result, however, as opposed to trying to tie specific financing to specific projects, so that the investment and financing decisions are not kept separate.

The Financing Proportions	Now that we know how to calculate the specific after-tax costs of debt, preferred stock, and common equity, we are almost ready to calculate the firm's cost of capital. Before doing that, however, it is necessary to determine the financing proportions to be employed by the firm. These proportions are a function of the firm's target capital structure, which is its desired mix of debt to total value. While many things influence target capital structure, it can be approximated by determining the current market value of the firm's outstanding securities. These current market values provide the best estimate of the firm's future financing mix.[9]

The Weighted Average Cost of Capital

Once we have the specific market costs and proportions, calculating the firm's cost of capital is straightforward. Let's return to the Ambassador example, and then we'll consider what happens if Ambassador decides to increase its capital substantially. Finally, we'll consider the question of how often the cost of capital should be calculated.

Calculating WACC for Ambassador	Earlier we calculated the specific costs of debt, preferred stock, and common equity for Ambassador Corporation. In addition to these after-tax costs, let's assume the market value proportions of financing to be employed are 30 percent debt, 10 percent preferred stock, and 60 percent common equity. Given these market value costs and proportions, Ambassador's weighted average cost of capital is 13.79 percent, as shown below:

Component	After-Tax Cost	× Market Value Weight	= Weighted Average Cost of Capital
Debt	7.8%	0.30	2.34%
Preferred stock	12.5	0.10	1.25
Common equity	17.0	0.60	10.20
		WACC =	13.79%

By using this as the discount rate for NPV calculations, or the hurdle rate for the IRR approach, Ambassador can make investment decisions for projects of average risk that maximize stockholder wealth.[10]

Jumps in the Cost of Capital	Until now we have assumed Ambassador could raise any amount of money needed at the prevailing expected costs. But does that apply in practice? The answer is "no." As Ambassador attempts to raise more and more capital at a given point in time, the cost of the last dollar of some or all of its various sources of funds will increase. This occurs because even though it is using the same percentage of debt and preferred stock, it is changing the size of the firm and therefore the dollar amount of fixed charges increases. The after-tax cost of both will increase as investors

[9] An alternative would be to employ a cash budget that provides an estimate of the expected sources of funds over the next 3 to 5 years.

[10] We are assuming Ambassador is at its target (or optimal) capital structure. Its WACC could be different (higher) if the firm used any other financing mix than 30 percent debt, 10 percent preferred stock, and 60 percent common equity. A different WACC may exist for every possible capital structure. This topic is explored in Chapter 15.

see that their risks have increased. In addition, as the risk of the firm increases and/or it has to sell common stock, the cost of common equity will also increase. While conceptually there would be many jumps in the WACC, for simplicity we change all the costs—debt, preferred stock, and common equity—at the same time.

Assume the new after-tax costs and financing proportions of Ambassador, if it wants to increase its capital substantially at a given point in time, are as follows:

Component	After-Tax Cost	×	Market Value Weight	=	Weighted Average Cost of Capital
Debt	8.5%		0.30		2.55%
Preferred stock	14.0		0.10		1.40
Additional common equity	19.0		0.60		11.40
				WACC =	15.35%

Figure 14.1 graphs Ambassador's cost of capital schedule. Note that as Ambassador increases the amount of financing required, its cost of capital increases. If Ambassador needed to raise even more capital at the same point in time, the costs of some or all of the sources would again rise. Conceptually, the cost of capital schedule could increase as a smoothed line if the firm raises small incremental amounts of capital. But since most firms raise capital in fairly large and discrete amounts, the acquisition process is lumpy. Firms are only concerned about one or possibly two costs of capital at any point in time.

Combining the Cost of Capital and Investment Opportunity Schedules

Now that we have determined the cost of capital schedule, we can use it to make capital budgeting decisions for projects of average risk. To do this, we need to consider the set of capital budgeting projects available to Ambassador. Assume they are as follows:

Project	Initial Investment, CF_0 (In millions)	IRR, or Discount Rate Where NPV = 0
A	$2	25%
B	1	21
C	3	19
D	4	18
E	2	15
F	3	12

When we graph them as in Figure 14.2, the schedule of possible capital investments is called the *investment opportunity schedule* (*IOS*). Combining the IOS schedule with Ambassador's cost of capital schedule (from Figure 14.1), we see that Ambassador should accept projects A, B, C, and D, which require a total capital investment of $10 million. All these projects have expected returns greater than the firm's cost of capital; accepting them maximizes the value of the firm, since the net present value for each project is greater than zero.

If Ambassador had more good investment opportunities, its IOS schedule would shift upward and to the right, and the intersection of the IOS and cost of capital schedules would occur farther to the right. If this happens, the cost of capital would still be 15.35 percent unless there was another increase in the cost of capital schedule (farther to the right). If Ambassador had fewer investment opportunities, its IOS

Figure 14.1 Cost of Capital Schedule for Ambassador

As the cost of the last dollar of a specific capital source increases, so does the firm's cost of capital.

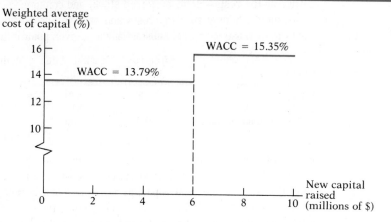

Figure 14.2 Combining Cost of Capital and IOS Schedules to Determine Ambassador's Optimal Capital Budget

When the WACC can increase, the actual discount rate employed for capital budgeting purposes is influenced by the set of projects available.

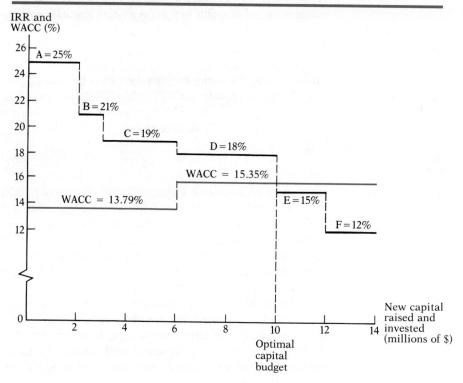

schedule would shift to the left and the intersection of the IOS and cost of capital schedules would occur at the lower discount rate of 13.79 percent. Hence, *when the cost of capital schedule increases or decreases, the discount rate used in making capital budgeting decisions is influenced by the set of projects available to the firm.*

Consider one other factor. What if Ambassador were reluctant to raise more than $6 million in additional capital because it did not want to experience an increase in its cost of capital? As noted in Chapter 9, Ambassador now faces a "soft," or internally imposed, capital rationing constraint. By refusing to raise additional capital, Ambassador accepts only projects A, B, and C (using up its $6 million in capital). But the analysis just conducted shows that even with the higher cost of capital for the next capital increment, Ambassador should accept project D. Failure to raise the additional capital, even at the higher cost, results in not accepting project D and reduces the long-run value of the firm.

How Often Should the WACC Be Calculated?

How often does the firm's weighted average cost of capital need to be recalculated? There is no hard and fast rule—we know firms that do it yearly, and others that estimated their WACC 5 years ago and have not really looked at it since. The best guide is to reexamine it periodically, especially when (1) the financing proportions have changed (or are expected to change), or (2) economic conditions have changed. In these rapidly changing economic times, firms would be wise to review their cost of capital at least every year. Given the rapid rise in actual and expected inflation in the late 1970s and early 1980s, firms that did not reestimate their WACC ended up underestimating their real cost of funds. Likewise, when inflation decreases, a downward revision is necessary.

Estimating Penney's WACC

In practice, calculating a firm's weighted average cost of capital follows the same process we have described. We will use J. C. Penney, and our calculations are made as of January 1988. This is an example of how to make the calculations, but obviously they would have to be reestimated to calculate today's WACC for Penney.

Market Value Proportions

The book value balance sheet for Penney as of January 30, 1988 (in millions) is as follows:

Assets		Liabilities and Stockholders' Equity	
Current	$7,130	Payables and accruals	$1,595
Long-term	3,712	Deferred taxes	1,511
Total	$10,842	Interest-bearing debt and lease obligations	3,563
		Stockholders' equity	4,173
		Total	$10,842

Note we have grouped the liabilities in a somewhat different manner than is usual for financial statement purposes. All accounts payable and accruals (for taxes, cash dividends, and so forth) are lumped together. These are typically ignored for cost of capital purposes. The reason is that for capital budgeting purposes, we netted out increases in current liabilities against increases in the current assets, and dealt only with incremental net working capital needs. Because of this netting out process (and assuming the firm pays these on time so their direct cost is zero), accounts payable and accruals are typically ignored. Deferred taxes are also excluded, since this is an accounting phenomenon that arises from using different depreciation methods for tax and accounting purposes. However, short-term debt is typically included when firms calculate their cost of capital. We will also follow this procedure. Also, lease obligations are included, since they represent a form of long-term financing.

Penney's interest-bearing debt and lease obligations are listed in Table 14.1. Its commercial paper and other short-term notes payable are not listed on any exchange, but we assume their current market value is approximately equal to their book value of $955 million. Then the long-term debentures and notes are listed along with their market prices. The 6 percent debentures of 2006 are deep discount bonds, and Penney also has three zero-coupon notes outstanding. The other long-term debt and lease obligations of $568.6 million were taken at their book value. Looking again at Table 14.1, we see that although the par value of Penney's debt is $3,975 million, its estimated market value as of January 1988 was $3,694.2 million.[11]

Looking further down Table 14.1, we see that the book value of Penney's common equity is $4,173 million, whereas the market value of the firm's common stock is $5,950.7 million. As is typical of most firms, the book value and market value for Penney's common equity are not very similar. Using these market value proportions, we estimate that Penney will raise approximately 38 percent of its new financing with debt; the other 62 percent will be raised through common equity financing. These are the proportions to use in calculating Penney's cost of capital. Obviously, Penney plans to rely on a reasonably balanced approach for its future financing.

Cost of Debt

The before-tax cost of debt for Penney is what the firm has to pay to raise additional debt. Penney had a number of bonds and notes outstanding, and all had an A1 rating according to Moody's. We can assume that any new long-term debt will have a 10-year or longer maturity. What rate of return would the market require on a new issue with this risk? One approach is to calculate the yield to maturity on Penney's existing long-term debt. Another is to determine what the market rate of return (or interest) was on comparable debt in January 1988. At that point in time, the yield to maturity on bonds rated A1 was about 10.0 percent. In our judgment, if Penney had decided to issue new intermediate to long-term debt in January 1988, the firm would have had to pay approximately 10.00 percent. This is the before-tax cost, k_b. We estimate that Penney's effective tax rate for 1987 was 30 percent. Our estimate of the after-tax cost of debt is

$$k_i = k_b(1 - T) = 10.00\%(1 - 0.30) = 7.00\%$$

Penney also had short-term debt and lease obligations in its capital structure. What should we do about them? The term structure of interest rates was upward sloping

---

[11] The par value is greater than Penney's accounting recorded book value due to the deep discount and zero-coupon notes, which *are not* recorded at par value for accounting purposes. As is fairly typical, the book value and market value of a firm's debt are often close together. This is especially true when current market interest rates are close to the coupon interest rates on the firm's debt.

Table 14.1 Calculation of Market Value Weights for Penney as of January 30, 1988

Where market prices are not available, judgment has to be employed to determine the estimated market value. For both short-term debt and other debt and lease obligations, the par (or book) value was employed.

Interest-Bearing Debt and Lease Obligations	Par (or Book) Value (In millions)	Market Price	Market Value (In millions)
J.C. Penney			
Short-term notes payable	$ 955	—	$ 955.0
$13\frac{3}{4}$% notes of '91	100	$102\frac{5}{8}$*	102.6
$12\frac{1}{8}$% notes of '93	150	$106\frac{1}{2}$	159.8
$9\frac{3}{4}$% notes of '95	100	$102\frac{1}{2}$	102.5
$8\frac{3}{8}$% notes of '96	150	$95\frac{1}{8}$	142.7
6% debentures of '06	200	$70\frac{7}{8}$	141.8
$8\frac{7}{8}$% sinking fund debentures of '95	72.5	$97\frac{1}{4}$	70.5
9% sinking fund debentures of '99	79.2	96	76.0
$9\frac{3}{8}$% sinking fund debentures of '16	150	$95\frac{1}{2}$	143.2
9% sinking fund debentures of '16	200	$92\frac{1}{4}$	184.5
Zero-coupon notes of '89	200	$89\frac{3}{4}$	179.5
Zero-coupon notes of '92	150	$66\frac{5}{8}$	99.9
$13\frac{5}{8}$% extendable notes of '99	100	$104\frac{1}{8}$	104.1
$6\frac{3}{4}$% Euronotes of '92	99.7	$104\frac{3}{4}$	104.4
J.C. Penney Financial			
$7\frac{7}{8}$% debentures of '91	75.0	$98\frac{3}{4}$	74.1
$12\frac{3}{4}$% Euronotes of '91	100.0	$106\frac{1}{8}$	106.1
10.2% sinking fund debentures of '94	75.0	$101\frac{1}{4}$	75.9
$10\frac{7}{8}$% guaranteed Euronotes of '90	100.0	$103\frac{1}{8}$	103.1
Zero-coupon Euronotes of '94	350.0	$57\frac{1}{8}$	199.9
Other long-term debt and lease obligations	568.6	—	568.6
Total debt	$3,975.0		$3,694.20
Common equity	$4,173	43	$5,950.7†

Market Value Proportions	**Dollars**	**Proportions**
Short-term debt	$ 955.0	0.099
Long-term debt and lease obligations	2,739.2	0.284
Common equity	5,950.7	0.617
Total	$9,644.9	1.000

* Bond price as a percent of par.
† 138,388,000 shares($43) = $5,950,684,000.

in January 1988, so short-term debt was cheaper than intermediate or long-term debt. We will use 8.50 percent for the approximate before-tax cost of short-term debt, or 5.95 percent on an after-tax basis. Finally, as we show in Chapter 17, the cost of both debt and lease financing should be the same for the firm. We will use 10.00 percent for the before-tax cost of leasing for Penney.

Cost of Common Equity

In recent years Penney has financed almost all its common equity needs through internally generated funds, so our approach is to ignore any possible sale of common stock. The first step is to estimate the growth rate in future dividends, as required by the dividend valuation approach. As Table 14.2 shows, the 10-year and 5-year historical growth rates in dividends per share are 7 and 8 percent, respectively. *Value Line* was projecting a 13.5 percent expected growth rate in dividends over the next 3 to 5 years. Note also that the historical and projected growth rates in earnings are 7 to 8 percent and 13 percent, respectively. While slightly lower than the *Value Line* estimate, 12 percent seems to be a reasonable estimate of the expected compound growth rate in cash dividends as of January 1988.

All three approaches discussed earlier were employed to estimate the cost of equity capital for Penney. First, using the dividend valuation approach (Table 14.3), the cost of internally generated equity capital is estimated to be 15.86 percent. Then, employing Penney's beta of 1.10 (from *Value Line*), a risk-free rate of 8 percent, and an expected return on the market of 16 percent, the CAPM approach produced an estimated cost of internally generated funds of 16.80 percent. Finally, the bond yield plus expected risk premium approach produced an estimated cost of 15.00 percent.

The three approaches produce very similar estimates of Penney's cost of equity capital. For simplicity, we averaged the three estimates to provide an estimate of

Table 14.2 Growth Rates of Earnings per Share and Dividends per Share for Penney

The historical growth rates are useful only as guides for the future. In this case there are some differences between historical and expected growth rates for both earnings and cash dividends.

Year	Earnings per Share	Dividends per Share
1977	$2.26	$0.74
1978	2.06	0.88
1979	1.76	0.88
1980	1.67	0.92
1981	2.75	0.92
1982	2.94	1.00
1983	3.13	1.08
1984	2.91	1.18
1985	2.66	1.18
1986	3.20	1.24
1987	4.39	1.48
10-year growth rate	$\dfrac{\$2.26}{\$4.39} = 0.515 = PV_{?\%,10yr}$ Closest PV is 7%	$\dfrac{\$0.74}{\$1.48} = 0.500 = PV_{?\%,10yr}$ Closest PV is 7%
5-year growth rate	$\dfrac{\$2.94}{\$4.39} = 0.670 = PV_{?\%,5yr}$ Closest PV is 8%	$\dfrac{\$1.00}{\$1.48} = 0.676 = PV_{?\%,5yr}$ Closest PV is 8%
Projected by *Value Line* for 1991–1993	13%	13.5%

Table 14.3 Calculation of Penney's Cost of Equity Capital as of January 1988

These three estimates provide some measure of the "reasonableness" of the final k_s figure.

Assumptions

$$\text{next year's cash dividends, } D_1 = \$1.48(1.12) = \$1.66$$

$$\text{current market price, } P_0 = \$43$$

$$\text{expected growth rate in dividends, } g = 12\%$$

$$\text{risk-free rate, } k_{RF} = 8\%$$

$$\text{market risk for Penney, } \beta_j = 1.10$$

$$\text{expected return on market portfolio, } k_M = \text{expected inflation} + \text{expected}$$
$$\text{real growth in economy} +$$
$$\text{expected risk premium}$$

$$= 8\% + 3\% + 5\% = 16\%$$

$$\text{expected bond yield} = 10\%$$

$$\text{expected long-term risk premium of stocks over bonds} = 5\%$$

Dividend Valuation Approach

$$k_s = \frac{D_1}{P_0} + g = \frac{\$1.66}{\$43.00} + 12\% = 0.0386 + 12\% = 3.86\% + 12\% = 15.86\%$$

CAPM Approach

$$k_s = k_{RF} + \beta_j(k_M - k_{RF}) = 8\% + 1.10(16\% - 8\%) = 8\% + 8.80\% = 16.80\%$$

Bond Yield Plus Expected Risk Premium

$$k_s = \text{bond yield plus expected risk premium} = 10.00\% + 5\% = 15.00\%$$

Penney's cost of equity capital of 15.89 percent [(15.86% + 16.80% + 15.00%)/3] and then rounded it up to 16 percent.

Penney's WACC Now that we have estimates of Penney's after-tax cost of short-term debt of 5.95 percent, long-term debt of 7 percent, and an estimated cost of equity of 16 percent, the cost of capital as of January 1988 can be calculated. As shown below, we estimate that Penney's WACC is 12.449 percent.

Component	After-Tax Cost	× Market Value Weight =	Weighted Average Cost of Capital
Short-term debt	5.95%	0.099	0.589%
Long-term debt	7.00	0.284	1.988
Common equity	16.00	0.617	9.872
		WACC =	12.449%

Given all the estimates that go into calculating a cost of capital, we would round this up to 12.50 percent. This is the minimum discount rate Penney should use as of January 1988 for projects of average risk; accepting projects with less than a 12.50 percent expected return is not consistent with the goal of maximizing the value of the firm.

This cost of capital can be used for making capital budgeting decisions (for projects of average risk) as long as Penney does not attempt to increase its level of financing substantially. If it seeks to secure a large increase in financing, then the cost of some or all of its capital sources would increase, and consequently Penney's cost of capital would also increase.

Divisional and Project-Specific Required Rates of Return

Up to now we have determined how to calculate the firm's cost of capital, which can be employed if new projects have a risk approximately equal to the firm's overall risk. We know, however, that each project must stand on its own legs if the firm is going to maximize its value. Firms must expect to receive a return sufficient to compensate them for the risk involved, and what they could get by investing in an equally risky project outside the firm. This is the stand-alone principle discussed in Chapter 10.

Divisional Required Rates of Returns

The essence of this approach is shown in Figure 14.3, where different discount rates will be employed depending on the riskiness of the division. If a firm employs a firmwide cost of capital when differences in risk exist, it makes the mistake of setting too high a required return for low-risk projects and too low a return for high-risk projects. The result is to underallocate capital to low-risk divisions and to overallocate funds to high-risk divisions.

The most widely used method in practice to implement risk adjustment is based on the assumption that project risks within divisions are somewhat similar, but that risk between divisions differs. If a firm has a furniture division, a paper division, and a data systems division, project risks may be the same within each division, but they may differ between divisions. To estimate divisional rates of return (or costs of capital), we proceed as follows:

STEP 1: Determine the firm's after-tax cost of debt, k_i, and use this as the cost of debt for each division. (Slightly more precision can be obtained by using separate after-tax costs for each division, but our approach is simpler and generally provides approximately the same answer.)

STEP 2: Identify one or more publicly traded firms that are similar in terms of product line to each separate division. These should be *pure play firms,* or publicly traded firms that are engaged solely in the same line of business as the division with the same operating risks. If the publicly traded firm has a different capital structure (or amount of financial risk) than the division, this will affect beta and an adjustment will be required. One way to estimate an *asset* (or unlevered) *beta* is as follows:

$$\beta_{asset} = \frac{\beta_{levered\ firm}}{1 + (1 - T)(B/S)} \tag{14.10}$$

where

$\beta_{levered\ firm}$ = the observed market beta for the publicly traded pure play firm
T = the publicly traded firm's marginal tax rate
B = market value of pure play firm's debt
S = market value of pure play firm's equity

Figure 14.3 Relating Risk to Divisional Costs of Capital for Capital Budgeting Purposes

Use of a firmwide WACC when risk differs results in underallocation of resources to low-risk divisions and overallocation to high-risk divisions.

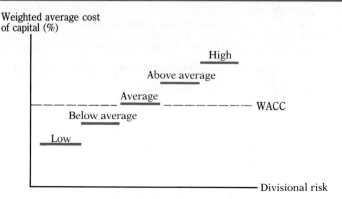

After calculating the unlevered asset beta, the divisional beta can be estimated by substituting in the β_{asset}, marginal tax rate for the division, T, and target capital structure proportions, B and S, and then solving for the levered β for the division.

STEP 3: Employing the beta of the publicly traded firm (with or without adjustment for differences in financial risk, as explained in Step 2), calculate each division's cost of equity capital as if each were a separate firm. Thus, each division's estimated cost of common equity is

$$\text{divisional cost of equity} = k_{RF} + \beta_{similar\ firm}(k_M - k_{RF}) \qquad (14.11)$$

STEP 4: Estimate the division's target or appropriate capital structure as if it were a freestanding firm. Due to differences in business risk between divisions, some may be able to employ substantially more debt than others.

STEP 5: Calculate the division's cost of capital using the costs and financing proportions estimated in steps 1, 3, and 4 above.

Consider the example of Wagner Industries. As shown in Table 14.4, with a beta of 1.25, k_{RF} of 10 percent, k_M = 18 percent, k_i = 8 percent, and using 40 percent debt and 60 percent common equity, we would estimate Wagner's firmwide cost of capital to be 15.20 percent. This would be the appropriate rate for capital budgeting purposes if all of Wagner's divisions were equally risky.

But what if Wagner has three very different divisions? The furniture division is in a very mature industry with low risk; the paper division has a risk that is close to the average risk of the firm; the data systems division is very risky. Due to the differences in risk, the divisions have different betas, which range from 0.75 for furniture to 1.25 for paper and 2.0 for data systems (as determined by examining publicly traded pure play firms with similar product lines). The financing proportions also differ, with the more risky divisions being less able to employ as much debt

Table 14.4 Calculation of Weighted Average Cost of Capital for Wagner Industries

This cost of capital is appropriate for divisions or projects whose risk is approximately equal to the average risk of new projects undertaken by the firm.

Assumptions

$$\text{after-tax cost of debt, } k_i = 8\%$$

$$\text{market risk, } \beta_j = 1.25$$

$$\text{risk-free rate, } k_{RF} = 10\%$$

$$\text{expected return on the market portfolio, } k_M = 18\%$$

Cost of Common Equity

$$k_s = k_{RF} + \beta_j(k_M - k_{RF}) = 10\% + 1.25(18\% - 10\%) = 10\% + 10\% = 20\%$$

Weighted Average Cost of Capital

Component	After-Tax Cost	×	Market Value Weight	=	Weighted Average Cost of Capital
Debt	8%		0.40		3.20%
Common equity	20		0.60		12.00
				WACC =	15.20%

financing. As shown in Table 14.5, these differences produce very different divisional costs of capital. The furniture division's cost of capital is 12 percent, while 15.20 percent is the appropriate discount rate for the paper division. The data services division's cost of capital is 22.40 percent, indicating that projects originating from that division must have a substantially higher expected return to compensate for the increased risk.

Estimating divisional costs of capital in practice requires a thorough understanding of the firm's divisions and identification of appropriate publicly traded firms that are similar to the divisions, following the steps as given here.

Project-Specific Required Rates of Return

The same basic steps employed to determine divisional required returns (or costs of capital) can be applied for specific projects. That is, we estimate the risk of the project, estimate an appropriate cost of equity capital, determine the amount of debt financing (and hence the debt/equity ratio) to be employed, and then calculate a project-specific required rate of return. If the project is really a major undertaking, we may be able to employ the pure play approach involving some other publicly traded firm in the same line. For smaller projects, however, we will have to estimate the project's beta. It is often difficult to come up with a good means of estimating project betas. One alternative would be to calculate an accounting beta for the project. However, given our understanding of the differences between accounting numbers, cash flows, and the value of the firm, we should immediately be wary of such an approach.

Table 14.5 Calculation of Divisional Costs of Capital for Wagner Industries

Using divisional costs of capital improves resource allocation decisions if risk differs substantially between a firm's divisions.

Furniture Division

$\beta_{furniture} = 0.75$

$k_{furniture} = k_{RF} + \beta_{furniture}(k_M - k_{RF})$

$\qquad = 10\% + 0.75(18\% - 10\%) = 10\% + 6\% = 16\%$

Divisional Cost of Capital

Component	After-Tax Cost	× Division's Financing Proportions	= Cost of Capital
Debt	8%	0.50	4.00%
Common equity	16	0.50	8.00
		Furniture division's cost of capital =	12.00%

Paper Division

$\beta_{paper} = 1.25$

$k_{paper} = 10\% + 1.25(18\% - 10\%) = 10\% + 10\% = 20\%$

Divisional Cost of Capital

Component	After-Tax Cost	× Division's Financing Proportions	= Cost of Capital
Debt	8%	0.40	3.20%
Common equity	20	0.60	12.00
		Paper division's cost of capital =	15.20%

Data Services Division

$\beta_{data\,services} = 2.00$

$k_{data\,services} = 10\% + 2.00(18\% - 10\%) = 10\% + 16\% = 26\%$

Divisional Cost of Capital

Component	After-Tax Cost	× Division's Financing Proportions	= Cost of Capital
Debt	8%	0.20	1.60%
Common equity	26	0.80	20.80
		Data services division's cost of capital =	22.40%

Finance theory doesn't help us much in terms of providing a simple procedure for estimating project-specific betas if the pure play approach doesn't work. Even subjective estimates by knowledgeable parties, however, are far better than no adjustment for risk. Generally, their estimates will provide a good idea of the direction of the adjustment required, even if the magnitude of the adjustment is subject to some unknown amount of error.

Summary

Calculating an appropriate required rate of return (whether it is a weighted average cost of capital, a divisional cost of capital, or a project-specific rate) is an integral part of the investment decision process. Costs of capital that are slightly different from the firm's "real" cost of capital do not normally influence investment decisions in practice. It is very important, however, to know if the firm's required rate of return is, for example, 13 percent or 18 percent. We must be able to estimate the firm's cost of capital accurately.

The cost of debt is typically the cheapest source, and common equity is the most expensive. By using the costs of new financing and the market value proportions, a firm can calculate its cost of capital. This is the minimum market-determined required rate of return for new projects of average risk undertaken by the firm. If a firm attempts to substantially increase its financing, its cost of capital will increase. In this case, the firm's discount (hurdle) rate and its optimum capital budget are determined simultaneously.

If a project's risk differs significantly from the average risk of projects undertaken, some alternative required rate of return should be employed as the discount rate. The most frequently used method in practice is to calculate divisional costs of capital. By doing this, the assumption is that risk is homogeneous within a division, but differs between divisions. Finally, project-specific required rates of return can also be employed.

Questions

14.1 Define or explain the following terms:

a. Opportunity cost of capital
b. Internally generated funds
c. Investment opportunity schedule (IOS)
d. Pure play firm
e. Asset beta

14.2 Explain the concept of a firm's required rate of return. What two ways can we approach this return?

14.3 Why is the cost of debt typically the lowest, and the cost of common equity the highest, of the specific costs?

14.4 "Internally generated funds are costless. Accordingly, the cost of new common stock is the only relevant cost of common equity for cost of capital purposes." Evaluate this statement.

14.5 Compare and contrast the dividend valuation, CAPM, and bond yield plus expected risk premium approaches to estimating the cost of common equity. Which do you believe is theoretically the best? The best in a practical sense?

14.6 Discuss the practical aspects of estimating a firm's cost of capital. Under what circumstances can you ignore payables and accruals? What about leases?

14.7 Under what circumstances will the cost of capital schedule increase? How can the schedule be employed to make capital investment decisions when capital rationing is thought to exist?

14.8 Explain how you might use the dividend valuation or bond yield plus expected risk premium approach to estimate the cost of common equity when calculating a divisional cost of capital. Do either of these approaches have any advantages or disadvantages compared to the CAPM approach for estimating a division's cost of common equity?

14.9 How would each of the following affect the firm's after-tax cost of debt, k_i, cost of equity, k_s, and weighted average cost of capital (WACC)? Use a plus sign (+) to indicate an increase, a minus sign (−) to indicate a decrease, and a zero to indicate either no effect or an indeterminant effect. (*Note:* Treat only the direct effect, not any secondary effects.)

	k_i	k_s	WACC
a. The corporate tax rate is decreased.	——	——	——
b. The firm begins to make substantial new investments in assets that are less risky than its present assets.	——	——	——
c. The firm is selling more bonds. Because Standard & Poor's decides the firm is more risky, it lowers the bond rating.	——	——	——
d. The firm decides to triple its financing.	——	——	——
e. Investors become less risk-averse.	——	——	——

Self-Test Problem   (Solution appears on page 729.)

Jump in Cost of Capital

ST 14.1 Jefferson Cement requires $15 million to fund its current year's capital projects. Jefferson will finance part of its needs with $9 million in internally generated funds. The firm's common stock market price is $120 per share. Dividends of $5 per share at t_0 are expected to grow at a rate of 11 percent per year for the foreseeable future. Another part will be funded with the proceeds (at $96 per share) from an issue of 9,375 shares of 12 percent $100 par preferred stock that will be privately placed. The remainder will be financed with debt. Five thousand 10-year $1,000 par bonds with a coupon rate of 15 percent will be issued to net the firm $1,020 each. Interest is paid annually on the bonds. The firm's tax rate is 30 percent.

a. What is Jefferson's WACC?

b. Jefferson has now decided to double its funding requirements. The financing proportions will remain as in (a). No additional internally generated funds are available. New common stock can be sold at $100 per share. Additional preferred stock and debt can be sold with all of the same conditions as in (a) *except* the dividend rate on preferred stock is 13.5 percent, while the coupon interest rate on bonds will be 17 percent. What is Jefferson's cost of capital for this second increment of financing?

Problems

After-Tax Cost of Debt

14.1 Calculate the after-tax cost of debt under the following conditions if the maturity value of the debt is $1,000, interest is paid annually, and the corporate tax rate is 35 percent.

a. Coupon interest rate is 8 percent, proceeds are $900, and the life is 20 years.

b. Bond pays $100 per year in interest, proceeds are $960, and the life is 10 years.

c. Coupon interest rate is 14 percent, proceeds are $1,120, and the bond has a 30-year life.

d. Proceeds are $1,000, coupon interest rate is 12 percent, and the life is 5 years.

14.2   What is the after-tax cost of preferred stock under the following circumstances?

a. Par is $80, dividend is $8 per year, and the proceeds are $76.
b. Proceeds are $46, and dividends are $7.
c. Par is $60, dividend is 9 percent (of par), and proceeds are $55.
d. Par is $40, dividend is 11 percent (of par), and proceeds are $40.

14.3   Given the following information, calculate the cost of common equity, k_s, under each of the following conditions.

a. P_0 is $80, $g = 8$ percent, and $D_1 = 5.
b. It is now January 1, 19X7; cash dividends in 19X2 were $2.05; they were $3 in 19X6. $P_0 = 47.
c. Historical growth in dividends is 4 percent, expected growth is 7 percent, D_0 is $4, and P_0 is $73.
d. $P_0 = 50 and the past dividends have been

Year	Dividends per Share
−5	$2.50
−4	2.80
−3	2.80
−2	3.10
−1	3.67
0	3.67

14.4   Calculate the cost of common equity, k_s, under the following conditions.

a. Expected return on the market portfolio = 16 percent, risk-free rate is 6 percent, and beta is 1.50.
b. $k_M = 18$ percent, $k_{RF} = 12$ percent, σ_M (standard deviation of the market) = 14 percent, σ_s (standard deviation of stock s) = 35 percent, and $Corr_{sM}$ (correlation between returns on stock s and returns on the market) = +0.80. (From Appendix 7B, remember that $\beta_s = \sigma_s Corr_{sM}/\sigma_M$.)
c. The current market interest rate on comparable long-term debt is 9 percent, and the expected risk premium differential of stocks over bonds is 4 percent.
d. The coupon rate on the firm's existing debt is 9 percent; current market yield on short-term debt is 10 percent; current market yield on long-term debt is 12 percent; and the expected risk premium differential of stocks over bonds is 5 percent.

14.5   Chesapeake Motors has called you in as a consultant to estimate its cost of common equity. After talking with its chief financial officer and consulting an econometric forecasting firm, you have come up with the following facts and estimates:

Estimates	Year	Dividends per Share
$P_0 = 85	−5	$1.21
$\beta_{Chesapeake\ Motors} = 1.50$	−4	1.21
U.S. Treasury bill rate = 10%	−3	1.30
market yield on comparable quality long-term debt = 13%	−2	1.40
expected return on the market portfolio = 16%	−1	1.71
expected risk premium of stocks over bonds = 4%	0	1.85
current earnings per share, EPS = $5.75		

Chesapeake plans to use 30 percent debt and 70 percent equity for its incremental financing. Also, the firm's marginal tax rate is 33 percent.

a. What do you estimate the past growth rate in cash dividends per share has been? Employ this as your estimate of g (round to the nearest whole number).

b. What is the estimated cost of common equity employing the following approaches: (1) dividend valuation, (2) CAPM, and (3) bond yield plus expected risk premium?

c. Explain why one of the estimates from (b) is substantially lower than the other two.

d. Take an average of all three answers from (b) for your estimate of Chesapeake's cost of common equity.

e. What is your estimate of Chesapeake's weighted average cost of capital? How confident of it are you?

WACC: Debt, Internally Generated, and New Common Stock

14.6 Schwendiman Tire plans to raise $20 million this year for expansion. The firm's current market value capital structure, shown below, is considered to be optimal.

Debt	$ 40,000,000
Common equity	60,000,000
	$100,000,000

New debt will have a market interest rate of 10 percent. Common stock is currently selling at $40 per share, expected growth in dividends is 7 percent, and $D_1 = \$3.60$. If new common stock is sold, the proceeds are expected to be $36 per share. Internally generated funds available for capital budgeting purposes are expected to be $6 million, and Schwendiman's marginal tax rate is 30 percent.

a. Calculate the market value proportions of debt and common equity.

b. Calculate the cost of the two relevant sources of capital. (*Note:* Remember it is the cost of the last dollar of each feasible source that is important. Firms tend to use internally generated funds before they issue additional common stock.)

c. What is Schwendiman's weighted average cost of capital?

WACC: Debt, Preferred Stock, and Common Equity (CAPM)

14.7 The chief financial officer of Portland Oil has given you the assignment of determining the firm's cost of capital. The present capital structure, which is considered optimal, is as follows:

	Book Value	Market Value
Debt	$50 million	$ 40 million
Preferred stock	10 million	5 million
Common equity	30 million	55 million
	$90 million	$100 million

The anticipated financing opportunities are these: Debt can be issued with a 15 percent before-tax cost. Preferred stock will be $100 par, carry a dividend of 13 percent, and can be sold to net the firm $96 per share. Common equity has a beta of 1.20, $k_M = 17$ percent, and $k_{RF} = 12$ percent.

a. If the firm's tax rate is 40 percent, what is its cost of capital?

b. What happens to its cost of capital if Portland's marginal tax rate is zero?

Cost of Capital

14.8 The management of Lincoln Hotel is considering further expansion. To evaluate the various alternatives, Lincoln's cost of capital needs to be estimated. Various financial data are given, as follows:

Balance Sheet (In millions)

Total assets $500		
	Accounts payable and accruals	$ 50
	Short-term debt	100
	Bonds ($1,000 par)	100
	Common stock (50 million shares)	50
	Retained earnings	200
	Total liabilities and stockholders' equity	$500

Estimates	Year	Dividends per Share
$P_0 = \$15.50$	−7	$1.00
expected return on the market portfolio = 12%	−6	1.00
risk-free rate (U.S. Treasury bills) = 7%	−5	1.05
market interest rate on comparable bonds = 9%	−4	1.05
beta for Lincoln Hotel = 0.80	−3	1.10
	−2	1.10
	−1	1.18
	0	1.23

a. Calculate the historical growth rate in cash dividends per share. Estimate the dividends to be paid in year +1.

b. Estimate the cost of common equity using both the dividend valuation and CAPM approaches. Average the two estimates and then round to the nearest whole number.

c. Calculate Lincoln Hotel's after-tax cost of long-term debt if the firm's marginal tax rate is 35 percent.

d. The short-term debt will carry a different cost. Using the U.S. Treasury bill rate and adding 1 percent to estimate Lincoln's before-tax cost of short-term debt, calculate the after-tax cost of Lincoln's short-term debt.

e. Determine the market value proportions if all of the following hold simultaneously:
   1. Accounts payable and accruals are ignored.
   2. Short-term debt is taken at face value.
   3. The current market value of long-term debt is $125 million.
   4. Common equity is determined by multiplying the number of shares times the stock price.

f. What is Lincoln's cost of capital?

Cost of Capital 14.9 Mendelson Markets is in the process of estimating their cost of capital. Financial data for the firm are as follows:

Balance Sheet (In millions)

Total assets $100,000		
	Accounts payables and accruals	$ 15,000
	Short-term debt	15,000
	Bonds ($1,000 par)	25,000
	Common stock (12,000 shares)	20,000
	Retained earnings	25,000
	Total liabilities and stockholders' equity	$100,000

Estimates	Year	Dividends per Share
$P_0 = \$8.00$	−5	$0.25
expected return on the market portfolio = 17%	−4	0.25
risk-free rate (U.S. Treasury bills) = 10%	−3	0.28
market interest rate on comparable bonds = 13%	−2	0.28
beta for Mendelson = 1.30	−1	0.36
	0	0.40

a. Calculate the historical growth rate in cash dividends per share. (*Note:* Round the growth rate to the nearest whole number.) Estimate the dividends to be paid in year +1.

b. Estimate the cost of equity capital using the dividend valuation, CAPM, and bond yield plus expected risk premium approaches. Assume the expected risk premium is 6 percent. Average the three estimates and then round to the nearest whole number.

c. Calculate Mendelson's after-tax cost of long-term debt if the firm's marginal tax rate is 40 percent.

d. For short-term debt, the before-tax cost is the U.S. Treasury Bill rate plus 1 percent. Calculate Mendelson's after-tax cost of short-term debt.

e. Determine the market value proportions if all of the following hold simultaneously:

1. Accounts payable and accruals are ignored.
2. Short-term debt is taken at face value.
3. The current market value of long-term debt is $21,000.
4. Common equity is determined by multiplying the number of shares times the stock price.

f. What is Mendelson's cost of capital?

Jump in Cost of Capital

14.10 Honeycutt is calculating its required rate of return. The following has been determined:

Debt. $1,000 par value, 20-year, 9 percent coupon-rate bond can be sold at a discount of $50 per bond. Interest is paid annually, and the marginal corporate tax rate is 40 percent.

Preferred stock. $100 par value 8.5 percent preferred stock can be sold at a discount of $9 per share.

Common equity. The present market price is $75 per share. The cash dividend next year is expected to be $5, and the growth rate is expected to be 7 percent for the foreseeable future.

Internally generated. All the common equity needs will be funded by internally generated funds.

Honeycutt's current market value capital structure is as follows:

Debt	30%
Preferred stock	20
Common equity	50
	100%

a. What is Honeycutt's required rate of return?

b. Assume now that Honeycutt decides to increase its financing substantially. Everything is the same as in (a) except:

Debt. 11 percent coupon interest rate.

Preferred stock. 10 percent dividend rate.

Common stock. Underpricing is $12 per share.

Internally generated. All used up, so none available.

What is Honeycutt's cost of capital (or required rate of return) for this increment of additional financing?

(Do only if using Pinches Disk.)

✗ **c.** Determine the firm's WACC in (a) and (b) if the marginal tax rate is (1) 20 percent; (2) zero percent.

✗ **d.** Now suppose Honeycutt's current market capital structure is

Debt	20%
Preferred stock	5
Common equity	75
	100%

and everything is the same as in (a) and (b) except the following: The cash dividend next year is $2.50, the stock price is $90, underpricing (for the second increment) is $10 per share, and the future growth rate is expected to be 10 percent. Determine the firm's cost of capital if the marginal tax rate is (1) 40 percent, (2) 20 percent, (3) zero percent.

X 14.11   Khilnani Products has three different divisions—A, B, and C. In estimating divisional costs of capital, it has been determined that $\beta_A = 1.20$, $\beta_B = 0.60$, and $\beta_C = 2.00$. Also, $k_{RF} = 8$ percent and $k_M = 13$ percent. If the after-tax cost of debt is 5 percent, and the appropriate capital structures for the divisions are given below, what are the three divisional costs of capital?

Target Financing Proportions

	Division A	Division B	Division C
Debt	0.50	0.20	0.60
Common equity	0.50	0.80	0.40

X 14.12   Gage Equipment has traditionally employed a firmwide cost of capital for capital budgeting purposes. However, its two divisions—machinery and farm implements—have different degrees of risk. Data on the firm and the divisions are as follows:

	Gage Equipment	Machinery Division	Farm Implement Division
Beta	1.4	1.0	2.0
Appropriate percentage of debt	40%	50%	20%
Appropriate percentage of common equity	60	50	80

The following estimates have been made: $k_i = 7$ percent, $k_{RF} = 10$ percent, and $k_M = 15$ percent. The firm is considering the following capital expenditures:

	Proposed Capital Projects	Initial Investment (In millions)	IRR
Machinery	M-1	$1	15%
	M-2	3	12
	M-3	2	9
Farm implements	F-1	4	16
	F-2	6	20
	F-3	5	12

a. Calculate Gage Equipment's firmwide cost of capital.
b. Based on your answer in (a), which projects should Gage select? What is the size of the capital budget?
c. Now calculate the costs of capital for the two divisions.
d. Which projects should now be selected? What is the size of the resulting capital budget?
e. What happens if a firm uses a firmwide cost of capital for capital budgeting purposes when it should be using divisional costs of capital?

References

Further information on the cost of capital is contained in

ARDITTI, FRED D., AND HAIM LEVY. "The Weighted Average Cost of Capital as a Cutoff Rate: A Critical Analysis of the Classical Textbook Weighted Average." *Financial Management* 6 (Fall 1977), pp. 24–34.

BEY, ROGER P., AND J. MARKHAM COLLINS. "The Relationship Between Before- and After-Tax Yields on Financial Assets." *Financial Review* 23 (August 1988), pp. 313–331.

BRIGHAM, EUGENE F., DELEP K. SHOME, AND STEVE R. VINSON. "The Risk Premium Approach to Measuring a Utility's Cost of Equity." *Financial Management* 14 (Spring 1985), pp. 33–45.

GITMAN, LAWRENCE J., AND VINCENT A. MERCURIO. "Cost of Capital Techniques Used by Major U.S. Firms: Survey and Analysis of Fortune's 1000." *Financial Management* 11 (Winter 1982), pp. 21–29.

HARRIS, ROBERT S., AND JOHN J. PRINGLE. "Risk-Adjusted Discount Rates—Extensions from the Average-Risk Case." *Journal of Financial Research* 8 (Fall 1985), pp. 237–244.

HAWAWINI, GABRIEL A., AND ASHOK VORA. "Yield Approximations: A Historical Perspective." *Journal of Finance* 37 (March 1982), pp. 145–156.

MILES, JAMES A., AND JOHN R. EZZELL. "The Weighted Average Cost of Capital, Perfect Capital Markets and Project Life: A Clarification." *Journal of Financial and Quantitative Analysis* 15 (September 1980), pp. 719–730.

Stocks, Bonds, Bills and Inflation, Chicago, Ill.: Ibbotson Associates (published yearly).

Divisional costs of capital are examined in

BOQUIST, JOHN A., AND WILLIAM T. MOORE. "Estimating the Systematic Risk of an Industry Segment: A Mathematical Programming Approach." *Financial Management* 12 (December 1983), pp. 11–19.

CONINE, THOMAS E., JR., AND MAURRY TAMARKIN. "Divisional Cost of Capital Estimation: Adjusting for Leverage." *Financial Management* 14 (Spring 1985), pp. 54–58.

FULLER, RUSSELL J., AND HALBERT S. KERR. "Estimating the Divisional Cost of Capital: An Analysis of the Pure-Play Technique." *Journal of Finance* 36 (December 1981), pp. 997–1009.

MILES, JAMES A., AND JOHN R. EZZELL. "Reformulating Tax Shield Valuation: A Note." *Journal of Finance* 40 (December 1985), pp. 1485–1492.

See Models five and seven in *Lotus 1-2-3® for Financial Management* by Pinches and Courtney for templates that calculate k_b (i.e., yield to maturity) and k_s.

15 Capital Structure

Overview

- A major determinant of the capital structure is the amount of the firm's business risk. An old adage is, "The more business risk, the less financial risk."

- In the absence of taxes and other financial market imperfections, the choice of capital structure may be "a mere detail." Once taxes and other factors are introduced, however, the firm may benefit from the judicious use of debt.

- The benefit derived from using debt wisely may lead to a firm increasing its overall value and lowering its cost of capital.

- The pecking order theory suggests a firm's financing, dividend, and capital expenditure decisions are interrelated. It also suggests that internally generated equity is used first, while new common stock is a last resort for financing.

I n 1988 Philip Morris acquired Kraft for $12.9 billion. In doing so it raised $9.6 billion by borrowing, driving its debt/equity ratio to 2.1 to 1. What enabled them to issue confidently so much more debt? It is Philip Morris's awesome ability to generate free cash flow—basically the amount left over after expenses, capital expenditures, and cash dividends. Over the next 5 years Philip Morris expects to generate about $12 billion in free cash flow. Only five firms, including IBM and General Motors, generate more cash. With this cash-generating ability, Philip Morris should be able to pay the $9.6 billion in debt off in only 4 years. Thus, they felt justified in issuing the debt and increasing their financial leverage.

Philip Morris is only one of a number of firms that have massively increased their use of debt. Other examples include Fairchild Industries, Coastal Corporation, and Medig, Inc. Yet, many others—such as Digital Equipment, National Presto, BIC Corporation, and Hi Shear Industries —rely much less on debt. What accounts for these vast differences? How much debt should a firm have? Some analysts suggest (only partially in jest) that the amount of debt employed depends on the age of the firm's chief financial officer; but many factors influence a firm's ratio of debt to total assets. There may be no precise answers; managers need a combination of expertise and judgment. In practice, most firms adopt a target capital structure. Once this is determined, the firm's cost of capital can be estimated and effective capital budgeting decisions can be made.

Risk and Capital Structure

Up to now we have taken the firm's debt/equity ratio, which signifies the amount of financial leverage being employed, as a given. For managers, however, it is not a given; it is one of the decisions firms have to make. The issue can be visualized as follows, where we have two different ways of slicing up the pie between stockholders and bondholders:

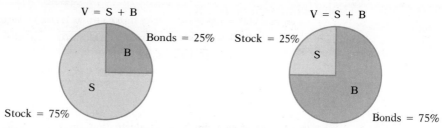

The question is this: Holding everything else constant, does how we slice the pie affect its size? By holding everything else constant, we are assuming that the firm's investments remain the same, as does its underlying cash flows, and everything else. If everything remains the same, then should the value of the firm be affected by how it is financed?

The answer to that simple question is *not* simple. In fact, there is a tremendous amount of controversy and discussion about that question. We begin by discussing two specific risk concepts further, then consider capital structure theory, and end with some practical considerations.

Determining a firm's financial structure means answering two basic questions: First, how should the firm's total sources of funds be divided among long-term and short-term financing? Second, what proportion of funds should be financed by debt and what proportion by equity? The first question, the maturity composition of the total sources of funds, requires focusing on the nature of the assets owned. We address it in Chapter 18, where we see that the matching principle provides some guidance.

Now, however, our attention is on the long-term sources of funds—debt, leases, preferred stock, internally generated funds, and common stock. The proportions of these long-term sources describe the *capital structure* of the firm. Our focus in this chapter is the second question above: How do we decide what proportion of various sources of long-term capital the firm should employ?

Business Risk

Business risk refers to the relative dispersion (or variability) in the firm's earnings before interest and taxes (EBIT). Consider Table 15.1, which presents the expected sales and resulting EBIT in three different states of the economy for one firm, Consolidated National. The expected EBIT for Consolidated is $10,000, and the standard deviation is $3,098. The coefficient of variation, which measures the relative variability of Consolidated's EBIT, is 0.31. If we were comparing it against another firm with an EBIT coefficient of variation of 0.80, we would conclude that Consolidated National has less business risk.

Another way of thinking about the impact of business risk is presented in Figure 15.1. If two firms have the same expected EBIT, then the one with more business

Table 15.1 Probabilities, Sales, and EBIT for Consolidated National

Business risk is measured by the coefficient of variation of EBIT. The higher the coefficient of variation, the more business risk exists.

Probability	0.30	0.40	0.30
Sales	$24,000	$32,000	$40,000
Costs	18,000	22,000	26,000
Earnings before interest and taxes (EBIT)	$ 6,000	$10,000	$14,000

expected EBIT = 0.30($6,000) + 0.40($10,000) + 0.30($14,000) = $10,000

standard deviation = $\sqrt{0.30(\$6,000 - \$10,000)^2 + 0.40(\$10,000 - \$10,000)^2 + 0.30(\$14,000 - \$10,000)^2}$

$= \sqrt{\$9,600,000} = \$3,098$

coefficient of variation = standard deviation/expected EBIT = $3,098/$10,000 = 0.31

---

risk will experience much wider fluctuations in EBIT as its sales fluctuate. Both Consolidated National and the other firm might experience a 10 percent change in sales in a given year. But if the other firm has higher business risk, its EBIT might change by 25 percent from last year's, whereas Consolidated National's only changes by, say, 15 percent. This greater fluctuation in EBIT for the other firm is directly attributable to its greater business risk. Now let's see where these differences in business risk come from.

Business risk is caused primarily by the nature of the firm's operations. As a first approximation, one may think about business risk as being a function of the

Figure 15.1 Probability Distributions of EBIT for Low and High Business Risk Firms

For simplicity, the same expected EBIT is assumed. Other things being equal, low business risk firms will experience much smaller fluctuations in EBIT than will high business risk firms.

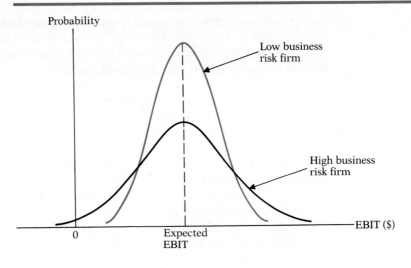

industry in which the firm operates. But business risk is more complex than that. Some of the primary determinants of business risk are the following:

1. SENSITIVITY OF SALES TO GENERAL ECONOMIC FLUCTUATIONS. Firms whose sales fluctuate more when general economic conditions change have more business risk.
2. DEGREE OF COMPETITION AND SIZE. The smaller the firm and its share of the market, the more business risk.
3. OPERATING LEVERAGE.[1] The higher the proportion of fixed relative to variable operating costs, the more *operating leverage* exists and hence the more business risk. Firms in service industries often have low fixed operating costs, and hence a low amount of operating leverage. Steel firms, on the other hand, have high fixed operating costs and more operating leverage and business risk.
4. INPUT PRICE VARIABILITY. The more uncertain the input prices for the firm's products, the more business risk.
5. ABILITY TO ADJUST OUTPUT PRICES. Firms that are in a monopolistic or oligopolistic situation, or that face an inelastic demand curve for their products, may have greater ability to adjust output prices and so be exposed to less business risk.

In general, business risk is a direct function of the firm's accumulated investment (capital budgeting) decisions. As these decisions are made, they affect both the nature of the firm's business and the composition of its assets. Firms with low business risk often exist in such industries as food processing and grocery retailing. Cyclical manufacturing industries and steel, copper, or aluminum firms are generally regarded as having high business risk.

An old adage is that business risk and financial risk are interrelated, so that "The more business risk, the less financial risk." Although the adage is not always true in practice (witness the commercial airline industry, for example), it is important to remember that business risk appears to have a major impact on the amount of financial risk a firm is willing or able to undertake.

Financial Risk

Financial risk is a result of the firm's long-term financing decisions. Financial risk refers to (1) the increased variability of earnings available to the firm's common stockholders, and (2) the increased probability of financial distress borne by the firm's owners if financial leverage is employed by the firm. Financial leverage refers to the use of fixed-cost types of financing.[2] The primary sources are debt, leases, and preferred stock. Although what we have to say applies equally to leases or preferred stock, for simplicity we restrict our analysis to the major source of financial leverage—debt. In terms of the capital structure decision, the question is this: How does the use of debt financing influence the risk and required return of the firm?

To begin answering this question, let's return to our example of Consolidated National. Assume it can employ three different capital structures, as follows:

[1] Operating leverage is considered in detail in Appendix 15A. Its relation to financial leverage is also examined there.

[2] Although some long-term bonds and leases have floating or variable rates, they are still a fixed-cost type of financing, since there are periodic payments required and they have a prior but limited claim before common stockholders receive anything. In addition, adjustable-rate preferred stock also exists; however, it still has the essential elements of a fixed-cost security.

Capital Structure A (zero debt)

Debt	$ 0
Common stock	30,000
Total liabilities and stockholders' equity	$30,000

Capital Structure B (20% debt at a 10% coupon rate)

Debt	$ 6,000
Common stock	24,000
Total liabilities and stockholders' equity	$30,000

Capital Structure C (40% debt at a 10% coupon rate)

Debt	$12,000
Common stock	18,000
Total liabilities and stockholders' equity	$30,000

Capital structure A has no debt; capital structure B has 20 percent of the firm's capital structure in debt. In capital structure C, 40 percent of it is debt, and the other 60 percent is equity. In this example, and throughout the chapter, *we examine the impact of shifting the proportions of debt and equity; the absolute dollar volume of the firm's required capital, however, remains the same.*

Table 15.2 shows the impact of the three different capital structures on Consolidated's earnings per share. (The three EBITs and associated probabilities are from Table 15.1.) For capital structure A, earnings per share ranges from $0.72 to $1.68. Under both B and C, the variation of the EPS is larger, ranging from $0.81 to $2.01 with 20 percent debt, and from $0.96 to $2.56 with 40 percent debt.

To determine the impact of financial risk, the coefficient of variation of Consolidated's EPS for the three different capital structures can be calculated. From the data in Table 15.2, the expected EPS and standard deviation of EPS are calculated (just like we calculated the expected EBIT and its standard deviation in Table 15.1). These are as follows:

	Expected EPS (1)	Standard Deviation of EPS (2)	Coefficient of Variation of EPS (2) ÷ (1) (3)
Capital structure A (zero debt)	$1.20	$0.37	0.31
Capital structure B (20% debt)	1.41	0.46	0.33
Capital structure C (40% debt)	1.76	0.62	0.35

Examining these data, we see that the EPS coefficient of variation when there is no debt (capital structure A) is 0.31, whereas it is 0.33 with 20 percent debt, and 0.35 with 40 percent debt. Since an increase in the coefficient of variation signifies an increase in relative variability, we see that financial risk increases as Consolidated National adds more debt to its capital structure. This increased riskiness is graphed in Figure 15.2 on p. 406, where we see that the dispersion of possible EPS outcomes increases substantially when 40 percent debt is employed, compared with no debt. (The impact of financial leverage is considered further in Appendix 15A.)

In Table 15.1 we calculated the coefficient of variation of Consolidated's EBIT to be 0.31. Note that the coefficient of variation of Consolidated's EPS under capital structure A is also 0.31. Is this just a coincidence? No! The reason these two are exactly the same is that they both represent the basic business risk of the firm.

Table 15.2 Earnings per Share for Three Capital Structures for Consolidated National

If there was preferred stock, those dividends would be subtracted from EAT to arrive at earnings available for common stockholders (EAC). Then EAC would be divided by the number of shares of common stock outstanding to arrive at the firm's EPS.

Probability	0.30	0.40	0.30
Capital Structure A (zero debt)			
EBIT	$6,000	$10,000	$14,000
Interest	0	0	0
EBT	6,000	10,000	14,000
Taxes (40%)	2,400	4,000	5,600
EAT	$3,600	$ 6,000	$ 8,400
EPS (based on 5,000 shares)	$0.72	$1.20	$1.68
Capital Structure B (20% debt)			
EBIT	$6,000	$10,000	$14,000
Interest	600	600	600
EBT	5,400	9,400	13,400
Taxes (40%)	2,160	3,760	5,360
EAT	$3,240	$5,640	$8,040
EPS (based on 4,000 shares)	$0.81	$1.41	$2.01
Capital Structure C (40% debt)			
EBIT	$6,000	$10,000	$14,000
Interest	1,200	1,200	1,200
EBT	4,800	8,800	12,800
Taxes (40%)	1,920	3,520	5,120
EAT	$2,880	$5,280	$7,680
EPS (based on 3,000 shares)	$0.96	$1.76	$2.56

Since capital structure A has no debt, it has no financial risk. Hence, the riskiness of the EPS under capital structure A reflects only business risk. The coefficients of variation for capital structures B and C, however, reflect the effects of *both* business and financial risk. *That part attributable only to financial risk is measured by the difference between the coefficient of variation of 0.31 and either 0.33 for capital structure B or 0.35 for C.*

This example confirms our earlier observation. Fluctuations in a firm's EPS are first and foremost a function of the firm's basic business risk. Once that is accounted for, the effects of the firm's capital structure on risk and required return can be seen. Our interest in the remainder of this chapter is on financial risk, assuming that business risk is held constant.

Impact on the Value of the Firm

The three capital structures produce differences in the expected EPS and its variability. Although these impacts on earnings per share may be significant, we know from our previous discussion that it is not earnings per share that is important. Rather, it is the market value of the firm, V. Remember, the manager's ultimate success or failure is determined in the marketplace. The capital structure question must be

Figure 15.2 **Probability Distributions of EPS for Different Capital Structures**

Favorable financial leverage results in an increase in the expected EPS and also in the dispersion of the possible EPSs.

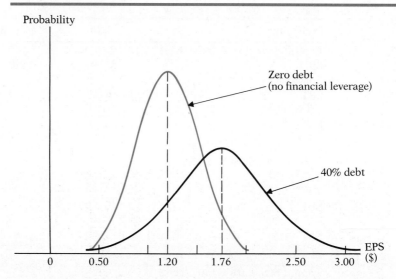

addressed from the standpoint of what impact different capital structures have on the market value of the firm—not on the firm's earnings per share.

The impact of changing capital structures on the value of the firm has been the subject of a tremendous amount of theoretical and empirical work. It all started with the argument that capital structure is a "mere detail." So, in order to understand how firms should address the capital structure decision, it is important to have some idea of the major elements of capital structure theory.

Capital Structure Theory

To highlight the issues involved, we start with a simplified example. The assumptions are as follows:

1. Only two types of securities are employed—long-term debt and common stock.
2. The firm is not expected to grow. Thus, the value of a share of stock can be determined by employing the basic no growth dividend valuation approach (from Chapter 6):

$$P_0 = \frac{D_1}{k_s} \tag{15.1}$$

where

P_0 = the current stock price
D_1 = the constant amount of cash dividends in perpetuity
k_s = the equity investor's required rate of return

3. All earnings are assumed to be paid out in the form of cash dividends. Accordingly, Equation 15.1 can be rewritten as

$$P_0 = \frac{EPS}{k_s} \qquad (15.2)$$

or for the firm as a whole

$$S = \frac{E}{k_s} \qquad (15.3)$$

where E is now the constant cash dividends (or earnings in perpetuity) and S is the total market value of the firm's stock.[3]

4. There are no costs or penalties (such as legal fees or the disruption of operations resulting from default) if the firm does not pay interest on the debt, although the bondholders may take over the firm.

Given this simplified situation, we are in a position to investigate what impact the firm's capital structure can have on the value of the firm. We begin with the no-tax case.

The Modigliani and Miller Model Without Corporate Taxes

In the simplest situation, a firm has only common stock and debt.[4] For the moment, we also assume there are no corporate taxes. Under these conditions, how does the firm's financing decision affect the value of the firm? To see, consider the example of Southern Industries, which is an all-equity-financed firm. Southern has an opportunity to receive $100,000 in cash flow from both its existing operations and a new investment. To receive the $100,000 in cash flow (or EBIT), Southern needs to make an additional $400,000 investment. The equity investor's required rate of return is 10 percent.

If only common stock financing is used to raise the additional $400,000, the total market value of Southern will be the present value of the dividends to the firm's stockholders. Since dividends will be a perpetual stream of $100,000, Equation 15.3 can be employed to find the stock value of Southern:

$$\text{value of Southern Industries stock} = S = \frac{\$100,000}{0.10} = \$1 \text{ million}$$

When only common stock is employed, the total value of the firm, V, is equal to the value of the firm's common stock, S, which is $1 million.

What happens if Southern Industries decides to raise the $400,000 by issuing debt instead of common stock? The debt has an interest rate, k_b, of 6 percent, so that the earnings (and dividends) now available to Southern's common stockholders are

---

[3] As we will see in Chapter 16, the impact of cash dividends on the value of the firm's common stock is also a subject of great debate. To avoid complicating this discussion, it is easier to assume that all earnings are paid out in the form of cash dividends.

[4] The following analysis could be presented in the context of the capital asset pricing model (CAPM), but it is less complicated to present it without introducing the CAPM.

EBIT	$100,000
Interest ($400,000)(0.06)	24,000
EBT	76,000
Taxes	zero for now
EAT	$ 76,000

If the earnings for common stockholders of $76,000 are *mistakenly* divided by the previous required rate of return of 10 percent, the *apparent* value of Southern's common stock is

$$\text{apparent value of Southern Industries stock} = S = \frac{\$76,000}{0.10} = \$760,000$$

Finally, with the value of Southern's debt equal to $400,000, the *apparent* total value of the firm would be

$$\text{total firm value} = \text{market value of common stock} + \text{market value of debt}$$

$$V = S + B \qquad\qquad (15.4)$$

$$= \$760,000 + \$400,000 = \$1,160,000$$

If the equity investor's required rate of return remains 10 percent, simply using debt instead of equity financing has apparently allowed Southern Industries to raise the value of the firm from $1 million to $1,160,000. At this point, Modigliani and Miller raised an important question: "Is it reasonable for the required rate of return demanded by equity investors to be the same when debt, as opposed to common stock, financing is employed?" Their answer is no, since *risk has increased because the use of debt places a drain on the cash flow stream before anything goes to the common stockholders*. This risk is composed of (1) the possibility of not receiving any earnings, and (2) increased variability in EPS due to increased financial leverage.

Modigliani and Miller (MM) developed their model given the following assumptions in addition to those already mentioned:

1. PERFECT CAPITAL MARKETS. In perfect capital markets, buying and selling securities involves no transaction costs (or brokerage fees). All investors have equal and costless access to information, and there are a large number of individual buyers and sellers, none of whom individually can affect market prices.
2. DEBT IS RISK-FREE. Any debt issued by investors and firms is always riskless debt no matter how much is issued. Therefore, the interest rate on all debt is the risk-free rate.
3. RISK CLASSES. All firms can be grouped into risk classes based on the variance of their EBITs.[5]
4. HOMOGENEOUS EXPECTATIONS. Individual investors agree on the expected value of future incomes of firms, that is, on each firm's average EBIT.

Accordingly, MM derived the following two propositions concerning the valuation of securities in firms with different capital structures:

---

[5] This assumption was required because when Modigliani and Miller developed their model, there was no complete model of risk and return such as the capital asset pricing model (CAPM).

Proposition I

The *equilibrium* market value of any firm is independent of its capital structure and is given by capitalizing its expected EBIT by the appropriate rate for an all-equity firm, k_s^U, in its risk class

$$V_L = S_L + B = \frac{\text{EBIT}}{k_s^U} = V_U \tag{15.5}$$

where

V_L = the market value of a levered firm

S_L = the market value of stock for a levered firm

k_s^U = the equity investor's required rate of return for an all-equity-financed firm

V_U = the market value of an unlevered firm

Proposition II

The cost of equity for a levered firm, k_s^L, is equal to the appropriate capitalization rate for an all-equity firm (in the risk class), k_s^U, plus a risk premium equal to the debt/equity ratio times the spread between k_s^U and the cost of debt, k_b,

$$k_s^L = k_s^U + (k_s^U - k_b)(B/S_L) \tag{15.6}$$

Taking the two propositions together, MM conclude in the no-tax case that there is no advantage or disadvantage to financing with common stock. Any "savings" from debt financing are immediately offset by a higher return required by common stockholders (due to greater financial risk), leaving the firm and its stockholders in the same position as before.

According to MM, the total market value of the firm must remain at $1 million (i.e., $V_L = V_U$), because nothing of value has been created. We can think of debt being a zero NPV project; that is why $V_L = V_U$. Subtracting the $400,000 in debt, we see that the value of the stock, S_L, is $600,000. Since the earnings before taxes (EBT) going to Southern's common stockholders are $76,000, Equation 15.3 can be solved for the levered required return on equity:

$$\text{levered required return on equity} = k_s^L = \frac{\text{earnings to stockholders}}{\text{market value of stock}}$$

$$= \frac{\$76,000}{\$600,000} = 0.1267 = 12.67 \text{ percent}$$

Alternately, we can use Equation 15.6 directly:

$$k_s^L = k_s^U + (k_s^U - k_b)(B/S_L)$$
$$= 10\% + (10\% - 6\%)(\$400,000/\$600,000) = 12.67 \text{ percent}$$

Common equity investors neither gained nor lost from the use of debt in the no-tax case. Thus, *the value of the firm does not change; rather, increased financial risk causes the stockholders' required rate of return to increase, so that any apparent gain from using cheaper debt financing is completely offset.*

Since the market value of the firm does not change with financial leverage, in the no-tax case the firm's weighted average cost of capital, WACC, is also constant

Figure 15.3 Value of the Firm and Cost of Capital with No Taxes According to Modigliani and Miller

As the firm moves to the right, it substitutes cheaper debt for more expensive equity capital. Because financial risk increases as you move to the right, the required rate of return increases, exactly offsetting any benefits of cheap debt financing.

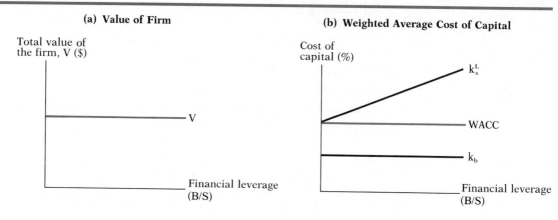

as financial leverage changes. When Southern Industries was all equity-financed, its WACC was equal to its unlevered cost of equity capital, k_s^U, which was 10 percent. In the no-tax case its WACC must remain at 10 percent when it shifts to 40 percent debt financing. Using Equation 14.1, we have

$$WACC = k_b W_{debt} + k_s^L W_{common\ equity}$$

$$= 6.00\%\left(\frac{\$400,000}{\$1,000,000}\right) + 12.67\%\left(\frac{\$600,000}{\$1,000,000}\right)$$

$$= 6.00\%(0.40) + 12.67\%(0.60) = 2.40\% + 7.60\% + = 10.00\%$$

In Figure 15.3, Modigliani and Miller's no-tax position is graphed. As the firm increases its financial leverage (by moving to the right), we see in Figure 15.3(a) that the value of the firm remains constant. In Figure 15.3(b) we see that the firm's cost of capital, WACC, is constant regardless of the amount of financial leverage employed. Both the value of the firm and its cost of capital are independent of financial leverage in the absence of taxes.

The Modigliani and Miller Model with Corporate Taxes

Suppose we now introduce corporate taxes into the example. We will assume that the marginal corporate tax rate, T, is 30 percent and to obtain the $100,000 EBIT, Southern still needs to raise the additional $400,000. The earnings after taxes are

EBIT	$100,000
Interest	0
EBT	100,000
Taxes (30%)	30,000
EAT	$ 70,000

This implies that the payment to *all* investors of the unlevered firm is

payments to investors = EBIT(1 − T) (15.7)

Because only common stock is employed, the required rate of return is still 10 percent, that is, $k_s^U = 10$ percent, and the total value of Southern, V_U, is equal to its stock value, which is

$$V_U = S = \frac{\text{EBIT}(1 - T)}{k_s^U} \tag{15.8}$$

$$= \frac{\$70,000}{0.10} = \$700,000$$

What happens when Southern uses $400,000 of debt financing instead of equity financing? With $400,000 of debt at 6 percent, interest is $24,000. Therefore, with debt financing and corporate taxes, the earnings are

EBIT	$100,000
Interest (k_bB)	24,000
EBT	76,000
Taxes (30%)	22,800
EAT	$ 53,200

In this situation the payment to *all* investors of the levered firm is made up of two components: (1) the $53,200 paid to stockholders, which may be represented as $(\text{EBIT} - k_bB)(1 - T)$, and (2) the $24,000 in interest, k_bB, paid to bondholders. Therefore, the payment to all investors of the levered firm may be written as

$$\text{payment to investors}_L = (\text{EBIT} - k_bB)(1 - T) + k_bB$$

which may be rearranged to read

$$\text{payment to investors}_L = (\text{EBIT})(1 - T) + Tk_bB \tag{15.9}$$

To find the value of the levered firm, V_L, we must determine the present value of Equation 15.9. Notice that the first term on the right-hand side of Equation 15.9, $(\text{EBIT})(1 - T)$, is identical to Equation 15.7. That is, this term is the same as the payment made to the investors of the unlevered firm and, therefore, must be discounted at the required rate of return for the unlevered firm, k_s^U, as we did in Equation 15.8. On the other hand, the second term on the right-hand side of Equation 15.9 represents the tax shield, or subsidy, provided by the interest payment on debt. Because all debt is riskless, and assuming it is perpetual, the present value of the debt tax shield can be found by dividing it by k_b. Thus, the value of the levered firm is

$$V_L = \frac{\text{EBIT}(1 - T)}{k_s^U} + \frac{Tk_bB}{k_b}$$

Because the first term on the right-hand side is identical to Equation 15.8, this can be rewritten as

$$V_L = V_U + TB \tag{15.10}$$

The value of a levered firm, according to MM, is equal to the value of the unlevered firm plus the debt tax shield. Therefore, the value of Southern with $400,000 of debt outstanding is

$$V_L = \$700{,}000 + (0.30)(\$400{,}000) = \$820{,}000$$

Since the total value of the firm, V_L, is also equal to the sum of its stock, S_L, and bonds, B, the value of the stock of the levered firm is $S_L = V_L - B$ and for Southern its stock will now be valued at $S_L = \$820{,}000 - \$400{,}000 = \$420{,}000$. If the debt/equity ratio, B/S_L, is prespecified at ($\$400{,}000/\$420{,}000$), the same result may be obtained by adjusting proposition II (Equation 15.6) for taxes as follows:

$$k_s^L = k_s^U + (k_s^U - k_b)(1 - T)(B/S_L) \tag{15.11}$$

$$= 10\% + (10\% - 6\%)(1 - 0.30)(\$400{,}000/\$420{,}000)$$

$$= 10\% + 2.8\%(95.2\%) = 10\% + 2.67\% = 12.67\%$$

$$S_L = \frac{(EBIT - k_b B)(1 - T)}{k_s^L} \tag{15.12}$$

$$= \frac{\$53{,}200}{0.1267} = \$420{,}000$$

By using financial leverage, Southern Industries has increased the total value of the firm from $700,000 to $820,000. This is composed of stock, S_L, valued at $420,000 and debt, B, valued at $400,000. Let's now see what happens to its cost of capital. With all common stock financing, Southern's WACC is still equal to its cost of equity capital, k_s^U, which is 10 percent. Once debt is introduced, we employ Equation 14.1 again to determine Southern's cost of capital:

$$WACC = k_b(1 - T)\left(\frac{B}{B + S}\right) + k_s^L\left(\frac{S}{B + S}\right)$$

$$= 6\%(1 - 0.30)\left(\frac{\$400{,}000}{\$820{,}000}\right) + 12.67\%\left(\frac{\$420{,}000}{\$820{,}000}\right)$$

$$= 2.05\% + 6.49\% = 8.54\%$$

Comparing the stock versus the debt financing plans once corporate taxes are introduced, we have

	All Stock Financing	Combination Stock and Debt Financing
Total stock value	$700,000	$420,000
Total debt value	0	$400,000
Total value of firm	$700,000	$820,000
Required return on equity	10%	12.67%
Weighted average cost of capital	10%	8.54%

Figure 15.4 shows the MM results once corporate taxes are introduced. Note that financial risk increases as debt is employed, as signified by the rising cost of common stock, k_s^L. Even with this increase in financial risk, *the presence of corporate taxes has the effect of subsidizing the use of debt, with the result that increases in financial leverage lead to increases in the total value of the firm and decreases in the firm's cost of capital.* As long as firms are profitable, there is an advantage to using debt financing. This advantage drives the total value, V_L, of the firm up and reduces the firm's cost of capital as more debt is employed.

Figure 15.4 Value of the Firm and Cost of Capital with Corporate Taxes According to Modigliani and Miller

Once corporate taxes are introduced, the government, in effect, supplies a subsidy for the use of debt as long as firms are profitable. This arises because interest is a tax-deductible expense. By using debt, the firm can increase its total value and decrease its cost of capital.

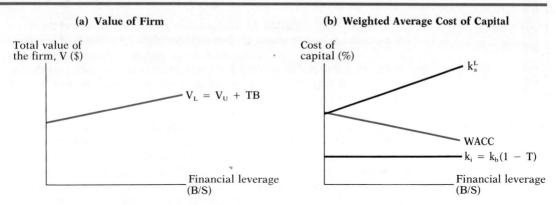

(a) Value of Firm

Total value of the firm, V ($)

$V_L = V_U + TB$

Financial leverage (B/S)

(b) Weighted Average Cost of Capital

Cost of capital (%)

k_s^L

WACC

$k_i = k_b(1 - T)$

Financial leverage (B/S)

Other Factors

The implication of the preceding analysis is that firms should finance almost exclusively with debt. Remember, however, that what we presented was highly simplified and based on a number of assumptions. Now we need to consider four other factors—(1) financial distress costs, (2) agency costs, (3) Miller's personal tax argument, and (4) signaling (or asymmetric information).

Financial Distress Costs

Not all firms succeed; some fail. *Bankruptcy costs* include legal and other direct costs associated with bankruptcy or reorganization proceedings. These are the "dead weight" costs of failing; only the lawyers benefit from them.

In addition to the direct costs, there are other indirect costs associated with financial difficulties, which include:

1. Cancelled orders (and lost sales) due to worried customers
2. Bypassed profitable (i.e., positive NPV) investment projects if they don't produce immediate cash inflows
3. Inefficiency caused by key employees leaving, or having their attention diverted from managing the firm as an ongoing entity
4. Loss of financial flexibility

The sum of the direct and indirect costs associated with bankruptcy and financial difficulties are the *financial distress costs*. Financial distress costs will affect the cost of both debt and equity. As bondholders and other creditors perceive the probability of financial distress increasing, they will require a higher return. Likewise, stockholders face the same concerns since if financial distress becomes too acute, the firm will file for bankruptcy and stockholders will lose everything (or almost everything). Accordingly, as stockholders perceive the probability of financial distress increasing, they will also require a higher return.

How big are these costs? Studies of the direct costs of bankruptcy do not indicate

Exchange Offers

     To determine the impact of a capital structure change on the value of the firm, a recent approach has been to look at intrafirm exchange offers. An exchange offer is where the firm offers to exchange its common stock for its debt, or vice versa. These events are unique in that they do not entail any direct cash inflows or outflows (with the exception of expenses), while they result in a major change in the firm's capital structure. As such, they are relatively clean and allow an analysis of the market impact of a drastic change in the capital structure, other things remaining constant.

     The first major study to look at this was by Masulis.[1] As the figure shows, where there was an increase in leverage (that is, where debt was exchanged for common stock) there was a significant positive abnormal return for the firm's common stock. Likewise, where there was a decrease in leverage, the value of the firm's common stock fell. These results indicate, at least for the time period studied, that an increase in debt led to an increase in the value of the shareholders' claim on the firm, whereas a decrease in debt adversely affected the value of the shareholders' claim.

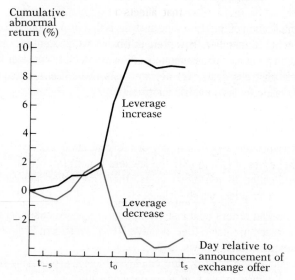

[1] Ronald W. Masulis. "The Effects of Capital Structure Change on Security Prices: A Study of Exchange Offers." *Journal of Financial Economics* 8 (June 1980).

they are large—perhaps 3 percent of the firm's value. But when indirect costs are included, some estimates place the financial distress costs at 10 to 15 percent of firm value. At that level, they are large enough to have an impact on the value of the firm. While the costs of financial distress and the tax shield discussed previously do not tell us what the firm's capital structure should be, they do suggest the following:

1. Firms with a greater probability of experiencing financial distress will borrow less.
2. Firms with high tax rates receive a larger tax subsidy and will borrow more.

However, there is still more to the story.

Agency Costs

Other costs may arise because of the presence of stockholders, managers, and bondholders. First, consider stockholders and managers. As long as the firm is owned and operated by a single entrepreneur, no complications arise because management and the owners are the same person. In this situation, the entrepreneur maximizes his or her wealth by balancing the combination of wages, perquisites (or "perks") such as a company car, company jet, luxurious office, and so on, and market value of the firm's common stock.

As the firm grows, however, the entrepreneur may meet financial needs by raising external funds either by sharing ownership with others (issuing common stock) or by incurring debt financing. Furthermore, as the firm grows the providers of new capital (the principals) delegate decision-making authority to a separate management group (the agent). This delegation of decision-making authority may result in an agency problem if a conflict of interest arises between the agent and principal, or among the principals, that affects the firm's operations. Such conflicts can be resolved only by incurring agency costs.

As sole owner the entrepreneur obtains part of his or her wealth through perks. In this situation, the owner not only receives all of the benefits of these perks but also bears all of their costs. However, if the entrepreneur sells part ownership of the firm to outsiders, while retaining the management capacity, he or she has an incentive to increase perks. Now the entrepreneur will receive all of the benefits of these perks but will pay only his or her ownership fraction of their costs. If the new co-owners realize this agency problem before they buy into the firm, they will not be willing to pay as much for each share. The difference between the price of the share without and with the agency problem represents an agency cost that serves to reduce the value of the firm. On the other hand, the entrepreneur and the new co-owners may enter into a monitoring agreement to ensure that the entrepreneur acts in the best interest of *all* stockholders. In either case an agency cost is incurred.

Another form of an agency problem occurs between stockholders and bondholders. Because the bondholders' claims on the firm's income are fixed, this creates an incentive for the stockholders to engage in riskier projects that transfer wealth from bondholders to stockholders. For example, assume there are two projects, A and B; both projects cost the same amount, and have the same expected return and market value. The variance of the returns of project B, however, is greater than that of project A. The shareholders of the firm may raise the needed funds through a bond issue by revealing only project A to potential lenders. If the firm has the ability to switch to project B, after it has raised the funds, it will do so. Because both projects have the same market value, this switch will not affect the total market value of the firm. It does make the debt more risky, however, thus redistributing value from bondholders to stockholders. To prevent such expropriation of their wealth,

Figure 15.5 Value of the Firm with Corporate Taxes, Financial Distress, and Agency Costs

The value of the levered firm with the inclusion of financial distress and agency costs, V_L', at first rises but then declines to be less than the value of the levered firm for the MM tax world, V_L. An optimal capital structure exists, B*/S, where the benefits of debt are exactly offset by the sum of the present values of the financial distress and agency costs.

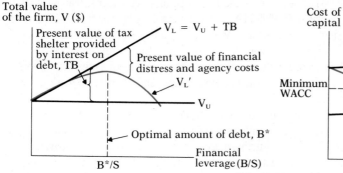

(a) Value of Firm

Total value of the firm, V ($)

Present value of tax shelter provided by interest on debt, TB

$V_L = V_U + TB$

Present value of financial distress and agency costs

V_L'

V_U

Optimal amount of debt, B*

B*/S

Financial leverage (B/S)

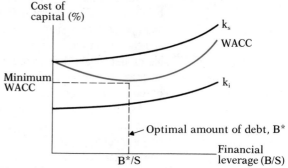

(b) Weighted Average Cost of Capital

Cost of capital (%)

k_s

WACC

Minimum WACC

k_i

Optimal amount of debt, B*

B*/S

Financial leverage (B/S)

bondholders will demand various types of restrictive covenants and monitoring devices. The cost of these instruments is another agency cost.

The analysis so far, which includes the tax subsidy associated with debt, financial distress costs, and agency costs, can be illustrated as in Figure 15.5. In the MM tax model (Equation 15.10), the value of the firm increases continuously as more debt is used. The value-maximizing firm would issue 100 percent debt. But with costs of financial distress and agency costs included, the total value of the firm becomes

$$V_L = V_U + \begin{array}{c} \text{present value} \\ \text{of tax} \\ \text{savings} \end{array} - \begin{array}{c} \text{present value} \\ \text{of financial} \\ \text{distress costs} \end{array} - \begin{array}{c} \text{present value} \\ \text{of agency} \\ \text{costs} \end{array} \qquad (15.13)$$

where the present value of the tax savings is equal to TB, the present value of the financial distress costs depends on the probability and costs associated with financial distress, and the present value of the agency costs depends on the monitoring and agency costs associated with both equity and debt. There is an optimal debt/equity ratio, B*/S, where the value of the firm is maximized and the WACC minimized. This optimum ratio exists such that substituting one more dollar of debt for equity will raise the costs more than the benefits. Similarly, cutting back will lower the costs by less than the benefits are reduced.

Introducing financial distress and agency costs leads to the conclusion that the firm will not be all equity financed, nor all debt financed. Now let's ignore financial distress and/or agency costs and consider another factor—personal taxes.

Corporate and Personal Taxes[6]

When MM developed their tax model they included corporate taxes but not personal taxes on either debt or stock income. As a result they determined the value

---

[6] This section may be omitted without loss of continuity.

of the levered firm to be $V_L = V_U + TB$. Consequently, the gain from leverage, G_L, is the difference between the value of the levered and unlevered firms.

$$G_L = V_L - V_U = TB \tag{15.14}$$

This gain from leverage, and consequently the value of the levered firm, increases as a firm uses more debt. Thus, the optimal capital structure is 100 percent debt.

What happens to the gain from leverage and the value of a firm that uses debt when both corporate and personal taxes exist? Merton Miller (one half of MM) addressed this question and developed the following equation.

$$V_L = V_U + \left[1 - \frac{(1 - T)(1 - T_{ps})}{(1 - T_{pb})} \right] B \tag{15.15}$$

where

T = the corporate tax rate
T_{ps} = the personal tax rate on stock income
T_{pb} = the personal tax rate on bond income (interest)

With this more realistic tax structure, the gain from leverage is now

$$G_L = \left[1 - \frac{(1 - T)(1 - T_{ps})}{(1 - T_{pb})} \right] B \tag{15.16}$$

If the personal tax rates are zero ($T_{ps} = 0$ and $T_{pb} = 0$) or if they are equal to one another ($T_{ps} = T_{pb}$), then this gain from leverage reduces to TB, the corporate benefits from the interest tax shelter developed by MM.

With the inclusion of personal taxes the objective is to maximize income after all taxes (corporate and personal). Thus, if T_{ps} is less than T_{pb}, then, other things being equal, the before-tax return on bonds must be high enough to compensate for the additional taxes that must be paid on bond income. If this were not true, investors would never hold bonds. Although the firm receives a subsidy because of the tax deductibility of the interest payment, this benefit is offset because the interest payment has been "grossed up" to compensate for the higher personal taxes that must be paid on the interest income. Consequently, the gain from leverage diminishes and, in fact, will disappear completely if $(1 - T_{pb}) = (1 - T)(1 - T_{ps})$. In this case, the results are the same as the MM model with no taxes because G_L will be zero, $V_U = V_L$, and, accordingly, the amount of debt used by a firm will not have any effect on its value or cost of capital. These relationships are graphed in Figure 15.6.

Under the Tax Reform Act of 1986, $T = 34$ percent, $T_{ps} = 28$ percent, and $T_{pb} = 28$ percent. If the *effective* tax rates on stock income and bond income are equal, then the gain from using debt is

$$G_L = \left[1 - \frac{(1 - 0.34)(1 - 0.28)}{(1 - 0.28)} \right] B = 0.34B$$

which is the same as given by the MM model with only corporate taxes. We would conclude there are substantial gains from using debt.

On the other hand, even with the stated personal tax rate on stock income and bond income at 28 percent, there is still one big tax advantage for stock. It arises

Figure 15.6   Gains from Financial Leverage: MM Models (With and Without Taxes) and Miller's Model

Depending on the effective rate of personal taxes on stock versus bond income, Miller's model may indicate an intermediate value for the firm.

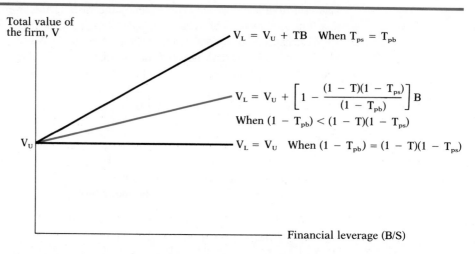

because over 50 percent of the return from investing in stock comes from capital gains, and an investor does not have to realize the capital gain (and pay taxes on it) immediately. This option to delay realizing capital gains means the effective tax rate on stock income is probably less than for bond income. What if the effective tax rate on stock income, T_{ps}, is 20 percent? Then the gain from using debt is

$$G = \left[1 - \frac{(1 - 0.34)(1 - 0.20)}{(1 - 0.28)}\right] B = 0.267B$$

While still substantial, there is somewhat less subsidy than when the effective personal rates on stock and bond income are equal. With the Miller model, the value of the tax benefits to the firm is a compromise between the MM model with no taxes and the MM tax model. This effect is shown in Figure 15.6.

When arriving at his result, Miller traded off the corporate benefits of debt against the personal tax disadvantage of the resulting interest income; he did not consider any corporate disadvantages to debt. DeAngelo and Masulis recognized this and extended Miller's work by including the effects of tax shields other than interest, such as depreciation and depletion. The existence of these "nondebt tax shelters" serves to decrease a firm's taxable income, thus causing a decline in the probability of being able to use all of the interest tax shield. Consequently, as more debt is used, the expected value of the interest tax shield declines. The firm is therefore forced to balance the use of debt substitutes against the use of debt in order to be able to use all tax deductions. Without considering any bankruptcy or agency cost, DeAngelo and Masulis demonstrated that this balancing procedure will also lead to a capital structure that entails less than 100 percent debt (and more than zero debt).

Signaling

An alternative approach to examining the capital structure issue is based on the belief that managers as insiders have information that outside investors do not have access to—this is often called "asymmetric information." This being the case, the choice of a capital structure by insiders can convey information about the firm to investors and cause a change in the value of the firm.

As an example, suppose a firm receives good news about the future (based on higher expected cash flows) and therefore issues more debt. Such a change would signal good news—providing the firm can validate it in the future. Another example has been proposed by Myers and Majluf. They developed a framework that suggests that managers will only issue equity when they know it is overvalued.

Under a signaling approach the capital structure becomes more of a dynamic, ongoing, evolving decision. There is not a single optimal level of debt, because managers continually have access to information before it is available to outside investors. And, depending on the nature of the information, managers may choose to issue debt, or equity, in amounts that will one time push the firm toward an optimal debt/equity ratio while another time they may push the firm away from an optimal debt/equity ratio.

Target Capital Structure and the Pecking Order Theory

Although there is still a great deal of controversy about the idea, many factors (both theoretical and practical) suggest the existence of capital structures that incorporate both debt and equity. This has lead to the development of the notion that firms have a *target capital structure*. This idea is illustrated in Figure 15.7. The target capital structure view does not suggest there is a single optimal debt level. Rather, it emphasizes there is a range of capital structures that are all approximately equally good; that is, within this range the value of the firm, V, is maximized and

Figure 15.7 Value of the Firm and Cost of Capital with a Target Capital Structure

Due to the impact of debt, the overall value of the firm initially increases with financial leverage. However, as more and more debt is employed, financial risk increases and value declines. Conversely, the cost of capital first falls and then rises. The target capital structure tends to maximize the value of the firm and minimize its cost of capital.

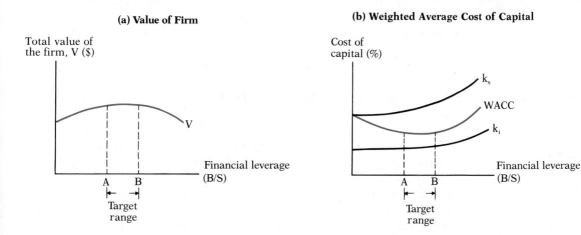

its weighted average cost of capital, WACC, minimized. Firms should stay within a few percentage points of their target. By doing so, their financing decisions will be consistant with the goal of maximizing the value of the firm.

The target capital structure idea is consistent with a theory recently proposed by Myers. His *pecking order theory,* which deals with the firm's investment, financing, and cash dividend decisions goes like this:

1. Firms prefer internal financing, either because of the lack of flotation (or issuance) costs, or to escape the disciplining influences of the financial markets.
2. They develop target cash dividend payout ratios, based on perceived investment opportunities. And, they want to avoid any sudden changes in dividends. (Dividend policy is explored in Chapter 16.)
3. Sticky cash dividend policies, and not completely predictable fluctuations in internally generated cash flows and investment opportunities, mean sometimes internally generated cash flow is greater than capital expenditures, and other times it is less. When cash flows are greater than needed, the firm builds up its cash balances, pays off debt, or repurchases some of its common stock. If it is less, the firm pulls down its cash reserve.
4. When external financing is needed, firms issue debt first. New common stock is viewed as a last resort.

In the pecking order theory there is no well-defined debt/equity ratio, because there are two kinds of equity—one at the top of the ladder and the other at the bottom. Each firm's actual debt ratio reflects its cumulative need for external financing, given its profitability (and internally generated cash flow), dividend policy, and capital investment opportunities. Under the theory the firm's debt/equity ratio will fluctuate over time—perhaps within some "target" range—based on the interplay between profitability, dividend policy, and capital investment opportunities. As such, the target capital structure idea, and the pecking order theory, provide a rationale for what we observe in practice.

Setting a Firm's Debt/Equity Ratio

It should be clear by now that there is no simple answer to the capital structure decision. We can't make a blanket statement that, for example, firms should have a debt/equity ratio of 1. But we can provide tools, guidelines, and some thoughts on planning ahead.

Tools for Digging

Some tools that can be employed to explore the capital structure issue include the following:

1. EPS-EBIT ANALYSIS. To employ *EPS-EBIT analysis,* we begin with the firm's estimated EBIT. Consider the example of Seaboard Industries, which currently has $2 million of 10 percent debt outstanding and 1 million shares of common stock with a market price of $20 each. Seaboard needs to raise $10 million in new capital and has two options. The first involves issuing 500,000 shares of additional common stock at $20 per share. The second would employ debt financing to raise the $10

million. The debt would carry a coupon interest rate of 12 percent. After the new investment, Seaboard's EBIT is $6 million. As shown below, at the $6 million EBIT, Seaboard's EPS would be $2.32 with common stock financing and $2.76 with the debt financing.

	Common Stock Financing (In millions)	Debt Financing (In millions)
EBIT	$6.00	$6.00
Interest	0.20	1.40*
EBT	5.80	4.60
Taxes (40%)	2.32	1.84
EAT	$3.48	$2.76
Number of shares of common stock (millions of shares)	1.50	1.00
EPS	$2.32	$2.76

* $200,000 on existing debt plus $1,200,000 interest on new debt.

Instead of simply calculating EPS, it is generally helpful to consider what happens to EPS at various EBIT levels. We can also calculate the crossover EBIT (EBIT*), which is the EBIT level that causes both financing alternatives to produce the same EPS, as follows:

$$\frac{(EBIT^* - I_1)(1 - T) - D_{ps1}}{N_1} = \frac{(EBIT^* - I_2)(1 - T) - D_{ps2}}{N_2} \tag{15.17}$$

where

$\quad$ EBIT* = the unknown crossover point in EBIT

$\quad$ I_1, I_2 = the annual total interest charges under the two financing plans

$\quad\quad$ T = the firm's marginal tax rate

$\quad$ N_1, N_2 = the number of shares of common stock outstanding under the two plans

$\quad$ D_{ps1}, D_{ps2} = the dollar amount of cash dividends on preferred stock under the two plans

The crossover EBIT idea is illustrated in self-test problem ST 15.3. EPS-EBIT analysis, while ignoring risk and the value of the firm, does provide some information on the impact of alternative financing plans on the firm's EPS.

2. COVERAGE RATIOS. Most firms and financial analysts calculate various coverage ratios to ascertain how the firm's EBIT relates to the cash outflows resulting from the use of fixed-cost financing. These ratios range from the times interest earned ratio (EBIT/interest) discussed in Chapter 3 to more complicated ratios that take into account principal repayments, sinking fund payments, cash dividends on preferred stock, and/or lease obligations. The basic intent of all these ratios is to ascertain how safe the firm is in terms of meeting its fixed-cost financing charges.

3. LENDER STANDARDS. Often a firm's lenders impose certain standards of financial performance. A debt issue (or term loan) may contain financial performance standards that have to be met before assets can be sold, cash dividends paid, and so on. In addition, many larger firms tie their target capital structure decision to the bond rating the firm desires to maintain. For example, a firm may decide it always wants to be able to issue reasonable amounts of new debt with an A bond rating. Accordingly,

the capital structure and other financial affairs are kept in a condition to achieve this result.

4. INDUSTRY NORMS. Many firms tend to follow what is commonly accepted among other firms in the same industry. For this reason, we see certain types of securities and commonly accepted capital structures within industry categories. Steel firms tend to have different capital structures from retail department stores, for example.

5. CASH FLOW ANALYSIS. A final approach is to investigate what happens to the ability of the firm to survive a severe recession. This involves a scenario analysis, where the firm focuses on the cash flow consequences under alternative assumed future states of the economy.

All these tools are guides for the manager in determining the firm's capital structure.

Guidelines for Setting Debt/ Equity Ratios

A three-pronged approach for making the capital structure decision is suggested.

1. RISK. With or without bankruptcy, financial distress is costly. While many factors affect risk, financial distress is more likely in firms that have high business risk. These firms tend to use less debt than low business risk firms. Business risk is often related to the type of assets employed. Where growth is high, and intangible assets play a major role, the value of the assets may erode quickly. Typically, firms that employ a lot of "brain power" or other intangible assets use less debt.

2. TAXES. For firms in a taxpaying position, an increase in the amount of debt reduces the taxes paid by the firm. Of course, it's not just whether the firm is in a taxpaying position; it's also whether they are expected to remain in a taxpaying position that is important. Firms with less assurance of being able to benefit from the interest tax shield will use less debt.

3. FINANCIAL SLACK. In the long run, a firm's value depends first and foremost on the investment and operating decisions made. These have the potential to add more value to the firm than its financing decisions. Therefore, firms want a certain amount of financial slack so they can react to new positive NPV opportunities. This is one of the reasons why high-growth firms tend to use less debt, because that posture provides greater financial slack.

Planning Ahead

The firm's capital structure decisions cannot be made in a vacuum. They have to be part of the firm's complete financial plan, which takes into account its investment opportunities, operating strategy, dividend plan, and so forth. That is why the capital structure decision cannot be made in complete isolation of the other activities of the firm.

In Chapter 4 we examined cash budgets and pro forma financial statements. While they don't tell you where to raise funds, they do provide insight into the anticipated amount and timing of the needs or surpluses. The use of sensitivity analysis is just as helpful when planning a firm's capital structure as it is for cash budgeting, or analyzing long-term investment decisions. In addition, simulation, which allows the whole probability distribution of financial consequences to be examined, is also useful. The overall impact of financial planning and strategy is explored in Chapter 23. For now, remember that planning ahead, and having some financial slack, is important when considering how much debt the firm should have.

Leveraging Up

By the end of 1988, nonfinancial companies had nearly doubled their debt within 6 short years to $1.8 trillion. At the same time they retired more than $400 billion in equity.[1] The interest paid by nonfinancial corporations equaled nearly 24 percent of corporate cash flows in 1988. What happened to cause American industry to leverage up?

While many factors contributed, the driving force behind most of the increase in leverage was management's desire to stay in charge. The increasingly competitive market for corporate control, where virtually any firm can be a potential takeover target, has made management look at actions that maximize the value of their firm. Faced with possible takeovers, which are financed in part by selling off underutilized assets and also by making use of excess debt capacity, many firms are restructuring, paying out large dividends, and increasing their debt. Debt is a tough taskmaster, but in today's competitive markets living with low rates of leverage is no longer feasible. Companies in Europe and Japan have long lived with debt burdens substantially higher than those carried by U.S. companies. Even today, U.S. companies have only about half the amount of financial leverage as their foreign counterparts.

All of this increase in financial leverage doesn't fall just on corporations. The financial system must also be able to handle this new mountain of debt. Wall Street must create new financial instruments, find customers, and work to keep capital markets liquid. Bankers are also involved, in terms of monitoring performance and insuring good things don't turn bad before they step in to rescue or liquidate corporations. Institutional investors will also have to take a more direct role and stake in corporate affairs by monitoring performance even more closely. Finally, the government plays an increasing role since the higher levels of debt means more firms are vulnerable to recessions.

[1] "Learning to Live with Leverage." *Business Week* (November 7, 1988).

International Capital Structure Issues

When investments are made on an international basis, they are often accomplished through the use of subsidiaries set up in various countries. The relevant capital structure in such a case is that of the subsidiary, not the parent firm. These local target capital structures may differ a good deal from those of the parent. For example, the debt load carried by most Japanese firms is far above the comparable debt load of a U.S firm in the same industry. This is due in part to direct government action, which favors loans to selected firms. The interrelated nature of firm ownership in Japan also leads to higher debt levels.

This same pattern of higher debt loads occurs in many countries. One of the primary reasons for it is the banking structure; banks are often encouraged to cooperate directly with firms in developing close ties and providing financing. A second reason for the high debt loads is related to the lack of highly developed equity capital markets. These differences must be taken into account when considering the target capital structure for use in countries outside the United States.

Summary

The firm's capital structure is the result of the interaction of many different factors. One primary factor is the business risk to which the firm is exposed. Other things being equal, the more business risk the firm faces, the less financial risk it wants to incur.

In the absence of taxes and other imperfections, the firm's capital structure does not influence the value of the firm or its cost of capital. However, once corporate taxes, financial distress costs, agency costs, personal taxes, and signaling are considered, the value of the firm does not appear to be independent of its capital structure. The judicious use of debt appears to raise the value of the firm and lower its cost of capital.

In practice, firms establish target capital structures. This practice is consistant with the pecking order theory, which states that a firm's capital structure, dividend, and capital budgeting decisions are interrelated. The pecking order theory also suggests why internally generated equity is used first, while new common stock is the last source employed. Once established, firms tend to fluctuate around their target capital structure over time. Given that a capital structure has been decided on, the required rate of return (or weighted average cost of capital) can be determined. Understanding the interrelationship of the firm's capital structure, its required rate of return, and its capital budgeting decisions is fundamental if we are to understand the manager's job when it comes to making effective long-term investment and financing decisions.

There is an appendix to this chapter, "Appendix 15A: Operating, Financial, and Total Leverage," at the back of the book.

Questions

15.1 Define or explain the following:

a. Capital structure
b. Operating leverage
c. Bankruptcy costs
d. Financial distress costs
e. Target capital structure

f. Pecking order theory
g. EPS-EBIT analysis
h. Degree of operating leverage (DOL)
i. Degree of financial leverage (DFL)
j. Degree of combined leverage (DCL)

15.2 Explain what causes business risk. What would you believe the relative business risk of the following would be: grocery stores, jewelers, farm equipment manufacturers, airlines? Why?

15.3 Financial leverage generally has two effects on earnings per share. Identify these two effects and then explain why they occur.

15.4 Why can firms with low business risk have high financial risk, and vice versa? From your observation, is this generally the case?

15.5 In a world of no corporate taxes, the capital structure is a "mere detail." Explain why and under what conditions this is so.

15.6 What happens when corporate taxes are introduced into the capital structure decision? And then financial distress and agency costs?

15.7 Explain Miller's personal tax model. Under what circumstances does it lead to the same conclusion as MM without corporate taxes? With corporate taxes?

15.8 Explain the pecking order theory. How does it relate to target capital structures?

15.9 How would you go about explaining why we see so many different capital structures in practice, both between and within industries?

Self-Test Problems   (Solutions appear on pages 730–731.)

No-Tax Case

ST 15.1 Scott Power is an electric utility that currently has $50 million in EBIT, $200 million in 5 percent coupon-rate bonds outstanding, and $400 million in stock outstanding.

a. Determine the firm's yearly interest and earnings, and the firm's cost of equity capital, k_s^L. What is its weighted average cost of capital?
b. Northern has decided to issue $100 million in stock and use the proceeds to buy back $100 million in bonds. What must the new cost of equity capital be according to Modigliani and Miller? What is the firm's cost of capital?

Gain from Leverage

ST 15.2 Benefit Mutual has $20 million of debt outstanding. The firm has a corporate tax rate of 40 percent. A survey by its investment banker has revealed that the marginal tax rate of the firm's common stockholders (average of dividends and capital gains) is 15 percent whereas the marginal tax rate on bond income is 28 percent.

a. What is the firm's gain from using the $20 million of debt?
b. What would the gain to the firm be if all of its investors paid no taxes?

Maximize EPS

ST 15.3 Outboard Equipment is an all-equity-financed firm with the following financial statements:

Balance Sheet		Income Statement	
Total assets	$1,000,000	Sales	$2,500,000
		Operating costs	2,100,000
Common stock ($5 par)	$ 250,000	EBIT = EBT (16%	
Retained earnings	750,000	of sales)	400,000
Total equity	$1,000,000	Taxes (40%)	160,000
		EAT	$ 240,000

Outboard Equipment is planning to raise $400,000 through the sale of common stock at $50 per share, or the issuance of debt with a 10 percent coupon rate. Once the expansion is completed, sales are expected to increase to $3 million; EBIT should be the same percentage of sales at this new level.

a. Determine the present number of shares of stock outstanding, and Outboard Equipment's present EPS.
b. What is the crossover EBIT between the two financing plans?
c. Determine the EPS under the two plans.

Problems

Business Risk

15.1 Two firms, A and B, have the following probability distributions of EBIT.

Probabilities	0.30	0.40	0.30
A's EBIT	$ 20,000	$ 40,000	$ 60,000
B's EBIT	$200,000	$280,000	$360,000

Which firm has the most business risk? Why?

Variability of EPS 15.2   State Systems is currently in the process of a substantial expansion program. The $3.5 million program will be financed by a stock issue (of 100,000 shares) or with a new 10 percent coupon rate bond issue. The firm's preexpansion income statement (in millions of dollars) is

Sales	$5.00
Operating costs	3.50
EBIT	1.50
Interest	0.25
EBT	1.25
Taxes (36%)	0.45
EAT	$0.80

EPS (200,000 shares) $4.00 per share

After the expansion, the EBIT is expected to be $1.5, $2.5, or $3.5 million, with associated probabilities of 0.30, 0.40, and 0.30.

a. Determine the EPS for both plans with each different probability.
b. Calculate the expected EPS, the standard deviation, and the coefficient of variation of EPS for each plan.
c. Which plan has the most risk? Explain.

Return on Unlevered Equity 15.3   Paul will invest $50,000 in a stock by borrowing (B) $30,000 and putting up $20,000 (S) himself. The cost of debt, k_b, is 8 percent and there are no taxes. Paul expects a return, k_s^L, of 17 percent. What would Paul's return be without the use of financial leverage?

Value of Firm 15.4   Assume the MM tax case holds. The market value of a firm that has $300,000 in debt is $1,200,000. The interest rate on debt is 12 percent and the marginal corporate tax rate is 30 percent. If the firm was all equity financed, the required return on equity would be 18 percent.

a. What is the firm's EBIT?
b. What would the market value be if the firm is all equity financed?

Levered and Unlevered Firms 15.5   Goering Brothers is an unlevered firm with an EBIT of $4 million, the tax rate is 40 percent, and the required rate of return on equity is 15 percent. Assume the MM tax case holds.

a. What is the market value of Goering?
b. Suppose Goering now issues $10 million of 8 percent bonds. What is the new market value of Goering?
c. Assume there are two firms, Y and Z, that are identical in all respects to the unlevered Goering and the levered Goering, respectively. Explain what will happen if the current market value of Y is $14 million, while that of Z is $23 million.

The Tax Case 15.6   Appalachian Industries is presently an all-common-stock-financed firm, with 8,000 shares of common stock outstanding and a tax rate of 35 percent. Assume the MM tax case holds. The firm is evaluating two different financing plans, as follows:

Common Stock	Debt
2,000 additional shares	$60,000 at an 8% coupon rate
$k_s^U = 10\%$	$k_s^L = 10.2727\%$
EBIT = $50,000	EBIT = $50,000

a. If common stock is employed, what is (1) the total stock value, S, (2) earnings per share (EPS), (3) the market price per share, P_0, (4) total value of the firm, V, and (5) its cost of capital (WACC)?

b. Rework (a) if debt financing is employed.

c. Explain why, in the absence of financial distress and agency costs, the firm may be able to lower its cost of capital and raise the total value of the firm by employing debt financing.

Personal and Corporate Taxes

✗ **15.7** Debt-Free Co. is an unlevered firm that has an equilibrium market value of $7 million. The firm is contemplating issuing $4 million of 10 percent coupon bonds. The firm has a corporate tax rate of 30 percent and has estimated that the tax rates for its investors are 20 percent on stock income and 25 percent on bond income:

a. If only corporate taxes exist, what is the new total value of the firm and the gain from leverage?

b. With both corporate and personal taxes, what is the gain from leverage and the total value of the firm?

c. Why is the gain from leverage (or, alternatively the total value of the firm) less in (b) than in (a)?

Target Capital Structure

15.8 Traynor Enterprises currently has $100 million of 13 percent (coupon rate) debt outstanding, its EBIT is $80 million, and its cost of equity capital, k_s^L, is 12 percent. Due to a decrease in interest rates, Traynor has decided to call the bond issue. (The bonds will be called at par.) Because Traynor is not at its target capital structure, it will issue either $150 million or $200 million of new debt at par. In either case, $100 million will be employed to refund the existing bond issue. The remainder will be employed to buy back outstanding shares of Traynor's common stock. If the $150 million bond issue is employed, the coupon interest rate will be 10 percent and k_s^L will increase to 12.5 percent. If the $200 million issue is employed, the coupon interest rate is 11 percent and k_s^L will be 14 percent. The marginal corporate tax rate is 30 percent, and all earnings are paid out as cash dividends.

a. If the bonds are selling at 115 percent of par, what is the current total value, V, of the firm (before any refinancing)?

b. What is the total value, V, of the firm if the $150 million bond issue is sold? The $200 million issue? (Assume the market value of the bonds is equal to their par value.)

c. What action should Traynor take?

Minimize WACC

15.9 Howell Graphics is doing some capital structure planning. Its investment bankers have estimated after-tax costs of equity and debt at various levels of debt as follows:

Total Debt to Total Assets	k_i	k_s
0	5.4%	12.0%
0.10	5.4	12.2
0.20	5.8	12.7
0.30	6.3	13.2
0.40	6.9	14.1
0.50	7.9	15.6
0.60	9.0	17.4

Based on this information, at what ratio of total debt to total assets is Howell's target capital structure?

Target Capital Structure, Market Value, and Cost of Capital

15.10 Big Three Enterprises is in the process of determining its target capital structure. The firm is currently all-equity-financed, but is thinking about issuing debt and using the proceeds to retire some of its common stock. The risk-free rate is 6 percent, there is no growth, and all earnings are paid out as cash dividends. Based on a good deal of internal discussion, and using some projections made by its investment bankers, Big Three has come up with the following schedule:

Total Debt to Total Assets (1)	EPS (2)	Beta (3)	$k_s^L = k_{RF} + \beta(k_M - k_{RF})$ (4)	Market Price, P_0 (2)/(4) (5)
0%	$2.00	0.80	10.8	$ ___
10	2.20	___	11.4	19.30
20	2.38	1.00	___	19.83
30	2.55	1.10	___	___
40	2.68	___	13.5	___
50	2.80	1.40	___	___
60	2.90	___	___	17.90

a. Fill in the schedule above. At what ratio of total debts to total assets is the market price maximized?

b. After completing (a), your boss asks: "What will be the impact on the firm's cost of capital?" To provide an answer, you have begun preparing the following schedule:

Proportion in Debt (1)	After-Tax Cost of Debt (2)	Weighted Debt Cost (1) × (2) (3)	Proportion in Equity (4)	k_s^L [from (a)] (5)	Weighted Equity Cost (4) × (5) (6)	Weighted Average Cost of Capital (3) + (6) (7)
0.00	4.8%	0	1.0	10.8%	10.8%	10.8%
0.10	4.8	___	___	___	___	___
0.20	5.1	___	___	___	___	___
0.30	5.4	___	___	___	___	___
0.40	6.0	___	___	___	___	___
0.50	6.9	___	___	___	___	___
0.60	7.8	___	___	___	___	___

Complete the schedule. Does the minimum WACC occur at the same total debt to total asset level where the market price of Big Three's stock is maximized? Explain.

Basic EPS-EBIT Analysis

15.11 Harrison Appliances is considering raising $5 million by selling 200,000 shares of stock or by issuing 8 percent coupon rate bonds at par. There are presently 100,000 shares of common stock outstanding, the tax rate is 35 percent, and Harrison already pays $100,000 in interest before any new financing.

a. What is the crossover point where the EPS will be the same for either financing plan? (*Note:* Don't forget the existing interest.)

b. If you are told there is a 50 percent chance EBIT will be $600,000, and a 50 percent chance it will be $1,000,000, which plan would you recommend? Why?

Crossover EBIT: Number of Shares

15.12 A firm is considering two different financing plans. Under plan I the interest is $8,000 and there are 1,000 shares of common stock outstanding. Under plan II the interest is $2,000. If the crossover EBIT (i.e., EBIT*) is $20,000 and the marginal tax rate is 30 percent, how many shares of common stock are outstanding for plan II?

Preferred Stock and Half Common Stock/ Half Debt

15.13 Joy Regulator currently has 100,000 shares of common stock outstanding with a market price of $60 per share. It also has $2 million (par value) in 6 percent coupon rate bonds outstanding. The firm is considering a $3 million expansion program that can be financed employing either (1) preferred stock sold at par with a 7 percent cash dividend, or (2) half common stock (sold at $60 per share) and half 8 percent coupon rate bonds (sold at par). The tax rate is 40 percent.

a. What is the indifferent EBIT between the two plans? (*Note:* Don't forget the existing interest.)

b. If EBIT is expected to be $1 million after the financing, what is the EPS under the two plans?

(Do only if using Pinches Disk.)

c. If the marginal tax rate is 20 percent, what are your answers to (a) and (b)?

d. What are your answers to (a), (b), and (c) if the expected EBIT is $1,500,000, instead of $1,000,000? [*Note:* The tax rate is 40 percent until (c).]

e. Now suppose plan (1) is to sell preferred stock at par with an 8 percent cash dividend, and plan (2) is to sell 60 percent common stock (at $60 per share) and 40 percent 9 percent coupon rate bonds (sold at par). How will these plans affect your answers to (a) through (d)? [*Note:* (a) through (c) have an expected EBIT of $1,000,000.]

Impact of Both Investment and Financing Decisions on Market Value

15.14 Louisiana General is an all-equity firm. The firm has 200,000 shares of common stock outstanding, the EPS is $2, and all earnings are paid out to the stockholders as dividends. The current market value of the stock is $20 per share, and the required rate of return on equity is 10 percent. Louisiana General is considering two alternative plans to raise $3 million for a new and highly promising investment project, as follows: common stock—issue 150,000 more shares at $20 per share; debt—issue $3 million of 9 percent coupon rate bonds. After the new investment, Louisiana General expects EBIT to be $1,400,000. The tax rate is 35 percent.

a. Calculate the EPS (and dividends per share) under each plan after the expansion.

b. If the required return on equity stays at 10 percent when common stock is employed, what is the new market price per share?

c. If bonds are used, the required return increases to 12 percent. What is the new market price per share if bonds are used?

d. Explain why the market price calculated in (b) is higher than the beginning market price of $20. Then explain why the market price calculated in (c) is greater than that calculated in (b). How does this relate to the basic business of the firm (business risk), and the financing employed (financial risk)?

e. Which financing plan do you recommend? Why?

Cash Flow Analysis ✕

15.15 Armour Motors is undertaking a thorough cash flow analysis. At present the firm has no debt or preferred stock outstanding. Although Armour is profitable and expects substantial long-run positive cash flows, it is experiencing a temporary problem. The forecasted financial information for next year, before any financing, is as follows:

Cash inflows from sales	$6 million
Cash wages and salaries	$2.2 million
Cash payments for materials used in production process	$2.8 million
Other cash outflows *including taxes*	$700,000

Even though the year is expected to be a poor one, Armour is considering expanding through a $5 million bond issue with a 13 percent coupon interest rate. Armour's current cash position is $600,000. Under no circumstances does it want to lower its cash balance to less than $300,000. The tax rate is 30 percent.

a. Based on the forecasted information, what is the projected addition to Armour's cash level?

b. What is the amount of cash outflow for interest on the new bond issue before and after taxes?

c. Based on your analysis, should Armour issue the bond?

References

Three classic articles in this area are

MILLER, MERTON H. "Debt and Taxes." *Journal of Finance* 32 (May 1977), pp. 261–275.

MODIGLIANI, FRANCO, AND MERTON H. MILLER. "Corporate Income Taxes and the Cost of Capital: A Correction." *American Economic Review* 53 (June 1963), pp. 433–443.

MODIGLIANI, FRANCO, AND MERTON H. MILLER. "The Cost of Capital, Corporation Finance, and the Theory of Investment." *American Economic Review* 48 (June 1958), pp. 261–297.

Of the many articles and books on capital structure, some recent ones include

BOQUIST, JOHN A., AND WILLIAM T. MOORE. "Inter-Industry Leverage Differences and the DeAngelo–Masulis Tax Shield Hypothesis." *Financial Management* 13 (Spring 1984), pp. 5–9.

DAVIS, ALFRED H. R. "Effective Tax Rates as Determinants of Canadian Capital Structure." *Financial Management* 16 (Autumn 1987), pp. 22–28.

DEANGELO, HARRY, AND RONALD W. MASULIS. "Optimal Capital Structure Under Corporate and Personal Taxation." *Journal of Financial Economics* 8 (March 1980), pp. 3–30.

EMERY, DOUGLAS R., AND ADAM K. GEHR, JR. "Tax Options, Capital Structure, and Miller Equilibrium: A Numerical Illustration." *Financial Management* 17 (Summer 1988), pp. 30–40.

MASULIS, RONALD W. *The Debt/Equity Choice.* Cambridge, Mass.: Ballinger, 1988.

MASULIS, RONALD W. "The Impact of Capital Structure Change on Firm Value: Some Estimates." *Journal of Finance* 38 (March 1983), pp. 107–126.

MYERS, STEWART C. "The Capital Structure Puzzle." *Journal of Finance* 39 (July 1984), pp. 575–592.

MYERS, STEWART C., AND NICHOLAS S. MAJLUF. "Corporate Financing and Investment Decisions When Firms Have Information that Investors Do Not Have." *Journal of Financial Economics* 13 (June 1984), pp. 187–22.

PREZAS, ALEXANDROS. "Effects of Debt on the Degrees of Operating and Financial Leverage." *Financial Management* 16 (Summer 1987), pp. 39–44.

SARIG, ODED, AND JAMES SCOTT. "The Puzzle of Financial Leverage Clienteles." *Journal of Finance* 40 (December 1985), pp. 1459–1467.

TALMOR, ELI, ROBERT HAUGEN, AND AMIR BARNEA. "The Value of the Tax Subsidy on Risky Debt." *Journal of Business* 58 (April 1985), pp. 191–202.

TITMAN, SHERIDAN, AND ROBERTO WESSELS. "The Determinants of Capital Structure Choice." *Journal of Finance* 43 (March 1988), pp. 1–19.

16 | Dividend Policy and Internal Financing

Overview

- Under the residual theory of dividends, firms make their investment decisions and then pay out any remaining funds as cash dividends. Accordingly, in theory, the market price of a firm's stock is not influenced by the firm's cash dividend policy.

- In practice, firms act as if cash dividends are important. Most adopt a smoothed residual dividend policy. This policy includes maintaining a target payout ratio and a target capital structure.

- Other things being equal, stock repurchases increase the earnings per share and market price of the remaining shares. Neither stock splits nor stock dividends by themselves benefit stockholders.

- Theoretical and empirical evidence suggests that changes in cash dividends, repurchases, and stock splits are viewed as signals about the firm's future cash flows.

Middle South Utilities failed to obtain rate increases in Louisiana and Mississippi to help finance its $3.5 billion Grand Gulf Unit 1 nuclear reactor. That announcement stirred rumors on Wall Street. Was Middle South's cash dividend in jeopardy? A spokesperson for Middle South was quick to respond: "We're certainly going to do all we can to make sure the dividend isn't interrupted. That is something to which we are truly and fully committed." Most firms treat cash dividends as important, yet there are vast differences in dividend policies. Such firms as TIE/Communications, Lotus Development, COMPAQ Computer, and Mack Trucks have never paid cash dividends on their common stock. On the other hand, Citicorp has paid cash dividends since 1813, Manufacturers Hanover since 1852, Bassett Furniture since 1935, and General Motors since 1915.

Other dividend-type decisions also have an impact on stockholders. In the past few years, many firms have started, or increased, stock repurchase plans. While technically not a dividend, we will see that repurchases have some of the same effects as paying cash dividends.

Dividends and Financing

In order to maximize the size of the pie, or value of the firm, we need to explore the firm's cash dividend policy. The question is, does a high or a low (or no) cash dividend policy maximize the value of the firm? Or should it simply repurchase shares of its common stock—which can be an alternative approach for distributing cash flows back to the owners? We will see that the answers to these questions are somewhat messy—and we are not completely sure how much a firm's dividend policy affects the value of the firm.

The decision to pay cash dividends is simultaneously a decision not to reinvest this same cash in the firm. To see this, consider the relationship between available cash flow and possible uses, shown in Figure 16.1. A firm's available cash comes

Figure 16.1 Relationship Between Available Cash Flow and Potential Uses

The more cash distributed to stockholders, the less available for maintaining ongoing operations and expansion or the more new external financing that must be obtained.

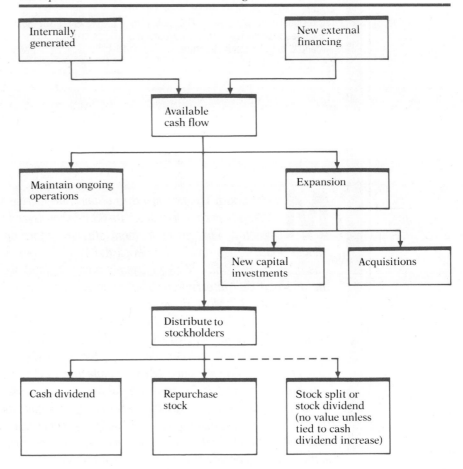

from two sources—internally generated and new external financing. Once cash is on hand, it has three general uses. First, ongoing operations must be maintained. These include paying salaries, the cost of materials, marketing expenses, taxes, financing charges, maintaining and updating equipment, and so forth. The remaining funds are then available for one of two other purposes: expansion—through new capital investments or the acquisition of other firms—or distribution to the firm's stockholders. Other things being equal, the more cash distributed to stockholders, the less internally generated equity capital is available (which affects the firm's capital structure) and the less that can be included in the firm's capital budget. Thus, the firm's cash dividend decision simultaneously affects its capital structure and capital budgeting decisions. For analytical purposes we often separate the three areas of investment decisions, financing decisions, and dividend policy, but their interrelationship must be kept in mind.

Once the firm decides to make a distribution to investors, it has two primary means of doing so. These also appear in Figure 16.1. The first and most direct is through cash dividends. The second is through stock repurchases. Many firms also declare stock splits and stock dividends that they would like you—as an investor—to consider valuable. As we shall see, however, neither a stock split nor a stock dividend by itself alters the value of the firm.

Before discussing these topics, it is useful to understand the magnitude of cash dividends. Table 16.1 presents a breakdown of total earnings, taxes, and cash dividends for firms during the 1979–1987 period. As we can see, taxes rose from 35 percent of earnings to 48 percent. The total amount of cash dividends increased every year—from $52.7 billion in 1979 to $95.5 billion in 1987. Over this period, the percentage increase in cash dividends was substantially in excess of the increase in earnings (before or after taxes); this was accomplished by increasing the dividend payout ratio (cash dividends divided by earnings after taxes). Also, consider the following data, which shows the percentage increase in both cash dividends and inflation.

Year	Total Cash Dividends (Percent Change)	Consumer Price Index (Percent Change)
1979	12.1%	11.3%
1980	10.2	13.5
1981	12.0	10.4
1982	6.3	6.0
1983	5.4	3.2
1984	8.4	4.0
1985	5.3	3.6
1986	6.0	1.9
1987	8.3	3.6
Mean	8.2	6.4

(SOURCE: *Federal Reserve Bulletin*, various issues.)

Many firms have expressly stated that one of their goals is to increase cash dividends at a rate at least equal to the inflation rate. An examination of this data indicates that total cash dividends increased faster than inflation in 8 out of the most recent 9 years.

Although there are many differences, firms in general pay out a sizable portion

Table 16.1   Total Earnings, Taxes, and Cash Dividends for Business Firms (In billions)

Dividend payout ratios have increased due to continued increases in total cash dividends being paid, coupled with little or no growth in earnings after taxes. (SOURCE: Federal Reserve Bulletin, *various issues.*)

Year	Taxes			Dividends		
	Taxes (1)	Earnings Before Taxes (2)	Taxes as a Percentage of Before-Tax Earnings (1)/(2) (3)	Cash Dividends Paid (4)	Earnings After Taxes (5)	Dividend Payout Ratio (4)/(5) (6)
1979	$ 87.6	$252.7	34.7%	$52.7	$165.1	31.9%
1980	84.7	242.4	34.9	58.1	157.8	36.8
1981	81.2	232.1	35.0	65.1	150.9	43.1
1982	60.7	165.5	36.7	69.2	104.8	66.0
1983	75.8	203.2	37.3	72.9	127.4	57.2
1984	93.9	239.9	39.1	79.0	146.1	54.1
1985	96.4	224.2	43.0	83.2	127.8	65.1
1986	106.6	236.3	45.1	88.2	129.8	68.0
1987	133.8	276.7	48.4	95.5	142.9	66.8

of their cash flows in the form of cash dividends. Also, the total dollar amount of dividends paid out continues to increase with each passing year and tends, over time, to exceed the rate of inflation. This understanding is important, given (1) the many factors that influence dividend policy, and (2) the tremendous differences of opinion concerning the importance of dividend policy. It is to a discussion of these topics that we now turn.

Does Dividend Policy Matter?

Next to the firm's appropriate capital structure and capital budgeting techniques, the dividend decision has probably generated the most discussion in financial management. The controversy centers around this question: Does the firm's cash dividend policy influence the value of its common stock? Alternatively, we could phrase the question as follows: Does dividend policy influence the required return on equity capital? To address this question, we begin by discussing the residual theory of dividends. Then we examine possible influences on the value of the firm's stock and other factors that influence dividend policy in practice.

The Residual Theory of Dividends

In previous chapters we discussed the role of investment opportunities, the firm's cost of capital, and the target capital structure. In general, we saw that the firm's optimal capital budget and its cost of capital were determined simultaneously, with the firm's capital structure taken as an intervening variable. The same basic approach can be employed to determine how much the firm should pay out in the form of cash dividends, and how much should be retained internally for capital investment.

The basis of the *residual theory of dividends* is that investors are as well or better off if the firm retains and reinvests internally generated funds, instead of paying them out, *provided* the investment opportunities facing the firm are at least as good as those facing investors. Under the residual theory, the firm's dividend policy would be the following:

1. Establish the optimum capital budget—that is, accept all projects with positive net present values.
2. Determine the amount of common equity needed to finance the new investments while maintaining the firm's target capital structure.
3. Use internally generated funds to supply this equity whenever possible.
4. Pay cash dividends only to the extent that internally generated funds remain after taking all appropriate capital investment opportunities.

The residual theory of dividends is concerned with the "left over" internally generated funds. Under this theory, cash dividends should be paid only if there is cash left over after making the investment decision.

Consider the example of Pacific Industries, which finances 40 percent of its investments via debt and the remaining 60 percent with common equity. The firm's internally generated funds are $12 million which, in part or total, can be distributed to the stockholders or reinvested in the firm. The investment opportunities facing Pacific are as follows:

Project	Initial Investment (In millions)	IRR
A	$5	25%
B	3	21
C	6	18
D	6	16
E	4	13
F	5	10

These are graphed in Figure 16.2, along with the firm's cost of capital of 14 percent. As shown, Pacific's WACC indicates that projects A, B, C, and D, requiring an initial outlay of $20 million, should be undertaken. Out of this $20 million, $12 million [i.e., ($20 million)(0.60)] in equity financing should be employed. Since the $12 million needed is exactly equal to the internally generated funds, Pacific would use these funds for capital investment and thus pay no cash dividends. The other $8 million required to finance the capital investments would be secured via debt financing.

If, on the other hand, Pacific's WACC had been higher so that only projects A, B, and C had been taken, a total of $14 million would be needed for capital investment. Sixty percent of this, or $8.4 million [i.e., ($14 million)(0.60)], would be provided via internally generated funds. The remainder, $12 million minus $8.4 million, or $3.6 million, would be distributed to the firm's common stockholders as a cash dividend.

Under the residual dividend theory, cash dividends are paid only if funds are left over after accepting all profitable capital budgeting projects. *The value of the firm is a function of its investment decisions. Thus, the residual theory suggests that dividend policy is a passive variable and therefore should have no influence on the value of the firm.*

Figure 16.2 Investment Opportunities and Cost of Capital Schedules for Pacific Industries

Pacific would accept all projects providing a return equal to or greater than its WACC of 14 percent. Hence, A, B, C, and D would be accepted, and E and F rejected.

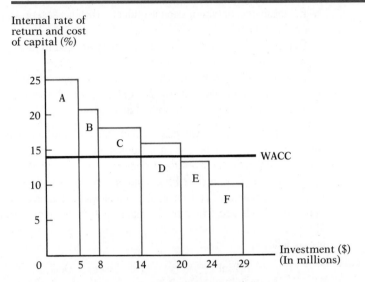

We should pause here and clarify one point before going on. In Chapter 6, we said that cash dividends are the foundation for the valuation of common stock. Thus, the market value of a share of stock is equal to the present value of all future cash dividends. Although this is true, the timing of the dividends can vary. When we say that dividend policy does not matter, we are simply saying that the present value of the future cash dividends remains unchanged even though dividend policy may influence their timing. Dividends, including liquidating dividends, can still be paid, but it is a matter of indifference *when* they are paid as long as their present value remains unchanged.

Arguments for Relevance

Before concluding that dividend policy has no impact on the value of the firm, it is necessary to consider whether there are factors that would suggest that a high or a low dividend payout ratio might influence the market value of the firm's stock, and thereby its cost of capital. First we consider factors suggesting that a high payout ratio increases the value of the stock. Then we consider arguments for a low payout ratio. In both cases, our concern is with the potential impact of the firm's cash dividend policy on the market price of its common stock.

High Payout

Four arguments are typically advanced to explain why there may be a preference among investors for high dividend payouts which, other things being equal, would be associated with a higher market value for the firm's common stock. These are (1) resolution of uncertainty, (2) signaling, (3) desire for current income, and (4) tax effects.

Resolution of Uncertainty. One argument presented in favor of a price effect is that by paying dividends, the firm resolves investor uncertainty. Since the retention of funds and promise of future dividends is uncertain, investors may prefer higher current dividends. Accordingly, they would bid up the market price for firms with high payout ratios. Although the basic business risk of the firm is not influenced, it is argued that investor perception of the riskiness decreases, thereby causing the market price to increase.

Our basic valuation framework is $P_0 = D_1/(k_s - g)$, where P_0 is the current market price, D_1 are the cash dividends expected at time $t = 1$, k_s is the investors' required rate of return, and g is the expected growth rate in cash dividends. If the investors' perception of risk decreases, their required rate of return, k_s, will decrease. If the cash dividend, D_1, is $3, k_s is 16 percent, and g is 8 percent, the initial price is

$$\text{price with no uncertainty resolution} = P_0 = \frac{\$3.00}{0.16 - 0.08} = \$37.50$$

On the other hand, if a higher payout ratio resolves investor uncertainty, and everything else remains the same, the required rate of return might decrease to 15 percent. In that case, the market price would be

$$\text{price with uncertainty resolution} = P_0 = \frac{\$3.00}{0.15 - 0.08} = \$42.86$$

Hence, if a high payout ratio reduces investor uncertainty, the market price of the firm's common stock increases.

Signaling. A second point often cited is that in a risky world with heterogeneous expectations and less than perfect markets, the cash dividend policy communicates information, or provides a signal, about the firm's future cash flows over and above any existing information. An increase in the payout ratio would be viewed as indicative of the future cash flows of the firm, and the market price of the firm's common stock would increase simply as a result of the increased cash dividends.

This viewpoint has been strengthened in recent years by a variety of theoretical and empirical evidence. All of it suggests that dividend initiations (that is, when a firm first starts to pay cash dividends) and unexpected increases in cash dividends lead to an increase in the value of the firm's stock. Additionally, there is evidence that dividend initiations are also associated with future increases in the firm's earnings (and hence, its cash flow). This suggests that dividends do signal unique information about the future prospects of the firm.

Desire for Current Income. Another factor might be investor preferences for current income. In Chapter 6 (Figure 6.6), the total returns on common stock investment between 1960 and 1987 were examined. Cash dividends provided almost 40 percent of the total returns from investing in common stock during this period. In addition, there is much less risk associated with cash dividends than with capital appreciation or loss, as evidenced by the much lower variability for the dividends. Investors with a preference for current income would favor a high-payout firm and hence might bid its price up.

Tax Effects. For corporations, as we have noted previously, 70 percent of the cash dividends received from the investment in another firm are excluded from the firm's income.[1] For a firm in the 34 percent marginal tax bracket, the tax rate on cash dividend income is only 10.2 percent [(1 − 0.70)(0.34)]. This is lower than the effective tax rate of 34 percent the same firm would pay on any gain realized from selling the stock. Although somewhat minor, this effect favors cash dividends, and hence might serve to drive up the price of the firm's common stock.

Low Payout

Two factors are often cited as favoring a low dividend payout. They are (1) flotation costs, and (2) other tax effects. Also, transaction costs may work both ways.

Flotation Costs. As we saw in Chapter 14, the presence of flotation costs makes the cost of internally generated common equity cheaper than the cost of issuing new common stock. If a firm's cost of internal common equity is 16 percent, its cost of external common stock may be 18 or 19 percent. This is due to the transaction costs and underpricing that occur when additional common stock is sold. Flotation costs may cause firms to favor retaining more via a low dividend payout policy, since it reduces their cost of capital.

Tax Effects. Prior to the Tax Reform Act of 1986, capital gains were taxed at a lower rate than ordinary income. This tax treatment created a bias toward low-payment firms since the firm, by retaining the cash flow and reinvesting it, should cause the market price to rise. When the investor sold the stock, he or she realized more after-tax income than if he or she had received the same present-value dollar amount via cash dividends. This tax effect did not affect tax-free institutional investors. Under the current tax code the different tax rates for ordinary income versus capital gains no longer exist. A tax effect may still exist, however, since the timing of when capital gains are to be realized (and taxes are paid) still exists. No such option exists when dividends are paid since the dividends must be reported and taxes paid.

Transactions Costs. In the absence of transactions costs, investors could always buy or sell securities to create their own cash "dividend" stream if they did not like the policy followed by the firm. The presence of transactions costs, however, means that investors receive less than 100 percent on the dollar when they buy or sell securities. Investors preferring high current income cannot, without incurring additional costs, sell stock. Likewise, those preferring a low level of current income also incur additional costs on reinvesting the cash dividends. The net effect may be to cut both ways—transactions costs may create a preference for either a high or a low level of cash dividends.

The Clientele Effect

Because of these factors, we see that certain investors might have a preference for high- or low-payout firms. Investors with low incomes and high current needs

[1] If the firm owns 20 percent or more of the firm, it may exclude 80 percent of the dividends.

would favor high-payout firms. Investors in high income brackets would favor low-payout firms. This has often been called the *clientele effect.* That is, depending on the cash dividend policy a firm establishes, it attracts a certain clientele of investors. Once that clientele is established, it may be that dividend policy does not directly influence the value of the firm's stock. A significant shift in the firm's cash dividend policy however, would disrupt the firm's clientele, causing price effects until a new investor clientele owns the firm's common stock. Some empirical testing lends support to the idea of a clientele effect.

Although there has been both extensive debate and substantial empirical testing, there is no consensus on another issue. That is, whether or not the firm's cash dividend policy *by itself* influences the value of the common stock. This is especially true when imperfect markets, investor heterogeneity, and after-tax returns are considered. The best we can say right now is that the firm's cash dividend policy may influence the market value of the firm's stock—and then again it may not! So most managers look at a number of other factors that come into play when the cash dividend decision is made.

Other Factors   In addition to possible price effects, other factors influence dividend policy in practice. These are (1) investment opportunities, (2) liquidity and profitability, (3) earnings stability, and (4) control.

Investment Opportunities

As indicated by the residual theory, the investment opportunities facing the firm may affect its cash dividend policy. We often see stable firms in mature industries paying out much more in cash dividends than smaller, fast-growing firms.

Liquidity and Profitability

The cash position of the firm can also influence cash dividends. Firms with a shortage of cash often restrict or discontinue cash dividends. Highly profitable firms with substantial cash positions often increase their cash dividends (or repurchase some of their own outstanding common stock). One reason for cash-rich firms to pay more dividends is to provide greater protection against a possible takeover by another firm. By paying higher dividends, the cash-rich firm accomplishes two things— it makes its current stockholders happy and reduces its cash position, thus becoming a less tempting takeover target.

Earnings Stability

Another factor often considered in practice is the stability of the firm's earnings. Other things being equal, more stable firms are often in a better position to pay larger cash dividends than less stable firms. This is because they can plan for the future with much more certainty than highly cyclical firms. Public utility firms, for example, pay high cash dividends. They can do this, in part, because of their relatively stable operating environment.

Control

For many smaller- and medium-sized firms, ownership control is an important issue. They may be reluctant to sell more common stock and will prefer to retain more internally generated funds to provide the equity capital needed for growth. By using internally generated common equity plus any borrowing required, they may be able simultaneously to maintain control *and* meet the firm's capital needs.

Constraints

Finally, there are some constraints that may inhibit the firm's ability to pay cash dividends. These involve (1) contractual restrictions, (2) legal restrictions, and (3) taxes on improperly accumulated earnings.

Contractual Restrictions

Bond indentures, term loan agreements, and even preferred stock provisions may often impose restrictions on the payment of cash dividends. These may include requirements for the maintenance of a certain level of working capital or minimum current or times interest earned ratios, to an inability to pay cash dividends on common stock until the preferred stockholders have received their dividends. Although these restrictions typically do not inhibit the firm's ability to pay dividends, they may when a firm is experiencing financial difficulties. From the creditors' or preferred stockholders' point of view, that is exactly what restrictions of this type are intended to do.

Legal Restrictions

Most state laws governing the incorporation of the firm provide statutory restrictions prohibiting the firm from paying cash dividends under certain conditions. These vary from state to state, but usually include a restriction on the firm's dividend-paying ability when the firm's liabilities exceed its assets, the anticipated dividend exceeds the retained earnings, or the dividend would be paid from the firm's invested capital.

Taxes on Improperly Accumulated Earnings

Firms do not have to pay cash dividends as long as the funds are used to purchase productive assets. But if the firm does not pay cash dividends and instead elects to keep increasing its level of cash and marketable securities, problems may arise. If the Internal Revenue Service finds the level of cash and marketable securities is beyond that deemed reasonable to meet liquidity needs, a special surtax is imposed on the improper accumulation. Although infrequently used, this requirement is designed to ensure that smaller firms do not avoid paying taxes through an excessive accumulation of cash.

Where Does That Leave Us?

Neither theory nor empirical testing provides a complete answer to the question of whether dividend policy influences the market value of the firm's common stock. But in practice firms (and their boards of directors) act as though dividend policy is an important decision. They view it as being important both in and of itself, and because of its signaling content. Stability of dividends is perceived as being important; firms prefer to maintain a steady and increasing level of cash dividends per share over time. Equally important, there is an extreme reluctance to reduce cash dividends. Most firms in practice follow what might be called a *smoothed residual dividend policy*. After taking into account many of the items discussed previously, they set the cash dividend policy based on the following considerations:

Timing of Cash Dividends

The timing of cash dividends is a known event because most firms establish a dividend policy and announce beforehand when they will pay the next dividend. Therefore, the dividend itself is not new, but the size may differ, or a firm occasionally may elect not to pay a dividend. In the face of a relatively known event, why do dividends provide information to investors?

Among a number of studies that have examined this issue, the results of a recent study are summarized in the figure.[1] We see firms that actually carry through with the anticipated dividends experience a significant positive abnormal return at day 0 and day +1, and even a few days subsequent to the announcement of the cash dividend. On the other hand, those firms that elect to omit a cash dividend suffer a significant decrease in their returns. In attempting to explain these results the study looked at the variances of stock returns and found them to be larger right around the event. This larger variance suggests part of the abnormal returns may be compensation for increased risk. Risk itself, however, does not entirely explain the abnormal returns. The authors concluded there are unknown factors still at work that cause returns to either increase or decrease substantially right around the dividend announcement date.

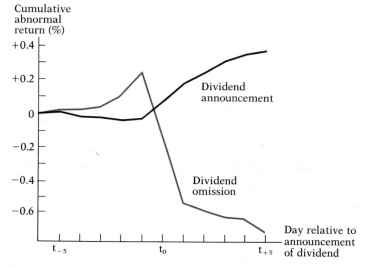

[1] Avner Kalay and Uri Loewenstein. "Predictable Events and Excess Returns: The Case of Dividend Announcements." *Journal of Financial Economics* 14 (September 1985).

1. The dividend is set at a constant dollar amount per share.
2. A target dividend payout ratio is established, which the firm plans to maintain over time.
3. Dividends will be increased when and if it appears the increased dollar amount per share can be maintained.

4. The dollar amount of cash dividends paid per share will be decreased only with great reluctance.
5. Over the long run, the firm attempts to finance capital expenditures with internally generated funds and debt (supplemented only occasionally, if at all, by new common stock), while fluctuating around its target capital structure.

This smoothed residual dividend policy is consistant with some early work done by Lintner. In addition, it is consistant with the pecking order theory suggested by Myers (as discussed in Chapter 15). A firm's dividend policy is determined simultaneously with its investment and financing decisions.

Dividend Policy in Practice

In assessing the firm's dividend policy in practice, it is useful to look at what firms do. In Table 16.2, the earnings per share, dividends per share, and payout ratios are presented for Alcan Aluminum, Baltimore Gas & Electric, and Union Pacific. Alcan Aluminum has had widely fluctuating dividends and payout ratios. The payout was around 20 percent for the 1979–1980 period, then increased substantially in the next 6 years in the presence of falling earnings. Baltimore Gas & Electric has had a very stable dividend policy that involves paying out 55 to 70 percent of earnings in the form of cash dividends. Union Pacific has had stable and increasing dividends, even though earnings per share suffered a slip in the 1982–1983 period. These are indicative of some of the intrafirm differences in cash dividends.

Industry Differences

Dividend payout policies also vary, to an extent, depending on the primary industry in which the firm is located. This is the result of different amounts of business risk between industries, the state of growth and maturity of the industry, investment

Table 16.2 Dividend Payout for Three Firms

Alcan Aluminum's cash dividends and dividend payout ratio have fluctuated widely due to wide swings in earnings. Both Baltimore Gas & Electric and Union Pacific have had more consistent payout ratios; however, both have changed some in recent years. (SOURCE: *Annual reports for each of the firms cited.*)

	Alcan Aluminum Limited			Baltimore Gas & Electric Company			Union Pacific Corporation		
Year	Dividends per Share	EPS	Dividend Payout	Dividends per Share	EPS	Dividend Payout	Dividends per Share	EPS	Dividend Payout
1979	$0.70	$3.35	21%	$1.20	$1.70	71%	$1.21	$4.01	30%
1980	0.90	4.47	20	1.25	1.82	69	1.45	4.22	34
1981	1.20	2.16	56	1.33	1.85	72	1.65	4.27	39
1982	0.90	(0.46)	*	1.40	2.04	69	1.80	2.94	61
1983	0.60	0.43	140	1.46	2.48	59	1.80	3.57	50
1984	0.80	1.51	53	1.55	2.77	56	1.80	4.01	45
1985	0.73	0.17	429	1.68	2.80	60	1.80	4.18	43
1986	0.53	1.18	45	1.78	3.15	57	1.85	4.20	44
1987	0.58	2.59	22	1.88	3.47	54	2.00	4.90	41

* Not a meaningful figure.

Table 16.3 Selected Industry Dividend Payout Ratios for 1987

Notice the differences from lows for firms in apparel and metals to highs for the electric utility industry. (SOURCE: Value Line Investment Service, *various issues. Reprinted by permission of the publisher. Copyright © 1989 by Value Line, Inc.*)

Industry	Payout Ratio
Apparel	27%
Chemical (basic)	44
Drug	43
Electric utility (West)	70
Food processing	37
Grocery store	36
Insurance (diversified)	38
Machinery	52
Metals and mining (general)	27
Newspaper	34
Retail store	34
Steel (general)	30
Textile	45

needs and profitability, and a follow-the-leader effect. In Table 16.3 we see a wide range of dividend payout ratios. The apparel, metals and mining, retail store, and steel industries paid out less than 35 percent of earnings in the form of cash dividends in 1987. On the other hand, the electric utility industry in the western part of the United States paid out 70 percent of its earnings in the form of cash dividends.

Not only do dividend payout ratios vary considerably between industries, they also vary among firms within a single industry. Consider the following data, which shows the 1987 dividend payout ratios for firms in the machine tool industry.

Firm	Dividends per Share	Payout Ratio
Acme-Cleveland	$0.40	*%
Brown & Sharpe	0.30	*
Cincinnati Milacron	0.72	*
Cross & Trecker	0	0
Gleason	0	0
Monarch Machine Tool	0.80	667
Norton	2.00	48
Snap-on Tools	0.70	33
Stanley Works	0.82	37
L. S. Starrett	0.55	27
Vermont American	0.35	19

* Not a meaningful figure.
(SOURCE: Value Line Investment Service, *November 18, 1988.* Reprinted by permission of the publisher. Copyright © 1989 by Value Line, Inc.)

We see that Acme-Cleveland paid cash dividends even though it suffered a loss, while Brown & Sharpe and Cincinnati Milacron paid out more than they earned. On the other hand, Cross & Trecker and Gleason continued their policy of not paying

Table 16.4 **Number of Firms Taking Action on Cash Dividends**

These data are based on approximately 9,500 publicly traded stocks. Note the increases relative to decreases, and the number of extras. (SOURCE: Moody's Dividend Record, various issues.)

Year	Action				
	Increased	**Resumed**	**Decreased**	**Omitted**	**Extra**
1979	3,045	85	70	115	917
1980	2,483	82	127	122	879
1981	2,513	82	136	226	900
1982	1,805	97	322	319	676
1983	2,006	183	137	172	630
1984	2,085	162	95	199	630
1985	1,898	88	104	231	627
1986	1,685	93	148	257	462
1987	1,822	114	84	186	533

any cash dividends. These vastly different policies within an industry reflect the substantial differences among firms. Thus, although there do appear to be industry differences that influence cash dividend policies, we must not let these differences obscure the sizable intra-industry differences that exist as well.

Dividend Changes

Instead of examining payout ratios, we can examine the action taken by firms relative to increasing or decreasing cash dividends. In Table 16.4, the number of firms increasing, resuming, decreasing, or omitting cash dividends is presented for the 1979–1987 period. In the last few years, we see that the number of firms increasing their cash dividends has fallen compared to earlier years. This is the result of the slowness in parts of the economy, with the attendant impact on earnings and internally generated funds. In 1987, we see that the number of firms resuming cash dividends climbed, while the number decreasing or omitting them fell. This indicates the somewhat stronger financial health of many firms. The extreme reluctance of firms to decrease or eliminate cash dividends, however, is vividly highlighted by the small number of decreases or omissions in comparison to the number of increases or resumptions.

One other aspect of Table 16.4 deserves attention—the "extra" column. Many firms follow the practice of paying a regular cash dividend, and then in good years declaring a *dividend extra*. This allows them to have a stated amount of cash dividends per share that can be supplemented, if desired, without raising the stated rate to a new higher level. In this way, the basic per share rate will not have to be cut in bad years.

Dividend Payment Procedures

Cash dividends are normally paid quarterly. Assume a firm has decided to pay a cash dividend of 75 cents each quarter. The relevant dates that stockholders would be concerned about if they owned or contemplated purchasing the stock, and the payment procedure, might be as follows:

Amount	Date Declared	Ex-Dividend Date	Date of Record	Date Payable
$0.75	January 21	February 8	February 14	March 12
0.75	April 15	May 4	May 10	June 11
0.75	July 15	August 4	August 10	September 9
0.75	October 14	November 4	November 10	December 10

1. DECLARATION (OR ANNOUNCEMENT) DATE. This is the date the board of directors meets and issues a statement declaring the next quarter's cash dividends. For our example this is January 21 in the first quarter, April 15 in the second quarter, and so on. Once the dividends are declared, they become a legal liability of the firm. For example, the announcement would indicate that a dividend of 75 cents a share will be paid on March 12 to stockholders of record as of February 14.

2. EX-DIVIDEND DATE. The *ex-dividend date* is an arbitrary date established for the convenience of the securities industry. The ex-dividend date is the fourth business day (i.e., Monday through Friday) preceding the record date as fixed by the firm. Establishing this date enables the firm (or its registrar, who is usually a bank) to obtain an accurate determination of all stockholders by the record date. All shares owned before the ex-dividend date receive the cash dividend. Stock purchased on or after the ex day will not be entitled to the next cash dividend, since they will not be listed as an owner of record on the record date. For the firm in our example, the first quarter's record date was February 14; accordingly, the ex day is February 8.[2] If you purchased the stock on or before February 7, you received the dividend of 75 cents per share when it was paid on March 12. If you bought the stock on February 8, or anytime thereafter, the former owner is entitled to the cash dividend paid on March 12.[3]

3. RECORD DATE. The *record date* is the date the stockholder books are closed to determine who the current stockholders are.

4. PAYMENT DATE. The *payment date* is when the firm actually mails the dividend checks to its common stockholders.

The record date is important, but the ex-dividend date is actually more important in terms of deciding who is the owner of the stock for dividend purposes. Because of its importance for determining who is entitled to the next cash dividend, we would expect to see an adjustment in the firm's common stock market price on the ex-dividend date. If you owned the stock in our example on the day before the ex date, you would receive 75 cents on the next pay date. But since you will be 75 cents better off and the firm will be 75 cents worse off, what should happen to the market price of the firm's common stock on the ex day? Other things being equal, it should decrease by an amount approximately equal to the value of the cash dividend to be received.

---

[2] Note that in most cases a weekend will be involved, so the ex-dividend day is typically 6 calendar days preceding the record date.

[3] Exactly the same ex day procedure is employed when a stock split or stock dividend occurs, or when stock rights (discussed in Chapter 12) are employed.

Dividend Reinvestment Plans

In recent years many firms have instituted *dividend reinvestment plans*. Under these plans stockholders can reinvest their cash dividends in additional shares of common stock. The stock can be existing or newly issued shares. Under the first plan, a bank acting as trustee accumulates funds from all stockholders electing this option and then purchases shares in the open market. Costs are borne on a pro rata basis but are generally small because of the volume of purchases.

In the second type of plan, the cash dividends go to buy newly issued shares of stock. This may be accompanied by a 3 to 5 percent reduction in the purchase price from the stock's current market price. Often no other fees are charged to the stockholders. A new issue dividend reinvestment plan enables firms gradually to raise substantial amounts of new common stock capital. It has been estimated that in recent years about 25 percent of all new common stock issued has been through dividend reinvestment plans. Due to their advantages, these plans have continued to grow in popularity; over 700 major firms now have dividend reinvestment plans.

But although dividend reinvestment plans have grown in popularity, they have one drawback from the stockholder's standpoint. Stockholders must pay taxes on the cash dividends each year, even though they never receive any cash. This factor more than any other has probably prevented more investors from signing up for dividend reinvestment plans.

Repurchasing Stock

In addition to paying cash dividends, firms sometimes repurchase their stock and hold it as treasury stock. Repurchasing may be accomplished by a tender offer to all the firm's stockholders, by purchasing stock in the secondary market, or by agreeing with one or a small group of the firm's major investors to buy their shares. Many repurchases are small in amount; others are very large. With fewer shares outstanding after a repurchase, and assuming the repurchase does not adversely affect the firm's earnings, the earnings per share of the remaining shares will increase. This increase should result in a higher market price.

To see this, consider the example of Northern Airlines, which has earnings after taxes of $10 million and plans to use 40 percent ($4 million) of it for cash dividends or for repurchasing some of the firm's common stock. Remember that neither usage affects the firm's reported net income. There are 4 million shares outstanding, and the market price of the stock is $15 per share. Northern can use the $4 million to repurchase 250,000 shares of common stock at $16 per share,[4] or it can pay a cash dividend of $1 per share. The net effect of the repurchase would be as follows:

$$\text{current EPS} = \frac{\text{total earnings}}{\text{number of shares outstanding}} = \frac{\$10 \text{ million}}{4 \text{ million}} = \$2.50 \text{ per share}$$

$$\text{current P/E} = \frac{\text{market price per share}}{\text{earnings per share}} = \frac{\$15}{\$2.50} = 6 \text{ times}$$

---

[4] The $16 figure is chosen because it is the price at which nonselling investors are neither better nor worse off than selling investors.

$$\frac{\text{EPS after repurchasing}}{250{,}000 \text{ shares}} = \frac{\$10 \text{ million}}{3.75 \text{ million}} = \$2.667 \text{ per share}$$

$$\frac{\text{expected market price}}{\text{after repurchasing}} = (\text{P/E})(\text{EPS}) = (6)(\$2.667) = \$16 \text{ per share}$$

From this example, we see that investors receive a $1 benefit either way. If cash dividends are paid they receive the dollar directly; with the repurchase, the market price of the common stock increases by $1 to $16 per share. This occurs because we assumed that (1) the shares would be repurchased at exactly $16 per share, and (2) the P/E ratio remained constant. *If the firm pays less than $16, the remaining (or nonselling) investors are better off; if more than $16 is paid, the remaining investors are worse off.*

Although this is a purely mechanical exercise so far, it serves to highlight some aspects of repurchasing. In fact, firms that repurchase their common stock almost always repurchase shares while maintaining their current cash dividend policy. With this background, it is now possible to consider some of the advantages and disadvantages of repurchasing.

Advantages

From the firm's standpoint, there are a number of possible advantages to stock repurchases.

1. If a firm had a temporary excess of cash being generated but did not want to adjust its stated cash dividend policy, it might decide to repurchase some of its stock. This provides nonselling stockholders with an alternative form of a dividend.
2. By repurchasing, a firm may reduce its future cash dividend requirements, or alternatively raise the dividends per share paid to its remaining stockholders without increasing the total cash dividend drain on the firm.
3. Repurchases can be used to effect an immediate and often large-scale change in the firm's capital structure. For example, if a firm previously had no debt and decided its target capital structure should include 20 percent debt, it could issue a bond and use the proceeds to repurchase common stock, thereby affecting the capital structure realignment.
4. Repurchasing can also be used to signal information about the firm's future cash flows. Empirical evidence indicates that a firm's stock price increases when it announces a repurchase.

Prior to the Tax Reform Act of 1986, one other advantage—this time for individuals—existed. If stock was repurchased, the gains on the shares were taxed at the capital gains rate, providing the stock had been owned for at least 6 months. Cash dividends, however, were treated as ordinary income. Under the current tax code, there is no difference in the tax rate applied to cash dividends and capital gains. Hence, this advantage favoring repurchasing no longer exists.

Disadvantages

From the firm's standpoint, some disadvantages may result from repurchasing its own shares.

1. In the past, firms that repurchased substantial amounts of stock often had poorer growth and investment opportunities than firms that did not. Announcing a repurchase program might signal to investors that good investment opportunities did

not exist. This negative impact appears to have lessened in recent years as different types of firms started viewing repurchases as an alternative to increasing their dividend payout ratio.

2. From a legal standpoint, the SEC may raise some questions if it appears the firm is using the repurchases to manipulate the price of its common stock. The Internal Revenue Service may become interested if it appears the repurchases are primarily for the avoidance of taxes on cash dividends. If this occurs, the IRS can impose penalties, since the firm's activities fall under Section 531 of the tax code, which deals with improper accumulation of earnings.

On net, it appears firms will continue to repurchase shares of their common stock. This is particularly true since repurchasing has gained favor as a means of attempting to fend off unwanted corporate suitors, and as a means of "leveraging up" the firm's capital structure. Note, however, that by reducing the proportion of cash or marketable securities in a firm's asset structure, the risk composition of the firm may increase. This increased risk, if it occurs, must be weighed against the benefits expected to be derived from the repurchase.

Stock Splits and Dividends

In addition to paying cash dividends, and sometimes repurchasing their own outstanding common stock, firms often issue more shares via a stock split or a stock dividend. In the absence of any other simultaneous occurrence, the effects of a stock split or dividend can be summarized as follows:

1. There is no change in the firm's total assets, liabilities, stockholders' equity, earnings, cash dividends, or total market value.
2. There is a drop in the per share earnings, cash dividends, and common stock market price, and a corresponding increase in the number of shares of common stock outstanding.

The consequence of a stock split or stock dividend is to increase the number of shares held by each investor. But each share is worth less, since nothing of value has been created. *The net effect would seem to neither increase or decrease the total market value of the firm.*

The Difference

Stock splits and stock dividends have exactly the same effect from an economic standpoint. For accounting purposes, however, there are differences between a stock split and a stock dividend.

Accounting Treatment

The accounting treatment for a *stock split* is straightforward. First, the stockholders must approve increasing the number of shares of common stock. Then, for a 2-for-1 split, for example, the number of shares of common stock is doubled and the par value is halved. As shown in Table 16.5, Wilbur Industries had 1 million shares at a

Table 16.5 Effect of Stock Split or Stock Dividend on Wilbur Industries Stockholders' Equity Accounts

In both cases, the total remains $7,000,000. However, a stock dividend involves capitalizing some of the firm's retained earnings by a transfer to the common stock and additional paid-in capital accounts.

Before Stock Split or Stock Dividend	
Common stock (1 million shares outstanding, $2 par)	$2,000,000
Additional paid-in capital	550,000
Retained earnings	4,450,000
Total stockholders' equity	$7,000,000
After 2-for-1 Stock Split	
Common stock (2 million shares outstanding, $1 par)	$2,000,000
Additional paid-in capital	550,000
Retained earnings	4,450,000
Total stockholders' equity	$7,000,000
After 10 Percent Stock Dividend	
Common stock (1.1 million shares outstanding, $2 par)*†	$2,200,000
Additional paid-in capital†	1,350,000
Retained earnings†	3,450,000
Total stockholders' equity	$7,000,000

* 100,000 shares are issued.
† Based on a market price of $10, ($2)(100,000 shares) = $200,000 is added to the common stock. Likewise, ($10 − $2)(100,000 shares) = $800,000 is added to the additional paid-in capital account. Retained earnings is reduced by $1,000,000 ($200,000 + $800,000).

par value of $2 per share before the split. After the split, Wilbur had 2 million shares at a par of $1 per share.

With a *stock dividend,* the par value is not reduced, but an accounting entry is made to transfer capital from the retained earnings account to the common stock and additional paid-in capital accounts. The amount to be transferred is determined by the size of the stock dividend and the current market price of the firm's common stock. If Wilbur declares a 10 percent stock dividend, it will issue 100,000 (10 percent of 1,000,000 shares) more shares of stock. With a current market price of $10 per share, the transfer out of retained earnings will be $1,000,000. Finally, as also shown in Table 16.5, the common stock account will be increased by $200,000 [i.e., ($2 par)(100,000 shares)], and the remaining $800,000 will be added to the additional paid-in capital account. Note that for both a stock split and a stock dividend, Wilbur's total stockholders' equity is $7 million both before and after the transaction.

Beware of False Gifts

By itself a stock split or stock dividend is valueless to an investor, since nothing has happened to influence the firm's short- or long-run earnings or its ability to generate cash flows. To see this, consider the example of Wilbur Industries again. In Table 16.6, we see that before the split Wilbur had total earnings of $1,150,000, total cash dividends of $460,000, and with a stock price of $10 per share, a total

Table 16.6 Effect of 2-for-1 Stock Split on both Wilbur Industries and an Individual Investor

There can be no benefit from a stock split unless it causes the total market value of the firm to increase. Stock dividends are similar.

Wilbur Industries		Investor
Before Stock Split		
Total earnings	$1,150,000	Owns 10,000 shares, which is equal to 1
Total cash dividends	460,000	percent of total shares outstanding
Total shares outstanding	1,000,000	

$$\text{EPS} = \frac{\$1,150,000}{1,000,000} = \$1.15$$

Cash dividends received
= (10,000 shares)($0.46)
= $4,600

$$\text{DPS} = \frac{\$460,000}{1,000,000} = \$0.46$$

Market value of stock
= (10,000 shares)($10)
= $100,000

$$\text{Dividend payout ratio} = \frac{\$0.46}{\$1.15} = 40\%$$

Market price per share = $10

Total market value, S = ($10)(1,000,000)

$$= \$10 \text{ million}$$

After Stock Split

Total earnings	$1,150,000	Owns 20,000 shares, which is equal to 1
Total cash dividends	460,000	percent of total shares outstanding
Total shares outstanding	2,000,000	

$$\text{EPS} = \frac{\$1,150,000}{2,000,000} = \$0.575$$

Cash dividends received
= (20,000 shares)($0.23)
= $4,600

$$\text{DPS} = \frac{\$460,000}{2,000,000} = \$0.23$$

Market value of stock
= (20,000 shares)($5)
= $100,000

$$\text{Dividend payout ratio} = \frac{\$0.23}{\$0.575} = 40\%$$

Market price per share = $5

Total market value, S = ($5)(2,000,000)

$$= \$10 \text{ million}$$

market value of $10,000,000. After the 2-for-1 split, Wilbur still has earnings of $1,150,000, cash dividends of $460,000, and a total market value of $10,000,000. Likewise, as also shown in Table 16.6, an investor owning 1 percent of Wilbur stock does not benefit directly from the stock split.[5]

---

[5] If a stockholder is entitled to a fractional share, the firm will pay cash in lieu of the fractional share. For example, if an investor held 25 shares and a 10 percent stock dividend was declared, the stockholder would be entitled to 2.5 shares. If the market price of the stock was $30 per share, the stockholder would receive 2 full shares and $15 cash in lieu of the fractional share.

Table 16.7 Stock Splits, Reverse Splits, and Dividends

These data are based on approximately 9,500 firms. Hence, 10 to 15 percent of the firms tabulated by Moody's are involved each year. A reverse split decreases the number of shares of common stock outstanding. (SOURCE: Moody's Dividend Record, *various years.*)

Year	Stock Splits	Reverse Stock Splits	Stock Dividends	Total
1979	337	32	948	1,317
1980	457	28	953	1,438
1981	493	39	943	1,475
1982	282	46	704	1,032
1983	705	55	903	1,663
1984	392	58	783	1,233
1985	516	84	763	1,363
1986	736	84	854	1,674
1987	602	128	791	1,521

Why Declare a Stock Split or Stock Dividend?

In the absence of any value-creating activities, it would seem that not many companies would want to declare stock splits or stock dividends. As Table 16.7 shows, however, over 1,000 companies every year declare one or the other.[6] Why is this so?

1. Some firms declare a stock split or stock dividend at the same time as a cash dividend. They view this action as an extension of the firm's cash dividend policy. If the firm actually increases its total cash dividend payout, then stockholders are receiving more total cash dividends. Note, however, that the firm's dividend payout could be increased without simultaneously declaring a stock split or stock dividend.

2. Many firms apparently believe their stock has an optimal trading range. Perhaps this is between $20 and $50 per share. If the market price of the firm's common stock increases to, say, $70, the firm may declare a 2-for-1 split to drive the price down to about $35 per share. Implicit in this idea is that the total value of the firm will be more when it is in its "trading range" than when it is outside it.

3. A third possible reason for declaring stock splits or stock dividends involves the signaling idea discussed earlier in the chapter when we considered cash dividend policy. The essence of the argument is that firms declaring stock splits or dividends communicate information about future cash flows over and above any existing information. Empirical evidence lends some support to this idea because the market value of a firm's stock tends, other things being equal, to increase when the firm has a stock split.

4. A final possible reason sometimes given is "to conserve the firm's cash." Firms in financial difficulty fairly frequently say they will declare the dividend in the form of stock rather than cash. By doing so they conserve cash, but stockholders are worse off. This occurs because stockholders suffer the loss of the cash dividend,

---

[6] A *reverse split* is just the opposite of a stock split. If a firm had 10,000 shares of stock outstanding selling at $5 per share, a 1-for-5 reverse split would reduce the number of shares to 2,000 and increase the market price to $25 per share.

Stock Splits and Stock Dividends

Stock splits and stock dividends do not directly affect the future cash flows of the firm. In addition, nothing else of direct benefit is created other than splitting the pie (or number of shares of ownership) into more pieces. Recent evidence (as shown in the figure) indicates, however, significant positive abnormal returns occur when stock dividends and stock splits are announced.[1] In this study the "all" category includes stock dividends and stock splits that may have other contemporaneous information, such as cash dividends, merger announcements, and stock issuances being announced at the same time. The "pure" stock dividend and stock split data had no other information announced, nor any cash dividends being paid, right around the announcement date. The study concluded there must be some information associated with stock distributions that provides insight about the firm's future cash flows. How else can we explain increases in the returns on stocks, when nothing of value appears to have been created?

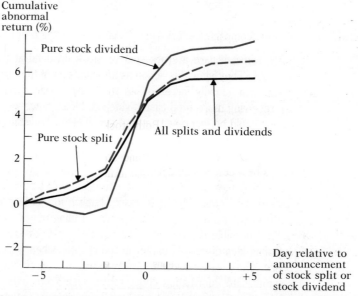

[1] Mark S. Grinblatt, Ronald W. Masulis, and Sheridan Titman. "The Valuation Effects of Stock Splits and Stock Dividends." *Journal of Financial Economics* 13 (December 1984).

and since the market value of each share of stock decreases proportionately as more shares are issued, the stockholders' total market value remains, at best, unchanged.

So why do firms continue to declare both stock dividends and stock splits? The answer appears to involve some elements of all the above. Although issuing additional shares of stock is much more expensive than issuing cash dividends, firms often use both stock splits and stock dividends to supplement their cash dividend policy and signal positive information about the future cash flows of the firm.

Summary

The firm's cash dividend decision involves determining how much of internally generated funds to pay out in the form of dividends, and how much to use for other corporate purposes. Two primary factors that influence the firm's dividend policy in practice are the level of the cash dividend and its stability. In determining cash dividend policy, firms consider many factors, including the policy's information (or signaling) content, stockholder desires, taxes, flotation costs, investment opportunities, liquidity and profitability, earnings stability, and control. In addition, some constraints exist relative to contractual restrictions and IRS regulations.

Most firms follow a policy consistent with the smoothed residual dividend approach. They establish both a dollar amount per share they plan to maintain and a percentage payout ratio around which they will fluctuate. Then the firm finances its corporate needs with internally generated funds and debt, while fluctuating around its target capital structure. Only under extreme circumstances do most firms issue new common stock to secure additional equity financing. With dividend reinvestment plans, however, firms are able to raise smaller amounts of new common stock financing on a continuous basis.

Some firms elect to repurchase shares of their own outstanding common stock. The primary reasons are to use excess cash, provide a form of dividend to stockholders, and "leverage up" the firm. Both stock splits and stock dividends provide additional shares to the firm's current stockholders on a pro rata basis. The firm's cash dividend policy, along with repurchases and stock splits or dividends are used by firms to signal information about the firm's future cash flows.

Questions

16.1 Define or explain the following:

a.	Residual theory of dividends	g.	Payment date
b.	Clientele effect	h.	Dividend reinvestment plan
c.	Smoothed residual dividend policy	i.	Stock split
d.	Dividend extra	j.	Stock dividend
e.	Ex-dividend date	k.	Reverse split
f.	Record date		

16.2 Explain the tradeoff between paying cash dividends versus retaining internally generated funds.

16.3 Discuss the residual dividend theory and how it relates to the value of the firm.

16.4 Discuss factors that would favor firms having high payout ratios. Do the same for factors favoring firms having low payout ratios.

16.5 Describe what other factors and constraints may also influence the firm's cash dividend decision.

16.6 How do you think the following conditions would affect dividend payout ratios, in general? (*Note:* For some, the direction may not be clear!) Explain your answer.

a. Interest rates fall.

b. A reduction in the corporate tax rate is coupled with increased depreciation allowances for tax purposes.

c. Taxes decrease for individuals.

d. The firm is in a mature industry and faces intense foreign competition. It decides to meet the competition head on.

e. The firm is repositioning itself into a new, young, growing industry.

16.7 Explain the smoothed residual dividend policy. How does this incorporate many of the observed practices of firms?

16.8 By using a time line illustrate the relationship among the declaration day, the ex-dividend date, the record day, and the payment date. What should the market price do on the ex-dividend date? Why?

16.9 When a firm repurchases shares of stock to hold as treasury stock, the shares are not viewed as an asset, since they never show up on the left-hand (or asset) side of the firm's balance sheet. Why do firms pay money for them if they are not an asset? Are nonselling stockholders better or worse off after the firm repurchases shares? Explain.

16.10 Explain the main differences between a stock split and a stock dividend from (a) an accounting viewpoint; (b) an investor's standpoint.

16.11 Theoretically, investors should not benefit directly from a stock split or stock dividend.

a. Explain fully why this is so.

b. How would you react if an investor said her investment had a price of $50 before a 2-for-1 split, and a price of $28 after the split? Is the market still efficient?

16.12 Summarize the signaling, or information content, aspects of a firm's dividend policy.

Self-Test Problems   (Solutions appear on pages 731–732.)

(Solutions appear on pages 731–732.)

Dividend Preference

ST 16.1 Kyle Mans just invested the same amount of money in two stocks, A and B, which have returns as follows:

	Dividends Expected D_1	Dividends Expected D_2	Capital Gain Expected When Sold at End of Year 2 (After receiving any cash dividend)
Stock A	$100	$100	$400
Stock B	0	0	600

Kyle's required rate of return is 10 percent, and he is in the 28 percent tax bracket for ordinary income.

a. Calculate the present value of his expected returns. Which stock provides higher returns? Why?

b. How much more would Kyle have to receive from stock B to be indifferent between the two stocks?

Stock Repurchase Price

ST 16.2 A firm has 1,000,000 shares of common stock outstanding selling at $90 per share. Its earnings after tax (EAT) is $6,000,000. Because it has excess cash, the firm has decided to buy back 200,000 shares of its common stock. However, since the excess cash has been invested in short-term marketable securities, the EAT will decrease to $5,000,000 once the repurchase is completed. If we assume the P/E ratio remains the same after the repurchase as it is now, what is the price per share that should be offered so that both selling and nonselling stockholders are indifferent to the repurchase?

Stock Split

ST 16.3 Markham Brothers has decided to go public. They have retained the services of an investment banker who has indicated that a P/E ratio for Markham of about 8 times earnings would be reasonable for a new offering of this type. In addition, the investment banker figured an offering price of $40 per share would be appropriate. Markham Brothers has earnings after taxes (EAT) of $7.5 million and presently has 500,000 shares of common stock. How large a stock split would you recommend for Markham before the firm goes public?

Problems

Dividends, Returns, and Inflation

16.1 Under FASB No. 33, "Financial Reporting and Changing Prices," firms must report both historical cost and constant dollar (inflation-adjusted) figures. Below is information on two firms—Central Energy, which is an energy resources firm, and Hoffman, which is a forest products concern.

	Year				
	1	**2**	**3**	**4**	**5**
Central Energy					
Cash dividends—as reported	$ —	$ 0.85	$ 0.95	$ 1.15	$ 1.35
Cash dividends—adjusted for general inflation	—	1.13	1.11	1.22	1.35
Market price—as reported	8.88	20.62	31.88	20.88	15.88
Market price—adjusted for general inflation	12.62	26.00	35.62	21.50	15.88
Hoffman					
Cash dividends—as reported	$ —	$ 1.13	$ 1.20	$ 1.20	$ 1.05
Cash dividends—adjusted for general inflation	—	1.50	1.40	1.27	1.05
Market price—as reported	24.25	26.38	25.00	20.13	26.25
Market price—adjusted for general inflation	34.55	33.20	27.97	20.67	26.25
Percent increase in inflation	—	11.5%	13.5%	10.2%	6.0%

a. Employing the return equation

$$R_t = \frac{P_t - P_{t-1} + D_t}{P_{t-1}}$$

compute the yearly returns for both Central Energy and Hoffman, for both the data as reported and the inflation-adjusted results. Do this for the four periods between year 1 and year 5.

b. Calculate the mean rate of return for both firms for both the historical cost and the inflation-adjusted data. Calculate the mean increase in inflation.

c. What can we say about (1) the effects of inflation on stockholder returns, and (2) the returns for the two firms vis-à-vis inflation?

Residual Dividend Policy

16.2 Husky Manufacturing follows a residual cash dividend policy. For the next year, the firm expects to have internally generated funds of $1 million, profitable investment opportunities are $2 million, and the firm's target capital structure is 40 percent equity and 60 percent debt.

a. How much should Husky pay out to its stockholders in cash dividends?

b. What if profitable investment opportunities are $3 million? $1.5 million?

Residual Dividend Policy

16.3 Alexander International is considering seven average-risk proposed capital expenditures, as follows:

Capital Investment	CF_0	Internal Rate of Return
A	$200	25%
B	300	22
C	150	17
D	450	16
E	350	14
F	250	12
G	100	9

The firm's target capital structure is 30 percent debt and 70 percent equity. Alexander's WACC is 15 percent, and there is $1,200 available in internally generated funds that can be reinvested in the firm or paid out in the form of cash dividends.

a. Which capital budgeting projects should be accepted? If the firm follows a residual dividend policy, how much is available to be paid out in the form of cash dividends?

b. How does your answer change if Alexander's WACC is only 11 percent?

Timing of Cash Dividends

16.4 Viscione Industries is planning to liquidate in 2 years; that is, at t_2. At t_0, the management was considering two alternative dividend policies. The first would be to pay a cash dividend of $2 at t_1, followed by a liquidating dividend of $29.35 at t_2. The second plan calls for a cash dividend of $10 at t_1 and a liquidating dividend of $19.83 at t_2.

a. If the required rate of return on Viscione Industries is 19 percent, which plan (if either) should *management* favor? (*Note:* Ignore any tax aspects and assume there is no uncertainty concerning whether the firm will actually have the cash to pay the dividends as indicated.)

b. Are there any practical considerations that need to be taken into account that might favor one over the other? Explain.

Flotation Costs and Value

16.5 McCormick Steel has a current stock market value of $4 million. It has 1 million shares of stock outstanding and currently pays no cash dividends. Two dividend policies are under consideration: Plan I is to continue paying no cash dividends. Plan II involves selling $500,000 of new stock (with no flotation costs) and immediately paying the $500,000 to the existing (but not the new) stockholders. Since there are presently 1 million shares of common stock outstanding, every current stockholder would receive 50 cents per share in cash dividends. The new stock would have to be sold at $3.50 per share (the current market value of $4 million divided by the current 1 million shares, less the cash dividend of 50 cents).

a. How many shares will have to be issued to raise the $500,000? Compare the per share value of the current stockholders' holdings, taking into account both market price and dividends under plan I versus plan II. (*Note:* Ignore taxes.)

b. Now assume that McCormick also has to incur flotation costs of 20 cents per share, so the new stock will sell at $3.30 per share. How many shares will now have to be issued to raise the $500,000? Compare the total per share value of the current stockholders' holdings for both plans now.

c. By comparing your answers to (a) and (b), what can we say about the impact of flotation costs on the dividend (and valuation) decision?

Dividend Payout

16.6 Westwood Corporation and Mayfair Company are in the same industry, are both publicly traded, and both have a large number of stockholders. Their characteristics are as follows:

	Westwood	Mayfair
Expected annual net cash flows (in thousands)	$75,000	$100,000
Standard deviation of cash flows (in thousands)	40,000	50,000
Annual capital expenditures (in thousands)	60,000	65,000
Existing long-term debt (in thousands)	80,000	100,000
Cash, marketable securities, and unused line of credit (in thousands)	40,000	50,000
Flotation costs and underpricing on common stock issue as a percentage of the gross proceeds	7%	4%

Which company is likely to have the higher dividend payout ratio? Why?

Dividend Extra

16.7 A firm has adopted a smoothed residual dividend policy. This is supplemented by declaring a dividend extra as follows:

1. Regular dividends paid out are presently 30 percent of earnings. The firm wants to keep its regular dividend payout at 30 percent, and will increase the regular payout only when net income increases for 2 consecutive years. (*Note:* For the data given below, this means that the regular cash dividend will not increase until t_4.)
2. Once the regular dividend is increased, it remains at that level until it can be raised again (based on 2 consecutive years' increases in net income).
3. Each year the firm pays out a total of 40 percent of earnings by declaring an extra dividend. The size of the extra dividend is then the difference between the 30 percent payout policy and the 40 percent payout policy.

   If the firm has earnings as follows, what are its regular and extra dividends per year?

t_1	t_2	t_3	t_4	t_5	t_6	t_7	t_8
$100	$100	$110	$140	$120	$160	$180	$220

Ex-Dividend Date

16.8 On March 1 (a Thursday), the board of directors of Save-More Enterprises met and declared a cash dividend of 50 cents per share payable April 18 (a Wednesday) to stockholders of record March 22 (a Thursday).

a. If you were going to purchase some stock in Save-More and wanted to receive this cash dividend, by what date would the purchase have to be made? (*Note:* Don't forget the weekend.)

b. Approximately how much should the market price of Save-More drop on the ex-dividend day?

c. What happens to the cash dividend if you already own the stock and the firm declares bankruptcy on March 12?

Repurchase of Common Stock

16.9 Nelson Drug has 50,000 shares of stock outstanding, total earnings of $600,000, a market price per share of $96, and pays a cash dividend of $4 per share.

a. Determine the (1) total market value, (2) EPS, (3) P/E ratio, (4) dividend payout ratio.

b. Gary Sargent, who owns 2,000 shares, has expressed great displeasure with the management policies of Nelson Drug. Management has approached him with the idea of buying back his shares.

    (1) If the firm offers Gary $100 per share instead of paying a cash dividend of $4 per share, are the remaining stockholders better off, worse off, or the same? Assume the P/E ratio remains the same.

    (2) If after the repurchase the firm elects to pay the same *total* dollar amount out in the form of cash dividends, what happens to the dividends per share? What, if anything, happens to the dividend payout ratio?

    (3) Discuss, but do not work out, what the general effect would be on the remaining stockholders if Nelson Drug had to pay $125 per share to repurchase the shares from Gary Sargent. (Assume the firm spends more than $200,000, so it purchases all of Gary's shares.)

Stock Split or Stock Dividend: Accounting Treatment

16.10 Van Horn Distributors lists the following on its annual report (dollars in thousands):

Common stock, $2.50 par; authorized, 6,000,000 shares; issued and outstanding, 3,589,970 shares	$ 8,975
Additional paid-in capital	2,239
Retained earnings	49,496
Total	$60,710

a. What changes would occur if Van Horn declared a 2-for-1 stock split? (*Note:* Assume the authorized shares double to 12,000,000.)

b. Independent of (a), what if Van Horn declared a 20 percent stock dividend and the market price was $25 per share?

Stock Split: Effect on Firm and Investor

16.11 Horizon Enterprises has 600,000 shares of common stock outstanding, and its EPS is $6. The firm has a dividend payout ratio of 20 percent, and a current market price of $90 per share.

a. Before the split, what is Horizon's (1) total earnings; (2) total cash dividends; (3) cash dividends per share; (4) total market value; (5) P/E ratio?

b. Jim Evans owns 50 shares of Horizon. What is his (1) total cash dividends, and (2) total market value?

c. Horizon declares a 3-for-1 stock split. What is the new (1) total earnings; (2) EPS; (3) total cash dividends; (4) dividends per share; (5) dividend payout ratio; (6) P/E ratio; (7) total market value? [Note: Assume there are no signaling effects in (c) or (d).]

d. After the split, what is Jim Evans' total cash dividends and total market value?

e. Under what circumstances (if any) might an investor be better off after a stock split?

Stock Dividend

16.12 The SLP Corporation had a market price of $60 per share on September 1. On September 5, the firm announced a 20 percent stock dividend payable October 20 to stockholders of record on September 30. You own 90 shares of SLP.

a. What is the ex-dividend date (*Remember:* Add 2 more days because of the weekend.)

b. If you sold your stock on September 20, what price would you receive? (Assume other things are equal and no brokerage costs.)

c. After the stock dividend, how many shares will you own?

d. What should be the market price per share, other things being equal, on September 28 if there are no signalling effects?

e. What is the total market value of your holdings both before and after the 20 percent stock dividend?

References

Recent articles on external financing and the relevance or impact of a firm's cash dividend policy, along with Lintner's early work, include

BARCLAY, MICHAEL J., AND CLIFFORD W. SMITH, JR. "Corporate Payout Policy: Cash Dividends Versus Open-Market Purchases." *Journal of Financial Economics* 22 (October 1988), pp. 61–82.

HEALY, PAUL M., AND KRISHNA G. PALEPU. "Earning's Information Conveyed by Dividend Initiations and Omissions." *Journal of Financial Economics* 21 (September 1988), pp. 149–175.

HUBERMAN, GUR. "External Financing and Liquidity." *Journal of Finance* 39 (July 1984), pp. 895–908.

LINTNER, JOHN. "Distribution of Incomes of Corporation Among Dividends, Retained Earnings, and Taxes." *American Economic Review* 46 (May 1956), pp. 97–113.

LITZENBERGER, ROBERT H., AND KRISHNA RAMASWAMY. "The Effects of Dividends on Common Stock Prices: Tax Effects or Information Effects." *Journal of Finance* 37 (May 1982), pp. 429–443.

LONG, JOHN B., JR. "The Market Valuation of Cash Dividends: A Case to Consider." *Journal of Financial Economics* 6 (June/September 1978), pp. 235–264.

MILLER, MERTON, AND KEVIN ROCK. "Dividend Policy and Asymmetric Information." *Journal of Finance* 40 (September 1985), pp. 1031–1051.

SHEFRIN, HERSH M., AND MEIR STATEMAN. "Explaining Investor Preference for Cash Dividends." *Journal of Financial Economics* 13 (June 1984), pp. 253–282.

Special dividends and stock splits are examined in

BRENNAN, MICHAEL J., AND THOMAS E. COPELAND. "Stock Splits, Stock Prices, and Transaction Costs." *Journal of Financial Economics* 22 (October 1988), pp. 83–101.

GRINBLATT, MARK S., RONALD W. MASULIS, AND SHERIDAN TITMAN. "The Valuation Effects of Stock Splits and Stock Dividends." *Journal of Financial Economics* 13 (December 1984), pp. 461–490.

WOOLRIDGE, J. RANDALL, AND DONALD R. CHAMBERS. "Reverse Splits and Shareholder Wealth." *Financial Management* 12 (Autumn 1983), pp. 5–15.

17

Leasing

Overview

- Leasing is a major source of long-term financing. It places a financial obligation on the firm leasing the asset similar to debt.

- The minimum lease rate quoted by the lessor can be determined using present value techniques.

- Financial leases are evaluated by lessees based on the net advantage of leasing,

- or NAL, which compares leasing with the possibility of purchasing the asset.

- The NAL approach separates the capital budgeting (or investment) decision from the financing decision. To neutralize risk between the lease and purchase options, the after-tax cost of borrowing is used as the discount rate.

BankAmerica sold its world headquarters complex in San Francisco and simultaneously leased back 60 percent of the space. The tower and two adjoining buildings had 1.8 million square feet and a depreciated book value of $80 million, but BankAmerica obtained a premium selling price—$660 million. Some real estate experts speculated that BankAmerica received that price by agreeing to pay inflated rents under the leaseback agreement. They noted that prime office space in San Francisco's financial district was renting for little more than $30 a square foot. BankAmerica, on the other hand, had agreed to pay $37 per square foot for the space. The deal, noted one real estate expert, was being made to look a lot better than it was: "It is obviously an earnings-driven deal and not a cash deal." Perhaps not so coincidentally, the anticipated boost in BankAmerica's earnings helped offset a $338 million operating loss for the second quarter. BankAmerica took a pretax profit of about 40 percent of the profit, or $230 million. The remaining $350 million was counted as earnings in later years.

Leasing has become one of the primary sources of financing in the United States in recent years. While not all the decisions are as big or complex as BankAmerica's, it is estimated that more than 20 percent of the investment in new assets during the next 5 years will be financed with leases. As we will see, the decision to lease or purchase must be consistent with the firm's objective of maximizing the value of the firm. Once again we base our analysis on the risks and cash flows involved.

Leasing and the Firm

Firms often enter into rental agreements that are called *leases.* The owner of the property is the *lessor,* who leases it to the user, or the *lessee.* Virtually anything that is needed by the firm—machinery, buildings, warehouses, airplanes, computers, ships, and so forth—can be leased. Our primary focus is from the standpoint of the lessee, but it is helpful to begin by understanding who provides lease financing. That is, who are the lessors?

Lease financing can be provided by manufacturers as part of their regular sales effort, or it can be provided by firms that specialize in lease financing. In the former category we find that GATX, a railroad car manufacturer, is the largest lessor of railcars, and that IBM is a major computer lessor. In recent years McDonnell Douglas agreed to lease planes to a number of airlines instead of selling them. Without the lease financing provided by McDonnell Douglas, it is unlikely the airlines would have proceeded to acquire the use of the new planes. In addition, lease financing is increasingly being provided by commercial banks, investment bankers, subsidiaries of other firms, and commercial finance companies.

Types of Leases

Leases come in many sizes, shapes, and forms, but in all cases the lessee (who has acquired use of the asset) is required to make periodic payments to the lessor. These payments generally are made monthly, quarterly, or semiannually, with the first payment due when the lease agreement is signed.

Service Lease

A *service lease* is a short-term lease that generally is cancellable. It is often employed to finance office machines, cars, and similar relatively inexpensive assets that require periodic maintenance. These leases often are called maintenance leases because the lessor generally is responsible for all service, as well as for any insurance or property taxes on the assets. The costs incurred by the lessor are passed on, since they are built into the lease payments. Large service leases should be subjected to financial evaluation; smaller ones, or leases of short duration, are typically not subjected to an extensive financial analysis like that discussed later in the chapter.

Financial Lease

The term *financial lease* is employed for tax purposes to identify a long-term, noncancellable contract between the lessor, who owns the asset, and the lessee, who agrees to lease the asset for some specified period of time. Financial leases are a form of long-term financing similar to borrowing. The lessee gains the use of the asset immediately, but in return has entered into a binding obligation to make payments as specified in the lease contract. Entering into a lease is similar to borrowing in terms of the cash flow consequences to the lessee. For this reason, the financial analysis employed by lessees presented later in the chapter will compare the cash flow consequences of leasing versus borrowing. Most financial leases are *net* leases; the lessee agrees to provide maintenance and pay for insurance coverage and/or property taxes related to the leased asset.

Sale and Leaseback

A *sale and leaseback* occurs when the owner of an asset decides to sell it to another party and then lease it back. This type of transaction occurs frequently when a firm wants to raise capital by selling a building or factory, but also wants to maintain the use of the facility for some specified period of time. The popularity of sale and leaseback agreements is growing as many firms attempt to translate the estimated 20 percent of their total assets in real estate into more productive uses. From the lessee's standpoint, the financial analysis of selling and leasing back versus borrowing is essentially the same as for other finance leases.

Leveraged Lease

A fourth major type of leasing, and one that has also become increasingly popular in recent years, is the *leveraged lease.* This arrangement involves three parties instead of two—the lender who puts up much of the money, the lessor (or equity participant) who owns the asset, and the lessee. Leveraged leases are complicated from the standpoint of both lender and lessor, but they remain a financial lease from the standpoint of the lessee. Table 17.1 summarizes the characteristics of the basic lease types.

Tax Considerations

From the lessee's standpoint, the lease payments are an expense of doing business and are deductible for tax purposes. Since the lessor owns the asset, depreciation is allowed as a tax-deductible expense.

Internal Revenue Service rules about what constitutes a lease for tax purposes were substantially modified under the Economic Recovery Tax Act of 1981. These rules were further modified by the Tax Equity and Fiscal Responsibility Act of 1982. Under the present rules, a lease is created under the following conditions:

1. The property qualifies for depreciation for tax purposes.
2. The transaction has economic substance independent of the tax benefits.
3. The lease is entered into within 90 days after the property is placed in service.
4. The lessee may be allowed to purchase the asset at the end of the lease if the option price is at least 10 percent of the original cost of the property.

Except in the next section, when accounting issues are discussed, we assume the leases under discussion in the remainder of the chapter are financial leases for tax purposes.

Accounting for Leases

Our primary concern is the evaluation of the financial consequences of leasing, but let's pause briefly to consider their accounting treatment. There are vast differences in both terminology and treatment for accounting versus tax purposes. The main terminology difference is that accountants refer to long-term leases that have to be capitalized on the firm's financial statements as *capital leases.* Any other leases are called *operating leases.*

Until 1976, all leases provided "off balance sheet" financing. That is, the fact that the firm had the use of the assets, as well as contractual obligations to make periodic lease payments, showed up (if at all) only as a footnote. Because lease obligations are as binding as debt, however, the reported financial statements tended to misrepresent a firm's true financial position if it leased long-term assets. Under

Table 17.1 Characteristics of the Major Types of Leases

*Service leases, often being of short duration, are usually not analyzed e⌐
financial impact. Financial leases, including sale and leasebacks and lever
similar from the standpoint of how the lessee evaluates them.*

Type of Lease	Parties Involved	Duration	Mai⌐ Payment or Insurance and Taxes
Service	Lessee and lessor	Short	Lessor
Financial	Lessee and lessor	Long	Lessee
Sale and leaseback	Lessee (seller) and lessor (buyer)	Long	Lessee
Leveraged	Lessee, lessor (equity participant), and lender	Long	Lessee

FASB No. 13[1] a capital lease exists if one or more of the following conditions are met:

1. The lease transfers ownership of the property to the lessee by the end of the lease term.
2. The lease gives the lessee the option to purchase the property, and it is likely the option will be exercised.
3. The lease term is equal to 75 percent or more of the estimated economic life of the property.

If these requirements (which are a good deal different from the tax requirements) are met, the present value of the lease payments must be entered as a liability on the right-hand side of the balance sheet. A corresponding entry must also be made on the left-hand side to record the value of the asset. This is typically lumped with other long-term assets of the firm. This asset is then amortized over its useful life, resulting in a reduction in reported income. Any lease that does not meet this criteria is considered an operating lease for accounting purposes.

To see the effect of these reporting requirements, consider Table 17.2. As of January 30, 1988 (the end of its fiscal year), J. C. Penney had more than $2,353 million in rent (or lease) obligations, but only about $213 million were capitalized (or appeared) on the firm's balance sheet as part of its long-term debt. In addition, although it is not broken out on Penney's income statement, we find that its total rent expense in 1987 was $444 million.

The net effect of FASB No. 13 has been for financial statements to reflect somewhat more accurately the firm's debt-type obligations. To get around this reporting requirement, many firms are structuring long-term leases so they are technically *not* capital leases as specified by FASB No. 13. These operating leases do not have to be shown on the firm's balance sheet and show up only in the footnotes. For Penney, most of their future lease (or rent) obligations do not appear on the firm's financial statements. While many firms are keeping substantial lease obligations off their balance

[1] *Financial Accounting Standards Board No. 13,* "Accounting for Leases" (Stamford, Conn.: FASB, 1976).

Table 17.2 Liabilities, Equity, and Lease (or Rent) Expenses for J. C. Penney as of January 30, 1988 (In millions)

Penney doesn't identify any lease obligations on their balance sheet. But many lease, or rent, obligations are shown in the supplemental information. (SOURCE: J. C. Penney Company, 1987 Annual Report.)

Balance Sheet: Liabilities and Stockholders' Equity
Current liabilities

Accounts payable and accrued expenses	$ 1,595
Short-term debt	955
Deferred taxes, principally installment sales	136
Total current liabilities	2,686
Long-term debt	2,608
Deferred taxes	1,375
Total stockholders' equity	4,173
Total liabilities and stockholders' equity	$10,842

Supplemental Information
Under the breakout of long-term debt, we find for 1987:

Present value of commitments under capital leases	$213

We also find rent expense for 1987 as follows:

Minimum rent on noncancellable operating leases	$193
Rent based on sales	42
Minimum rent in cancellable personal property leases	115
Real estate taxes and common area costs	94
Total	$444

Finally, we find the following minimum annual rents under noncancellable leases and subleases:

	Gross Rents	Net Rents*
1988	$ 189	$ 123
1989	183	118
1990	172	111
1991	164	105
1992	156	101
Thereafter	1,489	1,017
Total	$2,353	$1,575

* Rents are shown net of their estimated executory costs, which are principally real estate taxes, maintenance, and insurance.

sheets, the benefits from doing this are questionable unless (1) the lease is economically justified, as discussed subsequently, and (2) we assume that analysts, investors, and bankers are naive and do not adjust for this continued off-balance-sheet financing.

Setting Lease Rates

While our primary interest is from the lessee's standpoint, it is helpful to understand what factors lessors consider in setting lease rates. By understanding this process, lessees will be in a better position for knowledgeable lease bargaining.

For financial leases, the lessor wants to set a rate that pr[...]
return. This is done by focusing first on four items,[2] as follows:

1. The lessor's after-tax required rate of return on debt-type i[...]
2. The lessor's marginal tax rate, T
3. The cost of the leased asset, CLA_0
4. The depreciation scheme to be employed, and the depr[...]
   set, n

Once these items have been determined, the proper lease rate for the lessor to quote is determined using the following five-step procedure:

STEP 1: Determine cash-flow benefit. The tax benefit from owning the asset is the depreciation tax shield.

STEP 2: Calculate present value of benefit. Employing the lessor's after-tax required rate of return on debt-type investments, the present value of the ownership benefit is determined using Equation 17.1, as follows:

$$\text{present value of benefit} = \sum_{t=1}^{n} \frac{\text{Dep}_t(T)}{(1 + k_i)^t} \qquad (17.1)$$

STEP 3: Calculate amount to be recovered from lease payments. The net amount recoverable from lease payments is equal to the cost of the leased asset minus the present value of the benefit of ownership calculated in step 2, so that:

$$\text{net amount recoverable from lease payments} = CLA_0 - \text{present value of benefit} \qquad (17.2)$$

STEP 4: Determine the after-tax lease payment, ATL. Since lease payments are made in advance (at the beginning of each period), the after-tax lease payments are determined by solving for ATL in the following formula:

$$\text{net amount recoverable from lease payments} = \left[\sum_{t=1}^{n} \frac{\text{ATL}}{(1 + k_i)^t} \right] (1 + k_i) \qquad (17.3)$$

In Equation 17.3 ATL is an annuity due. The term $(1 + k_i)$ converts ATL from an ordinary annuity to an annuity due.

STEP 5: Determine the before-tax lease payment, L. To complete the process, the lessor adjusts the lease payment to its before-tax amount, as follows:

$$L = \frac{\text{ATL}}{1 - \text{lessor's marginal tax rate, T}} \qquad (17.4)$$

The lease rate L is what the lessor will quote to a prospective lessee. By doing so, the lessor will achieve the desired after-tax return on the leased asset. If any higher lease rate is quoted, the lessor's return increases accordingly.

[2] While resale values are important, for simplicity they are ignored. Resale values for lessors are examined in problem 17.2.

[3] The logic behind using k_i as the lessor's minimum discount rate is similar to that discussed later in the chapter for lessees. If markets are perfect and the tax status and all other factors are similar between lessors and lessees, then the returns to lessors from leasing are exactly equal to the cost of leasing to lessees.

Table 17.3 Setting a Lease Rate

Using this step-by-step procedure, we can determine the lease rates to quote for any leased asset.

Steps 1 and 2: Present Value of Ownership Benefit

Year	Depreciation* (Dep)	Depreciation × Tax Rate Dep(T)	× PV at 9% =	Present Value
1	$330,000	$115,500	0.917	$105,914
2	440,000	154,000	0.842	129,668
3	230,000	80,500	0.772	62,146

$$\sum_{t=1}^{n} \frac{Dep_t(T)}{(1+k_i)^t} = \$297,728$$

Step 3: Amount to be recovered from lease payments

$$\$1,000,000 - \$297,728 = \$702,272$$

Step 4: Determine after-tax lease payment, ATL

$$\$702,272 = ATL(\,PVA_{9\%,3yr}\,)(\,1.09\,)$$

$$\$702,272 = ATL(\,2.531\,)(\,1.09\,)$$

$$2.759\ ATL = \$702,272$$

$$ATL = \$702,272/2.759 = \$254,538.60$$

Step 5: Calculate before-tax lease payment, L

$$L = \frac{\$254,538.60}{1 - 0.35} = \frac{\$254,538.60}{0.65} = \$391,597.85 \approx \$391,598$$

---

* The simplified ACRS percentage for years 1 through 3 are 0.33, 0.44, and 0.23, respectively. The first year's depreciation is $1,000,000(0.33) = $330,000.

To illustrate setting lease rates, assume LeaseFirst has been approached to supply a 3-year lease on a $1,000,000 piece of specialized equipment. The equipment has a normal recovery period of 3 years, LeaseFirst's marginal tax rate is 35 percent, its before-tax required return on debt-type investments is 13.85 percent, and no resale value is assumed. What lease rate will LeaseFirst quote if the yearly lease payments are made in advance?[4]

The specific steps employed by LeaseFirst are shown in Table 17.3. In the first two, the present value of the ownership benefit to LeaseFirst is found to be $297,728. Then in step 3 the amount to be recovered from lease payments is simply $1,000,000 − $297,728, or $702,272. In steps 4 and 5 the after- and before-tax lease payments are determined. By collecting three annual lease payments of $391,598, each payable at the beginning of the year, LeaseFirst will receive its 13.85 percent before-tax (or 9 percent after-tax) required rate of return.

Other things being equal, the following actions will serve to increase the lease rates quoted by lessors:

---

[4] The same basic procedure would be employed in determining semiannual, quarterly, or monthly lease payments.

1. Using straight-line rather than ACRS depreciation for tax purposes
2. Raising the required rate of return
3. Increasing the number of payments by going to semiannual, quarterly or monthly payments instead of yearly payments.

In practice, three other factors must be considered. The first is that the lessor still owns the asset, and there will be some resale value for most assets after the lease terminates. Resale values serve to lower the quoted lease rate. Second, it is important to realize that information asymmetries generally exist between lessors and lessees. Lessors often know more about the asset than the lessee, and they may have economies of scale not enjoyed by the lessees. Finally, lessors will adjust the quoted lease rates upward to account for the transaction costs of setting up the lease agreement, and they will also factor in the costs incurred in obtaining information about potential lessees, and the lessee's risk of default. Thus, lease rates are actually set in a slightly more complex environment than the model outlined in Equations 17.1 through 17.4.

To Lease or Not to Lease?

If capital markets were perfect—that is, there were no transaction costs, financial distress costs, taxes, information asymmetries, and so forth—then debt and lease obligations would be valued exactly the same by lessors and lessees. The cost of debt or lease financing would be the same, and the lessee would be indifferent between leasing and borrowing. Given less than perfect markets, however, it is important to consider reasons for leasing. Some valid reasons exist; others often advanced are dubious, at best.

Good Reasons for Leasing

Tax Implications

One of the most important reasons for leasing is the tax implications associated with leasing. Lessees often benefit from leasing if they have a lower marginal tax rate than lessors. Due to the difference in tax rates, the IRS-based depreciation tax benefit may be worth more to the lessor with a higher tax bracket, resulting in savings to the lessee.

Flexibility and Convenience

A second reason for leasing is that it may increase the flexibility of the firm. It is often preferable to lease certain types of assets instead of purchasing them. In addition, the convenience of having the lessor secure, set up, and maintain assets may be a significant advantage at times, especially with highly technical pieces of equipment.

Dubious Reasons for Leasing

Conserve Capital

One argument often advanced to justify leasing is the conservation of the firm's working capital because the lease provides "100 percent" financing. Because virtually all lease agreements require the first payment in advance, however, even under the best of circumstances less than 100 percent financing is secured. For small firms there may be some validity in this argument, since they do not have the same access to the capital markets and therefore may have to finance the purchase with internally generated funds. Larger firms, however, can generally secure approximately the same amount of financing from the capital markets. For them, leasing does not appear to be a viable means of conserving working capital.

Increase Debt Capacity

Another argument often made is that the use of leases increases the firm's debt capacity. This is said to occur because the combination of leasing and borrowing results in more long-term financing (or debt capacity) than that achieved by borrowing alone. This argument assumes, however, that bankers, lenders, and the capital markets are naive and do not recognize that leasing places a financial obligation on the firm, just as borrowing does. If lease financing really increased borrowing capacity, lenders and the capital markets would be inefficiently assessing the risk and cash flow obligations of leases. This does not appear to be the case.

Avoid Restrictions

Bonds or term loans often impose restrictive covenants on the firm, potentially restricting its financial flexibility. By leasing the asset, the lessee may be able to avoid some of these restrictions. Although this argument often appears to have some justification in a technical sense, most of the time the actual restrictions on the firm due to bond or term loan covenants are substantially less than their perceived impact. This reason is not often of much importance as a reason for leasing instead of purchasing.

Evaluation of Financial Leases

The evaluation of leases from the lessee's standpoint is straightforward as long as certain basic ideas are understood. These relate to (1) the interaction between the firm's capital budgeting decision and the decision to lease or purchase the asset, (2) why debt financing is the appropriate standard of comparison, and (3) the fact that an incremental analysis of the lease versus purchase cash flows is employed.

What Decision Are We Concerned With?

When a firm makes a capital budgeting decision concerning the possible acquisition of an asset, it calculates the net present value of the proposed project. If the NPV is positive, the asset should be acquired because it will assist in maximizing the value of the firm. *Capital budgeting implicitly assumes that assets to be acquired will be purchased.* If leasing is a strong possibility, however, the basic capital budgeting decision must be supplemented by further analysis to determine whether the asset should be leased or purchased. To make this supplemental financing decision, the *net advantage of leasing (NAL)* is calculated.[5] If the net advantage of leasing is positive, the asset should be acquired by leasing; otherwise it should be purchased.

The capital budgeting (NPV) and lease evaluation (NAL) decisions interact. If some specialized machinery needed by a firm has a NPV value of $15,000, the capital budgeting decision has been reached. If the machinery can be either leased

---

[5] The internal rate of return, IRR, could also be employed, as noted later in the chapter.

Securitized Leases

The U.S. Army has teamed up with Wall Street. The army has an agreement with Bear, Stearns, and Chase Manhattan to track down and refinance $1 billion in equipment leases.[1] Each year the army pays out about $250 million for leased equipment. Much of this goes for leases that carry a relatively high cost. The firms say they can save the army about 10 percent of the current lease costs, and for every dollar saved the budget deficit can be shrunk by a dollar.

Here's how it works. First, Chase will dig through the file cabinets of over 20 command jurisdictions in the U.S. and overseas to identify the leases the army has entered into. The second step is to set up a trust. It will issue certificates of participation—COPs—for sale to institutional investors, like insurance companies, bank trust departments, and others. The money raised will be used to pay off old high-priced equipment leases. For example, if the army is 12 months into a 48-month lease ownership contract for a computer, proceeds from the COPs will pay off the rest. The army then enters into a new 36-month agreement with the trust and makes the lease payments to it. From this cash flow the trust pays the investors. The average maturity will be 2 to 3 years, after which time the army becomes the owner of the equipment.

By refinancing on Wall Street the army is replacing its retail leases with money it raises wholesale in the capital markets. The money raised, at, say, 10 percent, will be used to pay off old leases costing, say, 14 percent. While this approach sounds unusual it's the same type of thing that has been done in recent years with home mortgages, truck and computer leases, car loans, and even credit card receivables. All these assets have been securitized in recent years, by using them as collateral to back financing obtained on Wall Street.

[1] "Wall Street Is Building the Army a Debt-Bomber." *Business Week* (December 12, 1988).

or purchased, however, a subsequent calculation (the net advantage of leasing) must be made to determine the preferable means of financing. If the NAL is positive, the use of the specialized machinery should be gained by leasing. If the NAL is negative, the specialized machinery should be purchased.

One complication arises if the original net present value is negative. In this case, there may be instances in which the use of the assets should still be acquired if especially favorable lease terms are available. Consider a case where the NPV is −$5,000, but the subsequent NAL is $7,000. Since the net difference is a positive $2,000, the assets should be leased. If the NAL were negative, however, or positive but less than $5,000, the assets would not be leased or purchased. All these conditions are summarized in Figure 17.1. For simplicity, we assume the NPV is positive. Our concern is with the financing decision of whether the assets should be leased or purchased.

Figure 17.1 Interaction of Leasing and Capital Budgeting Decisions

If the NPV is positive, the firm leases if NAL is positive, or purchases if NAL is negative. If the NPV is negative, especially favorable lease terms can still lead to leasing.

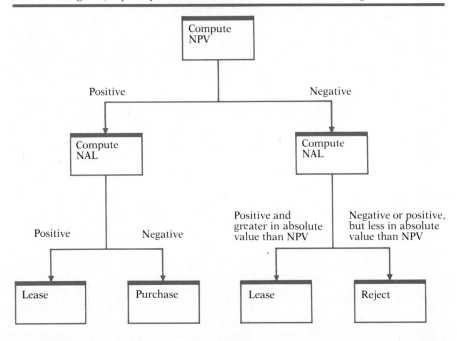

Why Compare Leasing with Borrowing?

To evaluate whether leasing is preferred to purchasing, it is necessary to make an assumption about the mode of financing employed if the asset is purchased. Leasing imposes the same kind of financial commitment on the firm that borrowing does. Hence, the relevant standard of comparison to use when evaluating leasing is to compare it with purchasing the asset and financing the capital needs via borrowing. We are interested in neutralizing the risk between the two alternatives. The most direct way to accomplish this is by establishing an equivalent borrowing amount that, in terms of the after-tax cash flows in each future period, is exactly the same as the after-tax lease cash flows. By doing so, the risk is neutralized.

Although this may sound complicated, it can be accomplished easily without ever calculating the implied loan. All that is required is that the discount rate employed be the after-tax borrowing rate of the firm. To neutralize risk differences in terms of the cash flow effects on the firm, we employ the lessee's after-tax borrowing rate, k_i, as the relevant discount rate. This after-tax borrowing rate is equal to k_b $(1 - T)$, where k_b is the lessee's before-tax borrowing rate and T is the firm's marginal tax rate.

Financial Lease Evaluation

A financial lease is evaluated in terms of the after-tax cash flows and opportunity costs incurred by leasing rather than purchasing the asset. The major elements of the NAL approach are these:

1. The lease payments, L, made periodically by the lessee on an after-tax basis. In line with industry practice, the first payment occurs at the time the lease is signed, t_0.
2. The depreciation tax shield, calculated by multiplying the annual IRS depreciation (Dep) by the lessee's marginal tax rate. By entering into a lease, the firm incurs an opportunity cost equal to the foregone depreciation tax shield.
3. The cost of the leased asset, CLA_0.

Employing these variables in an incremental framework, the net advantage of leasing is calculated as follows:

$$NAL = CLA_0 - \left[L_0(1-T) + \sum_{t=1}^{n-1} \frac{L_t(1-T)}{(1+k_i)^t} + \sum_{t=1}^{n} \frac{Dep_t(T)}{(1+k_i)^t} \right] \tag{17.5}$$

This model simply finds the cost of leasing the asset (the bracketed part of Equation 17.5, which includes both explicit and opportunity costs) versus the cost of the asset (represented by CLA_0). As long as the cost of leasing is less than the cost of the asset, Equation 17.5 will be positive and the asset should be leased.

To illustrate the use of this approach, look at the example of Digital Electronics, which is considering whether to lease or purchase some specialized equipment. Since the capital budgeting analysis indicating the equipment should be secured already has been completed, the question is whether to lease or purchase the equipment. The equipment has a 5-year economic and tax life, and the accelerated cost recovery system of depreciation will be employed. The equipment's resale value is zero, the marginal tax rate is 40 percent, and the firm's before-tax cost of borrowing is 15 percent. The equipment costs $800,000 if purchased or it can be leased for 5 years at $210,000 per year. The first lease payment is payable in advance.

To determine how to finance the equipment, the first step Digital undertakes is to calculate the after-tax cost of borrowing, k_i, which is the discount rate employed in Equation 17.5. Since k_b is 15 percent and the marginal tax rate is 40 percent, $k_i = k_b(1 - T) = 15\%(1 - 0.40) = 9$ percent. This is the discount rate that neutralizes the risk in terms of the after-tax cash flows under the two financing methods, and it should be used for the analysis. The net advantage of leasing equation is set up as follows:

NAL = cost of the asset − (after-tax cash flow of the first lease payment + present value of the subsequent lease payments + present value of the foregone depreciation tax shield)

$= \$800,000 - [\$210,000(1 - 0.40) + \$210,000(1 - 0.40)(PVA_{9\%,4yr})$
  $+ \text{present value of the depreciation tax shield}]$

$= \$800,000 - [\$126,000 + \$126,000(3.240) + \text{present value of the depreciation tax shield}]$

The present value of the depreciation tax shield is as follows:[6]

---

[6] The simplified ACRS percentages for years 1 through 5 are 0.20, 0.32, 0.19, 0.15, and 0.14, respectively. The first year's depreciation is $800,000(0.20) = $160,000.

Year	Depreciation (Dep)	Depreciation × Tax Rate Dep(T)	×	PV at 9%	=	Present Value
1	$160,000	$ 64,000		0.917		$ 58,688
2	256,000	102,400		0.842		86,221
3	152,000	60,800		0.772		46,938
4	120,000	48,000		0.708		33,984
5	112,000	44,800		0.650		29,120

$$\sum_{t=1}^{n} \frac{Dep_t(T)}{(1 + k_i)^t} = \$254,951$$

Substituting this value of $254,951 into the NAL equation, we have:

NAL = $800,000 − ($126,000 + $408,240 + $254,951)

= $800,000 − $789,191 = $10,809

Since the net advantage of leasing is positive, Digital Electronics should lease the assets.

The method just presented for evaluating the leasing decision is straightforward. In addition, it is practical to employ and theoretically correct, since it focuses attention on which means of financing is most consistent with the manager's goal. With this basic approach, the other complications often encountered can be readily incorporated into the NAL framework.[7]

Finding the Percentage Cost of a Lease

Instead of solving for the NAL, it is also possible to determine the percentage annual cost of the lease. This step is similar to solving for the internal rate of return, rather than the net present value, when making a capital budgeting decision. To solve for the cost of the lease, Equation 17.5 is rearranged as follows:

$$CLA_0 - L_0(1 - T) = \sum_{t=1}^{n-1} \frac{L_t(1 - T)}{(1 + IRR)^t} + \sum_{t=1}^{n} \frac{Dep_t(T)}{(1 + IRR)^t} \tag{17.6}$$

We then solve for the unknown percentage rate, IRR. This is the after-tax cost of the lease. The decision rule is as follows:

1. If cost of leasing, IRR, is less than cost of debt, k_i—accept.
2. If cost of leasing is greater than cost of debt—reject.
3. If cost of leasing is equal to cost of debt—you are indifferent.

Note that this relationship is exactly *opposite* that used in making capital budgeting decisions. Here, if the IRR is less than the specified rate, we accept; previously, it was just the reverse.

---

[7] Two other complications occur—incremental operating costs, O_t, if purchased, and resale value, RV_n, if the asset is purchased. Our original NAL equation becomes

$$NAL = CLA_0 - \left[L_0(1 - T) + \sum_{t=1}^{n-1} \frac{L_t(1 - T)}{(1 + k_i)^t} + \sum_{t=1}^{n} \frac{Dep_t(T)}{(1 + k_i)^t} - \sum_{t=1}^{n} \frac{O_t(1 - T)}{(1 + k)^t} + \frac{RV_n(1 - T)}{(1 + k)^n} \right]$$

The appropriate required rate of return, k, is employed for discounting the incremental operating expenses and resale value, since risk neutralization does not extend to these items. If the assets' risk is equal to the average firm risk, then k is the firm's weighted average cost of capital, WACC. These topics are examined in self-test problem ST 17.2 and problem 17.9.

To illustrate this calculation, consider the lease for Digital Electronics. The left-hand side of Equation 17.6 is

$$CLA_0 - L_0(1 - T) = \$800,000 - \$126,000 = \$674,000$$

The cash flows for the right-hand side are determined as follows:

Year	L(1 − T)	+	Dep(T)	=	After-tax Cash Flows
1	$126,000		$ 64,000		$190,000
2	126,000		102,400		228,400
3	126,000		60,800		186,800
4	126,000		48,000		174,000
5	0		44,800		44,800

The cash flow stream is:

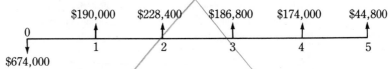

Solving for the internal rate of return, which is the effective after-tax percentage cost of the lease to Digital Electronics, we get 8.29 percent. Since this cost is less than Digital's after-tax cost of debt of 9 percent, we make the same decision as before. That is, Digital should lease the asset.

Summary

Leases come in many sizes, shapes, and forms, but all require periodic lease payments from the lessee (the user) to the lessor (the owner). These payments typically are made in advance. Leasing obligates firms to a series of legally enforceable payments similar to those required when debt financing is issued. Different requirements exist for capital leases for accounting purposes, and for financial leases for tax purposes. Our interest is solely in financial leases, since the tax consequences constitute a direct cash flow to the firm.

The decision to purchase or to lease an asset is a financial decision. The basis for comparison is the cash flows that occur if the asset is purchased versus those that arise if the asset is leased. This is accomplished by performing an incremental analysis to determine the net advantage of leasing, NAL. Risk is neutralized in terms of the cash flow demands on the firm by using the concept of an equivalent loan for the purchase alternative. Instead of having to calculate the equivalent loan, however, the use of the firm's after-tax cost of borrowing automatically accomplishes this equivalence. If the NAL is positive, the asset should be leased; otherwise (assuming the NPV is positive), the asset should be purchased.

Questions

17.1 Define or explain the following:

a. Lease
b. Lessor

c. Lessee
d. Service lease

e. Financial lease h. Capital lease
f. Sale and leaseback i. Operating lease
g. Leveraged lease j. Net advantage of leasing (NAL)

17.2 How does FASB No. 13, "Accounting for Leases," reduce the ability of firms to employ off-balance-sheet financing? Should a firm benefit by this financing?

17.3 What factors (both those discussed in the model covered by Equations 17.1 through 17.4 and others) affect the lease rates quoted by lessors? In which direction (an increase or a decrease in the quoted rate) do they each affect lease rates?

17.4 Explain some of the valid and some of the dubious reasons for leasing.

17.5 How do capital budgeting and financing decisions (to lease or buy) interact? Be sure to discuss the case in which the NPV is negative while the NAL is positive.

17.6 Explain why it is important to neutralize risk in terms of the cash flow obligations of the firm when conducting a lease or buy analysis. How does the after-tax cost of debt, k_i, relate to this issue?

17.7 The basic NAL equation is

$$NAL = CLA_0 - \left[L_0(1 - T) + \sum_{t=1}^{n-1} \frac{L_t(1 - T)}{(1 + k_i)^t} + \sum_{t=1}^{n} \frac{Dep_t(T)}{(1 + k_i)^t} \right]$$

Explain what each of the terms represents.

Self-Test Problems (Solutions appear on pages 732–733.)

Setting Lease Rates

ST 17.1 Vermont Capital is setting lease rates for a $600,000 asset with a 3-year normal recovery period where straight-line depreciation will be used. Vermont's tax rate is 40 percent and its before-tax required rate of return on debt-type investments is 10 percent. Determine the lease rate under the following conditions:

a. The annual lease payments are payable in advance. (*Note:* The payments occur at t_0, t_1, and t_2.)
b. The lease payments are semiannual and made in advance. (*Note:* Continue to use annual depreciation.)

Maximum Lease Payment

ST 17.2 Marsh Distributors is considering a lease arrangement as a means of acquiring the use of some new equipment. The equipment costs $150,000, has a 3-year normal recovery period, and straight-line depreciation will be employed. If purchased, the *after-tax* resale value will be $10,000. The marginal tax rate is 30 percent, the appropriate required rate of return, k, is 14 percent, and the before-tax cost of debt is 11.43 percent. If the three lease payments are made in advance, what is the maximum lease payment Marsh can make and still lease the asset? Assume the NPV is positive. (*Note:* Reference to footnote 7 is required.)

Problems

Setting Lease Rates

17.1 Coyne Financial is setting lease rates for two pieces of equipment:

	Loader	Digger
CLA$_0$	$600,000	$900,000
Normal recovery period	5 years	3 years
Depreciation method	Straight-line	ACRS

If the lease payments are made at the beginning of each period (that is, t_0, t_1, etc.), Coyne's marginal tax rate is 34 percent, and its before-tax return on debt-type investments is 16.67 percent, what lease rate, L, should be quoted on each piece of equipment?

Setting Lease Rates

17.2 TFX Leasing is assessing the impact of a number of different factors on the lease rates it quotes. Assume the asset costs $350,000 and it will be depreciated over its 5-year normal recovery period via straight-line. If TFX's marginal tax rate is 40 percent, determine the lease rate in each case below. (*Note:* Assume each part is independent of the other parts.)

a. TFX's required *after-tax* return on debt-type investments is 8 percent.

b. TFX's required after-tax return on debt-type investments is 10 percent.

c. TFX's required after-tax rate of return on debt-type investments is 8 percent, and the estimated before-tax resale value is $50,000. [*Note:* In calculating the present value of the resale value, use $RV_n(1 - T)(PV_{k,n})$ where $RV_n = \$50,000$ and the required rate of return, k, is 14 percent. The present value of the resale value, along with the present value of the depreciation, is subtracted from CLA_0 in Equation 17.2 to determine the net amount recoverable from lease payments.]

Basic Lease Evaluation

17.3 Norton Industries needs three trucks that cost $100,000 in total. Saveway Leasing has offered to lease the trucks to Norton for a total of $25,000 per year for each of 5 years, with the lease payments payable in advance. To evaluate this option, Norton will depreciate the trucks via straight-line depreciation over their 5-year normal recovery period, the firm's marginal tax rate is 30 percent, and Norton's before-tax cost of debt is 10 percent. Should Norton lease or purchase the trucks? (Assume the capital budgeting decision has already been made and the acquisition of the trucks is desirable.)

Lease Evaluation Under Alternative Conditions: ACRS Depreciation

17.4 Central Trust Bank has just completed a capital budgeting analysis on some automatic teller units. The conclusion was that the bank should acquire the units. They cost $250,000 and have a 3-year economic and tax life, and ACRS will be employed if they are purchased. Central Trust Bank has a 35 percent marginal tax rate, and its before-tax borrowing cost is 13.85 percent. Consider whether Central Trust Bank should purchase or lease the automatic tellers in each case below:

a. The lease payment is $100,000 for each of 3 years, payable in advance. (*Note:* The payments occur at t_0, t_1, and t_2.)

b. The lease payment is $100,000 for each of 3 years, payable at the end of each year. (*Note:* The payment occurs at t_1, t_2, and t_3.)

c. The lease rate is $90,000 for each of 3 years, payable at the beginning of each year (t_0 through t_2).

Sale and Leaseback

17.5 After completing a capital budgeting analysis, Great Pacific Railroad recently purchased some railroad cars for $10 million. The cars will be depreciated over their 10 year normal recovery period employing straight-line depreciation. Rebecca Hunt, one of the firm's directors, suggested that Great Pacific investigate a sale and leaseback agreement for the railroad cars, as many other railroads are doing. Upon checking, you find the railroad cars can be sold for $10 million and then leased back for 10 years at $1.6 million per year, with the lease payments being made in advance. Great Pacific's marginal tax rate is 40 percent and its before-tax cost of borrowing is 16.67 percent.

a. Should Great Pacific enter into the sale and leaseback agreement?

b. What is the maximum lease payment Great Pacific can pay?

Annual Versus Semiannual Lease Payments

17.6 Union Mutual is thinking about buying or leasing a piece of used equipment. It is still in good shape and can be used for another 5 years. The equipment will be depreciated over its 5-year normal recovery period via straight-line depreciation, the firm's tax rate is 30 percent, and the before-tax cost of borrowing is 14.30 percent. The equipment will cost $2 million, but it can be leased for $540,000 per year, payable at the beginning of each of the 5 years.

a. If the NPV is positive, should Union Mutual lease or purchase the equipment?

b. Rework the problem if 10 semiannual lease payments of $270,000 each (payable at the beginning of each 6-month period) are made. (*Note:* Continue to use annual depreciation.)

Basic Capital Budgeting and Lease Evaluation

17.7 A piece of equipment costs $300,000 and has a 5-year normal recovery period. For capital budgeting purposes the after-tax cash flows, CF, are estimated to be $98,000 per year, the firm's marginal tax rate is 40 percent, and the appropriate discount rate is 16 percent. For NAL purposes, straight-line depreciation will be employed, the lease rate, L, is $90,000 each year (at the beginning of the year) for 5 years, and the after-tax cost of borrowing, k_i, is 9 percent.

a. Should the use of the equipment be acquired?

b. After answering (a), determine if it should be leased or purchased.

Combination Capital Budgeting and Lease Evaluation

17.8 John Evans Labs is investigating whether new laboratory equipment is needed. The equipment, which requires an outlay of $550,000, has a 3-year normal recovery period and will be depreciated via ACRS. The net cash flows before taxes, CFBT, are $285,000 for each of 3 years. The firm's tax rate is 40 percent, and the appropriate discount rate is 14 percent.

a. Should John Evans acquire the new laboratory equipment?

b. After deciding the equipment should be acquired, John Evans is now considering whether to lease or purchase it. The lease would be $215,000 for each of 3 years, payable in advance. John Evans estimates its before-tax cost of borrowing is 15 percent. Should John Evans lease or purchase the equipment? [*Note:* Since the appropriate discount rate changes, the present value of the depreciation tax shield in (b) is different from that determined in (a).]

c. What decision should John Evans make in (b) if the net present value determined in (a) was −$15,000? Discuss the logic behind this decision.

Alternative Situations

17.9 Guaranteed Benefit is evaluating leasing or purchasing an asset that has a positive NPV. The following basic conditions exist: CLA_0 is $210,000, n is 3, depreciation is straight line, T is 35 percent, L is $82,000, k_i is 11 percent, lease payments are made annually in advance, and k is 15 percent.

a. Determine the base case NAL.

b. Employing the expanded NAL equation in footnote 7, determine the effect of the following conditions on the NAL for Guaranteed Benefit. (*Note:* Each part is independent of the other parts.)

   (1) If the asset is purchased, Guaranteed will incur incremental operating costs of $5,000 (before taxes) per year.

   (2) If the asset is purchased, Guaranteed estimates the before-tax resale value will be $40,000.

(Do only if using Pinches Disk.)

c. Suppose the CLA_0 is $400,000, L is $165,000, and everything else remains the same as in (a). What are your answers to (a) and (b)?

d. Now suppose CLA_0 is $325,000, L is $90,000, n is 5, depreciation is straight line, k_i is 10 percent, and k is 16 percent. Calculate the NAL for the following conditions: [*Note:* Each part is independent of the other parts until (5).]

   (1) The base case.

   (2) If the asset is purchased, Guaranteed will incur incremental operating costs of $10,000 (before taxes) per year.

   (3) Guaranteed estimates the before-tax resale value will be $75,000.

   (4) If k_i is 13 percent.

   (5) If (2), (3), and (4) hold at the same time.

Would you recommend to lease or purchase the asset in any of these conditions?

17.10 Quality Leasing needs to set a lease rate on the following equipment: CLA is $200,000, n is 5 years, depreciation is straight line, T is 40 percent, k_b is 15 percent, and lease payments are made at the beginning of the year.

a. Determine the lease rate Quality Leasing will quote. (*Note*: Carry the lease rate to two decimal places.)

b. Parkland Distributors needs to lease the equipment. Determine the NAL if everything is the same as for Quality, and L is as determined in (a).

17.11 LTI has decided to acquire a new computer, since the NPV on the project is positive. The cost of the computer is $500,000, and it can be leased at $120,000 per year with the five annual payments made in advance. LTI's before-tax cost of debt is 10 percent, the marginal tax rate is 30 percent, and the computer will be depreciated over 5 years via ACRS.

a. By computing the percentage cost of the lease, determine whether LTI should lease or purchase the computer.

b. Without calculating it, is the NAL positive or negative? Why?

c. What is LTI's percentage cost of the lease if it does not expect to be profitable for the next 5 years? Should it lease or buy the asset? (*Note:* Assume there is no carryback or carryforward, and that the NPV is still positive).

References

For an examination of different types of leases, see

COPELAND, THOMAS E., AND J. FRED WESTON. "A Note on the Evaluation of Cancellable Operating Leases." *Financial Management* 11 (Summer 1982), pp. 60–67.

GRIMLUND, RICHARD D., AND ROBERT CAPETTINI. "A Note on the Evaluation of Leveraged Leases and Other Investments." *Financial Management* 11 (Summer 1982), pp. 68–72.

KIM, E. HAN, WILBUR G. LEWELLEN, AND JOHN J. MCCONNELL. "Sale-and-Leaseback Agreements and Enterprise Valuation." *Journal of Financial and Quantitative Analysis* 13 (December 1978), pp. 871–883.

For theoretical, empirical, and practical aspects of leasing, see

ANG, JAMES, AND PAMELA P. PETERSON. "The Leasing Puzzle." *Journal of Finance* 39 (September 1984), pp. 1055–1065.

CASON, ROGER L. "Leasing, Asset Lives and Uncertainty: A Practitioner's Comments." *Financial Management* 16 (Summer 1987), pp. 13–16.

FRANKS, JULIAN R., AND STEWART D. HODGES. "Lease Valuation When Taxable Earnings Are a Scarce Resource." *Journal of Finance* 42 (September 1987), pp. 987–1005.

SCHALL, LAWRENCE D. "Analytic Issues in Lease vs. Purchase Decisions." *Financial Management* 16 (Summer 1987), pp. 17–20.

SCHALLHEIM, JAMES S., RAMON E. JOHNSON, RONALD C. LEASE, AND JOHN J. MCCONNELL. "The Determinants of Yields on Financial Leasing Contracts." *Journal of Financial Economics* 19 (September 1987), pp. 45–67.

SMITH, CLIFFORD W., JR., AND L. MACDONALD WAKEMAN. "Determinants of Corporate Leasing Policy." *Journal of Finance* 40 (July 1985), pp. 896–908.

WEINGARTNER, H. MARTIN. "Leasing, Asset Lives and Uncertainty: Guides to Decision Making." *Financial Management* 16 (Summer 1987), pp. 5–12.

See Model twelve in *Lotus 1-2-3® for Financial Management* by Pinches and Courtney for a template that values leases, using both the NAL and equivalent loan methods.

PART SIX

Working Capital Management

18 Working Capital Policy

Overview

- The goal of working capital management is to assist in maximizing the value of the firm. This is accomplished by focusing on the magnitude and timing of the cash flows and on the risks and required returns involved.

- The cash conversion cycle and other liquidity measures are important aids in formulating and monitoring an effective working capital policy.

- The firm's size, its major industry, the level and volatility of its sales, and the state of the economy are some of the major determinants of the firm's working capital needs.

- To finance its current assets, many firms follow the matching principle: Temporary assets are financed with temporary funds, permanent assets with long-term sources of funds.

Toyota Motor has a problem many firms would like to face—how to manage record cash flows. Toyota is reaping the benefits of heavy investment in model redesign, automation of its production facilities in the late 1970s, and increases in car prices, especially in the United States. But managing large amounts of cash effectively requires careful planning, and Toyota is one of the most financially conservative companies in the world; as one of Toyota's executives stated: "We like to remain independent." He means independence from both Japan's powerful banks and the ups and downs of the economy.

Toyota has chosen to repay all its long-term debt and has begun to invest in automobile production facilities in other countries, particularly in the United States. In the area of working capital Toyota emphasizes liquidity, short-term investments with stable returns, and minimal exposure to risk from fluctuating foreign exchange rates. Its aim is to avoid any investments that smack of speculation. This approach earns Toyota less on its short-term investments than other Japanese firms. But while some changes may come about, Toyota's approach will remain focused: "We don't really see ourselves in the business of making money from money. It takes away the focus from our main business, which is making cars."

This is a very conservative policy, and other firms are far more aggressive. In this chapter we examine working capital decisions by focusing on liquidity *and how both current assets and current liabilities can be managed aggressively or conservatively.*

Working Capital Management

To maximize the value of the firm, or the size of the pie, the firm must concentrate on providing quality products and/or services in a timely manner. In addition, they must do an effective job in marketing, employee relations, and so forth. From a financial perspective there are three crucial areas where decisions directly affect the value of the firm—its investment decisions, its financing decisions, and its working capital (or day-to-day management) decisions. To maximize the value of the firm we have:

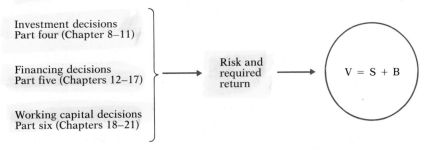

Investment decisions
Part four (Chapter 8–11)

Financing decisions
Part five (Chapters 12–17)

Working capital decisions
Part six (Chapters 18–21)

Risk and required return

$V = S + B$

Now it is time to examine the short-term, or working capital, decisions of the firm.

A firm's assets are normally classified as either current or long-term. Current assets include the cash and other assets that are expected to be converted into cash within 1 year. They are (1) cash and marketable securities, (2) accounts receivable, (3) inventory, and (4) other current assets. Liabilities also are split between current and long-term, with current liabilities those expected to be paid within 1 year. Current liabilities include (1) short-term debt, (2) accounts payable, (3) accruals (such as taxes or wages payable), (4) the current portion of long-term debt, and (5) other current liabilities. We use the term *working capital* to refer to both current assets and current liabilities. Thus, working capital management focuses on the coordinated control of the firm's current assets and current liabilities.

Working Capital Decisions

To gain some understanding of the types of decisions required in working capital management, consider Figure 18.1, which depicts the flow of cash through a firm. On the right-hand side of the figure are those long-term financial management areas that include capital investments, raising capital, and the related areas of determining the firm's cost of capital, capital structure, and dividend policy (discussed in Chapters 8–16). The other aspect of financial management, which focuses on the short-term day-to-day activities of the firm, is depicted on the left-hand side of Figure 18.1. The basic working capital decisions facing a firm include the following:

1. COLLECTIONS AND DISBURSEMENTS. One of the primary responsibilities is to manage the collection of funds from customers, and to pay suppliers, employees, marketing costs, taxes, and so forth. This frequently includes the implementation of some

Figure 18.1 Flow of Cash Through a Firm

Both working capital management and long-term financial management are important for achieving the goal of maximizing the value of the firm. Working capital management is more short run in nature, more operationally focused, and less theoretical than long-term financial management.

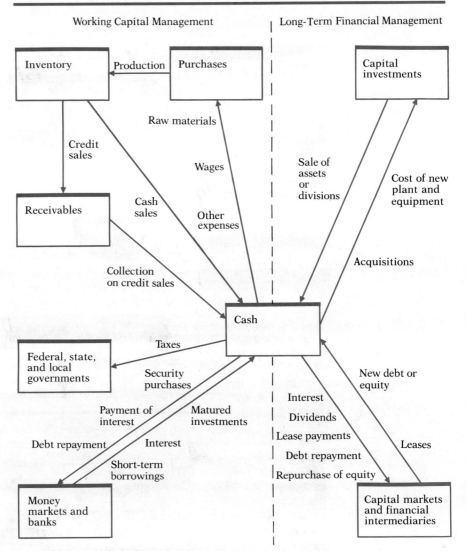

type of cash and check collection system, and the development of various systems for making cash disbursements cost effectively.

2. CASH CONCENTRATION. Managers also have the responsibility for designing and implementing a system to gather the funds from the many banks dealt with so they can be concentrated for better management and investment purposes.

3. LIQUIDITY MANAGEMENT. The firm's liquidity—both on the asset side and the liability side—must also be managed. Liquidity management includes decisions

regarding the determination of the expected surpluses or deficits of cash (via cash budgets as discussed in Chapter 4), along with managing the firm's portfolio of short-term marketable securities, and the type and maturity structure of the firm's short-term borrowings.

4. BANK RELATIONS. Another responsibility is that of designing the firm's banking network and managing its banking relationships. This category includes determining which banks to deal with and the services that will be secured from each.

5. RECEIVABLES. Management of the firm's credit policy and the resulting collection procedures are also important. While basic credit terms and customers must be determined in conjunction with marketing personnel, the ultimate responsibility for implementation and maintenance falls in the working capital management area.

6. INVENTORY. Inventory is the responsibility of many individuals within the firm. The major activities we are concerned with include the determination of how much investment in inventory is needed, and how to finance it.

We will examine each of these areas in Chapters 19 to 21, but before doing so it is important to understand more about working capital in general, why it is needed, and how firms can proceed with estimating how much working capital they need.

Why Do Firms Have Working Capital?

While it may seem obvious that firms need working capital, in a world of perfect markets where there are no transactions costs, no time delays in the production, marketing, and check-clearing system, and no financial distress costs, the value of the firm is independent of its working capital decisions. If that were true, there would be no need for us to study working capital management.

But, as in other areas of finance, we find that markets are not perfect, and that imperfect markets, and other delays and/or costs, are what create the need for a firm to concern itself with working capital management. Let's briefly consider some of the reasons why firms need working capital.

1. TRANSACTIONS COSTS. Transactions costs consist of (1) the service fees for buying and selling securities, or (2) the potential loss in value when a "fire sale" must be made at a price below what could be received if more time was available. Because of transactions costs, we see firms hold cash or marketable securities with a major emphasis on liquidity—that is, the ability quickly and cheaply to be available as cash in order to meet short-term needs.

2. TIME DELAYS. Time delays arise in the production, marketing, and cash collection aspects of a firm's business. Since transactions do not happen instantaneously, many activities affect working capital needs. These include steps such as (1) maintaining inventory (raw materials, work in process, or finished goods), (2) offering credit policies to help sell the product, (3) providing cash discounts for early payment, and (4) reducing the float when customers pay their bills. All these steps involve some costs that must be weighed against the benefits involved.

3. FINANCIAL DISTRESS COSTS. Financial distress costs include legal and other direct and indirect costs such as managerial time associated with reorganization, bankruptcy, or fending off financial difficulties. Because of the high cost most managers equate with financial distress, they tend to keep a significant amount of liquid balances, even though they generally earn less on these balances than on the firm's long-term asset investments. Alternatively, they may incur costs to have

access to credit markets, although they do not anticipate actually having to take advantage of this additional borrowing capacity.

Other items could be mentioned, but the point should be clear: In theory, working capital is not needed; in practice, it becomes one of the most important topics managers must deal with. As we will see in this and the next three chapters, effective working capital decisions involve the consideration of numerous specific items—all of which can assist in maximizing the value of the firm.

The Importance of Working Capital

Working capital typically comprises a large part of a firm's assets and liabilities. Consider the following data on the percentage breakdown of current assets and current liabilities (both compared to total assets) for manufacturing firms in 1981, 1984 and 1987:[1]

	1981	1984	1987
Current Assets			
Cash and marketable securities	5.1%	5.8%	5.9%
Accounts receivable	15.8	15.0	15.1
Inventory	19.4	17.5	15.5
Other	2.9	3.0	3.3
Total current assets	43.2%	41.3%	39.8%
Current Liabilities			
Short-term debt	4.2%	3.6%	3.7%
Accounts payable	9.4	8.7	8.2
Income tax payable	1.9	1.6	1.5
Current portion of long-term debt	1.1	1.4	1.8
Other	10.0	10.9	11.2
Total current liabilities	26.6%	26.2%	26.4%

Current assets account for about 40 percent of the total assets for manufacturing firms, while current liabilities comprise about 25 percent. Looking at the current assets, we see that the largest investment is in inventory, and the second largest is in receivables. For current liabilities, the largest percentages are in the "other" category (which includes accruals) and in accounts payable. Comparing the 3 years, we see that the investment in current assets decreased over this time period, while the amount of current liabilities remained constant.

Some of the more significant reasons why working capital management is important are as follows:

1. The size and volatility of working capital make it a major managerial concern. Managers spend much of their time on the day-to-day activities that revolve around working capital management.
2. The relationship between sales growth and working capital is both close and direct. As sales increase, firms must increase inventory and accounts payable. Increased sales generate a higher level of accounts receivable. So working capital must be managed as firms increase or decrease their scale of operations and

---

[1] *Quarterly Financial Report for Manufacturing, Mining and Trade,* Bureau of the Census, Fourth Quarter 1981, 1984 and 1987.

Certification

Three certification programs serve the corporate finance or investment professional. These are the certified cash manager (CCM), certified financial analyst (CFA), and certified management accountant (CMA).

The certified cash manager is the most recent entrant; it was started by the National Corporate Cash Management Association (NCCMA) in 1984. This certification is particularly important for those who have cash management responsibilities either in corporations or in banks. It is aimed at cash management and treasury professionals. In the 4 years it has been in existence, over 1,700 professionals have earned their CCM accreditation.

The certified financial analyst designation is granted by the Institute of Chartered Financial Analysts, an organization that serves investment professionals. This certification is particularly important for those in pension fund and portfolio management activities with corporations, and those with investment brokerage firms and investment management firms. Since the CFA was first started in the early 1960s, more than 10,000 professionals have earned their designation through the CFA program.

Finally, the certified management accountant designation is offered by the Institute of Management Accounting, which was established by the National Association of Accountants. This designation is primarily of interest to those concerned with the application of managerial accounting and financial management in corporations. Since its inception in 1972, over 8,500 professionals have earned the CMA designation.

In addition to these three broad-based certification programs, there are numerous others related to real estate, insurance, and personal financial planning. All of these programs have the purposes of raising the basic standard of knowledge, promoting professionalism, and increasing the stature of the profession in the eyes of others.

sales. At the same time, some of the current liabilities—especially accounts payable, tend to increase and decrease spontaneously as inventory and accounts receivable increase and decrease. This *spontaneous short-term financing* (due to the use of trade credit as discussed in Chapter 19) must be kept in mind as we consider both the current assets, and their financing (by both current and long-term sources).

3. The firm's well-being shows up first in its working capital accounts, especially its level of accounts receivable, inventory, and the flow of cash into and out of the firm. Firms that are doing well maintain control of their accounts receivable and inventory, and ensure the continual flow of cash.

4. Working capital is especially important for smaller firms, since they often carry a higher percentage of both current assets and current liabilities. Their survival is much more dependent on effective working capital management than that of larger firms.

Liquidity and the Cash Cycle

We start our analysis of working capital policy with the idea of liquidity. Marketable securities, which are short-term investments for excess cash, are highly liquid. Accounts receivable, which arise from the sale of the firm's goods or services, are less liquid than marketable securities. Inventory exists, but it is often even less liquid than accounts receivable. Liquidity is an important factor in determining a firm's working capital policy. It is a function of current asset and liability levels and composition, and the ability to raise cash when needed. While variability in current asset and liability levels is also important, for many firms the ongoing level of current assets and liabilities is fairly steady. Accordingly, we focus our primary attention on the level, not the variability, of the firm's working capital.

Liquidity has two major aspects—ongoing liquidity and protective liquidity. *Ongoing liquidity* refers to the inflows and outflows of cash through the firm as the product acquisition, production, sales, payment, and collection process takes place over time. *Protective liquidity* refers to the ability to adjust rapidly to unforeseen cash demands, and to have backup means available to raise cash. We begin by addressing ongoing liquidity, and defer a discussion of protective liquidity until later in the chapter.

The firm's ongoing liquidity is a function of its cash cycle. (The cash cycle is shown in the upper left corner of Figure 18.1.) As raw materials are purchased, the firm's current liabilities increase through accounts payable. Subsequently, the firm pays for these purchases. During the same time, the raw materials are converted into finished goods through the production process. After reaching the finished goods inventory, they can be sold—for cash or on credit. In the latter case, accounts receivable are created. Finally, the accounts receivable are collected, resulting in cash. Ongoing liquidity is influenced by all aspects of the cash cycle, since increases in purchases, inventory, or receivables will decrease liquidity. A decrease in any of the three, other things being equal, will increase ongoing liquidity.

A helpful way to look at the cash flow for the firm is to analyze the firm's cash conversion cycle. A *cash conversion cycle* reflects the net time interval in days between actual cash expenditures of the firm on productive resources and the ultimate recovery of cash. As shown in Figure 18.2, once the purchase of the raw materials is made, the *inventory conversion period* determines the average number of days it takes to produce and sell the product. The average collection period determines the average number of days it takes to collect credit sales. The *operating cycle,* which is

$$\begin{matrix} \text{operating} \\ \text{cycle} \end{matrix} = \begin{matrix} \text{inventory conversion} \\ \text{period} \end{matrix} + \begin{matrix} \text{average collection} \\ \text{period} \end{matrix} \qquad (18.1)$$

measures the total number of days from purchase to when cash is received. Because the raw materials typically are not paid for immediately, we must also determine how long the firm defers its payments. The difference between the operating cycle and the *payable deferral period* is the cash conversion cycle:

$$\begin{matrix} \text{cash conversion} \\ \text{cycle} \end{matrix} = \begin{matrix} \text{operating} \\ \text{cycle} \end{matrix} - \begin{matrix} \text{payable deferral} \\ \text{period} \end{matrix} \qquad (18.2)$$

As the cash conversion cycle lengthens, the firm's ongoing liquidity worsens; as the cycle is shortened, the firm's ongoing liquidity improves.

To determine a cash conversion cycle, the following steps are employed:

Figure 18.2 Cash Conversion Cycle for a Typical Firm

By focusing on both current assets and current liabilities, the cash conversion cycle the firm's ongoing liquidity.

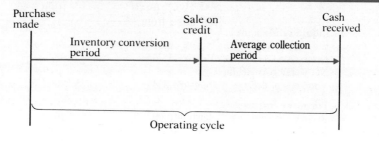

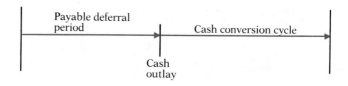

STEP 1: Calculate the receivables turnover, which is:

$$\text{receivables turnover} = \frac{\text{sales}}{\text{accounts receivable}} \tag{18.3}$$

STEP 2: Calculate the inventory turnover:

$$\text{inventory turnover} = \frac{\text{cost of goods sold}}{\text{inventory}} \tag{18.4}$$

STEP 3: Determine the payables turnover:

$$\frac{\text{cost of goods sold} + \text{general, selling, and administrative expenses}}{\text{accounts payable} + \text{salaries, benefits, and payroll taxes payable}} \tag{18.5}$$

STEP 4: Divide the three turnover ratios into 365 days to calculate the average collection period, inventory conversion period, and payable deferral period, respectively:

average collection period = 365/receivables turnover   (18.6)

inventory conversion period = 365/inventory turnover   (18.7)

payable deferral period = 365/payables turnover   (18.8)

STEP 5: Using Equations 18.1 and 18.2, and the values determined in step 4 above, calculate the cash conversion cycle.

These steps are shown in Table 18.1 for J. C. Penney, for 1985, 1986, and 1987. An examination of various liquidity measures (current ratio, quick ratio, and

Table 18.1 Cash Conversion Cycle for J. C. Penney

Although traditional liquidity measures indicate Penney's liquidity has remained relatively constant, its cash conversion cycle has actually decreased during this time period.

	1985	1986	1987
Liquidity Measures			
Current ratio	2.60	2.78	2.65
Quick ratio	1.76	1.98	1.78
Net working capital (in millions of dollars)	$4,354	$4,820	$4,440
Turnover Ratios			
Receivables turnover	3.05	3.19	3.38
Inventory turnover	4.02	4.51	4.32
Payables turnover	14.85	13.16	14.06
Cash Conversion Cycle			
Average collection period	119.59 days	114.25 days	107.99 days
Inventory conversion period	90.78	80.86	84.49
Operating cycle	210.37	195.11	192.48
Less: Payable deferral period	24.58	27.73	25.96
Cash conversion cycle	185.79 days	167.38 days	166.52 days

net working capital) in Table 18.1 indicates that Penney's liquidity appears to have remained fairly constant over this period. By calculating the cash conversion cycle, however, we see that its ongoing liquidity has improved some since 1985. While their cash conversion cycle is "high" due to carrying their accounts receivables (instead of having some other firm provide that financing), it has declined from 186 days in 1985 to 166 days in 1987.

The cash conversion cycle is a quick and convenient way to analyze the ongoing liquidity of the firm over time. Although it does not show how risky the cash flows are, it does focus on our main concern—cash flows. In the case of Penney, the traditional liquidity measures indicate constant liquidity. But the cash conversion cycle, by also incorporating Penney's payable policies, shows that ongoing liquidity is actually increasing. Thus, we see that the cash conversion cycle approach may pick up information hidden by other liquidity measures.

Strategy for Current Asset and Liability Management

Cash flows, liquidity, risk, and required return are essential elements that must be considered in establishing a working capital policy. We begin by analyzing first the strategy for current asset management and then that for current liabilities.

Current Assets　　The major current assets are cash, marketable securities, accounts receivable, and inventory. Before examining these assets in more detail in Chapters 19 and 20, it is helpful to consider the factors influencing a firm's investment in current assets.

The Level of Current Assets

Many factors influence the general level of current assets, but four of the most important are these:

1. NATURE OF THE FIRM'S BUSINESS. The specific activities pursued by the firm often have an important influence on the level of the firm's current assets. Retail firms have much larger inventories than manufacturing firms, leading to a larger percentage of current assets. On the other hand, fast-food chains always have more current liabilities than current assets. Due to the nature of the business, they operate—very successfully we might add—with a *negative* net working capital position.

2. SIZE OF THE FIRM. As shown below, smaller firms have a much higher percentage of current assets than larger firms.[2]

	Manufacturing Firms	
	Assets of $1,000 Million or Greater	Assets Under $25 Million
Assets		
Cash and marketable securities	4.6%	11.4%
Accounts receivable	12.1	26.4
Inventory	12.6	25.1
Other	3.3	3.6
Total	32.6%	66.5%
Current Liabilities		
Short-term debt	2.8%	8.4%
Accounts payable	9.5	14.2
Income tax payable	1.7	1.8
Current portion of long-term debt	1.5	3.4
Other	9.8	7.0
Total	25.3%	34.8%

This is evident in all the current asset accounts. The primary reasons for the differences are that: (a) large firms can devote the resources and attention necessary to manage their current assets; (b) larger firms may have some economies of scale in working capital, or more predictable cash flows; (c) larger firms have more access to the capital market than smaller firms; and (d) as firms get larger they become more capital-intensive. By capital-intensive we mean they tend to use more machines and equipment in the production and distribution process.

3. RATE OF INCREASE (OR DECREASE) IN SALES. As sales increase, there is generally an increase in both accounts receivable and inventory, along with a spontaneous increase in accounts payable. Consider the example of Crown Products, which has been analyzing its current assets and liabilities in relation to sales, as shown in Table 18.2. Current assets have averaged about 30 percent of sales, and current liabilities have been about 8 percent of sales. Note that as sales have increased, current assets have increased by roughly the same proportion. Likewise, current liabilities have tended to increase due to the spontaneous change in accounts payable as inventory expands.

[2] *Quarterly Financial Report for Manufacturing, Mining, and Trade,* Bureau of the Census, Fourth Quarter 1987.

Table 18.2 Working Capital for Crown Products

Although there have been year-to-year fluctuations, the relationships are stable enough for planning purposes.

Year	Current Assets (Thousands)	Current Liabilities (Thousands)	Net Working Capital (Thousands)	Sales (Thousands)	Current Assets/ Sales	Current Liabilities/ Sales	Net Working Capital/ Sales
1	$ 74	$20	$54	$250	29.6%	8.0%	21.6%
2	77	21	56	284	27.1	7.4	19.7
3	90	26	64	275	32.7	9.5	23.3
4	92	25	67	298	30.9	8.4	22.5
5	98	23	75	315	31.1	7.3	23.8
6	110	30	80	375	29.3	8.0	21.3
Average					30.1%	8.1%	22.0%

4. STABILITY OF THE FIRM'S SALES. The more stable the sales, the lower the level of current assets. On the other hand, firms with highly volatile sales must have more current assets, particularly cash and inventory.

Aggressive Versus Conservative Management

In examining the firm's current asset policies, we will concentrate on the composition of the firm's balance sheet. The effect changes in the firm's policies have on its asset composition, and hence its cash conversion cycle, expense levels, and risk and required return will be examined. For the time being, we are not concerned with how the firm finances its current assets; *our concern is solely with the composition of these assets.* A firm can manage its current assets conservatively or aggressively. To see this, consider Figure 18.3, which illustrates both conservative (with higher current asset levels) and aggressive (with lower current asset levels) approaches.

Since current assets never drop to zero, we can think of a firm having a need for some *permanent current assets* on an ongoing basis. At the same time Crown Products, and virtually all other firms, has needs for *seasonal, or temporary, current assets* that fluctuate over the year (or business cycle). The size of both the permanent and temporary current assets is determined, in part, by how aggressive a firm is toward the level of current assets it maintains.

Other things being equal, an aggressive asset management policy leads to (1) lower current assets, (2) a shorter cash conversion cycle, (3) lower expenses, and (4) higher risk and higher required return. Conservative asset management practices have just the opposite effects.

Current Assets. Aggressive asset management generally means lower levels of all current assets. The firm keeps only a minimal level of cash and marketable securities on hand, and relies on effective management and the possibility of short-term borrowing to meet any unexpected cash needs. Likewise, aggressive accounts receivable and inventory management will generally lead to lower levels of both.[3]

[3] In some circumstances, an aggressive accounts receivable or inventory policy could result in a high level of one or both. This is an exception to the general idea that the more aggressive the current asset policy, the lower their level. As noted in Chapter 20, a net present value, NPV, approach should be employed to determine the proper level of accounts receivable and inventory to maintain.

Figure 18.3 Aggressive Versus Conservative Asset Management for Crown Products

Aggressive management leads to higher risk and higher required returns; conservative management provides lower risk exposure and lower required returns.

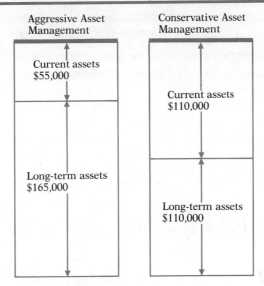

Characteristics of Aggressive Asset Management
1. Low levels of current assets, but effectively and aggressively managed.
2. Short cash conversion cycle.
3. Lower expenses and higher revenue leading to higher EBIT.
4. High risk–high required return strategy.

Characteristics of Conservative Asset Management
1. High levels of current assets.
2. Long cash conversion cycle.
3. Higher expenses and lower revenue leading to lower EBIT.
4. Low risk–low required return strategy.

Cash Conversion Cycle. More aggressive management shortens the cash conversion cycle. Remember from Equation 18.1 that the operating cycle is determined by adding the receivables conversion period to the inventory conversion period. Aggressive asset management, by lowering the average level of both receivables and inventory, increases turnover and shortens conversion periods. So an aggressive policy shortens the firm's operating cycle, which leads to a shorter cash conversion cycle. This increases a firm's ongoing liquidity, because it does not have as large a proportion of its assets tied up in accounts receivable and inventory.

Expense and Revenue Levels. Aggressive current asset management will have the effect of reducing expenses. Fewer accounts receivable will be carried, so there are lower carrying costs. In addition, fewer receivables will have to be written off as uncollectible. Likewise, by keeping inventory to a minimum, the carrying cost associated with inventory is avoided, as well as the possibility for loss due to obsolescence, theft, and so forth. This, in turn, leads to higher earnings before interest and taxes, EBIT, as compared with the results of a conservative asset management policy.

A further effect may be to increase expected revenues, which could also lead to a higher EBIT level. This can occur in two ways. First, if returns on long-term assets are higher than on short-term assets, which they typically are, total revenues should increase. Second, the firm could attempt to increase total revenues by tailoring its credit-granting policy to encourage sales. These presumably more lenient credit terms however, would be granted only if they were expected to lead to an even higher level of EBIT than without them.[4]

Risk and Required Return. Finally, let's consider what happens to the risk and required return for the firm. In Chapter 7 we developed the idea of the capital asset pricing model (CAPM) and nondiversifiable risk (beta) as a means of quantifying risk. Some of these ideas can be employed here, but it is easier to think of risk in terms of a scarcity of cash or other adverse consequences. We can still maintain the conceptual framework that (other things being equal) the higher the risk, the higher the required return, and vice versa.

The risks associated with an aggressive asset position include the possibility of running out of cash, or otherwise being so strapped for funds that effective management of the firm is impeded. Likewise, the firm might keep inventory so low that sales are lost when stockouts occur. The risk associated with an aggressive accounts receivable policy could also result in lost sales if too low a level is kept.

To see the effect of aggressive versus conservative asset management policies while holding other risks constant, consider Crown Products. It can adopt an aggressive or a conservative asset management position, with effects as follows:[5]

	Aggressive	Conservative
Sales	$375,000	$375,000
All expenses	325,000	335,000
EBIT	$ 50,000	$ 40,000

As shown previously in Figure 18.3, the aggressive approach has only $55,000 in current assets, whereas the more conservative approach has $110,000. The impact of fewer current assets and therefore less expenses shows up in EBIT of $50,000 for the aggressive plan, as opposed to only $40,000 with the conservative plan. Thus, by employing a more aggressive approach that exposes the firm to more risk, management has increased its expected EBIT.

Current Liabilities

Now that we have considered current assets, let's consider the financing needed to support these assets. There are two fundamental decisions the firm must make with regard to financing. First, how much will it secure from short-term versus

---

[4] Based on accepting positive NPV projects, the tendency would be for higher, rather than lower, accounts receivable. They would still be aggressively and effectively managed, however, so that they do not get out of control.

[5] For simplicity, we assume total assets and revenues are constant. An aggressive accounts receivable position employing looser credit policies is therefore excluded.

long-term debt (or liability) sources? Second, how much should the firm borrow in relation to what is put up by its owners? The first of these, the short-term versus the long-term question, is considered here. As we will see, the matching principle is widely employed to address this question. The second part, how much debt relative to equity should be employed, is discussed in Chapter 15. For now, we ignore this aspect of the problem and confine our attention to short-term financing.

The Level of Current Liabilities

Retail firms carry more current assets than manufacturing firms. This is primarily because retail firms have to carry more inventory. Because most merchandise for inventory is bought on credit, however, what would you expect the level of a typical retail firm's accounts payable to be compared to that of a typical manufacturing firm? It will be larger, simply because larger inventories lead spontaneously to larger accounts payable. So a major factor influencing the firm's level of current liabilities is its level of inventory and other current assets. Other things being equal, businesses that require high levels of current assets will have a tendency for fairly high levels of current liabilities.

A second element influencing the level of current liabilities is the amount of flexibility desired by the firm. If a firm has a low level of current liabilities it has flexibility, because short-term borrowing can generally be easily employed. Also, accounts payable can be built up in an emergency without endangering the firm. If the firm already has a high level of current liabilities, however, little flexibility is left. The more flexibility the firm wants, the less it will finance with current liabilities.

Aggressive Versus Conservative Management

Other things being equal, the lower the current liabilities, the more conservative the firm's liability management policies. As shown in Figure 18.4, the higher the level of current liabilities, the more aggressive the policy. This is exactly the opposite of an aggressive versus a conservative asset policy. In what follows *we focus on the liabilities, holding assets constant.* Then assets and liabilities will be considered together in the next section. An aggressive liability management policy results in (1) higher current liabilities, (2) a shorter cash conversion cycle, (3) lower interest costs (if short-term rates are less than long-term rates), and (4) higher risk and higher required return. Conservative policies have just the opposite effect.

Current Liabilities. Current liabilities consist of accounts payable, short-term loans or notes payable, various accrued expenses, and the current principal portion of long-term debt due.[6] An aggressive management approach increases the firm's reliance on short-term liabilities. Accounts payable will be used to the greatest extent possible—and payments on them will be made as late as possible without incurring a bad credit reputation. Short-term borrowing will also be used extensively.

Cash Conversion Cycle. By employing more accounts payable and accruals, aggressive liability management shortens the cash conversion cycle. Larger pay-

---

[6] The management of current liabilities is discussed in detail in Chapter 21.

The Savings and Loan Mess

In 1982 the savings and loan industry was deregulated. In the years since then many S&L's have used their new freedom recklessly and ended up in severe financial difficulty. Because of the deposit insurance guarantee, however, most depositors did not stand to lose even though the S&L's were making imprudent loans. As part of the bailout that started in 1988, many of the S&L's were taken over and sold to new investors. The process worked something like this. Federal regulators made deals with numerous private investors to rescue the ailing thrifts. The private investors then put up new capital for the insolvent or near-insolvent S&L's. The regulators in turn agreed to absorb big losses from the thrifts' bad loans. If the thrifts subsequently didn't make it, the new owners were out their money, but depositors didn't lose. On the other hand, if the new owners turned the S&L's around, they stood to benefit by collecting on many of the mortgages that were held by the S&L's.

The size of the deal was, and is, immense—it is estimated that at least $165 billion will need to be spent to rescue the beleaguered savings and loan industry. The rescue plan involves increased deposit insurance, tighter regulation, long-term government debt, and a restructuring that blurs the differences between S&L's and banks. In addition, an increase in the amount of cash that is held as part of the savings and loan capital is now required. (This cash is its reserve or cushion against losses on lending.) Two points are obvious from this mess. First, the savings and loan industry will never be the same as it was before the events of 1988. Second, taxpayers—that's you and I—are footing the bill for bailing out the savings and loan industry.

ables and accruals lead to a shorter payables turnover. This leads to a longer payable deferral period and a shorter cash conversion cycle. Aggressive liability management tends to increase the ongoing liquidity of the firm by shortening the cash conversion cycle—but it also has less future flexibility.

Interest Costs. To understand fully the impact of aggressive versus conservative liability management on a firm's interest costs, it is necessary to consider the term structure of interest rates presented in Chapter 2. At that time we discussed the yield curve, which plots the term to maturity versus the yield to maturity for borrowings that are equally risky, but which differ in terms of length to maturity. Yield curves are generally upward-sloping—which means that long-term debt financing is more expensive than short-term debt financing. An expected benefit of an aggressive liability management program is being able to borrow funds at a cheaper rate than the firm would pay for long-term debt financing.

To see the expected benefits of an aggressive versus conservative policy, consider again the example of Crown Products. In Figure 18.4, two different liability strategies were presented. The aggressive one employs $100,000 in current liabilities and only $30,000 in long-term liabilities. The conservative policy employs $30,000 in

Figure 18.4 Aggressive Versus Conservative Liability Management for Crown Products

Aggressive liability management is a high risk–high required return strategy, whereas a conservative approach produces lower risks and lower required returns.

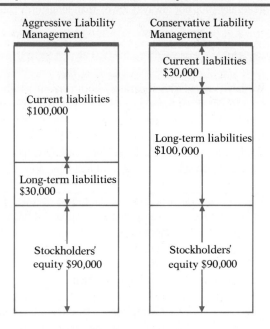

Characteristics of Aggressive Liability Management
1. High levels of current liabilities.
2. Short cash conversion cycle.
3. Lower interest costs if short-term rates are lower than long-term rates.
4. High risk–high required return strategy.

Characteristics of Conservative Liability Management
1. Low levels of current liabilities.
2. Long cash conversion cycle.
3. Higher interest costs if long-term rates are higher than short-term rates.
4. Low risk–low required return strategy.

current liabilities and $100,000 in long-term liabilities. If short-term interest rates are 10 percent and long-term rates are 14 percent, the total before-tax interest cost is $14,200 [(0.10)($100,000) + (0.14)($30,000)] for the aggressive policy, and $17,000 [(0.10)($30,000) + (0.14)($100,000)] for the conservative one. As long as long-term rates are higher than short-term rates, interest costs are reduced, leading to higher earnings for the firm.

Risk and Required Return. The main risk of an aggressive liability policy comes from general economic conditions and the continual need to refinance current liabilities. This is especially true if a firm is using extensive short-term financing through borrowing. Although the firm may be able to secure the financing, it is exposed to interest cost fluctuations. These fluctuating interest costs, and the continual need to refinance, increase the firm's risk exposure. An additional risk arises from reduced flexibility when the current liability level is high. Other things being equal, there are substantial risks associated with an aggressive liability policy that relies on large amounts of short-term debt. Greater returns are expected, however, by (1) reducing the cash conversion cycle, and (2) financing at interest rates that are generally (but not always) lower than long-term rates.

Putting It All Together

We have considered separately both current assets and current liabilities. Now it is time to put them together and discuss the management of the firm's working capital in total. The three basic strategies a firm could follow, as illustrated in Figure 18.5, are aggressive, conservative, or matched. The matched strategy, which is often cited as a guideline employed for working capital management, is embodied in the matching principle, or the idea of self-liquidating debt.

The Matching Principle

The *matching principle* can be stated as follows: Permanent investments in assets should be financed with permanent sources of financing, and temporary assets should be financed with temporary financing sources. The idea behind the matching principle is to match, or counterbalance, the cash-flow-generating characteristics of the assets with the maturity of the financing. A temporary buildup in current assets should be financed with current liabilities, which can be liquidated as the investment in current assets is reduced. A buildup in permanent current and long-term assets will take longer to convert to cash; hence, long-term financing will be needed.[7]

The matching principle can be applied to our previous discussion of aggressive versus conservative asset and liability policies. From Figure 18.5 we see that an aggressive asset policy calls for a low level of current assets and a conservative policy calls for a high level. Likewise, an aggressive liability policy calls for a high level of current liabilities and a conservative policy calls for a low level. To match them, the following rules apply:

1. If a firm has an aggressive current asset position (with a low level of current assets), it should counterbalance its risks by employing a conservative liability position (with a low level of current liabilities).
2. If a firm has a conservative current asset position (employing a high level of current assets), it should counterbalance its risks by employing an aggressive liability position (with a large amount of current liabilities).
3. If a firm has a moderate current asset position, it should counterbalance its risks by employing a moderate liability position.

The implication of the matching principle is that the firm should establish some *target* for its net working capital position that takes into account risks, required returns, and the appropriate current asset and current liability positions.

To see this, let's reconsider the example of Crown Products. With an aggressive asset approach it employs fewer current assets, so that expenses are reduced and

---

[7]Matching can be accomplished by matching on the basis of maturity, cash flows, or duration. These topics are beyond our coverage.

Figure 18.5 Alternative Working Capital Policies

By altering both its asset and its liability structure, the firm can vary its working capital policy considerably.

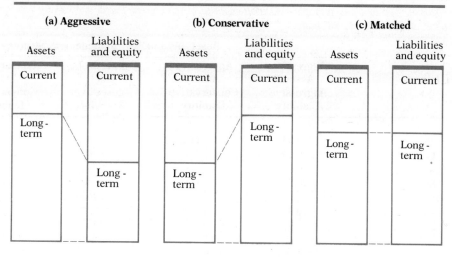

EBIT increases compared to a conservative approach. Likewise, an aggressive liability approach employs more current liabilities and results in lower total interest costs than a more conservative liability policy. As shown in Table 18.3, the following combinations exist for Crown Products: (1) a high risk–high required return policy employing both aggressive asset and aggressive liability strategies; (2) two intermediate strategies employing either an aggressive asset–conservative liability or a conservative asset–aggressive liability strategy;[8] and (3) a low risk–low required return policy employing both conservative asset and conservative liability policies. Note that the two intermediate strategies embody the matching principle. In line with the risks involved, the aggressive strategy has expected earnings of $23,270, whereas the conservative strategy has expected earnings of only $14,950.

Which working capital strategy should Crown select? As we know, it is not earnings that are most important, it is the market price of the firm's stock. Assume that Crown Products has 10,000 shares of stock outstanding. The earnings per share for the four strategies will be as follows:

	EAT	÷	Number of Shares	=	EPS
Aggressive asset; aggressive liability	$23,270		10,000		$2.327
Aggressive asset; conservative liability	21,450		10,000		2.145
Conservative asset; aggressive liability	16,770		10,000		1.677
Conservative asset; conservative liability	14,950		10,000		1.495

To determine the per share market value, we know that $P_0 = (EPS)(P/E)$, where P/E is the firm's price/earnings ratio. Since aggressive asset or liability policies are

---

[8] An alternative combination would be a more moderate position in both current assets and current liabilities.

Table 18.3 Impact of Alternative Current Asset and Liability Strategies on the Earnings of Crown Products

A high-risk strategy employs low current assets and high current liabilities, whereas a low-risk strategy is just the opposite. The matching principle, which attempts to match current assets and current liabilities, results in a tradeoff between risk and required return.

	Asset and Liability Management Strategy				
	Aggressive Asset; Aggressive Liability	Aggressive Asset; Conservative Liability	Conservative Asset; Aggressive Liability	Conservative Asset; Conservative Liability	
Sales	$375,000	$375,000	$375,000	$375,000	Impact of asset
Expenses	325,000	325,000	335,000	335,000	strategy
EBIT	50,000	50,000	40,000	40,000	
Interest	14,200	17,000	14,200	17,000	Impact of
EBT	35,800	33,000	25,800	23,000	liability
Taxes (35%)	12,530	11,550	9,030	8,050	strategy
EAT	$ 23,270	$ 21,450	$ 16,770	$ 14,950	
	High-risk, high-required return strategy	Intermediate positions more in line with matching principle		Low-risk, low-required return strategy	

viewed as being more risky by stockholders, other things being equal, they will have a lower P/E ratio than more conservative policies. Crown Products needs to estimate the potential impact of the various working capital strategies on its expected market value. One way is to forecast P/Es for various risk–required return strategies. For our example, assume these estimates are as follows:

	EPS	×	P/E	=	P_0
Aggressive asset; aggressive liability	$2.327		9		$20.94
Aggressive asset; conservative liability	2.145		10		21.45
Conservative asset; aggressive liability	1.677		11		18.45
Conservative asset; conservative liability	1.495		12		17.94

Based on these expected market values, Crown should implement one of the matching strategies (aggressive asset; conservative liability), since it provides the maximum market value for stockholders.

Recognizing and Dealing with Liquidity Problems

The firm's working capital policies need to take into account many factors. No matter how much planning is done, however, the firm must be able to recognize signs of declining liquidity and know how to deal with the situation. Some of the most important signs of deteriorating liquidity are these:

1. An unexpected buildup in inventory (an increase in the inventory conversion period).
2. An increase in the firm's level of outstanding accounts receivable (an increase in the average collection period).
3. A decline in the firm's daily or weekly cash inflows.
4. Increased costs the firm is unable to pass on to its customers.
5. A decline in the firm's net working capital, or an increase in its debt ratio.

These and similar occurrences indicate the firm has (or will have) a liquidity problem.

There are many different approaches for dealing with liquidity problems, depending on the source of the problem, its severity, and its expected length. Managers often take some of the following steps to deal with liquidity problems:

1. Control and reduce investment in inventory.
2. Reexamine and tighten up on credit and reduce the firm's level of accounts receivable.
3. Increase short-term or long-term debt, or issue equity.
4. Control overhead and increase awareness of the need for effective asset management.
5. Lay off employees.
6. Reduce planned long-term (capital) expenditures.
7. Reduce or eliminate cash dividends.

If these measures are not sufficient, more drastic steps will be necessary. The important point is that firms must plan for meeting ongoing liquidity problems as part of their working capital policies.

Protective Liquidity

Up to now we have been talking about the firm's ongoing liquidity. There is, however, another aspect of liquidity called protective liquidity, the ability to have liquid resources to meet unexpected cash demands. These demands may arise when, due to unforeseen circumstances, larger cash outflows (or smaller cash inflows) than expected occur. In some cases cash is needed to take advantage of unexpected opportunities. At other times, unexpected cash drains occur.

Planning the firm's working capital and liquidity needs involves uncertainty. Some of this uncertainty can be eliminated by effective cash budgeting (discussed in Chapter 4), but uncertainty still remains. Effective managers, whether they follow a conservative, aggressive, or matched working capital policy, always maintain some protective liquidity. This may be in the form of one or more *lines of credit,* which are just short-term borrowing agreements the firm has negotiated with a bank. At the firm's discretion, it may borrow or pay back on the line of credit.

Another strategy is to maintain a fairly large marketable securities portfolio, or have a bond or stock issue ready. Other firms establish bank relations and keep the bank informed about whether or not the firm will need to borrow from the bank. An alternative approach, to be discussed in Chapter 21, is to factor (or sell) the firm's accounts receivable. Effective management of the firm's working capital involves a continual tradeoff between risk and required return. To deal with risk, firms establish various means of ensuring protective liquidity as they formulate working capital policies.

Summary

Effective working capital management is at the core of financial management. Firms that are effective devote a lot of time and attention to working capital management. By doing so they are able to manage this portion of the firm's assets and liabilities in a manner that contributes to the overall goal of maximizing the value of the firm.

To understand working capital policy, it is important to understand the firm's cash cycle. By focusing on the cash conversion cycle, the manager's attention can be focused on the impact of various working capital decisions on liquidity. Both the asset and the liability sides may be managed in an aggressive or conservative manner. One guideline is the matching principle, whereby temporary assets are financed by temporary financing, and permanent assets are financed with permanent financing. Other things being equal, aggressive asset management lowers costs, whereas aggressive liability management lowers cash outflows related to interest. Both have the effect of increasing the returns required by the firm's stockholders, but they also increase the risk exposure of the firm.

We must also recognize that working capital management is not a one-time decision. The best strategy may vary, depending on the season of the year, the level of interest rates, or the stage of the business cycle. Working capital management is a dynamic area; the firm must be responsive to ongoing needs and goals, the state of the economy, trends in marketing and production, and risks and required returns. As these factors change, working capital policies must also change.

Questions

18.1 Define or explain the following:

a.	Working capital	**g.**	Operating cycle
b.	Spontaneous short-term financing	**h.**	Payable deferral period
c.	Ongoing liquidity	**i.**	Permanent current assets
d.	Protective liquidity	**j.**	Seasonal (temporary) current assets
e.	Cash conversion cycle	**k.**	Matching principle
f.	Inventory conversion period	**l.**	Line of credit

18.2 In a world of perfect markets, firms should not invest in working capital (since it lowers their value). What accounts for the sizable levels of current assets and current liabilities we observe?

18.3 Determine the impact of the following actions on a firm's cash conversion cycle:

a. It loosens its credit terms, leading to increased sales and accounts receivable. Sales increase more than receivables, on a percentage basis.

b. Payments on accounts owed are stretched from a 20-day average to a 35-day average.

c. It borrows on a short-term note instead of stretching payables, as in (b).

d. By introducing new control procedures, the firm reduces its inventory.

18.4 Explain why the basic nature of the firm's business, and its size, influence the amount of current assets required. Do the same factors also influence current liabilities?

18.5 Consider how an aggressive (versus a conservative) asset management position influences (a) the level of current assets, (b) the cash conversion cycle, (c) expense levels, and (d) risk and required return.

18.6 Consider how an aggressive (versus a conservative) liability management position influences (a) the level of current liabilities, (b) the cash conversion cycle, (c) interest costs, and (d) risk and required return.

18.7 At certain times the term structure of interest rates may be such that short-term rates are higher than long-term rates. Does it follow that the firm should finance entirely with long-term debt during such periods? Explain.

18.8 The firm faces two primary decisions with respect to its financing: (1) the percentage of short- or long-term financing to employ, and (2) the amount of borrowing to use relative to the owners' contribution. Discuss both decisions and how they might affect each other.

18.9 What is the matching principle? How does its use relate to the firm's cash conversion cycle, and its risk and required return?

Self-Test Problems (Solutions appear on pages 733–734.)

Cash Conversion Cycle

ST 18.1 A firm's cash conversion cycle is 40 days. If a 365-day year is employed, the receivables turnover is 8, and the payables turnover is 10, then consider the following questions:

a. What is the firm's inventory turnover?
b. What are accounts receivable if credit sales are $920,000?

Liquidity, New Common Stock, and Market Price

ST 18.2 Pittsburgh Distributors has the following balance sheet and income statement.

Balance Sheet		Income Statement	
Cash	$ 25,000	Sales	$900,000
Accounts receivable	60,000	Cost of goods sold	400,000
Inventory	65,000	General, selling, and	
Long-term assets	350,000	administrative expenses	100,000
Total assets	$500,000	All other expenses	250,000
		Net income (EAT)	$150,000
Accounts payable plus			
salaries, benefits, and			
payroll taxes payable	$ 80,000		
Other current liabilities	20,000		
Long-term debt	100,000		
Stockholders' equity			
(50,000 shares)	300,000		
Total liabilities and			
stockholders' equity	$500,000		

a. Determine Pittsburgh Distributors liquidity situation by calculating the current ratio, working capital, the ratio of current assets to total assets, the ratio of current liabilities to total assets, and the cash conversion cycle.
b. What is the current market price per share of Pittsburgh's stock if its P/E ratio is 8 times earnings?
c. David Sellers, Pittsburgh's chief financial officer, is very conservative and believes that the current ratio needs to be raised to 2.0. To accomplish this, he proposes to sell 2,500 shares of common stock to net the firm $20 per share. The proceeds will be added to the firm's cash account. Assuming everything else remains the same, determine the following:
   (1) Pittsburgh's new liquidity position, as in (a).
   (2) Its new market price per share.
   (3) Whether or not Pittsburgh should issue the stock.

Problems

18.1 Malott, Inc., is planning to make a $10 million investment in long-term assets and is attempting to estimate how much additional net working capital will be needed to support this expansion. The fixed asset turnover ratio on the new investment is estimated to be 2. From past experience, Malott estimates its total asset turnover ratio is 1. Also, for every dollar increase in current assets the firm experiences, about 60 percent of the increase can be financed through spontaneous increases in current liabilities. Determine the increase in net working capital that should accompany the anticipated increase in long-term assets.

18.2 San Francisco Systems has the following turnover ratios: receivables turnover, 6.0; inventory turnover, 4.0; payables turnover, 3.75.

a. Find San Francisco Systems' cash conversion cycle.

b. Now find its cash conversion cycle if receivables turnover improves to 7.0 and inventory turnover increases to 5.5.

c. Now assume the inventory conversion period is as determined in (b), and the payables turnover increases to 5.3. If the firm then wants a cash conversion cycle of no more than 35 days, what must the receivables turnover be?

18.3 Lee Corporation specializes in the design, manufacture, and marketing of products for the transmission and control of power. For 2 recent years, information is as follows:

	Year 1 (In thousands)	Year 0 (In thousands)
Sales	$2,711	$2,524
Cost of goods sold	2,224	2,106
Cost of goods sold plus general, selling, and administrative expenses	2,497	2,353
Accounts receivable	382	377
Inventory	602	619
Accounts payable plus accrued wages and employee benefits	245	223

Fresno Paper produces and markets a variety of paper products through its five divisions. Information for the same 2 years is as follows:

	Year 1 (In thousands)	Year 0 (In thousands)
Sales	$1,403	$1,233
Cost of goods sold	1,173	1,021
Cost of goods sold plus general, selling, and administrative expenses	1,286	1,123
Accounts receivable	136	138
Inventory	153	138
Accounts payable plus accrued wages and employee benefits	82	78

a. Calculate the cash conversion cycle for both firms for both years.

b. What trends, if any, are evident between year 0 and year 1?

c. Do you think part of these differences are caused by the industries they operate in? Why or why not?

18.4 Wood Management Group is attempting to determine its optimal level of current assets. It is considering three alternative policies, as follows:

	Aggressive	Average	Conservative
Current assets	$ 500	$ 700	$ 900
Long-term assets	1,000	800	600
Total	$1,500	$1,500	$1,500

In any case, the firm will employ the following financing: current liabilities of $700, long-term debt of $200, and common equity of $600. Sales are expected to be $2,500, but because of lower costs with the more aggressive policies, the ratio of EBIT to sales is 13 percent with the aggressive policy, 12 percent with the average risk policy, and 11 percent with the conservative policy. Interest is $65, and the tax rate is 30 percent.

a. Determine net income under the three different plans.

b. In this problem, we assumed that both total assets and sales are the same with any of the policies. Are these typically valid assumptions?

c. How, specifically, does the risk vary under the three plans? As part of your analysis, calculate the current ratio (current assets/current liabilities) and net working capital.

Reducing Inventory

18.5 LeCompte Software keeps a large inventory in order not to lose sales. Its new vice-president for finance has recommended that the firm's inventory be cut. Doing so would reduce the inventory level by $150,000 and allow the firm to forgo renewing a $150,000 note payable carrying a 12 percent interest rate that matures soon. An abbreviated income statement for LeCompte is as follows:

EBIT	$1,000,000
Interest	140,000
EBT	860,000
Taxes (35%)	301,000
Net Income (EAT)	$ 559,000

With 100,000 shares of stock outstanding and a P/E ratio of 10 times earnings, LeCompte's current stock price is $55.90.

a. Scenario 1: If EBIT and the P/E ratio are unaffected by the reduction in inventory and notes payable, what would the new market price be? (*Note:* Carry to three decimal places for EPS.)

b. Scenario 2: The marketing manager for LeCompte believes the inventory reduction will result in lower sales, and hence EBIT will decrease to $950,000. What would the market price be if this happens?

c. If there is a 60 percent chance that EBIT will stay at $1,000,000, and a 40 percent chance it will drop to $950,000, what action should LeCompte Software take?

(Do only if using Pinches Disk.)

d. If the note payable had a 14 percent coupon rate instead of 12 percent, what would be the new market price under scenarios 1 and 2? What action should the firm take if the percent chance of each scenario is the same as in (c)?

e. Recalculate the market price for both scenarios if the interest rate is again 12 percent and EBIT estimated for scenario 1 is $1,200,000 and for scenario 2 is $800,000. What action should the firm take if the weights are 70 percent for scenario 1 and 30 percent for scenario 2?

f. What are your answers to (a) through (e) if the marginal tax rate is only 20 percent? (*Note:* This also changes the original stock price of $55.90.)

Working Capital Management

18.6 Three companies—aggressive, average, and conservative—follow different working capital policies, as their names imply.

	Aggressive	Average	Conservative
Current assets	$ 300	$ 400	$ 600
Long-term assets	700	600	400
Total	$1,000	$1,000	$1,000
Current liabilities	$ 500	$ 350	$ 200
Long-term debt	100	250	400
Common equity	400	400	400
Total	$1,000	$1,000	$1,000

Selected income and balance sheet data are as follows:

	Aggressive	Average	Conservative
Sales	$1,800	$1,800	$1,800
Cost of goods sold	1,260	1,280	1,300
Cost of goods sold plus general, selling, and administrative expenses	1,560	1,580	1,600
Accounts receivable	120	160	240
Inventory	150	200	300
Accruals and accounts payable	250	200	100
Short-term borrowing	200	150	100

The interest rate on short-term debt is 10 percent, while on long-term debt it is 12 percent. The tax rate is 30 percent.

a. Determine the net income for each firm.
b. Calculate the cash conversion cycle for each firm.
c. What is the current ratio and the net working capital for each firm?
d. Are there other factors that would have to be taken into account in practice? What are the major ones?

Alternative Working Capital Policies

18.7 Salomon & Morgan is considering whether to adopt plan I or plan II for its current assets and liabilities. Adopting one plan versus the other is expected to affect sales, expenses, and interest. As a result, taxes and earnings after tax (EAT) will also vary. Based on a 50 percent probability of a good or bad year, Salomon & Morgan's finance department has made the following projections:

	Plan I		Plan II	
	Good Year	Bad Year	Good Year	Bad Year
Probability	0.50	0.50	0.50	0.50
Sales	$900,000	$800,000	$850,000	$760,000
All expenses except interest and taxes	750,000	710,000	730,000	690,000
EBIT	150,000	90,000	120,000	70,000
Interest	20,000	17,000	22,000	20,000
EBT	130,000	73,000	98,000	50,000
Taxes (40%)	52,000	29,200	39,200	20,000
Net income (EAT)	$ 78,000	$ 43,800	$ 58,800	$ 30,000

Salomon & Morgan has 10,000 shares of common stock outstanding. Risk will be measured by the coefficient of variation of earnings per share. (*Note:* The coefficient of variation is standard deviation/mean.)

a. Calculate the expected EPS, standard deviation of EPS, and coefficient of variation of EPS for both plans.

b. If Plan I carries a P/E ratio of 11 times earnings and Plan II a P/E of 10 times, which plan should Salomon & Morgan choose?

18.8 Williams, Inc., has the following income statement and balance sheet.

Balance Sheet			Income Statement	
Cash and marketable			Sales	$1,800
securities	$ 50		Cost of goods sold	
Accounts receivable	100		(70% of sales)	1,260
Inventory	100		General, selling, and	
Long-term assets	600		administrative expenses	190
Total assets	$850		EBIT	350
			Interest	25
Short-term debt	$ 50		EBT	325
Accounts payable	70		Taxes (36%)	117
Salaries, benefits, and			Net income (EAT)	$ 208
payroll taxes payable	40			
Other current liabilities	40			
Long-term debt	150			
Stockholders' equity				
(100 shares)	500			
Total liabilities and				
stockholders' equity	$850			

a. Determine Williams' current liquidity position by calculating its current ratio, net working capital, ratio of current assets to total assets, ratio of current liabilities to total assets, and cash conversion cycle.

b. If its current P/E ratio is 8 times earnings, what is Williams' present market price per share?

c. The marketing vice-president of Williams believes significant sales are being lost because of both not offering enough credit to customers and lack of inventory. In conjunction with the chief financial officer, the following plan has been prepared:

- $250 will be raised; $100 will be additional short-term debt with a 12 percent interest rate, and the other $150 will be additional long-term debt with a 14 percent interest rate.
- Cash will increase by $50, accounts receivable by $115, and inventory by $115; because of the increase in inventory, accounts payable will increase $30. (*Note:* Current assets increase by $30 more than the $250 due to the $30 of spontaneous short-term financing provided by the increase in accounts payable.)
- Sales are expected to be $2,200, cost of goods sold will remain 70 percent of sales, and general, selling, and administrative expenses will increase by $30.
- All other accounts remain the same.

Since investors are expected to view the new plan as being more risky, the new P/E ratio is estimated to be 7 times earnings.

(1) What is Williams' new liquidity position? [*Note:* Calculate the same information as you did in (a).]

(2) Calculate the new income statement. What is the new market price per share?

(3) Should Williams proceed with the plan?

18.9 Nashville Manufacturing is preparing a 2-year plan for its asset investments, as given in the following schedule. (For simplicity, long-term assets are assumed to be constant at

$40 million, as is stockholders' equity. Hence, you have to concern yourself only with current assets, current liabilities, and long-term debt.)

	Date	Total Current Assets per Period (In millions)
Year 1	3/31	$30
	6/30	36
	9/30	42
	12/31	39
Year 2	3/31	33
	6/30	39
	9/30	45
	12/31	42

a. Current liabilities tend to equal one-third of Nashville's current assets. If Nashville has $15 million in long-term debt, determine the amount of short-term borrowing required per quarter to complete the financing of the firm's current assets. (*Note:* The $15 million is constant and thus available each quarter.)

b. Instead of (a), assume that no long-term debt exists. How much short-term debt will be needed per quarter to match, or counterbalance, current assets?

c. If short-term interest rates are 9 percent and long-term rates are 11 percent, how much interest does Nashville save over the 2 years by matching its current assets? (*Note:* Remember that the interest is paid quarterly, so the quarterly amount is only one-fourth of the yearly amount.)

References

Recent books on working capital policy include

HILL, NED C., AND WILLIAM L. SARTORIS. *Short-Term Financial Management.* New York: Macmillan, 1988.

KALLBERG, JARL G., JOYCE R. OCHS, AND KENNETH L. PARKINSON (eds.) *Essentials of Cash Management.* 3rd ed. Newtown, Conn.: National Corporate Cash Management Association, 1989.

KALLBERG, JARL G., AND KENNETH PARKINSON. *Current Asset Management: Cash, Credit and Inventory.* New York: Wiley, 1984.

SCHERR, FREDERICK C. *Modern Working Capital Management.* Englewood Cliffs, N.J.: Prentice-Hall, 1989.

VANDER WEIDE, JAMES, AND STEVEN F. MAIER. *Managing Corporate Liquidity: An Introduction to Working Capital Management.* New York: Wiley, 1985.

Two articles attempting to show theoretically that firms should have working capital are

COHN, RICHARD A., AND JOHN J. PRINGLE. "Steps Toward an Integration of Corporate Financial Theory." In *Readings on the Management of Working Capital,* Keith V. Smith (ed.). St. Paul: West, 1980, pp. 35–41.

MORRIS, JAMES R. "The Role of Cash Balances in Firm Valuation." *Journal of Financial and Quantitative Analysis* 18 (December 1983), pp. 533–545.

The cash conversion cycle is discussed in

RICHARDS, VERLYN D., AND EUGENE J. LAUGHLIN. "A Cash Conversion Cycle Approach to Liquidity Analysis." *Financial Management* 9 (Spring 1980), pp. 32–38.

For more on recent developments, see

CRUM, ROY L., DARWIN D. KLINGMAN, AND LEE A. TAVIS. "An Operational Approach to Integrated Working Capital Planning." *Journal of Economics and Business* 35 (August 1983), pp. 343–378.

GENTRY, JAMES A. "State of the Art of Short-Run Financial Management." *Financial Management* 17 (Summer 1988), pp. 41–57.

GILMER, R. H., JR. "The Optimal Level of Liquid Assets: An Empirical Test." *Financial Management* 14 (Winter 1985), pp. 39–43.

HILL, NED C., AND DANIEL M. FERGUSON. "Cash Flow Timeline Management: The Next Frontier of Cash Management." *Journal of Cash Management* 5 (May–June 1985), pp. 12–22.

VISÇIONE, JERRY A. "How Long Should You Borrow Short Term?" *Harvard Business Review* 64 (March–April 1986), pp. 20–22, 24.

19 | Cash and Marketable Securities

Overview

- Total float time is comprised of mail float, processing float, and transit float.

- Because of float, firms attempt to speed the cash gathering process while controlling (or slowing) disbursement. The primary means for speeding collections are lockboxes and an efficient banking arrangement. Disbursements are managed by using controlled disbursing, zero balance accounts, and similar arrangements.

- The incremental costs and benefits are analyzed when comparing alternative cash and marketable security procedures.

- Risk and required return considerations determine both the amount of liquid assets held by a firm and the composition of its marketable securities portfolio.

I n 1985, E. F. Hutton, then the nation's fifth largest brokerage firm, pleaded guilty to 2,000 counts of bilking banks through an elaborate check overdraft scheme. It agreed to pay a fine of $2 million and prosecution costs of $750,000. In addition, Hutton agreed to pay back banks that may have been defrauded; it reserved some $8 million for that purpose. As a result of this case, the Justice Department has attempted to draw some legal limits around many cash management practices where none existed before. In so doing, it has sought to clarify the thin line between aggressive cash management—a tactic practiced by more and more firms—and outright fraud.

In the last decade cash management has become an increasingly important financial function. Higher interest rates were only one factor increasing the impact of successful cash management on bottom-line profits. Firms have been beefing up their cash management staffs, while technological advances have given cash managers ready access to information on cash inflows, outflows, and idle balances. Cash management is no longer a dead-end job, and cash managers are becoming part of the firm's overall planning function. One sign of this was the creation in 1980 of the National Corporate Cash Management Association (NCCMA).

These developments have created a dynamic area, one that will continue to undergo rapid change. The future will see further deregulation of financial institutions, the growth of regional and national financial service systems, and technological advances affecting both corporate payment systems and the information available to cash managers.

The Cash Management Function

Cash refers to currency on hand plus the demand deposits held in checking accounts at various commercial banks. *Marketable securities* are the short-term investments the firm may temporarily hold that can be quickly converted into cash. Together, cash and marketable securities form the *liquid assets* of the firm. There are three main questions relating to liquid asset management:

1. How should the firm design its cash-gathering and cash-disbursing system?
2. How should the investment in liquid assets be split between cash and marketable securities?
3. How should the marketable securities portfolio be managed?

Before discussing these, however, we need to consider some general aspects of the cash management function. Since liquid assets generally provide lower returns than long-term assets, we need to understand why firms hold liquid assets. Then we will discuss the general risk–required return aspects of liquid assets, followed by an examination of how much cash and how many marketable securities some typical firms hold.

Reasons for Holding Cash

The four basic reasons firms hold cash are as follows:

1. TRANSACTIONS PURPOSES. In the everyday course of business, firms need a certain minimum amount of cash on hand to meet cash outflow requirements. These include routine items such as paying the monthly bills, making payments to suppliers, and the like. In addition, cash is needed for major items such as tax payments, dividends, salaries, and paying interest and/or principal related to debt.
2. HEDGE AGAINST UNCERTAINTY. A second reason for holding liquid assets is as a hedge against uncertain future events. These funds often are held in the form of marketable securities. An alternative to holding liquid assets to hedge against uncertainty is to obtain a line of credit. With a line of credit, the firm can borrow up to a specified maximum amount from a bank over some time period. These lines of credit generally require a commitment fee, whether they are used or not.
3. CASH HOARD. Firms often hold liquid assets in anticipation of some future use. Many firms hold substantial amounts of liquid assets in anticipation of making future acquisitions of other firms or having the ability to fund, quickly and easily, positive net present value, NPV, capital investments. Likewise, during periods of economic downturn firms postpone capital expenditures and attempt to hoard liquid assets to "weather the storm."

4. COMPENSATING BALANCE REQUIREMENT. Banks perform many services for firms, including the collection and disbursement of funds, handling interbank transfers, providing lines of credit, and making loans. The compensation received by the bank comes from two sources—direct fees and *compensating balances*. A compensating balance is a certain amount the firm agrees to leave on deposit in its checking account. Typically this is set at some level related to the size of the loan or the amount of services provided.

Risk and Return

The main returns that can be expected from holding liquid assets are as follows:

1. The interest income earned by investing in marketable securities. Effective marketable security management can easily pay for itself and make an important contribution to the firm's overall profitability.
2. By having the cash on hand, firms can take advantage of *cash discounts* offered by suppliers and thereby lower the cost of items purchased. This topic is discussed in Chapter 21.
3. Occasionally the firm may find it can take advantage of special purchases by having cash on hand. The savings associated with these purchases represent a return for holding cash.
4. Finally, the firm's credit rating can be influenced by the amount of liquid assets the firm has. Holding too low a liquid asset level may adversely affect the firm's creditworthiness, and its credit rating will be lower, resulting in higher future costs for securing both short- and long-term funds.

The fundamental risk involved in holding too little cash relates to an inability to operate in the normal manner. If cash inflow is a problem, paying bills may have to be deferred, capital expenditures curtailed, short-term financing obtained, and assets sold. Other opportunities that present themselves will have to be bypassed. In an extreme case, the firm may be forced to file for protection under the bankruptcy code or forced into liquidation. The risk–required return tradeoff for liquid assets involves the following:

1. Having enough cash and liquid reserves (in the form of marketable securities or lines of credit) to meet all the firm's obligations.
2. Not holding excess liquid reserves, since investment in long-term assets generally provides higher returns than short-term investments.
3. Maintaining a minimum cash balance while actively managing the firm's portfolio of marketable securities to ensure as high a return as possible commensurate with the risk involved.

These tradeoffs will guide our discussion as we seek to maximize the value of the firm through liquid asset decisions.

Liquidity Policies in Practice

The amount of liquid assets held by a firm depends on many factors. Two of the main reasons for different liquid asset levels in practice are the following:

1. SIZE OF THE FIRM. As we saw in Chapter 18, large manufacturing firms held under 5 percent of their total assets in the form of cash and marketable securities,

while small ones held over 11 percent. Other things being equal, small firms hold more cash and marketable securities than large ones.

2. AGGRESSIVE VERSUS CONSERVATIVE MANAGEMENT. Data on two specific industries—and some selected firms within each industry for 1981, 1984, and 1987 are as follows:[1]

	Industry	Individual Firms	
Year	Retail Merchandise	May	J.C. Penney
1981	3.0%	2.1%	2.0%
1984	2.7	4.6	1.9
1987	3.3	2.8	1.0
Year	Aircraft, Guided Missiles and Parts	Boeing	Grumman
1981	6.5%	13.2%	6.2%
1984	6.3	18.9	6.5
1987	6.1	27.3	6.1

While both the retail merchandise and aircraft industries held about the same percentage amount of cash and marketable securities in all 3 years, there are sizable differences between firms. Boeing always held considerable liquid assets, while May and Penney were at the other end of the spectrum. Grumman occupied a middle position. These differences are due in part to the specific circumstances facing the firm and the amount of risk it is willing to undertake. As we saw in Chapter 18, a firm's aggressiveness or conservatism shows up in many facets of its working capital policy.

Cash Management Techniques

The flow of cash into and out of the firm is continual. Although the level at any point in time is a function of many factors, certain basic cash management ideas are fundamental to any firm, whatever its size, or industry, or the state of the economy. Two major aspects of cash management involve speeding the inflows through a cash-gathering system and controlling the outflows, via a cash-disbursing system.

Speeding the Inflows

The complexity of the cash-gathering system depends on the size of the firm and the scope of its operations. Small local firms will have very simple systems; large national or multinational firms will have very extensive systems. In the cash-gathering system, the concept of float is vital.

Float

Float is the length of time between when a check is written and when the recipient receives the funds and can draw upon them (when it has "good funds"). The *average*

---

[1] *Quarterly Financial Report for Manufacturing, Mining and Trade,* Bureau of the Census, Fourth Quarter, 1981, 1984 and 1987; and annual reports from the individual companies cited.

collection float is found by multiplying the number of days of float times the average daily dollar amount that is in the collection system.

For business firms, there are three sources of cash-gathering float. As shown in Figure 19.1, these are:

1. MAIL FLOAT. The time that elapses between when a customer places the check in the mail and when the selling firm receives it and begins to process it is the *mail float.*
2. PROCESSING FLOAT. The time it takes the selling firm to deposit the check in its bank after receiving the check is the *processing float.*
3. TRANSIT FLOAT. The time required for the check to clear through the banking system until the recipient can draw upon it (i.e., has "good funds") is the *transit float.*

Figure 19.1   Typical Payment System and Resulting Float

All three types of float are important and should be minimized as the firm strives to shorten its cash collection cycle.

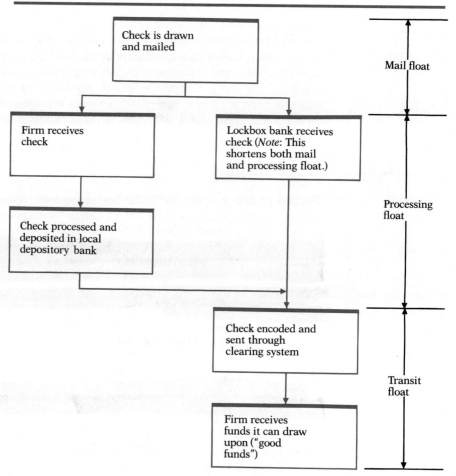

Figure 19.2 How Checks Are Cleared

The check clearing process has become more efficient in recent years as the Federal Reserve system has streamlined its operations and implemented a number of procedures to cut the transit float.

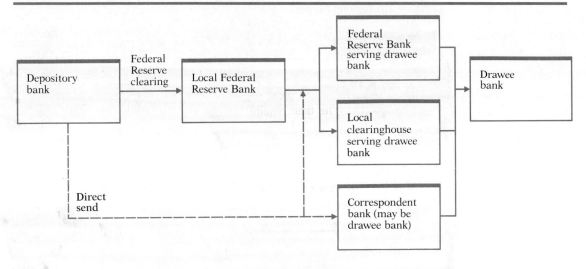

There are two primary ways that checks can be cleared. Under the first, the firm deposits the check in its local depository bank, which then forwards it to the local Federal Reserve bank. Then the check is sent to a Federal Reserve bank that serves the bank the check was drawn upon (the drawee bank), or to a local clearinghouse that serves the drawee bank. Finally, the check is presented to the drawee bank and funds are removed from the customer's account. To shortcut this system, especially if the volume or dollar amount of checks is large, the depository bank may use a *direct send.* With the direct send, the depository bank sends the check (often via commercial courier) directly to another bank or clearing system, thereby eliminating at least one step (the local Federal Reserve bank) in the check-clearing process. These steps are illustrated in Figure 19.2.

The Federal Reserve System has established a schedule specifying when funds will be available no matter where the check is deposited for collection. The float within the banking system has steadily declined due to requirements imposed on the Federal Reserve system by the Depository Institutions Deregulation and Monetary Control Act of 1980, and the use of more sophisticated clearing mechanisms.

A firm should focus first on the processing float. That is, the firm must establish an efficient internal system to minimize the delay between receipt of the customer's check (if it comes directly to the firm) and when it is deposited in the bank. After this has been accomplished, other techniques for reducing float can be considered.

Decentralized Collections

Mail float can be minimized by having decentralized collection points located in parts of the country where the firm has many customers. Two basic devices used for this purpose are local offices and lockboxes.

Local Offices. If the firm has local offices in the major regions in which it operates, it can have collections directed to these offices. Once the checks are received, they can be deposited in a local depository bank, which is tied into the firm's overall banking network.

Lockboxes. If the firm does not have local offices, or if it wants to keep collections out of the local offices, a widely used alternative is to establish lockboxes. With a *lockbox,* the customer is directed to send the payment to a post office box in a specified city. A bank picks up the mail several times a day and begins the clearing process while notifying the firm, via telecommunications, that the checks have been received. At the conclusion of the day, all check photocopies, invoices, deposit slips, and related materials are sent to the firm. To determine where to set up lockboxes, the firm can engage the services of banks or other cash management consulting services. Typically a national firm will establish lockboxes in various parts of the country depending on its customer base and the regional efficiency of the postal service.

The purpose of both local office and lockbox collection points is to keep mail float to a minimum. Lockboxes also reduce the processing float. The benefits gained from the reduced float, however, must be compared to the cost involved. With a local office arrangement, the costs involve personnel, equipment, and space. With a lockbox arrangement, the cost is the fee charged by the bank either directly or through a compensating balance requirement.

Banking Network

Large firms employ more than one bank for their gathering and disbursing systems. A typical "tiered" banking arrangement suitable for a large national firm is shown in Figure 19.3. Using a local office system, customers mail their checks to local offices that process and then forward them to local depository banks. The deposits are then transferred to regional concentration banks and finally to the firm's main account at its central concentration bank. The rationale for a tiered system is that the greatest check-clearing efficiency is often obtained by organizing the cash-gathering system in this manner.

If lockboxes are employed, they are generally set up at the regional concentration banks, and the local depository banks are bypassed. The regional concentration bank maintains the lockbox, forwards the funds to the firm's central concentration bank, and sends the supporting documents to the firm. The concentration banks typically are located in a Federal Reserve city in order to speed up the clearing process. In addition, the lockbox should be close to the customers to be served so that mail float is kept to a minimum.

Once the funds are at the firm's central concentration bank, they can be used to meet the cash outflows of the firm, and any extra funds can be quickly invested in marketable securities. If the firm is short of cash, it can draw on its lines of credit. (The typical firm's banking network will also include various disbursement accounts at one or more banks.)

With a banking network of the type presented in Figure 19.3, the transfer of funds between banks is necessary.

Figure 19.3 Typical Banking and Cash Movement System for a Large Firm

If the firm uses lockboxes, most of the deposits go directly to the regional concentration banks, speeding up the cash-gathering system.

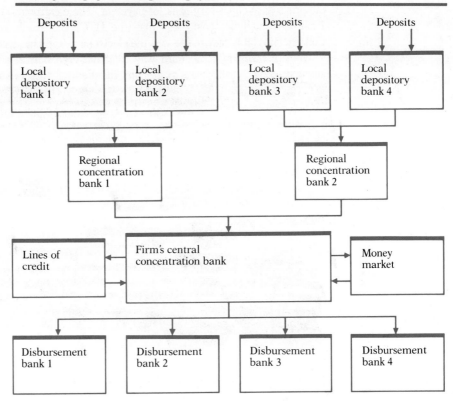

Bank Transfer Mechanisms. Three main transfer mechanisms for moving funds between banks are depository transfer checks, electronic DTCs, and wire transfers.

A *depository transfer check, DTC,* is a nonnegotiable instrument payable only to the bank of deposit (the firm's central concentration bank) for credit to the firm's specific account. In a mail-based system, the local office (after collecting and processing the checks received for the day) prepares a preprinted DTC and mails it with the deposit slip (for the funds put in the local depository bank) to the firm's central concentration bank. While the DTC is in the mail, the local depository bank processes the checks and then transfers them to the firm's central concentration bank. Funds are not available for use to the firm until the DTC has been received and cleared by the central concentration bank. This may involve 2 to 3 days or more.

The automation sweeping the banking industry has led to the creation of the electronic depository transfer check (see Figure 19.4). With the *electronic DTC,* a commercial collection center receives the deposit information from the firm. At specified times during the day, this information is transferred to the firm's central concentration bank. At this point, the concentration bank prepares a DTC and transmits it to the firm's local depository bank for payment. The electronic DTC involves a uniform 1-day clearing time, costs less than the DTC, and avoids the use of the mails. Consequently, it is easy to see why the electronic system has gained rapid acceptance.

A *wire transfer* is the third way to move cash between banks. This may be initiated using a bank wire system or the Federal Reserve's wire system. With wire transfer, the funds are transferred on a same-day basis. Transit float is eliminated. Wire transfers cost a good bit more, however, than either DTCs or electronic DTCs. Typically wire transfers are employed only for larger amounts, or used on a periodic basis (perhaps three times a week) to move funds from one bank to another.

Other Approaches

Some other approaches that could be employed to improve the efficiency of the collection process include the following:

1. SPECIAL HANDLING. With special handling, a courier might be dispatched to collect a large check directly to reduce mail and/or transit time.
2. PREAUTHORIZED CHECKS. A *preauthorized check* system might be created when the firm receives a large volume of payments in fixed amounts from the same customers. With the preauthorized procedure, the customer authorizes the firm to draw checks directly on the customer's demand deposit account. This method reduces mail and processing float and increases the regularity and certainty of cash inflows to the firm.

Figure 19.4 Electronic DTC System

Because of their relatively low cost and uniform one-day availability (for "good funds"), electronic DTCs have gained wide acceptance for moving funds between banks.

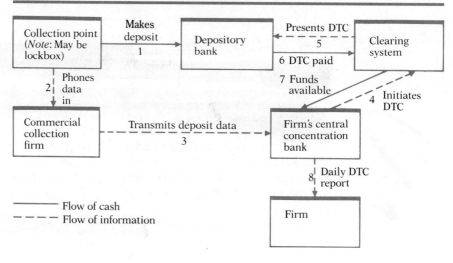

3. RECEIPT OF PAYMENT REQUIRED. A third alternative is for the firm to demand that the payment be received (not just mailed) by a certain date. This system can be used if a customer is going to take advantage of a cash discount. The receipt of payment approach eliminates mail float.
4. PAYMENT BY WIRE TRANSFER. A fourth alternative would be for the firm to demand payment by a wire transfer. This also eliminates float.

Since all these approaches have costs and benefits related to reducing the float, both must be considered when determining the most effective means of structuring the firm's cash-gathering system.

Analysis of Cash-Gathering Techniques

A basic model that can be employed to assess the cost effectiveness of various cash-gathering techniques compares the incremental costs with the incremental benefits:

$$\Delta C = \text{after-tax costs}$$
$$\Delta B = \text{benefits} = (\Delta t)(TS)(I)(1 - T) \tag{19.1}$$

where

ΔC = the incremental costs of a new method compared to an existing method
ΔB = the incremental benefits associated with a new method compared to an existing method
Δt = the time (in days) that float is changed
TS = the size of the transaction
I = the interest rate
T = the firm's marginal tax rate

Using this method, the following decisions will be made:

1. If ΔC is greater than ΔB—stay with the present method.
2. If ΔC is less than ΔB—switch to the proposed method.
3. If ΔC is equal to ΔB—you are indifferent.

This approach is extremely flexible. It can be conducted on a per unit or total basis, and on a daily or yearly basis. To illustrate its use, we first consider a lockbox example and then alternative transfer mechanisms.

Lockbox Example. Suppose your firm now has all collections sent to the home office. To increase efficiency and reduce float, a lockbox operation is being considered. You estimate that the reduction in float (both mail and processing) will be 3 days, the average check size is $440, the yearly rate of interest is 12 percent, and the firm's marginal tax rate is 30 percent. Employing Equation 19.1, we can find the approximate *per unit* benefits of the lockbox, as follows:[2]

---

[2] This is an approximation, since it is not compounded. We could convert the interest rate in Equation 19.1 to a compound annual percentage rate, APR, but the time frame is so short it generally does not change the decision. None of the rest of the benefits or rates computed in this chapter are based on compound APRs either.

$$\Delta B = (\,\Delta t\,)(\,TS\,)(\,I\,)(\,1 - T\,) = (\,3\,)(\,\$440\,)\left(\frac{0.12}{365}\right)(\,0.70\,) = \$0.304$$

On a per unit basis, the benefits are $0.304 per check processed. If the after-tax costs charged for the lockbox are less than this figure, the lockbox operation should be established, since the incremental benefits will be greater than the incremental costs. In addition, any employee time freed would be another benefit that also should be taken into account.

Instead of determining the benefits on a per unit basis, we could calculate them on a daily basis. If there are 300 checks per day, then the average daily volume of checks processed through the lockbox is $132,000 [i.e., (300)($440)]. The incremental benefits *per day* are then

$$\Delta B = (\,3\,)(\,\$132,000\,)\left(\frac{0.12}{365}\right)(\,0.70\,) = \$91.13$$

Thus, if the bank charged less than $91.13 per day after tax (on a 365-day year), the lockbox arrangement should be implemented.

Finally, we can also use Equation 19.1 to determine the incremental benefits *per year*. To do this, *either the daily volume, TS, must be converted to a yearly basis, or the daily interest rate, I/365, must be converted to a yearly interest rate.* The incremental after-tax benefits per year from the lockboxes are thus:

$$\Delta B = (\,3\,)[(\,365\,)(\,\$132,000\,)]\left(\frac{0.12}{365}\right)(\,0.70\,) = \$33,264$$

or

$$\Delta B = (\,3\,)(\,\$132,000\,)(\,0.12\,)(\,0.70\,) = \$33,264$$

Again, we would make our decision by comparing the incremental costs versus the incremental benefits. This time, however, we do it on a yearly basis, instead of on the per unit or per day basis determined previously.

Transfer Mechanisms. In the example above, we did not know the costs. We can also start out, however, by knowing what the incremental costs, ΔC, are, and then determine what the reduction in the float time, Δt, the average size, TS, or the interest rate, I, would have to be for us to be indifferent between the two methods. Suppose your firm is in the 40 percent tax bracket and is investigating whether a wire transfer should be employed instead of using a depository transfer check to move funds between two banks. The wire transfer costs $5 and the depository transfer check costs $1, so that $\Delta C = (\$5 - \$1)(1 - 0.40) = \$2.40$. The reduction in float time, Δt, is 2 days, and the yearly interest rate, I, is 10 percent. Setting ΔC equal to ΔB, we have

$$\Delta C = \Delta B$$

$$\$2.40 = (\,2\,)(\,TS\,)\left(\frac{0.10}{365}\right)(\,1 - 0.40\,)$$

$$TS = \frac{\$2.40}{(\,2\,)(\,0.10/365\,)(\,0.60\,)} = \$7,300 \text{ on a per unit basis}$$

Drexel Burnham Lambert

During the 1980s, Drexel Burnham Lambert emerged as one of the major investment banking firms in the United States. They literally created the junk (or high-yield) bond market, where "noninvestment" grade (Ba and B rated) corporate debt was issued directly by Wall Street. Some of their activities, however, aroused the interest of the Securities and Exchange Commission (SEC). In late 1988, culminating a 2-year investigation, the SEC filed a complaint against Drexel. The essence of the complaint was that Drexel had engaged in a number of illegal activities, many of them related to the head of Drexel's junk bond department, Michael R. Milken, and the famous investor, Ivan F. Boesky. Boesky had earlier agreed to plead guilty to insider trading charges and paid up to $100 million in fines and lawsuits.

On December 21, 1988 Drexel entered into an agreement with the SEC, pleaded guilty to six counts, and agreed to pay $650 million in fines and restitution. Five of the six counts involved illegal securities' "parking" between Boesky and Drexel between 1984 and 1986. Parking is a scheme between investors to disguise security ownership. In these parking schemes it is alleged that Milken would direct Boesky to buy some securities, while Drexel retained beneficial ownership. The securities involved include Fischbach, MCA, Phillips Petroleum, Harris Graphics, and Stone Container. In early 1989 Drexel discharged Milken.

While Drexel remained optimistic that they would not suffer any serious long-run damage, others thought that with Milken's departure, and the general uncertainty about the firm's future, Drexel would see a slow but devastating erosion of key employees. This could be particularly true in Drexel's junk bond department. While Drexel may survive, neither it nor Wall Street will be the same in the future.

If the average size of the check transferred between the two banks is at least $7,300, it pays to use a wire transfer. If the reduction in float time were only 1 day, the size of the average transfer would have to be $14,600 for the wire transfer to be justified.

In practice the models become more complex, because there are additional considerations such as having numerous locations and the service credits earned by having compensating balances at the banks. Nevertheless, the basic analytical concept of comparing the incremental costs versus the incremental benefits remains the same.

Controlling the Outflows

In designing the firm's cash-disbursement system, the emphasis is on controlling and slowing down the outflow of cash as long as possible without incurring the ill will of the firm's suppliers. The place to begin is with payment procedures. They should be designed so the firm pays just before the due date. Paying earlier simply reduces the time cash is available to the firm for investment.

Controlled Disbursing

Transit float is a function of the processing inefficiencies of various banks, their location, and the Federal Reserve System. To take advantage of transit float, firms may establish a *controlled disbursing* system. The idea is to locate the firm's disbursing banks so that payments to the firm's suppliers will remain outstanding as long as possible. The specific location of the controlled disbursing banks depends on the location and amount of billings by the firm, delays in transit time, and the costs involved. Generally the bank is located in a small or medium-sized city and receives only one delivery of checks from the Fed per day.

Controlled disbursing has become so advanced that twice a year Phoenix-Hecht, a consulting firm, conducts a nationwide survey of check clearance times between cities. In a recent survey, some of the longest transit floats were for checks drawn on banks in Portland, Maine; West Plains, Missouri; and Grand Junction, Colorado. Their average clearance time to all points in the United States was around 2.5 days.

The cost analysis of alternative cash-disbursing systems is similar to that employed for cash-gathering systems. Suppose a New Jersey-based firm in the 35 percent tax bracket is considering the establishment of two disbursing banks, one in northern California and the other in South Dakota. It expects that disbursement float will be increased by 2 days, the size of the average check is $5,000, and the yearly interest rate is 13 percent. Using Equation 19.1, we find that the incremental benefits are

$$\Delta B = (\,2\,)(\,\$5,\!000\,)\left(\frac{0.13}{365}\right)(\,1 - 0.35\,) = \$2.3151$$

As long as the two banks charge less than $2.3151 per check, the firm should go ahead. For example, if the firm writes 800 checks per month, it can afford to pay up to $1,852.08 [i.e., (800)($2.3151)] after-tax per month to establish the controlled disbursing system. By maximizing disbursement float, the firm can increase its cash level and employ the excess cash in other ways. The system does mean, however, that suppliers will be without payment for an additional number of days. The ill will created among suppliers must be taken into account when a controlled disbursing system is being established.

Zero Balance Accounts

When a large firm is organized on a divisional basis, invoices from suppliers often go to divisional finance offices for payment. If each division has its own disbursing bank, excess cash balances may build up, reducing the efficiency of the firm's cash-disbursing system. To prevent this buildup, the firm may establish a *zero balance account* system at its central concentration bank (see Figure 19.5). Each division continues to write its own checks, but they are all drawn on individual disbursing accounts at the concentration bank. Although these accounts are like individual demand deposit accounts, they contain no funds. Thus their name, "zero balance."

Each day the checks written on the individual disbursing accounts presented for payment are paid by the concentration bank. As they are paid, a negative balance builds up in the individual accounts. At the end of the day, the negative balances are restored to zero by means of a credit from the firm's master account at the central concentration bank. Each day, the firm receives a report summarizing the

Figure 19.5 Zero Balance Account System

Instead of divisional accounts, separate zero balance accounts could be kept for payroll, suppliers, cash dividends, and so forth.

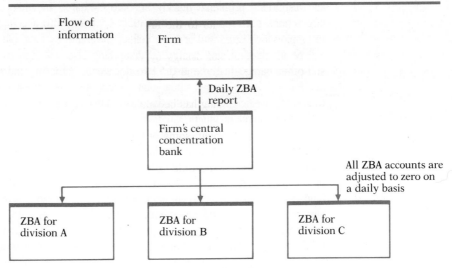

activity of the various accounts so that marketable securities can be bought or sold as needed, depending on the balance in the firm's master account. Zero balance accounts allow much more control, while maintaining divisional autonomy for payments. They are often an effective means of controlling the cash-disbursement system.

Other Approaches

Various other approaches for controlling cash disbursements include the following:

1. CENTRALIZED PAYABLES. When a firm has many divisions, it could have the invoices received and verified at the divisional level, but actually paid at the firm's headquarters. In this instance, all invoices must be forwarded to the central office for payment. Control can be maintained, and the disbursement cycle may be slowed by this procedure.
2. TIMING CHECK ISSUANCES. By issuing checks at certain times during the week, float may be increased. Thus, if average mail float is 1.5 days, by issuing checks on Wednesday or Thursday the firm may gain an extra 2 days (over the weekend) float. Likewise, issuing a payroll on Friday also means that not all the checks can clear the banking system before Monday or Tuesday of the next week.

The benefits and costs of all the cash-disbursing techniques must be analyzed. The basic framework to employ is the same as that presented earlier. In the disbursing situation, the benefit arises from the additional length of time the firm will have the funds available. This has to be weighed against the costs associated with better controlling the disbursement of cash.

Interactions	Up to now we have examined a number of techniques that could be used to improve the efficiency of the firm's cash-gathering system or to control the cash-disbursing system. In medium- to large-size firms, with various plants and offices, gathering and disbursing problems quickly become complex. In addition, there are obvious interactions between the two that must be taken into account. If the firm decides to employ lockboxes and/or have collections made by local offices, numerous banks will be involved. Using controlled disbursing also will lead to creating accounts at still other banks. In the end the two decisions, gathering and disbursing, cannot be made in isolation. Rather, their joint effects and costs must be considered in order to create an efficient, cost-effective cash management system that balances the risks and returns involved.

At the same time, there are advances in automation that are affecting the whole ordering and payment system. Increasingly, firms are using electronic data interchange, EDI, that affects everything from the ordering and manufacturing cycles, to the flow of documents related to shipment and payment. Likewise, electronic funds transfer, EFT, is slowly being implemented by more firms to handle payments electronically. These developments in EFT utilize either automated clearing houses, ACH, run by banks and the Federal Reserve, or private corporate trade payment, CTP, systems. On the disbursement side the substantial reduction in transit float has resulted in a decrease in the importance of controlled disbursing. The interaction between these various services, plus cost considerations, must be continually examined to decide on the best mix of cash management techniques for specific firms.

International Cash Management

In addition to managing domestic cash accounts, firms are paying increasing attention to the effective management of international cash flows.[3] The major international money movement techniques are as follows:

1. CONCENTRATION BANKING. To control the flow of funds internationally, firms concentrate their cash at a single bank within a country, or on a regional level. Often European-wide systems are established at a bank in London or Amsterdam, while Asian systems are located in Hong Kong or Singapore. Once this is done, funds can be controlled and invested, and a zero-balance-type of procedure can be implemented.

2. INTERNATIONAL TRANSFER. Using banks, firms can arrange for same-day settlement or other kinds of settlement procedures when funds move across country borders.

3. INTERNATIONAL LOCKBOX. This technique involves establishing one or more lockboxes in a country so that payments can be settled in the country where the currency is legal tender. With this system, cross-border check clearing is avoided, increasing the efficiency of the firm's cash system.

4. INTRACOMPANY NETTING. Many firms have large sums of money tied up in intracompany transactions. With these transactions, one subsidiary's payables are another

---

[3] In 1981 the Clearing House Interbank Payment System, CHIPS, moved to a one-day settlement procedure. Since this New York-based payment system handles many of the world's Eurodollar payments, the move increased the opportunities for effective multinational money management. Outside the United States the primary multinational bank transfer system is called SWIFT (Society for Worldwide Interbank Financial Telecommunications).

subsidiary's receivables. To avoid the physical transfer of funds, many international companies "net" the funds flowing between subsidiaries once a month.

In addition, due to fluctuating foreign exchange rates, many firms follow a practice of leading or lagging. Thus, if a firm has a net asset position in a weak or potentially depreciating currency, it should expedite the disposal of the asset—in other words, it should lead. Alternatively, a firm with a net liability position in a weak currency should delay payment, or lag, hoping that the currency will weaken further. Faced with a strong currency, the firm would lead, or make payments as soon as possible. Likewise, it would lag, or delay, collection as long as possible in a strong currency. Although leading and lagging cannot eliminate the risk caused by exchange-rate fluctuations, it is still an effective tool for international cash, accounts receivable, and short-term liability management.

Determining the Daily Cash Balance

Now that we have examined cash gathering and disbursing, the second question raised at the beginning of the chapter can be addressed: How should the investment in liquid assets be split between cash and marketable securities? The approach we examine is based on the idea that firms will attempt to keep as little cash in demand deposits as possible. It is assumed that the firm has a marketable securities portfolio of a sufficient size that funds can be transferred from it to the demand deposit account as needed. Because marketable securities typically earn higher returns than demand deposits, however, there is an incentive to leave excess funds in the marketable securities portfolio.

The following five-step procedure can be employed to determine the firm's daily cash balance. It involves estimating the major inflows and outflows and then modeling the routine cash flows.

1. Cash budgets are prepared on a monthly basis, as discussed in Chapter 4. Updates will be made, often weekly, as needed.
2. Major cash inflows and outflows are broken out of the cash budget. Major items would include such items as taxes, dividends, lease payments, debt service obligations, wages, and the like.
3. The timing of the major inflows and outflows expected to occur during the month are identified. From this information, we can estimate approximate times when daily transfers into or out of the marketable securities portfolio may be needed.
4. The remaining, or routine, cash inflows and outflows can be modeled[4] to determine when (based on historical patterns) we would expect their inflow and outflow to occur during the month. In this process it is important to consider seasonal influences, day-of-the-month effects, day-of-the-week effects, vacations, and the like. The output of this modeling process provides an estimate of the net daily inflow or outflow from routine items. Based on this information, and the timing of the major inflows and outflows from step 3, the planned times for adding to or selling marketable securities can be estimated. This step specifies the firm's estimated daily cash balance for each day of the month.

[4] See references list at end of chapter.

5. As the month progresses, the actual routine cash inflows and outflows are compared with the projected ones. Also, the exact timing of major cash inflows and outflows is known, or can be more accurately estimated. Other developments can be added as they occur. The actual dates and amounts of marketable security purchases and sales will be adjusted from those estimated in step 4 as the month progresses.

This approach to estimating the intramonth (or daily) cash balance is shown in Figure 19.6. The goal is to maintain the actual cash balance at some predetermined level. Obviously this level depends on the charges or credits the bank passes on to the firm. However, by breaking out the major items and then modeling the routine ones, the firm's monthly cash budget can easily be broken down into a day-by-day estimate of the necessary cash balance.

Transfers to and from the marketable securities portfolio employ the same balancing of incremental costs and benefits discussed earlier. Therefore, it may not be profitable to switch funds to and from the marketable securities portfolio every day. If it costs $50 to move funds in or out of the marketable securities portfolio, and the incremental interest, ΔI, from having funds in marketable securities is 4 percent, and the marginal tax rate is 40 percent, we can proceed as follows:

$$\Delta C = \Delta B$$

$$\Delta C = (\Delta t)(TS)(\Delta I)(1 - T)$$

$$\$50(1 - 0.40) = (1)(TS)\left(\frac{0.04}{365}\right)(1 - 0.40)$$

where Δt is specified as 1 day's gain in interest. Solving for TS, the amount of cash transferred, we have

$$TS = \frac{\$50(0.60)}{(0.04/365)(0.60)} = \$456{,}250$$

Therefore, there should be $456,250 that can be left in marketable securities for at least 1 day before the transfer is made. If we estimate, based on our daily cash balance model, that funds can be transferred from cash to marketable securities and left for 5 days, then

$$\$30 = (5)(TS)\left(\frac{0.04}{365}\right)(0.60)$$

$$TS = \frac{\$30}{5(0.04/365)(0.60)} = \$91{,}250$$

In this case the transfer should be made if there is more than $91,250 in excess funds in the firm's cash account. Similar calculations can be made if the differential interest rates (between that paid on demand deposits versus marketable securities) change, or if the cost of the transaction increases or decreases. The point, however, is that the same basic cost–benefit framework can be used to determine when to transfer funds into and out of the marketable securities portfolio.

Figure 19.6 Model for Estimating and Controlling the Firm's Cash Balance

In practice, other factors need to be addressed. These will cause the model to increase in complexity, but the basic concepts will remain the same.

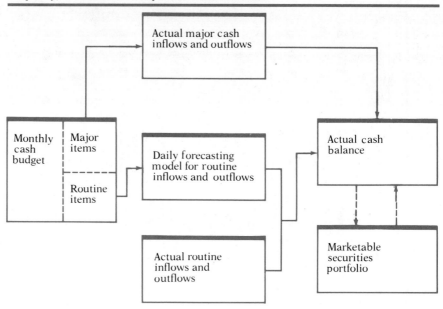

Management of the Marketable Securities Portfolio

Excess cash above that needed to meet the firm's cash balance requirement will be invested in marketable securities. Because of the need for liquidity, long-term bonds or common stock generally are not appropriate investments for temporary excess cash.

Investment Alternatives

Managers have a choice of many different marketable securities for short-term investments. These are shown in Table 19.1. U.S. Treasury bills are direct obligations of the U.S. government. They are typically considered the safest marketable security investment. The yield on Treasury bills is often used as a proxy for the risk-free rate, k_{RF}. All other marketable securities are viewed as being more risky, because they are not issued or backed directly by the U.S. government. Money market mutual funds are a pool of short-term marketable securities managed by an investment adviser. *Dutch auction (money market) preferred stock* may also be employed. Developed in the early 1980s the dividends, like other intrafirm cash dividends, qualify for the 70 percent tax exclusion.

Selection Criteria

In assessing the selection of alternative marketable securities, we look at (1) general economic risk, (2) inflation and disinflation risk, (3) firm- and issue-specific risk, and

Table 19.1 Characteristics of Marketable Securities

Given the wide variety of securities, maturities, and denominations, firms can tailor a marketable securities portfolio to meet their needs.

Instrument	Description	Maturity	Interest Basis	Marketability	Denomination
Treasury bills	Direct obligation of the U.S. government; exempt from state and local income tax	91 days to 1 year	Discount	Excellent secondary market	$10,000 and up
Federal agency issues	Notes issued by agencies created by the U.S. government; not explicitly backed by the government	5 days to several years; over half less than 1 year	Typically interest bearing, but may be discount	Good to excellent secondary market	$5,000 and up
Repurchase agreements (repos or buy-backs)	Sale of government securities by a bank or securities dealer with a simultaneous agreement to repurchase	1 day to 3 months	Repayment price set higher than selling price, paid at maturity	Limited	$500,000
Short-term tax exempts	Notes issued by states, municipalities, local housing agencies, and urban renewal agencies; exempt from federal income tax	2 months to 1 year	Interest bearing, paid at maturity, or discount	Good secondary market	$1,000
Finance paper	Unsecured notes issued by large finance companies or bank holding companies	3 to 270 days	Either discount or interest bearing, paid at maturity	No secondary market, but firm will usually redeem early	$100,000
Commercial paper	Unsecured notes issued by smaller finance companies or industrial firms; increasingly used by non-U.S.-based firms	30 to 270 days	Discount	No secondary market, but dealer may arrange buy-back	$100,000
Negotiable certificates of deposit (CDs)	Receipts for time deposits at commercial banks; very active market for overseas branches of U.S.-based banks	30 to 91 days or longer	Interest bearing, paid at maturity	Good secondary market	$1,000,000
Banker's acceptances	Time draft (or order to pay) issued by a business firm (usually an importer) that has been accepted by a bank	30 to 180 days	Discount	Good secondary market	$100,000
Eurodollars	Dollar-denominated time deposit at overseas banks	1 day to 1 year	Interest bearing, paid at maturity	No secondary market	$1,000,000
Money market mutual funds	Pool of short-term money market instruments	Shares may be sold anytime	Credited to account monthly	Good; provided by fund itself	$500
Dutch auction (money market) preferred stock	Specially designed preferred stock	Resold every 7 weeks	Dividend paying at maturity	No secondary market	$100,000

Dutch Auctions

When a firm decides to repurchase some of its outstanding shares, it has a number of ways of going about it. A technique used increasingly is a Dutch auction tender offer, in which the company states the number of shares it's going to buy during a stipulated period and sets a range within which shareholders can tender their stock. The shareholders then tender their stock and indicate what price they are willing to sell their stock at. For example, let's say a firm sets a price range of $35 to $40 a share. If investors tender enough stock between, say, $35 and $38, then the firm would buy all of the shares it set out to and would pay each investor the price they (i.e., the investors) stipulated when they tendered their stock. In this example, even though the firm set a range of $35 to $40, they ended up paying only $35 to $38 for the tendered shares.

From the company's point of view the Dutch auction tender offer has a special advantage. That is, the firm lets the market tell it what the price should be, rather than the firm telling the market. As such, the firm does not have to set a specific price, and instead it simply lets supply and demand in the marketplace determine the price.

The Dutch auction procedure has also been used to issue a short-term marketable security, called Dutch auction preferred stock. This security matures every 49 days, and is sold to firms at whatever they bid, in terms of the dividend they are willing to accept. The advantage of Dutch auction preferred stock is that every 49 days it is reauctioned, but by holding the stock for at least 45 days dividends received by the purchasing firm qualify for the 70 percent exclusion on cash dividends paid from one firm to another.

(4) international risk. In addition, we consider the liquidity and yield aspects of the alternative investments.

General Economic Risk

As general economic conditions change from boom to recession, market rates of interest change. In addition, the actions of the monetary and fiscal policies of the U.S. government can also influence market interest rates. As market interest rates go up, the market price of outstanding debt instruments decreases. As market interest rates go down, the market price of outstanding debt increases.

Figuring the Yield on Treasury Bills.[5] To examine this risk, let's consider one specific money market security—Treasury bills. U.S. Treasury bills are non-interest-bearing discount securities that are sold through regular weekly and monthly auctions, with 91- and 182-day maturity bills sold weekly, and 365-day maturity bills sold monthly. Since they are redeemed at full face value at maturity, the interest

[5] This section may be omitted without loss of continuity.

earned is the difference between the face value (if held to maturity) and the discounted price. Two interest rates are quoted for Treasury bills—the bank discount yield, k_{BD}, and the bond equivalent yield, k_{BE}.

The *bank discount yield* expresses the investor's expected return on a Treasury bill as a percent of the face value of the security, so that

$$k_{BD} = \left(\frac{P_M - P_0}{P_M} \right)\left(\frac{360}{n} \right) \tag{19.2}$$

where

k_{BD} = the bank discount yield
P_M = the maturity value of the Treasury bill
P_0 = the discounted price
n = the number of days until maturity

Note that the bank discount yield is based on 360 days.[6]

To illustrate, suppose you purchase a 182-day Treasury bill with a face value of $10,000 at a price of $9,500. What is your bank discount yield? Employing Equation 19.2, we have

$$k_{BD} = \left(\frac{\$10,000 - \$9,500}{\$10,000} \right)\left(\frac{360}{182} \right) = \frac{\$180,000}{\$1,820,000} = 0.0989 = 9.89\%$$

Alternatively, if someone told you that the bank discount yield on a 182-day $10,000 Treasury bill was 9.89 percent, and you wanted to find out how much you would pay for the security, we could rearrange Equation 19.2 and solve for P_0 as follows:

$$P_0 = P_M - P_M(k_{BD})(n/360) \tag{19.3}$$

$$= \$10,000 - \$10,000(0.0989)(182/360) = \$10,000 - \$500 = \$9,500$$

Since the bank discount yield is based on 360 days, and most interest rates are for 365 days, the *bond equivalent yield* for a Treasury bill is generally calculated. It is as follows:[7]

$$k_{BE} = \frac{(365)(k_{BD})}{360 - (k_{BD})(n)} \tag{19.4}$$

For our example, the bond equivalent yield is

$$k_{BE} = \frac{(365)(0.0989)}{360 - (0.0989)(182)} = \frac{36.0985}{342.0002} = 0.10555 \approx 10.56\%$$

Because of the difference between the 360- and 365-day years, the bond equivalent yield is always higher than the bank discount yield.

To illustrate the general economic risk that may exist with Treasury bills, let's

---

[6] Neither the bank discount nor the bond equivalent yield is calculated employing compound interest. Our presentation is in line with their use in practice.

[7] This formula applies only to Treasury bills with 182 days or less to maturity; another formula is used for longer-maturity bills.

continue with our example. If we buy the 182-day Treasury bill for $9,500 and hold it until maturity, our interest income is $500 ($10,000 − $9,500). But what happens if we have to sell before it matures, and if interest rates on Treasury bills have increased from the time we purchased the Treasury bill? Suppose we were forced to sell in 60 days, and the bank discount yield at that time was 11.00 percent.

To determine the effect of having to sell when interest rates have moved higher, we first have to figure out how much interest we *should* have earned over the 60 days (182 original days − 122 days left to maturity) we held the Treasury bill. Since our expected interest for the full 182 days was $500, we would expect to receive ($500)(60/182), or $164.84, in interest over the 60 days we held the bill. Alternatively, we would expect to be able to sell the bill for the original purchase price of $9,500 plus the $164.84 interest, or $9,664.84. But that does not take into account the increase in interest rates, which causes our Treasury bill to be worth less than expected when we sell it. Using Equation 19.3 and the new bank discount yield of 11 percent, we can solve for the actual selling price (ignoring transactions costs) with 122 days left as follows:

$$P_0 \text{ with 122 days left} = \$10,000 - \$10,000(\,0.11\,)(\,122/360\,)$$

$$= \$10,000 - \$372.78 = \$9,627.22$$

Comparing the price when we sold the security of $9,627.22 with our purchase price of $9,500, we see that our actual interest was only $127.22 ($9,627.22 − $9,500), not the $164.84 expected. Because of changes in general economic conditions, which adversely affected the market price of the Treasury bill when we sold prematurely, our actual return of $127.22 was less than our expected return of $164.84.

Inflation and Disinflation Risk

Changes in expected inflation can directly affect the market rate of interest. If expected inflation suddenly increases by 2 percent, the market rate of interest will also increase by about 2 percent. Likewise, disinflation will lead to decreases in market interest rates. Therefore, expected inflation is one part of the general economic conditions that may influence market prices and yields of marketable securities.

Firm- and Issue-Specific Risk

U.S. Treasury bills are issued and backed by the U.S. government. Many other marketable securities are issued by individual firms or banks. Commercial paper is issued by consumer finance companies, or by industrial, retail, or even public utility, firms. Likewise, many different banks issue negotiable certificates of deposit. The specific firm or issuer of the marketable security in these cases is responsible for payment. Managers must consider the ability of the firm issuing the marketable security to pay interest and principal on time.

International Risk

International risk comes into play if the marketable securities employed are Euro-dollar deposits, *certificates of deposit* issued by overseas branches of U.S. banks, or foreign firms issuing commercial paper in the United States. Although these risks are typically minimal for short-term investments, they must be considered when structuring the marketable securities portfolio.

Liquidity

Most marketable securities have excellent or good secondary markets. For commercial paper, however, it may be necessary to see if the issuing firm will redeem the security early if needed. Likewise, there is no secondary market for Eurodollars and only a limited secondary market for *repurchase agreements*. Since firms use their marketable securities portfolio as a source of ready cash, the liquidity aspect of the investment also requires careful consideration.

Yield

The final selection criterion is the yield on the marketable securities. Table 19.2 presents the yields on various securities during the 1981–1987 period. We see that yields fell dramatically between 1981 and 1987. Also notice that Eurodollar deposits always provide more returns than any other marketable security, while Treasury bills, being the least risky, provide the lowest returns.

The Marketable Securities Portfolio

The basic considerations for designing the firm's marketable securities portfolio are presented in Figure 19.7. The interaction of risk and liquidity determines the returns. The firm's risk–required return posture then determines the specific composition of the marketable securities portfolio. Very risk-averse firms might have a marketable securities portfolio composed almost entirely of U.S. Treasury bills. More aggressive firms will opt for a large portion in higher-yielding Eurodollars or certificates of deposit issued by overseas branches of U.S.-based banks. The impact of the returns on a big marketable securities portfolio, particularly when short-term interest rates are high, can be significant.

Table 19.2   Yields on 3-Month Money Market Instruments

Treasury bills, being the least risky, provide the lowest returns. Eurodollars, being more risky and less liquid, provide the highest returns. (SOURCE: Federal Reserve Bulletin, *various issues.*)

Instrument	Year						
	1981	1982	1983	1984	1985	1986	1987
Treasury bills	14.03%	10.61%	8.61%	9.52%	7.47%	5.97%	5.78%
Finance paper— directly placed	14.08	11.23	8.70	9.73	7.77	6.38	6.54
Commercial paper	15.32	11.89	8.88	10.10	7.95	6.49	6.82
Certificates of deposit	15.91	12.27	9.07	10.37	8.04	6.51	6.87
Banker's acceptances	15.32	11.89	8.90	10.14	7.91	6.38	6.75
Eurodollars	16.79	13.12	9.56	10.73	8.28	6.71	7.06

Figure 19.7 Considerations Influencing the Composition of the Marketable Securities Portfolio

The risk–required return posture of the firm plays a pivotal role in determining the final composition of its portfolio of marketable securities.

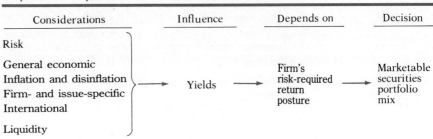

Considerations	Influence	Depends on	Decision
Risk			
General economic		Firm's	Marketable
Inflation and disinflation	Yields	risk-required	securities
Firm- and issue-specific		return	portfolio
International		posture	mix
Liquidity			

Summary

Effective management of the firm's cash and marketable securities requires that we understand techniques for cash gathering and disbursing, how the firm's cash balance can be minimized, and the basic instruments and techniques of marketable securities portfolio management. Adequate cash is needed for ordinary operating purposes, to take advantage of special purchases or cash discounts, and to maintain the firm's overall creditworthiness. Because demand deposits provide lower returns than marketable securities, however, the firm wants to minimize its cash balance while maintaining sufficient liquid reserves.

Because of mail, processing, and transit floats, special techniques can be employed to speed the gathering of cash coming into the firm. The primary techniques include decentralized collection points using local offices or lockboxes, along with an efficient banking network. For managing disbursements, firms can benefit from using controlled disbursing systems and zero balance accounts. In evaluating the effectiveness of these systems, the incremental costs must be compared with the incremental benefits. These same general considerations apply for the international aspects of a firm's cash management.

In determining the minimum cash balance to maintain, the firm's expected cash inflows and outflows can be broken down on a daily basis. By doing so, projected purchase or sale dates for marketable securities can be identified. The funds in the marketable securities portfolio must be invested for the highest possible return commensurate with the risk–required return posture of the firm, and the liquidity needs dictated by the projected inflows and outflows of cash. Since cash is the lifeblood of the firm, managers pay particular attention to its effective management.

Questions

19.1 Define or explain the following:

a. Marketable security
b. Liquid assets
c. Compensating balance
d. Cash discount

e.	Float	n.	Wire transfer
f.	Average collection float	o.	Preauthorized check
g.	Mail float	p.	Controlled disbursing
h.	Processing float	q.	Zero balance account
i.	Transit float	r.	Dutch auction (money market) preferred stock
j.	Direct send	s.	Bank discount yield
k.	Lockbox	t.	Bond equivalent yield
l.	Depository transfer check (DTC)	u.	Certificate of deposit
m.	Electronic DTC	v.	Repurchase agreement

19.2 The objective of the firm is to maximize the value of the firm. Since the return on real assets typically exceeds the return on marketable securities, explain why firms generally keep 5 to 10 percent of their assets in cash and marketable securities.

19.3 Explain the different types of float and how they affect the firm's cash-gathering system. Do these same types of float apply to the firm's disbursing system?

19.4 How can the firm speed up the cash-gathering process? Which float does each attempt to shorten?

19.5 Identify procedures the firm can employ to control the disbursement of cash. How does each serve to (a) reduce float, or (b) lower the firm's cash balance needs?

19.6 What impact would the following have on the firm's average cash balance?

a. Interest rates on marketable securities decrease.
b. Cost of trading marketable securities increases.
c. The firm's concentration bank raises its compensating balance requirement.
d. A zero balance account procedure is implemented.
e. New billing procedures allow a better correspondence between cash inflows and cash outflows.

19.7 Discuss the criteria that influence the firm's marketable securities selection procedure.

19.8 Treasury bills are widely employed by firms as an investment for temporary excess cash. Since they have the lowest yield of any marketable security, why are Treasury bills chosen?

19.9 During the last 25 years or so, many retail firms and others that issue credit cards have shifted from billing all customers on the last day of the month to "cycle billing." With cycle billing, customers are billed (often in alphabetical order) throughout the month. From the standpoint of the credit card issuer, what effect does cycle billing have on cash flows and average cash balances? Does it also have an impact on accounts receivable? Explain.

Self-Test Problems   (Solutions appear on pages 735–736.)

Lockbox

ST 19.1 A firm receives remittances totaling $27 million per year representing 90,000 checks. The firm currently has mail float of 3.2 days, a processing float of 1 day, and a transit float of 2 days. A 365-day year is assumed and the firm's marginal tax rate is 35 percent. The firm is examining a lockbox system to speed the collections by reducing float.

a. If the lockbox will cost $0.25 per check, and the funds freed can be invested at 9 percent, what is the reduction in float time necessary for the lockbox system to be adopted? What decision should be made if the reduction in float time is expected to be 2.5 days?
b. Instead of (a), the bank will provide the lockbox for a yearly fee of $10,000 plus $0.12 per check (all before taxes). If the reduction in float time is 2.5 days, and if the firm will

cut its own costs associated with processing the checks by $15,000 before taxes per year, should the lockbox system be implemented?

Wire Transfer **ST 19.2** A firm operating at a loss (so taxes are irrelevant) presently uses a wire transfer system to move funds between two banks. Each wire transfer costs $12. It can reduce its costs to $3 per transaction by going to an electronic DTC. The change will result in the loss of three-fourths of a day of float. If the net benefit ($\Delta B - \Delta C$) is $3.75 per transaction and the average transaction size is $62,050, what is the interest rate employed? Assume a 365-day year.

Market Price of Treasury Bill **ST 19.3** A $100,000 Treasury bill with 30 days to maturity has a bond equivalent yield of 10.48 percent. What is its current market price? (*Note:* Carry k_{BD} to five decimal places.)

Problems

Float **19.1** Melton & Sons projects its sales will be $120 million next year. All sales are for credit, but the credit policies are in good shape since there are very few bad debts and payments are mailed on time. Melton is concerned, however, about the cost of float time. Its marginal tax rate is 30 percent.

a. If funds could be invested to earn 7 percent, what is the incremental daily benefit of a 1-day reduction in float time using a 365-day year?

b. What is the daily benefit of a 1.5 day reduction in float if the funds could earn 8 percent?

Float **19.2** New Hampshire Healthcare currently has all incoming checks sent directly to its headquarters. The average mail time is 4 days, processing time is 2 days, and transit time is 1.5 days. The average cash inflow is $2 million per calendar day.

a. What is the average collection float in dollars?

b. While internal processing time is 2 days, New Hampshire is actually able to record the incoming checks for accounting purposes on its accounting records in 1 day. How much in dollars does New Hampshire have recorded on its accounting records that are not actually "good funds" in its bank account? (*Note:* Don't forget the 1.5 days of transit time.)

c. By modifying its system, New Hampshire Healthcare can reduce total float time *by* 2.25 days. The proposed system will cost $350,000 before taxes per year to operate, the interest rate is 12 percent, a 365-day year is assumed, and the marginal tax rate is 40 percent. Should New Hampshire implement the modified cash collection system? (*Note:* Solve for the yearly $\Delta B - \Delta C$.)

Lockbox **19.3** Mead-Tampa currently has a centralized cash receiving system located in Tampa, Florida. Its average float time on collections is 5.7 days. A North Carolina bank has approached Mead-Tampa, offering to establish a lockbox system that should reduce the float time to 2.9 days. (So the net reduction is 5.7 − 2.9 or 2.8 days.) Mead's daily collections are $600,000, and excess funds can be invested at 10 percent. If there are 800 checks per day, how much is the maximum Mead-Tampa can afford to pay *per check* for the lockbox operation? Assume a 365-day year and a tax rate of 30 percent.

Lockbox and Compensating Balance **19.4** Harcourt Supply presently uses a 2-lockbox system that has a total average daily transaction balance of $1 million (based on a 365-day year). The banks do not charge a direct fee, but they require Harcourt to keep a total of $2 million in compensating balances on which no interest is paid.

Fred Kahl, a recent finance graduate, has recommended that Harcourt switch to a new lockbox system. The savings in float time would be 1.2 days, the average check size is $500, the interest rate is 9 percent, and the firm's marginal tax rate is 34 percent. As compensation to the banks, Harcourt would have its compensating balance requirement reduced to $1.8 million (still no interest paid), pay $0.05 per check processed, and pay additional fixed fees of $50,000 to the banks each year. Based on the yearly incremental costs and benefits, should Harcourt make the switch recommended by Fred Kahl? (*Note:* Don't forget that interest can be earned on the freed compensating balances.)

Eliminating a Lockbox

19.5 Presently, Reuss Industries is using a lockbox arrangement. Reuss believes, however, it can save money by eliminating the lockbox system and handling the process internally. The lockbox costs $5 per day and $0.50 per check processed. Currently, 400 checks per day are being processed. If Reuss eliminates the lockbox, total costs will be $40,000 per year before taxes, and float time will increase by 2 days. Assume the average transaction size is $500 per check, the yearly interest rate is 11 percent, a 365-day year is employed, and the tax rate is 40 percent.

a. Should Reuss Industries eliminate the lockbox system? (*Note:* Compute the yearly incremental costs and benefits.)

b. At what incremental float time would Reuss be indifferent between the two approaches?

Transfer Mechanisms

19.6 Delaware Industries receives a periodic deposit of $20,000 at its San Juan, Puerto Rico, office. A mail depository transfer check that costs $1 and takes 3 days is presently used to transfer the funds to its concentration bank in Cleveland. Alternatively, a wire transfer system costing $9 where the funds are available immediately could be employed. Assume a 365-day year and a tax rate of 35 percent.

a. If Delaware earns 12 percent on excess funds once they reach the concentration bank, which transfer method should be employed?

b. What is the lowest dollar amount that should be transferred via wire transfer?

Lockbox and Concentration Banking

19.7 ElectroSystems has been growing so fast it has not examined its cash-gathering system. Presently, all cash comes into its corporate office. A downturn in the economy, however, has affected both sales and profitability. Now appears to be an appropriate time to review the cash-gathering system.

A consulting firm, for a fee of $100,000, has just presented the following information to ElectroSystems:

Present	**Proposed**
Home office collection system costing $75,000 per year.	Five lockboxes; the cost per check processed is $0.30.
Average daily volume is $900,000, with an average check size of $1,500, based on receipts for 270 days per year.	Twice-daily transfer of funds from *each* lockbox via electronic depository transfer check at a cost of $8 each.
	Reduction in float time, 2.6 days.
	Home office expenses of $50,000 per year.

a. If ElectroSystems can earn 9 percent on the excess funds and it is in the 40 percent marginal tax bracket, what are the yearly incremental after-tax costs and benefits of moving to the new system (ignoring the consultant's one-time fee of $100,000)? Should the switch be made? (*Note:* When calculating ∆C, assume that checks are processed only 270 days a year. When calculating ∆B, assume the $900,000 is available for all 365 days.)

b. Was the consultant's report worthwhile?

Controlled Disbursing

19.8 Andy of Hudson Valley Tire needs to know how much money would be saved by a controlled disbursing system. The average daily payables are $200,000, the controlled disbursing will add 1.5 days to the float, and the excess funds can be invested at 13 percent. Based on a 365-day year and a marginal tax rate of 30 percent, what are the yearly incremental benefits associated with the controlled disbursing system?

Controlled Disbursing

19.9 Sequoia Marine Supplies has set up a controlled disbursing system with two out-of-town banks. The net benefit ($\Delta B - \Delta C$) of the system to Sequoia is $28,700 per year. If Sequoia writes 200 checks per day with an average amount of $400, how many days of additional float will Sequoia obtain if the interest rate is 15 percent and the banks charge $0.10 per check cleared? Assume a 365-day year and that Sequoia is operating at a loss so that taxes are not relevant.

Zero Balance Accounts and Compensating Balances

19.10 Ketcham International maintains a number of checking accounts in various banks to allow its divisions to pay suppliers. The total average daily cash balance (over all the banks) is $480,000, on which no interest is earned. To control disbursements better, Ketcham is investigating whether to set up a series of zero balance accounts at the Second National Bank of Detroit. The bank will provide the service for a direct fee of $10,000 a year before taxes plus a daily average compensating balance of $400,000. By implementing the new arrangement, Ketcham would free $80,000 per day. No interest is earned on funds left with the bank in the $400,000 compensating balance arrangement.

Ketcham expects the float time to increase by 0.75 days with the zero balance account system. The average daily payables are $300,000, the excess funds can be invested at 12 percent, a 365-day year is assumed, and the marginal tax rate is 40 percent.

a. What is the yearly (before-tax) interest earned on the $80,000 freed?
b. What are the total yearly after-tax incremental costs and benefits of the zero balance accounts?

Treasury Bill

19.11 A 91-day Treasury bill with a $10,000 maturity value was purchased at 97.40 (as a percent of its maturity value).

a. What is the bank discount yield on the Treasury bill?
b. What is its bond equivalent yield?
c. Why is the bond equivalent yield always higher than the bank discount yield?

Interest on Treasury Bill

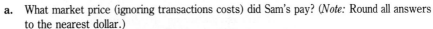

19.12 Sam's Supers has excess cash and purchased a $1 million (maturity value) 182-day Treasury bill when the bank discount yield was 7.9 percent.

a. What market price (ignoring transactions costs) did Sam's pay? (*Note:* Round all answers to the nearest dollar.)
b. After 80 days, Sam's had to sell the Treasury bill.
   (1) If the bank discount yield had not changed, how much interest (in dollars) would Sam's have earned on the Treasury bill over the 80 days?
   (2) Due to heavy government financing, the bank discount rate had climbed to 8.40 percent when Sam's sold the bill. What was the actual dollar amount of interest on the Treasury bill?
   (3) What dollar loss (compared with what it expected to receive) did Sam's incur due to the increase in the bank discount yield?

(Do only if using Pinches Disk.)
c. If Sam's sells the Treasury bill after 120 days, how do the answers in (a) and (b) change?
d. Suppose Sam's purchased the Treasury bill when the bank discount yield was 9 percent. What market price did it pay, assuming the same conditions as in (a)? How does this new rate affect (b) and (c)?
e. Now suppose Sam's purchased a 365-day Treasury bill. How would your answers change in (a) through (d)?

Marketable Securities Portfolio

19.13 Spivey Energy has the following schedule of excess cash available and cash needs over the next 6 months:

Time	Cash Availability/Needs
Now	$2 million excess cash
In 2 months	An additional $2 million excess cash
In 4 months	$2 million cash needed
In 6 months	An additional $2 million cash needed

The structure of short-term interest rates is as follows:

Now		Expected in 2 Months	
Maturity Period	**Yield (Annual)**	**Maturity Period**	**Yield (Annual)**
2 months	7.3%	2 months	8.0%
4 months	7.4	4 months	8.1
6 months	7.5		

Assume that once marketable securities are purchased, they are held to maturity. If it costs $100 every time marketable securities are purchased, which securities should be purchased to maximize the before-tax income from the added investment? [*Hint:* Remember the yields are on an annual basis. To convert to monthly, just divide the yearly figure by 12. For simplicity, (1) do *not* compound your results, and (2) take the transactions costs at the end of the time period.]

References

For some recent developments, see

"Corporate Treasury Services Offered by Commercial Banks." *Journal of Cash Management* 7 (July–August 1987), pp. 12–23.

HILL, NED C., AND DANIEL M. FERGUSON. "EDI and Payment Terms: Negotiating a Positive-Sum Game." *Journal of Cash Management* 7 (September–October 1987), pp. 21–26.

JOHNSON, THEODORE O., AND STEVEN F. MAIER. "Making the Corporate Decision: Paper Checks to Electronic Funds Transfer." *Journal of Cash Management* 5 (November–December 1985), pp. 30–38.

For more on cash gathering and disbursing, see

BATTIN, CARL ALAN, AND SUSAN HINKO. "A Game Theoretic Approach to Cash Management." *Journal of Business* 55 (July 1982), pp. 367–381.

MAIER, STEVEN F., AND JAMES H. VANDER WEIDE. "What Lockbox and Disbursement Models Really Do." *Journal of Finance* 38 (May 1983), pp. 361–371.

For more on cash flow forecasting and models, see

HEIKKI, RINNE, ROBERT A. WOOD, AND NED C. HILL. "Reducing Cash Concentration Costs by Anticipatory Forecasting." *Journal of Cash Management* 6 (March–April 1986), pp. 44–50.

STONE, BERNELL K., AND TOM W. MILLER. "Daily Cash Forecasting and Seasonal Resolution: Alternative Models and Techniques for Using the Distribution Approach." *Journal of Financial and Quantitative Analysis* 20 (September 1985), pp. 335–351.

STONE, BERNELL K., AND TOM W. MILLER. "Forecasting Disbursement Funding Requirements: The Clearing Pattern Approach." *Journal of Cash Management* 3 (October–November 1983), pp. 67 ff.

Marketable securities, and their management, is discussed in

ALDERSON, MICHAEL J., KEITH C. BROWN, AND SCOTT L. LUMMER. "Dutch Auction Rate Preferred Stock." *Financial Management* 16 (Summer 1987), pp. 68–73.

FIELITZ, BRUCE D. "Calculating the Bond Equivalent Yield for T-Bills." *Journal of Portfolio Management* 9 (Spring 1983), pp. 58–60.

FRANKLE, ALAN W., AND J. MARKHAM COLLINS. "Investment Practices of the Domestic Cash Manager." *Journal of Cash Management* 7 (May–June 1987), pp. 50–53.

RAMATH, RAVINDRA, SHAHRIAR KHAKSARI, HEIDI HYLTON MEIER, AND JOHN WINKLELECK. "Management of Excess Cash: Practices and Developments." *Financial Management* 14 (Autumn 1985), pp. 70–77.

See Model fourteen in *Lotus 1–2–3® for Financial Management* by Pinches and Courtney for a template for lockbox and disbursement site selection.

20

Accounts Receivable and Inventory

Overview

- Accounts receivable and inventory represent a significant investment. Funds tied up here are as costly as those employed elsewhere in the firm.

- Decisions on granting credit, or changing credit or collection policies, involve an analysis of the magnitude and timing of the cash flows and the risks and returns required.

- This analysis of cash flows is accomplished by calculating the net present value, NPV, of the proposed change in the firm's credit or collection policies.

- Decisions on the investment in inventory require exactly the same considerations and are also evaluated with an NPV framework.

Because of the beliefs of its founder, James Cash Penney, J. C. Penney for years and years never sold on credit—it was strictly a cash-and-carry operation. That policy has now changed dramatically. By 1987 over 58 percent of Penney's total sales were credit sales, with almost 50 percent accounted for by Penney's own credit card. The rest were based on Visa, MasterCard, or American Express. Credit card operations are so important to Penney that it now has 15 credit card service units and three processing centers, all equipped with state-of-the-art technology.

In addition to credit, inventory decisions can also affect a firm. Sawmills don't have inventory in the typical sense, but the supply of trees is their "inventory." Just as Pacific Northwest sawmills were recovering from earlier hard times, they have now been hit by severe "inventory" problems. There simply aren't enough "old-growth" logs. The cause is twofold—overcutting in prior years and increasing environmental concerns that are leading to more restrictions on harvesting logs from federal forests. As one industry participant observed: "People don't know where they'll get logs." The result will be an even faster reduction in sawmill employment and increasing lumber prices.

Whether it's a large retail firm like Penney's or a small firm like Larry's Auto Parts, the effective management of accounts receivable and inventory *is essential to financial well-being. In this chapter we explore how these decisions are made.*

Receivables, Inventory, and the Firm

To complete our analysis of the firm's current assets, we turn our attention to accounts receivable and inventory. Firms typically sell goods and services on both a cash and a credit basis. In the former, cash is received immediately; in the latter, the extension of *trade credit* leads to the establishment of accounts receivable. Receivables represent credit sales that have not been collected. Over time, as the customers pay these accounts, the firm receives the cash associated with the original sale. If the customer does not pay an account, a *bad debt* loss is incurred. To make sales, most firms carry various types of inventory. Firms carry inventory to ensure a smooth production cycle and to assist in the marketing effort. Without both receivables and inventory, most firms would cease to operate or would be much less efficient.

The investment in accounts receivable and inventory is similar to the long-term, or capital budgeting, decision discussed in Chapters 8–10, so many of the techniques used in this chapter are similar to those used in making capital budgeting decisions. Throughout, the emphasis is on the magnitude, timing, and riskiness of the cash flows resulting from the firm's investment in receivables and inventory. The effectiveness with which both are managed influences the firm's risk, required return, and stock price.

Importance of Receivables and Inventory

The financial goals of the firm must be coordinated with its marketing and production efforts. There is always a tradeoff between risk and required return, and different departments often want different policies. Nowhere is this more evident than in determining and maintaining proper levels of receivables and inventory. The marketing department may want lenient credit terms and collection policies in order to increase sales; the marketing effort also benefits from high inventory levels. The firm can promise immediate delivery, knowing that it will not lose sales because of stock outages. Higher inventory levels help the production department as well, enabling it to purchase in larger quantities, use longer production runs, and suffer less down time or unanticipated adjustments in the production schedule. These varying desires often conflict, however, with the objectives of the chief financial officer. Other things being equal, the CFO wants to minimize the firm's accounts receivable and inventory levels. Lower levels have two important financial benefits. First, less financing has to be secured, since the firm has less investment in receivables and inventory. Second, profits should be higher relative to sales or assets, because long-term investments are expected to generate higher returns than short-term assets.

The result must be a tradeoff between risk and required return. On the one hand, there is the risk of not granting enough credit or having enough inventory, thereby suffering sales losses. On the other hand, too high a level of receivables and inventory has a cost that may offset any sales or production benefits. A coordinated effort, involving marketing, production, and finance, is required to balance the risks against the required returns.

Most firms have substantial investments in receivables and inventory. Large manufacturing firms may have "only" 30 percent of total assets invested in receivables and inventory. But over 50 percent of the total assets of most retail and smaller manufacturing firms is invested in receivables and inventory, and that figure increases to over 60 percent for wholesale firms.

Although large firms carry the lowest levels of accounts receivable and inventory, there are substantial differences among firms. Consider Table 20.1, which shows the level of receivables held by firms in the retail merchandise and the machinery industries. As shown by the aggregate data, firms in the retail merchandise industry typically have a larger level of both receivables and inventory than their counterparts in the machinery industry. K mart and Penney, however, follow very different policies in terms of their relative amounts of both receivables and inventory. Likewise, Combustion Engineering and FMC also follow somewhat different policies.

The investment in both receivables and inventory is influenced by many factors. One primary determinant is the industry the firm is in. The industry effect is caused by competition, the characteristics of the product, the production process, and so forth. Recent surveys of credit policies have indicated that the actions of competitors are the major factor governing the credit terms granted. Likewise, a firm's investment in inventory is largely influenced by production processes and the requirements im-

Table 20.1 Receivables and Inventory to Total Assets, by Industry and Firm

Note the sizable differences between industries and firms. Also, over time, some differences within the same firm are evident. (SOURCE: Quarterly Financial Report for Manufacturing, Mining and Trade, Bureau of the Census, Fourth Quarter 1981, 1984 and 1987, and annual reports from the individual companies cited.)

| | | Industry | Individual Firms | |
	Year	Retail Merchandise	K mart	J.C. Penney
Receivables				
	1981	21.8%	1.3%	26.0%
	1984	24.6	2.5	41.0
	1987	23.1	3.2	41.8
Inventory				
	1981	28.8	47.0	25.4
	1984	28.0	49.5	24.3
	1987	26.8	29.1	21.7
	Year	Machinery	Combustion Engineering	FMC
Receivables				
	1981	18.6%	24.9%	21.3%
	1984	19.3	20.9	16.0
	1987	18.1	23.3	10.1
Inventory				
	1981	22.1	29.1	17.7
	1984	21.9	18.3	10.2
	1987	17.4	18.1	15.9

posed by competition. The importance of the industry effect cannot be minimized when examining a firm's investment in both receivables and inventory. Inventory management techniques are examined later in the chapter. For now, let's concentrate on receivables.

Size of Accounts Receivable

The size of the investment in accounts receivable is influenced by two other factors in addition to the industry effect. First, as shown in Figure 20.1, is total sales. Certain credit policies, such as liberal payment periods, encourage more sales. The state of the economy, the aggressiveness of the firm's marketing efforts, and other like factors all influence sales. As total sales increase, the level of credit sales and the investment in receivables usually increases. Second, the firm's credit and collection policies also influence the size of the investment in receivables. These policies can be broken down into four distinct aspects:

1. Terms and conditions of credit sales
2. Credit analysis
3. Credit decision
4. Collection policy

The decisions in these areas largely determine the length of time between the granting of credit and the receipt of cash. As the length of time before collection increases, the firm's investment in receivables increases. Shortening the average collection period reduces the firm's investment in receivables. The level of investment in accounts

Figure 20.1 Factors Affecting the Investment in Accounts Receivable

The level of sales, percentage of credit sales, and credit and collection policies determine the level of the firm's accounts receivable. Likewise, the credit management operation directly influences the flow of funds to the firm's cash account.

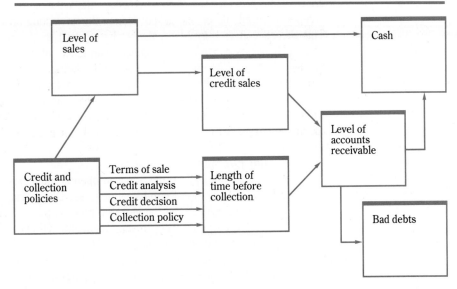

receivable is a function of the firm's industry, its total sales, and its credit and collection policies.

Credit and Collection Management

In this section, we will explore in more detail the four main aspects of credit and collection policies. In doing so, we want to see how they are established and the effect they can have on the value of the firm.

Terms and Conditions of Sale

Although most firms and industries grant trade credit, there are substantial variations. If the goods are produced to the customer's specifications, the selling firm may ask for cash before delivery. If the deliveries are irregular or some risk is involved, the seller may require *cash on delivery* (*COD*). If ordinary trade credit is granted, goods are on an open account, with payment due in some prespecified length of time, such as 30 or 60 days. As an inducement to encourage early payment, firms often offer a cash discount. If a firm sells on a 2/10, net 30 basis, customers who pay within 10 days receive a 2 percent discount; in any case, full payment is due within 30 days. In any open account agreement, the seller delivers the goods and provides an invoice, which constitutes the customer's bill and contains the terms of the arrangement.

If the goods are large in size, or the seller is unsure about the payment ability of the customer, other devices may be employed. The most common is the use of a draft, which is just a written order to pay a specified amount of money at a specified point in time to a given person (or to the bearer). The selling firm might agree to sell the goods only if the sale is made through a draft. If a *sight draft* is employed, the customer would have to pay the amount on presentation before receiving title to the goods. Alternatively, the draft could be a *time draft,* which states that payment will be made a certain number of days after presentation to the customer. A time draft can be accepted by the customer or the customer's bank. If the customer accepts the draft, he or she acknowledges this in writing on the back of the draft. This then becomes a *trade acceptance.* If the draft is accepted by the customer's bank, it becomes a *banker's acceptance.* The bank substitutes its creditworthiness for the customer's. As noted in Chapter 19, banker's acceptances are a major short-term marketable security; most of them arise from international trade.

The wide variety of terms and conditions have some logic to them, but tradition within an industry also plays a part. Sellers will demand early payment if the customers are in a high-risk class, if the accounts are small, or if the goods are perishable.

International Purchases or Sales

Although most domestic trade is on an open account basis, this is not true for firms involved in international purchases or sales. Due to lack of credit knowledge, communications difficulties, and the like, the process becomes more complex. Most international trade requires three main documents: (1) an order to pay, or draft, (2) a bill of lading, and (3) a letter of credit. We know about the draft, but let's briefly consider the other two documents.

A *bill of lading* is a shipping document that has a number of functions. Primary among these are to serve as a contract to order the shipment of goods from one party (the seller) to another (the customer), and to provide title to the goods. The bill of lading and the draft proceed together. Their use is recognized in international law, and banks or other financial institutions in virtually all countries handle these documents. By using the draft and bill of lading, a seller can sell the goods and still obtain protection, since title is not released until the draft has been accepted.

The letter of credit is the third document. A *letter of credit* is a written statement made by the customer's bank that it will pay out money (or honor a draft drawn on it) providing the bill of lading and other details are in order. Before the seller ships the goods, a letter of credit must be supplied. This letter is often irrevocable and confirmed by a bank in the seller's country. By obtaining the letter of credit, the seller ascertains before shipping the goods the creditworthiness and certainty of payment from the customer. Once the goods are shipped, they are covered by the bill of lading and accompanied by a draft (typically a time draft) that must be accepted by the customer's bank. All this may seem complicated, but it is routine in international trade.

Credit Analysis

Under the Robinson–Patman Act, firms cannot discriminate among customers by charging different prices. That same restriction applies to credit terms. Firms can, however, offer different terms of sale to different classes of customers or quantity discounts for large orders. Because of these legal considerations, the firm's primary means of protection is by determining who will be granted credit, and what the conditions of sale will be. Credit analysis forms the foundation for these decisions.

To conduct a credit analysis, information is needed on the creditworthiness and paying potential of the customer. Among the numerous sources that exist for securing this information are these:

1. FINANCIAL STATEMENTS. Based on financial statements provided by the potential customer, a credit-granting firm may judge the financial stability and cash-generating ability of the customer.
2. CREDIT RATINGS AND REPORTS. Dun & Bradstreet is probably the best known and most comprehensive credit agency. Its regular *Reference Book* provides credit ratings on about 3 million firms, both domestic and foreign. In addition, the National Association of Credit Management has enlisted TRW, Inc., to develop a computer-based credit retrieval system. A typical credit report includes the following information:
   a. Summary of recent financial statement(s)
   b. Key ratios and trends over time
   c. Information from the firm's suppliers indicating the firm's payment pattern
   d. Description of the firm's physical condition and unusual circumstances related to the firm or its owners
   e. A credit rating indicating the agency's assessment of the creditworthiness of the potential customer
3. BANKS. Most banks maintain credit departments and may provide credit information on behalf of their customers.
4. TRADE ASSOCIATIONS. Many trade associations provide reliable means of obtaining credit information.

5. COMPANY'S OWN EXPERIENCES. Based on the past experiences of the firm, some formal guidelines may have been developed of items to look for when gathering credit information and "sizing up" the creditworthiness of a potential customer.

Once the information is collected, a credit decision has to be made—that is, should credit be granted (and under what terms of sale), or not? To do this, many firms employ an approach based on classifying potential customers into risk classes. With such a system, a firm might form a number of risk classes, as follows:

Risk Class	Estimated Percentage of Uncollectible Sales	Percentage of Customers in This Class
1	0–1%	35%
2	1–$2\frac{1}{2}$	30
3	$2\frac{1}{2}$–4	20
4	4–6	10
5	More than 6	5

Firms in class 1 might be extended credit automatically and their status reviewed only once a year. Those in class 2 might receive credit within specific limits, with their status checked semiannually. Similar decisions could be made on the other categories. To protect against the possibility of loss, customers in class 5 might have to accept goods on a COD basis. This requirement for group 5 is perfectly legal, since it is the terms of the sale, *not* the sale price or cash discount (if any), that is affected. Some objective basis must exist, however, for placing a customer in one risk class as opposed to another.

To make the risk class judgment, many firms use *credit scoring models*. A typical model is as follows:

Variable	Weight	Credit Score*	Risk Class
Fixed charges coverage	4	Greater than 47	1
Quick ratio	11	40–47	2
Years in business (maximum of 15)	1	32–39	3
		24–31	4
		Less than 24	5

* Credit score = 4(fixed charges coverage) + 11(quick ratio) + 1(years in business).

Based on either statistical or some other method of analysis, firms determine the relevant variables that are reliable indicators of their customers' creditworthiness. In this example three variables—fixed charges coverage, quick ratio, and years in business—and their weights have been determined. Suppose a new customer with the following conditions applies for credit:

Fixed charges coverage   3.5
Quick ratio   0.8
Years in business   11

The customer's credit score would be 4(3.5) + 11(0.8) + 1(11) = 33.8 and it would be placed in risk category 3.

This type of approach is being supplemented by rapid advances in computer-based information systems in larger firms to limit risk exposure to credit losses.

Smaller firms often employ time-sharing computer facilities to achieve many of the same benefits.

Credit Decision

Once the firm has carried out the first two steps, it is ready to make the credit decision. There are many complexities that can be introduced, but let's start with the basic credit granting decision. To do this, we want to compare the costs of granting credit versus the benefits to be derived from granting credit, taking into account risk and the timing of the cash flows.

The Basic Model

To make the credit decision, the following items are needed:

cash inflows = the cash benefits expected to arise from the sale of goods on credit
cash outflows = the cash outflows associated with the goods to be sold (Note that any fixed costs are not relevant, since they will be incurred by the firm whether or not credit is granted.)
T = the firm's marginal tax rate

The after-tax cash flow, CF, received by a firm from a credit sale can be summarized by[1]

$$CF = (CFBT)(1 - T) \qquad (20.1)$$

where CFBT (cash flow before taxes) equals cash inflows minus cash outflows.

To determine whether to grant credit, we compare the present value of the benefits with the cost of granting credit, given the risks involved. The net present value, NPV, for the credit granting decision is

$$NPV = \frac{CF_t}{k} - CF_0 \qquad (20.2)$$

where[2]

CF_t = the after-tax cash flows in each time period
k = the after-tax required rate of return reflecting the risk class of the potential customer
CF_0 = the investment the firm makes in its accounts receivable

The decision rule for the net present value when making the credit-granting decision is as follows:

1. If NPV is greater than zero—grant credit.
2. If NPV is less than zero—do not grant credit.
3. If NPV is equal to zero—you are indifferent.

---

[1] This is the same as Equation 4.3, except no depreciation is shown. In this analysis, we are focusing on the variable cash flows associated with production and selling, assuming the firm already has the necessary long-term assets in place. Depreciation is not relevant. If the credit decision requires a sizable investment in new equipment, however, depreciation must be included.

[2] Equation 20.2 is the perpetuity form for the net present value (Equation 8.3) discussed in Chapter 8. If the benefits are not expected to continue until infinity, then NPV techniques for limited-life projects should be employed. The logic of the first term of Equation 20.2 is the same as discussed in Appendix 5A.

Making the Credit Decision

To use Equation 20.2, the granting firm's *investment in accounts receivable*, CF_0, and the net cash flows expected from granting credit,[3] CF_t, must be determined. These are:

$$CF_0 = (VC)(S)(ACP/365 \text{ days})$$ (20.3)

and

$$CF_t = [S(1 - VC) - S(BD) - CD](1 - T)$$ (20.4)

where

VC = the variable cash outflow of producing and selling the goods as a percentage of cash inflows

S = the cash inflows (sales) expected each period

ACP = average collection period in days

BD = bad debts as a percentage of cash inflows from sales

CD = the dollar amount of additional credit department cash outflow for administering or collecting the accounts receivable

T = the firm's marginal tax rate

To illustrate this approach to the credit-granting decision, consider Empire Electronics, which groups firms into risk categories. Two of these risk classes (X and Y) are shown below:

Risk Class	Required Rate of Return (k)	Average Collection Period (ACP)	Sales (S)	Bad Debts as a Percentage of Sales (BD)	Additional Collection Department Cash Outflows (CD)
X	18%	55 days	$200,000	9%	$10,000
Y	22	60	250,000	11	13,000

At present, Empire does not grant credit to firms in either class. The question is, should Empire modify its terms and now extend credit to firms in either or both risk classes? In addition to the data given above, Empire's variable cash outflows are 82 percent of sales, and its tax rate is 35 percent.

To make the decision, let's consider class X first. The additional initial investment (at cost) in accounts receivable is found using Equation 20.3, as follows:

$$CF_0 = (VC)(S)(ACP/365 \text{ days})$$
$$= (0.82)(\$200,000)(55/365) = \$24,712$$

The additional expected cash inflows, CF_t, are found using Equation 20.4, as follows:

$$CF_t = [S(1 - VC) - S(BD) - CD](1 - T)$$
$$= [\$200,000(1 - 0.82) - \$200,000(0.09) - \$10,000](1 - 0.35)$$
$$= (\$36,000 - \$18,000 - \$10,000)(0.65) = (\$8,000)(0.65) = \$5,200$$

---

[3] For simplicity, cash discounts are ignored in Equation 20.4.

Thus, if Empire grants credit to firms in risk class X, it benefits by receiving incremental expected after-tax cash inflows of $5,200 per period. To obtain these additional CFs, Empire must make an additional investment of $24,712 in accounts receivable. Employing a time line, the cash flows are as follows:

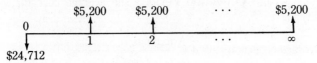

The net present value, which is the benefit to the firm from granting credit to firms in risk class X, employing Equation 20.2, is

$$NPV = \frac{CF_t}{k} - CF_0 = \frac{\$5,200}{0.18} - \$24,712 = \$28,889 - \$24,712 = \$4,177$$

Since the net present value is positive, Empire should grant credit to potential customers in risk class X. By doing so, it is making a decision that increases the value of the firm.

The same calculations can be carried out for firms in risk class Y.

$$CF_0 = (0.82)(\$250,000)(60/365) = \$33,699$$

and

$$CF_t = [\$250,000(1 - 0.82) - \$250,000(0.11) - \$13,000](1 - 0.35)$$
$$= (\$45,000 - \$27,500 - \$13,000)(0.65) = (\$4,500)(0.65) = \$2,925$$

The net present value is then

$$NPV = \frac{\$2,925}{0.22} - \$33,699 = \$13,295 - \$33,699 = -\$20,404$$

Since the net present value is negative, Empire would not grant credit to firms in risk class Y.

In the first case, the additional investment in accounts receivable was less than the present value of the expected cash inflows arising from granting credit.[4] In the second case, the investment was greater. Thus, credit should be granted to customers in risk class X, but not to those in risk class Y.

Collection Policy

Once the granting decision has been made, we cannot ignore the final step—namely, following up to ensure the collection of these receivables. The rate that receivables are converted into cash measures the efficiency of our collection policy. To ensure collections, we establish a collections department that is responsible for monitoring and following up on receivables. We first consider some techniques for monitoring accounts receivable; then we consider how to analyze changes in collection policies.

---

[4] In addition to the standard credit decision just discussed, the same basic approach can be employed to analyze the size of the cash discount offered or the terms of sale. Although these are also important issues, both the cash discount offered and the terms of sale are (1) influenced by competition and (2) subject to infrequent change.

Managing Collections

Two basic techniques for monitoring the receivables investment are (1) the collection period and (2) the receivables pattern approach.

Average Collection Period. The average collection period is calculated by dividing the firm's accounts receivable by average daily sales:

$$\text{average collection period} = \frac{\text{accounts receivable}}{\text{sales}/365} \tag{20.5}$$

If a firm's receivables are $1,800,000 and its sales for the year are $14,600,000, its average collection period, ACP, is

$$\text{ACP} = \frac{\$1,800,000}{\$14,600,000/365} = \frac{\$1,800,000}{\$40,000} = 45 \text{ days}$$

The ACP is easy to calculate, but it is not very effective for internal use in monitoring a firm's collections. This is because it is an aggregate measure and tends to hide many individual differences among customers in terms of payments. In addition, the ACP is influenced by changes in the level of receivables or changes in sales. If receivables increase to $2,000,000, the average collection period goes to 50 days in our example [$2,000,000 ÷ ($14,600,000/365)]. If receivables stay at the original level of $1,800,000, the collection period can increase to 50 days if sales drop to $13,140,000 [$1,800,000 ÷ ($13,140,000/365)]. From a control standpoint, the increase in the level of receivables to $2,000,000 might require different actions by the collection department from those needed if sales decreased to $13,140,000.

A Receivables Pattern Approach. Instead of using the average collection period or some other aggregate measure of accounts receivable, it is better to take a management-by-exception approach, using receivables pattern data for the firm's receivables. The *receivables pattern* is that percentage of credit sales remaining unpaid in the month of the sale, and in subsequent months. The key to understanding receivables patterns is to remember that *each* month's credit sales are kept separate, as well as the collections received on these credit sales. Consider a firm that has credit sales of $100,000 in January. Collections on the $100,000 are as follows:

Month	Collections from January Sales	Payment Pattern	Receivables from January Sales Outstanding at End of Month	Receivables Pattern
January	$10,000	10%	$90,000	90%
February	30,000	30	60,000	60
March	30,000	30	30,000	30
April	30,000	30	0	0

In January, 10 percent of the credit sales are paid, followed by 30 percent each in February, March, and April.[5] The receivables pattern, which is just 100 percent minus the cumulative percentage payments, declines from 90 percent in January to zero in April. This information is graphed in Figure 20.2.

---

[5] For simplicity, bad debts are ignored.

Figure 20.2 Graph of Payment and Receivables Pattern for January Credit Sales

The receivables pattern in (b) is derived from the payment pattern in (a). By focusing on the receivables pattern, it is easy to determine whether payments are being made in the manner expected.

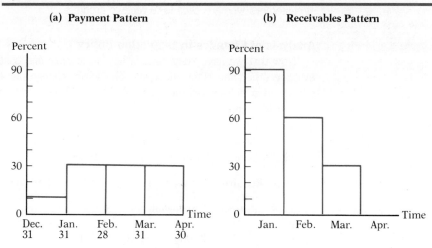

Since the receivables pattern approach relates uncollected accounts receivable to the months in which they arose, it has two significant advantages from a management standpoint. First, it disaggregates the receivables into their collection pattern relative to the month in which they occurred. Second, because accounts receivable are related to sales in the month of origin, they are not sales-dependent. No matter what the sales pattern, any changes in payment behavior can be recognized immediately.

To see how we might exercise control, consider Table 20.2, which provides both budgeted and actual receivable patterns over a 6-month period. Note that the budgeted receivables pattern was 91, 61, and 20 percent for January sales, whereas

Table 20.2 Budgeted Versus Actual Accounts Receivable Patterns

Looking across the bottom two rows, we see that since November, the actual receivables still outstanding both 1 and 2 months after the sales are greater than the budgeted receivables. The slow collection is not unique to the January credit sales.

	October	November	December	January	February	March
Budgeted						
% of same month sales	90%	91%	93%	91%	91%	90%
% of 1 month before	65	64	62	61	61	62
% of 2 months before	36	26	24	22	20	20
Actual						
% of same month sales	91%	93%	96%	90%	88%	89%
% of 1 month before	70	68	69	66	65	65
% of 2 months before	34	32	30	30	28	30

the actual receivables are 90, 65, and 30. In both the first and second months after the credit sales, the collections came in slower than expected. Further examination of Table 20.2 indicates this same pattern has been occurring since November. By focusing on the exceptions, or the deviations of the actual from the projected pattern, management is in a good position to change the collection policy or modify the classes of customers who are eligible to receive credit.

Analysis of Changes in Collection Policy

Now that we have some idea of how to analyze and control collections, we can evaluate other important questions. Should we change our existing credit granting or collection policies? To evaluate changing policies, and possibly curtailing credit previously granted, we simply employ the NPV approach discussed previously. A second decision is to tighten or loosen collection procedures related to existing customers. Consider the following, which shows the existing collection experience and proposed effects of improving our collection procedures.

Situa- tion	Required Rate of Return (k)	Average Collection Period (ACP)	Sales (S)	Bad Debts as a Percentage of Sales (BD)	Collection Department Cash Outflows (CD)
Old	15%	60 days	$1,000,000	10%	$50,000
New	15	55	1,000,000	7	90,000

Under the existing procedures, the average collection period is 60 days, sales are $1,000,000, bad debts are 10 percent of sales, and collection department cash outflows are $50,000. By expanding our collections department, we would be able to reduce the average collection period to 55 days, and bad debts would drop to only 7 percent. Our collection department cash outflows, however, would increase from $50,000 to $90,000. The question is this: Will the firm benefit from increasing its collection efforts?

To answer, we begin by calculating the incremental initial investment and incremental cash flows after taxes associated with the revised procedures. Then Equation 20.2 can be employed to determine whether the change adds to the profitability of the firm. The incremental investment, ΔCF_0, is equal to

$$\begin{array}{ll} \text{incremental} & = \text{investment,} - \text{investment,} \\ \text{investment, } \Delta CF_0 & \quad \text{new (N)} \quad \text{old (O)} \end{array} \qquad (20.6)$$

$$= (VC_N)(S_N)(ACP_N/365) - (VC_O)(S_O)(ACP_O/365)$$

If the variable cash outflows are 80 percent of sales in either case, then using the data given above, the incremental investment is

$$\Delta CF_0 = (0.80)(\$1,000,000)(55/365) - (0.80)(\$1,000,000)(60/365)$$

$$= \$120,548 - \$131,507 = -\$10,959$$

By reducing the average collection period from 60 to 55 days, the new collection plan frees $10,959 that can be used elsewhere in the firm.

The incremental cash flow after-tax, ΔCF_t, due to the change in the collection policy is

$$\text{incremental after-tax cash flow, } \Delta CF_t = \text{after-tax cash flow, new (N)} - \text{after-tax cash flow, old (O)}$$

$$= [S_N(1 - VC_N) - S_N(BD_N) - CD_N](1 - T)$$
$$- [S_O(1 - VC_O) - S_O(BD_O) - CD_O](1 - T) \qquad (20.7)$$

If the tax rate is 40 percent, the incremental after-tax cash flow due to implementing the new collection policy is

$$CF_t = [\$1,000,000(1 - 0.80) - \$1,000,000(0.07) - \$90,000](1 - 0.40)$$
$$- [\$1,000,000(1 - 0.80) - \$1,000,000(0.10) - \$50,000](1 - 0.40)$$

$$= (\$200,000 - \$70,000 - \$90,000)(0.60)$$
$$- (\$200,000 - \$100,000 - \$50,000)(0.60)$$

$$= (\$40,000)(0.60) - (\$50,000)(0.60) = \$24,000 - \$30,000 = -\$6,000$$

Implementing the tighter policy reduces cash inflows by \$6,000 per period. To determine if the firm should implement the proposed change, we calculate the NPV as follows:

$$\text{net present value} = \frac{-\$6,000}{0.15} - (-\$10,959)$$

$$= -\$40,000 + \$10,959 = -\$29,041$$

Since the net present value is negative, the firm is worse off with the new policy.

To carry this idea a little further, consider what would happen if everything was the same as in the preceding example, except that the average collection period decreases to 40 days if we undertake the new collection policy. The incremental after-tax cash flows are still −\$6,000 as before, but the firm is able to reduce its investment in receivables even more than before. With a 40-day average collection period, the incremental investment is

$$\Delta CF_0 = (0.80)(\$1,000,000)(40/365) - (0.80)(\$1,000,000)(60/365)$$
$$= \$87,671 - \$131,507 = -\$43,836$$

The NPV if the average collection period drops to 40 days is

$$NPV = \frac{-\$6,000}{0.15} - (-\$43,836) = -\$40,000 + \$43,836 = \$3,836$$

Since the NPV is positive, the firm would now proceed to implement the proposed change in collection policy.

Still other things might happen if the firm implements a new collection policy. One possibility is for the tighter collection policy to reduce sales. Any changes of this type can be investigated employing the approach just described. By focusing on the cash flows and the risks and required returns, we can determine whether a change in the firm's credit granting or collection policies will benefit the firm (those with positive NPVs) or not (those with negative NPVs). By making decisions that increase the value of the firm, credit and collection management decisions can assist us in achieving our goal of maximizing the value of the firm. Policies should be based on (1) maximizing net cash inflows, (2) spending time on large or risky accounts, and (3) looking beyond the immediate future. Then, the maximum benefits can be secured at the least possible cost.

Inventory Management

Inventory, like receivables, represents a sizable investment and must be managed effectively. Although the formal responsibility for the control of inventory lies with operating divisions, financial managers are also concerned about their management. The more efficiently the firm manages its inventory, the lower the investment required—which, other things being equal, will provide greater stockholder wealth.

Types of Inventory

Firms have different types of inventories. The three most common are (1) raw materials, (2) work-in-process, and (3) finished goods. Raw materials consist of goods that are used to manufacture a product. Work-in-process inventory consists of partially completed goods requiring additional work before they become finished goods. Finished goods are those goods on which production has been completed, and which are ready for sale.

For manufacturing firms, the purpose of holding inventory is to uncouple the acquisition of the goods, the stages of production, and selling activities. Without inventory, particularly work-in-process inventory, each stage of production would be dependent on the preceding stage finishing its operation. As a result, there would be delays and considerable idle time at certain stages of production. Likewise, the raw materials and finished goods inventory uncouples the purchasing and selling functions from the production function. Manufacturing firms hold all three types of inventory. Wholesale and retail firms typically hold only a finished goods inventory. Service firms may have no inventory except for a few supplies related to their activities.

Benefits from Inventory Investment

In addition to uncoupling the firm's operations, there may be a number of other benefits associated with the investment a firm makes in its inventory.

1. TAKING ADVANTAGE OF QUANTITY DISCOUNTS. Often suppliers will offer customers quantity discounts if they purchase a certain number of items at the same time. To take advantage of such discounts, firms need to hold inventory.
2. AVOIDING STOCK OUTAGES. When a firm runs out of inventory, it has a stock outage. If this occurs in the production process, it may disrupt the production cycle and even cause it to stop. If finished goods are not on hand, sales may be lost and the firm's reliability as a supplier comes into question.
3. MARKETING BENEFITS. Often there are distinct marketing benefits in terms of increased sales associated with having a full and complete line of merchandise. Also, developing the reputation for always being able to supply the needed items may be part of the firm's marketing strategy.
4. INVENTORY SPECULATION. In times of inflation, or if other factors are causing prices to increase, firms can benefit by increasing inventory. Other things being equal, this will increase the profitability of the firm.

Costs of Inventory Investment

The cost of a firm's investment in inventory consists of three main elements—carrying costs, ordering costs, and costs of running short.

1. CARRYING COSTS. Carrying costs include the direct investment the firm has in its inventory, including storage, insurance, property tax, and spoilage and deteriora-

Apple's Inventory

In the summer and fall of 1988, Apple Computer was experiencing a severe shortage in memory chips and high demand for their Macintosh computers. To alleviate the problem Apple rushed to buy memory chips on the spot, or current, market at any price. They bought the chips, and immediately thereafter the chips' availability started loosening up and prices fell dramatically. By early 1989 Apple still had millions of memory chips in inventory for which they had paid an average price of $38 each; they could, however, be bought on the open market at that time for $23 each. The impact on the prices of Apple's computers was that for the basic Macintosh II, Apple's cost of memory ended up being $120 higher than it should have been, while on a fully loaded Macintosh II the price ended up being $480 higher.

The net result was twofold. First, current earnings ended up being significantly lower because Apple had lower margins. Second, with their reluctance to discount the machines too much, Apple ended up losing sales. The day Apple announced the lower earnings the price of Apple's stock fell $4.125, to close at $37.625. Equally important, many of Apple's customers started opting for cheaper models, and putting in additional memory them-selves—at a substantial savings. This impact may be more long-term since purchasers realized there were cost-effective alternatives for obtaining extra memory on their Macintosh computers.

Apple learned a lesson that people in pork bellies, corn futures, and wheat futures already know. You can get badly burned betting on the direction of futures' prices. While Apple may or may not have suffered a long-term loss, it serves to indicate that Apple, like many other companies, isn't in complete control of their destiny, and sometimes makes serious miscalculations.

tion. In addition, there is an opportunity cost associated with having funds tied up in nonproductive or excess inventory. Thus, if it keeps $5 million in inventory when only $2 million is needed, the firm has $3 million tied up that could be used elsewhere.

2. ORDERING COSTS. The primary costs associated with ordering inventory include the clerical costs of placing the order, and transportation and shipping costs.

3. COSTS OF RUNNING SHORT. The main costs associated with running short (stock outages) include lost sales, loss of customer goodwill, and disruption of the firm's production process.

Because of these costs, firms attempt to control their inventory levels.

One approach is the *ABC method*. To illustrate, consider a firm that has thousands of inventory items, ranging from very expensive to very inexpensive. The A items require a high investment. As Figure 20.3 shows, 10 percent of the items may account for 50 percent of the dollar inventory investment. Category B items constitute 30 percent of the items and 35 percent of the dollar value, while the C items contribute

Figure 20.3 ABC Inventory Method

The ABC method provides a conceptual framework that suggests different control systems should be used for high- versus low-value items.

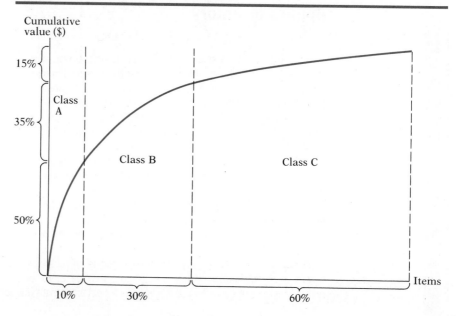

60 percent of the items but only 15 percent of the dollar investment. By separating the inventory into different groups, firms can concentrate on items where effective inventory control is most important. A formal system involving extensive and frequent monitoring is likely for category A items. Items in group B will be reviewed and adjusted less frequently—perhaps quarterly—and C items may be reviewed only annually. The ABC method has two advantages: (1) It focuses attention where it will do the most good, and (2) it makes the financial management of inventory paramount. That is, other considerations (marketing, production, purchasing) are met and then financial considerations are employed to control the firm's inventory investment.

Another approach being considered or implemented by many firms is based on the Japanese *just-in-time* approach. Under this system, the firm contracts with suppliers for both the goods and *when* they will be received. Since the firm wants to maintain almost zero inventory, the suppliers must be located nearby in order to make delivery on a daily or even hourly basis. From the firm's standpoint, the method requires a totally different approach to the production and management process. That is why it often takes new or completely redesigned plants and labor contracts to achieve the anticipated benefits of the just-in-time approach to controlling investment in inventory.

Effective management of the firm's inventory involves a balancing of the costs and benefits associated with the investment in inventory. A basic approach to deciding the size of the order to place is the *economic order quantity (EOQ)* model. The basic elements of the order quantity problem are presented in Appendix 20A. Investment in inventory is really just like any other investment a firm makes. So the NPV framework can also be employed to assist in deciding whether to increase or decrease inventory investment.

Analysis of Investment in Inventory

Often when a firm is considering an investment in some new long-term assets, such as building a new plant, streamlining storage facilities, and the like, part of that problem involves investment in current assets. As we saw in Chapters 8 and 9, any changes in net working capital (current assets minus current liabilities) must be analyzed as part of this larger problem.

However, some investments in inventory may not relate to the acquisition of long-term assets by the firm. Consider the example of Thrifty Stores. After an extensive study by its marketing and finance departments, the firm concluded that sales could be increased significantly if the firm increased its level of finished goods inventory. The increased sales would result from carrying a more complete line, resulting in multiple sales and increased customer traffic. In support of this plan, it has data from a pilot study in its Birmingham store. The firm's inventory would have to be increased by $4 million, while the increased after-tax cash flows, CF_t, are estimated to be $600,000 per year. Assuming the cash flows are expected to last for a long time, the time line for the cash flows is as follows:

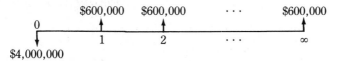

The question is this: Should the additional investment in the inventory be made?

After further evaluation, the firm has concluded that a 12 percent required rate of return is appropriate. Employing Equation 20.2, the net present value of this inventory buildup is

$$NPV = \frac{\$600,000}{0.12} - \$4,000,000 = \$5,000,000 - \$4,000,000 = \$1,000,000$$

Since the net present value is positive, the increased inventory investment should be made.

What happens, however, if Thrifty estimates there will be increased expenses (storage, losses, and so forth) resulting from the increased inventory level carried? These expenses are expected to reduce cash inflows by $70,000 per year. In addition, a senior vice-president believes that $80,000 of the estimated cash flows are extremely unlikely to come in. The additional investment is still $4 million, but the expected cash inflows are now $450,000 ($600,000 − $70,000 − $80,000) per year, which produces the following projected cash flow stream:

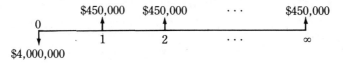

The net present value is now

$$\text{NPV} = \frac{\$450,000}{0.12} - \$4,000,000 = \$3,750,000 - \$4,000,000 = -\$250,000$$

Obviously, based on this set of expected cash flows and the 12 percent required rate of return, Thrifty should not increase its inventory investment.

In making inventory decisions, three items must be stressed. First, the emphasis has to be on cash flows. Second, since various types of inventory are held by firms, close attention should be devoted to the most important items. A management-by-exception framework can be used to control investment in all other items. Finally, the risks and required returns must be considered. For many firms, investment in inventory is their most important single investment.

Interaction of Accounts Receivable and Inventory Decisions

Up to now we have considered separately the management of receivables and the management of inventory. In practice, there are interactions between the firm's accounts receivable and its inventory. This interaction is often hard to see or to achieve, however, because the functions of inventory management and receivables management are typically in separate areas of responsibility within the firm. Inventory and receivables policies should be developed and evaluated on a joint basis, because there are cost and benefit tradeoffs between them. Combinations of tighter inventory control with relaxed credit, looser inventory policy and tighter credit, and varying mixes between these two can be evaluated in terms of the cash flow consequences to the firm. By viewing the investment in these two current assets in an integrated manner, the firm is in a better position to maximize its value.

Summary

Accounts receivable represents a sizable percentage of most firms' assets. The primary determinants of the receivables level are the industry, the level of total sales, and the firm's credit and collection policies. The latter policies include the terms and conditions of the sale, credit analysis, credit decisions, and collection management policies.

Firms cannot discriminate on price; however, they may offer different conditions of sale. Therefore, the most important credit granting decisions are (1) who will receive credit, and (2) what the conditions of the sale will be. Data for the credit analysis may come from financial statements, credit reports, banks, trade associations, and the firm's own experience. The actual credit decision involves an analysis of the size and timing of the cash flows involved, and the risks in a present value framework. Those with positive NPVs should be accepted while those with negative NPVs should be rejected.

The receivables pattern approach to managing collections focuses on the payment and receivables pattern relative to the month the sale occurred. As such, it is not influenced by the level of sales. Analysis of changes in a firm's collection policies, as well as its investment in inventory, also focuses on the magnitude and timing of the cash flows involved, as well as the risks. By employing net present values, managers can ensure that the firm's current asset investment decisions assist in maximizing the value of the firm. This is important, since for the average firm 30 to 65 percent (depending on the industry) of total assets are composed of accounts receivable and inventory.

There is an appendix to this chapter, "Appendix 20A: The Economic Order Quantity Model," at the back of the book.

Questions

20.1 Define or explain the following:

a. Trade credit	**h.** Bill of lading
b. Bad debt	**i.** Letter of credit
c. Cash on delivery (COD)	**j.** Credit scoring model
d. Sight draft	**k.** Receivables pattern
e. Time draft	**l.** ABC method
f. Trade acceptance	**m.** Just-in-time
g. Banker's acceptance	**n.** Economic order quantity (EOQ)

20.2 Firms sometimes sell their receivables at a discount to (1) a wholly owned "captive finance company," or (2) another firm that specializes in receivables management and collection. If it is a captive finance company, the parent provides part of the financing. The rest is obtained by issuing substantial amounts of debt. For both arrangements, what are the possible advantages?

20.3 Explain how the four parts of the firm's credit and collection policies interact.

20.4 What would be the effect of changes in the following on the level of accounts receivable?

a. The economy improves, and interest rates decline.
b. The credit manager tightens up on past due accounts.
c. The credit terms are changed from 3/10, net 30 to 2/10, net 30.
d. The firm's selling and production expenses decline relative to other firms.

20.5 Gail, the credit manager, is being criticized for the deterioration in her performance because the average collection period has increased, as have bad debts. Under what circumstances is this criticism unjustified?

20.6 Why is the receivables pattern approach superior to the average collection period in monitoring collections?

20.7 Compare the benefits and costs of investing in inventory.

20.8 What would be the effect of the following on the level of inventory held by the firm?

a. Inflation increases.
b. Our suppliers switch from truck to air freight delivery.
c. Competition increases in our sales market.
d. Our production cycle becomes shorter.

Self-Test Problems   (Solutions appear on page 736.)

Cash Discount

ST 20.1 Motan Furniture has been offered a one-time opportunity to purchase goods from a supplier at a bargain price of $50,000. The credit terms are 4/15, net 40. Motan does not have the cash on hand to take advantage of the offer, but it can secure the money from its bank at an annual rate of 14 percent. In 40 days it will have sufficient cash. Should Motan purchase the goods? Assume a 365-day year.

Investment in Receivables

ST 20.2 Cole United sells on a 1/10, net 30 basis and has sales of $18,250,000 per year. All sales are for credit. Fifteen percent of all sales are paid on the tenth day, and the rest are paid in an average of 40 days. Production costs are 80 percent of the sales price. Assume a 365-day year.

a. Employing these probabilities of occurrence, what is the average collection period?
b. What is the average investment in accounts receivable?
c. If Cole United can reduce the time the nondiscount customers take to pay to 30 days, what is its average investment in receivables?

Loosening the Collection Policy

ST 20.3 Sigma Systems has annual credit sales of $25 million. Its average collection period is 30 days, bad debts are 2 percent of sales, and its collection department expenses (cash outflows) are $500,000. Sigma is considering easing its collection policy. The result would be to increase the average collection period to 50 days, sales would increase to $27.5 million, and bad debts would increase to 4 percent. Collection department cash outflows, however, would decrease to $325,000. Sigma's variable cash outflows are 78 percent of sales, it is in the 30 percent tax bracket, and the discount rate is 20 percent. Should Sigma relax its collection policy? (Use a 365-day year.)

Problems

Average Collection Period and Sales

20.1 Deschamps Industries offers credit terms of 3/10, net 45. Twenty percent of its customers pay on the discount date, 40 percent pay on the net date, and the other 40 percent pay in 60 days. If Deschamp's average investment in accounts receivables is $500,000 and variable costs are 80 percent of sales, what is Deschamps annual sales? Assume a 365-day year. (*Note:* Carry to five decimal places.)

Cost of Credit Analysis (More Difficult)

20.2 Bulldog Industries makes and sells various pet equipment. The average order size is $100, and 25,000 orders are placed with Bulldog per year. (Assume each customer orders only once a year.) All sales are on credit on a net 30 basis, with an average collection period of 45 days, and production and selling cash flows are 80 percent of sales. Bad debts average 8.8 percent of sales. Assume a 365-day year and that there are no corporate taxes. (*Note:* This is not a NPV problem.)

a. What is Bulldog's profit per year, and its average investment in accounts receivable?
b. At present Bulldog does no credit analysis; however, for $1 per analysis, credit information can be obtained. With the new information, orders could be classified as follows:

	Order Category		
	Low Risk	**Average Risk**	**High Risk**
Bad debt loss	2%	7%	18%
Percentage of orders	30	40	30
Average collection period	10 days	45 days	80 days

(1) What would Bulldog's profits be, by category, with the credit analysis information? What would be its total profits over the first two categories, and for all three?

(2) Any funds freed by reducing its investment in receivables can be invested at 10 percent per year. How much could Bulldog earn on the money freed by the reduced investment in receivables?

(3) Should Bulldog secure the credit analysis?

20.3 Cincinnati Iron Works is in the process of evaluating its credit standards. Two potential classes of new customers exist, as follows:

Risk Class	Required Rate of Return (k)	Average Collection Period (ACP)	Sales (S)	Bad Debts as a Percentage of Sales (BD)	Additional Collection Department Cash Outflows (CD)
4	16%	45 days	$511,000	8%	$15,000
5	20	55	438,000	12	25,000

The variable cash outflows as a percentage of sales are 80 percent, and the tax rate is 30 percent. Should Cincinnati extend credit to potential customers in risk class 4? Risk class 5? (Assume a 365-day year.)

20.4 Madison Group makes all sales on a credit basis. It is evaluating the creditworthiness of its customers. The results of the analysis are as follows:

Risk Class	Required Rate of Return (k)	Average Collection Period (ACP)	Sales (S)	Bad Debts as a Percentage of Sales (BD)	Collection Department Cash Outflows (CD)
A	12%	20 days	$3 million	3%	$50,000
B	14	40	4	5	50,000
C	16	60	6	10	60,000
D	18	80	8	15	80,000

Variable cash outflows are 81 percent of sales, and taxes are 40 percent.

a. Analyze each of the present classes of customers. Should Madison continue to grant credit to all four risk classes? (Assume a 365-day year.)
b. What happens to the level of sales if Madison follows your recommendation in (a)? How would you proceed to convince Madison to follow your recommendation?

20.5 Marks is evaluating whether to grant credit to a risky class of potential customers. Variable cash outflows are 82 percent of sales, the average collection period is 65 days, sales per year (based on a 365-day year) are $10,950,000, bad debts are 12 percent of sales, additional collection department cash outflows are $300,000 per year, and the required rate of return is 12 percent. At what marginal tax rate is Marks indifferent between granting and not granting credit to this new class of customers?

20.6 Butcher Products is a new firm. All sales are on credit, and the sales and payments for the first 6 months are as follows:

	March	April	May	June	July	August
Credit sales	$1,500	$2,000	$2,400	$2,800	$3,700	$4,900
Payments—same month	200	400	500	600	700	800
Payments—1 month later		600	800	1,000	1,250	1,500
Payments—2 months later			500	700	800	850

After 2 months the uncollected sales are written off as bad debts. Calculate the receivables pattern for Butcher. Is it becoming more or less effective? What is happening to its bad debts? Are there any indications of change occurring in July and August?

20.7 Mutual Worldwide employs the average collection period (based on a 365-day year) to monitor its receivables. The sales and receivables pattern for the 4 months of February through May are as follows:

	February	March	April	May	June	July
Credit sales	$150,000	$200,000	$300,000	$300,000		
Receivables—same month sales	120,000	160,000	237,000	234,000		
Receivables—1 month before		60,000	80,000	114,000	108,000	
Receivables—2 months before			0	0	0	0	0

Total sales for the year are $2,555,000.

a. Calculate the average collection period (using the total yearly sales) for each of 3 months—March, April, and May.

b. What do your results from (a) suggest about the effectiveness of Mutual's collection policies?

c. Now calculate the receivables pattern for Mutual. Is its collection policy less effective in May than in March or April?

d. Explain why you got conflicting results from the average collection period versus the receivables pattern approach.

Easing the Collections Effort

20.8 Perry Air Conditioning has annual credit sales of $1.6 million. Current collection department cash outflows are $35,000, bad debts are 1.5 percent of sales, and the average collection period is 30 days. Perry is considering easing its collection efforts so that collection department outflows will be reduced to $22,000 per year. The change is expected to increase bad debts to 2.5 percent of sales and to increase the average collection period to 45 days. In addition, sales are expected to increase to $1.75 million. If the required rate of return is 16 percent, variable cash outflows are 75 percent of sales, and the marginal tax rate is 35 percent, should Perry make the change?

Tightening the Credit Policy

20.9 Little Rock Data believes its collection policy may be out of hand. Currently, the firm has sales of $6 million, an average collection period of 55 days, bad debts are 6 percent of sales, and yearly collection department cash outflows are $100,000. Its existing variable cash outflows are 80 percent of sales. If it tightens the collection policy significantly, it anticipates sales will drop to $5 million, the average collection period will become 25 days, bad debts will be 3 percent of sales, and collection department cash outflows will be $75,000 per year. At this level of sales, variable cash outflows will be 83 percent of sales. Assume the corporate tax rate is 30 percent, and use a 365-day year.

a. If Little Rock's required rate of return is 14 percent, should it tighten the collection policy?

b. What if the required rate of return is 20 percent?

Collecting Overdue Receivables

20.10 Gupta Sales has $500,000 in overdue receivables that it is considering writing off as worthless. It has been approached by a collection agency. The agency will charge $75,000 plus 50 percent of the first $200,000 collected by the agency and 25 percent of the rest collected. Gupta estimates there is a 60 percent probability that a total of $150,000 will be collected, a 30 percent probability that a total of $300,000 will be collected, and a 10 percent probability that a total of $450,000 will be collected.

a. Should Gupta Sales employ the collection agency?

(Do only if using Pinches Disk.)

b. If the collection agency's fixed charge is $125,000, instead of $75,000, should Gupta employ the agency?

c. If the charges are 50 percent for the first $250,000 collected, instead of the first $200,000 collected, should the firm employ the agency if everything remains the same as in (a)? As in (b)?

d. Now suppose the probabilities of collection are as follows:

Probability	Amount Collected
50%	$200,000
45	325,000
5	425,000

The variable charge by the collection agency is 40 percent on the first $200,000, while it is 30 percent for the rest. How would these estimates change your answers to (a) and (b)?

Inventory Investment

20.11 LaSalle Street Stores is considering three different mutually exclusive proposals for increasing its inventory level. The initial investments and after-tax cash flows are as follows:

Inventory Level	Initial Investment (CF_0)	Required Rate of Return (k)	After-Tax Cash Flow (CF_t)
A	$300,000	12%	$ 50,000
B	600,000	15	110,000
C	900,000	18	175,000

Which, if any, of the new inventory levels should LaSalle Street Stores adopt?

Reduction in Inventory

20.12 The Mukherjee Group presently carries an average inventory valued at $5 million. New management has proposed to reduce the inventory to $3.5 million. The expected loss in after-tax cash flows due to increased stock outages will be $200,000 per year if inventory is reduced, but losses due to theft and spoilage should decrease by $20,000 (after taxes). If the required return is 16 percent, should the inventory be reduced?

Interrelated Receivables and Inventory

20.13 Gordon Showrooms sells to its customers on a credit basis. It is considering loosening its credit granting standards to two additional risk classes, P and Q.

Risk Class	Required Rate of Return (k)	Average Collection Period (ACP)	Sales (S)	Bad Debts as a Percentage of Sales (BD)	Additional Collection Department Cash Outflows (CD)
P	15%	50 days	$ 800,000	6%	$20,000
Q	20	60	1,300,000	10	60,000

Variable costs are 75 percent of sales, a 365-day year is used, and Gordon's tax rate is 40 percent. In addition, granting credit to customers in risk class P would require an investment of an additional $60,000 in inventory. Extending credit to risk class Q would require an additional $150,000 investment in inventory (beyond that required for class P).

a. Should Gordon grant credit to customers in risk class P?
b. Assuming Gordon has already decided to grant credit to class P, should it also grant credit to customers in risk class Q?

References

For books that cover accounts receivables and/or inventory, see

CHRISTIE, GEORGE R., AND ALBERT E. BRACUTI. *Credit Management.* Lake Success, N.Y.: Credit Research Foundation, 1981.

EPPEN, G. D., AND F. J. GOULD. *Quantitative Concepts for Management: Decision Making Without Algorithms,* 3rd ed. Englewood Cliffs, N.J.: Prentice-Hall, 1989.

SCHONBERGER, RICHARD J., AND EDWARD M. KNOCH, JR. *Operations Management: Serving the Customer,* 3rd ed. Plano, Tx.: Business Publications, 1988.

For more on credit and receivables management, see

EMERY, GARY W. "A Pure Financial Explanation for Trade Credit." *Journal of Financial and Quantitative Analysis* 19 (September 1984), pp. 271–285.

FARRAGHER, EDWARD J. "Factoring Accounts Receivable." *Journal of Cash Management* 6 (March–April 1986), pp. 38–42.

GENTRY, JAMES A., AND JESUS M. DE LA GARZA. "A Generalized Model for Monitoring Accounts Receivable." *Financial Management* 14 (Winter 1985), pp. 28–38.

SARTORIS, WILLIAM L., AND NED C. HILL. "Evaluating Credit Policy Alternatives: A Present Value Framework." *Journal of Financial Research* 4 (Spring 1981), pp. 81–89.

SMITH, JANET K. "Trade Credit and Information Asymmetry." *Journal of Finance* 42 (September 1987), pp. 863–872.

SRINIVASAN, VENKAT, AND YONG H. KIM. "Credit Granting: A Comparative Analysis of Classification Procedures." *Journal of Finance* 42 (July 1987), pp. 665–681.

STONE, BERNELL K. "The Payments-Pattern Approach to the Forecasting and Control of Accounts Receivable." *Financial Management* 5 (Autumn 1976), pp. 65–82.

See Model thirteen in *Lotus 1–2–3® for Financial Management* by Pinches and Courtney for a template that evaluates a firm's credit policy.

21

Short-Term Financing

Overview

- Interest on most short-term financing is specified on an annual basis, often tied to the prime rate of interest.

- The annual percentage rate, APR, provides the before-tax cost of alternative financing sources.

- Other dollar costs in addition to interest, or sometimes benefits, often need to be considered in order to find the cost of financing.

- Trade credit, continuous factoring of accounts receivable, and field warehousing provide spontaneous short-term financing. Bank loans and commercial paper are negotiated short-term financing sources.

Gelco Corp., a billion-dollar Minnesota-based transportation firm, took a full year to put together a $90 million commercial paper issue. The firm maintains it was worth every day of the lengthy wait. That's because Gelco was pioneering an ingenious new credit-enhancement technique to reduce short-term financing costs. It set up a separate legal entity that held title to certain Gelco leases, making sure that even if Gelco failed, the leases in the separate entity would not be affected. Then Gelco had the separate entity issue commercial paper (backed by the leases) on its behalf. The net result was to raise the rating on Gelco's commercial paper from double B to A minus, thereby providing substantially cheaper financing.

Savings and loan associations employ a similar tactic: They use Treasury bills or notes they hold to provide collateral for commercial paper. Other lenders are turning to insurance firms—chiefly Aetna, INA, and Travelers—to guarantee their borrowings. These and other forms of credit enhancement are helping many firms significantly lower short-term borrowing costs.

However, not all businesses pay interest to borrow money. D'Hanis State Bank in Texas simply doesn't pay interest since it doesn't offer any interest-bearing accounts. Why don't depositors demand interest? "Three generations of folks don't miss something they never had." Not many firms are like the D'Hanis State Bank. In securing short-term financing our attention again focuses on risks, required returns, and cash flows.

Sources and Importance of Short-Term Financing

Among numerous sources of short-term financing are trade credit and short-term borrowing by the firm. Trade credit arises when one firm purchases goods from another firm and does not pay cash immediately. This creates an account payable for the purchasing firm. Trade credit often is called spontaneous short-term financing because it tends to expand automatically as firms purchase more goods and build up inventory. There are also *negotiated short-term financing* sources. Thus, to secure short-term borrowed funds, the firm must enter into negotiations with commercial banks, finance companies, and the like.

Aside from the matching principle discussed in Chapter 18, there are two other reasons firms use short-term financing. The first is to meet seasonal needs. As firms enter into that part of the year where accounts receivable and inventory expands, they employ short-term financing. Later, when cash inflows increase, they pay down the short-term financing. The second reason is to "roll" it into longer-term financing. Many firms use short-term financing until the total amount of financing needed becomes large enough to justify long-term debt (or equity) financing.

Size of Short-Term Financing

To see the importance of short-term financing, consider that small manufacturing firms (with assets of less than $25 million), retail firms, and wholesale firms all have current liabilities that are 35 percent or more of total assets. For larger manufacturing firms, the current liabilities drop to about 25 percent. The large size of current liabilities for small manufacturing firms, retail firms, and wholesale firms is because these firms have large amounts of current assets. Under the matching principle, we expect such firms to have large amounts of current liabilities, which they do. The majority of these current liabilities are in the form of accounts payable and short-term borrowings—the focus of this chapter. The other short-term liabilities include various accrued items, such as wages and taxes, and current maturities of long-term debt or lease obligations.

The amount of current liabilities varies both between industries and among firms in the same industry. As Table 21.1 shows, both the petroleum and retail merchandise industries had more current liabilities in 1987 than in 1984. Similarly, Atlantic Richfield increased its reliance on short-term financing, while Penney reduced its reliance. These changes were the result of both company policy and changing business and economic conditions.

Because of the firm's size, the varying nature of the firm's needs over the course of the year, changes in business conditions and interest rates, and changes in the money market and financing alternatives, short-term financing is more important than ever. Securing funds at the most cost-effective rate is vitally important. At the same time, the firm must ensure the availability of funds, no matter what the time of year or economic conditions. In this chapter we focus on the nature of short-term financing available, how to determine its cost, and the typical conditions surrounding alternative sources of short-term financing.

Cost of Short-Term Financing

In determining the cost of alternative sources of short-term financing, two important ideas must be kept in mind:

1. For the purpose of comparison, we express the costs in the same units over the same period of time. If one source costs $800 for a month's financing, while

Table 21.1 Accounts Payable, Short-Term Debt, and Other Current Liabilities as a Percentage of Total Assets, by Industry and Firm

Differences between industries affect the size and composition of current liabilities. In addition, many differences can only be explained by factors unique to individual companies. (SOURCES: Quarterly Financial Report for Manufacturing, Mining and Trade, *Bureau of the Census, Fourth quarter, 1984 and 1987; and annual reports from the individual companies cited.)*

Year	Industry Petroleum and Coal Products	Individual Firms Atlantic Richfield	Chevron
1984			
Accounts payable	7.9%	1.8%	4.5%
Short-term debt	3.1	8.6	14.6
Other current liabilities	5.7	3.0	6.2
Total current liabilities	16.7%	13.4%	25.3%
1987			
Accounts payable	6.7%	2.9%	2.7%
Short-term debt	5.0	13.9	8.3
Other current liabilities	7.2	2.9	13.7
Total current liabilities	18.9%	19.7%	24.7%

Year	Retail Merchandise	J. C. Penney	Wal-Mart
1984			
Accounts payable	12.3%	9.5%	0.1%
Short-term debt	5.2	11.7	20.5
Other current liabilities	11.9	6.4	10.6
Total current liabilities	29.4%	27.6%	31.2%
1987			
Accounts payable	12.1%	8.8%	0.1%
Short-term debt	6.8	4.8	23.5
Other current liabilities	11.4	11.1	10.5
Total current liabilities	30.3%	24.7%	34.1%

another charges a monthly rate of interest of 1.5 percent for the same amount of funds, it is not immediately obvious which is most expensive. To deal with this difference, all costs are expressed in the same units over the same time period. Because of simplicity and tradition, we convert all costs to an annual percentage rate.

2. The ultimate cost to the firm is influenced by the tax rate of the firm. If it is in a 35 percent bracket, and the firm's before-tax cost is 10 percent per year, the after-tax cost to the firm is only 6.5 percent [10%(1 − 0.35)]. The basic equation to calculate the before-tax *annual percentage rate* (APR), k_b, for any short-term financing is:

$$k_b = \left(1 + \frac{\text{costs} - \text{benefits}}{\text{net amount of financing}} \right)^m - 1 \qquad (21.1)$$

where m is the number of compounding periods per year. The after-tax cost to the firm is given by Equation 21.2, where

after-tax cost = (before-tax cost)(1 − the tax rate)

$$k_i = k_b(1 - T)$$ (21.2)

where k_i is the after-tax cost, k_b is the before-tax annual cost, and T is the firm's marginal tax rate. Although a firm can employ either the before- or after-tax cost for decision-making purposes, their ultimate cost is the after-tax cost given by Equation 21.2.

To see these ideas, consider the cost of a $100,000 loan on which the bank will charge interest of $3,500, where the interest will be paid in 90 days when the loan is repaid. The before-tax annual compound percentage cost of this loan, employing Equation 21.1 and a 365-day year, is[1]

$$k_b = \left(1 + \frac{\$3,500}{\$100,000} \right)^{365/90} - 1 = \left(1 + \frac{\$3,500}{\$100,000} \right)^{4.055556} - 1$$

$$= 1.1497 - 1 = 0.1497 = 14.97\%$$

The after-tax cost, if the firm is in the 35 percent marginal tax bracket, is

$$k_i = (14.97\%)(1 - 0.35) = 9.73\%$$

Thus, the firm's after-tax annual cost is 9.73 percent.

Consider what would happen to the same firm if its tax bracket was either 20 percent or zero percent. With a 20 percent tax bracket, the after-tax cost is

$$k_i \text{ with 20 percent tax bracket} = (14.97\%)(1 - 0.20) = 11.98\%$$

If the firm's tax bracket is zero, the after-tax cost is the same as the before-tax cost, so

$$k_i \text{ with zero tax bracket} = (14.97\%)(1 - 0) = 14.97\%$$

This example shows the importance of the firm's tax bracket for the cost of borrowing. As the tax bracket increases, other things being equal, the firm's after-tax cost of borrowing decreases.[2]

Accounts Payable, or Trade Credit

Most firms make purchases from other firms on credit. This shows up on the purchaser's accounting records as an account payable. Trade credit is a spontaneous source

---

[1] As discussed in Chapter 5, some loans employ a 360-day year. For simplicity, we use a 365-day year. (Occasionally, we use 12 equal periods.) To calculate this remember to use the y^x key on your calculator.

[2] If compounding is not employed, the simple interest cost is given by

$$k_b = \left(\frac{\text{costs} - \text{benefits}}{\text{net amount of financing}} \right)\left(\frac{365 \text{ days}}{\text{total number of days funds borrowed}} \right)$$

$$= \left(\frac{\$3,500}{\$100,000} \right)\left(\frac{365}{90} \right) = 0.1419 = 14.19\%$$

Simple interest always understates the annual percentage rate, APR.

of financing. If a firm typically makes purchases of $3,000 per day and pays its bills in 30 days, the average accounts payable outstanding are $90,000. What happens, however, if as the busy season of the year draws near, purchases increase to $5,000 per day? While the firm still pays in 30 days, the accounts payable have increased to $150,000. This difference of $60,000 ($150,000 − $90,000) in accounts payable occurred spontaneously as the firm geared up for its busy season. The firm generated $60,000 in additional financing just by increasing its purchases and taking advantage of the trade credit offered by its suppliers.

Cost of Trade Credit

Instead of being concerned about granting credit, as in Chapter 20, we are now the recipient of trade credit. Trade credit terms typically are expressed as 1/10, net 30, which means that a 1 percent discount applies if the account is paid within 10 days. If not, the account should be paid in full within 30 days. If the firm takes advantage of the 1 percent discount, there is no cost associated with the trade credit. That is, 10 days of credit is available at no cost to the purchaser. If the firm does not take the cash discount, there is a direct cost to the firm. This cost is

$$k_b = \left(1 + \frac{\text{discount percent}}{100\% - \text{discount percent}}\right)^{365/(\text{date paid} - \text{discount date})} - 1 \qquad (21.3)$$

The direct before-tax annual cost of not taking a 1 percent discount by paying in 10 days is

$$k_b = \left(1 + \frac{1}{100 - 1}\right)^{365/(30-10)} - 1 = (1 + 0.010101)^{18.25} - 1$$

$$= 1.2013 - 1 = 0.2013 = 20.13\%$$

In Equation 21.3 note that the discount not taken is related to the number of additional days for which credit is obtained. With terms of 1/10, net 30, the 1 percent cash discount is the interest cost for an additional 20 days of credit. This assumes the purchaser pays on the thirtieth day if the cash discount is not taken. Often firms "stretch" their payables by not paying on the net date. What happens to the direct annual cost if the firm stretches its payables by paying them 50 days after the invoice date? The cost is

$$k_b = (1 + 0.010101)^{365/40} - 1 = 1.0960 - 1 = 9.60\%$$

This is lower than before, since 40 (instead of 20) days of credit were obtained. As shown below, the effect of *stretching payables* is to reduce the direct cost of trade credit.

Credit Terms	If Paid on Net Date	If Paid 10 Days Past Net Date	If Paid 20 Days Past Net Date	If Paid 30 Days Past Net Date
½/10, net 30	9.58%	6.29%	4.68%	3.73%
1/10, net 30	20.13	13.01	9.60	7.61
2/10, net 30	44.59	27.86	20.24	15.89
2/10, net 60	15.89	13.08	11.11	9.66
3/10, net 60	24.90	20.36	17.21	14.91
4/10, net 60	34.72	28.19	23.72	20.47

Firms that pass up cash discounts can reduce the direct cost by stretching their payables. The effect of this practice, however, is to incur an opportunity cost. This is the loss of supplier goodwill resulting in possible curtailment of trade credit. Equally important, a firm that continually stretches its payables will suffer lower credit ratings, thereby raising the future cost of funds. Firms should always take advantage of the free credit period (10 days in our example). Nevertheless, in assessing the desirability of stretching payables (if the cash discount is not taken), both direct and opportunity costs must be considered.

Advantages of Trade Credit

Trade credit has a number of advantages as a source of short-term financing. First, it is readily available and can be conveniently obtained as a normal part of the firm's everyday activities. Second, it is free (and actually results in a reduction in the purchase price) if the discount is taken. Third, it is flexible and can expand or contract as purchases expand or contract. Finally, there are no restrictive terms (or formal agreements). For these reasons, all efficiently managed firms take advantage of trade credit. Not to do so would increase the financial burden on the firm, resulting in lower returns.

Unsecured Loans

Unsecured loans[3] occur in two forms—bank loans and commercial paper. Bank loans are short-term borrowings obtained from banks or finance companies; commercial paper is a short-term security sold in the money market to investors. In Table 21.2, we see that short-term borrowings have supplied substantially more funds than commercial paper. The relative importance of commercial paper, however, increased in 1981, 1984, and 1985 as more firms used this security. Short-term borrowing has generally supplied 35 to 80 percent of total external financing (excluding trade credit) obtained by firms between 1980 and 1987. Firms must negotiate a bank loan or issue commercial paper—as opposed to obtaining trade credit, which occurs spontaneously.

Bank Loans

Most bank loans have maturities of 1 year or less and often have a variable interest rate—that is, one that fluctuates over the life of the loan as interest rates change. The basic interest rate charged by banks is called the prime rate.[4] It is defined as the rate at which their best customers can borrow.[5] In Figure 21.1, the prime rate

---

[3] Some of these loans and even commercial paper may actually be backed by specific assets of the firm. For convenience, however, they will be considered unsecured loans.

[4] Each bank sets its own prime rate, but competition forces them to be similar. Generally, the major banks set prime a certain number of percentage points (typically 1 to 2 percent) above the rate on negotiable certificates of deposit issued by banks. Other banks typically follow suit; however, the prime may vary slightly, depending on the size and location of the bank. Increasingly, some banks are using other rates, such as the U.S. Treasury bill rate, or the London Interbank Offered Rate (LIBOR), instead of prime.

[5] Although prime is the rate banks supposedly charge their best customers, they also loan below prime to very important and financially strong firms. These firms have the option of issuing commercial paper which, as shown in Figure 21.1, has a yield below the prime rate. Because of this competitive factor, banks may occasionally "split the difference" between the prime rate and the commercial paper rate for loans to very sound major firms.

Table 21.2 Short-Term Borrowing by Nonfinancial Corporations (In billions)

Bank and finance company loans are the primary sources of short-term financing. Over this period, short-term financing provided over 65 percent of all external financing. (SOURCE: Flow of Funds Accounts, *Federal Reserve System, various issues.*)

Year	Bank Loans (1)	Finance Company Loans (2)	Commercial Paper (3)	Other (4)	Total (5) [(1) + (2) + (3) + (4)]	Total External Sources (6)	Short-Term as a Percentage of Total External (7) [(5)/(6)]
1980	$27.4	$ 3.8	$ 4.0	$ 4.4	$ 39.6	$ 92.7	42.7%
1981	34.6	10.2	14.7	12.3	71.8	94.5	76.0
1982	37.2	2.0	−6.1	3.4	36.5	80.4	45.4
1983	15.3	11.1	−0.8	5.7	31.3	88.6	35.3
1984	64.0	27.7	21.7	15.6	129.0	121.6	106.1
1985	35.9	21.6	14.6	−2.2	69.9	85.2	82.0
1986	56.1	16.9	−9.3	11.4	75.1	109.5	68.6
1987	12.9	30.9	2.3	7.1	53.2	77.4	68.7

and the rate on commercial paper are shown. The volatility of short-term interest rates is shown vividly. Between 1980 and 1982, the prime rate rose to more than 20 percent before falling off in the latter part of the period. Rates on loans are generally tied to prime, so the borrower pays prime plus half a percent, prime plus 1 percent, and so on. With a prime rate loan, as the bank's prime rate changes, so will the interest rate charged the borrowing firm.

Types of Bank Loans

A bank loan may be a single (transaction) loan or a line of credit. A *transaction loan* is made by the bank for a specific purpose. To obtain a transaction loan, a promissory note is signed. The note specifies (1) the amount borrowed, (2) the interest rate on the loan, (3) the maturity date and repayment schedule, (4) collateral (if any) involved, and (5) any other conditions agreed upon by the two parties. When the note is signed, the borrower receives the loan.

A line of credit is another type of agreement between a bank and a firm. A line of credit agreement means the firm can borrow up to some maximum amount over a specified time period. For example, the agreement may be that the firm can borrow, or "draw down," a $500,000 line of credit over the next year. This amount, or any portion of it, may be borrowed during this time period. Repayment can be made as desired, but by the end of the agreement all borrowings must be paid off. Although lines of credit can be informal agreements where the lender has no legal obligation to make the loan, often they are formal agreements for which the firm pays a *commitment fee* to the bank, whether or not it draws on the line of credit.[6]

---

[6] The commitment fee may be one-fourth to three-fourths of 1 percent per year. Thus, on a $5 million line of credit, the commitment fee could be $12,500 to $37,500 annually, whether or not the line was used. This arrangement generally involves a legal commitment from the lender to provide a loan up to the credit limit on the line.

Figure 21.1 Prime Rate and Yield on Commercial Paper

The rates are 3-month averages. Because banks key their prime rate to the yield on marketable securities, it is always one or two points above the yield on commercial paper. SOURCE: Federal Reserve Bulletin, *various issues.*

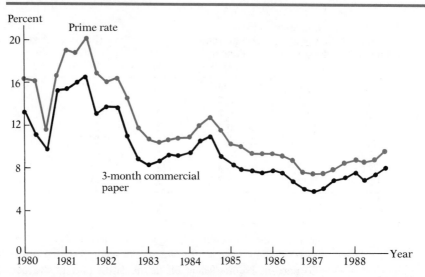

Cost of Bank Loans

The cost of bank loans depends on the conditions attached to the agreement. We illustrate three different types—(1) regular interest, (2) discount interest, and (3) installment interest. The effects of variable interest rates, compensating balance requirements, and interest for lines of credit are also considered.

Regular Interest. The cost of a loan with *regular interest* can be solved employing Equation 21.1. Assume there is a $10,000 loan, the bank will charge prime plus 1 percent, prime is 12 percent per year, and the loan is for 73 days. The two-step process to solve for the before-tax cost is as follows:

STEP 1: Determine the interest paid:

$$\frac{\text{interest}}{\text{paid}} = \left(\frac{\text{amount}}{\text{borrowed}}\right)\left(\frac{\text{annual interest}}{\text{rate}}\right)\left(\frac{\text{portion of year}}{\text{borrowed for}}\right)$$

$$= (\$10,000)(0.13)(73/365) = \$260$$

STEP 2: Employing Equation 21.1, determine k_b, which is

$$k_b = \left(1 + \frac{\$260}{\$10,000}\right)^{365/73} - 1 = 1.1369 - 1 = 13.69\%$$

Note that even though the stated rate is 13 percent, the annual percentage rate is 13.69 percent.

Discount Interest. Under *discount interest,* the bank deducts the interest at the beginning of the loan. In such a case, the borrower receives $9,740 ($10,000

− $260). From step 1 above, the interest is still $260. In step 2, $9,740 (the amount actually secured) replaces the $10,000 previously employed. The annual percentage cost of a discounted loan employing Equation 21.1 is

$$k_b = \left(1 + \frac{\$260}{\$9,740}\right)^{365/73} - 1 = 1.1408 - 1 = 14.08\%$$

Because the bank does not lend the full amount, the cost of a discounted loan is higher than with regular interest.

Installment Interest. Instead of paying the loan off in a lump sum, banks and many other financial institutions charge *installment interest,* with payments made monthly. In this case the total amount of interest is calculated and added to the original face value of the note. Then the monthly installment represents a payment of both principal and interest. Let's assume that we borrow $10,000 for 1 year, that we agree to pay interest at a 13 percent annual stated rate, and that 12 monthly payments will be made. The note will be for the principal of $10,000 plus the interest of $1,300 [i.e., ($10,000)(0.13)] for a total of $11,300. The monthly payment is $941.67 ($11,300/12).

To solve for the approximate annual rate of interest for an installment loan, we employ present value techniques for an annuity. Thus,

$10,000 = \$941.67(\, PVA_{k_b,n}\,)$

$PVA_{?\%,12} = \$10,000/\$941.67 = 10.619$

From Table F.4, this is slightly under 2 percent per month, or 24 percent per year. The cost of an installment loan is always slightly less than twice the stated rate.[7]

Variable Rate Loans. Now that we know how interest is calculated, we can consider some additional complications. The first is *variable rate* interest. What if a firm needed to borrow $10,000 for 150 days and was going to pay prime plus 1 percent? Interest will be figured employing the regular method. If prime was 12 percent annually for the first 73 days, $13\frac{3}{4}$ percent for the next 30 days, and $14\frac{1}{2}$ percent for the remaining 47 days, what is the cost to the firm? To solve this problem, the two-step procedure described above can be used.

STEP 1. Determine the interest paid:

Prime Rate	Prime Plus 1 Percent	Number of Days	Interest Cost in Dollars	
12%	13%	73	($10,000)(0.13)(73/365)	= $260.00
$13\frac{3}{4}$	$14\frac{3}{4}$	30	($10,000)(0.1475)(30/365) =	121.23
$14\frac{1}{2}$	$15\frac{1}{2}$	47	($10,000)(0.1550)(47/365) =	199.59
			Total interest =	$580.82

[7] Installment loans are similar to term loans, discussed in Chapter 5. With a financial calculator, we punch in PV = 10,000, PMT = 941.67, n = 12 and then hit the k_b = i button to solve for the exact rate of 1.932 percent per month. Multiplying by 12 to convert to a yearly rate, the before-tax cost is 23.18 percent.

The Uniqueness of Bank Loans

When firms need debt-type financing they have a variety of sources from which to select. They can issue longer-term debt either to the public markets or place it privately, or they can enter into a bank loan agreement. The latter is typically one of two types. It may be a credit agreement, which is typically a line of credit (i.e., a commitment to lend), or it may be a term loan. The typical bank agreement involves a line of credit where, at the firm's option, it can be converted into a term loan. Why should borrowing from a bank be different than borrowing from the public capital markets?

In addressing that question, James found the average 2-day (t_{-1} and t_0) abnormal returns were as follows:[1]

Type of Event	Announcement Period Abnormal Return
Bank loan agreement	1.93%
Private placement	−0.91
Public straight debt	−0.11
Bank loan agreement with borrowing indicated	1.71
Bank loan agreement with no borrowing indicated	3.68

We see that when firms enter into bank loan agreements they experience positive abnormal returns; when they borrow from the public markets they experience negative returns. In attempting to explain these differences the study analyzed differences in the length of maturity, borrower default risk, borrower size, and purpose of the borrowing. None of these explained the differences in a satisfactory manner. These results suggest that banks somehow provide a special service to firms not available from other sources.

[1] Christopher James. "Some Evidence on the Uniqueness of Bank Loans." *Journal of Financial Economics* 19 (December 1987).

STEP 2. Employing Equation 21.1, determine the before-tax annual cost, which is

$$k_b = \left(1 + \frac{\$580.82}{\$10,000} \right)^{365/150} - 1 = 1.1473 - 1 = 14.73\%$$

Compensating Balance. A compensating balance is an amount many banks require corporate customers to maintain in their demand deposit account if a loan is taken out. The compensating balance may be an average over some period, such as a month, or a minimum figure below which the account cannot drop. Average compensating balances are typical for firms. Two situations can be identified. The first is where the compensating balance requirement is less than the amount the firm typically keeps in the bank. In this case, the requirement does not change the cost to the firm. The second case is where the compensating balance requirement is above the amount the firm keeps in its demand deposit account. To illustrate this, let's use the same $10,000, 13 percent loan for 73 days employed when computing the cost of both regular and discount interest.

Assume the bank imposes a $2,000 compensating balance requirement, when the firm typically does not keep any money on deposit at the bank. The effect of the requirement is to reduce the proceeds of the loan by $2,000. If the loan is not discounted, the before-tax cost is

$$k_b = \left(1 + \frac{\$260}{\$10,000 - \$2,000} \right)^{365/73} - 1 = 1.1734 - 1 = 17.34\%$$

If the loan is discounted and a $2,000 compensating balance is required, the before-tax annual cost becomes:

$$k_b = \left(1 + \frac{\$260}{\$10,000 - \$2,000 - \$260} \right)^{365/73} - 1 = 1.1796 - 1 = 17.96\%$$

Line of Credit. Finally, let's consider a more complicated situation where a line of credit is involved. Suppose your firm negotiates a 91-day $1,000,000 line of credit with a bank that has a one-half of 1 percent annual commitment fee on the unused portion of the line, and an interest rate of prime plus 1 percent. Assume, for simplicity, there is no compensating balance requirement and that during the entire 91-day period, the prime rate is 10 percent. For the first 30 days your firm borrows $100,000 on the line of credit. For the remaining 61 days, an additional $300,000 is secured so that $400,000 in total short-term financing is obtained. What is the cost of the loan? To answer this, we can still use our two-step procedure. There are, however, a few other complications.

STEP 1: Determine the commitment fee and interest per period.

$$\frac{\text{commitment}}{\text{fee}} = (\text{unused portion})(\text{annual commitment fee})(\text{portion of year})$$

Using the equation, we obtain

first 30 days   ($1,000,000 − $100,000)(0.005)(30/365) = $369.86

next 61 days   ($1,000,000 − $400,000)(0.005)(61/365) =   501.37

Then the interest is determined as follows:

first 30 days   ($100,000)(0.11)(30/365) = $ 904.11

next 61 days   ($400,000)(0.11)(61/365) = 7,353.42

STEP 2: Employing a modification of Equation 21.1, we can determine the cost of the line of credit. This modification is necessary because the total costs and the average amount borrowed must be calculated and then annualized as follows:

$$k_b = \left(1 + \frac{\text{total commitment fee + interest}}{\text{average net amount of financing}} \right)^{365/\text{total number of days}} - 1 \qquad (21.4)$$

The total of the commitment fees and interest is $369.86 + $501.37 + $904.11 + $7,353.42 = $9,128.76. The average net amount of financing is determined as follows:

$$\text{average net amount of financing} = (\$100,000)\left(\frac{30}{91}\right) + (\$400,000)\left(\frac{61}{91}\right)$$

$$= \$32,967.03 + \$268,131.87 = \$301,098.90$$

The before-tax percentage cost of the credit line is

$$k_b = \left(1 + \frac{\$9,128.76}{\$301,098.90}\right)^{365/91} - 1 = 1.1273 - 1 = 12.73\%$$

If the bank imposes a 5 percent compensating balance on the total line of credit, the calculations will have to be redone if this reduces the net amount of financing obtained. Suppose the firm presently keeps no compensating balance in the bank. The effect of the 5 percent requirement is to reduce the net funds obtained by $50,000 [i.e., ($1,000,000)(0.05)]. Therefore, with the compensating balance requirement, the before-tax cost increases as follows:

$$k_b = \left(1 + \frac{\$9,128.76}{\$301,098.90 - \$50,000}\right)^{365/91} - 1 = 1.1540 - 1 = 15.40\%$$

Eurodollar Loans

Another kind of loan firms are increasingly taking advantage of is the Eurodollar loan. Eurodollars are dollars deposited in banks outside the United States. These banks may be chartered in the specific country in question, or they may be branches of U.S.-based banks. Obtaining a Eurodollar loan is similar to obtaining one in the United States. The one major difference is that the rate is not tied to the U.S. prime rate, but to the London Interbank Offered Rate (LIBOR). This rate fluctuates daily and reflects the strength of the world economy and foreign currency exchange rates. Rates on Eurodollar loans typically are comparable to those in the United States, although sometimes U.S. firms have been able to obtain cheaper financing overseas. Because of this, and the growing sophistication of managers and the world's money markets, we will continue to see an increasing role for the Eurodollar system.

Commercial Paper

Another important source of short-term borrowing is from *commercial paper,* a short-term promissory note sold by large firms to obtain financing. In recent years the market for commercial paper has grown rapidly, and is increasingly viewed as an alternative to short-term bank loans. As such, it tends to exert a downward pressure on borrowing costs for larger firms.

Nature and Use

The principal issuers of commercial paper include finance companies, bank holding companies, and large industrial firms. The issue size is commonly in multiples of $100,000. All commercial paper has a maturity of 270 days or less.[8] The paper is

---

[8] The maximum is because if the maturity exceeds 270 days, the issue will have to be registered with the Securities and Exchange Commission (SEC).

sold through dealers or via direct placement. Dealers, wh
eighth of 1 percent commission, typically are used by firms
commercial paper. Larger firms, such as consumer finance cc
part of their permanent financing from commercial paper, genera
paper directly.

Commercial paper is rated as to its quality. These ratings ar

Moody's		Standard & Poor's	
P-1	Superior capacity for repayment	A-1	Greatest capacity for timely repayment
P-2	Strong capacity	A-2	Strong capacity
P-3	Acceptable capacity	A-3	Satisfactory capacity
NP	Not prime	B	Adequate capacity
		C	Doubtful capacity
		D	In default or expected to be in default

The purpose of the ratings is to provide the commercial paper buyer some indication
of the riskiness of the investment. From the issuing firm's standpoint, ratings are
important because they influence the cost of financing. Other things being equal,
the higher the rating, the lower the cost to the firm.

Cost

As shown previously in Figure 21.1, the rate (or yield) on commercial paper
tends to be 1 to 2 percentage points below the prime rate. This differential fluctuates
as both general economic conditions and the level of interest rates change. Like
U.S. Treasury bills, commercial paper is sold at a discount from its par value. At
maturity, the difference between the selling price and the par value is the interest
earned by the investor. Consider a $100,000, 180-day issue of commercial paper
sold at $95,000. When it matures in 180 days, the firm will pay the holder $100,000.
Employing Equation 21.1, the before-tax cost to the firm is

$$k_b = \left(1 + \frac{\$5,000}{\$100,000 - \$5,000} \right)^{365/180} - 1 = 1.1096 - 1 = 10.96\%$$

This rate will be lower than the firm's annual cost of a bank loan due to the lower
yield on commercial paper than the prime rate charged by banks.

Other costs also enter into the picture. In most cases, issuers must back their
commercial paper 100 percent with lines of credit from commercial banks. This line
of credit may cost the firm from one-fourth to three-fourths of 1 percent annual
interest. Another common procedure is for the commercial paper issuer to have a
compensating balance at a bank, instead of paying the commitment fee for the line
of credit. In addition, there is a relatively small fee ($10,000 to $25,000) to have
the commercial paper rated. Because of these additional costs, the savings from
issuing commercial paper may not be as great as a firm originally thought. Suppose
the commercial paper issue just analyzed was backed by a line of credit that had a
commitment fee of one-half of 1 percent a year. The total fee would be

($100,000)(0.005)(180/365) = $246.58

[9] From *Moody's Bond Record* and *Standard & Poor's Creditweek*.

Adding this fee to the interest of $5,000 results in a total cost of $5,246.58. Employing Equation 21.1, the before-tax cost of the commercial paper is now[10]

$$k_b = \left(1 + \frac{\$5,246.58}{\$95,000} \right)^{365/180} - 1 = 1.1152 - 1 = 11.52\%$$

Although commercial paper may be an attractive form of short-term financing, it is available only to relatively large firms. Also, the commercial paper market may dry up occasionally, and firms are forced to use bank loans. Firms that make extensive use of commercial paper also keep their lines of communication open with banks, and typically borrow from banks in addition to using the commercial paper market.

Secured Loans

Because the lender requires it or to obtain cheaper financing, firms often use receivables or inventory to obtain short-term financing. Every state except Louisiana operates under the Uniform Commercial Code. Under the code, a security agreement or standardized document is provided for listing the assets pledged as collateral. Procedures for short-term financing are described below.

Financing with Accounts Receivable

Financing with accounts receivable involves pledging receivables or factoring them. The *pledging* of receivables involves the specific use of receivables as collateral for the loan. If the borrower defaults on the loan, the funds provided when the receivables are collected will go to repay the loan. *Factoring* involves the sale of accounts receivable. The factoring firm is responsible both for credit checking and for collection of the receivables. Many banks engage in making accounts receivable loans or in purchasing receivables. Commercial finance companies and other specialized factoring firms also provide accounts receivable financing to firms.

Pledging Accounts Receivable

Under a pledging agreement, the borrower uses the accounts receivable as collateral for the loan. The specific agreement between the borrower and the lending institution spells out the details of the transaction. The amount of the loan is stated as a percentage of the receivables pledged. In addition, the borrower typically pays a processing fee, which often is 1 percent of the total receivables pledged. This processing fee compensates the lending institution for the time involved in reviewing the pledged receivables.

If the loan agreement is on all receivables, then the lender has no control over

---

[10] Note that the commitment fee is *not* deducted from the financing received in the denominator. This treatment is based on the assumption that the commitment fee is an ongoing cost that is paid over time and is *not* a lump sum deduction at the outset. If the commitment fee is deducted at the outset, the net proceeds are $94,753.32 ($95,000 − $246.68), and the before-tax cost is

$$k_b = \left(1 + \frac{\$5,246.58}{\$94,753.32} \right)^{365/180} - 1 = 1.1155 - 1 = 11.55\%$$

This same assumption is made for the processing costs, factoring commissions, and warehousing fees discussed subsequently.

the quality of the receivables pledged. An alternative procedure is for the lender to review specific invoices to decide which ones it will lend against. This method is somewhat more expensive to the lender, since it must review each invoice and the creditworthiness of the customer, before deciding whether to lend against it. If the lender accepts all receivables, it may be willing to grant a loan for only 60 to 70 percent of the face value of the receivables. When it "screens" invoices, the loan agreement typically increases to 85 to 90 percent of the face value of the receivables.

The cost of accounts receivable financing is a function of both the processing fee and the annual interest rate charged. Because of the basic creditworthiness of the borrower, loans secured by receivables often have a stated interest rate of 2 to 4 percent above prime. To illustrate the cost, consider the example of Hammond Associates, which sells merchandise at a net 45 days basis. Its average credit sales are $9,000 per day and the average collection period is 60 days, resulting in accounts receivable averaging $540,000. All the receivables are pledged to the bank, which will lend 75 percent of the amount pledged at 2.5 percent over prime. The loan will be for $405,000 [i.e., ($540,000)(0.75)] for 60 days. There also is a three-quarters of 1 percent processing fee on all receivables pledged. If prime currently is 12.5

percent per year, the cost of this loan can be found by employing the same two-step approach described earlier.

STEP 1: Determine the interest paid and other costs:

$$\text{processing fee} = (0.0075)(\$9,000)(60 \text{ days}) = \$ \ 4,050$$
$$\text{interest} = (0.15)(\$405,000)(60/365) = \underline{9,986}$$
$$\text{total processing fee and interest} = \$14,036$$

STEP 2: Employing Equation 21.1, the annual before-tax cost is

$$k_b = \left(1 + \frac{\$14,036}{\$405,000} \right)^{365/60} - 1 = 1.2303 - 1 = 23.03\%$$

The processing fee increases the cost of the loan substantially above the nominal interest charge of 15 percent the bank levies for the loan.

Factoring Accounts Receivable

Instead of pledging its receivables, an alternative procedure employed in industries such as finished apparel, textiles, and home furnishings is to sell (or factor) them. Through factoring, a firm sells its accounts receivable to a bank or other firm engaged in factoring. The receivables are sold outright (without recourse), so the factor assumes the total credit risk and incurs any losses from nonpayment by the firm's customers.

Factoring operates in two basic ways. With *maturity factoring,* the factor purchases all receivables and once a month pays the seller for the receivables. The typical maturity factoring procedure is shown in Figure 21.2. Firms that employ maturity factoring are primarily interested in avoiding credit analysis and collection expenses, and the regularity of the cash flow. The charge for maturity factoring is the commission, which is between three-fourths of 1 percent and 2 percent of the total receivables factored.

To illustrate this type of factoring, consider the example of Gandy Wholesale. To avoid setting up a credit and collection department, it factors all its receivables. At the end of the month, the factor provides full payment on the average due date of the receivables. If the average month has $200,000 in receivables and the factoring commission is 1.5 percent per month, Gandy pays $3,000 per month [i.e., ($200,000)(0.015)], or $36,000 per year [($3,000)(12)], to the factor. For this, the factor assumes all bookkeeping and collection expenses. If this allows Gandy to reduce these expenses by $1,000 per month, then the net additional cost is $2,000 per month. The annual percentage rate, or cost, is then

$$k_b = \left(1 + \frac{\$2,000}{\$200,000} \right)^{12/1} - 1 = 1.1268 - 1 = 12.68\%$$

Under *advance factoring,* the factor provides a loan against the receivables. Thus, on the first of the month, a firm could borrow against the receivables it is selling. If the average due date is the twentieth of the month, the factor will charge interest from the first to the twentieth. This interest typically is 2 to 4 percent more than the annual prime rate. In addition, the factor still charges a factoring commission.

With advance factoring, the cost consists of both the factoring commission and the interest. To illustrate, Gandy Wholesale is now considering advance instead of

Figure 21.2 Maturity Factoring Procedure

Under maturity factoring the firm turns almost all of its credit and receivables management functions over to the factor.

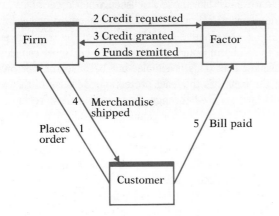

maturity factoring. The receivables to be sold total $400,000, and they have an average due date of 1 month. The factoring commission is one-half of 1 percent, the annual prime rate is 10 percent, and the loan is for 1 month at 4 percent over prime. The factor will loan an amount equal to 70 percent of the face value of the receivables, or $280,000 [i.e., ($400,000)(0.70)]. Employing the two-step procedure, we proceed as follows:

STEP 1: Determine the interest paid and all other costs:

$$\text{factoring commission} = (0.005)(\$400,000) = \$2,000$$
$$\text{interest} = (0.14)(\$280,000)(1/12) = \underline{3,267}$$
$$\text{total commission and interest} = \overline{\$5,267}$$

STEP 2: Using Equation 21.1, the before-tax cost is

$$k_b = \left(1 + \frac{\$5,267}{\$280,000}\right)^{12/1} - 1 = 1.2506 - 1 = 25.06\%$$

As we saw with selling receivables, the cost increases when a fee is charged in addition to the basic interest rate.

The advantages of factoring from the firm's standpoint can be fourfold. First, the entire credit and collection operation can be shifted to the factor. This can result in a sizable savings to the selling firm. Second, more effective and timely cash management can be obtained. Third, if advance factoring is employed, firms also may secure accelerated short-term financing from the factoring procedures. Finally, factors will often be willing to borrow money from the firm during periods when the firm has excess cash. For these reasons, factoring is continuing to become more common as an ongoing part of many firms' short-term financing strategy. Factoring is often a continuous process. Once the cycle is established, the firm automatically sends the receivables to the factor. Under continuous factoring, accounts receivable financing becomes a spontaneous source of short-term financing.

Financing with Inventory

A firm's inventory provides a second source of security for short-term loans. Because of the large size of the inventory for many firms and the associated carrying costs, firms often use part or all of their inventory to obtain short-term financing. The procedures are much like those discussed when receivables are employed. That is, the bank determines the percentage of the inventory value for which it will provide a loan. There are alternative methods, however, by which inventory can be secured.

Under the Uniform Commercial Code, the borrower can pledge all of its inventory under a blanket lien. This is simple, but because the borrower is free to sell the inventory, the bank has the least protection. Because of this weakness, some types of inventory are secured through the use of a trust receipt. This type of lending agreement, also known as floor planning, is used by automobile dealers, equipment dealers, and others who deal in "large ticket" items. With a trust receipt, an automobile dealer might reach an agreement with a bank to finance the inventory. When cars are shipped to the dealer, they are paid for in large part with funds borrowed from the bank. The trust receipt specifies that the goods are held in trust for the lender. When the cars are sold, the dealer obtains a release from the bank, and then applies the proceeds to pay the loan. Under a trust receipt agreement, the bank periodically inspects the automobile dealer's cars to ensure the security is still on hand.

Another method is warehouse financing. Under a public (or terminal) warehouse agreement, the inventory is stored on the premises of a third party. The third party releases the inventory to the borrower only when authorized to do so by the lender. The lender can then maintain strict control over the collateral. Sometimes the warehouse is set up as a field warehouse. This is accomplished by establishing a separate building or area directly on the borrower's premises. To provide inventory control, the bank employs a third party to run the field warehouse. A warehouse receipt is issued by the warehouse company when it receives additional inventory. This receipt goes to the bank, and inventory cannot be released without the bank's permission.

The basic cost of inventory loans typically consists of two parts. The first is the processing fee if a blanket lien is employed, or the cost of storing the inventory if a public or field warehouse agreement is employed. In addition, there is the interest cost, which is typically 2 to 4 percentage points above the prime rate. Consider a firm that employs a field warehouse agreement. The inventory loan is for 90 days, the amount of the inventory is $500,000, and the bank will lend 70 percent of the value of the collateral. The amount of the loan is $350,000 [i.e., ($500,000)(0.70)]. The field warehouse fee is $55 per day, the interest rate is 2 percent over prime, and prime is 11 percent. The annual before-tax cost is computed as follows:

STEP 1. Determine the interest paid and all other costs:

$$\text{field warehousing fee} = (\$55)(90) = \$\ 4,950$$
$$\text{interest} = (0.13)(\$350,000)(90/365) = \underline{\ 11,219}$$
$$\text{total warehousing fee and interest} = \overline{\$16,169}$$

STEP 2: The annual before-tax cost is determined using Equation 21.1, so that:

$$k_b = \left(1 + \frac{\$16,169}{\$350,000}\right)^{365/90} - 1 = 1.2010 - 1 = 20.10\%$$

Firms often enter into continuous agreements to finance their inventory through the use of field or terminal warehouse procedures. Like the use of factoring with accounts receivable, the continual use of these forms of inventory financing creates a spontaneous form of short-term financing.

Choosing Among Short-Term Financing Sources

In this chapter we have stressed the cost of alternative sources of short-term financing. Certain of these sources, such as trade credit and factoring or field warehouse loans, are spontaneous. That is, they tend to expand or contract automatically as the firm's accounts receivable and inventory expand or contract. Other sources of short-term financing are negotiated between the borrower and the lender.

To determine what sources of short-term financing to employ, four specific items should be considered. These are matching, cost, availability, and flexibility. By matching, we mean the firm must decide how much risk it is willing to incur in financing temporary assets with temporary liabilities. A more aggressive posture will require the firm to employ more sources and amounts of short-term financing than a conservative posture.

The second important item that influences the short-term financing selection is its cost. Employing the concepts developed in this chapter, we can determine the direct cost of alternative short-term financing sources. This is an important consideration, but there is more than the direct cost of the sources. Opportunity costs must also be considered. If firms anticipate the continued need to borrow from banks, good banking relations need to be maintained even if the bank charges a higher direct cost than some other source. Trade credit (if stretched) may be less costly than an inventory loan, but if stretching occurs continually, the firm may suffer from reduced credit ratings in the future. Opportunity costs must be considered along with the direct costs when considering the total cost of alternative sources of short-term financing.

The availability of credit is the third item that should be considered when evaluating financing sources. If a firm cannot borrow through an unsecured loan or commercial paper offering, then some type of secured means will have to be employed. Also, over the course of the business cycle, certain sources of funds may be more or less available. Availability refers to both the amount and the conditions attached to the short-term financing. Only by examining both features will managers be in a position to consider the firm's short-term financing sources over time.

Finally, there is the issue of flexibility. Flexibility refers to the ability of the firm to pay off a loan and still retain the ability to renew or increase it. With factoring, bank loans, and lines of credit, the firm can pay off the loan when it has surplus funds. Flexibility also refers to how easily the firm can secure or increase the financing on short notice. A line of credit can be increased quickly and easily, but a negotiated short-term loan may take longer to secure. Trade credit, factoring of receivables, and field warehousing provide spontaneous sources of short-term financing that increase the firm's flexibility.

All these items must be considered when a firm looks at its sources of short-term financing. Although the direct cost is a key element, it does not always provide the final answer. This arises because of opportunity costs relating to matching, availability, and flexibility. Because of the difficulty of quantifying opportunity costs, a practical approach is to rank sources according to their direct costs, and then consider these other factors. If the opportunity costs are significant, the ranking of the desirability of one source of short-term financing compared to another will change. Finally, since the firm's financing needs change over time, multiple sources of short-term financing must be considered even if some of them are not being employed presently.

Summary

Firms make extensive use of short-term financing. For some, it provides the major source of financing. The use of short-term financing is a function of both the nature of the firm's business, and how aggressive it wants to become in matching (financing) its temporary assets with temporary liabilities. Firms that are aggressive in their use of short-term financing employ substantially larger amounts than firms that adopt a conservative position.

Trade credit financing is readily available in most industries. It is costless if cash discounts are taken. Bank loans can be obtained through single transaction loans, a line of credit, or secured financing involving either receivables or inventory. Many finance companies also provide short-term loans to firms, especially when accounts receivable or inventory are involved. Larger firms have access to commercial paper. Although the direct costs of all these sources are available, this is only one item that requires attention. For this reason, effective managers assess both the risks and required returns associated with alternative sources of short-term financing as they strive to maximize the value of the firm.

Questions

21.1 Define or explain the following:

a.	Negotiated short-term financing	h.	Installment interest
b.	Annual percentage rate (APR)	i.	Variable rate (loan)
c.	Stretching payables	j.	Commercial paper
d.	Transaction loan	k.	Pledging
e.	Commitment fee	l.	Factoring
f.	Regular interest	m.	Maturity factoring
g.	Discount interest	n.	Advance factoring

21.2 The equation for calculating the before-tax annual percentage rate (APR), or cost of short-term financing, is

$$k_b = \left(1 + \frac{\text{costs} - \text{benefits}}{\text{net amount of financing}} \right)^m - 1.$$

Discuss why this approach must be employed.

21.3 Discuss the advantages and costs of trade credit.

21.4 Why is the rate on commercial paper typically below the prime rate? Are there other factors that tend to increase the cost of commercial paper to overcome some of its interest rate advantages?

21.5 Other things being equal, how would changes in the following conditions affect a firm's after-tax cost of funds?

a. The prime rate increases.
b. The bank goes to regular from discount interest.
c. The bank's compensating balance requirement decreases.
d. Tax rates increase (assume the firm is profitable).

21.6 With discount interest, the interest is deducted at the beginning of the loan, thereby reducing the net amount of financing obtained.

a. Discuss the effect of discount interest on the yearly percentage cost of the loan.
b. What if a compensating balance requirement exists? Or commitment fees or loan processing (origination) fees are deducted at the start of the loan? Is the effect on the cost of the loan the same as with discount interest?

21.7 Differentiate completely between maturity factoring and advance factoring.

21.8 For many of the short-term financing sources, the direct cost is made up of the interest plus some other charge (or requirement). Explain this other charge for the following:

a. Line of credit
b. Discount interest
c. Installment interest
d. Compensating balance
e. Commercial paper
f. Pledging accounts receivable
g. Advance factoring
h. Inventory loans

Self-Test Problems   (Solutions appear on page 737.)

Taking the Discount

ST 21.1 Alex Industries has annual purchases of $730,000 and average accounts payable of $60,000. Credit terms granted to Alex Industries are 1/10, net 30. Is the firm paying all of its bills in time to take advantage of the 1 percent discount? Assume a 365-day year.

Factoring Receivables

ST 21.2 Wildcat Industries is investigating the possibility of factoring its receivables via an advance factoring arrangement. The average receivables balance is $800,000 and the average collection period is 30 days. The loan would be for 30 days each time. The factor charges a 1 percent factoring commission on the average balance, and will loan 60 percent of the average balance at a rate of 15 percent per year. Use a 365-day year.

a. What is the before-tax cost (in annual percentage terms) of the factoring agreement?
b. After finishing (a), Wildcat realizes that the factoring agreement will reduce its credit and collection expenses, and its bad debts. It estimates the savings will be $7,000 every 30 days. What is the before-tax annual percentage cost of the factoring agreement, given this new information?

Alternative Loans

ST 21.3 Harbor Import needs $400,000 for the next 91 days. Two alternative sources are available:

a. A loan secured by accounts receivables. The bank has agreed to lend Harbor 70 percent of the value of its pledged receivables (which are just enough larger to provide the $400,000 loan). The interest rate is 11 percent per year. In addition, there is a processing fee of 1 percent (for the 91-day period) of the value of the *total* receivables pledged.
b. An insurance company has agreed to loan the $400,000 at a rate of 9 percent per year,

using a loan secured by Harbor's inventory. A field warehousing agreement will be used; it costs $2,100 per 30 days.

By calculating the before-tax annual percentage rate, determine which financing source should be employed.

Problems

Cost of Trade Credit

21.1 A firm receives trade credit terms of 2/15, net 45. Based on a 365-day year, what is the before-tax annual percentage cost if payment is made (a) by the fifteenth day, (b) on the forty-fifth day, (c) by stretching to 60 days past the invoice date, (d) 90 days past the invoice date? What other costs or considerations should be considered in addition to this direct cost?

Cost of Alternative Bank Loans

21.2 DeVito Industries has four choices for a $50,000, 1-year loan from a bank. Which one of the following has the lowest before-tax annual percentage cost?

a. A 14 percent annual interest rate with no compensating balance requirement. Interest is paid at the end of the year.
b. A 13 percent annual interest rate discounted, with no compensating balance requirement.
c. A 9 percent annual stated interest rate with installment interest, paid in 12 equal installments.
d. An 11 percent annual interest rate discounted, with a 10 percent compensating balance requirement. (*Note:* DeVito does not typically keep any funds in this bank.)

Discount Interest and Partial Compensating Balance

21.3 Key Computers has just received a *net* amount (after interest and any compensating balance requirement) of financing of $450,000 for 146 days. Its bank loaned the money at a 15 percent annual rate employing discount interest. The loan requires a $50,000 compensating balance, and Key keeps an average of $30,000 on deposit in the bank. If the tax rate is 40 percent, what is the after-tax annual percentage cost of the loan? Assume a 365-day year.

Line of Credit

21.4 Memphis Wholesalers has a 6-month, $1 million line of credit agreement with the Third National Bank. There is a one-half of 1 percent per year commitment fee charged on the unused portion of the line. The prime rate is 14 percent per year, and the interest rate on the line of credit is 1 percent over prime. Over the next 6 months, Memphis Wholesalers anticipates drawing on the line of credit as follows:

Month	Additional Borrowed (Repaid) per Month	Total Borrowed per Month
April	$100,000	$ 100,000
May	300,000	400,000
June	400,000	800,000
July	200,000	1,000,000
August	−300,000	700,000
September	−400,000	300,000

By October 1, the line is paid off in full.

a. What is the expected before-tax annual percentage cost to Memphis Wholesalers? (*Note:* Do not worry about a 365-day year; simply treat each month as one-twelfth of the total.)
b. If Memphis Wholesalers decides to borrow its full line of credit every month ($1,000,000 per month), what would its expected before-tax annual percentage cost be? What if Memphis borrows nothing during the 6 months?

(Do only if using Pinches Disk.)

c. Now suppose the prime rate (1) increased to 16 percent or (2) decreased to 12 percent. What are the expected before-tax annual percentage costs if the borrowing is as in (a)?

d. What happens to the expected before-tax annual percentage costs in (a) and (c) if nothing is borrowed in April and May, $300,000 is borrowed in June and July, and $100,000 in August and September?

Commercial Paper

21.5 Datatech is planning a $2 million issue of 270-day commercial paper. The interest rate is $11\frac{1}{2}$ percent per year, and Datatech will incur $15,000 in other issue-related expenses. Interest is to be discounted, and a 365-day year is to be used.

a. What is the before-tax annual percentage cost of the commerical paper issue?

b. What is the after-tax cost if Datatech's marginal tax rate is 35 percent? Twenty-five percent?

c. What are some other factors Datatech would need to consider in addition to the direct cost?

After-Tax Cost of Commercial Paper

21.6 Danley Transportation is going to issue $1,000,000 of commercial paper at a price of $940,822. If the issue is for 180 days and Danley's marginal tax rate is 30 percent, what is the after-tax percentage cost of the commercial paper? (Assume a 365-day year.)

Advance Factoring

21.7 Barnes & Field presently employs maturity factoring at a before-tax annual percentage cost of 23 percent. Under advance factoring, which is being considered, Barnes & Field would sell $1,200,000 of receivables with an average due date of 20 days. The factoring commission is one-fourth of 1 percent, the prime rate is 13 percent, and the factor will make the loan for 20 days at 3 percent over prime. The factor will loan 50 percent of the face value of the receivables. (Assume a 365-day year.)

a. By calculating the before-tax annual percentage cost, determine if Barnes & Field should switch to advance factoring.

b. What decision would be made if everything is the same as in (a) except the loan is at 2 percent over prime, and the factor will loan (or advance) $1,000,000?

Pledging Versus Factoring Receivables

21.8 Delta Industries has employed factoring for a number of years. Its sales average $1 million dollars every 30 days, with 80 percent being credit sales. The average collection period is 30 days, so the length of the loan is 30 days. The factor charges a 1 percent factoring commission on the total receivables. In addition, any loan, which may be up to 75 percent of credit sales, carries an interest rate of 15 percent per year. The factor employs a 365-day year. Delta Industries estimates that the factoring agreement results in two savings: (1) a $1,000 reduction in credit and collection expenses for every 30-day period, and (2) a reduction in bad debts equal to one-half of 1 percent of the credit sales.

Recently a finance company approached Delta about a loan involving the pledging of receivables. The loan could be up to 75 percent of receivables. The costs would be interest at 13 percent per year plus a three-fourths of 1 percent processing fee on the size of the loan. [So, the total processing fee on the receivables loan is (0.0075)($600,000) = $4,500.]

a. By computing the annual percentage cost, determine which plan is preferable.

b. If Delta Industries borrows only $200,000 per 30 days on average, which plan is preferable? (*Note:* If Delta factors the receivables, it still receives the $1,000 reduction in credit and collection expenses, plus the benefit of the one-half of 1 percent reduction in bad debts on the total receivables of $800,000, since it continues selling all the remaining receivables to the factor on a maturity factor basis.)

Inventory Loan

21.9 Charter United has to build up its inventory for a 4-month period each year to meet future sales demands. It is considering a bank loan with a field warehouse security agreement. The inventory during this 4-month period averages $500,000 per month. The bank will loan a maximum of 70 percent of the average inventory at prime plus 3 percent. Prime is 9 percent per year. The field warehousing agreement costs $2,400 per month. (*Note:* Use 12 months, not 365 days.)

a. If Charter United borrows $250,000, what is the before-tax annual percentage cost of the loan?

b. If Charter United borrows the maximum, what is the before-tax annual percentage cost of the loan?

Alternative Inventory Loans

21.10 Denver Press has experienced a severe cash squeeze and needs $300,000 for the next 75 days. The most likely source is to borrow against its inventory. Determine the best financing alternative from the two that are available. Use a 365-day year and calculate the before-tax annual percentage cost.

a. The Rocky Mountain Bank will lend the $300,000 at a rate of 12 percent per year. It requires, however, that a field warehouse security agreement be employed. The field warehousing costs are $30 per day. Finally, Denver Press believes that because of lower efficiency, before-tax cash flows will be reduced by $2,500 during this 75-day time period.

b. Bishop Finance will loan Denver Press the $300,000 at a rate of 18 percent per year under a blanket lien agreement. There are no other charges associated with this loan.

Alternative Inventory Loans

21.11 Green's Wholesalers presently employs a 90-day public warehouse agreement to finance most of its inventory. The average amount of inventory is $2,000,000, the bank lends Green's 75 percent of the value of the inventory, and the public warehousing fee is $200 per day. Total transportation costs for the 90-day period make up 1 percent of the average value of the inventory [that is, $(0.01)(\$2,000,000)$], the prime rate is 13 percent, and the bank will loan at 2 percent over prime. Green's is considering establishing a field warehouse on its premises, which would eliminate transportation costs, but cost $450 per day. The interest rate is 1 percent over prime, and the loan amount remains the same. (Assume a 365-day year.)

a. What is the before-tax annual percentage cost of the public warehouse financing agreement?

b. Does the annual percentage cost of the loan increase or decrease under the field warehousing agreement? By how much?

Alternative Short-Term Sources

21.12 The Clark Corporation has a need for $300,000 in short-term financing for the next 30 days. Based on the following four options, which source should Clark select to minimize its costs? (Calculate the before-tax annual percentage cost.)

a. A 91-day line of credit with a bank in the amount of $500,000. There is a 1 percent per year commitment fee on the unused portion, and the rate of interest on borrowed funds is 14 percent per year.

b. Forego cash discounts on $300,000 of payables. The terms are 2/10, net 40.

c. Issue commercial paper with a 30-day maturity. To borrow the entire $300,000, the maturity value of the issue will be $305,000. The firm incurs $1,000 additional expenses.

d. Obtain a 30-day loan against $400,000 worth of receivables. The factor will loan an amount equal to 75 percent of the receivables. The factoring commission is one-half of 1 percent, and the interest rate is 15 percent per year.

References

For general discussion, see

BROSKY, JOHN J. *The Implicit Cost of Trade Credit and Theory of Optimal Terms of Sale.* New York: Credit Research Foundation, 1969.

MACPHEE, WILLIAM A. *Short-Term Business Borrowing: Sources, Terms and Techniques.* Homewood, Ill.: Dow Jones-Irwin, 1984.

MOSKOWITZ, L. A. *Modern Factoring and Commercial Finance.* New York: Thomas Y. Crowell, 1977.

Trade credit is considered further in

SCHWARTZ, ROBERT A. "An Economic Analysis of Trade Credit." *Journal of Financial and Quantitative Analysis* 9 (September 1974), pp. 643–658.

For more on lines of credit, see

CAMPBELL, TIM S. "A Model of the Market for Lines of Credit." *Journal of Finance* 33 (March 1978), pp. 231–243.

HAWKINS, GREGORY. "An Analysis of Revolving Credit Agreements." *Journal of Financial Economics* 10 (March 1982), pp. 59–81.

HILL, NED C., WILLIAM L. SARTORIS, AND SUE L. VISSCHER. "The Components of Credit Line Borrowing Costs." *Journal of Cash Management* 3 (October–November 1983), pp. 47–56.

Factoring and secured lending is discussed in

FARRAGHER, EDWARD J. "Factoring Accounts Receivable." *Journal of Cash Management* 6 (March–April 1986), pp. 38–42.

QUILL, GERALD D., JOHN C. CRESCI, AND BRUCE D. SHUTER. "Some Considerations About Secured Lending." *Journal of Commercial Bank Lending* 57 (April 1977), pp. 41–56.

See Model fifteen in *Lotus 1–2–3® for Financial Management* by Pinches and Courtney for a template that prices various parts of a line of credit.

PART SEVEN

Financial Strategy

22 | Mergers and Corporate Restructuring

Overview

- Mergers should be undertaken only if they are expected to produce economic benefits in the form of increased economies or tax savings.

- Merger analysis is another net present value, NPV, problem. However, the benefits are computed a little differently than we did in Chapters 8–10. The costs differ depending on whether cash or stock is employed.

- Corporate restructuring focuses on value creation and/or the increased use of debt.

- A divestiture is another NPV problem. It involves comparing the NPV of continuing to operate the division with the after-tax divestiture proceeds.

In 1981 du Pont acquired Conoco for $7.4 billion. It was the largest acquisition of all time—but not for long. Suddenly megamergers became a fact of life. Since then RJR Nabisco was purchased for over $25 billion, Chevron purchased Gulf Oil for more than $13 billion, and Philip Morris acquired Kraft for over $11 billion. However, not all mergers involve large firms. Every year numerous large and small firms are acquired. Likewise, many divestitures take place where firms sell off part of their existing assets.

It has also been the era of the takeover artist. One of the most famous, T. Boone Pickens of Mesa Petroleum, made runs at Cities Service, General American Oil, Superior Oil, Phillips Petroleum, and Gulf Oil. He ended up with profits from his investments in these firms, but not the firms themselves. Carl Icahn, on the other hand, ended up acquiring Trans World Airlines—after runs at a number of other firms.

To some observers, these corporate raiders are the worst thing that has ever happened to American business. Some managers and employees may lose their jobs, or various divisions of the firm may be sold off if the takeover is successful. From a different perspective, the same raiders are viewed as the new entrepreneurs, helping stockholders maximize their returns, shaking up entrenched management, and seeing that firms make better *use of their assets. In this chapter we must put aside some of the rhetoric and emotion that accompanies mergers. The megamergers attract attention, but a vast number of mergers—large, medium, and small—occur every year. We need to know what makes mergers possible and when they are sound financial management.*

The Market for Corporate Control

Let's go back to our basic objective—to maximize the value of the firm or the size of the pie, which represents the market value of both equity and debt. Until now we have examined how managers make decisions in terms of acquiring and financing assets and managing ongoing operations—from determining the firm's capital structure to dividend policy and working capital strategy. In this part we examine three very important aspects of financial strategy—mergers and corporate restructuring (Chapter 22), financial planning and strategy (Chapter 23), and international financial management (Chapter 24). Instead of focusing on the micro, or area-by-area, firm decisions, we shift the emphasis to a more macro emphasis. By macro, we simply mean the emphasis is on the firm as a whole, rather than on some subpart of the financial decision-making process. Our framework remains the same, however, in terms of maximizing the total market value of the firm by concentrating on risk, required return, and cash flows.

In addition to managing their internal affairs efficiently, which includes all aspects of the investment, financing, and operating decisions, firms can also grow or shrink over time. Corporate restructuring is the most controversial, widely talked about, and analyzed area in financial management today. As depicted in Figure 22.1, it includes the acquisition of other firms (or portions of firms), defensive tactics that (hopefully) are designed to maximize the value of the firm, and actual restructuring via leveraging up, going private, leveraged buyouts, limited partnerships, and divestitures. In recent years this area has become known as the *market for corporate control,* where various management teams vie for the right to acquire and manage corporate activities and assets. The whole practice of financial management has undergone a dramatic shift in emphasis. Managers are more concerned now than ever with maximizing the size of the pie, and with the impact of their actions on the value of the firm. Critics contend that all this emphasis on value creation has wasted management time and effort by drawing it away from the main operating activities of the firm, and has further eroded the competitive position (and research and development emphasis) of American business. Supporters are quick to point out that the developments in the market for corporate control have really increased the efficiency of the resource allocation process by reducing waste and the misuse of corporate cash flows and assets. This debate is still going on—in board rooms, management suites, legislative halls, the press, and the classroom.

To better understand the issues, we focus first on acquisitions by examining sources of potential gains and how to value them, along with some procedural issues. Then we look at defensive tactics, after which we consider other aspects of restructuring, including divestitures. Our focus is from the standpoint of the *bidding firm.*

Figure 22.1 Market for Corporate Control

The market for corporate control involves widely divergent activities including expansion via a merger or tender offer, defensive tactics of many types, and restructuring via leveraging up, going private, limited partnerships, and even the divestiture of the firm's assets.

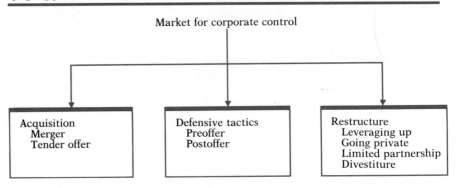

The company it seeks to acquire is the *target firm.* Even though there are different legal means of accomplishing an acquisition (as discussed later), we will refer to any acquisition of another firm, or the division of another firm, as a *merger.* It's important to keep in mind, however, that many acquisitions are accomplished via tender offers. In a tender offer, cash is often offered by the bidding firm directly to the shareholders of the target firm. Often the management of the target firm is not consulted before the tender offer is made. Hence, many tender offers are viewed as a hostile takeover attempt by the management of the target firm.

The level of merger activity in the United States is not constant over time; instead, there are waves of mergers that are generally related to stock prices and economic activity. In the early to mid-1970s, mergers fell off before increasing again dramatically in the last few years. Table 22.1 shows the level of merger activity for the 1980–1988 period. During this time period, merger activity was on the rise, with both domestic and foreign firms active in acquiring U.S.-based firms.

This trend for foreign firms to be active in acquiring U.S.-based firms can be seen by examining the largest mergers that occurred during 1988:

Bidding Firm	Target Firm	Value (In billions)
Philip Morris	Kraft	$12.64
Campeau	Federated Department Stores	6.51
B.A.T. Industries	Farmers Group	5.12
Eastman Kodak	Sterling Drug	5.09
Amoco	Dome Petroleum	3.77
News Corp.	Triangle Publications	3.59
Bridgestone	Firestone Tire & Rubber	2.66
Maxwell Communications	Macmillan	2.64
American Stores	Lucky Stores	2.51

Five of the bidding firms—Campeau, B.A.T. Industries, News Corp., Bridgestone, and Maxwell Communications—were foreign firms. While the vast majority of merger activity in the United States involves U.S. firms, there are international factors that play a role in the extent and types of mergers taking place.

Table 22.1　Number of Mergers Involving U.S. Firms

All acquisitions of at least $1 million in size, including the acquisition of 5 percent or more of a firm if the value was at least $1 million, are shown. SOURCE: Mergers & Acquisitions, various issues.

Year	U.S. Firm Acquiring Another U.S. Firm	Non-U.S. Firm Acquiring U.S. Firm	U.S. Firm Acquiring Non-U.S. Firm	Total
1980	1,239	165	113	1,517
1981	1,964	267	83	2,314
1982	1,960	222	139	2,321
1983	2,075	116	148	2,339
1984	2,625	182	139	2,946
1985	2,773	206	174	3,153
1986	3,799	358	166	4,323
1987	3,198	326	177	3,701
1988	2,875	446	158	3,479

Reasons for Merging

Attempting to grow by merging is a part of corporate strategy for many firms. So, it is important for managers to understand the potential benefits arising from a merger, as well as the danger signals in a deal. Let's look at some of the reasons for merging, both sensible and dubious.

Sensible Reasons

Any reasonable motive for merging has to provide economic gains. These gains occur when the value of the combined firm (AB) is more than the sum of the two separate firms (A,B) before the merger, so that:

$$value_{AB} > value_A + value_B$$

Two sensible reasons relate to increased economies and tax considerations.

Increased Economies

A merger should improve economic performance. This improvement may come from economies of scale so that the combined firm may be of sufficient size to be able to drive down production costs, distribution expenses, research and development costs, or whatever. The attempt to secure economies of scale is a primary reason why many mergers are undertaken. A separate but somewhat related motive is to seek economies by integrating vertically. Vertical integration refers to ensuring a continuous flow from acquisition of raw materials, through the various stages of production, to distribution and ultimate sale. A chemical firm that uses petroleum as a key raw material may decide to acquire an oil firm to achieve better vertical integration. By doing so, the chemical firm is attempting simultaneously to ensure adequate supplies of raw materials and to become more efficient by cutting the cost of raw materials acquisition.

Another possible economic benefit could come by merging two firms having overlapping expertise that may not be utilized when both are separate. For example, merging an electronics firm and a medical research firm may produce technology that neither firm operating independently could produce. Another benefit, market protection,

Mergers

Over the years there have been a number of studies analyzing the impact of mergers and tender offers on the returns of both bidding and target firms. A recent study of tender offers provides results (in the figure) that are indicative of the findings.[1] Target shareholders earn significantly abnormal returns, while the bidding firm's shareholders earn little or nothing.

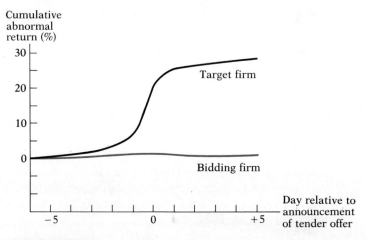

Further information on this can be seen by looking at the table below, which provides 2-day (t_{-1} and t_0) abnormal returns for target firms.[2]

Classification	Announcement Period Abnormal Returns
A. Type of Acquisition	
Tender offer	27.5%
Merger	22.6
Not disclosed	16.7
B. Payment Method	
Cash	29.3
Stock	14.4
Mixed	23.3
Not disclosed	15.4
C. Target Management's Reaction	
Resisted	28.3
Friendly	22.6
Not disclosed or neutral	23.1

We see higher premiums for tender offers, for cash, and where there is resistance. The higher returns for tender offers and cash basically go hand-in-hand because most tender offers are all or part cash.

[1] Michael Bradley, Anand Desai, and E. Han Kim. "Synergistic Gains from Corporate Acquisitions and Their Division Between the Stockholders of Target and Acquiring Firms." *Journal of Financial Economics* 21 (May 1988).

[2] Yen-Sheng Huang and Ralph A. Walking. "Target Abnormal Returns Associated with Acquisition Announcements: Payment, Acquisition Form, and Managerial Resistance." *Journal of Financial Economics* 19 (December 1987).

may be achieved by acquiring competitors in order to increase revenues and profit margins. While there may be some antitrust considerations, these are much less important now than previously, so there is less likelihood of the merger being challenged by the Justice Department or the Federal Trade Commission. The higher profits resulting from such a merger will, however, tend to attract more competition in the future. Consequently, the market protection may be temporary.

Finally, a merger may create increased economies by removing inefficient management and taking a fresh (and unbiased) look at the utilization of the firm's cash flows and other resources. Bidding firms are often more open to an in-depth analysis of the economic consequences of alternative uses of the firm's assets, or even selling off part of the assets, than is a firm's current management.

All attempts to secure increased economies relate to *synergism*. Synergism, or the "2 + 2 = 5 effect," refers to the idea that the sum of two parts, or firms, is worth more than the two firms are worth apart. Synergistic benefits are the primary objective of sensible mergers. It is easy (and very tempting), however, to overestimate the anticipated benefits and to underestimate the costs and problems involved. For this reason, managers must take special care to ensure that the difficulties of integrating two firms into a smoothly flowing operation are recognized at the time the merger is considered.

Tax Considerations

The other sensible reason for merging is to obtain tax benefits. If either the bidding or the target firm has incurred losses for tax purposes in the past, those losses can be carried back and then forward to offset the firm's tax liability. Sometimes, however, the losses are so severe that even after carrying them back or forward they are still not used up. The firm will lose these benefits unless it merges with another firm.

A case in point is Penn Central Corporation. Penn Central, which was primarily in the railroad business in the eastern part of the United States, had such severe losses that it filed for protection under the bankruptcy court in 1970. After reorganization, during which Penn Central restructured its financing and sold off the railroad properties, it again became a profitable firm. But the previous tax losses were so great they could never be used up before the carryforward time ran out. Penn Central's solution was to start acquiring other profitable firms so the tax losses could be used.

A second tax benefit may be due to the write up of assets to a new tax basis; if this occurs, the combined firm will be allowed to write off more depreciation for tax purposes, thereby lowering its cash outflows for taxes.

A third, and controversial, tax effect relates to the possible increase in debt, due to the unused debt capacity of the target firm. If the target firm does not have too much debt, the bidding firm may be able to finance a large portion of the merger via issuing debt. Because interest is a tax-deductible expense, the combined firm can reduce taxes. An alternative, and non-tax, benefit of using debt financing is that it provides additional incentives for management to create operating efficiencies so the debt can be repaid.

Dubious Reasons

In addition to the sensible reasons for merging, many dubious reasons are often given. Among the more important are these:

1. DIVERSIFICATION. It is often argued that the risk of the firm can be lowered by diversifying into two or more industries. Although such a move can reduce the risk, there is no evidence the bidding firm gains. The reason is that in an efficient market, such as the capital markets in the United States, it is easier and cheaper for individual investors to obtain diversification directly, instead of having the firm do it. In effect, the combined firm performs a redundant service that is not valued by investors. In addition, any benefits secured by either the bidding or target firm's bondholders through a coinsurance-type effect, may be the result of a simple transfer of value from the firm's stockholders.

2. GROWTH FOR GROWTH'S SAKE. Firms often attempt to justify an acquisition by suggesting it will enable the firm to keep growing in overall size and presumable earnings, and therefore the firm and its employees, managers, and stockholders will gain. But this growth does not produce anything of value unless it is accompanied by anticipated economies or tax benefits.

3. EARNINGS PER SHARE EFFECT. By acquiring another company, a firm often can achieve an immediate increase in EPS reported for financial statement purposes. This occurs because of the procedure accountants use to record the transaction—but it is, in fact, an illusion. This *EPS illusion,* unless it is accompanied by economic or tax benefits, does not serve the goal of maximizing the value of the firm.

Deciding Whether to Merge

Another NPV Problem

From the bidding firm's standpoint, a merger is another capital budgeting problem. To make the decision whether to merge, the bidding firm estimates the benefits in terms of the firm acquired and the incremental cash flows resulting from the acquisition, the costs in terms of the cash or securities to be offered, and the risks and return required. Thus, the basic framework is

$$NPV = benefits - costs \tag{22.1}$$

where

$$benefits = \Delta value + value_B$$
$$costs = the\ price\ paid,\ in\ cash\ or\ stock$$

The $\Delta value$ represents the present value of the incremental economic and/or tax benefits expected to arise due to the merger. $Value_B$ is the current (or pre-offer) market value of the target firm. Note that in an efficient market and with no incremental benefits, the NPV would be zero since the bidding firm would not be willing to pay more than the current market value for the target firm. For a positive NPV to exist, the bidding firm must be able to realize economic or tax benefits not available to the target firm.

Benefits

For a publicly traded target, its current value ($value_B$) is simply the market price of its outstanding securities. The incremental benefits, $\Delta value$, can be determined via

$$\Delta value = \sum_{t=1}^{n} \frac{\Delta CF_t}{(1 + k)^t} \tag{22.2}$$

where ΔCF_t are the incremental after-tax cash flows resulting from the acquisition of firm B by firm A, and k is the required rate of return appropriate for the incremental cash flows.

The incremental after-tax cash flows, ΔCF, are made up of the following items:

1. Incremental cash operating inflows, incremental operating cash outflows, and the incremental depreciation. Therefore (as we did in Chapter 9 for a replacement capital budgeting decision), we have

$$\Delta after\text{-}tax\ operating\ cash\ flows\ (\Delta CF) = \Delta CFBT(1 - T) + \Delta Dep(T)$$

where

$\Delta CFBT$ = the incremental operating cash inflows minus any incremental operating cash outflows

T = the firm's marginal tax rate

ΔDep = the incremental depreciation

2. Any additional outlays for new equipment (including required increases in net working capital).

3. Finally, consideration of the sale of any of the target firms assets, where the after-tax proceeds of the sale are anticipated to be greater or less than their going concern value (which is already reflected in value$_B$).

The total ΔCF from the merger is the net incremental benefits, where for any year t,

$$\Delta CF = \Delta CFBT(1 - T) + \Delta Dep(T) - \Delta after\text{-}tax\ investment\ in\ long\text{-}term$$
assets and net working capital $\pm$ after-tax gain or loss on the
disposition of some of the target firm's assets (when above or below
their going concern value)   (22.3)

Costs

The cost to firm A is the value of the cash or securities (i.e., the offer price) firm A will incur. Cash is easier to consider than stock, so we will start with it first.

If cash is employed, the cost of the acquisition is simply the amount of cash itself. For example, assume firm A and firm B are both publicly traded all-equity firms that have market values of $1,000,000 and $150,000, respectively. Firm A estimates, based on a detailed analysis, that the incremental value, $\Delta value$, resulting from the acquisition will be $100,000. The total benefits from the merger will be

$$benefits = \Delta value + value_B$$
$$= \$100,000 + \$150,000 = \$250,000$$

Suppose an agreement has been reached with firm B to be acquired for $200,000. The net present value, or increase in the value of firm A, due to the acquisition will be

$$NPV = benefits - costs$$
$$= \$250,000 - \$200,000 = \$50,000$$

The post-merger value of firm A will be $1,050,000 (i.e., $1,000,000 + $50,000).

In terms of firm A's shareholders, assume there were 10,000 shares of stock outstanding. The premerger market value per share was $1,000,000/10,000 = $100 per share. The post-merger value will be $1,050,000/10,000 = $105 per share. We see that if cash is employed, all of the net benefit (i.e., the NPV) from the merger goes to firm A's shareholders.

What if common stock is employed to finance the merger? In this case, the benefits are shared, since firm B's shareholders end up owning part of the combined firm. The purchase price was $200,000. Suppose firm A offers stock instead of cash. Since firm A's share price before the announcement was $100, and the offer price was $200,000, A will exchange 2,000 (i.e., $200,000/$100) shares for firm B, the *apparent* cost is as before:

apparent cost with stock = 2,000($100) = $200,000

This apparent cost is erroneous, however, since now the shareholders of firm B will share in the fortunes of the combined firm. If there are gains from the merger—which there were of $50,000—these are now shared with firm B's shareholders. The percent of the merged firm owned by firm B's shareholders, represented by W, is

$$W = \frac{\text{shares held by firm B}}{\text{total shares}} \qquad (22.4)$$

$$= \frac{2,000}{10,000 + 2,000} = 0.167$$

The *true* cost is

$$\text{true cost with stock} = W(\text{value}_{AB}) \qquad (22.5)$$
$$= 0.167(\$1,250,000) = \$208,750$$

instead of $200,000. Note that the postmerger combined value (value$_{AB}$) is employed in Equation 22.5. This occurs because the true cost must reflect the percentage ownership of the total market value of the combined firm. The NPV when stock is employed is

NPV = $250,000 − $208,750 = $41,250

Because the NPV is positive the merger is still feasible. Due to the sharing of the benefits with the shareholders of the target firm, however, the NPV is lower with stock than with cash (i.e., $41,250 versus $50,000).

The use of stock has implications for the market value per share for firm A's shareholders, summarized as follows:

| | Before Acquisition | | After Acquisition | |
	Firm A	Firm B	Cash	Stock
Market value	$1,000,000	$150,000	$1,050,000	$1,250,000
Number of shares	10,000	1,000	10,000	12,000
Price per share, P_0	$100	$150	$105	$104.17

We see that the total value of the combined firm is greater when stock is employed. This occurs because firm A did not incur the cash outflow of $200,000 for the acquisition. But, due to the sharing of the benefits between the shareholders of firm A and firm

B, the market value per share of $104.17 for firm A's ongoing shareholders is less with stock than with cash.

This distinction between cash and common stock financing is an important one. If cash is used, the cost of the acquisition is not dependent on the acquisition benefits. But, if common stock is used, the true cost is higher because of the sharing of the benefits between the shareholders of the two firms. In recent years, more and more use of cash has been made for financing mergers. These steps for evaluating a target are depicted in Figure 22.2.

Often the term exchange ratio is used in discussing merger terms. The *exchange ratio* is

$$\frac{\text{market value of cash and/or securities offered by bidding firm}}{\text{market value of target firm's stock}} \qquad (22.6)$$

In our example the exchange ratio with either cash or stock is $200,000/$150,000 = 1.33. A higher exchange ratio is often required when cash is employed. This occurs because the target firm's shareholders give up ownership if cash is employed and immediate income tax consequences (as discussed shortly) will result when cash, instead of stock, is employed.

Trying to Avoid Mistakes

In analyzing any proposed merger there are numerous mistakes that can be made. Perhaps this is why so many mergers that look good before completion turn out so poorly. Some of the mistakes, and ways to avoid them, are as follows:

1. RELY ON MARKET VALUES. It is often difficult to determine all of the value to be created using a present value approach. While conceptually this is just a capital budgeting problem, and we could attempt to value the entire firm to be acquired, it is sounder to rely on the established market value for firm B. In reasonably efficient markets the best estimate of the going concern value of firm B, given the current use of its cash flows and assets, is given by its present market value.

2. ESTIMATE INCREMENTAL CASH FLOWS. Only the incremental cash flows resulting from the proposed acquisition should be estimated. This simplifies the problem, but it is still easy to forget some of the incremental flows, or to overestimate inflows and underestimate outflows. Remember to ask, "How will my use of the cash flows and assets be different than their present use?"

3. USE THE RIGHT REQUIRED RATE OF RETURN. The proper required rate of return to employ relates to the incremental use of the cash flows and assets. If they are more risky than your firm's present cash flows and assets, then a higher required rate of return is necessary.

4. DON'T FORGET TRANSACTIONS COSTS. The costs incurred by lawyers, accountants, and investment bankers often run into the millions of dollars. These cannot be ignored in the process.

5. BE CRITICAL. Often it is tempting to get carried away with a proposed acquisition. This is especially true if a bidding war breaks out, where more than one firm wants to acquire firm B. In most bidding wars your shareholders will actually be better off if you lose—the "winner's curse" of overpaying often accompanies the firm that is "successful" and makes the winning bid.

Figure 22.2 Steps in Merger Valuation

The basic steps are the same whether cash or stock is employed. Due to cost differences, however, a slightly different approach is required to determine the cost for a stock-financed merger.

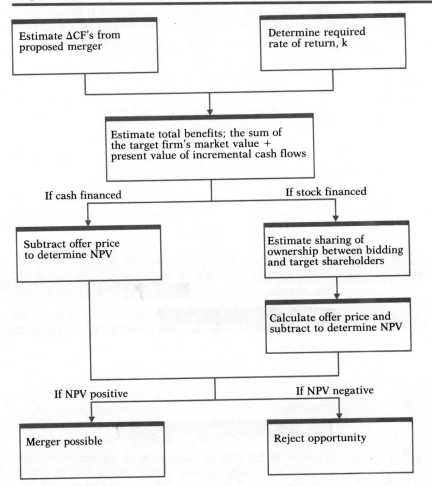

6. CONSIDER THE FORM OF THE FINANCING. The cash-versus-stock issue, and the amount of leverage the combined firm will have, are crucial decisions. While this seems obvious, often firms wake up a year or two later wondering if they should have structured the deal differently.

The RJR Nabisco Deal

Mergers and other restructuring activities come in all sizes and shapes. The largest deal of all time occurred in late 1988 involving RJR Nabisco. In 1988, F. Ross Johnson, Chief Executive Officer of RJR Nabisco, led a management-initiated proposal to take RJR private. That move touched off a bidding war ultimately won by the firm of Kohlberg Kravis Roberts & Co. (KKR). The final bid was a record $25 billion; that amounted to $109 per share for each share of RJR's stock. Seventy-four percent, or $81 per share, was paid in cash; the rest was in new preferred stock and convertible debentures. These additional securities, often called payment-in-kind (or PIK), represented $28 per share of the package.

To finance the deal KKR needed to raise $18.9 billion in cash. The money was raised as follows. Two billion dollars, the smallest part of the financing, came from KKR's equity investors and represented ownership in RJR Nabisco after the deal was completed. The second chunk, $11.9 billion in bank loans, came from 45 United States, Japanese, European, and Canadian banks. Finally, the last chunk, $5 billion, was raised by Drexel Burnham by selling notes to other investors. On February 9, 1989, an intricate system was devised to funnel the entire $18.9 billion to KKR with four banks—Manufacturers Hanover, Bankers Trust, Citibank, and Chase Manhattan—all assisting. One interesting sidelight was that the Federal Reserve's interbank wire transfer system cannot cope with amounts larger than $999 million. Most days that isn't a problem, but on February 9 it was. The solution was simply to break up some of the larger RJR transfers into batches of, say, a mere $900 million or so.

As soon as the money was gathered KKR wanted to make sure it was invested before nightfall so it could earn interest on the funds until they were paid out to RJR shareholders. At the then current short-term interest rates of about 9 percent, the return on $18.9 billion amounted to roughly $4.7 million a day. While it was "small change," it was nothing to be sneezed at. On February 21, 1989, the almost $19 billion was disbursed to the RJR shareholders. Then in March the approximately $6.5 billion in new payment-in-kind securities were also distributed to the former shareholders of RJR Nabisco.

Financing the deal was only part of the problem, since the bigger issue was how to manage RJR Nabisco effectively, sell off certain assets, and squeeze additional cash flow out of the existing operations. This was essential to pay the interest, pay debt, and make sure the whole deal didn't sink. The annual interest burden was estimated to be around $3 billion a year. KKR expected RJR Nabisco to produce about $4.5 billion in cash flow each year. That was up from $2.4 billion before the acquisition. Part of the increase was made up of a savings of roughly $560 million in cash dividends that would no longer have to be paid.

Other possibilities for increasing cash flow included terminating the "smokeless" cigarette that RJR Nabisco had experimented with. In addition, KKR took a hefty bite out of the company's estimated $150 million in corporate overhead each year, a move that is typical after a transaction of this type. In addition, RJR Nabisco's fleet of nine corporate planes was cut back. Other places for possible savings involved slashing the company's lavish $100 million sports-marketing program. Likewise, the company's annual $1.3 billion capital spending program was reassessed. In cutting this program, however, KKR had to make sure not to slash the capital budgeting program too dramatically.

Even after boosting the cash flow, KKR will not be home free, particularly if a serious economic downturn occurs or interest rates go up dramatically. Over the next few years, RJR Nabisco will have to start selling off a number of businesses to start paying its debt. They had an initial 6-month grace period, but after that lapsed some of the fixed-rate financing moved to a floating rate, and they had to start repaying principal on some of the debt. The pressure will increase steadily during the first 5 years. KKR estimated it would sell about $6 billion in food company assets within the first 2 years after the acquisition.

While the size of the RJR Nabisco deal is far larger than other mergers or leveraged buy-outs, the basic procedures and financing employed are not unusual. Most deals involve a lot of debt, with repayment coming from tighter operations that are designed to boost cash flows, and from the selling off of "undesirable" assets or divisions.

Who Benefits from Mergers?

There has been a lot of merger activity in recent years, but it is doubtful that everyone gains. Here is what we do know about mergers.

1. Stockholders of the target companies almost always gain, since most mergers involve a premium being paid over the target firm's premerger market value. Premiums often average 20 to 30 percent above the premerger market value, and sometimes go as high as 100 percent.
2. Numerous studies concerning the postmerger value of the bidding firms indicate little or no increase in value. Even though economic benefits leading to expected increases in value is the criterion that should be used for decision making, the empirical evidence fails to show that the stockholders of bidding firms consistently experience long-run benefits.
3. Investment bankers, and others who offer merger valuation services, have benefited by the many mergers in recent years.

Mechanics of a Merger

Buying another firm is much more complicated than many other business transactions. The details and the various options and factors affecting the merger can expand rapidly.

Form of the Acquisition

Up to now, we have used the term merger to refer to any acquisition or combination of companies. A merger, however, may take various forms:

1. A consolidation occurs when two or more firms combine to form a completely new firm. A new legal entity is formed, and there is no bidding and no target firm.
2. A merger can be accomplished through the acquisition of the stock of the target firm. The essential feature is that the bidding firm acquires both the target's assets and its liabilities by exchanging stock, cash, or other securities for the target firm's stock.
3. A merger may also be accomplished by acquiring the assets of the target firm. If the target sells all its assets, the proceeds from the sale (after paying off any liabilities) can be distributed to the target firm's stockholders, and the firm can be dissolved.
4. A holding company is another way to acquire control over another firm, although complete ownership may not be held. A firm may acquire 40 to 50 percent ownership in another firm. Though it does not control all or even a majority of shares, it can exercise effective control over the other firm.

Tax Implications

An acquisition can be taxable or tax-free for the target firm's stockholders. If it is a taxable transaction, the target's stockholders must treat the transaction as a sale for tax purposes and report any gains or losses. If you purchased stock originally for $10 per share and sold out through a merger at $50 per share your gain is $40 per share. You would pay taxes during the current period on this $40 gain. If the merger is tax-free, you retain your original $10 cost in the shares of the new firm. Only when you subsequently sell the new stock at some later date will any gain or loss in value have to be reported.

To qualify as tax-free, the transaction must meet the following conditions:

1. In a consolidation, three conditions hold. First, the acquisition must be for business purposes and not just for tax reasons. Second, there must be some continuity of the organization. Third, the stockholders of the target firm must receive a continuing interest in the new firm. The IRS has interpreted this to mean that at least 50 percent of the purchase price must be in the form of common stock.
2. In an acquisition of stock, the requirement is that only voting stock be employed, and that the bidding firm must purchase at least 80 percent of the target's total voting stock.
3. In an acquisition of assets, the bidding firm must acquire at least 80 percent of the assets of the target in exchange for voting stock.

The key requirement for a merger to be tax-free is that the target firm's stockholders receive common stock of the bidding firm.

Accounting Treatment

There are two basic accounting treatments for mergers: (1) *pooling of interests* and (2) *purchase*. The method employed can have a significant impact on the balance sheet and the profits reported for accounting purposes.

For a merger to be a pooling of interests, the following conditions must hold:[1]

1. Both the bidding and the target firm must have been autonomous for the 2 years preceding the merger. No more than 10 percent of the stock of the target could have been held by the bidding firm, or vice versa.
2. The merger must be effected in a single transaction or in accordance with a specific plan within 1 year after the plan is initiated. No contingent payments are permitted.
3. The bidding firm must issue voting common stock for substantially all the voting common stock of the target firm. "Substantially" means 90 percent or more.
4. The bidding firm must not dispose of a significant portion of the assets of the combined firms for 2 years after the merger.

If common stock is used, and if all other conditions are met, the merger is treated as a pooling of interests; otherwise, it is accounted for as a purchase.

Balance Sheet Effects

In a pooling of interests, the consolidated balance sheet is constructed by simply adding together the two preexisting balance sheets. In a purchase, the assets acquired

---

[1] "Business Combinations," APB No. 16 (New York: American Institute of Certified Public Accountants, 1970).

must be revalued to indicate the actual purchase price paid for the target firm. If a price greater than the book value of the assets is paid for the target company, the purchased assets must be revalued to reflect their fair market value. If the purchase price is more than the total fair market value of the assets acquired due to trade names, marketing or managerial expertise, and the like, goodwill is created.

To see the difference, consider two firms—X, the bidding firm, and Y, the target firm. Their premerger balance sheets are shown in Table 22.2. Firm X's assets are recorded at $1,000; Y's are recorded at $200. Because Y has some assets not reflected by its GAAP-based balance sheet, however, X actually paid $500 for Y. If the merger is concluded through the exchange of stock and the other requirements for a pooling of interests are met, column 3 of Table 22.2 shows the postmerger combined balance sheet. All that has happened is that the two premerger balance sheets have been added together. If cash or debt is used to finance the merger, then the $500 paid for firm Y has to be recorded as the purchase price. With the purchase method, long-term assets are written up to reflect their fair market value. Goodwill is also recorded. The postmerger combined balance sheet under the purchase method is as shown in column 4. The combined assets are recorded at $1,200 with the pooling of interest treatment; they are valued at $1,500 if accounted for as a purchase.

Income Statement Effects

The two different methods of accounting for a merger can also have an impact on the earnings reported by the combined firm. This occurs because under pooling of interests, assets are brought over at their current depreciated book value. Under

Table 22.2 Impact of Pooling of Interests Versus Purchase Accounting on the Postmerger Balance Sheet

As long as the price paid is more than the target's accounting book value, the purchase method results in an increased postmerger book value for the combined firm.

| | Premerger Balance Sheets | | Postmerger Combined Balance Sheet | |
	Firm X (1)	Firm Y (2)	Pooling of Interests (1) + (2) (3)	Purchase* (4)
Current assets	$ 300	$100	$ 400	$ 400
Long-term assets	700	100	800	1,000
Goodwill	0	0	0	100
Total	$1,000	$200	$1,200	$1,500
Debt	$ 400	$ 80	$ 480	$ 480
Stockholders' equity	600	120	720	1,020
Total	$1,000	$200	$1,200	$1,500

* Purchase price of firm Y is $500, versus its book value of $200. The long-term assets are revalued to their fair market value of $300 (representing a $200 upward revaluation from their book value of $100). The other $100 is shown as goodwill.

Table 22.3 Impact of Pooling of Interests Versus Purchase Accounting on the Postmerger Income Statement

If the purchase price paid is more than the target firm's book value, reported net income and earnings per share will be less with purchase accounting than with pooling of interests.

| | Premerger Income Statements | | Postmerger Combined Income Statement | |
	Firm X (1)	Firm Y (2)	Pooling of Interests (1) + (2) (3)	Purchase* (4)
Sales	$3,000.00	$600.00	$3,600.00	$3,600.00
Cash expenses	1,800.00	360.00	2,160.00	2,160.00
Depreciation	600.00	120.00	720.00	740.00
EBIT	600.00	120.00	720.00	700.00
Interest	40.00	8.00	48.00	48.00
EBT	560.00	112.00	672.00	652.00
Taxes (35%)	196.00	39.20	235.20	228.20
EAT	364.00	72.80	436.80	423.80
Writeoff of goodwill	—	—	—	10.00†
Net income	$ 364.00	$ 72.80	$ 436.80	$ 413.80
Number of shares of common stock	100	20	120	120‡
EPS	$ 3.64	$ 3.64	$ 3.64	$ 3.45

* The additional $200 in long-term assets is assumed to be written off over 10 years with straight-line depreciation. The $100 in goodwill is also written off over 10 years via the straight-line method.
† Goodwill is not a tax-deductible item and therefore is written off after EAT.
‡ For consistency we assume that common stock was employed to finance the merger, even though purchase accounting is employed.

the purchase method, assets are revalued to reflect the value of the merger. In our previous example, if the merger was accounted for as a purchase, firm Y's long-term assets were revalued upward to $300. This means that more depreciation will be charged off in future years than under pooling of interests. Goodwill was also created, and it must be written off over a period not to exceed 40 years.[2]

To see the effect on reported net income, the previous example is continued in Table 22.3. For simplicity, there is no impact on earnings per share if the pooling of interests method is employed: EPS is $3.64 both before and after the merger. If the purchase method is used, an additional $200 in depreciation must be charged off, and the $100 in goodwill must also be written off. Assuming both are done on a straight-line basis over 10 years, the resulting postmerger EPS is only $3.45 with the purchase method, versus $3.64 with pooling of interests. This accounting effect

[2] "Intangible Assets," APB No. 17 (New York: American Institute of Certified Public Accountants, 1970). One other technical point is important. Under pooling of interests, the income of the target firm for the entire year in which it was acquired is included in the combined firm's income. Under purchase accounting, only the appropriate pro rata income for the target firm is included. For simplicity, we include the entire year's income in any examples and problems.

is part of the EPS illusion mergers can have. So we see that earnings per share is subject to changes unrelated to the economic benefits of a merger.

Defensive Tactics

Preoffer Defenses

Firms have attempted to fend off unwanted takeovers through a number of actions. These basically fall into two main classifications—(1) preoffer and (2) postoffer defenses.

In the premerger group, defenses can be broken into three categories: general; shark repellent charter amendments; and other repellents.

GENERAL DEFENSES

1. PRIVATE COMPANY. The best defense of all may be to be a private company, such as Canadian-based Olympia & York Developments.
2. BLOCKING STAKES. Companies with 50 percent or more of their stock owned by one individual or a tight-knit group can be all but invulnerable. Thus, 70 percent of the voting control of Hershey Foods is in the hands of a foundation. In recent years many firms have instituted or enlarged ESOPs (employee stock ownership plans) in order to boost the percent of the firm owned by employees.
3. SIZE AND POLITICS. For a very few firms, such as IBM and Exxon, size alone may still be a valid defense. Likewise, certain companies, such as AT&T or defense-oriented high-tech firms may be immune to takeover due to potential political ramifications.
4. STRONG STOCK PRICE. One of the best defenses is a strong stock price, which signifies the investment community already believes in the firm, its management and growth prospects. While this is no barrier to a determined bidder who wants the company at all costs, it will still fend off many suitors.

SHARK REPELLENT CHARTER AMENDMENTS

5. STAGGERED BOARD. Under this tactic the board of directors is classified into three groups, with only one group elected every 3 years. Though a bidder can acquire majority ownership via a tender offer, it cannot obtain complete control of the board and the firm immediately.
6. SUPERMAJORITY. Instead of needing only one vote over 50 percent to approve a merger, many firms have asked their stockholders to change the bylaws and redefine the majority required to approve a merger. This *supermajority* is typically between two-thirds and 80 percent.
7. FAIR PRICE AMENDMENT. The supermajority provision may often be waived if the bidder pays all stockholders the same price; this prevents "two-tiered bids" where the first 80 percent of the shares tendered receive one price, while the last 20 percent receive a lower price for their stock.

OTHER DEFENSES

8. DUAL CLASS RECAPITALIZATION. A good many firms, such as Ford, have a class of supervoting stock that keeps control among the descendants of the founder or the builders of the business.

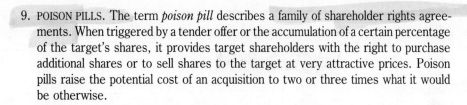

9. POISON PILLS. The term *poison pill* describes a family of shareholder rights agreements. When triggered by a tender offer or the accumulation of a certain percentage of the target's shares, it provides target shareholders with the right to purchase additional shares or to sell shares to the target at very attractive prices. Poison pills raise the potential cost of an acquisition to two or three times what it would be otherwise.

Postoffer Defenses

If all of the preoffer defenses fail to work, the target still has some postoffer defenses to call into play. These include the following:

1. LITIGATION. Many firms are filing suits to protect some of their defenses that have been challenged by a bidder, or they accuse the bidding firm of violating antitrust or securities laws.
2. ASSET RESTRUCTURING. Some firms purchase assets, or make another quick merger, to acquire assets the bidder does not want or that will create an antitrust problem. An alternative is for the firm to sell its "crown jewels," that is, the assets most desired by the bidder.
3. LIABILITY RESTRUCTURING. The targeted firm sells some shares to a friendly third party, called a *white squire,* or leverages up by issuing debt and/or buying back equity.
4. PACMAN. The targeted firm makes a counteroffer for the stock of the bidder.

These cover the majority of the defensive tactics used by firms fending off takeover bids, but new ones are always being devised. Two other items should be mentioned. The first is *greenmail* (or targeted repurchases) where an unfriendly bidder has purchased a significant stake in a target firm. Often to get rid of the unwanted suitor, the target firm buys back the common stock at a premium over its current market value. As part of the deal the suitor agrees not to purchase any new shares in the target for some specific period in time.

A final controversial item also deserves mention—golden parachutes. A *golden parachute* is a supplemental compensation agreement for senior management that provides substantial additional compensation in case of a takeover and the resignation (forced or voluntary) of the covered executives. In 1984 the amount of the compensation was restricted by law to no more than three times the executive's annual compensation; also, a special 20 percent excise tax was placed on the executive when he or she claimed the parachute.

Both greenmail and golden parachutes have received a lot of attention in recent years. Depending on how they are structured, they have both critics and supporters. Finally, if all fails, target firms often try to find a "friendly" firm—a *white knight*—to merge with. This strategy also involves risk however, because some white knights have turned out to be less chivalrous after the merger than the target anticipated.

Corporate Restructuring

Much of the recent merger activity in this country has involved mature, cash-rich firms. Because of this, many firms are rethinking how they use the cash flows generated by the firm. Instead of simply plowing the funds back into the same kinds

Poison Pills

A popular antitakeover device employed by many companies is known as a poison pill. One type lets shareholders of a target firm obtain newly issued shares at a deep discount, or even for free. The need for these poison pills is usually set off when an outsider buys a certain percent, say 20 percent, of the shares of the target firm. If the takeover attempt is not desired by the targeted firm, the existing shareholders, but not the bidding firm, then benefits from the poison pill. Because of the way they're structured, poison pills can double and even triple the price of an acquisition, making it prohibitive for a bidding firm to carry through with the acquisition.

Most firms are incorporated in the state of Delaware. There have been a number of lawsuits brought recently in the Delaware courts regarding whether poison pills can be used to thwart an acquisition. The upshot of the rulings is that when a bid is determined to be inadequate, the poison pill can be a very effective device for fending off a takeover proposal. For an all-cash, all-share offering however, the rulings indicate the target company has to provide a level playing field where all potential bidders, including the possibility of the target firm recapitalizing, must have the same opportunities.

Poison pills can protect firms against inadequate bids. In the presence of other bids, they can provide additional time and a good bit of leverage, and also encourage an open auction of the assets of a firm. Poison pills balance some of the needs of management and the firm, versus the needs of shareholders who have the objective of maximizing their returns. If legitimate takeover bids were completely prohibited by poison pills, then shareholders, quite legitimately, could bring suit that they were not being given the opportunity to sell their stock to the highest bidder, and therefore to maximize their returns.

---

of activities, or diversifying into areas in which they have no expertise, the motivation now—more than ever—is toward maximizing the value of the firm. There are two main points behind this emphasis on creating value. First, there is the recognition that corporate "fit" and maximizing NPV are all important. This recognizes the increased attention that needs to be given to the questions of "When and how should I get into positive NPV projects where my unique strengths provide the best opportunity to create value?" and "When and how should I get out of certain projects that no longer offer unique value-creating NPV opportunities?"

Second, there is recognition of the disciplining role of debt, and the strong impact it can have on focusing the firm's attention on cash flows, instead of accounting earnings. In short, debt provides a much stronger motivation than stock to concentrate attention on the really important activities of the firm. This motivation has been summed up as follows:

Equity is soft, debt hard. Equity is forgiving, debt insistent. Equity is a pillow, debt a sword. Equity and debt are the yin and yang of corporate finance.

Equity lulls management to sleep, forgiving their sins more readily than a death-bed priest. A surplus of stock muffles the alarms that should be heard when earnings decline. Forgive and forget is equity's creed.

Debt's edge jabs management awake, demanding attention. A staggering debt load is a credible threat, compelling necessary changes and exceptional performance.[3]

Leveraging Up

To increase efficiency and impose the discipline created by additional debt, as well as make themselves less attractive takeover candidates, many firms are leveraging up. In a *leveraging up* operation the firm dramatically shrinks the number of shares of common stock outstanding (through stock repurchases), and increases the amount of debt financing employed. These moves often result in the company shifting from a 20 to 30 percent debt to total asset ratio up to 60 or even 70 percent. The two activities can be combined in a leveraged repurchase, in which the firm issues substantial amounts of debt and uses the proceeds to buy back some of its common stock. Leveraging up forces a firm to become even more conscious of its cash flows, and imposes a discipline for the on-going operations of the firm that is often missing without the additional debt. While debt was often in the past viewed as disadvantageous, it is increasingly being viewed as a way to impose market discipline and encourage firms to become more efficient and productive. At the same time there is an additional benefit to the transaction. That is, the firm becomes a less tempting takeover candidate because there is not any "unused debt capacity" for a bidder to take advantage of.

Going Private and Leveraged Buyouts

Many firms are *going private*—that is, going from a publicly owned firm where common stock is actively traded on a stock exchange or in the over-the-counter market, to a privately held one controlled by a small group of owners. One of the reasons for going private is to avoid being acquired by another firm. Often the act of going private involves a management buyout. In a *management buyout* the top management of the firm usually bands together, often with an outside partner, to take all or part of the business and turn it into a private company. Usually these management buyouts are highly leveraged deals that are known as leveraged buyouts, LBOs. In a leveraged buyout a firm is acquired in a transaction that is financed largely by borrowing— often provided by institutional investors. The LBO debt can either be privately placed, or oftentimes it is supplied by the use of junk (or high-yield) bonds (see Chapter 13). Other leveraged buyouts may not involve the management of the firm, but may in fact be triggered by outside investors. While leveraged buyouts and management buyouts can be one and the same, it is possible for either one to occur separately.

Another tactic often used in conjunction with the act of going private is an *employee stock ownership* (*ESOP*). An ESOP is essentially an employee trust fund to which a firm may contribute stock or cash at no direct cost to the employee. Under a typical ESOP-based going-private deal, the firm tenders for its own stock using a bank loan. The firm then repays the loan by the ESOP, channeling periodic cash contributions to it through which the loan is paid. The result is that both principal and interest is repaid with money that is fully tax deductible—as long as the firm's contribution to the ESOP does not exceed 25 percent of its annual payroll.

Limited Partnerships

Sometimes corporate restructuring involves a fundamental change in the legal structure of the business. Some firms, for example, have reorganized themselves as limited partnerships. In this case the shareholders are replaced by partners and the firm's

---

[3] G. Bennett Stewart III, and David M. Glassman. "The Motives and Methods of Corporate Restructuring: Part II." *Journal of Applied Corporate Finance* 1 (Summer 1988), p. 81.

revenues and expenses are credited directly to the individual partners' accounts. These partnerships are generally known as master limited partnerships. A number of limited partnerships exist in the oil and gas industry, where producing properties have actually been spun off to partnerships. These partnership interests are then distributed to the firm's shareholders, thereby taking some of the assets out of the firm itself and distributing them to the firm's shareholders.

Typically, the management of a limited partnership is directly involved in how the firm is financed and where the cash flows go. This creates additional incentives to make sound use of the cash flows generated. Finally, there is a tax advantage to a limited partnership. Shareholders really pay taxes twice; once at the corporate level where the corporation pays taxes, and again at the personal level. Under a limited partnership the proceeds are taxed only once, when it appears on the partners' personal income tax forms.

Divestitures[4]

Firms not only acquire businesses, they continually have to ask the question "Should we continue to be in this business?" Too often in the past, divestitures carried with them negative connotations about how well the firm had done in managing the unit. But a *divestiture* should really be viewed as the product of good management, which is harvesting the fruits of past successful investments. The only question remaining should be "Can the firm create more value holding on to the unit due to some unique competitive advantage that a buyer does not have?"

The same basic ideas used when we considered the acquisition of assets are also of concern when a sale is contemplated. But instead of concerning ourselves with how much the firm can afford to pay to acquire assets, the issue now becomes how much can the firm sell the assets for. The steps to be used in making the decision to keep or divest a division (or any group of assets) are as follows (see Figure 22.3):

STEP 1: Estimate the operating after-tax cash flow stream associated with the division. Be sure to consider any impacts on the cash flows arising from complementary or substitute effects with other aspects of the firm's operations, as well as any future cash investments required in the division.

STEP 2: Determine the required rate of return, k, that reflects the risk associated with the division.

STEP 3: Calculate the present value of the CFs expected to accrue to the firm by keeping the division.

STEP 4: Subtract the current market value of the division's associated liabilities.[5] This produces the NPV to the firm of keeping the division, which is

$$NPV = \sum_{t=1}^{n} \frac{CF_t}{(1+k)^t} - B \qquad (22.7)$$

where

CF_t = the after-tax cash flows expected in year t from retention of the division

---

[4] This section may be omitted without loss of continuity.

[5] Debt should be valued at today's market value, since that is the present value of the firm's future obligation, discounted at the appropriate required rate of return.

Figure 22.3 Steps in Making the Divestiture Decision

These steps are similar to those employed when considering a merger or calculating the NPV of a proposed product.

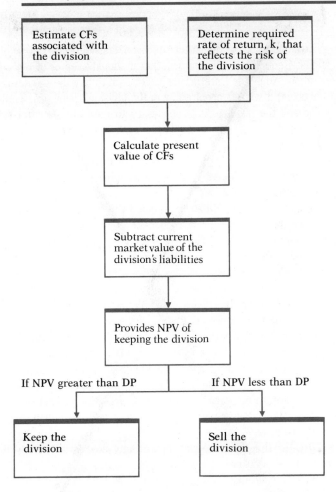

k = the required rate of return appropriate for the division

B = the current market value of the liabilities associated with the division

STEP 5: Compare the NPV of keeping the division with the net after-tax divestiture proceeds, DP, to be received if the division is sold. The decision rule is as follows:

1. If NPV is greater than DP—keep the division.
2. If NPV is less than DP—sell the division.
3. If NPV is equal to DP—you are indifferent.

In calculating the after-tax divestiture proceeds, two situations may exist. If the purchaser *acquires both the division's assets and associated liabilities,* the net after-tax amount received by the seller represents the divestiture proceeds, DP. But if the purchaser acquires only the division's assets, then the seller retains the division's liabilities, which must—sooner or later—be paid off. To make a consistent comparison *when the seller retains the division's liabilities,* the net divestiture proceeds are calculated as follows:

$$DP\left(\begin{array}{c}\text{if seller retains}\\\text{division's liabilities}\end{array}\right) = \begin{array}{c}\text{after-tax divestiture proceeds}\\\text{offered for the division}\end{array} - B \qquad (22.8)$$

To understand the divestiture decision, consider the example of General Communications. General is evaluating whether it should keep or divest a small movie theater operation. American Enterprises has offered to buy the theater division for $7 million after taxes; it will not acquire any of the division's liabilities. To determine if General should sell the division, it is necessary to estimate the after-tax cash flows (CFs) expected if it holds on to it. These cash flows should reflect (or be net of) any additional investments General will have to make in the future. The after-tax cash flows are shown in Table 22.4. Note that we have estimated year-by-year cash flows for the first 5 years, and then assumed they grow at a constant percentage growth rate to infinity.

In addition, General has determined that the required return rate is 12 percent and that the division's associated debt is $1 million. In years 2 and 3, additional investment is required if General keeps the theater division. Based on its projected cash flows, the NPV of keeping the theater division (after taking into account the division's debt) is $9.949 million, as shown in Table 22.4. Since this value far exceeds the after-tax divestiture proceeds of $6 million ($7 million from American Enterprises minus $1 million in the division's debt), General should retain the theater division. By doing so, it maximizes the value of the firm.

In considering whether to keep or liquidate assets, the decision facing the firm is exactly the opposite of the capital budgeting or merger decision. In an acquisition decision, the firm determines the present value of the benefits and compares it with the cost. If the benefits are greater than the cost, the firm acquires the assets. In a divestiture decision, the firm makes the same kind of analysis in reverse. It calculates the NPV of retaining the assets and continuing to operate them versus the after-tax cash proceeds from selling. If the benefits from keeping the assets are greater than the foregone opportunity cost arising from divesting, the assets are retained. Otherwise, they are disposed of.

This type of analysis is applicable for any kind of asset held by the firm. Typically, only fairly large projects are analyzed in this manner. These can include divisions, or possibly the whole firm. Even if the firm is not in financial difficulty, it might still consider liquidating. In the case of a voluntary liquidation, the NPV of continuing to operate is estimated with Equation 22.6. The liquidation proceeds represent the net after-tax proceeds available for distribution to the firm's stockholders, after all the firm's liabilities have been met.

Summary

Companies grow both internally and externally. Although many reasons are advanced to justify a merger, there are two primary benefits to be derived. The first and

Table 22.4 Net Present Value of Theater Division If Retained

Since the NPV of $9.949 million is greater than the divestiture proceeds of $6 million, General should retain its theater division.

Cash Flow Stream

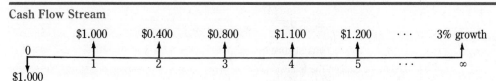

$1.000

Present Value of Expected Cash Inflows

Year	Cash Flow (In millions)	−	Additional Investment (In millions)	=	CF (In millions)	×	PV at 12%	=	Present Value (In millions)
1	$1.000		0		$ 1.000		0.893		$ 0.893
2	1.000		0.600		0.400		0.797		0.319
3	1.000		0.200		0.800		0.712		0.570
4	1.100		0		1.100		0.636		0.700
5	1.200		0		1.200		0.567		0.680
Beyond 5	3% per year		0		13.733*		0.567		7.787

Present value of future cash inflows = 10.949
Less: Present market value of associated debt, B = 1.000
NPV = $ 9.949

$$* V_5 = \frac{D_5(1 + g)}{k - g} = \frac{\$1.200(1.03)}{0.12 - 0.03} = \frac{\$1.236}{0.09} = \$13.733$$

most important is the expected economies, or synergism. A second is that in some cases there may be tax advantages that make merging desirable.

A merger is just another capital budgeting problem. To assess its economic desirability, managers must estimate the incremental expected cash inflows and outflows related to the merger. These projected net cash inflows are then discounted at the appropriate required rate of return and added to the current market value of the target firm. Then the cost, which differs depending on whether cash or stock is used, is determined. Once the costs are subtracted from the benefits, the NPV of the acquisition has been determined.

Numerous complexities exist in practice. An important one is related to the impact that accounting has on a merger. Others relate to the legal form of the merger, and the tax status for the target firm's stockholders. Through it all, it is important to remember that mergers are simply one way, and not necessarily the most effective way, to contribute to the goal of maximizing the value of the firm.

Many defensive tactics can be employed by potential target firms. These consist of both preoffer and postoffer defenses. All have the goal of (1) keeping the firm independent, or, if the firm is acquired, (2) making sure the target's shareholders maximize their value.

Corporate restructurings have increased dramatically in recent years. They are based on a two-pronged emphasis—recognition of corporate "fit" and maximizing NPV, and increasing the discipline imposed when more debt is employed. Some typical restructuring activities involve leveraging up, going private, limited partnerships, and divestitures. All focus on value creation and a better alignment of the interests of management with those of the firm's stockholders.

Questions

22.1 Define or explain the following:

a.	Market for corporate control	l.	White squire
b.	Bidding firm	m.	Greenmail
c.	Target firm	n.	Golden parachute
d.	Merger	o.	White knight
e.	Synergism	p.	Leveraging up
f.	EPS illusion	q.	Going private
g.	Exchange ratio	r.	Management buyout
h.	Pooling of interests	s.	Employee stock ownership plan
i.	Purchase		(ESOP)
j.	Supermajority	t.	Divestiture
k.	Poison pill		

22.2 There are both sensible and dubious reasons for merging. What are they? What distinguishes them?

22.3 Two firms, X and Y, are in unrelated fields and are planning to merge. No synergy is expected, but the standard deviation of the combined companies' returns will be lower than the standard deviation of either firm's separate returns. Is this a valid reason for merging? Why or why not?

22.4 A merger is another NPV problem. Explain:

a. What Δvalue is, and what cash flows must be included.
b. Why we don't use a discounted cash flow analysis to estimate the total benefits from the proposed acquisition.
c. Why the costs are different if stock is employed instead of cash.

22.5 What are some of the typical mistakes made in evaluating proposed mergers?

22.6 Who benefits from a merger? Do you think anyone loses?

22.7 Identify the different legal forms for acquiring another firm.

22.8 A merger can be taxable or tax-free to the target firm's stockholders. Why is this important? How does a merger qualify to be tax-free?

22.9 Clyde's acquired Zebra Pictures for $750 million, when Zebra's book value was only $185 million. From the standpoint of reported EPS, would Clyde's rather report this as a purchase or as a pooling of interests? Why?

22.10 Identify the defensive tactics a firm may employ. Are greenmail and golden parachutes also defensive tactics in the same sense as the others?

22.11 What are the two prongs (or points) behind value creation via corporate restructuring? How do the various forms of restructuring relate to this two-pronged emphasis?

22.12 How should a firm go about deciding whether or not to divest one of its divisions? What role does the division's debt play in the decision?

Self-Test Problems (Solutions appear on pages 737–739.)

Incremental Cash Flows and Merger Analysis

ST 22.1 Toepfer Products has estimated the following anticipated incremental benefits and investments for a potential target:

Year	ΔCFBT	ΔDep*	ΔInvestment
1	$ 80,000	$20,000	$150,000
2	80,000	50,000	100,000
3	135,000	50,000	50,000
4	190,000	50,000	0
5	195,000	50,000	0
6–10	200,000	20,000	0

* Δdepreciation is for the Δinvestment in the column immediately to the right.

a. If Toepfer's tax rate is 0.40, calculate the incremental after-tax cash flows, ΔCF, from the target.

b. The value of Toepfer before the merger is $2.4 million, while the target's market value is $1 million. The market price per share of Toepfer's stock is $50, and the required rate of return is 15 percent. Calculate the NPV for both a cash-financed and a stock-financed acquisition if Toepfer anticipates paying a 15 percent premium above the current market value of the target. (*Note:* Retain the negative sign for the first two ΔCFs.)

Synergism

ST 22.2 Buffalo Enterprises has agreed to merge into Gerard. To accomplish the merger, 2 shares of Gerard will be exchanged for every share of Buffalo. Before the merger, the firms were as follows:

	Gerard	Buffalo
Earnings	$1,000,000	$1,500,000
Shares of common stock outstanding	500,000	500,000
EPS	$2	$3
P/E ratio	10	8

After the merger, the P/E ratio is 9.

a. Calculate the postmerger EPS.

b. How much of the value of the combined firm can be attributed to synergistic effects?

c. Did the stockholders of Buffalo Enterprises gain? How about Gerard's stockholders?

Divestiture

ST 22.3 Automation Industries has an offer of $8 million after taxes for its plastics machine division. The cash flows from the division presently are constant at $2 million per year and are expected to remain that way. The division's present debt is $11 million; it will be assumed by the buyer. However, Automation has been considering modernizing the division, with the following expected consequences:

Year	After-Tax Cash Flows Without Modernization (In millions)	− Additional Investment (In millions)	+ Additional After-Tax Cash Flows (In millions)	= Postmodernization CFs (In millions)
1	$2.0	$3.0	$ 0	_____
2	2.0	2.0	0	_____
3	2.0	1.0	1.0	_____
4	2.0	0	1.5	_____
5	2.0	0	2.0	_____
Beyond year 5	2.0	0	2.0	8% growth to infinity

If the modernization is done, the division's debt will increase to $15 million. The appropriate discount rate is 14 percent either way. The proposed purchaser will offer $24 million after-tax, contingent on the modernization being done and the purchaser assuming the $15 million in debt.

a. If Automation does not modernize, should it divest or keep the plastics machine division?
b. What if the division is modernized?
c. Based on your answers to (a) and (b), what course of action should Automation take?

Problems

Basic Merger Analysis

22.1 Dellva Printing is analyzing the possible acquisition of Big Sky Electric. Dellva's market value is $3,000,000 and its market price per share is $40. Big Sky's market value is $800,000; Dellva estimates the incremental value, Δvalue, is $250,000, and the total purchase price would be $1,000,000.

a. If cash is used, what is the NPV of the proposed acquisition?
b. What is the NPV if stock is employed?
c. Why is the NPV for a cash-financed merger greater than if stock is employed? How much more cash could be offered if the NPV for a cash-financed deal just equaled the NPV for the stock-financed deal?

Incremental Value

22.2 West Virginia Foods is investigating a possible acquisition financed with cash. They estimate the incremental benefits and investment as follows:

Year	ΔCFBT	ΔDep*	ΔInvestment
0	$ 0	$ 0	$300,000
1	40,000	60,000	—
2	50,000	96,000	—
3	60,000	57,000	—
4	100,000	45,000	—
5	100,000	42,000	—
6	70,000	0	—
7	20,000	0	—

* Δdepreciation is for the Δinvestment in the column immediately to the right.

Without the incremental investment West Virginia Foods estimates there will be very few benefits from the acquisition. Should they proceed with plans for the acquisition if the marginal tax rate is 35 percent and the required return is 18 percent?

Incremental Cash Flows and Merger Analysis

22.3 Bill's Sporting Goods is examining the possible acquisition of Malatesta Industries. Bill's has estimated the following anticipated incremental benefits and investments:

Year	ΔCFBT	ΔDep*	ΔInvestment
0	$ 0	$ 0	$ 50,000
1	80,000	30,000	100,000
2	150,000	60,000	25,000
3	150,000	60,000	—
4	150,000	25,000	—
5	60,000	—	—

* Δdepreciation is for the Δinvestment in the column immediately to the right.

a. If Bill's tax rate is 0.30, calculate the incremental after-tax cash flows, ΔCF, expected from Malatesta.

b. The market value of Bill's before the merger is $900,000, while Malatesta Industries premerger market value is $400,000. The market price per share of Bill's stock is $100, and the required rate of return is 12 percent. Calculate the NPV for both a cash-financed and a stock-financed merger if Bill's pays a premium of 25 percent above Malatesta's current market value. (*Note:* Retain the negative sign for years 0 and 1.)

Effect of Merger on Value

22.4 Longfellow has agreed to acquire Sherman Brothers. The following information is for the two firms prior to the merger:

	Longfellow	Sherman Brothers
Earnings	$600,000	$900,000
Shares of common stock outstanding	400,000	250,000
EPS	$1.50	$3.60
P/E ratio	21	18

The merger terms provide that 2 shares of Longfellow will be issued for every share of Sherman Brothers common stock.

a. Josh Webber owns 100 shares of Longfellow stock. If the P/E of the combined firm is estimated to be 19, will he gain or lose from the transaction?

b. Are synergistic benefits evident?

c. How do you reconcile the answers to (a) and (b), which appear to conflict with one another?

Merger Analysis Versus EPS

22.5 Lamoureux Engine is evaluating four possible targets, which have the following financial data:

	W	X	Y	Z
Benefits	$2,800,000	$3,900,000	$3,100,000	$4,500,000
Shares of common stock outstanding	200,000	300,000	100,000	400,000
Stock price per share	$10	$18	$30	$7
Expected earnings	$400,000	$600,000	$700,000	$600,000

Lamoureux presently has 800,000 shares of stock outstanding, its stock price is $14, and its expected earnings are $1.6 million without any merger. Assume the target firms have no debt, no premium is paid, and cash is used to finance the mergers.

a. Based on the current market value of the four target firms, are any of the mergers infeasible?

b. Calculate the postmerger EPS for the feasible merger candidates.

c. If only one merger can be undertaken, which one is it? Why?

EPS Impact and Total Value

22.6 The Jones Company is in the process of acquiring Imperial Valley Industries. Prior to the merger, the following information existed:

	Jones	Imperial Valley
Total earnings	$3,000,000	$1,000,000
Shares of common stock outstanding	1,000,000	500,000
P/E ratio	15 times	10 times

a. Find the premerger EPS, market price per share, and total market value for both firms.

b. If Jones exchanges one share of common stock for every two shares of Imperial Valley, how many shares of stock will be issued? What is the postmerger EPS for the combined firms? What percentage premium did Jones pay over Imperial Valley's premerger market value?

c. If the P/E stays at 15 times, what is the total value of the combined firm? At 14 times? Is any evidence of synergism indicated by the resulting market values?

Merger Analysis: Alternative Conditions

22.7 Biller Textile is considering the acquisition of Omega Industries. Biller has estimated the following anticipated incremental benefits and investments:

Year	ΔCFBT	ΔDep*	ΔInvestment	ΔNet Working Capital
0	$ 0	$ 0	$ 70,000	$ 0
1	200,000	30,000	200,000	30,000
2	200,000	90,000	100,000	10,000
3	300,000	90,000	—	10,000
4	300,000	90,000	—	10,000
5	200,000	70,000	—	—
6	100,000	0	—	—

* Δdepreciation is for the Δinvestment in the column immediately to the right.

Omega's present market value is $600,000 while Biller's is $2,000,000. The marginal tax rate is 30 percent, the required rate of return is 15 percent, and Biller has 80,000 shares of stock outstanding.

a. If the exchange ratio is 1.4 what is the NPV if cash is used? If stock is employed?

(Do only if using Pinches Disk.)

b. What is the NPV for both a cash-financed and a stock-financed merger if each of the following occurs independently [while everything else remains as in (a)]?
   (1) CFBT for years 7–10 become $100,000 each.
   (2) Omega's present market value is $1,000,000.
   (3) The marginal tax rate is 40 percent.
   (4) The required rate of return is 18 percent.
   (5) The exchange ratio is 1.3.

c. What is the NPV for both cash-financed and stock-financed if all of the conditions in (b) occur simultaneously?

Market Value and Beta

22.8 Two firms, Ralston (R) and Sizemore (S), are going to merge. Ralston's market value is $11.75 million and its beta is 1.40; Sizemore has a market value of $25.50 million and a beta of 1.05. Both firms are all-equity financed, no premium or synergism is involved, and the new firm will be all-equity financed. After merging, a new project with a NPV of $6.50 million and a beta of 1.50 will be undertaken. What will be the market value of firm RS, and its beta? (*Note:* There are no transactions costs, and the new project is not reflected in the existing market values or betas.)

Beta and Premium

22.9 Louisburg has just announced a tender offer for Davis Industries at a price of $100 per share. Six months ago Davis's market price per share was $50. During the last 6 months, the market portfolio, k_M, has risen from 1,000 to 1,200.

a. What is the *percentage increase* in the market portfolio during the last 6 months?
b. If the market is efficient and Davis's beta is 1.3, what is the dollar premium per share being offered for Davis?
c. If the actual market price of Davis's stock was $70 at the time of the offer, does this necessarily mean the market is inefficient?

Tax Status of Target

22.10 Carol Cumpton started her own company many years ago. She owns all 80,000 shares of stock in the firm, and her cost basis for individual income tax purposes is $1 per share. She recently received an offer to sell out at $50 per share—in stock or in cash. If she elects stock, she will receive one share of stock with a market value of $50 per share for each share of her stock. If we assume Carol is in the 28 percent tax bracket for ordinary income and does not need any of the proceeds to live on, which form of payment should she favor? What are her net after-tax proceeds if she accepts cash? Are there any other factors she should consider?

Purchase Versus Pooling of Interests

22.11   Long Beach Laboratories is acquiring Omaha Drug. The premerger balance sheets and income statements for both firms are as follows:

Balance Sheets as of December 31

	Long Beach Laboratories	Omaha Drug
Current assets	$ 300,000	$20,000
Long-term assets	700,000	70,000
Total	$1,000,000	$90,000
Debt	$ 400,000	$10,000
Equity	600,000	80,000
Total	$1,000,000	$90,000

Income Statements for Period Ending December 31

	Long Beach Laboratories	Omaha Drug
Sales	$4,000,000	$900,000
Cash expenses	3,000,000	688,700
Depreciation	100,000	20,000
EBIT	900,000	191,300
Interest	56,000	1,400
EBT	844,000	189,900
Taxes (40%)	337,600	75,960
EAT	$ 506,400	$113,940
Shares of common stock outstanding	506,400	113,940

Long Beach will pay $450,000 in stock for Omaha, and no matter what accounting treatment is employed, the number of shares of common stock outstanding after the merger will be the sum of the two premerger share amounts. If purchase accounting is employed, current assets for Omaha will be $20,000, long-term assets will be $230,000, and goodwill will be $200,000. Debt will be $10,000, and equity will be $440,000. The additional depreciation and goodwill is written off via the straight-line method over 5 years.

a.   Determine the postmerger combined balance sheet under both the purchase and pooling of interests treatments.

b.   Determine the postmerger combined income statement under both purchase and pooling of interests. Then calculate EPS for both.

c.   Why does EPS decrease with the purchase method of accounting, but not when pooling of interests is employed?

Divestiture

22.12   LEM is evaluating the possibility of divesting its African division. It estimates the division's after-tax flows for the next 4 years as follows: $CF_1 = \$200$, $CF_2 = \$215$, $CF_3 = \$230$, and $CF_4 = \$240$. After year 4, the cash flows are estimated to grow at 2 percent per year to infinity. The appropriate discount rate is 13 percent, the division's debt is $500, and the division can be divested for $2,200 (after taxes), but LEM retains the division's liabilities. Should LEM divest or keep the division?

Voluntary Liquidation

22.13   Delores and Anita are trying to decide whether to liquidate their catering business or to continue with it. They can agree on the following estimated cash flows: $CF_1 = \$680$,

$CF_2 = \$680$, $CF_3 = \$740$, and $CF_4 = \$760$. They think growth will continue at 4 percent per year after year 4. The market value of the firm's debt is $1,500, and they estimate the firm's liquidation value is $5,200 after subtracting the $1,500. They cannot agree, however, on the proper discount rate to employ. Delores thinks 12 percent is relevant; Anita believes it should be 15 percent. Does the difference in discount rates have any impact on their decision? What course of action should they take?

References

Three recent books that cover a wide range of topics in this area are

AUERBACH, ALAN J. (ed.) *Corporate Takeovers: Causes and Consequences.* Chicago: University of Chicago Press, 1988.

COFFEE, JOHN C., JR., LOUIS LOWENSTEIN, AND SUSAN ROSE-ACKERMAN (eds.) *Knights, Raiders, and Targets: The Impact of the Hostile Takeover.* New York: Oxford University Press, 1988.

STERN, JOEL M., G. BENNETT STEWART III, AND DONALD H. CHEW (eds.) *Corporate Restructuring and Executive Compensation.* Cambridge, Mass.: Ballinger, 1989.

Here are some recent articles on mergers and corporate restructuring

BROWN, DAVID T. "The Construction of Tender Offers: Capital Gains Taxes and the Free Rider Problem." *Journal of Business* 61 (April 1988), pp. 183–196.

HUANG, YEN-SHENG, AND RALPH A. WALKING. "Target Abnormal Returns Associated With Acquisition Announcements: Payment, Acquisition Form, and Managerial Resistance." *Journal of Financial Economics* 19 (December 1987), pp. 329–349.

JENSEN, MICHAEL C., "Takeovers: Their Causes and Consequences." *Journal of Economic Perspectives* 2 (Winter 1988), pp. 21–48.

JENSEN, MICHAEL C., AND RICHARD S. RUBACK. "The Market for Corporate Control: The Scientific Evidence." *Journal of Financial Economics* 11 (April 1983), pp. 5–50.

RUBACK, RICHARD S. "The Cities Service Takeover: A Case Study." *Journal of Finance* 38 (May 1983), pp. 319–330.

SICHERMAN, NEIL W., AND RICHARD H. PETTWAY. "Acquisition of Divested Assets and Shareholder Wealth." *Journal of Finance* 42 (December 1987), pp. 1261–1273.

SMILEY, ROBERT H., AND SCOTT D. STEWART. "White Knights and Takeover Bids." *Financial Analysts Journal* 41 (January–February 1985), pp. 19–26.

STEWART, G. BENNETT, III, AND DAVID M. GLASSMAN. "The Motives and Methods of Corporate Restructuring, Parts I and II." *Journal of Applied Corporate Finance* 1 (Spring 1988), pp. 85–99 and (Summer 1988), pp. 79–88.

23

Financial Planning and Strategy

Overview

- Financial planning focuses on identifying positive net present value investment opportunities and financing strategies that create value for the firm while avoiding (or abandoning) those that lessen the value of the firm.

- In the short run, the emphasis of financial planning is on how to meet cash needs (or use excess cash) while retaining flexibility.

- In the longer run, the emphasis of financial planning shifts to value creation by maximizing returns, subject to the risks involved, and to liquidity and flexibility requirements.

- Financial and strategic planning is by necessity a trial-and-error activity that does not attempt to minimize risk. Rather, it is the process of deciding which risks to take and which are not worth taking.

In the computer industry NCR was a maverick—it had a very conservative, me-too strategy, yet it grew faster and was more profitable than many of its competitors. But no strategy works forever, and NCR now faces multiple threats. First, it generates over half of its sales and profits overseas. The dollar's recent strength has cut its revenue growth almost in half. Second, its main computer line is under mounting pressure from many competitors. Finally, NCR underestimated the difficulty in moving into another market area. It got there late and with an underpowered machine. The net result has made NCR more vulnerable to possible takeover and is forcing it to reassess its financial strategy.

Other firms have adopted different strategies. Sensing that large pharmaceutical firms often ignore certain drugs that have been developed, many start-up firms are interested. By licensing what has become known as "Lazarus drugs," a handful of newcomers—like U.S. Bioscience, Oclassen Pharmaceuticals, and Chemex Pharmaceuticals—hope to pare development costs and burst onto the pharmaceutical scene. Venture capitalists are providing much of the funding in the hopes of faster returns at a fraction of the cost compared to biotechnological firms.

Likewise, many of the New York money-center banks are also refocusing *their strategy. Citicorp has sold most of its Manhattan real estate and will halve its rent bill by relocating its retail headquarters in a new tower in Queens. Chase Manhattan is also moving—its back-office operations will be located in Brooklyn, not on Wall Street. Finally, Chemical Bank now sees itself as a superregional, with strongholds in Texas and the New York–New Jersey metropolitan area.*

Previous chapters have considered financial decisions taken one at a time. Our focus shifts now to financial and strategic planning and how firms can, and must sometimes, make broad, large-scale decisions that create value for their stockholders.

The Impact of Financial and Strategic Factors on the Value of the Firm

Until now we have approached the problem of maximizing the size of the pie, or value of the firm, V, as a series of bottom-up decisions. Now we need to shift the focus, and take an overall, or top-down, view. All of the ingredients, and their effect on one another, must be considered if we are to maximize the size of the pie.

All firms engage in some type of planning. Large ones, such as Holiday Inn, Eastman Kodak, or Gulf States Utilities, use complex procedures, forms, planning sessions, budgets, and models to develop plans. The plans of small firms like Joe's Service Station or Queen Bee Ladies Shoppe may simply be in the heads of one or two people or written down on scratch paper. But they are still plans.

The essence of planning is to ensure that the firm is following a dynamic policy that emphasizes the creation of value for its owners, and avoids options that destroy value. In terms of investment decisions, the firm's planning process must actively seek areas where positive net present values are possible. On the financing side, it must follow policies that minimize its cost. In addition, planning helps managers avoid surprises. It gives them a chance to think about how they will react to disruptions that may result in altered financial consequences. And planning helps establish concrete goals for motivating employees, and provides standards for measuring performance.

Factors Affecting the Value of the Firm

Many factors affect the value of the firm. Some are internal to the firm and can be dealt with as financial and strategic plans are developed; others are external to the firm. Within our four-part risk framework—general economic, inflation and disinflation, firm- and issue-specific, and international—some of these factors are as follows.

General Economic Risk

1. The robustness of the economy and how dependent the firm's cash flows are on the state of the economy will affect financing costs and the returns required by investors.
2. As the state of the economy changes, the cost of financing goes up or down. Accordingly, the level of capital investment made by the firm will also change.
3. The "tone" of the administration in Washington, how it views a balanced budget,

equal opportunity employment practices, mergers and leveraged buyouts, and the like will influence the actions taken.

4. Legislation can also have a significant impact. For example, if corporate taxes increase, firms have less cash for other purposes. The cost of financing will also be affected.

5. The local or regional economy can also have an impact. For example, the fall in oil prices during the last few years had a direct impact on the economy in the Southwest and on the fortunes of firms that depended on the robustness of that economy.

Inflation and Disinflation Risk

The rate of inflation or disinflation has a direct bearing on the firm in at least two ways. Higher expected inflation raises the required rate of return, which, other things being equal, cuts into capital investments. It may also put the firm under cost pressure due to a higher cost of goods and higher demands from labor, unless these can be passed on to customers. On the other hand, for many firms high expected inflation may be beneficial, since they can raise prices, without losing many sales, more than enough to compensate for the increased costs.

Firm- and Issue-Specific Risk

BUSINESS RISK

1. The position of the firm in its industry is a function of past investment decisions. Is it positioned in a fast- or slow-growing industry? Is it a market leader? What about production costs and expertise in research and development? More important, what is competition doing to hurt the firm's position, market share, and future cash flows?

2. Future investment decisions are a function of the firm's investment opportunities. In slow-growing, stable industries where few high-NPV projects are available, the primary emphasis often is to maintain what the firm already has. Emerging industries provide opportunities for making investment opportunities with high NPVs. What is the position of the firm? Should it abandon slow-growing industries and redeploy its assets?

3. The nature of the firm's operations and the products it sells determines its investment in both short- and long-term assets. What kinds of returns are we securing on our assets? Do we have too much or too little invested?

FINANCIAL RISK

1. The amount of debt a firm employs is determined by its capital structure. The judicious use of debt may lower the required rate of return, lower its cash outflows, increase its capital investments, and increase the value of the firm.

2. Financial risk also embodies the matching concept. An aggressive strategy uses fewer temporary assets, but more temporary liabilities. What strategy is adopted affects the expected cash flows; it also may affect the firm's required rate of return.

ISSUE-SPECIFIC RISK

1. Different types of financing, whether a line of credit, common stock, bonds, or whatever, have their own specific costs and risks. These issues must be considered,

since certain financing may be appropriate at one time and not at another. How about dilution effects, repayments, and all the new securities being developed?

2. The timing of the issue also may affect the firm's cash flows. Should short- or long-term funds be secured? What about waiting 6 months for more debt or equity financing?

International Risk

1. Firms selling overseas have unique problems. Such factors as the world economy, exchange rates, social and political structures, and taxes all serve to increase the complexity. Generally, the risks are higher, especially if the firm is engaged in doing business in many of the world's less developed countries.
2. Financing has taken on an international dimension. Should the firm raise funds in the Eurobond market the next time?
3. Increasing competition facing many domestic firms, such as those in the automobile, electronic, and steel industries, is causing both short- and long-run problems. Because of cost differentials, market share is being gained by foreign firms. What strategies should firms take to combat these pressures? Or should they abandon these markets altogether?

Other items could be mentioned, but the point is that the firm's financial and strategic planning process must take into account both the external environment—competition, labor and capital markets, politics, and so forth—and internal decisions already made or to be made. Before proceeding, however, let's pause for a review of how various actions—either taken by the firm, or due to external factors—can influence the market value of its stock.

The Basic Valuation Model

The basic valuation model for the constant growth case is[1]

$$S = \frac{D_1}{k_s - g} \tag{23.1}$$

where

S = the market value of the firm's stock

D_1 = the cash dividends expected to be received at time t_1

k_s = the required rate of return on the stock based on the risk-free rate and a risk premium appropriate to the firm in question. Using the capital asset pricing model (CAPM), $k_s = k_{RF} + \beta_j(k_M - k_{RF})$, k_{RF} = the risk-free rate, β_j = the nondiversifiable risk of stock j, and k_M = the expected return on the market portfolio

g = the expected (compound) rate of growth in the cash dividends

Instead of using Equation 23.1 directly, let's make a change so the equation is more useful for our present purposes. To do this, we define the cash dividends as being equal to the firm's *free cash flow*, which is

---

[1] More complex and realistic models are generally needed in practice; for simplicity, we employ the constant growth model.

free cash flow = cash inflow − cash outflow − capital investment $\quad\quad$ (23.2)

where free cash flow is what can be paid out in the form of cash dividends, cash inflow is what comes from revenues and new external financing, cash outflow is both ordinary expenses and repayments, and capital investment is the amount required in net working capital and long-term investments to sustain (or in some cases increase) the growth rate, g. Thus, we can redefine Equation 23.1 as[2]

$$S = \frac{\text{cash inflow}_1 - \text{cash outflow}_1 - \text{capital investment}_1}{k_s - g} \quad\quad (23.3)$$

Defined in this manner, the model allows us to see the impact of many factors on the value of the firm.

Consider the example of Mayco, an all-equity-financed firm that has expected cash inflows of $1,000, expected cash outflows of $600, and expected capital investments of $200. In addition, the expected return on the market, k_M, is 14 percent, the risk-free rate is 8 percent, and Mayco's nondiversifiable risk is 1.5. Cash dividends are expected to grow at 7 percent per year. As shown in Table 23.1, the market value of Mayco for the base case is $2,000. What happens to the value of the firm as factors internal or external to the firm change?

Increase in Expected Cash Inflow

Consider what happens to the market value of Mayco if, due to increased production efficiency, better sales efforts, or external market conditions, expected cash inflows go up to $1,100, while everything else remains the same. The new market value of Mayco is

$$S = \frac{\$1,100 - \$600 - \$200}{0.17 - 0.07} = \frac{\$300}{0.10} = \$3,000$$

This is considerably higher than the original $2,000. As would be expected, an increase in cash inflows increases the value of the firm.

Increase in Expected Cash Outflow

What happens now if everything stays the same except that cash outflows increase due to increased labor costs or poor management? If cash outflows are expected to be $700 instead of $600, the new market price is

$$S = \frac{\$1,000 - \$700 - \$200}{0.17 - 0.07} = \frac{\$100}{0.10} = \$1,000$$

An increase in cash outflows without any other change leads to a decrease in the firm's market value.

Increase in Expected Capital Investment

When we look at capital investments by the firm, the situation becomes slightly more complicated. Consider two basic situations. The first are "poor" investments

---

[2] Although capital investments are also a cash outflow, it is helpful now to break them out as a separate item.

Table 23.1 Base Case Market Value for Mayco

This approach, except for defining the expected dividends as being equal to the cash inflows minus cash outflows and capital investments, is the same as originally presented in Chapter 6.

Given

$$\text{expected cash inflow at } t_1 = \$1,000$$
$$\text{expected cash outflow at } t_1 = \$\ \ 600$$
$$\text{expected capital investment at } t_1 = \$\ \ 200$$
$$\text{expected dividend at } t_1, D_1 = \$1,000 - \$600 - \$200 = \$200$$
$$\text{risk-free rate, } k_{RF} = \ \ 8\%$$
$$\text{expected return on the market portfolio, } k_M = 14\%$$
$$\text{nondiversifiable risk for the firm (beta)} = 1.5$$
$$\text{required rate of return, } k_s = k_{RF} + \beta_j(\,k_M - k_{RF}\,) = \ \ 8\% + 1.5(\,14\% - 8\%\,) = 17\%$$
$$\text{expected constant growth in cash dividends} = \ \ 7\%$$

Market Value

$$S = \frac{D_1}{k_s - g} = \frac{\$200}{0.17 - 0.07} = \frac{\$200}{0.10} = \$2,000$$

that were made with inadequate analysis, had negative NPVs but were "necessary," or performed below expectations. The second are "good" investments that had a positive net present value when accepted and subsequently performed as expected. In the case of a poor capital investment, assume Mayco increases its investment to $250, but no additional cash inflows or outflows arise. The value of Mayco declines to $1,500:

$$S = \frac{\$1,000 - \$600 - \$250}{0.17 - 0.07} = \frac{\$150}{0.10} = \$1,500$$

However, what happens if a "good" investment decision has been made? Assume that as a result of the additional investment, cash inflows increase to $1,020 and g increases to 9 percent. The value of the firm increases to

$$S = \frac{\$1,020 - \$600 - \$250}{0.17 - 0.09} = \frac{\$170}{0.08} = \$2,125$$

The function of the firm's capital budgeting process is to create value by ensuring that projects that contribute to the maximization of the market value of the firm are accepted.

Increase in Required Rate of Return

An increase in the return required by investors will cause Mayco's market value to decline. If the required rate of return for Mayco increases to 20 percent while everything else is the same, Mayco's value declines from $2,000 to

$$S = \frac{\$1,000 - \$600 - \$200}{0.20 - 0.07} = \frac{\$200}{0.13} = \$1,538$$

As shown in Figure 23.1, there may be three different reasons why k_s increases. In Figure 23.1(a), the entire security market line (SML), including the risk-free rate, shifted up 3 percent. This might be the result of a 3 percent increase in expected inflation. In Figure 23.1(b), a general increase in risk aversion caused the

Figure 23.1 Three Ways for the Required Rate of Return to Increase

Although all three cause k_s to increase from 17 to 20 percent, the causes of the increase are different. The effects in (a) and (b) are caused by factors external to the firm; in (c) beta increases due to the increased risk of the firm itself.

(a) Increase in the Risk-Free Rate

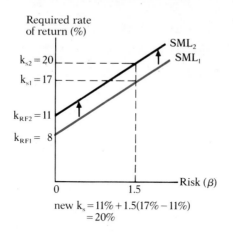

new $k_s = 11\% + 1.5(17\% - 11\%)$
$= 20\%$

(b) Increase in Risk Aversion

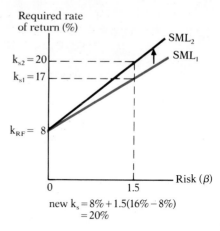

new $k_s = 8\% + 1.5(16\% - 8\%)$
$= 20\%$

(c) Increase in Beta

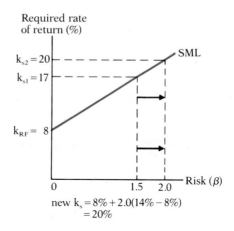

new $k_s = 8\% + 2.0(14\% - 8\%)$
$= 20\%$

security market line to pivot upward. Both effects are caused by marketwide factors affecting all stocks. In Figure 23.1(c), the risk of the firm, represented by its nondiversifiable risk (beta), increased to 2.00. Although the required rate of return still increased to 20 percent, in the last case the increase was caused by factors unique to the firm that affected its nondiversifiable risk.

Increase in Expected Growth in Dividends

The last item that can affect the value of the firm is a change in the expected rate of growth in dividends. What happens if g increases from 7 percent to 8, while everything else remains the same as in the base case? The value of Mayco increases to

$$S = \frac{\$1,000 - \$600 - \$200}{0.17 - 0.08} = \frac{\$200}{0.09} = \$2,222$$

With these ideas in mind, let's consider financial and strategic planning.

Financial and Strategic Planning

Financial and strategic planning focuses on the anticipated results of actions taken by the firm as they interact with external forces affecting the firm. The planning process results in the firm's *financial plan,* which encompasses both financial and strategic considerations. Much has and can be written about planning, but the reality varies tremendously from firm to firm. Our approach is to emphasize the key elements of any plan. As the plan develops, potential impacts on the creation or destruction of value from any proposed or continuing action must be analyzed.

What Is It?

Financial and strategic planning is a dynamic process that involves:

1. Analyzing the interaction of all the firm's decisions—investment, financing, short term, long term—to find the "best" plan for the firm. This plan stresses maximization of the value of stockholder claims and the value of the firm, but it also provides sufficient liquidity to meet current and anticipated needs. And it has flexibility to deal with unexpected consequences.
2. Projecting the consequences of decisions to avoid surprises. In addition, it provides the means to see the links between past, present, and future decisions. Forecasting is part of the planning process, but it is not the sole, or necessarily the most important, element.
3. Determining which alternative(s) to undertake. This decision involves goals for financing, marketing, production, labor relations, and the like. Most important, it defines the firm's strategy for the future.
4. Measuring performance against the plan. The performance of the firm, its managers, and its employees should be evaluated against the stated goals.

What Is Emphasized?

The main factors emphasized are these:

1. CASH FLOWS. Cash flows form the basis for any successful financial and strategic plan. By focusing on cash flows, the necessary interaction between liquidity, flexibility, risk, and the value of the firm is the center of attention.
2. DIVISIONAL ANALYSIS. Large firms break down the planning process on the basis of divisions or "strategic business units." The focus is on each division's aggregate cash flows, investments, and financing.
3. SCENARIO ANALYSIS. To determine the possible effects of various outcomes, most plans employ scenario analysis.
4. SHORT- AND LONG-RUN TIME FRAMES. Financial and strategic planning involves both short-run (typically a year or less) and long-run considerations. The long run is often 5 years, but it may be as long as 10.

Strategic Decisions

In reading the popular press we often get the impression that the United States does not value long-term decision making by firms. Rather, the emphasis is put on short-term performance results. In an attempt to investigate this topic, a recent study examined the market reaction to a number of strategic events.[1] The events that were studied, and the findings for the 2-day (t_{-1} and t_0) announcement period are as follows:

Type of Decision	Announcement Period Abnormal Return
Joint venture formation	0.78%
Research and development expenditure	1.20
Product strategy decision	0.84
Capital expenditures	0.35

The strategic investment decisions analyzed provided significant support for the proposition that these announcements are interpreted as decisions with expected positive NPVs. Thus, the results support the contention that management should be encouraged (by the market's reaction) to make strategic long-term investment decisions aimed at maximizing shareholder wealth. These results tend to contradict the popular press accounts, which claim that the competitive decline by U.S. industry is partially a function of a short-term orientation caused by the stock market.

[1] J. Randall Woolridge. "Competitive Decline in Corporate Restructuring: Is a Myopic Stock Market to Blame?" *Journal of Applied Corporation Finance* 1 (Spring 1988).

What About Accounting Statements?

We have not emphasized using the firm's GAAP-based accounting statements for planning purposes, nor will we. Why not? The basic reason is the same as we noted earlier. A firm's financial statements are accrual-based, allow for different generally accepted treatments, incorporate vastly different depreciation (and other treatments) than those employed for tax purposes, and are produced after the fact. They do not provide an accurate estimate of cash flows, profitability in a financial or economic sense, and the risks and required returns. Basing a firm's financial and strategic plans on accounting-based statements provides only a partial and incomplete analysis. Pro forma accounting statements should be developed (if desired) *after* the firm has formulated its financial and strategic plans.

The financial models used by many firms start with a firm's accounting statements and attempt to arrive at plans by projecting them. Due to all the assumptions inherent in the GAAP accounting process, however, and to its lack of emphasis on maximizing the market value of the firm, this is inconsistent with a financial management approach. *The best that can be said about many financial models presently in use is that they contain little finance!*

What Is Assumed?	Firms should start with explicit or implicit assumptions when they develop plans. Although all these assumptions should be subject to change as the planning process evolves, some primary decisions have already been made:

1. Capital budgeting procedures
2. The required rate of return (i.e., cost of capital or divisional screening rates)
3. Capital structure
4. Cash dividend policy
5. Aggressiveness or conservatism toward financing temporary assets with temporary liabilities
6. The efficiency and appropriateness of cash gathering and disbursing systems
7. Sale and collection terms and policies
8. Appropriate investment in inventory

One item that should not be *assumed* is the firm's complete corporate strategy. This should be a *result* of the planning process. Unfortunately, many firms establish their corporate strategy and then employ NPV to determine which projects should be taken. These firms have the cart before the horse—NPV should determine the strategy, not the other way around. The firm should evaluate alternative strategies and then select the one with the highest NPV.

What Should the Outcome Be?

The planning process should produce a number of tangible items. Among them are these:

1. CASH FLOW PROJECTIONS. Both short- and long-run cash flow projections and statements will be produced. In the short run, the emphasis is more on using short-term financing to meet cash flow needs, but as the time period lengthens, longer-term sources may be considered.
2. AN ARTICULATED CORPORATE STRATEGY. Certain areas for expansion, based on risks and required returns, will be identified. Areas for retrenchment or liquidation will also be identified.
3. SHORT- AND LONG-TERM CAPITAL BUDGETS. Planned capital expenditures typically are broken down by division and by expansion or replacement.
4. AMOUNT AND APPROXIMATE TIMING OF NEEDED FINANCING. The firm's present financing, planned repayments, capital structure, and forecasted financial market conditions are considered in drawing up these plans, along with retaining sufficient flexibility for the unexpected.
5. VALUE OF THE FIRM. The impact on the firm's expected free cash flows and their riskiness is also an outcome. In assessing the impact on the value of the firm, the reaction of the investment community to the firm's plans must be considered.

Developing Financial and Strategic Plans

Financial and strategic planning processes and models come in many sizes and shapes. In any model, however, there is an important relationship between the short- and long-run aspects. Consider Figure 23.2, which shows the relationships between the firm's short- and long-term cash inflows. The firm is experiencing cash inflows and outflows during the current period. At the end of this period, the net inflow or

Figure 23.2 Relationship Between Short- and Long-Term Financial and Strategic Planning

In the short term, the emphasis is on quarterly cash flows. In the longer term, the emphasis is on the cumulative cash inflows or outflows and the financial and strategic aspects.

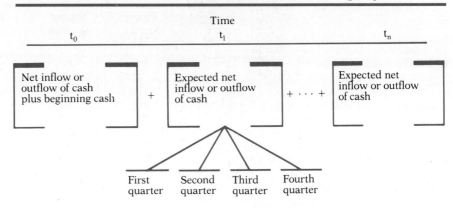

outflow, plus the beginning cash balance, determines how much cash is available at the start of period 1. Short-run planning is concerned with the net inflows in the next few periods. Although monthly cash flows could be used, we focus on quarterly flows.

For most firms, there will be times during the year when excess cash is available; at other times, the firm may be a net borrower. Short-term planning focuses on these short-run excesses or shortages of cash. In the long term, cumulative net cash flows must be considered in light of capital expenditure plans, financing plans, and all the other factors that influence the firm's cash flows and its value.

Short-Term Planning

To understand financial and strategic planning, consider the example of Keystone Industries. In the short term, *assume Keystone is a no-growth firm in a cyclical industry and is making just enough replacement investments to maintain itself at a constant level of profitability and cash flows.* Its free cash flows for paying cash dividends are $24 million per year. It is all-equity financed, and its market-determined required rate of return, k_s, is 12 percent. Using Equation 23.1, its value is

$S = \$24 \text{ million}/0.12 = \$200 \text{ million}$

Table 23.2 shows Keystone's expected net cash inflow or outflow per quarter and the amount of short-term financing needed.[3] This statement is the result of the cash budgeting process, discussed in Chapter 4. We see that Keystone expects a cash outflow the first quarter and then another sizable outflow the second quarter. In both the third and fourth quarters, cash should be generated to pay off any short-term borrowing. Table 23.2 defines Keystone's short-term financing needed. Note

---

[3] The cash inflows, cash outflows, funds for capital investment, and resulting free cash flow discussed at the beginning of the chapter are partially "buried" in a cash budget. The free cash flow (or dividends) of $24 million per year ($6 million per quarter) for Keystone is included in the first line 3—"Other net inflow or outflow."

Table 23.2 Keystone Industries Cash Budget (In millions) Showing Its Cash Flows and Short-Term Financing Needs

Even though Keystone suffers a net cash outflow of $10 million the first quarter, it has $5 million in marketable securities, reducing the amount of external financing needed.

	First Quarter	Second Quarter	Third Quarter	Fourth Quarter
Calculating Net Cash Inflow or Outflow				
1. Total operating cash inflow	$80	$95	$140	$130
2. Total operating cash outflow	− 55	− 80	− 90	− 60
3. Other net inflow or outflow	− 35	− 70	− 30	− 35
4. Net cash inflow (+) or outflow (−) (1 + 2 + 3)	−$10	−$55	$ 20	$ 35
Calculating Short-Term Financing Needed				
1. Cash and marketable securities at start of period	$10	$ 0	−$ 55	−$ 35
2. Change in cash balance (net cash inflow or outflow)	− 10	− 55	20	35
3. Cash at end of period (1 + 2)	0	− 55	− 35	0
4. Minimum cash balance required	− 5	− 5	− 5	− 5
5. Cumulative short-term financing needed (−) or surplus (+) (3 + 4)	−$ 5	−$60	−$ 40	−$ 5

that at the start of the planning period, Keystone has $5 million in cash and marketable securities in excess of its minimum needs. The question is "What is the 'best' way to secure the additional short-term financing?"

The First Alternative

There are many possible ways to meet these short-term financing needs, but we will investigate two alternative plans. The first makes use of the following sources of financing: (1) A bank line of credit that has a before-tax rate of interest of 12 percent per year. The maximum that can be drawn on this line of credit is $30 million. (2) An inventory loan that has a yearly interest rate of 15 percent. This can be paid back in part or full, as desired. For both loans, interest costs incurred one quarter are paid the next. With these two sources of financing, the strategy should be obvious. Draw on the line of credit until it is used up; then take out the inventory loan. The inventory loan should be paid off before the line of credit, because it has a higher cost.

Table 23.3 shows the resulting short-term plan. The bottom part indicates that in the first quarter Keystone will raise $5 million by selling its existing marketable securities. Then it will draw on the line of credit for the additional $5 million needed. Notice that since it had no interest-bearing debt outstanding, and since interest lags by one quarter, no interest payments show up for the first quarter in the top part of the table.

In the second quarter, Keystone must meet its $55 million outflow (from the first line 5 in Table 23.3), plus pay the interest of $150,000 on the line of credit.[4] On an after-tax basis, Keystone needs $55.090 million. Twenty-five million comes

---

[4] For simplicity, the specific number of days in a quarter are ignored when calculating the interest.

Table 23.3 Keystone Industries First Short-Term Plan (In millions)

The amount of cash raised interacts with the amount of cash needed due to interest cash outflows. A one-quarter lag is assumed for the interest outflows.

	First Quarter	Second Quarter	Third Quarter	Fourth Quarter
Cash Needed				
Interest				
1. Bank line of credit	$ 0	$ 0.150†	$ 0.900‡	$ 0.900
2. Inventory loan	0	0	1.128	0.424§
3. Total	0	0.150	2.028	1.324
4. After-tax interest outflow [3 × (1 − 0.40)]	0	0.090	1.217	0.794
Additional needs				
5. Net cash inflow or outflow*	10.000	55.000	−20.000	−35.000
6. Total cash needed (+) or surplus generated (−) (4 + 5)	$10.000	$55.090	−$18.783	−$34.206
Cash Raised				
New borrowing				
1. Bank line of credit	$ 5.000	$25.000	$ 0	$ 0
2. Inventory loan	0	30.090	0	0
3. Total	5.000	55.090	0	0
Repayments				
4. Bank line of credit	0	0	0	22.899**
5. Inventory loan	0	0	18.783	11.307
6. Total	0	0	18.783	34.206
7. Net new borrowing (3 − 6)	5.000	55.090	−18.783	−34.206
Marketable securities				
8. Sale of marketable securities	5.000	0	0	0
9. Less purchase of marketable securities	0	0	0	0
10. Total cash raised (+) or paid off (−) (7 + 8 + 9)	$10.000	$55.090	−$18.783	−$34.206

* From Table 23.2. Note that the signs are reversed in this table for the net cash inflows or outflows.
† ($5.000)(0.12/4)
‡ ($5.000 + $25.000)(0.12/4)
§ ($30.090 − $18.783)(0.15/4)
** $34.206 − $11.307

from drawing down the rest of the line of credit, while the remaining amount comes from borrowing $30.090 million on the inventory loan. In the third and fourth quarters, Keystone is able to pay back all of the inventory loan and most of the line of credit. The net result is that by the end of the year the line of credit will be paid down so that only $7.101 million is still borrowed.[5]

In evaluating this first alternative, a number of points should be considered. Among them are the following:

1. Has the cheapest form of financing been obtained? As we will see, the answer is "no."

[5] ($5.000 million + $25.000 million) − $22.899 million = $7.101 million. In addition, interest of $213,030 [$7.101 million(0.12/4)] is due the first quarter of next year.

Financial Management Today

Changes in the Firm's Managers

Does a change in the firm's chairman, vice chairman, president, or chief executive officer have any impact on the value of the firm? This issue was addressed recently where the management changes were not undertaken at the same time as major company events, like corporate restructurings, mergers, or divestments.[1] The results indicated that for internal appointments (i.e., where the incoming office holder was promoted from within the company) the 2-day (t_{-1} and t_0) abnormal return was a positive 1.05 percent. Where the appointment was external, that is, the individual was hired from outside the firm, the return was a positive 0.72 percent. When examining the results for large versus small firms, the study found more impact on stock returns for smaller firms. Overall these results indicate a change in top management is viewed as a positive move by the stock market.

Dismissals also were examined in this same study; the abnormal returns were a positive 1.03 percent. There is no evidence that dismissals decrease wealth; in fact, stock prices tend to rise. This suggests that the officers dismissed were apparently associated with policies viewed as harming the shareholders' interests.

[1] Eugene P. H. Furtado and Michael S. Rozeff. "The Wealth Effects of Company Initiated Management Changes." *Journal of Financial Economics* 18 (March 1987).

2. Does Keystone need more (or less) than a $5 million cash reserve? If it needs more, the plan should be revised to include a larger cash reserve. A smaller cash reserve would have the opposite effect.
3. Does the plan leave Keystone in good shape for the next year? The answer to this is only partially positive, since it entered the year with a $5 million cash and marketable security surplus and will enter next year with no cash surplus and $7.101 million borrowed on the line of credit.
4. Does Keystone need additional long-term financing? The answer to this depends on the prospects for the next year, plus Keystone's willingness to adopt a more aggressive position relative to financing temporary assets with temporary liabilities. Long-term financing might be needed now, but short-term financing probably will be sufficient unless Keystone maintains a very conservative working capital strategy, or if financial market conditions or other factors dictate long-term financing.
5. Can something be done to the firm's operating and capital investment plans to reduce the cash outflows? This might save the firm from borrowing so heavily.

The Second Alternative
The second plan involves the use of the following two financing sources: (1) An accounts receivable loan that carries an annual interest rate of 11 percent. The firm can borrow or pay back at will. (2) A $30 million issue of commercial paper at 9

percent interest. The issue would have a 6-month maturity. Since commercial paper is issued on a discount basis, Keystone would receive only $28.708 million.[6] The difference between $30 million and $28.708 million is the interest earned by the purchaser of the commercial paper. Given the before-tax costs, which are lower than in the first alternative, the second should be better. Let's see if it is.

Table 23.4 shows the details of the second alternative. The first quarter is exactly the same as before. In the second quarter, Keystone first issues commercial paper before drawing on the accounts receivable loan. In addition, interest of $138,000 on the first quarter's receivables loan must be paid. In the third quarter, it pays back part of the accounts receivable loan. In the fourth quarter, the commercial paper is paid off and the accounts receivable loan is also paid down. At the end of the fourth quarter, Keystone still has a $6.572 million accounts receivable loan outstanding.[7]

Because of the lower interest costs, Keystone is better off with the second plan. An easy way to see this is by comparing the interest charges under the two plans. Thus, the before-tax interest is

Interest per Quarter (In millions)

	1	2	3	4	Total Interest
First plan	0	$0.150	$2.028	$1.324	$3.502
Second plan	0	0.138	0.863	1.619	2.620

Keystone is better off by $882,000 in interest before tax, or $529,200 after tax. It can save over $500,000 in after-tax cash outflows by adopting the second plan.

Market Value Impact

The final item to consider is what happens to the market value of Keystone Industries if it adopts the first alternative rather than the more cost-effective second one. Previously, Keystone had $24 million in free cash flow for cash dividends. But since the first alternative results in over $500,000 more in after-tax cash outflows, the free cash flows, assuming nothing else changes, would decrease to about $23.5 million. If the required return stays at 12 percent, Keystone's market value with the first alternative is

$$S = \$23.5 \text{ million}/0.12 = \$195.833 \text{ million}$$

versus $200 million if it adopts the second and cheaper alternative. The value of Keystone decreases if it chooses the less-cost-effective short-run financing plan. While this example was designed to be simple, the basic result is general: *Ineffective short-run planning has a direct negative impact on the value of the firm.*

It is also important to remember that in both short- and long-run planning, a fairly simple straightforward analysis is often best. In evaluating various plans, it is

[6] This is determined as follows:

$$\text{principal} + (0.09/2)\text{principal} = \$30 \text{ million}$$
$$1.045 \text{ principal} = \$30 \text{ million}$$
$$\text{principal} = \$30 \text{ million}/1.045 = \$28.708 \text{ million}$$

[7] ($5.000 million + $26.375 million) − ($19.482 million + $5.321 million) = $6.572 million. Interest of $180,730 [$6.572 million(0.11/4)] is also due on the receivables loan in the first quarter of next year.

Table 23.4 Keystone Industries Second Short-Term Plan (In millions)

Comparing this to Table 23.3, we see that in quarter 2 Keystone borrows less, in quarter 3 it repays a lot more, and in quarter 4 it repays almost the same amount. Hence, this plan must be better than the first one.

	First Quarter	Second Quarter	Third Quarter	Fourth Quarter
Cash Needed				
Interest				
1. Accounts receivable loan	$ 0	$ 0.138†	$ 0.863‡	$ 0.327
2. Commercial paper	0	0	0	1.292§
3. Total	0	0.138	0.863	1.619
4. After-tax interest outflow [3 × (1 − 0.40)]	0	0.083	0.518	0.971
Additional needs				
5. Net cash inflow or outflow*	10.000	55.000	− 20.000	− 35.000
6. Total cash needed (+) or surplus generated (−) (4 + 5)	$10.000	$55.083	−$19.482	−$34.029
Cash Raised				
Net borrowing				
1. Accounts receivable loan	$ 5.000	$26.375	$ 0	$ 0
2. Commercial paper	0	28.708	0	0
3. Total	5.000	55.083	0	0
Repayments				
4. Accounts receivable loan	0	0	19.482	5.321**
5. Commercial paper	0	0	0	28.708
6. Total	0	0	19.482	34.029
7. Net new borrowing (3 − 6)	5.000	55.083	− 19.482	− 34.029
Marketable securities				
8. Sale of marketable securities	5.000	0	0	0
9. Less purchases of marketable securities	0	0	0	0
10. Total cash raised (+) or paid off (−) (7 + 8 + 9)	$10.000	$55.083	−$19.482	−$34.029

* From Table 23.2. Note that the signs are reversed in this table for the net cash inflows or outflows.
† ($5.000)(0.11/4)
‡ ($5.000 + $26.375)(0.11/4)
§ All the interest ($30.000 − $28.708) is paid in quarter 4. For tax purposes, some of it will be claimed in quarter 3, but for simplicity that complication is ignored.
** $34.029 − $28.708

much better not to become fascinated with detail. The KISS (Keep It Simple Stupid) principle should always be kept in mind when evaluating financial and strategic plans.

The determination of a firm's short-term plan is by necessity a trial-and-error procedure. We have illustrated two such plans, but many more exist and need to be evaluated. For a small firm with few options, the short-run plan can be developed by hand. In more complicated situations, the use of the computer and a spreadsheet program can facilitate the evaluation of alternative plans. Also, the short-term plans just analyzed incorporated many assumptions. If these assumptions change, the short-term plan also changes.

Long-Term Planning

Long-term planning, in a sense, is just a continuation of the ideas discussed for short-term planning. But there are some differences in emphasis. Consider Figure 23.3, which depicts the firm's long-term needs. Note that the long-term requirements

Figure 23.3 How Short- and Long-Term Financing Meet a Firm's Needs

Spontaneous short-term financing (through accounts payable, factoring of receivables, and continuous inventory loans) meets part of its needs. The rest are met by short-term borrowings and long-term financing.

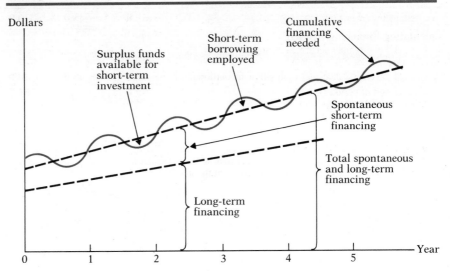

are dependent on the amount of spontaneous short-term financing secured, along with the amount of short-term borrowing employed. Firms that adopt an aggressive working capital strategy will, other things being equal, need less long-term financing. Also, in the long run the firm's strategic plan, its ability to forecast accurately, and the need for flexibility all become more important than in the short run, although the basic emphasis remains the same.

The long-term approach begins by continuing what was done in the short term. Instead of having a cash budget for 1 year, cash budgets are needed for longer time periods. Obviously, the further in the future, the less detail in the cash budget. Likewise, the further in the future, the more uncertainty concerning the projected cash flows. Table 23.5 presents Keystone's net cash flows and projected needs for the next 5 years. As part of the long-run plan, the firm is committed to a series of capital investments that will move it from its current no-growth situation, to a small positive growth estimated to be 2 percent per year to infinity.

Before proceeding, it is helpful to pause and consider what the net cash inflow or outflow row in Table 23.5 includes. Among other things, it incorporates the following:

1. The difference between net cash generated from operations less cash dividends, which represents the funds retained for reinvestment in the firm. Therefore, *internally generated equity funds are already considered when a long-term cash budget is developed.*
2. Any needed investment in current assets. If this is not taken into account, the firm may experience even greater cash needs if it plans to build up its investment in current assets.

Table 23.5 Keystone Industries Long-Term Cash Budget (In millions)

Large expected cash outflows in years 2 and 4 indicate the need for substantial increases in financing over the next five years.

	Year 1	Year 2	Year 3	Year 4	Year 5
Net cash inflow (+) or outflow (−)	−$12.0*	−$45.0	−$10.0	−$ 80.0	$ 30.0
Calculating Financing Needed					
1. Cash and marketable securities at start of period	$10.0	−$ 2.0	−$47.0	−$ 57.0	−$137.0
2. Change in cash balance (net cash inflow or outflow)	− 12.0	− 45.0	− 10.0	− 80.0	30.0
3. Cash at end of period (1 + 2)	− 2.0	− 47.0	− 57.0	− 137.0	− 107.0
4. Minimum cash balance required	− 5.0	− 5.0	− 7.5	− 7.5	− 10.0
5. Cumulative financing needed (−) or surplus (+) (3 + 4)	−$ 7.0	−$52.0	−$64.5	−$144.5	−$117.0

*Assumes Keystone adopts the second short-run plan, which leaves the firm with an accounts receivable loan of under $7 million to pay off. In addition, it sold $5 million in marketable securities in year 1.

3. Projected capital expenditures, including their timing and magnitude. Any planned acquisition or liquidation of assets has also been considered.
4. Repayment of the principal part of any debt due.
5. Short-term financing costs incurred to meet any short-term financing needs.
6. The firm's cash dividend policy.

Table 23.5 thus summarizes Keystone's best estimates of its financing needs over the next 5 years.

Earlier we decided that the market value of Keystone Industries was $200 million. If there are 4 million shares of common stock outstanding, then the market price per share is $200 million/4 million shares = $50. Based on its projected cash flows over the next 5 years, we see from Table 23.5 that Keystone estimates it needs to secure an additional $117 million in new external financing over this period.[8] This amount is in addition to the $40 million in internally generated financing the firm expects over this period. Keystone's current balance sheet (in millions) is as follows:

Cash and marketable securities	$ 10	Current liabilities	$ 25
		Long-term debt	0
Other current assets	90	Total debt	25
Total current assets	100	Common stock and additional paid-in capital	75
Net long-term assets	200	Retained earnings	200
Total assets	$300	Total liabilities and stockholders' equity	$300

[8] For simplicity, we ignore the buildup to $144.5 million needed by year 4.

All current liabilities are accounts payable and accruals on which no interest is charged. Also, the total book value of Keystone of $300 million is greater than its market value of $200 million. This is not an uncommon occurrence for a no growth firm. Based on this, the current ratio is 4.00 ($100/$25), while the ratio of total debt to total assets is 0.08 ($25/$300).

While Keystone has always avoided long-term debt, or an aggressive working capital strategy, its new chief financial officer believes that both should be investigated, since they should move the firm closer to its target capital structure. The board of directors has agreed and decided that two alternative financing plans should be considered—part common stock and part debt, and all debt.

The First Alternative

The first alternative considered to finance Keystone's capital needs employs both common stock and long-term debt. This involves issuing $50 million in common stock while raising the other $67 million with long-term debt. For simplicity, assume the common stock will sell for $50 per share. Keystone will therefore have to issue 1.0 million ($50 million/$50) additional shares of common stock. The $67 million in long-term debt will be issued at par and carry a coupon interest rate of 10 percent. Keystone's marginal tax rate is 40 percent.

By looking at Table 23.6 we see that this plan, along with the spontaneous growth in current assets and current liabilities, results in $475 million in total assets by year 5, $43 million in current liabilities, $67 million in long-term debt, and $365 million in stockholders' equity.[9] With the common stock/debt plan, Keystone keeps its current ratio at 4.0, while the ratio of total debt to total assets increases from 0.08 to 0.23.

The Second Alternative

The second alternative uses all debt—part short term and the rest long term. As shown in Table 23.6, $25 million in notes payable will be used and "rolled over" when needed, with $92 million in long-term debt employed. This is a substantially more aggressive policy, as shown by the current ratio of 2.53 and the total debt to total asset ratio of 0.34.

Market Value Impact

To complete the analysis, we need to move beyond the cash needs and examine the impact of the two alternative plans on Keystone's market value. First, let's examine the common stock/debt plan. Due to the growth aspects of the capital investments, Keystone estimates its free cash flow will increase to $29 million. As we found out in Chapter 15, introducing debt into a firm's capital structure increases the required rate of return—for Keystone the estimate is that k_s will go from 0.12 to 0.13. With compound growth of 2 percent per year due to the positive NPV nature of the capital investments, Keystone's estimated total common equity value is:

$$S_{common/debt} = \$29 \text{ million}/(0.13 - 0.02) = \$263.636 \text{ million}$$

---

[9] In Table 23.6 the $40 million in internally generated funds is assumed to be equal to the increase in retained earnings.

**Table 23.6 Keystone Industries Projected Balance Sheet (In millions)
for Two Long-Term Plans**

Both plans employ a lot more debt than Keystone currently uses; this increases the risk, but it also increases the required returns.

	Common Stock and Debt		All Debt	
	t_5	Amount of Financing	t_5	Amount of Financing
Item				
Assets				
Cash and marketable securities	$ 17		$ 17	
Other current assets	155		155	
Total current assets	172		172	
Net long-term assets	303		303	
Total assets	$475		$475	
Liabilities and Stockholders' Equity				
Current liabilities	$ 43		$ 68	$ 25
Long-term debt	67	$ 67	92	92
Total debt	110		160	
Common stock and additional paid-in capital	125	50	75	
Retained earnings	240		240	
Total liabilities and stockholders' equity	$475		$475	
Total external financing		$117		$117
Current assets/current liabilities	$172/$43 = 4.00		$172/$68 = 2.53	
Total debt/total assets	$110/$475 = 0.23		$160/$475 = 0.34	

Based on the total number of shares now outstanding of 5 million (4 million original plus 1 million new) Keystone's per share market price is

$P_{common/debt}$ = $263.636 million/5 million shares = $52.73

Thus, we see that by financing the expansion with a combination of debt and equity, Keystone's per share market price is expected to rise from $50 to $52.73.

What about the all-debt plan? Since both short-term debt and additional long-term debt is employed, the risk common stockholders are exposed to increases. This results in a required rate of return of 0.14. With the all-debt financing plan, Keystone has more fixed interest charges resulting in free cash flow of $26 million. Keystone's estimated common equity value is

S_{debt} = $26 million/(0.14 − 0.02) = $216.667 million

Because no additional common stock is issued, Keystone's estimated per share market price is

P_{debt} = $216.667 million/4 million shares = $54.17

Comparing the common stock/debt versus the all-debt plan, we have

	Common Stock/Debt	All Debt
Free cash flow	$29 million	$26 million
Shares of common stock outstanding	5 million	4 million
Total stock value, S	$263.636 million	$216.667 million
Total debt value[10], B	$67.000 million	$117.000 million
Total value of firm, V	$330.636 million	$333.667 million
Market price per share, P_o	$52.73	$54.17
Required return on equity, k_s	13%	14%
Cost of capital,[11] WACC	11.59%	11.19%

Based on these two plans, Keystone should employ all debt. By doing so it creates the most value for its stockholders, and maximizes the value of the firm.

Keystone is now in a position to plan both its capital needs and how it wants to finance them. Over the next 5 years, Keystone will have to raise some $117 million. If Keystone decides to adopt the all-debt approach, that does not mean it will raise all its financing at the same time, or use only one means of financing. It might consider various means for raising debt capital, including both coupon and zero-coupon bonds, term loans, leases, shelf registration, and so forth. The debt could be raised domestically or internationally. In addition, if financial markets are especially favorable, Keystone might use *prefinancing;* it could obtain funds 6 to 12 months before they are expected to be needed. In the interim, the funds will be invested in marketable securities.

Various other plans could also be considered. Whatever the final plan adopted, the important point to remember is that long-term planning forces the firm to consider its goals and needs in advance. By doing so, Keystone can ensure its flexibility while keeping its attention focused on the goal of creating value by maximizing stockholder claims on the firm.

What Remains?

We have only scratched the surface of financial and strategic planning. And since this is a book on financial management, we have focused more on the financial aspects, as opposed to the firm's strategic plans. In practice, both the financial and the strategic aspects must be examined in more detail. The same framework can be employed, since (1) it forces us to consider the creation and destruction of value for the firm; (2) it focuses attention where it should be—on the cash flows, risks, and required returns; and (3) it can be kept simple.

Other areas where planning can be extremely helpful are these:

---

[10] Consistent with Chapter 14, we have not included accounts payable and accruals when figuring the market value of the firm's debt. From a cost standpoint, this implies it pays accounts on time and therefore incurs no direct out-of-pocket cost for the financing provided from these sources.

[11] $\text{WACC}_{\text{common stock/debt}} = \left(\dfrac{\$67.000}{\$330.636} \right)(0.10)(1 - 0.40) + \left(\dfrac{\$263.636}{\$330.636} \right)(0.13) = 1.22 + 10.37 = 11.59$ percent

$\text{WACC}_{\text{debt}} = \left(\dfrac{\$117.000}{\$333.667} \right)(0.10)(1 - 0.40) + \left(\dfrac{\$216.667}{\$333.667} \right)(0.14) = 2.10 + 9.09 = 11.19$ percent

1. PROFIT PLANNING. This focuses attention on the prices we sell our products for, our costs, and the anticipated effects of inflation and disinflation on the firm's future cash flows. Should we raise prices? Should we automate, thereby raising our fixed operating costs while lowering our variable operating costs? What about changing suppliers to ensure greater reliability, quality, or lower prices? Should we revise our production and inventory control procedures by switching to the just-in-time approach? The potential impact of all these actions can best be evaluated by assessing their impact on the firm's future cash flows, the amount of risk involved, and the returns required.

2. CORPORATE STRATEGY. This area focuses on the basic businesses, or lines, we are in. Should we keep or discontinue a product line? What about modernizing, thereby increasing quality, driving our production costs down, and gaining market share? Should we stop making investments in a given line, since it is expected to perform poorly no matter what we do? How about redeploying assets by selling some divisions and moving into other areas? The financial impacts of these and other related questions need to be assessed *before* the decisions are made, not after.

3. THE GROWING FIRM. Growth is a desirable state of affairs for most firms, but it can have important financial and strategic consequences. How long can we continue to grow this fast before competitors enter the field and reduce the profitability of our business? What about economies of scale in research and development, marketing and sales, production, and financing? How much control are we willing to give up by selling more stock? Again, the impacts of all these questions can be examined with the procedures outlined in this chapter.

The important point to remember is this: Financial and strategic planning is an ongoing dynamic process. It must be *flexible, simple, and yet provide a reliable framework* for assessing the estimated impact of all decisions faced by the firm. Otherwise, unintended consequences could result in the destruction, rather than the creation, of value for the firm's stockholders.

Summary

Financial planning and strategy focuses on the anticipated results of actions undertaken by the firm as these actions interact with the effect of external forces. It is a process that stresses analysis, projections, alternatives, and the determination of goals or performance standards. The primary emphasis is on cash flows, divisions or subunits of the firm, scenario analysis, and short- and long-run considerations. The outcome includes cash flow projections, a corporate strategy, the firm's capital budget, and both short- and long-term financial plans.

To develop a plan, the factors that affect the firm's value must be understood. Other things being equal, the following events will increase the value of the firm:

1. An increase in cash inflows
2. A reduction in cash outflows
3. Accepting "good" capital expenditure projects that take advantage of temporary growth opportunities

4. A reduction in risk
5. An increase in the growth rate of expected cash dividends

Many factors both internal and external to the firm can interact to affect one or more of these events. For this reason, managers must understand and assess the possible effects of these factors on the value of the firm.

There is no model or theory that leads directly to the optimum financial and strategic plan. Consequently, the process involves trial and error. In the short run (1 year or less), the emphasis is primarily on the acquisition or investment of short-term funds. In the longer run, which builds on the short run, the procedure is much the same. The emphasis, however, is on the long-term investment, strategy, and financing of the firm. By focusing on the magnitude and timing of the expected cash flows, the risk and value of the firm, and liquidity and flexibility, managers use financial and strategic planning to meet the future needs of the firm.

Questions

23.1 Define or explain the following:

a. Free cash flow
b. Financial plan
c. Prefinancing

23.2 Explain what free cash flow is and how it relates to the firm's cash dividends.

23.3 Other things being equal, how would each of the following affect the value of the firm?

a. By increasing its maintenance costs by $50,000 per year, the firm can increase efficiency and reduce downtime by $80,000 per year.
b. The firm's major product is suddenly challenged by numerous health groups as being a possible cause of cancer.
c. The government institutes a mandatory job program that requires the firm to train and employ the unemployable.
d. The firm is in the forefront of a new major growth development requiring substantial capital investment.
e. The nation solves its economic and employment problems, leading to a significant increase in investor optimism.
f. Inflation is expected to increase dramatically during the next 2 years.

23.4 Why might the constant growth dividend model overestimate the value of the firm's stock, S?

23.5 Discuss the planning process. Be sure to indicate what is emphasized and the expected outcomes.

23.6 Why shouldn't traditional accounting statements form the basis for financial and strategic planning?

23.7 What are the differences between short-run and long-run financial and strategic planning?

23.8 Explain how the firm's decision about financing temporary assets with temporary liabilities relates to planning.

23.9 How would you go about distinguishing *after the fact* between good and bad financial and strategic planning versus good or bad luck?

Self-Test Problems (Solutions appear on pages 739–740.)

Impact on Market Value

ST 23.1 Ryan International has the following values for its base case: expected cash inflow$_1$ = \$5,000, expected cash outflow$_1$ = \$3,000, expected capital investment$_1$ = \$800, k_M = 14 percent, k_{RF} = 9 percent, β = 1.2, and g = 4 percent.

a. Determine the value of Ryan's stock for the base case.

b. Determine its market value under the following conditions (*Note:* Each part is independent of other parts, and variables not specified stay the same as in the base case):

(1) Political risk increases in a number of countries where Ryan is active. The result is that beta increases to 1.6.

(2) The government raises corporate taxes, causing expected cash outflows to increase to \$3,150 and expected capital investment to drop to \$750.

(3) The firm's outflows for pension liabilities increase by \$200 per year.

(4) Foreign competition increases, cutting expected cash inflows to \$4,600.

(5) The industry is mature, causing growth to slow by 2 percent.

(6) The expected rate of inflation drops 2 percent, causing k_{RF} to decrease by 2 percent. Because of increased investor confidence, the expected return on the market portfolio drops by 3 percent. (*Note:* Round k_s to the nearest whole number.)

Short-Term Planning

ST 23.2 Pathfinder United is forecasting its short-term financing needs. For the next 4 quarters, the cash flows are as follows:

	Quarter			
	1	2	3	4
Net cash inflow (+) or outflow (−)	−\$20	−\$30	−\$15	\$40
Calculating Short-Term Financing Needed				
1. Cash and marketable securities at start of period	\$15	−\$ 5	−\$35	−\$50
2. Change in cash balance (net cash inflow or outflow)	− 20	− 30	− 15	40
3. Cash at end of period (1 + 2)	− 5	− 35	− 50	− 10
4. Minimum cash balance required	− 10	− 10	− 10	− 10
5. Cumulative short-term financing needed (−) or surplus (+) (3 + 4)	−\$15	−\$45	−\$60	−\$20

Pathfinder has a line of credit it can draw down to meet this short-term financing need. The interest rate is 4 percent per quarter. The interest incurred one quarter is paid the next quarter and the tax rate is 30 percent.

a. Prepare a table like Table 23.3 that shows Pathfinder United's cash needs and surplus by quarter.

b. How much is still borrowed on the line of credit at the end of quarter 4?

Problems

Impact on Market Value

23.1 El Paso Mexican Products wants to determine its current market value. The expected cash inflow at t_1 = \$750, expected cash outflow at t_1 = \$500, and capital investment at t_1 = \$100. The expected rate of growth in cash dividends is 6 percent. The expected market rate of return is 15 percent, the risk-free rate is 7 percent, and El Paso's beta is 1.5.

a. Determine the value of El Paso's stock for the base case, given the data above.

b. What is the value of El Paso under each of the following? (*Note:* Each part is independent of other parts, and variables not specified stay the same as in the base case.)

(1) The firm is in a mature industry, so that the expected inflow is $600, expected capital investment is $50, and growth is 3 percent.

(2) The firm is faced with a major lawsuit that affects cash outflow and risk. Cash outflow increases to $550 and beta increases to 2.0.

(3) El Paso expects substantial growth, so that cash inflow increases to $800, capital investment increases to $150, and g increases to 9 percent.

(4) An economic downturn is expected that will decrease cash inflow to $675, capital investment to $50, growth to 5 percent, and raise k_M to 17 percent.

(5) The firm has too much debt and is beyond its target capital structure. It issues equity and retires debt, with the consequence that the firm's cost of capital decreases. Capital investment increases to $150, cash inflow increases to $775, and beta decreases to 1.0.

Constant Growth Rate

23.2 Moon's Bay Area Wholesalers has expected cash inflow of $780,000 next year, expected cash outflow of $475,000 and expected capital investment of $80,000.

a. If k_{RF} is 8 percent, k_M is 14 percent, and Moon's beta is 1.15, what is the market's expectation as to the future constant growth rate of cash dividends (that is, what is g) if the current market value of the firm's stock is $2,500,000?

b. Suppose Moon's can undertake a new project requiring an increase in its capital investment in both working capital and long-term assets totaling $75,000. The project will increase Moon's expected cash inflow *by* $90,000 next year and its expected cash outflow *by* $20,000. Also, Moon's common stock beta will drop to 1.05. If the firm's stock value remains at $2,500,000, what is the market's expectations as to the new constant percentage growth rate for Moon's cash dividends?

c. Without attempting to work it out, what can we infer about the NPV of the proposed project in (b)? Should Moon's undertake the project?

Nonconstant Growth

23.3 Victoria Shipping has a current market value, S, of $1.85 million. It is contemplating a major renovation that will depress near-term free cash flow, but help it in the longer term. The projections for the total firm are as follows:

Year	Cash Inflows	Cash Outflows	Capital Investment
1	$500,000	$300,000	$200,000
2	500,000	325,000	200,000
3	525,000	350,000	100,000
4	600,000	350,000	50,000
Beyond year 4 to infinity	7% per year	8% per year	12% per year

Victoria's required rate of return is 13 percent, and its constant growth rate in cash dividends (or free cash flow) after year 4 is 4 percent. By solving for the new market value, S, determine whether Victoria Shipping should embark on the major renovation.

Short-Term Cash Needs and Financing

23.4 Columbia Precision Products has forecast its cash flows for the next year as follows:

	First Quarter	Second Quarter	Third Quarter	Fourth Quarter
Total operating cash inflow	$175	$195	$220	$200
Total operating cash outflow	−120	−140	−180	−120
Other net inflow or outflow	− 50	− 90	− 60	− 30

a. Determine Columbia's net cash inflow or outflow per quarter and its cumulative short-term financing needs by quarter, if its beginning cash balance is $25 and its minimum cash balance is $15.

b. What is the maximum amount of short-term financing needed? In what quarter does it occur?

c. Ignoring any costs of short-term financing, is Columbia as well off at the end of the year as at the beginning?

d. The effective before-tax costs of alternative short-term financing sources are given below. Which one would be chosen? Is there any reason why the cheapest source might not be chosen?

Bank line of credit	16%	Accounts receivable loan	13%
Inventory loan	15	Factoring receivables	18
Stretching payables	20	Commercial paper (six months)	12

Short-Term Financing Costs

23.5 Baltimore Publishing has estimated its *cumulative* short-term financing needs (in millions) for the next 4 quarters as follows:

Quarter			
1	2	3	4
−$20	−$90	−$70	−$60

Two banks have offered to meet Baltimore's short-term needs as follows:

Bank A: $40 million line of credit at 12 percent
Inventory loan at 15 percent for the remainder
Bank B: $25 million line of credit at 10 percent
Inventory loan at 16 percent for the remainder

In both cases the interest incurred one quarter is paid the next, and Baltimore's marginal tax rate is 35 percent. There are no marketable securities available to meet any of the financing needs.

a. Calculate the net cash inflow (+) or outflow (−) per quarter.
b. Prepare a table like Table 23.3 for both alternatives.
c. Which plan is preferable (has the lowest total after-tax interest)?
d. How much is still borrowed under either option at the end of quarter 4?

(Do only if using Pinches Disk.)

e. Assume the banks' terms are now as follows:

Bank A: $30 million line of credit at 10 percent
Inventory loan at 15 percent for the remainder
Bank B: $30 million line of credit at 11 percent
Inventory loan at 14 percent for the remainder

How have your answers to (a), (c), and (d) changed?

f. Now suppose the cumulative short-term financing is

Quarter (in millions)			
1	2	3	4
+$20	−$70	−$90	−$50

(1) What are your answers under the original bank terms for (a), (c), and (d)?
(2) Under the terms in (e)?

Long-Term Needs

23.6 Jamaica Minerals is planning to meet its long-term needs. To arrive at its needs, it has come up with the following estimates:

	Year				
	1	2	3	4	5
Net cash inflow (+) or outflow (−) before short-term financing cash flows	$20	−$15	−$30	−$60	−$10
Short-term financing cash flows	− 3	− 4	− 4	− 6	− 2
Total cash inflow (+) or outflow (−)	$17	−$19	−$34	−$66	−$12

Jamaica's beginning cash balance is $30. The minimum cash balance is $15 in years 1 and 2, $20 in year 3, and $25 in years 4 and 5. Prepare a year-by-year statement to show the maximum amount of long-term financing Jamaica will need.

Capital Structure Proportions

23.7 Tate Systems is completing its long-run planning process. As a part of this, it has estimated the following needs for long-term funds and the amount it expects to provide out of internally generated equity funds:

	Year				
	1	2	3	4	5
Long-term financing needed per period	$5	$20	$15	$30	$43
To be provided by internally generated equity funds per period	− 6	− 7	− 7	− 8	−10
To be raised externally (+) or surplus (−) per period	−$1	$13	$ 8	$22	$33

Tate's present capital structure contains $40 in debt and $60 in common equity. A primary goal when raising long-term capital is to remain as close as possible to this percentage target capital structure. Either long-term debt or common stock can be issued in amounts of $15 each. (*Note:* If it raises too much long-term capital in any period it is okay and those funds are carried forward to the next year, but it cannot have a shortfall. That is, Tate cannot borrow on a short-term basis to cover any shortfall in long-term capital.)

a. Determine in which years Tate needs to secure additional long-term financing.
b. Indicate, by year, whether long-term debt or common stock should be issued. (Remember that the additional internally generated funds each year are added to the firm's equity base.)
c. What is the resulting capital structure at the end of year 5 and the ratio of total debt to total assets?

Stock Buyback Versus Redeployment: Mini Case

23.8 Heaton Fabrics is a no growth firm that just sold off one of its divisions for $300 million, after tax. The division was viewed as a zero-NPV operation, at best. Heaton's required rate of return is 10 percent. At the present time a raging debate is going on concerning what to do with the cash from the sale.

One group of Heaton's board of directors favors a buyback of shares of the firm's common stock. Their arguments are twofold. First, since part of the firm was sold, and it is owned by the common stockholders, this group believes the proceeds should be returned to the firm's owners. The cheapest way to do this is through a buyback. Second, by buying some of the stock back the firm's future obligations for cash dividends will be reduced, thereby alleviating the future need to raise funds. In support of their argument, the buyback proponents note the following:

1. The firm has $200 million in debt outstanding. There are 20 million shares of common stock outstanding and it is selling for about $60 per share. By paying a slight premium ($62.50 a share), the $300 million could be used to buy back 4.8 million [($62.50)(4,800,000 shares) = $300 million] shares of common stock.
2. The firm pays cash dividends of $6 per share, or $120 million in total. By retiring 4.8 million shares future cash dividends will drop *by* $28.8 million per year.

3. The firm's projected cumulative financing needs (just to maintain their position) for the next few years are as follows (in millions):

	Year				
	1	2	3	4	5
Cumulative financing needed (−)	−$15	−$50	−$100	−$125	−$145

By eliminating the future cash dividend requirements on the 4.8 million shares retired, Heaton Fabrics will not have to raise any long-term financing.

Another group on the board of directors favors taking the $300 million and using it, along with some additional funds, and moving into "magic velvet"—a new area that has both higher risks, but higher expected growth. In support of their position the redeployment proponents note the following:

1. Unless the funds are reinvested in the firm, the firm is actually shrinking away; that is bad for the morale of employees, customers, and the board. None of these board members want to be associated with a dying firm, and will resign if their position is not adopted.
2. To fund magic velvet, the $300 million will be needed, along with another $100 to $150 million. To meet these needs, as well as provide for the additional cumulative financing needs of $100 million over the next 3 years (from item 3 above), cash dividends will be cut to $45 million for the next 3 years.
3. In year 4 the dividends will be restated to $120 million *plus* any growth expected. [*Note:* $D_4 = D_3(1 + g) = \$120$ million$(1 + g)$.] The best estimates of the constant growth (to infinity) expected after year 3 are as follows:

Growth	Probability of Occurrence
8%	0.60
6	0.40

Due to the high-risk nature of magic velvet, the required rate of return for the firm could be as follows:

k_s	Probability of Occurrence
13%	0.40
17	0.60

Due to the intense feeling developing on the board, you have been hired to analyze the situation and make your recommendation. In making your recommendation you should focus on both an analysis of the data given, as well as other nonquantifiable factors. To accomplish this, you have decided to proceed as follows:

a. Determine what the effect of the stock retirement would be on the equity value of the firm, S.
   (1) As a first approximation you have decided to keep k_s at 10 percent. But you also need to consider whether, and in what direction, it might change.
   (2) Also, would the firm be better off paying out the same total cash dividends in the future, versus using the savings to meet future cumulative cash needs?
b. Determine what the effect of the asset redeployment would be on the equity value of the firm, S.
   (1) To do this, you first decide to look at the four possible combinations of growth, g, and required return, k_s.
   (2) Then you need to look at the expected outcome, which is an average of the four possible outcomes weighted by their joint probabilities of occurrence.

Based on your analysis, what is your recommendation? (*Note:* There is not a single precise answer to this problem.)

References

For some interesting examples of the effects of alternative financial strategies, see

ARZAC, ENRIQUE R. "Do Your Business Units Create Shareholder Value?" *Harvard Business Review* 64 (January–February 1986), pp. 121–126.

COOPER, KERRY, AND R. MALCOLM RICHARDS. "Investing the Alaskan Project Cash Flows: The Sohio Experience." *Financial Management* 17 (Summer 1988), pp. 58–70.

CORNELL, BRADFORD, AND ALAN C. SHAPIRO. "Financing Corporate Growth." *Journal of Applied Corporate Finance* 1 (Summer 1988), pp. 6–22.

DONALDSON, GORDON. "Financial Goals and Strategic Consequences." *Harvard Business Review* 63 (May–June 1985), pp. 56–66.

FRUHAN, WILLIAM E., JR. *Financial Strategy: Studies in the Creation, Transfer, and Destruction of Shareholder Value.* Homewood, Ill.: Irwin, 1979.

HARRINGTON, DIANA R. "Stock Prices, Beta, and Strategic Planning." *Harvard Business Review* 83 (May–June 1983), pp. 157–164.

MCINNES, J. MORRIS, AND WILLARD T. CARLETON. "Theory, Models and Implementation in Financial Management." *Management Science* 28 (September 1982), pp. 957–978.

MICHEL, ALLEN, AND ISRAEL SHAKED. "Airline Performance Under Deregulation: The Shareholders' Perspective." *Financial Management* 13 (Summer 1984), pp. 5–14.

MYERS, STEWART C. "Finance Theory and Financial Strategy." *Midland Corporate Finance Journal* 5 (Spring 1987), pp. 6–13.

24

International Financial Management

Overview

- A key difference in international financial management relates to exchange rates between currencies.

- Hedging can be employed to minimize losses due to unfavorable exchange rate fluctuations.

- Capital budgeting decisions should be based on the cash flows after considering

- all taxes and the ability to remit funds to the parent.

- The goal remains to maximize the value of the firm by focusing on the magnitude and timing of cash flows, the risks incurred, and the returns required.

Many firms around the world are concerned about the coming plans for integration in the European Community in 1992. With a more protectionist attitude and a freer flow of goods and services within the 12 member countries of the Common Market, perhaps an acquisition of a firm in one of those countries should be made. But now the Common Market is formulating a set of truly European merger rules and policies. The result would be to give the European Community's Competition Directorate a mandate to concentrate on larger cross-border mergers, leaving smaller deals to the national governments.

On the other side of the world, W. R. Grace, Minnesota Mining & Manufacturing, and Hilton International have all made investments in China. Unlike many firms, these three decided to enter the arena without a Chinese partner. Without a partner, it can be difficult to maneuver through the bureaucracy, or develop connections with government agencies. But investing alone permits greater freedom in decision making, hiring and firing employees, and duplicating home-office operating standards.

International business and financial activities affect all of us. Whether it's an insider-trading scandal in Japan, political maneuvering in Italy that may ruin AT&T's chances for a major contract, economic reform in Mexico, or *the acquisition by Federal Express of Tiger International, all have their impact on us.*

Firms, even those that invest and raise capital only in North America, are not isolated from international considerations. Whether it's foreign firms competing with them or international factors that cause the costs of financing to change, all businesses must be aware of the impact of international aspects on their business. Failure to do so exposes the firm to additional risks and puts it at a competitive disadvantage.

Foreign Exchange

Thus far we have talked principally about doing business in the United States. But many firms have significant foreign operations. The essential elements of international financial management are exactly as we have discussed for U.S. based firms. That is, we want to maximize the value of the firm by focusing on the after-tax cash flows, the risk, and the required returns. Thus, we come back to maximizing the size of the pie—this time by focusing our attention on those activities outside the United States. In applying the basic concepts we have discussed previously, we come up with some additional problems that have not been faced before.

The unique feature of international financial management is that we need to deal with more than one currency. Therefore, we need to look at how foreign exchange markets operate, why exchange rates change, and how we can attempt to protect ourselves against exchange rate risks. Then we consider the topic of making investment decisions in an international context. How do international companies make their capital budgeting decisions? How do they estimate the cash flows to use? How do they choose the required rate of return? Then we will briefly comment on other areas of international financial management by indicating where in the book certain topics are covered. We will see that the essential elements of financial management apply to the international section, but there are some additional pitfalls to watch out for.

A fundamental difference between international and domestic financial management is that international transactions are conducted in more than one currency. The dollar is used in the United States, the franc in France, the rupee in India, the yen in Japan, and the peso in Mexico. *Foreign exchange rates* are the conversion rates between currencies. They depend on the relative supply and demand for two currencies, inflation in the countries, and other factors. The exchange rate between the U.S. dollar and several other currencies in early 1989 is shown in Table 24.1.

Until the early 1970s, the world was on a fixed exchange rate system. Since 1973, it has operated on a "managed" floating system. Major world currencies move (or float) freely with market forces. Nevertheless, the central banks of countries intervene by buying or selling in the foreign exchange market to smooth out some of the fluctuations. Each central bank also attempts to keep its exchange rates within prescribed government limits to help the country's export or import situation. Floating exchange rates are a fact of life with which all managers must be prepared to cope.

Table 24.1 Selected Foreign Exchange Rates, February 16, 1989

Exchange rates can be stated two different ways; however, conversion from one to the other is straightforward. Exchange rates may change on a daily basis as conditions change in either of the countries, or as events throughout the world influence the rates. (SOURCE: Wall Street Journal, *February 17, 1989, p. C10.*)

Country	Currency	U.S. Dollars Required to Buy One Unit (1)	Number of Units of Foreign Currency per U.S. Dollar* (2)
Austria	schilling	0.07733	12.93
Britain	pound	1.7708	0.5647
Canada	dollar	0.8430	1.1862
France	franc	0.1592	6.2800
Hong Kong	dollar	0.128188	7.8010
India	rupee	0.0656598	15.23
Japan	yen	0.007929	126.11
Saudia Arabia	riyal	0.2666	3.7505
Venezuela	bolivar	0.02684	37.25
West Germany	mark	0.5441	1.8377

* Column 2 equals 1.0 divided by column 1.

Spot and Forward Rates

The exchange rates shown in Table 24.1 are called *spot rates,* which means the price paid for delivery of the currency today. In addition to spot rates there are also *forward rates.* These arise when the purchaser contracts to take delivery of the foreign currency some time in the future, but the rate of exchange is agreed upon today. Spot and forward rates for the British pound and Japanese yen in relation to the U.S. dollar on February 16, 1989, in the *Wall Street Journal* were as follows:

	U.S. Dollars Required to Buy One Unit	
Rate	British Pound	Japanese Yen
Spot	1.7708	0.007929
30-day forward	1.7663	0.007957
90-day forward	1.7576	0.008030
180-day forward	1.7471	0.008137

When the forward rate is above the current spot rate, the forward rate is said to be at a premium. When the forward rate is below the current spot rate, a discount exists. Examining these data, we see that the Japanese yen forward rate shows a premium over the spot rate, whereas the British pound forward rate is at a discount. Why is this so? Many factors affect the relationship, and this area becomes complicated fast, but a primary factor is the expected rate of inflation in the two countries. Other things being equal, a foreign currency will appreciate in relation to the U.S. dollar (i.e., its forward rate will increase) at a percentage rate approximately equaling the amount by which inflation in the United States exceeds the rate of inflation in the foreign country.[1] Conversely, a foreign currency will depreciate relative to the

---

[1] This relationship, which suggests that the price level of goods must be the same in two countries, is called the purchasing power parity, or the law of one price.

Financial Management Today

Top Companies and Countries

The largest companies in the world in 1988 covered a number of countries. In terms of sales, profits, and especially market values, however, Japanese firms topped the list.

Sales*		Profits*		Market Value*	
C. Itoh	$118.0	IBM	$5.26	Nippon T&T	$295.7
Mitsu	113.3	Exxon	4.84	Sumitomo	68.8
Marubeni	105.9	Royal Dutch/Shell	4.74	IBM	67.5
Sumitomo	104.4	Ford Motor	4.63	Dai-Ichi Kangyo	63.2
General Motors	101.8	General Motors	3.55	Fuji	62.8
Mitsubishi	101.2	British Petroleum	2.56	Exxon	61.9
Exxon	82.1	British Telecom	2.32	Tokyo Electric	61.5
Royal Dutch/Shell	78.3	Nomura Securities	2.17	Nomura Securities	56.1
Ford Motor	71.6	General Electric	2.12	Industrial Bank of Japan	55.9
Nissho Iwai	61.5	Toyota Motor	2.09	Mitsubishi	55.8
Mobil	56.7	AT&T	2.04	Sanwa	51.4
IBM	54.2	Fiat	1.85	Royal Dutch/Shell	51.3
Toyota Motor	53.4	Philip Morris	1.84	Toyota Motor	48.0
British Petroleum	50.8	du Pont	1.79	General Electric	38.2
Sears, Roebuck	48.4	Bellsouth	1.66	Matsushita Electric	37.4

* Billions of U.S. dollars.

In terms of overall stock market value we see the Japanese were also ahead:

Country	Billions of U.S. Dollars	Price Earnings (P/E)
Japan	$2,721	94
United States	1,708	22
Britain	466	13
West Germany	147	23
Canada	102	15
France	74	13
Switzerland	73	23
Italy	62	21
Netherlands	59	10
Australia	58	15

While Japanese companies have the highest market value, that's not surprising given their price/earnings ratio is four to six times higher than P/E ratios in other countries. This reflects both the robustness of the Japanese market and the fact that Japanese shares are traditionally higher priced than those in other parts of the world.

Source: "Who's Sitting on Top of the World?" *Business Week,* July 18, 1988.

U.S. dollar by approximately the rate at which that country's inflation exceeds the rate in the United States. Looking at the spot and forward rates above, we see that expected inflation rates in Britain were higher than in the United States, since the British pound was depreciating relative to the U.S. dollar. Conversely, expected inflation in Japan was lower than in the United States, as shown by the premium in the forward over the spot rate for the yen.

Hedging

Since exchange rates change continuously, that is, day-by-day, financial managers must deal with them directly. For example, assume an American exporter bills a customer in a foreign currency. The exporter has taken a risk since the exchange rate may change before the bill can be paid. Most of this exchange rate risk can be hedged. There are two basic ways of *hedging*. The first is through the use of the forward market, while the second involves the currency options market.

Forward Market Hedge

Consider a simple example. Suppose our U.S. exporter sells machinery to a French firm with the payment of 2 million francs due in 3 months. The payment will be made in francs. At the same time, assume the 3-month forward rate of exchange between the franc and the dollar is 6.25 francs for every dollar. An exporter who expects the receipt of this amount could hedge as follows; sell 3-month francs forward to lock in the dollar value of the francs. The amount it will net, after transactions cost, in 3 months is (2 million francs)(1/6.25) = $320,000. Once the rate is fixed in this way the exchange risk of the transaction is said to be *covered*. The exporter no longer stands to gain or lose as a result of subsequent changes in the foreign exchange rate. If the exporter does not cover the risk, he or she is said to have an *open* (or uncovered) position in the foreign currency.

Let's see what might happen if the risk is not hedged. Assume the actual rate of exchange in 3 months is 6.4 francs for 1 dollar. Then the net amount received by the exporter is (2 million)(1/6.4) = $312,500. We see that by not hedging, the exporter ended up losing $7,500 ($320,000 − $312,500) on the transaction. On the other hand, if the actual exchange rate is 6 francs for each dollar, in 3 months the amount received is ($2 million)(1/6) = $333,333.

The key point to remember from this example is that, by hedging, an exporter can take most of the risk out of the transaction. If exchange rates become more favorable the exporter suffers some loss or regret because the hedge was not needed; however, if exchange rates move against the exporter, he or she benefits. The possibility of actual exchange rates moving in either direction needs to be kept constantly in mind when considering the use of any kind of hedge.

Currency Options Market Hedge

The currency options market operates in a manner similar to the foreign exchange market, except it allows the firm the choice of exercising the option or letting it expire. Currency options are similar to insurance against downside risk that may be obtained by paying a fee. For example, if our U.S. firm expected to receive payment in francs in 3 months, it may wish to buy a put option. (*Remember:* Put options—as discussed in Chapter 11—give the holder the right to sell the currency at a given rate, while call options give the holder the right to buy the currency at a given rate.) In 3 months, if the spot exchange rate is less than the exchange rate specified in the option the exporter would exercise the option to convert. Conversely, if the spot rate in 3 months is greater than the exchange rate specified in the option the exporter would allow the option to expire.

Other

Perfect hedges are not obtainable because there are always some inefficiencies and uncertainties involved. The use of hedges, however, can take much of the risk out of international transactions. In addition to the two methods of hedging, there are numerous other ways of dealing with exchange rate fluctuations:

1. INVOICE IN THE HOME CURRENCY. This involves billing in U.S. dollars; now the customer bears the risk.
2. SELL THE RECEIVABLE. Instead of holding it, the exporter could sell the receivable.
3. LEADING AND LAGGING. Paying earlier or later depending on the strength or weakness of the two securities.
4. CENTRALIZED MANAGEMENT. This involves coordinating all of a firm's transactions in numerous countries, and only settling up, or hedging, the next exposure.
5. BORROWING ABROAD. Firms with investments abroad often try to borrow in the same currency in order to match assets and liabilities.

All of these, and other, techniques are employed by firms to protect themselves against the effects of exchange rate risk.

International Capital Budgeting

We have examined how capital budgeting decisions are made for firms in the United States. When investments are made in other countries, the basic steps are the same; that is, we identify the relevant incremental cash flows, determine the required rate of return, and accept all projects with positive net present values. While the steps are the same, there are some additional elements to consider. These revolve primarily around exchange rates, taxes, and the ability to repatriate (or bring back) funds to the parent company.

The Net Present Value

Assume a firm's export business has risen to the point that it is worth establishing a subsidiary in West Germany. Ignoring certain complications for a minute, there are two basic ways to calculate the net present value, NPV, of its West German venture:

1. The project's NPV can be evaluated entirely in terms of the West German mark. Then this figure can be converted into dollars at the current exchange rate.
2. A company could estimate the West German mark cash flows on a per year basis and convert these into dollars at the expected exchange rate. These dollar cash flows can then be discounted at a dollar-based required rate of return to give the investment's NPV in dollars.

To examine both approaches, assume the cash flows, CFs, in marks are as follows:

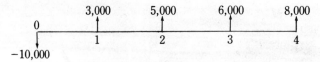

The appropriate U.S. required rate of return, k, on this project is 18 percent and the risk-free rate, k_{RF}, is 9 percent. The 9 percent is obtained simply by looking in the newspaper for the rate on U.S. Treasury bills. Likewise, assume the risk-free rate in West Germany is 6 percent. The following relationship holds between nominal interest rates and any required rate of return:

$$1 + \text{required return} = (1 + \text{nominal interest rate})(1 + \text{risk premium}) \qquad (24.1)$$

Since we know the required return is 18 percent and the nominal interest rate in the U.S. is 9 percent, we can use Equation 24.1 to solve for the risk premium as follows:

$$1 + \text{risk premium} = (1 + \text{required return})/(1 + \text{nominal interest rate})$$
$$= 1.18/1.09 = 1.0826$$

Thus, we have determined the risk premium required, in U.S. dollars, is 8.26 percent above the risk-free rate.

Using this information, and knowing the nominal interest rate in West Germany is 6 percent, we can employ Equation 24.1 to determine the required rate of return in West German marks as follows:

$$1 + \text{required return} = (1 + \text{nominal interest rate})(1 + \text{risk premium})$$
$$= (1.06)(1.0826) = 1.1476$$

So, the appropriate discount rate, or required return, in marks is 14.76 percent.

To use the first method we discount the West German mark cash flows by the West German mark required rate of return as follows:[2]

$$NPV = \frac{CF_1}{(1+k)} + \frac{CF_2}{(1+k)^2} + \frac{CF_3}{(1+k)^3} + \frac{CF_4}{(1+k)^4} - CF_0$$

$$= \frac{3{,}000}{(1.1476)} + \frac{5{,}000}{(1.1476)^2} + \frac{6{,}000}{(1.1476)^3} + \frac{8{,}000}{(1.1476)^4} - 10{,}000 = 4{,}993 \text{ marks}$$

If the spot rate is 1.5 marks to the dollar, we can now convert to dollars at the spot rate so that:

NPV in dollars = 4,993/1.5 = $3,329

Thus, since the NPV is greater than zero, we would accept the project.

Instead of using the first method, we can convert the West German mark cash flows into U.S. dollars before discounting. To do this we need to forecast what the exchange rates will be in the future. Rather than attempting to predict future exchange rates directly, it is generally preferable to assume markets are reasonably efficient, and that the *current difference* between the U.S. and West German interest rates

---

[2] Because the discount rate is not an even percent, we cannot use the $PV_{k,n}$ table in determining the NPV.

reflects the likely difference in future inflation rates. With the U.S. risk-free rate at 9 percent and the West German risk-free rate at 6 percent, we see there is a 3 percent difference in nominal interest rates. Let's assume the real interest rate is estimated to be approximately 2 percent and it is the same in West Germany as in the United States.[3] That means that *expected* inflation is approximately 7 percent $(9 - 2)$ in the United States, while it is approximately 4 percent $(6 - 2)$ in West Germany.

We said the current spot rate was 1.5 West German marks to the dollar. But since the expected inflation rate in West Germany is somewhat lower than in the United States, the mark is expected to appreciate against the dollar as follows:

$$\begin{pmatrix} \text{expected spot rate} \\ \text{at end of year 1} \end{pmatrix} = \begin{pmatrix} \text{spot rate at} \\ \text{start of year} \end{pmatrix}\begin{pmatrix} \text{inflation rate} \\ \text{differential} \end{pmatrix} \tag{24.2}$$

$$= (1.50)\left(\frac{1.04}{1.07}\right) = 1.458 \text{ marks per dollar}$$

At the end of year 2 the expected rate of exchange would be:

$$= (1.50)\left(\frac{1.04^2}{1.07^2}\right) = 1.417$$

The expected rates of exchange for years 3 and 4 are calculated in a similar manner. The forecasted cash flows and expected exchange rates are then:

	Year				
	0	**1**	**2**	**3**	**4**
1. Cash flow in marks, CF	−10,000	3,000	5,000	6,000	8,000
2. Forecasted spot exchange rate	1.500	1.458	1.417	1.377	1.339
3. Cash flow in dollars, CF (1/2)	−6,667	2,058	3,529	4,357	5,975

Because we have converted these cash flows into dollars, we use the dollar-denominated required rate of return of 18 percent to calculate the net present value as follows:

$$\begin{aligned} \text{NPV} = \ &\$2,058(PV_{18\%,1\text{yr}}) + \$3,529(PV_{18\%,2\text{yr}}) + \$4,357(PV_{18\%,3\text{yr}}) \\ &+ \$5,975(PV_{18\%,4\text{yr}}) - \$6,667 \end{aligned}$$

$$\begin{aligned} = \ &\$2,058(0.847) + \$3,529(0.718) + \$4,357(0.609) + \$5,975(0.516) \\ &- \$6,667 = \$10,013 - \$6,667 = \$3,346 \end{aligned}$$

Except for a rounding difference of $17 (i.e., $3,346 − $3,329), we see that both methods provide us with the same net present value. Therefore, it appears that either one can be used.

Unremitted Funds

So far we have assumed all cash flows can be remitted (or brought) back to the parent company. The ability to remit funds is not as easy as we have assumed. A foreign subsidiary can remit funds to a parent in many ways including the following: (1) dividends; (2) management fees; (3) interest and principal payments on debt; and (4) royalties on the use of trade names and patents. This topic becomes complex

---

[3] Both nominal and real interest rates were discussed in Chapter 2. The nominal interest rate = real rate of interest + expected inflation.

quickly, and many differences occur in different countries. Firms must pay special attention to remittance for two reasons. First, there may be current and/or future exchange controls. Many governments are sensitive to the charge of being exploited by foreign firms. They have therefore attempted to limit the ability of international firms to take funds out of the host country. The second reason is taxes. Not only do taxes have to be paid in the foreign country, the amount of taxes paid on funds remitted to the United States depends on whether it is a management fee, a royalty, a dividend, or simply the payment of interest or principal.

To illustrate some of the complexity, we will employ the second method (which is typically employed in practice) by converting all cash flows to dollars and then discounting at the dollar required rate of return of 18 percent. Assume West Germany has a corporate tax rate of 30 percent, and it also withholds taxes on funds transferred out of the country at 5 percent. The withholding tax is not really "withheld" since it is never returned to the payer. In Table 24.2 we show the same initial cash flows in West German marks as before, but *this time we assume they are before taxes.* Taking into account the West German corporate taxes and the taxes withheld on remitted funds, line 5 provides the remitted cash flows in West German marks. Then in line 8 we show the impact of U.S. taxes, followed in line 9 by the credit for taxes paid in West Germany. (See "International Tax Considerations" in Chapter 2 for additional discussion on taxes and tax credits.) Finally, in line 10 the after-tax flows, CFs, in dollars are shown. The NPV is then

$$NPV = \$1,510(\,0.847\,) + \$2,590(\,0.718\,) + \$3,199(\,0.609\,) + \$4,385(\,0.516\,)$$
$$- \$6,667 = \$7,349 - \$6,667 = \$682$$

Since the NPV is positive, the project would still be accepted.

This example is representative of some of the issues involved in determining the proper after-tax cash flows that the parent evaluates in an international capital budgeting decision. In practice the issue becomes more complex depending on taxes, and how the funds can be brought out of the host country in order to channel them to the parent. These complications make the determination of the after-tax cash flows stream for international capital budgeting decisions even more challenging than for domestic capital budgeting projects.

The Required Rate of Return

When discussing capital budgeting decisions for domestic firms we indicated the stand alone principle should apply. That is, the project should stand alone in terms of cash flows, and the discount rate used to apply to those cash flows should signify the amount of risk related to the cash flows. An important question for firms with international capital investments is whether the required rate of return, k, should be different from that for similar risk domestic projects. The answer to that question depends on two items. First, are international financial markets segmented? Second, what are the expropriation and creditor risks?

While investors in both the United States and overseas are beginning to view the whole world as their investment vehicle, available evidence indicates that shareholders do not typically diversify around the world. This means there is a certain amount of international segmentation taking place. Some estimates indicate that American investors are suffering a lower return by restricting their investments to firms in the United States as opposed to investing directly overseas. If this is true, that is

Table 24.2   After-Tax Cash Flows Remitted to Parent After West German and U.S. Taxes

Because of restrictions on how funds are brought out of the host country and taxes, cash flows in the parent countries' currency are required in order to make effective capital budgeting decisions.

	Year				
	0	1	2	3	4
1. Cash flow before taxes, in marks	−10,000	3,000	5,000	6,000	8,000
2. West German corporate tax at 30% (1 × 0.30)		−900	−1,500	−1,800	−2,400
3. Cash flow available for remittance to parent (1 − 2)		2,100	3,500	4,200	5,600
4. Tax withheld at 5% (3 × 0.05)		−105	−175	−210	−280
5. Remittance after West German taxes, in marks (3 − 4)		1,995	3,325	3,990	5,320
6. Forecasted spot exchange rate	1.500	1.458	1.417	1.377	1.339
7. Remittance received by parent, in dollars (5/6)	−6,667	1,368	2,347	2,898	3,973
8. U.S. corporate tax at 40% (7 × 0.40)		−547	−939	−1,159	−1,589
9. Foreign tax credit [(2 + 4)/6]		+689	+1,182	+1,460	+2,001
10. Cash flow in dollars, CF (7 + 8 + 9)	−6,667	1,510	2,590	3,199	4,385

Americans are willing to accept two to four points less by restricting their investments largely to U.S. firms, then we should see American firms being able to acquire capital somewhat more cheaply overseas. Therefore, the required rate of return for international capital projects would be lower than for a similar project here in the United States.

This potential advantage of raising capital and investing overseas may be offset because of the increased possibility of expropriation (of part or all of the firm's investment in a foreign subsidiary). We view expropriation broadly to include not only pure nationalization, but lesser forms such as increased ownership by the host country. In either case, the parent loses part or all of its investment or claim on cash flows from its subsidiary. Expropriation may be gradual, with an increase in demand for participation by locals or the host government in the ownership of the business. Initially, it may take the form of a high tax, or the right to buy the equity of the firm at some price. Often this price is extremely low relative to the market-determined worth of the subsidiary. A more dramatic form of expropriation is that suffered by some American firms with investments in Iran.

Firms can use various strategies in attempting to minimize the risk of expropriation. Generally, these fall into two categories. The first involves positive approaches, such as joint ventures, local participation, prior agreements for sale, and the like. All are designed to foster a positive long-term relationship. The second involves limiting the investment of the parent, or controlling the raw material, production, or sales process so the subsidiaries' success is fully dependent on the parent.

It should also be noted that default risk is often more serious than in the United States. Since bankruptcy laws similar to those in the United States often do not exist, creditors have little recourse to recoup losses. This factor must also be considered when firms make capital budgeting decisions and then market the goods produced in other countries.

If increased expropriation and/or creditor risk is present, this would offset, in part or total, any reduced required return from investing overseas. The net result is that the required rate of return may be the same, lower, or higher, for an international capital budgeting project. It all depends on the project itself, and the country where the investment is made. We know of no general guidelines that hold up across countries, except to know the territory, and evaluate all possible legal, tax, and political ramifications.

International Financing and Operating Decisions

Once a firm decides to invest in a foreign project, additional considerations are involved. The primary ones relate to financing the venture, and operating and reporting for the venture.

Financing Decisions

In raising capital and undertaking capital projects in other countries, the host company typically invests a relatively modest amount in equity capital and then raises the rest of the funds in some other manner. Three methods basically available for securing the majority of the funds are (1) to raise them at home and export them, (2) to raise cash by borrowing in a foreign country, or (3) to borrow wherever interest rates are cheapest.

If the U.S. firm raises cash by borrowing in the United States, it has an exchange rate risk. This has to be taken into account. An alternative is to borrow in the country where the foreign project is located. In this manner the firm receives a direct hedge against exchange rate fluctuations because they are borrowing in the same currency where the investment has been made. The final alternative is to finance where interest rates are cheapest. Again, one has to look at exchange rate risk between where the financing is done and the U.S. parent.

While each decision must take into account the specifics of the country, current and prospective international conditions, the length of financing needed, and the particular project, it is often best to use some combination of funds raised in the host country along with some provided in U.S. dollars. In raising short- and long-term funds the basic elements discussed in the "International Financing" section in Chapter 13, the "Eurodollar Loans" section in Chapter 21, and the "International Capital Structure Issues" section in Chapter 15 apply. Often funds raised in other countries are tied to LIBOR (London Interbank Offered Rate), which is the international equivalent of the prime rate used in the United States.

Operating and Accounting Aspects

Once the foreign subsidiary is up and running, the operation of it and the accounting for it become important. The essential elements of transferring funds and selling across borders were covered in the "International Cash Management" section in Chapter 19 and "International Purchases or Sales" section in Chapter 20. Finally, there are accounting considerations, since the functional currency, as discussed in the "International Accounting Aspects" section in Chapter 3, can be either the host country's currency or the U.S. dollar. Depending on which is selected, this can have a direct impact on the U.S. parent's year-by-year accounting statements. While these effects do not flow through the income statement, they do impact the balance sheet and can affect the level of assets and liabilities reported on a firm's financial statements.

Dividends in Japan

In the United States and most of the Western world, firms pay out 50 to 60 percent of their earnings in the form of cash dividends. A recent study of Japanese companies, however, shows they pay out only 30 percent of their firms' earnings in the form of cash dividends.[1] In addition, Japanese firms report lower earnings than do Western firms—presumably due to expensing more investments, faster write offs, and so forth. Even with lower earnings, a far lower percent is paid out in dividends to shareholders.

Japanese dividend policy can be explained largely in terms of their tax laws (since capital gains are not taxed), and the view that the obligation of the shareholder is met by a reasonable dividend with the balance of the funds being retained on behalf of other stakeholders in the company—its employees, suppliers, customers, and others who are concerned with the firms' well being and continued strength.

Dividend policy alone cannot explain why the Japanese are so successful, because they also use more debt and have a lower cost of capital. It does appear, however, to offer a partial explanation concerning Japanese firms. With the reluctance of Western firms to raise much external equity capital, the higher payouts by Western firms mean they have less to invest in terms of capital expenditures and research and development projects. For Western firms, assuming they have growth prospects and competitive pressures, the question may be why should they pay out 50 to 60 percent of earnings in the form of cash dividends?

[1] James C. Abegglen. "The Poor Japanese Shareholder." *Tokyo Business Today* (November 1988).

Summary

The fundamental difference between international and domestic financial management decisions is the introduction of foreign exchange fluctuations. Foreign exchange impacts all decisions; therefore, some understanding of the difference between spot and forward rates is essential.

In making investment decisions in an international context two methods can be employed that lead to the same NPV, provided there are no major tax and other implications. Once taxes and questions of how to remit the funds to the United States are considered, however, then the cash flow stream is directly affected. For this reason cash flows are typically converted into the currency of the parent companies' country before capital budgeting decisions are made. In addition, the required rate of return for a project may be the same, less, or more in a foreign country than in the United States. The net effect is that the required return, and/or the cash flows need to be adjusted to reflect any difference in risk as compared with a similar domestic capital budgeting project.

In financing projects overseas there are three choices of where to raise funds: in the U.S., in the host country, or in another country where interest rates are cheapest. The actual choice depends on the specifics of the situation. Operating and accounting considerations also must be taken into consideration when firms deal in the international arena. Thus, while the essential elements of financial management remain the same—that is, to maximize the value of the firm by focusing on the magnitude and timing of the cash flows, the risks incurred, and the returns required—additional complications must be dealt with in international financial management.

Questions

24.1 Define or explain the following:

a. Foreign exchange rate
b. Spot rate
c. Forward rate
d. Hedging
e. Covered
f. Open

24.2 Explain the difference between spot and forward exchange rates.

24.3 The average exchange rate (in terms of the number of U.S. dollars required to buy one unit) in year 1 and year 2 for three countries was

	Year 1	Year 2
Mexico (peso)	0.044	0.014
Singapore (dollar)	1.030	1.330
Belgium (franc)	0.596	0.492

What can you conclude about the worth of the U.S. dollar vis-à-vis the currencies of these other countries in year 1 and in year 2? What about the expected rate of inflation in these countries compared to the expected rate of inflation in the United States?

24.4 What alternative methods are available for hedging exchange rate risk? How are they similar? Different?

24.5 What two general methods are available for determining the NPV for an international capital budgeting project? Why is one method generally used more than the other?

24.6 How can we estimate future exchange rates by using presently available data and assuming the market is efficient?

24.7 Explain how foreign exchange risk, repatriation of funds, expropriation risk, and credit risk all influence international capital budgeting decisions.

24.8 What factors influence the required rate of return used when international capital budgeting decisions are made? What conclusions can be reached?

Self-Test Problems   (Solutions appear on pages 740–741.)

Different Currencies   ST 24.1 The current spot rate for the Israel shekel is 1.817 shekels to the U.S. dollar, while it is 7.15 Chinese yuan to the U.S. dollar. What is the spot rate of exchange between the shekel and the yuan?

ST 24.2 The expected cash flows in pounds from an investment in Britain are as follows:

	100,000	125,000	150,000	150,000
0				
	1	2	3	4
200,000				

Taxes in Britain have already been taken into account. The U.S. required rate of return, k, is 16 percent, the U.S. corporate tax rate is 35 percent, and the current spot rate is 0.560 pounds to the dollar. The U.S. risk-free rate is 8 percent, while it is 11 percent in Britain, and the real rate of interest is 2 percent in both countries.

a. Determine the expected spot rate of exchange for the next four years between the pound and the dollar.

b. What are the after-tax cash flows in dollars? (*Note:* Ignore any foreign tax credits.)

c. Should the project be undertaken?

Problems

24.1 Spot and forward rates for Canada and Switzerland relative to the U.S. dollar are:

	U.S.Dollars Required to Buy One Unit	
Rate	**Canadian Dollar**	**Swiss Franc**
Spot	0.848	0.640
30-day forward	0.846	0.642
90-day forward	0.843	0.646
180-day forward	0.839	0.652

a. What can we say about the expected rate of inflation in both countries relative to the expected rate of inflation in the United States?

b. How about the expected rate of inflation in Canada relative to the expected rate of inflation in Switzerland?

24.2 If the British pound has a spot rate of 1.771 U.S. dollars per pound while the West German mark has a spot rate of 0.544 dollars per West German mark, what is the spot rate of exchange between the pound and the mark?

24.3 Hunt Industries has just made a major sale to a Japanese firm. The payment will be made in yen, and is for 100 million yen. The payment will be in 180 days, and the 180-day forward rate is 123.24 yen per dollar.

a. How can Hunt lock in the dollar amount it will receive? What is the amount in dollars?

b. What if Hunt does not hedge and the actual rate of exchange in 180 days is 125.80 yen per dollar, or alternatively 121.20 yen per dollar? How much would Hunt gain or lose by going unhedged, versus if they had hedged?

24.4 Given a spot rate of 0.159 Swedish krona per dollar and expected rates of inflation of 9 percent in Sweden and 5 percent in the United States, what is the expected spot rate of exchange in 1 year, 3 years, and 6 years?

24.5 Douglas Communications is exploring whether to make an investment in Kuwait. The expected cash flows, in the Kuwait dinar, are:

	100,000	110,000	120,000
0			
	1	2	3
200,000			

The spot rate is 0.300 dinars per U.S. dollar, while the required rate of return, k, in U.S. dollars is 25 percent. The U.S. risk-free rate, k_{RF}, is 7 percent while it is 12 percent in Kuwait. The real rate of interest in both countries is estimated to be 2 percent.

a. Using the first method discussed in the chapter, calculate the NPV in U.S. dollars.
b. Now calculate the NPV in U.S. dollars using the second method.
c. Why do the two methods provide approximately the same NPV? (*Note:* Due to rounding, your answers can easily be a few hundred dollars off.)

Basic NPV

24.6 Lytle Productions is evaluating whether to invest in a project in the Netherlands. The expected cash flows, in guilders, are as follows:

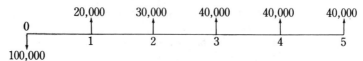

The spot rate is 2.086 guilders per U.S. dollar. The required rate of return, k, in dollars is 20 percent, and the U.S. risk-free rate, k_{RF}, is 10 percent while it is 8 percent in the Netherlands. The real rate of interest is estimated to be 3 percent in both countries.

a. Using the first method described in the chapter calculate the NPV in U.S. dollars.
b. Now calculate it using the second method.
c. Why do the two methods provide approximately the same NPV? (*Note:* Due to rounding, your two answers can easily be a few hundred dollars off.)

Taxes and Cash Flows

24.7 The before-tax cash flows in Austrian schillings and the forecasted spot exchange rates between the schilling and the dollar are as follows:

	Year			
	0	**1**	**2**	**3**
Cash flow before taxes, in schillings	−40,000	20,000	40,000	50,000
Forecasted spot exchange rate	0.600	0.658	0.724	0.800

The corporate tax rate in Austria is 20 percent, and the tax rate for funds withheld is 6 percent; the U.S. corporate tax rate is 35 percent. The U.S. grants a full tax credit for both foreign corporate taxes and taxes withheld.

a. Calculate after-tax cash flows in U.S. dollars.
b. If the required rate of return, k, in U.S. dollars is 15 percent, should the project be undertaken?
c. Independent of (a) and (b), now assume that everything remains the same except the United States allows a tax credit for only 40 percent of the foreign corporate income taxes and taxes withheld. Should the project now be undertaken?

Exchange Rates, Taxes, and Cash Flows

24.8 Austin Petroleum is considering an investment in Malaysia. The expected before-tax cash flows in the Malaysian ringgit are as follows:

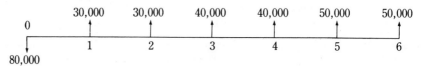

The required rate of return, k, in U.S. dollars is 14 percent, the spot rate is 0.700 ringgits per U.S. dollars, the nominal risk-free rate, k_{RF}, is 8 percent in the United States and 13 percent in Malaysia, and the real rate of interest is 2 percent in both countries. Malaysia's corporate tax rate is 25 percent, and it has a 5 percent withholding tax. The U.S. corporate tax rate is 40 percent.

a. Calculate the expected spot rates of exchange for years 1 through 6.

b. What are the expected after-tax cash flows in U.S. dollars?

c. Should the project be accepted?

d. Independent of (a) through (c), what if every thing remains the same, but Austin fears the project may be expropriated after 4 years, and this would result in little or no compensation. What is the project's NPV?

References

International financial management covers many topics; for more extensive coverage see, for example,

EITEMAN, DAVID K., AND ARTHUR I. STONEHILL. *Multinational Business Finance* 5th ed. Reading, Mass.: Addison-Wesley, 1989.

MADURA, JEFF. *International Financial Management* 2nd ed. St. Paul, Minn.: West, 1987.

SHAPIRO, ALAN C. *International Corporate Finance* 2nd ed. Cambridge, Mass.: Ballinger, 1988.

Numerous articles cover aspects of international financial management including

BRIYS, ERIC, AND MICHEL CROUHY. "Creating and Pricing Hybrid Foreign Currency Options." *Financial Management* 17 (Winter 1988), pp. 59–65.

CHOI, FREDERICK D. S. "International Data Sources for Empirical Research in Financial Management." *Financial Management* 17 (Summer 1988), pp. 80–98.

KHOURY, SARKIS J., AND K. HUNG CHAN. "Hedging Foreign Exchange Risk: Selecting the Optimal Tool." *Midland Corporate Finance Journal* 5 (Winter 1988), pp. 40–52.

LESSARD, DONALD R. "Finance and Global Competition: Exploiting Financial Scope and Coping with Volatile Exchange Rates." *Midland Corporate Finance Journal* 4 (Fall 1986), pp. 6–29.

MEESE, RICHARD, AND KENNETH ROGOFF. "Was It Real? The Exchange Rate–Interest Differential Relation over the Modern Floating-Rate Period." *Journal of Finance* 43 (September 1988), pp. 933–948.

ROLL, RICHARD. "The International Crash of October 1987." *Financial Analysts Journal* 44 (September–October 1988), pp. 19–35.

WHEATLEY, SIMON. "Some Tests of International Equity Integration." *Journal of Financial Economics* 21 (September 1988), pp. 177–212.

Appendixes

Appendix 4A

Linear Forecasting

Simple linear regression techniques can be used to forecast sales. Sales is the dependent variable (indicated by Y), while time is the independent variable (designated X). The regression model to be estimated, ignoring the residual error term, is

$$Y_t = \alpha + \beta X_t \tag{4A.1}$$

where

Y_t = the forecasted sales in time period t
α = (alpha) is the intercept of the fitted regression equation
β = (beta) is the slope of the fitted regression equation
X_t = the time period

This method is easy to employ. Let's use the data from Figure 4.2 and forecast Bartley's 19X7 sales. The historical sales are as follows:

Year	Sales (Y_i) (In millions)	Period (X_i)
19X1	$2.10	1
19X2	1.85	2
19X3	3.00	3
19X4	2.90	4
19X5	4.05	5
19X6	4.15	6

The time periods are converted to 1 for the first year through 6 for 19X6. The exact procedure, formulas employed, and calculations are shown in Table 4A.1. Based on this, the estimated regression equation is

$$Y_t = \$1.332 + 0.479X_t$$

Since we want to forecast sales for the next year, which is period 7, we substitute as follows

next year's forecasted sales = $1.332 + (0.479)(7)

$$= \$1.332 + 3.353 = \$4.685 \text{ million}$$

If we wanted to forecast 19X8 sales, the same procedure would be employed, except the time period would be 8, resulting in forecasted sales of $5.164 million.

This approach is simple to implement. For a firm (or divisions of a firm) in a stable environment, it may provide a reasonable degree of accuracy. However, since it ignores any factor *not* captured by a simple linear extrapolation of past sales, it can be very misleading. This is why other forecasting techniques and managerial expertise are also employed when forecasting sales.

Table 4A.1 Estimated Regression Equation to Forecast Sales of Bartley Instruments

Linear regression provides a simple means of projecting sales. However, since it is a linear method based solely on past sales it ignores any other factors (such as the state of the economy) that may influence actual sales.

Sales (Y_i) (1)	Period (X_i) (2)	Y_iX_i (1)(2) (3)	X_i^2 (2)^2 (4)
2.10	1	2.10	1
1.85	2	3.70	4
3.00	3	9.00	9
2.90	4	11.60	16
4.05	5	20.25	25
4.15	6	24.90	36
Totals 18.05	21	71.55	91

Means:

$$\overline{Y} = \Sigma Y_i/n = 18.05/6 = 3.008$$

$$\overline{X} = \Sigma X_i/n = 21/6 = 3.50$$

Calculation of β (slope):

$$\beta = \frac{\Sigma Y_iX_i - (n)(\overline{Y})(\overline{X})}{\Sigma X_i^2 - n(\overline{X}^2)} = \frac{71.550 - (6)(3.008)(3.50)}{91 - (6)(3.50^2)}$$

$$= \frac{71.550 - 63.168}{91 - 73.500} = \frac{8.382}{17.500} = 0.479$$

Calculation of α (intercept):

$$\alpha = \overline{Y} - \beta\overline{X} = 3.008 - (0.479)(3.50) = 3.008 - 1.676 = 1.332$$

Problem

Forecasting Sales

4A.1 J. C. Penney's sales (in millions) for 1980 through 1984 are as below:

1980	$10,824	1983	$12,078
1981	11,369	1984	13,451
1982	11,414		

a. Based on the linear extrapolation method, forecast 1985 sales.

b. How close is this to actual 1985 sales of $13,747?

c. Based on actual sales for 1980–1985, plus actual sales for 1986 and 1987 of $14,750 and $15,332, respectively, forecast 1988 sales.

d. How close is this to actual 1988 sales of $14,833? What does this suggest about the use of the linear extrapolation method for forecasting Penney's sales?

Appendix 5A

Deriving Time Value Equations

Future Value of an Ordinary Annuity

The future value of an ordinary annuity with both payments of size PMT received at the end of n periods and a compound rate of k can be written as follows:

$$FV_n = PMT(1 + k)^{n-1} + PMT(1 + k)^{n-2} + \cdots + PMT(1 + k)^1 + PMT(1 + k)^0$$

$$= PMT[(1 + k)^{n-1} + (1 + k)^{n-2} + \cdots + (1 + k)^1 + (1 + k)^0] \tag{5A.1}$$

We can express this more compactly as

$$FV_n = PMT \sum_{t=0}^{n-1} (1 + k)^t$$

which is just Equation 5.5. To derive Equation 5.6, the following steps are taken. First, since the term $(1 + k)^0$ equals 1, Equation 5A.1 can be written as follows:

$$FV_n = PMT[(1 + k)^{n-1} + (1 + k)^{n-2} + \cdots + (1 + k)^1 + 1] \tag{5A.2}$$

Multiplying both sides of Equation 5A.2 by the term $(1 + k)$, we have

$$(1 + k)FV_n = PMT[(1 + k)^n + (1 + k)^{n-1} + \cdots + (1 + k)^2 + (1 + k)^1] \tag{5A.3}$$

Subtracting Equation 5A.2 from Equation 5A.3 and simplifying, the result is Equation 5.6:

$$(1 + k)FV_n - FV_n = PMT[(1 + k)^n - 1]$$

$$FV_n[(1 + k) - 1] = PMT[(1 + k)^n - 1]$$

$$FV_n(k) = PMT[(1 + k)^n - 1]$$

$$FV_n = PMT\left[\frac{(1 + k)^n - 1}{k}\right]$$

Present Value of an Annuity

To find the present value of an annuity, we can write out the following equation:

$$PV_0 = \frac{PMT}{(1 + k)^1} + \frac{PMT}{(1 + k)^2} + \cdots + \frac{PMT}{(1 + k)^n}$$

$$= PMT\left[\frac{1}{(1 + k)^1} + \frac{1}{(1 + k)^2} + \cdots + \frac{1}{(1 + k)^n}\right] \tag{5A.4}$$

Summing the terms in brackets, we have Equation 5.8, which is

$$PV_0 = PMT \sum_{t=1}^{n} \frac{1}{(1+k)^t}$$

To derive Equation 5.9, we multiply both sides of Equation 5A.4 by the term $(1+k)$, so that

$$(1+k)(PV_0) = PMT \left[1 + \frac{1}{(1+k)^1} + \cdots + \frac{1}{(1+k)^{n-1}} \right] \qquad (5A.5)$$

Subtracting Equation 5A.4 from Equation 5A.5 and simplifying, the result is Equation 5.9:

$$(1+k)(PV_0) - PV_0 = PMT \left[1 - \frac{1}{(1+k)^n} \right]$$

$$PV_0[(1+k) - 1] = PMT \left[1 - \frac{1}{(1+k)^n} \right]$$

$$PV_0(k) = PMT \left[1 - \frac{1}{(1+k)^n} \right]$$

$$PV_0 = PMT \left\{ \frac{1 - [1/(1+k)^n]}{k} \right\}$$

Perpetuity

The present value of an annuity, as expressed in Equation 5.9, is

$$PV_0 = PMT \left\{ \frac{1 - [1/(1+k)^n]}{k} \right\}$$

By taking the k in the denominator outside the brackets, we have

$$PV_0 = \frac{PMT}{k} \left[1 - \frac{1}{(1+k)^n} \right]$$

As the number of years, n, approaches infinity, the term in brackets goes to 1. We are left with the value of a perpetuity given by Equation 5.12, which is

$$present\ value\ of\ a\ perpetuity_0 = \frac{PMT_1}{k}$$

Appendix 6A

Reading the Financial Pages

Being able to read and understand the financial pages is one of the first things students of finance want to learn to do. This appendix presents a brief overview of stock and bond quotations. Many sources of financial quotations exist, and local newspapers also provide varying coverage of the financial markets. But the most comprehensive daily listing is provided in the *Wall Street Journal* (*WSJ*). The *WSJ* provides information on all listed stocks that are traded on any given day, plus a variety of other financial information on other stocks, bonds, money market instruments, foreign exchange rates, options, and the like.

Quotation information from the *WSJ* for one day is provided below for two listed stocks—GTE (formerly General Telephone and Electronics) common stock and Duke Power $7.80 preferred stock.

52 Weeks					Yld		Vol				Net
Hi	Lo	Stock	Sym	Div	%	P/E	100s	Hi	Lo	Close	Chg
$44\frac{1}{2}$	$38\frac{1}{8}$	GTE	GTE	3.16	7.1	9	6099	$44\frac{3}{8}$	$43\frac{7}{8}$	$44\frac{1}{4}$	$+\frac{1}{4}$
$77\frac{1}{8}$	$61\frac{1}{2}$	DukePwr pf		7.80	10	...	z9220	$78\frac{3}{8}$	$76\frac{1}{2}$	$76\frac{7}{8}$	$+\frac{3}{8}$

We can tell the Duke Power stock is preferred by the "pf" after its name. The first two columns indicate the high and low stock prices for the last 52 weeks. Note that stocks are typically traded in 1/8's, so $38\frac{1}{8}$ means $38.125. "Sym" stands for the ticker symbol for the stock. The "Div" column indicates the yearly cash dividend. The "Yld" column is calculated by dividing the cash dividend by the stock price and is expressed as a percentage. The "P/E" (price/earnings) ratio is calculated by dividing the market price by the earnings available for common stockholders (after any preferred dividends are paid). This ratio is not calculated for preferred stocks. The "Vol" column indicates that 609,900 shares [(6,099)(100)] of GTE traded on this day. The "z9220" means that the total number of Duke Power preferred shares traded was 9,220. The next three columns indicate the high, low, and closing (or last) price for the day. "Net Chg" indicates the difference in the quoted closing price and the closing price on the preceding day. In this case, GTE closed up $\frac{1}{4}$ (or $0.25), whereas the $7.80 Duke Power preferred closed up $\frac{3}{8}$ (or $0.375).

Next, let's consider unlisted stocks. Information for Braniff is shown for one day as follows:

Stock & Div	Sales 100s	Bid	Asked	Net Chg
Branif	168	$5\frac{7}{8}$	6	$+\frac{1}{8}$

Prices for over-the-counter (OTC) stocks differ from those for listed stocks because unlisted quotations reflect transactions between security dealers, not actual sales or purchases by investors.[1] Braniff did not pay a cash dividend and had sales of 16,800 shares [i.e., (168)(100)]. The *bid price* (Bid) represents what security dealers would pay to buy the stock; the *asked price* (Asked) is what they would sell it for. From the standpoint of an investor, the asked price is what he or she would pay to acquire the stock, while the bid price is what they could sell it for. The "Net Chg" column shows that the bid price for Braniff was up $\frac{1}{8}$ (or $0.125) from its close on the previous day.

Some corporate bonds are also listed on the New York Exchange. Those for a Texaco (Texco) $8\frac{1}{2}$ percent coupon rate bond and a $7\frac{1}{4}$ percent coupon rate convertible ("cv") bond of Wendy's for one day are as follows:

Bonds	Cur Yld	Vol	Close	Net Chg
Texco $8\frac{1}{2}$06	10.6	41	80	+1
Wendys $7\frac{1}{4}$10	cv	45	68	+1$\frac{1}{2}$

The vast majority of bonds have a face (and maturity) value of $1,000. The coupon rate signifies how much interest will be paid per bond per year. Someone holding one Texaco bond will receive $85.00 [i.e., (0.0850)($1,000)] in interest each year. This interest is typically paid semiannually. The "06" after the coupon rate for the Texaco bond indicates it matures in 2006. The Wendy's bond matures in 2010. The "Cur Yld" (i.e., current yield) is simply the coupon rate divided by the closing price. The "cv" for the Wendy's bond means it is convertible into common stock. Since each bond has a maturity value of $1,000, we see that $41,000 [i.e., (41)($1,000)] face value in Texaco bonds changed hands, and $45,000 [i.e., (45)($1,000)] face value in Wendy's bonds were traded. The "Close" column indicates the price of the bond expressed as a percentage of the $1,000 face or maturity value. Thus, the closing price for the Texaco bond was $800 [i.e., (80%)($1,000)]. The "Net Chg" column shows that the Texaco bond closed up 1 point (or $10) from the close on the previous day, whereas the Wendy's convertible bond closed up 1$\frac{1}{2}$ points, for an increase of $15.00.

Direct obligations of the U.S. government exist in the form of U.S. Treasury bills, notes, and bonds. Because government issues are traded in the OTC market, "Bid" and "Asked" prices are quoted for both Treasury bills and longer-term securities, as follows:

U.S. Treasury Bills

Mat. Date	Bid Discount	Asked Discount	Yield
6–12	7.21	7.17	7.54

U.S. Treasury Bonds and Notes

Rate	Mat. Date	Bid	Asked	Bid Chg	Yld.
$11\frac{3}{4}$	1993 Nov n	109-11	109-14	−01	9.29
$14\frac{1}{4}$	2002 Feb	138-13	138-19	+03	9.14

U.S. Treasury bills are short-term (one year or less) borrowings of the government that pay $10,000 per bill to the owner upon maturity. They are issued at a discount, which means

---

[1] Information on another OTC market is also presented in the *WSJ*. This is the NASDAQ National Market. NASDAQ is an abbreviation for the National Association of Security Dealers Automated Quotation System, a computerized network that provides current price quotations for OTC stocks that enjoy a national following. Yearly high-low data, along with the day's high, low, and last prices, are provided in addition to dividend and net change information.

the investor pays less than the face value when the bill is purchased. If held to maturity, the interest earned by the investor is equal to the difference between what was paid and the $10,000 face value. The bill shown above matures in about 6 months. The "Bid" and "Asked" prices are annualized percentage discounts from the face value. Thus, a bid of 7.21 (with a 6-month bill) means the discount is 3.605 percent (7.21/2). Hence, the bid price is approximately $9,639.50 ($10,000 − $360.50). Likewise, the asked price is approximately $9,641.50. Even though the Treasury bill will mature in about 6 months, the yield is expressed on an annual basis. An investor purchasing the bill and holding it to maturity will earn an annualized return of 7.54 percent (ignoring any transaction costs).

U.S. government notes and bonds are longer-term securities that pay interest every 6 months. The $11\frac{3}{4}$ percent coupon rate issue due in November 1993 is a note, as denoted by "n." Notes typically have a maturity of 10 years or less when they are issued; a bond has a longer maturity. The $14\frac{1}{4}$ percent issue is a bond. Since government notes and bonds trade in 1/32's, the "Bid" of 109-11 means the bid price of the note was $109\frac{11}{32}$ percent of par, or $1,093.44 per note. The "Bid Chg" indicates the difference between the successive closing prices. The "Yld" column indicates the return (stated on an annualized basis) on both the note and the bond. As we see, the note provided a return of 9.29 percent, and the bond has a lower rate of return of 9.14 percent per year.

Problems

<table>
<tr><td>Listed Stock
Quotations</td><td>

6A.1 On one day the *Wall Street Journal* reported the following information for Burlington Northern, Federal Express, and Illinois Power:

</td></tr>
</table>

$30\frac{1}{4}$	23	BurlgtnNthn	BNI	1.64	5.7	—	669	$28\frac{7}{8}$	$27\frac{7}{8}$	$28\frac{3}{4}$	$+1\frac{1}{8}$
$52\frac{1}{4}$	$31\frac{1}{4}$	FedlExp	FDX		—	31	1160	$50\frac{1}{2}$	$49\frac{3}{4}$	$50\frac{1}{8}$	$+\frac{1}{8}$
20	$13\frac{3}{4}$	IllPow pf		2.04	11	—	z80	$18\frac{3}{4}$	$18\frac{5}{8}$	$18\frac{5}{8}$	$-\frac{1}{8}$

a. Which firm had the widest stock price range in the previous 52 weeks?
b. Which stock is a preferred stock?
c. What is a dividend yield? Why doesn't one of the stocks listed above have a dividend yield?
d. Which firm is operating at a loss?
e. What does the price/earnings ratio signify?
f. What were the total number of shares of each stock traded?
g. Which stock fluctuated most in price during the day?
h. What was the closing price of each stock on the *previous* day?

<table>
<tr><td>Listed Bond
Quotations</td><td>

6A.2 Information on two separate IBM bonds from the *Wall Street Journal* on one day were as follows:

</td></tr>
</table>

IBM	$9\frac{3}{8}$04	9.4	88	$99\frac{3}{8}$	. . .
IBM	$7\frac{7}{8}$04	cv	289	$101\frac{1}{2}$	$+\frac{1}{4}$

a. What are the coupon rates and the year each bond matures? How many dollars in interest would you receive each year from owning *one* of each of the bonds?
b. Which bond is convertible into IBM common stock?
c. What is the difference between the current yield and the coupon rate?
d. What bond sold more during the day?
e. How many dollars did the price of each bond increase or decrease from the previous day's close?
f. Why does the lower coupon rate bond trade at a higher price than the higher coupon rate bond? (*Hint:* Does it have something to do with the convertible feature?)

Appendix 7A

Calculating Covariances and Correlations

The covariance is

$$Cov_{AB} = \sigma_A \sigma_B Corr_{AB} \tag{7A.1}$$

where

σ_A, σ_B = the standard deviations for securities A and B, respectively
$Corr_{AB}$ = the degree of correlation between the respective returns on securities A and B

Like the correlation coefficient, the covariance is a measure of the degree of linear relationship between two variables. However, the covariance may take on any value (positive or negative) while the correlation coefficient can take on values only from $+1.0$ through zero to -1.0.

The formula for calculating the covariance from the expected returns is

$$Cov_{AB} = \sum_{i=1}^{n} (k_{Ai} - \bar{k}_A)(k_{Bi} - \bar{k}_B)P_i \tag{7A.2}$$

where

k_{Ai}, k_{Bi} = the outcome associated with the ith state for securities A and B, respectively
$\bar{k}_A$, $\bar{k}_B$ = the expected value for securities A and B, respectively
P_i = the probability associated with the ith state

To illustrate the calculation of the covariance, let's continue with the two stocks from Figure 7.1 in the chapter, Houston International and American Chemical. The mean, or expected rate of return, is 20 percent for Houston International and 15 percent for American Chemical. To determine the covariance, the following calculations are needed:

State of the Economy (1)	Houston International's Deviations from the Mean $(k_{HI} - \bar{k}_{HI})$ (2)		American Chemical's Deviations from the Mean $(k_{AC} - \bar{k}_{AC})$ (3)		Probability of State Occurring P_i (4)		Product of Probability × Deviations (5)
		×		×		=	
Boom	$(60 - 20)$		$(25 - 15)$		0.30		120
Normal	$(20 - 20)$		$(15 - 15)$		0.40		0
Recession	$(-20 - 20)$		$(5 - 15)$		0.30		120
						$Cov_{HI:AC} =$	$+240$

Once we know the covariance is $+240$, we can calculate the correlation between Houston International's and American Chemical's returns using Equation 7A.1. Since Houston International's standard deviation is 30.98 percent, while American Chemical's is 7.75 percent, we have

$$Cov_{HI:AC} = \sigma_{HI}\sigma_{AC}Corr_{HI:AC}$$

$$+240 = (30.98)(7.75)Corr_{HI:AC}$$

$$\text{Corr}_{HI:IC} = \frac{+240}{(30.98)(7.75)} = \frac{+240}{240.095} = +1.00$$

Hence, the correlation between the expected returns on Houston International and American Chemical is +1.00. As we should have expected by inspecting Figure 7.1, their returns tend to move together (even though those of Houston International have wider fluctuations than those for American Chemical).

Using Historical Data

Instead of having discrete probabilities of occurrence, we might want to calculate the covariance between the returns for two securities using historical data. The formula for calculating the covariance in that case is

$$\text{Cov}_{FG} = \frac{\displaystyle\sum_{t=1}^{n}(k_{Ft} - \bar{k}_F)(k_{Gt} - \bar{k}_G)}{n-1} \tag{7A.3}$$

where

k_{Ft}, k_{Gt} = the outcome associated with the tth time period for securities F and G, respectively
$\bar{k}_F, \bar{k}_G$ = the expected value for securities F and G, respectively
n = the total number of time periods

To illustrate this, let's calculate the covariance between the historical, or *ex post*, returns for stocks F and G with the data as given in Figure 7.5. These data were as follows:

Year	Stock F k_{Ft}	Stock G k_{Gt}
19X3	5%	25%
19X4	30	15
19X5	−10	0
19X6	15	40
Average return	10%	20%
Standard deviation	16.83%	16.83%

The calculations necessary to calculate the covariance are as follows:

Year	Stock F's Deviations from the Mean $(k_{Ft} - \bar{k}_F)$ (1)	×	Stock G's Deviations from the Mean $(k_{Gt} - \bar{k}_G)$ (2)	=	Product of the Deviations $(k_{Ft} - \bar{k}_F)(k_{Gt} - \bar{k}_G)$ (3)
19X3	(5 − 10)		(25 − 20)		−25
19X4	(30 − 10)		(15 − 20)		−100
19X5	(−10 − 10)		(0 − 20)		400
19X6	(15 − 10)		(40 − 20)		100

$$\sum_{t=1}^{n}(k_{Ft} - \bar{k}_F)(k_{Gt} - \bar{k}_G) = +375$$

From Equation 7A.3, the covariance is:

$$\text{Cov}_{FG} = \frac{+375}{4-1} = \frac{+375}{3} = +125$$

Knowing the covariance between the historical returns on stocks F and G, we can calculate the correlation between them using Equation 7A.1 as follows:

$$Cov_{FG} = \sigma_F \sigma_G Corr_{FG}$$

$$+125 = (16.83\%)(16.83\%)Corr_{FG}$$

$$Corr_{FG} = \frac{+125}{283.2489} = +0.4413 \approx +0.44$$

Problems

Covariance and
Correlation

7A.1 Two securities have probability distributions of returns as follows:

Security A		Security B	
Probability	**Return**	**Probability**	**Return**
0.2	40%	0.2	30%
0.4	25	0.4	60
0.4	10	0.4	20
0.2	0	0.2	−10

a. Calculate the mean and standard deviation of the returns for both securities.
b. What is their covariance and their correlation?

Covariance and
Correlation

7A.2 Hull Brothers and Tubbs Trucking have returns as follows:

Year	**Hull Brothers**	**Tubbs Trucking**
1	3%	15%
2	−8	10
3	15	−3
4	22	16
5	−2	7

a. Calculate the mean and standard deviation of the returns for both securities.
b. What is their covariance and their correlation?

Appendix 7B

Calculating Security Betas

To calculate beta, we begin with the returns for the stock in question, k_j, and the market portfolio, k_M. Consider the returns presented in Table 7B.1. To determine beta for stock j, we can begin by plotting the data as in Figure 7B.1. Note that the returns on the market are on the horizontal axis and the returns on stock j are on the vertical axis. We want to fit a least-squares regression line of the form $Y = \alpha + \beta X$, where α is the intercept on the vertical axis and β is the slope of the fitted line. Employing the same basic approach described in Appendix 4A, or a calculator with a linear regression function, the fitted regression line is:

$$k_j = \alpha + \beta k_M \tag{7B.1}$$

$$= 1.44 + 1.40 k_M$$

where

$\alpha = 1.44 =$ alpha, the intercept on the vertical axis

$\beta = 1.40 =$ beta, the sensitivity of the returns on security j relative to the returns on the market portfolio

Beta for stock j is 1.40, meaning that its nondiversifiable risk is 40 percent more than the average nondiversifiable risk. As such, security j is more risky than the market.

Instead of fitting a least-squares regression line, beta may also be determined if we know the standard deviation of the stock's returns, the standard deviation of the market's returns, and the correlation between the two returns. Employing this approach, beta equals the covariance (or comovement) between the stock's and market's returns divided by the variance of the market's returns, or

$$\text{beta} = \beta_j = \frac{\text{covariance}_{jM}}{\text{variance}_M} = \frac{\text{Cov}_{jM}}{\sigma_M^2} \tag{7B.2}$$

Table 7B.1   Historical Rates of Return on Stock j and the Market Portfolio
The returns encompass both cash dividends and any capital gain or loss for the year.

Year	Stock j (k_j)	Market (k_M)
19X2	22.51%	8.78%
19X3	14.96	4.06
19X4	−10.05	−3.99
19X5	26.46	20.70
19X6	5.12	7.45
Mean	11.80	7.40
Standard deviation	14.68%	8.94%
Correlation$_{jM}$	0.85	

Figure 7B.1 Plot and Fitted Regression Line of the Returns on Security j and the Market

The least-squares regression line can be determined using the procedure described in Appendix 4A, or a calculator with a regression function.

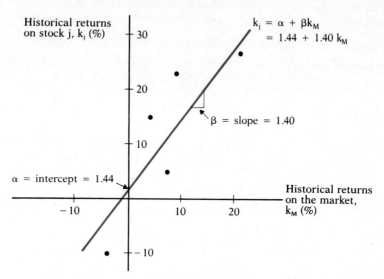

However, the covariance of the returns between security j and the market is equal to the standard deviation of security j, σ_j, times the standard deviation of the market, σ_M, times the correlation between security j and the market M, Corr_{jM}, so

$$\text{Cov}_{jM} = \sigma_j \sigma_M \text{Corr}_{jM} \tag{7B.3}$$

Inserting Equation 7B.3 into Equation 7B.2 and simplifying, we have:

$$\beta_j = \frac{\text{Cov}_{jM}}{\sigma_M{}^2} = \frac{\sigma_j \sigma_M \text{Corr}_{jM}}{\sigma_M{}^2} = \frac{\sigma_j \text{Corr}_{jM}}{\sigma_M} \tag{7B.4}$$

Note that the standard deviation, σ_M, of the market returns appeared in the numerator of Equation 7B.4 before simplifying, while the variance of the market returns, $\sigma_M{}^2$, appeared in the denominator. By dividing through, we are left with the result that beta is equal to the standard deviation of the security's returns times the correlation between the returns on the security and the market's returns, divided by the standard deviation of the market's returns. Returning to the data given in Table 7B.1, beta could be calculated as follows:

$$\beta_j = \frac{\sigma_j \text{Corr}_{jM}}{\sigma_M} = \frac{(14.68)(0.85)}{8.94} = \frac{12.478}{8.94} = 1.396 \approx 1.40$$

Hence, employing either a linear regression approach, or Equation 7B.4, the beta is 1.40. In practice, adjustments are made when deriving expected, as opposed to historical, betas.

Self-Test Problem   (Solution appears on page 741.)

CAPM, Beta, and Variance

ST 7B.1 If a security's required rate of return is 18 percent, the return on the market portfolio is 15 percent, the risk-free rate is 9 percent, the correlation between the security's and the market's return is +0.50, and the standard deviation of the security's return is 16 percent, what is the variance about the expected market return?

Problems

Calculation of Beta

7B.1 The returns and probabilities for a stock and the market are as follows:

Probability of Occurrence	Stock Returns	Market Returns
0.20	45%	50%
0.30	0	20
0.30	−5	10
0.20	−15	−10

a. What is the expected rate of return for each?
b. What is the standard deviation of each?
c. If the correlation between the stock's and the market's returns is +0.95, what is the beta for the stock?

Beta and Required Return

7B.2 Given the following data, what is the required rate of return for security j?

$$k_M = 10\% \qquad \sigma_j = 20\% \qquad k_{RF} = 4\%$$

$$\sigma_M = 15\% \qquad Corr_{jM} = +0.80$$

Risk, Return, and Correlation

7B.3 Assume you hold the following two securities, A and B:

Security A		Security B	
Probability P_i	Return k_i	Probability P_i	Return k_i
0.40	40%	0.30	65%
0.40	10	0.40	15
0.20	−10	0.30	−15

The correlation between security A and the market, M, is +0.50.

a. Calculate the expected return and standard deviation for each security.
b. What must the value of $Corr_{BM}$ be to make the two securities equally risky in terms of their beta coefficients? (*Note:* You are not given the standard deviation of the market, σ_M, but it is the same for each security and therefore does not affect your answer.)

Calculating Beta from Historical Data

7B.4 Year-end stock prices and dividends for J.C. Penney and the level of the S&P 500 stock index for the period 1981–1988 are as follows:

	J.C. Penney		S&P 500
Year	Dividend	Ending Price	Ending Value
1981	—	$14.312	122.55
1982	$1.00	24.188	140.64
1983	1.08	28.312	164.93
1984	1.18	23.188	167.24
1985	1.18	27.750	211.28
1986	1.24	36.125	242.17
1987	1.48	43.375	247.08
1988	2.00	50.625	277.72

a. Using the formula, return $=(D_1 + P_1 - P_0)/P_0$, calculate the returns for 1982 through 1988 for Penney and the S&P 500. (*Note:* Ignore dividends for the index.)
b. What is beta for Penney?

Appendix 8A

Important Depreciation and Tax Ideas

To calculate the relevant cash flows for capital budgeting decision making, both depreciation and corporate taxes must be understood.

Depreciation

Depreciation is a means of charging the original cost of long-term assets against revenues. Under generally accepted accounting principles, the purpose of depreciation is to match revenues and associated expenses in the same time periods. This is not the meaning of depreciation for tax purposes, especially since the enactment of the Economic Recovery Tax Act of 1981, as modified by the Tax Reform Act of 1986. The major impact of these laws was to (1) simplify the treatment of depreciation for tax purposes, and (2) shorten the period over which depreciation is charged.

Personal Property

The key to the tax depreciation scheme, called the modified *Accelerated Cost Recovery System* (*ACRS*), is the use of six different property classes that apply to everything except real estate. These six property classes, as shown in Table 8A.1, cover all depreciable assets purchased by firms, whether new or used. An asset has a 3-, 5-, 7-, 10-, 15-, or 20-year

Table 8A.1 Normal Recovery Period and Personal Property Classes

Notice that most equipment has a 7-year normal recovery period. Instead of modified ACRS, straight-line depreciation may be used over the normal recovery period.

Normal Recovery Period (Years)	Property
3	Certain short-lived property and special-purpose tools
5	Automobiles; light trucks; buses; technological equipment; information systems; construction equipment and electronic and semiconductor manufacturing equipment
7	Most manufacturing equipment; office furniture and equipment; railroad cars and locomotives; amusement parks
10	Some manufacturing equipment; cement plants; petroleum refineries; barges and tugs
15	Industrial steam and electric generation equipment; sewage treatment plants; telephone distribution plants; pipelines
20	Most public utility property; railroad structures

life, or *normal recovery period* for tax purposes. The key point is that all new or used equipment acquired by the firm falls into one of these six normal recovery periods regardless of the expected useful economic or accounting life of the item.

The amount of depreciation charged off for tax purposes is based on the applicable class, employing the declining balance method of depreciation, switching to straight-line. *For tax purposes all assets are depreciated to zero.* Also, a half-year convention is employed—that is, all assets (excluding real estate) are assumed to be purchased halfway through the year in which they were acquired so that the first year's depreciation is half of the full rate for that year. For 3-, 5-, 7-, and 10-year assets, the 200 percent (or double) declining balance method is used, while the 150 percent declining balance method is used for 15- and 20-year assets.

To illustrate this modified ACRS procedure, consider the depreciation on a $60,000 asset with a 5-year normal recovery period. The 200 percent declining balance method involves depreciating the undepreciated value of an asset at twice the rate of the straight-line method. Thus, in year 1 twice the straight-line amount of 0.20, or 0.40, would be depreciated normally. However, with the half-year convention, only one-half of 0.40, or 0.20, is depreciated in year 1. In year 2, 0.40 of the undepreciated balance, which is 100 percent minus 20 percent, or 80 percent, is depreciated. This is $(0.40)(80\%) = 32\%$, or 0.32. The same procedure is used in year 3. When it is appropriate, based on a higher depreciation value, the switch is made from the 200 percent declining balance method to straight-line depreciation. For 5-year assets this switch occurs in the fourth year. Note that the half-year convention also applies to the ending (or sixth year), so that all assets are depreciated over a life *one year longer* than the class they are in.

The calculations are as follows:

Year	Calculation	Proportion of Original Cost to Be Depreciated
1	200 percent declining balance $(100\%)(0.40)(\frac{1}{2})$	20%, or 0.2000
2	$(100\% - 20\%)(0.40)$	32%, or 0.3200
3	$(100\% - 20\% - 32\%)(0.40)$	19.2%, or 0.1920
4	Switch to straight-line $(100\% - 20\% - 32\% - 19.2\%)/$ 2.5 years remaining	11.52%, or 0.1152
5	same as year 4	11.52%, or 0.1152
6	half of year 4	5.76%, or 0.0576

For our $60,000 5-year asset, the amount of depreciation charged off for tax purposes using the modified ACRS method is

Year	Original Cost	×	Factor	=	Depreciation
1	$60,000		0.2000		$12,000
2	60,000		0.3200		19,200
3	60,000		0.1920		11,520
4	60,000		0.1152		6,912
5	60,000		0.1152		6,912
6	60,000		0.0576		3,456

Simplified ACRS Factors

While the method for calculating depreciation under the modified ACRS method given above is correct, it is also somewhat complicated—and it takes us away from our main focus, which is understanding financial concepts, theories, and practices. Accordingly, we use the simplified

Table 8A.2 Simplified ACRS Depreciation Factors by Normal Recovery Period and Year

The first year's factors are lower because a half-year convention is employed—that is, all assets are assumed to be purchased halfway through the fiscal year.

| Year | Normal Recovery Period | | | |
	3-Year	5-Year	7-Year	10-Year
1	0.33	0.20	0.14	0.10
2	0.44	0.32	0.25	0.18
3	0.23*	0.19	0.17	0.14
4		0.15*	0.13	0.12
5		0.14*	0.11*	0.09
6–7			0.10*	0.08*
8–10				0.07*

* Simplified to ignore the half-year convention at the end of the asset's normal recovery period.

ACRS factors given by Table 8A.2.[1] The essence of the simplification is to ignore the half-year convention applied at the end of an asset's life. For example, *for a 5-year asset we assume that all of the depreciation occurs over 5 years.* The first three depreciation factors are as specified by the tax code (rounded to two decimal points). When the switch to straight-line depreciation is made, in year 4, the remaining undepreciated amount of the asset's value is depreciated over 2 years rather than $2\frac{1}{2}$ years as specified by the tax code. This same type of adjustment is made for the other property classes as well. This change is made for pedagogical purposes: Do not use the simplified ACRS factors in Table 8A.2 when filing a tax return with the Internal Revenue Service!

In addition to using the ACRS method, the firm has the option of employing straight-line depreciation over the asset's normal recovery period.[2] Throughout this text we will employ either the simplified ACRS factors or straight-line depreciation over the asset's normal recovery period.

Real Estate

Real estate is covered by two special depreciation classes. The $27\frac{1}{2}$-year class includes residential rental property, defined as buildings or structures with 80 percent or more of their rental income from dwelling units. The $31\frac{1}{2}$-year class includes nonresidential real estate. For both classes the straight-line method of depreciation is required. We ignore real estate throughout the text.

Corporate Taxes

The top marginal corporate tax rate is now 34 percent. In addition, the Tax Reform Act of 1986 did away with different tax rates for ordinary income versus capital gains, and the investment tax credit.

---

[1] Table 8A.2 is reproduced as Table F.5.

[2] The half-year convention also applies if straight-line depreciation is employed. We ignore this complication also and with a 5-year asset simply depreciate 20 percent per year.

Sale of Assets

Depreciable assets acquired by the firm are generally subject to taxes when they are sold. No matter how long the asset is held, any gain is treated as an ordinary, or operating, gain; likewise, any loss on the sale of assets is treated as an ordinary loss.

To illustrate this, suppose Metroplex Distributors acquired some equipment 3 years ago for $20,000 that has now been depreciated to $8,800 for tax purposes. It plans to sell the equipment and wants to determine its tax liability and net cash proceeds (after paying taxes) from the sale. First, let us consider the simplest case: It sells the equipment for its depreciated book value of $8,800. In this case there is no tax liability, and the net cash proceeds are simply the $8,800 received from the sale.

Next, consider the sale of the equipment for more, or less, than its depreciated tax value. As shown below, two different situations are presented.

	Sold at a Gain (1)	Sold at a Loss (2)
Selling price	$12,000	$2,000
Remaining book value	8,800	8,800
Gain (loss) on sale	$ 3,200	($6,800)
Tax at 34%	$ 1,088	($2,312)
Net proceeds	$12,000 − $1,088 = $10,912	$2,000 + $2,312 = $4,312

In column (1), the equipment is sold for $12,000. Note that since the selling price is greater than the remaining book value, the IRS says Metroplex overdepreciated the asset, and thus underreported its taxable income and underpaid its taxes. The difference between the $12,000 selling price and the remaining book value of $8,800 is subject to recapture. At a 34 percent marginal corporate tax rate, Metroplex's additional tax is $1,088, resulting in net proceeds from the sale of $10,912. Now consider column (2), when the asset is sold for $2,000, while its book value for tax purposes is $8,800. In this case, the firm underdepreciated the asset, with the result that it realizes a tax savings *if the firm as a whole is profitable.* At a 34 percent marginal tax rate, the tax loss of $6,800 ($8,800 − $2,000) results in a $2,312 [i.e., ($6,800)(0.34)] reduction in the firm's tax liability. The net cash flow due to selling the asset is the $2,000 plus the $2,312 reduction in cash outflow for taxes, for a total of $4,312.

Operating Losses

An operating loss refers to the situation in which the firm has a negative taxable income. In this case, the firm has no income tax liability. These losses will first be carried back and then forward. For simplicity, we ignore carryback and carryforward in the text.

The Investment Tax Credit

The *investment tax credit (ITC)* is a provision that has been in and out of the tax code over time. Its purpose is to encourage capital investment by providing a direct reduction in the firm's tax liability when depreciable equipment, except real property like buildings, is purchased. The investment tax credit was repealed by the Tax Reform Act of 1986.

Self-Test Problem   (Solution appears on page 741.)

200 Percent Declining Balance Depreciation

ST 8A.1 An asset that falls in the 7-year class was just purchased for $140,000. What is its depreciation using both the 200 percent declining balance and straight-line methods, and *using the half-year convention for both the first and last (eighth) years?*

Problems

ACRS Depreciation

8A.1 A firm has just purchased two trucks: a light-duty one with a 5-year normal recovery period and a heavy-duty one with a 7-year normal recovery period. The cost of the light-duty truck was $15,000; the heavy-duty truck was $27,500. What is the per year depreciation charged for tax purposes using the simplified ACRS factors for both trucks?

True ACRS Versus
Simplified ACRS
Depreciation

8A.2 A 5-year normal recovery period asset costs $200,000.
a. Calculate the true ACRS depreciation per year.
b. Then calculate the depreciation per year using the simplified ACRS factors given by Table 8A.2.
c. If the marginal tax rate is 34 percent, and the required rate of return is 15 percent, find the present value of the depreciation tax shield, $\sum_{t=1}^{7} Dep_t(T)/(1 + k)^t$, for both (a) and (b). How close are the two figures? What does this indicate about the error introduced by using the simplified ACRS factors?

Tax on Asset Sold

8A.3 An asset has a remaining book value for tax purposes of $48,000. The marginal tax rate is 34 percent. Find the tax liability (or credit) if the asset is sold for (a) $60,000, (b) $20,000. (Assume the firm is profitable.)

Appendix 10A

Certainty Equivalents

Proponents of the certainty-equivalent method of risk adjustment object to changing the required rate of return because it combines the adjustment for risk with the adjustment for time. With the *certainty-equivalent* method, the adjustment for risk is handled by adjusting the cash flows, and the adjustment for time is accomplished by discounting the "certain" cash flows at the risk-free rate, k_{RF}. The certainty-equivalent cash flows are what the firm would be willing to receive *for certain* in lieu of the distributions of cash flows that are possible for each year.

To determine the net present value employing the certainty-equivalent method, the following steps are required:

1. Determine the most likely cash flows for each year.
2. Calculate the certainty equivalent factors, α_t, for each year. They range from 0 to 1, with 1 implying perfect certainty and progressively smaller values signifying greater risk.
3. Calculate the net present value, where

$$\text{certainty equivalent NPV} = \sum_{t=1}^{n} \frac{\alpha_t \overline{CF}_t}{(1 + k_{RF})^t} - \alpha_0 \overline{CF}_0 \qquad (10A.1)$$

Although both theoretically and conceptually the certainty-equivalent approach has much to recommend as a means of dealing with risk, it has one important drawback. How do managers derive the certainty-equivalent-factors, α_t? The same type of question can be raised with determining the required rate of return, but most managers find estimating certainty-equivalents even more difficult than estimating required rates of return.

To use the certainty-equivalent approach, assume we have the following CFs and certainty-equivalent factors:

Year	$\overline{CF}_t$	Certainty-Equivalent Factor, α_t
Initial investment	$15,000	1.0
1	8,000	0.9
2	9,000	0.9
3	10,000	0.8

Since both years 1 and 2 have the same certainty equivalent of 0.9, the cash flows for those 2 years are viewed as being equally risky. The certainty-equivalent NPV, with a risk-free rate of 6 percent is:

$$\begin{aligned}
\text{NPV} &= \$8,000(\,0.9\,)(\,PV_{6\%,1yr}\,) + \$9,000(\,0.9\,)(\,PV_{6\%,2yr}\,) \\
&\quad + \$10,000(\,0.8\,)(\,PV_{6\%,3yr}\,) - \$15,000(\,1.0\,) \\[6pt]
&= \$7,200(\,0.943\,) + \$8,100(\,0.890\,) + \$8,000(\,0.840\,) - \$15,000 \\[6pt]
&= \$6,789.60 + \$7,209 + \$6,720 - \$15,000 = \$5,718.60
\end{aligned}$$

Since the certainty-equivalent NPV is greater than zero, the project should be accepted.

In Chapter 10 we mentioned the implicit assumption incorporated in the required rate of return method—that risk increases solely as a function of time. One way to show this increase in risk is to calculate what happens to the certainty-equivalent factors, α_t, *implied* by using a constant required rate of return. If these implied certainty equivalents decrease, then the required rate of return method does indeed assume risk increases solely as a function of time. If both the certainty-equivalent and required return methods give the same value, we can set them equal so that for any time period t

$$\frac{\alpha_t \overline{CF}_t}{(1 + k_{RF})^t} = \frac{CF_t}{(1 + \text{required return})^t} \tag{10A.2}$$

By factoring out the cash flows, we have

$$\alpha_t \left[\frac{1}{(1 + k_{RF})^t} \right] = \frac{1}{(1 + \text{required return})^t} \tag{10A.3}$$

and using PVs, we have

$$\alpha_t \, PV_{\text{risk-free}_t} = PV_{\text{risky}_t}$$

or

$$\alpha_t = PV_{\text{risky}_t}/PV_{\text{risk-free}_t} \tag{10A.4}$$

To equate the certainty-equivalent and required rate of return solutions, the implied certainty coefficient, α_t, is equal to the risky PV factor divided by the risk-free PV factor. If t equals 1 year, $k_{RF} = 6$ percent, and the required return = 8 percent, the implied certainty equivalent necessary to equate the solution from the two methods is $\alpha_1 = PV_{8\%,1yr}/PV_{6\%,1yr} = 0.926/0.943 = 0.982$. If we do this for t equals 5, as shown in Table 10A.1, the implied $\alpha_5 = 0.912$, while for t = 10 the implied certainty-equivalent factor, α_{10}, is 0.830. Notice that the implied certainty-equivalent factors, α_t, decrease with time. This decrease is caused by the compounding of the risk premium (the difference between the risk-free rate and the required return) over time. Since the implied certainty equivalents for this risk premium decrease

Table 10A.1 Calculations Necessary to Derive Implied Certainty Coefficients, α_t, When the Risk-Free Rate Is 6 Percent

The implied certainty coefficients in columns 4 and 5 decrease over time. This shows that the use of an 8 or 15 percent discount rate, when the risk-free rate is 6 percent, assumes the risk premium increases over time with the required return approach.

| | Risk-Free | Risky | | Implied Certainty Coefficients, α_t | |
| | $PV_{6\%,t}$ | $PV_{8\%,t}$ | $PV_{15\%,t}$ | 8% (2)/(1) | 15% (3)/(1) |
Time, t	(1)	(2)	(3)	(4)	(5)
0	1.000	1.000	1.000	1.000	1.000
1	0.943	0.926	0.870	0.982	0.923
5	0.747	0.681	0.497	0.912	0.665
10	0.558	0.463	0.247	0.830	0.443
15	0.417	0.315	0.123	0.755	0.295
20	0.312	0.215	0.061	0.689	0.196
25	0.233	0.146	0.030	0.627	0.129
30	0.174	0.099	0.015	0.569	0.086

Figure 10A.1 Implied Certainty Coefficients, α_t, over Time with 6 Percent Risk-Free Rate

The decrease in the 8 and 15 percent implied certainty coefficients is due to the inherent assumption in the required rate of return method that risk increases over time.

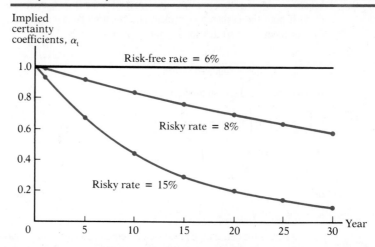

over time, we see that the required return approach implicitly assumes risk increases solely as a function of time. In Figure 10A.1, the results for both 8 and 15 percent required rates of return compared to a risk-free rate of 6 percent are graphed. The downward slope of the implied certainty-equivalent curve illustrates graphically the required return method assumes the risk premium increases solely as a function of time.

Problems

Certainty Equivalents

10A.1 Drzycimski, Inc., has decided to use the certainty-equivalent method to determine if it should purchase an $8,000 delivery truck. Cash flow and certainty equivalent estimates are given below.

Year	$\overline{CF}_t$	α_t
Initial investment	$8,000	1.00
1	2,200	0.95
2	2,100	0.91
3	2,000	0.87
4	1,800	0.83
5	1,800	0.80

If the risk-free rate is 7 percent, should the truck be purchased?

Determining the Risk-Free Rate

10A.2 Alliance Products uses the certainty-equivalent approach for making capital budgeting decisions. For a new project, the cash flows and certainty equivalents are

Year	$\overline{CF}_t$	α_t
Initial investment	$50,000	1.0
1	33,000	0.8
2	31,000	0.7
3	29,000	0.6
4	27,000	0.5

What is the risk-free rate, if the certainty equivalent NPV is $18,127?

(*Note:* It is easier to solve this problem by trial-and-error, rather than algebraically.)

Implied Certainty Coefficients

10A.3 If the risk-free rate is 7 percent, and the required return is 12 percent, calculate the implied certainty coefficients for years zero, 5, 10, 15, 20, and 25. Do the same if the required return now increases to 16 percent. Why do the certainty coefficients decrease over time, and why do those implied by the 16 percent rate decrease faster than those implied by the 12 percent required rate of return?

Appendix 11A

Valuing the Firm Using the Option Pricing Model

So far we have looked at examples using what we know about calls and puts. In a broader perspective, we can also value the whole firm—and we can view the firm as a large asset in which the stockholders' and bondholders' values can be expressed in terms of combinations of claims. We will see that the common stock of a levered firm (that is, one that has debt) is a call option written on the firms' assets. One of the primary advantages of this approach is that, unlike traditional valuation theory, it shows the interactions between the value of the firm's stock and its bonds.

In Chapter 11 (footnote 6) we introduced the put call parity, which says that

$$\text{value of a call} + \frac{\text{present value of the}}{\text{exercise price}} = \text{value of put} + \text{share price}$$

or in terms of the notation used previously,

$$V_c + \frac{X}{e^{k_{RF}t}} = V_P + P_0 \tag{11A.1}$$

Now we want to broaden this approach and notation as follows:

Value of calls and puts → becomes → Value of equity and debt

V_c	S: the market value of the equity claims on the firm
$\dfrac{X}{e^{k_{RF}t}}$	V_B: the present value of the promised payments to zero-coupon[1] bondholders discounted at the risk-free rate; the value of bonds if there is no risk of default
V_p	Default option: the value of the limited liability of stockholders; that is, the value of the stockholders' right to walk away from the debt of the firm and hand it over to the firm's creditors
P_0	V: value of the firm's assets

Thus, when valuing the whole firm, Equation 11A.1 becomes

$$S + V_B = \text{default option} + V \tag{11A.2}$$

or

---

[1] Zero-coupon bonds, as discussed in Chapter 13, do not pay periodic interest. Instead they are issued at a discount (from the par value of $1,000 per bond). The interest is simply the difference between their issuance price and their par, or maturity, value.

value of + value of riskless = stockholders' right + market value
stock   bonds   to default   of the firm's
                                                   assets

In this context the value of the stockholders' claim is

$$S = V - V_B + \text{default option} \qquad (11A.3)$$

In effect, stockholders have (1) bought the firm's assets, (2) borrowed the present value of the bondholders' claims on the firm, and (3) bought a put (or default) option that allows them to walk away from the firm and give it to the bondholders. Similarly, the market value of the bondholders' claim, B, on the firm is

$$V_B - \text{default option} = V - S \qquad (11A.4)$$

The left-hand side of Equation 11A.4 recognizes that the market value of the firm's debt, which is risky, is equal to the riskless market value of the firm's debt, V_B, *minus* the default (or put) option held by the stockholders, whereas the right-hand side is simply the total value of the firm minus the stockholders' claims. Either side of Equation 11A.4 can be employed to determine the market value of the bondholders' claims, B.

To understand this usage of option theory an example is helpful. Suppose a firm's total market value, V, is $500, the firm issues $200 face value of eight-year zero-coupon bonds, the risk-free rate is 0.12, and the annual standard deviation of the firm's value is 0.50. What is the value of the stockholders' claim on the firm, what is the value of the bondholders' risky claim on the firm, and what is the value of the default option held by the stockholders?

Assuming continuous compounding, the riskless value of the zero-coupon bonds is equal to[2]

$$V_B = \frac{\$200}{e^{k_{RF}t}} = \frac{\$200}{e^{0.12 \times 8}} = \$76.58$$

The value of the default option is simply the value of the put option. However, we cannot calculate this directly because we do not know the value of the stockholders' claim, S. Instead, we must first calculate the value of the stockholders' claim; it is

$$d_1 = \frac{\ln(V/\text{face value of bonds}) + [k_{RF} + 0.5(\sigma)^2]t}{\sigma\sqrt{t}}$$

$$= \frac{\ln(500/200) + [0.12 + 0.5(0.50)^2]8}{0.50\sqrt{8}}$$

$$= \frac{0.91629 + 1.96000}{1.41421} = \frac{2.87629}{1.41421} = 2.0338$$

$$d_2 = d_1 - \sigma\sqrt{t} = 2.0338 - 1.4142 = 0.6196$$

From Table 11.1, the cumulative distribution table, $N(d_1)$ is approximately 0.9788 and $N(d_2)$ is approximately 0.7257. The value of the stock is

$$S = V\,N(d_1) - \frac{\text{face value of bond}}{e^{k_{RF}t}}\,N(d_2)$$

$$= \$500(0.9788) - \frac{\$200}{e^{0.12 \times 8}}\,(0.7257)$$

$$= \$489.40 - \$76.5786(0.7257) = \$489.40 - \$55.57 = \$433.83$$

[2] The Black–Scholes equations are used directly because Table F.7 does not provide sufficient accuracy.

Now that we know the value of the stockholders' claim, S, along with the total value of the firm, V, and the riskless claim of the bondholders, we can determine the value of the default option. Using Equation 11A.2 it is

$$S + V_B = \text{default option} + V$$

$$\$433.83 + \$76.58 = \text{default option} + \$500$$

$$\text{default option} = \$433.83 + \$76.58 - \$500 = \$10.41$$

Finally, the value of the bondholders' risky claim on the firm is equal to

$$B = V_B - \text{default option}$$

$$= \$76.58 - \$10.41 = \$66.17$$

or alternatively, it is

$$B = V - S$$

$$= \$500 - \$433.83 = \$66.17$$

In this example we made a number of simplifying assumptions, such as that the firm paid no cash dividends and that it could declare default only at the end of 8 years. In reality there are other complexities that may affect the value of the firm. However, many of these additional complexities can be incorporated into more complete option pricing approaches to valuing a firm.

Problems

Stock, Debt and Default Option

11A.1 A firm has $40 million in outstanding zero-coupon debt that matures in 4 years. The market value of the firm's assets is $60 million, their standard deviation is 0.60, and the risk-free rate is 0.14.
a. What is the value of the firm's stock? Its debt?
b. The default option?

Stock, Debt and Default Option

11A.2 Bagamery's has $1,000 in zero-coupon bonds outstanding that mature in 5 years. The market value of Bagamery's assets is $1,400, their standard deviation is 0.40, and the risk-free rate is 0.08.
a. What is the value of Bagamery's stock, debt, and the default option held by the stockholders?
b. Now assume everything stays the same as in (a) except unexpected inflation increases the riskless rate to 0.13. What is the new value of Bagamery's stock, debt, and the default option? Explain your results.
c. Finally, assume everything is the same as in (a), except the standard deviation of the assets is reduced to 0.25 from 0.40. What is the new value of Bagamery's stock, debt, and the default option? Explain your results.

Appendix 13A

Refunding a Bond or Preferred Stock Issue

Refunding is the issuance of new securities to replace an existing bond or preferred stock issue. A firm occasionally refunds to get rid of overly restrictive provisions associated with the existing issue, but the primary motive is if the cost of new financing is substantially less than the cost of existing financing. This would occur if the coupon rate on a new bond issue (or dividend rate on preferred stock) was substantially less than the coupon (or dividend) rate on the existing issue. In this circumstance, firms may be able to secure the same long-term financing with a reduced level of cash outflows. To refund an issue, firms call it.

The decision to refund can be approached in essentially the same manner as the replacement capital budgeting decision. To do this, the incremental (new minus old) after-tax cash flows must be calculated and then discounted to determine the net present value, NPV, of the proposed refunding. Thus,

$$NPV = \sum_{t=1}^{n} \frac{\Delta CF_t}{(1 + k_i)^t} - \Delta CF_0 \qquad (13A.1)$$

where

ΔCF_t = the incremental after-tax cash flows resulting because of the refunding
$\quad k_i$ = the after-tax cost of the new bond issue
ΔCF_0 = the after-tax initial investment associated with the refunding

The decision rule is as follows:

1. If NPV is greater than zero—refund.
2. If NPV is less than zero—don't refund.
3. If NPV is equal to zero—you are indifferent.

In discounting the CFs, the current after-tax cost of the new issue is employed as the discount rate because it represents the appropriate rate for the risk involved. Since one issue is simply replacing another and there is little risk involved, the use of a higher rate such as the firm's cost of capital is inappropriate.

To understand refundings, consider the example of Albany Oil, which issued a 30-year, $50 million, $11\frac{1}{4}$ percent coupon-rate bond 5 years ago at par, with flotation costs of $480,000. Because these flotation costs are being amortized over the life of the bond, $16,000 ($480,000/30) is charged off per year. Since 5 years have gone by, the remaining unamortized flotation costs are $480,000 - [(5 years)($16,000)] = $400,000. The bonds can be called at 106, so the call premium is 6 percent of $50 million. Because of a drop in long-term market interest rates, Albany can now issue $50 million of 10 percent coupon-rate bonds at par, with flotation costs of $875,000. To ensure that funds will be available when needed, the new bonds will be issued 1 month before the existing bonds are retired. The net proceeds from the new issue can be invested for 1 month at the Treasury bill rate of 6 percent. Albany's marginal tax rate is 40 percent. The relevant data are as follows:

	Existing Issue	New Issue
Face value	$50 million	$50 million
Coupon interest rate	$11\frac{1}{4}\%$	10%
Original life	30 years	25 years
Remaining life	25 years	25 years
Flotation costs (remaining or total)	$400,000	$875,000
Marginal tax rate	40%	
Interest overlap	1 month	
Call premium on existing bonds	6%	
Treasury bill rate	6%	

To determine the NPV, the following steps are employed.

STEP 1. *Determination of the Incremental Initial Investment Associated with Refunding.* This involves the call premium, the flotation costs, write-off for tax purposes of the unamortized flotation costs on the existing issue, and interest during the overlap period. First, we calculate the before-tax initial investment, as follows:

Before-Tax:

Call price on old bonds (106% of par)	$53,000,000
Additional interest paid during overlap period*	468,750
Less: Net proceeds of new issue†	49,125,000
Interest earned on new issue proceeds during overlap period‡	245,625
Before-tax initial investment	$ 4,098,125

* One month's interest on old bonds = $(\$50,000,000)(0.1125)(\frac{1}{12}) = \$468,750$.
† Face value less flotation costs = $\$50,000,000 - \$875,000 = \$49,125,000$.
‡ One month's interest on proceeds = $(\$49,125,000)(0.06)(\frac{1}{12}) = \$245,625$.

Next, the tax consequences must be taken into account. This involves the following items: the call premium and unamortized flotation costs on the old bond that can be written off for tax purposes, and the additional interest during the overlap period. For Albany Oil, the tax consequences affecting the initial investment are as follows:

Tax-Deductible Expenses:

Call premium on old bond ($53,000,000 − $50,000,000)	$3,000,000
Unamortized flotation costs on old bond	400,000
Additional interest paid during overlap period	468,750
Less: Additional interest earned on new issue proceeds	245,625
Total tax-deductible expenses	3,623,125
Tax savings ($3,623,125)(0.40)	$1,449,250

Initial Investment:

Before-tax outlay	$4,098,125
Less: Tax savings	1,449,250
Initial Investment, ΔCF_0	$2,648,875

STEP 2: *Determination of the Incremental Cash Savings Resulting from the Refunding.* This involves the interest cash flows, the tax savings on them, and the tax impacts of the different amortization rates for the flotation costs of the two issues. For the old bonds, the following after-tax cash flow existed:

Interest on old bond ($50,000,000)(0.1125)		$5,625,000
Tax deductions:		
Interest	$5,625,000	
Amortization of flotation costs ($480,000/30)	16,000	
Total	$5,641,000	

Tax savings ($5,641,000)(0.40)	2,256,400
After-tax cash outflow on old bond	$3,368,600

For the new bonds Albany proposes to issue, the after-tax cash outflow is as follows:

Interest on new bond ($50,000,000)(0.10)		$5,000,000
Tax deductions:		
Interest	$5,000,000	
Amortization of flotation costs ($875,000/25)	35,000	
Total	$5,035,000	
Tax savings ($5,035,000)(0.40)		2,014,000
After-tax cash outflow on new bond		$2,986,000

The incremental cash savings that will occur for each of the next 25 years is as follows:

Cash outflow on old bond	$3,368,600
Less: Cash outflow on new bond	2,986,000
Annual cash saving, ΔCF_t	$ 382,600

STEP 3. *Calculating the Net Present Value.* Now that the incremental initial investment and the annual cash savings are available, the NPV of refunding can be calculated using the after-tax interest rate on the new bond issue as the discount rate. This after-tax rate is $0.10(1 - T)$, or 6 percent. With the after-tax cash flow stream as follows:

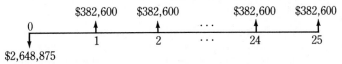

the net present value is

$$NPV = \$382,600(PVA_{6\%, 25yr}) - \$2,648,875$$

$$= \$382,600(12.783) - \$2,648,875 = \$2,241,900.80$$

Since the NPV is positive, the existing $11\frac{1}{4}$ percent bonds should be refunded.[1] If the NPV were negative, Albany would not want to refund the issue unless it wanted to remove some overly restrictive covenants imposed on the firm by the present bond issue. Refunding (or refinancing) a preferred stock issue uses the same concepts, except that the dividends on preferred stock are not tax deductible.

Problems

Bond Refunding

13A.1 Johnson Management is considering whether to refund a $50 million, 20-year, 12 percent coupon-rate bond issue that was sold 5 years ago. It is amortizing $2 million in flotation costs on the 12 percent bonds over their 20-year life. The $50 million in new 15-year bonds

---

[1] As presented, the refunding analysis keeps the firm's debt/equity ratio the same, but changes the cash flows to the firm. It can be argued that to neutralize risk, the cash flows (or the financial strain) on the firm should be kept the same. The present value of the cash savings, which is $4,890,775.80, represents the size of a loan that could be borrowed (with principal and interest, at 10 percent, being paid over 25 years) with the same after-tax cash flow impact on the firm. If the size of this term loan, which neutralizes the cash flow risk differential, is larger than the initial investment required to refund the old bond, refunding should take place. The decision whether or not to refund remains the same if it is viewed in this manner, as opposed to the approach described in the text. This risk-neutralization approach is used for the lease versus purchase analysis considered in Chapter 17.

would carry an annual interest rate of 10 percent. A call premium of 7 percent would be required to retire the old bonds, and flotation costs of $1.75 million would apply to the new issue. The marginal tax rate is 30 percent, and there is a 1-month overlap. The Treasury bill rate is 8 percent.

a. Should Johnson refund the bonds?

(Do only if using Pinches Disk.)

b. Suppose the bond issue in (a) has an original maturity of 30 years, there are 20 years remaining to maturity, and the new bond issue has a 20-year maturity. Should the firm still refund?

c. What if flotation costs for the new issue were estimated to be $3.5 million? Should the firm still refund if everything else remains the same as in (a)?

d. If the new bonds carry an interest rate of 11 percent, what should the decision be in (a), (b), and (c)?

Bond Refunding

13A.2 Micro Computers currently has $150 million of 14 percent coupon-rate bonds outstanding, with a remaining life of 25 years. They were issued 5 years ago with a flotation cost of $1.5 million; the unamortized flotation cost is now $1.25 million. Right now, $150 million of 25-year, 12.5 percent coupon-rate bonds could be issued at par to refund these bonds. Interest rates are not expected to decline further, flotation costs on the new bonds are $2.25 million, the call premium on the old bonds is 12 percent, there is a 1-month overlap, and Micro's tax rate is 36 percent. The Treasury bill rate is 9 percent. Should the firm refund the existing bonds?

Refinancing a
Preferred Stock Issue

13A.3 Central Florida Power & Light is considering refinancing $100 million of existing 13 percent dividend-rate preferred stock. The preferred does not have a maturity date, but it can be called at 106.5 percent of par. The $100 million new preferred issue would carry a 12 percent dividend rate, require $2 million in flotation costs, and there is a 1-month overlap. The Treasury bill rate is 8 percent. Central Florida's tax rate is 40 percent. The $2 million in flotation costs are completely deductible for tax purposes in the current year. Thus, flotation costs are *not* amortized, as with bonds. Also, the call premium is *not* deductible for tax purposes when a preferred stock refinancing occurs. Should Central Florida refinance the preferred issue? (*Note:* Remember that dividends are an after-tax expense. This influences both the cash savings and the discount rate employed.)

Appendix 15A

Operating, Financial, and Total Leverage

In Chapter 15 the topic of operating leverage was mentioned as one of the elements affecting business risk. Financial leverage was also discussed at length as we considered the firm's capital structure. The concepts of operating leverage and financial leverage can both be carried further.

Operating Leverage

Operating leverage arises if a firm experiences fixed operating costs for such things as labor, rent, executive salaries, and the like. If a firm has only variable operating expenses, by definition it has no operating leverage. Operating leverage is the responsiveness of the firm's earnings before interest and taxes (EBIT) to fluctuations in sales. To understand operating leverage, let's continue with the example of Consolidated National from the chapter. In Table 15A.1, sales and other data are given for Consolidated. The present sales level is $32,000. This is the base level of sales at time period t_0. Also shown are two possible sales levels for next year. Case 1 is an $8,000 decrease in sales; case 2 represents an $8,000 increase. The question to be examined is this: How does EBIT respond to a 25 percent change in Consolidated's sales?

The 25 percent change in sales is determined as follows:

$$\text{percentage change in sales} = \frac{\$40,000 - \$32,000}{\$32,000} = \frac{\$8,000}{\$32,000} = 0.25 = 25\%$$

The percentage change in EBIT can be determined in a similar manner:

$$\text{percentage change in EBIT} = \frac{\$14,000 - \$10,000}{\$10,000} = \frac{\$4,000}{\$10,000} = 0.40 = 40\%$$

As Consolidated's sales change 25 percent, we see that its EBIT changes by 40 percent. This magnification in the percentage change in EBIT due to a given percentage change in sales is called operating leverage. The *degree of operating leverage, DOL*, is defined as

$$\begin{aligned}\text{degree of operating leverage} \\ \text{from base level sales}\end{aligned} = \text{DOL} = \frac{\text{percentage change in EBIT}}{\text{percentage change in sales}}$$

$$= \frac{\Delta \text{EBIT}/\text{EBIT}}{\Delta \text{sales}/\text{sales}} \qquad (15\text{A}.1)$$

Using Equation 15A.1, the degree of operating leverage for Consolidated is

$$\text{DOL}_{\$32,000} = 40\%/25\% = 1.6 \text{ times}$$

Table 15A.1 Base Level and Forecasted Sales and EBIT for Consolidated National

Operating leverage arises from the magnification of the fluctuation in sales, leading to a larger change in EBIT due to the presence of fixed operating costs.

	Case 1: Decrease Forecasted Sales, $t + 1$	Base Level Sales, t_0	Case 2: Increase Forecasted Sales, $t + 1$
	$\overbrace{\hspace{2cm}}^{-25\%}$	$\overbrace{\hspace{2cm}}^{+25\%}$	
Sales	$24,000	$32,000	$40,000
Variable operating costs	12,000	16,000	20,000
Revenue before fixed operating costs	12,000	16,000	20,000
Fixed operating costs	6,000	6,000	6,000
EBIT	$ 6,000	$10,000	$14,000
	$\underbrace{\hspace{2cm}}_{-40\%}$	$\underbrace{\hspace{2cm}}_{+40\%}$	

Thus, from the base sales of $32,000, a given percentage change in sales leads to a percentage change in EBIT that is 1.6 times as large.

A second way to determine the degree of operating leverage at any base level of sales is

$$\text{degree of operating leverage from base level sales} = \text{DOL} = \frac{\text{sales} - \text{variable costs}}{\text{EBIT}} \qquad (15\text{A}.2)$$

Using $32,000 as our base level of sales again, employing Equation 15A.2 and the data from Table 15A.1, DOL is

$$\text{DOL}_{\$32,000} = \frac{\$32,000 - \$16,000}{\$10,000} = \frac{\$16,000}{\$10,000} = 1.6 \text{ times}$$

Using either Equation 15A.1 or 15A.2, the degree of operating leverage is 1.6.

As the firm's sales increase, and assuming everything else stays constant, the degree of operating leverage declines, as shown below:

Sales	Degree of Operating Leverage*
$12,000 or below	Undefined
18,000	3.00
24,000	2.00
32,000	1.60
40,000	1.43
46,000	1.35

* Calculated using Equation 15A.2.

Thus, as sales become higher and higher, there are lower percentage fluctuations in EBIT. However, as long as some fixed operating expenses exist, the concept of operating leverage indicates that percentage changes in EBIT will exceed percentage changes in sales.

Financial Leverage

Financial leverage is the responsiveness of the firm's earnings per share to fluctuations in EBIT. Using data from Table 15.2, Table 15A.2 shows the impact of changes in Consolidated's EBIT on the reported EPS. When no debt is used, we see that a 40 percent change in EBIT leads to exactly a 40 percent change in EPS. With 20 percent of the capital structure in debt, however, a 40 percent change in EBIT leads to a 42.55 percent change in EPS. Finally, with 40 percent debt, a 40 percent change in EBIT leads to a 45.45 percent change in EPS. The magnification in EPS under capital structures B and C is caused by financial leverage.

Like the degree of operating leverage, the *degree of financial leverage, DFL,* can be calculated. Thus, DFL is

$$\frac{\text{degree of financial leverage}}{\text{from base level EBIT}} = \text{DFL} = \frac{\text{percentage change in EPS}}{\text{percentage change in EBIT}}$$

$$= \frac{\Delta EPS/EPS}{\Delta EBIT/EBIT} \qquad (15A.3)$$

Using this equation and the information from Table 15A.2, the degree of financial leverage when EBIT is $10,000, and capital structure C (which has 40 percent debt) is employed, is

Table 15A.2   Impact of Three Different Capital Structures on Consolidated National's Earnings per Share

The base case remains $32,000 in sales, which lead to EBIT of $10,000, as shown in Table 15A.1. All percentages are measured relative to this base.

	EBIT	Earnings per Share	
Capital structure A (zero debt)			
−40% {	$ 6,000	$0.72	} −40%
	10,000	1.20	
+40% {			} +40%
	14,000	1.68	
Capital structure B (20% debt)			
−40% {	$ 6,000	$0.81	} −42.55%
	10,000	1.41	
+40% {			} +42.55%
	14,000	2.01	
Capital structure C (40% debt)			
−40% {	$ 6,000	$0.96	} −45.45%
	10,000	1.76	
+40% {			} +45.45%
	14,000	2.56	

$DFL_{\$10,000} = 45.45\%/40\% = 1.14$ times

From a base of $10,000 EBIT, a given percentage change in EBIT will bring about a percentage change in EPS that is 1.14 times as large.

A second way to determine the degree of financial leverage is this:

$$\text{degree of financial leverage from base level EBIT} = DFL = \frac{EBIT}{EBIT - interest} \qquad (15A.4)$$

For Consolidated, we can again calculate its degree of financial leverage

$$DFL_{\$10,000} = \frac{\$10,000}{\$10,000 - \$1,200} = \frac{\$10,000}{\$8,800} = 1.14 \text{ times}$$

which is the same as we determined previously using Equation 15A.3.

Combining Operating and Financial Leverage

We have seen that operating leverage causes a change in the volume of sales to have a magnified effect on the firm's EBIT. Likewise, financial leverage causes a change in the firm's EBIT to have a magnified effect on the firm's EPS. When operating and financial leverage are combined, even small changes in the level of sales can have a large impact on EPS. For capital structure C this is shown in Table 15A.3. A 25 percent increase (decrease) in sales leads to a 45.45 percent increase (decrease) in EPS.

The *degree of combined leverage, DCL*, can be determined by using any one of the following equations. Thus, DCL is

Table 15A.3 Combined Leverage Effects for Consolidated National

Operating leverage arises from fixed costs of operation; financial leverage arises from fixed costs associated with financing. Combining both produces potentially wide swings in EPS as sales volume changes.

	Base Level Sales, t_0	Forecasted Sales, $t + 1$		
	+25%			
Sales	$32,000	$40,000		
Variable costs	16,000	20,000		
Revenues before fixed costs	16,000	20,000	DOL =	
Fixed costs	6,000	6,000	$\frac{40\%}{25\%} = 1.6$ times	
EBIT	$10,000	$14,000		
	+40%			DCL = $\frac{45.45\%}{25\%} = 1.82$
Interest	1,200	1,200		or $(1.6)(1.14) = 1.82$
EBT	8,800	12,800	DFL =	
Taxes (40%)	3,520	5,120	$\frac{45.45\%}{40\%} = 1.14$ times	
EAT	$ 5,280	$ 7,680		
Earnings per share	$5,280/3,000 = $1.76	$7,680/3,000 = $2.56		
	+45.45%			

Figure 15A.1 Graphic Depiction of the Relationship Between Operating and Financial Leverage

Firms like those in the airline industry have both high operating and high financial leverage. As the sales, or load factor, changes, EPS fluctuates widely.

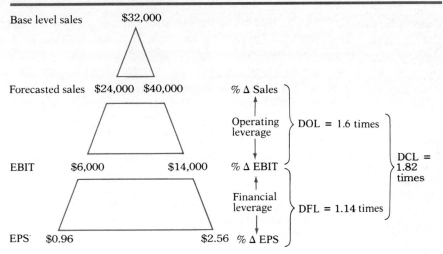

degree of combined leverage from base level sales $= DCL = \dfrac{\text{percentage change in EPS}}{\text{percentage change in sales}}$

$$= \frac{\Delta\text{EPS/EPS}}{\Delta\text{sales/sales}} \qquad (15A.5)$$

or

$$DCL = \frac{\text{sales} - \text{variable costs}}{\text{EBIT} - \text{interest}} \qquad (15A.6)$$

or

$$DCL = (DOL)(DFL) \qquad (15A.7)$$

Using Equation 15A.6 at sales of $32,000 and capital structure C, the DCL is

$$DCL_{\$32,000} = \frac{\$32,000 - \$16,000}{\$10,000 - \$1,200} = \frac{\$16,000}{\$8,800} = 1.82 \text{ times}$$

Likewise, using Equation 15A.7, the DCL is

$$DCL = (1.6)(1.14) = 1.82 \text{ times}$$

This interrelationship between operating and financial leverage can be depicted as in Figure 15A.1. The triangle represents the magnification of sales fluctuations and the effect they have on both EBIT and EPS when both fixed operating costs and fixed financing costs are present.

Problems

Operating Leverage   **15A.1** Ann Arbor Industries produces various wood products. Their average selling price is $10 per unit. The variable cost is $6 per unit, and total fixed costs are $60,000.

a. What would the firm's EBIT be if the number of units sold were 20,000, 30,000 or 40,000?

b. Using Equation 15A.2, find the degree of operating leverage for each of the three production and sales levels given in (a).

c. What conclusion can we draw about the degree of operating leverage as the sales increase?

Financial Leverage

15A.2 Miami Press is a specialized publisher of high-quality books. Its EBIT is $3 million, interest is $500,000, the tax rate is 35 percent, and there are 1 million shares of common stock outstanding.

a. What is Miami's EPS?

b. What is its degree of financial leverage?

c. If EBIT increases by 50 percent, what are the absolute and percentage changes in EPS?

d. Does the percentage change from (c) divided by the percentage change in EBIT of 50 percent (or 0.50) give you the same answer as calculated in (b)? Explain why this is so.

Combining Operating and Financial Leverage

15A.3 Tallman Brothers has the following income statement (in millions of dollars):

Sales	$50
Variable operating costs	24
Revenues before fixed operating costs	26
Fixed operating costs	13
EBIT	13
Interest	3
EBT	10
Taxes (30%)	3
EAT	$ 7

a. At this level of sales, what is Tallman's degree of operating leverage?

b. What is the degree of financial leverage?

c. What is the degree of combined leverage?

d. If sales should increase by 20 percent, by what percent would earnings increase after taxes? [*Note:* To answer this, simply multiply the 20 percent by the DCL from (c).]

e. If sales increase by 20 percent, what is the new dollar level of EAT?

Combined Leverage

15A.4 British Replications makes metal replicas of famous British buildings, people, and the like. Its current income statement (in millions of dollars) is

Sales	$20.0
Variable operating costs	8.0
Revenue before fixed operating costs	12.0
Fixed operating costs	4.0
EBIT	8.0
Interest	2.0
EBT	6.0
Taxes (40%)	2.4
EAT	$ 3.6

Earnings per share (1 million shares) is $3.60.

a. Calculate the following:
  (1) Degree of operating leverage
  (2) Degree of financial leverage
  (3) Degree of combined leverage

b. British Replications is considering changing to a new production process. Highly capital-intensive, the new process will double fixed costs to $8 million while lowering variable costs to $4 million at the current level of sales. If the investment required is financed by bonds, interest will increase by $600,000. If common stock is employed, 100,000 new shares will be issued. If sales remain constant, calculate the following for each financing method:

(1) Earnings per share

(2) Degree of combined leverage

c. If we expected sales to increase substantially, which plan would we favor if we are interested in maximizing EPS?

Appendix 20A

The Economic Order Quantity Model

Effective management of inventory is a complex and constant problem for all organizations. In this appendix we highlight some of the main elements of inventory management by examining the basic decision, the economic order quantity model, the assumptions involved, quantity discounts, and safety stocks. The primary purpose of the economic order quantity model is to determine how often and what quantity to order, and the average inventory to have on hand.

The Basic Inventory Decision

Although inventories differ substantially, all inventories share three costs—ordering, carrying, and shortage. Initially, we focus on ordering and carrying costs; the costs of running short will be considered when we add "safety stocks" to the inventory model. To consider the inventory problem, the following symbols and terms are employed:

C = carrying costs expressed in dollars per unit of inventory, $20

O = ordering costs expressed in dollars per order placed, $250

Q = order quantity expressed in units

S = sales per year expressed in units, 3,600

Consider an example: Reynolds Industries sells 3,600 units per year of a given item and is trying to determine the number of times per year and the quantity, Q, to order. If inventory usage is constant over time, and no safety stocks are kept, Reynolds' inventory will go to zero just before an order is received. With an order size of Q, the average inventory on hand is simply Q divided by 2, or $Q/2$. The total carrying costs are then the average inventory times the carrying cost per unit, C, or:

$$\text{carrying costs} = \left(\frac{Q}{2}\right)(C) = \frac{QC}{2} \tag{20A.1}$$

Likewise, we can determine the total ordering costs. With sales of S units per year, the number of orders placed per year is simply S divided by Q (the order size), or S/Q. Since each order costs an amount O to place, the total ordering costs are[1]

$$\text{ordering costs} = \left(\frac{S}{Q}\right)(O) = \frac{SO}{Q} \tag{20A.2}$$

---

[1] Some portion of the ordering costs may be fixed while the rest vary, depending on the number of units ordered. This modification can easily be included, but for simplicity the ordering costs are assumed to be $250 regardless of the number of units per order.

Table 20A.1 Carrying, Ordering, and Total Costs for Reynolds Industries

An order size of 300 units appears to minimize total costs. If either 310 or 290 units are ordered, for example, total costs increase to $6,003.

Size of Order (Q)	Average Inventory (Q/2)	Carrying Cost (Q/2)(C)	Number of Orders per Year (S/Q)	Ordering Cost (S/Q)(O)	Total Cost (3) + (5)
(1)	(2)	(3)	(4)	(5)	(6)
100	50	$1,000	36.0	$9,000	$10,000
200	100	2,000	18.0	4,500	6,500
300	150	3,000	12.0	3,000	6,000
400	200	4,000	9.0	2,250	6,250
500	250	5,000	7.2	1,800	6,800
600	300	6,000	6.0	1,500	7,500

Thus, Reynolds' total costs are equal to the carrying costs plus the ordering costs, so

total costs = carrying costs + ordering costs

$$= \frac{QC}{2} + \frac{SO}{Q} \tag{20A.3}$$

To maximize its market price, Reynolds must minimize the total cost of ordering and carrying inventory. How can we determine when Reynolds should order inventory, and what size, Q, the order should be? One way would be to employ a trial-and-error approach. As shown in Table 20A.1, if the order quantity is assumed to be 100 units, both the carrying costs of $1,000 and the ordering costs of $9,000 can be determined, leading to total costs of $10,000.

Likewise, by increasing the order quantity to 200, 300, and so forth, the other total costs in Table 20A.1 can be calculated. By inspection, it appears the total costs are minimized at $6,000, which occurs when the order quantity is 300 units and orders are placed 12 times a year. Plotting these data in Figure 20A.1 also suggests that total costs are minimized when the order quantity is 300 units.

The EOQ Model

There is a more direct way to determine the optimal order quantity, which is called the economic order quantity or EOQ. This is done by differentiating Equation 20A.3 with respect to Q and setting the result equal to zero.[2] The optimum value of Q is

[2] The first derivative with respect to Q defines the slope of the total cost curve. Setting this equal to zero specifies the minimum (zero slope) point. Thus,

$$\frac{d\,TC}{d\,Q} = \frac{C}{2} - \frac{SO}{Q^2} = 0$$

$$\frac{C}{2} = \frac{SO}{Q^2}$$

$$Q^2 = \frac{2SO}{C}$$

$$Q = \sqrt{\frac{2SO}{C}}$$

To verify that this is a minimum instead of a maximum value, the second derivative must be positive— which it is.

Figure 20A.1 Determination of the Minimum Total Costs and Economic Order Quantity

In the absence of safety stocks, the minimum total costs occur when the total ordering costs just equal the total carrying costs. This then determines the optimum size of the order, or EOQ.

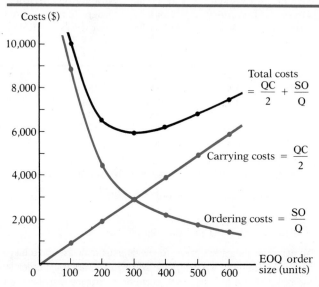

$$EOQ = \sqrt{\frac{2S0}{C}} \qquad (20A.4)$$

Employing the EOQ formula for Reynolds, we have

$$EOQ = \sqrt{\frac{2(\,3,600\,)(\,\$250\,)}{\$20}} = \sqrt{90,000} = 300 \text{ units}$$

which is the same as obtained by the trial-and-error approach in Table 20A.1.

Once the EOQ quantity is determined, we can see how the inventory for Reynolds Industries varies over time. As shown in Figure 20A.2, the inventory varies from a high of 300 units to a low of zero. The average number of units on hand at any point in time will be 150 units. Likewise, since 12 (3,600 divided by the EOQ of 300) orders will be placed a year, the firm will place an order approximately every 30 days. The slope of the line in Figure 20A.2 indicates the rate of sales per week. As it becomes steeper, sales are increasing per unit of time. A more gentle slope signifies fewer sales per unit of time. For Reynolds, the slope indicates that 70 units are sold per week. Since the delivery time is 7 days, Reynolds will order additional inventory every time its stock on hand falls to 70 units. By doing so, the inventory should reach zero on the same day the next delivery is received.

Quantity Discounts

Often the firm can take advantage of quantity discounts when it orders. Suppose Reynolds Industries does not receive any quantity discount when it orders 300 units at a time. If Reynolds increases the order to 400 units, the supplier will reduce the purchase price by $0.35 per unit. To determine whether Reynolds should take advantage of this discount, the incremental

Figure 20A.2 Inventory Position and Order Point Without Safety Stock

With a lead time of 7 days, Reynolds Industries places an order when the inventory level drops to 70 units.

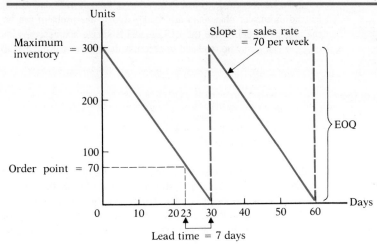

benefits must be examined in relationship to the incremental costs involved. The savings to Reynolds due to the lower purchase price is

savings from quantity discount = (discount per unit)(number of units)

$$= \$0.35(\,3,600\,) = \$1,260$$

The cost is the additional carrying cost less the savings in ordering costs due to cutting the number of orders per year from 12 to 9. The additional carrying costs can be calculated by employing a modification of Equation 20A.1 (where Q' is the new order size). This is

$$\frac{Q'C}{2} - \frac{(\,EOQ\,)(\,C\,)}{2} = \frac{(\,400\,)(\,\$20\,)}{2} - \frac{(\,300\,)(\,\$20\,)}{2} = \$4,000 - \$3,000 = \$1,000$$

The savings in ordering costs, employing a modification of Equation 20A.2, is

$$\frac{SO}{EOQ} - \frac{SO}{Q'} = \frac{(\,3,600\,)(\,\$250\,)}{300} - \frac{(\,3,600\,)(\,\$250\,)}{400} = \$3,000 - \$2,250 = \$750$$

The net increase in costs to Reynolds is $1,000 − $750, or $250.[3] Since the incremental costs are $250, while the incremental benefits are $1,260, Reynolds should increase the order size to 400 units. Thus, the EOQ approach serves as a point of departure to determine the benefits of quantity discounts and other changes in costs to the firm.

EOQ Assumptions

The three major assumptions of the EOQ model are these:

1. Constant or uniform demand
2. Constant carrying costs
3. Constant ordering costs

[3] This increase in costs of $250 can be seen in Table 20A.1, where the total costs are $6,000 when the order size is 300 units, whereas they are $6,250 at an order size of 400 units.

To make the EOQ approach useful when uncertainty exists and demand is not constant, safety stocks must be added. Carrying costs are often not constant per unit, but may vary due to the size of the inventory carried. This situation may be handled through a modification of the original total cost model. Finally, ordering costs may vary due to economies achieved if larger instead of smaller shipments are made. Again, this problem can be dealt with by modifying the original model. While the EOQ model is simple and assumes both certainty and constant costs, it can easily be modified to accommodate more realistic conditions.

Safety Stocks

Up to now we have not allowed for uncertainty—in terms of demand or in terms of delivery time. To deal with uncertainty, most firms employ a safety stock. Let's assume that Reynolds decides a safety stock of 100 units is needed to meet these uncertainties. Although the inclusion of this safety stock does not change the EOQ of 300 units, it does increase the level of inventory held. This idea is illustrated in Figure 20A.3(a). Note that with a safety stock of 100 units, the order point is set at 170 units instead of the previous 70.

In Figure 20A.3(b) the actual experience of Reynolds Industries is shown. In the first segment, we see that the sales rate is somewhat less than expected. [The slope of the line

Figure 20A.3 Inventory Position and Order Point with Uncertainty and Safety Stock

Uncertain demand and delivery times are cushioned by the safety stock. Without it, Reynolds Industries would have experienced three stock outages.

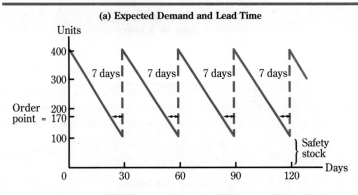

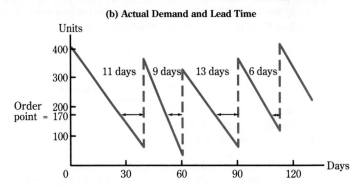

is less than in Figure 20A.3(a).] At the order point of 170, an order is placed for 300 more units. Instead of taking 7 days for delivery, however, it actually takes 11 days. The inventory has been depleted to 70 units before the order is received. In the second segment, sales are more than expected. [A steeper slope than in Figure 20A.3(a).] With the time of 9 days from placing the order until its receipt, the stock falls to 30 units before the next order of 300 is received. As a result of the heavy demand and slow delivery, the safety stock has virtually been depleted. During the third and fourth segments, both demand and delivery times continue to fluctuate. By the receipt of the fourth shipment, however, the inventory has been built back up. The important part of this example is to emphasize the role of the safety stock in absorbing random fluctuations in both demand and delivery times.

Determining the amount of the safety stock is not always easy. But some points should be mentioned. First, the greater the uncertainty concerning either demand or delivery times, the larger the safety stock should be. Second, how critical is it if we run out of inventory? Will we incur substantial lost sales, lose customer goodwill, or have to shut down the production line? Finally, how much do we incur in additional carrying costs by increasing safety stock? Ultimately, the amount of safety stock carried involves a balancing of the costs incurred if we run out versus those arising from carrying more inventory. To maximize the market value of the firm, we should not add safety stock beyond the point where the additional carrying costs equals the benefits derived from avoiding a stock outage.

Self-Test Problem   (Solution appears on page 742.)

EOQ and Reorder Point   **ST 20A.1**   Cameron Industries sells high-quality equipment. Cameron has a yearly demand of 45,000 units, carrying costs are $0.30 per unit, and the cost of placing an order with its supplier is $30. The lead time for placing an order is 5 days (assume a 365-day year). Cameron keeps a 6-day supply on hand as a safety stock. (*Note:* Carry calculations to two decimal places.)

a. What is the economic order quantity (EOQ)?
b. On average, how many units are sold per day?
c. How much safety stock does Cameron have on hand?
d. What is the firm's reorder point?

Problems

Inventory Costs   **20A.1**   A firm has a demand for 5,600 units per year, the carrying cost per unit is $10, and the ordering cost is $70 per order.

a. Fill in the blanks in the table below.

Size of Order (Q) (1)	Average Inventory (Q/2) (2)	Carrying Cost (Q/2)(C) (3)	Number of Orders per Year(S/Q) (4)	Ordering Cost (S/Q)(O) (5)	Total Cost (3 + 5) (6)
80					
160					
280					
400					
700					

b. What is the EOQ?

| EOQ and Quantity Discounts | **20A.2** King's Drug Stores sells 225,000 rolls of camera film a year. Its carrying costs are $0.10 cents per roll, and ordering costs are $200 per order. |

a. What is the economic order quantity?

b. Its supplier now offers King's a quantity discount of $0.01 per roll if the order size is increased to 90,000 rolls. Should King's take advantage of the quantity discount?

c. What other factors might also influence the decision to take or not take the quantity discount?

EOQ and Safety Stock

20A.3 New Orleans Tool needs 122,500 units per year. The carrying costs per unit are $5, ordering costs are $1,000 per order, and the safety stock (already on hand) is 4,000 units. The expected delivery time is 5 days.

a. What is the economic order quantity?

b. What is the optimal number of orders to place per year?

c. Assuming a 365-day year, at what inventory level should a reorder be placed?

EOQ, Reorder Point, and Average Inventory

20A.4 Dewitt Lawn and Garden Center sells 50,000 bags of potting soil annually. The firm keeps a safety stock of 1,000 bags on hand, carrying costs are $0.10 per bag, and ordering costs are $25 per order. The lead time is 9 days. Assume a 365-day year. (*Note:* Carry calculations to two decimal places.)

a. What is Dewitt's EOQ?

b. How often is an order for more potting soil placed?

c. What is the reorder point?

d. What is Dewitt's average potting soil inventory?

Solutions to
Self-Test Problems

Chapter 2

ST 2.1   **a.**   total taxable income = $30,000 + $1,900 [i.e., ($20,000)(0.095)] = $31,900

tax liability = ($18,550)(0.15) + ($31,900 − $18,550)(0.28) = $6,520.50

b.   after-tax cash flow

with corporate bond = $31,900 − $6,520.50 = $25,379.50

with municipal bond = $30,000 − tax on $30,000

+ interest on municipal bond of $1,400 [i.e., ($20,000)(0.07)]

tax on $30,000 = $2,782.50 + ($30,000 − $18,550)(0.28) = $5,988.50

after-tax cash flow = $30,000 − $5,988.50 + $1,400 = $25,411.50

Fritz is better off by $32 ($25,411.50 − $25,379.50) with the municipal bond.

c.   tax-exempt yield = (taxable yield)(1 − marginal tax rate)

7% = (taxable yield)(1 − 0.28)

7% = (taxable yield)(0.72)

(indifferent) taxable yield = 7%/0.72 = 9.72%

ST 2.2   For simplicity, in this problem cash inflows are assumed to equal taxable income, while cash outflows equal taxable expenses. This is not generally the case—so this assumption *will not* be maintained later in the book.

Issuing common stock

Income	$14.00 million
Expenses	8.00
Taxable income (EBT)	6.00
Taxes (40%)	2.40
Earnings after tax	3.60
Cash dividends	1.80
After-tax cash flow	$ 1.80 million

Issuing debt

Income	$14.00 million
Expenses (other than interest)	8.00
Interest ($30 million)(0.08)	2.40
Taxable income (EBT)	3.60
Taxes (40%)	1.44
After-tax cash flow	$ 2.16 million

Joehnk Hotel has $360,000 ($2.16 million − $1.80 million) more in after-tax cash flow by using debt financing.

Chapter 3

ST 3.1

$$\text{average collection period} = \frac{\text{accounts receivable}}{\text{sales}/365}$$

So

$$\text{sales} = \frac{(\text{accounts receivable})(365)}{\text{average collection period}} = \frac{(\$500)(365)}{10} = \$18,250$$

$$\text{gross margin} = \frac{\text{gross margin on sales}}{\text{sales}} = \frac{\text{sales} - \text{cost of goods sold}}{\text{sales}}$$

So

$$\text{cost of goods sold} = \text{sales} - [(\text{gross margin})(\text{sales})]$$

$$= \$18{,}250 - [(0.20)(\$18{,}250)] = \$14{,}600$$

$$\text{inventory turnover} = \frac{\text{cost of goods sold}}{\text{inventory}}$$

So

$$\text{inventory} = \text{cost of goods sold/inventory turnover}$$

$$= \$14{,}600/29.2 = \$500$$

$$\text{quick ratio} = \frac{\text{current assets} - \text{inventory}}{\text{current liabilities}}$$

So

$$\text{current assets} = [(\text{quick ratio})(\text{current liabilities})] + \text{inventory}$$

$$= [(2.0)(\$400)] + \$500 = \$1{,}300$$

Since

$$\text{current assets} = \text{cash} + \text{accounts receivable} + \text{inventory}$$

then

$$\text{cash} = \text{current assets} - \text{accounts receivable} - \text{inventory}$$

$$= \$1{,}300 - \$500 - \$500 = \$300$$

$$\text{return on total assets} = \frac{\text{net income}}{\text{total assets}}$$

So

$$\text{total assets} = \text{net income/return on total assets}$$

$$= \$200/0.08 = \$2{,}500$$

Since

$$\text{total assets} = \text{current assets} + \text{net plant and equipment}$$

then

$$\text{net plant and equipment} = \text{total assets} - \text{current assets}$$

$$= \$2{,}500 - \$1{,}300 = \$1{,}200$$

$$\text{return on equity} = \frac{\text{net income}}{\text{stockholders' equity}}$$

So

$$\text{stockholders' equity} = \text{net income/return on equity}$$

$$= \$200/0.20 = \$1{,}000$$

Since

$$\text{stockholders' equity} = \text{common stock} + \text{retained earnings}$$

then

$$\text{common stock} = \text{stockholders' equity} - \text{retained earnings}$$

$$= \$1{,}000 - \$300 = \$700$$

Since

$$\text{total liabilities} = \text{total assets}$$

and

$$\text{total liabilities and} = \text{current liabilities} + \text{long-term debt}$$
$$\text{stockholders' equity} \quad + \text{stockholders' equity}$$

then

$$\text{long-term debt} = \text{total liabilities} - \text{current liabilities} - \text{stockholders' equity}$$
$$= \$2,500 - \$400 - \$1,000 = \$1,100$$

The balance sheet is as follows:

Cash	$ 300	Current liabilities	$ 400
Accounts receivable	500	Long-term debt	1,100
Inventory	500	Common stock	700
Net plant and equipment	1,200	Retained earnings	300
Total assets	$2,500	Total liabilities and	
		stockholders' equity	$2,500

ST 3.2

a. (1)
$$\text{total asset turnover} = \frac{\text{sales}}{\text{total assets}}$$

$$\text{sales} = (\text{total asset turnover})(\text{total assets})$$
$$= (5)(\$5,000,000) = \$25,000,000$$

Then
$$\text{net profit margin} = \frac{\text{net income}}{\text{sales}} = \frac{\$500,000}{\$25,000,000} = 2.0\%$$

(2)
$$\text{return on total assets} = (\text{net profit margin})(\text{total asset turnover})$$
$$= (2.0\%)(5) = 10.0\%$$

(3)
$$\text{return on equity} = \text{return on total assets} \bigg/ \left(1 - \frac{\text{total debt}}{\text{total assets}}\right)$$

$$= 10.0\%/(1 - 0.20) = 12.5\%$$

b. (1)
$$\text{total asset turnover} = \frac{\text{sales}}{\text{total assets}} = \frac{\$25,000,000}{\$6,000,000} = 4.167$$

So
$$\text{return on total assets} = (3.0\%)(4.167) = 12.5\%$$

(2)
$$\text{return on equity} = \text{return on total assets} \bigg/ \left(1 - \frac{\text{total debt}}{\text{total assets}}\right)$$

$$= 12.5\%/0.80 = 15.625\%$$

c. Letting W be the new ratio of total debt to total assets, we have

$$\text{return on equity} = \text{return on total assets}/(1 - W)$$

$$15.625\% = 10.0\%/(1 - W)$$

$$1 - W = 10.0\%/15.625\%$$

$$1 - W = 0.64$$

$$W = 1 - 0.64 = 0.36$$

Thus, by increasing W (the ratio of total debt to total assets) to 0.36, or 36 percent, the return on total assets could stay at 10 percent and still achieve a 15.625 percent return on equity.

Chapter 4

ST 4.1

Parkwest Hotel

	GAAP Income Statement	Taxable Income Statement	Actual Cash Flow
Revenues	$180,000	$180,000	$180,000
All operating expenses except depreciation	142,000	142,000	142,000
Depreciation	15,000	20,000	
EBIT	23,000	18,000	
Interest	11,000	11,000	11,000
EBT	12,000	7,000	
Taxes (30%)	3,600	2,100	2,100
Net income	$ 8,400	$ 4,900	
Actual cash flow			$ 24,900

ST 4.2

a. For quarter 1:

$$\text{cost of goods sold} = \$40,000 + (\text{sales})(0.20)$$
$$= \$40,000 + (\$100,000)(0.20) = \$60,000$$

selling, general, and
administrative expenses $= \$10,000 + (\$100,000)(0.05) = \$15,000$

$$\text{taxes} = (\text{cash inflows} - \text{cash outflows})(0.40)$$
$$= (\$100,000 - \$60,000 - \$15,000 - \$5,000)(0.40) = \$8,000$$

Total operating inflows are $100,000, while total operating outflows are $88,000 ($60,000 + $15,000 + $5,000 + $8,000). After calculating the same information for the other 3 quarters, the net cash inflow or outflow per quarter is

	Quarter			
	1	**2**	**3**	**4**
1. Total operating cash inflow	$100,000	$120,000	$140,000	$100,000
2. Total operating cash outflow	− 88,000	− 99,000	− 110,000	− 88,000
3. Other net inflow (+) or outflow (−)	+ 10,000	− 50,000	− 60,000	+ 20,000
4. Net cash inflow (+) or outflow (−) (1 + 2 + 3)	$ 22,000	−$ 29,000	−$ 30,000	$ 32,000

The short-term financing needed is calculated as follows:

	Quarter			
	1	**2**	**3**	**4**
1. Cash at start of period	$20,000	$42,000	$13,000	−$17,000
2. Change in cash balance	+ 22,000	− 29,000	− 30,000	+ 32,000
3. Cash at end of period (1 + 2)	42,000	13,000	− 17,000	15,000
4. Minimum cash balance required	− 15,000	− 15,000	− 15,000	− 15,000
5. Cumulative short-term financing needed (−) or surplus (+) (3 + 4)	$27,000	−$ 2,000	−$32,000	0

Under the most likely scenario, CRF has to borrow in quarters 2 and 3, and will just break even in quarter 4. It will not violate the loan agreement.

b. Under the pessimistic sales forecast, the final figures (you calculate them!) are as follows:

	\ Quarter			
	1	**2**	**3**	**4**
Net cash inflow (+) or outflow (−)	$13,000	−$28,000	−$29,000	$23,000
Cumulative short-term financing needed (−) or surplus (+)	$18,000	−$10,000	−$39,000	−$16,000

Since it will still be borrowing to meet the negative cumulative outflow in quarter 4, CRF would violate the loan agreement (unless some cash inflows other than borrowing are found).

c. For the optimistic forecast, we have

	\ Quarter			
	1	**2**	**3**	**4**
Net cash inflow (+) or outflow (−)	$31,000	−$40,000	−$36,000	$41,000
Cumulative short-term financing needed (−) or surplus (+)	$36,000	−$ 4,000	−$40,000	$ 1,000

Yes, CRF can increase the other net cash outflows as planned.

ST 4.3

Cash is ($50,000)(0.05)	$ 2,500
Accounts receivable are ($50,000)(0.15)	7,500
Inventory is ($50,000)(0.20)	10,000
Net long-term assets are ($50,000)(0.30)	15,000
Current liabilities are half of current assets [($2,500 + $7,500 + $10,000)/2]	10,000
Long-term debt is a "plug" figure	
Common stock is the same as last year	5,000
After-tax profits are ($50,000)(0.05)	2,500
Dividends are ($2,500)(0.40)	1,000
Accordingly, the transfer to retained earnings is $2,500 − $1,000	1,500
Total retained earnings = $10,000 + $1,500	11,500
Total financing needed, excluding any debt, is $35,000 − ($10,000 + $5,000 + $11,500)	8,500

Ciliotta, Inc.
Pro Forma Balance Sheet
December 31

Assets		Liabilities and Stockholders' Equity	
Cash	$ 2,500	Current liabilities	$10,000
Accounts receivable	7,500	Long-term debt	8,500
Inventory	10,000	Common stock	5,000
Net long-term assets	15,000	Retained earnings	11,500
Total assets	$35,000	Total liabilities and stockholders' equity	$35,000

Chapter 5

ST 5.1

a. $FV_n = PV_0(FV_{k,n})$

$FV_6 = \$1,000(FV_{11\%,6yr}) = \$1,000(1.870) = \$1,870$

Total interest = $1,870 - $1,000 = $870

b. The certificate is worth $1,000. Thus,

$$FV_1 = \$1,000(\,FV_{11\%,1yr}\,) = \$1,000(\,1.110\,) = \$1,110$$

Each year the interest will be $1,110 - $1,000 = $110. Since there are 6 years, the total interest withdrawn is (6)($110) = $660.

c. This arises since interest is earned on interest (i.e., it is compounded) in (a), but not in (b).

ST 5.2

Stream A at 11 Percent

$$PV_0 = \$100(\,PV_{11\%,1yr}\,) + \$200(\,PVA_{11\%,2yr}\,)(\,PV_{11\%,1yr}\,) + \$300(\,PVA_{11\%,2yr}\,)(\,PV_{11\%,3yr}\,)$$

$$= \$100(\,0.901\,) + \$200(\,1.713\,)(\,0.901\,) + \$300(\,1.713\,)(\,0.731\,) = \$774.44$$

Stream B at 11 Percent

$$PV_0 = \$400(\,1.713\,) + \$100(\,2.444\,)(\,0.812\,) = \$883.65$$

At zero percent the present value is just the sum of the cash flows, which is $1,100 for stream A and also $1,100 for stream B.

ST 5.3

$$PV_0 = FV_1(\,PV_{k,1yr}\,) + FV_2(\,PV_{k,2yr}\,)$$

$$\$5,893 = \$3,000(\,PV_{?\%,1yr}\,) + \$5,000(\,PV_{?\%,2yr}\,)$$

Trial-and-error must be employed to find the discount rate that makes the present value of the inflows (the right-hand side of the equation) equal the cash outflow (the left-hand side).

Year	CF	× PV at 21% =	Present Value
1	$3,000	0.826	$2,478
2	5,000	0.683	3,415
		PV_0 =	$5,893

Since 21 percent makes the present value of the inflows exactly equal to the cash outflow of $5,893, the annual compound rate is exactly 21 percent.

ST 5.4

To find the total payment per year, we have:

$$PV_0 = PMT(\,PVA_{13\%,20yr}\,)$$

A = $70,250/7.025 = $10,000

Year 1   Interest = ($70,250)(0.13) = $9,132.50
Principal repayment = $10,000 - $9,132.50 = $867.50
Remaining balance   = $70,250 - $867.50 = $69,382.50

Year 2   Interest = ($69,382.50)(0.13) = $9,019.72
Principal repayment = $10,000 - $9,019.72 = $980.28
Remaining balance   = $69,382.50 - $980.28 = $68,402.22

Year 3   Interest = ($68,402.22)(0.13) = $8,892.29
Principal repayment = $10,000 - $8,892.29 = $1,107.71

ST 5.5

The size of the loan payment is based on the $80,000, so:

$$PV_0 = PMT(\,PVA_{12\%,30yr}\,)$$

PMT = $80,000/8.055 = $9,931.72

Since Linda Jackson received only $74,448 net, her yearly cost is

$$PV_0 = PMT(\,PVA_{?\%,30yr}\,)$$

$$PVA_{?\%,30yr} = \$74,448/\$9,931.72 = 7.496$$

Looking across the row for year 30 in Table F.4, a PVA of 7.496 gives an annual cost of 13 percent.

a. $PV_0 = \dfrac{FV_n}{\left(1+\dfrac{k}{m}\right)^{mn}} = \dfrac{\$750}{\left(1+\dfrac{0.20}{1}\right)^{1(5)}} = \dfrac{\$750}{(1.20)^5} = \$301.41$

b. $PV_0 = \dfrac{\$750}{\left(1+\dfrac{0.20}{2}\right)^{2(5)}} = \dfrac{\$750}{(1.10)^{10}} = \$289.16$

c. $PV_0 = \$282.67$

a. $k_{effective} = \left(1+\dfrac{k_{nom}}{m}\right)^m - 1 = \left(1+\dfrac{0.09}{1}\right)^1 - 1 = (1.09)^1 - 1 = 9.000\%$

b. $k_{effective} = \left(1+\dfrac{0.09}{4}\right)^4 - 1 = (1.022500)^4 - 1 = 9.308\%$

c. $k_{effective} = 9.416\%$
d. $k_{effective} = 9.417\%$

Chapter 6

Annually

a. $B_0 = I(PVA_{k_b,n}) + M(PV_{k_b,n})$

$\quad = \$120(PVA_{12\%,10\,yr}) + \$1,000(PV_{12\%,10\,yr})$

$\quad = \$120(5.650) + \$1,000(0.322) = \$1,000$

b. $B_0 = \$895.92$

c. $B_0 = \$1,268.20$

Semiannually

a. $B_0 = \dfrac{I}{2}(PVA_{k_b/2,\,2 \times n}) + M(PV_{k_b/2,\,2 \times n})$

$\quad = \$60(PVA_{6\%,20}) + \$1,000(PV_{6\%,20}) = \$688.20 + \$312 = \$1,000.20 \approx \$1,000$

b. $B_0 = \$893.64$

c. $B_0 = \$1,271.40$

This problem requires that we reinvest the interest payments and compound them forward to the end of the 20th year (40 periods). Then, by knowing the beginning price of $1,000 and the terminal value (which is the compound value of the interest received plus the $1,000 par), we can solve for the realized return. All calculations must take the semiannual nature of the bond into account.

$FV_{40} = \begin{matrix}\text{future value of}\\\text{interest for}\\\text{first 10 periods}\\\text{at 7\%}\end{matrix} + \begin{matrix}\text{future value of}\\\text{interest for}\\\text{next 10 periods}\\\text{at 5\%}\end{matrix} + \begin{matrix}\text{future value of}\\\text{interest for}\\\text{last 20 periods}\\\text{at 4\%}\end{matrix} + \begin{matrix}\text{maturity}\\\text{value}\end{matrix}$

$= \$70(FVA_{7\%,10})(FV_{7\%,30}) + \$70(FVA_{5\%,10})(FV_{5\%,20})$
$+ \$70(FVA_{4\%,20}) + \$1,000$

$$= \$70(\,13.816\,)(\,7.612\,) + \$70(\,12.578\,)(\,2.653\,) + \$70(\,29.778\,) + \$1{,}000$$

$$= \$7{,}361.72 + \$2{,}335.86 + \$2{,}084.46 + \$1{,}000 = \$12{,}782.04$$

$$PV_{?\%,\,40} = PV_0/FV_n = \$1{,}000/\$12{,}782.04 = 0.078$$

Looking up this PV factor and eyeballing it, the semiannual rate is 6.60 percent. (Via financial calculator, it is 6.58 percent.) Converting this to a yearly rate, we see that Homer's realized return is 13.20 percent [i.e., (6.60 percent)(2)], versus an expected return of 14 percent when he purchased the bond. The difference is due to the fact that Homer could not reinvest the interest payments at 14 percent.

ST 6.3

a.

Dividend (or Price)		$\times$	PV at 14% =	Present Value
$D_1 = \$2.00(1.12)$	$= \$\ 2.24$		0.877	$\$\ 1.96$
$D_2 =\ \ 2.00(1.12)^2$	$=\ \ 2.51$		0.769	1.93
$D_3 =\ \ 2.00(1.12)^3$	$=\ \ 2.81$		0.675	1.90
$D_4 =\ \ 2.81(1.06)$	$=\ \ 2.98$		0.592	1.76
$D_5 =\ \ 2.81(1.06)^2$	$=\ \ 3.16$		0.519	1.64
$P_5 = \dfrac{3.16(1.02)}{0.14 - 0.02} = \dfrac{3.2232}{0.12}$	$=\ \ 26.86$		0.519	13.94
			$P_0 =$	$\$23.13$

b. D_1 through D_5 are the same. Thus $P_5 = \$3.16/0.14 = \$22.57$, and P_0 is therefore $\$20.90$.

Chapter 7

ST 7.1

a. $\bar{k} = \displaystyle\sum_{i=1}^{n} k_i P_i$

$$\bar{k}_A = 0.2(\,40\%\,) + 0.5(\,0\%\,) + 0.3(\,-10\%\,) = 5\%$$

For stock B the expected rate of return is 11 percent, while it is 8 percent for the portfolio AB.

b. $\sigma = \sqrt{\displaystyle\sum_{i=1}^{n} (\,k_i - \bar{k}\,)^2 P_i}$

For stock A, we have:

$(\,(k_i - \bar{k}\,)$	$(k_i - \bar{k})^2$	$\times$	P_i	$= (k_i - \bar{k})^2 P_i$
$(40 - 5)$	1,225		0.2	245.0
$(0 - 5)$	25		0.5	12.5
$(-10 -5)$	225		0.3	67.5
		variance $= \sigma^2 =$		325.0

$$\sigma = \sqrt{325.0} = 18.0278\% \approx 18.03\%$$

For stock B and the portfolio AB, the standard deviations are 19.97 percent and 19.00 percent, respectively.

From the discussion in the chapter we know that when the correlation between two securities is perfectly positive, there is no reduction in risk by forming a portfolio. Thus, when the correlation is +1.00, the following must hold: $\sigma_P = W_A\sigma_A + W_B\sigma_B$. The simple average of the standard deviations for the two securities is $(18.03\% + 19.97\%)/2 =$

19.00%, which is the same as the standard deviation for portfolio AB. Hence the correlation between the returns on stocks A and B is +1.00.

c. The expected return on the market portfolio is

$$\bar{k}_M = 0.2(\,40\%\,) + 0.5(\,15\%\,) + 0.3(\,-15\%\,) = 11\%$$

d. $k_j = k_{RF} + \beta_j(\,k_M - k_{RF}\,)$

Taking the data available, we have

$$8\% = 5\% + \beta_{AB}(\,11\% - 5\%\,)$$

$$8\% = 5\% + 6\%(\,\beta_{AB}\,)$$

$$\beta_{AB} = \frac{8\% - 5\%}{6\%} = \frac{3\%}{6\%} = 0.50$$

ST 7.2 Saying the asset is 60 percent riskier than the market is the same as saying that the beta for the asset is 1.6. Thus

$$k_j = k_{RF} + \beta_j(\,k_M - k_{RF}\,)$$

$$= 6\% + 1.6(\,12\% - 6\%\,) = 15.6\%$$

ST 7.3 a. $k_s = k_{RF} + \beta_j(\,k_M - k_{RF}\,)$

$$= 6\% + 1.20(\,12\% - 6\%\,) = 6\% + 7.2\% = 13.2\%$$

b. $k_s = 16.2\%$

c. $k_s = 16.8\%$

d. (1) $k_s = 18\%$

(2) $k_s = 9\%$

ST 7.4 $$k_j = k_{RF} + \beta_j(\,k_M - k_{RF}\,)$$

$$k_{(Miller)} = 9\% + 1.7(\,14\% - 9\%\,) = 17.5\%$$

$$k_{(India)} = 12\%$$

$$k_{(Royal)} = 15\%$$

Stock	Expected Return	Required Return	Conclusion
Miller Aviation	18%	17.5%	Undervalued
India Imports	11	12	Overvalued
Royal Communications	15	15	Correctly valued

Chapter 8

ST 8.1 $$NPV_X = \$70{,}000(\,PV_{11\%,1yr}\,) + \$40{,}000(\,PV_{11\%,2yr}\,) + \$30{,}000(\,PV_{11\%,3yr}\,)$$
$$+ \$10{,}000(\,PVA_{11\%,2yr}\,)(\,PV_{11\%,3yr}\,) - \$120{,}000$$

$$= \$70{,}000(\,0.901\,) + \$40{,}000(\,0.812\,) + \$30{,}000(\,0.731\,)$$
$$+ \$10{,}000(\,1.713\,)(\,0.731\,) - \$120{,}000$$

$$= \$63{,}070 + \$32{,}480 + \$21{,}930 + \$12{,}522.03 - \$120{,}000 = \$10{,}002.03$$

$$NPV_Y = \$10,000(\,0.901\,) + \$20,000(\,0.812\,) + \$30,000(\,0.731\,)$$
$$+ \$50,000(\,0.659) + \$90,000(\,0.593\,) - \$120,000$$

$$= \$9,010 + \$16,240 + \$21,930 + \$32,950 + \$53,370 - \$120,000 = \$13,500$$

Using the NPV approach, project Y should be selected.

IRR$_X$

Year	CF (1)	PV at 15% (2)	Present Value [(1) × (2)] (3)	PV at 16% (4)	Present Value [(1) × (4)] (5)
1	$70,000	0.870	$ 60,900	0.862	$ 60,340
2	40,000	0.756	30,240	0.743	29,720
3	30,000	0.658	19,740	0.641	19,230
4	10,000	0.572	5,720	0.552	5,520
5	10,000	0.497	4,970	0.476	4,760
Present value of inflows			$121,570		$119,570

Since the IRR is the rate that makes the present value of the cash inflows equal the initial investment, CF_0, we have bracketed the IRR—it is between 15 and 16 percent, and closer to 16 percent (as seen by comparing $121,570 and $119,570 versus $120,000). By financial calculator, the IRR is 15.78 percent.

IRR$_Y$

The IRR for project Y (via financial calculator) is 14.19 percent.

Using the IRR criterion, project X would be chosen, since its IRR is larger than project Y's. The difference in rankings between NPV and IRR is due to different assumptions concerning reinvestment rates. To maximize the value of the firm, the NPV criterion should be used in mutually exclusive decisions. Hence, project Y should be chosen.

ST 8.2

a. **Initial Investment**

Investment in finished inventory	$150,000
Purchase of assets	80,000
Initial investment, CF_0	= $230,000

Operating Cash Flow

Depreciation = $80,000/5 = $16,000

$$CF = CFBT(\,1 - T\,) + Dep(\,T\,)$$
$$= (\,\$100,000 - \$40,000\,)(\,1 - 0.40\,) + \$16,000(\,0.40\,) = \$36,000 + \$6,400$$
$$= \$42,400$$

Terminal Cash Flow

This is just the release of the $150,000 tied up in inventory.

Cash Flow Stream

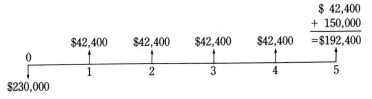

Net Present Value

$$NPV = \$42,400(\, PVA_{13\%,4yr}\,) + \$192,400(\, PV_{13\%,5yr}\,) - \$230,000$$
$$= \$42,400(\, 2.974\,) + \$192,400(\, 0.543\,) - \$230,000$$

$$= \$126,098 + \$104,473 - \$230,000 = \$571$$

Since the NPV is positive, Norris Electronics should expand its inventory.

b. Although the initial and terminal CFs remain unchanged, the operating cash flow stream must be adjusted. The CFBT becomes $10,000 instead of $60,000, and the final CF stream is as follows:

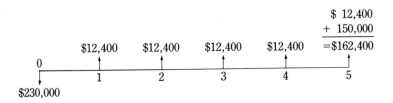

The NPV is −$104,939. Due to the opportunity cost of $50,000 per year, the investment is not warranted.

Chapter 9

ST 9.1

a. Depreciated Book Value
The current depreciated book value of the old asset is: $80,000 − $80,000(0.20 + 0.20) = $80,000 − $32,000 = $48,000.

b. Incremental Initial Investment

Purchase new machine	$120,000
Plus: Increase in net working capital	5,000
Tax on gain from sale of old machine for greater than book value [(0.40)($72,000 − $48,000)]	9,600
Less: Sell old machine	−72,000
Incremental initial investment, $\Delta CF_0 = $	$ 62,600

c. Incremental Depreciation

Year	Simplified ACRS Factors	× Original Cost of New Asset	= New Depreciation	Remaining Depreciation on Old*	Incremental Depreciation (3) − (4)
	(1)	**(2)**	**(3)**	**(4)**	**(5)**
1	0.20	$120,000	$24,000	$16,000	$ 8,000
2	0.32	120,000	38,400	16,000	22,400
3	0.19	120,000	22,800	16,000	6,800
4	0.15	120,000	18,000	—	18,000
5	0.14	120,000	16,800	—	16,800

* ($80,000)(0.20) = $16,000.

Incremental Operating Cash Flows

Year	ΔCFBT (1)	ΔCFBT(1 – T) (2)	ΔDep (3)	ΔDep(T) (4)	ΔCF (2) + (4) (5)
1	$22,000	$13,200	$ 8,000	$3,200	$16,400
2	22,000	13,200	22,400	8,960	22,160
3	22,000	13,200	6,800	2,720	15,920
4	22,000	13,200	18,000	7,200	20,400
5	22,000	13,200	16,800	6,720	19,920

d. Incremental Terminal Cash Flow

This is just the $5,000 release in net working capital. Therefore, the incremental CF stream is:

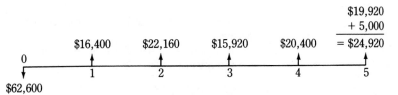

$$\begin{array}{c} \$19,920 \\ + 5,000 \\ \hline = \$24,920 \end{array}$$

e. The NPV at a 15 percent rate is $2,950. Since it is positive, the asset should be replaced.

ST 9.2 The NPV for Project I is

Year	CF	× PV at 14% =	Present Value
1	$ 60,000	0.877	$ 52,620
2	80,000	0.769	61,520
3	100,000	0.675	67,500
	Sum of discounted cash inflows		181,640
	Less: Initial investment		150,000
	NPV$_I$ =		$ 31,640

Since Projects I and II are interrelated, the total CF must be used. It is

	t_0	t_1	t_2	t_3
CFs, project I	−$150,000	$ 60,000	$ 80,000	$100,000
CFs, project II	− 60,000	30,000	30,000	30,000
Less: Reduction in projects I's CFs		(10,000)	(10,000)	(10,000)
Relevant CF stream	−$210,000	$ 80,000	$100,000	$120,000

Considering both projects together, the NPV is

Year	CF	× PV at 14% =	Present Value
1	$ 80,000	0.877	$ 70,160
2	100,000	0.769	76,900
3	120,000	0.675	81,000
	Sum of discounted cash inflows		228,060
	Less: Initial investment		210,000
	NPV$_{I \& II}$ =		$ 18,060

Since Pisano Industries' goal is to maximize NPV, it should accept only project I.

Chapter 10

ST 10.1

First, the internal rate of return (IRR) on the project must be determined. (*Note:* This is where the NPV on the project equals zero.) At 18 percent we have

Year	CF	× PV at 18%	= Present Value
1	$14,000	0.847	$11,858
2	14,000	0.718	10,052
3	11,000	0.609	6,699
4	15,000	0.516	7,740
5	17,000	0.437	7,429
6	30,329.74	0.370	11,222

$$\text{Sum of discounted cash flows} = \$55,000$$

Since the present value of the cash inflows exactly equals the initial investment of $55,000, the IRR is 18 percent.

For the firm to be indifferent, the NPV must equal zero so the IRR of 18 percent must be exactly on the security market line. Thus:

$$k_{project} = k_{RF} + \beta_{project}(k_M - k_{RF})$$

$$18\% = 8\% + 1.25(k_M - 8\%)$$

$$18\% = 8\% + 1.25\, k_M - 10\%$$

$$1.25\, k_M = 20\%$$

$$k_M = 20\%/1.25 = 16\%$$

At any market rate above 16 percent, the slope of the SML is such that the project is unacceptable; below 16 percent the SML (with a beta of 1.25) lies below the IRR of 18 percent, and the project is acceptable.

ST 10.2

a. $\text{Mean}_{word\ processor} = 0.20(\$70,000) + 0.60(\$60,000) + 0.20(\$30,000)$

$$= \$14,000 + \$36,000 + \$6,000 = \$56,000$$

$SD_{word\ processor} = \sqrt{0.20(\$70,000 - \$56,000)^2 + 0.60 (\$60,000 - \$56,000)^2 + 0.20(\$30,000 - \$56,000)^2}$

$$= \sqrt{\$39,200,000 + \$9,600,000 + \$135,200,000}$$

$$= \sqrt{\$184,000,000} = \$13,565$$

$CV_{word\ processor} = \$13,565/\$56,000 = 0.24$

$CV_{computer} = \$32,000/\$76,000 = 0.42$

Based on the coefficient of variation, the computer project is riskier than the word processing project.

b. $\text{Required return}_{word\ processor} = 8\% + 18\%(0.24) = 8\% + 4.32\% = 12.32\%$ or 12%

$NPV_{word\ processor} = \$56,000(PVA_{12\%, 5\,yr}) - \$215,000$

$$= \$56,000(3.605) - \$215,000 = \$201,880 - \$215,000 = -\$13,120$$

Reject the word processing system, since the NPV is negative.

Required return$_{computer}$ = 15.56% or 16%

NPV$_{computer}$ = −$21,176

Reject the microcomputer project also.

ST 10.3   **a.**   NPV = $23 million(PVA$_{10\%,15yr}$) − $150 million

= $23 million(7.606) − $150 million

= $174.938 million − $150 million = $24.938 million

Albany should build the resort.

b.   Expected CF = 0.2($30 million) + 0.7($23 million) + 0.1(0) = $22.1 million

NPV = $22.1 million(7.606) − $150 million = $18.093 million.

No, it does not change the decision.

Chapter 11

ST 11.1   **a.** $\sigma\sqrt{t} = 0.20\sqrt{0.65} = 0.1612$

$$\frac{P_0}{X/e^{k_{RF}t}} = \frac{\$35}{\$40/e^{0.11\times0.65}} = \frac{\$35}{\$40/e^{0.0715}}$$

$$= \$35/\$37.23985 = 0.9399$$

From Table F.7, the tabled value is 0.0349 and V_c is approximately $35(0.0349) = $1.22.

b.   Given the same two values calculated above, the tabled value from Table F.8 is 0.0988, and V_p is approximately $35(0.0988) = $3.46.

c. $\sigma\sqrt{t} = 0.20\sqrt{0.30} = 0.1095$

$$\frac{P_0}{X/e^{k_{RF}t}} = \frac{\$35}{\$40/e^{0.11\times0.30}} = \frac{\$35}{\$40/e^{0.0330}}$$

$$= \$35/\$38.70154 = 0.9044$$

From Table F.7, the tabled value is 0.0079 and V_c is approximately $35(0.0079) = $0.28.

ST 11.2

$$\text{lower limit} = \left(\begin{array}{c}\text{market price of}\\\text{common stock} -\\\text{exercise price}\end{array}\right)\left(\begin{array}{c}\text{number of shares}\\\text{purchased with}\\\text{one warrant}\end{array}\right)$$

lower limit when purchased = ($15 − $10)(2) = $10

lower limit now = ($35 − $10)(2) = $50

percentage return = ($50 − $10)/$10 = 400%

ST 11.3

Year (1)	Present Value of Free Cash Flows Discounted at 25 Percent, P_0 (2)	Standard Deviation Times the Square Root of Time (3)	Price (or Asset Value) Divided by the Present Value of the Exercise Price (4)
1	$5.5/e^{0.25 \times 1} = \$4.28$	$0.32\sqrt{1} = 0.3200$	$\dfrac{\$4.28}{\$6/e^{0.11 \times 1}} = 0.7963$
2	$9.5/e^{0.25 \times 2} = \$5.76$	$0.32\sqrt{2} = 0.4525$	$\dfrac{\$5.76}{\$7/e^{0.11 \times 2}} = 1.0253$
3	$12/e^{0.25 \times 3} = \$5.67$	$0.32\sqrt{3} = 0.5543$	$\dfrac{\$5.67}{\$8/e^{0.11 \times 3}} = 0.9858$

From Table F.8 the tabled values are given in column (2) below:

Year (1)	Tabled Put Option Factor (2)	×	P_0 (3)	=	Value of Guarantee (In millions) (4)
1	0.2942		$4.28		$1.26
2	0.1666		5.76		0.96
3	0.2292		5.67		1.30
			Value of guarantee =		$3.52

Santiago should charge an additional $3.52 million, above and beyond the base price for the division, due to the free cash flow guarantees.

Chapter 12

ST 12.1

a. The proceeds to Consumers Power equals ($80,000,000)(0.99125) = $79,300,000.

b. Total underwriting costs = $80,000,000 − $79,300,000 = $700,000.
Percentage underwriting costs = $700,000/$80,000,000 = 0.00875 = 0.875%.
The cost per bond was $1,000(0.00875) = $8.75.

c. (1) The amount was $2.50 per bond, or $125 [i.e., ($2.50)(50)].
(2) The bonds sold for $1,000 per bond so for 50 bonds, the gross proceeds equal $50,000. With a total of $125, the dealer paid $50,000 − $125 = $49,875 for the 50 bonds.

ST 12.2

$D_1 = \$4$

$$P_0 = \frac{D_1}{k_s - g} = \frac{\$4}{0.19 - 0.09} = \frac{\$4}{0.10} = \$40$$

Let X be the number of shares to be issued. The net proceeds of $16,560,000 are equal to

$16,560,000 = \$40(1 - 0.08)X$

$16,560,000 = \$40(0.92)X$

$16,560,000 = \$36.80X$

$X = \$16,560,000/\$36.80 = 450,000$

The number of shares to be issued is 450,000.

ST 12.3

N, the number of rights to buy one additional share, is given by

$$N = \frac{\text{existing shares}}{\text{additional shares}} = \frac{200,000}{20,000} = 10$$

Setting Equation 12.5 equal to Equation 12.6, we have

$$\frac{P_0 - P_s}{N + 1} = \frac{P_x - P_s}{N}$$

$$\frac{P_0 - \$12}{10 + 1} = \frac{\$16 - \$12}{10}$$

$$10(P_0 - \$12) = 11(\$4)$$

$$10(P_0) = \$44 + \$120$$

$$P_0 = \$164/10 = \$16.40$$

The rights-on stock price is $16.40.

Chapter 13

ST 13.1

EBIT must be four times greater than total interest so,

total interest = EBIT/4 = $200,000/4 = $50,000

The interest on the existing bonds is $16,000 [i.e., (0.10)($160,000)], so the amount of additional interest that can be paid and stay within the constraint is $50,000 − $16,000 = $34,000.

Interest = (coupon rate)(par value)

$34,000 = 0.08(par value)

Par value = $34,000/0.08 = $425,000

The maximum amount of new bonds that can be issued is $425,000.

ST 13.2

a.

$$\begin{array}{c}\text{size of each payment} \\ \text{to retire one-tenth} \\ \text{of the issue}\end{array} = \frac{\begin{array}{c}\text{total value of} \\ \text{bond issue}\end{array}}{\begin{array}{c}\text{number of years} \\ \text{to maturity}\end{array}} = \frac{\$30 \text{ million}}{10} = \$3 \text{ million per year}$$

b.

Year	Bonds Outstanding at Beginning of Year (In millions) (1)	After-Tax Interest (In millions) (1) × (0.10)(1 − T) (2)	Sinking Fund Payment (In millions) (3)	After-Tax Debt Service Obligation (In millions) (2) + (3) (4)
1	$30	$1.950	$3	$4.950
2	27	1.755	3	4.755
3	24	1.560	3	4.560
4	21	1.365	3	4.365
5	18	1.170	3	4.170
6	15	0.975	3	3.975
7	12	0.780	3	3.780
8	9	0.585	3	3.585
9	6	0.390	3	3.390
10	3	0.195	3	3.195

ST 13.3   **a.** The cost is the discount rate that equates the present value of the interest payments and the maturity value to the net proceeds to the firm of $9,850,000:

$9.85 \text{ million} = \$0.80 \text{ million}(PVA_{?\%,20yr}) + \$10 \text{ million}(PV_{?\%,20yr})$

At 8%	**At 9%**
PV = $10 million	$ 0.80 million(9.129) = $7.303 million
	10.00 million(0.178) = <u> 1.780 million</u>
	$PV_0 = \overline{\$9.083} \text{ million}$

The before-tax cost is slightly over 8 percent. Using a financial calculator, it is 8.15 percent.

b. Since the issue is sold at par, the before-tax cost is simply the coupon rate of 8.5 percent.

c. $9.80 \text{ million} = \$0.40 \text{ million}(PVA_{?\%,20yr}) + \$25 \text{ million}(PV_{?\%,20yr})$

At 7%	**At 8%**
$ 0.40 million(10.594) = $ 4.238 million	$ 0.40 million(9.818) = $3.927 million
25.00 million(0.258) = <u> 6.450 million</u>	25.00 million(0.215) = <u> 5.375 million</u>
$PV_0 = \overline{\$10.688} \text{ million}$	$PV_0 = \overline{\$9.302} \text{ million}$

The before-tax cost is between 7 and 8 percent, and by inspection appears closer to 8 percent. Using a financial calculator, it is 7.62 percent.

d. $9.90 \text{ million} = \$45 \text{ million}(PV_{?\%,20yr})$

Using a financial calculator the before-tax cost is 7.86 percent.

Since option c, the deep discount bond (at 7.62%), has the lowest percentage cost to maturity, it is the cheapest financing source.

ST 13.4   This problem is typical of what actually happens because market interest rates are constantly changing. When calculating the yield to maturity, YTM, in Chapter 6, we made an implicit assumption about the rate the future interest payments could be reinvested at. That assumed reinvestment rate was the calculated YTM. (This is exactly the same implied reinvestment rate assumption made when calculating IRRs in Chapter 8.)

a. Pam's expected yield to maturity is the 16 percent, because she bought the bond at par.

b. The interest received per year is $160 [i.e., ($1,000)(0.16)]. To calculate Pam's actual (compound) percentage return, the $160 received at both t_1 and t_2 must be compounded forward and added to the $160 received at t_3. Thus:

$$\text{future value at } t_3 = \text{interest}(FVA_{6\%,3yr}) + \$1,000$$

$$= \$160(3.184) + \$1,000 = \$1,509.44$$

The cash flow stream is

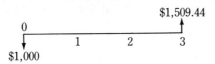

To solve for Pam's realized return, we have

$$\$1,000 = \$1,509.44(PV_{?\%,3yr})$$

$$PV_{?\%,3yr} = \$1,000/\$1,509.44 = 0.6625$$

Looking across the 3-year row on our PV table (Table F.3), the value is 0.675 at 14 percent and 0.658 at 15 percent. So the rate is between 14 and 15 percent, but closer to 15 percent. By financial calculator, the rate is 14.71 percent.

Pam's realized return of 14.71 percent is much less than her expected return of 16 percent. This is because of the reinvestment rate assumption embedded in the original YTM—that the interest payments at t = 1 and t = 2 would be reinvested at a 16 percent interest rate. When the actual reinvestment rate dropped to 6 percent, that resulted in a lower realized return for Pam. (*Note:* The drop all the way to 6 percent is not realistic, but it serves to illustrate the impact of varying the interest rate.)

Chapter 14

ST 14.1 **a. Specific Costs**

Debt

The bonds will net $1,020. Hence, the before-tax cost, k_b, is given by:

$$B_0 = I(PVA_{k_b,n}) + M(PV_{k_b,n})$$

$$\$1,020 = \$150(PVA_{?\%,10\,yr}) + \$1,000(PV_{?\%,10\,yr})$$

Via financial calculator, $k_b = 14.61\%$. $k_i = k_b(1 - T) = 14.61\%(1 - 0.30) = 10.23\%$.

Preferred stock

$$k_{ps} = D_1/P_0 = \$12/\$96 = 12.50\%$$

Internally generated common equity

$$k_s = \frac{D_1}{P_0} + g = \frac{\$5.00(1.11)}{\$120} + 11\% = 4.63\% + 11\% = 15.63\%$$

Financing proportions

common equity (internally generated) = $9 million/$15 million = 0.60

preferred stock = [(9,375 shares)($96)]/$15 million = $900,000/$15,000,000 = 0.06

Debt is the remainder, or

$$1.00 - (0.60 + 0.06) = 0.34$$

The WACC is

Component	After-Tax Cost	× W$_i$	=	Weighted Average Cost of Capital
Debt	10.23%	0.34		3.48%
Preferred stock	12.50	0.06		0.75
Common equity	15.63	0.60		9.38
				WACC = 13.61%

b. Specific Costs

Via financial calculator, $k_b = 16.58\%$, and $k_i = (16.58\%)(1 - 0.30) = 11.61\%$. Then, $k_{ps} = 14.06\%$ and k_s (external common equity) = 16.55%. The WACC is 14.72 percent; it is slightly over 1 percent higher than for the first increment.

Chapter 15

ST 15.1

a. The interest is ($200 million)(0.05) = $10 million per year.

EBIT	$50 million
Interest	10 million
Earnings	$40 million

$$k_s^L = \frac{E}{S} = \frac{\$40 \text{ million}}{\$400 \text{ million}} = 0.1000 = 10\%$$

$$\text{WACC} = k_b W_{\text{debt}} + k_s W_{\text{common equity}}$$

$$= (5\%)\left(\frac{\$200 \text{ million}}{\$600 \text{ million}}\right) + (10\%)\left(\frac{\$400 \text{ million}}{\$600 \text{ million}}\right)$$

$$= 1.67\% + 6.67\% = 8.34\%$$

b. The firm will now have $100 million debt and $500 million equity. The interest will be $5 million, and the earnings are as follows:

EBT	$50 million
Interest	5 million
Earnings	$45 million

$$k_s^L = \frac{\$45 \text{ million}}{\$500 \text{ million}} = 0.0900 = 9\%$$

The cost of capital should be the same as before. Thus,

$$\text{WACC} = (5\%)\left(\frac{\$100 \text{ million}}{\$600 \text{ million}}\right) + (9\%)\left(\frac{\$500 \text{ million}}{\$600 \text{ million}}\right) = 8.33\%$$

The difference between 8.34 percent and 8.33 percent is caused by rounding.

ST 15.2

a. $$G_L = \left[1 - \frac{(1-T)(1-T_{ps})}{(1-T_{pb})}\right]B = \left[1 - \frac{(1-0.40)(1-0.15)}{(1-0.28)}\right]\$20 \text{ million}$$

$$= [1 - 0.7083]\$20 \text{ million} = \$5.834 \text{ million}$$

b. $G_L = TB = 0.40(\$20 \text{ million}) = \$8 \text{ million}$

ST 15.3

a. $$\text{number of shares} = \frac{\text{common stock}}{\text{par value (per share)}} = \frac{\$250,000}{\$5} = 50,000 \text{ shares}$$

$$\text{EPS} = \frac{\text{EAT}}{\text{number of shares}} = \frac{\$240,000}{50,000} = \$4.80$$

b. If common stock is used, the number of additional shares is $400,000/$50 = 8,000. The total shares are 58,000 (i.e., 50,000 + 8,000).

If debt is employed, the interest is $40,000 [i.e., ($400,000)(0.10)]. The common stock remains at 50,000 shares.

$$\frac{(\text{EBIT}^* - I_1)(1-T)}{N_1} = \frac{(\text{EBIT}^* - I_2)(1-T)}{N_2}$$

$$\frac{(\text{EBIT}^* - 0)(0.60)}{58,000} = \frac{(\text{EBIT}^* - \$40,000)(0.60)}{50,000}$$

$$\frac{0.60 \text{ EBIT*}}{58,000} = \frac{0.60 \text{ EBIT*} - \$24,000}{50,000}$$

Cross-multiplying, we have

$$30,000 \text{ EBIT*} = 34,800 \text{ EBIT*} - \$1,392,000,000$$

$$4,800 \text{ EBIT*} = \$1,392,000,000$$

$$\text{EBIT*} = \$1,392,000,000/4,800 = \$290,000$$

c. New EBIT = (sales)(EBIT percentage) = $3,000,000(0.16) = $480,000

	Common Stock Financing	Debt Financing
EBIT	$480,000	$480,000
Interest	0	40,000
EBT	480,000	440,000
Taxes (40%)	192,000	176,000
EAT	$288,000	$264,000
EPS	$\dfrac{\$288,000}{58,000} = \$4.97$	$\dfrac{\$264,000}{50,000} = \$5.28$

Chapter 16

ST 16.1

a. return on stock A = $100(1 - 0.28)($PVA_{10\%,2yr}$) + $400(1 - 0.28)($PV_{10\%,2yr}$)

$$= \$72(1.736) + \$288(0.826) = \$124.992 + \$237.888 = \$362.88$$

return on stock B = $600(1 - 0.28)($PV_{10\%,2yr}$) = $432(0.826) = $356.832

Stock B provides lower returns than stock A because of the timing of the cash flows.

b. $362.880/$356.832 = 1.01695; so you need a return of 1.01695($600) = $610.169 from stock B in year 2 to be indifferent between the two stocks.

ST 16.2

The current earnings per share, EPS, is $6,000,000/1,000,000 = $6. The P/E is then:

$$P_0 = (\text{EPS})(\text{P/E})$$

$$\$90 = \$6(\text{P/E})$$

$$\text{P/E} = \$90/\$6 = 15 \text{ times}$$

After the repurchase, 800,000 shares of common stock will be outstanding, and the new EPS = $5,000,000/800,000 = $6.25. The market price of the outstanding shares after the repurchase is ($6.25)(15) = $93.75. Because a present stockholder should be indifferent in a fair repurchase, the price to be offered is $93.75.

ST 16.3

The current earnings per share is EAT/number of shares = $7,500,000/500,000 = $15. Based on the estimated P/E of 8 times earnings and a market price of $40, the required EPS is:

$$P_0 = (\text{required EPS})(\text{P/E})$$

$$\$40 = \text{required EPS}(8)$$

Required EPS = $40/8 = $5 per share

The earnings per share needs to drop from \$15 to \$5; this can be accomplished by increasing the number of shares to 1,500,000 (i.e., \$7,500,000/1,500,000 total shares = \$5). Hence, a 3-for-1 stock split is required.

Chapter 17

ST 17.1 **a.** $k_i = 10\%(1 - 0.40) = 6\%$

depreciation = \$600,000/3 = \$200,000

Present Value of Ownership Benefit

depreciation = \$200,000(0.40)($PVA_{6\%,3yr}$) = \$200,000(0.40)(2.673) = \$213,840

Amount to Be Recovered
\$600,000 − \$213,840 = \$386,160

After-Tax Lease Payment

$\$386,160 = ATL(PVA_{6\%,3yr})(1 + k_i)$

$\$386,160 = ATL(2.673)(1.06)$

2.833 ATL = \$386,160

ATL = \$386,160/2.833 = \$136,307.80

Before-Tax Lease Payment
L = \$136,307.80/(1 − 0.40) ≈ \$227,180

b. $k_i(\text{semiannual}) = 6\%/2 = 3\%$

Present value of ownership benefit is the same as in (a)—\$213,840; amount to be recovered is the same as in (a)—\$386,160.

Semiannual After-Tax Payment

$\$386,160 = ATL(PVA_{3\%,6})(1 + k_i)$

$\$386,160 = ATL(5.417)(1.03)$

5.580 ATL = \$386,160

ATL = \$386,160/5.580 = \$69,204.30

Semiannual Before-Tax Lease Payment

L = \$69,204.30/(1 − 0.40) ≈ \$115,341

ST 17.2 Two differences are illustrated in this problem, as follows:
1. Resale value and the required return, k, per footnote 7, must be added to the basic NAL equation. (*Note:* The resale value is already an after-tax figure.)
2. Because the lease payments are not given, they must be solved for by assuming the NAL is zero. Hence,

$$0 = -CLA_0 + L_0(1 - T) + \sum_{t=1}^{n-1} \frac{L_t(1 - T)}{(1 + k_i)^t} + \sum_{t=1}^{n} \frac{Dep_t(T)}{(1 + k_i)^t} + \frac{RV_n(1 - T)}{(1 + k)^n}$$

$CLA_0 = \$150,000$

$$k_i = k_b(1 - T) = 11.43\%(1 - 0.30) = 8.001\% \approx 8\%$$

The depreciation tax shield is

Depreciation $= \$150,000/3 = \$50,000$
Present value of depreciation tax shield $= \$50,000(T)(PVA_{8\%,3yr})$
$$= \$50,000(0.30)(2.577) = \$38,655$$

$$0 = -\$150,000 + L(1 - 0.30) + L(1 - 0.30)(PVA_{8\%,2yr}) + \$38,655$$
$$+ \$10,000(PV_{14\%,3yr})$$

$$0 = -\$150,000 + 0.70L + 0.70L(1.783) + \$38,655 + \$10,000(0.675)$$

$$0 = -\$150,000 + 0.70L + 1.2481L + \$38,655 + \$6,750$$

$1.9481L = \$104,595$

$$L = \$104,595/1.9481 = \$53,690.78$$

If Marsh Distributors can negotiate a lease of less than $53,690.78 per year, it should lease the equipment; otherwise, it should purchase.

Chapter 18

ST 18.1

a. cash conversion cycle $= \dfrac{365}{\text{inventory turnover}} + \dfrac{365}{\text{receivables turnover}} - \dfrac{365}{\text{payables turnover}}$

$$40 = \frac{365}{\text{inventory turnover}} + \frac{365}{8} - \frac{365}{10}$$

$$40 = \frac{365}{\text{inventory turnover}} + 45.625 - 36.500$$

$365/\text{inventory turnover} = 30.875$
$\text{inventory turnover} = 365/30.875 = 11.82$

b. receivables turnover $=$ sales/accounts receivable

$$8 = \$920,000/\text{accounts receivable}$$

accounts receivable $= \$920,000/8 = \$115,000$

ST 18.2   **a.**   current assets $=$ cash $+$ accounts receivable $+$ inventory

$$= \$25,000 + \$60,000 + \$65,000 = \$150,000$$

current liabilities $=$ accounts payable plus salaries, benefits, and payroll taxes payable $+$ other current liabilities

$$= \$80,000 + \$20,000 = \$100,000$$

current ratio $=$ current assets/current liabilities

$$= \$150,000/\$100,000 = 1.5$$

$$\text{net working capital} = \$150{,}000 - \$100{,}000 = \$50{,}000$$

$$\text{current assets/total assets} = \$150{,}000/\$500{,}000 = 0.30$$

$$\text{current liabilities/total assets} = \$100{,}000/\$500{,}000 = 0.20$$

Cash Conversion Cycle:

$$\text{receivables turnover} = \text{sales/accounts receivable} = 15.00$$

$$\text{inventory turnover} = \text{cost of goods sold/inventory} = 6.15$$

$$\text{payables turnover} = \frac{\begin{array}{c}\text{cost of goods sold} + \text{general,}\\ \text{selling, and administrative}\\ \text{expenses}\end{array}}{\begin{array}{c}\text{accounts payable} + \text{salaries,}\\ \text{benefits, and payroll taxes}\\ \text{payable}\end{array}} = 6.25$$

$$\text{average collection period} = 365/\text{receivables turnover} = 24.33 \text{ days}$$

$$\text{inventory conversion period} = 365/\text{inventory turnover} = 59.35 \text{ days}$$

$$\text{payable deferral period} = 365/\text{payables turnover} = 58.40 \text{ days}$$

$$\text{cash conversion cycle} = 25.28 \text{ days}$$

b. EPS = EAT/shares of stock = $\$150{,}000/50{,}000 = \$3.00$

$$P_0 = (\text{EPS})(\text{P/E}) = (\$3.00)(8) = \$24$$

c. By issuing the common stock, cash is increased to $75,000, current assets to $200,000, total assets to $550,000, stockholders' equity to $350,000, and total liabilities and stockholders' equity to $550,000. No other balance sheet accounts are affected, nor are any income statement accounts affected.

(1) $\qquad\qquad\qquad$ current ratio = 2.00

$$\text{net working capital} = \$100{,}000$$

$$\text{current assets/total assets} = 0.36$$

$$\text{current liabilities/total assets} = 0.18$$

The cash conversion cycle remains exactly as it was in (a).

(2) The total number of shares outstanding is $50{,}000 + 2{,}500 = 52{,}500$

$$\text{EPS}_{\text{new}} = \$150{,}000/52{,}500 = \$2.857$$

$$P_{0\text{new}} = (\$2.857)(8) = \$22.856 \approx \$22.86$$

(3) While Pittsburgh Distributors liquidity (as measured by its current ratio, net working capital, ratio of current assets to total assets, and ratio of current liabilities to total assets) looks better, its ongoing liquidity as measured by the cash conversion cycle is unchanged. At the same time, issuing more shares of stock while not increasing earnings after tax has resulted in a decrease in the firm's market value. David Sellers may sleep better if the common stock is issued, but his recommendation is not in the best interests of the firm's stockholders. Pittsburgh should not issue the common stock.

Chapter 19

ST 19.1 **a.**
$$\Delta C = \Delta B$$
$$\Delta C = (\Delta t)(TS)(I)(1-T)$$
$$\$0.25(1-0.35) = \Delta t(\$27,000,000/90,000)(0.09/365)(1-0.35)$$
$$\Delta t = \frac{\$0.25(0.65)}{\$300(0.09/365)(0.65)} = 3.3796, \text{ or } 3.38 \text{ days}$$

This represents the change in the float time required to afford paying the $0.25 check charge. If the expected reduction in float time is only 2.5 days, it should not be done.

b. Incremental costs (ΔC)

Yearly fee	$10,000
Per check charge (0.12)(90,000)	10,800
Charges by bank	20,800
Less: Reduced costs for firm	15,000
ΔC before taxes per year	5,800
Taxes	2,030
Net ΔC	$3,770

Incremental benefits (ΔB)
$$\Delta B = (\Delta t)(TS)(I)(1-T)$$
$$= (2.5)(\$27,000,000)(0.09/365)(1-0.35) = \$10,819$$

Since the incremental benefits exceed the incremental costs, the lockbox system should be implemented.

ST 19.2 Because the firm is operating at a loss, we simply ignore taxes in the solution. Thus, the incremental cost (or savings in this case) per transaction is $12 - \$3 = \$9$. If the net benefit of $3.75 = \Delta B - \Delta C$, then $\Delta B = \$3.75 + \Delta C = \$3.75 + \$9 = \$12.75$. Therefore,

$$\Delta B = (\Delta t)(TS)(I/365)$$
$$\$12.75 = (0.75)(\$62,050)(I/365)$$
$$\$12.75 = \$127.50(I)$$
$$I = \$12.75/\$127.50 = 0.10, \text{ or } 10\%$$

ST 19.3 To solve for the bank discount yield, we have

$$k_{BE} = \frac{(365)(k_{BD})}{360 - (k_{BD})(n)}$$

$$0.1048 = \frac{(365)(k_{BD})}{360 - (k_{BD})(30)}$$

$$0.1048 = \frac{365k_{BD}}{360 - 30k_{BD}}$$

$$37.728 - 3.144k_{BD} = 365\,k_{BD}$$

$$368.144k_{BD} = 37.728$$

$$k_{BD} = 37.728/368.144 = 0.10248$$

Now we can solve for the market price, P_0, using

$$P_0 = P_M - P_M(k_{BD})(n/360)$$

$$= \$100,000 - \$100,000(0.10248)(30/360) = \$100,000 - \$854 = \$99,146$$

Chapter 20

ST 20.1

While the \$50,000 purchase price may be a bargain, Motan also needs to consider the effect of *not* taking advantage of the cash discount. The dollar amount of the discount is $(0.04)(\$50,000) = \$2,000$. If Motan takes out the loan to take advantage of the cash discount, it will need it for 40 days $-$ 15 days $=$ 25 days. The amount borrowed will be \$50,000 $-$ \$2,000 $=$ \$48,000. The dollar amount of the interest paid on the loan will be $(0.14)(\$48,000)(25/365) = \$460.27$. Motan will save \$1,539.73 $(\$2,000 - \$460.27)$ by taking out the loan to take advantage of the cash discount. It should purchase the goods and take out the 25-day bank loan.

ST 20.2

a. average collection period $= 0.15(10) + 0.85(40) = 1.5 + 34 = 35.5$ days

b. sales per day $= \$18,250,000/365 = \$50,000$

$$\text{average investment} = (\text{average collection period})(\text{sales per day})$$
$$(\text{production costs})$$

$$= (35.5 \text{ days})(\$50,000)(0.80) = \$1,420,000$$

c. new average collection period $= 0.15(10) + 0.85(30) = 1.5 + 25.5 = 27$ days

average investment in receivables $= (27)(\$50,000)(0.80) = \$1,080,000$

ST 20.3

The incremental investment is

$$\Delta CF_0 = (VC_N)(S_N)(ACP_N/365) - (VC_O)(S_O)(ACP_O/365)$$

$$= (0.78)(\$27,500,000)(50/365) - (0.78)(\$25,000,000)(30/365)$$

$$= \$2,938,356 - \$1,602,740 = \$1,335,616$$

The incremental expected cash inflows are

$$\Delta CF_t = [S_N(1 - VC_N) - S_N(BD_N) - CD_N](1 - T)$$
$$- [S_O(1 - VC_O) - S_O(BD_O) - CD_O](1 - T)$$

$$= [\$27,500,000(1 - 0.78) - \$27,500,000(0.04) - \$325,000](1 - 0.30)$$
$$- [\$25,000,000(1 - 0.78) - \$25,000,000(0.02) - \$500,000](1 - 0.30)$$

$$= (\$6,050,000 - \$1,100,000 - \$325,000)(0.70)$$
$$- (\$5,500,000 - \$500,000 - \$500,000)(0.70)$$

$$= (\$4,625,000)(0.70) - (\$4,500,000)(0.70) = \$87,500$$

The net present value is

$$NPV = \frac{CF_t}{k} - CF_0 = \frac{\$87,500}{0.20} - \$1,335,616 = -\$898,116$$

Since the NPV is negative, Sigma should not relax its collection policy.

Chapter 21

ST 21.1

The average daily purchases are $730,000/365 = $2,000 per day. If the firm is taking advantage of the cash discount, there would be an average of no more than $20,000 [i.e.,(10 days)($2,000 per day)] in accounts payable. Because the accounts payable are $60,000, the firm has an average of $60,000/$2,000 = 30 days purchases on hand. It must reduce its accounts payable by at least $40,000, or 20 days' purchases, to be taking advantage of all of the cash discounts.

ST 21.2

a.   Factoring commission = (0.01)($800,000) = $8,000. The amount the factor will loan is $480,000 [i.e., ($800,000)(0.60)]. The interest is (0.15)($480,000)(30/365) = $5,918. Therefore, the total cost per 30 days is $8,000 + $5,918 = $13,918.

$$k_b = \left(1 + \frac{\$13,918}{\$480,000} \right)^{365/30} - 1 = 1.4159 - 1 = 41.59\%$$

b.   The $7,000 savings reduces the cost from $13,918 to $6,918:

$$k_b = \left(1 + \frac{\$6,918}{\$480,000} \right)^{365/30} - 1 = 1.1902 - 1 = 19.02\%$$

ST 21.3

a.   The total receivables pledged, W, is determined by:

$$0.70W = \$400,000$$

$$W = \$400,000/0.70 = \$571,429$$

The interest and processing fees are:

$$
\begin{aligned}
\text{interest} &= (\$400,000)(0.11)(91/365) = \$10,969.86 \\
\text{processing fee} &= (\$571,429)(0.01) \qquad = \underline{\ 5,714.29} \\
\text{total interest and processing fee} &= \$16,684.15
\end{aligned}
$$

$$k_b = \left(1 + \frac{\$16,684.15}{\$400,000} \right)^{365/91} - 1 = 1.1781 - 1 = 17.81\%$$

b.   The interest and field warehousing fees are:

$$
\begin{aligned}
\text{interest} &= (\$400,000)(0.09)(91/365) = \$\ 8,975.34 \\
\text{warehousing fee} &= (\$2,100)(91/30) \qquad = \underline{\ 6,370.00} \\
\text{total interest and warehousing fee} &= \$15,345.34
\end{aligned}
$$

$$k_b = \left(1 + \frac{\$15,345.34}{\$400,000} \right)^{365/91} - 1 = 1.1630 - 1 = 16.30\%$$

The loan from the insurance company has the lowest cost and should be employed.

Chapter 22

ST 22.1

a. $\Delta CF_t = \Delta CFBT_t(1 - T) + \Delta Dep_t(T) - \Delta investment_t$

$\Delta CF_1 = \$80,000(1 - 0.40) + \$20,000(0.40) - \$150,000 = -\$94,000$

$\Delta CF_2 = \$80,000(0.60) + \$50,000(0.40) - \$100,000 = -\$32,000$

$\Delta CF_3 = \$51,000$

$\Delta CF_4 = \$134,000$

$\Delta CF_5 = \$137,000$

$\Delta CF_{6-10} = \$128,000$

b. $\Delta\text{value} = \displaystyle\sum_{t=1}^{n} \frac{\Delta CF_t}{(1+k)^t}$

$\quad = -\$94,000(0.870) - \$32,000(0.756) + \$51,000(0.658)$
$\quad\quad + \$134,000(0.572) + \$137,000(0.497) + \$128,000(3.352)(0.497)$

$\quad = -\$81,780 - \$24,192 + \$33,558 + \$76,648 + \$68,089 + \$213,241 = \$285,564$

The NPV if cash-financed is:

$NPV_{cash} = \text{benefits} - \text{costs}$

$\quad = \$285,564 + \$1,000,000 - 1.15(\$1,000,000)$

$\quad = \$1,285,564 - \$1,150,000 = \$135,564$

The NPV if stock-financed is:

Shares of Toepfer outstanding $= \$2,400,000/\$50 = 48,000$

Shares offered for target $= \$1,150,000/\$50 = 23,000$

$W = \dfrac{\text{shares held by target}}{\text{total shares}} = \dfrac{23,000}{48,000 + 23,000} = 0.324$

true cost with stock $= W(\text{value}_{AB}) = 0.324(\$2,400,000 + \$1,285,564) = \$1,194,123$

$NPV = \$1,285,000 - \$1,194,123 = \$90,877$

ST 22.2

a. The number of additional shares of Gerard after the merger is $(2)(500,000) = 1,000,000$. Hence, the total number of shares is 1,500,000.

$EPS = \text{total earnings/shares of common stock outstanding}$

$\quad = (\$1,500,000 + \$1,000,000)/1,500,000 = \$1.6667$

b.
$\quad\quad\quad P_0 \text{ after merger} = (P/E)(EPS) = 9(\$1.6667) = \$15$

market value of firm after merger $= (\$15)(1,500,000 \text{ shares}) = \$22.5 \text{ million}$

premerger value of Gerard $= (EPS)(P/E)(\text{number of shares})$

$\quad\quad = (\$2)(10)(500,000) = \$10 \text{ million}$

premerger value of Buffalo $= (\$3)(8)(500,000) = \$12 \text{ million}$

gain in value due to synergism $= \text{value}_{combined} - (\text{value}_{Gerard} + \text{value}_{Buffalo})$

$\quad\quad = \$22.5 \text{ million} - (\$10 \text{ million} + \$12 \text{ million})$

$\quad\quad = \$0.5 \text{ million}$

c. Of the 1,500,000 shares outstanding after the merger, Buffalo's former stockholders control two-thirds of them, or $15 million [($\frac{2}{3}$)($22.5 million)] worth. Since the firm was worth only $12 million before, they benefited by $3 million.

Gerard's stockholders ended up with only one-third of the merged firm, which is worth $7.5 million. They lost $2.5 million ($10 million − $7.5 million). While the overall merger looks beneficial, the present Gerard stockholders should be upset.

ST 22.3

a. Since the CFs are $2 million until infinity, their present value is $2/0.14 = $14.286 million. The NPV is $14.286 million − $11 million = $3.286 million. Because the divestiture proceeds are $8 million, Automation is better off by $4.714 million ($8 − $3.286) by divesting.

b.

Year	CF (In millions)	× PV at 14% =	Present Value (In millions)
1	−$ 1.0	0.877	−$ 0.877
2	0	0.769	0
3	2.0	0.675	1.350
4	3.5	0.592	2.072
5	4.0	0.519	2.076
Beyond 5	72.0*	0.519	37.368
	Present value of future cash inflows =		41.989
	Less: Present market value of associated debt, B =		15.000
	NPV =		$26.989

$$*V_5 = \frac{\$4(1.08)}{0.14 - 0.08} = \frac{\$4.32}{0.06} = \$72.0$$

Since the NPV is greater than the after-tax divestiture proceeds of $24 million, Automation is better off by $2.989 million if it retains and modernizes the division.

c. Automation maximizes stockholders' wealth by choosing the option that provides the largest difference between the NPV and DP. This is accomplished by divesting the division immediately.

Chapter 23

ST 23.1

a. $k_s = k_{RF} + \beta_j(k_M - k_{RF})$

$= 9\% + 1.2(14\% - 9\%) = 9\% + 6\% = 15\%$

$$S = \frac{\text{cash inflow}_1 - \text{cash outflow}_1 - \text{capital investment}_1}{k_s - g}$$

$$S = \frac{\$5,000 - \$3,000 - \$800}{0.15 - 0.04} = \frac{\$1,200}{0.11} = \$10,909$$

b. (1) $k_s = 17\%$; $S = \$9,231$

(2) $k_s = 15\%$; $S = \$10,000$

(3) $k_s = 15\%$; $S = \$9,091$

(4) $k_s = 15\%$; $S = \$7,273$

(5) $k_s = 15\%$; $S = \$9,231$

(6) $k_s = 11.8\%$ (round to 12%); $S = \$15,000$

ST 23.2

a. The statement is as follows. Note that in quarter 1 Pathfinder can draw down the cash account by $5, so only $15 is borrowed on the line of credit.

	Quarter			
	1	2	3	4
Cash Needed				
1. Interest on line of credit	$ 0	$ 0.600*	$ 1.817†	$ 2.468‡
2. After-tax interest				
[1 × (1 − 0.30)]	0	0.420	1.272	1.728

3. Net cash inflow or outflow	20.000	30.000	15.000	− 40.000
4. Total cash needed (+) or surplus generated (−) (2 + 3)	$20.000	$30.420	$16.272	−$38.272

Cash Raised
1. Draw down cash	$ 5.000	$ 0	$ 0	$ 0
2. Borrow on line of credit	15.000	30.420	16.272	0
3. Repay line of credit	0	0	0	− 38.272
4. Total cash raised (+) or paid off (−) (1 + 2 + 3)	$20.000	$30.420	$16.272	−$38.272

* $15.000(0.04)

† ($15.000 + $30.420)(0.04)

‡ ($15.000 + $30.420 + $16.272)(0.04)

b. amount still borrowed = $15.000 + $30.420 + $16.272 − $38.272 = $23.420

Chapter 24

ST 24.1

The spot rates are: 1.817 shekels per U.S. dollar

7.15 yuan per U.S. dollar

Dividing 1.817 by 7.15 = 0.254; the rate of exchange is 1 yuan for 0.254 shekels, or 3.935 yuan for 1 shekel.

ST 24.2

a. Expected inflation in the U.S. is 8 − 2 = 6 percent, while it is 11 − 2 = 9 percent in Britain.

$$\begin{pmatrix} \text{Expected spot rate} \\ \text{at end of year 1} \end{pmatrix} = \begin{pmatrix} \text{spot rate at} \\ \text{start of year} \end{pmatrix}\begin{pmatrix} \text{inflation rate} \\ \text{differential} \end{pmatrix}$$

$$= 0.560\left(\frac{1.09}{1.06}\right) = 0.576$$

$$\begin{matrix} \text{Expected spot rate} \\ \text{at end of year 2} \end{matrix} = 0.560\left(\frac{1.09^2}{1.06^2}\right) = 0.592$$

$$\begin{matrix} \text{Expected spot rate} \\ \text{at end of year 3} \end{matrix} = 0.560\left(\frac{1.09^3}{1.06^3}\right) = 0.609$$

$$\begin{matrix} \text{Expected spot rate} \\ \text{at end of year 4} \end{matrix} = 0.560\left(\frac{1.09^4}{1.06^4}\right) = 0.626$$

b.

		Year			
	0	1	2	3	4
1. Remittance in pounds	−200,000	100,000	125,000	150,000	150,00
2. Forecasted spot exchange rate	0.560	0.576	0.592	0.609	0.62
3. Remittance received by parent, in dollars (1/2)	−357,143	173,611	211,149	246,305	239,61
4. U.S. corporate tax at 35% (3 × 0.35)		60,764	73,902	86,207	83,86
5. Cash flow in dollars, CF (3 − 4)	−357,143	112,847	137,247	160,098	155,75

c. NPV = $112,847(0.862) + $137,247(0.743) + $160,098(0.641) + $155,751(0.552)
$- $357,143 = $30,703$

Since the NPV is positive, the investment should be made.

Appendix 7B

ST 7B.1

$$k_j = k_{RF} + \beta_j(k_M - k_{RF})$$

$$18\% = 9\% + \beta_j(15\% - 9\%)$$

$$\beta_j = (18\% - 9\%)/6\% = 1.5$$

Equation 7B.4 tells us that:

$$\beta_j = \frac{\sigma_j Corr_{jM}}{\sigma_M}$$

$$1.5 = \frac{(16\%)(+0.50)}{\sigma_M}$$

$$\sigma_M = \frac{(16\%)(+0.50)}{1.5} = 5.333\%$$

Since the variance is the square of the standard deviation, the variance about the expected market return is $\sigma_M^2 = (5.333\%)^2 = 28.44$ percent.

Appendix 8A

ST 8A.1

200 percent declining balance

Year 1   ($140,000)($\frac{2}{7}$)($\frac{1}{2}$) = $20,000.00
Year 2   ($140,000 - $20,000)($\frac{2}{7}$) = ($120,000)($\frac{2}{7}$) = 34,285.71
Year 3   ($120,000 - $34,285.71)($\frac{2}{7}$) = ($85,714.29)($\frac{2}{7}$) = $24,489.80
Year 4   ($85,714.29 - $24,489.80)($\frac{2}{7}$) = ($61,224.49)($\frac{2}{7}$) = $17,492.71
Year 5   if 200 percent declining balance is used
        ($61,224.49 - $17,492.71)($\frac{2}{7}$) = ($43,731.78)($\frac{2}{7}$) = $12,494.79
        if straight-line (over the 3.5 years remaining) is used
        $43,731.78/3.5 years remaining = $12,494.79

Since the same depreciation is charged off with either method it doesn't make any difference which method is employed. But, for the next year switch to straight-line depreciation.

Year 6   ($43,731.78 - $12,494.79)/2.5 years remaining
        = ($31,236.99)/2.5 years = $12,494.796 ≈ $12,494.80
Year 7 $12,494.80
Year 8 $12,494.796/2 = $6,247.398 ≈ $6,247.39*

* Rounded down so the sum of the depreciation over all 8 years is $140,000.

Straight-line

Year 1   ($140,000/7)($\frac{1}{2}$)   = $10,000
Years 2–7 $140,000/7   = $20,000
Year 8   ($140,000/7)($\frac{1}{2}$)   = $10,000

Appendix 20A

ST 20A.1

a. $\text{EOQ} = \sqrt{\dfrac{2S0}{C}} = \sqrt{\dfrac{2(45,000)(\$30)}{\$0.30}} = 3,000 \text{ units}$

b. Average daily sales = 45,000/365 = 123.29 units. Alternatively, the firm places 15 (45,000/3,000) orders per year, or an order every 24.33 (365/15) days. Dividing the EOQ of 3,000 by 24.33 days equals 123.30 units, which is the same except for a 0.01 rounding difference.

c. safety stock = (6 days)(123.29 units per day) = 739.74 units

d. reorder point = safety stock + (lead time)(daily sales)

$$= 739.74 + (5)(123.29) = 1,356.19 \approx 1,356 \text{ units}$$

Answers to
Selected Problems

Chapter 2

2.6 $883,344.30.

Chapter 3

3.1

Cash	$ 17,542
Accounts receivable	63,836
Inventory	156,230
Other	13,675
Property, plant, and	
equipment	188,900
Depreciation	(69,467)
Total	$ 370,716
Accounts and notes	
payable	$ 65,377
Accrued expenses	81,797
Long-term debt and	
leases	108,962
Deferred taxes	11,372
Common stock	22,776
Retained earnings	80,432
Total	$ 370,716
Sales	$1,093,611
Cost of goods sold	875,727
Gross margin	217,884
Selling, general, and	
administrative	
expenses	170,505
EBIT	47,379
Interest	14,122
EBT	33,257
Taxes	15,230
EAT	$ 18,027

3.4
 a. Average collection period: 29.2 days.
  Inventory turnover: 7.5 times.
  Quick ratio: 1.0.
 b. Inventory: $37,500.
 c. Accounts receivable: $30,000.

3.6
 a. Current ratio: 1.91.
  Quick ratio: 0.28.
  Average collection period: 2.68 days.
  Inventory turnover: 3.71.
  Long-term asset turnover: 5.74.
  Total asset turnover: 2.49.
  Total debt to total assets: 0.70.
  Times interest earned: 2.88.
  Net profit margin: 2.19%.
  Return on total assets: 5.43%.
  Return on equity: 18.19%.

3.10
 a. Total asset turnover: 2.0.
  Net profit margin: 5.0%.
  Return on total assets: 10.0%.
  Return on equity: 20.0%.
 b. Return on equity: 22.2%.

3.13
 a. Return on equity: 20%.
 b. Return on equity: 12.5%.

Chapter 4

4.2 $22.50.

4.6
 a. Cash at end of period:
  $0; − $55,000; $70,000;
  $140,000.
 b. $105,000 in February.

4.8
 a.

Sales	$5,432.2
Operating	
expenses	4,862.4

Income from	
operations	569.8
+ Other	42.4
EBIT	612.2
Interest	202.6
EBT	409.6
Taxes	93.4
EAT	$ 316.2

Chapter 5

5.1
 a. $216.
 b. $251.94 or $252.
 c. $185.19 or $185.20.
 d. $158.77 or $158.80.

5.4
 a. 14 years.
 b. 7 years.
 c. 5 years.

5.6	$8,415.38.			**c.**	Approximately 10.0%.
				d.	7.27%.
5.9	Series A: $483.00; $815.79.		**5.20**	**a.**	17%.
	Series B: $390.90; $660.23.			**b.**	40%.
	Series C: $443.75; $749.49.			**c.**	25%.
5.12	**a.**	6%.		**5.27**	Over 24%.
	b.	9%.		**5.29**	**a.** 11.04%.
	c.	8%.			
	d.	12%.			
5.16	**a.**	7.23%.			
	b.	6.04%.			

Chapter 6

6.3	**a.**	7%.		**6.9**	**a.** $33.33.
	b.	12%.			**b.** $108.
6.5	**a.**	14%.			**c.** $36.57.
	b.	14.59%.		**6.12**	$11.70.
	c.	14.17%.			

Chapter 7

7.1	$\bar{k}$: 20%.			**7.13**	**a.** k_{RF}: 7%.
	σ: 10.95%.				k_M: 12.6%.
7.3	**b.**	AB: $\bar{k} = 35\%$; $\sigma = 15.49\%$.		**7.17**	**a.** $22.50.
		AC: $\bar{k} = 45\%$; $\sigma = 7.75\%$.			**b.** $26.25.
7.6	**a.**	12.5%.			**c.** $35.00.
	b.	9%; 7.81%; 4.58%.			**d.** $34.67.
7.11	**a.**	17%.		**7B.2**	10.40%.
	b.	14.5%.			

Chapter 8

8.2	**a.**	$105,000.		**8.9**	**a.** NPV$_A$: $2,122.
	b.	$70,000.			NPV$_B$: $1,259.
8.4	**a.**	A: 1.75 years.			**b.** IRR$_A$: 17.80%.
		B: 3.14 years.			IRR$_B$: 14.96%.
	b.	NPV$_A$: $97.05.		**8.11**	**a.** NPV$_C$: $11,160.
		NPV$_B$: $320.90.			NPV$_D$: $13,254.
8.6	**a.**	$34,080.			**b.** IRR$_C$: 20.82%.
	b.	−$6,144.			IRR$_D$: 17.04%.
				8.15	−$24,882.

Chapter 9

9.2	Incremental: $920; $4,000; $1,760;		**9.7**	NPV$_{apartment}$: $824,000.
	$640; $3,080; $2,800; $2,800.			NPV$_{recreation}$: −$70,400.
9.5	$8,969.			NPV$_{both}$: $1,275,200.

9.8   Equivalent annual NPV:
       One-speed: $81.93.
       Three-speed: $71.12.

9.15 **a.** NPV_A: $13,646.
       NPV_B: −$3,332.
       NPV_C: $10,558.

NPV_D: $4,320.
NPV_E: $10,825.
NPV_F: $7,225.

b. Projects A, D, and E.
c. NPV: $28,791.
    Loss: $17,783.

Chapter 10

10.1 **a.** $1,983.

10.5 $579,328.

10.7 **a.** (1) $1,769.
       (2) −$88.

(3) $492.
(4) $926.

10A.1 −$791.07.

Chapter 11

11.2 **a.** (1) $12.15. ($12.95 using Table F.7)
       (2) $15.35. ($14.77)
    b. (1) $21.75. ($20.83)
       (2) $5.99. ($6.39)

11.6 $13.98 ($13.80 using Table F.7)

11.9 **a.** −$56,827 (−$57,155 using Table F.7)
    b. approximately 0.77 to 0.78.

11A.1 **a.** S = $41.91 million. ($41.26 using Table F.7)
       B = $18.09 million. ($18.74)
    b. $4.76 million. ($4.11)

Chapter 12

12.1 **a.** $29,515,000.
    b. 1.62%.

12.4 **a.** $10 to $40 million.
    b. Selling price: $80; $20.
       Proceeds: $16 million; $4 million.

12.7

Cash	$ 9 million
Other	62 million
Total	$71 million

Liabilities	$25 million
Common stock	5 million
Additional paid-in	15 million
Retained earnings	26 million
Total	$71 million

12.11 **a.** $4; $80.
      b. Value is $58,800 unless the rights expire; then the value is only $56,000.

Chapter 13

13.1 $14 million.

13.5 **a.** 14%.
    b. 14.75%.
    c. 13.75%.

13.8 **a.** $88.889.
    b. 112,500.

13.10 **a.** Plan I: $2.47; $29.64.
      Plan II: $2.27; $29.51.

13A.2 NPV: $1,794,920.

Chapter 14

14.5
   a. 9%.
   b. 11.37%; 19%; 17%.
   d. 15.79%.
   e. 13.66%.

14.7
   a. 14.18%.
   b. 16.58%.

14.11 Cost of capital$_A$: 9.50%.
Cost of capital$_B$: 9.80%.
Cost of capital$_C$: 10.20%.

Chapter 15

15.1 CV$_A$: 0.39.
CV$_B$: 0.22.

15.4
   a. $285,429.
   b. $1,110,000.

15.12 1,500 shares.

15.15
   a. $300,000.
   b. Before tax: $650,000.
      After tax: $455,000.

   c. The cash flows will decrease by $155,000, but are still above $300,000.

15A.3
   a. 2.00.
   b. 1.30.
   c. 2.60.
   d. 52%.
   e. $10.64.

Chapter 16

16.1
   a. Central Energy—as reported: 141.78%; 59.21%; −30.90%; −17.48%.
      Inflation adjusted: 114.98%; 41.27%; −36.22%; −19.86%.
      Hoffman—as reported: 13.44%; −0.68%; −14.68%; 35.62%.
      Inflation adjusted: 0.43%; −11.54%; −21.56%; 32.08%.
   b. Central Energy: 38.15%; 25.04%.
      Hoffman: 8.42%; −0.15%.
      Inflation: 10.30%.

16.5
   a. $4 with either plan.
   b. Plan I: $4.00.
      Plan II: $3.97.

16.8
   a. March 15.
   b. $0.50.

16.11
   a. $3,600,000; $720,000; $1.20; $54,000,000; 15 times.
   b. $60; $4,500.
   c. $3,600,000; $2.00; $720,000; $0.40; 20%; 15 times; $54,000,000.
   d. $60; $4,500.

Chapter 17

17.2
   a. $92,067.
   b. $97,463.
   c. $86,049.

17.8
   a. $19,155.
   b. $6,946.

   c. Do not lease since NAL of $6,946 is less than the NPV of −$15,000.

17.10
   a. $54,150.95.
   b. 0.

Chapter 18

18.2
   a. 54.75 days.
   b. 21.17 days.
   c. 9.73.

18.4
   a. Aggressive: $182.
      Average: $164.5.
      Conservative: $147.

c.	Current ratio: 0.71; 1.00; 1.29.
Net working capital: −$200;
$0; $200.

18.9	**a.**	Year 1: $5; $9; $13; $11.
Year 2: $7; $11; $15; $13.
b.	Year 1: $20; $24; $28; $26.
Year 2: $22; $26; $30; $28.
c.	Savings: $600,000.

Chapter 19

19.1	**a.**	$44.14.
b.	$75.66.

19.6	**a.**	Incremental costs: $5.20.
Incremental benefits: $12.82.
b.	$8,111.

19.11	**a.**	10.29%.
b.	10.71%.

19.13	Optimal: Invest $2 million for 2 months; reinvest this $2 million for another 2 months; in 2 months invest $2 million for 4 months. Revenue: $104,700.

Chapter 20

20.3	Class 4: $152,250.
Class 5: −$17,660.

20.7	**a.**	March: 31.43 days.
April: 45.29 days.
May: 49.71 days.

c.

	March	April	May	June
Sales	100%	100%	100%	
Received as % of same-month sales	80	79	78	

Received as % of 1 month before	40	38	36

20.9	**a.**	−$135,959.
b.	$36,541.

20.12	$375,000.

20A.3	**a.**	7,000.
b.	17.5.
c.	5,678.

Chapter 21

21.1	**a.**	No cost.
b.	27.86%.
c.	17.81%.
d.	10.33%.

21.6	9.22%.

21.9	**a.**	25.41%.
b.	21.62%.

21.12	**a.**	19.63%.
b.	27.86%.
c.	27.24%.
d.	25.73%.

Chapter 22

22.1	**a.**	$50,000.
b.	$37,500.
c.	$12,500.

22.4	**a.**	Gain of $16.70.
b.	No: loss of approximately $300,000.

22.9	**a.**	20%.
b.	$37.

22.13	At 12%: $6,943.12.
At 15%: $4,637.14.

Chapter 23

23.4   **a.** $15; −$20; −$40; $10.
         b. $40 in quarter three.

23.6 $32; $13; −$26; −$97; −$109.

Chapter 24

24.4   1 year: 0.165.
       3 years: 0.178.
       6 years: 0.199.

24.6   **a.**   NPV: $681.
         b.   NPV: $754.

Financial Tables

Table F.1 Future Value Factors for $1 Compounded at k Percent for n Periods:

$$FV_{k,n} = (1 + k)^n$$

Period, n	Compound Rate, k																			
	1%	2%	3%	4%	5%	6%	7%	8%	9%	10%	11%	12%	13%	14%	15%	16%	17%	18%	19%	20%
1	1.010	1.020	1.030	1.040	1.050	1.060	1.070	1.080	1.090	1.100	1.110	1.120	1.130	1.140	1.150	1.160	1.170	1.180	1.190	1.200
2	1.020	1.040	1.061	1.082	1.102	1.124	1.145	1.166	1.188	1.210	1.232	1.254	1.277	1.300	1.323	1.346	1.369	1.392	1.416	1.440
3	1.030	1.061	1.093	1.125	1.158	1.191	1.225	1.260	1.295	1.331	1.368	1.405	1.443	1.482	1.521	1.561	1.602	1.643	1.685	1.728
4	1.041	1.082	1.126	1.170	1.216	1.262	1.311	1.360	1.412	1.464	1.518	1.574	1.630	1.689	1.749	1.811	1.874	1.939	2.005	2.074
5	1.051	1.104	1.159	1.217	1.276	1.338	1.403	1.469	1.539	1.611	1.685	1.762	1.842	1.925	2.011	2.100	2.192	2.288	2.386	2.488
6	1.062	1.126	1.194	1.265	1.340	1.419	1.501	1.587	1.677	1.772	1.870	1.974	2.082	2.195	2.313	2.436	2.565	2.700	2.840	2.986
7	1.072	1.149	1.230	1.316	1.407	1.504	1.606	1.714	1.828	1.949	2.076	2.211	2.353	2.502	2.660	2.826	3.001	3.185	3.379	3.583
8	1.083	1.172	1.267	1.369	1.477	1.594	1.718	1.851	1.993	2.144	2.305	2.476	2.658	2.853	3.059	3.278	3.511	3.759	4.021	4.300
9	1.094	1.195	1.305	1.423	1.551	1.689	1.838	1.999	2.172	2.358	2.558	2.773	3.004	3.252	3.518	3.803	4.108	4.435	4.785	5.160
10	1.105	1.219	1.344	1.480	1.629	1.791	1.967	2.159	2.367	2.594	2.839	3.106	3.395	3.707	4.046	4.411	4.807	5.234	5.695	6.192
11	1.116	1.243	1.384	1.539	1.710	1.898	2.105	2.332	2.580	2.853	3.152	3.479	3.836	4.226	4.652	5.117	5.624	6.176	6.777	7.430
12	1.127	1.268	1.426	1.601	1.796	2.012	2.252	2.518	2.813	3.138	3.498	3.896	4.335	4.818	5.350	5.936	6.580	7.288	8.064	8.916
13	1.138	1.294	1.469	1.665	1.886	2.133	2.410	2.720	3.066	3.452	3.883	4.363	4.898	5.492	6.153	6.886	7.699	8.599	9.596	10.699
14	1.149	1.319	1.513	1.732	1.980	2.261	2.579	2.937	3.342	3.797	4.310	4.887	5.535	6.261	7.076	7.988	9.007	10.147	11.420	12.839
15	1.161	1.346	1.558	1.801	2.079	2.397	2.759	3.172	3.642	4.177	4.785	5.474	6.254	7.138	8.137	9.266	10.539	11.974	13.590	15.407
16	1.173	1.373	1.605	1.873	2.183	2.540	2.952	3.426	3.970	4.595	5.311	6.130	7.067	8.137	9.358	10.748	12.330	14.129	16.172	18.488
17	1.184	1.400	1.653	1.948	2.292	2.693	3.159	3.700	4.328	5.054	5.895	6.866	7.986	9.276	10.761	12.468	14.426	16.672	19.244	22.186
18	1.196	1.428	1.702	2.026	2.407	2.854	3.380	3.996	4.717	5.560	6.544	7.690	9.024	10.575	12.375	14.463	16.879	19.673	22.901	26.623
19	1.208	1.457	1.754	2.107	2.527	3.026	3.617	4.316	5.142	6.116	7.263	8.613	10.197	12.056	14.232	16.777	19.748	23.214	27.252	31.948
20	1.220	1.486	1.806	2.191	2.653	3.207	3.870	4.661	5.604	6.727	8.062	9.646	11.523	13.743	16.367	19.461	23.106	27.393	32.429	38.338
21	1.232	1.516	1.860	2.279	2.786	3.400	4.141	5.034	6.109	7.400	8.949	10.804	13.021	15.668	18.822	22.574	27.034	32.324	38.591	46.005
22	1.245	1.546	1.916	2.370	2.925	3.604	4.430	5.437	6.659	8.140	9.934	12.100	14.714	17.861	21.645	26.186	31.629	38.142	45.923	55.206
23	1.257	1.577	1.974	2.465	3.072	3.820	4.741	5.871	7.258	8.954	11.026	13.552	16.627	20.362	24.891	30.376	37.006	45.008	54.649	66.247
24	1.270	1.608	2.033	2.563	3.225	4.049	5.072	6.341	7.911	9.850	12.239	15.179	18.788	23.212	28.625	35.236	43.297	53.109	65.032	79.497
25	1.282	1.641	2.094	2.666	3.386	4.292	5.427	6.848	8.623	10.835	13.585	17.000	21.231	26.462	32.919	40.874	50.658	62.669	77.388	95.396
26	1.295	1.673	2.157	2.772	3.556	4.549	5.807	7.396	9.399	11.918	15.080	19.040	23.991	30.167	37.857	47.414	59.270	73.949	92.092	114.48
27	1.308	1.707	2.221	2.883	3.733	4.822	6.214	7.988	10.245	13.110	16.739	21.325	27.109	34.390	43.535	55.000	69.345	87.260	109.59	137.37
28	1.321	1.741	2.288	2.999	3.920	5.112	6.649	8.627	11.167	14.421	18.580	23.884	30.633	39.204	50.066	63.800	81.134	102.97	130.41	164.84
29	1.335	1.776	2.357	3.119	4.116	5.418	7.114	9.317	12.172	15.863	20.624	26.750	34.616	44.693	57.575	74.009	94.927	121.50	155.19	197.81
30	1.348	1.811	2.427	3.243	4.322	5.743	7.612	10.063	13.268	17.449	22.892	29.960	39.116	50.950	66.212	85.850	111.06	143.37	184.68	237.38
35	1.417	2.000	2.814	3.946	5.516	7.686	10.677	14.785	20.414	28.102	38.575	52.800	72.068	98.100	133.18	180.31	243.50	328.00	440.70	590.67
40	1.489	2.208	3.262	4.801	7.040	10.286	14.974	21.725	31.409	45.259	65.001	93.051	132.78	188.88	267.86	378.72	533.87	750.38	1051.7	1469.8
45	1.565	2.438	3.782	5.841	8.985	13.765	21.002	31.920	48.327	72.890	109.53	163.99	244.64	363.68	538.77	795.44	1170.5	1716.7	2509.7	3657.3
50	1.645	2.692	4.384	7.107	11.467	18.420	29.457	46.902	74.358	117.39	184.56	289.00	450.74	700.23	1083.7	1670.7	2566.2	3927.4	5988.9	9100.4

Table F.1 FV$_{k,n}$ (Continued)

Period, n	21%	22%	23%	24%	25%	26%	27%	28%	29%	30%	31%	32%	33%	34%	35%	40%	45%	50%	55%	60%
1	1.210	1.220	1.230	1.240	1.250	1.260	1.270	1.280	1.290	1.300	1.310	1.320	1.330	1.340	1.350	1.400	1.450	1.500	1.550	1.600
2	1.464	1.488	1.513	1.538	1.563	1.588	1.613	1.638	1.664	1.690	1.716	1.742	1.769	1.796	1.823	1.960	2.103	2.250	2.403	2.560
3	1.772	1.816	1.861	1.907	1.953	2.000	2.048	2.097	2.147	2.197	2.248	2.300	2.353	2.406	2.460	2.744	3.049	3.375	3.724	4.096
4	2.144	2.215	2.289	2.364	2.441	2.520	2.601	2.684	2.769	2.856	2.945	3.036	3.129	3.224	3.322	3.842	4.421	5.063	5.772	6.554
5	2.594	2.703	2.815	2.932	3.052	3.176	3.304	3.436	3.572	3.713	3.858	4.007	4.162	4.320	4.484	5.378	6.410	7.594	8.947	10.486
6	3.138	3.297	3.463	3.635	3.815	4.002	4.196	4.398	4.608	4.827	5.054	5.290	5.535	5.789	6.053	7.530	9.294	11.391	13.867	16.777
7	3.797	4.023	4.259	4.508	4.768	5.042	5.329	5.629	5.945	6.275	6.621	6.983	7.361	7.758	8.172	10.541	13.476	17.086	21.494	26.844
8	4.595	4.908	5.239	5.590	5.960	6.353	6.768	7.206	7.669	8.157	8.673	9.217	9.791	10.395	11.032	14.758	19.541	25.629	33.316	42.950
9	5.560	5.987	6.444	6.931	7.451	8.005	8.595	9.223	9.893	10.604	11.362	12.166	13.022	13.930	14.894	20.661	28.334	38.443	51.640	68.719
10	6.728	7.305	7.926	8.594	9.313	10.086	10.915	11.806	12.761	13.786	14.884	16.060	17.319	18.666	20.107	28.925	41.085	57.665	80.042	109.95
11	8.140	8.912	9.749	10.657	11.642	12.708	13.862	15.112	16.462	17.922	19.498	21.199	23.034	25.012	27.144	40.496	59.573	86.498	124.06	175.92
12	9.850	10.872	11.991	13.215	14.552	16.012	17.605	19.343	21.236	23.298	25.542	27.983	30.635	33.516	36.644	56.694	86.381	129.75	192.30	281.47
13	11.918	13.264	14.749	16.386	18.190	20.175	22.359	24.759	27.395	30.288	33.460	36.937	40.745	44.912	49.470	79.371	125.25	194.62	298.07	450.36
14	14.421	16.182	18.141	20.319	22.737	25.421	28.396	31.691	35.339	39.374	43.833	48.757	54.190	60.182	66.784	111.12	181.62	291.93	462.00	720.58
15	17.449	19.742	22.314	25.196	28.422	32.030	36.062	40.565	45.587	51.186	57.421	64.359	72.073	80.644	90.158	155.57	263.34	437.89	716.10	1152.9
16	21.114	24.086	27.446	31.243	35.527	40.358	45.799	51.923	58.808	66.542	75.221	84.954	95.858	108.06	121.71	217.80	381.85	656.84	1110.0	1844.7
17	25.548	29.384	33.759	38.741	44.409	50.851	58.165	66.461	75.862	86.504	98.540	112.14	127.49	144.80	164.31	304.91	553.68	985.26	1720.4	2951.5
18	30.913	35.849	41.523	48.039	55.511	64.072	73.870	85.071	97.862	112.46	129.09	148.02	169.56	194.04	221.82	426.88	802.83	1477.9	2666.7	4722.4
19	37.404	43.736	51.074	59.568	69.389	80.731	93.815	108.89	126.24	146.19	169.10	195.39	225.52	260.01	299.46	597.63	1164.1	2216.8	4133.4	7555.8
20	45.259	53.358	62.821	73.864	86.736	101.72	119.14	139.38	162.85	190.05	221.53	257.92	299.94	348.41	404.27	836.68	1688.0	3325.3	6406.7	12089
21	54.764	65.096	77.269	91.592	108.42	128.17	151.31	178.41	210.08	247.06	290.20	340.45	398.92	466.88	545.77	1171.4	2447.5	4987.9	9930.4	19342
22	66.264	79.418	95.041	113.57	135.53	161.49	192.17	228.36	271.00	321.18	380.16	449.39	530.56	625.61	736.79	1639.9	3548.9	7481.8	15392	30948
23	80.180	96.889	116.90	140.83	169.41	203.48	244.05	292.30	349.59	417.54	498.01	593.20	705.65	838.32	994.66	2295.9	5145.9	11222	23857	49517
24	97.017	118.21	143.79	174.63	211.76	256.39	309.95	374.14	450.98	542.80	652.40	783.02	938.51	1123.4	1342.8	3214.2	7461.6	16834	36979	79228
25	117.39	144.21	176.86	216.54	264.70	323.05	393.63	478.90	581.76	705.64	854.64	1033.6	1248.2	1505.3	1812.8	4499.9	10819	25251	57318	126765
26	142.04	175.94	217.54	268.51	330.87	407.04	499.92	613.00	750.47	917.33	1119.6	1364.3	1660.1	2017.1	2447.2	6299.8	15688	37876	88843	202824
27	171.87	214.64	267.57	332.95	413.59	512.87	634.89	784.64	968.10	1192.5	1466.6	1800.9	2208.0	2702.9	3303.8	8819.8	22747	56815	137706	324518
28	207.97	261.86	329.11	412.86	516.99	646.21	806.31	1004.3	1248.9	1550.3	1921.3	2377.2	2936.6	3621.9	4460.1	12347	32984	85222	213445	519229
29	251.64	319.47	404.81	511.95	646.23	814.23	1024.0	1285.6	1611.0	2015.4	2516.9	3137.9	3905.7	4853.3	6021.1	17286	47826	127834	330840	830767
30	304.48	389.76	497.91	634.82	807.79	1025.9	1300.5	1645.5	2078.2	2620.0	3297.2	4142.1	5194.6	6503.5	8128.6	24201	69348	191751	512803	*
35	789.75	1053.4	1401.8	1861.1	2465.2	3258.1	4296.7	5653.9	7424.0	9727.9	12720	16599	21617	28097	36448	130161	444508	*	*	*
40	2048.4	2847.0	3946.4	5455.9	7523.2	10347	14195	19426	26520	36118	49074	66520	89963	121392	163437	700037	*	*	*	*
45	5313.0	7694.7	11110	15994	22958	32860	46899	66749	94740	134106	189325	266579	374389	524464	732857	*	*	*	*	*
50	13780	20796	31279	46890	70064	104358	154948	229349	338443	497929	730406	*	*	*	*	*	*	*	*	*

* FV is greater than 999999.

Table F.2 Future Value Factors for an Annuity of $1 Compounded at k Percent for n Periods:

$$FVA_{k,n} = \sum_{t=0}^{n-1}(1+k)^t = \frac{(1+k)^n - 1}{k}$$

Compound Rate, κ

Period, n	1%	2%	3%	4%	5%	6%	7%	8%	9%	10%	11%	12%	13%	14%	15%	16%	17%	18%	19%	20%
1	1.000	1.000	1.000	1.000	1.000	1.000	1.000	1.000	1.000	1.000	1.000	1.000	1.000	1.000	1.000	1.000	1.000	1.000	1.000	1.000
2	2.010	2.020	2.030	2.040	2.050	2.060	2.070	2.080	2.090	2.100	2.110	2.120	2.130	2.140	2.150	2.160	2.170	2.180	2.190	2.200
3	3.030	3.060	3.091	3.122	3.152	3.184	3.215	3.246	3.278	3.310	3.342	3.374	3.407	3.440	3.473	3.506	3.539	3.572	3.606	3.640
4	4.060	4.122	4.184	4.246	4.310	4.375	4.440	4.506	4.573	4.641	4.710	4.779	4.850	4.921	4.993	5.066	5.141	5.215	5.291	5.368
5	5.101	5.204	5.309	5.416	5.526	5.637	5.751	5.867	5.985	6.105	6.228	6.353	6.480	6.610	6.742	6.877	7.014	7.154	7.297	7.442
6	6.152	6.308	6.468	6.633	6.802	6.975	7.153	7.336	7.523	7.716	7.913	8.115	8.323	8.536	8.754	8.977	9.207	9.442	9.683	9.930
7	7.214	7.434	7.662	7.898	8.142	8.394	8.654	8.923	9.200	9.487	9.783	10.089	10.405	10.730	11.067	11.414	11.772	12.142	12.523	12.916
8	8.286	8.583	8.892	9.214	9.549	9.897	10.260	10.637	11.028	11.436	11.859	12.300	12.757	13.233	13.727	14.240	14.773	15.327	15.902	16.499
9	9.369	9.755	10.159	10.583	11.027	11.491	11.978	12.488	13.021	13.579	14.164	14.776	15.416	16.085	16.786	17.519	18.285	19.086	19.923	20.799
10	10.462	10.950	11.464	12.006	12.578	13.181	13.816	14.487	15.193	15.937	16.722	17.549	18.420	19.337	20.304	21.321	22.393	23.521	24.709	25.959
11	11.567	12.169	12.808	13.486	14.207	14.972	15.784	16.645	17.560	18.531	19.561	20.655	21.814	23.045	24.349	25.733	27.200	28.755	30.404	32.150
12	12.683	13.412	14.192	15.026	15.917	16.870	17.888	18.977	20.141	21.384	22.713	24.133	25.650	27.271	29.002	30.850	32.824	34.931	37.180	39.581
13	13.809	14.680	15.618	16.627	17.713	18.882	20.141	21.495	22.953	24.523	26.212	28.029	29.985	32.089	34.352	36.786	39.404	42.219	45.244	48.497
14	14.947	15.974	17.086	18.292	19.599	21.015	22.550	24.215	26.019	27.975	30.095	32.393	34.883	37.581	40.505	43.672	47.103	50.818	54.841	59.196
15	16.097	17.293	18.599	20.024	21.579	23.276	25.129	27.152	29.361	31.772	34.405	37.280	40.417	43.842	47.580	51.660	56.110	60.965	66.261	72.035
16	17.258	18.639	20.157	21.825	23.657	25.673	27.888	30.324	33.003	35.950	39.190	42.753	46.672	50.980	55.717	60.925	66.649	72.939	79.850	87.442
17	18.430	20.012	21.762	23.698	25.840	28.213	30.840	33.750	36.974	40.545	44.501	48.884	53.739	59.118	65.075	71.673	78.979	87.068	96.022	105.93
18	19.615	21.412	23.414	25.645	28.132	30.906	33.999	37.450	41.301	45.599	50.396	55.750	61.725	68.394	75.836	84.141	93.406	103.74	115.27	128.12
19	20.811	22.841	25.117	27.671	30.539	33.760	37.379	41.446	46.018	51.159	56.939	63.440	70.749	78.969	88.212	98.603	110.28	123.41	138.17	154.74
20	22.019	24.297	26.870	29.778	33.066	36.786	40.996	45.762	51.160	57.275	64.203	72.052	80.947	91.025	102.44	115.38	130.03	146.63	165.42	186.69
21	23.239	25.783	28.676	31.969	35.719	39.993	44.865	50.423	56.765	64.002	72.265	81.699	92.470	104.77	118.81	134.84	153.14	174.02	197.85	225.03
22	24.472	27.299	30.537	34.248	38.505	43.392	49.006	55.457	62.873	71.403	81.214	92.503	105.49	120.44	137.63	157.41	180.17	206.34	236.44	271.03
23	25.716	28.845	32.453	36.618	41.430	46.996	53.436	60.893	69.532	79.543	91.148	104.60	120.20	138.30	159.28	183.60	211.80	244.49	282.36	326.24
24	26.973	30.422	34.426	39.083	44.502	50.816	58.177	66.765	76.790	88.497	102.17	118.16	136.83	158.66	184.17	213.98	248.81	289.49	337.01	392.48
25	28.243	32.030	36.459	41.646	47.727	54.865	63.249	73.106	84.701	98.347	114.41	133.33	155.62	181.87	212.79	249.21	292.10	342.60	402.04	471.98
26	29.526	33.671	38.553	44.312	51.113	59.156	68.676	79.954	93.324	109.18	128.00	150.33	176.85	208.33	245.71	290.09	342.76	405.27	479.43	567.38
27	30.821	35.344	40.710	47.084	54.669	63.706	74.484	87.351	102.72	121.10	143.08	169.37	200.84	238.50	283.57	337.50	402.03	479.22	571.52	681.85
28	32.129	37.051	42.931	49.968	58.403	68.528	80.698	95.339	112.97	134.21	159.82	190.70	227.95	272.89	327.10	392.50	471.38	566.48	681.11	819.22
29	33.450	38.792	45.219	52.966	62.323	73.640	87.347	103.97	124.14	148.63	178.40	214.58	258.58	312.09	377.17	456.30	552.51	669.45	811.52	984.07
30	34.785	40.568	47.575	56.085	66.439	79.058	94.461	113.28	136.31	164.49	199.02	241.33	293.20	356.79	434.75	530.31	647.44	790.95	966.71	1181.9
35	41.660	49.994	60.462	73.652	90.320	111.43	138.24	172.32	215.71	271.02	341.59	431.66	546.68	693.57	881.17	1120.7	1426.5	1816.7	2314.2	2948.3
40	48.886	60.402	75.401	95.026	120.80	154.76	199.64	259.06	337.88	442.59	581.83	767.09	1013.7	1342.0	1779.1	2360.8	3134.5	4163.2	5529.8	7343.9
45	56.481	71.893	92.720	121.03	159.70	212.74	285.75	386.51	525.86	718.90	986.64	1358.2	1874.2	2590.6	3585.1	4965.3	6879.3	9531.6	13203	18281
50	64.463	84.579	112.80	152.67	209.35	290.34	406.53	573.77	815.08	1163.9	1668.8	2400.0	3459.5	4994.5	7217.7	10435	15089	21813	31515	45497

Table F.2 FVA$_{k,n}$ *(Continued)*

Period, n	Compound Rate, k																			
	21%	22%	23%	24%	25%	26%	27%	28%	29%	30%	31%	32%	33%	34%	35%	40%	45%	50%	55%	60%
1	1.000	1.000	1.000	1.000	1.000	1.000	1.000	1.000	1.000	1.000	1.000	1.000	1.000	1.000	1.000	1.000	1.000	1.000	1.000	1.000
2	2.210	2.220	2.230	2.240	2.250	2.260	2.270	2.280	2.290	2.300	2.310	2.320	2.330	2.340	2.350	2.400	2.450	2.500	2.550	2.600
3	3.674	3.708	3.743	3.778	3.813	3.848	3.883	3.918	3.954	3.990	4.026	4.062	4.099	4.136	4.173	4.360	4.553	4.750	4.952	5.160
4	5.446	5.524	5.604	5.684	5.766	5.848	5.931	6.016	6.101	6.187	6.274	6.362	6.452	6.542	6.633	7.104	7.601	8.125	8.676	9.256
5	7.589	7.740	7.893	8.048	8.207	8.368	8.533	8.700	8.870	9.043	9.219	9.398	9.581	9.766	9.954	10.946	12.022	13.188	14.448	15.810
6	10.183	10.442	10.708	10.980	11.259	11.544	11.837	12.136	12.442	12.756	13.077	13.406	13.742	14.086	14.438	16.324	18.431	20.781	23.395	26.295
7	13.321	13.740	14.171	14.615	15.073	15.546	16.032	16.534	17.051	17.583	18.131	18.696	19.277	19.876	20.492	23.853	27.725	32.172	37.262	43.073
8	17.119	17.762	18.430	19.123	19.842	20.588	21.361	22.163	22.995	23.858	24.752	25.678	26.638	27.633	28.664	34.395	41.202	49.258	58.756	69.916
9	21.714	22.670	23.669	24.712	25.802	26.940	28.129	29.369	30.664	32.015	33.425	34.895	36.429	38.029	39.696	49.153	60.743	74.887	92.073	112.87
10	27.274	28.657	30.113	31.643	33.253	34.945	36.723	38.593	40.556	42.619	44.786	47.062	49.451	51.958	54.590	69.814	89.077	113.33	143.71	181.59
11	34.001	35.962	38.039	40.238	42.566	45.031	47.639	50.398	53.318	56.405	59.670	63.122	66.769	70.624	74.697	98.739	130.16	171.00	223.75	291.54
12	42.142	44.874	47.788	50.895	54.208	57.739	61.501	65.510	69.780	74.327	79.168	84.320	89.803	95.637	101.84	139.23	189.73	257.49	347.82	467.46
13	51.991	55.746	59.779	64.110	68.760	73.751	79.107	84.853	91.016	97.625	104.71	112.30	120.44	129.15	138.48	195.93	276.12	387.24	540.12	748.93
14	63.909	69.010	74.528	80.496	86.949	93.926	101.47	109.61	118.41	127.91	138.17	149.24	161.18	174.06	187.95	275.30	401.37	581.86	838.19	1199.3
15	78.330	85.192	92.669	100.82	109.69	119.35	129.86	141.30	153.75	167.29	182.00	198.00	215.37	234.25	254.74	386.42	582.98	873.79	1300.2	1919.9
16	95.780	104.93	114.98	126.01	138.11	151.38	165.92	181.87	199.34	218.47	239.42	262.36	287.45	314.89	344.90	541.99	846.32	1311.7	2016.3	3072.8
17	116.89	129.02	142.43	157.25	173.64	191.73	211.72	233.79	258.15	285.01	314.64	347.31	383.30	422.95	466.61	759.78	1228.2	1968.5	3126.2	4917.5
18	142.44	158.40	176.19	195.99	218.04	242.59	269.89	300.25	334.01	371.52	413.18	459.45	510.80	567.76	630.92	1064.7	1781.8	2953.8	4846.7	7868.9
19	173.35	194.25	217.71	244.03	273.56	306.66	343.76	385.32	431.87	483.97	542.27	607.47	680.36	761.80	852.75	1491.6	2584.7	4431.7	7513.4	12591
20	210.76	237.99	268.79	303.60	342.94	387.39	437.57	494.21	558.11	630.17	711.38	802.86	905.88	1021.8	1152.2	2089.2	3748.8	6648.5	11646	20147
21	256.02	291.35	331.61	377.46	429.68	489.11	556.72	633.59	720.96	820.22	932.90	1060.8	1205.8	1370.2	1556.5	2925.9	5436.7	9973.8	18053	32236
22	310.78	356.44	408.88	469.06	538.10	617.28	708.03	812.00	931.04	1067.3	1223.1	1401.2	1604.7	1837.1	2102.3	4097.2	7884.3	14961	27983	51579
23	377.05	435.86	503.92	582.63	673.63	778.77	900.20	1040.4	1202.0	1388.5	1603.3	1850.6	2135.3	2462.7	2839.0	5737.1	11433	22443	43375	82527
24	457.22	532.75	620.82	723.46	843.03	982.25	1144.3	1332.7	1551.6	1806.0	2101.3	2443.8	2840.9	3301.0	3833.7	8033.0	16579	33666	67233	132045
25	554.24	650.96	764.61	898.09	1054.8	1238.6	1454.2	1706.8	2002.6	2348.8	2753.7	3226.8	3779.5	4424.4	5176.5	11247	24040	50500	104213	211273
26	671.63	795.17	941.46	1114.6	1319.5	1561.7	1847.8	2185.7	2584.4	3054.4	3608.3	4260.4	5027.7	5929.7	6989.3	15747	34860	75751	161531	338038
27	813.68	971.10	1159.0	1383.1	1650.4	1968.7	2347.8	2798.7	3334.8	3971.8	4727.9	5624.8	6687.8	7946.8	9436.5	22046	50548	113628	250374	540862
28	985.55	1185.7	1426.6	1716.1	2064.0	2481.6	2982.6	3583.3	4302.9	5164.3	6194.5	7425.7	8895.8	10649	12740	30866	73295	170443	388081	865381
29	1193.5	1447.6	1755.7	2129.0	2580.9	3127.8	3789.0	4587.7	5551.8	6714.6	8115.8	9802.9	11832	14271	17200	43214	106279	255666	601527	*
30	1445.2	1767.1	2160.5	2640.9	3227.2	3942.0	4813.0	5873.2	7162.8	8730.0	10632	12940	15738	19124	23221	60501	154106	383500	932368	*
35	3755.9	4783.6	6090.3	7750.2	9856.8	12527	15909	20188	25596	32422	41029	51869	65504	82636	104136	325400	987794	*	*	*
40	9749.5	12936	17154	22728	30088	39792	52571	69377	91447	120392	158300	207874	272613	357033	466960	*	*	*	*	*
45	25295	34971	48301	66640	91831	126382	173697	238387	326688	447019	610723	833058	*	*	*	*	*	*	*	*
50	65617	94525	135992	195372	280255	401374	573877	819103	*	*	*	*	*	*	*	*	*	*	*	*

*FVA is greater than 999999.

Table F.3 Present Value Factors for $1 Discounted at k Percent for n Periods:

$$PV_{k,n} = \frac{1}{(1+k)^n}$$

Period, n	Discount Rate, k																			
	1%	2%	3%	4%	5%	6%	7%	8%	9%	10%	11%	12%	13%	14%	15%	16%	17%	18%	19%	20%
1	0.990	0.980	0.971	0.962	0.952	0.943	0.935	0.926	0.917	0.909	0.901	0.893	0.885	0.877	0.870	0.862	0.855	0.847	0.840	0.833
2	0.980	0.961	0.943	0.925	0.907	0.890	0.873	0.857	0.842	0.826	0.812	0.797	0.783	0.769	0.756	0.743	0.731	0.718	0.706	0.694
3	0.971	0.942	0.915	0.889	0.864	0.840	0.816	0.794	0.772	0.751	0.731	0.712	0.693	0.675	0.658	0.641	0.624	0.609	0.593	0.579
4	0.961	0.924	0.888	0.855	0.823	0.792	0.763	0.735	0.708	0.683	0.659	0.636	0.613	0.592	0.572	0.552	0.534	0.516	0.499	0.482
5	0.951	0.906	0.863	0.822	0.784	0.747	0.713	0.681	0.650	0.621	0.593	0.567	0.543	0.519	0.497	0.476	0.456	0.437	0.419	0.402
6	0.942	0.888	0.837	0.790	0.746	0.705	0.666	0.630	0.596	0.564	0.535	0.507	0.480	0.456	0.432	0.410	0.390	0.370	0.352	0.335
7	0.933	0.871	0.813	0.760	0.711	0.665	0.623	0.583	0.547	0.513	0.482	0.452	0.425	0.400	0.376	0.354	0.333	0.314	0.296	0.279
8	0.923	0.853	0.789	0.731	0.677	0.627	0.582	0.540	0.502	0.467	0.434	0.404	0.376	0.351	0.327	0.305	0.285	0.266	0.249	0.233
9	0.914	0.837	0.766	0.703	0.645	0.592	0.544	0.500	0.460	0.424	0.391	0.361	0.333	0.308	0.284	0.263	0.243	0.225	0.209	0.194
10	0.905	0.820	0.744	0.676	0.614	0.558	0.508	0.463	0.422	0.386	0.352	0.322	0.295	0.270	0.247	0.227	0.208	0.191	0.176	0.162
11	0.896	0.804	0.722	0.650	0.585	0.527	0.475	0.429	0.388	0.350	0.317	0.287	0.261	0.237	0.215	0.195	0.178	0.162	0.148	0.135
12	0.887	0.788	0.701	0.625	0.557	0.497	0.444	0.397	0.356	0.319	0.286	0.257	0.231	0.208	0.187	0.168	0.152	0.137	0.124	0.112
13	0.879	0.773	0.681	0.601	0.530	0.469	0.415	0.368	0.326	0.290	0.258	0.229	0.204	0.182	0.163	0.145	0.130	0.116	0.104	0.093
14	0.870	0.758	0.661	0.577	0.505	0.442	0.388	0.340	0.299	0.263	0.232	0.205	0.181	0.160	0.141	0.125	0.111	0.099	0.088	0.078
15	0.861	0.743	0.642	0.555	0.481	0.417	0.362	0.315	0.275	0.239	0.209	0.183	0.160	0.140	0.123	0.108	0.095	0.084	0.074	0.065
16	0.853	0.728	0.623	0.534	0.458	0.394	0.339	0.292	0.252	0.218	0.188	0.163	0.141	0.123	0.107	0.093	0.081	0.071	0.062	0.054
17	0.844	0.714	0.605	0.513	0.436	0.371	0.317	0.270	0.231	0.198	0.170	0.146	0.125	0.108	0.093	0.080	0.069	0.060	0.052	0.045
18	0.836	0.700	0.587	0.494	0.416	0.350	0.296	0.250	0.212	0.180	0.153	0.130	0.111	0.095	0.081	0.069	0.059	0.051	0.044	0.038
19	0.828	0.686	0.570	0.475	0.396	0.331	0.277	0.232	0.194	0.164	0.138	0.116	0.098	0.083	0.070	0.060	0.051	0.043	0.037	0.031
20	0.820	0.673	0.554	0.456	0.377	0.312	0.258	0.215	0.178	0.149	0.124	0.104	0.087	0.073	0.061	0.051	0.043	0.037	0.031	0.026
21	0.811	0.660	0.538	0.439	0.359	0.294	0.242	0.199	0.164	0.135	0.112	0.093	0.077	0.064	0.053	0.044	0.037	0.031	0.026	0.022
22	0.803	0.647	0.522	0.422	0.342	0.278	0.226	0.184	0.150	0.123	0.101	0.083	0.068	0.056	0.046	0.038	0.032	0.026	0.022	0.018
23	0.795	0.634	0.507	0.406	0.326	0.262	0.211	0.170	0.138	0.112	0.091	0.074	0.060	0.049	0.040	0.033	0.027	0.022	0.018	0.015
24	0.788	0.622	0.492	0.390	0.310	0.247	0.197	0.158	0.126	0.102	0.082	0.066	0.053	0.043	0.035	0.028	0.023	0.019	0.015	0.013
25	0.780	0.610	0.478	0.375	0.295	0.233	0.184	0.146	0.116	0.092	0.074	0.059	0.047	0.038	0.030	0.024	0.020	0.016	0.013	0.010
26	0.772	0.598	0.464	0.361	0.281	0.220	0.172	0.135	0.106	0.084	0.066	0.053	0.042	0.033	0.026	0.021	0.017	0.014	0.011	0.009
27	0.764	0.586	0.450	0.347	0.268	0.207	0.161	0.125	0.098	0.076	0.060	0.047	0.037	0.029	0.023	0.018	0.014	0.011	0.009	0.007
28	0.757	0.574	0.437	0.333	0.255	0.196	0.150	0.116	0.090	0.069	0.054	0.042	0.033	0.026	0.020	0.016	0.012	0.010	0.008	0.006
29	0.749	0.563	0.424	0.321	0.243	0.185	0.141	0.107	0.082	0.063	0.048	0.037	0.029	0.022	0.017	0.014	0.011	0.008	0.006	0.005
30	0.742	0.552	0.412	0.308	0.231	0.174	0.131	0.099	0.075	0.057	0.044	0.033	0.026	0.020	0.015	0.012	0.009	0.007	0.005	0.004
35	0.706	0.500	0.355	0.253	0.181	0.130	0.094	0.068	0.049	0.036	0.026	0.019	0.014	0.010	0.008	0.006	0.004	0.003	0.002	0.002
40	0.672	0.453	0.307	0.208	0.142	0.097	0.067	0.046	0.032	0.022	0.015	0.011	0.008	0.005	0.004	0.003	0.002	0.001	0.001	0.001
45	0.639	0.410	0.264	0.171	0.111	0.073	0.048	0.031	0.021	0.014	0.009	0.006	0.004	0.003	0.002	0.001	0.001	0.001	*	*
50	0.608	0.372	0.228	0.141	0.087	0.054	0.034	0.021	0.013	0.009	0.005	0.003	0.002	0.001	0.001	0.001	*	*	*	*

* PVIF is zero to three decimal places.

Table F.3 $PV_{k,n}$ (Continued)

Period, n	Discount Rate, k																			
	21%	22%	23%	24%	25%	26%	27%	28%	29%	30%	31%	32%	33%	34%	35%	40%	45%	50%	55%	60%
1	0.826	0.820	0.813	0.806	0.800	0.794	0.787	0.781	0.775	0.769	0.763	0.758	0.752	0.746	0.741	0.714	0.690	0.667	0.645	0.625
2	0.683	0.672	0.661	0.650	0.640	0.630	0.620	0.610	0.601	0.592	0.583	0.574	0.565	0.557	0.549	0.510	0.476	0.444	0.416	0.391
3	0.564	0.551	0.537	0.524	0.512	0.500	0.488	0.477	0.466	0.455	0.445	0.435	0.425	0.416	0.406	0.364	0.328	0.296	0.269	0.244
4	0.467	0.451	0.437	0.423	0.410	0.397	0.384	0.373	0.361	0.350	0.340	0.329	0.320	0.310	0.301	0.260	0.226	0.198	0.173	0.153
5	0.386	0.370	0.355	0.341	0.328	0.315	0.303	0.291	0.280	0.269	0.259	0.250	0.240	0.231	0.223	0.186	0.156	0.132	0.112	0.095
6	0.319	0.303	0.289	0.275	0.262	0.250	0.238	0.227	0.217	0.207	0.198	0.189	0.181	0.173	0.165	0.133	0.108	0.088	0.072	0.060
7	0.263	0.249	0.235	0.222	0.210	0.198	0.188	0.178	0.168	0.159	0.151	0.143	0.136	0.129	0.122	0.095	0.074	0.059	0.047	0.037
8	0.218	0.204	0.191	0.179	0.168	0.157	0.148	0.139	0.130	0.123	0.115	0.108	0.102	0.096	0.091	0.068	0.051	0.039	0.030	0.023
9	0.180	0.167	0.155	0.144	0.134	0.125	0.116	0.108	0.101	0.094	0.088	0.082	0.077	0.072	0.067	0.048	0.035	0.026	0.019	0.015
10	0.149	0.137	0.126	0.116	0.107	0.099	0.092	0.085	0.078	0.073	0.067	0.062	0.058	0.054	0.050	0.035	0.024	0.017	0.012	0.009
11	0.123	0.112	0.103	0.094	0.086	0.079	0.072	0.066	0.061	0.056	0.051	0.047	0.043	0.040	0.037	0.025	0.017	0.012	0.008	0.006
12	0.102	0.092	0.083	0.076	0.069	0.062	0.057	0.052	0.047	0.043	0.039	0.036	0.033	0.030	0.027	0.018	0.012	0.008	0.005	0.004
13	0.084	0.075	0.068	0.061	0.055	0.050	0.045	0.040	0.037	0.033	0.030	0.027	0.025	0.022	0.020	0.013	0.008	0.005	0.003	0.002
14	0.069	0.062	0.055	0.049	0.044	0.039	0.035	0.032	0.028	0.025	0.023	0.021	0.018	0.017	0.015	0.009	0.006	0.003	0.002	0.001
15	0.057	0.051	0.045	0.040	0.035	0.031	0.028	0.025	0.022	0.020	0.017	0.016	0.014	0.012	0.011	0.006	0.004	0.002	0.001	0.001
16	0.047	0.042	0.036	0.032	0.028	0.025	0.022	0.019	0.017	0.015	0.013	0.012	0.010	0.009	0.008	0.005	0.003	0.002	0.001	0.001
17	0.039	0.034	0.030	0.026	0.023	0.020	0.017	0.015	0.013	0.012	0.010	0.009	0.008	0.007	0.006	0.003	0.002	0.001	0.001	*
18	0.032	0.028	0.024	0.021	0.018	0.016	0.014	0.012	0.010	0.009	0.008	0.007	0.006	0.005	0.005	0.002	0.001	*	*	*
19	0.027	0.023	0.020	0.017	0.014	0.012	0.011	0.009	0.008	0.007	0.006	0.005	0.004	0.004	0.003	0.002	0.001	*	*	*
20	0.022	0.019	0.016	0.014	0.012	0.010	0.008	0.007	0.006	0.005	0.005	0.004	0.003	0.003	0.002	0.001	0.001	*	*	*
21	0.018	0.015	0.013	0.011	0.009	0.008	0.007	0.006	0.005	0.004	0.003	0.003	0.003	0.002	0.002	0.001	*	*	*	*
22	0.015	0.013	0.011	0.009	0.007	0.006	0.005	0.004	0.004	0.003	0.003	0.002	0.002	0.002	0.001	0.001	*	*	*	*
23	0.012	0.010	0.009	0.007	0.006	0.005	0.004	0.003	0.003	0.002	0.002	0.002	0.001	0.001	0.001	*	*	*	*	*
24	0.010	0.008	0.007	0.006	0.005	0.004	0.003	0.003	0.002	0.002	0.002	0.001	0.001	0.001	0.001	*	*	*	*	*
25	0.009	0.007	0.006	0.005	0.004	0.003	0.003	0.002	0.002	0.001	0.001	0.001	0.001	0.001	0.001	*	*	*	*	*
26	0.007	0.006	0.005	0.004	0.003	0.002	0.002	0.002	0.001	0.001	0.001	0.001	0.001	*	*	*	*	*	*	*
27	0.006	0.005	0.004	0.003	0.002	0.002	0.002	0.001	0.001	0.001	0.001	0.001	*	*	*	*	*	*	*	*
28	0.005	0.004	0.003	0.002	0.002	0.002	0.001	0.001	0.001	0.001	0.001	*	*	*	*	*	*	*	*	*
29	0.004	0.003	0.002	0.002	0.002	0.001	0.001	0.001	0.001	0.001	*	*	*	*	*	*	*	*	*	*
30	0.003	0.003	0.002	0.002	0.001	0.001	0.001	0.001	*	*	*	*	*	*	*	*	*	*	*	*
35	0.001	0.001	0.001	0.001	*	*	*	*	*	*	*	*	*	*	*	*	*	*	*	*
40	*	*	*	*	*	*	*	*	*	*	*	*	*	*	*	*	*	*	*	*
45	*	*	*	*	*	*	*	*	*	*	*	*	*	*	*	*	*	*	*	*
50	*	*	*	*	*	*	*	*	*	*	*	*	*	*	*	*	*	*	*	*

* PV is zero to three decimal places.

Table F.4 Present Value Factors for an Annuity of $1 Discounted at k Percent for n Periods:

$$PVA_{k,n} = \sum_{t=1}^{n} \frac{1}{(1+k)^t} = \frac{1 - [1/(1+k)^n]}{k}$$

Period, n	Discount Rate, k																			
	1%	2%	3%	4%	5%	6%	7%	8%	9%	10%	11%	12%	13%	14%	15%	16%	17%	18%	19%	20%
1	0.990	0.980	0.971	0.962	0.952	0.943	0.935	0.926	0.917	0.909	0.901	0.893	0.885	0.877	0.870	0.862	0.855	0.847	0.840	0.833
2	1.970	1.942	1.913	1.886	1.859	1.833	1.808	1.783	1.759	1.736	1.713	1.690	1.668	1.647	1.626	1.605	1.585	1.566	1.547	1.528
3	2.941	2.884	2.829	2.775	2.723	2.673	2.624	2.577	2.531	2.487	2.444	2.402	2.361	2.322	2.283	2.246	2.210	2.174	2.140	2.106
4	3.902	3.808	3.717	3.630	3.546	3.465	3.387	3.312	3.240	3.170	3.102	3.037	2.974	2.914	2.855	2.798	2.743	2.690	2.639	2.589
5	4.853	4.713	4.580	4.452	4.329	4.212	4.100	3.993	3.890	3.791	3.696	3.605	3.517	3.433	3.352	3.274	3.199	3.127	3.058	2.991
6	5.795	5.601	5.417	5.242	5.076	4.917	4.767	4.623	4.486	4.355	4.231	4.111	3.998	3.889	3.784	3.685	3.589	3.498	3.410	3.326
7	6.728	6.472	6.230	6.002	5.786	5.582	5.389	5.206	5.033	4.868	4.712	4.564	4.423	4.288	4.160	4.039	3.922	3.812	3.706	3.605
8	7.652	7.325	7.020	6.733	6.463	6.210	5.971	5.747	5.535	5.335	5.146	4.968	4.799	4.639	4.487	4.344	4.207	4.078	3.954	3.837
9	8.566	8.162	7.786	7.435	7.108	6.802	6.515	6.247	5.995	5.759	5.537	5.328	5.132	4.946	4.772	4.607	4.451	4.303	4.163	4.031
10	9.471	8.983	8.530	8.111	7.722	7.360	7.024	6.710	6.418	6.145	5.889	5.650	5.426	5.216	5.019	4.833	4.659	4.494	4.339	4.192
11	10.368	9.787	9.253	8.760	8.306	7.887	7.499	7.139	6.805	6.495	6.207	5.938	5.687	5.453	5.234	5.029	4.836	4.656	4.486	4.327
12	11.255	10.575	9.954	9.385	8.863	8.384	7.943	7.536	7.161	6.814	6.492	6.194	5.918	5.660	5.421	5.197	4.988	4.793	4.611	4.439
13	12.134	11.348	10.635	9.986	9.394	8.853	8.358	7.904	7.487	7.103	6.750	6.424	6.122	5.842	5.583	5.342	5.118	4.910	4.715	4.533
14	13.004	12.106	11.296	10.563	9.899	9.295	8.745	8.244	7.786	7.367	6.982	6.628	6.302	6.002	5.724	5.468	5.229	5.008	4.802	4.611
15	13.865	12.849	11.938	11.118	10.380	9.712	9.108	8.559	8.061	7.606	7.191	6.811	6.462	6.142	5.847	5.575	5.324	5.092	4.876	4.675
16	14.718	13.578	12.561	11.652	10.838	10.106	9.447	8.851	8.313	7.824	7.379	6.974	6.604	6.265	5.954	5.668	5.405	5.162	4.938	4.730
17	15.562	14.292	13.166	12.166	11.274	10.477	9.763	9.122	8.544	8.022	7.549	7.120	6.729	6.373	6.047	5.749	5.475	5.222	4.990	4.775
18	16.398	14.992	13.754	12.659	11.690	10.828	10.059	9.372	8.756	8.201	7.702	7.250	6.840	6.467	6.128	5.818	5.534	5.273	5.033	4.812
19	17.226	15.678	14.324	13.134	12.085	11.158	10.336	9.604	8.950	8.365	7.839	7.366	6.938	6.550	6.198	5.877	5.584	5.316	5.070	4.843
20	18.046	16.351	14.877	13.590	12.462	11.470	10.594	9.818	9.129	8.514	7.963	7.469	7.025	6.623	6.259	5.929	5.628	5.353	5.101	4.870
21	18.857	17.011	15.415	14.029	12.821	11.764	10.836	10.017	9.292	8.649	8.075	7.562	7.102	6.687	6.312	5.973	5.665	5.384	5.127	4.891
22	19.660	17.658	15.937	14.451	13.163	12.042	11.061	10.201	9.442	8.772	8.176	7.645	7.170	6.743	6.359	6.011	5.696	5.410	5.149	4.909
23	20.456	18.292	16.444	14.857	13.489	12.303	11.272	10.371	9.580	8.883	8.266	7.718	7.230	6.792	6.399	6.044	5.723	5.432	5.167	4.925
24	21.243	18.914	16.936	15.247	13.799	12.550	11.469	10.529	9.707	8.985	8.348	7.784	7.283	6.835	6.434	6.073	5.746	5.451	5.182	4.937
25	22.023	19.523	17.413	15.622	14.094	12.783	11.654	10.675	9.823	9.077	8.422	7.843	7.330	6.873	6.464	6.097	5.766	5.467	5.195	4.948
26	22.795	20.121	17.877	15.983	14.375	13.003	11.826	10.810	9.929	9.161	8.488	7.896	7.372	6.906	6.491	6.118	5.783	5.480	5.206	4.956
27	23.560	20.707	18.327	16.330	14.643	13.211	11.987	10.935	10.027	9.237	8.548	7.943	7.409	6.935	6.514	6.136	5.798	5.492	5.215	4.964
28	24.316	21.281	18.764	16.663	14.898	13.406	12.137	11.051	10.116	9.307	8.602	7.984	7.441	6.961	6.534	6.152	5.810	5.502	5.223	4.970
29	25.066	21.844	19.188	16.984	15.141	13.591	12.278	11.158	10.198	9.370	8.650	8.022	7.470	6.983	6.551	6.166	5.820	5.510	5.229	4.975
30	25.808	22.396	19.600	17.292	15.372	13.765	12.409	11.258	10.274	9.427	8.694	8.055	7.496	7.003	6.566	6.177	5.829	5.517	5.235	4.979
35	29.409	24.999	21.487	18.665	16.374	14.498	12.948	11.655	10.567	9.644	8.855	8.176	7.586	7.070	6.617	6.215	5.858	5.539	5.251	4.992
40	32.835	27.355	23.115	19.793	17.159	15.046	13.332	11.925	10.757	9.779	8.951	8.244	7.634	7.105	6.642	6.233	5.871	5.548	5.258	4.997
45	36.095	29.490	24.519	20.720	17.774	15.456	13.606	12.108	10.881	9.863	9.008	8.283	7.661	7.123	6.654	6.242	5.877	5.552	5.261	4.999
50	39.196	31.424	25.730	21.482	18.256	15.762	13.801	12.233	10.962	9.915	9.042	8.304	7.675	7.133	6.661	6.246	5.880	5.554	5.262	4.999

Table F.4 PVA$_{k,n}$ (Continued)

Period, n	Discount Rate, k																			
	21%	22%	23%	24%	25%	26%	27%	28%	29%	30%	31%	32%	33%	34%	35%	40%	45%	50%	55%	60%
1	0.826	0.820	0.813	0.806	0.800	0.794	0.787	0.781	0.775	0.769	0.763	0.758	0.752	0.746	0.741	0.714	0.690	0.667	0.645	0.625
2	1.509	1.492	1.474	1.457	1.440	1.424	1.407	1.392	1.376	1.361	1.346	1.331	1.317	1.303	1.289	1.224	1.165	1.111	1.061	1.016
3	2.074	2.042	2.011	1.981	1.952	1.923	1.896	1.868	1.842	1.816	1.791	1.766	1.742	1.719	1.696	1.589	1.493	1.407	1.330	1.260
4	2.540	2.494	2.448	2.404	2.362	2.320	2.280	2.241	2.203	2.166	2.130	2.096	2.062	2.029	1.997	1.849	1.720	1.605	1.503	1.412
5	2.926	2.864	2.803	2.745	2.689	2.635	2.583	2.532	2.483	2.436	2.390	2.345	2.302	2.260	2.220	2.035	1.876	1.737	1.615	1.508
6	3.245	3.167	3.092	3.020	2.951	2.885	2.821	2.759	2.700	2.643	2.588	2.534	2.483	2.433	2.385	2.168	1.983	1.824	1.687	1.567
7	3.508	3.416	3.327	3.242	3.161	3.083	3.009	2.937	2.868	2.802	2.739	2.677	2.619	2.562	2.508	2.263	2.057	1.883	1.734	1.605
8	3.726	3.619	3.518	3.421	3.329	3.241	3.156	3.076	2.999	2.925	2.854	2.786	2.721	2.658	2.598	2.331	2.109	1.922	1.764	1.628
9	3.905	3.786	3.673	3.566	3.463	3.366	3.273	3.184	3.100	3.019	2.942	2.868	2.798	2.730	2.665	2.379	2.144	1.948	1.783	1.642
10	4.054	3.923	3.799	3.682	3.571	3.465	3.364	3.269	3.178	3.092	3.009	2.930	2.855	2.784	2.715	2.414	2.168	1.965	1.795	1.652
11	4.177	4.035	3.902	3.776	3.656	3.543	3.437	3.335	3.239	3.147	3.060	2.978	2.899	2.824	2.752	2.438	2.185	1.977	1.804	1.657
12	4.278	4.127	3.985	3.851	3.725	3.606	3.493	3.387	3.286	3.190	3.100	3.013	2.931	2.853	2.779	2.456	2.196	1.985	1.809	1.661
13	4.362	4.203	4.053	3.912	3.780	3.656	3.538	3.427	3.322	3.223	3.129	3.040	2.956	2.876	2.799	2.469	2.204	1.990	1.812	1.663
14	4.432	4.265	4.108	3.962	3.824	3.695	3.573	3.459	3.351	3.249	3.152	3.061	2.974	2.892	2.814	2.478	2.210	1.993	1.814	1.664
15	4.489	4.315	4.153	4.001	3.859	3.726	3.601	3.483	3.373	3.268	3.170	3.076	2.988	2.905	2.825	2.484	2.214	1.995	1.816	1.665
16	4.536	4.357	4.189	4.033	3.887	3.751	3.623	3.503	3.390	3.283	3.183	3.088	2.999	2.914	2.834	2.489	2.216	1.997	1.817	1.666
17	4.576	4.391	4.219	4.059	3.910	3.771	3.640	3.518	3.403	3.295	3.193	3.097	3.007	2.921	2.840	2.492	2.218	1.998	1.817	1.666
18	4.608	4.419	4.243	4.080	3.928	3.786	3.654	3.529	3.413	3.304	3.201	3.104	3.012	2.926	2.844	2.494	2.219	1.999	1.818	1.666
19	4.635	4.442	4.263	4.097	3.942	3.799	3.664	3.539	3.421	3.311	3.207	3.109	3.017	2.930	2.848	2.496	2.220	1.999	1.818	1.666
20	4.657	4.460	4.279	4.110	3.954	3.808	3.673	3.546	3.427	3.316	3.211	3.113	3.020	2.933	2.850	2.497	2.221	1.999	1.818	1.667
21	4.675	4.476	4.292	4.121	3.963	3.816	3.679	3.551	3.432	3.320	3.215	3.116	3.023	2.935	2.852	2.498	2.221	2.000	1.818	1.667
22	4.690	4.488	4.302	4.130	3.970	3.822	3.684	3.556	3.436	3.323	3.217	3.118	3.025	2.936	2.853	2.498	2.222	2.000	1.818	1.667
23	4.703	4.499	4.311	4.137	3.976	3.827	3.689	3.559	3.438	3.325	3.219	3.120	3.026	2.938	2.854	2.499	2.222	2.000	1.818	1.667
24	4.713	4.507	4.318	4.143	3.981	3.831	3.692	3.562	3.441	3.327	3.221	3.121	3.027	2.939	2.855	2.499	2.222	2.000	1.818	1.667
25	4.721	4.514	4.323	4.147	3.985	3.834	3.694	3.564	3.442	3.329	3.222	3.122	3.028	2.939	2.856	2.499	2.222	2.000	1.818	1.667
26	4.728	4.520	4.328	4.151	3.988	3.837	3.696	3.566	3.444	3.330	3.223	3.123	3.028	2.940	2.856	2.500	2.222	2.000	1.818	1.667
27	4.734	4.524	4.332	4.154	3.990	3.839	3.698	3.567	3.445	3.331	3.224	3.123	3.029	2.940	2.856	2.500	2.222	2.000	1.818	1.667
28	4.739	4.528	4.335	4.157	3.992	3.840	3.699	3.568	3.446	3.331	3.224	3.124	3.029	2.940	2.857	2.500	2.222	2.000	1.818	1.667
29	4.743	4.531	4.337	4.159	3.994	3.841	3.700	3.569	3.446	3.332	3.225	3.124	3.030	2.941	2.857	2.500	2.222	2.000	1.818	1.667
30	4.746	4.534	4.339	4.160	3.995	3.842	3.701	3.569	3.447	3.332	3.225	3.124	3.030	2.941	2.857	2.500	2.222	2.000	1.818	1.667
35	4.756	4.541	4.345	4.164	3.998	3.845	3.703	3.571	3.448	3.333	3.226	3.125	3.030	2.941	2.857	2.500	2.222	2.000	1.818	1.667
40	4.760	4.544	4.347	4.166	3.999	3.846	3.703	3.571	3.448	3.333	3.226	3.125	3.030	2.941	2.857	2.500	2.222	2.000	1.818	1.667
45	4.761	4.545	4.347	4.166	4.000	3.846	3.704	3.571	3.448	3.333	3.226	3.125	3.030	2.941	2.857	2.500	2.222	2.000	1.818	1.667
50	4.762	4.545	4.348	4.167	4.000	3.846	3.704	3.571	3.448	3.333	3.226	3.125	3.030	2.941	2.857	2.500	2.222	2.000	1.818	1.667

Table F.5 Simplified ACRS Depreciation Factors by Normal Recovery Period and Year

Year	Normal Recovery Period			
	3-Year	5-Year	7-Year	10-Year
1	0.33	0.20	0.14	0.10
2	0.44	0.32	0.25	0.18
3	0.23*	0.19	0.17	0.14
4		0.15*	0.13	0.12
5		0.14*	0.11*	0.09
6–7			0.10*	0.08*
8–10				0.07*

* Simplified to ignore the half-year convention at the end of the asset's normal recovery period.

Table F.6 Cumulative Normal Distribution Function

d	N(d)	d	N(d)	d	N(d)
		−1.00	0.1587	1.00	0.8413
−2.95	0.0016	−0.95	0.1711	1.05	0.8531
−2.90	0.0019	−0.90	0.1841	1.10	0.8643
−2.85	0.0022	−0.85	0.1977	1.15	0.8749
−2.80	0.0026	−0.80	0.2119	1.20	0.8849
−2.75	0.0030	−0.75	0.2266	1.25	0.8944
−2.70	0.0035	−0.70	0.2420	1.30	0.9032
−2.65	0.0040	−0.65	0.2578	1.35	0.9115
−2.60	0.0047	−0.60	0.2743	1.40	0.9192
−2.55	0.0054	−0.55	0.2912	1.45	0.9265
−2.50	0.0062	−0.50	0.3085	1.50	0.9332
−2.45	0.0071	−0.45	0.3264	1.55	0.9394
−2.40	0.0082	−0.40	0.3446	1.60	0.9452
−2.35	0.0094	−0.35	0.3632	1.65	0.9505
−2.30	0.0107	−0.30	0.3821	1.70	0.9554
−2.25	0.0122	−0.25	0.4013	1.75	0.9599
−2.20	0.0139	−0.20	0.4207	1.80	0.9641
−2.15	0.0158	−0.15	0.4404	1.85	0.9678
−2.10	0.0179	−0.10	0.4602	1.90	0.9713
−2.05	0.0202	−0.05	0.4801	1.95	0.9744
−2.00	0.0228	0.00	0.5000	2.00	0.9773
−1.95	0.0256	0.05	0.5199	2.05	0.9798
−1.90	0.0287	0.10	0.5398	2.10	0.9821
−1.85	0.0322	0.15	0.5596	2.15	0.9842
−1.80	0.0359	0.20	0.5793	2.20	0.9861
−1.75	0.0401	0.25	0.5987	2.25	0.9878
−1.70	0.0446	0.30	0.6179	2.30	0.9893
−1.65	0.0495	0.35	0.6368	2.35	0.9906
−1.60	0.0548	0.40	0.6554	2.40	0.9918
−1.55	0.0606	0.45	0.6736	2.45	0.9929
−1.50	0.0668	0.50	0.6915	2.50	0.9938
−1.45	0.0735	0.55	0.7088	2.55	0.9946
−1.40	0.0808	0.60	0.7257	2.60	0.9953
−1.35	0.0885	0.65	0.7422	2.65	0.9960
−1.30	0.0968	0.70	0.7580	2.70	0.9965
−1.25	0.1057	0.75	0.7734	2.75	0.9970
−1.20	0.1151	0.80	0.7881	2.80	0.9974
−1.15	0.1251	0.85	0.8023	2.85	0.9978
−1.10	0.1357	0.90	0.8159	2.90	0.9981
−1.05	0.1469	0.95	0.8289	2.95	0.9984

Table F.7 Call Option Value for Non-Dividend-Paying Stocks (in Decimal Form) Relative to Share Price

Standard Deviation Times the Square Root of Time

	0.05	0.10	0.15	0.20	0.25	0.30	0.35	0.40	0.45	0.50	0.55	0.60	0.65	0.70	0.75	0.80	0.85	0.90	0.95	1.00
0.50	*	*	*	*	0.0003	0.0015	0.0044	0.0094	0.0167	0.0261	0.0375	0.0506	0.0651	0.0808	0.0976	0.1151	0.1333	0.1520	0.1712	0.1906
0.60	*	*	*	0.0004	0.0024	0.0070	0.0144	0.0243	0.0366	0.0506	0.0661	0.0827	0.1003	0.1185	0.1373	0.1565	0.1761	0.1958	0.2157	0.2356
0.70	*	*	0.0005	0.0035	0.0103	0.0204	0.0333	0.0482	0.0645	0.0820	0.1003	0.1191	0.1384	0.1580	0.1778	0.1977	0.2176	0.2376	0.2575	0.2773
0.75	*	0.0001	0.0018	0.0077	0.0178	0.0310	0.0463	0.0632	0.0810	0.0997	0.1188	0.1383	0.1580	0.1779	0.1978	0.2178	0.2377	0.2575	0.2772	0.2968
0.80	*	0.0005	0.0050	0.0148	0.0283	0.0442	0.0615	0.0799	0.0989	0.1183	0.1380	0.1578	0.1777	0.1977	0.2176	0.2374	0.2572	0.2768	0.2963	0.3156
0.82	*	0.0010	0.0072	0.0186	0.0334	0.0502	0.0682	0.0870	0.1063	0.1259	0.1457	0.1657	0.1856	0.2055	0.2254	0.2452	0.2648	0.2843	0.3037	0.3228
0.84	*	0.0018	0.0099	0.0230	0.0390	0.0566	0.0752	0.0943	0.1139	0.1337	0.1536	0.1735	0.1935	0.2133	0.2331	0.2528	0.2724	0.2918	0.3110	0.3300
0.86	*	0.0031	0.0133	0.0280	0.0450	0.0633	0.0824	0.1019	0.1216	0.1415	0.1614	0.1814	0.2013	0.2211	0.2408	0.2604	0.2798	0.2991	0.3181	0.3370
0.88	0.0001	0.0051	0.0175	0.0336	0.0516	0.0705	0.0899	0.1096	0.1295	0.1494	0.1693	0.1892	0.2091	0.2288	0.2484	0.2679	0.2872	0.3063	0.3252	0.3439
0.90	0.0003	0.0079	0.0225	0.0399	0.0586	0.0779	0.0976	0.1175	0.1374	0.1573	0.1772	0.1971	0.2168	0.2364	0.2559	0.2752	0.2944	0.3134	0.3321	0.3507
0.92	0.0010	0.0118	0.0283	0.0467	0.0660	0.0857	0.1055	0.1255	0.1454	0.1653	0.1852	0.2049	0.2245	0.2440	0.2634	0.2825	0.3016	0.3204	0.3390	0.3574
0.94	0.0027	0.0169	0.0349	0.0542	0.0738	0.0937	0.1136	0.1336	0.1535	0.1733	0.1931	0.2127	0.2322	0.2515	0.2707	0.2898	0.3086	0.3272	0.3457	0.3639
0.96	0.0060	0.0232	0.0424	0.0622	0.0821	0.1020	0.1219	0.1418	0.1616	0.1813	0.2010	0.2204	0.2398	0.2590	0.2780	0.2969	0.3156	0.3340	0.3523	0.3704
0.98	0.0116	0.0309	0.0507	0.0707	0.0906	0.1105	0.1304	0.1501	0.1698	0.1894	0.2088	0.2282	0.2473	0.2664	0.2852	0.3039	0.3224	0.3407	0.3588	0.3767
1.00	0.0199	0.0399	0.0598	0.0797	0.0995	0.1192	0.1389	0.1585	0.1780	0.1974	0.2167	0.2358	0.2548	0.2737	0.2923	0.3108	0.3292	0.3473	0.3652	0.3829
1.02	0.0311	0.0501	0.0695	0.0891	0.1086	0.1281	0.1476	0.1670	0.1862	0.2054	0.2245	0.2434	0.2622	0.2809	0.2994	0.3177	0.3358	0.3538	0.3715	0.3890
1.04	0.0445	0.0613	0.0799	0.0988	0.1180	0.1372	0.1563	0.1754	0.1945	0.2134	0.2323	0.2510	0.2696	0.2880	0.3063	0.3244	0.3424	0.3601	0.3777	0.3951
1.06	0.0595	0.0734	0.0907	0.1090	0.1276	0.1463	0.1651	0.1839	0.2027	0.2214	0.2400	0.2585	0.2769	0.2951	0.3132	0.3311	0.3489	0.3664	0.3838	0.4010
1.08	0.0754	0.0863	0.1020	0.1193	0.1373	0.1556	0.1740	0.1925	0.2109	0.2293	0.2477	0.2659	0.2841	0.3021	0.3200	0.3377	0.3552	0.3726	0.3898	0.4068
1.10	0.0914	0.0996	0.1136	0.1299	0.1472	0.1649	0.1829	0.2010	0.2191	0.2372	0.2553	0.2733	0.2912	0.3090	0.3267	0.3442	0.3615	0.3787	0.3957	0.4125
1.12	0.1073	0.1132	0.1255	0.1407	0.1572	0.1743	0.1918	0.2095	0.2273	0.2451	0.2629	0.2806	0.2983	0.3158	0.3333	0.3506	0.3677	0.3847	0.4015	0.4181
1.14	0.1229	0.1270	0.1376	0.1516	0.1672	0.1837	0.2007	0.2180	0.2354	0.2529	0.2704	0.2878	0.3052	0.3226	0.3398	0.3569	0.3738	0.3906	0.4072	0.4236
1.16	0.1380	0.1407	0.1497	0.1626	0.1773	0.1932	0.2096	0.2264	0.2435	0.2606	0.2778	0.2950	0.3121	0.3292	0.3462	0.3631	0.3798	0.3964	0.4128	0.4291
1.18	0.1525	0.1544	0.1619	0.1736	0.1874	0.2026	0.2185	0.2349	0.2515	0.2683	0.2852	0.3021	0.3190	0.3358	0.3525	0.3692	0.3857	0.4021	0.4184	0.4344
1.20	0.1667	0.1679	0.1741	0.1846	0.1975	0.2120	0.2273	0.2432	0.2595	0.2759	0.2925	0.3091	0.3257	0.3423	0.3588	0.3752	0.3916	0.4077	0.4238	0.4397
1.25	0.2000	0.2004	0.2040	0.2119	0.2227	0.2353	0.2492	0.2639	0.2791	0.2946	0.3104	0.3262	0.3422	0.3581	0.3741	0.3900	0.4058	0.4214	0.4370	0.4524
1.30	0.2308	0.2309	0.2329	0.2385	0.2473	0.2583	0.2707	0.2842	0.2983	0.3129	0.3278	0.3429	0.3582	0.3735	0.3888	0.4042	0.4194	0.4346	0.4497	0.4647
1.35	0.2593	0.2593	0.2604	0.2643	0.2713	0.2806	0.2916	0.3039	0.3169	0.3306	0.3447	0.3591	0.3736	0.3883	0.4031	0.4178	0.4326	0.4473	0.4619	0.4765
1.40	0.2857	0.2857	0.2863	0.2889	0.2944	0.3023	0.3120	0.3230	0.3351	0.3478	0.3611	0.3747	0.3886	0.4026	0.4168	0.4310	0.4453	0.4595	0.4737	0.4878
1.45	0.3103	0.3103	0.3106	0.3124	0.3166	0.3232	0.3316	0.3416	0.3526	0.3645	0.3769	0.3898	0.4030	0.4165	0.4301	0.4438	0.4575	0.4713	0.4851	0.4987
1.50	0.3333	0.3333	0.3335	0.3346	0.3378	0.3432	0.3506	0.3595	0.3696	0.3806	0.3923	0.4044	0.4170	0.4298	0.4429	0.4561	0.4693	0.4826	0.4959	0.5092
1.75	0.4286	0.4286	0.4286	0.4287	0.4294	0.4313	0.4347	0.4395	0.4457	0.4530	0.4613	0.4703	0.4799	0.4900	0.5005	0.5112	0.5222	0.5334	0.5447	0.5560
2.00	0.5000	0.5000	0.5000	0.5000	0.5001	0.5007	0.5022	0.5047	0.5083	0.5131	0.5188	0.5253	0.5326	0.5404	0.5488	0.5575	0.5666	0.5760	0.5856	0.5953
2.50	0.6000	0.6000	0.6000	0.6000	0.6000	0.6001	0.6003	0.6009	0.6021	0.6041	0.6067	0.6101	0.6142	0.6190	0.6243	0.6301	0.6363	0.6430	0.6499	0.6571

Share Price Divided by the Present Value of the Exercise Price

* Value is zero to four decimal places.

Table F.7 Call Option (*Continued*)

Standard Deviation Times the Square Root of Time

	1.05	1.10	1.15	1.20	1.25	1.30	1.35	1.40	1.45	1.50	1.75	2.00	2.25	2.50	2.75	3.00	3.50	4.00	4.50	5.00
0.50	0.2103	0.2301	0.2500	0.2700	0.2899	0.3098	0.3295	0.3491	0.3686	0.3878	0.4803	0.5651	0.6412	0.7080	0.7655	0.8143	0.8883	0.9364	0.9657	0.9826
0.60	0.2555	0.2754	0.2953	0.3150	0.3346	0.3540	0.3731	0.3921	0.4109	0.4293	0.5174	0.5973	0.6684	0.7306	0.7840	0.8291	0.8973	0.9416	0.9686	0.9840
0.70	0.2964	0.3165	0.3358	0.3550	0.3739	0.3926	0.4111	0.4293	0.4472	0.4649	0.5485	0.6239	0.6907	0.7490	0.7989	0.8410	0.9046	0.9458	0.9708	0.9852
0.75	0.3162	0.3355	0.3545	0.3733	0.3919	0.4102	0.4283	0.4461	0.4636	0.4808	0.5623	0.6356	0.7005	0.7570	0.8054	0.8462	0.9077	0.9476	0.9718	0.9857
0.80	0.3347	0.3535	0.3722	0.3906	0.4088	0.4268	0.4444	0.4618	0.4789	0.4957	0.5751	0.6464	0.7095	0.7643	0.8113	0.8509	0.9106	0.9492	0.9727	0.9861
0.82	0.3418	0.3605	0.3790	0.3973	0.4153	0.4331	0.4506	0.4678	0.4847	0.5014	0.5799	0.6505	0.7129	0.7671	0.8135	0.8527	0.9116	0.9498	0.9730	0.9863
0.84	0.3488	0.3674	0.3857	0.4039	0.4217	0.4393	0.4566	0.4737	0.4904	0.5069	0.5847	0.6545	0.7162	0.7698	0.8157	0.8544	0.9127	0.9504	0.9733	0.9865
0.86	0.3557	0.3741	0.3923	0.4103	0.4279	0.4454	0.4625	0.4794	0.4960	0.5123	0.5893	0.6583	0.7194	0.7724	0.8178	0.8560	0.9137	0.9510	0.9736	0.9866
0.88	0.3624	0.3807	0.3987	0.4165	0.4340	0.4513	0.4683	0.4850	0.5014	0.5176	0.5938	0.6621	0.7225	0.7749	0.8198	0.8577	0.9146	0.9515	0.9739	0.9868
0.90	0.3690	0.3872	0.4050	0.4226	0.4400	0.4571	0.4739	0.4905	0.5068	0.5227	0.5981	0.6658	0.7255	0.7774	0.8218	0.8592	0.9156	0.9521	0.9742	0.9869
0.92	0.3755	0.3935	0.4112	0.4287	0.4459	0.4628	0.4795	0.4958	0.5119	0.5278	0.6024	0.6693	0.7284	0.7798	0.8237	0.8607	0.9165	0.9526	0.9745	0.9871
0.94	0.3819	0.3997	0.4172	0.4345	0.4516	0.4683	0.4848	0.5011	0.5170	0.5327	0.6066	0.6728	0.7313	0.7821	0.8256	0.8622	0.9174	0.9531	0.9748	0.9872
0.96	0.3882	0.4058	0.4232	0.4403	0.4572	0.4738	0.4901	0.5062	0.5220	0.5375	0.6106	0.6762	0.7341	0.7844	0.8274	0.8636	0.9182	0.9536	0.9750	0.9873
0.98	0.3944	0.4118	0.4290	0.4460	0.4627	0.4791	0.4953	0.5112	0.5268	0.5422	0.6146	0.6795	0.7368	0.7866	0.8292	0.8650	0.9191	0.9540	0.9753	0.9875
1.00	0.4004	0.4177	0.4347	0.4515	0.4680	0.4843	0.5003	0.5161	0.5315	0.5467	0.6184	0.6827	0.7394	0.7887	0.8309	0.8664	0.9199	0.9545	0.9756	0.9876
1.02	0.4064	0.4234	0.4403	0.4569	0.4733	0.4894	0.5053	0.5209	0.5362	0.5512	0.6222	0.6858	0.7420	0.7908	0.8325	0.8677	0.9207	0.9549	0.9758	0.9877
1.04	0.4122	0.4291	0.4458	0.4623	0.4785	0.4944	0.5101	0.5255	0.5407	0.5556	0.6259	0.6889	0.7445	0.7928	0.8342	0.8690	0.9214	0.9554	0.9760	0.9878
1.06	0.4179	0.4347	0.4512	0.4675	0.4835	0.4993	0.5149	0.5301	0.5452	0.5599	0.6295	0.6919	0.7469	0.7948	0.8357	0.8702	0.9222	0.9558	0.9763	0.9879
1.08	0.4236	0.4401	0.4565	0.4726	0.4885	0.5041	0.5195	0.5346	0.5495	0.5641	0.6330	0.6948	0.7493	0.7967	0.8373	0.8715	0.9229	0.9562	0.9765	0.9881
1.10	0.4291	0.4455	0.4617	0.4776	0.4933	0.5088	0.5241	0.5390	0.5538	0.5682	0.6364	0.6976	0.7517	0.7986	0.8388	0.8726	0.9236	0.9566	0.9767	0.9882
1.12	0.4345	0.4508	0.4668	0.4826	0.4981	0.5134	0.5285	0.5434	0.5579	0.5722	0.6398	0.7004	0.7539	0.8005	0.8403	0.8738	0.9243	0.9570	0.9769	0.9883
1.14	0.4399	0.4559	0.4718	0.4874	0.5028	0.5180	0.5329	0.5476	0.5620	0.5762	0.6431	0.7031	0.7562	0.8023	0.8417	0.8749	0.9250	0.9574	0.9771	0.9884
1.16	0.4451	0.4610	0.4767	0.4922	0.5074	0.5224	0.5372	0.5517	0.5660	0.5801	0.6463	0.7058	0.7583	0.8040	0.8431	0.8760	0.9257	0.9578	0.9773	0.9885
1.18	0.4503	0.4660	0.4815	0.4968	0.5119	0.5268	0.5414	0.5558	0.5699	0.5838	0.6495	0.7084	0.7605	0.8057	0.8445	0.8771	0.9263	0.9581	0.9775	0.9886
1.20	0.4554	0.4709	0.4863	0.5014	0.5163	0.5310	0.5455	0.5598	0.5738	0.5876	0.6526	0.7110	0.7626	0.8074	0.8458	0.8782	0.9269	0.9585	0.9777	0.9887
1.25	0.4677	0.4828	0.4978	0.5125	0.5271	0.5414	0.5555	0.5694	0.5831	0.5965	0.6600	0.7171	0.7676	0.8115	0.8490	0.8807	0.9284	0.9594	0.9782	
1.30	0.4796	0.4943	0.5088	0.5231	0.5373	0.5513	0.5651	0.5786	0.5920	0.6051	0.6671	0.7230	0.7723	0.8153	0.8521	0.8831	0.9299			
1.35	0.4909	0.5052	0.5193	0.5333	0.5471	0.5608	0.5742	0.5874	0.6005	0.6133	0.6739	0.7285	0.7768	0.8189	0.8550	0.8854				
1.40	0.5018	0.5157	0.5295	0.5431	0.5565	0.5698	0.5829	0.5958	0.6086	0.6211	0.6804	0.7338	0.7811	0.8224	0.8577					
1.45	0.5123	0.5258	0.5392	0.5524	0.5656	0.5785	0.5913	0.6039	0.6163	0.6286	0.6865	0.7389	0.7852	0.8257						0.9897
1.50	0.5224	0.5355	0.5485	0.5614	0.5742	0.5869	0.5993	0.6116	0.6238	0.6357	0.6924	0.7437								0.9899
1.75	0.5674	0.5788	0.5902	0.6015	0.6128	0.6240	0.6350	0.6460	0.6568	0.6675	0.7186									0.9907
2.00	0.6051	0.6151	0.6250	0.6350	0.6450	0.6549	0.6648	0.6746	0.6843											0.9913
2.50	0.6645	0.6721	0.6798	0.6877	0.6956	0.7035														0.9923

Share Price Divided by the Present Value of the Exercise Price

Table F.8 Put Option Value for Non-Dividend-Paying Stocks (in Decimal Form) Relative to Share Price

Standard Deviation Times the Square Root of Time

	0.05	0.10	0.15	0.20	0.25	0.30	0.35	0.40	0.45	0.50	0.55	0.60	0.65	0.70	0.75	0.80	0.85	0.90	0.95	1.00
0.50	1.0000	1.0000	1.0000	1.0000	1.0003	1.0015	1.0044	1.0094	1.0167	1.0261	1.0375	1.0506	1.0651	1.0808	1.0976	1.1151	1.1333	1.1520	1.1712	1.1906
0.60	0.6667	0.6667	0.6667	0.6671	0.6691	0.6736	0.6810	0.6910	0.7032	0.7172	0.7327	0.7494	0.7669	0.7852	0.8040	0.8233	0.8427	0.8625	0.8823	0.9023
0.70	0.4286	0.4286	0.4291	0.4321	0.4388	0.4490	0.4618	0.4767	0.4931	0.5106	0.5289	0.5477	0.5670	0.5866	0.6064	0.6263	0.6462	0.6661	0.6860	0.7058
0.75	0.3333	0.3334	0.3352	0.3411	0.3511	0.3643	0.3796	0.3965	0.4144	0.4330	0.4522	0.4716	0.4914	0.5112	0.5312	0.5511	0.5710	0.5908	0.6106	0.6301
0.80	0.2500	0.2505	0.2550	0.2648	0.2783	0.2942	0.3115	0.3299	0.3489	0.3683	0.3880	0.4078	0.4277	0.4477	0.4676	0.4874	0.5072	0.5268	0.5463	0.5656
0.82	0.2195	0.2205	0.2267	0.2381	0.2529	0.2697	0.2877	0.3065	0.3258	0.3454	0.3653	0.3852	0.4051	0.4250	0.4449	0.4647	0.4843	0.5038	0.5232	0.5423
0.84	0.1905	0.1923	0.2004	0.2135	0.2295	0.2471	0.2656	0.2848	0.3044	0.3242	0.3441	0.3640	0.3839	0.4038	0.4236	0.4433	0.4628	0.4822	0.5014	0.5205
0.86	0.1628	0.1659	0.1761	0.1908	0.2078	0.2261	0.2452	0.2647	0.2844	0.3043	0.3242	0.3442	0.3641	0.3839	0.4036	0.4232	0.4426	0.4619	0.4809	0.4998
0.88	0.1365	0.1414	0.1538	0.1700	0.1879	0.2068	0.2262	0.2460	0.2658	0.2858	0.3057	0.3256	0.3454	0.3652	0.3848	0.4042	0.4235	0.4426	0.4616	0.4803
0.90	0.1114	0.1190	0.1336	0.1510	0.1697	0.1890	0.2087	0.2286	0.2485	0.2684	0.2884	0.3082	0.3279	0.3476	0.3670	0.3864	0.4055	0.4245	0.4433	0.4618
0.92	0.0880	0.0988	0.1152	0.1337	0.1530	0.1726	0.1925	0.2124	0.2324	0.2523	0.2721	0.2919	0.3115	0.3310	0.3503	0.3695	0.3885	0.4073	0.4259	0.4443
0.94	0.0665	0.0807	0.0988	0.1180	0.1377	0.1575	0.1775	0.1974	0.2173	0.2372	0.2569	0.2765	0.2960	0.3154	0.3346	0.3536	0.3724	0.3911	0.4095	0.4278
0.96	0.0476	0.0649	0.0841	0.1038	0.1237	0.1437	0.1636	0.1835	0.2033	0.2230	0.2426	0.2621	0.2815	0.3007	0.3197	0.3385	0.3572	0.3757	0.3940	0.4120
0.98	0.0320	0.0513	0.0711	0.0911	0.1110	0.1309	0.1508	0.1705	0.1902	0.2098	0.2292	0.2486	0.2677	0.2868	0.3056	0.3243	0.3428	0.3611	0.3792	0.3971
1.00	0.0199	0.0399	0.0598	0.0797	0.0995	0.1192	0.1389	0.1585	0.1780	0.1974	0.2167	0.2358	0.2548	0.2737	0.2923	0.3108	0.3292	0.3473	0.3652	0.3829
1.02	0.0115	0.0305	0.0499	0.0695	0.0890	0.1085	0.1280	0.1474	0.1666	0.1858	0.2049	0.2238	0.2426	0.2613	0.2798	0.2981	0.3162	0.3342	0.3519	0.3694
1.04	0.0061	0.0228	0.0414	0.0604	0.0795	0.0987	0.1179	0.1370	0.1560	0.1750	0.1938	0.2125	0.2311	0.2496	0.2679	0.2860	0.3039	0.3217	0.3392	0.3566
1.06	0.0029	0.0168	0.0341	0.0523	0.0710	0.0897	0.1085	0.1273	0.1461	0.1648	0.1834	0.2019	0.2203	0.2385	0.2566	0.2745	0.2923	0.3098	0.3272	0.3444
1.08	0.0013	0.0122	0.0279	0.0453	0.0632	0.0815	0.0999	0.1184	0.1368	0.1553	0.1736	0.1919	0.2100	0.2280	0.2459	0.2636	0.2812	0.2985	0.3157	0.3327
1.10	0.0005	0.0087	0.0227	0.0390	0.0563	0.0740	0.0920	0.1101	0.1282	0.1463	0.1644	0.1824	0.2003	0.2181	0.2357	0.2533	0.2706	0.2878	0.3048	0.3216
1.12	0.0002	0.0061	0.0184	0.0336	0.0500	0.0672	0.0847	0.1024	0.1201	0.1379	0.1557	0.1735	0.1911	0.2087	0.2261	0.2434	0.2606	0.2775	0.2944	0.3110
1.14	0.0001	0.0042	0.0148	0.0288	0.0444	0.0609	0.0779	0.0952	0.1126	0.1301	0.1476	0.1650	0.1824	0.1998	0.2170	0.2340	0.2510	0.2678	0.2844	0.3008
1.16	*	0.0028	0.0118	0.0246	0.0394	0.0552	0.0717	0.0885	0.1055	0.1227	0.1399	0.1571	0.1742	0.1913	0.2083	0.2251	0.2419	0.2585	0.2749	0.2911
1.18	*	0.0019	0.0094	0.0210	0.0349	0.0501	0.0660	0.0823	0.0990	0.1158	0.1326	0.1495	0.1664	0.1832	0.2000	0.2167	0.2332	0.2496	0.2658	0.2819
1.20	*	0.0012	0.0074	0.0179	0.0309	0.0453	0.0607	0.0766	0.0928	0.1092	0.1258	0.1424	0.1590	0.1756	0.1921	0.2086	0.2249	0.2411	0.2571	0.2730
1.25	*	0.0004	0.0040	0.0119	0.0227	0.0353	0.0492	0.0639	0.0791	0.0946	0.1104	0.1262	0.1422	0.1581	0.1741	0.1900	0.2058	0.2214	0.2370	0.2524
1.30	*	0.0001	0.0021	0.0078	0.0165	0.0275	0.0399	0.0534	0.0675	0.0821	0.0970	0.1121	0.1274	0.1427	0.1581	0.1734	0.1887	0.2039	0.2190	0.2339
1.35	*	*	0.0011	0.0050	0.0120	0.0213	0.0324	0.0446	0.0577	0.0714	0.0854	0.0998	0.1144	0.1291	0.1438	0.1586	0.1733	0.1881	0.2027	0.2172
1.40	*	*	0.0005	0.0032	0.0087	0.0165	0.0263	0.0373	0.0494	0.0621	0.0754	0.0890	0.1029	0.1169	0.1311	0.1453	0.1596	0.1738	0.1880	0.2021
1.45	*	*	0.0003	0.0020	0.0062	0.0128	0.0212	0.0312	0.0423	0.0541	0.0666	0.0795	0.0927	0.1061	0.1197	0.1334	0.1472	0.1609	0.1747	0.1883
1.50	*	*	0.0001	0.0013	0.0045	0.0099	0.0173	0.0262	0.0363	0.0473	0.0589	0.0711	0.0837	0.0965	0.1096	0.1227	0.1360	0.1493	0.1626	0.1758
1.75	*	*	*	0.0001	0.0008	0.0027	0.0061	0.0110	0.0171	0.0245	0.0327	0.0417	0.0513	0.0614	0.0719	0.0827	0.0937	0.1048	0.1161	0.1275
2.00	*	*	*	*	0.0001	0.0007	0.0022	0.0047	0.0083	0.0131	0.0188	0.0253	0.0326	0.0404	0.0488	0.0575	0.0666	0.0760	0.0856	0.0953
2.50	*	*	*	*	*	0.0001	0.0003	0.0009	0.0021	0.0041	0.0067	0.0101	0.0142	0.0190	0.0243	0.0301	0.0363	0.0430	0.0499	0.0571

Share Price Divided by the Present Value of the Exercise Price

* Value is zero to four decimal places.

Table F.8 Put Option (*Continued*)

Standard Deviation Times the Square Root of time

Share Price / PV of Exercise Price	1.05	1.10	1.15	1.20	1.25	1.30	1.35	1.40	1.45	1.50	1.75	2.00	2.25	2.50	2.75	3.00	3.50	4.00	4.50	5.00
0.50	1.2103	1.2301	1.2500	1.2700	1.2899	1.3098	1.3295	1.3491	1.3686	1.3878	1.4803	1.5651	1.6412	1.7080	1.7655	1.8143	1.8882	1.9364	1.9657	1.9826
0.60	0.9222	0.9421	0.9619	0.9817	1.0012	1.0206	1.0398	1.0588	1.0775	1.0960	1.1840	1.2640	1.3351	1.3973	1.4507	1.4958	1.5640	1.6083	1.6353	1.6507
0.70	0.7255	0.7450	0.7644	0.7835	0.8025	0.8212	0.8397	0.8579	0.8758	0.8934	0.9770	1.0525	1.1193	1.1776	1.2275	1.2696	1.3332	1.3744	1.3994	1.4138
0.75	0.6496	0.6688	0.6878	0.7066	0.7252	0.7435	0.7616	0.7794	0.7969	0.8141	0.8956	0.9689	1.0338	1.0903	1.1387	1.1795	1.2410	1.2809	1.3052	1.3190
0.80	0.5847	0.6035	0.6222	0.6406	0.6588	0.6768	0.6944	0.7118	0.7289	0.7457	0.8251	0.8964	0.9595	1.0143	1.0613	1.1009	1.1606	1.1992	1.2227	1.2361
0.82	0.5613	0.5800	0.5986	0.6168	0.6349	0.6526	0.6701	0.6873	0.7042	0.7209	0.7994	0.8700	0.9324	0.9866	1.0330	1.0722	1.1311	1.1693	1.1925	1.2058
0.84	0.5392	0.5579	0.5762	0.5943	0.6122	0.6298	0.6471	0.6642	0.6809	0.6974	0.7751	0.8450	0.9066	0.9603	1.0062	1.0448	1.1031	1.1409	1.1638	1.1769
0.86	0.5185	0.5369	0.5551	0.5730	0.5907	0.6082	0.6253	0.6422	0.6588	0.6751	0.7521	0.8211	0.8821	0.9352	0.9806	1.0188	1.0764	1.1138	1.1364	1.1494
0.88	0.4988	0.5171	0.5351	0.5529	0.5704	0.5877	0.6047	0.6214	0.6378	0.6540	0.7301	0.7985	0.8588	0.9113	0.9562	0.9940	1.0510	1.0879	1.1103	1.1231
0.90	0.4802	0.4983	0.5161	0.5338	0.5511	0.5682	0.5851	0.6016	0.6179	0.6339	0.7092	0.7769	0.8366	0.8885	0.9329	0.9703	1.0267	1.0632	1.0854	1.0980
0.92	0.4625	0.4805	0.4982	0.5156	0.5328	0.5497	0.5664	0.5828	0.5989	0.6147	0.6894	0.7563	0.8154	0.8667	0.9107	0.9477	1.0034	1.0395	1.0615	1.0740
0.94	0.4458	0.4635	0.4811	0.4984	0.5154	0.5322	0.5487	0.5649	0.5808	0.5965	0.6704	0.7366	0.7951	0.8459	0.8894	0.9260	0.9812	1.0169	1.0386	1.0510
0.96	0.4299	0.4475	0.4648	0.4820	0.4988	0.5154	0.5318	0.5478	0.5636	0.5791	0.6523	0.7178	0.7757	0.8260	0.8691	0.9053	0.9599	0.9952	1.0167	1.0290
0.98	0.4148	0.4322	0.4494	0.4664	0.4831	0.4995	0.5157	0.5316	0.5472	0.5626	0.6350	0.6999	0.7572	0.8070	0.8496	0.8854	0.9395	0.9744	0.9957	1.0079
1.00	0.4004	0.4177	0.4347	0.4515	0.4680	0.4843	0.5003	0.5161	0.5315	0.5467	0.6184	0.6827	0.7394	0.7887	0.8309	0.8664	0.9199	0.9545	0.9756	0.9876
1.02	0.3868	0.4038	0.4207	0.4373	0.4537	0.4698	0.4857	0.5013	0.5166	0.5316	0.6026	0.6662	0.7224	0.7712	0.8129	0.8481	0.9011	0.9353	0.9562	0.9681
1.04	0.3737	0.3907	0.4073	0.4238	0.4400	0.4560	0.4716	0.4871	0.5023	0.5172	0.5874	0.6504	0.7060	0.7544	0.7957	0.8305	0.8830	0.9169	0.9376	0.9494
1.06	0.3613	0.3781	0.3946	0.4109	0.4269	0.4427	0.4582	0.4735	0.4886	0.5033	0.5729	0.6353	0.6903	0.7382	0.7791	0.8136	0.8656	0.8992	0.9197	0.9313
1.08	0.3495	0.3661	0.3824	0.3985	0.4144	0.4300	0.4454	0.4606	0.4754	0.4900	0.5589	0.6207	0.6753	0.7227	0.7632	0.7974	0.8488	0.8821	0.9024	0.9140
1.10	0.3382	0.3546	0.3708	0.3867	0.4024	0.4179	0.4331	0.4481	0.4628	0.4773	0.5455	0.6067	0.6608	0.7077	0.7479	0.7817	0.8327	0.8657	0.8858	0.8973
1.12	0.3274	0.3436	0.3596	0.3754	0.3910	0.4063	0.4214	0.4362	0.4508	0.4651	0.5327	0.5933	0.6468	0.6933	0.7331	0.7667	0.8172	0.8499	0.8698	0.8811
1.14	0.3171	0.3331	0.3490	0.3646	0.3800	0.3952	0.4101	0.4248	0.4392	0.4534	0.5203	0.5803	0.6334	0.6795	0.7189	0.7521	0.8022	0.8346	0.8543	0.8656
1.16	0.3072	0.3231	0.3388	0.3542	0.3695	0.3845	0.3993	0.4138	0.4281	0.4421	0.5084	0.5679	0.6204	0.6661	0.7052	0.7381	0.7877	0.8198	0.8394	0.8505
1.18	0.2978	0.3135	0.3290	0.3443	0.3594	0.3742	0.3889	0.4033	0.4174	0.4313	0.4969	0.5559	0.6079	0.6532	0.6919	0.7246	0.7738	0.8056	0.8250	0.8360
1.20	0.2887	0.3043	0.3196	0.3347	0.3497	0.3644	0.3789	0.3931	0.4071	0.4209	0.4859	0.5443	0.5959	0.6408	0.6792	0.7115	0.7603	0.7918	0.8110	0.8220
1.25	0.2677	0.2828	0.2978	0.3125	0.3271	0.3414	0.3555	0.3694	0.3831	0.3965	0.4600	0.5171	0.5676	0.6115	0.6490	0.6807	0.7284	0.7594	0.7782	0.7889
1.30	0.2488	0.2635	0.2780	0.2924	0.3065	0.3205	0.3343	0.3479	0.3612	0.3743	0.4364	0.4922	0.5416	0.5845	0.6213	0.6523	0.6991	0.7294	0.7478	0.7584
1.35	0.2316	0.2459	0.2601	0.2741	0.2879	0.3015	0.3149	0.3282	0.3412	0.3540	0.4147	0.4693	0.5176	0.5597	0.5957	0.6261	0.6720	0.7017	0.7197	0.7301
1.40	0.2161	0.2300	0.2438	0.2574	0.2708	0.2841	0.2972	0.3101	0.3229	0.3354	0.3947	0.4481	0.4954	0.5367	0.5720	0.6018	0.6468	0.6759	0.6937	0.7038
1.45	0.2019	0.2155	0.2288	0.2421	0.2552	0.2682	0.2810	0.2936	0.3060	0.3182	0.3762	0.4285	0.4749	0.5153	0.5500	0.5792	0.6234	0.6520	0.6694	0.6794
1.50	0.1890	0.2022	0.2152	0.2281	0.2409	0.2535	0.2660	0.2783	0.2904	0.3024	0.3591	0.4104	0.4558	0.4955	0.5295	0.5582	0.6016	0.6297	0.6468	0.6566
1.75	0.1389	0.1503	0.1616	0.1730	0.1842	0.1954	0.2065	0.2174	0.2283	0.2389	0.2900	0.3364	0.3778	0.4141	0.4452	0.4716	0.5114	0.5373	0.5531	0.5621
2.00	0.1051	0.1151	0.1250	0.1350	0.1450	0.1549	0.1648	0.1746	0.1843	0.1939	0.2402	0.2826	0.3206	0.3540	0.3828	0.4072	0.4441	0.4682	0.4829	0.4913
2.50	0.0645	0.0721	0.0798	0.0877	0.0956	0.1035	0.1115	0.1195	0.1274	0.1354	0.1740	0.2100	0.2427	0.2716	0.2967	0.3180	0.3505	0.3718	0.3848	0.3923

*Value is zero to four decimal places.

Share Price Divided by the Present Value of the Exercise Price

Glossary

Terms italicized within definitions are also defined in this glossary. Numbers in parentheses following the definition give the principal chapters in which the term is used.

abandonment decision *Capital budgeting* decision where the *net present value* of continuing to operate is compared with the after-tax proceeds if the project is discontinued. (9)

ABC method Inventory control procedure where items are grouped in categories by their value. Group A items require high investment and the most control. (20)

abnormal return Difference between the actual stock market performance for a firm (or group of firms) and its expected performance on a given day. Determined when an *event study* is conducted. (2)

accelerated cost recovery system (ACRS) *Depreciation* system set up by the Economic Recovery Tax Act of 1981 and modified by the Tax Reform Act of 1986. All assets (except real estate) are divided into six *normal recovery periods*—3-year, 5-year, 7-year, 10-year, 15-year, and 20-year. Assets are depreciated to zero if held to the end of the normal recovery period. (8)

acid test ratio See *quick ratio*.

adjustable rate preferred stock *Preferred stock* where the *cash dividend* rate is tied to a U.S. Treasury security index and is adjusted quarterly. Since the dividend adjusts, there is little fluctuation in the market value of the security. (13)

advance factoring Short-term financing in which a lender (factor) provides a loan against a firm's receivables. (21)

agency cost The costs associated with monitoring the actions of management to ensure they are consistent with any contractual agreements among management, stockholders, and *creditors*. These costs are ultimately borne by the firm's common stockholders. (1, 15)

agent Someone who acts on behalf of another. The firm's managers are the agent of its stockholders. (1)

American option A *call* or *put option* that can be exercised at any time up to its expiration date. (11)

amortization schedule Schedule that shows how a *term loan* will be paid off by specifying both the *principal* and *interest* payments made per payment. The size of the payment is constant, but with each successive payment more goes to principal and less to interest. (5)

announcement period A time period of interest examined in an *event study*. Often is the 2-day period $(-1, 0)$, but can be longer. (2)

annual percentage rate (APR) Compound percent rate of *interest* stated on an annual basis. $k_b = \{1 + [(\text{costs} - \text{benefits})/\text{net amount of financing}]\}^m - 1$. (21)

annual report Report issued to stockholders by *corporations* that contains basic financial statements as well as management's opinion of the past year's operations and prospects for the future. (3)

annuity A series of equal payments for a specified number of periods with each payment occurring at the end of the period; also called an *ordinary annuity*. (5)

annuity due A series of equal payments for a specified number of periods, with each payment occurring at the beginning of the period. (5)

arbitrage pricing theory Theory that specifies the *risk premium* for stocks is a function of a number of risk factors, not just the *expected return* on the *market portfolio* as given by the *capital asset pricing model*. (7)

asked price Price at which a dealer or specialist in securities will sell shares of stock. (6)

arrearages An overdue payment; used to describe *cash dividends* on *cumulative preferred stock* that have not been paid. (13)

asset beta Unlevered *beta* that indicates the riskiness of the firms' assets, without regard for how the firm is financed. Beta for an all-equity firm. (14)

assignment An out-of-court procedure for liquidating a firm. (13)

average collection float The number of days of *float* times the average daily dollar amount in the collection system. (19)

average collection period Accounts receivable divided by the average sales per day (sales/365 days). A measure of the length of time from when goods are sold on credit until cash is received from the customer. (3, 18, 20)

average tax rate The rate found by dividing the total taxes paid by taxable income. (2)

bad debt Occurs when a seller extends credit to a buyer, and the buyer fails to pay the account. (20)

balance sheet Accounting statement that records the assets of the firm and claims against them (liabilities and equities), as of a specific moment in time. (3)

bank discount yield How yields are figured on *Treasury bills*. $k_{BD} = [(P_M - P_0)/P_M](360/n)$. (19)

banker's acceptance A short-term security that typically arises through international trade; a draft drawn on a specific bank by a seller to obtain payment for goods that have been shipped (sold) to a customer. The bank, by accepting (or endorsing), assumes the obligation of payment at the due date. (20)

bankruptcy costs Includes legal and other direct costs associated with bankruptcy or *reorganization* procedures. (15)

bearer form *Bonds* that are not registered (or recorded) by the firm (or its *agent*). No owner's name appears on the bond certificate, so whoever holds it is the owner. Coupons must be "clipped" and sent in to receive *interest* payments. (13)

best efforts Procedure for selling a new security issue in which an *investment banking* firm agrees to try and market the issue, but the issue is not *underwritten* and there is no guarantee the full amount of the issue will be sold. (12)

beta A statistical measure of an asset's *nondiversifiable risk*. Calculated by (1) regressing the *returns* for an asset against the returns for the *market portfolio* or (2) dividing the *covariance* between the returns on an asset and the market portfolio by the *variance* of the market's return: $\beta_j = \text{Cov}_{jM}/\sigma_M^2 = \sigma_j \text{Corr}_{jM}/\sigma_M$. (7, 10, 14, 23)

bid price The price a dealer or specialist in securities will pay to buy a security. (6)

bidding firm The firm that is buying another firm in a *merger* or acquisition. (22)

bill of lading Shipping document that authorizes the shipment of goods from one party (the seller) to another (the customer). Typically, the bill of lading provides title to the goods. (20)

blue sky laws State laws pertaining to security market regulation. (12)

bond A long-term (typically 10 years or more) promissory note issued by the borrower promising to pay a specified *interest* per year and/or *maturity* value. (1, 6, 13)

bond equivalent yield Means of converting *bond discount yield* on *Treasury bills* to an approximate 365-day annualized yield. $k_{BE} = [(365)(k_{BD})]/[360 - (k_{BD})(n)]$. (19)

bond rating Estimates supplied (primarily by Moody's or Standard & Poor's) of the *probability* of repayment of *principal* and *interest* on a *bond*. The higher the rating, the less *risk* and the lower the *yield to maturity*, other things being equal. (13)

book value Assets minus liabilities, or stockholders' equity. (1)

book value per share Stockholders' equity divided by the number of shares of *common stock* outstanding. (3, 12)

break-even analysis Analysis of the level of sales at which a project will just cover its costs, or break even. (10)

business risk Source of *risk* because of the basic nature of the industry in which the firm operates. Measured by the uncertainty of the future *earnings before interest and taxes* (EBIT) of the firm. (7, 15)

call option The right—but not the obligation—to purchase a certain number of shares of stock at a stated price within a specified time period. (11)

call premium The difference between a *bond's* or *preferred stock's par value* and what the firm has to pay to call them for retirement. The call price is greater than or equal to the par value, so the call premium is either positive or zero. (13)

call provision Stipulation in a *bond* or *preferred stock* issue allowing the firm to repurchase the securities before *maturity* for the purpose of retiring them. (13)

capital asset pricing model (CAPM) A model of *required rates of return* for financial assets. The required rate of return is equal to the *risk-free rate* plus a *risk premium* based on the *expected return* on the *market portfolio* and the asset's *nondiversifiable risk* as measured by *beta:* $k_j = k_{RF} + \beta_j(k_M - k_{RF})$. (7, 10, 14, 23)

capital budget A statement of the firm's planned long-term investment projects, usually done annually. (8)

capital budgeting The procedure by which long-term investments are generated, analyzed, and placed on the *capital budget.* (8, 9, 10, 24)

capital budgeting process The four *capital budgeting* steps are: (1) search and identification; (2) estimating the magnitude, timing, and riskiness of cash flows; (3) selection or rejection; and (4) control and postcompletion audit. (8)

capital gain The difference between the selling price of an asset and its original cost, provided the selling price is greater than the original cost. Under the Tax Reform Act of 1986, both capital gains and ordinary income are taxed at the same rate. (2, 8)

capital lease A *lease* that meets certain *GAAP* requirements and accordingly must be capitalized and shown as both an asset and a liability on the firm's *balance sheet.* (17)

capital market Financial market where long-term (longer than 1-year) financial assets such as *bonds, preferred stock,* or *common stock* are bought or sold. (2, 12)

capital market line (CML) Set of all *efficient portfolios* consisting of various combinations of the *risk-free rate* and the *market portfolio.* (7)

capital rationing A situation where a constraint (either external or internal) is placed on the funds available such that some wealth-maximizing *capital budgeting* projects cannot be accepted. (9)

capital structure The long-term financing of the firm, typically represented by *bonds, leases, preferred stock,* and *common stock.* (15)

carryback, carryforward For income tax purposes, operating losses are first carried back 3 years and then carried forward for up to 15 years. Serves to reduce cash outflows for taxes. (2)

cash budget A detailed forecast of all expected cash inflows and outflows by the firm for some period of time. (4, 23)

cash conversion cycle The net time interval in days between actual cash expenditure by the firm on its productive resources and the ultimate recovery of cash. Calculated by subtracting the *payable deferral period* from the *operating cycle.* (18)

cash discount A provision often included in a firm's credit terms. Payment within the discount period allows the customer to reduce the cost of the purchase. (19, 21)

cash dividend (dividend) The distribution to investors who own *common* or *preferred stock* of some of the firm's cash. Typically paid quarterly, if declared by the firm's board of directors. (3, 6, 16)

cash flow The actual dollars coming into a firm (cash inflow) or paid out by a firm (cash outflow). (1, 4, 8, 20, 22)

cash flow after tax (CF) Equals *cash flow before tax* minus taxes (CFBT − taxes); or cash flow before tax times 1 minus the *marginal tax rate,* plus *depreciation* times the marginal tax rate [CFBT(1 − T) + Dep(T)]. (4, 8, 9, 20, 22)

cash flow before tax (CFBT) Equals cash inflows minus cash outflows. (4, 8, 20, 22)

cash on delivery (COD) Term of sale where payment is required at the time the goods are delivered to the buyer. (20)

certainty equivalent Method of dealing with *risk* in *capital budgeting* decisions whereby *cash flows* are adjusted to their "certain" amount, and then *discounted* at the *risk-free rate.* Has the advantage of adjusting for risk as a separate step from any adjustment for the *timing* of the cash flows. (10)

certificate of deposit (CD) A short-term time deposit issued by a bank. (19)

chief financial officer The individual ultimately responsible for making and implementing financial decisions in a firm. (1)

clientele effect The tendency of firms to attract a certain kind of stockholder, depending on the *cash dividend* policy maintained by the firm. Investors desiring high current income invest in high *dividend payout* stocks, and vice versa. (16)

coefficient of variation A measure of relative riskiness calculated by dividing the *standard deviation* by the *expected value* (or *mean*) of the distribution. Useful when the *risk* of two variables with different means is being considered. (7, 15)

commercial paper Short-term nonsecured promissory notes issued by commercial finance and industrial firms. The maximum maturity is 270 days. (19, 21)

commitment fee A fee charged by the lender on a *line of credit;* generally charged on the unused balance of the line. (21)

common-size statement Financial statement expressed in percentage terms. A common-size *income statement* expresses all items as a percentage of net sales, whereas a common-size *balance sheet* expresses everything as a percentage of total assets. (3)

common stock A document that represents (residual) ownership in a corporation. The common stockholder is the last to receive any distribution of earnings or assets. (1, 6, 12)

compensating balance Money on deposit with a bank to compensate the bank for services rendered. Such a balance tends to raise the *annual percentage rate*, or cost, of a loan, unless the firm always keeps that much cash in the bank. (19, 21)

complementary projects Two or more *capital budgeting* projects that interact positively so that the total *cash flows*, if all are undertaken, are more than the simple sum of their individual cash flows. (9)

composition Out-of-court agreement between a firm and its *creditors* whereby the creditors receive less than the total amount due them in full settlement of their claim. (13)

compound rate Rate applicable when *interest* is earned not only on the initial *principal*, but also on the accumulated interest from previous periods. (5)

compounding The process of finding the *future value* of a series of *cash flows*. It is the inverse of *discounting*. (5)

consol Perpetual coupon-paying *bond*. (6)

constant growth model Form of the *dividend valuation model* in which *cash dividends* are expected to grow at a constant percentage *growth rate* (g) until

infinity. The value of the stock is $P_0 = D_1/(k_s - g)$. (6, 14, 23)

controlled disbursing System in which the firm directs checks to be drawn on a bank that is in a small- or medium-size city to maximize the amount of *transit float* before the check is finally deducted from the firm's demand deposit account. (19)

controller The individual in a firm who is responsible for preparing financial statements, for cost accounting, for internal auditing, for budgeting, and for the tax department. (1)

convertible security *Bond* or *preferred stock* that, at the option of the owner, may be exchanged for a predetermined number of shares of *common stock*. (3, 13)

convertible subordinated debenture Unsecured long-term *bonds* that have a junior (or subordinated) claim to other debt and are convertible into *common stock*. Virtually all convertible bonds are convertible subordinated debentures. (13)

corporation A legal entity formed to conduct business and given the power to act as an individual and limited liability. (1)

correlation A statistical measure of the degree of linear relationship between two random variables. It can vary from +1.0 (perfect positive correlation), to 0.0 (independent), to −1.0 (perfect negative correlation). The sign indicates the direction of the relationship, and the size of the correlation coefficient indicates the degree (or closeness) of the co-movement between the two variables. (7)

coupon interest rate The stated percentage rate of *interest* on a *bond* relative to its *par value*. By multiplying the coupon rate by the par value, the interest per year is determined. (6, 13)

covariance A statistical measure of the degree of linear relationship between two random variables. Similar to *correlation* except the covariance is not bounded by plus and minus one. Calculated by multiplying the *standard deviation* of an asset times the standard deviation of the market times the correlation between the asset and the market: $Cov_{jM} = \sigma_j \sigma_M Corr_{jM}$. (7)

covered The act of *hedging* a *foreign exchange rate* exposure so little or no loss or gain occurs if exchange rates change. (24)

credit scoring model Point-based system used to determine the creditworthiness of customers based on key financial and credit characteristics. (20)

creditor Persons or firms to which money is owed. The firm's creditors include those that have fixed-type financial claims on the firm arising from short- or long-term debt. (1)

cumulative Provision in many *preferred stocks* and *income bonds* that requires that all past *cash dividends* or *interest* be paid in full before any additional dividend or interest is paid. (13)

cumulative abnormal return Cumulative sum of day-by-day *abnormal returns*. Calculated in an *event study* to see if new information causes stock market prices to increase of decrease. (2)

cumulative voting System of electing the board of directors whereby each share is entitled to one vote. By voting more than once for a single director, cumulative voting encourages minority representation on the board of directors. (12)

current ratio Current assets divided by current liabilities; a measure of liquidity. (3)

days purchases outstanding Accounts payable divided by credit purchases per day. Important for creditors; but often purchases (credit or total) are not available, so they must be estimated. (3)

debenture Unsecured long-term borrowing by a firm backed only by its full faith and credit. (13)

debt capacity The amount of debt or debt-type securities (like *leases* and *preferred stock*) a firm can service. The larger the debt capacity, the more fixed financing charges the firm can handle. (3, 15, 17)

deep discount bond *Bond* whose *coupon interest rate* is set substantially below the prevailing market interest rate at the time of issue. Accordingly, the bond must be sold at a *discount* from its *par (maturity) value.* (13)

default premium Additional *return* required to compensate investor for the *risk* that the bond issuer will not be able to make *interest* payments or repay *principal* amount on schedule; the difference between the interest rate on a corporate *bond* and a Treasury security of equal *maturity* and marketability. (2, 6)

defeasance To "render null and void." Procedure whereby a firm, through a trustee, sets aside enough Treasury securities to meet the *interest* and *principal* payments on some of the firm's outstanding debt. (13)

deferred taxes A liability account on the *balance sheet* that represents the additional income tax due in the future arising because the firm has claimed larger expenses (primarily *depreciation*) for tax purposes than for financial reporting purposes. (3, 4)

degree of combined leverage (DCL) Measure of the responsiveness of percentage changes in *earnings per share* (EPS) to percentage changes in sales. Caused by both *operating leverage* and *financial leverage*. Calculated as follows: (ΔEPS/EPS) ÷ (Δsales/sales), or (sales − variable costs)/(*EBIT − interest*), or (*degree of operating leverage*)(*degree of financial leverage*). (15)

degree of financial leverage (DFL) Measure of the responsiveness of percentage changes in *earnings per share* (EPS) to percentage changes in *EBIT*. Calculated as follows: (ΔEPS/EPS) ÷ (ΔEBIT/EBIT), or EBIT/(EBIT − *interest*). (15)

degree of operating leverage (DOL) A measure of the responsiveness of percentage changes in *EBIT* to percentage changes in sales. Calculated as follows: (ΔEBIT/EBIT) ÷ (Δsales/sales), or -(sales − variable costs)/EBIT. (15)

depository transfer check (DTC) Means of moving funds between banks. The DTC is nonnegotiable and payable only to the bank of deposit for credit to the firm's account. (19)

depreciable life An asset's *normal recovery period* specified by the Internal Revenue Service for tax purposes. (8)

depreciation (Dep) For accounting purposes, an annual charge against current income to record the wear and tear of assets; a portion of the historical cost of an asset is written off each year. For tax purposes, depreciable lives and amounts are provided by the modified *Accelerated Cost Recovery System* (ACRS). (4, 8)

direct placement Sale of securities from the firm to the ultimate purchaser, without the services of an *investment banker*. Often this is done with *common stock* via a *rights offering.* (12)

direct send When the depositing bank sends a check to another bank or clearing system (thereby eliminating the local Federal Reserve bank) to speed the check clearing process. (19)

discount (on a bond) Difference between the current market price on a bond selling below its *par value,* and its par value. (6)

discounting (discount) The process of finding the *present value* of a series of future *cash flows;* the inverse of *compounding.* (5)

discount interest Process whereby a lender deducts the *interest* at the start; by doing so, the borrower receives less than the *principal*, and the actual interest rate paid increases. (21)

discount rate The rate used to calculate the *present value* of future *cash flows.* (5)

disinflation A slowing down in the rate of *inflation*. Although there may still be inflation, it is at a lower rate than before. (2)

disinflation risk Source of *risk* due to a slowing down in the rate of *inflation.* (7)

diversifiable risk That part of a security's *total risk* that can be eliminated in a diversified *portfolio.* Also called unsystematic or firm-specific risk. This risk arises within a firm, but since events that affect one firm will not typically affect others, the risk can be eliminated by *diversifying.* (7)

diversifying Investing in more than one asset where the assets do not move proportionally in the same direction at the same time. (7)

divestiture Decision by a firm to sell off some of its assets. (22)

dividend extra Practice of paying an extra or special *cash dividend* in addition to the regular *dividend per share.* Generally done yearly, if at all. (16)

dividend payout *Dividends per share* divided by *earnings per share,* or total *cash dividends* divided by net income. The proportion of the firm's reported earnings distributed to common stockholders in the form of cash dividends. (3, 16)

dividend reinvestment plan Plan in which stockholders can elect to have their *cash dividends* reinvested in order to purchase additional shares of *common stock.* (16)

dividends per share Calculated by dividing total *cash dividends* to common stockholders by the number of shares of *common stock* outstanding. Reflects how much cash the investor will receive for owning one share of stock. Typically, dividends are paid quarterly. (3, 16)

dividend valuation model Model that says the current market value of *common stock* is equal to the *present value* of all expected *cash dividends* discounted at the investor's *required rate of return:* $P_0 = \Sigma_{t=1}^{\infty} [D_t/(1+k)^t]$. (6, 14, 23)

dividend yield *Dividend per share* divided by market price per share. Part of the *return* investors expect from most stocks. The other part of the *required return* is price appreciation. (3, 16)

divisional cost of capital Cost of capital for a specific division of a firm, or for a group of projects that have been grouped together; the minimum *required rate of return* for projects as risky as those faced by the division. (10, 14)

du Pont system *Net profit margin* times *total asset turnover* equals *return on total assets.* Dividing return on total assets by 1 minus the *total debt to total asset* ratio results in *return on equity.* An accounting-based system of analysis that focuses on profitability, asset utilization, and *financial leverage.* (3)

Dutch auction preferred stock *Marketable security* that is resold every 49 days. Firms bid (in terms of the lowest return they are willing to accept) for the security. Because its holding period is longer than 45 days, the *dividends* qualify for the 70 percent tax exclusion for interfirm cash dividends. Also called *money market preferred stock.* (19)

earnings after tax (EAT) Calculated by subtracting cost of goods sold; general, selling, and administrative expenses; *depreciation; interest;* and taxes from sales. Also called net income. (3)

earnings available for common stockholders (EAC) Used when *preferred stock* is outstanding to indicate what portion of earnings go to the benefit of the common stockholders after *cash dividends* on preferred stock are accounted for. Equals net income minus cash dividends on preferred stock. (3)

earnings before interest and taxes (EBIT) Earnings before *interest* on debt and income taxes are deducted; also called net operating income. (3, 15)

earnings before tax (EBT) Earnings before income taxes are deducted. (3)

earnings per share (EPS) Calculated by taking net income minus any *cash dividends* on *preferred stock,* and then dividing by the number of shares of *common stock* outstanding. (3, 15)

economic life The length of time an asset will be economically useful. (8)

economic order quantity (EOQ) The optimal inventory order size that minimizes total cost, which is the sum of the ordering plus the carrying costs. $EOQ = \sqrt{2SO/C}$. (20)

effective interest rate Actual interest rate earned (paid) after adjusting the *nominal interest rate* for the frequency of compounding employed and the number of days assumed in a year. (5)

efficient frontier That part of the *feasible set* that contains only *efficient portfolios.* (7)

efficient market Market in which security prices adjust rapidly to the announcement of new information so that current market prices fully reflect all available information, including *risk.* (2, 7)

efficient market hypothesis Proposition that states in an *efficient market* prices react quickly and unambiguously to new information. (7)

efficient portfolio A *portfolio* that provides the highest *expected return* for a given amount of *risk*, or the lowest risk for a given expected return. (7)

electronic DTC A *depository transfer check* sent via telecommunications between banks; has a uniform 1-day clearing time. (19)

employee stock ownership plan (ESOP) Employee

trust fund to which a firm may contribute stock or cash at no direct cost to the firm. (22)

EPS-EBIT analysis A technique used when examining the effect of alternative *capital structures* on a firm's *earnings per share*. To solve for the unknown indifferent point, EBIT*, the following formula is employed: $\{[(\text{EBIT}^* - I_1)(1 - T) - D_{ps1}]/N_1\} = \{[(\text{EBIT}^* - I_2)(1 - T) - D_{ps2}]/N_2\}$. (15)

EPS illusion The increase in *earnings per share* that can result solely from a *merger*. (22)

equilibrium When the *expected return* equals the *required rate of return,* assets are neither *overpriced* nor *underpriced*. (7)

equipment trust certificate Form of security often used to finance railroad equipment or similar "rolling stock." The trustee holds title to the assets until the security is paid off in full by the firm employing the financing. (13)

equivalent annual NPV The *net present value* (NPV) of a *capital budgeting* project divided by the $PVA_{k,n}$ over the project's life. This produces a yearly equivalent NPV that allows *mutually exclusive* projects with unequal lives to be compared. (9)

Eurobond *Bond* underwritten by an international syndicate and sold primarily in countries other than the country in which the issue is denominated. (13)

Eurocurrency system The worldwide system in which one country's currency is on deposit in another country; often called *Eurodollars,* since a major part of the system is composed of U.S. dollars on deposit in foreign banks. (13)

Eurodollar U.S. dollars deposited in a U.S. branch bank located outside the United States or in a foreign bank. (13)

European option A *call* or *put option* that can only be exercised at its expiration date. (11)

event risk *Risk* caused by a drastic, unanticipated, increase in a firm's debt that causes the market price of its outstanding *bonds* to fall. (6)

event study Empirical study that focuses on *abnormal returns* and/or *cumulative abnormal returns* to see whether new information causes stock market prices to increase or decrease. (2)

ex ante rate of return The return expected before the fact from investing in stocks, bonds, or real assets; same as the *expected rate of return*. (6)

exchange ratio The relationship of the market value of the cash and securities offered by the *bidding firm* divided by the market value of the *target firm* in a proposed *merger*. (22)

ex-dividend date The date set by the securities industry to determine who is entitled to receive a *cash dividend, stock dividend, stock split,* or *rights offering;* four business days (Monday through Friday) before the *record date*. Purchasers must buy stock before the ex-dividend date to receive the dividend (or stock or right). (16)

exercise price Price at which the owner of an option can buy (a *call option*) or sell (a *put option*) the underlying stock. Also called *strike price*. (11)

expansion project *Capital budgeting* project designed to improve the firm's ability to produce or market its goods by expanding its scale of operations. (8)

expected NPV The *mean* or average *net present value* obtained from a *probability distribution* of possible *cash flows*. (10)

expected rate of return See *ex ante rate of return*.

expected return on a portfolio, $\bar{K}_p$ The average of the *expected returns* for a group of securities weighted by the proportion of the *portfolio* devoted to each security. (7)

expected value See *mean*.

ex post rate of return The *return* realized after the fact from investing in stocks, *bonds*, or real assets; same as the *realized rate of return*. (6)

extension An out-of-court procedure by which *creditors* grant a debtor additional time before paying the full amount of past-due obligations. (13)

factoring The sale of a firm's accounts receivables as a means of speeding up the inflow of funds, or to obtain a loan. There are two main types—*advance factoring* and *maturity factoring*. (21)

feasible set The set of all possible *portfolios*. (7)

Federal Reserve system The central banking system in the United States. (2)

finance The money resources available to governments, firms, or individuals, and the management of these monies. (1)

financial distress Situation in which a firm is having difficulty meeting its financial obligations. It may be temporary, or it may be the first sign of impending bankruptcy. (13)

financial distress costs The sum of the direct and indirect costs associated with bankruptcy and financial difficulties. These effect both debt and equity. (15)

financial intermediaries Financial institutions such as banks, savings and loan associations, insurance companies, pension funds, and investment companies that assist in the transfer of funds from suppliers to demanders of these funds. (2)

financial lease Long-term *lease* that meets certain criteria as set by the Internal Revenue Service. Because the *lessee* commits to a series of fixed payments, some of its *debt capacity* is used up.   (17)

financial leverage The use of securities bearing a fixed charge to finance a portion of the firm's assets in order to increase (decrease) earnings and *required returns* to common stockholders. Arises from using *bonds, preferred stock,* or *leases,* which all have a fixed but limited charge.   (3, 15)

financial management The acquisition, management, and financing of resources for firms by means of money, but with due regard for prices in external economic markets.   (1)

financial manager Anyone directly engaged in making or implementing financial decisions.   (1)

financial plan Plan, based on *cash flow* projections, that specifies where the firm is going and how it anticipates getting there. The outcome, in addition to cash flow projections, includes the firm's corporate strategy, its *capital budget,* and its planned financing.   (23)

financial risk A source of *risk* arising if the firm uses financing sources that have a fixed but prior claim relative to *common stock.* Arises from the use of *bonds, preferred stock,* or *leases.*   (7, 15)

firm- and issue-specific risk A source of *risk* that encompasses *business risk, financial risk,* and *issue-specific risk.* This risk can largely be diversified away.   (7, 15)

Fisher effect The relationship between the *nominal interest rate,* the *real rate of interest,* and expected *inflation.* Formally, nominal interest rate = real rate of interest + expected inflation.   (2)

fixed asset turnover See *long-term asset turnover.*

fixed charges coverage *Earnings before interest and taxes* plus *lease* expenses, divided by the sum of *interest* charges plus lease expenses. A ratio that measures the firm's ability to meet its fixed charges.   (3)

float The length of time between when a check is written and when the recipient receives the funds and can draw upon them (has "good funds"). Made up of *mail, processing,* and *transit floats.*   (19)

flotation cost Cost of issuing new stock or *bonds.* The difference between what the securities are sold for to the public and what the firm receives, plus any other costs such as accounting and legal fees.   (12, 14)

foreign bond *Bond* issued by a foreign borrower, but *underwritten,* sold, and denominated in one country.   (13)

foreign exchange rate The price of a unit of a country's currency relative to the price of a unit of another country's currency; the rate at which one currency can be exchanged for another.   (24)

forward rate The rate of exchange between two currencies as set today, but with the transaction to occur at some specified future date.   (24)

free cash flow The difference between cash inflows, cash outflows, and capital investments made by the firm; equal to *cash dividends.*   (23)

fully diluted EPS Earnings that would result by dividing *earnings available for common shareholders* by the total number of shares of *common stock* that would be outstanding after all *convertible securities* were converted.   (3)

fully registered Process whereby *bonds* are issued and registered with respect to *principal* and *interest.* The registration *agent* for the issue keeps a list of owners and mails out interest checks to the bondholders.   (13)

functional currency Primary currency in which a foreign subsidiary operates. The functional currency is used when accounting for the results of foreign operations.   (3)

future value The amount to which a lump sum, or series of payments, will grow by a given future date when compounded at a given *interest* rate. Often called *compounding,* or compound interest.   (5)

future value factor ($FV_{k,n}$) Set of factors that for different rates, k, and periods, n, converts a *present value* into a larger *future value.*   (5)

future value factor for an annuity ($FVA_{k,n}$) Set of factors that for different rates, k, and periods, n, converts an *annuity* into a single *future value.*   (5)

general cash offering *Primary market* transaction in which a firm sells securities to the general public for cash.   (12)

general economic risk A source of *risk* due to the effects of overall economic conditions like recessions, monetary and fiscal policies, tax adjustments, and so forth.   (7, 23)

generally accepted accounting principles (GAAP) Financial reporting requirements established by the Financial Accounting Standards Board that determine the rules by which firms produce the financial statements provided to investors and creditors.   (3)

going private Process by which a publicly owned firm whose *common stock* is actively traded becomes a privately held firm owned and controlled by a small group of investors.   (22)

golden parachute Special employment contract, including a generous severance package, granted to key executives in case of resignation when a firm is acquired in a *merger.*   (22)

greenmail Practice whereby a stake in a *target firm* is purchased, and then sold back to the firm at some price above its current market value.   (22)

gross margin Net sales minus cost of goods sold. (3)

gross profit margin *Gross margin* divided by net sales; the percentage of each dollar of sales remaining after the cost of goods sold is taken into account. (3)

growth rate (g) Compound percentage growth rate in *cash dividends*. Used in the *constant growth model*. (6, 14, 23)

hedging Taking some action using the forward market or options to guard against fluctuations in *foreign exchange rates;* establishing a *covered* position. (24)

hurdle rate In *capital budgeting,* the minimum acceptable return. It is the *discount rate* used when *net present value* is calculated, or the rate against which a project's *internal rate of return* is compared. The hurdle rate is the firm's *cost of capital* for projects of average risk, or some *required rate of return.* (8)

income bond *Bond* that will pay *interest* only to the extent it has the earnings to do so; failure to pay does not result in bankruptcy. (13)

income statement Accounting statement that records the results of the firm's operations over some period of time, typically a year; shows revenues, expenses, and resulting net income (or loss). (3)

incremental cash flow The *cash flows* from a new project minus the cash flows on an old or existing project. Designated ΔCF. (9, 20)

incremental IRR approach Method used to evaluate *mutually exclusive projects* to ensure the same ranking is obtained using the *internal rate of return* (IRR) as with *net present value* (NPV). (8)

indenture Legal agreement between the issuing firm and the bondholders. Provides the specific terms of the *bond.* (13)

independent projects *Capital budgeting* projects whose *cash flows* are unrelated. Acceptance of one has no bearing on whether another project is accepted or rejected. (8, 9)

inflation A condition in which the price level increases rapidly. (2, 6, 7, 9)

inflation premium A premium for expected *inflation* that investors require in addition to the *real rate of interest.* (2)

inflation risk Source of *risk* related to the change in the price level, or purchasing power. (7, 9, 23)

initial investment The net after-tax cash outflow associated with a *capital budgeting* project to get it started. This outflow typically occurs immediately (at time t_0), but for large projects may be spread out over a number of time periods. (8, 9, 20)

initial public offering (IPO) The original sale of a firm's securities to the public. A *primary market* transaction. (12)

installment interest A method of computing *interest* on the total *principal* for the total life of the loan; then, using *annuities,* a fixed payment per period is made, with part of it going to principal and part to interest. (21)

interest The rate paid on money that is borrowed, or received on money lent; usually stated as a percentage rate per year. (2, 6, 13, 19, 21)

interest rate risk Change in market price of a *bond* as general interest rates change. Long-term bonds have more interest rate risk than short-term bonds, thereby leading to a *maturity premium* on long-term bonds. (6, 13)

interest rate swap Agreement between two parties to swap *interest,* but not *principal,* payments. (13)

internally generated funds Those *cash flows* generated by the firm's operations that are free to be paid out to stockholders or reinvested in the business. (14, 16)

internal rate of return (IRR) The rate of *interest* that equates the *present value* of a series of cash inflows with the *initial investment* at time t = 0. (5, 6, 8, 9, 14, 17)

international bond A *bond* sold outside the country of the borrower. (13)

international risk Source of *risk* that arises due to a firm marketing and/or producing internationally. (7, 10, 23, 24)

interrelated projects *Capital budgeting* projects in which the *cash flows* are intertwined so they cannot be examined separately. To evaluate interrelated projects, the combined cash flows (after taking account of interrelationships) must be considered. (9)

inventory conversion period The number of days of the year (365) divided by the *inventory turnover.* A measure of how long it takes to produce and sell a product. (18)

inventory turnover Cost of goods sold divided by inventory. A ratio that measures how many times a year the firm's inventory is turned over, or sold and replaced. (3, 18)

investment banker A firm that serves as a middleperson between the financial markets and the demanders of capital. The investment banker specializes in *underwriting* and selling new securities, and advising corporate clients. (2, 12)

investment opportunity schedule (IOS) Schedule that shows possible capital investments ranked in order by their *internal rate of return.* (14)

investment tax credit (ITC) A direct dollar-for-dollar credit against income tax when new equipment is purchased; was repealed in 1986. (8)

issue-specific premium Compensation for *risk* that arises from the characteristics of the securities and the provisions attached to them. (2, 6)

junk bond Corporate *bond* rated Ba or below; one that is not an investment grade bond (not Aaa, Aa, A or Baa). Sometimes called high-yield bonds. (13)

just-in-time Inventory (and production) system where inventory is minimized by contracting with suppliers so deliveries are made, often daily or hourly, as needed for production. (20)

lease A rental agreement whereby the *lessee* obtains the use of an asset in exchange for an agreement to make fixed payments to the *lessor*. What constitutes a lease for tax purposes may differ substantially from what is accounted for as a lease in the firm's financial statements. (17)

lessee The user of a leased asset. (17)

lessor The owner of an asset that is leased to someone else. (17)

letter of credit An agreement sent by one party (generally a bank) to another, concerning funds that will be made available. Usually a buyer supplies a letter of credit to the seller when they are unknown to each other, thereby guaranteeing payment upon receipt of the goods. (20)

leveraged buyout (LBO) Transaction in which a publicly owned firm is acquired by someone else (or a group); financed largely by borrowing—typically from banks or institutional investors. (1, 22)

leveraged lease A *lease* in which the *lessor* supplies 20 to 30 percent of the funds and borrows the rest from a lender. (17)

leveraging up Firm dramatically increases its amount of debt and at the same time shrinks the number of shares of *common stock* outstanding. (22)

line of credit Agreement between a firm and a bank whereby the firm can borrow up to a maximum amount. Typically this is an informal agreement, sometimes accompanied by a *commitment fee*. Generally the bank is not legally obligated to provide the credit. (18, 21)

liquid assets A firm's cash and *marketable securities*. (19)

liquidation The process of dissolving the firm by selling its assets. This may be out-of-court (an *assignment*) or in-court under Chapter 7 of the Bankruptcy Reform Act of 1978. (13)

liquidity premium Additional *return* to compensate investors for investing in less liquid stocks or *bonds*. (2, 6)

lockbox An arrangement whereby a firm has its customers make payments to a post office box. A local bank makes collections from the post office box, processes the checks, and forwards the money to the firm's central bank, with supporting documentation to the firm. (19)

London Interbank Offered Rate (LIBOR) Interest rate that banks in different countries trade at. Used in place of the U.S. *prime rate* when *Eurodollar* loans are made. (13, 21)

long-term asset turnover Sales divided by long-term (fixed) assets. A ratio that indicates how much sales a firm generates relative to its long-term assets. Also called *fixed asset turnover*. (3)

mail float The time that elapses between when a customer places a check in the mail, and when the selling firm receives it and begins to process it. (19)

majority voting A system of electing the board of directors whereby a simple majority (one-half of all votes plus 1) is required to elect each director. (12)

management buyout Top management, usually with the assistance of an outside partner, takes all or part of a firm and turns it into a private firm. Generally done using primarily debt via a *leveraged buyout*. (22)

marginal tax rate The rate at which the last dollar of income is taxed. (2)

marketable security Short-term debt security that can quickly be converted into cash with little or no loss of *principal*. (19)

market for corporate control Market where various management teams vie for the right to acquire and manage corporate activities and assets. Includes *mergers*, defensive tactics, and restructuring via *leveraging up*, *going private*, limited partnerships, and *divestitures*. (22)

market portfolio (k_M) The *portfolio* of all securities. For the stock market, the New York Stock Exchange (NYSE) or Standard & Poor's 500 stock indices are often used as a proxy for the market portfolio. (7)

market price of risk The slope of the *capital market line;* the *equilibrium* expected reward per unit of *risk*. (7)

matching principle A guideline for *working capital* management that holds that temporary assets should be financed by temporary financing and permanent assets should be financed by permanent sources of financing. (18)

maturity The length (or term) to maturity for a *bond*

expressed in years. At maturity, the borrower must redeem the bond at its *par value*. (6, 13)

maturity factoring Short-term financing in which the factor purchases all a firm's receivables and pays for them once a month. The advantages to the firm are reduced bookkeeping and collection expenses and regularity of cash inflow. (21)

maturity premium Additional *return* required on longer-term *bonds* to compensate the investor for the greater price fluctuation as market *interest* rates change. (2, 6)

mean The weighted average of all possible outcomes, where the weights are the *probabilities* assigned to the expected outcomes; also called the *expected value*. (7, 10, 15)

merger The acquisition of a firm, a division of a firm, or part or all of its assets by another firm. (22)

money market A financial market in which funds are borrowed or lent for short periods of time (up to 1 year). (2, 19)

money market preferred stock See *Dutch auction preferred stock.*

Monte Carlo simulation See *simulation.*

mortgage bond *Bond* secured by a lien on real property of the firm, such as buildings or equipment. In the event of default, the proceeds from selling the mortgaged assets go first to pay the mortgage bondholders. (13)

multiple internal rates of return Condition that may arise when calculating the *internal rate of return* (IRR) if there are *nonsimple cash flows;* that is, where the sign of the *cash flow after tax* stream changes from negative to positive (or vice versa) more than once. (8)

mutually exclusive projects *Capital budgeting* alternatives of which only one can be selected. By selecting the one, others are eliminated from consideration. (8, 9)

negotiated short-term financing Short-term financing such as bank loans or loans secured by accounts receivable or inventory that are negotiated and have a specific length. (21)

net advantage of leasing (NAL) Method to decide whether an asset should be leased or purchased. The NAL equals the cost of the asset minus the *present value* of the after-tax *lease* payments and foregone *depreciation* tax shield, where the after-tax cost of borrowing is used as the *discount rate*. (17)

net present value (NPV) The *present value* of the future *cash flows, discounted* at the *required rate of return* minus the *initial investment* for the project. (8, 9, 10, 20, 22, 24)

net profit margin Net income divided by sales. Profitability ratio that shows how much net income the firm generates per dollar of sales. (3)

net working capital Current assets minus current liabilities. (8, 18)

no growth model Form of the *dividend valuation model* in which no growth in future *cash dividends* is expected. Therefore, $P_0 = D_1/k_s$. (6)

nominal interest rate Stated or observed interest rate; equal to the *real rate of interest* plus an *inflation premium*. (2, 5)

nondiversifiable risk That part of a security's *total risk* that cannot be eliminated in a diversified *portfolio;* also called market or systematic risk. This risk is due to general factors that affect all risky assets to a greater or lesser extent and is measured by *beta*. (7)

nonsimple cash flow A set of *cash flows* whose sign changes from positive to negative (and vice versa) more than once. For every change in sign, there may be one *internal rate of return*. (8)

normal recovery period Property classes established under the *accelerated cost recovery system* of *depreciation*. The six classes are 3-year, 5-year, 7-year, 10-year, 15-year, and 20-year. (8)

ongoing liquidity A function of the expected inflows and outflows of cash through the firm as the product acquisition, production, sales, payment, and collection process takes place over time. (18)

open Not *hedging* a *foreign exchange rate* exposure. (24)

operating cash flows *Cash flows after tax* (CF) expected to occur over the *economic life* of a *capital budgeting* project. Typically these are positive, but occasionally CFs for some years are negative. (8, 9, 20)

operating cycle Part of the *cash conversion cycle;* equal to the *inventory conversion period* plus the *average collection period*. (18)

operating lease Term used in accounting to describe any *lease* that does not meet the criteria established for *capital leases*. (17)

operating leverage The responsiveness of the firm's *earnings before interest and taxes* to fluctuations in sales. Operating leverage arises from the presence of fixed operating costs like executive salaries and rent. (15)

operating profit Net sales minus all expenses except *interest* and taxes, but before any adjustments. If there are no adjustments, operating profit equals *earnings before interest and tax*. (3)

opportunity cost The cost associated with an alternative or foregone opportunity that a firm or individual bypasses. (8, 9)

opportunity cost of capital *Required return* that is foregone by investing in a *capital budgeting* project rather than in a similar *risk* investment, such as financial securities. (14)

ordinary annuity See *annuity.*

organized security exchange Formal organizations that have a physical location and exist to bring together buyers and sellers of securities in the *secondary market.* (2)

overpriced Situation where the *expected return* is less than the *required rate of return.* (7)

over-the-counter (OTC) market A market for securities based on telecommunications facilities that bring together buyers and sellers of securities; a part of the *secondary market.* Many stocks and most *bonds* trade in the OTC market. (2)

partnership An unincorporated business owned by two or more individuals. (1)

par (maturity) value (of a bond) The stated or face value of a *bond,* typically $1,000 per bond. This is the amount to be repaid by the borrower at *maturity.* (6)

par value (of a stock) An arbitrary value employed for accounting purposes; has no economic significance except in rare circumstances. (3, 12)

payable deferral period The number of days in the year (365) divided by payables turnover [(cost of goods sold + general, selling, and administrative expenses)/(accounts payables + salaries, benefits, and payroll taxes payable)]. (18)

payback period The amount of time T (in years) for the expected cash inflows from a *capital budgeting* project to just equal the *initial investment* (or outflow) at time t = 0. (8)

payment date The date set by a firm when a *cash dividend, stock split,* or *stock dividend* will be paid. (16)

pecking order theory *Capital structure* and financing theory that suggests firms value the flexibility associated with financial slack; *internally generated funds* will be used first, then debt, and finally new *common stock.* (15, 16)

percentage of sales method Method of developing *pro forma statements* where historical percentages of items to sales or assets are used for projection purposes. (4)

permanent current assets The minimum current assets the firm always needs to have on hand to maintain its operations. (18)

perpetuity A stream of equal payments expected to continue forever; an infinite *annuity.* (5)

pledging Short-term borrowing when the loan is secured by the borrower's accounts receivable. (21)

poison pill Tactic used to make a *merger* more difficult. When triggered by a *tender offer* or the accumulation of a certain percent of ownership, target shareholders have the right to purchase additional shares, or to sell shares to the target at very attractive prices. (22)

pooling of interests An accounting method employed when firms *merge.* The assets of the two firms are simply added together on an account-by-account basis to form the combined firm's postmerger *balance sheet.* (22)

portfolio A combination of various securities owned for investment. (7)

portfolio beta A weighted average of the *betas* for the securities in the *portfolio,* where the weights are determined by the proportion devoted to each security. (7)

preauthorized check A check that does not require the signature of the person on whose account it is drawn. If authorized by the customer, the use of a preauthorized check can ensure the firm of regularity of receipt of payments. (19)

preemptive right A provision that allows current common stockholders to purchase additional shares offered by the firm before they are offered to outsiders; also called a *rights offering.* (12)

preferred stock Stock that has a prior but limited claim on assets and income before *common stock,* but after debt. *Cash dividends* may not be paid on common stock until all dividends on preferred stock have been paid. (2, 6, 13)

prefinancing Obtaining financing early—6 to 12 months before it is expected to be needed. In the interim, the funds are rolled over in short-term *marketable securities.* (23)

premium (on a bond) Difference between the current market price of a *bond* selling above its *par value,* and its par value. (6)

present value The value today of a given future lump sum, or series of receipts, when *discounted* at a given *discount rate.* (5)

present value factor ($PV_{k,n}$) Set of factors that for different rates, k, and periods, n, converts a *future value* into a smaller *present value.* (5)

present value factor for an annuity ($PVA_{k,n}$) Set of factors that for different rates, k, and periods, n, converts an *annuity* into its *present value.* (5)

present value profile A graph that plots the relationship between a project's *net present value* and the *discount rate* employed. The point at which the present value profile cuts the horizontal (discount rate) axis is the project's *internal rate of return.* (8)

price/earnings (P/E) Market price per share of *common stock* divided by *earnings per share;* shows how much investors are paying for one dollar of current earnings. (3, 12)

primary EPS Accounting calculation whereby *earnings available for common stockholders* are divided by the number of shares of *common stock* that would have been outstanding if all "likely to be converted" securities were converted. (3)

primary market Market in which financial assets are originally sold, with the proceeds going to the issuing firm (or government). (2)

prime rate An administered *interest* rate the bank's best customers are supposedly charged. Most customers will pay more than prime, such as "prime plus 2 percent." (13, 21)

principal The amount of money that must be repaid by a borrower. *Interest* is figured on the principal. Alternatively, the amount lent by a lender. The lender will receive the principal and interest upon *maturity*. (2, 21)

private market purchase Purchase by a firm of its own *bonds* (or stock) directly from an institutional investor. Typically done to retire the securities. (13)

private placement Financing directly between a demander of funds and a supplier of funds that bypasses the public. Private placements do not have to be registered with the Securities and Exchange Commission. (2, 12)

probability The chance of a single event's occurrence. A probability distribution is a listing of all possible outcomes and their chances of occurrence. (7)

probability of success Likelihood that the *net present value* will be positive, or the *internal rate of return* will be greater than the *required rate of return* when *simulation* is employed. (10)

processing float The length of time it takes a firm to process and deposit a customer's check after receiving it. (19)

profitability index The *present value* of future *cash flows*, *discounted* at the *required rate of return* divided by the *initial investment* for the project. (9)

pro forma statements Forecasted financial statements; typically an *income statement* and a *balance sheet*. (4)

proprietorship An unincorporated business owed by one individual. (1)

prospectus See *registration statement.*

protective liquidity The ability to adjust rapidly to unforeseen cash demands, and to have backup sources of cash available. (18)

proxy fight An attempt by an outside group to obtain control of the firm's board of directors. This is done by soliciting proxies, which are authorizations given by

a stockholder that let someone else exercise the stockholder's voting rights at a stockholder meeting. (1)

public offering Sale of securities to the general public by a firm; can be either a *general cash offer* or a *rights offering*; a *primary market* transaction, where the proceeds go to the firm. (12)

purchase (accounting) A method employed when firms *merge*. The assets of the *target firm* are revalued to their fair market value, and any remaining difference between the purchase price and the revalued assets is recorded as goodwill. (22)

pure play firm Firm in the same line of business with the same operating *risk* as a division of a firm, or a specific *capital budgeting* project. Employed to estimate the *beta* for the division or project. (14)

put option The right—but not the obligation—to sell a certain number of shares of stock at a stated price within a specified time period. (11)

quick ratio Current assets minus inventory divided by current liabilities—a measure of liquidity; also called the *acid test ratio*. (3)

realized rate of return See *ex post rate of return.*

real rate of interest Interest rates in the absence of *inflation*; i.e., *nominal interest rate* adjusted for inflation. (2, 24)

receivables pattern Method for analyzing a firm's receivables calculated by determining the percentage of credit sales still outstanding in the month of the sale and in subsequent months. (20)

record date The date determined by a firm when the stockholder books are closed to determine who the current stockholders are. It is important when *cash dividends, stock splits, stock dividends,* or a *rights offering* are scheduled. (16)

red herring Preliminary *registration statement* that can be distributed when a proposed security offering is being reviewed by the Securities and Exchange Commission. (12)

refunding Process of replacing an old *bond* issue with a new one; often done if market *interest* rates have dropped so that the firm can save on interest costs. The same basic process is applicable for *preferred stock*, but it is called refinancing. (13)

registration statement Statement filed with the Securities and Exchange Commission when a firm plans to issue securities to the public. The statement contains all the pertinent facts concerning the firm and the proposed issue. (12)

regular interest Process whereby the lender charges

interest as a percentage of the *principal.* Either periodically, or at the *maturity* of the loan (if short term), the interest is paid.   (21)

regulatory project *Capital budgeting* project that is required for which no measurable cash inflows are expected to occur.   (8)

reinvestment rate risk *Risk* that arises when a *bond* is *called* or *matures* and investors have to reinvest in a lower *coupon interest rate* bond.   (6)

reorganization An in-court procedure under Chapter 11 of the Bankruptcy Reform Act of 1978 under which the firm is revitalized. Assets are sold off and the firm's liabilities and *capital structure* are restructured in an attempt to ensure a healthy, profitable firm after reorganization.   (13)

replacement project *Capital budgeting* project that replaces existing assets that are physically or technologically obsolete. The *incremental cash flows* between the two projects are evaluated.   (8, 9)

repurchase agreement Sale of government securities by a bank or a government securities dealer with a simultaneous agreement to repurchase them in a certain number of days at a specified price. A very flexible short-term *marketable security.*   (19)

required rate of return The minimum *return* necessary to attract a firm or investor to make an investment. Equals the risk-free rate plus a risk premium. In *equilibrium,* the required rate of return equals the *ex ante* (or *expected*) *rate of return.*   (2, 6, 7, 14)

residual theory of dividends A theory that specifies firms should first make all their *capital budgeting* decisions. After the necessary financing has been secured based on the firm's *target capital structure,* any remaining *internally generated funds* would be paid out as *cash dividends.*   (16)

retained earnings An equity account on the *balance sheet* that reflects the sum of the firm's net income (losses) over its life, less all *cash dividends* paid.   (3)

return For any period, the sum of *cash dividends, interest,* and so forth, and any capital appreciation or loss (the difference between the beginning and ending market values).   (6)

return on equity Net income divided by stockholders' equity; or *return on total assets* divided by 1 minus the *total debt to total asset* ratio. A profitability ratio that shows how much net income the firm generates per dollar of equity.   (3)

return on investment See *return on total assets.*

return on total assets Net income divided by total assets; or *net profit margin* times *total asset turnover.* A profitability ratio that shows how much net income the firm generates per dollar of total assets; also called *return on investment.*   (3)

reverse split An action to decrease the number of shares of *common stock* outstanding and simultaneously increase their *par value.* The opposite of a *stock split.*   (16)

rights offering Means of selling *common stock* whereby current stockholders have the first opportunity of buying the issue; also called a privileged subscription.   (12)

risk The degree of *uncertainty* associated with something happening, or a situation in which there is exposure to possible loss. Frequently used interchangeably with the term uncertainty.   (1, 7, 10)

risk aversion A dislike for *risk.*   (7)

risk-free rate (k_{RF}) The *interest* rate on assets that are viewed as being free of any *risk premium.* In nominal terms, the risk-free rate equals the *real rate of interest* plus an *inflation premium.* It is often approximated by the return on *Treasury bills.*   (2, 7)

risk premium The difference between the *required rate of return* on an asset and the *risk-free* rate.   (2, 6)

rolling forecast Process in which *cash budgets* are updated (monthly or quarterly) by dropping the most recent period and adding another period in the future.   (4)

sale and leaseback An arrangement arising when a firm sells an asset to another and simultaneously agrees to *lease* the property back for a specified period of time.   (17)

scenario analysis The process of changing a number of input variables or assumptions simultaneously to see what the effect is on the outcome. Often the assumptions used are most likely, optimistic, and pessimistic.   (4)

seasonal (temporary) current assets The difference between the firm's total current assets and its *permanent current assets.* Fluctuates over the year or business cycle.   (18)

secondary market Market for financial assets that have already been issued. The transactions occur between two parties, with the original issuer not having any part in the sale or purchase. This market includes both the *organized exchanges* and the *over-the-counter market.*   (2)

security market line (SML) Graphic representation of the *capital asset pricing model* (CAPM). Based on investor expectations, their degree of *risk aversion,* the *risk-free rate,* and the *expected return* on the *market portfolio.* Shows the relationship between *nondiversifiable risk* (*beta*) and *required rates of return* for individual assets or *portfolios* of assets.   (7, 23)

semistrong-form efficiency Form of the *efficient market* *hypothesis* in which the relevant information is all publicly available data.   (7)

sensitivity analysis An analysis of the effect of changing one or more of the input variables (or assumptions) at a time to ascertain how much the result is affected. Also called *what if analysis*.   (10, 23)

sequential analysis Method of analyzing *capital budgeting* projects when *risk,* and therefore the *required rate of return,* varies over the life of the project.   (10)

serial bonds *Bonds* issued at the same time, but with different years to *maturity*. Typically, the *coupon interest rate* may vary depending on the maturity.   (13)

service lease A short-term *lease* that can be canceled at any time after proper notice has been given to the *lessor*.   (17)

shelf registration Process whereby large firms can gain prior approval from the Securities and Exchange Commission for public offerings of securities to be issued over the next 2 years. Then, as needed, the firm can take part or all of the securities "off the shelf" and sell them.   (12)

sight draft An order to pay on sight. A customer would have to pay a sight draft before receiving title to goods purchased.   (20)

simple cash flow A sequence of *cash flows* where there is only one change in sign (from positive to negative, or vice versa). There will be no more than one *internal rate of return*.   (8)

simple EPS Value calculated by dividing the *earnings available for common stockholders* by the number of shares of *common stock* outstanding. The same as *earnings per share* when no *convertible securities* exist.   (3)

simulation Method of calculating the *probability* distribution of possible outcomes from a project. Also called *Monte Carlo simulation*.   (10)

sinking fund Required payments to retire part of a *bond* or *preferred stock* issue before *maturity*.   (13)

smoothed residual dividend policy *Cash dividend* policy whereby the firm sets a long-run target *dividend payout* ratio and ties it to a specific *dividend per share*. The firm attempts to stabilize dividends per share while generating the bulk of equity funds needed for investment from *internally generated funds* while fluctuating around its *target capital structure*.   (16)

spontaneous short-term financing Short-term financing such as *trade credit, maturity factoring* of receivables, and inventory warehouse loans that tend to expand (contract) as the firm's current assets expand (contract).   (18, 21)

spot rate The current rate of exchange (*foreign exchange rate*) between two currencies for immediate delivery.   (24)

spreadsheet program Computer program that allows financial data to be manipulated or forecasted. Popular versions include Lotus 1-2-3® and Excel.   (4)

stand-alone principle A *capital budgeting* project should be evaluated by comparing it with the *return* that could be secured by investing in a similar *risk* project. The foregone returns from the bypassed investment are captured by using the appropriate *required rate of return*.   (10)

standard deviation (σ) A statistical measure of the spread of a distribution from its *mean* or *expected value*. Calculated by taking the square root of the sum of the squared deviations from the mean, weighted by the *probabilities* of each outcome occurring. The square root of the *variance*.   (7, 10, 15)

statement of cash flows Accounting statement that reports the flow of cash into and out of the firm during the year. It is broken down into three categories of flows—those arising from operating activities, investing activities, and financing activities.   (4)

stock dividend A means of issuing additional shares of *common stock*. From an accounting standpoint, it involves a transfer from *retained earnings* to the common stock and additional paid-in capital accounts.   (16)

stockholder wealth maximization The objective of the firm—to maximize the value of stockholder claims on the firm by maximizing the market value of the firm, S, or per share price, P_0.   (1)

stock split An action to increase the number of shares of *common stock* outstanding and simultaneously reduce their *par value*.   (16)

stretching payables Practice of not paying an account by its net date, but taking longer to pay the bill. Lowers the direct cost of *trade credit* when the *cash discount* is not taken.   (21)

strike price See *exercise price*.

strong-form efficiency Form of the *efficient market hypothesis* in which the relevant information is all public and private data.   (7)

subchapter S corporation Provision of the Internal Revenue Service code that allows small business *corporations* (with no more than 35 stockholders) to be taxed at the individual tax rate.   (2)

subordinated debenture Unsecured long-term borrowing of the firm that has a lower claim than other unsecured claims.   (13)

substitute projects Two or more *capital budgeting* projects where the acceptance of all of them results in total *cash flows* less than the sum of the individual cash flows. (9)

supermajority Provision requiring more than 50 percent (often two-thirds or even 80 percent) approval when a *merger* is approved. (22)

syndicate A group of *investment bankers* that has agreed to cooperate in purchasing and then reselling a security issue. (12)

synergism The idea that the value of two firms is greater than the sum of their separate values. In *mergers,* this is the "2 + 2 = 5 effect." (22)

systemwide project *Capital budgeting* projects where all of them have to be accepted or rejected as a package, since they are 100 percent *complementary projects.* (9)

target capital structure The planned-for *capital structure,* or mixture of debt and equity, around which the firm attempts to fluctuate; the structure that simultaneously maximizes the firm's value and minimizes its *weighted average cost of capital.* (15)

target firm A firm that is being pursued or is bought out in a *merger.* (22)

temporary current assets See *seasonal current assets.*

tender offer An offer by a firm or group directly to stock- or bondholders to purchase their stock or *bonds* at a certain price. (13, 22)

terminal cash flow The net after-tax cash inflow or outflow that occurs when a *capital budgeting* project is terminated. (8, 9)

term loan Loans with *maturities* of 1 to 10 years that are paid off by periodic payments over the life of the loan. Generally the payment is fixed at a given dollar amount per period, with more going to pay *interest* in the early payments and more to pay *principal* in the late payments. (5, 13)

term structure The relationship between the *yield to maturity* and the length to *maturity* for *bonds* that are equally risky. (2)

time draft A draft that must be paid at a stated future date. If accepted by a firm, it becomes a *trade acceptance.* If accepted by a bank, it becomes a *banker's acceptance.* (20)

times interest earned *Earnings before interest and taxes* divided by *interest* charges. A ratio that measures the ability of the firm to meet its interest charges. (3)

timing The specific point in time (t_0 to t_∞) when cash inflows or outflows occur. (1, 5)

total asset turnover Sales divided by total assets; a ratio that indicates how much sales a firm generates relative to its total assets. (3)

total debt to total assets A ratio that indicates how much of the firm's funds are being supplied by its *creditors.* A high ratio is indicative of greater use of *financial leverage.* (3)

total risk For a security or *portfolio,* total *risk* is measured by its *standard deviation;* for a portfolio, it is composed of *diversifiable risk* plus *nondiversifiable risk.* (7)

trade acceptance *Time draft* drawn upon and accepted by a firm. (20)

trade credit Interfirm credit that arises when one firm sells to another through a credit sale. It appears as an account receivable on the seller's books and as an account payable on the buyer's records. (20, 21)

transaction loan Bank loan made for a specific purpose for a predetermined length of time. (21)

transit float The length of time it takes for a check to clear through the banking system until the recipient can draw upon it (have "good funds"). (19)

treasurer The individual in a firm who is responsible for seeing that funds are obtained as needed, for making sure cash is collected and invested, for maintaining relations with banks and other financial institutions, and for seeing that bills are paid on time. (1)

Treasury bill Short-term security issued by the U.S. government. Issued weekly, T-bills mature in 1 year or less and are often used as a proxy for the *risk-free rate.* (2, 19)

uncertainty In a statistical sense, the situation in which the *probabilities* can be ascertained only subjectively. In *finance,* the terms *risk* and uncertainty are typically used interchangeably. (7)

underpriced Situation where the *expected return* is greater than the *required rate of return.* (7)

underpricing Issue of securities below their fair market value. (12)

underwritten The process whereby an *investment banker* purchases securities from an issuing firm and then immediately resells them. The investment banker bears all the *risks* and assumes the marketing function. (12)

valuation The process of determining what an asset (or liability) is worth based on the magnitude and timing of the *cash flows* expected and the *risks* involved. (1, 6)

variable rate (loan) Loan on which the *interest* rate is not fixed, but fluctuates based on the *prime rate, LIBOR,* or some other rate. (21)

variance (σ^2) A statistical measure of the spread of a distribution from its *mean* or *expected value.* Calculated by summing the average squared deviations from the mean, weighted by the *probabilities* of each outcome occurring. The square of the *standard deviation.* (7)

warrant A long-lived *call option* to purchase a fixed number of shares of *common stock* at a predetermined price during some specified time period. (11)

weak-form efficiency Form of the *efficient market hypothesis* in which the relevant information is past price or return data. (7)

weighted average cost of capital (WACC) The cost of the last dollar of additional funds secured, or the firm's *required rate of return* for projects of average *risk*. It is calculated by multiplying the after-tax cost of specific financing sources by their market-value-determined weights of financing. (10, 14, 15)

what if analysis See *sensitivity analysis*.

white knight The friendly third firm in a situation in which one firm (the potential *bidding firm*) is attempting to take over a *target firm*. The target firm will often seek out another firm to merge with, thereby thwarting the bidding firm. (22)

white squire Friendly firm where a large percentage of another firm's *common stock* is placed to ward off any potential takeover by a third firm. (22)

wire transfer Means of transferring money between banks using a commercial bank wire system or the *Federal Reserve's* wire system (if both banks are members of the Federal Reserve system). (19)

working capital The firm's current assets and current liabilities. (18)

yield curve A plot of the relationship between *yield to maturity* and length (or term) to *maturity* for equally risky *bonds*. (2)

yield to call (YTC) The compound *return* earned on a *bond* purchased at a given price and held until it is called. The call date is before the *maturity* date, and a *call premium* is often paid (over and above the *par value* of the bond). (6)

yield to maturity (YTM) The compound *return* earned on a *bond* if it is purchased at a given price and held to *maturity*. The rate of return that equates the *present value* of the anticipated *interest* and *principal* to its current market value; the *internal rate of return* on a bond. (6, 13, 14)

zero balance account System whereby the bank and the firm create a demand deposit account that contains no funds. Each day the bank transfers enough funds into the account to meet all checks presented for payment. (19)

zero-coupon bond Long-term *bond* issued at a *discount* from its *par value*, for which *interest* each period is simply the difference in the market value at the beginning and end of the period. Similar to *Treasury bills*, which are also issued at a discount, but of much longer *maturity*. (13)

Index

Essential Equations *(Number in brackets indicates principal chapters in text)*

I. Cash Flow [4, 8, 9, 20]

$$CF = CFBT(1 - T) + Dep(T)$$

II. Future and Present Values [5]

A. Future value of a single amount

$$FV_n = PV_0(1 + k)^n$$

B. Present value of a single amount

$$PV_0 = \frac{FV_n}{(1 + k)^n}$$

C. Future value of an annuity

$$FV_n = PMT \sum_{t=0}^{n-1} (1 + k)^t = PMT \left[\frac{(1 + k)^n - 1}{k} \right]$$

D. Present value of an annuity

$$PV_0 = PMT \sum_{t=1}^{n} \frac{1}{(1 + k)^t} = PMT \left\{ \frac{1 - [1/(1 + k)^n]}{k} \right\}$$

E. Present value of a perpetuity

$$PV_0 = PMT_1/k$$

F. Effective interest rate

$$k_{effective} = \left(1 + \frac{k_{nom}}{m} \right)^m - 1$$

III. Valuation [6]

A. Bond (with annual interest)

$$B_0 = \sum_{t=1}^{n} \frac{I}{(1 + k_b)^t} + \frac{M}{(1 + k_b)^n}$$

B. Common stock (dividend valuation model)

$$P_0 = \sum_{t=1}^{\infty} \frac{D_t}{(1 + k_s)^t}$$

C. Common stock—no growth

$$P_0 = D_1/k_s$$

D. Common stock—constant growth

$$P_0 = D_1/(k_s - g)$$

IV. Risk and Return [7]

A. Expected value (or mean)

$$\bar{k} = \sum_{i=1}^{n} k_i P_i$$

B. Standard deviation

$$\sigma = \sqrt{\sum_{i=1}^{n} (k_i - \bar{k})^2 P_i}$$

C. Expected return on two-security portfolio

$$\bar{K}_p = W_A \bar{k}_A + W_B \bar{k}_B$$

D. Standard deviation for a two-security portfolio

$$\sigma_p = \sqrt{W_A^2 \sigma_A^2 + W_B^2 \sigma_B^2 + 2W_A W_B \sigma_A \sigma_B Corr_{AB}}$$

E. Capital market line

$$\bar{K}_p = k_{RF} + \left(\frac{k_M - k_{RF}}{\sigma_M} \right) \sigma_p$$

F. Capital asset pricing model

$$k_j = k_{RF} + \beta_j(k_M - k_{RF})$$

V. Capital Budgeting [8]

A. Net present value, finite life

$$NPV = \sum_{t-1}^{n} \frac{CF_t}{(1 + k)^t} - CF_0$$

B. Internal rate of return

$$\sum_{t=1}^{n} \frac{CF_t}{(1 + IRR)^t} = CF_0$$